Gender Law
and Policy

ASPEN COLLEGE SERIES

Gender Law and Policy

Second Edition

KATHARINE T. BARTLETT
A. Kenneth Pye Professor of Law

Duke University

DEBORAH L. RHODE
Ernest W. McFarland Professor of Law

Director, Stanford Center on the Legal
Profession Stanford University

JOANNA L. GROSSMAN
Sidney and Walter Siben Distinguished
Professor of Family Law

Hofstra University School of Law

SAMANTHA L. BUCHALTER
Duke University School of Law Class of 2013

Printed in the United States of America.

4 5 6 7 8 9 0

ISBN 978-1-4548-4128-9

Library of Congress Cataloging-in-Publication Data

Bartlett, Katharine T., author.
    Gender law and policy / Katharine T. Bartlett, A. Kenneth Pye Professor of Law, Duke University; Deborah L. Rhode, Ernest W. McFarland Professor of Law Director, Stanford Center on the Legal Profession Stanford University; Joanna L. Grossman, Sidney and Walter Siben Distinguished Professor of Family Law, Hofstra University School of Law; Samantha L. Buchalter, Duke University School of Law Class of 2013. — Second Edition.
        pages cm
    Includes bibliographical references and index.
    ISBN 978-1-4548-4128-9 (per : alk. paper)
    1. Sex discrimination against women—Law and legislation—United States—Cases. 2. Women—Legal status, laws, etc.—United States—Cases. 3. Equality before the law—United States—Cases. I. Rhode, Deborah L., author. II. Grossman, Joanna L., author. III. Buchalter, Samantha L., author. IV. Title.

KF4758.B37 2014
342.7308'78—dc23

2014011146

About Wolters Kluwer Law & Business

Wolters Kluwer Law & Business is a leading global provider of intelligent information and digital solutions for legal and business professionals in key specialty areas, and respected educational resources for professors and law students. Wolters Kluwer Law & Business connects legal and business professionals as well as those in the education market with timely, specialized authoritative content and information-enabled solutions to support success through productivity, accuracy and mobility.

Serving customers worldwide, Wolters Kluwer Law & Business products include those under the Aspen Publishers, CCH, Kluwer Law International, Loislaw, Best Case, ftwilliam.com and MediRegs family of products.

CCH products have been a trusted resource since 1913, and are highly regarded resources for legal, securities, antitrust and trade regulation, government contracting, banking, pension, payroll, employment and labor, and healthcare reimbursement and compliance professionals.

Aspen Publishers products provide essential information to attorneys, business professionals and law students. Written by preeminent authorities, the product line offers analytical and practical information in a range of specialty practice areas from securities law and intellectual property to mergers and acquisitions and pension/benefits. Aspen's trusted legal education resources provide professors and students with high-quality, up-to-date and effective resources for successful instruction and study in all areas of the law.

Kluwer Law International products provide the global business community with reliable international legal information in English. Legal practitioners, corporate counsel and business executives around the world rely on Kluwer Law journals, looseleafs, books, and electronic products for comprehensive information in many areas of international legal practice.

Loislaw is a comprehensive online legal research product providing legal content to law firm practitioners of various specializations. Loislaw provides attorneys with the ability to quickly and efficiently find the necessary legal information they need, when and where they need it, by facilitating access to primary law as well as state-specific law, records, forms and treatises.

ftwilliam.com offers employee benefits professionals the highest quality plan documents (retirement, welfare and non-qualified) and government forms (5500/PBGC, 1099 and IRS) software at highly competitive prices.

MediRegs products provide integrated health care compliance content and software solutions for professionals in healthcare, higher education and life sciences, including professionals in accounting, law and consulting.

Wolters Kluwer Law & Business, a division of Wolters Kluwer, is headquartered in New York. Wolters Kluwer is a market-leading global information services company focused on professionals.

To our students

Summary of
Contents

Contents

CHAPTER 1
Formal Equality

CHAPTER 3
Nonsubordination   291

CHAPTER 6
Identity

Preface

This is a book about sex, and what law has to do with it. It touches virtually every area of life, and issues that deeply affect everyone, including jobs, family, education, pay equity, reproductive rights, military service, sexual identity, sexual violence, and social justice. The book both examines what the law is, and helps you think more deeply about what it should be. It could also stimulate your interest in pursuing a career in law, policy, or public service. But whatever work you choose, these readings can help you think about the life you want to lead, and the legal and social changes that will make it possible.

The book has two goals. One is to survey the most significant legal and policy issues relating to gender. For each of the many topics covered, the book defines the significant issues, identifies the relevant law (often through excerpts of court cases), and provides commentary by leading academics and policymakers. For each section, notes provide background, "reading questions" identify key issues, definition boxes explain legal terms, and problems ("Putting Theory Into Practice") challenge you to apply legal principles to concrete, often "real-life," situations.

The other goal of the book is to identify and compare different theoretical frameworks that will help you to think systematically (as opposed to impulsively) about gender issues. These frameworks organize the book, and enable you to identify and rethink the factual and normative assumptions of your own views. Each framework offers a different "handle" on the relationship between law and gender. The formal equality perspective assumes the basic sameness of men and women, and mandates that both sexes be treated identically, whatever the outcome. The substantive equality framework assumes some significant differences between men and women and urges accommodations (usually for women) in order to eliminate the negative consequences of those differences. Nonsubordination theory assumes that law is structured to make women's subordination look natural and inevitable, and seeks to expose and challenge this subordination. Difference theory looks at women's differences from men not so much as disadvantages to be eliminated, but as models for a more just and caring society. The autonomy framework explores legal issues from the standpoint of how to provide women better, and freer, choices.

Finally, the identity perspective highlights fundamental questions about what we mean by "woman" and "man," "sex" and "gender," and feminism.

These theoretical perspectives are not mutually exclusive, nor are they "total" theories that are intended to answer every doctrinal and policy question. Rather, they represent major lenses through which to view the relationship between law and gender. We believe that each theoretical framework has significant value and limitations. The approach of this book works best if readers attempt to be both open to, and critical of, each perspective.

The book is drawn from a longer and somewhat more technical textbook designed for law school courses on law and gender: Gender and Law: Theory, Doctrine, Commentary, now in its sixth edition. Its intended use is for undergraduate courses in gender, law, and public policy. Most of the sources in the book have been heavily edited. Additions to, deletions from, and other substantive alterations to quoted materials are indicated by brackets and ellipses; footnotes and citations are generally deleted without such designations. Where footnotes are retained, the original numbers are used. Paragraph breaks and the order of paragraphs are occasionally modified to make edited excerpts coherent.

Our approach to teaching law and gender is committed to multiple ways of looking at an issue. For this reason, the book is an ongoing unraveling and reweaving of interconnected designs, rather than a straight-seamed assembly of a single, finished fabric. This approach enables you to reconsider problems examined earlier in the book in light of perspectives presented later, and to keep your own mind open to views that may affect your previous judgments.

Katharine T. Bartlett
Duke University School of Law

Deborah L. Rhode
Stanford Law School

Joanna L. Grossman
Hofstra University School of Law

Samantha L. Buchalter
Duke University School of Law Class of 2013

March 2014

Acknowledgments

This book has been a truly collaborative effort, involving an expanding circle of colleagues, friends, and students. We thank those instructors who have used the book and pass on to us useful comments. We especially appreciate the able administrative assistance of Gladys Bethea from Duke.

We also thank the following authors and copyright holders for permission to use their works:

Kathryn Abrams, The Second Coming of Care, Illinois Institute of Technology Chicago-Kent College of Law, 76 Chi.-Kent L. Rev. 1605, 1607-1608, 1610-1611 (2001). Reprinted with permission.

Elvia R. Arriola, Law and the Gendered Politics of Identity: Who Owns the Label "Lesbian," 8 Hastings Women's L.J. 1-3, 5-6, 8-9 (1997). Reprinted from Hastings Women's Law Journal, © 1997 by University of California, Hastings College of the Law.

Leslie Bender, A Lawyer's Primer on Feminist Theory and Tort, 38 J. Legal Educ. 3, 31-36 (1988). Copyright © 1988 by the Association of American Law Schools. Reprinted with permission.

Deborah L. Brake, Getting in the Game: Title IX and the Women's Sports Revolution, NYU Press 16-17, 112-118, 170, 219-220 (2010). Reprinted with permission of the author and publisher.

Kingsley R. Browne, Sex and Temperament in Modern Society: A Darwinian View of the Glass Ceiling and the Gender Gap, 37 Ariz. L. Rev. 971, 984, 1016, 1065-1066, 1071, 1081-1082 (1995). Copyright 1995 by Arizona Board of Regents and Kingsley R. Browne. Reprinted with permission by the author and publisher.

Kingsley R. Browne, Women at War: An Evolutionary Perspective, 49 Buff. L. Rev. 51, 54-57 (2001). Reprinted by permission.

Devon W. Carbado and Mitu Gulati, The Fifth Black Woman, 11 J. Contemp. Legal Issues 701, 710-715, 717-720 (2001). Reprinted by permission of authors.

Donna K. Coker, Heat of Passion and Wife Killing: Men Who Batter/Men Who Kill, 2 S. Cal. Rev. L. & Women's Stud. 71, 93-94, 116, 117-120, 123, 128 (1992). Reprinted by permission.

Frank Rudy Cooper, "Who's the Man?" Masculinities Studies, Terry Stops, and Policy Training, 18 Colum. J. Gender & L. 671, 671-672, 674-676, 741 (2009). Reprinted with permission by the author.

Nancy E. Dowd, Asking the Man Question: Masculinities Analysis and Feminist Theory, 33 Harv. J.L. & Gender 415, 416-419 (2010). Reprinted with permission of the author and publisher.

Susan Estrich, Rape, 95 Yale L.J. 1087, 1102-1105 (1986). Reprinted by permission of the author.

Martha Albertson Fineman, Cracking the Foundational Myths: Independence, Autonomy, and Self-Sufficiency, 8 Am. U. J. Gender Soc. Pol'y & L. 13, 22-23, 25-26 (2000). Reprinted by permission of the author and American University Journal of Gender, Social Policy and Law.

Karla Fischer, Neil Vidmar & René Ellis, The Culture of Battering and the Role of Mediation in Domestic Violence Cases, 46 SMU L. Rev. 2117, 2121-2130, 2133, 2136-2138, 2141 (1993). Reprinted by permission of the authors, the SMU Law Review and the Southern Methodist University Dedman School of Law.

Joanna L. Grossman, Pregnancy, Work, and the Promise of Equal Citizenship, 98 Geo. L.Rev. 567, 615-617 (2010). Reprinted with permission of author.

L. Camille Hébert, The Economic Implications of Sexual Harassment for Women, 3 Kan. J.L. & Pub. Pol'y 41, 47-50 (Spring 1994). Reprinted by permission of the author and Kansas Journal of Law and Public Policy.

Ronald Henry, "Primary Caretaker": Is It a Ruse?, 17 Fam. Advoc. 53, 53-56 (Summer 1994). Copyright © 1995 American Bar Association. Reprinted by permission.

Nan D. Hunter and Sylvia A. Law, Brief Amici Curiae of Feminist Anti-Censorship Taskforce et al., in American Booksellers Association v. Hudnut, 21 U. Mich. J.L. Reform 69, 126-131 (Fall 1987-Winter 1988). Reprinted with permission.

Herma Hill Kay, Equality and Difference: The Case of Pregnancy, 1 Berkeley Women's L.J. 1, 26-31 (1985). Reprinted with permission of the author and the Regents of the University of California.

Michael Kimmel, Integrating Men into the Curriculum, 4 Duke J. Gender L. & Pol'y 181, 181-182, 184, 186-188 (1997). Reprinted with permission of the author and Duke Journal of Gender Law and Policy.

Judith E. Koons, Motherhood, Marriage, and Morality: The Pro-Marriage Moral Discourse of American Welfare Policy, 19 Wis. Women's L.J. 1, 2-3, 6-8, 10-14, 20-24, 41-42 (2004). Reprinted with permission of the author.

Karen M. Kramer, Note, Rule by Myth: Note, Rule by Myth: The Social and Legal Dynamics Governing Alcohol-Related Acquaintance Rapes, 47 Stan. L. Rev. 115, 141-143 (1994). Copyright © 1994 by the Board of Trustees of Leland Stanford Junior University.

Linda Hamilton Krieger, The Content of Our Categories, 47 Stan. L. Rev. 1161, 1188-1190 (1995). Copyright © 1995 by the Board of Trustees of Leland Stanford Junior University.

Dorchen Leidholdt, Prostitution: A Violation of Women's Human Rights. 1 Cardozo Women's L.J. 133, 135-138 (1993). Reprinted with permission of the author.

Catharine A. MacKinnon, Feminism Unmodified: Discourses on Life and Law. 32-38, 40-41 (1987). Reprinted by permission from FEMINISM UNMODIFIED: DISCOURSES ON LIFE AND LAW by Catharine MacKinnon, Cambridge, Mass.: Harvard University Press, Copyright © 1987 by President and Fellows of Harvard College.

Catharine A. MacKinnon, Women's Lives, Men's Laws, Harvard University Press. 86-90 (2005). Reprinted by permission from WOMEN'S LIVES, MEN'S LAWS by Catharine MacKinnon, Cambridge, Mass.: Harvard University Press, Copyright © 2005 by Catharine A. MacKinnon.

Martha R. Mahoney, Legal Images of Battered Women: Redefining the Issue of Separation, 90 Mich. L. Rev. 1, 2-3, 5-7 (1991). Reprinted with permission of the author and publisher.

L. Amede Obiora, Bridges and Barricades: Rethinking Polemics and Intransience in the Campaign Against Female Circumcision, 47 Case W. Res. L. Rev. 275, 288-290, 295-299, 316-317, 329 (1997). Reprinted with permission of the author.

Richard A. Posner, Conservative Femanism, 1989 U. Chi. Legal F. 191, 195-198, 214 (1989). Reprinted with permission of the author.

Margaret Jane Radin, The Pragmatist and the Feminist, 63 Southern California Law Review, pp. 1688-1701 (1990). Reprinted with the permission of the Southern California Law Review.

Judith Resnik, On the Bias: Feminist Reconsiderations of the Aspirations for Our Judges, 61 S. Cal. L. Rev. 1877, 1879, 1921-1926 (1988). Reprinted with the permission of author.

Deborah L. Rhode, Speaking of Sex: The Denial of Gender Inequality (1997), Cambridge, MA: Harvard University Press, 1997, pp. 133-137. Reprinted with the permission of the author and the Harvard University Press.

Dorothy Roberts, Spiritual and Menial Housework, 9 Yale J.L. & Feminism 51, 55-59 (1997). Reprinted with the permission of the author.

Darren Rosenblum, Unsex Mother: Toward a New Culture of Parenting, 35 Harv. J.L. & Gender 57, 58 (2012). Reprinted with permission of the author and publisher.

Vicki Schultz, Life's Work, 100 Colum. L. Rev. 1881, 1883-1886, 1914-1915, 1928-1935 (2000). Reprinted by permission of the author.

Reva B. Siegel, Reasoning from the Body: A Historical Perspective on Abortion Regulation and Questions of Equal Protection, 44 Stan. L. Rev. 261, 267, 361-363, 370 (1992). Copyright © 1992 by the Board of Trustees of Leland Stanford Junior University.

Reva B. Siegel, Dignity and the Politics of Protection: Abortion Restrictions Under Casey/Carhart, 117 Yale L.J. 1694, 1699-1700, 1715, 1718-1719, 1721-1722, 1783-1784, 1794, 1796 (2008). Reprinted by permission of the author and Yale Law Journal Company, Inc.

Jeannie Suk, The Trajectory of Trauma: Bodies and Minds of Abortion Discourse, 110 Colum. L. Rev. 1193, 1193-1201 (2010). Reprinted with the permission of the author and Directors of the Columbia Law Review Association, Inc.

Madhavi Sunder, Piercing the Veil, 112 Yale L.J. 1399, 1401-1405 (2003). Reprinted with the permission of the author and the Yale Law Journal Company, Inc.

Susan Sturm, Second Generation Employment Discrimination: A Structural Approach, 101 Colum. L. Rev. 458, 460 (2001). Reprinted with the permission of the author and the Directors of the Columbia Review Association, Inc.

Leti Volpp, Framing Cultural Difference: Immigrant Women and Discourses of Tradition 90, 93-97, 106 (2011). Reprinted with permission of author.

Robin West, Jurisprudence and Gender, University of Chicago, 55 U. Chi. L. Rev. 1, 1-3, 14-15, 58-59 (1988). Reprinted with the permission of the author.

Robin L. West, The Supreme Court 1989 Term, Foreword: Taking Freedom Seriously, 104 Harv. L. Rev. 43, 82-85 (1990). Reprinted with the permission of the author.

Joan Williams, Toward a Reconstructive Feminism: Reconstructing the Relationship of Market Work and Family Work, 19 N. Ill. U. L. Rev. 89, 89-93 (1998). Reprinted with the permission of the author and the Board of Regents for Northern Illinois University.

Joan Williams, Do Wives Own Half? Winning for Wives After *Wendt,* 32 Conn. L. Rev. 249, 253, 265-268 (1999). Reprinted with the permission of the author and The Connecticut Law Review.

Joan C. Williams, Femmes, Tomboys, and Real Men: Placing Masculinity at the Core of a Feminist Analysis. William E. Massey Sr., Lecture in the History of American Civilization, Harvard University, May 8, 2008. Reprinted with the permission of the author.

Gender Law
and Policy

CHAPTER 1

Formal Equality

Formal equality is the principle of treating like people alike. In determining whether people are alike and thus deserve the same treatment, formal equality demands that people be judged according to their actual characteristics rather than on the basis of assumptions — "stereotypes" — about who they are or who they ought to be. In the context of sex, formal equality requires the state to provide men and women the same opportunity to exercise civic responsibility, such as voting and serving on juries. It requires that public benefits such as Social Security and unemployment compensation be made available to men and women on the same terms, and that property rules, tax liabilities, and alimony rules be sex-neutral. Formal equality also dictates that employers apply the same hiring and promotion criteria to men and women.

Chapter 1 begins with several cases illustrating traditional legal restrictions against women. It then explores the constitutional and statutory doctrines that evolved to dismantle these restrictions. These doctrines emerged from a series of decisions by the U.S. Supreme Court beginning in the early 1970s, and drew heavily from earlier civil rights cases brought under the Fourteenth Amendment of the United States Constitution and from the formal equality model that undergirded these cases.

One central issue for sex discrimination law involves the appropriate "standard of review" that courts should use in considering constitutional challenges to any governmental use of sex-based classifications. The standard of review determines how strong the governmental interest supporting a classification must be, and how tight the fit must be between that interest and the sex-based classification. This test is not simply a legal technicality; the standard of review has significant practical consequences. Classifications involving state action that discriminate against racial minorities require the most rigorous standard of review under the Equal Protection Clause of the Fourteenth Amendment, known as "strict scrutiny." Few classifications survive strict scrutiny. In contrast, ordinary economic and social legislation — for example, legislation regarding minimum wage laws or food and safety regulation — are considered constitutionally acceptable as long as they are "reasonable" or have "any rational basis." Since the 1920s, few laws have ever been invalidated under this rational basis review.

The **standard of review** refers to the weight of the state's burden to justify a challenged statute or practice. Courts utilize different standards of review when considering different types of legislation. A **rational basis** standard of review means that courts will give deference to the decisions made by the legislature and overturn them only if they lack a reasonable justification. A **strict scrutiny** standard of review requires the state to show that the statute or practice is necessary to achieve a compelling state interest. **Intermediate scrutiny** falls between these two standards, requiring the state to show that the rule or practice is substantially related to an important governmental objective.

Traditionally, courts evaluated the constitutionality of sex-based classifications involving state action under the rational basis test and virtually always upheld them. Muller v. Oregon and Goesart v. Cleary, set forth in Part A, illustrate this approach. Starting with Reed v. Reed in 1971,[1] however, the Supreme Court moved to a more stringent "intermediate" standard. Craig v. Boren, decided in 1976,[2] held that a classification based on sex "must serve important governmental objectives and . . . be substantially related to achievement of those objectives." Subsequently, the Court has stated that a sex-based classification must be supported by "an exceedingly persuasive justification."[3] Although many sex-based classifications have been invalidated under this intermediate standard, a number of sex-based rules have survived as well.

A court's **holding** is the legal decision in the case. What the court **holds** is important because it constitutes the principle that can be applied to other, similar cases as **precedent**.

A statement by the court in a case that is not necessary to the holding is **dictum** (plural: **dicta**). Dicta, while not binding in subsequent cases, can nonetheless be persuasive to other courts.

In addition to a holding, the court may also make **findings**. Generally, a finding relates to a fact determined by the court, as compared to the legal holding of the case.

In reviewing the legitimacy of sex-based classifications, a chief concern under both the U.S. Constitution and various civil rights statutes has been the accuracy of the underlying assumptions. Many of the laws and practices successfully challenged in courts have been based on stereotypes about women.

Some stereotypes are *descriptive* generalizations that are overbroad or factually unsupported, such as the stereotype that women do not have the strength or ability to work in certain jobs. Other stereotypes are *prescriptive*, such as the normative assumption that women belong in the home, not the workplace. Some assumptions about women have some factual basis, but statutes or practices based on these assumptions are impermissible under the formal equality principle because they are not drawn narrowly enough to support sufficiently important state objectives. Women *on average* may be less strong than men, but not *all women* are less strong than *all men*; thus, ordinarily, formal equality requires that individual women have the opportunity to prove that they have the strength required for a particular job. This opportunity follows from not only fairness concerns, but also the danger that limiting women's opportunities will reinforce and perpetuate the stereotypes on which the limitations are based.

Sometimes job requirements that appear neutral in fact rest on traditional stereotypes. So, for example, a workplace may use equipment designed with the average heights and weights of men in mind, since the work in question traditionally has been considered "men's work." Similarly, an employer may require all of its employees — male and female — to work from 8 a.m. to 5 p.m. or attend evening events, even though those hours may be relatively disadvantageous to women because of the greater family obligations they tend to assume. A continuing dilemma within the formal equality framework is what to do about rules and practices that are "formally" equal in their application to men and women, but in practice have a disparate impact on women. Chapter 1 focuses on claims for identical treatment; Chapter 2 focuses on claims for a broader equality that takes into account the practical realities of men's and women's lives.

Formal equality applies to sex-based classifications that discriminate against men as well as those that discriminate against women. As a result, women's rights advocates have often supported male litigants in their challenges to sex-based rules and practices. As these advocates note, equality for men is justified not only as a matter of fair treatment for men, but also as a means of reducing stereotypes that restrict opportunities for women. For example, a policy that gives parental leaves only to women deprives men of a benefit and also reinforces a domestic division of labor that penalizes women in the world outside of work.

The materials in this chapter address challenges to policies and practices that treat the sexes differently, with formal equality principles that call for the same treatment for men and women. As you read this chapter, identify both the strengths and limitations of formal equality. Clearly this framework has facilitated substantial progress for women, but are there problems that it does not adequately address? What additional theoretical tools would be necessary to support an appropriate remedy in those cases?

A. HISTORICAL FOUNDATIONS FOR WOMEN'S CLAIM TO FORMAL EQUALITY

1. The Historical Legacy: Women as Different and in Need of Protection

a. *Economic and Social Legislation to Protect Women*

Throughout this nation's history, the conventional view has been that women are unfit for many occupations, and that their biological characteristics and reproductive role make it necessary to limit their employment. This section includes two cases illustrating this conventional view. Muller v. Oregon, decided in 1908, upheld an Oregon statute that limited the maximum number of hours women could work in a single day to ten, based largely on women's assumed physical limitations. The case was decided during a period between 1905 and 1937 when the U.S. Supreme Court routinely invalidated statutes that interfered with the ability of individuals and businesses to make contracts controlling their own commercial relationships. This period is sometimes referred to as the *Lochner* era, based on a 1905 case, Lochner v. New York,[4] which is referenced in the *Muller* case, set forth below. In upholding economic legislation that limited the terms upon which an employer and employee could contract, the *Muller* case is an exception to the *Lochner*-era cases. Its outcome demonstrates the special strength of the claim, extensively briefed by future Supreme Court Justice Louis Brandeis, that women need special protection in the workplace. The *Lochner* era ended in 1937 with West Coast Hotel Co. v. Parrish,[5] in which the Court upheld a state's Minimum Wage for Women Act, and established the modern principle that courts should defer to legislatures when they enact economic and social legislation unless the legislation has no rational basis. In Goesart v. Cleary, decided in 1948, the Supreme Court upheld a Michigan law that prevented the licensing of women as bartenders unless the woman was the wife or daughter of a male who owned the bar where she worked, stressing the moral dangers for women who are without the protection of their fathers or husbands. *Goesart* was decided after the *Lochner* period, and while its deference to legislatures was typical of that period, the decision is also striking for what it assumed about women's "difference."

Reading Questions

1. Under what circumstances should women welcome, or reject, legislation intended specifically to protect them?
2. Note that the laws in *Muller* and *Goesart* were challenged by employers, not the women negatively affected by the law. Should that matter?
3. What assumptions does the *Muller* decision make about women? Are any of these assumptions true?

4. What appears to be the purpose of the statute in *Goesart*? Can you guess why the statute at issue in the case applies to bartenders, but not waitresses?
5. What role does marriage play in *Goesart*?

Muller v. Oregon

208 U.S. 412 (1908)

Mr. Justice BREWER delivered the opinion of the court.

On February 19, 1903, the legislature of the State of Oregon passed an act, [providing that it would be a misdemeanor to employ any female in any mechanical establishment, or factory, or laundry more than ten hours in any one day. Defendant was charged with violation of the statute for ordering Mrs. E. Gotcher to work more than ten hours per day in defendant's laundry]. . . .

A trial resulted in a verdict against the defendant, who was sentenced to pay a fine of $10. The Supreme Court of the State affirmed the conviction . . . whereupon the case was brought here on writ of error.

The single question is the constitutionality of the statute under which the defendant was convicted so far as it affects the work of a female in a laundry. . . .

It is the law of Oregon that women, whether married or single, have equal contractual and personal rights with men. . . .

[Yet the] legislation and opinions referred to [above, including a brief by Mr. Louis D. Brandeis,] are significant of a widespread belief that woman's physical structure, and the functions she performs in consequence thereof, justify special legislation restricting or qualifying the conditions under which she should be permitted to toil. Constitutional questions, it is true, are not settled by even a consensus of present public opinion, for it is the peculiar value of a written constitution that it places in unchanging form limitations upon legislative action, and thus gives a permanence and stability to popular government which otherwise would be lacking. At the same time, when a question of fact is debated and debatable, and the extent to which a special constitutional limitation goes is affected by the truth in respect to that fact, a widespread and long continued belief concerning it is worthy of consideration. We take judicial cognizance of all matters of general knowledge.

That woman's physical structure and the performance of maternal functions place her at a disadvantage in the struggle for subsistence is obvious. This is especially true when the burdens of motherhood are upon her. Even when they are not, by abundant testimony of the medical fraternity continuance for a long time on her feet at work, repeating this from day to day, tends to injurious effects upon the body, and as healthy mothers are essential to vigorous offspring, the physical well-being of woman becomes an object of public interest and care in order to preserve the strength and vigor of the race.

Still again, history discloses the fact that woman has always been dependent upon man. He established his control at the outset by superior physical strength, and this control in various forms, with diminishing intensity, has continued to the present. As minors, though not to the same extent, she has been looked upon in the courts as needing especial care that her rights may be preserved. Education was long denied her, and while now the doors of the school room are opened and her opportunities for acquiring knowledge are great, yet even with that and the consequent increase of capacity for business affairs it is still true that in the struggle for subsistence she is not an equal competitor with her brother. Though limitations upon personal and contractual rights may be removed by legislation, there is that in her disposition and habits of life which will operate against a full assertion of those rights. She will still be where some legislation to protect her seems necessary to secure a real equality of right. Doubtless there are individual exceptions, and there are many respects in which she has an advantage over him; but looking at it from the viewpoint of the effort to maintain an independent position in life, she is not upon an equality. Differentiated by these matters from the other sex, she is properly placed in a class by herself, and legislation designed for her protection may be sustained, even when like legislation is not necessary for men and could not be sustained. It is impossible to close one's eyes to the fact that she still looks to her brother and depends upon him. Even though all restrictions on political, personal and contractual rights were taken away, and she stood, so far as statutes are concerned, upon an absolutely equal plane with him, it would still be true that she is so constituted that she will rest upon and look to him for protection; that her physical structure and a proper discharge of her maternal functions — having in view not merely her own health, but the well-being of the race — justify legislation to protect her from the greed as well as the passion of man. The limitations which this statute places upon her contractual powers, upon her right to agree with her employer as to the time she shall labor, are not imposed solely for her benefit, but also largely for the benefit of all. Many words cannot make this plainer. The two sexes differ in structure of body, in the functions to be performed by each, in the amount of physical strength, in the capacity for long-continued labor, particularly when done standing, the influence of vigorous health upon the future well-being of the race, the self-reliance which enables one to assert full rights, and in the capacity to maintain the struggle for subsistence. This difference justifies a difference in legislation and upholds that which is designed to compensate for some of the burdens which rest upon her.

We have not referred in this discussion to the denial of the elective franchise in the State of Oregon, for while it may disclose a lack of political equality in all things with her brother, that is not of itself decisive. The reason runs deeper, and rests in the inherent difference between the two sexes, and in the different functions in life which they perform.

For these reasons, and without questioning in any respect the decision in Lochner v. New York, we are of the opinion that it cannot be adjudged that the act in question is in conflict with the Federal Constitution, so far as it respects the work of a female in a laundry, and the judgment of the Supreme Court of Oregon is affirmed.

> When a judgment is **affirmed**, the ruling of the court whose decision is being reviewed (the **lower court**) has been upheld. A judgment that has been **reversed** has been overturned. A case that is **reversed and remanded** is one that is sent back to the lower court for further action consistent with the **reviewing court's** decision.

Goesart v. Cleary

335 U.S. 464 (1948)

Mr. Justice FRANKFURTER delivered the opinion of the Court.

As part of the Michigan system for controlling the sale of liquor, bartenders are required to be licensed in all cities having a population of 50,000 or more, but no female may be so licensed unless she be "the wife or daughter of the male owner" of a licensed liquor establishment. The case is here on direct appeal from an order of the District Court of three judges, . . . denying an injunction to restrain the enforcement of the Michigan law. The claim, denied below, one judge dissenting, and renewed here, is that Michigan cannot forbid females generally from being barmaids and at the same time make an exception in favor of the wives and daughters of the owners of liquor establishments. Beguiling as the subject is, it need not detain us long. To ask whether or not the Equal Protection of the Laws Clause of the Fourteenth Amendment barred Michigan from making the classification the State has made between wives and daughters of owners of liquor places and wives and daughters of non-owners, is one of those rare instances where to state the question is in effect to answer it.

We are, to be sure, dealing with a historic calling. We meet the alewife, sprightly and ribald, in Shakespeare, but centuries before him she played a role in the social life of England. The Fourteenth Amendment did not tear history up by the roots, and the regulation of the liquor traffic is one of the oldest and most untrammeled of legislative powers. Michigan could, beyond question, forbid all women from working behind a bar. This is so despite the vast changes in the social and legal position of women. The fact that women may now have achieved the virtues that men have long claimed as their prerogatives and now indulge in vices that men have long practiced, does not preclude the States from drawing a sharp line between the sexes, certainly in such matters as the regulation of the liquor traffic. The Constitution does not require legislatures to reflect sociological insight, or shifting social standards, any more than it requires them to keep abreast of the latest scientific standards.

While Michigan may deny to all women opportunities for bartending, Michigan cannot play favorites among women without rhyme or reason. The Constitution in enjoining the equal protection of the laws upon States precludes irrational discrimination as between persons or groups of persons in the incidence of a law. But the Constitution does not require situations "which are different in fact or opinion to be treated in law as though they were the same." . . . Since bartending by women may, in the allowable legislative judgment, give rise to moral and social problems against which it may devise preventive measures, the legislature need not go to the full length of prohibition if it believes that as to a defined group of females other factors are operating which either eliminate or reduce the moral and social problems otherwise calling for prohibition. Michigan evidently believes that the oversight assured through ownership of a bar by a barmaid's husband or father minimizes hazards that may confront a barmaid without such protecting oversight. This Court is certainly not in a position to gainsay such belief by the Michigan legislature. If it is entertainable, as we think it is, Michigan has not violated its duty to afford equal protection of its laws. We cannot cross-examine either actually or argumentatively the mind of Michigan legislators nor question their motives. Since the line they have drawn is not without a basis in reason, we cannot give ear to the suggestion that the real impulse behind this legislation was an unchivalrous desire of male bartenders to try to monopolize the calling. . . .

Nor is it unconstitutional for Michigan to withdraw from women the occupation of bartending because it allows women to serve as waitresses where liquor is dispensed. The District Court has sufficiently indicated the reasons that may have influenced the legislature in allowing women to be waitresses in a liquor establishment over which a man's ownership provides control. Nothing need be added to what was said below as to the other grounds on which the Michigan law was assailed.

Judgment affirmed.

Mr. Justice RUTLEDGE, with whom Mr. Justice DOUGLAS and Mr. Justice MURPHY join, dissenting.

While the equal protection clause does not require a legislature to achieve "abstract symmetry" or to classify with "mathematical nicety," that clause does require lawmakers to refrain from invidious distinctions of the sort drawn by the statute challenged in this case.

The statute arbitrarily discriminates between male and female owners of liquor establishments. A male owner, although he himself is always absent from his bar, may employ his wife and daughter as barmaids. A female owner may neither work as a barmaid herself nor employ her daughter in that position, even if a man is always present in the establishment to keep order. This inevitable result of the classification belies the assumption that the statute was motivated by a legislative solicitude for the moral and physical well-being of women who, but for the law, would be employed as barmaids. Since there could be no other conceivable justification for such discrimination against women owners of liquor establishments, the statute should be held invalid as a denial of equal protection.

Putting Theory Into Practice

1-1. An Oregon statute enacted in the mid-1950s makes it a crime for women to "participat[e] in wrestling competition and exhibition." A woman is charged under the statute and offers as a defense that the statute violates her rights under the federal Constitution's Equal Protection Clause. *Defend* the statute, and her prosecution, in light of the arguments in *Muller* and *Goesart*.

1-2. In enacting the statute described in Problem 1-1 above, a court found that:

> [the Oregon legislature] intended that there should be at least one island on the sea of life reserved for man that would be impregnable to the assault of woman. It had watched her emerge from long tresses and demure ways to bobbed hair and almost complete sophistication; from a creature needing and depending upon the protection and chivalry of man to one asserting complete independence. She had already invaded practically every activity formerly considered suitable and appropriate for men only. In the field of sports she had taken up, among other games, baseball, basketball, golf, bowling, hockey, long distance swimming, and racing, in all of which she had become more or less proficient, and in some had excelled. In the business and industrial fields as an employe[e] or as an executive, in the professions, in politics, as well as in almost every other line of human endeavor, she had matched her wits and prowess with those of mere man, and . . . in many instances had outdone him.[6]

Does this rationale have any continuing resonance in U.S. society? Assuming the rationale would no longer be a constitutionally sufficient justification for a sex-based classification, is there another purpose that might justify the statute?

b. Women's Differences and the Practice of Law

For most of this nation's history, the conventional view was that women's "difference" made women unfit for law and law unfit for women. In the colonial era, when labor was scarce and relatively few occupations required formal licenses, a few women did manage to participate in legal transactions either by acting as their husband's representative or by obtaining special authorization to proceed independently. During the late eighteenth century, however, the gradual formalization of bar admission criteria made it increasingly difficult for women to act as lawyers. The inability of married women to make contracts reinforced the barriers to any independent career. And, of course, African-American women under slavery had no capacity to assert even their own legal rights, let alone represent others.

After the Civil War, the rise in women's educational and political activism contributed to a growing stream of female applicants to the bar. In 1867, Iowa became the first state to license a woman attorney, Belle Babb Mansfield, and the following decades witnessed a gradual increase in female candidates from largely white, middle- and upper-middle-class backgrounds. Women's initial reception as lawyers in most jurisdictions was less than enthusiastic. Many nineteenth-century lawmakers invested the sexes' "separate spheres" with both spiritual and constitutional significance.[7] The following excerpt from Justice Bradley's concurring opinion in Bradwell v. Illinois was typical in rooting women's domesticity in "the divine ordinance." In addition to raising concerns over women's proper role and "peculiar sensibilities," commentators linked female professional careers to infertility, frigidity, and "race suicide." "Theories about the deadly 'brain-womb' conflict warned that women who diverted their scarce energies to cognitive rather than reproductive pursuits risked permanent physical and psychological damage."[8]

Myra Bradwell based her claim for entrance to the bar on the Privileges and Immunities Clause of the Fourteenth Amendment of the U.S. Constitution. This clause provides that "No State shall make or enforce any law which shall abridge the privileges or immunities of citizens of the United States." Her claim arose before other provisions of the Fourteenth Amendment, notably the Equal Protection Clause and the Due Process Clause, became the more important legal foundations for women's rights in the twentieth century.

Bradwell v. Illinois

83 U.S. (16 Wall.) 130 (1872)

Mrs. Myra Bradwell, residing in the State of Illinois, made application to the judges of the Supreme Court of that State for a license to practice law. . . .

[The Supreme Court of Illinois denied the application because she was a married woman. Mrs. Bradwell challenged the denial under the Privileges and Immunities Clause of the Fourteenth Amendment of the U.S. Constitution, but the decision of the Illinois Supreme Court was upheld. The opinion of the Court is omitted here; what follows is the concurring opinion of Justice Bradley.]

Mr. Justice BRADLEY, concurring: . . .

The claim of the plaintiff, who is a married woman, to be admitted to practice as an attorney and counsellor-at-law, is based upon the supposed right of every person, man or woman, to engage in any lawful employment for a livelihood. The Supreme Court of Illinois denied the application on the ground that, by the common law, which is the basis of the laws of Illinois, only men were admitted to the bar, and the legislature had not made any change in this respect. . . .

The claim that, under the fourteenth amendment of the Constitution, which declares that no State shall make or enforce any law which shall abridge the privileges and immunities of citizens of the United States, the statute law of Illinois, or the common law prevailing in that State, can no longer be set up as a barrier against the right of females to pursue any lawful employment for a livelihood (the practice of law included), assumes that it is one of the privileges and immunities of women as citizens to engage in any and every profession, occupation, or employment in civil life.

It certainly cannot be affirmed, as an historical fact, that this has ever been established as one of the fundamental privileges and immunities of the sex. On the contrary, the civil law, as well as nature herself, has always recognized a wide difference in the respective spheres and destinies of man and woman. Man is, or should be, woman's protector and defender. The natural and proper timidity and delicacy which belongs to the female sex evidently unfits it for many of the occupations of civil life. The constitution of the family organization, which is founded in the divine ordinance, as well as in the nature of things, indicates the domestic sphere as that which properly belongs to the domain and functions of womanhood. The harmony, not to say identity, of interests and views which belong, or should belong, to the family institution is repugnant to the idea of a woman adopting a distinct and independent career from that of her husband. So firmly fixed was this sentiment in the founders of the common law that it became a maxim of that system of jurisprudence that a woman had no legal existence separate from her husband, who was regarded as her head and representative in the social state; and, notwithstanding some recent modifications of this civil status, many of the special rules of law flowing from and dependent upon this cardinal principle still exist in full force in most States. One of these is, that a married woman is incapable, without her husband's consent, of making contracts which shall be binding on her or him. This very incapacity was one circumstance which the Supreme Court of Illinois deemed important in rendering a married woman incompetent fully to perform the duties and trusts that belong to the office of an attorney and counsellor.

It is true that many women are unmarried and not affected by any of the duties, complications, and incapacities arising out of the married state, but these are exceptions to the general rule. The paramount destiny and mission of woman are to fulfil the noble and benign offices of wife and mother. This is the law of the Creator. And the rules of civil society must be adapted to the general constitution of things, and cannot be based upon exceptional cases.

The humane movements of modern society, which have for their object the multiplication of avenues for woman's advancement, and of occupations adapted to her condition and sex, have my heartiest concurrence. But I am not prepared to say that it is one of her fundamental rights and privileges to be admitted into every office and position, including those which require highly special qualifications and demanding special responsibilities. In the nature of things it is not every citizen of every age, sex, and condition that is qualified for every calling and position. It is the prerogative of the legislator to prescribe regulations founded on nature, reason, and experience for the due admission of qualified persons to professions and callings demanding special skill and confidence. This fairly belongs to the police power of the State; and, in my opinion, in view of the peculiar characteristics, destiny, and mission of woman, it is within the province of the legislature to ordain what offices, positions, and callings shall be filled and discharged by men, and shall receive the benefit of those energies and responsibilities, and that decision and firmness which are presumed to predominate in the sterner sex.

For these reasons I think that the laws of Illinois now complained of are not obnoxious to the charge of abridging any of the privileges and immunities of citizens of the United States. . . .

A judicial opinion that expresses the views of the majority of the court is an **opinion of the court**, which is also referred to as the **majority opinion**. A **concurring opinion** agrees with the result of the majority opinion, but not the entirety of its reasoning. If the holding of the case depends upon the agreement of judges who do not agree on the grounds for decision, there will no majority opinion, but only a **plurality opinion**, representing the views of the majority of judges voting in favor of the court's holding. (For an example, see Frontiero v. Richardson, excerpted on p. 26.)

A **dissenting opinion** disagrees with the court's holding.

Judges participating in the decision must sign one opinion, and sometimes sign more than one opinion that is consistent with their views of the case.

The **common law** consists of rules adopted by court, and maintained through judicial precedent, rather than enacted by a legislature.

---

2. The Case for Women's Suffrage

Modern feminism has its roots in the nineteenth-century movement for women's suffrage. Although several states briefly allowed women to cast ballots in state and local elections, women did not achieve the vote until the passage of the Nineteenth Amendment in 1920. Efforts to include women in the Civil Rights Amendments that enfranchised former slaves were unsuccessful.

A key document in the history of women's suffrage is the Declaration of Sentiments, adopted at the Seneca Falls Convention in Seneca Falls, New York, in July 1848. As historian Gerda Lerner notes, this convention was the "first forum in which women gathered together to publicly air their own grievances, not those of the needy, the enslaved, orphans, or widows." The declaration quite clearly uses the Declaration of Independence as the template. Lerner suggests that naming of "man" as the culprit, which anticipated the subsequent, radical feminist critique of patriarchy detailed in Chapter 3 of this casebook, was probably intended more as part of the declaration's "rhetorical flourishes" than an "actual analysis of women's situation."[9] The Declaration of Sentiments, as well as all of the other documents excerpted in this section, can be found in a multivolume collection of women's suffrage documents, History of Woman Suffrage, edited by Elizabeth Cady Stanton, Susan B. Anthony, and Matilda Joslyn Gage (reprint edition 1985).

The women's suffrage movement was intertwined with the campaign to abolish slavery. Indeed, the idea for the Seneca Falls Convention was inspired by a London antislavery convention a few years earlier at which two American participants, Lucretia Mott, a Quaker minister, and Elizabeth Cady Stanton, were barred from participation and required to sit behind a curtain.[10] Some suffragettes also had close ties to other social movements, such as campaigns to protect children from abuse, to criminalize sale and consumption of liquor, to combat "vices" such as prostitution and obscenity, and to improve the conditions of the working poor.

The case of United States v. Anthony, excerpted below, involves the conviction of women's suffrage leader Susan B. Anthony for violation of an 1870 federal civil rights statute intended to prohibit multiple voting by white voters in order to dilute black votes. The excerpt includes Anthony's statements in her defense. After dedicating much of her life to the suffrage struggle, Anthony died in 1906, 14 years before the Nineteenth Amendment was passed.

Another prominent suffragette was Elizabeth Cady Stanton, whose address in the New York State legislature in 1854 forms another basic document in the history of women's suffrage. This reading demonstrates the breadth of the feminist social agenda of the period.

After the turn of the twentieth century, women's rights supporters attracted a mass movement and pursued tactics of escalating pressure, including parades, White House pickets, and hunger strikes. Such strategies, together with women's increasing role in public life and gratitude for their service during World War I, led in 1920 to passage of the Nineteenth Amendment. After that victory, the women's movement dissolved. Although many women remained active in progressive causes and a few continued to struggle for a constitutional equal rights amendment, an organized feminist campaign did not reemerge until the 1960s.

To what extent do the arguments by leading suffragettes assume that women are the same as men and to what extent do they assume women are different? Which assumptions about sameness and difference are reflected in contemporary debates? Was it "racist" for women to argue that educated women were even more deserving of the vote than illiterate former slaves?

Declaration of Sentiments, Seneca Falls Convention, Seneca Falls, New York

(July 1848)

When, in the course of human events, it becomes necessary for one portion of the family of man to assume among the people of the earth a position different from that which they have hitherto occupied, but one to which the laws of nature and of nature's God entitle them, a decent respect to the opinions of mankind requires that they should declare the causes that impel them to such a course.

We hold these truths to be self-evident: that all men and women are created equal; that they are endowed by their Creator with certain inalienable rights; that among these are life, liberty, and the pursuit of happiness; that to secure these rights governments are instituted, deriving their just powers from the consent of the governed. Whenever any form of government becomes destructive of these ends, it is the right of those who suffer from it to refuse allegiance to it, and to insist upon the institution of a new government, laying its foundation on such principles, and organizing its powers in such form, as to them shall seem most likely to effect their safety and happiness. Prudence, indeed, will dictate that governments long established should not be changed for light and transient causes; and accordingly all experience hath shown that mankind are more disposed to suffer, while evils are sufferable, than to right themselves by abolishing the forms to which they were accustomed. But when a long train of abuses and usurpations, pursuing invariably the same object evinces a design to reduce them under absolute despotism, it is their duty to throw off such government, and to provide new guards for their future security. Such has been the patient sufferance of the women under this government, and such is now the necessity which constrains them to demand the equal station to which they are entitled.

The history of mankind is a history of repeated injuries and usurpations on the part of man toward woman, having in direct object the establishment of an absolute tyranny over her. To prove this, let facts be submitted to a candid world.

He has never permitted her to exercise her inalienable right to the elective franchise.

He has compelled her to submit to laws, in the formation of which she had no voice.

He has withheld from her rights which are given to the most ignorant and degraded men — both natives and foreigners.

Having deprived her of this first right of a citizen, the elective franchise, thereby leaving her without representation in the halls of legislation, he has oppressed her on all sides.

He has made her, if married, in the eye of the law, civilly dead.

He has taken from her all right in property, even to the wages she earns. He has made her, morally, an irresponsible being, as she can commit many crimes with impunity, provided they be done in the presence of her husband. In the covenant of marriage, she is compelled to promise obedience to her husband, he becoming, to all intents and purposes, her master — the law giving him power to deprive her of her liberty, and to administer chastisement.

He has so framed the laws of divorce, as to what shall be the proper causes, and in case of separation, to whom the guardianship of the children shall be given, as to be wholly regardless of the happiness of women — the law, in all cases, going upon a false supposition of the supremacy of man, and giving all power into his hands.

After depriving her of all rights as a married woman, if single, and the owner of property, he has taxed her to support a government which recognizes her only when her property can be made profitable to it.

He has monopolized nearly all the profitable employments, and from those she is permitted to follow, she receives but a scanty remuneration. He closes against her all the avenues to wealth and distinction which he considers most honorable to himself. As a teacher of theology, medicine, or law, she is not known.

He has denied her the facilities for obtaining a thorough education, all colleges being closed against her.

He allows her in Church, as well as State, but a subordinate position, claiming Apostolic authority for her exclusion from the ministry, and with some exceptions, from any public participation in the affairs of the Church.

He has created a false public sentiment by giving to the world a different code of morals for men and women, by which moral delinquencies which exclude women from society, are not only tolerated, but deemed of little account in man.

He has usurped the prerogative of Jehovah himself, claiming it as his right to assign for her a sphere of action, when that belongs to her conscience and to her God.

He has endeavored, in every way that he could, to destroy her confidence in her own powers, to lessen her self-respect, and to make her willing to lead a dependent and abject life.

Now, in view of this entire disfranchisement of one-half the people of this country, their social and religious degradation—in view of the unjust laws above mentioned, and because women do feel themselves aggrieved, oppressed, and fraudulently deprived of their most sacred rights, we insist that they have immediate admission to all the rights and privileges which belong to them as citizens of the United States.

In entering upon the great work before us, we anticipate no small amount of misconception, misrepresentation, and ridicule; but we shall use every instrumentality within our power to effect our object. We shall employ agents, circulate tracts, petition the State and National legislatures, and endeavor to enlist the pulpit and the press in our behalf. We hope this Convention will be followed by a series of Conventions embracing every part of the country.

United States v. Anthony

(1873)

Miss ANTHONY: All my prosecutors, from the 8th Ward corner grocery politician, who entered the complaint, to the United States Marshal,

Commissioner, District Attorney, District Judge, your honor on the bench, not one is my peer, but each and all are my political sovereigns; and had your honor submitted my case to the jury, as was clearly your duty, even then I should have had just cause of protest, for not one of those men was my peer; but, native or foreign, white or black, rich or poor, educated or ignorant, awake or asleep, sober or drunk, each and every man of them was my political superior; hence, in no sense, my peer. Even, under such circumstances, a commoner of England, tried before a jury of lords, would have far less cause to complain than should I, a woman, tried before a jury of men. Even my counsel, the Hon. Henry R. Selden, who has argued my cause so ably, so earnestly, so unanswerably before your honor, is my political sovereign. Precisely as no disfranchised person is entitled to sit upon a jury, and no woman is entitled to the franchise, so, none but a regularly admitted lawyer is allowed to practice in the courts, and no woman can gain admission to the bar—hence, jury, judge, counsel, must all be of the superior class.

Judge HUNT: The Court must insist—the prisoner has been tried according to the established forms of law.

Miss ANTHONY: Yes, your honor, but by forms of law all made by men, interpreted by men, administered by men, in favor of men, and against women; and hence, your honor's ordered verdict of guilty, against a United States citizen for the exercise of "that citizen's right to vote," simply because that citizen was a woman and not a man. But, yesterday, the same man-made forms of law declared it a crime punishable with $1,000 fine and six months' imprisonment, for you, or me, or any of us, to give a cup of cold water, a crust of bread, or a night's shelter to a panting fugitive as he was tracking his way to Canada. And every man or woman in whose veins coursed a drop of human sympathy violated that wicked law, reckless of consequences, and was justified in so doing. As then the slaves who got their freedom must take it over, or under, or through the unjust forms of law, precisely so now must women, to get their right to a voice in this Government, take it; and I have taken mine, and mean to take it at every possible opportunity.

Judge HUNT: The Court orders the prisoner to sit down. It will not allow another word.

Miss ANTHONY: When I was brought before your honor for trial, I hoped for a broad and liberal interpretation of the Constitution and its recent amendments, that should declare all United States citizens under its protecting aegis—that should declare equality of rights the national guarantee to all persons born or naturalized in the United States. But failing to get this justice— failing, even, to get a trial by a jury not of my peers—I ask not leniency at your hands—but rather the full rigors of the law.

Judge HUNT: The Court must insist—(Here the prisoner sat down.)

Judge HUNT: The prisoner will stand up. (Here Miss Anthony arose again.) The sentence of the Court is that you pay a fine of one hundred dollars and the costs of the prosecution.

Miss ANTHONY: May it please your honor, I shall never pay a dollar of your unjust penalty. All the stock in trade I possess is a $10,000 debt, incurred by publishing my paper—The Revolution—four years ago, the sole object of which was to educate all women to do precisely as I have done, rebel against your man-made, unjust unconstitutional forms of law, that tax, fine, imprison, and hang women, while they deny them the right of representation in the Government; and I shall work on with might and main to pay every dollar of that honest debt, but not a penny shall go to this unjust claim. And I shall earnestly and persistently continue to urge all women to practical recognition of the old revolutionary maxim, that "Resistance to tyranny is obedience to God."

Elizabeth Cady Stanton, Address to the Legislature of the State of New York

(February 14, 1854)

The tyrant, Custom, has been summoned before the bar of Common-Sense. His majesty no longer awes his multitude—his sceptre is broken—his crown is trampled in the dust—the sentence of death is pronounced upon him. . . . [A]nd now, that the monster is chained and caged, timid woman, on tiptoe, comes to look him in the face, and to demand of her brave sires and sons, who have struck stout blows for liberty, if, in this change of dynasty, she, too, shall find relief. Yes, gentlemen, in republican America, in the nineteenth century, we, the daughters of the revolutionary heroes of '76, demand at your hands the redress of our grievances—a revision of your State Constitution—a new code of laws. Permit us then, as briefly as possible, to call your attention to the legal disabilities under which we labor.

1st. Look at the position of woman as woman. . . . We are persons; native, free-born citizens; property-holders, tax-payers; yet we are denied the exercise of our right to the elective franchise. We support ourselves, and, in part, your schools, colleges, churches, your poor-houses, jails, prisons, the army, the navy, the whole machinery of government, and yet we have no voice in your councils. . . . We are moral, virtuous, and intelligent, and in all respects quite equal to the proud white man himself and yet by your laws we are classed with idiots, lunatics, and negroes; and though we do not feel honored by the place assigned us in fact, our legal position is lower than that of either; for the negro can be raised to the dignity of a voter if he possess himself of $250; the lunatic can vote in his moments of sanity, and the idiot, too, if he be a made one, and not more than nine-tenths a fool; but we, who have guided great movements of charity, established missions, edited journals, published works on history, economy, and statistics; who have governed nations, led armies, filled the professor's chair, taught philosophy and mathematics to the savants of our age, discovered planets, piloted ships across the sea, are denied the most sacred rights of citizens, because, forsooth, we came not into this republic crowned with the dignity of manhood! . . .

Now, gentlemen, who would fain know by what authority you have disfranchised one-half the people of this State? You who have so boldly taken possession of the bulwarks of this republic, show us your credentials, and thus prove your exclusive right to govern, not only yourselves, but us. . . . Can it be that here, where we acknowledge no royal blood, no apostolic descent, that you, who have declared that all men were created equal—that governments derive their just powers from the consent of the governed, would willingly build up an aristocracy that places the ignorant and vulgar above the educated and refined—the alien and the ditch-digger above the authors and poets of the day—an aristocracy that would raise the sons above the mothers that bore them? Would that the men who can sanction a Constitution so opposed to the genius of this government, who can enact and execute laws so degrading to womankind, had sprung, Minerva-like, from the brains of their fathers, that the matrons of this republic need not blush to own their sons! . . .

[Y]ou place the negro, so unjustly degraded by you, in a superior position to your own wives and mothers; for colored males, if possessed of a certain amount of property and certain other qualifications, can vote, but if they do not have these qualifications they are not subject to direct taxation; wherein they have the advantage of woman, she being subject to taxation for whatever amount she may possess. . . .

[W]e demand in criminal cases that most sacred of all rights, trial by a jury of our own peers. . . .

Shall an erring woman be dragged before a bar of grim-visaged judges, lawyers, and jurors, there to be grossly questioned in public on subjects which women scarce breathe in secret to one another? Shall the most sacred relations of life be called up and rudely scanned by men who, by their own admission, are so coarse that woman could not meet them even at the polls without contamination? [A]nd yet shall she find there no woman's face or voice to pity and defend? Shall the frenzied mother, who, to save herself and child from exposure and disgrace, ended the life that had but just begun, be dragged before such a tribunal to answer for her crime? How can man enter into the feelings of that mother? How can he judge of the agonies of soul that impelled her to such an outrage of maternal instincts? How can he weigh the mountain of sorrow that crushed that mother's heart when she wildly tossed her helpless babe into the cold waters of the midnight sea? Where is he who by false vows thus blasted this trusting woman? Had that helpless child no claims on his protection? Ah, he is freely abroad in the dignity of manhood, in the pulpit, on the bench, in the professor's chair. The imprisonment of his victim and the death of his child, detract not a tithe from his standing and complacency. His peers made the law, and shall law-makers lay nets for those of their own rank? Shall laws which come from the logical brain of man take cognizance of violence done to the moral and affectional nature which predominates, as is said, in woman?

Statesmen of New York, whose daughters guarded by your affection, and lapped amidst luxuries which your indulgence spreads, care more for their nodding plumes and velvet trains than for the statute laws by which their persons and properties are held—who, blinded by custom and prejudice to the degraded position which they and their sisters occupy in the civil scale, haughtily claim that they already have all the rights they want, how, think ye, you would feel to see a daughter summoned for such a crime—and remember these daughters are but human—before such a tribunal? Would it not, in that hour, be some consolation to see that she was surrounded by the wise and virtuous of her own sex; by those who had known the depth of a mother's love and the misery of a lover's falsehood; to know that to these she could make her confession, and from them receive her sentence? . . .

2d. Look at the position of woman as wife. Your laws relating to marriage—founded as they are on the old common law of England, a compound of barbarous usages, but partially modified by progressive civilization—are in open violation of our enlightened ideas of justice, and of the holiest feelings of our nature. If you take the highest view of marriage, as a Divine relation, which love alone can constitute and sanctify, then of course human legislation can only recognize it. Men can neither bind nor loose its ties, for that prerogative belongs to God alone, who makes man and woman, and the laws of attraction by which they are united. But if you regard marriage as a civil contract, then let it be subject to the same laws which control all other contracts. Do not make it a kind of half-human, half-divine institution, which you may build up, but can not regulate. Do not, by your special legislation for this one kind of contract, involve yourselves in the grossest absurdities and contradictions. . . .

The wife who inherits no property holds about the same legal position that does the slave on the Southern plantation. She can own nothing, sell nothing. She has no right even to the wages she earns; her person, her time, her services are the property of another. She can not testify, in many cases, against her husband. She can get no redress for wrongs in her own name in any court of justice. She can neither sue nor be sued. She is not held morally responsible for any crime committed in the presence of her husband so completely is her very existence supposed by the law to be merged in that of another. Think of it; your wives may be thieves, libelers, burglars, incendiaries, and for crimes like these they are not held amenable to the laws of the land, if they but commit them in your dread presence. For them, alas! there is no higher law than the will of man. . . .

4th. Look at the position of woman as mother. There is no human love so strong and steadfast as that of the mother for her child; yet behold how ruthless are your laws touching this most sacred relation. Nature has clearly made the mother the guardian of the child; but man, in his inordinate love of power, does continually set nature and nature's laws at open defiance. The father may apprentice his child, bind him out to a trade, without the mother's consent—yea, in direct opposition to her most earnest entreaties, prayers and tears.

He may apprentice his son to a gamester or rum-seller, and thus cancel his debts of honor. By the abuse of this absolute power, he may bind his daughter to the owner of a brothel, and, by the degradation of his child, supply his daily wants; and such things, gentlemen, have been done in our very midst. Moreover, the father, about to die, may bond out all his children wherever and to whomsoever he may see fit, and thus, in fact, will away the guardianship of all his children from the mother. . . . [B]y your laws, the child is the absolute property of the father, wholly at his disposal in life or at death.

In case of separation, the law gives the children to the father; no matter what his character or condition. At this very time we can point you to noble, virtuous, well-educated mothers in this State, who have abandoned their husbands for their profligacy and confirmed drunkenness. All these have been robbed of their children, who are in the custody of the husband, under the care of his relatives, whilst the mothers are permitted to see them but at stated intervals. . . .

Many times and oft it has been asked us, with unaffected seriousness, "What do you women want? What are you aiming at?" Many have manifested a laudable curiosity to know what the wives and daughters could complain of in republican America, where their sires and sons have so bravely fought for freedom and gloriously secured their independence, trampling all tyranny, bigotry, and caste in the dust, and declaring to a waiting world the divine truth that all men are created equal. What can woman want under such a government? Admit a radical difference in sex, and you demand different spheres—water for fish, and air for birds. . . .

When we plead our cause before the law-makers and savants of the republic, they can not take in the idea that men and women are alike; and so long as the mass rest in this delusion, the public mind will not be so much startled by the revelations made of the injustice and degradation of woman's position as by the fact that she should at length wake up to a sense of it.

If you, too, are thus deluded, what avails it that we show by your statute books that your laws are unjust—that woman is the victim of avarice and power? . . .

Would to God you could know the burning indignation that fills woman's soul when she turns over the pages of your statute books, and sees there how like feudal barons you freemen hold your women. Would that you could know the humiliation she feels for sex, when she thinks of all the beardless boys in your law offices, learning these ideas of one-sided justice—taking their first lessons in contempt for all womankind—being indoctrinated into the incapacities of their mothers, and the lordly, absolute rights of man over all women, children, and property, and to know that these are to be our future presidents, judges, husbands, and fathers; in sorrow we exclaim, alas! for that nation whose sons bow not in loyalty to woman. . . .

But if, gentlemen, you take the ground that the sexes are alike, and, therefore, you are our faithful representatives—then why all these special laws for woman? Would not one code answer for all of like needs and wants? Christ's golden rule is better than all the special legislation that the ingenuity of man can devise: "Do unto others as you would have others do unto you." This, men and brethren, is all we ask at your hands. We ask no better laws than those you have made for yourselves. We need no other protection than that which your present laws secure to you.

In conclusion, then, let us say, in behalf of the women of this State, we ask for all that you have asked for yourselves in the progress of your development, since the *Mayflower* cast anchor beside Plymouth Rock; and simply on the ground that the rights of every human being are the same and identical. You may say that the mass of the women of this State do not make the demand; it comes from a few sour, disappointed old maids and childless women.

You are mistaken; the mass speak through us. A very large majority of the women of this State support themselves and their children, and many their husbands too. . . .

Now, do you candidly think these wives do not wish to control the wages they earn—to own the land they buy—the houses they build? To have at their disposal their own children, without being subject to the constant interference and tyranny of an idle, worthless profligate? Do you suppose that any woman is such a pattern of devotion and submission that she willingly stitches all day for the small sum of fifty cents, that she may enjoy the unspeakable privilege, in obedience to your laws, of paying for her husband's tobacco and rum? Think you the wife of the confirmed, beastly drunkard would consent to share with him her home and bed, if law and public sentiment would release her from such gross companionship? Verily, no! Think you the wife with whom endurance has ceased to be a virtue, who, through much suffering, has lost all faith in the justice of both heaven and earth, takes the law in her own hand, severs the unholy bond, and turns her back forever upon him whom she once called husband, consents to the law that in such an hour tears her child from her—all that she has left on earth to love and cherish? The drunkards' wives speak through us, and they number 50,000. Think you that the woman who has worked hard all her days in helping her husband to accumulate a large property, consents to the law that places this wholly at his disposal? Would not the mother whose only child is bound out for a term of years against her expressed wish, deprive the father of this absolute power if she could?

For all these, then, we speak. If to this long list you add the laboring women who are loudly demanding remuneration for their unending toil; those women who teach in our seminaries, academies, and public schools for a miserable pittance; the widows who are taxed without mercy; the unfortunate ones in our work-houses, poor-houses, and prisons; who are they that we do not now represent? But a small class of the fashionable butterflies, who, through the short summer days, seek the sunshine and the flowers; but the cool breezes of autumn and the hoary frosts of winter will soon chase all these away; then they, too, will need and seek protection, and through other lips demand in their turn justice and equity at your hands.

NOTE ON THE BIRTH AND REBIRTH OF MODERN FEMINISM

The women's movement resurfaced in the 1960s in response to a variety of social, economic, and political trends. One was demographic: the increase in women's life expectancy and control over reproduction, and the rise in divorce rates, meant that domesticity was a less stable basis for an entire life. At the turn of the twentieth century, a woman's average life expectancy was 48, and she could contemplate living only 10 to 15 years after her last child left home. By the 1960s, the average woman could contemplate living two-thirds of her adult life with no children under 18.[11] So, too, women's increasing education and employment experience, particularly during World War II, made them less content with full-time domesticity. Rising economic expectations also propelled more women into the paid labor force and led to frustration with the discrimination they encountered there. Women's discontent was captured in Betty Friedan's widely read publication, The Feminine Mystique. The book, which became an instant bestseller, reported the results of Friedan's interviews with affluent fellow graduates of Smith College, then suburban housewives like Friedan herself. Despite their material privilege and the attainment of their lifelong dreams to be wives and mothers, these women felt deeply isolated, bored, and empty. Many women suffered from anxiety and depression, which they treated with tranquilizers. Others had affairs, kept redecorating the house, made gourmet meals, dieted excessively, or had more babies, in a desperate search to find real meaning and fulfillment. Friedan labeled their disaffection "the problem that has no name."[12]

So, too, as was true of the first wave of feminism, the contemporary women's rights movement drew inspiration and supporters from the civil rights struggle and other progressive social movements. Female activists who encountered gender discrimination in those movements began increasingly to turn their energy to the emerging struggle for "women's liberation," based on a fundamental equality between the sexes.[13] Materials in this chapter represent many of the key legal outcomes of these efforts, while subsequent chapters reflect theories that developed once the basic civil rights framework for gender equality was in place.

Putting Theory Into Practice

1-3. Think of an injustice in U.S. society. Does the injustice exist because some people are (wrongly) treated differently than other people? Or would it be an injustice even if everyone were treated the same way? Can you define the injustice in noncomparative terms?

B. FORMAL QUALITY AND THE CONSTITUTIONAL RIGHT TO EQUAL PROTECTION

1. The Right to Equal, Individualized Treatment

Equality claims often arise in the context in which a person asks to be treated as an individual, and without regard to membership in a particular category. The state cannot avoid categories when it makes laws. For example, the state sets age limits concerning rights to vote, drink alcoholic beverages, and marry, even though maturity levels vary, because it would be too difficult to make an individual determination of maturity in every case. So too, employers' hiring decisions may depend on applicants' educational levels, years of experience, or test scores, even though these are not perfect measures of job fitness.

The state is not allowed to rely on some categories, however, regardless of administrative convenience. Such is the case with classifications based on race and national origin. These classifications are subject to strict scrutiny, which means they must be based on a compelling state interest that cannot be achieved through other, more tailored means. The Supreme Court has never held that strict scrutiny is required for sex-based classifications. Instead, the Court has opted for the "intermediate standard of review," developed in the cases that follow.

The three cases in this section reflect the early evolution of this intermediate standard of review. In Reed v. Reed, the Supreme Court invalidated a gender classification for the first time. Sally Reed had custody of her son, Richard, but his father's visitation rights had increased as Richard got older. Richard had a troubled adolescence, involving depression and juvenile crime, and eventually he committed suicide with his father's gun. His mother blamed her former husband for the difficulties. She applied to administer his limited estate, which included only a few personal belongings (clothes, a clarinet, and less than $500 in savings). The father filed a competing application, which was granted under an Idaho statute giving men a preference. In reviewing that statute, the Court articulated the traditional rational basis test, but determined that the male preference was not reasonably related to the statute's objective.

In Frontiero v. Richardson, the Court struck down a law requiring female military personnel to demonstrate a spouse's dependency before receiving economic benefits to which married male personnel were automatically entitled. The statute assumed that all female spouses were dependent, although employment statistics at the time showed that 60 percent of all married women living with their husbands were employed outside the home. Sharron Frontiero's husband was going through college on the GI Bill, receiving a stipend of $205/month. The Air Force, for whom Sharron worked as an officer, refused to recognize him as her dependent, so the couple had no right to either married quarters on the base or the supplemental housing allowance available to married men. Sharron's husband was also not entitled to use medical facilities available to female spouses. While four Justices thought that strict scrutiny should be used to review gender classifications in the law, this position did not get a majority of the Justices' votes.

In Orr v. Orr, the Supreme Court declared Alabama's alimony statutes unconstitutional because they were based on a gender stereotype that women, but not men, are financially dependent on their spouses.

Each of these cases involves government or "state action"—either at the federal or state level. The Fourteenth Amendment of the U.S. Constitution applies to the states. The Due Process Clause of the Fifth Amendment, which incorporates the protections of the Fourteenth Amendment, applies to the federal government. Discrimination by private individuals or entities is not covered by the Constitution and can be prohibited only through legislation or executive action. An example is Title VII of the Civil Rights Act of 1964, which was passed by Congress, and which is addressed later in this chapter.

State action refers to official activity on the part of the state, including its laws, policies, and decisions by state officials, as well as behavior by state employees in the course of their authorized duties.

Reading Questions

1. The plaintiff in *Orr* and one of the plaintiffs in *Frontiero* are male. Should courts treat laws discriminating against men with the same level of scrutiny as laws discriminating against women (intermediate scrutiny)?
2. What is the best argument that laws discriminating against men warrant the same level of constitutional protection as laws discriminating against women? Does the same argument apply in the race context (i.e., that laws discriminating against whites warrant the same constitutional protection as laws discriminating against members of racial minorities)?
3. How unreasonable are the statutes invalidated in the cases that follow? Is it clear to you that each of them should be unconstitutional?

Reed v. Reed

404 U.S. 71 (1971)

Mr. Chief Justice BURGER delivered the opinion of the Court.

[This case challenges an Idaho statute that designates an order of priority for courts to designate the administrator of an estate of a person who dies intestate (without a will). Parents are one priority group, and for all priority groups, Idaho law provides that males are preferred to females. The case is brought by the mother of a child who died intestate, after the probate court issued an order naming the child's father as the administrator of the child's estate.]

In issuing its order, the probate court implicitly recognized the equality of entitlement of the two [parent] applicants; . . . the court ruled, however, that appellee, being a male, was to be preferred to the female appellant [under Idaho law]. In stating this conclusion, the probate judge gave no indication that he had attempted to determine the relative capabilities of the competing applicants to perform the functions incident to the administration of an estate. It seems clear the probate judge considered himself bound by statute to give preference to the male candidate over the female, each being otherwise "equally entitled." . . .

The **appellant** is the party who has appealed the ruling of the court below. The party who prevailed at the court below and opposes the appellant on appeal is the **appellee**.

[W]e have concluded that the arbitrary preference established in favor of males . . . cannot stand in the face of the Fourteenth Amendment's command that no State deny the equal protection of the laws to any person within its jurisdiction.

In applying that clause, this Court has consistently recognized that the Fourteenth Amendment does not deny to States the power to treat different classes of persons in different ways. . . . The Equal Protection Clause of that amendment does, however, deny to States the power to legislate that different treatment be accorded to persons placed by a statute into different classes on the basis of criteria wholly unrelated to the objective of that statute. A classification "must be reasonable, not arbitrary, and must rest upon some ground of difference having a fair and substantial relation to the object of the legislation, so that all persons similarly circumstanced shall be treated alike. . . ." . . .

The **Equal Protection Clause** of the Fourteenth Amendment of the U.S. Constitution provides that "No state shall make or enforce any law which shall . . . deny to any person within its jurisdiction the equal protection of the laws." Most cases challenging sex-based discrimination by a state are brought under the Equal Protection Clause. Most cases challenging sex discrimination by the federal government (e.g., Frontiero v. Richardson, excerpted below) are brought under the **Due Process Clause** of the Fifth Amendment. The Due Process Clause provides that "No person shall be . . . deprived of life, liberty, or property, without due process of law." The privileges and immunities clause of the Fourteenth Amendment provides that "No state shall make or enforce any law which shall abridge the privileges or immunities of citizens of the United States." This provision has also been used to challenge discrimination based on sex (see, e.g., Bradwell v. Illinois, excerpted above).

In upholding the [Idaho statute], the Idaho Supreme Court concluded that its objective was to eliminate one area of controversy when two or more persons, equally entitled under [Idaho law], seek letters of administration and thereby present the probate court "with the issue of which one should be named." The court also concluded that where such persons are not of the same sex, the elimination of females from consideration "is neither an illogical nor arbitrary method devised by the legislature to resolve an issue that would otherwise require a hearing as to the relative merits . . . of the two or more petitioning relatives. . . ." . . .

Clearly the objective of reducing the workload on probate courts by eliminating one class of contests is not without some legitimacy. The crucial question, however, is whether [Idaho law] advances that objective in a manner consistent with the command of the Equal Protection Clause. We hold that it does not. To give a mandatory preference to members of either sex over members of the other, merely to accomplish the elimination of hearings on the merits, is to make the very kind of arbitrary legislative choice forbidden by the Equal Protection Clause of the Fourteenth Amendment; and whatever may be said as to the positive values of avoiding intrafamily controversy, the choice in this context may not lawfully be mandated solely on the basis of sex. . . .

Reversed and remanded.

Reversed and remanded. When a case is reversed and remanded, the appellate court has overruled the decision under review (the **reversal**), and sent it back to an appropriate lower court for further appropriate action (the **remand**). In this case, an estate remains to be probated and an administrator must be appointed. In Reed v. Reed, the case was sent back to the probate court to appoint an administrator without using the priority in favor of males, which the Supreme Court had found unconstitutional.

Frontiero v. Richardson

411 U.S. 677 (1973)

Mr. Justice BRENNAN announced the judgment of the Court in an opinion in which Mr. Justice DOUGLAS, Mr. Justice WHITE, and Mr. Justice MARSHALL join.

The question before us concerns the right of a female member of the uniformed services to claim her spouse as a "dependent" for the purposes of obtaining increased quarters allowances and medical and dental benefits under [federal law] on an equal footing with male members. Under the [federal statutes at issue], a serviceman may claim his wife as a "dependent" without regard to whether she is in fact dependent upon him for any part of her support. . . . A servicewoman, on the other hand, may not claim her husband as a "dependent" under these programs unless he is in fact dependent upon her for over one-half of his support. . . . [T]he question for decision is whether this difference in treatment constitutes an unconstitutional discrimination against servicewomen in violation of the Due Process Clause of the Fifth Amendment. . . .

In an effort to attract career personnel through reenlistment, Congress established . . . a scheme for the provision of fringe benefits to members of the uniformed services on a competitive basis with business and industry. [Under this scheme] a member of the uniformed services with dependents is entitled to an increased "basic allowance for quarters" and . . . a member's dependents are provided comprehensive medical and dental care.

Appellant Sharron Frontiero, a lieutenant in the United States Air Force, sought increased quarters allowances, and housing and medical benefits for her husband, appellant Joseph Frontiero, on the ground that he was her "dependent." Although such benefits would automatically have been granted with respect to the wife of a male member of the uniformed services, appellant's application was denied because she failed to demonstrate that her husband was dependent on her for more than one-half of his support. [In a footnote, Justice Brennan notes that it was clear that Joseph Frontiero, a student who received veterans' benefits, was not dependent upon Sharron Frontiero.] Appellants then commenced this suit, contending that, by making this distinction, the statutes unreasonably discriminate on the basis of sex in violation of the Due Process Clause of the Fifth Amendment. In essence, appellants asserted that the discriminatory impact of the statutes is twofold: first, as a procedural matter, a female member is required to demonstrate her spouse's dependency, while no such burden is imposed upon male members; and, second, as a substantive matter, a male member who does not provide more than one-half of his wife's support receives benefits, while a similarly situated female member is denied such benefits. Appellants therefore sought a permanent injunction against the continued enforcement of these statutes and an order directing the appellees to provide Lieutenant Frontiero with the same housing and medical benefits that a similarly situated male member would receive.

Although the legislative history of these statutes sheds virtually no light on the purposes underlying the differential treatment accorded male and female members, a majority of the three-judge District Court [which voted to uphold the statutes] surmised that Congress might reasonably have concluded that, since the husband in our society is generally the "breadwinner" in the family—and the wife typically the "dependent" partner—"it would be more economical to require married female members claiming husbands to prove actual dependency than to extend the presumption of dependency to such members." Indeed, given the fact that approximately 99% of all members of the uniformed services are male, the District Court speculated that such differential treatment might conceivably lead to a "considerable saving of administrative expense and manpower."

At the outset, appellants contend that classifications based upon sex, like classifications based upon race, alienage, and national origin, are inherently suspect and must therefore be subjected to close judicial scrutiny. We agree and, indeed, find at least implicit support for such an approach in our unanimous decision only last Term in Reed v. Reed. . . .

[The Court reviews the attitude of "romantic paternalism" discussed in *Reed*.] As a result of notions such as these, our statute books gradually became laden with gross, stereotyped distinctions between the sexes and, indeed, throughout much of the 19th century the position of women in our society was, in many respects, comparable to that of blacks under the pre-Civil War slaves codes. Neither slaves nor women could hold office, serve on juries, or bring suit in their own names, and married women traditionally were denied the legal capacity to hold or convey property or to serve as legal guardians of their own children. . . . And although blacks were guaranteed the right to vote in 1870, women were denied even that right . . . until adoption of the Nineteenth Amendment half a century later.

It is true, of course, that the position of women in America has improved markedly in recent decades. Nevertheless, it can hardly be doubted that, in part because of the high visibility of the sex characteristic, women still face pervasive, although at times more subtle, discrimination in our educational institutions, in the job market and, perhaps most conspicuously, in the political arena. . . .

Moreover, since sex, like race and national origin, is an immutable characteristic determined solely by the accident of birth, the imposition of special disabilities upon the members of a particular sex because of their sex would seem to violate "the basic concept of our system that legal burdens should bear some relationship to individual responsibility. . . . " And what differentiates sex from such non-suspect statuses as intelligence or physical disability, and aligns it with the recognized suspect criteria, is that the sex characteristic frequently bears no relation to ability to perform or contribute to society. As a result, statutory distinctions between the sexes often have the effect of invidiously relegating the entire class of females to inferior legal status without regard to the actual capabilities of its individual members.

We might also note that, over the past decade, Congress has itself manifested an increasing sensitivity to sex-based classifications. In [Title VII] of the Civil Rights Act of 1964, for example, Congress expressly declared that no employer, labor union, or other organization subject to the provisions of the Act shall discriminate against any individual on the basis of "race, color, religion, sex, or national origin." Similarly, the Equal Pay Act of 1963 provides that no employer covered by the Act "shall discriminate . . . between employees on the basis of sex." And §1 of the Equal Rights Amendment, passed by Congress on March 22, 1972, and submitted to the legislatures of the States for ratification, declares that "(e)quality of rights under the law shall not be denied or abridged by the United States or by any State on account of sex." Thus, Congress itself has concluded that classifications based upon sex are inherently invidious, and this conclusion of a coequal branch of Government is not without significance to the question presently under consideration. . . .

With these considerations in mind, we can only conclude that classifications based upon sex, like classifications based upon race, alienage, or national origin, are inherently suspect, and must therefore be subjected to strict judicial scrutiny. Applying the analysis mandated by that stricter standard of review, it is clear that the statutory scheme now before us is constitutionally invalid.

The sole basis of the classification established in the challenged statutes is the sex of the individuals involved. . . .

[T]he Government concedes that the differential treatment accorded men and women under these statutes serves no purpose other than mere "administrative convenience." In essence, the Government maintains that, as an empirical matter, wives in our society frequently are dependent upon their husbands, while husbands rarely are dependent upon their wives. Thus, the Government argues that Congress might reasonably have concluded that it would be both cheaper and easier simply conclusively to presume that wives of male members are financially dependent upon their husbands, while burdening female members with the task of establishing dependency in fact.[22]

The Government offers no concrete evidence, however, tending to support its view that such differential treatment in fact saves the Government any money. In order to satisfy the demands of strict judicial scrutiny, the Government must demonstrate, for example, that it is actually cheaper to grant increased benefits with respect to all male members, than it is to determine which male members are in fact entitled to such benefits and to grant increased benefits only to those members whose wives actually meet the dependency requirement. Here, however, there is substantial evidence that, if put to the test, many of the wives of male members would fail to qualify for benefits. And in light of the fact that the dependency determination with respect to the husbands of female members is presently made solely on the basis of affidavits rather than through the more costly hearing process, the Government's explanation of the statutory scheme is, to say the least, questionable.

In any case, our prior decisions make clear that, although efficacious administration of governmental programs is not without some importance, "the Constitution recognizes higher values than speed and efficiency. . . ." And when we enter the realm of "strict judicial scrutiny," there can be no doubt that "administrative convenience" is not a shibboleth, the mere recitation of which dictates constitutionality. . . . We therefore conclude that, by according differential treatment to male and female members of the uniformed services for the sole purpose of achieving administrative convenience, the challenged statutes violate the Due Process Clause of the Fifth Amendment insofar as they require a female member to prove the dependency of her husband. Reversed.

---

22. It should be noted that these statutes are not in any sense designed to rectify the effects of past discrimination against women. . . . On the contrary, these statutes seize upon a group—women—who have historically suffered discrimination in employment, and rely on the effects of this past discrimination as a justification for heaping on additional economic disadvantages.

Mr. Justice POWELL, with whom THE CHIEF JUSTICE and Mr. Justice BLACKMUN join, concurring in the judgment. . . .

It is unnecessary for the Court in this case to characterize sex as a suspect classification, with all of the far-reaching implications of such a holding. Reed v. Reed, [1971], which abundantly supports our decision today, did not add sex to the narrowly limited group of classifications which are inherently suspect. . . . In my view, we can and should decide this case on the authority of *Reed* and reserve for the future any expansion of its rationale.

There is another, and I find compelling, reason for deferring a general categorizing of sex classifications as invoking the strictest test of judicial scrutiny. The Equal Rights Amendment, which if adopted will resolve the substance of this precise question, has been approved by the Congress and submitted for ratification by the States. If this Amendment is duly adopted, it will represent the will of the people accomplished in the manner prescribed by the Constitution. . . . It seems to me that this reaching out to pre-empt by judicial action a major political decision which is currently in process of resolution does not reflect appropriate respect for duly prescribed legislative processes. . . .

Orr v. Orr

440 U.S. 268 (1979)

Mr. Justice BRENNAN delivered the opinion of the Court.

The question presented is the constitutionality of Alabama alimony statutes which provide that husbands, but not wives, may be required to pay alimony upon divorce.

The fact that the classification expressly discriminates against men rather than women does not protect it from scrutiny. . . . "To withstand scrutiny" under the Equal Protection Clause, "classifications by gender must serve important governmental objectives and must be substantially related to achievement of those objectives." . . .

Appellant [husband, who was ordered to pay alimony and challenges the Alabama alimony statutes as a violation of the Equal Protection Clause in a contempt action brought against him for being in arrears on his alimony obligations] views the Alabama alimony statutes as effectively announcing the State's preference for an allocation of family responsibilities under which the wife plays a dependent role, and as seeking for their objective the reinforcement of that model among the State's citizens. . . .

The opinion of the Alabama Court of Civil Appeals suggests other purposes that the statute may serve. Its opinion states that the Alabama statutes were "designed" for "the wife of a broken marriage who needs financial assistance." This may be read as asserting either of two legislative objectives. One is a legislative purpose to provide help for needy spouses, using sex as a proxy for need. The other is a goal of compensating women for past discrimination during marriage, which assertedly has left them unprepared to fend for themselves in the working world following divorce. We concede, of course, that assisting needy spouses is a legitimate and important governmental objective. We have also recognized "[r]eduction of the disparity in economic condition between men and women caused by the long history of discrimination against women . . . as . . . an important governmental objective." It only remains, therefore, to determine whether the classification at issue here is "substantially related to achievement of those objectives."

Ordinarily, we would begin the analysis of the "needy spouse" objective by considering whether sex is a sufficiently "accurate proxy" . . . for dependency to establish that the gender classification rests "upon some ground of difference having a fair and substantial relation to the object of the legislation." [Reed v. Reed (1971)] . . . Similarly, we would initially approach the "compensation" rationale by asking whether women had in fact been significantly discriminated against in the sphere to which the statute applied a sex-based classification, leaving the sexes "not similarly situated with respect to opportunities" in that sphere. . . .

But in this case, even if sex were a reliable proxy for need, and even if the institution of marriage did discriminate against women, these factors still would "not adequately justify the salient features of" Alabama's statutory scheme. . . . Under the statute, individualized hearings at which the parties' relative financial circumstances are considered already occur. . . . There is no reason, therefore, to use sex as a proxy for need. Needy males could be helped along with needy females with little if any additional burden on the State. In such circumstances, not even an administrative-convenience rationale exists to justify operating by generalization or proxy. Similarly, since individualized hearings can determine which women were in fact discriminated against vis-à-vis their husbands, as well as which family units defied the stereotype and left the husband dependent on the wife, Alabama's alleged compensatory purpose may be effectuated without placing burdens solely on husbands. Progress toward fulfilling such a purpose would not be hampered, and it would cost the State nothing more, if it were to treat men and women equally by making alimony burdens independent of sex. "Thus, the gender-based distinction is gratuitous; without it, the statutory scheme would only provide benefits to those men who are in fact similarly situated to the women the statute aids," . . . and the effort to help those women would not in any way be compromised.

Moreover, use of a gender classification actually produces perverse results in this case. As compared to a gender-neutral law placing alimony obligations on the spouse able to pay, the present Alabama statutes give an advantage only to the financially secure wife whose husband is in need. Although such a wife might have to pay alimony under a gender-neutral statute, the present statutes exempt her from that obligation. Thus, "[t]he [wives] who benefit from the disparate treatment are those who were . . . nondependent on their husbands." . . . They are precisely those who are not "needy spouses" and who are "least likely to have been victims of . . . discrimination," . . . by the institution of marriage. A gender-based classification which, as compared to a gender-neutral one, generates additional benefits only for those it has no reason to prefer cannot survive equal protection scrutiny.

Legislative classifications which distribute benefits and burdens on the basis of gender carry the inherent risk of reinforcing the stereotypes about the "proper place" of women and their need for special protection. . . . Thus, even statutes purportedly designed to compensate for and ameliorate the effects of past discrimination must be carefully tailored. Where, as here, the State's compensatory and ameliorative purposes are as well served by a gender-neutral classification as one that gender classifies and therefore carries with it the baggage of sexual stereotypes, the State cannot be permitted to classify on the basis of sex. And this is doubly so where the choice made by the State appears to redound — if only indirectly — to the benefit of those without need for special solicitude. Reversed and remanded.

Putting Theory Into Practice

1-4. The following exchange is reported as part of a voir dire examination conducted by a judge in a criminal case in a municipal court in California:

The Court: Miss Bobb, what is your occupation?

Miss Bobb: I'm an attorney.

The Court: And in your practice do you practice criminal law as well as civil law?

Miss Bobb: No, I practice entirely bankruptcy law.

The Court: All right. Is there a Mr. Bobb?

Miss Bobb: I have some difficulty with that question because I've noticed only the women have been asked to answer that.

The Court: Yes, I know. Do you have a Mr. Bobb — is there a Mr. Bobb?

Miss Bobb: Are you going to [poll] the men to see if they care to disclose —

The Court: No, I'm just going to ask you if you have a husband or not. Do you have a husband?

Miss Bobb: I don't care to answer it then. What's relative to women is relative to men.

The Court: Yes, I know. What is your husband's occupation?

Miss Bobb: I don't care to answer that.

The Court: I instruct you to answer.

Miss Bobb: I don't think I should.

The Court: I've got — you understand that you'll be in contempt of Court — jury — you're an attorney, you understand these rules, don't you?

Miss Bobb: No, I do not understand why only the women are asked certain questions and the men aren't asked the same questions.

> *The Court:* The question to you, Mrs. Bobb—you're an attorney at law, you understand the rules and regulations of—of—of being an attorney. And the question to you now simply is: What is your husband's occupation?
>
> *Miss Bobb:* I refuse to answer.
>
> *The Court:* You're held in contempt of Court, Mrs. Bobb.[14]

Is Mrs. Bobb's resistance reasonable? To what extent will formal equality principles provide relief to Mrs. Bobb?

Upon appeal, the Court of Appeals of California decided that Carolyn Bobb was improperly held in contempt of court. The reviewing court found no compelling state interest for posing some questions to female jurors, but not to male jurors; it therefore held that requiring Mrs. Bobb to answer the question denied her equal protection of the law. Is this ruling good for women? Does it prevent the court from learning the information, or is there another way to get an answer that is consistent with formal equality principles?

Voir dire is a preliminary interview with a prospective juror by a judge, or by the parties' counsel, to decide whether the individual is qualified and suitable to serve on a jury.

---

2. The Right to Equal Group Treatment

In *Reed* and *Orr*, the state had in place a system of individualized fact-finding; the only question was whether part of that fact-finding could be abbreviated by using sex as a proxy—in *Reed*, a proxy for ability and interest in administering an estate, and in *Orr*, a proxy for financial dependency. In both of these contexts, eliminating sex as a proxy (as the Supreme Court did) does not impose a great administrative burden and is likely to produce more accurate results in terms of the goals of the statutes.

However, in many contexts the state needs to draw lines to decide questions that do not lend themselves to individualized fact-finding. Common examples include the right to vote, marry, drive, serve in the military, and attend public schools. This section examines two other examples. In Stanton v. Stanton, the Supreme Court declared unconstitutional a Utah law requiring parents to support their female children only until age 18, while male children had to be supported until age 21. The Court invalidated the statute because it was based on outdated and stereotypical notions of gender roles. In Craig v. Boren, the Court found unconstitutional a law that set different drinking ages for men and women. With these cases, the Supreme Court was faced with stereotypes that have some basis in fact. At the same time, acting on those stereotypes tended to reinforce and perpetuate the inequality that has traditionally accompanied them.

Although the cases are only one year apart, note the different review standards. The Court in the 1975 *Stanton* decision finds the different support ages for boys and girls unreasonable, parroting the rational basis test the Court purported to apply in *Reed*. In *Craig*, the Court elevates the standard, requiring that sex-based classifications "serve important government objectives and . . . be substantially related to achievement of those objectives." Justice Stevens in his concurring opinion states that the classification "is not totally irrational" but is unacceptable under this higher standard. Justice Rehnquist in his dissenting opinion criticizes the new standard as coming "out of thin air," and particularly inappropriate in a case in which the disadvantaged sex is male.

Reading Questions

1. To what extent are the statutes at issues in these cases based on stereotypes? What stereotypes? Is the problem that these stereotypes are inaccurate? If not, what is the problem?
2. In *Stanton*, should the equal protection problem be eliminated by raising the age of support to 21 for both male and female children, or by lowering the age of support for all to 18? Does it matter, for constitutional purposes? Who should decide—courts or legislatures?
3. Should sex-based classifications disadvantaging males be subject to the same heightened review applied to review sex-based classifications disadvantaging females, or is Justice Rehnquist correct that the more lenient rational basis test is more appropriate?

Stanton v. Stanton

421 U.S. 7 (1975)

Mr. Justice BLACKMUN delivered the opinion of the Court.

This case presents the issue whether a state statute specifying for males a greater age of majority than it specifies for females denies, in the context of a parent's obligation for support payments for his children, the equal protection of the laws. . . .

[The case is an appeal arising from divorce proceedings, following a . . . judgment requiring the father to pay child support to the mother for a daughter and a son. The father discontinued support payments for the daughter when she turned 18, pursuant to Utah law which set the age of majority for girls at 18 and the age of majority for boys at 21. The trial court denied the mother's motion for further support, which the Supreme Court of Utah affirmed.]

We find it unnecessary in this case to decide whether a classification based on sex is inherently suspect. . . . [Reed v. Reed (1971)] we feel, is controlling here. . . . "A classification 'must be reasonable, not arbitrary, and must rest upon some ground of difference having a fair and substantial relation to the object of the legislation, so that all persons similarly circumstanced shall be treated alike.'" . . . The test here, then, is whether the difference in sex between children warrants the distinction in the appellee's obligation to support that is drawn by the Utah statute. We conclude that it does not. It may be true, as the Utah court observed and as is argued here, that it is the man's primary responsibility to provide a home and that it is salutary for him to have education and training before he assumes that responsibility; that girls tend to mature earlier than boys; and that females tend to marry earlier than males. The last mentioned factor, however, under the Utah statute loses whatever weight it otherwise might have, for the statute states that "all minors obtain their majority by marriage"; thus minority, and all that goes with it, is abruptly lost by marriage of a person of either sex at whatever tender age the marriage occurs.

Notwithstanding the "old notions" to which the Utah court referred, we perceive nothing rational in the distinction drawn by [the statute] which, when related to the divorce decree, results in the appellee's liability for support for Sherri only to age 18 but for Rick to age 21. This imposes "criteria wholly unrelated to the objective of that statute." A child, male or female, is still a child. No longer is the female destined solely for the home and the rearing of the family, and only the male for the marketplace and the world of ideas. . . . Women's activities and responsibilities are increasing and expanding. Coeducation is a fact, not a rarity. The presence of women in business, in the professions, in government and, indeed, in all walks of life where education is a desirable, if not always a necessary, antecedent is apparent and a proper subject of judicial notice. If a specified age of minority is required for the boy in order to assure him parental support while he attains his education and training, so, too, is it for the girl. To distinguish between the two on educational grounds is to be self-serving: if the female is not to be supported so long as the male, she hardly can be expected to attend school as long as he does, and bringing her education to an end earlier coincides with the role-typing society has long imposed. And if any weight remains in this day to the claim of earlier maturity of the female, with a concomitant inference of absence of need for support beyond 18, we fail to perceive its unquestioned truth or its significance, particularly when marriage, as the statute provides, terminates minority for a person of either sex. . . .

A court takes **judicial notice** of a matter when it takes into account a fact that neither party has formally placed into evidence. Under the Federal Rules of Evidence, judicial notice is reserved for matters generally known within the jurisdiction of the trial court or capable of accurate determination through sources whose accuracy cannot reasonably be questioned.

[Whether the common law age of 21 applies to both children or the remedy for the unconstitutional inequality is to treat males as adults at age 18] is an issue of state law to be resolved by the Utah courts on remand. . . .

Craig v. Boren

429 U.S. 190 (1976)

Mr. Justice BRENNAN delivered the opinion of the Court, with whom Mr. Justice POWELL, Mr. Justice STEVENS, Mr. Justice BLACKMUN (in part), and Mr. Justice STEWART concurred.

The interaction of two sections of an Oklahoma statute . . . prohibits the sale of "nonintoxicating" 3.2% beer to males under the age of 21 and to females under the age of 18. The question to be decided is whether such a gender-based differential constitutes a denial to males 18-20 years of age of the equal protection of the laws in violation of the Fourteenth Amendment.

This action was brought in the District Court for the Western District of Oklahoma on December 20, 1972, by appellant Craig, a male then between 18 and 21 years of age, and by appellant Whitener, a licensed vendor of 3.2% beer. The complaint [alleged] that [the law] constituted invidious discrimination against males 18-20 years of age. A three-judge court . . . sustained the constitutionality of the statutory differential and dismissed the action. . . . We reverse. . . .

An action for **declaratory relief** is one in which a person seeks to adjudicate the legality of a statute before it is enforced or acted upon. Here, an under-age male and a seller both seek to determine whether a statute is constitutional without either of them first violating the statute. An action for **injunctive relief** is one that seeks a court order requiring a party to do something, or preventing a party from doing something. Here, the appellant asks the court to **declare** the statute unconstitutional, and **enjoin** (i.e., prevent) the state from enforcing it.

To withstand constitutional challenge . . . classifications by gender must serve important governmental objectives and must be substantially related to achievement of those objectives. . . . We accept for purposes of discussion the District Court's identification of the objective underlying [the statutes in question] as the enhancement of traffic safety. Clearly, the protection of public health and safety represents an important function of state and local governments. However, appellees' statistics in our view cannot support the conclusion that the gender-based distinction closely serves to achieve that objective and therefore the distinction cannot under [Reed v. Reed (1971)] withstand equal protection challenge.

The appellees introduced a variety of statistical surveys. First, an analysis of arrest statistics for 1973 demonstrated that 18–20-year-old male arrests for "driving under the influence" and "drunkenness" substantially exceeded female arrests for that same age period. Similarly, youths aged 17-21 were found to be overrepresented among those killed or injured in traffic accidents, with males again numerically exceeding females in this regard. Third, a random roadside survey in Oklahoma City revealed that young males were more inclined to drive and drink beer than were their female counterparts. Fourth, Federal Bureau of Investigation nationwide statistics exhibited a notable increase in arrests for "driving under the influence." Finally, statistical evidence gathered in other jurisdictions, particularly Minnesota and Michigan, was offered to corroborate Oklahoma's experience by indicating the pervasiveness of youthful participation in motor vehicle accidents following the imbibing of alcohol. Conceding that "the case is not free from doubt" . . . , the District Court nonetheless concluded that this statistical showing substantiated "a rational basis for the legislative judgment underlying the challenged classification." . . .

Even were this statistical evidence accepted as accurate, it nevertheless offers only a weak answer to the equal protection question presented here. The most focused and relevant of the statistical surveys, arrests of 18–20-year-olds for alcohol-related driving offenses, exemplifies the ultimate unpersuasiveness of this evidentiary record. Viewed in terms of the correlation between sex and the actual activity that Oklahoma seeks to regulate—driving while under the influence of alcohol—the statistics broadly establish that .18% of females and 2% of males in that age group were arrested for that offense. While such a disparity is not trivial in a statistical sense, it hardly can form the basis for employment of a gender line as a classifying device. Certainly if maleness is to serve as a proxy for drinking and driving, a correlation of 2% must be considered an unduly tenuous "fit." Indeed, prior cases have consistently rejected the use of sex as a decisionmaking factor even though the statutes in question certainly rested on far more predictive empirical relationships than this.

Moreover, the statistics exhibit a variety of other shortcomings that seriously impugn their value to equal protection analysis. Setting aside the obvious methodological problems,[14] the surveys do not adequately justify the salient features of Oklahoma's gender-based traffic-safety law. None purports to measure the use and dangerousness of 3.2% beer as opposed to alcohol generally, a detail that is of particular importance since, in light of its low alcohol level, Oklahoma apparently considers the 3.2% beverage to be "nonintoxicating." . . . Moreover, many of the studies, while graphically documenting the unfortunate increase in driving while under the influence of alcohol, make no effort to relate their findings to age-sex differentials as involved here. Indeed,

14. The very social stereotypes that find reflection in age-differential laws, see *Stanton*, are likely substantially to distort the accuracy of these comparative statistics. Hence, "reckless" young men who drink and drive are transformed into arrest statistics, whereas their female counterparts are chivalrously escorted home. . . . Moreover, the Oklahoma surveys, gathered under a regime where the age-differential law in question has been in effect, are lacking in controls necessary for appraisal of the actual effectiveness of the male 3.2% beer prohibition. In this regard, the disproportionately high arrest statistics for young males—and, indeed, the growing alcohol-related arrest figures for all ages and sexes—simply may be taken to document the relative futility of controlling driving behavior by the 3.2% beer statute and like legislation, although we obviously have no means of estimating how many individuals, if any, actually were prevented from drinking by these laws.

the only survey that explicitly centered its attention upon young drivers and their use of beer—albeit apparently not of the diluted 3.2% variety—reached results that hardly can be viewed as impressive in justifying either a gender or age classification.[16]

. . . [T]he showing offered by the appellees does not satisfy us that sex represents a legitimate, accurate proxy for the regulation of drinking and driving. In fact, when it is further recognized that Oklahoma's statute prohibits only the selling of 3.2% beer to young males and not their drinking the beverage once acquired (even after purchase by their 18-20-year-old female companions), the relationship between gender and traffic safety becomes far too tenuous to satisfy *Reed*'s requirement that the gender-based difference be substantially related to achievement of the statutory objective.

We hold, therefore, that under *Reed*, Oklahoma's 3.2% beer statute invidiously discriminates against males 18-20 years of age. . . .

Mr. Justice STEVENS, concurring.

There is only one Equal Protection Clause. It requires every State to govern impartially. It does not direct the courts to apply one standard of review in some cases and a different standard in other cases. Whatever criticism may be leveled at a judicial opinion implying that there are at least three such standards applies with the same force to a double standard. . . .

In this case, the classification is not as obnoxious as some the Court has condemned, nor as inoffensive as some the Court has accepted. It is objectionable because it is based on an accident of birth, because it is a mere remnant of the now almost universally rejected tradition of discriminating against males in this age bracket, and because, to the extent it reflects any physical difference between males and females, it is actually perverse [because males are on average heavier than females and thus have a greater capacity to consume alcohol without impairing their ability to drive]. The question then is whether the traffic safety justification put forward by the State is sufficient to make an otherwise offensive classification acceptable.

16. The random roadside survey of drivers conducted in Oklahoma City during August 1972 found that 78% of drivers under 20 were male. Turning to an evaluation of their drinking habits and factoring out nondrinkers, 84% of the males versus 77% of the females expressed a preference for beer. Further 16.5% of the men and 11.4% of the women had consumed some alcoholic beverage within two hours of the interview. Finally, a blood alcohol concentration greater than .01% was discovered in 14.6% of the males compared to 11.5% of the females. "The 1973 figures, although they contain some variations, reflect essentially the same pattern." . . . Plainly these statistical disparities between the sexes are not substantial. Moreover, when the 18-20 age boundaries are lifted and all drivers analyzed, the 1972 roadside survey indicates that male drinking rose slightly whereas female exposure to alcohol remained relatively constant. Again, in 1973, the survey established that "compared to all drivers interviewed, . . . the under-20 age group generally showed a lower involvement with alcohol in terms of having drunk within the past two hours or having a significant BAC (blood alcohol content)." [Id.] In sum, this survey provides little support for a gender line among teenagers and actually runs counter to the imposition of drinking restrictions based upon age.

The classification is not totally irrational. For the evidence does indicate that there are more males than females in this age bracket who drive and also more who drink. Nevertheless, there are several reasons why I regard the justification as unacceptable. It is difficult to believe that the statute was actually intended to cope with the problem of traffic safety, since it has only a minimal effect on access to a not very intoxicating beverage and does not prohibit its consumption. Moreover, the empirical data submitted by the State accentuate the unfairness of treating all 18–20-year-old males as inferior to their female counterparts. The legislation imposes a restraint on 100% of the males in the class allegedly because about 2% of them have probably violated one or more laws relating to the consumption of alcoholic beverages. It is unlikely that this law will have a significant deterrent effect either on that 2% or on the law-abiding 98%. But even assuming some such slight benefit, it does not seem to me that an insult to all of the young men of the State can be justified by visiting the sins of the 2% on the 98%. . . .

Mr. Justice REHNQUIST, dissenting. . . .

I think the Oklahoma statute challenged here need pass only the "rational basis" equal protection analysis . . . and I believe that it is constitutional under that analysis.

Most obviously unavailable to support any kind of special scrutiny in this case, is a history or pattern of past discrimination, such as was relied on by the plurality in [Frontiero v. Richardson (1973)] to support its invocation of strict scrutiny. There is no suggestion in the Court's opinion that males in this age group are in any way peculiarly disadvantaged, subject to systematic discriminatory treatment, or otherwise in need of special solicitude from the courts.

The Court does not discuss the nature of the right involved, and there is no reason to believe that it sees the purchase of 3.2% beer as implicating any important interest, let alone one that is "fundamental" in the constitutional sense of invoking strict scrutiny. . . .

It is true that a number of our opinions contain broadly phrased dicta implying that the same test should be applied to all classifications based on sex, whether affecting females or males. . . . However, before today, no decision of this Court has applied an elevated level of scrutiny to invalidate a statutory discrimination harmful to males, except where the statute impaired an important personal interest protected by the Constitution. There being no such interest here, and there being no plausible argument that this is a discrimination against females,[2] the Court's reliance on our previous sex-discrimination

2. I am not unaware of the argument from time to time advanced, that all discriminations between the sexes ultimately redound to the detriment of females, because they tend to reinforce "old notions" restricting the roles and opportunities of women. As a general proposition applying equally to all sex categorizations, I believe that this argument was implicitly found to carry little weight in our decisions upholding gender-based differences. . . . Seeing no assertion that it has special applicability to the situation at hand, I believe it can be dismissed as an insubstantial consideration.

cases is ill-founded. It treats gender classification as a talisman which — without regard to the rights involved or the persons affected — calls into effect a heavier burden of judicial review.

The Court's conclusion that a law which treats males less favorably than females "must serve important governmental objectives and must be substantially related to achievement of those objectives" apparently comes out of thin air. The Equal Protection Clause contains no such language, and none of our previous cases adopt that standard. I would think we have had enough difficulty with the two standards of review which our cases have recognized — the norm of "rational basis," and the "compelling state interest" required where a "suspect classification" is involved — so as to counsel weightily against the insertion of still another "standard" between those two. How is this Court to divine what objectives are important? How is it to determine whether a particular law is "substantially" related to the achievement of such objective, rather than related in some other way to its achievement? Both of the phrases used are so diaphanous and elastic as to invite subjective judicial preferences or prejudices relating to particular types of legislation, masquerading as judgments whether such legislation is directed at "important" objectives or, whether the relationship to those objectives is "substantial" enough. I would have thought that if this Court were to leave anything to decision by the popularly elected branches of the Government, where no constitutional claim other than that of equal protection is invoked, it would be the decision as to what governmental objectives to be achieved by law are "important," and which are not. As for the second part of the Court's new test, the Judicial Branch is probably in no worse position than the Legislative or Executive Branches to determine if there is any rational relationship between a classification and the purpose which it might be thought to serve. But the introduction of the adverb "substantially" requires courts to make subjective judgments as to operational effects, for which neither their expertise nor their access to data fits them. And even if we manage to avoid both confusion and the mirroring of our own preferences in the development of this new doctrine, the thousands of judges in other courts who must interpret the Equal Protection Clause may not be so fortunate. . . .

Notes

1. **"Simple Little Case"?**   At a distance of three decades, the cases in this section do not seem so difficult, but at the time they were decided, most members of the all-male Court did not perceive them as straightforward. Justice Blackmun's papers offer a window into how one of those who voted ultimately to overturn the gender preference in *Reed* viewed the case and the arguments underlying it. The brief in *Reed*, on which now-Justice Ruth Bader Ginsburg had collaborated as an advocate, argued that the probate code compounded the "subordination of women." It claimed that "American women have been stigmatized historically as an inferior class and are today subject to pervasive discrimination. . . . A person born female continues to be branded inferior for

this congenital and unalterable condition of birth." Justice Blackmun found the brief "mildly offensive and arrogant" and out of proportion in what he considered "a very simple little case." It was "much ado about nothing" since the estate in dispute amounted to less than $1,000. However, Justice Blackmun also recognized that it was meant as a "test case," and he was prepared to join the majority because "there can be no question that women have been held down in the past in almost every area." He advised the Court to write a "brief and simple opinion" and hoped that "we do not get into a long and emotional discussion about women's rights."[15]

Was the Court's decision to write a "brief and simple" opinion in *Reed* the right choice? How much guidance does it provide about the kinds of classifications that do not pass constitutional scrutiny? Does Justice Blackmun's reference to "emotional" arguments about women's rights reflect the very same stereotypes that underpinned the classifications in *Reed*, *Orr*, and the cases that followed?

As in *Reed*, an irony of Craig v. Boren is that one of the nation's most important sex discrimination cases arose in one of the least important factual contexts. Ruth Bader Ginsburg, then director of the Women's Rights Project of the American Civil Liberties Union, filed an amicus curiae brief in the case and noted later: "It was a petty law, mercifully terminated. One might wish the Court had chosen a less frothy case" for announcing a crucial principle.[16]

An **amicus curiae** ("friend of the court") brief is filed by a nonparty in the case to present additional information or perspectives. In important cases, the Supreme Court may receive dozens of briefs from amici organizations, groups, and government officials.

2. The Role of Stereotyping in Formal Equality Analysis. The articulated standard in these cases, at least from Craig v. Boren forward, is that the challenged classification must bear a substantial relationship to important governmental objectives. Note the frequency with which the Supreme Court's analysis focuses on the fact of stereotyping by the legislature. What is the problem with stereotyping? Is it that stereotypes are "archaic" and "overbroad," and therefore too often inaccurate? Or is the problem that individuals are harmed by stereotypical assumptions even when they are at least partially true about women, or men, as a group? Or is the concern that stereotypes, even when they are accurate, perpetuate the inequalities that they reflect? What stereotypes underlie the classification in *Craig*?

3. Remedying Inequality in Formal Treatment. Problems of formal equality often can be eliminated in more than one way. Formal gender neutrality could be achieved in *Orr* either by eliminating alimony for both husbands and wives, or by leaving the state's system of individualized alimony determinations in place and extending eligibility to husbands who can prove their dependency. The latter alternative, which is the option Alabama chose, presents the classic "won the battle but lost the war" scenario for Mr. Orr: he prevails on the constitutional point, but remains liable for alimony under a different, gender-neutral regime. The formal equality principle applied in *Craig* and *Stanton* also did not compel any particular resolution: the state could use the higher age or the lower age or some other age altogether, just so long as they used the same age for both males and females.

Frontiero v. Richardson also presents the rule-maker with options — either require all employees to demonstrate dependency, or extend dependency benefits to all spouses. The first option would have the same effect as the ultimate result in *Orr*: all spouses would have to show dependency in order to receive the benefits. Instead, the court extended the presumption of dependency to all spouses, putting the burden on Congress to eliminate the presumption if it so chose. Thus, in *Orr*, a benefit previously available only to women was extended to men, but only if they could prove dependency (which Mr. Orr could not). By contrast, in *Frontiero*, the effect of extending the benefit was to give a windfall to some employees — female as well as male. It seems clear enough why Mr. Orr should not have relief — escape from alimony obligations — simply because other husbands (dependent ones) were victims of unconstitutional discrimination: Mr. Orr was not like those other, dependent husbands. But should Sharron Frontiero and her husband receive dependency benefits when her husband was not a dependent, simply because some other potential claimants, who also were not dependent, were receiving them? Another way of looking at this issue is that while in *Reed*, *Orr*, *Craig*, and *Stanton* the Court forces the state to abandon gender-based stereotypes and adopt an approach that is *more* accurate, in *Frontiero*, extension of the presumption actually renders the fringe-benefit scheme *less* accurate. Should this be a problem, constitutionally speaking? Alternatively, does it reflect legitimate differences in the administrative burdens associated with individualized determinations of eligibility?

4. Who Is the Protected Victim?   One question in some of these cases is who the victim of discrimination is. In *Frontiero*, for example, is it the female wage-earner whose benefits are lower because her husband is not presumed to be a dependent, or the male dependent himself?

What are the consequences of the answer to this question? None, if you think that discrimination against men should be analyzed the same as discrimination against women. But Justice Rehnquist's view in his dissenting opinion in *Craig* (and other early cases) was that when the "victim" of the discrimination is male, the constitutional standard of review appropriate to other forms of "social welfare legislation" — i.e., the rational basis test — is all that is required (and that administrative convenience satisfies this standard). Consider this position, in light of the Court's view, shared by Chief Justice Rehnquist and explored in Chapter 2 of this book, that affirmative action plans designed to eliminate the effects of past discrimination against racial minorities be subject to the same strict standard as rules and practices that exclude or disadvantage those minorities.

One approach to the "victim" problem is reflected in such cases as *Orr* and *Craig*, but found frivolous by Justice Rehnquist in Footnote 2 to his dissent in *Craig*. That approach assumes that women are harmed not only by discrimination against them, but also by discrimination that favors them, when this benign discrimination reflects and thus perpetuates traditional stereotypes. How would you evaluate this claim? Are women harmed by preventing men from buying 3.2 percent beer? How? Does it matter what the legislative history of the statute suggests about the role of stereotypes? In *Craig*, the sparse information available on the state legislature's 1972 retention of different ages for alcohol purchases suggests the influence of religious fundamentalist concerns. The principal testimony opposing equalization of ages came from a minister who wanted to protect young men from the "pool, beer, and girls syndrome."[17]

Finally, Footnote 22 of Justice Brennan's opinion in *Frontiero* notes that the statutes at issue in that case were not designed to rectify the effects of past discrimination against women. If they had been so designed, should the result in the case be different? This issue is explored in Chapter 2.

5. The Equal Rights Amendment. The Equal Rights Amendment (ERA), discussed in both Justice Brennan's and Justice Powell's opinions in *Frontiero*, failed by three states to gain the support of two-thirds (38) of the states by the 1982 congressional deadline (a date extended three years beyond the original 1979 deadline). The proposed amendment read: "Equality of rights under the law shall not be denied or abridged by the United States or by any state on account of sex." The text of the amendment did not resolve when differences between the sexes justify different treatment. However, debate over the amendment generally assumed that it would require "strict scrutiny" of sex-based classifications, along the lines favored by four Justices in *Frontiero*.

The amendment, initially proposed in 1923, has been reintroduced in every congressional session since 1982, but it never emerged from committee. The United States is one of a small number of nations that does not have an explicit guarantee of women's rights in its Constitution. Opinion polls find support for such a guarantee; in one national survey, 82 percent of Americans believed that women's rights were already protected under the U.S. Constitution, and 69 percent supported amending the Constitution to include language that specifically protects women.[18]

Given such support, what has prevented passage? Opponents such as Concerned Women for America claim that women already have equal opportunity, and that the ERA will strip women of laws and institutions that protect them. One writer states that the ERA would eliminate the Violence Against Women Act, the Women's Bureau, the Office of Women's Health, National Women's History Month, and Mother's Day.[19] Commentator Christina Hoff Sommers believes the Amendment would "hand radical feminist groups . . . a powerful weapon" to achieve other "terrible" outcomes: "Boy Scouts would be forced to 'integrate,' sororities and fraternities would be eliminated or required to merge. . . . Single sex schools and summer camps for boys would be phased out."[20] The ERA website responds that the Amendment would not make all single-sex institutions unconstitutional, only those that "perpetuate the historical dominance of one sex over another."[21]

Supporters of the amendment have stepped up efforts in response to recent political pressure to roll back women's rights, especially with respect to reproductive health issues.[22]

Twenty states have enacted versions of an equal rights amendment in their own constitutions. While a few states have incorporated the same review standards as the federal Equal Protection Clause, and while numerous decisions interpreting state ERAs have not had the effect proponents may have desired,[23] one comprehensive review of state ERAs concluded that they have been "an extremely important tool in advancing sex equality for women,"[24] especially with respect to women's reproductive autonomy, disparate impact cases, and discrimination based on sexual orientation.[25] One commentator argues that state ERAs have often been deployed to protect men's rights instead of women's and to this extent are ineffective for women "except as symbols."[26] Formal equality, of course, does not distinguish between men's rights and women's rights. Is this a strength, or a weakness, of the formal equality principle?

Putting Theory Into Practice

1-5. In response to acts of violence in and around school by rival gangs, a school board instituted a ban on students wearing or displaying any gang symbol. This ban is interpreted in one school to bar males, but not females, from wearing earrings, because some males who wear earrings do so as a sign of gang allegiance, while earrings on females do not have any gang significance. Should the rule be allowed to stand? Does it offend formal equality principles? Would a dress code by a state employer that prevented males but not females from wearing earrings be permissible? Would it depend on the nature of the job (teacher versus police officer)?

1-6. In the United States today, women are excluded from the obligation to register with the military at age 18, and from some military combat positions. Based on the principles articulated in these materials, do you think these exclusions are constitutional?

1-7. A female U.S. Air Force fighter pilot challenges the constitutionality of regulations requiring female military personnel to be accompanied by a male companion and to wear a full-length dark abaya on trips off base in Saudi Arabia. The pilot claims that these regulations violate her equal rights.[27] Should she win?

3. Indirect Discrimination: Discrimination Based on Impact, Not Intent

The cases examined so far are examples of "facial" or "direct discrimination," which means that the classifications are explicitly based on sex. When an employer fires or fails to promote someone because of her sex, this is also a case of direct discrimination. Examples of direct discrimination under employment discrimination law are explored later in this chapter.

Discrimination can also be indirect, such as when a state acts on a basis other than sex, but the impact of its laws or practices disproportionately affects members of one sex. Personnel Administrator of Massachusetts v. Feeney, excerpted below, concerns the disproportionate effect of a veterans' preference system for state civil service positions.

Reading Questions

1. When a statute explicitly provides that only women may receive alimony, or assumes that only wives, not husbands, of service members are likely to be dependent, it is clear that the legislature "intends" to draw lines based on sex. A critical aspect of the *Feeney* case is whether the Massachusetts legislature "intended" to discriminate against women. Did it?
2. Give the best argument that it matters, for constitutional purposes, whether or not the Massachusetts legislature *meant to* disadvantage women. Give the best argument why intent should be irrelevant, as long as discriminatory impact is clear.
3. Justice Stewart's opinion states that "discriminatory intent is . . . either . . . a factor that has influenced the legislative choice or it is not." Is it that simple?

Personnel Administrator of Massachusetts v. Feeney

442 U.S. 256 (1979)

Mr. Justice STEWART delivered the opinion of the Court.

This case presents a challenge to the constitutionality of the Massachusetts veterans' preference statute . . . on the ground that it discriminates against women in violation of the Equal Protection Clause of the Fourteenth Amendment. Under [this statute], all veterans who qualify for state civil service positions must be considered for appointment ahead of any qualifying nonveterans. The preference operates overwhelmingly to the advantage of males.

The appellee Helen B. Feeney is not a veteran. She brought this action pursuant to 42 U.S.C. §1983, alleging that the absolute preference formula established in [the Massachusetts statute] inevitably operates to exclude women from consideration for the best Massachusetts civil service jobs and thus unconstitutionally denies them the equal protection of the laws. The three-judge District Court agreed, one judge dissenting. . . .

---

42 U.S.C. §1983, commonly referred to as **Section 1983** (or §1983), is part of the Civil Rights Act of 1871, which creates a civil damages action against anyone who, under color of any statute, regulation, or custom, causes anyone to be deprived of any rights, privileges, or immunities secured by the Constitution and laws. The "42" preceding the U.S.C. reference in the citation indicates the volume number of the United States Code.

Under color of law refers to action taken under state or federal law. Section 1983 has generated a vast and complex body of doctrine about what legal violation can serve as the basis of a §1983 action. In *Feeney*, the potential legal violation involved the Equal Protection Clause of the U.S. Constitution.

The Federal Government and virtually all of the States grant some sort of hiring preference to veterans. The Massachusetts preference, which is loosely termed an "absolute lifetime" preference, is among the most generous. It applies to all positions in the State's classified civil service, which constitute approximately 60% of the public jobs in the State. It is available to "any person, male or female, including a nurse," who was honorably discharged from the United States Armed Forces after at least 90 days of active service, at least one day of which was during "wartime." Persons who are deemed veterans and who are otherwise qualified for a particular civil service job may exercise the preference at any time and as many times as they wish. . . .

[The record shows that Ms. Feeney, who entered the state civil service system in 1963, did quite well in the competitive civil service examinations she took in order to obtain a promotion, but was "consistently eclipsed by veterans."] . . .

The sole question for decision on this appeal is whether Massachusetts, in granting an absolute lifetime preference to veterans, has discriminated against women in violation of the Equal Protection Clause of the Fourteenth Amendment. . . .

The cases of Washington v. Davis, [1976], and Arlington Heights v. Metropolitan Housing Dev. Corp., [1977], recognize that when a neutral law has a disparate impact upon a group that has historically been the victim of discrimination, an unconstitutional purpose may still be at work. But those cases signaled no departure from the settled rule that the Fourteenth Amendment guarantees equal laws, not equal results. *Davis* upheld a job-related employment test that white people passed in proportionately greater numbers than Negroes, for there had been no showing that racial discrimination entered into the establishment or formulation of the test. *Arlington Heights* upheld a zoning board decision that tended to perpetuate racially segregated housing patterns, since, apart from its effect, the board's decision was shown to be nothing more than an application of a constitutionally neutral zoning policy. Those principles apply with equal force to a case involving alleged gender discrimination.

When a statute, gender-neutral on its face, is challenged on the ground that its effects upon women are disproportionably adverse, a twofold inquiry is thus appropriate. The first question is whether the statutory classification is indeed neutral in the sense that it is not gender-based. If the classification itself, covert or overt, is not based upon gender, the second question is whether the adverse effect reflects invidious gender-based discrimination. . . . In this second inquiry, impact provides an "important starting point," but purposeful discrimination is "the condition that offends the Constitution." . . .

Veteran status is not uniquely male. Although few women benefit from the preference the nonveteran class is not substantially all female. To the contrary, significant numbers of nonveterans are men, and all nonveterans—male as well as female—are placed at a disadvantage. Too many men are affected by [the statute] to permit the inference that the statute is but a pretext for preferring men over women. . . .

Discriminatory intent is . . . either . . . a factor that has influenced the legislative choice or it is not. The District Court's conclusion that the absolute veterans' preference was not originally enacted or subsequently reaffirmed for the purpose of giving an advantage to males as such necessarily compels the conclusion that the State . . . intended nothing more than to prefer "veterans." Given this finding, simple logic suggests that an intent to exclude women from significant public jobs was not at work in this law. To reason that it was, by describing the preference as "inherently nonneutral" or "gender-biased," is merely to restate the fact of impact, not to answer the question of intent. . . .

The basic distinction between veterans and nonveterans, having been found not gender-based, and the goals of the preference having been found worthy, [the statute] must be analyzed as is any other neutral law that casts a greater burden upon women as a group than upon men as a group. The enlistment policies of the Armed Services may well have discriminated on the basis of sex. . . . But the history of discrimination against women in the military is not on trial in this case. . . .

"Discriminatory purpose" . . . implies more than intent as volition or intent as awareness of consequences. . . . It implies that the decisionmaker, in this case a state legislature, selected or reaffirmed a particular course of action at least in part "because of," not merely "in spite of," its adverse effects upon an identifiable group. Yet, nothing in the record demonstrates that this preference for veterans was originally devised or subsequently re-enacted because it would accomplish the collateral goal of keeping women in a stereotypic and predefined place in the Massachusetts Civil Service. . . .

Veterans' hiring preferences represent an awkward—and, many argue, unfair—exception to the widely shared view that merit and merit alone should prevail in the employment policies of government. After a war, such laws have been enacted virtually without opposition. During peacetime, they inevitably have come to be viewed in many quarters as undemocratic and unwise. Absolute and permanent preferences, as the troubled history of this law demonstrates, have always been subject to the objection that they give the veteran more than a square deal. But the Fourteenth Amendment "cannot be made a refuge from ill-advised . . . laws." . . . . The substantial edge granted to veterans by [the Massachusetts statute] may reflect unwise policy. The appellee, however, has simply failed to demonstrate that the law in any way reflects a purpose to discriminate on the basis of sex.

The judgment is reversed, and the case is remanded for further proceedings consistent with this opinion. . . .

Mr. Justice MARSHALL, with whom Mr. Justice BRENNAN joins, dissenting. . . .

In the instant case, the impact of the Massachusetts statute on women is undisputed. Any veteran with a passing grade on the civil service exam must be placed ahead of a nonveteran, regardless of their respective scores. The District Court found that, as a practical matter, this preference supplants test results as the determinant of upper level civil service appointments. . . . Because less than 2% of the women in Massachusetts are veterans, the absolute-preference formula has rendered desirable state civil service employment an almost exclusively male prerogative. . . .

As the District Court recognized, this consequence follows foreseeably, indeed inexorably, from the long history of policies severely limiting women's participation in the military. . . .

The legislative history of the statute reflects the Commonwealth's patent appreciation of the impact the preference system would have on women, and an equally evident desire to mitigate that impact only with respect to certain traditionally female occupations. Until 1971, the statute and implementing civil service regulations exempted from operation of the preference any job requisitions "especially calling for women." . . . In practice, this exemption, coupled with the absolute preference for veterans, has created a gender-based civil service hierarchy, with women occupying low-grade clerical and secretarial jobs and men holding more responsible and remunerative positions. . . .

Thus, for over 70 years, the Commonwealth has maintained, as an integral part of its veterans' preference system, an exemption relegating female civil service applicants to occupations traditionally filled by women. Such a statutory scheme both reflects and perpetuates precisely the kind of archaic assumptions about women's roles which we have previously held invalid. . . . The Court's conclusion to the contrary — that "nothing in the record" evinces a "collateral goal of keeping women in a stereotypic and predefined place in the Massachusetts Civil Service" — displays a singularly myopic view of the facts established below.

To survive challenge under the Equal Protection Clause, statutes reflecting gender-based discrimination must be substantially related to the achievement of important governmental objectives. . . . Appellants here advance three interests in support of the absolute-preference system: (1) assisting veterans in their readjustment to civilian life; (2) encouraging military enlistment; and

(3) rewarding those who have served their country. . . . Although each of those goals is unquestionably legitimate, the "mere recitation of a benign, compensatory purpose" cannot of itself insulate legislative classifications from constitutional scrutiny. . . . And in this case, the Commonwealth has failed to establish a sufficient relationship between its objectives and the means chosen to effectuate them. . . .

[The statute is "overinclusive" in allowing veterans to use the advantage repeatedly, without regard to their date of discharge. It is not well suited to inducing enlistment because it bestows benefits on men drafted as well as those who volunteered. It operates by exacting a substantial price from a discrete group of individuals instead of distributing its costs across the taxpaying public. Finally, there are less discriminatory means of accomplishing the Commonwealth's goal.]

I would affirm the judgment of the court below.

NOTE ON DISCRIMINATORY INTENT

Did the Idaho and Alabama legislatures in *Reed* and *Orr* "intend" to disadvantage people because of their sex? Probably not, but the point of these cases is that laws based on stereotyped thinking about women are unacceptable, even if — perhaps *especially* if — they are unintentional.

Why, then, in *Feeney*, does the Court allow to stand a system that has a substantially disproportionate impact against women — a much greater practical impact, indeed, than the statutes in *Reed* and *Orr*? One explanation is that an explicit sex-based distinction is, by definition, discriminatory (whether or not it is justified), while it is less clear that a rule or practice that does not make an explicit sex-based distinction has, in fact, discriminated based on sex.

Does it follow that intent should be required in order to establish sex discrimination in cases such as *Feeney* where the challenged statute is neutral on its face? On the one hand, as noted above, without such a requirement it is harder to know if the classification reflects discrimination or some more benign explanation. On the other hand, rules and practices that are not explicitly sex-based but that have a disproportionate, negative impact against women may be even more dangerous than cases of explicit sex-based discrimination; the stereotypes that guide decisionmaking in such cases may be more hidden and thus easier to perpetuate. In fact, Title VII of the Civil Rights Act of 1964, explored later in this chapter, requires that rules and practices in the employment context that have a disparate impact on women and minorities be job-related, regardless of the "intent" of the employer.

Ironically, some direct or explicit sex-based classifications are actually "saved" by the intention to discriminate. For example, in the 1981 case of Rostker v. Goldberg (discussed in Chapter 3), the Supreme Court upheld a male-only draft registration system on the theory that, since females could not serve in combat, they were not likely to be subjected to future drafts.[28] Because reasons for the exclusion of women were well reviewed in the legislative history, the statute was not an "accidental by-product" of narrow, outmoded stereotypes about women, but a deliberate, reasoned choice. Similarly, in Mississippi University for Women (MUW) v. Hogan, discussed in Chapter 2, the Court's conclusion that an all-female state-supported nursing school was a violation of equal protection turned in part on the origins of the school and stereotyped notions about what it was appropriate to train women to do.[29] Justice O'Connor suggests in her opinion for the Court that if the intent had been to compensate women for the disadvantage they experienced in their educational or employment opportunities, another result might have followed. An example in the affirmative action context is Contractors Ass'n of Eastern Pennsylvania v. City of Philadelphia, which held that an affirmative action plan favoring women will pass intermediate scrutiny if it is shown to be "a product of analysis rather than a stereotyped reaction based on habit."[30]

To the extent that a showing of discriminatory intent seems desirable, how should it be demonstrated? In Feeney, the fact that few women qualified as veterans is taken as a neutral fact that disproves discriminatory intent. Is this analysis sound?

Putting Theory Into Practice

1-8. A Veterans Administration rule requires that all chaplains at VA hospitals be "ordained" clergy members. The requirement is shown to have a disparate impact on women because the Roman Catholic Church, among others, will not ordain women as priests. Does the rule offend formal equality principles? Is this an example of direct, or indirect discrimination, or neither?

1-9. Although women make up about 50 percent of medical school graduates, only about 15 percent of surgeons are women. A significant part of the gender gap is thought to be attributable to the high stress and irregular hours involved in the surgical profession.[31] Is this a problem? If so, does a public medical school or public hospital have any responsibility for addressing it?

C. FORMAL EQUALITY IN EMPLOYMENT

The preceding cases involve constitutional challenges to classifications by Congress or state legislatures. The U.S. Constitution, of course, is but one legal tool to address sex-based discrimination—one that, as noted above, only applies to the state or someone acting under authority of the state. Other important sources of authority are laws passed by Congress or a state or local legislative body, executive orders, and administrative regulations. Important federal statutes include the Equal Pay Act of 1963,[32] which requires employers to give women and men equal pay for equal work, and Title VII of the Civil

Rights Act of 1964 (Title VII),[33] which prohibits employers from discriminating with respect to the compensation, terms, conditions, or privileges of employment based on the individual's race, color, religion, sex, or national origin. Both of these statutes track formal equality principles in ways that are illustrated in the discussion that follows.

Equal Pay Act:

Employers must pay women and men equal pay for equal work.

Title VII:

Employers may not discriminate in compensation or terms and conditions of employment based on race, color, religion, sex, or national origin.

---

1. The Equal Pay Act: Formal Equality Paradigm

The Equal Pay Act requires that men and women receive "equal pay" for "equal work." Equal work is defined as "jobs the performance of which requires equal skills, effort, and responsibility, and which are performed under similar working conditions." The Act includes some exceptions for factors not related to sex, such as a seniority or merit system.

EEOC v. Madison Community Unit School District No. 12, set forth below, concerns whether high school coaches of female athletic teams must be paid the same as the coaches of male athletic teams. In examining possible differences between the jobs (to ascertain whether the jobs were equal, as claimed by plaintiffs), the court attempts to steer a course between allowing any small difference between jobs to justify pay differentials, which would defeat the purpose of the Act, and requiring pay equity between "comparable" male and female jobs, which is more than the Act explicitly mandates. Applying the usual standard of deference to trial court findings unless they are "clearly erroneous," the appellate court accepts the trial court's conclusion that the coaching jobs for boys' and girls' teams in the same sport amounted to "equal work," but not the coaching jobs for boys' and girls' teams in different sports.

The school district claimed that the pay differential did not violate the Act because it was based on the sex of the teams, not the sex of the coaches. The appellate court rejected this argument, stating that while, under the right circumstances, this defense might be viable, it was not credible in this case because the school district had discouraged females from applying for coaching positions for male teams. "An employer cannot divide equal work into two job classifications that carry unequal pay, forbid women to compete for one of the classifications, and defend the resulting inequality in pay between men and women by reference to a 'factor other than [the] sex' of the employees."[34]

Reading Questions

1. Is coaching a girls' softball team and a boys' hardball team "equal work"? Are the two sports the same? How about girls' basketball and boys' track? What significance, if any, should be placed on the number of assistant coaches the teams have, or differences in the athletic ability of girls and boys?
2. Is coaching a male college basketball team that draws a large crowd, attracts attention from the media, and raises substantial revenue a different job than coaching a female team that is less popular? If so, does this justify large differences in pay between the two coaches?

EEOC v. Madison Community Unit School District No. 12

818 F.2d 577 (7th Cir. 1987)

POSNER, Circuit Judge.

The Equal Employment Opportunity Commission brought this suit against the school district of Madison, Illinois, charging that the district was paying female athletic coaches in its high school and junior high school less than male coaches, in violation of the Equal Pay Act of 1963. . . .

The **Equal Employment Opportunity Commission (EEOC)** is the federal agency charged with enforcing Title VII and other employment discrimination laws. Ordinarily, claimants must file a claim with the EEOC before they can bring a lawsuit in court. The EEOC issues regulations to guide employers, employees, and the courts about how to interpret Title VII.

The trial brought out the following facts:

[Luvenia] Long was paid substantially less for coaching girls' track than Steptoe, a man, was paid for coaching boys' track. Although the boys' track program included more students and had more meets than the girls', Steptoe had two assistant coaches compared to Long's one, and as a result Long and Steptoe devoted approximately equal time to their coaching jobs. Long also coached the girls' tennis team, and Jakich, a man, the boys' tennis team; and Jakich was paid more than Long even though there were no significant differences between the teams in number of students, length of season, or number of practice sessions; however, the boys' team played almost twice as many matches as the girls' team. Long was also assistant coach of the girls' basketball team one year and received lower pay than Tyus, the male assistant coach of the boys' track team. The district judge found that the work of the two assistant coaches was substantially equal and required the same skill, effort, and responsibility—except that Long worked longer hours than Tyus. [Carol] Cole, who coached the girls' volleyball, girls' basketball, and girls' softball teams, was paid less for coaching volleyball than the male coach of the boys' soccer team, less for coaching basketball than the male coach of the boys' soccer team, and less for coaching softball than the male coach of the boys' baseball team. Also, as assistant coach of the girls' track team she was paid less than the assistant coach of the boys' track team. In all of these cases the judge found that the work of the female coach and her male counterpart was the same in skill, effort (including time), and responsibility. Any potential differences in effort and responsibility stemming from the fact that the boys' teams were sometimes larger and played longer seasons were, he found, offset by the fact that the head coaches of the boys' teams had more assistants than their female counterparts. . . .

The first question we must decide is whether the pairs of jobs that the district judge compared in finding unequal pay are sufficiently similar to be "equal work" within the meaning of the Equal Pay Act. The Act is not a general mandate of sex-neutral compensation. It does not enact "comparable worth" — the principle that wages should be based on "objective" factors, rather than on market conditions of demand and supply which may depress wages in jobs held mainly by women relative to wages in jobs held mainly by men. . . . A female secretary paid less than a male janitor cannot complain under the Equal Pay Act that the disparity in their wages is not justified by "objective" factors such as differences in skill, responsibility, and effort. . . . The Act requires equal pay only when men and women are performing "equal work on jobs the performance of which requires equal skill, effort, and responsibility, and which are performed under similar working conditions." The working conditions of a janitor are different from those of a secretary, and so are the skills and responsibilities of the two jobs. The Act does not prohibit paying different wages even if the result is to pay a woman less than a man and by doing so "underpay" her because the difference in the wage rate is greater than necessary to compensate the male for any greater skill, effort, or responsibility required by, or any inferior working conditions encountered in, his job.

Thus the jobs that are compared must be in some sense the same to count as "equal work" under the Equal Pay Act; and here we come to the main difficulty in applying the Act: whether two jobs are the same depends on how fine a system of job classifications the courts will accept. If coaching an athletic team in the Madison, Illinois school system is considered a single job rather than a congeries of jobs, the school district violated the Equal Pay Act prima facie by paying female holders of this job less than male holders, and the only question is whether the district carried its burden of proving that the lower wages which the four female coaches received were lower than the wages of their male counterparts because of a factor other than sex. If on the other hand coaching the girls' tennis team is considered a different job from coaching the boys' tennis team, and a fortiori if coaching the girls' volleyball or basketball team is considered a different job (or jobs) from coaching the boys' soccer team, there is no prima facie violation. So the question is how narrow a definition of job the courts should be using in deciding whether the Equal Pay Act is applicable.

. . . The Act requires that the jobs compared have "similar working conditions," not the same working conditions. This implies that some comparison of different jobs is possible. It is true that similarity of working conditions between the jobs being compared is not enough to bring the Act into play — the work must be "equal" and the jobs must require "equal" skill, effort, and responsibility, as well as similar working conditions. But since the working conditions need not be "equal," the jobs need not be completely identical.

Estimating and comparing the skill, effort, responsibility, and working conditions in two jobs are factual determinations. . . . We can overturn them, therefore, only if they are clearly erroneous. . . . The district judge found (among other things) that coaching a girls' tennis team is sufficiently like coaching a boys' tennis team, coaching a girls' softball team is sufficiently like coaching a boys' hardball team, and, indeed, coaching a girls' volleyball or basketball team is sufficiently like coaching a boys' soccer team, to allow each pair of jobs to be described as involving equal work, as requiring equal skill, effort, and responsibility, and as being performed under similar working conditions. . . .

There are pitfalls in allowing any comparisons between different jobs, and they are illustrated by this case. One is a tendency to focus entirely on the measurable differences and ignore the equally or more important but less readily measurable ones. The witnesses in this case concentrated on the amount of skill and time required for coaching girls' and boys' teams and paid little attention to responsibility. It may be true that because the boys' teams tend to have more assistant coaches than the girls' teams, the head coaches of the boys' teams put in no more time than the head coaches of the girls' teams even when the boys' teams are larger and play more matches. But normally there is greater responsibility (one of the dimensions in which the statute requires equality between the jobs compared) if you have a staff than if you don't. That is one reason why the president of a company is paid more than a junior executive who, lacking staff assistance, may work longer hours. . . .

Another difference tends to be ignored when effort, which is hard to measure, is equated to time, which is easy to measure. Boys and girls differ on average in strength, speed, and perhaps other dimensions of athletic ability; there may also be important differences in their attitudes toward athletic competition. The differences between boys and girls in athletic aptitude and interest may make coaching a boys' team harder — or easier — than coaching a girls' team; there can be no confidence that the two jobs require equal effort. . . . The Act did not seek to eliminate whatever differences between the sexes might make it harder to coach a boys' team than a girls' team. If it is harder (we are not saying it is harder — we are just discussing possibilities), the statutory requirement of equal effort is not met and the differential in pay is outside the scope of the Act.

Nevertheless, we are unwilling to hold that coaches of girls' and boys' teams can never be found to be doing equal work requiring equal skill, effort, and responsibility and performed under similar working conditions. Above the lowest rank of employee, every employee has a somewhat different job from every other one, even if the two employees being compared are in the same department. So if "equal work" and "equal skill, effort, and responsibility" were taken literally, the Act would have a minute domain. . . .

But the words "very much alike," "closely related," or, as the cases sometimes say, "substantially equal" — even the words "virtually identical" — are not synonymous with "identical." . . . There is a gray area, which we must be vigilant to police, between "very much alike," which is within the scope of the Act, and "comparable," which is outside; for it is plain that Congress did not want to enact comparable worth as part of the Equal Pay Act of 1964. . . .

[The court upholds the trial court's determination that coaching a girls' team and a boys' team are sufficiently alike to be equal work with the Equal Pay Act, but that coaching teams of different sports is not. It also holds that even if there were reasons unrelated to the sex of the coaches that coaches of male teams were paid more than coaches of female teams, the failure of the school district to allow women to apply to be coaches of male teams would "[cast] doubt on the bona fides of the school district's claim. . . ."]

The reason for discouraging women from coaching boys' teams was that the school authorities were concerned about the "locker room problem." This may or may not be a good reason . . . but it does suggest that women receive less pay than men for doing what the district court found was equal work within the meaning of the Equal Pay Act because they are women; their sex makes them ineligible to receive the higher wage that men receive for equal work. Even if the school district is entitled to insist that coaches and coached be of the same sex, if the work of each coach is the same and the reason for the difference in pay is the difference in the sex of the coach, the Equal Pay Act is violated. An employer cannot divide equal work into two job classifications that carry unequal pay, forbid women to compete for one of the classifications, and defend the resulting inequality in pay between men and women by reference to a "factor other than [the] sex" of the employees. . . . It would not be the sexual segregation that had caused the inequality in pay, but a decision to pay men more for doing the same work as women (albeit with a "clientele" of a different sex from the women's "clientele").

Notes

1. **The Formal Equality Paradigm.**   The Equal Pay Act of 1963 is a paradigmatic application of formal equality principles. The main interpretative task is defining what work is equal. It obviously would be unfair to allow employers to circumvent the Act by minor variations in job titles or job descriptions. Thus, the Act has been applied to require the same wages for different job classifications entailing substantially equal duties and involving comparable skill, responsibility, and effort, such as female "cleaners" and male "janitors," "beauticians" and "barbers," and "seamstresses" and "tailors."[35]

Successful Equal Pay Act cases, however, are relatively rare, particularly in cases involving upper-level employees. The main problem with administrative and executive positions is the difficulty of finding a close enough comparison. Courts generally require the plaintiff in an Equal Pay Act suit to identify a particular employee who is earning more for the same work, and it is more difficult to compare the substance of white-collar jobs than lower-level positions.[36] A representative example is Georgen-Saad v. Texas Mutual Insurance Co.[37] There, the plaintiff, a Senior Vice President of Finance, alleged underpayment in comparison with other senior vice presidents in the company. The court dismissed that claim on the ground that "the assertion that any one of these jobs requires 'equal skill, effort, and responsibility' . . . cannot be taken seriously. . . . These are Senior Vice Presidents in charge of different aspects of Defendant's operation; these are not assembly-line workers or customer-service representatives." In the court's view, the Equal Pay Act could deal with "commodity-like" work, not the functions of high-level executives.

The Equal Pay Act addresses unjustified wage differentials based on sex but does not deal with gender biases that underlie the disparities. For example, the Act would not encompass discriminatory behavior that may have prevented women from becoming coaches of male sports teams at Madison Community Unit School. Such claims would need to proceed under Title VII, discussed below. Moreover, the law allows employers to raise four affirmative defenses to proven pay disparities, one of which is proof that the decision was based on a "factor other than sex."

Plaintiffs can bring wage discrimination claims under Title VII as well as the Equal Pay Act, but specific legislation applies the Equal Pay Act's affirmative defenses to compensation claims brought under Title VII.

2. Lilly Ledbetter and Pay Discrimination Claims under Title VII. Plaintiffs can bring wage discrimination claims under Title VII as well as the Equal Pay Act. The Equal Pay Act has some advantages, including a longer statute of limitations and the lack of an intent requirement, but under Title VII, a plaintiff can prove wage discrimination without necessarily proving that a man was being paid more than a woman for the same job.

The Supreme Court considered a Title VII wage discrimination claim in Ledbetter v. Goodyear Tire & Rubber Co. in 2006, a case that captured the public attention and led to Congressional action.[38] The lawsuit was brought by Lilly Ledbetter, the only female production supervisor at a Goodyear plant in Gadsen, Alabama. She proved to a jury that she suffered illegal pay discrimination on the basis of sex—her salary was as much as 40 percent lower than that of the lowest-paid male supervisor—and was awarded the maximum available damages under Title VII. On appeal, Goodyear successfully argued before the Eleventh Circuit that her claim was time-barred because every discriminatory pay decision occurred more than 180 days prior to when she first filed a charge with the EEOC.[39] Title VII provides that an EEOC charge must be brought within 180 or 300 days (depending on the jurisdiction) "after the alleged unlawful employment practice occurred." There are three possible dates from which the 180-/300-day clock could run: (1) from the date of the pay decision that sets a discriminatory wage, (2) from the date an employee learns her pay is discriminatory (a "discovery" rule), or (3) from the date any paycheck that contains an amount affected by a prior discriminatory pay decision is issued (this is deemed a "paycheck accrual" rule). The Supreme Court opted for the first approach, holding that a plaintiff has 180/300 days after the pay decision that sets the discriminatory wage to file her charge with the EEOC in compliance with Title VII's statute of limitations. The majority flatly rejected the paycheck accrual rule, reasoning that a paycheck containing a discriminatory amount of money is not a present violation, but, instead, is merely the present effect of a prior act of discrimination. "[C]urrent effects alone cannot breathe life into prior, charged discrimination," the Court wrote; "such effects have no present legal consequences."[40]

Statute of Limitations. A statute of limitations is the period after which the wrong complained of occurred within which a lawsuit must be filed. As the *Ledbetter* case illustrates, some difficult questions can arise over the date from which a statute of limitations begins to run.

The Supreme Court's ruling in *Ledbetter* provoked public outrage, and efforts to overrule it by legislation began immediately. Although *Ledbetter* dealt with a rather technical rule, it promised significantly adverse effects for victims of pay discrimination unless they were able to quickly perceive and promptly complain about pay disparities. After President Barack Obama was elected, a new version of the bill, the Lilly Ledbetter Fair Pay Act of 2009, was passed and it became the first bill signed into law during his presidency.[41] The new law provides that an

> unlawful employment practice occurs, with respect to discrimination in compensation in violation of this title, when a discriminatory compensation decision or other practice is adopted, when an individual becomes subject to a discriminatory compensation decision or other practice, or when an individual is affected by application of a discriminatory compensation decision or other practice, including each time wages, benefits, or other compensation is paid, resulting in whole or in part from such a decision or other practice.

In effect, the Act takes a broad view of the employment practices that trigger the limitations period under Title VII, adopting the "paycheck accrual" rule that the Supreme Court rejected in *Ledbetter*. Lilly Ledbetter, who campaigned for the Act and testified before Congress, received no benefit from the law in her name, since her jury verdict was vacated and subject to no further appeals. But she became a civil rights folk hero who does extensive public speaking and published a memoir in 2012, entitled Grace and Grit: My Fight for Equal Pay at Goodyear and Beyond.

Litigation over the meaning of the Act has continued. Regardless of how broadly the Ledbetter Act is construed, however, it deals only with the narrow issue of the statute of limitations and does nothing to deal with other obstacles to successful proof of pay discrimination.[42] Pay secrecy, a well-documented phenomenon, is just one of those obstacles.[43] The Paycheck Fairness Act (PFA) has been introduced in several sessions of Congress to make it easier to prove wage discrimination.[44] Among other changes, the PFA would expand damages under the EPA and narrow the fourth affirmative defense, which allows employers to justify pay disparities by "any factor other than sex." It also calls for data collection and voluntary guidelines for employers to evaluate jobs in order to eliminate unfair pay disparities. The bill was introduced in the Senate most recently in January 2013.

3. The Wage Gap.   Although the wage gap between women's and men's earnings has been slowly eroding, it remains significant. Adjusting for hours worked (but not for differences in education, experience, or time in the work force), women's median weekly earnings are about 81 percent those of men, as compared to 62 percent in 1979. The gap is narrower among African-Americans (93.5 percent), Hispanics (90.7 percent), and Asians (83 percent).[45] The bulk of the reduction occurred in the 1970s and 1980s; very little has changed since 1990.[46] At current rates of change, it would take an estimated half-century to achieve gender parity.[47]

The disparity for older women is greater than for younger men. For example, full-time working women in the 16-24 age bracket earned on average 95 percent of what men earn; women in the 55-64 age range earn only 75 percent.[48] Particularly in higher paid occupations, including law, the gender gap increases over women's life cycle.

Part of the explanation for the overall gender gap in wages is the occupational distribution of male and female workers. As compared to men, women are much less likely to work in construction, production, utilities, or transportation jobs and are more likely to work in administrative support occupations.[49] Although women are more likely than men to work in professional and related occupations, they are concentrated in the lower-paying positions within this job group such as elementary school teaching. Only 8 percent of working women are employed in the high-paying occupations within computer and engineering fields, compared with 43 percent of working men. Instead, 69 percent of professional women work in the lower-paying fields of education and health care, compared with 31 percent of male professionals in these occupational groups.[50] Women comprise 12.9 percent of engineers, but 86 percent of paralegals.[51]

Even in jobs in which women are concentrated, women earn less than men. For example, female elementary and middle school teachers earn 90.9 percent of what men earn; female registered nurses earn 86.5 percent of what men earn; and women administrative assistants earn 90.6 percent.[52] On average, among full-time, year-round workers, U.S. women earn $36,877 annually, as compared to $47,905 for men—resulting in an average disparity of $425,000 over a 40-year career.[53] For a woman with a bachelor's degree or higher, the difference can be more than $700,000; in law, the career wage gap averages almost $1.5 million.[54]

Moreover, women have not all benefited equally from the shrinking of the wage gap. For instance, although earnings for women with college degrees have increased more than earnings for males with college degrees, the wage disparity between men and women with higher education continues to be larger than it is for the overall population (74 percent those with college or doctoral degrees, and 72 percent for professional degrees).[55] Similarly, while women now constitute about half of the workforce in occupations typified by high earnings (executive, administrative, and managerial positions), these female employees earn only 73.5 percent of what their male colleagues earn and are underrepresented in the best-paid positions.[56] With the exception of Asians, women of color are at the bottom of the economic scale. In 2010, the median weekly earnings for men and women broken down by race were Asian men, $936; Asian women, $773; white men, $850; white women, $684; African-American men, $633; African-American women, $592; Hispanic or Latino men, $560; Hispanic or Latino women, $508.[57]

The wage disparity between male and female employees is greater if part-time employees are included; approximately one-quarter of women are part-time employees, compared with only 13 percent of men. These jobs tend to be paid less on a pro rata basis than full-time jobs, and carry fewer benefits. Women are also more likely to take time out of the labor force for caregiving or other household responsibilities, which disrupts their earning potential.[58] (The relationship between women's choices and pay equity is explored more fully in Chapter 2.) But, even in the aggregate, nothing explains the full wage gap; discrimination accounts for some of it.[59] For example, part of the wage gap is sometimes attributed to differing degrees of labor force attachment between men and women. Yet, women who work year-round and full time during at least 12 of 15 consecutive years earn only 64 percent of what men with a similar attachment to the labor force earn.[60] There is also affirmative evidence of discrimination, including a well-documented "wage premium" for married men that is not evident in the pay of married women; a wage penalty for mothers, but not fathers; and a penalty for women's leaves based on the expectation that they will take longer and more frequent leaves than they typically do.[61]

4. Factors Justifying Differences in Pay. How should courts treat pay disparities that are attributable to market conditions and practices? Consider an employer's willingness to match a worker's salary at a previous position. This common practice is, on the one hand, a practical response to competitive market conditions; on the other hand, it serves to immunize pay disparities that begin elsewhere and to perpetuate the social conditions that the Equal Pay Act was designed to eliminate.

The problem is aggravated by the fact that women do not negotiate as effectively as men for their own salaries. One illustrative study found that male Carnegie Mellon graduates were eight times more likely to negotiate a starting salary than their female classmates.[62]

Courts have not been uniform in their approach to wage disparities based on matching offers and similar market forces.[63] Where there is evidence of past discrimination, however, market forces are not usually adequate to prove that the discrimination was for a reason other than sex. In Corning Glass Works v. Brennan, for example, the Supreme Court rejected an employer's claim that market forces justified paying more to night workers than day workers given that women had previously been excluded from such positions.[64]

A case study in the difficulties of applying equal pay principles involves athletic coaches. Women hold fewer than 3.5 percent of the coaching jobs in men's sports in all divisions and the coaches for men's teams are paid more than twice the amount paid to coaches for women's teams.[65] The percentage of women who are head coaches of women's teams has also declined from 90 percent to 42 percent since enactment of Title IX, largely due to the increase in resources and status of women's sports.[66] What might justify the substantial pay differential between male and female coaches? Should differences in athletic team revenues justify differences in salaries? Judge Posner in *Madison* sees no problem with a revenue-based criterion as long as women have equal access to the higher paid coaching jobs. Under his analysis, however, failure to treat male and female applicants equally would not only violate Title VII, but it would also help establish an equal pay claim because (1) it means the woman's sex *is* a reason for the difference in pay; and (2) it "casts doubt on the bona fides" of the employer's justifications for gender disparities in compensation.

In an effort to clarify the treatment of sex-based pay disparities in coaching under the Equal Pay Act and Title VII discussed below, the federal Equal Employment Opportunity Commission has promulgated guidelines providing that relevant factors justifying pay differences include experience, duties, and working conditions. Under the guidelines, however, where job responsibilities are equivalent and the primary justification for a salary disparity is the profitability of the sport or prevailing wage rates, then sex-based disparities can constitute an equal pay violation. To justify differential salaries based on differential revenues, the institution must demonstrate that the revenue discrepancy in no way relates to (1) institutional discrimination in opportunity, or (2) societal discrimination. In effect, the school must show that the female coach received the same opportunities as the male coach to be a revenue producer, and that the differences in revenue did not relate to lower interest in female sports or fewer resources for female athletic programs. The Guidelines also made clear that that "[s]ex discrimination in the marketplace which results in lower pay for jobs done by women will not support the marketplace value defense."[67]

5. "Comparable Worth" or "Pay Equity." Should teachers and secretaries be paid less than sanitation workers, maintenance staff, and mechanics?

Should child care workers be paid less than gas station attendants and pet sitters? What do you suppose explains the differences? Can they be successfully challenged through the principle of formal equality?

As noted above, the Equal Pay Act covers only "equal pay" for "equal work." An alternative concept, referred to as comparable worth or pay equity, seeks not only to ensure equal pay for equal work, but also to achieve salary comparability for workers in different, sex-segregated job classifications requiring equivalent degrees of training, experience, and effort. In EEOC v. Madison Community Unit School District No. 12, Justice Posner makes clear that the Equal Pay Act does not encompass comparable worth.[68] Chapter 2 discusses state and federal efforts to review the pattern of low salaries in job categories in which women have been traditionally concentrated.

Putting Theory Into Practice

1-10. As head coach of the University of Southern California women's basketball team, Marianne Stanley led her team to four national championships. In 1993, she sought a salary increase from $60,000 to $150,000, to match that paid to George Raveling, the head coach of the men's basketball team. At that time, she had brought her team to the previous three NCAA Tournaments, where it advanced to the round of 16 in 1993 and the final eight in 1992. She was named PAC-10 Coach-of-the-Year in 1993. Raveling's team had never won a national championship and did not have as good an NCAA Tournament record. Stanley had 17 years of coaching experience, as compared to Raveling's 31 years' coaching experience and nine years of marketing and promotional experience outside of coaching.

Both head coaches recruited student athletes, coached basketball, provided academic guidance to team members and supervised their coaching staffs. Coach Raveling was under more pressure to increase the number of spectators in order to help alleviate the million-and-a-half dollar deficit in the athletic department. The pressure was created by the media, the public, and the school's administration and donors, which made the men's basketball team a far more significant source of funds and school loyalty than the women's team. The average number of spectators for a men's basketball game, was 4,103; for a women's game, the average was 762. Stanley made herself available for public appearances but was not required to make any specific number of them, while Raveling's contract required participation in at least 12 outside speaking engagements per year and availability to the media for interviews.

While Stanley was head coach, the USC women's basketball program produced just under $60,000 in revenue. During the same period, the men's basketball program produced revenue of over $4.5 million from ticket sales, broadcast right fees, cable television right fees, PAC-10 conference revenue sharing, guarantees from away games, post-season revenue sharing, and endowment income. Supporters of the men's team donated close to $100,000, as compared to under $13,000 by supporters of the women's team.

Should the Equal Pay Act require that USC pay Stanley as much as it pays Raveling?

What if Raveling argues that he could obtain competing job offers much higher than Stanley because male, but not female, college teams compete for talent with professional sports? Is your answer affected by the fact that when Pat Summit of the University of Tennessee became the first coach in Division 1 college basketball history—man or woman—to coach a team to 1,000 wins, she still made less than half of the salaries of the highest paid men's coaches?[69]

1-11. Since 2007, all of the Grand Slam tennis events have paid men and women winners the same prize money. In 2012, the thirteenth-seeded male tennis player at Wimbledon, Gilles Simon, made news when he complained that men should be paid more than women because "men spend twice as long on court as women do."[70] Men play best-of-five set matches, while women play best-of-three, which means men's matches are longer and more demanding. Men's tennis is also arguably more competitive than women's in the top ranks and, for this reason, some fans and sports commentators believe, more entertaining. If the standard of the Equal Pay Act was applied to Grand Slam tennis tournaments, would it require that men and women be paid the same? What should the law be? Assuming it is not required by law, is it good policy to equalize tennis tournament winnings? Give your reasons.

1-12. A national clothing store chain has separate departments for women's and men's clothing. The merchandise in the men's department is, on average, of higher price and better quality than the merchandise in the women's department, and the store's gross revenues and profit margin is greater for men's clothing. Only male sales personnel work in the men's department; only female personnel work in the women's department. Their salaries reflect base payments plus incentives pegged to the value of the garments sold. Female saleswomen, who receive lower salaries than male salesmen, have challenged the compensation system under the Equal Pay Act. They do not challenge the job segregation, which the store justifies in terms of customer's discomfort at having sales personnel of a different sex in fitting rooms. The company acknowledges that the basic functions of male and female sales personnel is the same, but defends its incentive system as a practice "other than sex," and one that is widespread in the sales industry. What are the best arguments in defense of store policy? Against? How should the court decide?[71]

1-13. The all-female nursing faculty at a major university sues the university for violation of the Equal Pay Act, arguing that the skill, effort, and responsibility of their jobs are functionally equivalent to the salaries of the majority-male, higher-paid faculties at the university's architecture, urban planning, and environmental health schools. Should they prevail?[72]

2. Title VII: Finding the Limits of Formal Equality

The linchpin of employment discrimination law is Title VII of the Civil Rights Act of 1964. Two theories of employment discrimination have emerged under Title VII. The *disparate treatment* theory addresses employment rules or decisions that treat an employee less favorably than others because of the employee's race, sex, religion, or national origin. When plaintiffs challenge a formal policy that discriminates on the basis of sex, the employer's only statutory defense is to prove that a sex-based requirement or restriction is a bona fide occupational qualification (BFOQ). While a number of different tests for the BFOQ defense exist, the standard basically requires the employer to show that "the essence of the business operation would be undermined" by hiring employees without the qualification in question and that either virtually all members of the excluded sex lack the qualification or it is impossible to test for it individually. When plaintiffs challenge adverse employment actions that are not rooted in a formal policy, they must prove that the decisions were made "because of sex." In systemic cases, they do so through a combination of statistical evidence and individual anecdotes that reveal the underlying discriminatory motive;[73] in individual cases, they utilize the proof structures laid out below.

The second theory under Title VII is *disparate impact* discrimination. Under this theory, the plaintiff must show that a facially neutral job requirement or policy disproportionately affects women. Unlike discrimination cases brought under the U.S. Constitution, like Massachusetts v. Feeney (excerpted earlier), the plaintiff in a Title VII disparate impact case need not show discriminatory intent. Once the plaintiff introduces facts showing disparate impact, the employer must either refute those facts, or demonstrate that the facially neutral job requirement is both job-related and consistent with business necessity. Even then, the plaintiff has the opportunity to show that the employer's goals could be met in a less restrictive manner. To the extent that the discriminatory impact approach focuses on the *effects* of a rule rather than its *form*, it more closely fits the model of substantive, rather than formal, equality — a model examined more closely in Chapter 2.

Title VII has been a significant tool in helping women gain access to areas of employment previously closed to them. The statute has had greater difficulty, however, with rules that are based on women's actual differences from men. Such questions tend to divide into two separate phases of Title VII analysis: (1) whether the claimed discrimination constitutes "discrimination on the basis of sex"; and (2) whether, if a classification constitutes sex discrimination, it is nonetheless justified because of its relationship to legitimate business concerns.

a. What Is Discrimination "Based on Sex"?

When an employer considers only women for flight attendant positions, or only men for road maintenance positions, there is no question but that the employer is discriminating "based on sex." The only question, then, is whether the sex-based discrimination is justified (see next section). Many cases, however, are not so clear about whether discrimination has occurred.

Courts have recognized two proof structures for individual disparate treatment claims: pretext and mixed-motives. In pretext claims, the plaintiff bears the burden of proof that the discrimination complained of was based on sex. The first step (the "prima facie case") is to establish that an adverse employment decision was made because of the plaintiff's sex, whatever the employer's stated reason. If the defendant then offers a legitimate, nondiscriminatory reason for the decision, the plaintiff has the burden of proving that the reason is a pretext for sex discrimination. Ezold v. Wolf, Block, Schorr & Solis-Cohen, excerpted below, is an example. In *Ezold*, the plaintiff alleged that she was not promoted to partnership in a law firm because of her sex; the firm claimed that she was not promoted because of a lack of analytical ability and other qualifications. The plaintiff claimed that this reason was a pretext, and that the real reason for her failure to be promoted was sex discrimination. Was Nancy Ezold discriminated against based on her sex? Why or why not?

Burden of Proof. In each case, the plaintiff has the **burden of proof**, or the duty to provide sufficient facts to support a claim. If the plaintiff meets her burden of establishing a basis for her claim, the burden of proof **shifts** to the defendant, who then has the opportunity to establish a defense. To prove something by a **preponderance of the evidence**, a party must show that the greater weight of the evidence—i.e., more than 50 percent—supports its assertion.

In *mixed-motive* claims, both discriminatory and nondiscriminatory reasons are present. Price Waterhouse v. Hopkins, excerpted below, is an example. The case involves an accounting firm that denied the plaintiff's promotion to partner, and tried to justify the denial based on criticisms of her interpersonal skills.

Reading Questions

1. Was Nancy Ezold discriminated against based on her sex? Why or why not?
2. To what extent is an employee's personality or appearance relevant in promotion and retention decisions? What if an employee is abrasive and difficult, but nonetheless is effective for clients and highly profitable for the employer? Why did Price Waterhouse lose the case below? Do you agree with the decision? If you had been the lawyer for Price Waterhouse, what would you have argued? If you had been the judge, would you have been persuaded?
3. Is the likely result of the *Price Waterhouse* case an expansion of employment opportunities for women? Or does it simply make people more careful about what they say in the workplace?

Ezold v. Wolf, Block, Schorr & Solis-Cohen

983 F.2d 509 (3d Cir. 1992), cert. denied, 510 U.S. 826 (1993)

HUTCHINSON, Circuit Judge.

Wolf, Block, Schorr and Solis-Cohen (Wolf) appeals from a judgment of the United States District Court for the Eastern District of Pennsylvania granting relief in favor of Nancy O'Mara Ezold (Ezold) on her claim that Wolf intentionally discriminated against her on the basis of her sex in violation of Title VII . . . when it decided not to admit her to the firm's partnership effective February 1, 1989. . . .

The district court held that the nondiscriminatory reason articulated by Wolf for its rejection of Ezold's candidacy—that her legal analytical ability failed to meet the firm's partnership standard—was a pretext. . . .

Ezold was hired by Wolf as an associate on a partnership track in July 1983. She had graduated in the top third of her class from the Villanova University School of Law in 1980 and then worked at two small law firms in Philadelphia. . . . Ezold was hired at Wolf by Seymour Kurland, then chairman of the litigation department. The district court found that Kurland told Ezold during an interview that it would not be easy for her at Wolf because "she was a woman, had not attended an Ivy League law school, and had not been on law review." . . . [She] was assigned to the firm's litigation department. From 1983-87, Kurland was responsible for the assignment of work to associates in the department. He often delegated this responsibility to partner Steven Arbittier. . . . The district court found that Arbittier assigned Ezold to actions that were "small" by Wolf standards. . . .

Senior associates within two years of partnership consideration are evaluated annually; non-senior associates are evaluated semi-annually. The firm's partners are asked to submit written evaluations on standardized forms. . . . Ten criteria of legal performance are listed on the forms in the following order:

legal analysis, legal writing and drafting, research skills, formal speech, informal speech, judgment, creativity, negotiating and advocacy, promptness and efficiency. Ten personal characteristics are also listed: reliability, taking and managing responsibility, flexibility, growth potential, attitude, client relationship, client servicing and development, ability under pressure, ability to work independently, and dedication. As stated by Ian Strogatz, Chairman of the Associates Committee: "The normal standards for partnership include as factors for consideration all of the ones . . . that are contained [on] our evaluation forms." . . .

The firm's partners evaluated Ezold twice a year as an associate and once a year as a senior associate from October 1983 until the Associates Committee determined that it would not recommend her for partnership in September 1988. The district court found that "in the period up to and including 1988, Ms. Ezold received strongly positive evaluations from almost all of the partners for whom she had done any substantial work." . . . Ezold's overall score in legal skills in the 1988 bottom line memorandum before the Associates Committee was a "G" for good [the second highest rating on a 5-part scale ranging from exceptional to unacceptable]. . . .

Evaluations in Ezold's file not mentioned by the district court show that concerns over Ezold's legal analytical ability arose early during her tenure at the firm. In an evaluation covering the period from November 1984 through April 1985, Arbittier wrote:

> I have discussed legal issues with Nancy in connection with [two cases]. I found her analysis to be rather superficial and unfocused. I am beginning to doubt that she has sufficient legal analytical ability to make it with the firm. . . . She makes a good impression with people, has common sense, and can handle routine matters well. However these traits will take you just so far in our firm. I think that due to the nature of our practice Nancy's future here is limited. . . .

That same year Schwartz wrote:

> I have worked a great deal with Nancy since my last evaluation. . . . Both cases are complex, multifaceted matters that have presented novel issues to us. While her enthusiasm never wanes and she keeps plugging away—I'm often left with a product that demonstrates uncertainty in the analysis of a problem. After extensive discussions with me, the analysis becomes a little more focused, although sometimes I get the sense that Nancy feels adrift and is just marching as best she can to my analytical tune. . . . In my view her energy, enthusiasm and fearlessness make her a valuable asset to us. While she may not be as bright as some of our best associates, her talents will continue to serve us well.

. . . Also in 1985, partner Donald Joseph rated Ezold's legal analytical ability as marginal and wrote "its [sic] too early to tell but I have been disappointed on her grasp of the problem, let alone performance." . . .

During her next evaluation period from April through November 1985, Ezold received similar negative evaluations. Arbittier, Robert Fiebach and Joseph rated her legal analytical abilities as marginal. Arbittier wrote:

> She took a long time getting [a summary judgment brief] done and I found it to be stilted and unimaginative. One of the main issues—dealing with the issue of notice—she missed completely and did not grasp our position. . . . Also, in considering whether to file a defensive motion . . . she failed to cite me to a clause in the agreement that was highly relevant leaving me with the impression that the motion could not succeed. I think Nancy tries hard and can handle relatively straight-forward matters with a degree of maturity and judgment, but when she gets into more complicated areas she lacks real analytical skill and just does what she is told in a mechanical way. She is not up to our minimal Wolf, Block standards. . . .

Boote made the following report on his performance review with Ezold after this evaluation period:

> Nancy appeared to accept the judgment, albeit a little grudgingly, that her analytical, research and writing ability was not up to our standards and that she should focus on the types of matters that she can handle effectively. . . . We made it very clear to Nancy that if she pursues general civil litigation work she is not on track toward partnership and that her only realistic chance for partnership in our opinion is to develop a good reputation for herself in one of the specialized areas of practice. . . .

In the evaluation period covering November 1985 to April 1986, Boote wrote the following to the Associates Committee:

> Nancy continues to get mixed reviews. Her pluses are that she is mature, courageous, pretty good on her feet and has the capacity to inspire confidence in clients. Her minuses are that there is doubt about her analytic and writing ability. . . . In considering Nancy's prospects for the long range, I think we should bear in mind that we have made mistakes in the past in letting people go to other firms who really could have filled a valuable niche here. Whether Nancy is such a person, of course, remains to be seen. . . .

A summary of Ezold's performance review from October 1986 prepared by Schwartz stated:

> Nancy was advised that several of the lawyers feel she has made very positive progress as a lawyer, Sy [Kurland] being one of them. However, he told her that other lawyers had strong negative sentiments about her capabilities and they feel she has a number of shortcomings in the way of complicated analysis of legal problems and in being able to handle the big complicated corporate litigation, and therefore, does not meet the standard for partnership at Wolf, Block. . . . Both Sy and I urged Nancy to seriously consider looking for employment elsewhere as she may not be able to turn the tide. . . .

Although several partners saw improvement in Ezold's work, negative comments about her analytical ability continued up until, and through, her 1988 senior associate evaluation, the year she was considered for partnership. . . . [In the 1988 review] the Associates Committee voted 9-1 not to recommend Ezold for . . . partnership. . . .

Out of a total of eight candidates in Ezold's class, five male associates and one female associate were recommended for regular partnership. One male associate, Associate X, was not recommended for either regular or special partnership. . . . Ezold resigned from the firm on June 7, 1989. . . .

Ezold claims Wolf intentionally discriminated against her because of her sex. Intentional discrimination in employment cases falls within one of two categories: "pretext" cases and "mixed-motives" cases. See Price Waterhouse v. Hopkins, 490 U.S. 228, 247 n.12 (1989) (plurality). . . . [She] litigated this case as a pretext case. . . . The plaintiff must first establish by a preponderance of the evidence a prima facie case of discrimination. . . . The plaintiff can establish a prima facie case by showing that she is a member of a protected class; that she was qualified for and rejected for the position; and that non-members of the protected class were treated more favorably. . . . The parties do not dispute the district court's conclusion of law that Ezold demonstrated a prima facie case. . . .

The defendant may rebut the presumption of discrimination arising out of the plaintiff's prima facie case by producing evidence that there was a "legitimate, nondiscriminatory reason" why the plaintiff was rejected. . . . The burden then shifts to the plaintiff to show that the defendant's articulated reasons are pretextual. This burden merges into the plaintiff's ultimate burden of persuading the court that she has been the victim of intentional discrimination. The plaintiff must demonstrate "by competent evidence that the presumptively valid reason[] for [the alleged unlawful employment action was] in fact a coverup for a . . . discriminatory decision." . . . Explicit evidence of discrimination—i.e., the "smoking gun"—is not required. . . . A plaintiff can establish pretext in one of two ways: "either directly by persuading the court that a discriminatory reason more likely motivated the employer or indirectly by showing that the employer's proffered reason is unworthy of credence." . . .

In proving that the employer's motive was more likely than not the product of a discriminatory reason instead of the articulated legitimate reason, sufficiently strong evidence of an employer's past treatment of the plaintiff may suffice. . . . The employer's "general policy and practice with respect to minority employment" may also be relevant. . . . Alternately, if a plaintiff produces credible evidence that it is more likely than not that "the employer did not act for its proffered reason, then the employer's decision remains unexplained and the inferences from the evidence produced by the plaintiff may be sufficient to prove the ultimate fact of discriminatory intent." . . .

Wolf's articulated nondiscriminatory reason for denying Ezold's admission to the partnership was that she did not possess sufficient legal analytical skills to handle the responsibilities of partner in the firm's complex litigation practice. Ezold attempted to prove that Wolf's proffered explanation was "unworthy of credence" by showing she was at least equal to, if not more qualified than, similarly situated males promoted to partnership. She also contended that her past treatment at the firm showed Wolf's decision was based on a discriminatory motive rather than the legitimate reason of deficiency in legal analytical ability that the firm had articulated.

The district court compared Ezold to eight successful male partnership candidates. . . . It found:

> The test that was put to the plaintiff by the Associates Committee that she have outstanding academic credentials and that before she could be admitted to the most junior of partnerships, she must demonstrate that she had the analytical ability to handle the most complex litigation was not the test required of male associates. . . .

The district court then concluded:

> Ms. Ezold has established that the defendant's purported reasons for its conduct are pretextual. The defendant promoted to partnership men having evaluations substantially the same or inferior to the plaintiff's, and indeed promoted male associates who the defendant claimed had precisely the lack of analytical or writing ability upon which Wolf, Block purportedly based its decision concerning the plaintiff. The defendant is not entitled to apply its standards in a more "severe" fashion to female associates. . . . Such differential treatment establishes that the defendant's reasons were a pretext for discrimination. . . .

[The district court was wrong.]

The record does not show that anyone was taken into the partnership without serious consideration of their strength in the category of legal analytic ability. . . . Wolf reserves for itself the power to decide, by consensus, whether an associate possesses sufficient analytical ability to handle complex matters independently after becoming a partner. It is Wolf's prerogative to utilize such a standard. . . . The partnership evaluation process at Wolf, though formalized, is based on judgment, like most decisions in human institutions. A consensus as to that judgment is the end result of Wolf's formal process. In that process, the Associates Committee has the role of collecting and weighing hundreds of evaluations by partners with diverse views before reaching its consensus as to a particular associate's abilities. . . . The differing evaluations the partners first submit to the Associates Committee are often based on hearsay or reputation. No precise theorem or specific objective criterion is employed. . . .

Were the factors Wolf considered in deciding which associates should be admitted to the partnership objective, as opposed to subjective, the conflicts in various partners' views about Ezold's legal analytical ability that this record shows might amount to no more than a conflict in the evidence that the district court as factfinder had full power to resolve. . . . [The difficulty in this case] is the lack of an objective qualification or factor that a plaintiff can use as a yardstick to compare herself with similarly situated employees. . . .

When an employer relies on its subjective evaluation of the plaintiff's qualifications as the reason for denying promotion, the plaintiff can prove the articulated reason is unworthy of credence by presenting persuasive comparative evidence that non-members of the protected class were evaluated more favorably, i.e., their deficiencies in the same qualification category as the plaintiff's were overlooked for no apparent reason when they were promoted to partner.

A plaintiff does not establish pretext, however, by pointing to criticisms of members of the non-protected class, or commendation of the plaintiff, in categories the defendant says it did not rely upon in denying promotion to a member of the protected class. . . .

The district court's failure to consider the negative evaluations of Ezold's legal analytic ability because the partners making them had little contact with Ezold cannot be excused in the face of the credence the district court gave to positive comments about Ezold's ability from those who likewise had little or no contact with her. While a factfinder can accept some evidence and reject other evidence on the basis of credibility, it should not base its credibility determination on a conflicting double standard.

Moreover, . . . [t]here is no evidence that Wolf's practice of giving weight to negative votes and comments of partners who had little contact and perhaps knew nothing about an associate beyond the associate's general reputation was not applied equally to female and male associates. . . .

This Court has recognized that when an employer discriminatorily denies training and support, the employer may not then disfavor the plaintiff because her performance is affected by the lack of opportunity. . . . Even if we assume that Ezold received "small" cases at the beginning of her tenure at Wolf, however, there is no evidence this was the result of sex discrimination. Her evaluations indicate, rather, that it may have been her academic credentials that contributed to her receipt of less complex assignments. For example, Davis stated that "the Home Unity case was the first really fair test for Nancy. I believe that her background relegated her to . . . matters (where she got virtually no testing by Wolf, Block standards) and small matters." . . . It is undisputed that Arbittier opposed hiring Ezold because of her academic history and lack of law review experience. In one of Ezold's early evaluations, Kurland wrote: "She has not, in my view, been getting sufficiently difficult matters to handle because she is not the Harvard Law Review type. . . . We must make an effort to give her more difficult matters to handle." . . . He also stated: "I envisioned . . . her when I hired her as a 'good, stand-up, effective courtroom lawyer.'" . . . In urging the Executive Committee to reconsider Ezold's candidacy Magarity wrote:

> [The] perception [that she is not able to handle complex cases] appears to be a product of how Sy Kurland viewed Nancy's role when she was initially hired. For the first few years Sy would only assign Nancy to non-complex matters, yet, at evaluation time, Sy, and some other partners, would qualify their evaluations by saying that Nancy does not work on complex matters. . . .

Nancy was literally trapped in a Catch 22. The Chairman of the Litigation Department would not assign her to complex cases, yet she received negative evaluations for not working on complex matters. . . . While it would be unfortunate if these academic and intellectual biases were perpetuated after the decision was made to hire Ezold, academic or intellectual bias is not evidence of sex discrimination. The district court made no finding that Ezold was given small assignments because of her sex. . . .

The district court found that when Ezold suggested to Schwartz in her early years at Wolf that an unfairness in case assignments may have occurred because she was a woman, Schwartz replied: "Nancy, don't say that around here. They don't want to hear it. Just do your job and do well." . . . This statement, made years before the 1988 decision to deny Ezold partnership, does not show that Wolf's evaluation of her legal ability was pretextual. . . .

Finally, the district court found that by allowing partners to bypass the formal assignment system, Kurland and Arbittier "prevented the plaintiff from securing improved assignments . . . [and] impaired her opportunity to be fairly evaluated for partnership." . . . The fact that Wolf's formal assignment process was often bypassed does not support the district court's finding of pretext. Title VII requires employers to avoid certain prohibited types of invidious discrimination, including sex discrimination. It does not require employers to treat all employees fairly, closely monitor their progress and insure them every opportunity for advancement. "Our task is not to assess the overall fairness of [Wolf's] actions." . . . It is a sad fact of life in the working world that employees of ability are sometimes overlooked for promotion. Large law firms are not immune from unfairness in this imperfect world. The law limits its protection against that unfairness to cases of invidious illegal discrimination. This record contains no evidence that Wolf's assignment process was tainted by a discriminatory motive. . . .

The district court found that Ezold was "evaluated negatively for being 'very demanding,' while several male associates who were made partners were evaluated negatively for lacking sufficient assertiveness in their demeanors." . . . The criticisms of Ezold's assertiveness related to the way in which she handled administrative matters such as office and secretarial space, and not legal matters. . . . In particular, David Hofstein's evaluation of Ezold in 1984 stated:

> My one negative experience did not involve legal work. When my group moved to the south end of the 21st floor, Nancy had a fit because she had to move. As I, Strogatz and our [Office Manager] know, Nancy's behavior was inappropriate and I think affected everyone's perception of her. Dealing with administrative matters professionally is almost as important as dealing with legal matters competently, and at least in that instance, Nancy blew it. . . .

The district court refers to criticisms of male associates for lacking assertiveness, but in connection with their handling of legal matters. The district court was comparing apples and oranges. The record shows that male associates were also criticized for their improper handling of administrative problems. . . . The district court also quotes an evaluation of Ezold as a "prima donna" on administrative matters, but leaves out the full context of the statement which compares her to a male associate: "Reminds me of [a male associate]—very demanding, prima donna-ish, not a team player." . . .

The district court's finding that this evidence supports its conclusion that Ezold was treated differently because of her gender is clearly erroneous. An "unfortunate and destructive conflict of personalities does not establish sexual discrimination." . . . Further, by the time of Ezold's final evaluation in 1988, there was no mention of her attitude on administrative matters. Rosoff testified that in independently reviewing the Associate Committee's decision not to recommend Ezold for partnership, he disregarded the criticisms of her handling of administrative matters from earlier years as "ancient history." . . .

We have reviewed the evidence carefully and hold that it is insufficient to show pretext. Despite Ezold's disagreement with the firm's evaluations of her abilities, and her perception that she was treated unfairly, there is no evidence of sex discrimination here. . . .

Accordingly, we will reverse the judgment of the district court in favor of Ezold and remand for entry of judgment in favor of Wolf.

Price Waterhouse v. Hopkins

490 U.S. 228 (1989)

Justice BRENNAN announced the judgment of the Court and delivered an opinion, in which Justice MARSHALL, Justice BLACKMUN, and Justice STEVENS join.

Ann Hopkins was a senior manager in an office of Price Waterhouse when she was proposed for partnership in 1982. . . . When the partners in her office later refused to repropose her for partnership, she sued Price Waterhouse under Title VII . . . charging that the firm had discriminated against her on the basis of sex in its decisions regarding partnership. Judge Gesell in the Federal District Court for the District of Columbia ruled in her favor on the question of liability . . . and the Court of Appeals for the District of Columbia Circuit affirmed. . . . We granted certiorari to resolve a conflict among the Courts of Appeals concerning the respective burdens of proof of a defendant and plaintiff in a suit under Title VII when it has been shown that an employment decision resulted from a mixture of legitimate and illegitimate motives. . . .

Ann Hopkins had worked at Price Waterhouse's Office of Government Services in Washington, D.C., for five years when the partners in that office proposed her as a candidate for partnership. Of the 662 partners at the firm at that time, 7 were women. Of the 88 persons proposed for partnership that year, only 1—Hopkins—was a woman. Forty-seven of these candidates admitted to the partnership, 21 were rejected, and 20—including Hopkins—were "held" for reconsideration the following year. Thirteen of the 32 partners who had submitted comments on Hopkins supported her bid for partnership. Three partners recommended that her candidacy be placed on hold, eight stated that they did not have an informed opinion about her, and eight recommended that she be denied partnership.

In a jointly prepared statement supporting her candidacy, the partners in Hopkins' office showcased her successful 2-year effort to secure a $25 million contract with the Department of State, labeling it "an outstanding performance" and one that Hopkins carried out "virtually at the partner level." Despite Price Waterhouse's attempt at trial to minimize her contribution to this project, Judge Gesell specifically found that Hopkins had "played a key role in Price Waterhouse's successful effort to win a multi-million dollar contract with the Department of State." Indeed, he went on, "[n]one of the other partnership candidates at Price Waterhouse that year had a comparable record in terms of successfully securing major contracts for the partnership."

The partners in Hopkins' office praised her character as well as her accomplishments, describing her in their joint statement as "an outstanding professional" who had a "deft touch," a "strong character, independence and integrity." Clients appear to have agreed with these assessments. At trial, one official from the State Department described her as "extremely competent, intelligent," "strong and forthright, very productive, energetic and creative." Another high-ranking official praised Hopkins' decisiveness, broadmindedness, and "intellectual clarity"; she was, in his words, "a stimulating conversationalist." Evaluations such as these led Judge Gesell to conclude that Hopkins "had no difficulty dealing with clients and her clients appear to have been very pleased with her work" and that she "was generally viewed as a highly competent project leader who worked long hours, pushed vigorously to meet deadlines and demanded much from the multidisciplinary staffs with which she worked."

On too many occasions, however, Hopkins' aggressiveness apparently spilled over into abrasiveness. Staff members seem to have borne the brunt of Hopkins' brusqueness. Long before her bid for partnership, partners evaluating her work had counseled her to improve her relations with staff members. Although later evaluations indicate an improvement, Hopkins' perceived shortcomings in this important area eventually doomed her bid for partnership. Virtually all of the partners' negative remarks about Hopkins—even those of partners supporting her—had to do with her "interpersonal skills." Both "[s]upporters and opponents of her candidacy," stressed Judge Gesell, "indicated that she was sometimes overly aggressive, unduly harsh, difficult to work with and impatient with staff."

There were clear signs, though, that some of the partners reacted negatively to Hopkins' personality because she was a woman. One partner described her as "macho"; another suggested that she "overcompensated for being a woman"; a third advised her to take "a course at charm school." Several partners criticized her use of profanity; in response, one partner suggested that those partners objected to her swearing only "because it's a lady using foul language." Another supporter explained that Hopkins "ha[d] matured from a tough-talking somewhat masculine hard-nosed mgr to an authoritative, formidable, but much more appealing lady ptr candidate." But it was the man who, as Judge Gesell found, bore responsibility for explaining to Hopkins the reasons for the Policy Board's decision to place her candidacy on hold who delivered the coup de grace: in order to improve her chances for partnership, Thomas Beyer advised, Hopkins should "walk more femininely, talk more femininely, dress more femininely, wear make-up, have her hair styled, and wear jewelry."

Dr. Susan Fiske, a social psychologist and Associate Professor of Psychology at Carnegie-Mellon University, testified at trial that the partnership selection process at Price Waterhouse was likely influenced by sex stereotyping. Her testimony focused not only on the overtly sex-based comments of partners but also on gender-neutral remarks, made by partners who knew Hopkins only slightly, that were intensely critical of her. One partner, for example, baldly stated that Hopkins was "universally disliked" by staff, and another described her as "consistently annoying and irritating"; yet these were people who had had very little contact with Hopkins. According to Fiske, Hopkins' unique-ness (as the only woman in the pool of candidates) and the subjectivity of the evaluations made it likely that sharply critical remarks such as these were the product of sex stereotyping—although Fiske admitted that she could not say with certainty whether any particular comment was the result of stereotyping. Fiske based her opinion on a review of the submitted comments, explaining that it was commonly accepted practice for social psychologists to reach this kind of conclusion without having met any of the people involved in the deci-sionmaking process.

In previous years, other female candidates for partnership also had been evaluated in sex-based terms. As a general matter, Judge Gesell concluded, "[c]andidates were viewed favorably if partners believed they maintained their femin[in]ity while becoming effective professional managers"; in this environment, "[t]o be identified as a women's lib[b]er" was regarded as [a] negative comment. In fact, the judge found that in previous years "[o]ne part-ner repeatedly commented that he could not consider any woman seriously as a partnership candidate and believed that women were not even capable of functioning as senior managers—yet the firm took no action to discourage his comments and recorded his vote in the overall summary of the evaluations."

Judge Gesell found that Price Waterhouse legitimately emphasized inter-personal skills in its partnership decisions, and also found that the firm had not fabricated its complaints about Hopkins' interpersonal skills as a pretext for discrimination. Moreover, he concluded, the firm did not give decisive emphasis to such traits only because Hopkins was a woman; although there were male candidates who lacked these skills but who were admitted to part-nership, the judge found that these candidates possessed other, positive traits that Hopkins lacked.

The judge went on to decide, however, that some of the partners' remarks about Hopkins stemmed from an impermissibly cabined view of the proper behavior of women, and that Price Waterhouse had done nothing to disavow reliance on such comments. He held that Price Waterhouse had unlawfully discriminated against Hopkins on the basis of sex by consciously giving credence and effect to partners' comments that resulted from sex stereotyping. Noting that Price Waterhouse could avoid equitable relief by proving by clear and convincing evidence that it would have placed Hopkins' candidacy on hold even absent this discrimination, the judge decided that the firm had not carried this heavy burden.

Equitable relief. Plaintiffs in most cases seek **legal relief**, or money damages. In some cases, a plaintiff also seeks **equitable relief**, typically an injunction requiring specific action. In this case, Ann Hopkins wants to be made a partner. Equitable relief generally requires evidence that a monetary compensation alone would be inadequate.

The Court of Appeals affirmed the District Court's ultimate conclusion, but departed from its analysis in one particular: it held that even if a plaintiff proves that discrimination played a role in an employment decision, the defendant will not be found liable if it proves, by clear and convincing evidence, that it would have made the same decision in the absence of discrimination. Under this approach, an employer is not deemed to have violated Title VII if it proves that it would have made the same decision in the absence of an impermissible motive, whereas under the District Court's approach, the employer's proof in that respect only avoids equitable relief. We decide today that the Court of Appeals had the better approach, but that both courts erred in requiring the employer to make its proof by clear and convincing evidence. . . .

Justice KENNEDY, with whom THE CHIEF JUSTICE and Justice SCALIA join, dissenting. . . .

The ultimate question in every individual disparate-treatment case is whether discrimination caused the particular decision at issue. Some of the plurality's comments with respect to the District Court's findings in this case, however, are potentially misleading. As the plurality notes, the District Court based its liability determination on expert evidence that some evaluations of respondent Hopkins were based on unconscious sex stereotypes,[5] and on the

5. The plaintiff who engages the services of Dr. Susan Fiske should have no trouble showing that sex discrimination played a part in any decision. Price Waterhouse chose not to object to Fiske's testimony, and at this late stage we are constrained to accept it, but I think the plurality's enthusiasm for Fiske's conclusions unwarranted. Fiske purported to discern stereotyping in comments that were gender neutral—e.g., "overbearing and abrasive"—without any knowledge of the comments' basis in reality and without having met the speaker or subject. "To an expert of Dr. Fiske's qualifications, it seems plain that no woman could be overbearing, arrogant, or abrasive: any observations to that effect would necessarily be discounted as the product of stereotyping. If analysis like this is to prevail in federal courts, no employer can base any adverse action as to a woman on such attributes." . . . Today's opinions cannot be read as requiring factfinders to credit testimony based on this type of analysis. . . .

fact that Price Waterhouse failed to disclaim reliance on these comments when it conducted the partnership review. The District Court also based liability on Price Waterhouse's failure to "make partners sensitive to the dangers [of stereotyping], to discourage comments tainted by sexism, or to investigate comments to determine whether they were influenced by stereotypes."

Although the District Court's version of Title VII liability is improper under any of today's opinions, I think it important to stress that Title VII creates no independent cause of action for sex stereotyping. Evidence of use by decisionmakers of sex stereotypes is, of course, quite relevant to the question of discriminatory intent. The ultimate question, however, is whether discrimination caused the plaintiff's harm. Our cases do not support the suggestion that failure to "disclaim reliance" on stereotypical comments itself violates Title VII. Neither do they support creation of a "duty to sensitize." As the dissenting judge in the Court of Appeals observed, acceptance of such theories would turn Title VII "from a prohibition of discriminatory conduct into an engine for rooting out sexist thoughts."

Notes

1. Assessing the Facts in *Ezold*. The evidence showed that only 1 of 55 litigation partners in the law firm in *Ezold* was a woman, that most of the law firm partners had gone to a more prestigious law school than the plaintiff, that some male associates with less favorable evaluations than the plaintiff had made partner, and that the plaintiff was involved with women's issues at the firm, especially concerning the firm's treatment of paralegals. Although the trial court ruled in the plaintiff's favor, the appellate court reversed because it was persuaded by evidence that two-thirds of the partners voted against the plaintiff primarily because she lacked the analytic ability to handle complex litigation. The only woman litigation partner voted against her, no women testified in her favor, and several gave evidence concerning the firm's fairness toward women. How would you assess such evidence? Which factors seem the most important?[74]

2. The Significance of Stray Remarks. In evaluating claims of sex discrimination, what significance should be given to "stray remarks" concerning the plaintiff? The district court had found that Nancy Ezold "was evaluated negatively for being too involved with women's issues . . . specifically her concern about the [firm's] treatment of paralegals." How significant is this finding? Although a partner had written in one evaluation that Ezold's "[j]udgment is better, although it still can be clouded by over-sensitivity to what she misperceives as 'womens' [sic] issues," the appellate court concluded that the criticism was for her misperception that the firm's treatment of paralegals was a women's issue, rather than for her over-sensitivity to such issues. What do you think? The Supreme Court in *Price Waterhouse* found that certain remarks by partners about Ann Hopkins were based on sex-role stereotypes, and thus discriminatory. Is there a difference in the way courts treat "stray remarks" in the two cases?

In other cases involving such comments, courts have reached inconsistent results. In one 2005 case, the Tenth Circuit Court of Appeals held that evidence that male supervisors referred to a woman physician as "Jane" instead of "Dr." and called her a "femi-Nazi" were relevant and precluded summary judgment, even though they were not directly related to the termination decision.[75] Another case, decided in 1999, upheld a judgment against a terminated surgical resident, finding irrelevant various remarks about her based on her sex and national origin. These remarks included: statements that "her difficulties in the program were 'cultural'"; concerns by one superior about women putting themselves through surgical residency particularly if they plan on having children because "they're constantly tired, and they don't have time to put on their makeup and put on clothes and do a lot of things girls need to do. . . . "; and the observation of one superior that the plaintiff was "not accepted well by the 'good old boys.'"[76]

A federal district court recently dismissed a systemic disparate treatment case brought by the EEOC against Bloomberg, L.P., on grounds that the plaintiff's anecdotal evidence of pregnancy discrimination was insufficient, given the lack of statistical data to support the claim, to show a pattern and practice of discrimination. In the words of the court, " 'J'accuse!' is not enough in court."[77] While the EEOC presented evidence of comments that the court viewed as stereotyped or biased—such as the CEO's asking "is every fucking woman in the company having a baby or going to have a baby?"—it concluded that they were not sufficient to support an inference of systemic discrimination. "Isolated remarks by a handful of executives . . . do not show that Bloomberg's standard operating procedure was to discriminate against pregnant women and mothers."[78] And remarks such as a threat by a manager to " 'kill your children and burn down your house' if a deadline was missed ha[ve] nothing to do with the type of discrimination the EEOC allege[d]. . . ."[79]

3. "Mixed-Motive" Discrimination.   The plaintiff in *Price Waterhouse*, Ann Hopkins, presented evidence of the partners' discriminatory motivation. The firm presented evidence of nondiscriminatory reasons for denying her partnership. The Supreme Court decided that if a plaintiff could show that sex was a substantial motivating factor for the employment action at issue, the burden would shift to the employer, who must then prove by clear and convincing evidence that it would have made the same decision even in the absence of a discriminatory motive.

After the decision in *Price Waterhouse*, Congress enacted the Civil Rights Act of 1991, which modified the relief available in mixed-motive cases. Whereas the Court in *Price Waterhouse* was prepared to relieve the defendant of liability and damages if it could have shown that it would have reached the same decision on nondiscriminatory grounds, Title VII now provides that if sex or any other protected characteristic is "a motivating factor for any employment practice, even though other factors also motivated the practice," the employer is liable for committing an unlawful employment practice.[80] The employer can avoid monetary damages and certain other remedies, however, by proving that it "would have taken the same action in the absence of the impermissible motivating factor."[81] In such cases, remedies are limited to declaratory relief, injunctive relief, and attorney's fees. Financial damages, reinstatement, hiring, or promotion—available in other disparate treatment cases—are not available.

4. Determining and Proving Intent in Disparate Treatment Cases. Sex discrimination may be based on hostility against women but, more often, it is based on stereotypes. Stereotypes, themselves, come in different shapes and sizes. For example, some stereotypes are *descriptive*, in the sense that they assume (often inaccurate) facts about women that lead people to misjudge women's abilities and qualifications. The assumption of women's dependency in *Orr* and *Frontiero* is an example, and Nancy Ezold's claim of sex discrimination was also based, at least in part, on the allegation that the firm made judgments on her analytical ability because she was a woman, and because of the law school she attended. Ann Hopkins may also have been the victim of descriptive stereotypes, but her claim also involved *prescriptive* stereotypes, meaning expectations of how women *should* act. Women are damaged by descriptive stereotypes when others assume that they don't have the necessary qualifications. *Price Waterhouse* recognized that women can also be harmed by prescriptive stereotypes when they do not conform to gender expectations—in Ann Hopkins' case, by being more aggressive and outspoken than a woman "should" be.

Note that decisions based on stereotypes—either descriptive or prescriptive—are often unconscious or unintended. The fact that the partners were not aware that they were discriminating against Ann Hopkins because of her sex does not mean that their behavior was not sex discrimination. Title VII protects victims of unconscious or non-deliberate discrimination, as well as intentional discrimination, as long as it is shown to be "because of sex." In recognizing the harm of imposing different prescriptive expectations on individuals because of their sex in the workplace context, *Price Waterhouse* broke new ground. Its sex stereotyping theory has been useful (although not always successful) in a variety of different contexts, including discrimination against gays and lesbians (see Chapter 3).

In *Price Waterhouse*, the trial court found that the firm had discriminated against Hopkins on the basis of sex "by consciously giving credence and effect to partners' comments that resulted from sex stereotyping." The statements provided "circumstantial" evidence of intent. Was it appropriate for the court to infer discriminatory intent from this evidence? Can the low percentage of women among the employer's partners itself be probative of discrimination? One commentator notes:

Glass ceiling cases are rarely stronger than this. At the time when Price Waterhouse withheld her promotion, all but 7 of the firm's 662 partners were male. Hopkins billed more hours and brought in more business than any other person nominated for partnership in the year of her reject, and clients generally had given her high rankings. . . . Several men who obtained partnerships [in the year that Hopkins did not] were characterized as "abrasive," "overbearing," or "cocky." No one mentioned charm school for them.[82]

Is this analysis convincing, even without expert evidence about unconscious discrimination?

What constitutes unconscious gender bias? Consider the following analysis by the American Bar Association's Commission on Women in the Profession, which references both descriptive and prescriptive stereotypes.

[T]he characteristics traditionally associated with women are at odds with many characteristics traditionally associated with professional success such as assertiveness, competitiveness, and business judgment. Some lawyers and clients still assume that women lack sufficient aptitude for complex financial transactions or sufficient combativeness for major litigation. Particularly in high stakes matters, risk averse managers are often reluctant to gamble on female practitioners.

Yet professional women also tend to be rated lower when they depart from traditional stereotypes and adopt "masculine," authoritative styles. Negative evaluations are particularly likely when the evaluators are men, or the role is one typically occupied by men.

As a consequence, female lawyers often face a double standard and a double bind. They risk appearing too "soft" or too "strident," too "aggressive" or "not aggressive enough." And what appears assertive in a man often appears abrasive in a woman. . . .

The force of traditional stereotypes is compounded by the subjectivity of performance evaluations and by other biases in decisionmaking processes. People are more likely to notice and recall information that confirms prior assumptions than information that contradicts them. Attorneys who assume that working mothers are less committed tend to remember the times they left early, not the nights they stayed late.

A related problem is that people share what psychologists label a "just world" bias. They want to believe that, in the absence of special treatment, individuals generally get what they deserve and deserve what they get. Perceptions of performance are frequently adjusted to match observed outcomes. Individuals are also motivated to interpret information in ways that maintain their own status and self-esteem.[83]

A substantial body of research indicates that the likelihood of bias in performance evaluations is greater in settings where women constitute a minority of the workforce, the applicant pool, and the senior management.[84] The expert testimony of Professor Susan Fiske in the *Price Waterhouse* case, introduced to explain the influence of gender stereotypes, drew on the influential research of Harvard Professor Rosabeth Moss Kanter. Kanter's research on tokenism found that groups constituting 15 percent or less of an organization are particularly vulnerable to stereotyping.

> Fiske stated that when there is dramatic underrepresentation of a group, the token individuals are much more likely to be thought about in terms of their social category. People expect token individuals to fit preconceived views about the traits of the group. . . . When a token person behaves in a way that is counterstereotypical—for example, when a woman acts in an aggressive, competitive, ambitious, independent, or active way—she is more likely to be regarded as uncaring or lacking in understanding. This does not mean that women can play safe by conforming to conventional stereotypes. The Catch 22 or double bind of the powerless group is that stereotypes associated with nondominant groups are also traits that are not highly valued in the organization. A woman who acts womanly acts in a way that may cast doubt on her competence and effectiveness; a woman who is thought to be too masculine may be regarded as deviant.

> In describing how persons respond to an individual whose behavior is incongruent with prevailing stereotypes, Fiske referred to Kanter's four "role traps." Under this scheme, the dominant male group perceives token women as mothers, seductresses, iron maidens, or pets. . . . The role trap most applicable to Hopkins was that of the "iron maiden." . . . Under Fiske's theory, the explicitly sex-based comments describing Hopkins were a predictable response to her status as a token woman who did not fit the conventional feminine mold. . . .

> An additional cue Fiske found which indicated that stereotyping was influencing decisionmaking was the intensity of the negative reaction toward Hopkins. . . . Claims were made, for example, that Hopkins was universally disliked, potentially dangerous, and likely to abuse authority. Fiske contrasted these extremely negative comments with positive comments by others in the organization who seemed to describe the same behavior. Supporters found Hopkins as "outspoken, sells her own ability, independent, [has] the courage of her convictions." Detractors found her "overbearing, arrogant, abrasive, runs over people, implies she knows more than anyone in the world about anything and is not afraid to let anybody know it." Fiske's testimony on this phenomenon of "selective perception" suggested that the differing reactions to Hopkins were not simply a function of the slice of Hopkins' behavior that each individual evaluator had witnessed. Instead, when all the evidence was in, the "real" Ann Hopkins might still not clearly emerge from putting all the pieces together. Fiske's use of Kanter's role traps also demonstrated how other people can contribute to the social construction of the personality of an individual. This made it more difficult to separate Hopkins' "real" personality from the environment in which she worked.[85]

Is this testimony persuasive? Of what? Would it have helped Nancy Ezold? If Dr. Fiske's theory is accepted, would employers safely be able to suggest ways for an employee to improve deficiencies that could be associated with traditional gender roles? What if a woman *is* ineffective because she is too assertive? Or not assertive enough? Or does not maintain a professional appearance?

5. Upper-Level Employees.   Lawsuits such as *Ezold* and *Price Waterhouse* demonstrate the difficulties for plaintiffs in proving discrimination in professional and upper-level employment positions. Such cases are costly to litigate and "smoking guns" like the charm school comments in *Hopkins* are rare. Human resources personnel advise managers to ensure that written performance reviews include concrete examples of employee weaknesses and avoid stereotypical characterizations. Many researchers believe that unconscious bias in evaluations, mentoring, and assignments, along with inflexible workplace structures, have largely replaced deliberate sex discrimination in employment, particularly for managerial and professional positions.[86]

A threshold question in *Price Waterhouse* and *Ezold* is the extent to which Title VII regulates employment practices by partnerships. The United States Supreme Court, in Hishon v. King & Spalding, held that the decision by a private law firm whether to offer partnership to a law associate falls under Title VII because opportunities for partnership constituted a term or privilege "linked directly with an [associate's] status as an employee."[87] It is not clear, however, whether Title VII covers an employment package that, from the outset, decouples partnership consideration from performance as an associate. Justice Powell, in a concurring opinion in *Hishon*, stated his view that absent a claim based on the law firm's promise of partnership consideration, Title VII would not apply to such decisions.

> The relationship among law partners differs markedly from that between employer and employee—including that between the partnership and its associates. The judgmental and sensitive decisions that must be made among the partners embrace a wide range of subjects [including participation in profits; work assignments; approval of commitments in bar association, civic or political activities; questions of billing; and acceptance of new clients]. The essence of the law partnership is the common conduct of a shared enterprise.[88]

Subsequent cases have confirmed that even if Title VII covers the partnership decision, it does not necessarily cover treatment of partners by the partnership, at least when the partner has equity in the partnership, has a significant degree of management over the partnership, and is subject to liability.[89] Similarly, the EEOC issued guidelines in 2000 that would bring Title VII into play when "the individual is subject to the organization's control," although they would not apply when "the individual acts independently and participates in managing the organization."[90]

6. Systemic Bias.   Many commentators have argued that employment discrimination today is more a problem of the "structure" of the workplace, rather than individual acts of bias.[91] Employee search processes, for example, may not access the best sources of female or minority candidates, or they may use selection criteria that are incomplete in a way that disfavors candidates who are not already well represented in the workforce. Workplaces may lack strong mentoring for workers who feel isolated by reason of their sex or minority status. Work groups may be organized to reinforce rather than reduce status differentials and other factors that facilitate stereotyping. "Diversity" programs are often poorly designed and mere window dressing that obscures institutional bias.

The law recognizes that employers may engage in systemic discrimination practices that affect multiple employees. The theory of the systemic disparate treatment claim is that, left unexplained, a significant gap between members of the plaintiff class in the at-issue jobs and in the qualified labor pool raises an inference of discrimination.[92] Title VII allows the EEOC to sue employers for such a "pattern and practice" of discrimination. In addition, class actions may be brought on behalf of groups of individuals under the Federal Rules of Civil Procedure Rule 23 if there are sufficiently common questions of fact or law and if the rule's other requirements (e.g., numerosity, representativeness) are met.

In fact, however, even though Title VII contemplates collective claims, the theories it provides, as interpreted by courts, are not particularly conducive to the recognition of systemic claims of discrimination. Disparate treatment law addresses treating a woman worse than a man, but it is inconsistent in addressing discrimination where evidence of discriminatory intent is absent, and it does not hold employers responsible for failing to use "best practices" in gender equity. In theory, disparate impact analysis should apply where women fare badly in a particular workplace in a systematic way, but a disparate impact claim requires that plaintiffs identify a specific practice that disproportionately disadvantages women; an employer's failure to adopt any particular practice that might curtail the exercise of unconscious bias or otherwise eliminate disparities in the workplace generally is not sufficient. The law imposes a duty on employers not to discriminate, but it does not require them to address disparities that cannot be traced to an employer policy, or that arise from broader, societywide dynamics.

The difficulties of framing a case of systemic discrimination are apparent in, and made more difficult by, the Supreme Court's 2011 ruling in Wal-Mart Stores, Inc. v. Dukes.[93] Plaintiffs in *Wal-Mart* alleged in 2001 that Wal-Mart's personnel system was plagued by several factors that set the stage for biased and stereotyped decisionmaking, including a highly subjective and discretionary system that allowed mostly male supervisors to make biased pay and promotion decisions. Their evidence included statistical studies showing disparities in women's pay, which was on average $1,100 less annually for women who were in hourly positions and $14,500 less for women in salaried management positions. Plaintiffs also presented evidence that the women, despite being paid less, had greater seniority and higher performance ratings on average. With respect to promotion, while women composed 67 percent of hourly workers and 78 percent of hourly department managers, only 35.7 percent of assistant managers, 14.3 percent of store managers, and 9.8 percent

of district managers were women. Plaintiffs showed that women were significantly less likely to be promoted than men in the same position and had to
wait longer for promotions. They also showed that competitor big-box stores
had significantly higher percentages of women in higher management positions than Wal-Mart. Plaintiffs sought certification of a class of approximately
1.5 million women who were employed at any Wal-Mart domestic retail store
at any time since December 26, 1998, and who had been or may have been
subjected to Wal-Mart's challenged pay and management track promotions
policies and practices.

Class Action. In a class action, the plaintiff sues on behalf of herself and other
similarly situated individuals. Before a class action may move forward, the court
must "certify" that the requirements of a class action exist, under Federal Rule of
Civil Procedure 23. The rules for class certification are complex and provide for
different types of classes, with different requirements and consequences. If the
court certifies a class, it also defines the criteria for membership in the class, and
the type of class it is certifying.

After years of litigation, in 2010, the Ninth Circuit Court of Appeals meeting en banc affirmed the district court's certification of a class.[94] The Supreme
Court reversed on two different grounds, the most important of which being
that class certification was inappropriate, insofar as the plaintiffs did not adequately establish a companywide policy of discrimination against women, or
a common source of discrimination, and thus did not present sufficiently common questions of law and fact. According to the Court's majority, individuals were free to make their own discrimination claims, subject to individual
defenses Wal-Mart might assert, but they could not sue as a class for Wal-
Mart's allegedly discriminatory personnel practices.

Under prior case law, systemic (or "pattern and practice") discrimination
claims may be proven through statistical evidence of gaps between, for example, the percentage of women in particular jobs in an employer's work force
and the percentage of women in the qualified labor pool. Left unexplained,
such a gap raises an inference of discrimination, especially when supported by
anecdotal evidence of discriminatory motives.[95] Many recent cases also rely on
so-called social framework evidence, which draws on social science research
about the types of structures and conditions that give rise to biased or stereotyped decisionmaking, as a way of bolstering the inference that the disparity
reflects discriminatory decisionmaking. The testimony in *Price Waterhouse* by
Susan Fiske, drawing on the work of Rosabeth Moss Kanter, discussed above,
is an example of such evidence. Although the *Wal-Mart* ruling was technically
interpreting Federal Rule of Civil Procedure 23, the Court's reasoning throws
the substantive theory of systemic discrimination into question. Can plaintiffs
in a future case prove unlawful discrimination based on statistical evidence
and bolstered by anecdotal evidence? The Court's opinion reveals skepticism

about systemic, institutional bias, and narrowly defines discrimination as the product of an individual actor with a conscious bad intent. The Court also heavily criticizes the social framework evidence offered by the plaintiffs.[96] With this precedent, absent a companywide policy of discrimination, plaintiffs can win only by showing that individual decisions were the product of discriminatory motive. Yet individual plaintiffs are unlikely to be able to prove discrimination on their own facts alone; the discrimination becomes apparent only when the evidence is viewed collectively.

Why wasn't the broad discretion Wal-Mart gave to its supervisors itself a "policy" of discrimination? Probably because the company's stated, official policy was one of nondiscrimination. Can an employer have a policy of discrimination without knowing it? Should employers be held responsible even for "innocent" discrimination? Arguably, the disparate impact theory is intended to cover discrimination not motivated by discriminatory intent. Yet there is an understandable reluctance to treat employers who do not mean to discriminate the same as those who do. Some commentators have suggested reformulations of the disparate treatment and disparate impact theories to more fully recognize discrimination when employers do not intend to discriminate but fail to take steps to restructure a workplace that they should realize does not promote gender equity and inclusiveness.[97] Is it reasonable to expect employers affirmatively to identify potential sources of discrimination in the workplace and take steps to eliminate them? Or to structure decisionmaking in a way that reduces the chance that bias will infect it? Why or why not?

7. Strategies for Countering Bias in the Workplace. Some scholars, such as Richard Epstein, have argued that employer self-interest is a sufficient check against gender bias. Their assumption is that a free market rewards efficiency, and it is inefficient for employers to discriminate against qualified women. If they are not advancing at the same rate as men, the reason must be sex-based differences in female employees' choices and capabilities.[98] Other experts respond that the market is not always efficient and that unconscious biases and preferences for individuals who are like them restrict opportunities and cause subordinate groups to chose workplaces with less discrimination.[99]

Approaches to dealing with employment bias involve both individual and managerial initiatives. Commonly recommended strategies for employees are to be clear about their values and goals, seek mentors, negotiate for what they need, and adopt a style with which they and others are comfortable. Members of groups who perceive themselves as subject to negative stereotypes often feel the need to do what Devon Carbado and Mitu Gulati label "identity work to counter those stereotypes." Examples include acting harried and tired to overcome the impression that they are not busy, or sending emails late at night to indicate that they have worked late. Some strategies may compromise individuals' identities or have other psychic costs: heterosexual "performances" to counter suspicions of homosexuality; avoidance of social events that might suggest racial "cliquishness"; laughing at racist or sexist jokes to demonstrate a sense of humor, prevent discomfort, and indicate a lack of obsession with "outsider status."[100]

Evidence suggests that when members of subordinate groups do succeed at climbing the employment ladder, incentives exist for them to differentiate themselves from less successful members of these groups and to conform with existing workplace landscapes instead of trying to change them.[101] What are these incentives? If the only women and minorities who succeed in the workplace are the individuals who are most like those already there, what kind of equality (or diversity, for that matter) is achieved? Is it enough to level the playing field, or do the rules of the game also need to change?

Some commentators believe that the most promising approach to reducing gender inequality in the workforce is to shift emphasis away from after-the-fact enforcement of antidiscrimination prohibitions and to rely more on improving an employer's capacities to identify, prevent, and redress unconscious bias and exclusionary practices. Consider Susan Sturm's analysis:

> [Current inequalities] frequently involve patterns of interaction among groups within the workplace that, over time, exclude nondominant groups. This exclusion is difficult to trace directly to intentional, discrete actions of particular actors. . . .
>
> [Take the example of a large law firm that] aggressively recruits women at the entry level and [yet] fails to track patterns in work assignment and promotion so [that] the firm's management [was] largely unaware of any problem until [the following] complaints arose: . . . differences in patterns of work assignment and training opportunities among men and women; tolerance of a sexualized work environment by partners who are otherwise significant "rainmakers"; routine comments by male lawyers, particularly in the predominantly male departments, on the appearance, sexuality, and competence of women; harsh assessments of women's capacities and work styles based on gender stereotypes; avoidance of work-related contact with women by members of particular departments; and hyper-scrutiny of women's performance by some, and the invisibility of women's contributions to others. These complaints coincide with a concern about low morale and productivity among diverse work teams. Upon examination, the firm discovers dramatic differences in the retention and promotion rates of men and women in the firm.
>
> The problems of bias described in this scenario result from ongoing patterns of interaction shaped by organizational culture. These interactions influence workplace conditions, access, and opportunities for advancement over time, and thus constitute the structure for inclusion or exclusion. They cannot be traced solely to the sexism of a single "bad actor." Nor can they be addressed by disaggregating the problem into discrete legal claims. The overall gender impact of this conduct may be discernible only if examined in context and in relation to broader patterns of conduct and access. The absence of systematic institutional reflection about these patterns and their impact on workplace conditions, access, and opportunity for advancement contributes to their cumulative effect. The overall organizational culture affects the extent to which particular acts produce bias in a given workplace. Comments or

behavior occurring in conjunction with sex segregation and marginalization may be discriminatory, while the same statements may produce little gender exclusion in a more integrated context. . . .

[These] second generation problems cannot be reduced to a fixed code of specific rules or commands that establishes clear boundaries governing conduct. Instead, their resolution requires a different process, namely problem solving. That process identifies the legal and organizational dimensions of the problem, encourages organizations to gather and share relevant information, builds individual and institutional capacity to respond, and helps design and evaluate solutions that involve employees who participate in the day-to-day patterns that produce bias and exclusion. An effective system of external accountability, including judicial involvement as a catalyst, would encourage organizations to identify and correct these problems without creating increased exposure to liability, and to learn from other organizations that have engaged in similar efforts.

A rule-enforcement approach . . . discourages this type of proactive problem solving. That approach treats regulation as punishing violations of predefined legal rules and compliance as the absence of identifiable conduct violating those rules. . . .

In a rule-enforcement process, problems tend to be redefined as discrete legal violations with sanctions attached. Fear of liability for violation of ambiguous legal norms induces firms to adopt strategies that reduce the short-term risk of legal exposure rather than strategies that address the underlying problem. They accomplish this in significant part by discouraging the production of information that will reveal problems, except in the context of preparation for litigation. Under the current system, employers producing information that reveals problems or patterns of exclusion increase the likelihood that they will be sued. Thus, lawyers counsel clients not to collect data that could reveal racial or gender problems or to engage in self-evaluation, because that information could be used to establish a plaintiff's case. . . .

Fundamentally, the rule-enforcement model encourages lawyers to see issues as potential legal claims, rather than as problems in need of systemic resolution. This narrow focus on avoiding liability diverts attention from the structural dimensions underlying the legal violations, as well as the organizational patterns revealed through aggregating claims.[102]

Professor Sturm, like other experts, proposes that employers should be obligated to establish systems to collect information on recruitment, hiring, promotion, retention, and quality of life issues; monitor evaluation, assignment, and mentoring practices; provide adequate diversity training, family leave, and alternative schedule policies; and hold managers accountable for their performance in achieving diversity-related goals.[103] Many commentators urge more expansive liability for implicit bias or "unconscious" discrimination.[104] Will stronger legal standards coerce more egalitarian behavior by employers? Katharine Bartlett draws on social science research to suggest that measures that affirm people's intentions to act in nondiscriminatory ways may be more effective in reducing discrimination than legal coercion that assumes the worst in people. She argues that:

> threat and confrontation about race and gender bias, which people do not want to possess or exhibit, may inadvertently provoke shame, guilt, and resentment, which lead to avoidance and resistance, and ultimately to more stereotyping. In other words, pressure and threat will often deepen bias rather than correct it. Positive strategies that affirm people's good intentions, in contrast, engage people constructively in defining their better, nondiscriminatory selves and aligning their conduct accordingly. While coercion and threat make people defensive, opportunity and engagement leverage people's good intentions into a deeper commitment to a more inclusive, nondiscriminatory workplace. It is this type of commitment—not legal coercion—that will best address the implicit bias that is most characteristic of today's workplace. . . . [A]ttention needs to be given to the means by which internal commitment to those standards, or what I refer to as good intentions, is generated. . . . [P]eople who have an internal commitment to nondiscrimination norms will combat implicit discrimination more effectively than those motivated by traditional legal sanctions.[105]

Is she right? What are the implications for law?

Putting Theory Into Practice

1-14. Plaintiff, who was the only female among her employer's four top-level executives, brought a lawsuit for sex discrimination after she was terminated. The employer claims that the dismissal was because of unsatisfactory performance. The plaintiff presents evidence of remarks by one vice president that questioned the ability of women to have children and still remain committed to work. She also presents evidence of a company hiring goal (or "profile") in favor of hiring unmarried, childless women, which another vice president said was justified by the fact that such women are more committed to their work and available for long hours and travel. Should this evidence be sufficient to prove that the employer's performance concerns were pretextual and that the real reason for termination was motherhood?[106] Would you need other facts to decide that issue?

1-15. At one point during the *Ezold* litigation, the plaintiff would have accepted an offer of $75,000 (one year's pay) to settle the matter. That was less than the cost of just one of the lawyers who worked on the firm's appeal, and the costs in reputation, acrimony, and time, as well as fees, were considerable. Ezold later noted, "it was ironic that the partners criticized me for lack of analytic ability when any lawyers in their right mind would have advised settlement." In a press interview after the trial, however, the co-chair of the firm's executive committee indicated that he felt there was "no choice" but to challenge the "impression that maybe there was sex discrimination," which would have hurt recruiting efforts and tarnished the firm's reputation as a champion of civil rights. By contrast, even after the firm won its appeal, Robert Segal, another firm leader, expressed doubts about whether he would have made the same judgment again. The litigation was "very expensive and very painful. This may have been a case that wasn't worth winning."[107]

If you had been a member of the firm's executive committee, would you have advised settlement? If you had been a female associate at the firm who had experienced sexist comments, would you have been willing to disclose them to Ezold's lawyer?

b. What Is Discrimination? The Special Case of Appearance Regulation

Many workplaces require their employers to meet certain appearance standards, which are often sex-based—for example, only women may be required to wear skirts, while only men may be required to have short hair. These cases often present difficult issues about what constitutes sex discrimination. On the one hand, a rule that allows (or requires) only women to wear skirts explicitly discriminates on the basis of sex. On the other hand, it may seem reasonable to give employers some latitude in regulating appearance, and courts do not want to spend scarce resources micromanaging workplace dress codes.

Courts have avoided finding sex discrimination through various approaches. The first federal appellate case on the subject upheld a hair length requirement imposed only on male employees on the grounds that the "discrimination" was based not on the "immutable characteristics" of sex, but rather characteristics over which the individual had control.[108] Other courts have determined that appearance regulations discriminate not on the basis of sex but rather on "neutral" generally accepted community grooming standards (that happen to be sex-specific).[109] Such reasoning is explored more fully in the notes below. The following case, Jespersen v. Harrah's Operating Company, takes a still different approach. There, the federal appellate court holds that sex-specific appearance rules are acceptable so long as the rules do not impose "unequal burdens" on men and women. In this case, the court found that although Harrah's required female employees, but not male employees, to wear makeup, the plaintiff failed to show that this policy posed an unequal burden on women.

How important a part do you think dress and appearance rules play in the disadvantages experienced by women? Do the standards challenged below perpetuate stereotypes that reduce women's opportunity?

Reading Questions

1. How important a part do you think dress and appearance rules play in the disadvantages experienced by women? Do the standards challenged below perpetuate stereotypes that reduce women's opportunities?
2. Should an employer be permitted to require only women to wear skirts in the workplace, and prohibit only men from wearing earrings?
3. Are any women advantaged by conventional expectations related to dress and appearance? What about men? Are the benefits worth the costs?
4. Who has the better argument concerning Harrah's policy? Does it impose an unequal burden on women? If so, should that be a violation of anti-discrimination law?
5. Should the *Jespersen* case have come out the other way, based on the sex stereotyping theory approved in *Price Waterhouse*?

Ordinarily in the federal court system, a case is heard by a panel of three judges who are members of that geographical circuit. An **en banc** opinion involves a decision by all the judges of the circuit, typically after a three-judge panel has made a decision, and a majority of the circuit believes that the circumstances warrant reconsideration by the entire court.

Jespersen v. Harrah's Operating Company, Inc.

444 F.3d 1104 (9th Cir. 2006) (en banc)

SCHROEDER, Chief Judge:

We took this sex discrimination case en banc in order to reaffirm our circuit law concerning appearance and grooming standards, and to clarify our evolving law of sex stereotyping claims.

The plaintiff, Darlene Jespersen, was terminated from her position as a bartender at the sports bar in Harrah's Reno casino not long after Harrah's began to enforce its comprehensive uniform, appearance and grooming standards for all bartenders. The standards required all bartenders, men and women, to wear the same uniform of black pants and white shirts, a bow tie, and comfortable black shoes. The standards also included grooming requirements that differed to some extent for men and women, requiring women to wear some facial makeup and not permitting men to wear any. Jespersen refused to comply with the makeup requirement and was effectively terminated for that reason.

The district court granted summary judgment to Harrah's on the ground that the appearance and grooming policies imposed equal burdens on both men and women bartenders because, while women were required to use makeup and men were forbidden to wear makeup, women were allowed to have long hair and men were required to have their hair cut to a length above the collar. The district court also held that the policy could not run afoul of Title VII because it did not discriminate against Jespersen on the basis of the "immutable characteristics" of her sex. The district court further observed that the Supreme Court's decision in *Price Waterhouse v. Hopkins*, prohibiting discrimination on the basis of sex stereotyping, did not apply to this case because in the district court's view, the Ninth Circuit had excluded grooming standards from the reach of *Price Waterhouse*. The district court granted summary judgment to Harrah's on all claims. [The en banc court affirmed.]

Summary judgment. A summary judgment means that the court decides the case on the allegations of the complaint and the response, without a trial. Summary judgment is appropriate when courts determine that even if plaintiffs are able to prove the facts they allege, they would not have a right to the relief they claim.

I. BACKGROUND

Plaintiff Darlene Jespersen worked successfully as a bartender at Harrah's for twenty years and compiled what by all accounts was an exemplary record. During Jespersen's entire tenure with Harrah's, the company maintained a policy encouraging female beverage servers to wear makeup. The parties agree, however, that the policy was not enforced until 2000. In February 2000, Harrah's implemented a "Beverage Department Image Transformation" program at twenty Harrah's locations, including its casino in Reno. Part of the program consisted of new grooming and appearance standards, called the "Personal Best" program. The program contained certain appearance standards that applied equally to both sexes, including a standard uniform of black pants, white shirt, black vest, and black bow tie. Jespersen has never objected to any of these policies. The program also contained some sex-differentiated appearance requirements as to hair, nails, and makeup.

In April 2000, Harrah's amended that policy to require that women wear makeup. Jespersen's only objection here is to the makeup requirement. The amended policy provided in relevant part (emphasis added):

> All Beverage Service Personnel, in addition to being friendly, polite, courteous and responsive to our customer's needs, must possess the ability to physically perform the essential factors of the job as set forth in the standard job descriptions. They must be well groomed, appealing to the eye, be firm and body toned, and be comfortable with maintaining this look while wearing the specified uniform. Additional factors to be considered include, but are not limited to, hair styles, overall body contour, and degree of comfort the employee projects while wearing the uniform. . . .
>
> Beverage Bartenders and Barbacks will adhere to these additional guidelines:
>
> Overall Guidelines (applied equally to male/female):

Appearance: Must maintain Personal Best image portrayed at time of hire.

Jewelry, if issued, must be worn. Otherwise, tasteful and simple jewelry is permitted; no large chokers, chains or bracelets.

No faddish hairstyles or unnatural colors are permitted.

Males:

Hair must not extend below top of shirt collar. Ponytails are prohibited.

Hands and fingernails must be clean and nails neatly trimmed at all times. No colored polish is permitted.

Eye and facial makeup is not permitted.

Shoes will be solid black leather or leather type with rubber (non skid) soles.

Females:

Hair must be teased, curled, or styled every day you work.

Hair must be worn down at all times, no exceptions.

Stockings are to be of nude or natural color consistent with employee's skin tone. No runs.

Nail polish can be clear, white, pink or red color only. No exotic nail art or length.

Shoes will be solid black leather or leather type with rubber (non skid) soles.

Make up (face powder, blush and mascara) must be worn and applied neatly in complimentary colors. Lip color must be worn at all times.

Jespersen did not wear makeup on or off the job, and in her deposition stated that wearing it would conflict with her self-image. It is not disputed that she found the makeup requirement offensive, and felt so uncomfortable wearing makeup that she found it interfered with her ability to perform as a bartender. Unwilling to wear the makeup, and not qualifying for any open positions at the casino with a similar compensation scale, Jespersen left her employment with Harrah's.

. . . In her complaint, Jespersen sought damages as well as declaratory and injunctive relief for discrimination and retaliation for opposition to discrimination, alleging that the "Personal Best" policy discriminated against women by "(1) subjecting them to terms and conditions of employment to which men are not similarly subjected, and (2) requiring that women conform to sex-based stereotypes as a term and condition of employment."

Harrah's moved for summary judgment, supporting its motion with documents giving the history and purpose of the appearance and grooming policies. Harrah's argued that the policy created similar standards for both men and women, and that where the standards differentiated on the basis of sex, as with the face and hair standards, any burdens imposed fell equally on both male and female bartenders.

In her deposition testimony, attached as a response to the motion for summary judgment, Jespersen described the personal indignity she felt as a result of attempting to comply with the makeup policy. Jespersen testified that when she wore the makeup she "felt very degraded and very demeaned." In addition, Jespersen testified that "it prohibited [her] from doing [her] job" because "it affected [her] self-dignity . . . [and] took away [her] credibility as an individual and as a person." . . .

The record therefore does not contain any affidavit or other evidence to establish that complying with the "Personal Best" standards caused burdens to fall unequally on men or women, and there is no evidence to suggest Harrah's motivation was to stereotype the women bartenders. Jespersen relied solely on evidence that she had been a good bartender, and that she had personal objections to complying with the policy, in order to support her argument that Harrah's "'sells' and exploits its women employees." Jespersen contended that as a matter of law she had made a prima facie showing of gender discrimination, sufficient to survive summary judgment on both of her claims.

II. UNEQUAL BURDENS

. . . [T]his case involves an appearance policy that applied to both male and female bartenders, and was aimed at creating a professional and very similar look for all of them. All bartenders wore the same uniform. The policy only differentiated as to grooming standards.

In Frank v. United Airlines, Inc. [2000], we dealt with a weight policy that applied different standards to men and women in a facially unequal way. The women were forced to meet the requirements of a medium body frame standard while men were required to meet only the more generous requirements of a large body frame standard. In that case, we recognized that "an appearance standard that imposes different but essentially equal burdens on men and women is not disparate treatment." The United weight policy, however, did not impose equal burdens. On its face, the policy embodied a requirement that categorically "'applied less favorably to one gender[,]'" and the burdens imposed upon that gender were obvious from the policy itself.

This case stands in marked contrast, for here we deal with requirements that, on their face, are not more onerous for one gender than the other. Rather, Harrah's "Personal Best" policy contains sex-differentiated requirements regarding each employee's hair, hands, and face. While those individual requirements differ according to gender, none on its face places a greater burden on one gender than the other. Grooming standards that appropriately differentiate between the genders are not facially discriminatory. . . .

Not every differentiation between the sexes in a grooming and appearance policy creates a "significantly greater burden of compliance." For example, . . . this court upheld Safeway's enforcement of its sex-differentiated appearance standard, including its requirement that male employees wear ties, because the company's actions in enforcing the regulations were not "overly burdensome to its employees." Similarly, as the Eighth Circuit has recognized, "where, as here, such [grooming and appearance] policies are reasonable and are imposed in an evenhanded manner on all employees, slight differences in the appearance requirements for males and females have only a negligible effect on employment opportunities." . . .

Jespersen asks us to take judicial notice of the fact that it costs more money and takes more time for a woman to comply with the makeup requirement than it takes for a man to comply with the requirement that he keep his hair short, but these are not matters appropriate for judicial notice. . . .

. . . Jespersen did not submit any documentation or any evidence of the relative cost and time required to comply with the grooming requirements by men and women. As a result, we would have to speculate about those issues in order to then guess whether the policy creates unequal burdens for women. This would not be appropriate.

III. SEX STEREOTYPING

In *Price Waterhouse*, the Supreme Court considered a mixed-motive discrimination case. There, the plaintiff, Ann Hopkins, was denied partnership in the national accounting firm of Price Waterhouse because some of the partners found her to be too aggressive. While some partners praised Hopkins's "'strong character, independence and integrity,'" others commented that she needed to take "a course at charm school,". . . .

The stereotyping in *Price Waterhouse* interfered with Hopkins' ability to perform her work; the advice that she should take "a course at charm school" was intended to discourage her use of the forceful and aggressive techniques that made her successful in the first place. Impermissible sex stereotyping was clear because the very traits that she was asked to hide were the same traits considered praiseworthy in men.

Harrah's "Personal Best" policy is very different. The policy does not single out Jespersen. It applies to all of the bartenders, male and female. It requires all of the bartenders to wear exactly the same uniforms while interacting with the public in the context of the entertainment industry. It is for the most part unisex, from the black tie to the non-skid shoes. There is no evidence in this record to indicate that the policy was adopted to make women bartenders conform to a commonly-accepted stereotypical image of what women should wear. The record contains nothing to suggest the grooming standards would objectively inhibit a woman's ability to do the job. The only evidence in the record to support the stereotyping claim is Jespersen's own subjective reaction to the makeup requirement.

Judge Pregerson's dissent improperly divides the grooming policy into separate categories of hair, hands, and face, and then focuses exclusively on the makeup requirement to conclude that the policy constitutes sex stereotyping. This parsing, however, conflicts with established grooming standards analysis. . . . The requirements must be viewed in the context of the overall policy.

The dissent's conclusion that the unequal burdens analysis allows impermissible sex stereotyping to persist if imposed equally on both sexes . . . is wrong because it ignores the protections of *Price Waterhouse* our decision preserves. If a grooming standard imposed on either sex amounts to impermissible stereotyping, something this record does not establish, a plaintiff of either sex may challenge that requirement under *Price Waterhouse*.

We respect Jespersen's resolve to be true to herself and to the image that she wishes to project to the world. We cannot agree, however, that her objection to the makeup requirement, without more, can give rise to a claim of sex stereotyping under Title VII. If we were to do so, we would come perilously close to holding that every grooming, apparel, or appearance requirement that an individual finds personally offensive, or in conflict with his or her own self-image, can create a triable issue of sex discrimination.

This is not a case where the dress or appearance requirement is intended to be sexually provocative, and tending to stereotype women as sex objects. See, e.g., EEOC v. Sage Realty Corp., [1981]. In *Sage Realty*, the plaintiff was a lobby attendant in a hotel that employed only female lobby attendants and required a mandatory uniform. . . . There, the plaintiff was required to wear a uniform that was "short and revealing on both sides [such that her] thighs and portions of her buttocks were exposed." Jespersen, in contrast, was asked only to wear a unisex uniform that covered her entire body and was designed for men and women. The "Personal Best" policy does not, on its face, indicate any discriminatory or sexually stereotypical intent on the part of Harrah's. . . . Jespersen's claim here materially differs from Hopkins' claim in *Price Waterhouse* because Harrah's grooming standards do not require Jespersen to conform to a stereotypical image that would objectively impede her ability to perform her job requirements as a bartender.

We emphasize that we do not preclude, as a matter of law, a claim of sex-stereotyping on the basis of dress or appearance codes. Others may well be filed, and any bases for such claims refined as law in this area evolves. This record, however, is devoid of any basis for permitting this particular claim to go forward, as it is limited to the subjective reaction of a single employee, and there is no evidence of a stereotypical motivation on the part of the employer. This case is essentially a challenge to one small part of what is an overall apparel, appearance, and grooming policy that applies largely the same requirements to both men and women. . . . [T]he touchstone is reasonableness. A makeup requirement must be seen in the context of the overall standards imposed on employees in a given workplace.

PREGERSON, Circuit Judge, with whom Judges KOZINSKI, GRABER, and W. FLETCHER join, dissenting:

. . . I believe that the "Personal Best" program was part of a policy motivated by sex stereotyping and that Jespersen's termination for failing to comply with the program's requirements was "because of" her sex. Accordingly,

I dissent from Part III of the majority opinion and from the judgment of the court.

The majority contends that it is bound to reject Jespersen's sex stereotyping claim because she presented too little evidence — only her "own subjective reaction to the makeup requirement." I disagree. Jespersen's evidence showed that Harrah's fired her because she did not comply with a grooming policy that imposed a facial uniform (full makeup) on only female bartenders. Harrah's stringent "Personal Best" policy required female beverage servers to wear foundation, blush, mascara, and lip color, and to ensure that lip color was on at all times. Jespersen and her female colleagues were required to meet with professional image consultants who in turn created a facial template for each woman. Jespersen was required not simply to wear makeup; in addition, the consultants dictated where and how the makeup had to be applied. . . .

This policy did not, as the majority suggests, impose a "grooming, apparel, or appearance requirement that an individual finds personally offensive," but rather one that treated Jespersen differently from male bartenders "because of" her sex. I believe that the fact that Harrah's designed and promoted a policy that required women to conform to a sex stereotype by wearing full makeup is sufficient "direct evidence" of discrimination.

The majority contends that Harrah's "Personal Best" appearance policy is very different from the policy at issue in *Price Waterhouse* in that it applies to both men and women. . . . The fact that a policy contains sex-differentiated requirements that affect people of both genders cannot excuse a particular requirement from scrutiny. By refusing to consider the makeup requirement separately, and instead stressing that the policy contained some gender-neutral requirements, such as color of clothing, as well as a variety of gender-differentiated requirements for "hair, hands, and face," the majority's approach would permit otherwise impermissible gender stereotypes to be neutralized by the presence of a stereotype or burden that affects people of the opposite gender, or by some separate non-discriminatory requirement that applies to both men and women. . . . But the fact that employees of both genders are subjected to gender-specific requirements does not necessarily mean that particular requirements are not motivated by gender stereotyping.

Because I believe that we should be careful not to insulate appearance requirements by viewing them in broad categories, such as "hair, hands, and face," I would consider the makeup requirement on its own terms. Viewed in isolation — or, at the very least, as part of a narrower category of requirements affecting employees' faces — the makeup or facial uniform requirement becomes closely analogous to the uniform policy held to constitute impermissible sex stereotyping in Carroll v. Talman Federal Savings & Loan Ass'n of Chicago, [1979]. In *Carroll*, the defendant bank required women to wear employer-issued uniforms, but permitted men to wear business attire of their own choosing. The Seventh Circuit found this rule discriminatory because it suggested to the public that the uniformed women held a "lesser professional status" and that women could not be trusted to choose appropriate business attire.

Just as the bank in *Carroll* deemed female employees incapable of achieving a professional appearance without assigned uniforms, Harrah's regarded women as unable to achieve a neat, attractive, and professional appearance without the facial uniform designed by a consultant and required by Harrah's. The inescapable message is that women's undoctored faces compare unfavorably to men's, not because of a physical difference between men's and women's faces, but because of a cultural assumption—and gender-based stereotype—that women's faces are incomplete, unattractive, or unprofessional without full makeup. We need not denounce all makeup as inherently offensive, just as there was no need to denounce all uniforms as inherently offensive in *Carroll*, to conclude that *requiring* female bartenders to wear full makeup is an impermissible sex stereotype and is evidence of discrimination because of sex. Therefore, I strongly disagree with the majority's conclusion that there "is no evidence in this record to indicate that the policy was adopted to make women bartenders conform to a commonly-accepted stereotypical image of what women should wear."

I believe that Jespersen articulated a classic case of *Price Waterhouse* discrimination and presented undisputed, material facts sufficient to avoid summary judgment. Accordingly, Jespersen should be allowed to present her case to a jury.

KOZINSKI, Circuit Judge, with whom Judges GRABER and W. FLETCHER join, dissenting:

I agree with Judge Pregerson and join his dissent—subject to one caveat: I believe that Jespersen also presented a triable issue of fact on the question of disparate burden.

The majority is right that "the [makeup] requirements must be viewed in the context of the overall policy." But I find it perfectly clear that Harrah's overall grooming policy is substantially more burdensome for women than for men. Every requirement that forces men to spend time or money on their appearance has a corresponding requirement that is as, or more, burdensome for women: short hair v. "teased, curled, or styled" hair; clean trimmed nails v. nail length and color requirements; black leather shoes v. black leather shoes. The requirement that women spend time and money applying full facial makeup has no corresponding requirement for men, making the "overall policy" more burdensome for the former than for the latter. The only question is how much.

It is true that Jespersen failed to present evidence about what it costs to buy makeup and how long it takes to apply it. But is there any doubt that putting on makeup costs money and takes time? Harrah's policy requires women to apply face powder, blush, mascara and lipstick. You don't need an expert witness to figure out that such items don't grow on trees.

Nor is there any rational doubt that application of makeup is an intricate and painstaking process that requires considerable time and care. Even those of us who don't wear makeup know how long it can take from the hundreds of hours we've spent over the years frantically tapping our toes and pointing to our wrists. It's hard to imagine that a woman could "put on her face," as they say, in the time it would take a man to shave—certainly not if she were to do the careful and thorough job Harrah's expects. Makeup, moreover, must be applied and removed every day; the policy burdens men with no such daily ritual. While a man could jog to the casino, slip into his uniform, and get right to work, a woman must travel to work so as to avoid smearing her makeup, or arrive early to put on her makeup there.

It might have been tidier if Jespersen had introduced evidence as to the time and cost associated with complying with the makeup requirement, but I can understand her failure to do so, as these hardly seem like questions reasonably subject to dispute. We could—and should—take judicial notice of these incontrovertible facts.

Alternatively, Jespersen did introduce evidence that she finds it burdensome to *wear* makeup because doing so is inconsistent with her self-image and interferes with her job performance. My colleagues dismiss this evidence, apparently on the ground that wearing makeup does not, as a matter of law, constitute a substantial burden. This presupposes that Jespersen is unreasonable or idiosyncratic in her discomfort. Why so? Whether to wear cosmetics—literally, the face one presents to the world—is an intensely personal choice. Makeup, moreover, touches delicate parts of the anatomy—the lips, the eyes, the cheeks—and can cause serious discomfort, sometimes even allergic reactions, for someone unaccustomed to wearing it. If you are used to wearing makeup—as most American women are—this may seem like no big deal. But those of us not used to wearing makeup would find a requirement that we do so highly intrusive. Imagine, for example, a rule that all judges wear face powder, blush, mascara and lipstick while on the bench. Like Jespersen, I would find such a regime burdensome and demeaning; it would interfere with my job performance. I suspect many of my colleagues would feel the same way.

Everyone accepts this as a reasonable reaction from a man, but why should it be different for a woman? It is not because of anatomical differences, such as a requirement that women wear bathing suits that cover their breasts. Women's faces, just like those of men, can be perfectly presentable without makeup; it is a cultural artifact that most women raised in the United States learn to put on—and presumably enjoy wearing—cosmetics. But cultural norms change; not so long ago a man wearing an earring was a gypsy, a pirate or an oddity. Today, a man wearing body piercing jewelry is hardly noticed. So, too, a large (and perhaps growing) number of women choose to present themselves to the world without makeup. I see no justification for forcing them to conform to Harrah's quaint notion of what a "real woman" looks like.

Nor do I think it appropriate for a court to dismiss a woman's testimony that she finds wearing makeup degrading and intrusive, as Jespersen clearly does. Not only do we have her sworn statement to that effect, but there can be no doubt about her sincerity or the intensity of her feelings: She quit her job—a job she performed well for two decades—rather than put on the makeup. That is a choice her male colleagues were not forced to make. To me, this states a case of disparate burden, and I would let a jury decide whether an employer can force a woman to make this choice.

Finally, I note with dismay the employer's decision to let go a valued, experienced employee who had gained accolades from her customers, over what, in the end, is a trivial matter. Quality employees are difficult to find in any industry and I would think an employer would long hesitate before forcing a loyal, long-time employee to quit over an honest and heart-felt difference of opinion about a matter of personal significance to her. Having won the legal battle, I hope that Harrah's will now do the generous and decent thing by offering Jespersen her job back, and letting her give it her personal best — without the makeup.

Notes

1. Judicial Ideology. The lineup of votes in *Jespersen* is somewhat surprising. Judge Mary Schroeder, who wrote the majority decision, is widely viewed as liberal, while Judge Alex Kozinski, one of the nation's most prominent conservative judges, dissented. Some have speculated that Judge Schroeder was aware that Jespersen would lose and voted with the majority in order to assign herself the opinion and to minimize its negative impact on discrimination law. Others have suggested that she decided that the burdens involved were relatively trivial and wanted to discourage comparable litigation. If either of those reasons is true, how would you evaluate it? Is your view affected by research finding that although Harrah's changed its policy, the decision has not significantly influenced practices in the casino industry and has not triggered further lawsuits? Part of the reason is that female workers generally see makeup as a way to ensure good tips, and lawyers do not believe these cases are sufficiently remunerative to file.[110]

2. The Importance of Appearance. Beauty may be only "skin deep," but that is deep enough to confer significant advantages.[111] Attractive individuals are more likely to be hired and promoted, and it is estimated that they make 14 percent more per hour than their less attractive counterparts.[112] Even in fields like law, where appearance bears no obvious relation to job performance, one study found that attractive attorneys, regardless of qualification and experience, earned significantly more than their less attractive counterparts, and that the disparity increases over time.[113] In a national poll, about 16 percent of individuals believed that they had been subject to appearance-related discrimination, a higher percentage than those in other polls reporting gender or racial discrimination (12 percent).[114]

What are the costs of appearance-related bias to employees, employers, and society generally? Are they justified or inevitable? Is a person's appearance like intelligence, which produces different opportunities that we must simply accept? Or is it an unfair basis for discrimination that we should attempt to reduce through legal remedies? Does it matter that research shows that some appearance preferences such as facial symmetry and unblemished skin appear to be innate?[115] If so, should it matter that the "in-group" preferences underlying racial and ethnic discrimination also appear to be hard-wired? Should we expect employers to take reasonable steps to avoid using attractiveness as a proxy for effective job performance?

3. Legal Standards.   The unequal burden test endorsed in *Jespersen* marks an advance over prior law, which saw grooming codes as neutral and acceptable as long as they merely reflected "community standards." Commentators often had pointed out that reliance on community standards, discussed further below, only served to reinforce the very stereotypes that Title VII was intended to eliminate.[116] Does the unequal burden test do much better? What would Jespersen have needed to show to demonstrate that the makeup requirement imposed an unequal burden on women? Couldn't a court take judicial notice of the fact that cosmetics don't grow on trees and that it takes time to style hair? Does the equal burden test capture all that is objectionable in Harrah's policy? Consider Rhode's claim:

> The problem with this prevailing approach to appearance regulation is not only that judges often seem clueless about the disproportionate demands that many codes impose on women. The difficulty is also that a framework comparing male and female burdens fails to capture all of what makes these regulations objectionable. Darlene Jespersen resisted Harrah's makeup requirement not because it took more time and money for her to be presentable than her male counterparts, but because she felt that being "dolled up" was degrading and undermined her credibility with unruly customers. Dress codes that require women to wear skirts and high heels are problematic for similar reasons, regardless of what the codes demand of men.[117]

In Rhode's view,

> Justifications for banning appearance discrimination rest on three basic claims. The first is that such discrimination offends principles of equal opportunity; individuals should be judged on merit and performance, not irrelevant physical characteristics. A second rationale is that appearance-related bias reinforces group subordination; it exacerbates disadvantages based on gender, race, ethnicity, class, age, and sexual orientation. A third justification is that some decisions based on appearance unduly restrict self-expression and cultural identity. Although opponents of prohibiting appearance discrimination raise some legitimate concerns, these can be met through well-designed statutory schemes. The excessive liability and business backlash that critics have predicted have not in fact materialized in the few jurisdictions that have prohibited appearance-related bias.[118]

What is your view? Should judges take a less permissive view toward appearance discrimination? In general, courts have upheld sex-specific requirements even when the standards are stricter or more burdensome for one sex (although not when they also discriminate by race).[119] Are these rulings defensible? What would happen in most workplaces if courts held that sex-specific grooming codes constituted unlawful discrimination? Would it have a major effect on dress and grooming practices? Would there be any significant negative consequences?

Claims of discrimination by plaintiffs that they were discriminated against for being too attractive and dressing too sexy have also been largely unsuccessful.[120] However, a few courts have been willing to see standards of attractiveness as a form of sex stereotyping. In v. Heartland Inns of America (2010), the Eighth Circuit Court of Appeals found that the plaintiff had established a prima facie case of sex discrimination based on allegations that she had lost her position as a front desk hotel clerk because she was not "pretty," and lacked the "Midwestern girl look."[121]

Why do businesses want to control the appearance of their employees? Ordinarily, a business cannot discriminate on the basis of race, sex, or other prohibited factors just because customers may prefer it. The reasons are obvious, and explored more fully in Wilson v. Southwest Airlines, discussed below. Often these preferences reflect precisely the biases that anti-discrimination laws seek to address. Are dress and appearance standards just a version of this? A highly publicized example is Craft v. Metromedia, Inc.[122] There, a local television station anchorwoman, Christine Craft, filed suit against her employer after she was moved to another, off-camera position because producers found her hair and makeup to be inappropriate. Craft claimed that she was judged by harsher standards than male anchors. The station responded with audience research including focus groups and a scientific telephone survey, which showed that the plaintiff's appearance had an adverse impact on her acceptance among viewers. The court determined that she was properly reassigned due to the demonstrated negative viewer response.[123] By that logic, could television stations require that female but not male anchors look young and attractive because viewers will accept a Larry King but not a female equivalent?

One problem with such double standards is that they can become self-perpetuating. Viewers may expect youth and beauty in female newscasters partly because they lack exposure to an alternative: women who gained their position through merit-related qualifications. Reconsider how to approach this question after reading Wilson v. Southwest Airlines.

4. Weight. One of the most common forms of appearance discrimination concerns weight. A wide array of research finds that women are judged more harshly than men for being overweight, that a majority of overweight women report experiencing discrimination, and that those who are obese or significantly overweight earn less than average-sized women.[124] Because being overweight is most common in African-American and low income women, weight requirements have a disproportionate impact based on race and class.

Weight limits have been a common appearance requirement in some occupations. Flight attendants were the most widely noted examples. Courts initially upheld strict restrictions even though the standards for men took into account large frame sizes while the standards for women presupposed small or medium builds. One court relied on the "fact" that the weight restrictions for women at issue in that case did not concern an "immutable characteristic": weight, unlike height, is subject to the "reasonable control" of most individuals.[125] Frank v. United Airlines, Inc., cited in *Jespersen*, reversed such rulings. There, the Ninth Circuit Court of Appeals found that a policy permitting men's weight to vary within a broader range of frame sizes than women constituted unlawful sex discrimination.

Despite the commonly held view that weight is a matter of personal choice and discipline, a wide array of research indicates that it is also influenced by genetic and environmental factors and that over 90 percent of individuals are unable to achieve long-term weight loss through dieting.[126] Discrimination based on weight contributes to eating disorders, which disproportionately affect women and girls.[127] Over 90 percent of those suffering from anorexia or bulimia are female, although some recent research suggests that the problems are growing among men.[128]

Some plaintiffs have successfully sued for weight discrimination under the federal Americans with Disabilities Act (ADA) and analogous state provisions. However, governing regulations under the ADA interpret the Act to cover only extremely severe obesity (100 percent over average weight) caused by a physiological disorder.[129] Although a few state and local ordinances offer broader protections, the vast majority of individuals remain unprotected.[130]

A few jurisdictions have specific prohibitions on appearance discrimination. Michigan and San Francisco ban discrimination based on height and weight. Local ordinances in Madison, Wisconsin, Urbana, Illinois, Santa Cruz, California, and Howard County, Maryland, ban appearance discrimination more generally, although with certain exceptions such as for grooming requirements or for characteristics within an individual's control.[131]

Should more jurisdictions enact such prohibitions? In one opinion poll, 33 percent of Americans thought that laws should protect unattractive people from hiring discrimination, while 39 percent believed that employers should be allowed to discriminate based on appearance.[132] Scholars are also divided. Some worry that extending civil rights acts to such claims will erode support for such legislation and trivialize more serious forms of bias. Stanford law professor Richard Ford frames a common objection:

> [T]here are practical limits of human attention and sympathy. The good-natured humanitarian who listens attentively to the first claim of social injustice will become an impatient curmudgeon after multiple similar admonishments. . . . And a business community united in frustration at a bloated civil rights regime could become a powerful political force for reform or even repeal. . . . The growing number of social groups making claims to civil rights protection threatens the political and practical viability of civil rights for those who need them most.
>
> The law can identify a small set of social prejudices—race, sex, religion, national origin, age and disability—that are so unjustified and so socially

destructive that we're confident that the benefits of prohibiting them out-weigh the costs. . . . But there are limits. . . . It's a mistake to turn civil rights against truly invidious discrimination into an omnibus requirement that we reward intrinsic merit. . . . The fantastic aspiration to somehow make soci-ety perfectly "fair" through force of law reflects a dangerous combination of gauzy idealism, narcissistic entitlement and reckless hubris.[133]

Is this a fair point? One survey of appearance discrimination laws found no evidence of such backlash, but also highly limited enforcement activity, partly due to the costs and difficulties of proof and the limited remedies avail-able. Such regulation did, however, remedy some of the worst abuses, increase complainants' bargaining leverage, and attract public attention to the prob-lems.[134] The same appears true for the one other jurisdiction abroad, Victoria, Australia, that explicitly prohibits appearance discrimination.[135] Is this an ade-quate justification for the laws? What other policy strategies might be useful? Would modifying the employment-at-will doctrine to require just cause for dismissals or demotion be a partial solution?[136]

5. Sex and Age. Sex and age can be a devastating combination, particu-larly for women. Even in jobs where appearance is considered less important, older women earn lower salaries than men and younger women, and they may lack opportunities to obtain higher-paying and more prestigious jobs.[137] A few high-profile cases have rendered successful verdicts for women claiming age and appearance discrimination.[138] In one recent lawsuit, nine Atlantic City cocktail servers, including women ages 54, 57, and 66, claimed that they had been dismissed after having to audition in "skimpy flapper" costumes. Gloria Allred, who represented the women, maintained that maybe owners believed that "they can profit by using young women as bait to hook in young men to buy drinks, but it's wrong. Women are not just sex objects."[139] One commen-tator responded, "[t]he whole point of being a cocktail waitress in a casino is to be a sex object. . . . And eventually, grandma needs to take off the cocktail underwear."[140] Who is right?

6. Feminism and Appearance. Issues of appearance have long been divisive issues for feminists. While some leaders of the women's movement have denounced makeup, high heels, and cosmetic surgery as forms of objec-tification and subordination, other feminists see them as a source of pleasure and agency. Where do you fall in this debate? Is there a way to find common ground by focusing not on individual practices but on social forces that shame and stigmatize women, and that fail to provide sufficient safeguards against unsafe or fraudulent cosmetic practices?[141] Consider Rhode's view:

> The overemphasis on attractiveness diminishes women's credibility and diverts attention from their capabilities and accomplishments. In the long run, these are more stable sources of self-esteem and social power than appear-ance. Prevailing beauty standards also place women in a double bind. They are expected to conform, yet condemned as vain and narcissistic for attempts

to do so. Neither should they "let themselves go," nor look as if they were trying too hard not to. Beauty must seem natural, even, or especially, when it can only be accomplished through considerable unnatural effort. . . . Feminists are in a particularly problematic situation. Those who defy conventional standards are ridiculed as homely harpies; those who comply are dismissed as hypocrites.

Whatever their other disagreements on these issues, most individuals appear to share certain core values. Appearance should be a source of pleasure, not of shame. Individuals should be able to make decisions about whether to enhance their attractiveness without being judged politically incorrect or professionally unacceptable. Our ideals of appearance should reflect diversity across race, ethnicity, age, and body size. In this ideal world, the importance of appearance would not be overstated. Nor would it spill over to employment and educational contexts in which judgments should be based on competence, not cosmetics. Women would not be held to higher standards than men. Neither would they be subject to sexualized grooming requirements unless sex is the commodity being sold. Women's self-esteem would be tied to accomplishment, not appearance. In order for appearance to be a source of enjoyment rather than anxiety, it cannot dictate women's self-worth.[142]

Do you agree? Is a unifying agenda for feminists possible on this issue?

Putting Theory Into Practice

1-16. Can a retail cosmetic saleswoman be fired for "not being hot enough"? Could a casino impose weight and appearance requirements on its Borgata "Babes" who serve cocktails?[143]

1-17. A prestigious uptown law firm in Manhattan requires women in its receptionist and secretarial positions to wear high heels. Does this violate Title VII? Does it matter, under Title VII, that high-heeled shoes are largely responsible for the fact that 90 percent of all forefoot surgery is performed on women, and that "seventy-five percent of the problems eventuating in [the foot] corrections performed annually in the United States either result from or are greatly aggravated by the use of high-fashion footwear"?[144] Or that, in addition to the adverse health consequences, high heels have long been used as a symbol of idleness or, in Thorstein Veblen's words, of "the wearer's abstinence from productive employment"?[145]

1-18. At the Seventh Circuit Annual Judicial Conference, some judges complained of distracting attire—"blouses so short there's no way the judges wouldn't look" and a velour outfit that looked as if the lawyer was "on her way home from the gym."[146] Is it appropriate for firms to monitor what lawyers wear to court on the grounds that some judges have complained about overly sexy or informal attire? Is there a difference between overly sexy and informal attire that might justify an employer's stronger regulation of one or the other?

1-19. Jazzercise refused a franchise to Jennifer Portnick, a 245-pound aerobics instructor, on the ground that the company sold "fitness." According to its lawyer, "[o]ne of the keys to success is extending franchises to instructors with a fit, toned body. Being able to portray this image inspires students. The fit and toned body image is a necessary part of what students seek to achieve." Portnick was in fact fit. She worked out six days a week, taught back-to-back exercise classes, and had no history of performance problems or lack of students. Can she win a lawsuit against Jazzercise under San Francisco's ordinance banning discrimination based on height and weight, or does a company have a legitimate reason for refusing to be associated with an overweight instructor?[147]

c. When Is Sex a "Bona Fide Occupational Qualification"?

Once plaintiffs demonstrate that they have been treated differently on the basis of sex, employers are liable under Title VII unless they can meet the high burden of showing that sex is a "bona fide occupational qualification," or BFOQ. For cases brought under the disparate impact theory of Title VII, the employer must meet the somewhat lower burden of "business necessity."

Dothard v. Rawlinson, excerpted below, considers two different sets of requirements for applicants to be correctional counselors in the Alabama state prison system. The first are height and weight requirements that are neutral on their face, and discriminatory only in their disproportionate effects in excluding women from job eligibility; Title VII reaches these job requirements only through the disparate impact theory. The second is an explicit exclusion of women from maximum-security contact positions, and thus that issue is analyzed under Title VII as disparate treatment. In *Dothard*, the Supreme Court found unconstitutional the height and weight requirements, which were not shown to be sufficiently job-related, but it upheld the exclusion of women from "contact positions" in all-male prisons.

In Wilson v. Southwest Airlines Co., a class of male job applicants challenged the employer's policy against hiring men for flight attendant and ticket agent positions. The Texas court held that although the employer used female allure successfully to market its business, being female was not a necessary qualification to perform these jobs.

Reading Questions

1. Can you think of particular jobs where sex should be either a BFOQ or a business necessity?
2. What if the only plausibility for the offered BFOQ defense reflects stereotypes held by others? Should it matter whether these other people are prisoners, or customers?

Dothard v. Rawlinson

433 U.S. 321 (1977)

Mr. Justice STEWART delivered the opinion of the Court.

Appellee Dianne Rawlinson sought employment with the Alabama Board of Corrections as a prison guard, called in Alabama a "correctional counselor." After her application was rejected, she brought this class suit under Title VII of the Civil Rights Act of 1964. . . .

At the time she applied for a position as correctional counselor trainee, Rawlinson was a 22-year-old college graduate whose major course of study had been correctional psychology. She was refused employment because she failed to meet the minimum 120-pound weight requirement established by an Alabama statute. The statute also establishes a height minimum of 5 feet 2 inches. [Rawlinson subsequently amended her complaint to challenge Alabama Administrative Regulation 204 that established a "gender criteria" for assigning correctional counselors to "contact positions" requiring close physical proximity to inmates.] . . .

Like most correctional facilities in the United States, Alabama's prisons are segregated on the basis of sex. . . . A correctional counselor's primary duty within these institutions is to maintain security and control of the inmates by continually supervising and observing their activities. . . .

At the time this litigation was in the District Court, the Board of Corrections employed a total of 435 people in various correctional counselor positions, 56 of whom were women. Of those 56 women, 21 were employed at the Julia Tutwiler Prison for Women. . . . Because most of Alabama's prisoners are held at the four maximum-security male penitentiaries, 336 of the 435 correctional counselor jobs were in those institutions, a majority of them concededly in the "contact" classification. Thus, even though meeting the statutory height and weight requirements, women applicants could under Regulation 204 compete equally with men for only about 25% of the correctional counselor jobs available in the Alabama prison system. . . .

It is asserted . . . that these facially neutral qualifications standards work . . . disproportionately to exclude women from eligibility for employment by the Alabama Board of Corrections. [Our prior cases involving racial bias] make clear that to establish a prima facie case of discrimination, a plaintiff need only show that the facially neutral standards in question select applicants for hire in a significantly discriminatory pattern. Once it is thus shown that the employment standards are discriminatory in effect, the employer must meet "the burden of showing that any given requirement (has) . . . a manifest relationship to the employment in question [Griggs]." If the employer proves that the challenged requirements are job related, the plaintiff may then show that other selection devices without a similar discriminatory effect would also "serve the employer's legitimate interest in 'efficient and trustworthy workmanship.'" . . .

A **prima facie** case is established when a party has produced sufficient evidence for the judge or jury to rule in the party's favor unless the evidence is rebutted.

. . . In considering the effect of the minimum height and weight standards on this disparity in rate of hiring between the sexes, the District Court found that . . . [w]hen the height and weight restrictions are combined, Alabama's statutory standards would exclude 41.13% of the female population while excluding less than 1% of the male population. Accordingly, the District Court found that Rawlinson had made out a prima facie case of unlawful sex discrimination.

The appellants argue that a showing of disproportionate impact on women based on generalized national statistics should not suffice to establish a prima facie case. They point in particular to Rawlinson's failure to adduce comparative statistics concerning actual applicants for correctional counselor positions in Alabama. There is no requirement, however, that a statistical showing of disproportionate impact must always be based on analysis of the characteristics of actual applicants. . . . The application process might itself not adequately reflect the actual potential applicant pool, since otherwise qualified people might be discouraged from applying because of a self-recognized inability to meet the very standards challenged as being discriminatory. . . . A potential applicant could easily determine her height and weight and conclude that to make an application would be futile. Moreover, reliance on general population demographic data was not misplaced where there was no reason to suppose that physical height and weight characteristics of Alabama men and women differ markedly from those of the national population.

For these reasons, we cannot say that the District Court was wrong in holding that the statutory height and weight standards had a discriminatory impact on women applicants. . . .

We turn, therefore, to the appellants' argument that they have rebutted the prima facie case of discrimination by showing that the height and weight requirements are job related. These requirements, they say, have a relationship to strength, a sufficient but unspecified amount of which is essential to effective job performance as a correctional counselor. In the District Court, however, the appellants produced no evidence correlating the height and weight requirements with the requisite amount of strength thought essential to good job performance. Indeed, they failed to offer evidence of any kind in specific justification of the statutory standards. . . .

[T]he District Court was not in error in holding that Title VII . . . prohibits application of the statutory height and weight requirements to Rawlinson and the class she represents.

III

Unlike the statutory height and weight requirements, Regulation 204 [excluding women from maximum security "contact positions"] explicitly discriminates against women on the basis of their sex. In defense of this overt discrimination, the appellants rely on [Title VII's BFOQ defense], which permits sex-based discrimination "in those certain instances where . . . sex . . . is a bona fide occupational qualification reasonably necessary to the normal operation of that particular business or enterprise." . . .

We are persuaded by the restrictive language of [Title VII], the relevant legislative history, and the consistent interpretation of the Equal Employment Opportunity Commission that the BFOQ exception was in fact meant to be an extremely narrow exception to the general prohibition of discrimination on the basis of sex. In the particular factual circumstances of this case, however, we conclude that the District Court erred in rejecting the State's contention that Regulation 204 falls within the narrow ambit of the BFOQ exception.

The environment in Alabama's penitentiaries is a peculiarly inhospitable one for human beings of whatever sex. Indeed, a Federal District Court has held that the conditions of confinement in the prisons of the State, characterized by "rampant violence" and a "jungle atmosphere," are constitutionally intolerable. . . . The record in the present case shows that because of inadequate staff and facilities, no attempt is made in the four maximum-security male penitentiaries to classify or segregate inmates according to their offense or level of dangerousness—a procedure that, according to expert testimony, is essential to effective penological administration. Consequently, the estimated 20% of the male prisoners who are sex offenders are scattered throughout the penitentiaries' dormitory facilities.

In this environment of violence and disorganization, it would be an oversimplification to characterize Regulation 204 as an exercise in "romantic paternalism." [Frontiero v. Richardson]. In the usual case, the argument that a particular job is too dangerous for women may appropriately be met by the rejoinder that it is the purpose of Title VII to allow the individual woman to make that choice for herself. More is at stake in this case, however, than an individual woman's decision to weigh and accept the risks of employment in a "contact" position in a maximum-security male prison.

The essence of a correctional counselor's job is to maintain prison security. A woman's relative ability to maintain order in a male, maximum-security, unclassified penitentiary of the type Alabama now runs could be directly reduced by her womanhood. There is a basis in fact for expecting that sex offenders who have criminally assaulted women in the past would be moved to do so again if access to women were established within the prison. There would also be a real risk that other inmates, deprived of a normal heterosexual environment, would assault women guards because they were women.[22] In a prison system where violence is the order of the day, where inmate access to

---

22. The record contains evidence of an attack on a female clerical worker in an Alabama prison, and of an incident involving a woman student who was taken hostage during a visit to one of the maximum-security institutions.

guards is facilitated by dormitory living arrangements, where every institution is understaffed, and where a substantial portion of the inmate population is composed of sex offenders mixed at random with other prisoners, there are few visible deterrents to inmate assaults on women custodians.

Appellee Rawlinson's own expert testified that dormitory housing for aggressive inmates poses a greater security problem than single-cell lockups, and further testified that it would be unwise to use women as guards in a prison where even 10% of the inmates had been convicted of sex crimes and were not segregated from the other prisoners. The likelihood that inmates would assault a woman because she was a woman would pose a real threat not only to the victim of the assault but also to the basic control of the penitentiary and protection of its inmates and the other security personnel. The employee's very womanhood would thus directly undermine her capacity to provide the security that is the essence of a correctional counselor's responsibility. . . .

The judgment is accordingly affirmed in part and reversed in part, and the case is remanded to the District Court for further proceedings consistent with this opinion. . . .

Mr. Justice MARSHALL, with whom Mr. Justice BRENNAN joins, concurring in part and dissenting in part. . . .

The Court properly rejects two proffered justifications for denying women jobs as prison guards. It is simply irrelevant here that a guard's occupation is dangerous and that some women might be unable to protect themselves adequately. Those themes permeate the testimony of the state officials below, but as the Court holds, "the argument that a particular job is too dangerous for women" is refuted by the "purpose of Title VII to allow the individual woman to make that choice for herself." . . . Some women, like some men, undoubtedly are not qualified and do not wish to serve as prison guards, but that does not justify the exclusion of all women from this employment opportunity. . . .

What would otherwise be considered unlawful discrimination against women is justified by the Court, however, on the basis of the "barbaric and inhumane" conditions in Alabama prisons, conditions so bad that state officials have conceded that they violate the Constitution. . . . To me, this analysis sounds distressingly like saying two wrongs make a right. It is refuted by the plain words of [Title VII, which] requires that a BFOQ be "reasonably necessary to the normal operation of that particular business or enterprise." But no governmental "business" may operate "normally" in violation of the Constitution. . . .

The Court's error in statutory construction is less objectionable, however, than the attitude it displays toward women. Though the Court recognizes that possible harm to women guards is an unacceptable reason for disqualifying women, it relies instead on an equally speculative threat to prison discipline supposedly generated by the sexuality of female guards. There is simply no evidence in the record to show that women guards would create any danger to security in Alabama prisons significantly greater than that which already exists. All of the dangers with one exception discussed below are inherent in a prison setting, whatever the gender of the guards.

The Court first sees women guards as a threat to security because "there are few visible deterrents to inmate assaults on women custodians." . . . In fact, any prison guard is constantly subject to the threat of attack by inmates, and "invisible" deterrents are the guard's only real protection. No prison guard relies primarily on his or her ability to ward off an inmate attack to maintain order. Guards are typically unarmed and sheer numbers of inmates could overcome the normal complement. Rather, like all other law enforcement officers, prison guards must rely primarily on the moral authority of their office and the threat of future punishment for miscreants. As one expert testified below, common sense, fairness, and mental and emotional stability are the qualities a guard needs to cope with the dangers of the job. . . . Well qualified and properly trained women, no less than men, have these psychological weapons at their disposal.

The particular severity of discipline problems in the Alabama maximum-security prisons is also no justification for the discrimination sanctioned by the Court. . . . If male guards face an impossible situation, it is difficult to see how women could make the problem worse, unless one relies on precisely the type of generalized bias against women that the Court agrees Title VII was intended to outlaw. For example, much of the testimony of appellants' witnesses ignores individual differences among members of each sex and reads like "ancient canards about the proper role of women." . . . The witnesses claimed that women guards are not strict disciplinarians; that they are physically less capable of protecting themselves and subduing unruly inmates; that inmates take advantage of them as they did their mothers, while male guards are strong father figures who easily maintain discipline, and so on. Yet the record shows that the presence of women guards has not led to a single incident amounting to a serious breach of security in any Alabama institution.[3] And, in any event, "[g]uards rarely enter the cell blocks and dormitories" . . . where the danger of inmate attacks is the greatest.

It appears that the real disqualifying factor in the Court's view is "[t]he employee's very womanhood." . . . The Court refers to the large number of sex offenders in Alabama prisons, and to "[t]he likelihood that inmates would assault a woman because she was a woman." . . . In short, the fundamental justification for the decision is that women as guards will generate sexual assaults. With all respect, this rationale regrettably perpetuates one of the most insidious of the old myths about women that women, wittingly or not, are seductive sexual objects. The effect of the decision, made I am sure with the best of intentions, is to punish women because their very presence might provoke sexual assaults. It is women who are made to pay the price in lost job opportunities

---

3. The Court refers to two incidents involving potentially dangerous attacks on women in prisons. . . . But these did not involve trained corrections officers; one victim was a clerical worker and the other a student visiting on a tour.

for the threat of depraved conduct by prison inmates. Once again, "[t]he pedestal upon which women have been placed has . . . , upon closer inspection, been revealed as a cage." . . . It is particularly ironic that the cage is erected here in response to feared misbehavior by imprisoned criminals.

The proper response to inevitable attacks on both female and male guards is not to limit the employment opportunities of law-abiding women who wish to contribute to their community, but to take swift and sure punitive action against the inmate offenders. Presumably, one of the goals of the Alabama prison system is the eradication of inmates' antisocial behavior patterns so that prisoners will be able to live one day in free society. Sex offenders can begin this process by learning to relate to women guards in a socially acceptable manner. To deprive women of job opportunities because of the threatened behavior of convicted criminals is to turn our social priorities upside down.[5] . . .

Wilson v. Southwest Airlines Co.

517 F. Supp. 292 (N.D. Tex. 1981)

HIGGINBOTHAM, District Judge.

This case presents the important question whether femininity, or more accurately female sex appeal, is a bona fide occupational qualification ("BFOQ") for the jobs of flight attendant and ticket agent with Southwest Airlines. Plaintiff Gregory Wilson and the class of over 100 male job applicants he represents have challenged Southwest's open refusal to hire males as a violation of Title VII. . . .

At the phase one trial on liability, Southwest conceded that its refusal to hire males was intentional. . . . Southwest contends, however, that the BFOQ exception to Title VII's ban on sex discrimination justifies its hiring only females for the public contact positions of flight attendant and ticket agent. The BFOQ window through which Southwest attempts to fly permits sex discrimination in situations where the employer can prove that sex is a "bona fide occupational qualification reasonably necessary to the normal operation of

---

5. The appellants argue that restrictions on employment of women are also justified by consideration of inmates' privacy. It is strange indeed to hear state officials who have for years been violating the most basic principles of human decency in the operation of their prisons suddenly become concerned about inmate privacy. It is stranger still that these same officials allow women guards in contact positions in a number of non-maximum-security institutions, but strive to protect inmates' privacy in the prisons where personal freedom is most severely restricted. I have no doubt on this record that appellants' professed concern is nothing but a feeble excuse for discrimination. As the District Court suggested, it may well be possible, once a constitutionally adequate staff is available, to rearrange work assignments so that legitimate inmate privacy concerns are respected without denying jobs to women. Finally, if women guards behave in a professional manner at all times, they will engender reciprocal respect from inmates, who will recognize that their privacy is being invaded no more than if a woman doctor examines them. The suggestion implicit in the privacy argument that such behavior is unlikely on either side is an insult to the professionalism of guards and the dignity of inmates.

that particular business or enterprise." Southwest reasons it may discriminate against males because its attractive female flight attendants and ticket agents personify the airline's sexy image and fulfill its public promise to take passengers skyward with "love." Defendant claims maintenance of its females-only hiring policy is crucial to the airline's continued financial success. . . .

FACTUAL BACKGROUND . . .

Southwest was incorporated in March of 1967 and . . . as a result of the defensive tactics of Southwest's competitors . . . [i]n December of 1970, Southwest had $143 in the bank and was over $100,000 in debt, though no aircraft had ever left the ground.

Barely intact, Southwest, in early 1971, called upon a Dallas advertising agency, the Bloom Agency, to develop a winning marketing strategy. Planning to initiate service quickly, Southwest needed instant recognition and a "catchy" image to distinguish it from its competitors.

The Bloom Agency evaluated both the images of the incumbent competitor airlines as well as the characteristics of passengers to be served by a commuter airline. Bloom determined that the other carriers serving the Texas market tended to project an image of conservatism. The agency also determined that the relatively short haul commuter market which Southwest hoped to serve was comprised of predominantly male businessmen. Based on these factors, Bloom suggested that Southwest break away from the conservative image of other airlines and project to the traveling public an airline personification of feminine youth and vitality. A specific female personality description was recommended and adopted by Southwest for its corporate image: This lady is young and vital . . . she is charming and goes through life with great flair and exuberance . . . you notice first her exciting smile, friendly air, her wit . . . yet she is quite efficient and approaches all her tasks with care and attention. . . .

From the personality description suggested by The Bloom Agency, Southwest developed its now famous "Love" personality. Southwest projects an image of feminine spirit, fun, and sex appeal. Its ads promise to provide "tender loving care" to its predominantly male, business passengers. The first advertisements run by the airline featured the slogan, "AT LAST THERE IS SOMEBODY ELSE UP THERE WHO LOVES YOU." Variations on this theme have continued through newspaper, billboard, magazine and television advertisements during the past ten years.[4] . . .

Over the years, Southwest gained national and international attention as the "love airline." Southwest Airlines' stock is traded on the New York Stock Exchange under the ticker symbol "LUV." During 1977 when Southwest

4. Unabashed allusions to love and sex pervade all aspects of Southwest's public image. Its T.V. commercials feature attractive attendants in fitted outfits, catering to male passengers while an alluring feminine voice promises in-flight love. On board, attendants in hot-pants (skirts are now optional) serve "love bites" (toasted almonds) and "love potions" (cocktails). Even Southwest's ticketing system features a "quickie machine" to provide "instant gratification."

opened five additional markets in Texas, the love theme was expanded to "WE'RE SPREADING LOVE ALL OVER TEXAS."

As an integral part of its youthful, feminine image, Southwest has employed only females in the high customer contact positions of ticket agent and flight attendant. From the start, Southwest's attractive personnel, dressed in high boots and hot-pants, generated public interest and "free ink." Their sex appeal has been used to attract male customers to the airline. Southwest's flight attendants, and to a lesser degree its ticket agents, have been featured in newspaper, magazine, billboard and television advertisements during the past ten years. Some attendants assist in promotional events for other businesses and civic organizations. Southwest flight attendants and ticket agents are featured in the company's in-flight magazine and have received notice in numerous other national and international publications. The airline also encourages its attendants to entertain the passengers and maintain an atmosphere of informality and "fun" during flights. According to Southwest, its female flight attendants have come to "personify" Southwest's public image.

Southwest has enjoyed enormous success in recent years.[6] This is in no small part due to its marketing image. . . . The evidence was undisputed that Southwest's unique, feminized image played and continues to play an important role in the airline's success.

Less certain, however, is Southwest's assertion that its females-only hiring policy is necessary for the continued success of its image and its business. Based on two on-board surveys, one conducted in October, 1979, before this suit was filed, and another in August, 1980, when the suit was pending, Southwest contends its attractive flight attendants are the "largest single component" of its success. In the 1979 survey, however, of the attributes considered most important by passengers, the category "courteous and attentive hostesses" ranked fifth in importance behind (1) on time departures, (2) frequently scheduled departures, (3) friendly and helpful reservations and ground personnel, and (4) convenient departure times. . . . Apparently, one of the remaining eight alternative categories, "attractive hostesses," was not selected with sufficient frequency to warrant being included in the reported survey results. . . .

[R]ather than Southwest's female personnel being the "sole factor" distinguishing the airline from its competitors, as Defendant contends, the 1980 survey lists Southwest's "personnel" as only one among five characteristics contributing to Southwest's public image. . . . Accordingly, there is no persuasive proof that Southwest's passengers prefer female over male flight attendants and ticket agents, or, of greater importance, that they would be less likely to fly Southwest if males were hired.

In evaluating Southwest's BFOQ defense, therefore, the Court proceeds on the basis that "love," while important, is not everything in the relationship

---

6. From 1979 to 1980, the company's earnings rose from $17 million to $28 million when most other airlines suffered heavy losses. As a percentage of revenues, Southwest's return is considered to be one of the highest in the industry.

between Defendant and its passengers. Still, it is proper to infer from the airline's competitive successes that Southwest's overall "love image" has enhanced its ability to attract passengers. To the extent the airline has successfully feminized its image and made attractive females an integral part of its public face, it also follows that femininity and sex appeal are qualities related to successful job performance by Southwest's flight attendants and ticket agents. The strength of this relationship has not been proved. It is with this factual orientation that the Court turns to examine Southwest's BFOQ defense.

INTERPRETATIONS OF THE BONA FIDE OCCUPATIONAL QUALIFICATION . . .

Southwest concedes with respect to the *Weeks* test that males are able to perform safely and efficiently all the basic, mechanical functions required of flight attendants and ticket agents. . . . Southwest's position, however, is that females are required to fulfill certain non-mechanical aspects of these jobs: to attract those male customers who prefer female attendants and ticket agents, and to preserve the authenticity and genuineness of Southwest's unique, female corporate personality.

A similar, though not identical, argument that females could better perform certain non-mechanical functions required of flight attendants was rejected in Diaz v. Pan American World Airways, Inc., [1971]. There, the airline argued and the trial court found that being female was a BFOQ because women were superior in "providing reassurance to anxious passengers, giving courteous personalized service and, in general, making flights as pleasurable as possible within the limitations imposed by aircraft operations." . . . Although it accepted the trial court findings, the Court of Appeals reversed, holding that femininity was not a BFOQ, because catering to passengers' psychological needs was only "tangential" to what was "reasonably *necessary*" for the business involved (original emphasis). . . . Characterizing the "essence" or "primary function" of Pan American's business as the safe transportation of passengers from one point to another, the court explained:

> While a pleasant environment, enhanced by the obvious cosmetic effect that female stewardesses provide as well as, according to the findings of the trial court, their apparent ability to perform the non-mechanical functions of the job in a more effective manner than most men, may all be important, they are tangential to the essence of the business involved. No one has suggested that having male stewards will so seriously affect the operation of the airline as to jeopardize or even minimize its ability to provide safe transportation from one place to another. . . .

Similar reasoning underlay the appellate court's rejection of Pan American's claim that its customers' preference for female attendants justified its refusal to hire males. Because the non-mechanical functions that passengers preferred females to perform were tangential to the airline's business, the court held, "the fact that customers prefer (females) cannot justify sex discrimination."

. . . The Fifth Circuit in *Diaz* did not hold that customer preference could never give rise to a sex BFOQ. Rather, consistent with the EEOC's exception for authenticity and genuineness, the Court allowed that customer preference could "be taken into account only when it is based on the company's inability to perform the primary function or service it offers," that is, where sex or sex appeal is itself the dominant service provided.

Diaz and its progeny establish that to recognize a BFOQ for jobs requiring multiple abilities, some sex-linked and some sex-neutral, the sex-linked aspects of the job must predominate. Only then will an employer have satisfied [the] requirement that sex be so essential to successful job performance that a member of the opposite sex could not perform the job. An illustration of such dominance in sex cases is the exception recognized by the EEOC (Equal Employment Opportunity Commission) for authenticity and genuineness. In the example given in [EEOC Regulations], that of an actor or actress, the primary function of the position, its essence, is to fulfill the audience's expectation and desire for a particular role, characterized by particular physical or emotional traits. Generally, a male could not supply the authenticity required to perform a female role. Similarly, in jobs where sex or vicarious sexual recreation is the primary service provided, e.g. a social escort or topless dancer, the job automatically calls for one sex exclusively; the employee's sex and the service provided are inseparable. Thus, being female has been deemed a BFOQ for the position of a Playboy Bunny, female sexuality being reasonably necessary to perform the dominant purpose of the job which is forthrightly to titillate and entice male customers. . . . One court has also suggested, without holding, that the authenticity exception would give rise to a BFOQ for Chinese nationality where necessary to maintain the authentic atmosphere of an ethnic Chinese restaurant. . . .

APPLICATION OF THE BONA FIDE OCCUPATIONAL QUALIFICATION TO SOUTHWEST AIRLINES

Applying the first level test for a BFOQ, with its legal gloss, to Southwest's particular operations results in the conclusion that being female is not a qualification required to perform successfully the jobs of flight attendant and ticket agent with Southwest. Like any other airline, Southwest's primary function is to transport passengers safely and quickly from one point to another.[24] To do this, Southwest employs ticket agents whose primary job duties are to ticket passengers and check baggage, and flight attendants, whose primary duties are to assist passengers during boarding and deboarding, to instruct

---

24. Southwest's argument that its primary function is "to make a profit," not to transport passengers, must be rejected. Without doubt the goal of every business is to make a profit. For purposes of BFOQ analysis, however, the business "essence" inquiry focuses on the particular service provided and the job tasks and functions involved, not the business goal. If an employer could justify employment discrimination merely on the grounds that it is necessary to make a profit, Title VII would be nullified in short order.

passengers in the location and use of aircraft safety equipment, and to serve passengers cocktails and snacks during the airline's short commuter flights. Mechanical, non-sex-linked duties dominate both these occupations. Indeed, on Southwest's short-haul commuter flights there is time for little else. That Southwest's female personnel may perform their mechanical duties "with love" does not change the result. "Love" is the manner of job performance, not the job performed.

While possession of female allure and sex appeal have been made qualifications for Southwest's contact personnel by virtue of the "love" campaign, the functions served by employee sexuality in Southwest's operations are not dominant ones. According to Southwest, female sex appeal serves two purposes: (1) attracting and entertaining male passengers and (2) fulfilling customer expectations for female service engendered by Southwest's advertising which features female personnel. As in *Diaz*, these non-mechanical, sex-linked job functions are only "tangential" to the essence of the occupations and business involved. Southwest is not a business where vicarious sex entertainment is the primary service provided. Accordingly, the ability of the airline to perform its primary business function, the transportation of passengers, would not be jeopardized by hiring males.

Southwest does not face the situation . . . where an established customer preference for one sex is so strong that the business would be undermined if employees of the opposite sex were hired. Southwest's claim that its customers prefer females rests primarily upon inferences drawn from the airline's success after adopting its female personality. But according to Southwest's own surveys, that success is attributable to many factors. There is no competent proof that Southwest's popularity derives directly from its females-only policy to the exclusion of other factors like dissatisfaction with rival airlines and Southwest's use of convenient Love and Hobby Fields. Nor is there competent proof that the customer preference for females is so strong that Defendant's male passengers would cease doing business with Southwest as was the case in [Fernandez v. Wynn Oil Co.]. In short, Southwest has failed in its proof to satisfy Diaz's business necessity requirement, without which customer preference may not give rise to a BFOQ for sex. . . .

It is also relevant that Southwest's female image was adopted at its discretion, to promote a business unrelated to sex. Contrary to the unyielding South American preference for males encountered by the Defendant company in *Fernandez*, Southwest exploited, indeed nurtured, the very customer preference for females it now cites to justify discriminating against males. . . . Moreover, the fact that a vibrant marketing campaign was necessary to distinguish Southwest in its early years does not lead to the conclusion that sex discrimination was then, or is now, a business necessity. Southwest's claim that its female image will be tarnished by hiring males is, in any case, speculative at best. . . .

[S]ex does not become a BFOQ merely because an employer chooses to exploit female sexuality as a marketing tool, or to better insure profitability. . . .

CONCLUSION . . .

Rejecting a wider BFOQ for sex does not eliminate the commercial exploitation of sex appeal. It only requires, consistent with the purposes of Title VII, that employers exploit the attractiveness and allure of a sexually integrated workforce. Neither Southwest, nor the traveling public, will suffer from such a rule. More to the point, it is my judgment that this is what Congress intended.

Notes

1. The Business Necessity Defense. The Supreme Court reasoned in *Dothard* that the height and weight requirements were proxies for strength, which could have been more directly measured without gender discrimination. How likely do you think it is that substantially more women could qualify under a strength test? Of course, if a disproportionate impact remained, that rule, too, would need to be justifiable under the business necessity test. What if the defendant had shown that the height and weight restrictions were necessary to create the *appearance* of strength, as vital to prison security as strength itself? (Justice Rehnquist, concurring in the opinion, raises this possibility.)

2. BFOQs and Sexual Authenticity. As facially discriminatory exclusions based on sex, the prison regulation excluding women as prison guards in maximum-security areas in *Dothard* and the exclusion of men as flight attendants in *Wilson* are examples of disparate treatment discrimination, which are justified under Title VII only if the sex of the employee in each case is shown to be a bona fide occupational qualification or BFOQ. One application of the BFOQ arises in the entertainment industry, in circumstances in which an actor's or actress's plausibility depends on sexual identity with the character portrayed. Another context is the sex entertainment industry. According to *Wilson*, sex may be used to establish a climate of female sex appeal only when the "essence" of the business relates to that sex appeal.[148] Thus, while a family restaurant cannot discriminate between men and women for waiter positions, it generally is assumed that a topless bar may hire only women dancers, and may discharge an employee for failure to meet the employer's criteria relating to sexual image. Ironically, then, the more explicitly the employer's business exploits sex for money, the more easily sex will be viewed as a BFOQ. Is this perverse? Does it fail to protect women when they most need it? This issue is explored in Chapter 3.

Some expensive New York French restaurants hire only male waiters, in line with the tradition of the "classiest" Continental establishments. Are they violating Title VII? What if they hire only French waiters, and thereby exclude waiters of color? What is the "essence" of such a job?

3. BFOQs and Customer Preferences. Under what circumstances might customer preference justify discriminatory conduct? In the lower court decision in *Diaz*, the airline introduced evidence of a survey indicating that 79 percent of all passengers, male and female, preferred being served by female flight attendants. Expert psychological evidence was also introduced to explain the general preference of airline passengers for female attendants. It posited that: the unique experience of being levitated off the ground and transported through the air at high speeds creates feelings of apprehension, boredom, and excitement; females were psychologically better equipped to cope with these conflicting states and especially adept at relieving passenger apprehension; and passengers of both sexes responded better to the presence of females. This and other evidence persuaded the district court that sex was a BFOQ for flight attendants. The Fifth Circuit Court of Appeals, however, held that the airline could take the interpersonal skills of flight attendant applicants into account, but that it could not do so by categorically excluding all men.

As noted in the previous section, the court in Craft v. Metromedia came to a different conclusion. There, the court determined that a television anchor-woman could be properly reassigned due to the demonstrated negative viewer response. Is the rejection of the survey evidence in *Diaz* and *Wilson* reconcilable with its use in *Craft*? Fernandez v. Wynn Oil Co., cited in *Wilson*, held that an oil company could not refuse to hire female executives because its South American clients would refuse to deal with them.[149] Is this the correct decision? Is it reconcilable with *Craft*? When does positive viewer or customer response become a "business necessity"?

4. BFOQs and Privacy Considerations. Courts have also found the BFOQ test satisfied in some cases in which sex-specific hiring accommodates privacy or other related interests. In Fesel v. Masonic Home of Delaware, Inc., for example, nine of the nursing home's female residents signed an affidavit objecting "most strenuously" to male nurses or nurses' aides, though apparently not to male physicians.[150] The court accepted the employer's defense that female sex was a BFOQ for the nursing positions. Quite a number of cases in the context of hospitals and nursing homes have reached the same conclusion. Does it seem reasonable to hire only men, or only women, when the employment at issue implicates sex-specific privacy or therapeutic interests?[151] UAW v. Johnson Controls, excerpted in Chapter 2, includes suggestions that the Court was prepared to endorse a privacy application of the BFOQ defense.

Yet allowing the BFOQ exception in this context would seem to perpetuate age-old stereotypes that Title VII was meant to condemn—i.e., that a woman's role is to wash and clean up after people, and a man's role is that of the skilled professional.[152] A more recent case suggests that the BFOQ privacy defense is narrow, and only comes into play when hiring members of one sex would undermine the institution's safety and effectiveness. In Slivka v. Camden-Clark Memorial Hospital, the West Virginia state supreme court struck down a hospital policy to hire only female obstetrics nurses, despite evidence that 80 percent of patients demanded female nurses and female nurses were needed as chaperones for male physicians. The *Slivka* court noted the importance of not deferring to personal preferences based on dated world views.[153]

When the privacy claim is by a prisoner, it is unlikely to prevail.[154] Courts that do recognize a right to privacy for inmates tend to give more respect to women's privacy than to men's.[155] Are there compelling justifications for giving special solicitude to women?

5. BFOQs and Formal Equality Analysis. Justice Stewart's opinion upholding the female ban on maximum security positions in *Dothard* articulates the most common defense to a formal equality claim: women are different from men in ways that justify different treatment. The reasoning of the opinion leaves no room for a woman to become qualified for the position. Safety at the prison—safety of the woman and the prison population more generally—would be compromised by their "womanhood," referring to both women's relative weakness and their vulnerability to sexual assault. Viewed this way, women's unsuitability for the position reflects inherent sex differences, not ones that the state has produced or perpetuated by excluding them from the position.

Justice Marshall's dissent challenges the majority's assumptions about women's differences on multiple grounds. It (1) disputes the factual premises of the rule—for example, that woman guards would create a danger to the prison's basic security; (2) identifies the stereotypes about women as "seductive sexual objects" that are reinforced through the exclusion; (3) insists that some women will be able to protect themselves and should be given the chance to prove their individual ability despite the average characteristics of their sex; and (4) claims that improvements in staffing (as a prior case had already required) was essentially a less restrictive alternative to excluding women from the positions.

If you think *Dothard* is wrongly decided, is it because the Court failed to apply standard formal equality principles correctly? Or because formal equality does not provide the tools necessary to analyze an exclusion based on factors "unique" to women?

Is excluding women where they might present temptation for the prisoners comparable to giving in to "consumer preference"? Is the concern for prison safety and security sufficiently distinguishable from the kinds of business justifications rejected in other cases? Isn't it just a question of economics? Why should Southwest Airlines be required to forego the income attributable to being the "LUV" airline, while the state of Alabama may defend its exclusion of women based on inadequate protection of their safety under present staffing arrangements? Should courts be more sympathetic when taxpayers are footing the bill and underfunding causes chronic security problems?

Is *Dothard* less troubling if courts require a detailed "basis in fact" for assumptions about how men or women are likely to behave on the job? A number of courts in recent years have denied employer motions for summary judgment in BFOQ cases because the factual predicate was insufficient.[156] One court observed that "the BFOQ defense generally requires a 'case-by-case' analysis."[157] Are juries any less likely than judges to be convinced that a gender-based BFOQ is justified?

6. His Very Manhood? The majority in *Dothard* allowed the prison's BFOQ defense in part because a female correctional officer's "very woman-hood" would "directly undermine her capacity to provide the security that is the essence of a correctional counselor's responsibility."[158] Can the "very manhood" of male correctional counselors undermine their ability to carry out the essence of a prison's business? In several cases over the last decade, several prisons have been sued over policies that exclude men from certain positions in women's prisons as a means of curbing the sexual abuse of female prisoners.[159]

In Everson v. Michigan Dep't of Corrections, the Sixth Circuit upheld such a policy of the Michigan Department of Corrections (MDOC) on the theory that being female was a BFOQ for 250 designated positions in housing units at female prisons.[160] This policy was enacted as part of the response to a prob-lem of female inmates that had "long plagued the MDOC." In addition to the prevalence of sexual abuse (189 allegations of sexual abuse by male officers over a 6-year period), the problem was exacerbated by a fear of reporting inci-dents of abuse and tolerance of sexual misconduct by higher-ups. The court relied heavily on *Dothard* for the proposition that excluding officers of one gender can be an appropriate response to an "inhospitable" environment in which security cannot be otherwise maintained.[161] The court concluded that "a basis in fact exists that privacy screens preclude proper surveillance of inmates and that allegations of sexual abuse engender hesitancy in male officers and mistrust between inmates and guards, and thus the 'very manhood' of male [officers] undermines their capacity to provide security."[162] And even though most male officers will "conduct themselves professionally," the MDOC "can-not predict which officers will engage in sexual abuse." Based on the data pro-vided by MDOC, the court was persuaded that "some male officers possess a trait precluding safe and efficient job performance—a proclivity for sexually abusive conduct—that cannot be ascertained by means other than the knowl-edge of the officer's gender."[163] Thus gender was a "legitimate proxy for a safety-related job qualification" given "the endemic problem of sexual abuse in Michigan's female facilities."[164]

In Breiner v. Nevada Dep't of Corrections (NDOC), the Ninth Circuit considered a similar policy, in which men could not be hired as "correctional lieutenants," but reached the opposite conclusion.[165] NDOC argued that the exclusion of male officers would reduce sexual misconduct because male offi-cers are more likely to "condone sexual abuse by their male subordinates"; are "themselves likely to sexually abuse female inmates"; and lack the "instinct" that female officers possess that makes them less susceptible to manipulation by inmates.[166] The court rejected all three justifications for the exclusion of men and held that NDOC had not established a gender BFOQ. For the policy to stand, NDOC had to show a "high correlation between sex and the ability to perform job functions" that are "reasonably necessary" to the business of running pris-ons. NDOC did not meet its burden of showing "a basis in fact" (required by *Dothard*) for concluding that "all male correctional lieutenants would tolerate

sexual abuse by their subordinates; that all men in the correctional lieutenant role would themselves sexually abuse inmates; or that women, by virtue
of their gender, can better understand the behavior of female inmates." Nor
did NDOC refute "the viability of alternatives that would achieve [the goal of
reducing abuse] without impeding male employees' promotional opportunities."[167] Moreover, NDOC's explanation for its policy "relies on the kind of
unproven and invidious stereotype that Congress sought to eliminate from
employment decisions when it enacted Title VII."[168] The court was particularly
disturbed by NDOC's suggestion that "all men are inherently apt to sexually
abuse, or condone sexual abuse of, female inmates."[169]

Which of these courts has the better of the argument? Is reliance on a
guard's "very manhood" to predict his likelihood to commit or tolerate sexual abuse equally reliant on stereotypes as reliance on a female officer's "very
womanhood" to predict her likelihood of being victimized? Does the protection of female inmates offset any harm from the possible perpetuation of gender stereotypes?

Putting Theory Into Practice

1-20. A mid-size law firm handles, among other things, insurance and
employment discrimination defense. A number of the firm's oldest and
best clients prefer to work with male attorneys, because they have more
confidence in their abilities. Most recently, an insurance client threatened
to take his business elsewhere if a Jewish female lawyer, who was assigned
to handle a personal injury trial for his company, was not replaced by one
of the firm's "bright, new" (male) attorneys. The client claims that the man
will be more effective in the "redneck" Southern town where the case is
scheduled for trial. The law firm makes the reassignment to please the client. Is this discrimination based on sex? Is use of sex valid as a BFOQ?[170]

1-21. The firm in Problem 1-19 above also has a practice of assigning
women attorneys to employment discrimination cases brought by women
claiming sex discrimination, and assigning minority attorneys to employment discrimination cases in which race is an issue. A white male attorney with the firm believes that this policy in assigning cases reduces his
opportunities to excel at the firm. Is this discrimination based on sex? Is
it justified? Would the issue be different if a black woman is assigned as
defense counsel in a rape trial before a largely black jury on the theory that
she would have the most credibility in cross examining the black woman
complainant?

1-22. Assume that a psychiatric hospital has credible evidence that
an emotionally disturbed and sexually abused female child will open up
more in a counseling setting to a woman counselor than to a male one. Is it
appropriate, then, to assign the patient only to female counselors?[171]

1-23. Transition House, New England's first battered women's shelter, caused controversy by hiring a man as the interim executive director. About Women, a collective of psychologists and social workers who were influential in creating shelters, including Transition House, wrote a public letter of protest. In their view, the decision constituted a "flagrant violation" of the organization's founding principle to establish a space where women could feel safe from male intrusion and could openly unburden themselves of the experiences of male violence they had undergone without fear of censure, criticism, or inhibition by male presence. The male interim director responded by noting that he spent his time in administrative offices in a separate location from the shelter and had limited contact with residents.[172] Who is right? If the male director is fired based on the rationale of About Women, would he have a sex discrimination claim under Title VII?

1-24. Professor V. works for a state university and conducts many research projects under grants obtained through the university. One of these projects is a study of women who have rejected settlement offers by a trust fund set up to satisfy the claims of women injured by the Dalkon Shield interuterine birth-control device and who must pursue their claims through non-judicial adjudicatory hearings. The purpose of the project is to study the effectiveness of those hearings and the surrounding process. The research requires lengthy interviews of women claimants both before and after the hearings, with questions that probe, among other things, the intimate details of their sex lives, their sex partners, their contraception histories, and other matters relating to their experiences with the Dalkon Shield. Most of these women have suffered substantial distress and harm as a result of these experiences, and many find it understandably difficult to discuss these experiences with strangers.

Professor V. wants to hire only white women, ages 35 to 45, to conduct these interviews. His reason is that the validity of his research requires the interviewer to create a neutral, nonjudgmental atmosphere in which the interviewees feel comfortable talking about one of the most private aspects of their lives. Research has shown that people of virtually every race, sex, and background, including blacks, Hispanics, men, and women, feel most comfortable talking about the intimate details of their lives with middle-aged, white women between the ages of 35 and 45.

He asks your advice. May he hire only white women ages 35 to 45 as interviewers without violating any law?

1-25. Hooters is an Atlanta-based restaurant chain that hires only female food servers, bartenders, and hosts. These women wear tight short-shorts and tank tops or half-tees with a large-eyed owl on the front. Some shirt backs read "More than a Mouthful." Hooters sells food, drink, posters, T-shirts, calendars, and other products. It also offers an atmosphere of what a spokeswoman described as "good–humored, wholesome sex appeal" that the Hooters girls embody. Although it "welcomes" children, the sexy cheerleader image of the Hooters' girls is designed to attract its target audience of adult males.

Does Hooters have a BFOQ defense to a sex discrimination suit brought by male applicants who were rejected for jobs because of their sex?

1-26. An airline adopts a policy that requires pregnant flight attendants to stop flying by the fourth month of pregnancy. Defending a lawsuit, the airline argues that nonpregnancy is a BFOQ because the essence of an airline's business is safe travel, that the ability of flight attendants to operate at full capacity is vital to emergency management, and that pregnant attendants are more likely to be impaired during an emergency due to fatigue, nausea, vomiting, or miscarriage. Should the airline prevail?[173]

D. STATE PUBLIC ACCOMMODATIONS LAWS AND ASSOCIATIONAL FREEDOMS

In addition to federal and state laws prohibiting sex discrimination in employment, many states have passed civil rights acts prohibiting sex discrimination in public accommodations and in private clubs and organizations. Challenges to the application of these statutes have claimed infringement of rights of expression, association, and privacy protected by the federal and state constitutions. Such rights have long served to protect the activities and privacy of politically unpopular groups, including those involved in the civil rights movement. The question is how far this protection extends, and to whom.

In 1984, the United States Supreme Court faced this issue with respect to sex discrimination in the case of Roberts v. United States Jaycees. There, the Court rejected a First Amendment challenge to a Minnesota anti-discrimination statute under which the Jaycees were ordered to admit women as full voting members.[174] Three years later, in Board of Directors of Rotary International v. Rotary Club of Duarte, (1987), the Court upheld application of California's Unruh Act to California's Rotary Clubs, requiring them to admit women.[175]

These cases articulated criteria for determining when an association was sufficiently "private" to remain constitutionally protected from sex discrimination challenges. The more personal and intimate the association in terms of its size, purpose, selectivity, and agenda, and the more it pursues a specific political, social, or religious agenda, the greater the First Amendment protection. By contrast, the larger, more open to the public, and less attached to a specific political or religious agenda, the less protection the First Amendment affords. In Foster v. Back Bay Spas, the court held in favor of James Foster, who claimed that the spa's refusal to allow men membership was a violation of state public accommodation laws.[176]

Reading Questions

1. Is it appropriate that the more exclusive the association, the greater autonomy it will enjoy? Is it perverse that a neo-Nazi group but not a Little League may be able to exclude Jews, and that a women's health club cannot exclude men?
2. Does the court in Foster v. Back Bay Spas, below, reach the right result?
3. Should the Boy Scouts be able to exclude girls? The Girl Scouts to exclude boys? Are your answers to these questions consistent with formal equality principles?

Board of Directors of Rotary International v. Rotary Club of Duarte

481 U.S. 537 (1987)

Mr. Justice POWELL delivered the opinion of the Court.

We must decide whether a California statute that requires California Rotary Clubs to admit women members violates the First Amendment.

I

Rotary International (International) is a nonprofit corporation founded in 1905, with headquarters in Evanston, Illinois. It is "an organization of business and professional men united worldwide who provide humanitarian service, encourage high ethical standards in all vocations, and help build goodwill and peace in the world." . . . Individual members belong to a local Rotary Club rather than to International. In turn, each local Rotary Club is a member of International. . . . In August 1982, shortly before the trial in this case, International comprised 19,788 Rotary Clubs in 157 countries, with a total membership of about 907,750. . . .

Individuals are admitted to membership in a Rotary Club according to a "classification system." The purpose of this system is to ensure "that each Rotary Club includes a representative of every worthy and recognized business, professional, or institutional activity in the community." . . . Each active member must work in a leadership capacity in his business or profession. The general rule is that "one active member is admitted for each classification, but he, in turn, may propose an additional active member, who must be in the same business or professional classification." Thus, each classification may be represented by two active members. In addition, "senior active" and "past service" members may represent the same classifications as active members. . . . There is no limit to the number of clergymen, journalists, or diplomats who may be admitted to membership. . . . Subject to these requirements, each local Rotary Club is free to adopt its own rules and procedures for admitting new members. . . .

Membership in Rotary Clubs is open only to men. . . . Herbert A. Pigman, the General Secretary of Rotary International, testified that the exclusion of women results in an "aspect of fellowship . . . that is enjoyed by the present male membership," . . . and also allows Rotary to operate effectively in foreign countries with varied cultures and social mores. Although women are not admitted to membership, they are permitted to attend meetings, give speeches, and receive awards. Women relatives of Rotary members may form their own associations and are authorized to wear the Rotary lapel pin. Young women between 14 and 28 years of age may joint Interact or Rotaract, organizations sponsored by Rotary International. . . .

In 1977 the Rotary Club of Duarte, California, admitted Donna Bogart, Mary Lou Elliott, and Rosemary Freitag to active membership. International notified the Duarte Club that admitting women members is contrary to the Rotary constitution. After an internal hearing, International's board of directors revoked the charter of the Duarte Club and terminated its membership in Rotary International. The Duarte Club's appeal to the International Convention was unsuccessful.

The Duarte Club and two of its women members filed a complaint in the California Superior Court for the County of Los Angeles. The complaint alleged, inter alia, that appellants' actions violated the Unruh Civil Rights Act.[2] . . .

II

In Roberts v. United States Jaycees, [468 U.S. 609 (1984)], we upheld against First Amendment challenge a Minnesota statute that required the Jaycees to admit women as full voting members. *Roberts* provides the framework for analyzing appellants' constitutional claims. As we observed in *Roberts*, our cases have afforded constitutional protection to freedom of association in two distinct senses. First, the Court has held that the Constitution protects against unjustified government interference with an individual's choice to enter into and maintain certain intimate or private relationships. Second, the Court has upheld the freedom of individuals to associate for the purpose of engaging in protected speech or religious activities. In many cases, government interference with one form of protected association will also burden the other form of association. In *Roberts* we determined the nature and degree of constitutional protection by considering separately the effect of the challenged state action on individuals' freedom of private association and their freedom of expressive association. We follow the same course in this case. . . .

2. The Unruh Civil Rights Act provides, in part: "All persons within the jurisdiction of this state are free and equal, and no matter what their sex, race, color, religion, ancestry, or national origin are entitled to the full and equal accommodations, advantages, facilities, privileges, or services in all business establishments of every kind whatsoever." Cal. Civ. Code Ann. §51 (West 1982).

A

The Court has recognized that the freedom to enter into and carry on certain intimate or private relationships is a fundamental element of liberty protected by the Bill of Rights. Such relationships may take various forms, including the most intimate. . . . We have not attempted to mark the precise boundaries of this type of constitutional protection. The intimate relationships to which we have accorded constitutional protection include marriage . . . the begetting and bearing of children . . . child rearing and education . . . and cohabitation with relatives. . . . In determining whether a particular association is sufficiently personal or private to warrant constitutional protection, we consider factors such as size, purpose, selectivity, and whether others are excluded from critical aspects of the relationship. [468 U.S. at 620.]

The evidence in this case indicates that the relationship among Rotary Club members is not the kind of intimate or private relation that warrants constitutional protection. The size of the local Rotary Clubs ranges from fewer than 20 to more than 900. . . . There is no upper limit on the membership of any local Rotary Club. About 10 percent of the membership of a typical club moves away or drops out during a typical year. . . . The clubs therefore are instructed to "keep a flow of prospects coming" to make up for the attrition and gradually to enlarge the membership. . . . The purpose of Rotary "is to produce an inclusive, not exclusive, membership, making possible the recognition of all useful local occupations, and enabling the club to be a true cross section of the business and professional life of the community." . . . The membership undertakes a variety of service projects designed to aid the community, to raise the standards of the members' businesses and professions, and to improve international relations. Such an inclusive "fellowship for service based on diversity of interest," . . . however beneficial to the members and to those they serve, does not suggest the kind of private or personal relationship to which we have accorded protection under the First Amendment. To be sure, membership in Rotary Clubs is not open to the general public. But each club is instructed to include in its membership "all fully qualified prospective members located within its territory," to avoid "arbitrary limits on the number of members in the club," and to "establish and maintain a membership growth pattern."

Many of the Rotary Clubs' central activities are carried on in the presence of strangers. Rotary Clubs are required to admit any member of any other Rotary Club to their meetings. Members are encouraged to invite business associates and competitors to meetings. At some Rotary Clubs, the visitors number "in the tens and twenties each week." . . . Joint meetings with the members of other organizations, and other joint activities, are permitted. The clubs are encouraged to seek coverage of their meetings and activities in local newspapers. In sum, Rotary Clubs, rather than carrying on their activities in an atmosphere of privacy, seek to keep their "windows and doors open to the whole world." . . . We therefore conclude that application of the Unruh Act to local Rotary Clubs does not interfere unduly with the members' freedom of private association.

B

The Court also has recognized that the right to engage in activities protected by the First Amendment implies "a corresponding right to associate with others in pursuit of a wide variety of political, social, economic, educational, religious, and cultural ends." Roberts v. United States Jaycees, [468 U.S. at 622]. . . . For this reason, "[i]mpediments to the exercise of one's right to choose one's associates can violate the right of association protected by the First Amendment. . . ." Hishon v. King & Spalding, [467 U.S. 69, 80 n.4 (1984)] (Powell, J., concurring) (citing NAACP v. Button, [371 U.S. 415 (1963)]; NAACP v. Alabama ex rel. Patterson, [357 U.S. 449 (1958)]). In this case, however, the evidence fails to demonstrate that admitting women to Rotary Clubs will affect in any significant way the existing members' ability to carry out their various purposes.

As a matter of policy, Rotary Clubs do not take positions on "public questions," including political or international issues. . . . To be sure, Rotary Clubs engage in a variety of commendable service activities that are protected by the First Amendment. But the Unruh Act does not require the clubs to abandon or alter any of these activities. It does not require them to abandon their basic goals of humanitarian service, high ethical standards in all vocations, good will, and peace. Nor does it require them to abandon their classification system or admit members who do not reflect a cross section of the community. Indeed, by opening membership to leading business and professional women in the community, Rotary Clubs are likely to obtain a more representative cross section of community leaders with a broadened capacity for service.

Even if the Unruh Act does work some slight infringement on Rotary members' right of expressive association, that infringement is justified because it serves the State's compelling interest in eliminating discrimination against women. See Buckley v. Valeo, [424 U.S. 1, 25 (1976)] (per curiam) (right of association may be limited by state regulations necessary to serve a compelling interest unrelated to the suppression of ideas). On its face the Unruh Act, like the Minnesota public accommodations law we considered in *Roberts*, makes no distinctions on the basis of the organization's viewpoint. Moreover, public accommodations laws "plainly serv[e] compelling state interests of the highest order." [468 U.S. at 624.] In *Roberts* we recognized that the State's compelling interest in assuring equal access to women extends to the acquisition of leadership skills and business contacts as well as tangible goods and services. [Id. at 626.] The Unruh Act plainly serves this interest. We therefore hold that application of the Unruh Act to California Rotary Clubs does not violate the right of expressive association afforded by the First Amendment. . . .

Justice SCALIA concurs in the judgment.

Justice BLACKMUN and Justice O'CONNOR took no part in the consideration or decision of this case.

Foster v. Back Bay Spas

1997 Mass. Super. LEXIS 194 (Superior Court, Suffolk, Sept. 29, 1997)

Judge Nonnie S. BURNS . . .

This motion for summary judgment arises out of plaintiff James Foster's action to require the defendant . . . to allow him to join the health club. The club does not admit men. Foster argues that this policy violates [the Massachusetts public accommodations statute that prohibits discrimination based on sex].

BACKGROUND

Plaintiff James Foster [lives] in Boston. Defendant Back Bay Spas, Inc. d/b/a Healthworks Fitness Center ("Healthworks") owns and operates a health club facility in the Back Bay area of Boston which accepts only women. Foster is a member of the Marriott Health Club at Copley Place, directly across the street from a Healthworks facility. There exist a large number of other, co-ed exercise facilities in the Boston area with similar resources as Healthworks. Nevertheless, Foster seeks membership at Healthworks Fitness Center, the one facility which caters only to women.

Healthworks was developed and designed for use by women, and thus its programs and facilities—including locker rooms and restrooms—cater to women. Healthworks, in addition to providing a full range of exercise equipment and facilities, offers various fitness and health classes, including classes tailored towards female concerns such as pre-natal programs and special nutrition counseling for women. Healthworks has also contracted with the YWCA Boston so that its members may use its facility. Healthworks promotes itself as an all women's facility, by its advertising and facility window displays.

Healthworks opened its Back Bay facility in February 1996 and its membership is now over 3,500. Foster inquired about membership at Healthworks in February 1996 and was turned away because he is a man.

Affidavits submitted by Healthworks reveal that many of the club's members based their decision to join and to remain members of the facility because it is only open to women. Moreover, Healthworks submitted an affidavit of a Robert Tanenbaum, Ph.D., an expert on areas that impact exercise behavior and fitness including knowledge of gender differences, human sexuality, and reduction of performance anxiety. Dr. Tanenbaum served as an expert on a similar case in Pennsylvania. In his affidavit, Dr. Tanenbaum concludes that over 80% of the members he interviewed stated that the all female aspect of the club was the most important reason for joining Healthworks; that many of the members are of "post-childbearing age and have experienced bodily changes resulting from pregnancy and childbirth which alter their appearance . . . older members who have recently gone through menopause . . . feel intimidated exercising in a coed environment"; that many of the women expressed concern about being watched by members of the opposite sex while exercising; and, that several were recovering from past physical or sexual abuse, or had specific religious concerns about exercising in a coed facility. Most significantly, Dr. Tanenbaum concluded that "approximately 87% of the women . . . said that they would stop exercising at Healthworks if men were permitted to join. . . . Healthworks meets an existing need among the women described and minimizes the hurdles typically found in a coed setting, particularly for women who do not have a consistent fitness history."

Discussion

No material facts are in dispute. The Court, therefore, is charged with determining whether Foster has proved, as a matter of law, that Healthworks' refusal to allow men membership in its facility is in violation of the Massachusetts Public Accommodation Law, . . . and, if so, whether there is any exception to the anti-discrimination provisions in that law.

[Massachusetts law] provides [that]:

> No . . . place of public accommodation, resort or amusement shall, directly or indirectly . . . distribute or display . . . any . . . notice or sign, . . . intended to discriminate against or actually discriminating against persons of any . . . sex . . . in the full enjoyment of the accommodations, advantages, facilities or privileges offered to the general public by such places of public accommodation. . . .

The statute further defines a "place of public accommodation" [to include]:

> any place, . . . which is open to and accepts or solicits the patronage of the general public and . . . (8) a place of public amusement, recreation, sport, exercise or entertainment. . . .

[The law provides]:

> Whoever makes any distinction, discrimination or restriction on account of . . . sex . . . relative to the admission of any person to, or his treatment in any place of public accommodation, resort or amusement, as defined in Section ninety-two A, . . . shall be punished. . . . All persons shall have the right to the full and equal accommodations, advantages, facilities and privileges of any place of public accommodation, resort or amusement subject only to the conditions and limitations established by law and applicable to all persons.

Healthworks has stipulated that it is "a place of public accommodation." . . . On its face, therefore, there is no dispute that the exclusion of males from this place of public accommodation is in violation of the public accommodation law. Healthworks claims, however, that women have a privacy right to exercise in an all female environment.

The privacy statute grants a right to privacy. [The statute provides that] "a person shall have a right against unreasonable, substantial or serious interference with his privacy." The central issue in this case, therefore, is whether a privacy right exists, or can be read into the public accommodations statute, which would permit the exclusion of all men from an all women's exercise facility.

Healthworks claims that its customers' privacy rights are protected by [the law]; that there exists within the public accommodations statute an implied right of privacy for all women to exercise in an all women environment; and that the public accommodation statute was amended to protect women, not men. Specifically, Healthworks argues that a privacy right exists, based on the customer gender preferences of Healthworks's membership. [In a Pennsylvania case identical to this one] that case, the Commonwealth Court of Pennsylvania held that based on a "customer gender privacy" defense, an all women's health club would be permitted to exclude all men from its facility, stating that "this defense recognizes a pervasive public policy that certain conduct that relates to and between genders is inappropriate." . . . In determining that the membership had a privacy interest in exercising in a single sex club the court concluded that "they [members] expose parts of the body about which they are most sensitive, assume awkward and compromising positions, and move themselves in a way which would embarrass them if men were present."

This Court recognizes the difficulty in defining what constitutes "privacy rights." Nevertheless, it is clear that the cases relied upon [in the Pennsylvania case] all involve the exposure or the touching of intimate body parts. This case, on the other hand, involves exercising—an activity—performed before numerous other people, in full exercise attire. Moreover, as Foster points out, at the Healthworks facility in Boston's Back Bay area, the exercisers can be seen from the street as there are two large windows at the front of the facility. Healthworks argues that although there is little nudity involved, and recognizes that any such nudity is voluntary, the compromising positions and contours the customers must invariably assume while exercising raises this clothed activity to a level of exposure akin to nudity or physical contact and thus requires the protection of a privacy right. Again, this Court disagrees. No exercise position, performed while dressed, would result in the sort of exposure of intimate body parts which has been protected by the privacy right.

. . . Here, the putative privacy right is only the right to exercise in a same-sex facility. No private information is being disclosed, and no highly personal or intimate facts are being revealed. The only basis for the claimed right is the exposure of one's clothed anatomy while exercising. Massachusetts case law supports no such right.

Healthworks' affidavits and personal statements describe the sense of intimidation certain women, including post-menopausal women, and women who have undergone mastectomies or who have suffered abuse, will feel in a coed exercise atmosphere, such that they would cease their exercise program. While the Court recognizes the impact that the admission of men into the club may have on these women, intimidation and the assumption that all male Healthworks members will harass and leer at their exercise compatriots is still an insufficient ground on which to create a privacy exception. Absent the unclothed exposure of intimate body parts, or the touching of body parts by members of the opposite sex, this Court can find no basis for overriding the public accommodations statute's mandate.

Further, an affidavit from a member of the Islamic faith stated that Islamic women, who are forbidden from revealing any part of their body (except for their face and hands) while in the presence of men, would no longer be able to use the Healthworks facility at all if men were allowed to join. Healthworks, however, is not a religious facility providing exercise facilities only to Islamic women. It is a public health club. And while this Court recognizes the disparate impact the inclusion of men will have on women of the Islamic faith, this Court cannot allow Healthworks to discriminate against men by allowing women of all faiths access to a single-sex exercise space on the basis of the religious beliefs of a portion of its members.

Because this Court concludes that there is no legitimate privacy interest to be recognized or protected which would excuse the discriminatory exclusion of males in violation of the public accommodations statute, the inquiry need not go further. Since the customers of Healthworks have no privacy right to be protected, the Court is not required, indeed cannot, consider whether Healthworks' policy is reasonable.

For the reasons set forth above, [Foster's motion for summary judgment is granted].

Notes

1. First Amendment Challenges.   Antidiscrimination statutes similar to the one applied in the Healthworks case also have faced First Amendment challenges. An important early case involved a successful challenge to the exclusion of girls by the Boys' Club of Santa Cruz. The Club's mission was to combat delinquency in boys, who were four times more likely than girls to get into trouble with the law. Club owners, and the principal donor, had determined that male juvenile delinquency could be most effectively addressed in an all-male setting.[177] After the Club lost on its First Amendment claim, the donor attempted to cancel the $15 million trust fund that brought in 75 percent of the club's annual budget. She was unable to because her original gift had not required the exclusion of girls. A few years after the litigation, girls constituted almost a third of the members of the Boys' Club and were involved in all aspects of the club, including football and baseball. According to one report, there were "no signs of tension" as a result of the change in admission policy.[178]

In California, similar litigation was unsuccessful in forcing the Boy Scouts to admit girls.[179] The Boy Scouts still exclude girls, although the Explorers allow female adolescents between 14 and 20 to join. Moreover, since 1988, adult women have been allowed to become Boy Scout troop leaders. Until 2014, the Boy Scouts excluded homosexual youth, a policy the organization successfully defended in the United States Supreme Court, which held that its membership policy was protected by the organization's First Amendment right of expressive association.[180] The Boy Scouts began admitting gay youth on January 1, 2014, but continue to exclude "open and avowed homosexuals" as employees or troop leaders. Should the Boy Scouts, like the Boys' Club, be required to integrate by gender? Sexual orientation discrimination is discussed at some length in Chapter 3.

Financial as well as legal pressures have led a number of formerly all-male associations to expand their membership to women. And the Boy Scouts have experienced considerable economic repercussions due to their decision to exclude gays.[181] The federal government, however, has continued to support the Boy Scouts.[182] The Girl Scouts have avoided these consequences by adopting a national guideline against discrimination based on sexual orientation, along with a policy against "'sexual displays' or advocacy of personal lifestyles." Local Girl Scout councils apparently are not dechartered if they violate the national policy.[183] After some initial resistance, the Girl Scouts of Colorado admitted a transgendered boy to a troop. The organization said it would welcome a child who "lives life as a girl" and would not require any proof of anatomical gender from parents requesting membership for a daughter.[184]

2. Separate But Equal. At the time the Jaycees and Rotary Club cases were decided, there were no comparable organizations for women that provided the same networking advantages. Should it have made a difference if there were? Is the Boy Scouts' exclusionary policy justifiable because the Girl Scouts offers similar opportunities? Does "separate but equal"—a now-discredited doctrine that once justified racial segregation—seem different in the context of same sex associations? If the Boy Scouts should be required to admit girls, should the Girl Scouts be required to admit boys? Does it matter whether the purpose of the organization is to remedy past discrimination against girls, or to provide for girls' "special needs"? Which case would be the stronger one? The problems set forth below should be considered again in the context of Chapter 2, which addresses both of these rationales for all-female schools. If Massachusetts wanted to allow all-women's health clubs, was it also required to allow all-men's health clubs, or could the legislature have allowed only all-women's clubs?

3. The Scope of State and Local Public Accommodations Laws. Federal law prohibits discrimination in public accommodations on the basis of race, color, religion, national origin or disability, but not sex.[185] Federal constitutional guarantees of equal protection apply only to public entities. Thus, challenges to sex-based exclusions from private associations, as in *Rotary Club*, or private business or retail establishments have been brought under state civil rights acts. The public accommodations laws in some states do not apply to sex-based exclusions at all.[186] Among the many that do, however, the scope varies. Some prohibit discrimination only as to places of public accommodation, construed to mean entities that exist at a particular place, such as hotels or restaurants, and thereby excluding organizations that may meet in different locations, such as the Jaycees, Rotary Clubs, and some scouting organizations. Others apply to private clubs only in areas or at functions where nonmembers are present. Some apply only to businesses, although business may be quite broadly construed. Some statutes specifically exempt "private" or "distinctly private" clubs.[187] Although the plaintiff won his case against Healthworks, the Massachusetts legislature then passed legislation exempting fitness facilities from its general public accommodations law. A handful of other states have also carved out narrow exemptions for health clubs, changing rooms, bath houses, and other places where privacy concerns might be relevant.[188] Are targeted exemptions a reasonable compromise?

4. Law v. Public Pressure: Integrating Golf and Country Clubs. All-male golf and country clubs have been the subject of many public accommodations lawsuits, as well as several highly public controversies. Public pressure has been at least as great a factor as the law in integrating private clubs. One widely publicized effort involved the Augusta National Golf Club, one of the nation's most prestigious all-male associations, which hosted the 2002 Masters tournament.[189] The National Council of Women's Organizations sought to force major corporate sponsors to withdraw their support if the club did not admit women. Similar pressure by civil rights organizations in the 1970s had forced the racial integration of the club that hosted the prestigious Professional Golf Association tournament. After the Augusta effort, CBS broadcast the event with no commercial sponsorship in 2003 and 2004. When major companies again began supporting the event, the National Council organized shareholder resolutions charging that the corporate sponsorship violated company antidiscrimination policy.[190] In April 2012, the club reaffirmed its all-male policy, with chairman Billy Payne calling it a "private matter." But later that year, the club admitted its first two female members—former secretary of state Condoleezza Rice and business executive Darla Moore.[191] The Arizona state attorney general's office has recently issued an advisory legal opinion that the Phoenix Country Club is violating state antidiscrimination laws by excluding women.[192] Why do you suppose that it has been harder to get clubs and corporate sponsors to take sex discrimination as seriously as race discrimination?

5. Gender-Based Pricing. In states with broad public accommodations laws, men and women have challenged pricing differentials that benefit the other sex.[193] The California Supreme Court ruled, in Koire v. Metro Car Wash, that several car washes and a bar violated the public accommodations law by providing "ladies' day" discounts to women.[194] The legislature later adopted a law making clear that price differentials cannot be based on sex and requiring certain businesses, including dry cleaners and hair salons, to post a notice informing customers that state law prohibits discrimination "with respect to the price charged for services of similar or like kind, against a person because of the person's gender."[195] In 2004, the New Jersey Director of Civil Rights issued a ruling that a bar's "ladies' night"—a night each week when it admitted women without a cover charge and charged them less for drinks— violated the state's antidiscrimination law.[196] The restaurant argued that it had a legitimate purpose for the promotion—to increase patronage and revenue by bringing more women to the restaurant because of the reduced prices and more men because of the greater number of women. It also argued that this type of discrimination was too trivial to matter and, in any event, was canceled out by similar promotions on different nights for men. The director rejected all these arguments and held that the New Jersey law contained no exceptions. Some courts, however, have found that gender-based pricing does not necessarily violate public accommodations laws. A Michigan court, for example, held that the public accommodations statute was not violated by a reduced-price membership for women at a racquet club because both men and women had access to the club.[197] Other courts have allowed price differentials as long as they were not motivated by animus or other improper motive.[198]

Are gender-based price differentials ever justified? Are some forms of discrimination too trivial to bother with? Is equality served more by strict interpretation of antidiscrimination laws or by focusing only on the most severe types of discrimination? Are women helped or harmed by a policy that charges them less for alcoholic drinks?

6. Sexual Orientation and Public Accommodations.   A new frontier in public accommodations law has been challenges to exclusion based on sexual orientation. A growing number of states ban discrimination by public accommodations on grounds of sexual orientation and, in a smaller number of states, gender identity.[199] The Supreme Court of California held that California's Unruh Act, invoked in *Koire* and *Isbister*, was violated by a medical group's refusal to provide infertility treatment to lesbian women.[200] The statute had been amended in 2005 to provide protection for sexual orientation and gender identity and expression. But even before that amendment, the list of protected characteristics in the statute was treated as illustrative rather than exhaustive, and courts had repeatedly applied it to exclusions on the basis of sexual orientation. The court in North Coast Women's Care Medical Group, Inc. v. Superior Court rejected the argument that the doctors' religious objections to inseminating a lesbian, unmarried woman were sufficient to excuse the clear violation of the public accommodations law. Medical practices, like other business establishments, must provide all patients with "full and equal" access. A 2009 report by the American Society for Reproductive Medicine concluded that there is no ethical basis for physicians to deny access to fertility services on the basis of marital status or sexual orientation.[201] The American College of Obstetrics and Gynecology gives doctors more room to exercise conscientious objection by refusing to provide particular services or to treat particular patients.[202] Regardless of the ethics, however, surveys suggest that many fertility specialists do indeed discriminate on the basis of sexual orientation and marital status.[203]

7. Social Stigma Harms.   Victims of sex discrimination will sometimes be ostracized by the members of the clubs and associations they must sue in order to gain admittance, which seriously undermines the value of the protection public accommodations statutes are able to offer. One revealing *New York Times* account of a lawsuit to end discriminatory practices at a Massachusetts country club described the ostracism and frustration of plaintiffs, which contributed to divorce and the loss of clients and business, among other things.[204] These difficulties also occur in the employment context when a plaintiff sues to protect her rights, but there, employers have an obligation to protect an employee from retaliation as a result of pursuing her employment rights; they also tend to have greater control over the other employees than private clubs may have over their members. Is this problem a necessary price of litigation? Should the law address it?

Putting Theory Into Practice

1-27. Should a private law firm specializing in women's rights litigation be allowed to hire only women associates and partners? Can it decide to take only women clients? Hire only women who fit in with its own female tone and atmosphere? Contribute only to pro-women's political organizations and pro bono activities?[205]

If so, should a private law firm specializing in men's rights litigation be able to make comparable choices?

1-28. Under the Massachusetts law cited in *Foster*, could a Massachusetts public golf course run all-male tournaments if it also holds all-female tournaments?[206]

1-29. The Las Vegas Athletic Club offers cheaper sign-up rates for women than for men, because it has more trouble attracting women as members and seeks to increase its female clientele. Nevada has a law prohibiting discrimination based on sex in public accommodations.[207] Does the Athletic Club policy violate that statute? Should this practice be illegal? What about its offering of a women-only workout room? What about the sex-segregated topless swimming pools also available in some Las Vegas fitness centers?[208] Is it legal for the Nevada Hard Rock Hotel and Casino to promise that "ladies dressed in schoolgirl outfits drink free Champagne all night"?[209]

1-30. Nineteenth-century hotels used to have separate floors for women. These were abandoned by the 1980s, but they are returning, as customer research has indicated that many women prefer the privacy and special amenities of floors that cater especially to women, like cookies, extra-soft socks, massages, and skin moisturizers.[210] Is this a positive development, or a throwback to a discriminatory era?

1-31. The Black Women's Health Imperative is a membership organization dedicated to "health education, research, advocacy and leadership development" for black women and girls. Its website describes itself as follows:

> Founded in 1983 by health activist Byllye Y. Avery, it has been a pioneer in promoting the empowerment of African American women as educated health care consumers and a strong voice for the improved health status of African American women. The organization is gaining the well-earned reputation as the leading force for health for African American women. Black Women's Health Imperative possesses national stature as the only national organization devoted solely to the health of the nation's 19 million Black women and girls.[211]

The organization's services and programs are all geared toward black women and girls. Should this organization be subject to state legislation banning race and sex discrimination? How would you respond to the view propounded in relation to the organization's predecessor organization, the National Black Women's Health Project?

> If African-American women do not exclude white women from their association, their sharing will be chilled by the presence of white women. African-American women will spend valuable time listening to white women defend their actions. In essence, African-American women will spend time concentrating on white women, instead of focusing on themselves. Their communications will become stilted until they are effectively silenced in their own associations.[212]

1-31. The relevant state public accommodations statute prohibits discrimination based on, among other things, sexual orientation. Your Faith, Your Health is a health club that caters to religious conservatives, although there are no religious restrictions on membership. The clientele is not comfortable with gay customers. Not only do most customers disapprove of the "gay lifestyle," but they are also anxious around gays, especially in changing rooms, showers, saunas, and other intimate settings. On this basis, may Your Faith, Your Health exclude gay customers?

1-32. How do the identity-based student organizations on your campus handle membership and leadership? Under formal equality principles, do you see any problem with their approaches?

---

1. 404 U.S. 71 (1971).
2. 429 U.S. 190 (1976).
3. See Mississippi Univ. for Women v. Hogan, 458 U.S. 718, 724 (1982); United States v. Virginia, 518 U.S. 515, 531 (1996).
4. 198 U.S. 45 (1905).
5. 300 U.S. 379 (1937).
6. State v. Hunter, 300 P.2d 455, 458 (Or. 1956).

7. See Deborah L. Rhode, Justice and Gender 20-24 (1989); Karen Morello, The Invisible Bar: The Woman Lawyer in America (1986); Cynthia Epstein, Women in Law 66-67 (1981).

8. Deborah L. Rhode, Midcourse Corrections: Women in Legal Education, 53 J. Legal Educ. 475, 477 (2003).

9. Gerda Lerner, The Meaning of Seneca Falls, 1848-1998, Dissent at 35, 37-39 (Fall 1998).

10. See Sara M. Evans, Born for Liberty: A History of Women in America 81 (1989).

11. Rhode, Justice and Gender, supra note 7 at 54.

12. Betty Friedan, The Feminine Mystique 15-32 (1963).

13. For further reading, see Gail Collins, America's Women (2003); A Companion to American Women's History (Nancy A. Hewitt ed., 2002); No Small Courage: A History of Women in the United States (Nancy F. Cott ed., 2000); William H. Chafe, The Road to Equality: 1962–Today, in No Small Courage, supra, at 529-586; Eleanor Flexner & Ellen Fitzpatrick, Century of Struggle: The Woman's Rights Movement in the United States (enlarged ed. 1996); Joan Hoff, Law, Gender, and Injustice: A Legal History of U.S. Women (1991); Sara M. Evans, supra note 10; Nancy Woloch, Women and the American Experience (1984); Linda K. Kerber, Women of the Republic: Intellect and Ideology in Revolutionary America (1980); Gerda Lerner, The Majority Finds Its Past (1979); Ellen Carol DuBois, Feminism and Suffrage: The Emergence of an Independent Women's Movement in America 1848-1869 (1978); Barbara J. Harris, Beyond Her Sphere: Women and the Professions in American History (1978).

14. Bobb v. Municipal Court, 192 Cal. Rptr. 270, 270-271 (Cal. App. 1983).

15. For the full story, see Linda Greenhouse, Becoming Justice Blackmun: Harry Blackmun's Supreme Court Journey 209-211 (2005).

16. Ruth Bader Ginsburg, Remarks for the Celebration of 75 Years of Women's Enrollment at Columbia Law School, 102 Colum. L. Rev. 1441, 1445 (2002).

17. Brief of Appellants at 11, Craig v. Boren, No. 75-628 (1976).

18. Chris Lombardi, Women's Equality Day Poll Finds Support for ERA, Aug. 27, 2002, available at www.womensnews.org/story/washington-outlookcongresswhite-house/030712/women's-equality-day-poll-finds-support-era.

19. Sarah Rode, The Equal Rights Amendment: A Case for Rejection, available at http://www.cwfa.org/articledisplay.asp?id=13163&department=CWA&categoryid=life.

20. Christina Hoff Sommers, "Equal Rights" Time Warp, Wall St. J., Apr. 3, 2007, at A15.

21. http://www.equalrightsamendment.org/faq.htm.

22. See, e.g., Paul Abrams, The Equal Rights Amendment: Now Is the Time, available at http://www.huffingtonpost.com/paul-abrams/the-equal-rights-amendmen_b_1312339.html (state laws requiring medically unnecessary ultrasound exams without their consent and federal efforts to permit employers to withdraw health care coverage for contraceptives demonstrate the need for an ERA).

23. See Linda J. Wharton, State Equal Rights Amendments Revisited: Evaluating Their Effectiveness in Advancing Protection Against Sex Discrimination, 36 Rutgers L.J. 1201, 1243-1247 (2005) (discussing Rhode Island and Florida).

24. Id. at 1204.

25. Id. at 1248-1268.

26. See Paul Benjamin Linton, State Equal Rights Amendments: Making a Difference or Making a Statement?, 70 Temp. L. Rev. 907, 941 (1997) (arguing that the "ultimate irony" of state ERAs is that "in many respects women have given up 'privileges' they always enjoyed in exchange for 'rights' that never were in jeopardy").

27. The Department of Defense agreed to change the regulations to "strongly advise" rather than require women to wear the abaya. They still may not drive off base alone. The pilot remained unsatisfied and claimed that American women are more likely to be harassed if they wear the abaya than if they are dressed in Western clothes and that the policy was not requested by the Saudi government. Congressional legislation subsequently prohibited the military from requiring or strongly encouraging servicewomen to wear the abaya. See Megan Twohey, Taking Off the Abaya, Salon.com, May 16, 2002; Bob Stump National Defense Authorization Act for Fiscal Year 2003, Pub. L. No. 107-314, Section 563, 116 Stat. 2458 (2002).

28. 453 U.S. 57 (1981).

29. 458 U.S. 718 (1982).

30. 6 F.3d 990, 1010 (3d Cir. 1993).

31. See Suvarna Bhatt, Is There a Glass Ceiling for Female Surgeons?, Health Careers Network, Nov.2,2010,athttp://www.healthecareers.com/article/is-there-a-glass-ceiling-for-female-surgeons/158279.

32. 29 U.S.C. §206 (2012).

33. 42 U.S.C. §2000e et seq. (2012).

34. EEOC v. Madison Cmty. Unit Sch. Dist. No. 12, 818 F.2d 577, 585 (7th Cir. 1987) (quoting 29 C.F.R. §800.114(a)).

35. See, e.g., Aldrich v. Randolph Central Sch. Dist., 963 F.2d 520 (2d Cir. 1992).

36. See, e.g., Juliene James, The Equal Pay Act in the Courts: A De Facto White-Collar Exemption, 79 N.Y.U. L. Rev. (2004); Mary E. Graham & Julie L. Hotchkiss, A Systematic Assessment of Employer Equal Employment Opportunity Efforts as a Means of Reducing the Gender Earnings Gap, 12 Cornell J.L. & Pub. Pol'y 169 (2002).

37. 195 F. Supp. 2d 853 (W.D. Tex. 2002).

38. 550 U.S. 618 (2007).

39. 421 F.3d 1169 (11th Cir. 2005).

40. 550 U.S. at 628.

41. See Lilly Ledbetter Fair Pay Act of 2009, Pub. L. No. 111-2, 123 Stat. 5 (codified as amended at 42 U.S.C. §2000e-5(e)(3)(A) (2012)).

42. On the "glass ceiling" of the EPA, see Deborah Thompson Eisenberg, Shattering the Equal Pay Act's Glass Ceiling, 63 SMU L. Rev. 17 (2010).

43. Leonard Bierman & Rafael Gely, "Love, Sex and Politics? Sure. Salary? No Way": Workplace Social Norms and the Law, 25 Berkeley J. Emp. & Labor L. 167, 168, 171 (2004) (explaining that social norms discourage discussion of salaries in the workplace and observing that one-third of U.S. private sector employers have policies which, although illegal, bar employees from discussing their salaries, while many other employers informally communicate an expectation of salary confidentiality).

44. See Paycheck Fairness Act, S. 84, available at https://www.govtrack.us/congress/bills/113/s84.

45. U.S. Department of Labor, Bureau of Labor Statistics, Rep. No. 1034, Women in the Labor Force: A Databook (Dec. 2011), at 52, Table 16, available at http://www.bls.gov/cps/wlf-databook-2011 .pdf.

46. See Francine D. Blau & Lawrence M. Kahn, The U.S. Gender Pay Gap in the 1990s: Slowing Convergence, 60 Indus. & Lab. Relations Rev. 45 (2007).

47. Institute for Women's Policy Research, Women's Economic Status in the States: Wide Disparities by Race, Ethnicity, and Region (2004).

48. U.S. Department of Labor, Bureau of Labor Statistics, Highlights of Women's Earnings in 2010, Rep. 1031, at 9 (July 2011), available at http://www.bls.gov/cps/cpswom2010.pdf.

49. Women in the Labor Force, supra note 45, at 1 & Table 14.

50. Highlights of Women's Earnings, supra note 48, at 2.

51. Women in the Labor Force, supra note 45, at Table 11, at 30.

52. Id. at 59-67, Table 18; see also Men Outearn Women in Almost All Occupations, Institute for Women's Policy Research, April 28, 2009, available at http://news.yahoo.com/s/usnw/20090428/pl_usnw/men_outearn_women_in_almost_all_occupations.

53. Carmen DeNavas-Walt, Bernadette D. Proctor, & Jessica C. Smith, Income, Poverty, and Health Insurance Coverage in the United States: 2010, at 5 (Sept. 2011), available at http://www.census.gov/prod/2011pubs/p60-239.pdf; Jessica Arons, Lifetime Losses: The Career Wage Gap, Center for American Progress (Jan. 6, 2009), http://www.american-progress.org/issues/2009/01/wage_gap_numbers.html, at 1.

54. See Arons, supra note 53, at 4, 5.

55. Women in the Labor Force, supra note 45, at 53-54, Table 17.

56. Id. at 55, Table 18.

57. Id. at 16, at 51-52.

58. Highlights of Women's Earnings, supra note 48, at 2.

59. See AAUW, Behind the Pay Gap, at 3, 17-18, available at http://www.aauw.org/learn/research/upload/behindPayGap.pdf (concluding, after regression analysis, that "the portion of the pay gap that remains unexplained after all other factors are taken into account is 5 percent one year after graduation and 12 percent 10 years after graduation"); Francine D. Blau & Lawrence M. Kahn, The Gender Pay Gap: Have Women Gone as Far as They Can?, 21 Acad. Mgmt. Persp. 7 (2007) (finding an unexplained pay gap of 9 percent); see also Deborah Thompson Eisenberg, Money, Sex, and Sunshine: A Market-Based Approach to Pay Discrimination, 43 Ariz. St. L.J. 951, 972-982 (2011) (reviewing wage gap data and explanations); Daniel H. Weinberg, U.S. Dep't of Commerce, Census 2000 Special Reports, Evidence from Census 2000 About Earnings by Detailed Occupation for Men and Women 7 (May 2004) ("There is a substantial gap in median earnings between men and women that is unexplained, even after controlling for work experience . . . education, and occupation."); U.S. Gen. Acct. Office, Women's

Earnings: Work Patterns Partially Explain Difference Between Men's and Women's Earnings, GAO-04-35 at 2 (Oct. 2003) (examining nationally representative longitudinal data set and concluding that women in 2000 earned only 80 percent of what men earned even after accounting for differing work patterns and other "key factors"); Michael Selmi, Family Leave and the Gender Wage Gap, 78 N.C. L. Rev. 707, 719-743 (2000) (reviewing data).

60. See Stephen J. Ro.se & Heidi I. Hartmann, Inst. For Women's Pol'y Res., Still a Man's Labor Market: The Long-Term Earnings Gap 10 (2004).

61. See AAUW, The Simple Truth About the Gender Pay Gap, 10 (2012); Shelley J. Correll & Stephen Benard, Getting a Job: Is There a Motherhood Penalty?, 112 Amer. J. Sociol. 1297 (2007); Selmi, supra note 59, at 726, 745-750.

62. See Linda Babcock & Sara Laschever, Women Don't Ask: Negotiation and the Gender Divide (2003); Shankar Vedantam, Salary, Gender and the Social Cost of Haggling, Wash. Post, July 30, 2007.

63. Compare, e.g., Wernsing v. Illinois Dep't of Human Servs., 427 F.3d 466 (7th Cir. 2005) (court "not even slightly tempted" to change its longstanding position that prior salary may be taken into account when setting an employee's starting pay) with Glenn v. General Motors Corp., 841 F.2d 1567 (11th Cir. 1988) (rejecting employer justification for wage disparity based on male clerks' transfer from higher paying positions than female clerks).

64. 417 U.S. 188, 205-207 (1974).

65. Linda Jean Carpenter & R. Vivian Acosta, Women in Intercollegiate Sport: A Longitudinal, National Study — Thirty-Five Year Update 1977-2012, at 17-18 (2012), available at http://acostacarpenter.org/AcostaCarpenter2012.pdf; see also NCAA, Gender-Equity Report 2004-2010. Some evidence suggests that if football, basketball, and ice hockey were excluded, the salaries for male and female head coaches would be nearly equal. Robert Drago et al., Final Report for Cage: The Coaching and Gender Equity Report 11 (2005), available at http://lser.la.psu.edu/workfam/CAGEfinalreport.doc.

66. Carpenter & Acosta, supra note 65.

67. Enforcement Guidance on Sex Discrimination in the Compensation of Sports Coaches in Educational Institutions (1997), available at http://www.eeoc.gov/policy/docs/coaches.html. For discussion, see Deborah L. Rhode & Christopher J. Walker, Gender Equity in College Athletics, 4 Stan. J. C.R. & C.L. 101, 117-119 (2008).

68. See also Am. Nurses' Ass'n v. Illinois, 783 F.2d 716 (7th Cir. 1986) (Title VII does not require state to review wage scales in predominantly male and predominantly female jobs).

69. See Stanley v. Univ. of S. Cal., 13 F.3d 1313 (9th Cir. 1994) (rejecting equal pay claim). For a critique of the case, see Andrew M. Giampetro-Meyer, Recognizing and Remedying Individual and Institutional Gender-Based Wage Discrimination in Sport, 37 Am. Bus. L.J. 343 (2000). After a college coaching career that included Southern Cal, Berkeley, Stanford, and Penn, Stanley moved on to the pros, where she coached the Washington Mystics for two seasons, and then became an assistant coach for the New York Liberty. See Vicki L. Friedman, Where Are They Now?, The Virginian Pilot, Feb. 26, 2005, at C7. For Summitt's salary, see Milestones, Ms., Spring 2009, at 11.

70. The Associated Press, France's Gilles Simon Says Men Should Be Paid More Than Women at Tennis' Grand Slam Tournaments, June 27, 2012, available at www.nydailynews.com/sports/more-sports/france-gilles-simon-men-paid-women-tennis-grand-slam-tournaments-article-1.1103224.

71. See Hodgson v. Robert Hall Clothes, Inc., 473 F.2d 589 (3d Cir. 1973) (rejecting Equal Pay Act claim).

72. Spaulding v. Univ. of Wash., 749 F.2d 686 (9th Cir. 1994).

73. Most systemic disparate treatment claims are litigated as class actions. The likelihood of obtaining class certification in an employment discrimination case is less likely after the Supreme Court's ruling in Wal-Mart Stores, Inc. v. Dukes, 131 S. Ct. 2541 (2011), in which it rejected certification of a class of more than 1.5 million plaintiffs who alleged pay and promotion discrimination on the basis of sex. The impact of this case is discussed in detail below.

74. For a case history of the litigation, see Deborah L. Rhode, What's Sex Got to Do with It: The Challenge of Diversity in the Legal Profession, in Legal Ethics: Law Stories 233 (Deborah L. Rhode & David Luban eds., 2005).

75. Plotke v. White, 405 F.3d 1092 (10th Cir. 2005).

76. Sreeram v. La. State Univ. Med. Ctr., 188 F.3d 314 (5th Cir. 1999). See also Heim v. State of Utah, 8 F.3d 1541, 1546 (10th Cir. 1993) (holding that a supervisor's comment, "Fucking women, I hate having fucking women in the office," was insufficient to show discrimination because it appeared directed at "women in general," rather than at plaintiff).

77. EEOC v. Bloomberg, L.P., 778 F. Supp. 2d 458, 461 (S.D.N.Y. 2011).

78. Id. at 478-481.

79. Id. at 479.

80. 42 U.S.C. §2000e-2(m) (2012).

81. Id. at §2000e-5(g)(2)(B).

82. Deborah Rhode, Speaking of Sex: The Denial of Gender Equality 161 (1997).

83. ABA Commission on Women in the Profession, The Unfinished Agenda: A Report on the Status of Women in the Legal Profession 15-16 (2001). See also Deborah L. Rhode & Barbara Kellerman, Gender Differences and Gender Stereotypes—Crossing the Bridge: Reflections on Women and Leadership, in Women and Leadership: The State of Play and Strategies for Change 1, 6-11 (Barbara Kellerman & Deborah L. Rhode eds., 2007).

84. Virginia Valian, Why So Slow?: The Advancement of Women 139-141 (1998).

85. Martha Chamallas, Listening to Dr. Fiske: The Easy Case of *Price Waterhouse v. Hopkins*, 15 Vt. L. Rev. 89, 96-99 (1990).

86. See Susan Sturm, Second Generation Employment Discrimination: A Structural Approach, 101 Colum. L. Rev. 458, 460 (2001). For more on unconscious bias, see Jerry Kang, Trojan Horses of Race, 118 Harv. L. Rev. 1489 (2005); Linda Hamilton Krieger, The Content of Our Categories: A Cognitive Bias Approach to Discrimination and Equal Employment Opportunity, 47 Stan. L. Rev. 1161 (1995).

87. 467 U.S. 69, 76 (1984).

88. Id. at 79-80 & n.3 (Powell, J., concurring).

89. See, e.g., EEOC v. Sidley Austin Brown & Wood, 315 F.3d 696, 703-707 (7th Cir. 2002) (partners may still be employees when they lack equity in the partnership, receive regular salary, and lack meaningful management over the partnership).

90. See EEOC Compliance Manual, ¶7110, §2-III-A.1.d (2000).

91. See, e.g., Sturm, supra note 86; Tristin K. Green, Insular Individualism: Employment Discrimination Law After Ledbetter v. Goodyear, 43 Harv. C.R.-C.L. L. Rev. 353 (2008); Tristin K. Green, A Structural Approach as Antidiscrimination Mandate: Locating Employer Wrong, 60 Vand. L. Rev. 849 (2007). See also discussion of unconscious bias in note 4 on p. 78.

92. Teamsters v. United States, 431 U.S. 324 (1977).

93. 131 S. Ct. 2541 (2011).

94. 603 F.3d 571 (9th Cir. 2010) (en banc).

95. Teamsters v. United States, 431 U.S. 324 (1977).

96. For opposing views on the admissibility and usefulness of social framework evidence, compare Melissa Hart & Paul M. Secunda, A Matter of Context: Social Framework Evidence in Employment Discrimination Class Actions, 78 Fordham L. Rev. 37 (2009) (arguing that social framework evidence should be admissible in many employment class actions) with John Monahan et al., Contextual Evidence of Gender Discrimination: The Ascendance of "Social Frameworks," 94 Va. L. Rev. 1715 (2008) (arguing that court should not allow expert witness to link the general research findings of social framework evidence to the facts of a particular case).

97. See, e.g., David Benjamin Oppenheimer, Negligent Discrimination, 141 U. Pa. L. Rev. 899 (1993) (suggesting a theory of "negligent discrimination"); Deborah M. Weiss, A Grudging Defense of Wal-Mart v. Dukes, 24 Yale J. Law & Feminism 119 (2012) (developing a "notice theory" of discrimination); Tristin K. Green, The Future of Systemic Disparate Treatment Law, 32 Berkeley J. Employment & Labor Law 395 (2011) (suggesting a "context" model of systemic discrimination).

98. Richard A. Epstein, Forbidden Grounds: The Case Against Employment Discrimination Laws (1992).

99. See, e.g., Scott A. Moss, Women Choosing Diverse Workplaces: A Rational Preference with Disturbing Implications for Both Occupational Segregation and Economic Analysis of Law, 27 Harv. Women's L.J. 1 (2004).

100. Devon W. Carbado & Mitu Gulati, Working Identity, 85 Cornell L. Rev. 1259, 1262 (2000) (excerpted in Chapter 6).

101. See Devon W. Carbado & Mitu Gulati, Race to the Top of the Corporate Ladder: What Minorities Do When They Get There, 61 Wash. & Lee L. Rev. 1645 (2004).

102. Sturm, supra note 86, at 468, 470-471, 475-476. See also Green, supra note 91 (noting a "potentially devastating conceptual shift" in employment discrimination law based on "the belief that discrimination can be reduced to the action of an individual decisionmaker (or group of decisionmakers) isolated from the work environment and the employer").

103. Sturm, supra note 86; Rhode & Kellerman, supra note 83, at 29-31; Tristin K. Green, Work Culture and Discrimination, 93 Cal. L. Rev. 623, 684 (2005).

104. See, e.g., Russell K. Robinson, Perceptual Segregation, 108 Colum. L. Rev. 1093 (2008); Tristin K. Green & Alexandra Kalev, Discrimination-Reducing Measures at the Relational Level, 59 Hastings L.J. 1435, 1457 (2008); Ivan Bodensteiner, The Implications of Psychological Research Related to Unconscious Discrimination and Implicit Bias in Proving Intentional Discrimination, 73 Mo. L. Rev. 83, 108, 120-127 (2008); Ann C. McGinley, ¡Viva La Evolucion!: Recognizing Unconscious Motive in Title VII, 9 Cornell J.L. & Pub. Pol'y 415, 482 (2000).

105. Katharine T. Bartlett, Making Good on Good Intentions: The Critical Role of Motivation in Reducing Implicit Workplace Discrimination, 95 Va. L. Rev. 1893, 1901-1902 (2009).

106. Santiago-Ramos v. Centennial P.R. Wireless Corp., 217 F.3d 46 (1st Cir. 2000).

107. Rhode, What's Sex Got to Do with It, supra note 74, at 245.

108. See Baker v. Cal. Land Title Co., 507 F.2d 895 (9th Cir. 1974).

109. See, e.g., Willingham v. Macon Tel. Publ'g Co., 507 F.2d 1084 (5th Cir. 1975).

110. Tracy E. George et al., The New Old Legal Realism, 105 Nw. U. L. Rev. 689, 715-716, 723, 727 (2011) (noting lack of change); Deborah L. Rhode, The Beauty Bias 14 (2010) (noting change in Harrah's policy).

111. See Rhode, Beauty Bias, supra note 110, at 23-44; Daniel S. Hamermesh, Beauty Pays (2011).

112. See the studies reviewed in Deborah L. Rhode, The Injustice of Appearance, 61 Stan. L. Rev. 1033, 1038-1039 (2009); Megumi Hosoda et al., The Effects of Physical Attractiveness on Job Related Outcomes: A Meta-Analysis of Experimental Studies, Personnel Psychol. 56 (2003), at 4311; Kristie M. Engemann & Michael T. Owyang, So Much for That Merit Raise: The Link Between Wages and Appearance, Q. Rev. Bus. & Econ. Conditions (Apr. 2005), at 10 (14 percent estimate).

113. See Jeff E. Biddle & Daniel S. Hamermesh, Beauty, Productivity and Discrimination: Lawyers' Looks and Lucre, 16 J. Lab. Econ. 172, 185-190 (1998).

114. See polls cited in Rhode, The Injustice of Appearance, supra note 112, at 1068-1069.

115. See Nancy Etcoff, Survival of the Prettiest: The Science of Beauty 31-32 (1999) (describing study of babies).

116. See, e.g., Katharine T. Bartlett, Only Girls Wear Barrettes: Dress and Appearance Standards, Community Norms, and Workplace Equality, 92 Mich. L. Rev. 2541 (1994).

117. Rhode, Beauty Bias, supra note 110, at 121.

118. Id. at 93.

119. See, e.g., Jordan D. Bello, Attractiveness as a Hiring Criteria: Savvy Business Practice or Racial Discrimination, 8 J. Gender, Race & Just. 483, 483 (2004). Abercrombie & Fitch ultimately settled a case charging discrimination based on its policy of hiring attractive "All American" white sales personnel. Steven Greenhouse, Abercrombie & Fitch Bias Case Is Settled, N.Y. Times, Nov. 17, 2004, at A16.

120. See Goodwin v. Harvard College, No. 03-11797-JLT (D. Mass. 2005).

121. 591 F.3d 1033, 1036 (2010).

122. 572 F. Supp. 868 (W.D. Mo. 1983), rev'd in part, 776 F.2d 1205 (8th Cir. 1985).

123. For Craft's own account of her experience, see Craft, Too Old, Too Ugly, and Not Deferential to Men (1988).

124. Rhode, The Injustice of Appearance, supra note 112, at 1039; Dalton Conley & Rebecca Glauber, Gender, Body Mass, and Socioeconomic Status: New Evidence from the PSID, 17 Advances in Health Econ. & Health Servs. 253 (2007) (finding that women earn 0.6 percent less family income for each 1 percent increase in body mass); John Cawley, The Impact of Obesity on Wages, 39 J. Hum. Res. 451, 468 (2004) (finding that obese women average 9 percent less per hour than average-sized women).

125. Jarrell v. Eastern Airlines, Inc., 430 F. Supp. 884, 892 (E.D. Va. 1977), aff'd mem., 577 F.2d 869 (4th Cir. 1978).

126. Sunaina Assanand, John P. J. Pine, & Darrin R. Lehman, Personal Theories of Hunger and Eating, 28 J. Applied Soc. Psych. 998 (1998) (discussing popular assumptions). For the role of genetic and environmental factors, see Gina Kolata, Rethinking Thin (2007); John C. Peters et al., From Instinct to Intellect: The Challenge of Maintaining Healthy Weight in the Modern World, 3 Obesity Revs. 69, 70 (2002). On the ineffectiveness of diets, see Rhode, supra note 112, at 1042, 1063.

127. See http://www.cbsnews.com/stories/2005/10/25/health/webmd/main972825.shtml.

128. Id. Research shows that up to 25 percent of men are on diets at any given time.

129. 29 C.F.R. §1630 (2012).

130. Rhode, The Injustice of Appearance, supra note 112, at 1078-1079; Elizabeth E. Theran, Legal Theory of Weight Discrimination, in Weight Bias: Nature, Consequences and Remedies 195, 206 (Kelly D. Brownell et al. eds., 2005).

131. For the impact of these laws, see Rhode, The Injustice of Appearance, supra note 112, at 1081-1090. For further discussion of the problem of obesity discrimination, see Lucy Wang, Weight Discrimination: One Size Fits All Remedy?, 117 Yale L.J. 1900 (2008); Kari Horner, A Growing Problem: Why the Federal Government Needs to Shoulder the Burden in Protecting Workers from Weight Discrimination, 54 Cath. U. L. Rev. 589 (2005).

132. Press Release, Employment Law Alliance, National Poll Shows Public Opinion Sharply Divided on Regulating Appearance—From Weight to Tattoos—in the Workplace, Mar. 22, 2005 (on file with the Employment Law Alliance).

133. Richard Ford, The Race Card 176-177 (2007).

134. Rhode, The Injustice of Appearance, supra note 112, at 1095-1096.

135. Rhode, Beauty Bias, supra note 110, at 134-136.

136. William R. Corbett, Hotness Discrimination: Appearance Discrimination as a Mirror for Reflecting on the Body of Employment Discrimination Law, 60 Cath. U. L. Rev. 615, 657 (2011).

137. See Nicole Buonocore Porter, Sex Plus Age Discrimination: Protecting Older Women Workers, 81 Denv. U. L. Rev. 79, 94-99 (2003).

138. See, e.g., Eduardo Porter, UBS Ordered to Pay $29 Million in Sex Bias Lawsuit, N.Y. Times, Apr. 15, 2005, at C4 (reporting on case against bank where plaintiff was called "old and ugly").

139. Elie Mystal, Women Are Not Sex Objects; Cocktail Waitresses, On the Other Hand . . . , May, 31, 2011, http://abovethelaw.com/2011/05/women-are-not-sex-objects-cock-tail-waitresses-on-the-other-hand (quoting Allred).

140. Id.

141. Rhode, Beauty Bias, supra note 110, at 69-89.

142. Id. at 76, 87.

143. Yanowitz v. L'Oreal U.S.A., 131 Cal. Rptr. 2d 575, 588 (Cal. App. 2003); Gersh Kuntzman, Casino Gal's Fat Chance—Hotel's Waitress Rule: Gain Pounds, Lose a Job, N.Y. Post, Feb. 18, 2005, at 3.

144. See Marc Linder, Smart Women, Stupid Shoes, and Cynical Employers: The Unlawfulness and Adverse Health Consequences of Sexually Discriminatory Workplace Footwear Requirements for Female Employees, J. Corp. L. 295, 296 (Winter 1997).

145. Thorstein Veblen, The Theory of the Leisure Class: An Economic Study of Institutions 121 (1899).

146. John Schwartz, At a Symposium of Judges, a Debate of the Laws of Fashion, N.Y. Times, May 22, 2009, at A10.

147. Letter from C. Robert Sturm, Law Firm of Littler Mendelson, to the San Francisco Commission on Human Rights, Oct. 26, 2001, at 6. The case was mediated to a successful resolution and the complaint dismissed.

148. On when sex constitutes the essence of the business, see Kimberly Yuracko, Private Nurses and Playboy Bunnies: Explaining Permissible Sex Discrimination, 92 Cal. L. Rev. 147 (2004).

149. 653 F.2d 1273 (9th Cir. 1981).

150. 447 F. Supp. 1346 (D. Del. 1978), aff'd mem., 591 F.2d 1334 (3d Cir. 1979).

151. See Emily Gold Waldman, The Case of the Male OB-GYN: A Proposal for the Expansion of the Privacy BFOQ in the Healthcare Context, 6 U. Pa. J. Lab. & Emp. L. 357, 366-392 (2004) (proposing that employers should be able to hire, for example, only female obstetricians and gynecologists).

152. See Amy Kapczynski, Same-Sex Privacy and the Limits of Antidiscrimination Law, 112 Yale L.J. 1257 (2003).

153. 594 S.E.2d 616 (W. Va. 2004).

154. See, e.g., Gunther v. Iowa State Men's Reformatory, 612 F.2d 1079 (8th Cir. 1980).

155. Compare, e.g., Oliver v. Scott, 276 F.3d 736 (5th Cir. 2002) (holding that privacy rights did not bar cross-sex surveillance of male prisoners or require shower partitions and that such conditions did not violate equal protection rights), with Everson v. Michigan Department of Corrections, 391 F.3d 737 (6th Cir. 2004) (upholding sex as a BFOQ in Michigan's women's prisons, because the duties required officers to patrol sleeping, shower, and bathroom areas, and Michigan sought to address a deplorable record in caring for its female inmates).

156. See, e.g., White v. Dep't of Correctional Svcs., 814 F. Supp. 2d 374 (S.D.N.Y. 2011) (denying summary judgment because a reasonable jury could find that the prison could find less restrictive ways to ensure that strip frisks and urine tests were performed by an officer of the same gender as the

prisoner); Reese v. Mich. Dep't of Corrections, 105 Fair Empl. Prac. Cas. (BNA) 1584 (E.D. Mich. 2009) (denying summary judgment because factual record was not clear on how frequently male officers would have to perform pat-downs on female prisoners); Inscore v. Doty, 2009 WL 2753049 (E.D. Ark.) (denying summary judgment to employer who refused to hire women for undercover positions in narcotics unit because there was genuine issue of material fact "as to whether being a young black male was an essential qualification to the investigation unit's business of infiltrating the culture of crack cocaine dealers").

157. *Reese*, 105 Fair Empl. Prac. Cas. (BNA) at *4.

158. *Dothard*, 433 U.S. at 336.

159. In addition to the cases discussed below, see Henry v. Milwaukee County, 539 F.3d 573 (7th Cir. 2008) (invalidating gender-based staffing policy in juvenile detention center because insufficient evidence of sexual abuse problem and same-gender mentoring/rehabilitation plan did not require same-gender staffing at night).

160. 391 F.3d 737 (6th Cir. 2004).

161. Id. at 754.

162. Id. at 755.

163. Id.

164. Id. at 755, 762.

165. 601 F.3d 1202 (9th Cir. 2010).

166. Id. at 1211.

167. Id. at 1216.

168. Id. at 1211.

169. Id. at 1215.

170. This case is modeled on Karen Horowitz, a video vignette from Stephen Gillers's series, Adventures in Legal Ethics (1992).

171. Compare Healey v. Southwood Psychiatric Hospital, 78 F.3d 128 (3d Cir. 1996) (sex is a BFOQ) with EEOC v. Physicians Weight Loss Centers, 953 F. Supp. 301 (W.D. Mo. 1996) (although 95 percent of customers at a weight loss center were women and some objected to having their measurements taken by a man and did not feel comfortable discussing emotional and physiological issues associated with weight loss with a man, sex was not a BFOQ for center's counselors).

172. Courtney E. Martin, Violence Shelter Considers Hiring Male Director, www.womensenews .org, Aug. 22, 2005.

173. See Harriss v. Pan Am World Airways, Inc., 437 F. Supp. 413 (N.D. Cal. 1977).

174. 468 U.S. 609 (1984).

175. 481 U.S. 537 (1987).

176. 1997 Mass. Super. LEXIS 194 (Sup. Ct., Suffolk, Sept. 29, 1997).

177. Isbister v. Boys' Club of Santa Cruz, 707 P.2d 212 (Cal. 1985).

178. Jill Zuckman, Boys' Club Finds Sugar and Spice, San Jose Mercury News, Aug. 14, 1987, at 1B.

179. See Yeaw v. Boy Scouts of America, 64 Cal. Rptr. 2d 85 (Ct. App. 1997).

180. Boy Scouts of America v. Dale, 530 U.S. 640 (2000). On the organization's current membership policies, see http://www.scouting.org/sitecore/content/membershipstandards/resolution/resolution.aspx.

181. See Kate Zernike, Scouts' Successful Ban on Gays Is Followed by Loss in Support, N.Y. Times, Aug. 29, 2000, at A1 (reporting on withdrawal by cities, corporations, a state-run charity, and some United Way agencies, of various types of support including use of parks and schools and funding, as a result of its policy against gay members); David France, Scouts Divided, Newsweek, Aug. 6, 2001, at 44, 47 (noting a 4.5 percent drop in Boy Scout membership in year following *Dale* decision).

182. See Boy Scouts of America Equal Access Act (2001); Support Our Scouts Act (2005).

183. Peg Tyre, Where the Girls Are: The Girl Scouts Try a Version of "Don't' Ask, Don't Tell," Newsweek, Aug. 6, 2001, at 51.

184. See Phil Gast, Parents Urged to Support, Safeguard Children as They Explore Gender, CNN .com, Oct. 28, 2011.

185. 42 U.S.C. §2000a (2012); 42 U.S.C. §12182 (2012).

186. For a comprehensive listing of public accommodations laws, see Joseph William Singer, No Right to Exclude: Public Accommodations and Private Property, 90 Nw. U. L. Rev. 1283, 1478-1495 (1996).

187. Examples of each of these types of statutes are discussed in Sally Frank, The Key to Unlocking the Clubhouse Door: The Application of Antidiscrimination Laws to Quasi-Private Clubs, 2 Mich. J. Gender & L. 27 (1994).

188. See Mass. Gen. Laws ch. 272 §92A (2012); 775 Ill. Comp. Stat. 5/5-103 (West 2012); Tenn. Code Ann. §4-21-503 (2012). See also Michael R. Evans, The Case for All-Female Health Clubs: Creating a Compensatory Purpose Exception to State Public Accommodation Laws, 11 Yale J.L. & Feminism 307 (1999).

189. On the controversy, see Frank J. Ferraro, Prerogative or Prejudice?: The Exclusion of Women from Augusta National, 1 DePaul J. Sports L. Contemp. Probs. 39 (2003).

190. See Elizabeth Dwoskin, Burk Swings at Exxon, www.womensenews.org, Apr. 17, 2006; Martha Burk, Cult of Power: Sex Discrimination in Corporate America and What Can Be Done About It (2005).

191. Karen Crouse, Touchy Day at Augusta National Men's Club, N.Y. Times, Apr. 4, 2012, at B11; Elisabeth Bumiller, Avid Golfer Rice Jumps a Barrier Again, N.Y. Times, Aug. 20, 2012, at B9.

192. See Jennifer Steinhauer, A Cozy Spot to Eat After Golf, But Out of Bounds to Women, N.Y. Times, June 28, 2008, at A1.

193. See Mark Allan Herzberg, "Girls Get in Free": A Legal Analysis of the Gender-Based Door Entry Policies, 19 S. Cal. Rev. L. & Soc. Just. 479 (2010).

194. 707 P.2d 195 (Cal. 1985). See also Ladd v. Iowa W. Racing Ass'n, 438 N.W.2d 600 (Iowa 1989) (race track's policy of giving free admission and discounted concessions to women constituted unlawful discrimination).

195. Cal. Civ. Code §51.6 (2012).

196. Gillespie v. Coastline Restaurant, CRT 2579-03, Order, N.J. Dep't of Law & Public Safety (June 1, 2004), available at http://www.state.nj.us/lps/Gillespie.Order.06.01.04.html.

197. Tucich v. Dearborn Indoor Racquet Club, 309 N.W.2d 615, 619 (Mich. Ct. App. 1981).

198. See The Dock Club, Inc. v. Illinois Liquor Control Comm'n, 428 N.E.2d 735 (Ill. App. Ct. 1981); MacLean v. First Northwest Indus., 635 P.2d 683 (Wash. 1981).

199. A map of current state laws on this subject is available at http://www.aclu.org/maps/non-discrimination-laws-state-state-information-map.

200. North Coast Women's Care Medical Group, Inc. v. Superior Court, 44 Cal. 4th 1145 (2008).

201. ASRM-Ethics Committee, Access to Fertility Treatment by Gays, Lesbians, and Unmarried Persons, 92 Fertility & Sterility 1190 (2009).

202. ACOG-Committee on Ethics, The Limits of Conscientious Refusal in Reproductive Medicine, 110 Obstetrics & Gynecology 1203 (2007, aff'd 2010).

203. See Liza Mundy, Everything Conceivable: How the Science of Assisted Reproduction is Changing Men, Women, and the World 202 (2008) (citing 2005 study of doctors finding that half would refuse infertility services to a lesbian woman).

204. Marcia Chambers, The High Price of Victory, N.Y. Times, Apr. 2, 2001, at D1.

205. In Nathanson v. Commonwealth, 16 Mass. L. Rep. 761 (Super. Ct. 2003), the court affirmed a ruling of the Massachusetts Commission Against Discrimination that fined a female matrimonial lawyer $5,000 for refusing to accept male clients. For discussion, see the symposium in 20 W. New Eng. L. Rev. 5 (1998).

206. See Joyce v. Town of Dennis, 705 F. Supp. 2d 74 (D. Mass. 2010).

207. See Steve Friess, A Las Vegas Gym Faces a "Ladies' Night" Bias Case, N.Y. Times, Dec. 12, 2007, at A27.

208. See Phillips v. Las Vegas Athletic Club, Nev. Dep't Empl., Training and Rehab., Charge No. 0828-07-0563L.

209. Id. (describing Nevada litigation); Lauren Collins, Hey LA-A-A-Dies!, New Yorker, Aug. 6, 2007, at 22-23 (describing New York litigation).

210. See Paul Burnham Finney, Women-Friendly Hotel Floors Return, with Modern Twists, http://www.nytimes.com/2008/08/05/business/worldbusiness/05iht-05women.15010505.html.

211. http://www.blackwomenshealth.org/site.

212. Pamela J. Smith, We Are Not Sisters: African-American Women and the Freedom to Associate and Disassociate, 66 Tul. L. Rev. 1467, 1511 (1992).

CHAPTER 2

Substantive Equality

When men and women are similarly situated, requiring that they be treated equally often opens up opportunities for women that were previously unavailable to them. To the extent that men and women are differently situated, however, applying the same rules to them may produce different, unequal outcomes. Theories of substantive equality seek to avoid these unequal outcomes by taking differences into account and eliminating their negative effects on women. Deciding which differences matter and what alternative approach will best accommodate women can involve complex, contested judgments.

One source of unequal outcomes for women is past discrimination. Women historically have been excluded, either by law or by gender roles and customs, from obtaining jobs equal to men in status and compensation. Examples of remedial measures intended to reverse the effects of past discrimination include "affirmative action" plans designed to increase female representation in traditionally male occupations and "pay equity" schemes designed to restructure wage scales.

Biological differences are another potential target of substantive equality strategies. Only women become pregnant, for example, and pregnancy can disadvantage workers in current work environments with respect to hiring, promotion, and job security. Disability leave provisions specifically designed for pregnant women and flexible work schedules aim to neutralize this disadvantage.

Many differences between men and women are matters of averages, rather than definitional or categorical differences. Formal equality rules level the playing field for the exceptional or "non-average" woman who can compete successfully for an opportunity on the same basis as the average man. Other more result-oriented approaches may be necessary, however, if the goal is to ensure that women and men have functionally equivalent opportunities. In the educational context, for example, some argue that all-female classrooms or sports teams are necessary to ensure equal opportunities for girls. In the family law context, some commentators claim that special rules are required at divorce to recognize women's economic vulnerability and their greater investment in their children.

In considering the examples of substantive equality in this chapter, it is important to note (1) which differences in circumstances or characteristics between men and women are, or should be, significant, (2) what outcomes are just, and (3) what strategies are most likely to lead to those outcomes. How different is a substantive equality approach from formal equality? To what extent is it necessary to choose between the two?

A. REMEDYING THE EFFECTS OF PAST DISCRIMINATION

1. Sex-Specific Public Benefits to Remedy Past Societal Discrimination

One of the circumstances that might justify different treatment for otherwise similarly situated people is past discrimination that has disadvantaged members of one group. This rationale has been at the heart of affirmative action programs for racial and ethnic minorities. In Kahn v. Shevin, excerpted below, the Supreme Court upheld a state tax exemption that was available to widows, but not widowers, on the ground that Florida was fairly attempting to compensate for disparities between economic capabilities of men and women. It is doubtful that this case would be decided the same today, but the opinion is an important historical marker for use of affirmative remedies to address gender inequalities.

Reading Questions

1. Under what circumstances, if any, do you think the state is justified in giving economic advantages to women in order to reduce the effects of past discrimination?
2. When, if ever, should an employer be allowed to address past societal discrimination by favoring women for jobs that they have not traditionally held?

Kahn v. Shevin

416 U.S. 351 (1974)

Mr. Justice DOUGLAS delivered the opinion of the Court.

Since at least 1885, Florida has provided for some form of property tax exemption for widows. The current law granting all widows an annual $500 exemption . . . has been essentially unchanged since 1941. Appellant Kahn is a widower who lives in Florida and applied for the exemption to the Dade

County Tax Assessor's Office. It was denied because the statute offers no analogous benefit for widowers. [T]he Circuit Court for Dade County, Florida, held the statute violative of the Equal Protection Clause of the Fourteenth Amendment. . . . The Florida Supreme Court reversed. . . .

There can be no dispute that the financial difficulties confronting the lone woman in Florida or in any other State exceed those facing the man. Whether from overt discrimination or from the socialization process of a male-dominated culture, the job market is inhospitable to the woman seeking any but the lowest paid jobs. There are, of course, efforts under way to remedy this situation. . . . But firmly entrenched practices are resistant to such pressures, and, indeed, data compiled by the Women's Bureau of the United States Department of Labor show that in 1972 a woman working full time had a median income which was only 57.9% of the median for males—a figure actually six points lower than had been achieved in 1955. . . . The disparity is likely to be exacerbated for the widow. While the widower can usually continue in the occupation which preceded his spouse's death, in many cases the widow will find herself suddenly forced into a job market with which she is unfamiliar, and in which, because of her former economic dependency, she will have fewer skills to offer.

There can be no doubt, therefore, that Florida's differing treatment of widows and widowers "rest[s] upon some ground of difference having a fair and substantial relation to the object of the legislation." [Reed v. Reed (1971)] . . .

This is not a case like Frontiero v. Richardson . . . where the Government denied its female employees both substantive and procedural benefits granted males "solely . . . for administrative convenience." We deal here with a state tax law reasonably designed to further the state policy of cushioning the financial impact of spousal loss upon the sex for which that loss imposes a disproportionately heavy burden. . . .

Affirmed.

Mr. Justice BRENNAN, with whom Mr. Justice MARSHALL joins, dissenting. . . .

In my view . . . a legislative classification that distinguishes potential beneficiaries solely by reference to their gender-based status as widows or widowers, like classifications based upon race, alienage, and national origin, must be subjected to close judicial scrutiny, because it focuses upon generally immutable characteristics over which individuals have little or no control, and also because gender-based classifications too often have been inexcusably utilized to stereotype and stigmatize politically powerless segments of society. See Frontiero v. Richardson [1973]. . . .

I agree that, in providing special benefits for a needy segment of society long the victim of purposeful discrimination and neglect, the statute serves the compelling state interest of achieving equality for such groups. No one familiar with this country's history of pervasive sex discrimination against women can doubt the need for remedial measures to correct the resulting economic imbalances. . . . [T]he purpose and effect of the suspect classification are ameliorative; the statute neither stigmatizes nor denigrates widowers not also benefited by the legislation. Moreover, inclusion of needy widowers within the class of beneficiaries would not further the State's overriding interest in remedying the economic effects of past sex discrimination for needy victims of that discrimination. While doubtless some widowers are in financial need, no one suggests that such need results from sex discrimination as in the case of widows.

The statute nevertheless fails to satisfy the requirements of equal protection, since the State has not borne its burden of proving that its compelling interest could not be achieved by a more precisely tailored statute or by use of feasible, less drastic means. [The statute] is plainly overinclusive, for the $500 property tax exemption may be obtained by a financially independent heiress as well as by an unemployed widow with dependent children. The State has offered nothing to explain why inclusion of widows of substantial economic means was necessary to advance the State's interest in ameliorating the effects of past economic discrimination against women. . . .

By merely redrafting that form to exclude widows who earn annual incomes, or possess assets, in excess of specified amounts, the State could readily narrow the class of beneficiaries to those widows for whom the effects of past economic discrimination against women have been a practical reality.

Mr. Justice WHITE, dissenting.

The Florida tax exemption at issue here is available to all widows but not to widowers. The presumption is that all widows are financially more needy and less trained or less ready for the job market than men. It may be that most widows have been occupied as housewife, mother, and homemaker and are not immediately prepared for employment. But there are many rich widows who need no largess from the State; many others are highly trained and have held lucrative positions long before the death of their husbands. At the same time, there are many widowers who are needy and who are in more desperate financial straits and have less access to the job market than many widows. Yet none of them qualifies for the exemption. . . .

I find the discrimination invidious and violative of the Equal Protection Clause. There is merit in giving poor widows a tax break, but gender-based classifications are suspect and require more justification than the State has offered. . . .

It may be suggested that the State is entitled to prefer widows over widowers because their assumed need is rooted in past and present economic discrimination against women. But this is not a credible explanation of Florida's tax exemption; for if the State's purpose was to compensate for past discrimination against females, surely it would not have limited the exemption to women who are widows. Moreover, even if past discrimination is considered to be the criterion for current tax exemption, the State nevertheless ignores all those widowers who have felt the effects of economic discrimination, whether as a member of a racial group or as one of the many who cannot escape the cycle of poverty. It seems to me that the State in this case is merely conferring an economic benefit in the form of a tax exemption and has not adequately explained why women should be treated differently from men.

I dissent.

NOTE ON "BENIGN" CLASSIFICATIONS FAVORING WOMEN

As a result of the statute upheld in Kahn v. Shevin, a wealthy widow could receive a $500 property tax exemption while an impoverished widower could not. Can this result be justified under equal treatment principles?

Justice Douglas, one of the Court's most liberal members and strongest supporters of gender equality, was convinced that Florida's preference for women was justifiable. Some commentators have attributed this view to Douglas' own experience. At age six, his mother was left destitute by the death of his father, a rural preacher. Douglas and his older sister washed store windows and picked fruit to earn the nickels and dimes that, as he later recalled, "often meant the difference between dinner and no dinner."[1] At oral argument, the lawyer for the widower, Ruth Bader Ginsburg, attempted to convince the Court that the preference was an inadequate way of responding to widows' plight: "if need is the concern, then sex should not substitute for an income test. And if widowed state is the concern, then it is irrational to distinguish between taxpayers based on their sex."[2] Does Justice Douglas' opinion respond to this argument? Is this a case that Ginsburg and the ACLU Women's Rights Project should not have brought?

Kahn v. Shevin is one of a few benefits decisions that have allowed group-based treatment more favorable to women than to men. The other principal case along this line is Califano v. Webster (1977), a case that upheld a Social Security provision applicable to retirements before 1972 and computed old-age benefits under a formula more favorable to women than to men. The benefits for both sexes were determined according to an average monthly wage earned during certain years, but women were given the opportunity of excluding three additional lower earning years than men. In a per curiam opinion, the Court concluded:

> The more favorable treatment of the female wage earner enacted here was not a result of "archaic and overbroad generalizations" about women . . . or of "the role typing society has long imposed" upon women . . . such as casual assumptions that women are "the weaker sex" or are more likely to be child-rearers or dependents. . . . Rather, "the only discernible purpose of [the statute's more favorable treatment is] the permissible one of redressing our society's longstanding disparate treatment of women."

> The challenged statute operated directly to compensate women for past economic discrimination. Retirement benefits under the Act are based on past

earnings. But as we have recognized: "Whether from overt discrimination or from the socialization process of a male-dominated culture, the job market is inhospitable to the woman seeking any but the lowest paid jobs." [Kahn v. Shevin] Thus, allowing women, who as such have been unfairly hindered from earning as much as men, to eliminate additional low-earning years from the calculation of their retirement benefits works directly to remedy some part of the effect of past discrimination.[3]

How "benign" is the classification that *Kahn* upheld? In an illuminating international study by Peter Glick and Susan Fiske, some 15,000 men and women were rated on attitudes of hostile sexism and benevolent sexism (an example of the latter would be "women should be cherished and protected by men"). They found that the two forms of sexism were related and together were better predictors of gender inequality than either alone.[4] What are the policy implications of this research?

How good are benign classifications for women? Consider Catharine MacKinnon's criticism of both equal treatment and "special benefits" approaches to equality:

> The special benefits side of the difference approach has not compensated for the differential of being second class. . . . Under its double standard, women who stand to inherit something when their husbands die have gotten the exclusion of a small percentage of the inheritance tax to the tune of Justice Douglas waxing eloquent about the difficulties of all women's economic situation. If we're going to be stigmatized as different, it would be nice if the compensation would fit the disparity.[5]

Is MacKinnon's criticism fair to Justice Douglas? Should legislatures have to "fix" a problem of inequality in order to address it? Or was this an example of tokenism that reflects stereotypical assumptions that in the long run do more to hurt than benefit women?

Putting Theory Into Practice

2-1. The U.S. Navy at one time had a policy in which male officers were terminated after they were passed over for promotion a second time after 9 years, while female officers were discharged for nonpromotion only after 13 years. The rationale was that women could only be assigned to hospital ships and transports and not to vessels involved in combat, so they did not have the same opportunities as men to compile records warranting promotion.[6] Was this a reasonable policy? To the extent that many women in the military have had fewer opportunities in their careers because of limitations on their participation in combat, is the policy still justified?

2. "Affirmative Action" in Employment

Under certain circumstances, Title VII permits affirmative action to redress a significant gender imbalance in the workplace. An affirmative action plan might give preference to qualified women for a job they previously would not have obtained because of past discrimination, or because of patterns of sex segregation that channeled male and female workers into separate and unequal positions.

Litigation sometime forces employers to implement an affirmative action plan to remedy past discrimination, but some employers wish to voluntarily integrate their workforce even in the absence of legal liability. The latter situation was the case in Johnson v. Transportation Agency. There, the Supreme Court held that the agency could appropriately take into account the sex of the female employee in its promotion decisions, even though past discrimination by the Agency could not be proved.

Reading Questions

1. Should Santa Clara County be able to voluntarily adopt an affirmative action plan, even though there is no finding that it previously engaged in sex discrimination? Why or why not?
2. What limits on affirmative action does the Court in *Johnson* place on employers that want to address a gender imbalance in their workforce? What differences among the Justices exist on this question?
3. Should sex-based affirmative action plans be evaluated under the same standard as race-based affirmative action plans?
4. By what reasoning does Justice Scalia conclude that the Court has converted Title VII from being a law prohibiting discrimination based on race or sex to one requiring it? Is he correct that (1) the elimination of discrimination and (2) the alteration of social attitudes that cause women themselves to avoid certain jobs and favor others are two distinct phenomena?

Johnson v. Transportation Agency

480 U.S. 616 (1987)

Justice BRENNAN delivered the opinion of the Court.

Respondent, Transportation Agency of Santa Clara County, California, unilaterally promulgated an Affirmative Action Plan . . . pursuant to which the Agency passed over petitioner Paul Johnson, a male employee [for promotion to road dispatcher], and promoted a female employee applicant, Diane Joyce. The question for decision is whether in making the promotion the Agency impermissibly took into account the sex of the applicants in violation of Title VII of the Civil Rights Act of 1964. [No constitutional issue was raised.] The

District Court for the Northern District of California . . . held that respondent had violated Title VII. The Court of Appeals for the Ninth Circuit reversed. . . . We affirm.[2]

I

In December 1978, the Santa Clara County Transit District Board of Supervisors adopted an Affirmative Action Plan (Plan) for the County Transportation Agency. The Plan implemented a County Affirmative Action Plan, which had been adopted, declared the County, because " 'mere prohibition of discriminatory practices is not enough to remedy the effects of past practices and to permit attainment of an equitable representation of minorities, women and handicapped persons." . . . Relevant to this case, the Agency Plan provides that, in making promotions to positions within a traditionally segregated job classification in which women have been significantly underrepresented, the Agency is authorized to consider as one factor the sex of a qualified applicant.

In reviewing the composition of its work force, the Agency noted in its Plan that women were represented in numbers far less than their proportion of the County labor force in both the Agency as a whole and in five of seven job categories. Specifically, while women constituted 36.4% of the area labor market, they composed only 22.4% of Agency employees. Furthermore, women working at the Agency were concentrated largely in EEOC job categories traditionally held by women: women made up 76% of Office and Clerical Workers, but only 7.1% of Agency Officials and Administrators . . . . As for the job classification relevant to this case, none of the 238 Skilled Craft Worker positions was held by a woman. . . . The Plan noted that this underrepresentation of women in part reflected the fact that women had not traditionally been employed in these positions, and that they had not been strongly motivated to seek training or employment in them "because of the limited opportunities that have existed in the past for them to work in such classifications." . . . The Plan also observed that, while the proportion of ethnic minorities in the Agency as a whole exceeded the proportion of such minorities in the County work force, a smaller percentage of minority employees held management, professional, and technical positions.

The Agency stated that its Plan was intended to achieve "a statistically measurable yearly improvement in hiring, training, and promotion of minorities and women throughout the Agency in all major job classifications where they are underrepresented." . . . As a benchmark by which to evaluate progress, the Agency stated that its long-term goal was to attain a work force whose composition reflected the proportion of minorities and women in the area labor force. . . . Thus, for the Skilled Craft category in which the road dispatcher position at issue here was classified, the Agency's aspiration was that eventually about 36% of the jobs would be occupied by women. . . .

---

2. No Constitutional issue was either raised or addressed in the litigation below. . . . We therefore decide in this case only the issue of the prohibitory scope of Title VII. . . .

The Agency's Plan . . . set aside no specific number of positions for minorities or women, but authorized the consideration of ethnicity or sex as a factor when evaluating qualified candidates for jobs in which members of such groups were poorly represented. . . .

On December 12, 1979, the Agency announced a vacancy for the promotional position of road dispatcher in the Agency's Roads Division. Dispatchers assign road crews, equipment, and materials, and maintain records pertaining to road maintenance jobs. . . .

Twelve County employees applied for the promotion, including Joyce and Johnson. Joyce had worked for the County since 1970, serving as an account clerk until 1975. She had applied for a road dispatcher position in 1974, but was deemed ineligible because she had not served as a road maintenance worker. In 1975, Joyce transferred from a senior account clerk position to a road maintenance worker position, becoming the first woman to fill such a job. . . . During her four years in that position, she occasionally worked out of class as a road dispatcher.

Petitioner Johnson began with the County in 1967 as a road yard clerk, after private employment that included working as a supervisor and dispatcher. He had also unsuccessfully applied for the road dispatcher opening in 1974. In 1977, his clerical position was downgraded, and he sought and received a transfer to the position of road maintenance worker. . . . He also occasionally worked out of class as a dispatcher while performing that job.

Nine of the applicants, including Joyce and Johnson, were deemed qualified for the job, and were interviewed by a two-person board. Seven of the applicants scored above 70 on this interview, which meant that they were certified as eligible for selection by the appointing authority. The scores awarded ranged from 70 to 80. Johnson was tied for second with a score of 75, while Joyce ranked next with a score of 73. A second interview was conducted by three Agency supervisors, who ultimately recommended that Johnson be promoted. Prior to the second interview, Joyce had contacted the County's Affirmative Action Office because she feared that her application might not receive disinterested review.[5] The Office in turn contacted the Agency's Affirmative Action

_____

5. Joyce testified that she had had disagreements with two of the three members of the second interview panel. One had been her first supervisor when she began work as a road maintenance worker. In performing arduous work in this job, she had not been issued overalls, although her male co-workers had received them. After ruining her pants, she complained to her supervisor, to no avail. After three other similar incidents, ruining clothes on each occasion, she filed a grievance, and was issued four pairs of overalls the next day. . . . Joyce had dealt with a second member of the panel for a year and a half in her capacity as chair of the Roads Operation Safety Committee, where she and he "had several differences of opinion on how safety should be implemented." . . . In addition, Joyce testified that she had informed the person responsible for arranging her second interview that she had a disaster preparedness class on a certain day the following week. By this time about 10 days had passed since she had notified the person of her availability, and no date had yet been set for the interview. Within a day or two after this conversation, however, she received a notice setting her interview at a time directly in the middle of her disaster preparedness class. . . . This same panel member had earlier described Joyce as a "rebel-rousing, skirt-wearing person." . . .

Coordinator, whom the Agency's Plan makes responsible for, *inter alia*, keeping the Director informed of opportunities for the Agency to accomplish its objectives under the Plan. At the time, the Agency employed no women in any Skilled Craft position, and had never employed a woman as a road dispatcher. The Coordinator recommended to the Director of the Agency, James Graebner, that Joyce be promoted.

Graebner, authorized to choose any of the seven persons deemed eligible, thus had the benefit of suggestions by the second interview panel and by the Agency Coordinator in arriving at his decision. After deliberation, Graebner concluded that the promotion should be given to Joyce. As he testified: "I tried to look at the whole picture, the combination of her qualifications and Mr. Johnson's qualifications, their test scores, their expertise, their background, affirmative action matters, things like that. . . . I believe it was a combination of all those." . . .

The certification form naming Joyce as the person promoted to the dispatcher position stated that both she and Johnson were rated as well qualified for the job. . . . Graebner testified that he did not regard as significant the fact that Johnson scored 75 and Joyce 73 when interviewed by the two-person board. . . .

Petitioner Johnson filed a complaint with the EEOC alleging that he had been denied promotion on the basis of sex in violation of Title VII. . . .

II

As a preliminary matter, we note that petitioner bears the burden of establishing the invalidity of the Agency's Plan. . . .

The assessment of the legality of the Agency Plan must be guided by our decision in Steelworkers v. Weber, [1979]. In that case, the Court [held that] a voluntary affirmative action plan designed to "eliminate manifest racial imbalances in traditionally segregated job categories" [did not violate Title VII]. As we stated:

> It would be ironic indeed if a law triggered by a Nation's concern over centuries of racial injustice and intended to improve the lot of those who had "been excluded from the American dream for so long" constituted the first legislative prohibition of all voluntary, private, race-conscious efforts to abolish traditional patterns of racial segregation and hierarchy. . . .

We noted that the plan did not "unnecessarily trammel the interests of the white employees," since it did not require "the discharge of white workers and their replacement with new black hirees." Nor did the plan create "an absolute bar to the advancement of white employees," since half of those trained in the new program were to be white. . . . Finally, we observed that the plan was a temporary measure, not designed to maintain racial balance, but to "eliminate a manifest racial imbalance." . . . As Justice Blackmun's concurrence made clear, *Weber* held that an employer seeking to justify the adoption of a plan need not point to its own prior discriminatory practices, nor even to evidence of an "arguable violation" on its part. Rather, it need point only to a "conspicuous . . . imbalance in traditionally segregated job categories." Our decision was grounded in the recognition that voluntary employer action can play a crucial role in furthering Title VII's purpose of eliminating the effects of discrimination in the workplace, and that Title VII should not be read to thwart such efforts.

The first issue [in this case] is therefore whether consideration of the sex of applicants for Skilled Craft jobs was justified by the existence of a "manifest imbalance" that reflected underrepresentation of women in "traditionally segregated job categories." In determining whether an imbalance exists that would justify taking sex or race into account, a comparison of the percentage of minorities or women in the employer's work force with the percentage in the area labor market or general population is appropriate in analyzing jobs that require no special expertise. . . . Where a job requires special training, however, the comparison should be with those in the labor force who possess the relevant qualifications. . . .

A manifest imbalance need not be such that it would support a prima facie case against the employer . . . since we do not regard as identical the constraints of Title VII and the Federal Constitution on voluntarily adopted affirmative action plans. Application of the "prima facie" standard in Title VII cases would be inconsistent with *Weber*'s focus on statistical imbalance, and could inappropriately create a significant disincentive for employers to adopt an affirmative action plan. . . .

As the Agency Plan recognized, women were most egregiously underrepresented in the Skilled Craft job category, since none of the 238 positions was occupied by a woman. . . .

[H]ad the Plan simply calculated imbalances in all categories according to the proportion of women in the area labor pool, and then directed that hiring be governed solely by those figures, its validity fairly could be called into question. This is because analysis of a more specialized labor pool normally is necessary in determining underrepresentation in some positions. If a plan failed to take distinctions in qualifications into account in providing guidance for actual employment decisions, it would dictate mere blind hiring by the numbers. . . .

The Agency's plan emphatically did not authorize such blind hiring. It expressly directed that numerous factors be taken into account. . . .

We next consider whether the Agency Plan unnecessarily trammeled the rights of male employees or created an absolute bar to their advancement. In contrast to the plan in *Weber*, which provided that 50% of the positions in the craft training program were exclusively for blacks, . . . the Plan sets aside no positions for women. The Plan expressly states that "[t]he 'goals' established for each Division should not be construed as 'quotas' that must be met." . . . Rather, the Plan merely authorizes that consideration be given to affirmative action concerns when evaluating qualified applicants. As the Agency Director testified, the sex of Joyce was but one of numerous factors he took into account in arriving at his decision. . . . Similarly, the Agency Plan requires women to compete with all other qualified applicants. No persons are automatically excluded from consideration; all are able to have their qualifications weighed against those of other applicants.

In addition, petitioner had no absolute entitlement to the road dispatcher position. Seven of the applicants were classified as qualified and eligible, and the Agency Director was authorized to promote any of the seven. Thus, denial of the promotion unsettled no legitimate, firmly rooted expectation on the part of petitioner. . . .

Finally, the Agency's Plan was intended to attain a balanced work force, not to maintain one. The Plan contains 10 references to the Agency's desire to "attain" such a balance, but no reference whatsoever to a goal of maintaining it. . . .

Express assurance that a program is only temporary may be necessary if the program actually sets aside positions according to specific numbers. . . . In this case, however, substantial evidence shows that the Agency has sought to take a moderate, gradual approach to eliminating the imbalance in its work force, one which establishes realistic guidance for employment decisions, and which visits minimal intrusion on the legitimate expectations of other employees. . . .

Justice STEVENS, concurring. . . .

. . . I see no reason why the employer has any duty, prior to granting a preference to a qualified minority employee, to determine whether his past conduct might constitute an arguable violation of Title VII. Indeed, in some instances the employer may find it more helpful to focus on the future. Instead of retroactively scrutinizing his own or society's possible exclusions of minorities in the past to determine the outer limits of a valid affirmative-action program — or indeed, any particular affirmative-action decision — in many cases the employer will find it more appropriate to consider other legitimate [diversity-related] reasons to give preferences to members of under-represented groups. Statutes enacted for the benefit of minority groups should not block these forward-looking considerations. . . . The Court today does not foreclose other voluntary decisions based in part on a qualified employee's membership in a disadvantaged group. Accordingly, I concur.

Justice O'CONNOR, concurring in the judgment. . . .

As I read *Weber* . . . the Court . . . determined that Congress had balanced [its intent to root out invidious discrimination against any person on the basis of race or gender, and its goal of eliminating the lasting effects of discrimination against minorities] by permitting affirmative action only as a remedial device to eliminate actual or apparent discrimination or the lingering effects of this discrimination.

Contrary to the intimations in Justice Stevens' concurrence, this Court did not approve preferences for minorities "for any reason that might seem sensible from a business or a social point of view." . . . I concur in the judgment of the Court.

Justice SCALIA, with whom THE CHIEF JUSTICE joins, and with whom Justice WHITE joins in Parts I and II, dissenting. . . .

The Court today completes the process of converting [Title VII] from a guarantee that race or sex will *not* be the basis for employment determinations, to a guarantee that it often *will*. Ever so subtly, without even alluding to the last obstacles preserved by earlier opinions that we now push out of our path, we effectively replace the goal of a discrimination-free society with the quite incompatible goal of proportionate representation by race and by sex in the workplace. . . .

I . . .

. . . In a discrimination-free world, it would obviously be a statistical oddity for every job category to match the racial and sexual composition of even that portion of the county work force *qualified* for that job; it would be utterly miraculous for each of them to match, as the plan expected, the composition of the entire work force. Quite obviously, the plan did not seek to replicate what a lack of discrimination would produce, but rather imposed racial and sexual tailoring that would, in defiance of normal expectations and laws of probability, give each protected racial and sexual group a governmentally determined "proper" proportion of each job category. . . .

II

The most significant proposition of law established by today's decision is that racial or sexual discrimination is permitted under Title VII when it is intended to overcome the effect, not of the employer's own discrimination, but of societal attitudes that have limited the entry of certain races, or of a particular sex, into certain jobs. . . .

In fact, . . . today's decision goes well beyond merely allowing racial or sexual discrimination in order to eliminate the effects of prior societal discrimination. The majority opinion often uses the phrase "traditionally segregated job category" to describe the evil against which the plan is legitimately (according to the majority) directed. As originally used in *Weber*, that phrase described skilled jobs from which employers and unions had systematically and intentionally excluded black workers—traditionally segregated jobs, that is, in the sense of conscious, exclusionary discrimination. But that is assuredly not the sense in which the phrase is used here. It is absurd to think that the nationwide failure of road maintenance crews, for example, to achieve the Agency's ambition of 36.4% female representation is attributable primarily, if even substantially, to systematic exclusion of women eager to shoulder pick and shovel. It is a "traditionally segregated job category" not in the *Weber* sense, but in the sense that, because of longstanding social attitudes, it has not been regarded by women themselves as desirable work. . . . There are, of course, those who believe that the social attitudes which cause women themselves to avoid certain jobs and to favor others are as nefarious as conscious, exclusionary discrimination. Whether or not that is so (and there is assuredly no consensus on the point equivalent to our national consensus against intentional discrimination), the two phenomena are certainly distinct. And it is the alteration of social attitudes, rather than the elimination of discrimination, which today's decision approves as justification for state-enforced discrimination. This is an enormous expansion, undertaken without the slightest justification or analysis.

III . . .

It is impossible not to be aware that the practical effect of our holding is . . . effectively [to require] employers, public as well as private, to engage in intentional discrimination on the basis of race or sex. This Court's prior interpretations of Title VII, especially the decision in Griggs v. Duke Power Co., [1971], subject employers to a potential Title VII suit whenever there is a noticeable imbalance in the representation of minorities or women in the employer's work force. Even the employer who is confident of ultimately prevailing in such a suit must contemplate the expense and adverse publicity of a trial. . . . If, however, employers are free to discriminate through affirmative action, without fear of "reverse discrimination" suits by their nonminority or male victims, they are offered a threshold defense against Title VII liability premised on numerical disparities. Thus, after today's decision the failure to engage in reverse discrimination is economic folly, and arguably a breach of duty to shareholders or taxpayers, wherever the cost of anticipated Title VII litigation exceeds the cost of hiring less capable (though still minimally capable) workers. (This situation is more likely to obtain, of course, with respect to the least skilled jobs — perversely creating an incentive to discriminate against precisely those members of the nonfavored groups least likely to have profited from societal discrimination in the past.) . . . A statute designed to establish a color-blind and gender-blind workplace has thus been converted into a powerful engine of racism and sexism, not merely permitting intentional race- and sex-based discrimination, but often making it, through operation of the legal system, practically compelled.

It is unlikely that today's result will be displeasing to politically elected officials, to whom it provides the means of quickly accommodating the demands of organized groups to achieve concrete, numerical improvement in the economic status of particular constituencies. Nor will it displease the world of corporate and governmental employers (many of whom have filed briefs as amici in the present case, all on the side of Santa Clara) for whom the cost of hiring less qualified workers is often substantially less — and infinitely more predictable — than the cost of litigating Title VII cases and of seeking to convince federal agencies by nonnumerical means that no discrimination exists. In fact, the only losers in the process are the Johnsons of the country, for whom Title VII has been not merely repealed but actually inverted. The irony is that these individuals — predominantly unknown, unaffluent, unorganized — suffer this injustice at the hands of a Court fond of thinking itself the champion of the politically impotent. I dissent.

Notes

1. Affirmative Action: Definitions and Background.   Affirmative action plans vary across multiple dimensions: which employees are covered; whether the plans are voluntarily adopted or imposed under law or court order; and what measures they require. Some plans seek to expand the group of qualified applicants through recruitment and training, but do not show any preference in terms of hiring or promotion to members of the underrepresented group. At the other end of the spectrum are "quotas" that go so far as to compel the hiring or promotion of a certain number or percentage of group members. In between are various forms of goals, timetables, and tie-breaking preferences that favor members of the underrepresented group without changing the applicable qualification standards.

Affirmative action became part of U.S. law in 1965, when President Lyndon Johnson approved Executive Order 11246. It was then strengthened under President Nixon, and further modified under President Clinton. The Order requires firms over a certain size doing a certain level of business with the federal government to employ qualified individuals from targeted groups in percentages roughly proportional to their representation in the available applicant pool. If those groups are underrepresented, the employer must develop a corrective plan and make good-faith efforts to implement it. Another form of affirmative action involves "set-asides" — preferences for targeted groups in the government contracting process. The concept originated in the 1950s as a way to help small businesses. Set-asides were expanded in the 1970s to encompass minority-owned businesses, and further extended in the 1980s to include women-owned businesses. The federal government has between 150 and 200 other laws and regulations supporting some form of affirmative action. Most are aspirational: they express a desire for proactive strategies but not methods of implementation or sanctions for noncompliance. About one-fifth of American employees work for the U.S. government or for contractors and subcontractors who are subject to federal affirmative action requirements. Many more workers are covered by state or local mandates or voluntary private sector plans.[7]

The different opinions in *Johnson* represent the range of judicial perspectives about when affirmative action on behalf of women is justified. Justice Scalia believes that voluntary affirmative action should be permitted only by employers who previously engaged in discrimination against the group in question. Justice O'Connor believes that the disparity that the state is attempting to correct should be substantial and provide a "firm basis for believing that remedial action is required." Justice Brennan, writing for a plurality of the Court, maintains that a voluntary affirmative action plan is justified to address a "manifest imbalance" (or substantial underrepresentation of women in "traditionally segregated job categories"). Justice Stevens thinks that the employer should be given even more leeway, in order to achieve a "forward-looking" diversity.

Note that in Kahn v. Shevin, the Court seemed satisfied that Florida was attempting to address societal discrimination rather than any past acts by the state itself. A difference in *Johnson*, besides the applicability of Title VII, is the existence of a specific "victim" who, according to the district court, would have gotten the job at issue were it not for Santa Clara's "affirmative action" plan. Even Justice Brennan's opinion seeks to protect the interests of the nonminority employees from being "unnecessarily trammeled." Should the cause of significant underrepresentation matter? Under an approach of formal equality, would the employer's own actions be conclusive? If women "choose" not to take advantage of an opportunity to enter a particular male-dominated occupation, does it matter why?

2. Affirmative Action and Gender: A Separate Standard?   Shifts in the makeup of the Court, as well as changes in public attitudes about affirmative action, have created considerable uncertainty about the continued legality of preferential treatment. Since the *Johnson* case was decided, the Supreme Court has held that race-based minority set-aside programs must be reviewed under the same strict scrutiny standard of review that is applicable for laws and practices that disfavor racial minorities, and that this level of scrutiny is not satisfied in voluntary affirmative action cases except to correct proven instances of past discrimination.[8]

A pivotal question is whether the standard for reviewing affirmative action plans is the same for gender as for race. As noted in Chapter 1, the standard for gender is intermediate review, not strict scrutiny: a sex-based classification must serve important governmental objectives and be substantially related to those objectives or, more recently, supported by "an 'exceedingly persuasive justification.'"[9] However, given the objective of affirmative action — to reverse the effects of past discrimination and/or to enhance diversity — there is no obvious reason why gender-based affirmative action should be treated more leniently than race-based plans. Indeed, if race is the more suspect category, it may be perverse to impose greater barriers to ending past race discrimination than to eliminating past sex discrimination. Courts have not been entirely consistent in dealing with this issue, and there is conflicting authority on the question. Cases allowing gender-based affirmative action plans have generally required some showing of past discrimination, but not necessarily discrimination by the employer whose affirmative action plan is in dispute.[10] Moreover, to an extent not apparent in judicial analysis of race-based affirmative action plans, courts emphasize that the purpose for reviewing gender-based discrimination is less to "smoke out" hidden, invidious discrimination than to make sure that sex-based rules are not based unintentionally on archaic stereotypes.[11] Does this difference justify a different legal standard?[12]

Most surveys reflect between 10 and 20 percent greater popular support for affirmative action programs on behalf of women than for programs on behalf of African Americans. In both cases, whether people say they support affirmative action depends upon the way the plan is described, and how the question is asked. In general, support is much lower for quotas or for "preferential treatment" than for other strategies that seek to equalize opportunities or take qualifications into account. Support for affirmative action is greater when specific practices are described, when policies are characterized in terms of promoting diversity rather than giving preferences, and when socially useful functions are presented.[13]

Popular opposition to government-sponsored affirmative action plans and judicial decisions has led to the reversal of some plans. For example, in 1996, California voters passed the California Civil Rights Initiative (Proposition 209), which prohibits "discrimination against, or . . . preferential treatment to, any individual on the basis of race, sex, color, ethnicity, or national origin in the operation of public employment, public education, or public contracting." Proposition 209 was upheld in both federal and state courts. It has had significantly more negative impact on racial diversity than on gender diversity, with the number of African-American men and women enrolled at the University of California at Berkeley and UCLA falling from 469 (out of 7,100) in 1995 to 218 (out of 7,350) in 2004.[14] A number of states, including Texas, Washington, Nebraska, and Michigan, enacted initiatives similar to Proposition 209, and affirmative action was ended by executive order from Governor Jeb Bush in Florida. California, Texas, and Florida substituted their affirmative action plans with "percentage plans" designed to require students who rank in a specified percentage of their high school graduating class to be admitted to a campus in the state university system, but these plans did not achieve the same level of student body diversity that was achieved under their prior affirmative action plans.[15]

In Grutter v. Bollinger,[16] the U.S. Supreme Court upheld an affirmative action plan from the University of Michigan on the basis of the educational benefits of a diverse educational setting. Following *Grutter*, and upon finding that its percentage plan had not produced sufficient diversity to end racial isolation and racial tensions at the University of Texas at Austin, Texas reinstated its affirmative action plan. In Fisher v. University of Texas, the Supreme Court in a 7-1 decision set aside a lower appellate court's upholding the plan because it had not applied the appropriate standard of strict scrutiny articulated in *Grutter*. The case was remanded for further consideration.[17] The case is not applicable to sex-based affirmative action, which presumably would be evaluated under the less rigorous, intermediate scrutiny standard.

One reason race-based affirmative action is more of a hot-button issue than sex-based affirmative action in the educational setting is that women earn about 57 percent of all bachelor's degrees[18] and represent 59 percent of enrollment in graduate programs.[19] Except in programs like science and engineering, where women are still underrepresented, some schools favor men in the application process in order to avoid having more than 60 percent women.[20] Is such a male preference justified?

3. Women's "Choices": Explanation or Symptom of Gender Inequality? In his dissent in *Johnson*, Justice Scalia attributes women's underrepresentation in traditionally male job categories to women's choices. In his view, it is "absurd" to think that women could be "eager to shoulder pick and shovel." Could he be right? If so, should a "lack of interest" by women generally in certain jobs be a defense to the absence, or severe underrepresentation, of women in those jobs?

This defense was the focus of an important lawsuit by the Equal Employment Opportunity Commission (EEOC) against Sears, Roebuck & Co. in the late 1980s. The suit alleged a nationwide pattern and practice of discriminating against women for commission sales positions. To support its claim, the EEOC offered extensive statistical evidence that women who applied for sales positions were less likely than men with similar qualifications to receive high-paying commission jobs involving "big ticket" items, such as major appliances, furnaces, roofing, and tires. Rather, women disproportionately ended up in non-commission lower-paying jobs selling apparel, linen, toys, paint, and cosmetics. In defending its employment practices, Sears introduced testimony by a female historian, Rosalind Rosenberg, that such patterns were consistent with women's traditional preferences, including their reluctance to work irregular hours, their desire for "social contact and friendship," and their discomfort with the stress of competitive pay structures. The trial court found such evidence more credible than testimony by other historians called by the EEOC, who asserted that women are influenced by the opportunities presented to them, and have been eager to take higher-paying nontraditional jobs when such options have been available.

Other evidence in the case showed that Sears relied on tests measuring applicants' "vigor" by reference to their views on boxing, wrestling, and swearing. One witness explained that female employees weren't in higher-paid retail sales positions because they "didn't like going outside when it's snowing, raining, or whatever." In addition, Sears had taken no steps that might have made the higher-paid positions more attractive to women, such as flexible schedules or outreach and support programs.[21] Should this evidence have concerned the court? The judgment for Sears was affirmed on appeal, over the dissent of Judge Cudahy who challenged the stereotypes implicit in the court's analysis and its failure to recognize the employer's role in shaping the interests of applicants.

Is the *Sears* case about the failure of courts to recognize stereotypes at work? Or does it simply recognize reality and decline to impose responsibility on employers to alter that reality? According to one commentator:

> The liberal prohibition against stereotyping assumes that the problem is that the employer has inaccurately identified the job interests of (at least some exceptional) women who have already formed preferences for nontraditional work. By stopping at this level of analysis, however, liberal courts fail to inquire into or discover the deeper process through which employers actively shape women's work aspirations along gendered lines. . . . [For example, through] their recruiting strategies, employers do more than simply publicize job vacancies to those who are already interested: They actually stimulate interest among those they hope to attract to the jobs.[22]

To what extent does the affirmative action plan at issue in *Johnson* address this concern?

Women do disproportionately "choose" lower-paying jobs, resulting in sex segregation in many occupation categories. For example, women constitute 97 percent of preschool and kindergarten teachers, 96 percent of secretaries and administrative assistants, and 80 percent of social workers, but only 4 percent of firefighters, 3 percent of truck drivers, and less than 2 percent of electricians, carpenters, and other construction trades.[23] Should these disparities be a concern?

4. Affirmative Action and the "Merit" Principle. To what extent is "merit" compromised by affirmative action plans? Justice Scalia assumes that every affirmative action hire violates the merit principle. Justice Brennan, citing an amicus curiae brief from the American Society for Personnel Administration, disputes that underlying assumption:

> It is a standard tenet of personnel administration that there is rarely a single, "best qualified" person for a job. An effective personnel system will bring before the selecting official several fully-qualified candidates who each may possess different attributes which recommend them for selection. Especially where the job is an unexceptional, middle-level craft position, without the need for unique work experience or educational attainment and for which several well-qualified candidates are available, final determinations as to which candidate is "best qualified" are at best subjective.[24]

Justice Scalia rejects entirely the view cited by Justice Brennan:

> [Acceptance of the brief's contention] effectively constitutes appellate reversal of a finding of fact by the District Court in the present case ("[P]laintiff was more qualified for the position of Road Dispatcher than Diane Joyce. . . ."). More importantly, it has staggering implications for future Title VII litigation, since the most common reason advanced for failing to hire a member of a protected group is the superior qualification of the hired individual.[25]

Are you persuaded that Joyce was less "qualified" than Johnson? Note that her quantitative score included subjective interview evaluations. Is there an argument that a woman who compiled her record in a workplace with so much gender bias is at least as qualified as a man who ranked marginally higher? What do you make of Footnote 5 in the opinion?

The debate about the meaning of merit was at the heart of a highly contested case, Ricci v. DeStefano, which concerned the constitutionality of the City of New Haven's failure to certify the results of a promotion exam that relied 60 percent on scores from written tests.[26] The results of the exam would have excluded all African Americans and all but one Hispanic from promotion. In holding that an employer cannot abandon a test that produced disparate results based on a good faith fear of liability for that disparate impact, the Supreme Court assumed that the test was a valid predictor of performance. In her dissenting opinion, Justice Ginsburg concluded that the heavy reliance on written tests to select fire officers was "flawed," "dubious," and "a questionable practice, to say the least."

> Successful fire officers, the City's description of the position makes clear, must have the "[a]bility to lead personnel effectively, maintain discipline, promote harmony, exercise sound judgment, and cooperate with other officials." These qualities are not well measured by written tests. [As testified by one expert, l]eadership skills, command presence, and the like "could have been identified and evaluated in a much more appropriate way."[27]

Justice Ginsburg's skepticism about the value of written tests to judge leadership skills is supported by the research of Susan Sturm and Lani Guinier, who argue that standardized paper-and-pencil tests leave out criteria indicative of potential future success, such as discipline, emotional intelligence, commitment, drive to succeed, reliability, creativity, judgment, honesty, courage, the ability to manage anger, and leadership. The criteria that are overvalued in relation to their correlation with preparation for higher education or employment are the willingness to guess, conformity, and docility.[28] Along these lines, Professor Marjorie Shultz at the University of California at Berkeley School of Law and others have questioned the over-reliance of law school admissions on the LSAT, and argued for criteria that better measure potential as an effective lawyer.[29] What criteria do you think might be more relevant?

5. The Problem of Stigma.   One primary objection to affirmative action is that singling out women for special assistance risks reinforcing the very assumptions of inferiority that society should be trying to eliminate. Even when women perform effectively, their success may be devalued and their advancement may be assumed to reflect preferential treatment rather than individual merit. However, as one commentator notes:

> Assumptions of inferiority predate preferential treatment and would persist without it. Affirmative action is not responsible for adverse stereotypes. Racism and sexism are. White males who long benefited from preferences in schools, jobs, and clubs have suffered no discernible loss of self-esteem. What, moreover, is the likely alternative to affirmative action programs? A return to the "neutral" policies that have perpetuated gender and racial hierarchies is scarcely preferable. Women who benefit from preferential treatment may experience some stigma, but the absence of women is stigmatizing as well.

Many members of underrepresented groups find it demeaning to lose affirmative action on the ground that they will find it demeaning.[30]

Do you agree? Why or why not?

6. "Positive Action" in European Law. The European Union (as well as Canada) has explicit constitutional commitments to "positive action," or affirmative action programs for women. Tax breaks are available to firms who hire women in traditionally men-dominated fields, and advancement plans for women are sometimes mandatory. Still, these commitments are mixed with legal rules that reflect the same tensions apparent in U.S. debates on affirmative action, particularly when a man objects that he would have gotten a job but for gender preferences. In one case, the European Court of Justice struck down an affirmative action plan under facts strikingly similar to *Johnson*.[31] Yet European Union countries are considerably more generous in providing social and economic support for women when they are pregnant or raising small children (explored later in this chapter). Are the two approaches to "special treatment" consistent? What do you make of the fact that sex segregation remains high even in Scandinavian countries with the most progressive work/family policies?

The European Union is considering affirmative action mandates to improve the representation of women on corporate boards, which in 2012, was 15 percent among Britain's top 100 companies. Viviane Reding, the EU's justice commissioner, said that at the current rate of improvement, it would take more than 40 years for women to hold 40 percent of board positions in Europe's publicly traded companies.[32] Norway, Iceland, France, Spain, Italy, and Belgium already have enacted binding quotas for women.[33] Are these a good idea?

7. Diversity as an Alternative Rationale for Affirmative Action. Does the goal of diversity offer a better theory for affirmative action than remedies for past discrimination? Some advocates believe that forward-looking justifications are preferable because they ascribe no guilt, require no admission of prior discrimination, and focus on the benefits to individuals and institutions. What is your view?

Critics of the diversity approach argue that it deflects focus from responsibility for prior discrimination, ignores diversity within groups, and offers no justification for the favored treatment of certain groups rather than others. For example, Yale Law Professor Peter Schuck contends that "[a] group can only create diversity value if it possesses certain desired qualities *qua* group. . . . To affirm that a quality inheres in a racial group, however, is to essentialize race in a way that utterly contradicts liberal egalitarian, legal, scientific, and religious values." Moreover, Schuck asks, how much diversity is enough and whose diversity counts? "Doesn't the perspective of a Muslim or fundamentalist Christian applicant have at least as much diversity value as that of a middle-class black or Hispanic?"[34] Do you have an answer to Schuck's argument? Does it apply to women?

8. Pay Equity and Women's Choices.   As noted in Chapter 1, the Equal Pay Act requires that women and men be paid the same for the same work, but it does not require pay equity between job categories. In other words, it demands that male and female nurses be paid the same, but not that the wage structures for traditionally female occupations like nurses, teachers, and secretaries be fair in relation to wage structures for traditionally male occupations like sanitation workers, mechanics, or appliance repair workers. Arguments for and against pay equity tend to turn on assumptions about the causes of occupational segregation, and on the form of equality to which one is committed. If occupational segregation follows from the different priorities and lifestyle choices of men and women, there is arguably no problem to solve. Human capital theorists posit that women anticipate working fewer years than men with more interruptions, and so "self-select" into occupations requiring lower levels of skill and less educational investment. They may also choose jobs that offer lower pay in exchange for more pleasant and less hazardous working conditions, and more flexible schedules.[35] Some argue that these choices are, at least in part, hard-wired into women's biology.[36] Opponents of pay equity argue also that free markets will operate to eliminate pay structures that are unequal: If men are overpaid, women will move into those fields, creating surpluses in those occupations and shortages in traditionally female occupations. The result will be the elimination of pay discrepancies that are not justified by the nature and demands of the work. Under this market view, women not satisfied to be teachers at existing salary levels should seek higher pay as sanitation workers or mechanics. Are you persuaded by these points?

Women also leave the paid labor force at a rate approximately three times that of men. Economists Stephen Rose and Heidi Hartmann, using national data from the Michigan Panel Study of Income Dynamics, found that over a 15-year period, 52 percent of women, but only 16 percent of men, had at least one full calendar year with no earnings.[37]

To what extent do women's "choices" in the paid labor market simply reflect the same broader patterns of societal discrimination that affirmative action in the hiring context is designed to overcome—i.e., gendered definitions of work and past discrimination? Will supply and demand take care of job segregation and low pay in traditionally female occupations due to these factors? Some say not, especially given the social reason why men tend to invest more heavily in their human capital and do not participate as much in the family responsibilities that constrain the job choices of many women.

If affirmative action is justified to overcome these factors on the hiring side, should wage structures be proactively examined with the goal of recalibrating the wage scales for job categories that have been historically dominated by women? A number of states have done so, undertaking pay equity studies and making adjustments in various pay categories in state employment where bias was identified. In addition, Minnesota and Iowa have passed legislation requiring pay equity in state employment, and Maine requires it for private sector jobs as well. Other countries, including Sweden, England, and Australia, and Ontario, Canada, also have pay equity requirements. European Council Directive 75.117, Article I, provides that the principle of equal pay under Article 119 of the EEC Treaty requires equal pay for "work to which equal value is attributed." Pay equity legislation has been introduced at the federal level in this country for a number of years, so far without success.

Finally, while sex-segregated job categories help to explain why women's earnings are only 81 percent of men's,[38] they do not explain why, within the same occupational category, significant salary disparities exist. Women lawyers, for example, make 77 percent what men make; women physicians and surgeons make 71 percent; and women truck drivers make 71 percent of what their male counterparts earn.[39] Do these figures demonstrate the fundamental failure of the Equal Pay Act to eliminate discrimination in wages? Or do they show that women are making trade-offs not only between occupational categories, but also within them? Is your answer consistent with the fact that women represent close to 60 percent of all advanced degrees earned in the United States?[40]

9. Women and Contingent Work.   A significant sector of the U.S. workforce is made up of "contingent workers"—i.e., those employed other than on a full-time, permanent basis. This group includes part-time workers, temporary workers, independent contractors, day laborers, and home-based workers. Part-time workers have lower wages and fewer benefits than full-time workers. According to data from the Bureau of Labor Statistics, almost 20 percent of the American workforce works part time, with women making up 67 percent of the part-time workforce.[41] In 2011, 27 percent of employed women worked part time, compared with about 13 percent of employed men.[42] Contingent work has been growing, and some researchers argue that it is increasingly necessary to provide flexibility in a global environment characterized by cheap overseas labor and "just in time" production methods. Does women's role in the contingent workforce raise gender equity concerns? If so, how should they be addressed?

Putting Theory Into Practice

2-2. Grounds maintenance and information technology occupations at your university are 80 percent male. Is this a problem? If so, can it be fixed without violating constitutional and statutory prohibitions on discrimination?

2-3. A state university typically provides financial incentives to encourage departments to make hires that are consistent with university priorities. The physics department faculty is all men. This year, the university is offering $10,000 in extra research funds to the physics department for every female it hires. Is this plan appropriate? Is it constitutional?

2-4. The Federal Communications Commission seeks to give preference to women in the granting of operation licenses for radio and television stations, on the theory that they have faced discrimination as a general population and thus have "separate needs and interests with respect to which the inclusion of women in broadcast ownership and operation can be of value."[43] Should such preferences be allowed?[44] Does women's ownership affect programming? What is "women's programming"? Is it good for women?

B. ELIMINATING THE DISADVANTAGES OF WOMEN'S DIFFERENCES

1. Pregnancy

Different treatment of women might also be justified on the basis of genuine differences (i.e., not stereotypes) between men and women. The most obvious difference between women and men is their reproductive capacity. Although this difference has a "real" biological basis, it has also given rise to gender stereotypes. Women's childbearing role was one of the nineteenth- and early twentieth-century justifications for excluding them from positions ranging from serving on juries to working as lawyers or bartenders. The question for contemporary sex discrimination law is whether different treatment based on pregnancy can reduce the disadvantages that childbearing produces, without also reinforcing other practices and attitudes that disadvantage women.

The first modern Supreme Court case concerning pregnancy discrimination, Cleveland Board of Education v. LaFleur, addressed the constitutionality of a rule requiring public school classroom teachers to take unpaid maternity leave once they reached the fourth month of pregnancy and to stay out of the classroom until their child was at least three months old. The Court invalidated the policy. Although the state could prevent an individual woman from working if she was not fit for the job as a result of pregnancy, the Court held that it could not compromise her procreative rights by conclusively presuming an inability to work.[45]

In the same year, however, the Court upheld a California law that excluded pregnancy from an otherwise comprehensive list of disabilities covered by the state disability insurance plan. In Geduldig v. Aiello, the Court distinguished the exclusion of pregnancy from prior precedents involving the exclusion of women, by characterizing the exclusion as one based on pregnancy, not sex:

[T]his case is . . . a far cry from cases like [*Reed*] and [*Frontiero*], involving discrimination based upon gender as such. The California insurance program does not exclude anyone from benefit eligibility because of gender but merely removed one physical condition—pregnancy—from the list of compensable disabilities. While it is true that only women can become pregnant, it does not follow that every legislative classification concerning pregnancy is a sex-based classification. . . . Normal pregnancy is an objectively identifiable physical condition with unique characteristics. Absent a showing that distinctions involving pregnancy are mere pretexts designed to effect an invidious discrimination against the members of one sex or the other, lawmakers are constitutionally free to include or exclude pregnancy from the coverage of legislation such as this on any reasonable basis, just as with respect to any other physical condition.

The lack of identity between the excluded disability and gender as such under this insurance program becomes clear upon the most cursory analysis. The program divides potential recipients into two groups—pregnant women and nonpregnant persons. While the first group is exclusively female, the second includes members of both sexes. The fiscal and actuarial benefits of the program thus accrue to members of both sexes.[46]

Is the distinction between women and non-pregnant persons persuasive?

The Court in General Electric Co. v. Gilbert (1976) applied the reasoning in *Geduldig* in the Title VII context, holding that pregnancy discrimination is not a form of actionable sex discrimination.[47] That decision was overruled by Congress by an amendment to Title VII known as the Pregnancy Discrimination Act of 1978 (PDA). The PDA explicitly declares that discrimination based on pregnancy is discrimination based on sex for purposes of Title VII:

The terms "because of sex" or "on the basis of sex" include, but are not limited to, because of or on the basis of pregnancy, childbirth, or related medical conditions; and women affected by pregnancy, childbirth, or related medical conditions shall be treated the same for all employment-related purposes, including receipt of benefits under fringe benefit programs, as other persons not so affected but similar in their ability or inability to work, and nothing in section 703(h) of this title shall be interpreted to permit otherwise.[48]

The PDA amended Title VII but not the U.S. Constitution. Pregnancy discrimination can still be lawful where Title VII or other statutes are inapplicable. Under the PDA, employers cannot treat pregnant workers worse than other workers who are temporarily disabled. Can it treat them better? Should employers be required to accommodate pregnant workers? Workers with small children? One could argue that accommodations to women for pregnancy, as well as the higher costs of insuring them for medical costs, amount to "subsidies." Is this a problem?

The PDA is the subject of each of the cases in this section. In California Federal Savings & Loan v. Guerra, the Court addressed the legality of a California statute requiring employers to provide pregnant employees with a pregnancy disability leave. The Court upheld the state statute as consistent with the PDA, because it was designed to accommodate pregnant employees, not discriminate against them.

Even if accommodation of women's pregnancy does not violate the PDA, should it be required of employers? Troupe v. May Department Stores Co., also excerpted below, holds that a pregnant woman must be treated the same as other temporarily disabled employees, but the employer is not required to treat her better. In concluding that the accommodation to pregnancy is not specifically required, *Troupe* follows a formal equality approach rather than substantive equality.

In holding that an employer's fetal-protection policy violated Title VII, UAW v. Johnson Controls, Inc. also follows the formal equality model. However, in treating women the same as other workers, it protects opportunities that otherwise may have been denied to them because of the risks to their unborn children.

Reading Questions

1. In what sense is pregnancy "unique"? Does it justify workplace rules different from those applicable to other disabled workers? For example, should pregnant women receive rest periods or relief from strenuous duties regardless of what other employees can receive?
2. If you believe that it is acceptable to give pregnant women certain special accommodations, would you extend that reasoning to women with young children? To all parents? Why or why not?
3. Should women's employment opportunities be the same as men's, even if certain jobs pose a special risk to their unborn children?

California Federal Savings & Loan Association v. Guerra

479 U.S. 272 (1987)

Justice MARSHALL delivered the opinion of the Court.

The question presented is whether Title VII of the Civil Rights Act of 1964, as amended by the Pregnancy Discrimination Act of 1978 (PDA), pre-empts a state statute that requires employers to provide leave and reinstatement to employees disabled by pregnancy.

Under the law of **preemption**, a state law that is inconsistent with a federal law on a subject matter that federal law is intended to "occupy" is not valid. Under these circumstances, the federal law will govern. In holding that the federal statute (FEHA) does not pre-empt state law in the *California Federal* case, the Court allows the state to compel more benefits to pregnant employees than the minimal requirements of federal law.

I

California's Fair Employment and Housing Act (FEHA) . . . is a comprehensive statute that prohibits discrimination in employment and housing. In September 1978, California amended the FEHA to proscribe certain forms of employment discrimination on the basis of pregnancy. [At issue in this case is a provision that] requires these employers to provide female employees an unpaid pregnancy disability leave of up to four months. [It has been construed] to require California employers to reinstate an employee returning from such pregnancy leave to the job she previously held, unless it is no longer available due to business necessity. In the latter case, the employer must make a reasonable, good-faith effort to place the employee in a substantially similar job. The statute does not compel employers to provide paid leave to pregnant employees. Accordingly, the only benefit pregnant workers actually derive . . . is a qualified right to reinstatement. . . .

II

Petitioner California Federal Savings & Loan Association (Cal Fed) is a federally chartered savings and loan association based in Los Angeles; it is an employer covered by both Title VII and [the relevant state FEHA law]. Cal Fed has a facially neutral leave policy that permits employees who have completed three months of service to take unpaid leaves of absence for a variety of reasons, including disability and pregnancy. Although it is Cal Fed's policy to try to provide an employee taking unpaid leave with a similar position upon returning, Cal Fed expressly reserves the right to terminate an employee who has taken a leave of absence if a similar position is not available.

Lillian Garland was employed by Cal Fed as a receptionist for several years. In January 1982, she took a pregnancy disability leave. When she was able to return to work in April of that year, Garland notified Cal Fed, but was informed that her job had been filled and that there were no receptionist or similar positions available. Garland filed a complaint with respondent Department of Fair Employment and Housing, which issued an administrative accusation against Cal Fed. . . . Prior to the scheduled hearing . . . , Fair Employment and Housing Commission, Cal Fed, joined by petitioners Merchants and Manufacturers Association and the California Chamber of Commerce, brought this action in the United States District Court for the Central District of California. They sought a declaration that [the California unpaid pregnancy disability leave requirement] is inconsistent with and pre-empted by Title VII and an injunction against enforcement of the section. The District Court granted petitioners' motion for summary judgment. . . .

The United States Court of Appeals for the Ninth Circuit reversed. . . .

We granted certiorari . . . and we now [uphold the statute]. . . .

III

Petitioners argue that the language of the federal statute itself unambiguously rejects California's "special treatment" approach to pregnancy discrimination. . . . They contend that the PDA forbids an employer to treat pregnant employees any differently from other disabled employees. . . .[6]

[S]ubject to certain limitations, we agree with the Court of Appeals' conclusion that Congress intended the PDA to be "a floor beneath which pregnancy disability benefits may not drop, not a ceiling above which they may not rise." . . .

The context in which Congress considered the issue of pregnancy discrimination supports this view of the PDA. Congress had before it extensive evidence of discrimination against pregnancy, particularly in disability and health insurance programs like those challenged in *Gilbert*. . . . Opposition to the PDA came from those concerned with the cost of including pregnancy in health and disability-benefit plans and the application of the bill to abortion, not from those who favored special accommodation of pregnancy. . . .

We . . . find it significant that Congress was aware of state laws similar to California's but apparently did not consider them inconsistent with the PDA. In the debates and Reports on the bill, Congress repeatedly acknowledged the existence of state antidiscrimination laws that prohibit sex discrimination on the basis of pregnancy. Two of the States mentioned [Connecticut and Montana] then required employers to provide reasonable leave to pregnant workers. . . . [B]oth the House and Senate Reports suggest that these laws would continue to have effect under the PDA.

Title VII, as amended by the PDA, and California's pregnancy disability leave statute share a common goal. The purpose of Title VII is "to achieve equality of employment opportunities and remove barriers that have operated in the past to favor an identifiable group of . . . employees over other employees." . . . Rather than limiting existing Title VII principles and objectives, the PDA extends them to cover pregnancy. As Senator Williams, a sponsor of the Act, stated: "The entire thrust . . . behind this legislation is to guarantee women the basic right to participate fully and equally in the workforce, without denying them the fundamental right to full participation in family life." . . .

[The California law at issue in the case] also promotes equal employment opportunity. By requiring employers to reinstate women after a reasonable pregnancy disability leave, [this law] ensures that they will not lose their jobs on account of pregnancy disability. California's approach is consistent with the dissenting opinion of Justice Brennan in General Electric Co. v. Gilbert . . . :

---

6. [The PDA provides that] [t]he terms "because of sex" or "on the basis of sex" include, but are not limited to, because of or on the basis of pregnancy, childbirth, or related medical conditions; and women affected by pregnancy, childbirth, or related medical conditions shall be treated the same for all employment-related purposes, including receipt of benefits under fringe benefit programs, as other persons not so affected but similar in their ability or inability to work, and nothing in [this law] shall be interpreted to permit otherwise.

[D]iscrimination is a social phenomenon encased in a social context and, therefore, unavoidably takes its meaning from the desired end products of the relevant legislative enactment, end products that may demand due consideration of the uniqueness of the "disadvantaged" individuals. A realistic understanding of conditions found in today's labor environment warrants taking pregnancy into account in fashioning disability policies. . . .

By "taking pregnancy into account," California's pregnancy disability-leave statute allows women, as well as men, to have families without losing their jobs.

We emphasize the limited nature of the benefits [this law] provides. The statute is narrowly drawn to cover only the period of *actual physical disability* on account of pregnancy, childbirth, or related medical conditions. Accordingly, unlike the protective labor legislation prevalent earlier in this century, [this law] does not reflect archaic or stereotypical notions about pregnancy and the abilities of pregnant workers. A statute based on such stereotypical assumptions would, of course, be inconsistent with Title VII's goal of equal employment opportunity. . . .

Moreover, even if we agreed with petitioners' construction of the PDA, we would nonetheless reject their argument that the California statute requires employers to violate Title VII. [The challenged statute] does not prevent employers from complying with both the federal law (as petitioners construe it) and the state law. This is not a case where "compliance with both federal and state regulations is a physical impossibility," . . . or where there is an "inevitable collision between the two schemes of regulation." . . . [The California law] does not compel California employers to treat pregnant workers better than other disabled employees; it merely establishes benefits that employers must, at a minimum, provide to pregnant workers. Employers are free to give comparable benefits to other disabled employees, thereby treating "women affected by pregnancy" no better than "other persons not so affected but similar in their ability or inability to work." Indeed, at oral argument, petitioners conceded that compliance with both statutes "is theoretically possible." . . .

Herma Hill Kay, *Equality and Difference: The Case of Pregnancy*

1 Berkeley Women's L. J. 1, 26-31 (1985)

Philosophers recognize that, just as the concept of equality requires that equals be treated equally, so it requires that unequals be treated differently. To treat persons who are different alike is to treat them unequally. The concept of formal equality, however, contains no independent justification for making unequals equal. A different concept, that of equality of opportunity, offers a theoretical basis for making unequals equal in the limited sense of removing barriers that prevent individuals from performing according to their abilities. The notion is that the perceived inequality does not stem from an innate difference in ability, but rather from a condition or circumstance that prevents certain uses or developments of that ability. As applied to reproductive behavior, the suggestion would be that women in general are not different from men in innate ability. During the temporary episode of a woman's pregnancy, however, she may become unable to utilize her abilities in the same way she had done prior to her reproductive conduct. Since a man's abilities are not similarly impaired as a result of his reproductive behavior, equality of opportunity implies that the woman should not be disadvantaged as a result of that sex-specific variation.

As applied to the employment context, the concept of equality of opportunity takes on the following form. Let us postulate two workers, one female, the other male, who respectively engage in reproductive conduct. Assume as well that prior to this activity, both were roughly equal in their ability to perform their similar jobs. The consequence of their having engaged in reproductive behavior will be vastly different. The man's ability to perform on the job will be largely unaffected. The woman's ability to work, measured against her prior performance, may vary with the physical and emotional changes she experiences during pregnancy. At times, her ability to work may be unaffected by the pregnancy; at other times, she may be temporarily incapacitated by it. Ultimately, she may require medical care to recover from miscarriage, or to complete her pregnancy by delivery, or to terminate it earlier by induced abortion. In order to maintain the woman's equality of opportunity during her pregnancy, we should modify as far as reasonably possible those aspects of her work where her job performance is adversely affected by the pregnancy. Unless we do so, she will experience employment disadvantages arising from her reproductive activity that are not encountered by her male co-worker. . . .

[P]regnancy differs from sex . . . in that pregnancy is an episodic occurrence, rather than an immutable trait. The category of pregnant persons is a sub-class within the larger category of women. . . . Employers must take those measures that may be reasonably necessary to permit pregnant workers to continue working until delivery, in order to avoid discrimination against them. Women returning from pregnancy leave must be allowed to resume their former status as workers. An episodic view of pregnancy requires that any benefits extended to pregnant workers or restrictions imposed on them be tailored to actual medical need resulting from the pregnancy, and not be triggered by stereotypical notions of what pregnant women should or should not do.

This interpretation of Title VII based on an episodic analysis of biological reproductive differences will permit pregnancy to be recognized as the normal consequence of reproductive behavior that can and should be accommodated in the workplace. Pregnancy is not itself a disability, although an individual pregnant woman may experience disabling symptoms and may require medical care. If she is temporarily impaired from performing at work up to her normal level of ability, the concept of equal employment opportunity embodied in Title VII requires not only that she remain free of resulting job reprisals, but also that she secure compensatory benefits to offset any potential work-related disadvantage. Under this analysis, women will be equal to men in their ability to work and to make reproductive choices. . . .

Richard A. Posner, *Conservative Feminism*

1989 U. Chi. Legal F. 191, 195-198

Where the libertarian is apt to part company with the liberal or radical feminist in the field of employment is over the question whether employers should be forced to subsidize female employees, as by being compelled to offer maternity leave or pregnancy benefits, or to disregard women's greater longevity when fixing pension benefits. To the extent that women workers incur higher medical expenses than men (mainly but not entirely due to pregnancy), or live longer in retirement on a company pension, they cost the employer more than male workers do. So the employer should not be required to pay the same wage *and* provide the same package of fringe benefits. (Of course, to the extent that women impose lower costs—for example, women appear to be more careful about safety than men, and therefore less likely to be injured on the job—they are entitled to a correspondingly higher wage or more extensive fringe benefits.) This is not to suggest—which would be absurd—that women are blameworthy for getting pregnant or for living longer than men. It is to suggest merely that they may be more costly workers and that, if so, the disparity in cost should be reflected in their net compensation. If this disparity is not reflected, then male workers are being discriminated against in the same sense in which women would be discriminated against if they received a lower wage than equally productive (and no less costly) male workers. What is sauce for the goose should be sauce for the gander. More than symmetry is involved; we shall see in a moment that laws designed to improve the welfare of women may boomerang, partly though not wholly because of the economic interdependence of men and women. . . .

It is not even clear, moreover, that women benefit, on balance, from laws that forbid employers to take into account the extra costs that female employees can impose. Such laws discourage employers from hiring, promoting, and retaining women, and there are many ways in which they can discriminate in these respects without committing detectable violations of the employment-discrimination laws. Sometimes there is no question of violation, as when an employer accelerates the substitution of computers for secretaries in response to an increase in the costs of his female employees.

There is an additional point. Most women are married—and many who are not currently married are divorced or widowed and continue to derive a benefit from their husband's earnings. The consumption of a married woman is, as I have noted, a function of her husband's income as well as of her own (in the divorce and widowhood cases as well, for the reason just noted). Therefore a reduction in men's incomes as a result of laws that interfere with profit-maximizing and cost-minimizing decisions by employers will reduce women's welfare as well as men's. Moreover, women who are not married are less likely to have children than women who are married; and where employer benefits are child-related—such as pregnancy benefits and maternity leave—their effect is not merely to transfer wealth from men to women but from women to women. The effect could be dramatic. Compare the situation of a married woman with many children and an unmarried woman with no children. Generous pregnancy benefits and a generous policy on maternity leave will raise the economic welfare of the married woman. Her and her husband's wages will be lower, because all wages will fall in order to finance the benefit, but the reduction will probably be smaller than the benefits to her—in part because the unmarried female worker will experience the same reduction in wages but with no offsetting benefit. Feminists who support rules requiring employers to grant pregnancy benefits and maternity leave may therefore, and I assume unknowingly, be discouraging women from remaining single or childless. Feminists of all persuasions would think it outrageous if the government required fertile women to have children, yet many feminists support an oblique form of such a policy—a subsidy to motherhood. They do this, I suspect, because they have not considered the economic consequences of proposals that *appear* to help women.

Troupe v. May Department Stores Co.

20 F.3d 734 (7th Cir. 1994)

POSNER, Chief Judge.

The plaintiff, Kimberly Hern Troupe, was employed by the Lord & Taylor department store in Chicago as a saleswoman in the women's accessories department. . . . Until the end of 1990 her work was entirely satisfactory. In December of that year, in the first trimester of a pregnancy, she began experiencing morning sickness of unusual severity. The following month she requested and was granted a return to part-time status, working from noon to 5:00 p.m. Partly it seems because she slept later under the new schedule, so that noon was "morning" for her, she continued to experience severe morning sickness at work, causing what her lawyer describes with understatement as "slight" or "occasional" tardiness. In the month that ended with a warning from her immediate supervisor, Jennifer Rauch, on February 18, she reported late to work, or left early, on nine out of the 21 working days. The day after the warning she was late again and this time received a written warning. After she was tardy three days in a row late in March, the company on March 29 placed her on probation for 60 days. During the probationary period Troupe was late eleven more days; and she was fired on June 7, shortly after the end of the probationary period. She testified at her deposition that on the way to the meeting with the defendant's human resources manager at which she was fired, Rauch told her that "I [Troupe] was going to be terminated because she [Rauch] didn't think I was coming back to work after I had my baby." Troupe was due to begin her maternity leave the next day. . . . [A]t argument Lord & Taylor's counsel said that employees of Lord & Taylor are entitled to maternity leave with half pay. . . .

The great, the undeniable fact is the plaintiff's tardiness. Her lawyer argues with great vigor that she should not be blamed—that she was genuinely ill, had a doctor's excuse, etc. That would be pertinent if Troupe were arguing that the Pregnancy Discrimination Act requires an employer to treat an employee afflicted by morning sickness better than the employer would treat an employee who was equally tardy for some other health reason. This is rightly not argued. If an employee who (like Troupe) does not have an employment contract cannot work because of illness, nothing in Title VII requires the employer to keep the employee on the payroll. . . .

Against the inference that Troupe was fired because she was chronically late to arrive at work and chronically early to leave, she has only two facts to offer. The first is the timing of her discharge: she was fired the day before her maternity leave was to begin. . . . Thus, her employer fired her one day before the problem that the employer says caused her to be fired was certain to end. If the discharge of an unsatisfactory worker were a purely remedial measure rather than also, or instead, a deterrent one, the inference that Troupe wasn't really fired because of her tardiness would therefore be a powerful one. But that is a big "if." We must remember that after two warnings Troupe had been placed on probation for sixty days and that she had violated the implicit terms of probation by being as tardy during the probationary period as she had been before. If the company did not fire her, its warnings and threats would seem empty. Employees would be encouraged to flout work rules knowing that the only sanction would be a toothless warning or a meaningless period of probation.

[I]t might appear to be an issue for trial whether it is superior to Troupe's interpretation. But what is Troupe's interpretation? Not (as we understand it) that Lord & Taylor wanted to get back at her for becoming pregnant or having morning sickness. The only significance she asks us to attach to the timing of her discharge is as reinforcement for the inference that she asks us to draw from Rauch's statement about the reason for her termination: that she was terminated because her employer did not expect her to return to work after her maternity leave was up. We must decide whether a termination so motivated is discrimination within the meaning of the pregnancy amendment to Title VII.

Standing alone, it is not. (It could be a breach of contract, but that is not alleged.) . . . We must imagine a hypothetical Mr. Troupe, who is as tardy as Ms. Troupe was, also because of health problems, and who is about to take a protracted sick leave growing out of those problems at an expense to Lord & Taylor equal to that of Ms. Troupe's maternity leave. If Lord & Taylor would have fired our hypothetical Mr. Troupe, this implies that it fired Ms. Troupe not because she was pregnant but because she cost the company more than she was worth to it.

The Pregnancy Discrimination Act does not, despite the urgings of feminist scholars . . . require employers to offer maternity leave or take other steps to make it easier for pregnant women to work . . . to make it as easy, say as it is for their spouses to continue working during pregnancy. Employers can treat pregnant women as badly as they treat similarly affected but nonpregnant employees. . . .

The plaintiff has made no effort to show that if all the pertinent facts were as they are except for the fact of her pregnancy, she would not have been fired. So in the end she has no evidence from which a rational trier of fact could infer that she was a victim of pregnancy discrimination. . . . The Pregnancy Discrimination Act requires the employer to ignore an employee's pregnancy, but . . . not her absence from work, unless the employer overlooks the comparable absences of nonpregnant employees. . . . Of course there may be no comparable absences . . . ; but we do not understand Troupe to be arguing that the reason she did not present evidence that nonpregnant employees were treated more favorably than she is that . . . there is no comparison group of Lord & Taylor employees. . . . We doubt that finding a comparison group would be that difficult. Troupe would be halfway home if she could find one nonpregnant employee of Lord & Taylor who had not been fired when about to begin a leave similar in length to hers. She either did not look, or did not find. Given the absence of other evidence, her failure to present any comparison evidence doomed her case.

UAW v. Johnson Controls, Inc.

499 U.S. 187 (1991)

Mr. Justice BLACKMUN delivered the opinion of the Court.

In this case we are concerned with an employer's gender-based fetal-protection policy. May an employer exclude a fertile female employee from certain jobs because of its concern for the health of the fetus the woman might conceive?

I

Respondent Johnson Controls, Inc., manufactures batteries. In the manufacturing process, the element lead is a primary ingredient. Occupational exposure to lead entails health risks, including the risk of harm to any fetus carried by a female employee.

Before [Title VII] became law, Johnson Controls did not employ any woman in a battery-manufacturing job. In June 1977, however, it announced its first official policy concerning its employment of women in lead-exposure work:

> [P]rotection of the health of the unborn child is the immediate and direct responsibility of the prospective parents. While the medical profession and

the company can support them in the exercise of this responsibility, it cannot assume it for them without simultaneously infringing their rights as persons. . . .

Since not all women who can become mothers wish to become mothers (or will become mothers), it would appear to be illegal discrimination to treat all who are capable of pregnancy as though they will become pregnant. . . .

Consistent with that view, Johnson Controls "stopped short of excluding women capable of bearing children from lead exposure," . . . but emphasized that a woman who expected to have a child should not choose a job in which she would have such exposure. The company also required a woman who wished to be considered for employment to sign a statement that she had been advised of the risk of having a child while she was exposed to lead. The statement informed the woman that although there was evidence "that women exposed to lead have a higher rate of [miscarriage]," this evidence was "not as clear . . . as the relationship between cigarette smoking and cancer," but that it was, "medically speaking, just good sense not to run that risk if you want children and do not want to expose the unborn child to risk, however small. . . ."

Five years later, in 1982, Johnson Controls shifted from a policy of warning to a policy of exclusion. Between 1979 and 1983, eight employees became pregnant while maintaining blood lead levels in excess of 30 micrograms per deciliter. . . . This appeared to be the critical level noted by the Occupational Health and Safety Administration (OSHA) for a worker who was planning to have a family. . . . The company responded by announcing a broad exclusion of women from jobs that exposed them to lead:

[I]t is [Johnson Controls'] policy that women who are pregnant or who are capable of bearing children will not be placed into jobs involving lead exposure or which could expose them to lead through the exercise of job bidding, bumping, transfer or promotion rights. . . .

The policy defined "women . . . capable of bearing children" as "[a]ll women except those whose inability to bear children is medically documented." . . . It further stated that an unacceptable work station was one where, "over the past year," an employee had recorded a blood lead level of more than 30 micrograms per deciliter or the work site had yielded an air sample containing a lead level in excess of 30 micrograms per cubic meter. . . .

In April 1984, petitioners filed in the United States District Court for the Eastern District of Wisconsin a class action challenging Johnson Controls' fetal-protection policy as sex discrimination that violated Title VII. . . . Among the individual plaintiffs were petitioners Mary Craig, who had chosen to be sterilized in order to avoid losing her job, Elsie Nason, a 50-year-old divorcee, who had suffered a loss in compensation when she was transferred out of a job where she was exposed to lead, and Donald Penney, who had been denied a request for a leave of absence for the purpose of lowering his lead level because he intended to become a father. . . .

A **class action** is a lawsuit on behalf of named plaintiffs and members of a class of persons that a court finds are "similarly situated" concerning the legal claim. Complex state and federal procedures govern class action lawsuits.

[The District Court granted summary judgment for defendant and the court of appeals affirmed.] . . .

III

The bias in Johnson Controls' policy is obvious. Fertile men, but not fertile women, are given a choice as to whether they wish to risk their reproductive health for a particular job. [Title VII] prohibits sex-based classifications in terms and conditions of employment, in hiring and discharging decisions, and in other employment decisions that adversely affect an employee's status. Respondent's fetal-protection policy explicitly discriminates against women on the basis of their sex. The policy excludes women with childbearing capacity from lead-exposed jobs and so creates a facial classification based on gender. . . .

[The assumption by the appellate courts that sex-specific fetal-protection policies do not involve facial discrimination was incorrect.]

First, Johnson Controls' policy classifies on the basis of gender and childbearing capacity, rather than fertility alone. Respondent does not seek to protect the unconceived children of all its employees. Despite evidence in the record about the debilitating effect of lead exposure on the male reproductive system, Johnson Controls is concerned only with the harms that may befall the unborn offspring of its female employees. . . . Johnson Controls' policy is facially discriminatory because it requires only a female employee to produce proof that she is not capable of reproducing.

Our conclusion is bolstered by the Pregnancy Discrimination Act of 1978 (PDA), in which Congress explicitly provided that, for purposes of Title VII, discrimination "on the basis of sex" includes discrimination "because of or on the basis of pregnancy, childbirth, or related medical conditions." . . . In its use of the words "capable of bearing children" in the 1982 policy statement as the criterion for exclusion, Johnson Controls explicitly classifies on the basis of potential for pregnancy. Under the PDA, such a classification must be regarded, for Title VII purposes, in the same light as explicit sex discrimination. Respondent has chosen to treat all its female employees as potentially pregnant; that choice evinces discrimination on the basis of sex.

. . . [T]he absence of a malevolent motive does not convert a facially discriminatory policy into a neutral policy with a discriminatory effect. Whether an employment practice involves disparate treatment through explicit facial discrimination does not depend on why the employer discriminates but rather on the explicit terms of the discrimination. . . .

We hold that Johnson Controls' fetal-protection policy is sex discrimination forbidden under Title VII unless respondent can establish that sex is a "bona fide occupational qualification."

IV . . .

The wording of the BFOQ defense contains several terms of restriction that indicate that the exception reaches only special situations. The statute thus limits the situations in which discrimination is permissible to "certain instances" where sex discrimination is "reasonably necessary" to the "normal operation" of the "particular" business. . . .

Johnson Controls argues that its fetal-protection policy falls within the so-called safety exception to the BFOQ. Our cases have stressed that discrimination on the basis of sex because of safety concerns is allowed only in narrow circumstances. In Dothard v. Rawlinson, . . . this Court indicated that danger to a woman herself does not justify discrimination. We there allowed the employer to hire only male guards in contact areas of maximum-security male penitentiaries only because more was at stake than the "individual woman's decision to weigh and accept the risks of employment." . . . Similarly, some courts have approved airlines' layoffs of pregnant flight attendants at different points during the first five months of pregnancy on the ground that the employer's policy was necessary to ensure the safety of passengers. . . . In two of these cases, the courts pointedly indicated that fetal, as opposed to passenger, safety was best left to the mother. . . .

We considered safety to third parties in Western Airlines, Inc. v. Criswell . . . in the context of the [Age Discrimination in Employment Act]. We focused upon "the nature of the flight engineer's tasks," and the "actual capabilities of persons over age 60" in relation to those tasks. Our safety concerns were not independent of the individual's ability to perform the assigned tasks, but rather involved the possibility that, because of age-connected debility, a flight engineer might not properly assist the pilot, and might thereby cause a safety emergency. . . .

Third-party safety considerations properly entered into the BFOQ analysis in *Dothard* and *Criswell* because they went to the core of the employee's job performance. Moreover, that performance involved the central purpose of the enterprise. . . . The concurrence attempts to transform this case into one of customer safety. The unconceived fetuses of Johnson Controls' female employees, however, are neither customers nor third parties whose safety is essential to the business of battery manufacturing. No one can disregard the possibility of injury to future children; the BFOQ, however, is not so broad that it transforms this deep social concern into an essential aspect of batterymaking. . . .

The PDA's amendment to Title VII contains a BFOQ standard of its own: unless pregnant employees differ from others "in their ability or inability to work," they must be "treated the same" as other employees "for all employment-related purposes." This language clearly sets forth Congress' remedy for discrimination on the basis of pregnancy and potential pregnancy. Women who are either pregnant or potentially pregnant must be treated like others "similar in their ability . . . to work." [Id.] In other words, women as capable of doing their jobs as their male counterparts may not be forced to choose between having a child and having a job. . . .

We conclude that the language of both the BFOQ provision and the PDA which amended it, as well as the legislative history and the case law, prohibit an employer from discriminating against a woman because of her capacity to become pregnant unless her reproductive potential prevents her from performing the duties of her job. We reiterate our holdings in *Criswell* and *Dothard* that an employer must direct its concerns about a woman's ability to perform her job safely and efficiently to those aspects of the woman's job-related activities that fall within the "essence" of the particular business.[4]

V

We have no difficulty concluding that Johnson Controls cannot establish a BFOQ. Fertile women, as far as appears in the record, participate in the manufacture of batteries as efficiently as anyone else. . . .

VI

A word about tort liability and the increased cost of fertile women in the workplace is perhaps necessary.

[The Court concedes the possibility that it may cost the employer more to protect pregnant women, at the risk of tort liability if it does not.] . . .

[T]he extra cost of employing members of one sex . . . does not provide an affirmative Title VII defense for a discriminatory refusal to hire members of that gender. . . . Indeed, in passing the PDA, Congress considered at length the considerable cost of providing equal treatment of pregnancy and related conditions, but made the "decision to forbid special treatment of pregnancy despite the social costs associated therewith." . . .

We, of course, are not presented with, nor do we decide, a case in which costs would be so prohibitive as to threaten the survival of the employer's business. We merely reiterate our prior holdings that the incremental cost of hiring women cannot justify discriminating against them.

VII

Our holding today that Title VII . . . forbids sex-specific fetal-protection policies is neither remarkable nor unprecedented. Concern for a woman's existing or potential offspring historically has been the excuse for denying women equal employment opportunities. See, e.g., Muller v. Oregon . . . . Congress in

---

4. The concurrence predicts that our reaffirmation of the narrowness of the BFOQ defense will preclude considerations of privacy as a basis for sex-based discrimination. . . . We have never addressed privacy-based sex discrimination and shall not do so here because the sex-based discrimination at issue today does not involve the privacy interests of Johnson Control's customers. Nothing in our discussion of the "essence of the business test," however, suggests that sex could not constitute a BFOQ when privacy interests are implicated. See, e.g., Backus v. Baptist Medical Center, [1981] (essence of obstetrics nurse's business is to provide sensitive care for patient's intimate and private concerns).

the PDA prohibited discrimination on the basis of a woman's ability to become pregnant. We do no more than hold that the Pregnancy Discrimination Act means what it says. . . .

The judgment of the Court of Appeals is reversed and the case is remanded for further proceedings consistent with this opinion.

A **tort** is a wrong committed against another person for which they can obtain a remedy by bringing a legal action in court. A **prenatal tort** is a wrong committed against a fetus. If born alive, a child can sue to compensate for injuries resulting from tortious conduct that harmed the child before birth.

Justice WHITE, with whom THE CHIEF JUSTICE and Justice KENNEDY join, concurring in part and concurring in the judgment. . . .

I . . .

Common sense tells us that it is part of the normal operation of business concerns to avoid causing injury to third parties, as well as to employees, if for no other reason than to avoid tort liability and its substantial costs. This possibility of tort liability is not hypothetical; every State currently allows children born alive to recover in tort for prenatal injuries caused by third parties . . . and an increasing number of courts have recognized a right to recover even for prenatal injuries caused by torts committed prior to conception. . . .

Dothard and *Criswell* make clear that avoidance of substantial safety risks to third parties is inherently part of both an employee's ability to perform a job and an employer's "normal operation" of its business. . . . On the facts of this case . . . protecting fetal safety while carrying out the duties of battery manufacturing is as much a legitimate concern as is safety to third parties in guarding prisons (*Dothard*) or flying airplanes (*Criswell*).[5]

Dothard and *Criswell* also confirm that costs are relevant in determining whether a discriminatory policy is reasonably necessary for the normal operation of a business. In *Dothard*, the safety problem that justified exclusion of women from the prison guard positions was largely a result of inadequate staff and facilities. . . . If the cost of employing women could not be considered, the employer there should have been required to hire more staff and restructure the prison environment rather than exclude women. Similarly, in *Criswell*

---

5. I do not, as the Court asserts, . . . reject the "essence of the business" test. Rather, I merely reaffirm the obvious—that safety to third parties is part of the "essence" of most if not all businesses. Of course, the BFOQ inquiry "'adjusts to the safety factor.'" *Criswell*. . . . As a result, more stringent occupational qualifications may be justified for jobs involving higher safety risks, such as flying airplanes. But a recognition that the importance of safety varies among businesses does not mean that safety is completely irrelevant to the essence of a job such as battery manufacturing.

the airline could have been required to hire more pilots and install expensive monitoring devices rather than discriminate against older employees. . . .

The Court's narrow interpretation of the BFOQ defense in this case . . . means that an employer cannot exclude even pregnant women from an environment highly toxic to their fetuses. It is foolish to think that Congress intended such a result, and neither the language of the BFOQ exception nor our cases require it.[8]

II

Despite my disagreement with the Court concerning the scope of the BFOQ defense, I concur in reversing the Court of Appeals because that court erred in affirming the District Court's grant of summary judgment in favor of Johnson Controls. First, the Court of Appeals erred in failing to consider the level of risk-avoidance that was part of Johnson Controls' "normal operation." . . . If the fetal protection policy insists on a risk-avoidance level substantially higher than other risk levels tolerated by Johnson Controls such as risks to employees and consumers, the policy should not constitute a BFOQ.

Second, even without more information about the normal level of risk at Johnson Controls, the fetal protection policy at issue here reaches too far. This is evident both in its presumption that, absent medical documentation to the contrary, all women are fertile regardless of their age . . . and in its exclusion of presumptively fertile women from positions that might result in a promotion to a position involving high lead exposure. . . .

Third, it should be recalled that until 1982 Johnson Controls operated without an exclusionary policy, and it has not identified any grounds for believing that its current policy is reasonably necessary to its normal operations. . . .

Finally, the Court of Appeals failed to consider properly petitioners' evidence of harm to offspring caused by lead exposure in males. . . . It seems clear that if the Court of Appeals had properly analyzed that evidence, it would have concluded that summary judgment against petitioners was not appropriate because there was a dispute over a material issue of fact.

Mr. Justice SCALIA, concurring in the judgment.

I generally agree with the Court's analysis, but have some reservations, several of which bear mention. . . . [T]he Court goes far afield, it seems to

8. The Court's cramped reading of the BFOQ defense is also belied by the legislative history of Title VII, in which three examples of permissible sex discrimination were mentioned—a female nurse hired to care for an elderly woman, an all-male professional baseball team, and a masseur. . . . In none of those situations would gender "actually interfer[e] with the employee's ability to perform the job," as required today by the Court. . . . The Court's interpretation of the BFOQ standard also would seem to preclude considerations of privacy as a basis for sex-based discrimination, since those considerations do not relate directly to an employee's physical ability to perform the duties of the job. The lower federal courts, however, have consistently recognized that privacy interests may justify sex-based requirements for certain jobs. . . .

me, in suggesting that increased cost alone—short of "costs . . . so prohibitive as to threaten survival of the employer's business" . . . —cannot support a BFOQ defense. . . . I think, for example, that a shipping company may refuse to hire pregnant women as crew members on long voyages because the on-board facilities for foreseeable emergencies, though quite feasible, would be inordinately expensive. In the present case, however, Johnson has not asserted a cost-based BFOQ.

Notes

1. The Feminist Debate over "Equal" vs. "Special" Treatment. A broad coalition of feminist groups advocated the passage of the PDA, but after its passage they split over its meaning. Dispute centered on the legality and desirability of rules that attempt to eliminate some of the special disadvantages associated with pregnancy and childbirth.

Supporters of "special" treatment, like Professor Kay, argued that neutral rules cannot ensure equality between men and women when their circumstances are different, as in the case of pregnancy. By contrast, opponents like Wendy Williams claimed:

> Pregnancy [is] the centerpiece, the linchpin, the essential feature of women's separate sphere. The stereotypes, the generalizations, the role expectations [are] at their zenith when a woman [becomes] pregnant. . . .
>
> [F]eminists who seek special recognition for pregnancy are starting from the same basic assumption, namely, that women have a special place in the scheme of human existence when it comes to maternity. . . .
>
> The special treatment model has great costs. . . . [T]he reality [is] that conceptualizing pregnancy as a special case permits unfavorable as well as favorable treatment of pregnancy. Our history provides too many illustrations of the former. . . .[49]

Judge Posner's analysis offers a market-based rationale against "special treatment." Does his analysis have the same consequences as Williams' rationale? To what extent is Judge Posner correct that maternity leave policies "subsidize" women? Are there ordinary employment policies that subsidize men?

Is *Cal Fed* consistent with *Johnson Controls*? *Cal Fed* permits special legislation that gives pregnant women employees unique protection, while *Johnson Controls* prohibits special protection. Is the rule that protections favoring pregnant women are permissible but that protections compromising their work opportunities are not? Is this distinction satisfactory?

2. Stereotypes v. Facts. *Troupe* represents the prevailing interpretation of the PDA as a mandate to treat pregnant women like other similarly situated non-pregnant employees—no worse, but not necessarily any better. But *LaFleur* and the first clause of the PDA make clear that employers must base decisions on a pregnant woman's actual work capacity, rather than on stereotypes about how pregnant women or mothers behave. Proving the basis for an employer's decision can be a challenge. Is it realistic to expect Ms. Troupe to show that she was treated worse, even if she was? Consider the view of Ruth Colker: "[w]hat was she supposed to find—a nonpregnant employee with a sudden record of tardiness after a nearly spotless work record who also had scheduled a lengthy leave?"[50] Kimberly Troupe argued unsuccessfully that the problem was not her lateness, but the fact that the employer had impermissibly assumed that she would not return to work after her pregnancy leave. If she had proved this fact, should she have won?

Defining a comparison group is an important feature of formal equality. But there are, of course, all kinds of ways to structure the comparison. Instead of comparing pregnant persons to non-pregnant persons, for example, the law could compare women engaged in reproductive activity to men engaged in reproductive activity, and check to ensure that rules and practices do not impede one group any more than the other. On this theory, should Kimberly Troupe have won?

In a case also from the Seventh Circuit Court of Appeals, Maldonado v. U.S. Bank,[51] a new part-time bank employee was terminated after notifying her supervisor that she was pregnant and due in July, because the bank needed a teller who could fill in for full-time tellers during summer vacations. The court held that the bank could not take advance adverse action against Maldonado, noting that Maldonado had not asked for leave and had even hinted to her supervisor that she might not carry the pregnancy to term. The court qualified its holding, however, by suggesting that

> under narrow circumstances that we are not convinced are present here, [an employer may] project the normal inconveniences of pregnancy and their secondary effects into the future and take actions in accordance with and in proportion to those predictions. . . . But an employer cannot take anticipatory action unless it has a good faith basis, supported by sufficiently strong evidence, that the normal inconveniences of an employee's pregnancy will require special treatment.[52]

A growing number of mothers also have had success where they were harmed by stereotypical assumptions about their work commitments. These cases are discussed in the next section on work/family conflicts.

3. Pregnancy as a Disability. Note that California's pregnancy leave requirement challenged in the *Cal Fed* case was a "disability leave." Should pregnancy be considered a disability under the Americans with Disabilities Act of 1990 (ADA)?[53] The ADA provides employees with a covered disability the right to reasonable accommodations that do not impose undue hardship for the employer.[54] The ADA does not expressly mention pregnancy, but most courts have interpreted it to exclude coverage for women who suffer temporary disability from the complications of normal pregnancy.[55] In 2008, Congress passed the Americans with Disabilities Act Amendments Act (ADAAA), which restores protections for the disabled that had been gutted by federal court rulings over two decades. Among other changes, the ADAAA expands the definition of disabled to include conditions that interfere with mundane, work-related tasks like standing, lifting, or bending.[56] It also directs courts to construe the statute broadly in favor of the disabled. In response, the EEOC issued an interpretive guidance stating that temporary disabilities can be covered if "substantially limiting," which is "not meant to be a demanding standard," and should be understood to encompass an employee with a "20-pound lifting restriction that lasts or is expected to last for several months." Yet, the EEOC guidance expressly excludes pregnancy from coverage under the ADAAA based on the theory that because "pregnancy is not the result of a physiological disorder," it is "not an impairment."[57] Given that the amended statute is designed to cover potentially short-term disabilities, including those whose only manifestation is a lifting restriction, can the continuing exclusion of pregnancy be justified? Is there any benefit to women to refusing to treat pregnancy as a disability? On the one hand, the purpose of the ADA is to eliminate stereotyped thinking about disability. On the other hand, this exclusion avoids associating pregnancy with the dependence implied in the notion of disability, upon which traditional legal restrictions against women were often based. Given the stereotypes associated with pregnancy, why exclude it from the Act, which requires reasonable accommodation?

4. Nondiscrimination vs. Accommodation Under the PDA. Unlike the ADA, the PDA provides only a comparative right of accommodation — employers need only accommodate the pregnant worker's needs if they accommodate the needs of those "similar in their ability or inability to work, but unaffected by pregnancy." In a recent case, Wal-Mart fired a pregnant woman who worked in the fitting room for carrying a water bottle throughout the day because her doctor had advised that she drink water regularly to prevent recurring bladder infections.[58] The case was litigated under the FMLA, but could the plaintiff have sought relief under the PDA? If Wal-Mart allows other employees to eat or drink on the job (say a diabetic in need of frequent snacks), then it would have to make a similar accommodation for a pregnant employee with a comparable medical need. But if the company makes no exceptions to its policy, can it deny her this medically indicated and costless accommodation?

What if the employer does provide accommodations to some temporarily disabled workers, but not to pregnant women? In Reeves v. Swift Transportation Co., the employer provided light-duty assignments to those temporarily unable to satisfy the lifting or other requirements of the truck driver position, but only if the injuries were incurred on the job.[59] Pregnant women are not otherwise eligible for light-duty assignment, but neither are employees with other medical conditions that developed off the job. The Sixth Circuit held that the policy did not violate the PDA because pregnant women were treated at least as well as some other employees — those also injured off the job. Other courts have reached similar conclusions about restrictive light-duty policies.[60] In one of the few cases in which a restrictive light-duty policy was invalidated, the plaintiffs showed that the policy was not applied evenhandedly (light-duty assignments were given to some men injured off the job) and that higher-ups bore animus towards women.[61] Is *Reeves* consistent with the PDA?

Is the PDA deficient insofar as it prevents explicit discrimination against pregnant women but stops short of requiring accommodations necessary to meet their needs? Should it be extended? How? A bill entitled the Pregnant Women's Fairness Act was recently introduced in Congress.[62] It proposes a right of reasonable accommodation for pregnancy-related disability, modeled after the ADA.[63] What objections might you expect to this bill from employers?

5. Disparate Impact Theory.   Another theory potentially available under existing law is that the failure to accommodate pregnancy has a disparate impact against women.[64] In *Cal Fed*, the Court specifically declined to address the issue, and few plaintiffs have succeeded under this theory.[65] Consider the following analysis of disparate impact claims under the PDA:

> In theory, disparate impact law should compensate for some of the shortcomings of the PDA's comparative right of accommodation by invalidating some of the harsh employment policies that make it difficult for women to work through pregnancy. . . . The reality is that plaintiffs almost never prevail on such claims in the pregnancy context.
>
> There are a number of reasons why disparate impact theory has not turned out to be more useful for pregnant workers. Although most courts acknowledge the theoretical existence of disparate impact theory under the PDA, some refuse to apply it in its true form. These courts treat the [PDA] . . . as a ceiling on what accommodations employers can be forced to provide. Judge Posner, for example, in *Troupe*, described disparate impact as a "permissible theory" under the PDA but cautioned that "properly understood," it was not a "warrant for favoritism" and could not be used to prevent employers from treating pregnant workers "as badly as they treat similarly affected but nonpregnant employees." Other courts have taken a similar tack—claiming to recognize disparate impact law but refusing to allow it to provide anything more than a comparative right to accommodation or leave. The Fifth Circuit . . . refused to apply disparate impact to claims "in which the plaintiff's only challenge is that the amount of sick leave granted to employees is insufficient to accommodate the time off required in a typical pregnancy. To hold otherwise would be to transform the PDA into a guarantee of medical leave for pregnant employees, something we have specifically held that the PDA does not do." . . .
>
> Even when courts are not openly dismissive of disparate impact claims, plaintiffs have not met with much success. One potential obstacle is the inability to identify, as required under the statute, a particular "employment practice" that produces the disparate impact. Courts have held, for example, that any discretionary decision—such as the decision to deny a particular woman's request for pregnancy-related leave—cannot be challenged as a practice. . . .
>
> A second obstacle arises when courts prejudge the merits of the claim by refusing to apply disparate impact analysis to "legitimate" job requirements

like attendance. As the Seventh Circuit reasoned in [a case challenging an absenteeism policy], the "concept of disparate impact was developed and is intended for cases in which employers impose eligibility requirements that are not really necessary for the job." Disparate impact theory can be used to challenge "rules or practices that arbitrarily exclude pregnant women," but not to argue "that the employer should be required to excuse pregnant employees from having to satisfy the legitimate requirements of their job." . . . It may well be that many of the job requirements that pregnant workers have difficulty satisfying indeed are justified by business necessity, but it is the employer's burden to prove it if a disparate impact has been shown. Not all policies that fall into legitimate categories—like leave or attendance policies—are in fact necessary to the normal operation of the employer's business.

A final, but important, obstacle is that courts tend to require statistical proof of a disparate impact. Courts have been largely unwilling to accept non-statistical showings of impact, or to rely on broader societal data to support a claim of disparate impact. And plaintiffs have been mostly unsuccessful in making the requisite statistical showing. . . . In many cases, the sample is just too small, particularly in so-called non-traditional occupations for women. It is unlikely that enough pregnant women will have been adversely affected by any particular policy to show a statistically significant impact. . . . In other cases, there seems to be confusion about the proper comparison groups for statistical analysis. . . . Given these specific obstacles and the incredibly small number of cases in which pregnant workers have prevailed on disparate impact claims, it seems fair to conclude that the theory provides little meaningful protection for pregnant workers beyond that provided by disparate treatment or formal policy models of discrimination.[66]

Should courts be more accepting of disparate impact claims in the pregnancy context? Is it consistent with the aims of the PDA? With its structure?

6. European Community Law.   European Community law has developed in a direction far more favorable to the claims of pregnant women than American law. One representative case found a violation of the nondiscrimination provisions of a Council Directive of the European Community Union when an employer discharged a pregnant woman who had been hired without knowledge of her pregnancy, even though the only reason she got the job was to replace another employee on maternity leave. The European cases go well beyond *Troupe* and the PDA by protecting pregnancy regardless of whether other disabilities are protected. As one commentator explains, the European "no comparison necessary" approach places a "badge of protection" on pregnant women, which shields them from adverse employment-related consequences whether or not other disabling conditions would receive similar treatment. Would this be a better approach than the one reflected in *Troupe*? Would it violate the PDA? As the following discussion indicates, European Union law also provides greater accommodation than the American law for caretaking responsibilities. What might account for this more favorable treatment?

7. *Johnson Controls* as a Reprieve of the Protective Legislation Debate.
In Muller v. Oregon, excerpted in Chapter 1, the famous Brandeis brief cited
the protective legislation of 19 states and 7 foreign countries, and then brought
to the Court's attention

> over ninety reports of committees, bureaus of statistics, commissioners of
> hygiene, inspectors of factories, both in this country and in Europe, to the
> effect that long hours of labor are dangerous for women, primarily because of
> their special physical organization. . . . Perhaps the general scope and charac-
> ter of all these reports may be summed up in what an inspector for Hanover
> says: "The reasons for the reduction of the working day to ten hours—(a) the
> physical organization of women, (b) her maternal functions, (c) the rearing
> and education of the children, (d) the maintenance of the home—are all so
> important and so far reaching that the need for such reduction need hardly
> be discussed."[67]

In *Muller*, the issue was whether the danger to women of a long work day
was sufficient enough to overcome the Fourteenth Amendment freedom of
contract rights of the employer. In *Johnson Controls*, the question was whether
the danger to women and their fetuses justified their exclusion from certain job
categories under Title VII (as a "bona fide occupational qualification" under
Title VII). Freedom of contract no longer has the recognition it once had, and
women's equality is now a protected value, both constitutionally and statutorily. Nonetheless, Justice Blackmun, and many legal commentators, have
drawn parallels between fetal protection policies and protective legislation of
the nineteenth century, which was also backed by "scientific" data.

What are the costs and benefits of contemporary protective legislation?
What, if anything, should be inferred from the fact that these policies are more
common in certain industries—typically those with higher pay and benefits
that have been traditionally dominated by men? Consider the following:

> The electronics industry . . . employs mostly women, and many of these
> women frequently come into contact with six of the seven substances [the
> presence of which was used to exclude women from traditionally male jobs
> in companies such as *Johnson Controls*]: lead, benzene, vinyl chloride, carbon
> tetrachloride, carbon monoxide, and carbon disulfide. Yet fetal vulnerability
> policies have not been instituted in this industry. Many women laundry work-
> ers and dry cleaners are exposed to carbon disulfide and benzene. Women
> laboratory technicians are often exposed to benzene and other dangerous
> chemicals. Infectious agents and chemicals create risks of fetal harm to health
> care workers and hospital laundry workers. Dental offices are often contami-
> nated by mercury. . . . Yet with the exception of hospitals that fire pregnant
> x-ray technicians or otherwise restrict their exposure, women are generally
> allowed to work in women's jobs without restrictions based on fetal safety.[68]

Some research also suggests significant risks to women's reproductive
health from extensive exposure to the electromagnetic fields produced by
video display terminals.[69] Yet employers generally have not attempted to place
restrictions on women's working eight-hour days in front of computer screens?

How should society respond to the selective nature of employers' concerns? Should workers receive more information about risks that state and federal safety regulations permit? Should fetal risks, to which the company in *Johnson Controls* said it was responding, be totally irrelevant to the legal validity of protection policies?

8. Women Workers and "Choice."   The issue of women's choice with respect to fetal protection policies can be posed in different ways. Fetal protection policies do give women one kind of choice—between sterilization and losing their jobs. Professor David Kirp reports on the circumstances under which many women have made such choices, including one woman, Betty Riggs, who submitted to sterilization although she wanted more children, because her marriage was breaking up and she needed the money. Not long after Betty Riggs and four other women were sterilized, the company shut down its pigments department and their jobs were eliminated.[70] The Court in *Johnson Controls*, in invalidating fetal protection policies, concludes that women workers should make their own decisions about whether to assume the risks of the workplace for themselves and their potential offspring. In fact, this has been the general industry response to the Court's decision in *Johnson Controls*. Is this the best approach for women?

Many commentators have pointed out measures Johnson Controls could have taken to make the workplace safer for pregnant women. Likewise, the law in the United Kingdom requires employers to assess risks to expectant mothers and their fetuses and then to control the risk if possible. If the risk cannot be controlled, then suitable alternative work or paid leave must be given until the woman is no longer pregnant.[71] Could this approach be justified under formal equality, or does the possibility of paid leave treat women too favorably?

9. Equality Analysis in *Johnson Controls*.   The *Johnson Controls* case offers a number of different ways to identify the groups to compare for purposes of equality analysis. The Seventh Circuit Court of Appeals, in effect, compared employees who could bear children against employees who could not. On that basis, the appellate court concluded that the policy was facially sex-neutral and justifiable as a way to protect women's unconceived offspring. This approach is similar to the one used by the U.S. Supreme Court when it concluded in Geduldig v. Aiello that discrimination on the basis of pregnancy (even though only women were thereby affected) was not discrimination between women and men but rather discrimination between pregnant and non-pregnant persons.[72]

For his part, Justice Blackmun in *Johnson Controls* compared fertile women to fertile men, concluding that the fetal protection policy violates Title VII because it treats these two groups differently. Justice Blackmun referred in his opinion to evidence that lead exposure may damage sperm as well as ova to strengthen his analysis that men and women are similarly situated and thus the relevant groups for comparison. Justice Scalia did not specify the groups to be compared. In his view, whether or not the Court thought the policy in question was a form of sex discrimination, Congress unequivocally had determined with the Pregnancy Discrimination Act that it was. For the same reason, Justice Scalia's analysis is not affected by whether or not there are any comparable fetal risks to be passed through male employees.

If the *Johnson Controls* case satisfies formal equality requirements, does it also satisfy substantive equality—i.e., does it ensure that women and men enjoy the same opportunities? Arguably so, except that women may face damage to their reproductive capacities that men do not face. Is it up to the employer to eliminate that potential difference in working conditions?

Is it unfair to employers to prevent them from excluding women but to hold them potentially liable for miscarriages or birth defects attributable to lead exposure? Or is this simply a cost to the employer of being engaged in a risky business, which is best dealt with by ordinary business means, such as insurance, or passing the risks of business along to the consumer?

Should mothers themselves be subject to tort liability for harm suffered by a child due to the mother's voluntary exposure to harmful substances during pregnancy? This issue is further discussed in Chapter 5.

Putting Theory Into Practice

2-5. Barbara works the 8-5 shift as a department store cashier. She is entitled to an hour break for lunch and two ten-minute breaks during the day. Ordinarily, the supervisor manages lunch hours and breaks for all employees by staggering the lunch hours on a rotating basis and trying to fit in the shorter breaks around lulls in store business. An employee may have her lunch hour at 11 a.m. one day, and 3 p.m. the next.

Barbara is returning to work after a maternity leave. She wants to have her breaks timed so that she can use her lunch break to breastfeed her baby (at an adjacent day-care center) and her short breaks to pump her breast milk. For this to work well, she needs a regular daily lunch hour and evenly spaced breaks. Should she be entitled to these accommodations? What if another mother returning to work wants a similar arrangement? Alternatively, what if such accommodations would prevent the supervisor from attending a management training seminar given over the lunch break? How should fairness to other workers be juggled?

2-6. Peggy was hired by UPS as an "air driver," charged with delivering packages that arrived by air rather than ground and thus tended to be "lighter letters and packs." Her job description, however, required that she be able to lift 70 pounds without assistance, and assist with the movement of packages up to 150 pounds. She sought a light-duty assignment when she became pregnant because of a lifting restriction imposed by her doctor, which UPS denied. The collective bargaining agreement required that light-duty assignments be given to those temporarily disabled because of on-the-job injuries. UPS also had a policy of granting light-duty to drivers who had lost their driver's license for any reason, including driving under the influence. Is the employer's policy valid under the PDA?[73]

2-7. An inner-city community center runs after-school programs for teenage girls, many of whom lack positive adult role models. The center has a policy against hiring unmarried pregnant woman, on the theory that these individuals present negative role models. Does the policy wrongfully discriminate on the basis of sex?[74]

2-8. The National Guard in New York adopted a policy requiring each female recruit to sign a form indicating her understanding that a pregnancy must be immediately disclosed to her commanding officer and will result in all cases in immediate discharge and cessation of medical benefits. Is this legal? If so, is it good policy?

2. Work and Family

Joan Williams, Toward a Reconstructive Feminism: Reconstructing the Relationship of Market Work and Family Work

19 N. Ill. U. L. Rev. 89, 89-93 (1998)

Domesticity remains the entrenched, almost unquestioned, American norm and practice. As a gender system it has two defining characteristics. The first is its organization of market work around the ideal of a worker who works full-time and overtime and takes little or no time off for childbearing or childrearing. Though this ideal-worker norm does not define all jobs today, it defines the good ones: full-time blue-collar jobs in the working-class context, and high level executive and professional jobs for the middle-class and above. When work is structured in this way, caregivers often cannot perform as ideal workers. Their inability to do so gives rise to domesticity's second defining characteristic: its system of providing for caregiving by marginalizing the caregivers, thereby cutting them off from most of the social roles that offer responsibility and authority.

Domesticity introduced not only a new structuring of market work and family work but also a new description of men and women. The ideology of domesticity held that men "naturally" belong in the market because they are competitive and aggressive; women belong in the home because of their "natural" focus on relationships, children, and an ethic of care. In its original context, domesticity's descriptions of men and women served to justify and reproduce its breadwinner/housewife roles by establishing norms that identified successful gender performance with character traits suitable for those roles.

Both the ideology and the practice of domesticity retain their hold. A recent survey found that fully two-thirds of Americans believe it would be best for women to stay home and care for family and children. Domesticity's descriptions of men and women persist in vernacular gender talk such as John Gray's Men Are from Mars, Women Are from Venus, as well as in the strain of feminist theory that associates women with an ethic of care. [For more on the ethic of care, see Chapter 4.]

Even more important, market work continues to be structured in ways that perpetuate the economic vulnerability of caregivers. Their vulnerability stems from the way we define the ideal worker, as someone who works at least forty hours a week year round. This ideal worker norm, framed around the traditional life patterns of men, excludes most mothers. Nearly two-thirds of mothers of child-bearing age are not ideal workers even in the minimal sense of working full-time full year. One quarter of mothers of child-bearing age still are homemakers. Single, as well as married mothers are affected: never married mothers are the group of women most likely to be at home.

Moreover, full-time work is no guarantee of avoiding economic vulnerability: even mothers who work full-time often find themselves on the "mommy track." In addition, full-time workers who cannot work overtime often suffer economically because many of the best jobs now require substantial overtime. A rarely recognized, but extraordinarily important fact is that jobs requiring extensive overtime exclude virtually all mothers (93 percent).

Our economy is divided into mothers and others. Having children has a very strong negative effect on women's income, an effect that actually increased in the 1980s despite the fact that women have become better educated. . . . As a result, in an era when women's wages are catching up with men's, mothers' wages lag behind. Given that nearly 90% of women become mothers during their working lives, this pattern is inconsistent with gender equality.

If mothers have failed to achieve equality in market work, equality in the family has proved equally elusive. Buying and cooking food, doing dishes and laundry, caring for children: on average mothers spend thirty-one hours a week on these tasks. Many commentators have noted the contradiction: despite our self-image of gender equality, American women still do 80% of child care and two-thirds of core housework.

In short, the basic elements of domesticity's organization of market work and family work remain intact. . . . Women still specialize in family work. Men still specialize in market work. Market work continues to be framed around the assumption that ideal workers have access to a flow of family work few mothers enjoy. Social and cultural norms still sustain and reproduce this organization of (market and family) work.

Domesticity did not die; it mutated. In the nineteenth century most married women were marginalized outside of the economy. Although women have reentered market work, most remain marginalized today. This is not equality.

Notes

1. Women's Disproportionate Caretaking Burdens. Sociologist Arlie Hochschild coined the term "second shift" to describe the social norm under which women who work for wages are also expected to take care of the house and the children.[75] Although men's share of family tasks has increased, government data indicate that employed mothers average five more hours of total unpaid and paid work a week than employed fathers. Men with children work more hours in outside employment than men without children, while the average number of hours worked by women declines when they have children.[76]

Surveys suggest that although domestic work is the highest source of discord in marriages after money, only about a third of wives are dissatisfied with the allocation of work in their households. The key to happiness appears not to be an equal split of chores but partners who are understanding and supportive, and willing to invest quality time in their relationships.[77] What accounts for these patterns? Is it that women just enjoy housework more, or hate it less?[78] Is it more a matter of expectations? Drawing on sociological theory, Naomi Cahn suggests that wives take responsibility for a disproportionate share of housework and child care as a way of "performing gender": since women are expected to mother and to take care of the house, doing so gives wives both social approval and interpersonal power.[79] By contrast, men may suffer social stigma when they are full-time "househusbands."

Responses to the recent economic downturn are consistent with that theory. When mothers lose their job and are looking for another, they devote about twice as much time to child care. Fathers' family work remains the same; they spend more time sleeping and watching television, along with searching for another job.[80] It is unclear whether labor market trends will ultimately force changes in these patterns. Because layoffs have disproportionately affected men's jobs, more women are in primary breadwinning roles, and it is projected that their labor force participation may soon surpass men's.[81] Do you think this will affect the allocation of household burdens?

2. Women's Choices. A common explanation for women's underrepresentation in positions of greatest status, power, and financial reward is women's different choices. In a study by the Center for Work-Life Policy of some 3000 high-achieving American women and men (defined as those with graduate or professional degrees or high honors undergraduate degrees), nearly four in ten women reported leaving the workforce voluntarily at some point over their careers. The same proportion reported sometimes choosing a job with lesser compensation and fewer responsibilities than they were qualified to assume in order to accommodate family responsibilities. By contrast, only one in ten men left the workforce primarily for family-related reasons.[82] Reports vary about the extent to which women opt out of the workforce to accommodate domestic obligations. The popular press reports that almost 20 percent of women with graduate or professional degrees are not in the labor force, compared with only 5 percent of similarly credentialed men, and that one in three women with MBAs are not working full time, compared with one in twenty men.[83] A recent study, however, concluded that fewer than 8 percent of professional women born since 1956 opt out of the labor force for a year or more during their prime childbearing years.[84] Moreover, the overwhelming majority of women who leave the workforce want to return to work, and most do so, although generally not without significant career costs and difficulties.[85] The same is true in other advanced industrial nations for which data is available.[86]

To the extent that more women are dropping out, some observers find it unproblematic—a function of priorities that society should respect. Others, like Linda Hirschman, believe that women are "cutting their ambitions off at the knees." In her view, those who put family first have "fewer opportunities for full human flourishing" in public life. Assigning this role to women "is unjust. Women assigning it themselves is equally unjust."[87] Leslie Bennetts argues that it has become "inescapably clear the choosing economic dependency as a lifestyle is the classic feminine mistake."[88] Other commentators fault the workplace for its failure to provide flexible, reduced hours and leave policies that do not penalize those who take advantage of them.[89] What is your view? This issue is more fully examined in Chapter 4.

How much responsibility do women bear for caretaking priorities that may restrict their job commitments? Consider the comments of a lawyer who defends employers in cases where plaintiffs claim that they were victims of "caretaker bias": "When someone says 'Gee, the reason I couldn't put in all those hours is because I have young children'—that's not holding someone's gender against them, it's holding their choice."[90]

3. Caregiver Discrimination Lawsuits. Lawsuits alleging discrimination against caregivers are on the rise. One study found verdicts in 170 caregiver discrimination suits between 2000 and 2005.[91] Caregiving is not one of the protected characteristics under Title VII or any other federal antidiscrimination law. In 2007, however, the EEOC issued an enforcement guidance to explain the circumstances under which caregiver discrimination might nonetheless be actionable.[92] For example, it is unlawful, as a form of illegal sex stereotyping, for an employer to assume that female employees will have caregiving responsibilities that interfere with job performance or labor force commitment. Employers cannot assume that women with young children will not work long hours or be available for travel or that they will be more likely to leave the workforce. This type of actionable discrimination is exemplified by Back v. Hastings on Hudson, for example, in which a school psychologist argued that she was denied tenure because school personnel had decided that, as a young mother, she would not be able to devote herself to the job.[93] The trial court granted summary judgment to the school district, but the Second Circuit Court of Appeals reversed. The court allowed the case to proceed on a gender discrimination theory based on sex-stereotyped comments about mothers, without any comparative evidence about the treatment of fathers. Evidence introduced included comments that maybe her hard work was "just an act" until she received tenure and would start going home mid-afternoon, and that maybe it was not possible to "do this job" and "be a good mother."[94]

In another case, Lust v. Sealy, the plaintiff was a sales representative who lost a promotion to a man. Evidence of discrimination included her supervisor's admission that he didn't consider recommending her for promotion because she had children. He didn't think she would want to relocate her family, even though she had not told him that and, in fact, had indicated frequently how much she wanted the promotion. When the plaintiff asked about that promotion, the supervisor also asked why her husband wasn't going to take care of her.[95] The plaintiff won at trial and the verdict was upheld on appeal in a decision written by Richard Posner, the same judge who wrote the opinion in *Troupe*. The court reduced the damages award to $150,000 — half the maximum statutorily allowed — because the employer had taken steps to remedy the discrimination.

A wide body of research, as well as reported cases, document adverse stereotypes that working mothers face, such as a presumed lack of dependability, productivity, and commitment.[96] Should such research be admissible in sex discrimination cases where women claim that they were subject to the "motherhood penalty" but lack explicit statements like those present in *Back* and *Sealy*? How else might this body of work be helpful in preventing workplace bias?

The EEOC guidance also makes clear that it is unlawful to treat male employees with caregiving responsibilities less favorably than female employees in the same situation (or vice versa), especially if motivated by the belief that men should not assume such responsibilities. For example, an employer who told a male employee that he was not eligible for leave to take care of a newborn unless his wife was "in a coma or dead" committed actionable discrimination of this nature.[97] Two years later, in 2009, the EEOC issued a "best practices" document that encourages employers to provide accommodations for caregiving beyond those required by law to promote a better work/life balance for all employees.[98] The EEOC recommends that employers adopt a "caregiver" policy that describes common stereotypes or biases about caregivers and provides examples of prohibited discriminatory conduct. It also encourages employers to take proactive efforts to purge the hiring process of unfair stereotypes about caregivers and to ensure that applicants are not evaluated or steered into particular jobs on the basis of caregiving responsibilities. Finally, the EEOC recommends a number of policies to alleviate common conflicts faced by caregiving employees. Flexible work arrangements are at the top of the list, along with voluntary overtime, reasonable leave time for caregiving obligations, and other "family-friendly" modifications of conventional workplace rules. Should such policies be mandated? What objections do you see to them?

4. Accommodation vs. Discrimination. Should policies concerning childrearing, like childbearing, be seen as *accommodations* to employees with special needs, or as necessary components of a *nondiscriminatory* workplace? Some scholars, drawing on frameworks applicable to religious beliefs or disabilities, argue that employers have an obligation to undertake some expense and inconvenience if necessary to enable caretakers to participate fully in the workforce. Viewed this way, as measures to overcome disadvantages women experience from engaging in gendered activities, such workplace accommodations reflect values of substantive, rather than formal, equality.

Other scholars have resisted the equal treatment/special treatment dichotomy. They argue that the workplace is not a neutral structure that needs restructuring to accommodate women, but rather a set of arrangements already favoring an ideal worker, typically male, who lacks substantial caretaking responsibilities. On this view, reforming the workplace to acknowledge employees' caretaking responsibilities is not "special treatment" for women, but rather a recognition of the fundamental reality of women's lives. Joan Williams' call for a "reconstructive feminism" is in this vein. Williams argued that the focus of discussion should be not on theories of equality, but on how household work should be allocated within the household, how the cost of childrearing should be shifted from the private to the public arena, and what workplace restructuring should occur.[99] Does this formulation escape the choice between nondiscrimination and accommodation?

How might this agenda be achieved? An important rationale for work/family reforms is that they can be effective for employers as well as society.

> [E]mployers who provide family-friendly workplaces often save money because of decreased attrition and absenteeism, as well as enhancing recruitment and productivity. Practices that employees deem to reflect business necessity may in fact reflect business-irrational practices driven by gender stereotypes.[100]

Are employers who do not provide family-friendly workplaces overemphasizing short-term costs at the expense of long-term savings? If so, will the market eventually provide correctives or do we need policy interventions?

5. Parenting Leave: The Family and Medical Leave Act. In 1993, Congress passed the federal Family and Medical Leave Act (FMLA). The FMLA requires employers of more than 50 workers to allow up to a three-month, unpaid leave for the care of a new infant or ill family member, with the right to return to the same or an equivalent position without loss of pre-leave benefits. The Act covers employees who have worked for the employer for at least 12 months and for 1,250 hours during the year preceding the start of the leave. Only half the workforce is covered by the Act, and the U.S. Department of Labor found that 88 percent of eligible employees who need time off do not take it largely because they cannot afford to go without a paycheck. Even many who can afford to take leave sometimes do not do so because of resistance by supervisors and colleagues. One study of highly educated individuals found that about a third of women and almost half of men reported that their workplace culture penalized employees for taking advantage of family-friendly policies.[101] Other research has indicated that many employees did not assert their rights because of well-founded concerns of informal retaliation and blacklisting; they feared being branded as a "troublemaker" or "slacker" and not getting favorable assignments, shifts, or recommendations if they changed jobs.[102] Fewer men take family leaves than women, and fewer employers offer paid leave to men. What accounts for this difference? Is it a problem that employers or public policy should address?[103]

Should the government require *paid* family leave? If so, who should subsidize it? In 2002, California became the first state to amend a state disability program to include up to six weeks of compensation for leaves to care for an ill family member, or the birth, adoption, or foster care placement of a new child. New Jersey and Washington followed suit, and a handful of other states have expanded their unemployment insurance programs to provide wage replacement for parental leave.[104] Should such legislation be a top priority?

An important legal precedent is the U.S. Supreme Court's decision in Nevada v. Hibbs, upholding the constitutionality of the FMLA as applied to state employees.[105] The primary legal issue in the case concerned sovereign immunity. The Eleventh Amendment to the U.S. Constitution prohibits money damages against a state except to the extent Congress has limited that immunity through specific legislation. *Hibbs* raised the question whether the FMLA constituted such a limitation, and whether it was valid under Section Five of the Fourteenth Amendment as a congruent and proportional response to a state-sponsored history of discrimination. The plaintiff was a man and the expansive language of then-Chief Justice Rehnquist, one of the court's most conservative justices, is noteworthy in its recognition of the power of gender stereotyping with respect to family care issues and the intent of the gender-neutral provisions of the FMLA to address the resulting disadvantages.

> The FMLA aims to protect the right to be free from gender-based discrimination in the workplace. . . . The history of the many state laws limiting women's employment opportunities is chronicled in—and, until relatively recently, was sanctioned by—this Court's own opinions. . . . Congress responded to this history of discrimination by abrogating States' sovereign immunity in Title VII of the Civil Rights Act of 1964. . . . According to the evidence that was before Congress when it enacted the FMLA, states continue to rely on invalid gender stereotypes in the employment context, specifically in the administration of leave benefits. . . . Congress . . . heard testimony that . . . "Even . . . [w]here child-care leave policies do exist, men, *both in the public and private sectors*, receive notoriously discriminatory treatment in their requests for such leave." . . . Many States offered women extended 'maternity' leave that far

exceeded the typical 4- to 8-week period of physical disability due to pregnancy and childbirth, but very few States granted men a parallel benefit: Fifteen States provided women up to one year of extended maternity leave, while only four provided men with the same. . . . This and other differential leave policies were not attributable to any differential physical needs of men and women, but rather to the pervasive sex-role stereotype that caring for family members is women's work.[106]

Note that the Act was inspired by a problem that disproportionately affected women, but by insisting that men receive the same parental leave benefits as similarly situated women, the FMLA reflects a clear application of formal equality principles. If women disproportionately use parenting leave, is this benefit a "subsidy" for women?

In an interesting twist, nine years after *Hibbs*, the Supreme Court distinguished the FMLA's family leave provisions from the FMLA's provision entitling a covered employee to leave when that employee's own "serious health condition . . . interferes with the employee's ability to perform at work." According to the Court in Coleman v. Maryland Court of Appeals,[107] the FMLA's "self-care" provision was not a response to any identified pattern of gender-based discrimination, and thus does not constitute a valid congressional abrogation of state sovereign immunity. Thus, while individuals under *Hibbs* can obtain money damages against a state for violations of the FMLA family-care provisions, sovereign immunity protects states against such suits under the FMLA's self-care provision. Is the Court's distinction between the FMLA's family-care and self-care persuasive? In a dissenting opinion, Justice Ginsburg emphasized the importance of job security for pregnant women with maternity-related disabilities before and after childbirth to the achievement of gender equality—an importance underlined in the legislative history of the Act. To Justice Ginsburg, an essential aspect of the FMLA is the way the family-care and the self-care provisions work together to protect women from discrimination on account of their pregnancies. "It would make scant sense to provide job-protected leave for a woman to care for a newborn, but not for her recovery from delivery, a miscarriage, or the birth of a stillborn baby."[108]

Does it matter that the plaintiff in *Coleman* was a man? According to Justice Ginsburg, the availability of FMLA rights to men was intended, among other things, to blunt the force of stereotypes of women as primary caregivers—in other words, to recognize the historic pattern of discrimination against pregnant women and female caregivers in a gender-neutral way. Does this intention supply the necessary connection between the self-care provision and an identified pattern of gender discrimination?

6. Parenting Leave: An International Perspective. Three years after the passage of the FMLA, the European Council adopted the European Union Directive on Parental Leave, which provides minimum standards with which the member states must comply. These standards include a right to parental leave for at least three months, protection against dismissal, and the right to return to the same or similar position. Most of the Member States of the European Union apply standards that exceed European Union standards for parental leave. For example, Finland allows "47.5 weeks of leave per child-birth: 17.5 weeks of maternity leave, 4 weeks of paternity leave, and 26 weeks of parental leave." Similarly, Sweden offers parents comparable amounts of leave—14 weeks of maternity leave, two weeks of paternity leave, and an additional 13 months of parental leave. In many Scandinavian countries, leaves may be split between parents or extended over a number of years. For example, Norway allows parents to spread 29 weeks of childcare over a two-year period following the birth of a child, and Sweden allows a parent to take a 25 percent reduction in working hours until the child is 8 years old.[109]

The comparative generosity of other countries' family leave policies, however, obscures complex issues about implementation and equity. In some countries, liberal leave policies foster employer resistance against women workers. In Mexico, for example, where women are guaranteed 12 weeks' paid maternity leave, many employers believe they have the right to deny employment to women if they state an intention to take a leave; others administer illegal pregnancy tests. These infractions are only weakly sanctioned. Similarly, Japan's Equal Employment Opportunity Law, effective in 1986, provides for equal opportunity and treatment in the job market for men and women. However, as one commentator notes, "the provisions of the law were not mandatory and no enforcement provisions were provided, resulting in minimal effectiveness."[110]

Some countries have achieved much higher rates of male involvement by a "use it or lose it approach." Sweden, for example, requires that 60 days of paid leave be taken by fathers; it is not transferable to mothers. That requirement, coupled with an extensive public education campaign, has resulted in 70 percent of fathers taking parental leave.[111] Sweden also pays a "gender-equality" bonus if parenting leave is shared. Studies of Scandinavian approaches find that when fathers take more leave, it results in shorter leaves by mothers and a smaller loss in their earning potential. However, Swedish fathers account for only about 12 percent of total benefit days claimed. One reason is employer resistance. Another is mothers' preferences: about half of those surveyed wanted all the days for themselves. Gender differences persist after the parental leave period. Sixty percent of mothers of young children work part time compared with only 5 percent of fathers.[112]

Drawing on such evidence, several American commentators argue that the FMLA should be amended to reward employers for encouraging men to take more parental leave.[113] Are these proposals worth considering? Should greater male use of parental leave be a policy priority? Should other family members also be eligible?

7. Child Care.   Another form of assistance to families involves child care. Early in the second wave of feminism, a common assumption was that the state would step in to provide quality child care for families.

> When Betty Friedan wrote [The Feminine Mystique (1963)], she assumed that
> very soon there would be a national system of subsidized child care centers
> that would be as free, accessible, and high in quality as public libraries. She
> actually believed this. Not only did she believe this, it was not an implausible
> vision. After all, that is what has happened in Belgium. That's what happened
> in France. . . . Ninety-five percent of nursery school age children in those coun-
> tries are in government-subsidized child care.[114]

Friedan's vision came nowhere close to realization. Instead, as Joan Williams
notes:

> In 1971, when Congress passed a Comprehensive Child Development Act,
> President Nixon vetoed it under pressure from an intense lobbying campaign
> that decried the proposal as "a radical piece of social legislation" designed to
> deliver children to "communal approaches to child-rearing over and against
> the family-centered approach." A 1975 proposal was also defeated, decried as
> an effort to "[s]ovietize the family." As a result, the U.S. offers less governmen-
> tal support for child care than does any other industrialized nation.[115]

Current law provides federal funds for various child-care assistance programs for disadvantaged children. The federal Child and Dependent Care Tax
Credit allows a credit for a percentage of money certain taxpayers spend on
child care. The Personal Responsibility and Work Opportunity Reconciliation
Act of 1996 offsets some of the losses to poor families under "welfare reform"
through a $4 billion increase in child-care funding. This Act is discussed more
broadly in Chapter 5. The funding for federal programs, however, has failed
to keep up with inflation and many states have reduced their commitment to
child-care subsidies, even as the number of eligible children has risen.[116]

Some employers also offer significant day-care assistance. According to a
National Compensation Survey, 3 percent of all workers receive employer subsidies for child care and 5 percent have access to on-site or off-site employer-
assisted day care. Others provide other support such as emergency child-care
services or referral networks. Workers in white-collar occupations are more
than twice as likely to have employer subsidies for child care as blue-collar
or service workers. Employers with 100 workers or more are five times more
likely to provide child-care subsidies, and more than four times more likely to
have on-site and off-site child-care facilities.[117]

Critics of current policies continue to advocate a comprehensive
government-supported child-care system available to all free of charge or at
progressive rates scaled to income.[118] As they note, most Western countries
have gone considerably further than the United States in assisting families
with children. Sweden, for example, not only provides paid caretaking leave,
but also a basic child allowance for all families, increased allowances for families with three or more children, and additional subsidies to replace support
that a non-custodial parent is unable or unwilling to pay. There are additional
income supports for post-childbirth leave and for care of children with disabilities, as well as an extensive publicly financed child-care system. Single

parents receive preferential treatment for housing and child care. The tax system encourages the entry of women into the workforce by taxing the second earner separately, rather than at the marginal rate of the primary wage earner. France, like Sweden, has a family allowance system, one that is particularly generous to large families. France also has a nearly universally available child care and preschool education system, regardless of whether the parent or parents are in the paid workforce.

However, even the most generous policies do not necessarily translate into gender equality. For example, Swedish women continue to do a disproportionate share of family work and took 52 days of leave for every day taken by a man.[119] Indeed, Sweden's level of sex segregation in the workforce is greater than that of the United States.[120]

Putting Theory Into Practice

2-9. How much responsibility should private employers have to support employees with families? Paid leave? Flex-time and part-time options? Child-care assistance? Benefit plans with choices that include family-related assistance? Does it depend on the employer's labor market position? What problems do you foresee in obtaining such initiatives? Are any of them unfair to workers who do not have families?

2-10. You are the head of the litigation department at a mid-size firm. A senior associate who has just had a second child asks not to be assigned to any cases requiring overnight travel. She also tends to avoid late or weekend hours at the firm, although she is accessible at home for conference calls and last-minute assignments. She is a hard-working and competent litigator but not a superstar. Other attorneys with families are annoyed that they are bearing a disproportionate share of document review work in other cities, and tasks that require office face time. You believe that the woman's choices may signal a lack of commitment that will hurt her at partnership. When you raise this concern, she claims that it reflects gender bias. How do you respond? How should the firm?

2-11. A program at the University of Michigan, funded in part by the National Science Foundation to address the acute shortage of female scientists, provides small grants to allow female scientists to hire

> . . . an extra set of hands in the lab or a substitute teacher in the classroom so they can spend more time at home without watching their careers stall. . . . Michigan has even paid for weekend day care so that female scientists have quiet time to write grants and journal articles. . . .
>
> [At Harvard, under a similar program,] the vast majority of the grants have gone to women with children. But [one male doctor] has turned his $25,000 fellowship over to the hospital to hire doctors to cover a portion

of his work week in the emergency room so that he can attend a new clinical-research training program at Harvard . . . and spend more time with his 2-year-old daughter. . . . [The doctor] says he initially felt guilty about taking a fellowship designed for women. "I'm sensitive to the idea that women have it harder than men in making their academic and family careers work, and I didn't want to be competing for an award with women who deserve it," he says. But his wife, who is pregnant with their second child, is a lawyer with the Office of the Massachusetts General. "Her career is just as demanding and high-powered as mine," says [the doctor,] so he felt he qualified for the grant.[121]

Are government grants to assist scientists manage the tough laboratory hours required of first-rate scientists a good policy? Should universities do the same in fields where women are significantly underrepresented? If so, does the acute underrepresentation of female scientists justify giving priority to women?

C. RECOGNIZING SEX-LINKED AVERAGE DIFFERENCES: EDUCATION AND SPORTS

Some sex-based differences affect matters where group-based judgments remain highly relevant. For example, on average, women live longer than men, have fewer driving-related accidents, have higher health costs, and stay out of the workforce for longer periods—which all affect the costs of insurance. Does our commitment to sex equality require that we ignore such average differences? Similar questions arise in education and sports. Researchers document some differences in the way girls and boys learn (again, on average). Does that justify "separate but equal" classroom treatment? Can athletic programs take account of average sex-based differences in strength, size, and speed? Even if only some girls can compete on equal terms with boys, should those who can have access to boys' teams? In sports where schools can only afford a girls team, should boys have a right to compete? What does gender equality require?

1. Sex-Segregated Schools

During much of early American history, it was often assumed that women needed no formal education; informal training in the household arts was thought sufficient. In the nineteenth century, as elementary and secondary education opportunities increased, prominent medical experts warned that women faced a deadly "brain womb conflict." Rigorous study assertedly would divert needed physical resources from reproductive organs to cognitive capacities. Even those who favored expanded female education, such as Catherine Beecher, generally believed that its primary objective should be "the preparation of woman for her distinctive profession as housekeeper, mother, nurse, and chief educator of infancy and childhood." Defenders of academic rigor emphasized that the point of women's instruction in traditional disciplines was not only to "enlarge their sphere of thought" but to render them "more interesting companions to men." Chemistry might be significant in its own right, but its principles were also applicable in the kitchen. Smith College's first president and early administrators denied that the college would produce competitors with men or diminish the "innate capacities which have been the glory and charm of true womanhood."[122]

These views are long out of date, but disputes still arise about whether girls and boys have different abilities, learning styles, and/or interests that should shape their educations. One issue concerns single-sex schools. In 1982, the U.S. Supreme Court held in Mississippi University for Women (MUW) v. Hogan that a traditionally all-female state nursing school could not exclude men. Underlying the Court's decision was evidence that the school's sex segregation reflected not legitimate educational or compensatory justifications, but rather stereotypical views of nursing as an exclusively female occupation.[123]

The Court did not, however, declare all single-sex schools unconstitutional. Justice O'Connor reserved the possibility that under "limited circumstances," a gender-based classification favoring one sex might be justified "if it intentionally and directly assists members of the sex that is disproportionately burdened." Justice Powell, joined by Justice Rehnquist, wrote a strong dissent emphasizing the "honored" tradition of single-sex education in this country, its benefits especially to women, and its contributions to educational diversity. Quoting from the Brief for the MUW Alumnae Association, Justice Powell noted the values of sex-segregated schools in freeing women from the distraction of romantic relationships:

> [I]n the aspect of life known as courtship or mate-pairing, the American female remains in the role of the pursued sex, expected to adorn and groom herself to attract the male. . . .

> An institution of collegiate higher learning maintained exclusively for women is uniquely able to provide the education atmosphere in which some, but not all, women can best attain maximum learning potential. It can serve to overcome the historic repression of the past and can orient a woman to function and achieve in the still male-dominated economy. It can free its students of the burden of playing the mating game while attending classes, thus giving academic rather than sexual emphasis.[124]

Fourteen years after *Hogan*, the Supreme Court was faced with another challenge—this time, to an all-male state military college, the Virginia Military Institute (VMI). In United States v. Virginia, the Supreme Court held that the exclusion of women by VMI was unconstitutional, despite Virginia's effort to develop a parallel leadership program for women at Mary Baldwin College.

Reading Questions

1. Assume that the presence of women will so alter the climate and teaching methods at VMI that it will not offer the same traditional benefits to men. Should this be of constitutional concern?
2. Would it have been possible for Virginia to establish a parallel institution for women that would have been "equal" to VMI? If so, what would that institution have looked like?

United States v. Virginia

518 U.S. 515 (1996)

GINSBURG, J., delivered the opinion of the court, in which STEVENS, O'CONNOR, KENNEDY, SOUTER, and BREYER, JJ., joined.

Virginia's public institutions of higher learning include an incomparable military college, Virginia Military Institute (VMI). The United States maintains that the Constitution's equal protection guarantee precludes Virginia from reserving exclusively to men the unique educational opportunities VMI affords. We agree. . . .

II

From its establishment in 1839 as one of the Nation's first state military colleges, VMI has remained financially supported by Virginia and "subject to the control of the [Virginia] General Assembly." . . .

VMI today enrolls about 1,300 men as cadets. Its academic offerings in the liberal arts, sciences, and engineering are also available at other public colleges and universities in Virginia. But VMI's mission is special. It is the mission of the school to produce educated and honorable men, prepared for the varied work of civil life, imbued with love of learning, confident in the functions and attitudes of leadership, possessing a high sense of public service, advocates of the American democracy and free enterprise system, and ready as citizen-soldiers to defend their country in time of national peril. . . .

In contrast to the federal service academies, institutions maintained "to prepare cadets for career service in the armed forces," VMI's program "is directed at preparation for both military and civilian life"; "[o]nly about 15% of VMI cadets enter career military service."

VMI produces its "citizen-soldiers" through "an adversative, or doubting, model of education" which features "[p]hysical rigor, mental stress, absolute equality of treatment, absence of privacy, minute regulation of behavior, and indoctrination in desirable values." . . .

VMI cadets live in spartan barracks where surveillance is constant and privacy nonexistent; they wear uniforms, eat together in the mess hall, and regularly participate in drills. Entering students are incessantly exposed to the rat line, "an extreme form of the adversative model," comparable in intensity to Marine Corps boot camp. Tormenting and punishing, the rat line bonds new cadets to their fellow sufferers and, when they have completed the 7-month experience, to their former tormentors.

VMI's "adversative model" is further characterized by a hierarchical "class system" of privileges and responsibilities, a "dyke system" for assigning a senior class mentor to each entering class "rat," and a stringently enforced "honor code," which prescribes that a cadet "'does not lie, cheat, steal nor tolerate those who do.'"

VMI attracts some applicants because of its reputation as an extraordinarily challenging military school, and "because its alumni are exceptionally close to the school." "[W]omen have no opportunity anywhere to gain the benefits of [the system of education at VMI]." . . .

In 1990, prompted by a complaint filed with the Attorney General by a female high-school student seeking admission to VMI, the United States sued the Commonwealth of Virginia and VMI, alleging that VMI's exclusively male admission policy violated the Equal Protection Clause of the Fourteenth Amendment. . . .

In the two years preceding the lawsuit, the District Court noted, VMI had received inquiries from 347 women, but had responded to none of them. "[S]ome women, at least," the court said, "would want to attend the school if they had the opportunity." The court further recognized that, with recruitment, VMI could "achieve at least 10% female enrollment"—"a sufficient 'critical mass' to provide the female cadets with a positive educational experience." And it was also established that "some women are capable of all of the individual activities required of VMI cadets." In addition, experts agreed that if VMI admitted women, "the VMI ROTC experience would become a better training program from the perspective of the armed forces, because it would provide training in dealing with a mixed-gender army."

[The District Court ruled in favor of VMI, because admission of women would require alterations of some of the distinctive and beneficial aspects of VMI; the Fourth Circuit Court of Appeals reversed and remanded, holding that the state could not achieve its purposes by favoring one gender and that VMI had to either admit women, establish a parallel institution or program, or abandon state support. In response to the Fourth Circuit's ruling, Virginia proposed a parallel program at Mary Baldwin College, a private liberal arts school for women: Virginia Women's Institute for Leadership (VWIL). The program was to be open, initially, to 25 to 30 students. The District Court decided that the program plan met the requirements of the Equal Protection Clause, and a divided Court of Appeals affirmed.]

III

The cross-petitions in this case present two ultimate issues. First, does Virginia's exclusion of women from the educational opportunities provided by VMI — extraordinary opportunities for military training and civilian leadership development — deny to women "capable of all of the individual activities required of VMI cadets," the equal protection of the laws guaranteed by the Fourteenth Amendment? Second, if VMI's "unique" situation — as Virginia's sole single-sex public institution of higher education — offends the Constitution's equal protection principle, what is the remedial requirement?

IV ...

To summarize the Court's current directions for cases of official classification based on gender: Focusing on the differential treatment or denial of opportunity for which relief is sought, the reviewing court must determine whether the proffered justification is "exceedingly persuasive." The burden of justification is demanding and it rests entirely on the State. [See Mississippi Univ. for Women v. Hogan, 1982.] The State must show "at least that the [challenged] classification serves 'important governmental objectives and that the discriminatory means employed' are 'substantially related to the achievement of those objectives.'" The justification must be genuine, not hypothesized or invented post hoc in response to litigation. And it must not rely on overbroad generalizations about the different talents, capacities, or preferences of males and females. . . .

The heightened review standard our precedent establishes does not make sex a proscribed classification. Supposed "inherent differences" are no longer accepted as a ground for race or national origin classifications. Physical differences between men and women, however, are enduring: "[T]he two sexes are not fungible; a community made up exclusively of one [sex] is different from a community composed of both." . . .

"Inherent differences" between men and women, we have come to appreciate, remain cause for celebration, but not for denigration of the members of either sex or for artificial constraints on an individual's opportunity. Sex classifications may be used to compensate women "for particular economic disabilities [they have] suffered," . . . to "promot[e] equal employment opportunity," . . . , to advance full development of the talent and capacities of our Nation's people. But such classifications may not be used, as they once were, . . . to create or perpetuate the legal, social, and economic inferiority of women.

Measuring the record in this case against the review standard just described, we conclude that Virginia has shown no "exceedingly persuasive justification" for excluding all women from the citizen-soldier training afforded by VMI. We therefore affirm the Fourth Circuit's initial judgment, which held that Virginia had violated the Fourteenth Amendment's Equal Protection Clause. Because the remedy proffered by Virginia — the Mary Baldwin VWIL program — does not cure the constitutional violation, i.e., it does not provide equal opportunity, we reverse the Fourth Circuit's final judgment in this case.

V . . .

Single-sex education affords pedagogical benefits to at least some students, Virginia emphasizes, and that reality is uncontested in this litigation.[8] Similarly, it is not disputed that diversity among public educational institutions can serve the public good. But Virginia has not shown that VMI was established, or has been maintained, with a view to diversifying, by its categorical exclusion of women, educational opportunities within the State. In cases of this genre, our precedent instructs that "benign" justifications proffered in defense of categorical exclusions will not be accepted automatically; a tenable justification must describe actual state purposes, not rationalizations for actions in fact differently grounded. . . .

Neither recent nor distant history bears out Virginia's alleged pursuit of diversity through single-sex educational options. In 1839, when the State established VMI, a range of educational opportunities for men and women was scarcely contemplated. Higher education at the time was considered dangerous for women; reflecting widely held views about women's proper place, the Nation's first universities and colleges—for example, Harvard in Massachusetts, William and Mary in Virginia—admitted only men. . . . VMI was not at all novel in this respect: In admitting no women, VMI followed the lead of the State's flagship school, the University of Virginia, founded in 1819. . . .

Debate concerning women's admission as undergraduates at the main university continued well past the century's midpoint. . . . If women were admitted, it was feared, they "would encroach on the rights of men; there would be new problems of government, perhaps scandals; the old honor system would have to be changed; standards would be lowered to those of other coeducational schools; and the glorious reputation of the university, as a school for men, would be trailed in the dust." . . .

Ultimately, in 1970, "the most prestigious institution of higher education in Virginia," the University of Virginia, introduced coeducation and, in 1972 [by court order], began to admit women on an equal basis with men. . . .

Virginia describes the current absence of public single-sex higher education for women as "an historical anomaly." But the historical record indicates action more deliberate than anomalous: First, protection of women against higher education; next, schools for women far from equal in resources and stature to schools for men; finally, conversion of the separate schools to coeducation. . . .

8. On this point, the dissent sees fire where there is no flame. "Both men and women can benefit from a single-sex education," the District Court recognized, although "the beneficial effects" of such education, the court added, apparently "are stronger among women than among men." The United States does not challenge that recognition. Cf. C. Jencks & D. Riesman, The Academic Revolution 297-298 (1968): "The pluralistic argument for preserving all-male colleges is uncomfortably similar to the pluralistic argument for preserving all-white colleges. . . . The all-male college would be relatively easy to defend if it emerged from a world in which women were established as fully equal to men. But it does not. It is therefore likely to be a witting or unwitting device for preserving tacit assumptions of male superiority—assumptions for which women must eventually pay."

[I]t is uncontested that women's admission would require accommodations, primarily in arranging housing assignments and physical training programs for female cadets. It is also undisputed, however, that "the VMI methodology could be used to educate women." The District Court even allowed that some women may prefer it to the methodology a women's college might pursue. "[S]ome women, at least, would want to attend [VMI] if they had the opportunity," the District Court recognized, and "some women," the expert testimony established, "are capable of all of the individual activities required of VMI cadets." The parties, furthermore, agree that "some women can meet the physical standards [VMI] now impose[s] on men." In sum, as the Court of Appeals stated, "neither the goal of producing citizen soldiers," VMI's *raison d'etre*, "nor VMI's implementing methodology is inherently unsuitable to women.

In support of its initial judgment for Virginia, a judgment rejecting all equal protection objections presented by the United States, the District Court made "findings" on "gender-based developmental differences." These "findings" restate the opinions of Virginia's expert witnesses, opinions about typically male or typically female tendencies." For example, "[m]ales tend to need an atmosphere of adversativeness," while "[f]emales tend to thrive in a cooperative atmosphere." "I'm not saying that some women don't do well under [the] adversative model," VMI's expert on educational institutions testified, "undoubtedly there are some [women] who do"; but educational experiences must be designed "around the rule," this expert maintained, and not "around the exception."

The United States does not challenge any expert witness estimation on average capacities or preferences of men and women. Instead, the United States emphasizes that time and again since this Court's turning point decision in Reed v. Reed, [1971], we have cautioned reviewing courts to take a "hard look" at generalizations or "tendencies" of the kind pressed by Virginia, and relied upon by the District Court. . . .

It may be assumed, for purposes of this decision, that most women would not choose VMI's adversative method. As Fourth Circuit Judge Motz observed, however, in her dissent from the Court of Appeals' denial of rehearing en banc, it is also probable that "many men would not want to be educated in such an environment." . . . (On that point, even our dissenting colleague might agree.) Education, to be sure, is not a "one size fits all" business. The issue, however, is not whether "women—or men—should be forced to attend VMI"; rather, the question is whether the State can constitutionally deny to women who have the will and capacity, the training and attendant opportunities that VMI uniquely affords.

The notion that admission of women would downgrade VMI's stature, destroy the adversative system and, with it, even the school, is a judgment hardly proved, a prediction hardly different from other "self-fulfilling prophec[ies]," . . . once routinely used to deny rights or opportunities. When women first sought admission to the bar and access to legal education, concerns of the same order were expressed. . . .

[Such] fear, according to a 1925 report, accounted for Columbia Law School's resistance to women's admission, although

> [t]he faculty . . . never maintained that women could not master legal learning. . . . No, its argument has been . . . more practical. If women were admitted to the Columbia Law School, [the faculty] said, then the choicer, more manly and red-blooded graduates of our great universities would go to the Harvard Law School! . . .

More recently, women seeking careers in policing encountered resistance based on fears that their presence would "undermine male solidarity," . . . deprive male partners of adequate assistance, and lead to sexual misconduct. . . .

Women's successful entry into the federal military academies, and their participation in the Nation's military forces, indicate that Virginia's fears for the future of VMI may not be solidly grounded. . . .

The Commonwealth's misunderstanding and, in turn, the District Court's, is apparent from VMI's mission: to produce "citizen-soldiers," individuals "imbued with love of learning, confident in the functions and attitudes of leadership, possessing a high sense of public service, advocates of the American democracy and free enterprise system, and ready . . . to defend their country in time of national peril. . . ."

Surely that goal is great enough to accommodate women, who today count as citizens in our American democracy equal in stature to men. Just as surely, the State's great goal is not substantially advanced by women's categorical exclusion, in total disregard of their individual merit, from the State's premier "citizen-soldier" corps. Virginia, in sum, "has fallen far short of establishing the 'exceedingly persuasive justification'" . . . that must be the solid base for any gender-defined classification.

VI

In the second phase of the litigation, Virginia presented its remedial plan—maintain VMI as a male-only college and create VWIL as a separate program for women. . . .

The constitutional violation in this case is the categorical exclusion of women from an extraordinary educational opportunity afforded men. A proper remedy for an unconstitutional exclusion, we have explained, aims to "eliminate [so far as possible] the discriminatory effects of the past" and to "bar like discrimination in the future." . . .

Virginia chose not to eliminate, but to leave untouched, VMI's exclusionary policy. For women only, however, Virginia proposed a separate program, different in kind from VMI and unequal in tangible and intangible facilities. . . .

VWIL affords women no opportunity to experience the rigorous military training for which VMI is famed. . . . Instead, the VWIL program "deemphasize[s]" military education, and uses a "cooperative method" of education "which reinforces self-esteem."

VWIL students participate in ROTC and a "largely ceremonial" Virginia Corps of Cadets, but Virginia deliberately did not make VWIL a military institute. The VWIL House is not a military-style residence and VWIL students need not live together throughout the four year program, eat meals together, or wear uniforms during the school day. VWIL students thus do not experience the "barracks" life "crucial to the VMI experience," the spartan living arrangements designed to foster an "egalitarian ethic." "[T]he most important aspects of the VMI educational experience occur in the barracks," the District Court found, yet Virginia deemed that core experience nonessential, indeed inappropriate, for training its female citizen-soldiers.

VWIL students receive their "leadership training" in seminars, externships, and speaker series, episodes and encounters lacking the "[p]hysical rigor, mental stress, . . . minute regulation of behavior, and indoctrination in desirable values" made hallmarks of VMI's citizen-soldier training. Kept away from the pressures, hazards, and psychological bonding characteristic of VMI's adversative training, VWIL students will not know the "feeling of tremendous accomplishment" commonly experienced by VMI's successful cadets.

Virginia maintains that these methodological differences are "justified pedagogically," based on "important differences between men and women in learning and developmental needs," "psychological and sociological differences" Virginia describes as "real" and "not stereotypes." The Task Force charged with developing the leadership program for women, drawn from the staff and faculty at Mary Baldwin College, "determined that a military model and, especially VMI's adversative method, would be wholly inappropriate for educating and training *most women*" . . . [and noted that] while some women would be suited to and interested in [a VMI-style experience]," VMI's adversative method "would not be effective for *women as a group*." . . .

As earlier stated, generalizations about "the way women are," estimates of what is appropriate for *most women*, no longer justify denying opportunity to women whose talent and capacity place them outside the average description. Notably, Virginia never asserted that VMI's method of education suits *most men*. It is also revealing that Virginia accounted for its failure to make the VWIL experience "the entirely militaristic experience of VMI" on the ground that VWIL "is planned for women who do not necessarily expect to pursue military careers." By that reasoning, VMI's "entirely militaristic" program would be inappropriate for men in general or *as a group*, for "[o]nly about 15% of VMI cadets enter career military service."

In contrast to the generalizations about women on which Virginia rests, we note again these dispositive realities: VMI's "implementing methodology" is not "inherently unsuitable to women," "some women . . . do well under [the] adversative model," "some women, at least, would want to attend [VMI] if they had the opportunity," "some women are capable of all of the individual activities required of VMI cadets," and "can meet the physical standards [VMI] now impose[s] on men." . . .

In myriad respects other than military training, VWIL does not qualify as VMI's equal. VWIL's student body, faculty, course offerings, and facilities hardly match VMI's. Nor can the VWIL graduate anticipate the benefits associated with VMI's 157-year history, the school's prestige, and its influential alumni network.

Mary Baldwin College, whose degree VWIL students will gain, enrolls first-year women with an average combined SAT score about 100 points lower than the average score for VMI freshmen. The Mary Baldwin faculty holds "significantly fewer Ph.D.'s," and receives substantially lower salaries than the faculty at VMI.

Mary Baldwin does not offer a VWIL student the range of curricular choices available to a VMI cadet. VMI awards baccalaureate degrees in liberal arts, biology, chemistry, civil engineering, electrical and computer engineering, and mechanical engineering. . . . VWIL students attend a school that "does not have a math and science focus," they cannot take at Mary Baldwin any courses in engineering or the advanced math and physics courses VMI offers. . . .

For physical training, Mary Baldwin has "two multi-purpose fields" and "[o]ne gymnasium." VMI has "an NCAA competition level indoor track and field facility; a number of multi-purpose fields; baseball, soccer and lacrosse fields; an obstacle course; large boxing, wrestling and martial arts facilities; an 11-laps-to-the-mile indoor running course; an indoor pool; indoor and outdoor rifle ranges; and a football stadium that also contains a practice field and outdoor track."

Although Virginia has represented that it will provide equal financial support for in-state VWIL students and VMI cadets, and the VMI Foundation has agreed to endow VWIL with $5.4625 million, the difference between the two schools' financial reserves is pronounced. Mary Baldwin's endowment, currently about $19 million, will gain an additional $35 million based on future commitments; VMI's current endowment, $131 million—the largest per-student endowment in the Nation—will gain $220 million.

The VWIL student does not graduate with the advantage of a VMI degree. Her diploma does not unite her with the legions of VMI "graduates [who] have distinguished themselves" in military and civilian life. . . . A VWIL graduate cannot assume that the "network of business owners, corporations, VMI graduates and non-graduate employers . . . interested in hiring VMI graduates," will be equally responsive to her search for employment. . . .

Virginia, in sum, while maintaining VMI for men only, has failed to provide any "comparable single-gender women's institution." Instead, the Commonwealth has created a VWIL program fairly appraised as a "pale shadow" of VMI in terms of the range of curricular choices and faculty stature, funding, prestige, alumni support, and influence.

Virginia's VWIL solution is reminiscent of the remedy Texas proposed 50 years ago, in response to a state trial court's 1946 ruling that, given the equal protection guarantee, African Americans could not be denied a legal education at a state facility. . . . Reluctant to admit African Americans to its flagship

University of Texas Law School, the State set up a separate school for Herman Sweatt and other black law students. [In holding that the all-black school was not equivalent to the University of Texas facility, the Court emphasized not only the size of the full-time faculty, library, and extracurricular offerings, but also the alumni network.]

More important than the tangible features, the Court [in *Sweatt*] emphasized, are "those qualities which are incapable of objective measurement but which make for greatness" in a school, including "reputation of the faculty, experience of the administration, position and influence of the alumni, standing in the community, traditions and prestige." Facing the marked differences reported in the *Sweatt* opinion, the Court unanimously ruled that Texas had not shown "substantial equality in the [separate] educational opportunities" the State offered. Accordingly, the Court held, the Equal Protection Clause required Texas to admit African Americans to the University of Texas Law School. In line with *Sweatt*, we rule here that Virginia has not shown substantial equality in the separate educational opportunities the State supports at VWIL and VMI.

[Reversed and remanded.]

Justice SCALIA, dissenting.

Today the Court shuts down an institution that has served the people of the Commonwealth of Virginia with pride and distinction for over a century and a half. To achieve that desired result, it rejects (contrary to our established practice) the factual findings of two courts below, sweeps aside the precedents of this Court, and ignores the history of our people. As to facts: it explicitly rejects the finding that there exist "gender-based developmental differences" supporting Virginia's restriction of the "adversative" method to only a men's institution, and the finding that the all-male composition of the Virginia Military Institute (VMI) is essential to that institution's character. As to precedent: it drastically revises our established standards for reviewing sex-based classifications. And as to history: it counts for nothing the long tradition, enduring down to the present, of men's military colleges supported by both States and the Federal Government.

Much of the Court's opinion is devoted to deprecating the closed-mindedness of our forebears with regard to women's education, and even with regard to the treatment of women in areas that have nothing to do with education. Closed-minded they were—as every age is, including our own, with regard to matters it cannot guess, because it simply does not consider them debatable. The virtue of a democratic system with a First Amendment is that it readily enables the people, over time, to be persuaded that what they took for granted is not so, and to change their laws accordingly. That system is destroyed if the smug assurances of each age are removed from the democratic process and written into the Constitution. So to counterbalance the Court's criticism of our ancestors, let me say a word in their praise: they left us free to change. The same cannot be said of this most illiberal Court, which has embarked on a course of inscribing one after another of the current preferences of the society (and in some cases only the counter-majoritarian preferences of the society's law-trained elite) into our Basic Law. Today it enshrines the notion that no substantial educational value is to be served by an all-men's military academy—so that the decision by the people of Virginia to maintain such an institution denies equal protection to women who cannot attend that institution but can attend others. Since it is entirely clear that the Constitution of the United States—the old one—takes no sides in this educational debate, I dissent.

I . . .

[I]n my view the function of this Court is to *preserve* our society's values regarding (among other things) equal protection, not to *revise* them; to prevent backsliding from the degree of restriction the Constitution imposed upon democratic government, not to prescribe, on our own authority, progressively higher degrees. For that reason it is my view that, whatever abstract tests we may choose to devise, they cannot supersede—and indeed ought to be crafted *so as to reflect*—those constant and unbroken national traditions that embody the people's understanding of ambiguous constitutional texts. More specifically, it is my view that "when a practice not expressly prohibited by the text of the Bill of Rights bears the endorsement of a long tradition of open, widespread, and unchallenged use that dates back to the beginning of the Republic, we have no proper basis for striking it down." . . .

The all-male constitution of VMI comes squarely within such a governing tradition. Founded by the Commonwealth of Virginia in 1839 and continuously maintained by it since, VMI has always admitted only men. And in that regard it has not been unusual. For almost all of VMI's more than a century and a half of existence, its single-sex status reflected the uniform practice for government-supported military colleges. Another famous Southern institution, The Citadel, has existed as a state-funded school of South Carolina since 1842. And all the federal military colleges—West Point, the Naval Academy at Annapolis, and even the Air Force Academy, which was not established until 1954—admitted only males for most of their history. Their admission of women in 1976 (upon which the Court today relies), came not by court decree, but because the people, through their elected representatives, decreed a change. . . . In other words, the tradition of having government-funded military schools for men is as well rooted in the traditions of this country as the tradition of sending only men into military combat. The people may decide to change the one tradition, like the other, through democratic processes; but the assertion that either tradition has been unconstitutional through the centuries is not law, but politics-smuggled-into-law.

And the same applies, more broadly, to single-sex education in general, which, as I shall discuss, is threatened by today's decision with the cut-off of all state and federal support. Government-run *non*military educational institutions for the two sexes have until very recently also been part of our national tradition. "[It is] [c]oeducation, historically, [that] is a novel educational theory. From grade school through high school, college, and graduate and professional training, much of the Nation's population during much of our history has been educated in sexually segregated classrooms." Mississippi Univ. for Women v. Hogan, [1982] (Powell, J., dissenting). These traditions may of course be changed by the democratic decisions of the people, as they largely have been.

Today, however, change is forced upon Virginia, and reversion to single-sex education is prohibited nationwide, not by democratic processes but by order of this Court. Even while bemoaning the sorry, bygone days of "fixed notions" concerning women's education, the Court favors current notions so fixedly that it is willing to write them into the Constitution of the United States by application of custom-built "tests." This is not the interpretation of a Constitution, but the creation of one.

II

To reject the Court's disposition today, however, it is not necessary to accept my view that the Court's made-up tests cannot displace longstanding national traditions as the primary determinant of what the Constitution means. It is only necessary to apply honestly the test the Court has been applying to sex-based classifications for the past two decades. . . . We have denominated this standard "intermediate scrutiny" and under it have inquired whether the statutory classification is "substantially related to an important governmental objective." . . .

Only the amorphous "exceedingly persuasive justification" phrase, and not the standard elaboration of intermediate scrutiny, can be made to yield this conclusion that VMI's single-sex composition is unconstitutional because there exist several women (or, one would have to conclude under the Court's reasoning, a single woman) willing and able to undertake VMI's program. Intermediate scrutiny has never required a least-restrictive-means analysis, but only a "substantial relation" between the classification and the state interests that it serves. . . .

Not content to execute a *de facto* abandonment of the intermediate scrutiny that has been our standard for sex-based classifications for some two decades, the Court purports to reserve the question whether, even in principle, a higher standard (i.e., strict scrutiny) should apply. . . . [The Court's] statements are misleading, insofar as they suggest that we have not already categorically *held* strict scrutiny to be inapplicable to sex-based classifications. . . . And the statements are irresponsible, insofar as they are calculated to destabilize current law. Our task is to clarify the law—not to muddy the waters, and not to exact over-compliance by intimidation. The States and the Federal Government are entitled to know *before they act* the standard to which they will be held, rather than be compelled to guess about the outcome of Supreme Court peek-a-boo.

The Court's intimations are particularly out of place because it is perfectly clear that, if the question of the applicable standard of review for sex-based classifications were to be regarded as an appropriate subject for reconsideration, the stronger argument would be not for elevating the standard to strict scrutiny, but for reducing it to rational-basis review. The latter certainly has a firmer foundation in our past jurisprudence: Whereas no majority of the Court has ever applied strict scrutiny in a case involving sex-based classifications, we routinely applied rational-basis review until the 1970's. . . .

It is hard to consider women a "discrete and insular minorit[y]" unable to employ the "political processes ordinarily to be relied upon," when they constitute a majority of the electorate. And the suggestion that they are incapable of exerting that political power smacks of the same paternalism that the Court so roundly condemns. Moreover, a long list of legislation proves the proposition false. . . .

III . . .

There can be no serious dispute that, as the District Court found, single-sex education and a distinctive educational method "represent legitimate contributions to diversity in the Virginia higher education system." As a theoretical matter, Virginia's educational interest would have been best served (insofar as the two factors we have mentioned are concerned) by six different types of public colleges—an all-men's, an all-women's, and a coeducational college run in the "adversative method," and an all-men's, an all-women's, and a coeducational college run in the "traditional method." But as a practical matter, of course, Virginia's financial resources, like any State's, are not limitless, and the Commonwealth must select among the available options. Virginia thus has decided to fund, in addition to some 14 coeducational 4-year colleges, one college that is run as an all-male school on the adversative model: the Virginia Military Institute.

Virginia did not make this determination regarding the make-up of its public college system on the unrealistic assumption that no other colleges exist. Substantial evidence in the District Court demonstrated that the Commonwealth has long proceeded on the principle that "'[h]igher education resources should be viewed as a whole—public and private'" —because such an approach enhances diversity and because "'it is academic and economic waste to permit unwarranted duplication.'" It is thus significant that, whereas there are "four all-female private [colleges] in Virginia," there is only "one private all-male college," which "indicates that the private sector is providing for th[e] [former] form of education to a much greater extent that it provides for all-male education." In these circumstances, Virginia's election to fund one public all-male institution and one on the adversative model—and to concentrate its resources in a single entity that serves both these interests in diversity—is substantially related to the State's important educational interests. . . .

IV . . .

In an odd sort of way, it is precisely VMI's attachment to such old-fashioned concepts as manly "honor" that has made it, and the system it represents, the target of those who today succeed in abolishing public single-sex education. The record contains a booklet that all first-year VMI students (the so-called "rats") were required to keep in their possession at all times. Near the end there appears the following period-piece, entitled "The Code of a Gentleman":

> Without a strict observance of the fundamental Code of Honor, no man, no matter how "polished," can be considered a gentleman. The honor of a gentleman demands the inviolability of his word, and the incorruptibility of his principles. He is the descendant of the knight, the crusader; he is the defender of the defenseless and the champion of justice . . . or he is not a Gentleman.
>
> A Gentleman . . .
>
> Does not discuss his family affairs in public or with acquaintances.
>
> Does not speak more than casually about his girl friend.
>
> Does not go to a lady's house if he is affected by alcohol. He is temperate in the use of alcohol.
>
> Does not lose his temper; nor exhibit anger, fear, hate, embarrassment, ardor or hilarity in public.
>
> Does not hail a lady from a club window.
>
> A gentleman never discusses the merits or demerits of a lady. Does not mention names exactly as he avoids the mention of what things cost.
>
> Does not borrow money from a friend, except in dire need. Money borrowed is a debt of honor, and must be repaid as promptly as possible. Debts incurred by a deceased parent, brother, sister or grown child are assumed by honorable men as a debt of honor.
>
> Does not display his wealth, money or possessions.
>
> Does not put his manners on and off, whether in the club or in a ballroom. He treats people with courtesy, no matter what their social position may be.
>
> Does not slap strangers on the back nor so much as lay a finger on a lady.
>
> Does not "lick the boots of those above" nor "kick the face of those below him on the social ladder."
>
> Does not take advantage of another's helplessness or ignorance and assumes that no gentleman will take advantage of him.
>
> A Gentleman respects the reserves of others, but demands that others respect those which are his.
>
> A Gentleman can become what he wills to be. . . .

I do not know whether the men of VMI lived by this Code; perhaps not. But it is powerfully impressive that a public institution of higher education still in existence sought to have them do so. I do not think any of us, women included, will be better off for its destruction.

Notes

1. What's at Stake Here?   The *VMI* case started with an anonymous complaint by a northern Virginia female high school student to the U.S. Department of Justice that the school did not accept applications from women. One of the issues in the case was whether women would really attend VMI, although the case record revealed that 347 women had made inquiries about VMI in the two years preceding the lawsuit.[125] Another subject of debate was whether the presence of women would significantly change the school, and eliminate its benefits for men. The government argued that women could thrive at VMI, without changing it. Was this a realistic claim? VMI contended, and the district court agreed, that women would change the fundamental dynamic of the school and ruin what was unique and valuable about it. Was this plausible? Or was it beside the point? Should women be excluded from a public institution simply because their presence might change that institution?

Despite a claim that VMI would not have to change, after the Supreme Court decided the case, the government pressured VMI to make changes to accommodate women, such as more privacy in bedrooms and bathrooms, and less severe haircuts. Was this appropriate?

A case parallel to the *VMI* case was filed against South Carolina's The Citadel, the only other state-supported all-male military college. Unlike the anonymous plaintiff in the VMI case, the case against The Citadel was brought by a named plaintiff, Shannon Faulkner, who had been accidentally admitted to the school because the admissions office did not realize that she was female. While the *VMI* litigation was still working its way through the courts, the Fourth Circuit Court of Appeals issued an injunction requiring her admission to day classes, pending final resolution of the case.[126] Less than a week later, Faulkner dropped out of The Citadel, "overcome by stress and terror as the only woman alone in the barracks with 1800 male cadets, most of whom hated her guts."[127] Physical conditioning was an issue, and some faulted Faulkner's attorneys for not ensuring that she was sufficiently prepared for the ordeal.[128] Other plaintiffs picked up the litigation after Faulkner's withdrawal.[129] The case was not fully resolved until the Supreme Court decided the *VMI* case, at which point The Citadel decided to admit women.

For a short period after the *VMI* case was decided, the school considered giving up its state support, in order to remain all-male. The motion to privatize failed by a 9-8 vote of the Board of Directors. An important factor was that VMI would have needed to raise $250-$300 million in endowment, after VMI alumni had already paid more than $14 million in legal fees, public relations, and payments to VWIL. Another factor was the threat by the Department of Defense to terminate the Reserve Officers' Training Corps (ROTC) at VMI, unless VMI integrated women.[130]

While the exclusion of women from VMI was the central legal issue, another concern, not directly addressed in the parties' briefs or in the Supreme Court decision, was the propriety of the adversative method itself.

> The adversative method, which defined the essence of the institution, was deliberately and pervasively gendered. Its purpose was to create leaders by giving them near-impossible challenges, and then equating success in meeting those challenges with masculinity. Given this purpose, the problem with admitting women to VMI was as much that they might succeed, as that they would fail. As one researcher put it, "if women could perform well on [the rat line], how could it continue to function as evidence of manhood?" Tellingly, sexual references saturated the VMI "official" vocabulary. Every rat was required to memorize such terminology as to "bone," or report someone for a violation; to "bust," or reduce in rank; and "running a period," or "going twenty-eight days without a demerit." To reinforce the machismo ethos, gendered obscenities and hostility toward women . . . served as official motivational techniques in the rat line. . . . Other familiar phrases [included] "raping your virgin ducks" (peeling apart the stiffly starched legs of a new pair of white trousers), [and] "rolling your hay tight as a tampon" (rolling up thin mattress in the morning).[131]

Given this highly gendered system, was VMI's exclusion of women the only constitutional defect? Or should it also be unconstitutional for a state-supported institution to implement such a pedagogy of male superiority, no matter who has access to that institution?

The VWIL program at Mary Baldwin College has consistently enrolled more students than the number of women enrolled at VMI—sometimes more than double. More VWIL graduates receive military commissions, and these women have been serving with distinction.[132] Does this surprise you? Does it indicate the VWIL is actually the superior program for women?

Mary Anne Case visited both VMI and VWIL after the *VMI* decision. She found the "rats" at VMI "a sorry lot—terrified, sweating, shaking, and exhausted . . . they were unable to tell their left feet from their right." By contrast, the female equivalents to rats (nULLS) in the VWIL program were working together, learning the same values of accountability and discipline in a more supporting, encouraging, and non-intimidating environment. She noted, however, that VMI was still the more prestigious, sought-after alternative, even by many women.

> The paradoxes here are many: First, the dominant class, men, have selected what appears to be the less attractive standard for themselves. Second, in part because they have selected it, this standard is assumed unquestionably to be desirable; inquiry into it is generally limited only to how far it will be extended to women. Much less attention is paid to whether the separate standard sought to be applied to women might in fact make some sense for women and men alike.[133]

What do you make of this analysis?

2. Single-Sex Schools at the Elementary and Secondary Level. While the number of women's colleges has declined from 300 in 1960 to about 50 today, single-sex education at the secondary level has increased significantly since the Supreme Court decided United States v. Virginia. In 1995, the nation had only two single-sex public high schools; by 2009 there were 95, and the number of single-sex classrooms is estimated to have grown from about a dozen in 2002 to more than 500 in 40 states in 2011.[134]

Changes in federal regulations reflected and reinforced the interest in single-sex approaches. In 2001, Congress passed the No Child Left Behind Act, which included a clause stating that "funds made available to local educational agencies . . . shall be used for innovative assistance programs, which may include . . . programs to provide same-gender schools and classrooms (consistent with applicable law)."[135] In 2006, the U.S. Department of Education amended its regulations under Title IX to allow elementary and secondary non-vocational schools that receive federal funding to be single-sex as long as there is a "substantially equal" single-sex or coeducational school for students of the excluded sex. They may also offer single-sex classes or extracurricular activities when they are voluntary, substantially related to improving students' educational achievement, as long as a "substantially equal" opportunity is available to the excluded sex. Funding recipients must conduct at least biennial evaluations to ensure that single-sex opportunities are "based on genuine justifications and do not rely on overly broad generalizations about the different talents, capacities, or preferences of either sex to ensure they remain constitutional."[136]

Some of the impetus for the revival of girls-only educational opportunities in the 1990s came from research by the American Association of University Women (AAUW) identifying significant differences between boys and girls as they progress through educational institutions, with girls experiencing a much steeper decline than boys in self-image and in career aspirations, especially those related to math and science:

> Girls, aged eight and nine, are confident, assertive, and feel authoritative about themselves. They emerge from adolescence with a poor self-image, constrained views of their future and their place in society, and much less confidence about themselves and their abilities. Sixty percent of elementary school girls say they are "happy the way I am," a core measure of personal self-esteem. More boys, 67 percent of those surveyed, also strongly agreed with the statement. Over the next eight years, girls' self-esteem falls 31 percentage points, with only 29 percent of high school girls saying they are happy with themselves. Almost half of the high school boys (46 percent) retain their high self-esteem. By high school, this gender gap increases from 7 points to 17 points.[137]

The AAUW findings have been challenged by other experts who claim that the conclusion that schools shortchange girls is based on "soft and slippery issues, like the 'silencing' of girls in the classroom," rather than on educational achievement tests, college entrance and graduation rates, and earnings. Self-esteem measures may in part reflect boys' self-deception, bravado, and immaturity.[138] Moreover, on many measures, female students do better. They receive higher grades and receive more honors in every field but science and sports. On standardized tests, although boys do better in mathematics, science, and geopolitics, the margins are small; girls do better in reading achievement, and surpass boys in writing skills by a significant amount. Boys are also more likely to be at the bottom of their class, or to be assigned to special education programs. Recent statistics show that boys are more likely to repeat a grade, have a learning disability, and create a discipline problem. They also participate less in extracurricular activities and attend college at lower rates than their female counterparts, suggesting a "new gender gap." What can be done about it is less clear.[139]

Also open to dispute is whether single-sex education is likely to address the disadvantages confronting either sex. Advocates argue that male and female students learn differently, and benefit from classrooms that are geared toward their special needs, and that remove the distractions related to sex.[140] Evidence on this point is mixed. Not all studies find fewer distractions or greater academic achievements in single-sex environments, and some school districts have discontinued such initiatives. However, other evidence, including studies of Catholic schools, indicates that single-sex schools significantly benefit some students, particularly those from poor and minority communities.[141] The most comprehensive meta-analysis of existing studies, by the Department of Education and American Institute for Research, found that 41 percent documented advantages, 45 percent found no influence, 8 percent favored coed schools, and 6 percent found mixed effects (positive results for one sex but not the other).[142] Authors of another meta-analysis criticized the "pseudoscience" of single-sex education, arguing that it "is deeply misguided, and often justified by weak, cherry-picked, or misconstrued scientific claims rather than by valid scientific evidence." According to their analysis of existing studies, "[t]here is no well-designed research showing that single-sex education improves students' academic performance, but there is evidence that sex segregation increases stereotyping and legitimizes institutional sexism."[143]

Women's rights groups, including the Women's Rights Project of the American Civil Liberties Union and the National Organization for Women, have opposed single-sex schools and classrooms, and have challenged the Department of Education regulations that allow them. These groups argue that the single-sex model reinforces stereotypes about differences between boys and girls. They also draw on evidence that the positive outcomes from single-sex schooling are due less to the single-sex quality of the school than to other factors, such as student background, small class size, favorable faculty-student ratio, or special mentoring programs—features that could be replicated in coed schools.[144] The AAUW believes "single-sex education without proper attention to civil rights protections can reinforce problematic gender stereotypes, increase discrimination, and restrict the educational opportunities open to both girls and boys. Where separate programs are established for boys and girls, such programs have tended to be distinctly unequal, with fewer resources allocated for girls programs."[145]

In 2012, the ACLU launched a campaign styled "Teach Kids, Not Stereotypes"; the group claims that many single-sex programs violate Title IX and the Equal Protection Clause and has filed complaints against several public school districts. A preliminary report documents widespread instances of reliance on stereotyped attitudes and discredited science, including the idea that "boys are better than girls in math because boys' brains receive several daily 'surges' of testosterone, whereas girls can perform well on tests only a few days per month when they experience 'increased estrogen during the menstrual cycle.'"[146] Is the ACLU right that the 2006 regulations green-lighting the establishment of more single-sex public schools and classes should be repealed?

3. Race and Single-Sex Schooling. Although female students routinely graduate from high school and college at a higher rate than their male counterparts, the most significant disparities in educational achievement are not based on gender but on race, ethnicity, and income levels.[147] In the 1980s and 1990s, the rise in single-sex secondary schools reflected a desire to assist racial and ethnic minorities. During this period, schools for boys in inner-city neighborhoods were founded, and a Young Women's Leadership School in East Harlem was launched. Other urban centers later followed suit. These schools have aimed to increase positive role models, raise self-esteem, and nurture academic values. All-female academies have been especially successful in achieving high levels of college enrollments and low dropout rates.[148] Opinion within the African-American community is mixed, with groups like the NAACP opposing sex-segregated schools, and others welcoming the extra help they might bring to at-risk children who suffer from disproportionate homicide and school dropout rates, as well as poor grades and test performance.

In Garrett v. Board of Education of School District of Detroit, plaintiffs (represented by the ACLU and the NOW Legal Defense and Education Fund) successfully challenged the exclusion of girls from the Detroit all-male academies.[149] A federal district court held that excluding girls served no substantial interest and violated both the federal and the state constitutions, as well as Title IX. Critics of the academies argued that

> the all-male black school is paternalistic. It stigmatizes boys, ignores girls, and brazenly discounts women as capable teachers of boys. In the minds of all-male black school advocates, only males can teach boys to become men.[150]

Is this a fair critique? Data at the time showed that the homicide rate for black males between 18 and 24 in Wayne County, Michigan, was 14 times the national rate, that the dropout rate for males was twice that of females, that boys were suspended three times as often as girls, and that scores on standardized tests were consistently lower.[151] Does this data change the picture?

Explicitly all-black academies would be difficult to sustain under existing race discrimination law, which requires the almost impossible task of showing that these schools are a narrowly tailored means to address specific prior intentional discrimination or to achieve a compelling state purpose.[152] General societal discrimination will not do. As a practical matter, however, given the small number of white residents in most inner-city school districts, de facto racial segregation is common.

Putting Theory Into Practice

2-12. In a footnote to her *VMI* opinion, Justice Ginsburg cites a claim by educational experts that: "The all-male college would be relatively easy to defend if it emerged from a world in which women were established as fully equal to men." Why would such a defense be easy? What would be the important societal justification for single-sex educational institutions in a world of gender equality?

2-13. A female Women's Studies professor at a coeducational college does not let men enroll in her feminist ethics course, arguing that, in her experience, male students inhibit the participation of women. As an alternative for male students, she offers one-on-one tutorials, which about two dozen men have taken since she began teaching in 1966. She is sued by a male student under Title IX, and under the Fourteenth Amendment's Equal Protection Clause. Who should win?

2-14. In 1983, the first public school in the United States was established geared specifically to gay and lesbian adolescents and their problems. The New York City Board of Education is operating the school in conjunction with the Institute for the Protection for Lesbian and Gay Youth (since renamed the Hetrick-Martin Institute)—an advocacy and counseling group for gays and lesbians, financed in part by the City and the State of New York. The Harvey Milk School (named after a gay member of the San Francisco board of supervisors who was shot and killed by a political rival) started with dropouts whose sexual orientation caused them difficulty in "fitting in at conventional high schools," says the director of clinical programs for the institute. "For the most part, the males are overtly effeminate, some are transvestites, and the girls are all tough," said one teacher. "All of them would be targets for abuse in regular schools."[153]

You have been asked to advise community leaders of another major city whether it should open a school based on the Harvey Milk model. Is it legal? Is it a good idea? See Chapter 3 for further discussion of discrimination based on sexual orientation.

2-15. King Abdalaziz University paid Virginia Tech $246,000 to design and operate a faculty development program for teachers from Saudi Arabia. In keeping with the preferences of the University, Virginia Tech created one class for about 30 male faculty members and a separate class for the 30 female faculty members. Eloise Coupey, an associate professor of marketing, filed a sex discrimination complaint.[154] Should she win?

2-16. In the early 1970s, college enrollments in the U.S. were roughly 43 percent female and 57 percent male. Today, these figures are reversed; about 58 percent of students are women. The widening gender gap is especially acute in lower-income categories.[155]

Should it be permissible for a university to enact an affirmative plan to boost male enrollment? Could private schools do the same under Title IX? One admissions officer explained the pressures: "gender balance matters in ways both large and small on a residential college campus. Once you become decidedly female in enrollment, fewer males, and, as it turns out, fewer females find your campus attractive."[156] Does this justify preferential treatment for male applicants? According to another admission officer, such treatment is "not an issue of equity; it's an issue of institutional prerogative [to create] a community that will best serve both the men and the women who elect to be members of that community."[157] Do you agree?

2. School Athletics

Some of the issues raised by single-sex education arise in the context of school athletics. Differences in boys' and girls' experiences with sport begin early and have lasting consequences. Is this justified by biological sex differences? Or is it a matter of stereotyping? What does the equality principle require?

One issue concerns whether school sports teams should be sex-segregated. Separate teams explicitly discriminate on the basis of sex, but they are generally thought to be justified because if female athletes had to compete with male athletes, their opportunities would be more limited. Given the physical differences between the sexes, it seems fair to let girls compete against girls, and boys against boys, as long as they each have equal opportunities to participate in sports. Separate girls' and boys' basketball teams would seem to benefit both. Opportunities may be separate, in other words, as long as they are equal. Is this reasoning consistent with the *VMI* case?

What happens, then, if because of student demand, a school only offers a particular sport to either girls or boys rather than separate teams for each? Should a boy, then, be able to compete for the girls' field hockey team, or a girl for the football team?

Title IX of the Education Amendments of 1972 exempts contact sports from its nondiscrimination provisions,[158] and many courts have assumed that the exemption is reasonable and that it forecloses constitutional claims.[159] However, a handful of judicial decisions in the context of wrestling, football, tennis, cross-country skiing, soccer, and golf have held that federal or state equal protection clauses prohibit the exclusion of girls from both contact and non-contact sports teams, if no girls' team is offered in the sport.[160] In sports like wrestling, some 6,500 women compete on high school teams, largely against male competitors on predominately male teams. These female athletes are not always welcome participants, and some boys have forfeited matches rather than compete against girls.[161] What accounts for this resistance, and how do you think it should be handled?

Another cluster of cases has involved boys suing to be on all-girls teams when there are no teams for boys in the same sport (e.g., volleyball or field hockey). These cases have been generally unsuccessful.[162] Under Title IX, only persons whose athletic opportunities have been limited historically by sex have the right to try out for a team offered to members of the other sex. This restriction has left male athletes with little hope of using Title IX to gain access to sports typically offered only to women, such as field hockey and volleyball. They have generally fared no better with constitutional equal protection rights (federal or state), on the grounds that their exclusion is substantially related to the important purpose of remedying athletic discrimination against girls and protecting their still-limited opportunities. Is this fair?

In an outlier case, the Massachusetts Supreme Judicial Court applied the state's equal rights amendment to permit boys to try out for female-only teams in sports not otherwise available to them such as field hockey.[163] The few boys who did so were often considerably larger, faster, and stronger than their female competitors, and parents, players, and coaches expressed safety as well as fairness concerns. And some team members complained that when "you win, people think it's only because of the boys on your team. It's so defeating."[164] Critics of allowing boys to play on girls' teams question whether such integration rights are fair to girls. For example, average height differences between boys and girls might create an unfair advantage in volleyball, where there is a nearly seven-inch difference in the height of the net used in girls' and boys' games. Skeptics also question whether letting boys onto a girls' team will change the experience of the game for girls, making it less fun and empowering for girls. How would you address these concerns?

Another group of cases involve girls who are especially talented and who want to compete on boys' teams instead of girls' teams where the school offers both (e.g., basketball). Plaintiffs in these cases have not fared well.[165] Title IX limits integration rights to sports that are offered only to one sex; constitutional claims also typically fail where there is already a girls' team in that sport. Should they succeed? Is the existence of a team for each sex a sufficient guarantee of equality for all players? Why might a girl prefer to play on a boys' team?

These two sets of cases are quite different. In the first, boys claim that, *as a group*, they are denied an opportunity that girls have. They lose because if boys were allowed on girls' teams, they could take over the team, and substantially reduce opportunities for girls. In the second, girls seek to be treated *as individuals*, rather than as members of a group. Few will qualify for boys' teams, so their presence will have only a slight impact on opportunities for boys. Are the two types of cases comparable? If the boys lose their claims to participate on girls' teams, should girls also lose their claims to participate on boys' teams?

Some scholars have argued that separate teams are not justified, even on biological terms.[166] Katherine M. Franke, for example, questions the rationality of athletic sex-segregation given studies showing that as a result of women's increased access to coaching, nutrition, fitness, and sports medicine, the gap between men's and women's performance has narrowed. As she notes, between 1964 and 1985, female marathon runners "knocked more than an hour-and-a-half off their running times, while men's times during the same period have decreased by only a few minutes." She predicts that if "the gap between highly trained male and female athletes were to continue to close at the current rate, in thirty to forty years men and women would compete in these sports on an equal basis."[167] Is this plausible? Eileen McDonagh and Laura Pappano argue against "coercive sex segregation in sports," which is embodied in law, custom, and tradition. The key problem they see with this system is

> that these policies are not based on the athletic ability of any particular girl or woman who seeks to "play with the boys," but are based solely on the sex categorization of girls and women as "female." Thus, coercive sex-segregated sports policies prescribe such segregation, regardless of the athletic talent or demonstrated qualifications of any particular girl or woman.[168]

McDonagh and Pappano argue that gender segregation turns primarily on stereotypes rather than physical differences and that separation perpetuates the notion that women's sports are not "real," but rather a watered-down version of men's sports. The norm of separation codifies "historic myths about female physical inferiority and fosters a system which, while offering women more opportunities than ever before, still keeps them from being perceived as equal athletes to men."[169] Deborah Brake counters that neither sex-separation nor integrated teams can solve the dilemma of difference as it plays out in this context:

Neither model is costless. Shifting to a framework that offers coed opportunities for all athletes with no attention to gender could potentially wipe out the biggest gains Title IX has produced: the burgeoning numbers of girls and women who participate in competitive school sports. With gender-blind team selection and competition, the majority of female athletes could well be relegated to second-tier teams or club and intramural games with only token representation at the varsity level. For many girls and women, such a shift would offer fewer paths to the success and status that so many female athletes have achieved under Title IX. Sport as a path to empowerment would become much narrower for most women, if not closed off completely. Although some individual female athletes might be better off with coed teams because of their ability to excel in competition with male athletes, women as a group would likely face diminished opportunities to play sports at the most elite levels.

On the other hand, accommodating gender difference has its costs, too. It reinforces an ideology that has historically been used to justify the outright denial of sports opportunities to women and, more recently, to place a lower value on women's sports. Having separate men's and women's teams risks sending the message that women are inherently lesser athletes. The existence of sex-segregated programs risks identifying female athletes as the second-class citizens of sport. It also sacrifices whatever benefits might be gained by having men and women, and boys and girls, compete with and against one another and the potential transformation in gender relations that might result. As the feminist sport historian Jennifer Hargreaves explains the dilemma, separation can increase women's control over sport, mobilize women to fight for equal resources, and enable them to participate in sports free from male domination, but it also re-creates social gender divisions and can exaggerate sexism, with the message that biological sex, rather than culture, defines athleticism.[1]

This is the classic dilemma of difference, leaving advocates for gender equality damned if they ignore gender and damned if they don't. Title IX negotiates this terrain with a flexible and pragmatic approach. As a starting point, Title IX allows schools to offer separate competitive teams for men and women. But this baseline can be altered in narrow circumstances recognized by Title IX and, in some cases, the U.S. Constitution's equal protection clause. The result is that individual athletes have a right to try out for an opposite-sex team, but only if they meet certain criteria—criteria that strongly favor tryout rights for women over those for men.[170]

How would you resolve this "dilemma of difference"? Does segregation or integration best serve equality?

This section explores additional questions of how to guarantee equality for women in sports within a particular educational institution. What are the obligations of a college or university to make equal opportunities available to men and women in school sports? How is equality to be evaluated: An equal number of spots for men and women on varsity teams? Equal expenditure of

---

1. Jennifer Hargreaves, Sporting Females: Critical Issues in the History and Sociology of Women's Sports (New York: Routledge Press, 1994), 25-34, 207, 208.

resources? Equal prestige? Equal pay for coaches? These questions are complicated by the fact that female students, on average, have shown less interest in competitive athletics than their male classmates. Does this mean that a university is justified in having fewer opportunities for them? Or is it a university's obligation to stimulate women's interest in sports?

These questions were addressed in Cohen v. Brown University, which interprets Title IX to require that the proportion of women served by varsity sports needs to be the same as the proportion of men served, even if that means that the needs of a higher proportion of women interested in sports are met than of men interested in sports. Does this seem fair to you? How would you justify this result?

Reading Questions

1. Are single-sex sports teams defensible in public schools under the *VMI* decision? Is it easier to justify single-sex sports teams than single-sex schools, or are we just more used to them?
2. If single-sex sports teams are constitutionally acceptable, how will equality be judged? Does there have to be a woman's team for every men's team? In the same sport? Do the resources have to be identical? What if twice as many men participate in sports as women?
3. If fewer women than men participate in sports, does the school system have an obligation to undertake efforts to increase women's interest in sports? Does the school system also have an obligation to try to reduce the disparity between men's and women's performance so that, to the extent possible, single-sex teams eventually can be eliminated?

Cohen v. Brown University

101 F.3d 155 (1st Cir. 1996), cert. denied, 520 U.S. 1186 (1997)

BOWNES, Senior Circuit Judge.

This is a class action lawsuit charging Brown University, its president, and its athletics director (collectively "Brown") with discrimination against women in the operation of its intercollegiate athletics program, in violation of Title IX of the Education Amendments of 1972, and its implementing regulations. . . . The plaintiff class comprises all present, future, and potential Brown University women students who participate, seek to participate, and/or are deterred from participating in intercollegiate athletics funded by Brown.

This suit was initiated in response to the demotion in May 1991 of Brown's women's gymnastics and volleyball teams from university-funded varsity status to donor-funded varsity status. Contemporaneously, Brown demoted two men's teams, water polo and golf, from university-funded to donor-funded varsity status. As a consequence of these demotions, all four teams lost, not only their university funding, but most of the support and privileges that accompany university-funded varsity status at Brown.

[Following a bench trial, the district court found Brown to be in violation of Title IX, and ordered a comprehensive plan for compliance be submitted. The court found that the plan submitted was not comprehensive and did not comply with the opinion. The court rejected the plan and ordered Brown to elevate and maintain the women's teams at university-funded varsity status.]

. . . Brown challenges on constitutional and statutory grounds the test employed by the district court in determining whether Brown's intercollegiate athletics program complies with Title IX. . . .

I . . .

As a Division I institution within the National Collegiate Athletic Association ("NCAA") with respect to all sports but football, Brown participates at the highest level of NCAA competition. Brown operates a two-tiered intercollegiate athletics program with respect to funding: although Brown provides the financial resources required to maintain its university-funded varsity teams, donor-funded varsity athletes must themselves raise the funds necessary to support their teams through private donations. The district court found . . . that it is difficult for donor-funded varsity athletes to maintain a level of competitiveness commensurate with their abilities and that these athletes operate at a competitive disadvantage in comparison to university-funded varsity athletes. . . .

Brown's decision to demote the women's volleyball and gymnastics teams and the men's water polo and golf teams from university-funded varsity status was apparently made in response to a university-wide cost-cutting directive. The district court found that Brown saved $62,028 by demoting the women's teams and $15,795 by demoting the men's teams, but that the demotions "did not appreciably affect the athletic participation gender ratio." . . .

Plaintiffs alleged that, at the time of the demotions, the men students at Brown already enjoyed the benefits of a disproportionately large share of both the university resources allocated to athletics and the intercollegiate participation opportunities afforded to student athletes. Thus, plaintiffs contended, what appeared to be the even-handed demotions of two men's and two women's teams, in fact, perpetuated Brown's discriminatory treatment of women in the administration of its intercollegiate athletics program.

The district court . . . summarized the history of athletics at Brown. . . . It found that, in 1993-94, there were 897 students participating in intercollegiate varsity athletics, of which 61.87% (555) were men and 38.13% (342) were women. During the same period, Brown's undergraduate enrollment comprised 5,722 students, of which 48.86% (2,796) were men and 51.14% (2,926) were women. . . . [I]n 1993-94, Brown's intercollegiate athletics program consisted of 32 teams, 16 men's teams and 16 women's teams. Of the university-funded teams, 12 were men's teams and 13 were women's teams; of the donor-funded teams, three were women's teams and four were men's teams. At the time of trial, Brown offered 479 university-funded varsity positions for men, as compared to 312 for women; and 76 donor-funded varsity positions for men, as compared to 30 for women. In 1993-94, then, Brown's varsity program—including both university- and donor-funded sports—afforded over 200 more positions for men than for women. Accordingly, the district court found that Brown maintained a 13.01% disparity between female participation in intercollegiate athletics and female student enrollment, and that "[a]lthough the number of varsity sports offered to men and women are equal, the selection of sports offered to each gender generates far more individual positions for male athletes than for female athletes." . . .

The district court found from extensive testimony that the donor-funded women's gymnastics, women's fencing and women's ski teams, as well as at least one women's club team, the water polo team, had demonstrated the interest and ability to compete at the top varsity level and would benefit from university funding. . . .

The district court did not find that full and effective accommodation of the athletics interests and abilities of Brown's female students would disadvantage Brown's male students.

II

Title IX provides that "[n]o person in the United States shall, on the basis of sex, be excluded from participation in, be denied the benefits of, or be subjected to discrimination under any education program or activity receiving Federal financial assistance." . . . As a private institution that receives federal financial assistance, Brown is required to comply with Title IX.

The agency responsible for administering Title IX is the United States Department of Education, through its Office for Civil Rights. Congress expressly delegated to Department of Education the authority to promulgate regulations for determining whether an athletics program complies with Title IX. . . .

At issue in this appeal is the proper interpretation of the . . . so-called three-part test [developed to implement these regulations], which inquires as follows:

(1) Whether intercollegiate level participation opportunities for male and female students are provided in numbers substantially proportionate to their respective enrollments; or

(2) Where the members of one sex have been and are underrepresented among intercollegiate athletes, whether the institution can show a history and continuing practice of program expansion which is demonstrably responsive to the developing interest and abilities of the members of that sex; or

(3) Where the members of one sex are underrepresented among intercollegiate athletes, and the institution cannot show a continuing practice of program expansion such as that cited above, whether it can be demonstrated that the

interests and abilities of the members of that sex have been fully and effectively accommodated by the present program. . . .

The district court held that, "because Brown maintains a 13.01% disparity between female participation in intercollegiate athletics and female student enrollment, it cannot gain the protection of prong one." Nor did Brown satisfy prong two. While acknowledging that Brown "has an impressive history of program expansion," the district court found that Brown failed to demonstrate that it has "maintained a *continuing practice* of intercollegiate program expansion for women, the underrepresented sex." The court noted further that, because merely reducing program offerings to the overrepresented gender does not constitute program expansion for the underrepresented gender, the fact that Brown has eliminated or demoted several men's teams does not amount to a continuing practice of program expansion for women. As to prong three, the district court found that Brown had not "fully and effectively accommodated the interest and ability of the underrepresented sex 'to the extent necessary to provide equal opportunity in the selection of sports and levels of competition available to members of both sexes.'" . . .

The district court found that Brown predetermines the approximate number of varsity positions available to men and women, and, thus, that "the concept of any measure of unfilled but available athletic slots does not comport with reality." The district court concluded that intercollegiate athletics opportunities "means real opportunities, not illusory ones, and therefore should be measured by counting *actual participants*." . . .

IV . . .

Brown contends that . . . the district court's interpretation and application of the test is irreconcilable with the statute, the regulation, and the agency's interpretation of the law, and effectively renders Title IX an "affirmative action statute" that mandates preferential treatment for women by imposing quotas in excess of women's relative interests and abilities in athletics. . . .

Brown's talismanic incantation of "affirmative action" has no legal application to this case and is not helpful to Brown's cause. . . . Title IX is not an affirmative action statute; it is an anti-discrimination statute. . . . No aspect of the Title IX regime at issue in this case—inclusive of the statute, the relevant regulation, and the pertinent agency documents—mandates gender-based preferences or quotas, or specific timetables for implementing numerical goals.

Like other anti-discrimination statutory schemes, the Title IX regime permits affirmative action. In addition, Title IX, like other anti-discrimination schemes, permits an inference that a significant gender-based statistical disparity may indicate the existence of discrimination. . . .

From the mere fact that a remedy flowing from a judicial determination of discrimination is gender-conscious, it does not follow that the remedy constitutes "affirmative action." Nor does a "reverse discrimination" claim arise every time an anti-discrimination statute is enforced. While some gender-conscious relief may adversely impact one gender—a fact that has not been demonstrated in this case—that alone would not make the relief "affirmative action" or the consequence of that relief "reverse discrimination." . . .

Brown maintains that the district court's decision imposes upon universities the obligation to engage in preferential treatment for women by requiring quotas in excess of women's relative interests and abilities. With respect to prong three, Brown asserts that the district court's interpretation of the word "fully" "requires universities to favor women's teams and treat them better than men's [teams]. . . . forces them to eliminate or cap men's teams. . . . [and] forces universities to impose athletic quotas in excess of relative interests and abilities." . . .

Brown simply ignores the fact that it is required to accommodate fully the interests and abilities of the underrepresented gender, not because the three-part test mandates preferential treatment for women *ab initio*, but because Brown has been found (under prong one) to have allocated its athletics participation opportunities so as to create a significant gender-based disparity with respect to these opportunities, and has failed (under prong two) to show a history and continuing practice of expansion of opportunities for the underrepresented gender. . . .

To adopt [Brown's] relative interests approach would be . . . to . . . entrench and fix by law the significant gender-based disparity in athletics opportunities found by the district court to exist at Brown. . . . According to Brown's relative interests interpretation of the equal accommodation principle, the gender-based disparity in athletics participation opportunities at Brown is due to a lack of interest on the part of its female students, rather than to discrimination, and any attempt to remedy the disparity is, by definition, an unlawful quota. This approach is entirely contrary to "Congress's unmistakably clear mandate that educational institutions not use federal monies to perpetuate gender-based discrimination" . . . and makes it virtually impossible to effectuate Congress's intent to eliminate sex discrimination in intercollegiate athletics. . . .

Interest and ability rarely develop in a vacuum; they evolve as a function of opportunity and experience. The Policy Interpretation recognizes that women's lower rate of participation in athletics reflects women's historical lack of opportunities to participate in sports. . . .

[T]here exists the danger that, rather than providing a true measure of women's interest in sports, statistical evidence purporting to reflect women's interest instead provides only a measure of the very discrimination that is and has been the basis for women's lack of opportunity to participate in sports. Prong three requires some kind of evidence of interest in athletics, and the Title IX framework permits the use of statistical evidence in assessing the level of interest in sports. Nevertheless, to allow a numbers-based lack-of-interest defense to become the instrument of further discrimination against the underrepresented gender would pervert the remedial purpose of Title IX. We conclude that, even if it can be empirically demonstrated that, at a particular time, women have less interest in sports than do men, such evidence, standing alone, cannot justify providing fewer athletics opportunities for women than for men. Furthermore, such evidence is completely irrelevant where, as here, viable and successful women's varsity teams have been demoted or eliminated. . . .

Finally, the tremendous growth in women's participation in sports since Title IX was enacted disproves Brown's argument that women are less interested in sports for reasons unrelated to lack of opportunity. . . .

V . . .

Of course, a remedy that requires an institution to cut, add, or elevate the status of athletes or entire teams may impact the genders differently, but this will be so only if there is a gender-based disparity with respect to athletics opportunities to begin with, which is the only circumstance in which prong three comes into play. Here, however, it has not been shown that Brown's men students will be disadvantaged by the full and effective accommodation of the athletic interests and abilities of its women students. . . .

There can be no doubt that Title IX has changed the face of women's sports as well as our society's interest in and attitude toward women athletes and women's sports. . . . In addition, there is ample evidence that increased athletics participation opportunities for women and young girls, available as a result of Title IX enforcement, have had salutary effects in other areas of societal concern. . . .

Affirmed in part, reversed in part, and remanded for further proceedings. . . .

TORRUELLA, Chief Judge (dissenting). . . .

As Brown rightly argues, the district court's application of the three-prong test requires Brown to allocate its athletic resources to meet the as-yet-unmet interest of a member of the underrepresented sex, women in this case, while simultaneously neglecting any unmet interest among individuals of the over-represented sex. To the extent that the rate of interest in athletics diverges between men and women at any institution, the district court's interpretation would require that such an institution treat an individual male student's athletic interest and an individual female student's athletic interest completely differently: one student's reasonable interest would have to be met, by law, while meeting the other student's interest would only aggravate the lack of proportionality giving rise to the legal duty. "The injury in cases of this kind is that a 'discriminatory classification prevent[s] . . . competition on an equal footing.'" . . . As a result, individual male and female students would be precluded from competing against each other for scarce resources; they would instead compete only against members of their own gender. . . .

A pragmatic overview of the effect of the three-prong test leads me to reject the majority's claim that the three-prong test does not amount to a quota because it involves multiple prongs. In my view it is the result of the test, and not the number of steps involved, that should determine if a quota system exists. Regardless of how many steps are involved, the fact remains that the test requires proportionate participation opportunities for both sexes (prong one) unless one sex is simply not interested in participating (prong three). It seems to me that a quota with an exception for situations in which there are insufficient interested students to allow the school to meet it remains a quota. All of the negative effects of a quota remain, and the school can escape the quota under prong three only by offering preferential treatment to the group that has demonstrated less interest in athletics. . . .

[T]he majority has put the power to control athletics and the provision of athletic resources in the hands of the underrepresented gender. Virtually every other aspect of college life is entrusted to the institution, but athletics has now been carved out as an exception and the university is no longer in full control of its program. Unless the two genders participate equally in athletics, members of the underrepresented sex would have the ability to demand a varsity level team at any time if they can show sufficient interest. Apparently no weight is given to the sustainability of the interest, the cost of the sport, the university's view on the desirability of the sport, and so on. . . .

Notes

1. Title IX and Women's Participation in Sports.   At one time, strenuous physical activity was thought to be harmful to women's reproductive capacities and competition antithetical to their femininity. "Unsexed Amazons" on the playing fields were widely viewed as unattractive, and some physicians worried that they would damage women's delicate nerves and physiques, or drain the "vital forces" necessary for reproduction.[171]

The passage of Title IX reflected the more modern understanding that "girls who play sports have higher self-esteem, less risk of depression, a lower likelihood of engaging in high-risk behaviors, and perform better in school than girls who do not play sports."[172] Girls who participate in sports are also less likely to develop osteoporosis and breast cancer, less likely to have an unintended pregnancy, more likely to graduate from high school, and less likely to engage in an array of health-risk behaviors.[173] Although Title IX enforcement got off to a slow start, it is now widely regarded as having led to substantially increased opportunities for female athletes.[174] Under Title IX, participation in high school sports went from approximately 294,000 girls in 1971 to 3,173,000 in the 2010-2011 school year.[175] Participation in intercollegiate sports went from 32,000 before Title IX to over 191,000 in 2011.[176]

2. Title IX and Women's Interest in Sports.   Since the ruling in *Cohen*, courts have uniformly upheld the three-part test against arguments from defendants that it amounts to reverse discrimination against men who, they argue, are more interested than women in playing sports.[177] Courts have ruled that men, as the overrepresented sex, are not protected by the three-part test, and that the test's focus on expanding opportunities for the underrepresented sex is constitutional. The three-part test has also been applied to high school sports, and the Office for Civil Rights (OCR) has repeatedly rebuffed requests by conservative groups to rescind its application in this context.[178] To the contrary, the OCR continues to actively enforce it against high schools.[179]

Despite courts' upholding of the three-part test, it remains controversial. President George W. Bush's administration made efforts to repeal or water-down the three-part test by making it difficult for women to show unmet interest in sports. In 2005, the OCR issued a policy clarification allowing schools to measure student interest via email surveys, which triggered major criticisms from the NCAA, the Women's Sports Foundation, the National Women's Law Center, and the scholarly community.[180] One objection involves the survey methodology, which targets only current students and infers a lack of interest from a lack of response. Women students who have the interest and ability to play a particular varsity sport are unlikely to attend an institution that fails to offer it. Finally, and most fundamentally, it is charged that this strategy ignores one of the most fundamental lessons of Title IX and related social research; as Billie Jean King has succinctly put it, "interest reflects opportunities."[181] The Bush administration guidance never gained widespread support and was short-lived; the Obama administration rescinded it in 2010.[182] Yet how else, apart from surveys, can institutions show that the interests and abilities of the underrepresented sex have been fully accommodated, as Title IX regulations require?

Some commentators continue to criticize the three-part test for failing to account for women's asserted lower athletic interest levels. Recently, some scholars have criticized the test from a cultural feminist perspective, arguing that the three-part test locks women into a model of sport that is designed for men's interests, and that women's athletic interests are more recreational and less competitive.[183] Do you agree? Are men inherently more interested (or well served by) a hyper-competitive model of sport? How can we know whether gender differences in interest are authentic rather than socially constructed?

3. Affirmative Action or Remedy for Past Discrimination? Is the three-part proportionality test adopted in *Cohen* an example of "affirmative action"? This depends, of course, on what one understands as a neutral fact or given, in relation to which some change might be understood as "affirmative" intervention.

Cohen rejects Brown's claim about the lack of greater women's interest in athletics based on factors controlled by Brown that historically seemed to have contributed to the problem. Scholars have identified numerous ways in which educational institutions have historically contributed to women's lack of interest. These include (1) the dominance of men in leadership positions in college athletics and the relegation of most women to token positions; (2) disparities in hiring, promotion, and pay between male and female coaches and resource inequalities in other expenditures for women's sports; (3) the linkage of sport with masculinity, which is evidenced in training methods built on norms of masculinity ("you throw like a girl"); (4) hostile or demeaning characterizations of female athletes; (5) lesbian-baiting; and (6) the objectification of women in sport (starting with the "quintessentially 'feminine' role" of cheerleaders who "[stand] at the periphery, offering unconditional support for the athletes who play the traditionally masculine role of competing in the primary athletic event").[184] One survey of *Sports Illustrated* coverage found that only 10 percent of the photographs were of women, and half of those were in provocative poses. Many female Olympic athletes appeared only in the swimsuit edition.[185]

Deborah Brake argues:

[N]othing about sports as played in today's educational institutions is "natural"—not even what counts as a "sport." The popularity and revenue-producing potential of a sport is certainly not natural; it is carefully promoted and nurtured by the machinery of college (and professional) athletics. It is a product of countless social and institutional factors, including longstanding and continuing investments in facilities, personnel, programs, recruiting, marketing, and coaching. . . . These investments contribute to a certain image and status of a sport that greatly affect its marketability. The existence of average differences in male and female bodies in height and upper body strength does not "naturally" translate into inequality in markets and spectatorship.[186]

If Brake is right, what can Brown University do to "affirmatively" reverse the effects of its past practices? Should more sports be co-educational?[187] Or would shifting to a coed model of sports only further marginalize female athletes? Are there other ways of structuring sport that would make it more open to women?

4. Title IX and Male Sports.   Over the last quarter century, men's overall participation in high school and college athletics has risen, but half of men's intercollegiate sports have experienced a decline in the number of teams.[188] Is Title IX to blame? Many reductions in sports offerings or team sizes are blamed on Title IX, but experts believe that the decreases are attributable to numerous other factors, such as fluctuations in the popularity of particular sports, and concerns about liability. The number of men's soccer teams, for example, has risen, while the number of gymnastics and wrestling teams has dropped. Experts also cite the escalating expenditures for revenue-producing male sports, particularly football and basketball, for the reductions in other male sports. In these sports, the large roster sizes, scholarships, and coaches' salaries have placed increasing strain on college budgets. At NCAA Division I schools, football and basketball consume three-quarters of male athletic budgets.[189] Although at some schools these sports finance other parts of the athletic budget, according to the most systematic analysis of NCAA data, about 60 percent of these college basketball and football programs operate at a deficit.[190] Still, many schools are reluctant to incur the loss in morale, publicity, reputation, and alumni support that might accompany cutbacks in these sports budgets. Is it reasonable to claim that the unique function of revenue sports make these sports incomparable to other sports for Title IX purposes? Or should efforts be made at the national level to curb the escalating arms' race in expenditures for male football and basketball programs?

5. Allocating Resources Under Title IX.   In addition to requiring equal participation opportunities—the issue litigated in *Cohen*—Title IX also requires equal treatment of men's and women's teams. Some of the litigated cases address matters of unequal scheduling, access to fields, and equipment. For example, one case involved schools that scheduled girls' soccer in the spring, and boys' soccer in the fall, in order to stagger use of field space. As a result of the spring schedule, the girls' team was unable to compete in the New York Regional and State Championships, while the boys' team could compete. The appellate court found that this practice denied equality of athletic opportunity to the female team members, in violation of Title IX.[191]

The most frequent Title IX issue relates to the allocation of resources. Title IX regulations reviewed in *Cohen* make it clear that Title IX does not require that women's sports receive equal expenditures. The allocation of scholarships must match women's participation rates. With respect to athletic programs more generally, however, equality must be measured by consideration of a variety of open-ended factors relating to the availability of teams and levels of competition, equipment, supplies, scheduling, travel, tutoring, locker rooms, practice facilities, housing, publicity, and the like. Women account for 57 percent of college enrollments, but only 42 percent of athletes and 37 percent of program expenditures.[192]

A major problem, say many Title IX advocates, is the federal review policy. The OCR does not audit or monitor the accuracy of data that schools report concerning gender equity, despite widespread evidence of error.[193] Nor does it routinely initiate Title IX compliance review proceedings on its own initiative. As a consequence, many experts worry that gender equity reports have become a "shell game," without strategies for holding the process accountable.[194] The insufficiency of penalties is another widespread concern. Funding cut-offs are available in principle but not in practice. Nor does the OCR routinely pursue other options, such as referral of cases to the Department of Justice for further legal proceedings.[195] Surveyed college administrators have estimated that as many as 80 percent of schools may be out of compliance.[196]

6. Pregnant Student Athletes.   Where do pregnant athletes fit in the male model of sport? This issue was thrust into the public eye in 2007 when ESPN's *Outside the Lines* ran a segment showcasing athletes who lost their athletic scholarships and dropped out of school when they became pregnant.[197] In response to the criticism and controversy that followed, the OCR issued a "Dear Colleague" letter explaining the obligations under Title IX with respect to pregnant athletes.[198] The NCAA, which was taken to task in the ESPN program for not addressing pregnancy in its scholarship or eligibility rules, also took action. In 2008, it amended its scholarship rules to require members to treat pregnancy like other injuries or illnesses, which means that a school cannot withdraw a scholarship based on pregnancy alone.[199] It also issued a model policy on the treatment of pregnant and parenting students that it urges its members to adopt.[200] What would you expect a model policy to include? Should pregnant athletes have any restrictions or be entitled to any accommodations?

7. Title IX and Race.   Girls and women of color have benefited from Title IX, but not as much as their white counterparts.[201] A report by the Women's Sports Foundation revealed that while the participation opportunities for women of color have increased dramatically since the passage of Title IX, they are still underrepresented when compared to enrollment—25 percent of the student body, but under 15 percent of the athletes.[202] One reason for this is that the new sports that schools have added to come into compliance with the three-part test are often "country club" or suburban sports like soccer, lacrosse, golf, and tennis. Women of color are also clustered in certain sports, such as basketball. As Deborah Brake notes, nine out of ten black female athletes are on basketball or track and field teams.[203] Because Title IX has not spurred much growth in these traditional sports, women of color have not benefitted as much from the expansion in participation opportunities. Another problem is that girls of color are concentrated in nearly all-black schools in urban areas; with little offered to boys in those schools, "equality" does not bring many new additions for girls. In contrast, rich, suburban schools with well-funded athletic programs have had to add substantially to the girls' athletic programs to keep up with what is available to boys.[204] Are there any obvious solutions to the racial gap in obtaining the benefits of Title IX?

8. Redefining Sport.   Is equality too limited a concept in college sports, if it means that women's intercollegiate sports will follow the road men's sports have taken? Some recognized early on that Title IX reproduced in female sports the same pressure to produce high visibility and powerhouse teams that is endemic to male sports, rather than to increase participation in intramural and club programs and the promotion of health and well-being of broad numbers of students. Before Title IX, the Association for Intercollegiate Athletics for Women (AIAW) pursued a less competitive model of sport than the NCAA. After passage of Title IX, against which the NCAA had initially opposed, the AIAW successfully managed to swallow up the AIAW and take control over women's sports. This takeover, some have contended, imposed an overly commercial system on a program that had superior athlete-centered, educationally oriented values.[205] Do you agree? Would most female athletes? Could improving opportunities for women mean producing a more cooperative model of sport that better promotes physical and psychological health, teamwork, friendship, and recreation, rather than replicating the "male model"?

Putting Theory Into Practice

2-17. It is typical for coed intramural teams at colleges and universities to have requirements for participation by women in every game (for example, that at least two women be on the field, or in the batting line-up, at all times). What intramural rules exist at your school for, say, softball or soccer? Do they make sense from a gender equality perspective? What type of equality do they help to achieve? What is the cost?

2-18. If the college sponsors female cheerleading teams that sexualize women, is it contributing to women's disadvantages? Or are the women who cheerlead in this form the ones responsible? Is this a gender equity issue?

2-19. Should a boys' wrestling team be required to accept girls if there is no separate girls' team? Should girls' field hockey teams be required to accept boys?

2-20. In the United States, field hockey is typically a girls' sport. But when Keeling Pilaro moved to Long Island from Ireland, where he had been taught to play, he asked to play on the girls' team. As a sixth grader, he was invited to play for the local high school varsity field hockey team. He was a high scorer and earned "all-conference" honors. After two years, he was told that he was now "too skilled" to play for the girls' team. At 4 foot 8 inches tall and 82 pounds, he is no larger than the average female player on his team. The school administrators said they looked only at his skill level, which gives him an "unfair advantage," and decided that his presence was interfering with meaningful athletic opportunities for girls. Should he be allowed to play? Does it matter that he has been playing for two years already?[206]

D. SUBSTANTIVE EQUALITY IN THE FAMILY

To the extent that women's role in the home traditionally limited their opportunities in the world outside it, the family has been seen as a principal site of women's social and economic vulnerability. Under early Anglo-American law, when a woman married, her identity became merged with that of her husband. He assumed an obligation to support his wife and, in return, obtained total control of her property. Because wives lost their separate identity on marriage, they could not form contracts, keep their own earnings, acquire property, or bring their own legal actions.

Gradually, throughout the nineteenth century, legislation known generally as "married women's property acts" loosened these restrictions. However, well into the second half of the twentieth century, family law still disfavored women. Only eight states provided for joint ownership of "community property" acquired during the marriage. In the others, property acquired by husbands and wives typically was the property of the spouse who earned it—the husband in traditional households. As a result, divorced women were often left with little or no property, even what they helped their husbands to acquire. At the same time, husbands typically owed their former wives continuing spousal support (often termed "maintenance" or "alimony"), unless the wife was determined to be at "fault" for the divorce.

Beginning in the late 1960s and 1970s, states began to pass no-fault divorce statutes and "equitable distribution" laws, designed to allow courts to divide property by taking into account a range of factors having to do with child care as well as the economic contributions of both spouses. In 1979, the *Orr* case, excerpted in chapter 1, decided that alimony had to be available on a gender-neutral basis to men as well as women. About the same time, often in the name of "equality," states moved to limit spousal support obligations to shorter periods in an effort to encourage women's economic independence and avoid reinforcing traditional stereotypes about women's role. Many states also moved to reduce the significance of fault in defining post-divorce obligations between the spouses.

With respect to parental rights, traditionally fathers had complete authority over their children, including the right to custody in the event of the parents' divorce. In the nineteenth century, during what is sometimes referred to as the "cult of domesticity," states reversed that practice, creating legal presumptions giving mothers custody unless they were shown to be unfit (due to adultery, drunkenness, neglect, and so forth). In the 1970s, explicit maternal presumptions were largely (although not entirely) eliminated in favor of the gender-neutral "best interests of the child" test.

Modern marriage and custody law reforms have been more controversial than one might expect, because they have limited traditional protections for women without eliminating the economic vulnerability that women experience disproportionately at divorce. Most of the materials in this section explore the tension between formal and substantive equality principles: the desire to promote equal treatment and at the same time to ensure fairness for weaker parties, typically women, at divorce.

It bears emphasis that regulation of the family is primarily a matter of state, not federal, law. State statutes and court decisions vary widely on many questions, making it sometimes difficult to generalize about national trends. The cases and statutes in this section should be viewed as representative of their own time and jurisdiction, but not necessarily of the nation as a whole.

1. The Traditional View

The traditional view of married women is reflected in the reading below by William Blackstone, a well-known eighteenth-century English jurist who undertook to set forth all of English common law. While his treatise does not represent the law in all states in early America, it expresses one of the underlying theories for many of the disabilities faced by married women.

William Blackstone, 1 Commentaries on the Laws of England

*430-431, 432

By marriage, the husband and wife are one person in law: that is, the very being or legal existence of the woman is suspended during the marriage, or at least is incorporated and consolidated into that of the husband; under whose wing, protection, and cover, she performs everything; . . . and her condition during her marriage is called her *coverture*. Upon this principle, of a union of person in husband and wife, depend almost all the legal rights, duties, and disabilities, that either of them acquire by the marriage. I speak not at present of the rights of property, but of such as are merely *personal*. For this reason, a man cannot grant any thing to his wife, or enter into covenant with her; for the grant would be to suppose her separate existence; and to covenant with her would be only to covenant with himself; and therefore it is also generally true, that all compacts made between husband and wife, when single, are voided by the intermarriage. . . . The husband is bound to provide his wife with necessaries by law, as much as himself; and, if she contracts debts for them, he is obliged to pay them; but for anything besides necessaries he is not chargeable. . . . If the wife be injured in her person or her property, she can bring no action for redress without her husband's concurrence, and in his name, as well as her own; neither can she be sued without making the husband a defendant. . . . In criminal prosecutions, it is true, the wife may be indicted and punished separately; for the union is only a civil union. But in trials of any sort they are not allowed to be evidence for, or against, each other. . . .

But though our law in general considers man and wife as one person, yet there are some instances in which she is separately considered; as inferior to him, and acting by his compulsion. And therefore all deeds executed, and acts done, by her, during her coverture, are void; except it be a fine, or the like matter of record, in which case she must be solely and secretly examined, to learn if her act be voluntary. She cannot by will devise lands to her husband, unless under special circumstances; for at the time of making it she is supposed to be under his coercion. And in some felonies, and other inferior crimes, committed by her, through constraint of her husband, the law excuses her; but this extends not to treason or murder.

2. Modern Divorce

The divorce reforms that began in the 1970s had several objectives. One was the elimination of explicit gender distinctions, such as the rule invalidated in *Orr* that only wives could receive alimony and the presumptions favoring mothers in child custody cases. One of the questions explored in the next two sections is the extent to which this move to formal equality promoted or undercut substantive equality between the sexes.

Not all aspects of the divorce reform movement explicitly concerned gender bias. One effort was to remove fault as a significant role in determining entitlement to divorce, custody, division of property, and spousal support. The requirement of fault often resulted in acrimony and false testimony, and was inconsistent with the modern notion of marriage as a complicated private relationship in which legal assignments of blame and innocence were often neither accurate nor constructive. It is not entirely clear whether the reduction of fault as a factor in divorce systematically favored, or disfavored, women. Although divorce is available now in every state on at least one ground that is not fault-based, fault continues to play a role in many divorces. Even in states that have only no-fault grounds for divorce, it is often hard to avoid fault considerations when discretion is permitted in the distribution of property or determination of spousal support.

About half of first marriages today end in divorce. Studies have consistently shown that women and children are, on average, worse off economically after divorce than men, although the extent of the measured disparity has declined over time and varies by study. Research based on the National Survey of Families and Households concluded that women who remain single after divorce now have, on average, only a 14 percent drop in median per capita income, and remarried or cohabiting women only a 3 percent decrease.[207] Women are also less dependent on others for economic support than in the past. Between 1980 and 2001, the percentage of divorced women who reported receiving spousal or child support declined from about one-third to one-fifth.[208]

The three major economic issues at divorce are property distribution, spousal support, and child support. **Property distribution** is a one-time distribution of the assets of the parties at divorce. **Spousal support** is an ongoing obligation of one spouse to the other after divorce. **Child support** is also a continuing obligation of one parent to the other for the support of children, at least until the child reaches the age of majority.

Property Distribution. As noted earlier, the traditional rule in most states (which have what are called "common law property regimes") was that ownership of property at divorce followed title of that property, which in turn usually reflected who earned the money with which the property was purchased.

The title rule caused substantial inequalities in cases where spouses acted as partners during the marriage, both contributing to the value of assets that were assigned at divorce to only one of them, usually the husband.[209] A minority of states have community property regimes that have long considered the earnings of each spouse to be the property of both marriage partners. With respect to property division, most women traditionally were better off at divorce in community property states than they were in common law property states.

Equitable distribution reform swept the nation in the 1970s and 1980s in an effort to promote greater fairness in the division of property. Implicit in most equitable distribution statutes is the principle of a marital partnership, similar to the premise of community property states. This principle assumes an equitable division of responsibility during the marriage, and thus the need for an equitable division of the property at divorce. However, the statutes often try to accommodate competing principles as well. One such principle, contribution, invites consideration of how the assets were acquired, and thus tends to favor the spouse whose earnings or efforts produced the property; the effect of this principle is sometimes relieved by also recognizing the "homemaker contribution" to the partnership. Still another principle—need—emphasizes the spouses' comparative abilities to support themselves after the marriage, and thus favors the more financially dependent spouse.

The law in many jurisdictions recites a range of factors to consider in dividing property "equitably," including contribution, need, and the duration of the marriage. Other states, particularly ones with community property, call for equal division of assets between the parties.

Spousal Support. Traditional theories of spousal support called for compensation to a dependent wife for her divorcing husband's breach of marital vows and responsibilities. With the rise of no-fault divorce, a needs-based rationale supplanted the fault-based rationale. However, commentators have had difficulty constructing a viable theory for why one spouse should be the permanent insurer of the financial security of the other, when modern marriage law generally allows either spouse to terminate the marriage. Need supplies a standard, but not an explanation for obligations that might define the contours of that standard.

The trend in the law has been (1) to disfavor spousal support, preferring to accomplish a "clean break" for the parties through property distribution alone, if possible; and (2) if spousal support is ordered, to favor short term or "rehabilitative" awards designed to get a dependent spouse back on her (or his) feet so that a "clean break" can eventually be accomplished. When need comes into play, courts have applied relatively open ended standards that produce widely varying results. About half of jurisdictions also consider fault in determining entitlement to support.

The American Law Institute proposes to treat spousal support as a return of noneconomic investments in the marital partnership on behalf of the family, investments that would otherwise be irrational or inefficient. The theory of this approach is that spousal support encourages (socially useful) investments in the marriage. The proposal provides for "compensatory spousal payments" to close the post-marriage gap between the parties' earning capacities attributable to lost opportunities by one spouse as a result of investments in the marriage. It uses length of marriage as a multiplier in the income-gap closing formula, thereby serving as a proxy for "lost opportunity." It further increases the amount when the dependent spouse assumed primary caretaking responsibilities for the couple's children during the marriage.[210] Does this approach reinforce marital role specialization? If so, is it good or bad for women?

Child Support. Child support has also been a target of extensive reform. Close to a third of American adults are either payors or beneficiaries of such awards. Traditionally, courts used their discretion in setting amounts, which led to inconsistent and often inadequate payments and increased the number of families needing welfare. In an effort to address these problems, federal law conditions funding of certain state programs on states' adoption of measures to improve the quantity, quality, and enforceability of child support. Among other things, states must have formula guidelines, which act as rebuttable presumptions of amounts owed, and they must implement automatic wage withholding of support payments in most cases. Federal law also provides for the interception of tax refunds, garnishment of federal wages, and locator services for delinquent parents. The Federal Child Support Recovery Act of 1992 makes it a federal crime to cross state lines to avoid payment of child support.

Aggressive state laws have been added to help improve child support collections. At least 15 states provide for the suspension, revocation, or denial of occupational or business licenses of individuals delinquent in their child support obligations. Fifteen states provide for the suspension or revocation of delinquents' driver's licenses. Other statutes provide for the suspension of permanent license plates or motor vehicle registrations, hunting or fishing licenses, and even passports and marriage licenses.

In choosing a formula for determining child support, most state guidelines either take a percentage of the obligor's income (percentage formula) or proportion liability based on the parents' relative incomes (income shares). Under both approaches, the level of support sought to be captured in a child support order is the marginal amount that a parent would be expected to spend on the child if the child still lived with the parent. Policymakers aim for this amount so that, theoretically at least, the obligor is paying only the child's expenses and not those of others in the household where the child primarily lives.

The perceived fairness of child support awards under existing child support formulas depends on the goals one thinks should be achieved and, among other things, the relative earning powers of the two parents. When the parties' incomes are substantially different, and the party with whom the child primarily lives is the lower-earning parent (as is typical), the standard of living enjoyed by the child in his or her primary residence is generally lower, sometimes far lower, than the standard of living enjoyed by the nonresidential parent. When the primary residential parent earns more, the child support order may require substantial sacrifice from the obligor parent in order to subsidize a household that is living quite comfortably. Remarriage of one or both parents further complicates the issue, since it introduces new obligations and/or resources. It is difficult for formulas to ensure results that are both consistent across cases and sensitive to such variations.[211] Some commentators believe that current guidelines mask value choices by treating amounts as technical matters, and often depart from popular intuitions of fairness. For example, percentage formulas that base parents' obligations solely on their own income seems to ignore a factor that surveyed individuals believe is relevant, namely their former spouses' financial resources. And income-shares approaches that allow parents to pay a declining share of their income as that income rises are out of step with popular intuitions that the share should be the same so that children don't experience a significantly lower standard of living in their custodial household than in the payor's household.[212]

Subsequent families pose especially difficult challenges. Should child support be refigured with each new family obligation, so that all children of the parent paying support are receiving equal treatment? Or when parents undertake new family responsibilities should their prior obligations remain intact? Should stepparent income be figured into the calculus? What if remarriage enables one of the parents with support obligations to reduce their work, and thus reduces their income available for support?

Should child support ever change hands when the child spends equal time with both parents? Should it matter whether one family has a substantially higher standard of living? What happens when a parent is laid off or quits and cannot or chooses not to find work at a comparable salary level?[213] These questions are difficult ones for courts, and are not always resolved consistently.

It is relatively easy to make divorce laws formally equal; they simply have to apply the same rules to both sexes. Does equality require more than this? For many women's rights advocates, formal equality does not go far enough to ensure that wives leave marriage on fair and equal terms. They seek equality not in form but in fact—in fair results. Joan Williams, in the reading below, for example, argues that women suffer under equitable distribution laws that take into account the ostensibly sex-neutral factor of whose earnings paid for marital assets. For Williams and other advocates, equality requires sex-neutral rules that ensure that women as a group do not leave marriage worse off than men.

Reading Questions

1. What should be the priority of divorce law? Protecting the mutual expectations of the married couple when they got married? A clean break that encourages parties to get on with their lives? Equality? Justice? Women's autonomy? Self-sufficiency? Holding a guilty party accountable? What consequences follow from each of these possible goals?
2. Is gender neutrality the principle objective of divorce law? Or should courts be trying to equalize the circumstances of the parties at divorce so that they can each make a fresh start on the same basis? If the latter, how should this be done?
3. Toward what economic standard should spousal support aim? As good a standard of living as during the marriage? Basic self-sufficiency? Or something else? Which goal is most likely to advance women's long-term interests? What about fairness to men?

Joan Williams, Do Wives Own Half?
Winning for Wives After **Wendt**

32 Conn. L. Rev. 249, 253, 265-268 (1999)

[D]omesticity's peculiar organization of market work and family work first marginalizes mothers from market work, then limits their access to entitlements based on family work. The result is a system that is inconsistent with our commitment to gender equality, and leads to the widespread impoverishment of mothers and the children who depend on them. . . . [W]e need to deconstruct domesticity and develop in its place a new vision of morality in family life. . . .

The joint property theory begins from the principle that ideal workers who are parents are supported by a flow of family work from the primary caregiver of their children. If the ideal worker's performance depends on a flow of family work from his wife, then "his" wage is the product of two adults: his market work, and her family work. If an asset is produced by two family members, it makes no sense to award ownership to only one of them. We should abandon the "he who earns it, owns it" rule as an outdated expression of coverture, and give the wife half the accumulated family wealth based on her family work, without which that wealth would not have been created.

This is true whether or not the children are in child care. In the vast majority of families, the primary caregiver provides much of the child care even when the children are cared for by relatives, a nanny, or a day care center. Recent studies show that mothers spend three times as much time as fathers interacting with children . . . Even when mothers' caregiving consists in part of finding child care and training and supervising child care workers, this, too, is work: managerial work. Studies show that women still do roughly 80% of the management work, even in families where men contribute substantially to the actual caretaking. We do not refuse to pay managers because their employees "really do all the work"; the same principle should apply to mothers.

The joint property theory has implications both for property division and for alimony. In the context of property division, it explains why wives should jointly own the family wealth, eliminating the unexplained jump in human capital theory between joint ownership and an enumeration of the specific contributions of the wife. It also provides the basis for arguing that the household of the custodial parent, often composed of three people, should have a greater share of family wealth than the household of the noncustodial parent, composed of only one. Certainly, in this context, a 50/50 split should be the floor, not the ceiling. In assessing how to split the family assets of a middle class family, the court should take into consideration how such families use their assets: to buy housing that offers a secure home environment and access to good schools, and to send children to college. Children should not lose these entitlements simply because their parents divorce and fathers prefer to found a new family rather than support the old one. In dividing family property, courts should begin from the principle that parents have the duty to share their wealth with their children. They should award more than 50% of family assets if that is necessary to ensure that the life chances of the family's children, to the extent possible, are unaffected by divorce.

In the context of very large estates consisting of more assets than are required to preserve the expectations of the family's children to decent housing and a good education, the joint property theory mandates a 50/50 split.

In most divorces, the key issue is not property division but human capital. This is true because no rule concerning property division makes much difference in most divorces: in our cash flow society, most families have accumulated few assets. Therefore, the key issue is income sharing: who owns the family wage after divorce. The joint property theory offers a new rationale for income sharing that begins from the observation that—after as well as before the divorce—the father can perform as an ideal worker only because the mother's family work allows him to do so. In an economy where ideal workers need to be supported by a flow of family work, a divorced father can continue to perform as an ideal worker only because his ex-wife continues to support his ability to be one by continuing as the primary caregiver of his children. Evidence of this is that divorced fathers with custody often cannot perform as ideal workers because they lack the flow of family work that supports fathers without custody. The joint property theory mandates not a 50/50 split but an equalization of the standard of living in the post-divorce two households.

Because the joint property theory mandates post-divorce sharing on the basis of its analysis of dependence in the modern family, it avoids the language of partnership and other commercial metaphors. . . .

The joint property theory also is quite different from the established theory that wives deserve half because of their contributions, particularly when lawyers focus on wives' direct contributions to husbands' businesses (as when a wife helps decorate the company offices). The joint property theory shifts the focus away from market work onto family work. The point is not that the wife helped the husband in business development, but that the husband could not have performed as an ideal worker without the marginalization of his wife.

If the joint property regime were put into effect, the next question is when it should end. I have proposed that joint property in wages should equalize the standard of living of the two post-divorce households for the period of the children's dependence, followed by a period of years designed to allow the wife to regain her ability to recover her earning potential (if she is young enough) or save for her future (if she is not). This additional period should be set at one additional year of income sharing for each two years of the marriage. . . . [T]his formula is designed to give the father an incentive to support his former wife's return to nonmarginalized market work: the more she earns, the less income he needs to provide her. The formula also gives the mother herself the incentive to develop a career. Because income sharing does not last for life, mothers who are young enough to do so will have to prepare themselves for a time when income sharing has ended.

Arneault v. Arneault

639 S.E.2d 720 (W. Va. 2006)

DAVIS, Chief Justice. . . .

[The parties divorced after a 33-year marriage that produced two children, now adults.] During the marriage, Mrs. Arneault stayed home with the children until 1990, when she returned to work on a part-time basis as a teacher. In 1995, Mrs. Arneault started her own business as a counselor providing college placement and career consulting services to high school students. While there is discord as to the effort Mrs. Arneault applied to her business, there is no dispute that Mrs. Arneault's business did not generate great income.

Mr. Arneault currently holds the same job position as he did at the time of the divorce. Mr. Arneault is Chairman, President, and Chief Executive Officer of MTR Gaming Group, Inc. (hereinafter "MTR"), which owns and controls Mountaineer Park, Inc., and operates video lottery terminals. Since 1995, Mr. Arneault has worked in Chester, West Virginia, away from the marital home. Prior to the divorce, he returned to Michigan on most weekends. There is no dispute that Mr. Arneault has been responsible for MTR's great success. In return for his achievements, Mr. Arneault has received a lucrative income from MTR, as well as MTR stock. . . .

[T]he family court determined that because Mr. Arneault had contributed significantly to the marital estate, a 50/50 split of the estate would be inequitable. Thus, the family court ordered that the parties' marital estate be divided 35/65, with Mr. Arneault receiving the larger share. . . . Mrs. Arneault now appeals to this Court. . . .

Mrs. Arneault argues that a 50/50 split of the marital estate is appropriate, and that Mr. Arneault has not overcome the presumption of an equal division of the marital property. Conversely, Mr. Arneault avers that his contribution to the marital estate has been so substantial that it would be inequitable to require him to divide the marital estate equally. The family court accepted Mr. Arneault's argument and found that it was unjust to divide equally the vast accumulation of wealth of the marital estate. Therefore, the family court split the marital estate 35/65, and the circuit court affirmed.

In a divorce proceeding, subject to some limitations, all property is considered marital property, which preference is reflected in our case law. . . .

With a few exceptions, all of the parties' property constituted marital property and should have been divided equally absent some compelling reason otherwise. Guidance is provided by . . . [West Virginia law], which provides as follows:

> In the absence of a valid agreement, the court shall presume that all marital property is to be divided equally between the parties, but may alter this distribution, without regard to any attribution of fault to either party which may be alleged or proved in the course of the action, after a consideration of the following:

(1) The extent to which each party has contributed to the acquisition, preservation and maintenance, or increase in value of marital property by monetary contributions, including, but not limited to:

(A) Employment income and other earnings; and
(B) Funds which are separate property.

(2) The extent to which each party has contributed to the acquisition, preservation and maintenance or increase in value of marital property by nonmonetary contributions, including, but not limited to:

(A) Homemaker services;
(B) Child care services;
(C) Labor performed without compensation, or for less than adequate compensation, in a family business or other business entity in which one or both of the parties has an interest;
(D) Labor performed in the actual maintenance or improvement of tangible marital property; and
(E) Labor performed in the management or investment of assets which are marital property.

(3) The extent to which each party expended his or her efforts during the marriage in a manner which limited or decreased such party's income-earning ability or increased the income-earning ability of the other party, including, but not limited to:

(A) Direct or indirect contributions by either party to the education or training of the other party which has increased the income-earning ability of such other party; and
(B) Foregoing by either party of employment or other income-earning activity through an understanding of the parties or at the insistence of the other party.

(4) The extent to which each party, during the marriage, may have conducted himself or herself so as to dissipate or depreciate the value of the marital property of the parties: Provided, That except for a consideration of the economic consequences of conduct as provided for in this subdivision, fault or marital misconduct shall not be considered by the court in determining the proper distribution of marital property.

The [family court] judge explained the rationale for the unequal [65/35] distribution by finding that . . . Mr. Arneault's contributions to the marital estate overwhelmed the contributions made by Mrs. Arneault. Specifically, the family court reasoned as follows:

Having considered the factors enumerated in [the statute], this Court finds that the presumption of equal division has been rebutted. The petitioner's own overwhelming contribution make it completely inequitable to divide the marital estate equally. Equity mandates that the petitioner be awarded a greater percentage of the marital estate. [A]s [Mrs. Arneault's expert] testified, the respondent engaged in service contributions which gave the petitioner the freedom to focus on his business pursuits. Those contributions and the other factors in ¶ 103 create the respondent's entitlement to a portion of the estate. This Court believes her contributions were substantial, but not as overwhelming as the petitioner's contributions. Thus it is equitable that her share of the estate be less, although still substantial, because of her service contributions, and this Court finds equity to require that she receive thirty-five percent (35%) of the marital estate. It is proper that the petitioner must receive an adequate award for his accomplishments, and, at the same time, the respondent be properly rewarded for her contributions to the environment which permitted him to use his personal talents to amass this fortune.

In that same order, the family court further explained that

[t]he petitioner's intelligence and ability are unique to him and the development of these attributes can not [sic] be attributed equally to the petitioner and respondent, regardless of the environment which the respondent created in order to allow the petitioner to achieve the estate that has been amassed. He must be given some additional weight and credit in equitable distribution for existence of those attributes, intelligence, and abilities, which helped him achieve the marital estate currently in question. This Court looks at these personal attributes as substantial service contributions to the marital estate. There are many persons who have obtained an MBA and become a CPA during their marriage, but they have not accomplished nearly the achievements of the petitioner. These achievements go beyond the acquisition of degrees or experience, and must be given additional consideration in equitable distribution.

In essence, it appears that the family court judge believed Mr. Arneault's intelligence and ability led to his great financial success, and while Mrs. Arneault's homemaking and child-rearing duties were substantial they did not compare to Mr. Arneault's contribution to the marital estate. . . .

Significantly, we disagree with the family court's undervaluement of the contributions made to the marital estate by Mrs. Arneault. In essence, the family court found that because Mrs. Arneault's contributions were not monetary in nature, they did not count as substantially as Mr. Arneault's contributions to the marital estate. This idea is contrary to West Virginia jurisprudence. We previously have held:

Under equitable distribution, the contributions of time and effort to the married life of the couple—at home and in the workplace—are valued equally regardless of whether the parties' respective earnings have been equal. Equitable distribution contemplates that parties make their respective contributions to the married life of the parties in that expectation.

We likewise have stated that "general contributions, rather than economic contributions [a]re to be the basis for a distribution" of a marital estate. . . .

The facts of the present case highlight how important the contributions of both parties were to the marital estate. It was conceded that Mr. Arneault and Mrs. Arneault did not have any unusual fortune at the time of their marriage. Mrs. Arneault had recently received an undergraduate degree, and Mr. Arneault earned his undergraduate degree soon after they married. Mrs.

Arneault then earned a masters degree, while Mr. Arneault went on to obtain his CPA license and a masters degree in business administration. The family court found that Mr. Arneault's innate abilities led to the financial wealth of the marital estate. However, the facts illustrate that the opposite is more probable. Mr. Arneault and Mrs. Arneault entered the marriage on fairly equal levels. Mr. Arneault earned a professional license and a graduate degree after the marriage commenced. It is very conceivable that this accumulation of knowledge, after the commencement of the marriage, led to the development of Mr. Arneault's innate abilities.

Even though Mrs. Arneault also had an advanced degree, she abandoned her own career in order to stay home with the couple's children. She also was responsible for the majority of the housework and the maintenance of the marital residence. Her responsibilities were manifestly increased by the fact that Mr. Arneault was completely absent from the marital home during the work week, leaving Mrs. Arneault with even greater responsibilities and household duties than is normally encountered in like circumstances. Rather than the conclusion made by the family court, the facts of this case show it is more likely that Mrs. Arneault's contributions to the marriage are precisely the reason that Mr. Arneault was able to succeed in his work.

While this Court has recognized that there are circumstances in which an unequal distribution of a marital estate is appropriate, this is not one of those cases. . . .

Thus, we conclude that the family court abused its discretion in fixing a 35/65 split of the marital estate. Mr. Arneault's intelligence and financial prowess is not sufficient justification for straying from the presumption of a 50/50 split. . . .

STARCHER, J., dissenting. . . .

This marriage was *not* a standard fifty/fifty marital partnership, where Mrs. Arneault was the homemaker/support mechanism and Mr. Arneault was the income earner outside the home. Although the couple lived together prior to Mr. Arneault's success (which has resulted in this dispute over the MTR Gaming stock), the Arneaults have lived and worked in separate states for more than a decade.

Since 1995, Mrs. Arneault lived in Michigan and Mr. Arneault spent the bulk of his time in West Virginia. He returned to Michigan a few days a week, being actively involved in various activities with his children, including coaching his son's teams in various sports, such as football, wrestling, basketball, and baseball, and performing household duties, while Mrs. Arneault engaged in her counseling business. Mrs. Arneault only visited West Virginia perhaps three times in ten years. The couple's children are now both emancipated adults and Mrs. Arneault, who received her masters' degree in 1971, works in her consulting business, which she has maintained on a full-time basis since 1995. There was no evidence that Mrs. Arneault's choices regarding work were compelled by Mr. Arneault or the couple's circumstances. Rather, since 1995, the couple pursued separate lives in separate states.

There is no evidence to support Mrs. Arneault's assertions that she provided substantial assistance in Mr. Arneault's success with MTR Gaming. For example, there is no evidence of record that Mrs. Arneault was a host for her husband's business functions. . . . Other than residing in the couple's Michigan home while Mr. Arneault toiled in West Virginia, Mrs. Arneault had nothing to do with MTR Gaming, even long after the children had gone to college.

The record is also undisputed that much of MTR's success was due to Mr. Arneault's considerable efforts. The evidence was undisputed that Mr. Arneault is not merely an employee of MTR. He is president, chief executive officer, and chairman of the board of directors. He is also the spokesman and public persona of the corporation. . . . The family court found that Mr. Arneault nearly single-handedly created the gaming industry in West Virginia. Plainly, Mr. Arneault's role in the success of MTR Gaming has been remarkable.

Essentially, Mrs. Arneault makes a "community property" argument, contending that because she was Mr. Arneault's long-time wife, she is automatically entitled to one-half of the stock of a corporation that Mr. Arneault built irrespective of their relative contributions to the corporation.

West Virginia, however, is *not* a "community property" state. Rather, West Virginia is an "equitable distribution" state in which its legislature has prescribed various factors to be considered in making, not an "equal" distribution of marital property, but an "equitable" distribution, based primarily upon the parties' relative contributions. . . .

Mrs. Arneault did almost nothing to refute the substantial evidence presented by Mr. Arneault which supported the thirty-five/sixty-five division of the stock. Consequently, there is a paucity of discussion in the majority opinion regarding her contributions to the marriage or the corporation.

No details are provided about Mrs. Arneault's contributions to MTR Gaming because Mrs. Arneault made no contributions to MTR Gaming. Few details are provided about Mrs. Arneault's contributions to the marital home and child rearing because third parties provided many housekeeping and child-care services, and despite Mr. Arneault's business travel, he shared the parenting duties. There is no evidence that Mrs. Arneault ever sacrificed her career for Mr. Arneault's. Instead, as was noted, Mr. Arneault's career involved great sacrifice on his part in leaving the marital residence to earn a living which allowed Mrs. Arneault to enjoy a comfortable lifestyle and to pursue her far less lucrative business interests. In contrast to the overwhelming evidence of Mr. Arneault's sacrifices, there was no evidence of Mrs. Arneault's sacrifices.

Rather, Mrs. Arneault took the position that as Mr. Arneault's long-time wife, she was automatically entitled to one-half of everything, including the subject stock, and contrary to this Court's previous cases, she argues that the [statutory] factors apply only "in some extraordinary circumstance" or in "peculiar cases."

The statute, of course, does not require a finding that a case is "extraordinary" or "peculiar" before a court can find facts warranting an equitable distribution that is not equal. . . .

While married to Mr. Arneault, Mrs. Arneault reaped the benefits of his success and would be a multi-millionaire under the judgment of the Circuit Court of Hancock County. It is simply inequitable for her also to receive fifty percent of the stock in light of her negligible contribution to the success of the company, merely as the result of her status as his wife. MTR is not a "lottery ticket," the cost of which was purchased with marital funds and the equal division of which would be equitable. Rather, the overwhelming evidence was that Mr. Arneault was the heart and soul of MTR and it was his extraordinary personal efforts that built the company into what it is today. . . .

There are spouses, both husbands and wives, whose contributions to the success of their spouse's businesses are more or less, particularly considering their other contributions to the marriage, such as homemaker services, equal. For those spouses, they absolutely deserve a fifty percent distribution of the value of those businesses. Where one spouse, however, as in the instant case, is so instrumental in building a business, and the other spouse's contributions are relatively insignificant, an unequal distribution of the value of that business is appropriate. Had Mrs. Arneault, in reality, served the role of "corporate spouse" that she alleges, she might be entitled to half of the value of MTR stock.

In most cases, in the ordinary circumstances of divorce—which is that neither party can afford it—a relatively strict application of the presumption of equal distribution may be more appropriate. "Let both parties suffer equally" is not an unreasonable principle. But when the "super rich" start dividing things up, and even a person with the shorter end of the stick will be "rich" after a divorce, then it is less harmful to let the equities have their way. The majority opinion is therefore additionally deficient in its discussion of equitable distribution because it pretends that the enormous wealth that Mr. Arneault has amassed through his work is just like the "house and pension and savings" that ninety-nine percent of us have. . . .

Putting Theory Into Practice

2-21. George has been a highly paid executive for a Fortune 50 company. As a result of his earnings at the time of his divorce from Kate, the couple has $50 million of assets. Kate never worked during the marriage, but she managed the household and did the majority of childrearing for their one child, who is now 30 years old.

Under what sex-neutral principle should the parties' assets be divided? In a similar fact situation, the husband complained about the division of the assets. "The biggest stress of the day for my wife was deciding what to tell the cook to make for dinner. There is a certain class of wealthy women who contribute nothing to the family wealth and then expect 50 percent on divorce. The court says she is entitled to continue the lifestyle you have provided. It's lunacy, absolute lunacy."[214] How would you respond to him?

In another similar case, the wife, who was a classic corporate spouse, rejected a settlement offer of $10 million from her corporate-executive husband whose net worth was close to $100 million. As she explained: "Marriage is a partnership, and I should be entitled to 50 percent. I gave thirty-one years of my life. I loved the defendant. I worked hard and I was very loyal." Although she admitted she could survive on $10 million, she asked "Why should he get $90 million? I entered this marriage as a partner. I don't know when he decided that it was not a partnership. [He] wanted to buy out my partnership, and I didn't want to be bought out. It's like a hostile takeover—he offered me a very small percentage, and I said that's not the price of a buyout."[215] Is her analogy persuasive?

2-22. Mary and Lewis both want to become lawyers and to open up a law practice together in their home town. They do not have enough funds to support themselves while both of them go to law school so they decide that Mary will support the couple as a data systems analyst while Lewis earns his law degree. Afterward, Lewis will support them while Mary goes to law school.

They follow the plan, except that on the day he gets his law degree, Lewis announces to Mary that he has fallen in love with someone else, and he now wants a divorce. They have no assets. Lewis has taken a Wall Street position making $140,000 a year.

What financial rights should Mary have? On what theory of equality should the court decide? What if she no longer wants to go to law school, and instead hopes to be a full-time painter?

2-23. Sanja and Maya divorce when their two children are ages six and eight. Maya has been a stay-at-home mother but will need to return to work now that the parties will be living in two different households. The children will spend an equal number of nights per month with each parent. Maya will be earning about $50,000 annually. Sanja will earn about twice that amount. Should he have to pay child support? What if he is remarrying a woman who is pregnant with his child, who plans to be a full-time homemaker for the new baby and a young son by a previous marriage? What principles for determining the amount of child support would be most fair to all involved?

2-24. J.S. v. J.S. involves a couple who has been married 38 years and has three grown children. The husband is 58, and has earned between $100,000 and $300,000 as a Jaguar dealer. His wife is 57, has a high school degree, and has worked intermittently, but not recently, largely because of health issues. She now receives about $700 in disability, but that is not enough to maintain her at the couple's current upper middle income level. The trial court divided the couple's assets equally and awarded the wife $3,000 a month in maintenance for 10 years. In declining to award permanent spousal support, the court concludes that although such an award "might assuage the Court's conscience for the wife's future financial being, it would do so at the expense of enslaving the historic wage earner to indefinite years of employment beyond any reasonable expected retirement. Only a balance of the realistic needs and abilities of both parties can result in an equitable maintenance determination."[216]

If you were the lawyer for the wife, what would you argue on appeal? If you were on the appellate panel, what would you decide? What factors would be most relevant to your decision?

3. Child Custody

Although today's child custody standards focus on the best interests of the child, mothers continue to have custody of their children the large majority of the time. About 85 percent of current custodial parents are mothers, a percentage largely unchanged over the past decade.[217] The prevailing rule in child custody cases is the best-interests-of-the-child test. This test encompasses a wide range of factors: the "quality of the emotional bonds between parent and child," "the ethical, emotional, and intellectual guidance the parent gives to the child throughout his formative years," the "moral fitness" and "ability" of the parents, and the best way to provide continuity of care. Such criteria have been criticized as overly subjective; they allow judges to act on their own instincts and biases (or those of the experts upon whom they rely), which results in uncertainty, inconsistency, recriminations among parents, and undesirable strategic behavior.[218]

Gender bias has been a particular problem. It can work both ways. Mothers sometimes benefit from traditional stereotypes and gender role expectations, but they also suffer if they fail to conform to idealized views of motherhood, or if fathers exceed the minimal expectations associated with fatherhood. In one case, for example, a father was awarded custody based on his "slightly more active engagement in their children's lives," even though the undisputed evidence showed that the father spent only 9 waking hours per week with the children, as compared with 20 hours by the working mother.[219] Bias against lesbians, mothers with demanding jobs, and wives who have had extra-marital affairs has also been apparent.

The difficulties of a standard focused on the best interests of the child have led many commentators, to support a primary caretaker presumption. Under this presumption, courts would award custody to the parent who has provided the day-to-day care of the child, including (1) preparing and planning of meals; (2) bathing, grooming, and dressing; (3) purchasing, cleaning, and care of clothes; (4) medical care, including nursing and trips to physicians; (5) arranging for social interaction among peers after school; (6) arranging alternative care; (7) putting child to bed at night, attending to child in the middle of the night, and waking child in the morning; (8) disciplining, teaching general manners, and toilet training; (9) educating; and (10) teaching elementary skills. This standard assumes that the best interests of the child favor custody with the primary caretaker, unless the other parent proves otherwise.

The main argument in favor of such a presumption is that it is a more determinate standard than the best interests test, and reduces the possibility of bias, stereotyping, uncertainty, and acrimonious litigation. It is also thought to encourage involvement in childrearing by rewarding parents who have assumed that responsibility. Is this test applied appropriately in the *Patricia Ann S.* case? Does the standard favor mothers, as some have claimed? Is there a better alternative?

In one of the readings below, fathers' rights advocate Ronald Henry criticizes the primary caretaker presumption because it favors mothers—not explicitly, but in practice. Note that Henry's charge takes the same form as claims made in favor of affirmative action and other measures intended to achieve substantive rather than formal equality goals. Analyze the analytical foundations of this critique. Does a primary caretaker presumption perpetuate gender bias, even though it is framed in gender-neutral terms?

Henry argues in favor of a joint custody presumption, a legal trend fueled in the 1980s by fathers' rights groups. Every state today permits some form of joint custody, but the statutory rules vary widely as to its meaning and application. Joint custody can mean physical custody, in which the child shares residences with both parents, or legal custody, in which parents share decision-making authority, but the child resides primarily with one parent. Arguments in favor of joint custody emphasize its potential to reinforce more egalitarian ideals of parenthood and to break down detrimental gender stereotypes. Joint custody can also offer economic and emotional benefits to women, who would have greater flexibility to pursue their own personal and employment interests than if they had sole custody. Critics, however, worry that the custody cases that go to court tend to be the ones that involve high conflict between parents, and those are the cases in which shared physical custody is likely to be detrimental to children.[164] They also object to joint legal custody relationships that give the noncustodial parent, usually the father, power over childrearing decisions without the actual day-to-day responsibility of living with those decisions.

Reading Questions

1. What should be the goal of custody law? How important should gender neutrality be? How important should it be that the child spends an equal amount of time with both parents after divorce?

2. Can you rewrite the primary caretaker presumption so that it is more "fair" to fathers? Is it a better rule?

3. If there is a problem with the *Patricia Ann S.* case, is it because the wrong legal standard is identified, or because that standard is misapplied? Does the court avoid subjective factors in applying this more "objective" standard? On what basis does it decide that neither parent is entitled to primary caretaker status? What are the consequences of that determination?

4. Is the *Patricia Ann S.* result fair to the mother? How important is fairness in custody decisions? How about fairness to the non-custodial father who has spent his time supporting the family? Should children's interests always trump those of their parents? What factors are most important in determining what is best for a child?

Patricia Ann S. v. James Daniel S.

435 S.E.2d 6 (W. Va. 1993)

PER CURIAM

Three children were born of the [parties'] marriage, [who are now ages 14, 11, and 7]. The [mother] was a kindergarten school teacher but left her employment upon the birth of their first child. The [father] is an architect. . . .

The primary issue in this case is the [mother]'s contention that she should be awarded custody of the parties' children. . . .

The parties agree that the guidelines for establishing custody are clearly set forth in Garska v. McCoy, [1981]. We defined primary caretaker . . . in *Garska*, as "that natural or adoptive parent who, until the initiation of divorce proceedings, has been primarily responsible for the caring and nurturing of the child." The law presumes that it is in the best interests of young children to be placed in the custody of the primary caretaker. . . .

It is the circuit court's responsibility to determine which parent is the primary caretaker. . . . In *Garska*, we listed the factors to be considered by the circuit court in making this determination. However, . . . we pointed out, "[i]f the trial court is unable to establish that one parent has clearly taken primary responsibility for the caring and nurturing duties of a child neither party shall have the benefit of the primary caretaker presumption."

It is clear from the evidence that the parties shared the primary caretaker duties as discussed in *Garska*. While the evidence presented established the fact that the [mother] was the homemaker and the [father] was the wage earner, this Court has recognized that the length of time a parent has alone with a child is not determinative of whether the primary caretaker presumption should attach. . . . The [mother] was at home for the children when they would return from school while the [father] would work throughout the day. However, the [father] was also a substantial participant in the child care duties once he came home from work.

With respect to the child care duties, the [mother] testified that she was a night person, meaning she would stay up late at night and sleep later in the morning. As a result, both parties testified that the [father] would be responsible for getting the boys ready for school and fixing their breakfast. Both parties further testified that the [mother] would primarily plan and prepare the evening meals on the weekdays, but on the weekends the [father] would often prepare the evening meals. The parties also testified that they shared the responsibility for getting the children ready for bed each night.

In terms of school and social activities for the children, the evidence is indicative of the fact that both parties were active in their children's social lives. . . . [The mother] participated in PTO (Parent Teacher Organization) meetings and school activities. [A teacher] also testified that the [father] was involved with the children's school activities; and, the [father] testified that he was instrumental in helping the children with their homework in the evenings.

Furthermore, each parent organized and participated in social activities with the children. [The mother] would organize birthday parties for the children, and she would often host pool parties for the children and their friends at the parties' home. On the other hand, the [father] would arrange and participate in camping, hiking, and biking trips as well as other sporting events with the children. . . .

Finally, the evidence suggests that the parties shared in the responsibility of disciplining the children. The [father] admitted that he used a belt to whip the boys, but he stated that he used his hand to whip Jennifer. The [mother], however, stated that she no longer uses the belt to whip the children. Rather, the [mother] testified that she had attended parenting classes, and as a result, she employed a new method of discipline such as taking away the children's privileges and grounding them for their wrongdoings. . . .

[W]e agree . . . that neither party is entitled to the status of primary caretaker because the child care duties were shared equally by the parties. Therefore, the issue of custody properly rests on the best interests of the child. . . .

With this in mind, we turn to the [mother's contention] that the circuit court erred in utilizing psychological expert witnesses prior to the circuit court's determination as to who was entitled to the status of primary caretaker. . . .

[The father] called psychologist, Mari Sullivan Walker, to testify before the family law master. Ms. Walker met with the [father] and the three children for approximately ninety minutes on September 22, 1990. Ms. Walker was of the opinion that the children perceive their father as the more nurturing person rather than their mother. Ms. Walker testified that all three children told her that the [mother] "beat" them. . . . Based upon the children's responses [to her question how they thought life would be with their father versus life with their mother,] Ms. Walker opined that the children have more faith in their father as opposed to their mother whom they were afraid of and with whom they were angry. . . .

Dr. Charles Yeargan, a child psychologist, . . . was initially hired by the [mother], but later the parties agreed to use him as a neutral expert to give his opinion regarding the welfare of the children. In October of 1990, Dr. Yeargan interviewed the entire S. family.

In response to questions asked by [father]'s counsel, Dr. Yeargan stated that he didn't ask the children where and with whom they wanted to live; however, based upon the children's comments, it was Dr. Yeargan's opinion that the children feel emotionally safer with the [father and that they would prefer to live with him].

Dr. Yeargan stated that the children perceive the [father] as emotional and supportive, and the [mother] is perceived as angry. Further, Dr. Yeargan testified that Jennifer told him that if her brothers live with the [father], then that is where she wants to live. Dr. Yeargan also opined that both parents have behavioral traits that they need to work out in order for them to be able to better cope with and relate to their children.

Ultimately, it was Dr. Yeargan's opinion that it was in the best interests of the two boys, Jason and Justin, that they live with the [father]. With respect to Jennifer, Dr. Yeargan admitted he did not have a lot to go on, but he recommended that Jennifer live with her mother because of "the interests of the two different parties," "the activity levels," "the socialization issues" and "the involvements."

Dr. Carl McGraw . . . interviewed all three children, the [father], and the [father]'s mother, because she had been helping care for the children. Dr. McGraw stressed the importance of keeping the children together in order to keep the family unit intact. Dr. McGraw noted that he had difficulty understanding Dr. Yeargan's reasoning for splitting the children between each parent. Dr. McGraw testified that the children told him they felt their mother was mean. Dr. McGraw stated he didn't ask the children who they wanted to live with, but he testified that they were adamant about wanting to live with their father. It was Dr. McGraw's opinion that the children would "have a better chance" if all three of them were to live with the [father], considering the rapport [he] has with [them]. . . .

The circuit court determined that the best interests of the children would be served by awarding custody to the [father]. There was an abundance of evidence presented in this case, which included the testimony of the parties, neighbors, teachers, family members, friends, and psychologists.

[In addition to the psychological testimony,] Jessica Halstead Sharp, a neighbor and friend of the parties, testified that she found the [father] to be loving and nurturing towards the children unlike the [mother] who, in Mrs. Sharp's opinion, had a problem dealing with the children. Mrs. Sharp also stated that, on more than one occasion, she overheard the [mother] calling the children vulgar names.

In addition, Nancy Jo S. and Reese and Ron Webb, Jr. testified that the children interact well with the [father]. However, they all felt the [mother] acted hostile with the children, and thus, the children did not respond well to her. All three witnesses further confirmed Mrs. Sharp's testimony that the [mother] called the children vulgar names, and they added, she used bad language around the children as well. . . .

Jason, the eldest son at fourteen years of age, is old enough to make a decision as to which parent he wants to live with, and the record clearly supports the circuit court's finding that Jason should live with his father. . . . Justin, on the other hand, is eleven years of age and not quite capable of making such a decision, but the evidence supports the circuit court's finding that he should live with his father. In addition, the [mother] admits that there is a lot of hostility between the boys and her, and because of this anger she might not be able to manage them. . . .

However, with respect to Jennifer, we do not believe that the record has been adequately developed. . . .

[W]e hold that the circuit court judge did not abuse his discretion by concluding that the best interests of the two boys would be served by awarding custody to the [father]. With respect to Jennifer, we remand the case to the circuit court for further development of the record in order to determine what is in her best interests. . . .

WORKMAN, CHIEF JUSTICE, dissenting.

The majority opinion marks a sharp departure from the primary caretaker rule which has been a viable and working concept in West Virginia for more than a decade. More disturbing, however, is the determination that it is in the best interests of children to place them in the custody of a parent who has abused both the wife and the children. In doing so, the majority implicitly places its stamp of approval on physical and emotional spousal abuse.

Deaths by domestic violence are increasing dramatically every year in West Virginia, and there is much discussion about the inefficacy of the judicial system in dealing with family violence. But until judicial officers on every level come to a better understanding of the phenomenon of family violence in its finer gradations, the response of the court system will continue to fall short. The majority demonstrates a tragic lack of understanding of the true nature of the dynamics that underlie family violence.

Erosion of Primary Caretaker Presumption

The primary caretaker rule as set forth in Garska v. McCoy . . . has been an important part of domestic relations law . . . for more than twelve years. . . .

> In setting the child custody law in domestic relations cases we are concerned with three practical considerations. First, we are concerned to prevent the issue of custody from being used in an abusive way as a coercive weapon to affect the level of support payments and the outcome of other issues in the underlying divorce proceeding. Where a custody fight emanates from this reprehensible motive the children inevitably become pawns to be sacrificed in what ultimately becomes a very cynical game. Second, in the average divorce

proceeding intelligent determination of relative degrees of fitness requires a precision of measurement which is not possible given the tools available to judges. . . . Third, there is an urgent need in contemporary divorce law for a legal structure upon which a divorcing couple may rely in reaching a settlement . . . .

After stating the rationale for implementing the primary caretaker rule, this Court [in *Garska*] ruled that: "in any custody dispute involving children of tender years it is incumbent upon the circuit court to determine as a threshold question which parent was the primary caretaker parent before the domestic strife giving rise to the proceeding began." . . .

In the instant case, it was clearly an abuse of discretion for the family law master and the circuit court to deny primary caretaker status to the mother. It is unfathomable that a woman who gives up her career (in this case, that of being a kindergarten teacher) to stay home to raise three children does not qualify as the primary caretaker, when as a full-time stay-at-home mother she breast-fed all three children; was so concerned about unnecessary additives and excess sugar that she processed her own baby food; was responsible for the majority of meal planning and preparation; was primarily responsible for laundering the family's clothing and housecleaning; was a Girl Scout troop leader; was a regular volunteer at her children's school and an active member of the parent-teacher organization; was responsible for scheduling and taking the children to their medical appointments; and was primarily responsible for managing the children's social activities. For some unarticulated reason, both the family law master and the circuit court appear to have been bowled over by the fact that the father helped in the evenings and weekends. Not unlike many modern fathers, the [father] did participate in some of the household and childrearing responsibilities. The mother and father jointly oversaw the bedtime routine of the children. Upon the birth of the third child, the father, by agreement of the parties, awoke the two oldest children and prepared their breakfasts, because the baby (Jennifer) was up a lot at night. As Jennifer grew older and began sleeping all night, the parties continued this routine. Although the mother stayed up late, during those evening hours she cleaned up from dinner, prepared lunches for the children to take to school the next day, and did other household duties. The [father] planned recreational activities such as camping and hiking trips, primarily for the boys. Given the father's admitted ten to twelve-hour work days combined with frequent business trips which took him away from home, it is difficult to conceive how he could ever qualify as having equal caretaking responsibility. The family law master and circuit court's conclusions that neither individual qualified as the primary caretaker has the effect of somehow elevating the father's necessarily limited hours with the children, given his lengthy work days, to accord him the same caretaker status as the full-time stay-at-home mother. The majority in essence places a higher value on a father's time and contribution.

By upholding the circuit court's ruling, the majority begins an erosion of the primary caretaker rule, or at least sends a signal to domestic relations practitioners that it will be situationally ignored when expedient. . . . Sadly, . . . this case boils down to . . . one expert versus another [which the primary caretaker presumption was intended to avoid.] We explained the dangers of relying on expert testimony in custody cases in [a previous case]:

> Expert witnesses are, after all, very much like lawyers: They are paid to take a set of facts from which different inferences may be drawn and to characterize those facts so that a particular conclusion follows. There are indeed cases in which a mother or father may appear competent on the surface, only to be exposed after perfunctory inquiry as a child abuser. . . . When both parents are good parents, the battle of the experts can result only in gibberish.

In this case, the testimony of three expert witnesses was admitted. Only one of the three, Dr. Charles Yeargan, was deemed by the court to be an independent expert. The [father] sought out Dr. Mari Walker, who has since been disciplined by the West Virginia Psychological Association for violation of the ethical principles of the American Psychological Association for her testimony in this case [that is, making a recommendation that the father receive temporary custody of the children on the basis of a single ninety-minute interview]. Later, the [father] sought out another expert, Dr. Carl McGraw, who concurred with the findings of Dr. Walker that custody should be placed with the father. Of primary interest to Dr. McGraw was his concern that the children not be split up among the parents. While this is certainly a laudable concern, it appears that this focus may have totally overshadowed Dr. McGraw's "objectivity" with regard to his ultimate recommendation. . . .

The family law master and circuit court . . . erred by permitting testimony on the issue of the relative fitness of the parties. Fitness, once it has properly been raised, does not involve a comparison of the parties, but instead requires a showing that the individual designated as the primary caretaker is unfit. . . . Because there was no showing of unfitness on the part of the mother, who clearly qualified as the primary caretaker, the majority opinion does great disservice to the primary caretaker rule in addition to exacerbating the pain of this family. . . .

Majority Okays Spousal Abuse

This father not only takes a belt to the three children regularly, but he also has taken a belt to his wife. Phenomenally, the family law master did not permit the wife to testify in detail to the physical abuse she endured throughout the marriage, as he apparently concluded it had nothing to do with the children. In fact, spousal abuse has a tremendous impact on children [in terms of both direct physical and psychological injuries to children, and the vulture of violence it breeds in future generations. Abused children are at great risk of becoming abusive parents.] . . .

There is yet another aspect of spousal abuse that judges and many others find difficult to understand. These relationships are characterized not only by physical abuse, but also by repeated humiliation and other psychological abuse that "'reaches the level of a campaign to reduce the partner's sense of self-worth and to maintain control'" [;] and "a pattern on the part of the abusive partner to control the victim's daily actions...."...

It is clear from Mr. S.'s testimony that he ran this family with an iron hand, a significant trait in abusive relationships being the total power and control of one party. The evidence reflects that for some period of time Mrs. S. was not allowed to have a cent, not even grocery money. She was permitted to write a grocery list, and if her husband was ever-so-gracious, he would include her requests.... Once she attempted to take $20 from his wallet and wound up in the emergency room after he wrestled with her over it. Mr. S. testified that he actually found the whole episode rather humorous, likening his wife clinging desperately to the $20 bill by hiding it in her mouth as resembling a lizard with lettuce sticking out of its mouth.

One of the complaints made about this mother is that she lacked the ability to manage the boys, ages twelve and ten at the time of the hearings, and surely the record is clear that it was difficult for her to manage these boys, especially Jason, the older of the two. In her petition for review, she pointed out that for several years, her husband had been "mentally, emotionally, and physically cruel" to her. Studies demonstrate that after ages five or six, children show strong indications of identifying with the aggressor and losing respect for the mother....

In her personal petition for review to the circuit court, she [the mother] stated:

> My two boys in particular identify with their father. Unfortunately, their father has downgraded me for years in front of them and continues to do so. I would become angry in response. The children have seen their father hit me with a belt. My oldest son Jason has bit me and kicked me so hard to have left bruises on me. Jason repeats to me in arguments what his father tells him happens in court.... My second son Justin is ten years old and is having difficulty adjusting. Since he has been with his father, his grades have gone from "A's" and "B's" to some "C's," "D's," and one "F." My six year old daughter, Jennifer is a 4.0 student in first grade. She is also in the gifted program. She has done fine under my care alone this past year.

The evidence reflects that Mr. S. modelled for these children the behavior of demeaning, discrediting, and otherwise disempowering the mother. For example, the father devised a point system to reward good behavior and punish bad behavior. When the mother attempted to participate in the system as a method of encouraging good behavior and managing the children, the children were told that "mommy's points don't count" and "mommy is crazy." The mother testified that the children's response was that "you're not the boss, daddy's the boss...." Furthermore, the father would tally the points and take the children to the toy store for the payoff, which the mother had no financial resources to do....

From Dr. Yeargan's report:

> Mr. S. reported that he can't see himself trying to tell the boys to be kinder and gentler to their mother for fear that he'll lose credibility with them. He said, "I'm not too interested in finding a way to help the enemy camp look good or better . . . until all three kids are together and this is resolved. My primary objective is to have the three kids."

Mrs. S. testified that she attended counselling, both in an effort to save the marriage and in an effort to get help in working with the children, and that she read a number of books on parenting and divorce. She admitted that she used bad language (as did the whole family) and that the husband's constant demeaning of her in front of the children made her angry. She acknowledged she had made mistakes and was working to correct them.

Mr. S., however, presents himself as the perfect father as demonstrated by his testimony that his rapport with the children was "exemplary," and "that it would be very difficult to improve upon." He described himself as "nurturing," "kind," "loving," "caring," "understanding," and "patient."

But a look at Dr. Yeargan's report presents a very different picture of this man:

> Some of the same parental behaviors that previously contributed to the children feeling torn between parents is continuing; those behaviors are (a) increasing the alienation between the children and their mother and (b) exacerbating the loneliness which the boys feel for their sister and vice versa. In this examiner's opinion the behaviors of Mr. [S.] . . . are of primary importance in the creation of more alienation and loneliness in the children. . . .

Mr. S. acknowledges that (although less frequently on five-year-old Jennifer), yes, he does use a belt on all three children, and according to unrefuted testimony he also has grabbed Jason by the shoulders and banged Jason's head against a tree. His own description of how he handles physical discipline shows best the kind of fear he uses to exert control over this family:

> Normally, the punishment is a smack on the behind with a belt. And I tell them what will happen if they transgress or exceed certain limitations; and, when they, on occasion—not recently, but on occasion—test an adult's authority, which all children are want (sic) to do, I have no choice but to follow through consistently with what I told them would happen. . . .

> On the occasions when I do smack their behinds with a belt, I will always make sure, after I have done it in a controlled and unemotional way—never in anger—that they understand what the punishment was for and why I had to do it, and I will always check their little bottoms to make sure that there is not sufficient force to seriously damage them, say bruising or whatever.

With all of these circumstances, one may wonder why the children were taken from the mother. A close reading of the record reveals that the most damaging things that can be said about Mrs. S. are that 1) she uses bad language;

2) she is very angry; 3) the children told the psychologists that they wanted to live with their father; and 4) one of the psychologists concluded that they "feel safer with their father."

Anger

What judges and indeed many therapists usually fail to understand is the behavior manifestations battered women frequently demonstrate. . . . Psychologists unfamiliar with all the circumstances and with the unique dynamics of family abuse may make these mistakes:

> 1. They fail to see that the victim's anger is appropriate and normal. . . . 2. They look to the victim's behavior and personality problems to explain the abuse. . . . Such blaming of the victim tends to reinforce the abuser's position that . . . the victim is crazy. 3. They seem to identify with the seemingly sociable, "appropriate" male as a man who has been pushed beyond his limits by an "angry woman." 4. They fail to see beneath the sincere, positive image of the abuser, but look instead for the "typical" abuser personality. . . . 7. Finally, they criticize [the woman] for focusing her anger on her husband. . . .

It does not appear that any of the psychologists had any information on the domestic abuse and none dealt with the physical abuse; only Dr. Yeargan seems to have had any information on the psychological abuse and domination. If family law masters and judges are to make decisions on the lives of troubled families, they must become sufficiently knowledgeable about physical and emotional domination to enable them to recognize that these factors are just as invidious, and probably more pervasive, than physical abuse alone. And we must begin to see anger on the part of the victim as healthy.

Children's Preference

These children learned from their father that their mother did not have even sufficient authority to purchase a package of Oreo cookies for them, that it was okay to demean, disobey, and verbally abuse her, and that physical violence awaited those who did not do as he said. The mother reacted with anger, and the father by word, deed, and dollar delivered the message that mommy's crazy and mommy's contemptible.

Jason was twelve years old at the time of the hearings before the family law master and thirteen by the time of the divorce. . . . Consequently, even though the mother was the primary caretaker, the circuit court cannot be said to have abused its discretion in giving weight to Jason's preference and placing him in the custody of his father. In all likelihood, and by all the evidence, this young man has already demonstrated a propensity to act out anger with violence, and we can only hope we do not see him in court in another generation.

Justin was ten years old and Jennifer six years old at the time their preferences were expressed. Although it could be argued that a ten-year-old's preference could be given some weight, Jennifer at six was too young to express a meaningful preference. Furthermore, a reading of the record makes it quite clear that Jennifer was spirited off to see psychologists by her father and instructed rather specifically on the way by her father and older brother regarding what to say. She related to her mother after-the-fact that she told lies and even Dr. Yeargan discerned that she had been coached.

Justin and Jennifer should have been placed in the custody of their mother. The majority wreaks further havoc on this family (especially Jennifer) by a remand for further evidence. It appears that anxiety and manipulation will again be the order of the day for this little girl, and life's most basic uncertainties will resume as the family is figuratively killed with due process. . . .

Ronald K. Henry, "Primary Caretaker": Is It a Ruse?

17 Fam. Advoc. 53, 53-56 (Summer 1994)

"Primary caretaker" is a warm, fuzzy phrase with a superficial appeal. Like all legal terms, however, the substance is in the definition; every definition that has been put forward for this term has systematically counted and recounted the types of tasks mothers most often perform while systematically excluding the ways that fathers most often nurture their children. No effort has been made to hide this bias.

In fact, in some definitions, the very first credit on the list of factors to be considered goes to that parent, regardless of gender, "who has devoted significantly greater time and effort than the other to . . . breast-feeding." The duration of the credit extended to the parent who has performed such services is unlimited according to some definitions, despite the obvious fact that an historic role as breast-feeder has little relevance to the determination of custody of an adolescent who is contemplating the merits of rival street gangs. The more fundamental problem, of course, is the lack of any consideration for the father's efforts on behalf of the child and his involvement throughout the child's life. No one seriously disputes the role of father absence in street gang formation, teenage pregnancy, and other pathologies. Yet, the primary caretaker theory remains fixated on "mothering" and ignores "fathering."

The primary caretaker theory aggressively asserts that traditional "men's work" is irrelevant. The typical definition of the primary caretaker gives credit for shopping but not for earning the money that permits the shopping; for laundering the Little League uniform but not for developing the interest in baseball; for vacuuming the floors but not for cutting the grass; and for chauffeuring the children, but not for driving to work. . . .

Generally, the tasks that count in accumulating primary caretaker points do not involve great skill or invoke debates about hormonal determination. For example, points are usually given for planning and preparing meals. In our house, the 8-year-old loves canned spaghetti in ABC shapes; the 6-year-old hates the ABCs and loves the Ninja Turtles; and the 3-year-old can finger paint equally well with either. To establish a custody preference on the basis of opened-can counts is an affront to all parents and hardly squares with our understanding that many women entered the paid workforce precisely because they were stupefied by the mindless tasks of daily child care.

Most unreasonable is the contempt for paid work that is apparent in the primary caretaker theory. Although time spent shopping counts, time spent doing work for pay does not. Often, grocery shopping, clothes shopping, and other shopping are counted separately. A single afternoon of shopping may be counted several times over, yet the paid work that makes the shopping possible is not counted at all. Which parent is really providing for the child's needs?

Going to work requires a parent's devotion and sacrifice. It is obscene to say that spending is nurturing while earning is mere, heartless cash waiting to be transferred under a child support order. I don't know any parent who is incapable of earning. Which is the better care giver?

In any childless, two-adult household, there is a division of the tasks necessary to simply carry on with life. Cooking, cleaning, and shopping are not counted as child care in a childless home any more than paid work, yard maintenance, and home repairs are so counted. The nature of these tasks does not change with the introduction of a child. Instead, all of the tasks—specifically *including* paid work—collectively support the child's environment.

The gender bias that is inherent in the primary caretaker theory is its insistence that the types of tasks most often performed by women—regardless of the presence of children—are more worthy than those most often performed by men. A child may increase the "task burden" in the household, but it does not cause one adult or one subset of tasks to suddenly become more valuable than the other: For every mother who reduces her hours doing paid work because of a "devotion to the child," there is a father who must increase his. . . .

Additionally, with an ever-increasing number of two-career couples, the primary caretaker is likely to be a day-care center. Should the day-care center be awarded custody? . . .

Even if it were possible to remove the gender bias from the selection of "primary care" factors, the theory still suffers from the fact the its "freeze frame" analysis of who-did-what during the marriage ignores the reality that children's needs change. The best breastfeeder may be a lousy soccer coach, math tutor, or spaghetti-can opener.

The historical division of labor during a marriage also says nothing about the abilities of the parents and their actual behavior before or after the marriage. Just as mom and dad had to fend for themselves before the marriage, so also will they be compelled to fend for themselves after the divorce. The "primary caretaker" father will have to get a job. The "wage slave" mother will have to cook more meals and wash her own laundry. Similarly, each will have to provide for the needs of the children during their periods of residence. We know this is necessary and we know that it happens even in cases of the minimalist "standard" visitation order.

The allocation of tasks that existed during the marriage necessarily must change upon divorce. The agreed specialization of labor during the joint enterprise of marriage cannot continue after divorce. Each former spouse will have to perform the full range of tasks, and the difficulties encountered by the former full-time homemaker who must now learn to earn a wage have been a central concern of feminists. The primary caretaker theory, with its imposition of single parent burdens upon the spouse least able to cope with the need for earning a living is thus tangibly damaging to the very class that its bias aims to aid. As growing number of leading feminists have come to understand [citing Karen DeCrow, former president of the National Organization for Women]:

> Shared parenting is not only fair to men and to children, it is the best option for women. After observing women's rights and responsibilities for more than a quarter-century of feminist activism, I conclude that shared parenting is great for women, giving time and opportunity for female parents to pursue education, training, jobs, careers, professions and leisure.
>
> There is nothing scientific, logical or rational to excluding the men, and forever holding the women and children, as if in swaddling clothes themselves, in eternal loving bondage. Most of us have acknowledged that women can do everything that men can do. It is now time to acknowledge that men can do everything women can do. . . .

No one will argue that America suffers from an excess of good parenting. Why, then, do we focus on finding easier ways to place children in single parent custody? The focus, instead, should be on developing a structure that demilitarizes divorce, that gets past winner-loser dichotomies, and that encourages the maximum continued involvement of both parents.

Children are born with and need two parents. In all but the small number of cases that involve a pathological parent, courts should strive to strengthen the child's relationship with both. If distance or other factors prevent substantially equal relationships, preference should be given to the parent who shows the greater willingness and ability to cooperate and nurture the child's relationship with the other parent.

In re Marriage of Elser

895 P.2d 619 (Mont. 1995)

Justice KARLA M. GRAY delivered the opinion of the court.

Cindy Ann Ansell . . . appeals from the findings, conclusions, and order . . . denying her motion for an order permitting her to remove her minor children to a permanent residence outside of Montana and granting Dan Roy Elser's (Dan) motion to appoint him primary residential custodian if Cindy proceeds with her relocation. We affirm.

The District Court dissolved Cindy's and Dan's marriage via a final decree of dissolution dated November 17, 1993. Pursuant to the terms of a separation agreement incorporated into the final decree, Cindy and Dan were awarded joint custody of Amber and Jaimie, their two minor daughters; Cindy was designated the children's primary residential custodian. Dan was granted visitation rights on alternating weekends and major holidays, residential custody for two months in the winter, and any other visitation agreed to by Cindy and Dan which would not interfere with the children's education and social activities. The separation agreement also provided that "neither party shall remove any of the minor children to a permanent residence outside the State of Montana without the other party's prior written consent or prior approval of a court having proper jurisdiction over the minor children. . . ."

Cindy resided in Hamilton with the children after the dissolution; Dan maintained a residence in Corvallis. Cindy, a radiology assistant, desired to continue her education and applied for admission to the radiology technician program at St. Patrick's Hospital in Missoula. After St. Patrick's denied her application, Cindy notified Dan of her intention to relocate with the children to Kansas and enroll in the University of Kansas' radiology technician program. Dan refused to consent to the relocation.

Cindy moved the District Court for an order permitting her to remove the children to a permanent residence outside of Montana. She included a proposed visitation modification whereby Dan would be allowed to have his two-month custody of the girls during the summer instead of the winter and visitation on alternating major holidays. Dan objected to the children's relocation and moved the court to designate him as their primary residential custodian in the event Cindy relocated out of state. The District Court denied Cindy's motion and ordered that Dan would become the children's primary residential custodian in the event Cindy left Montana. Cindy appeals. . . .

[T]he District Court's ruling on both motions ultimately rested on application of the best interest of the children standard. . . . [W]e need only review its findings that the move to Kansas is not in the children's best interests. Cindy argues that the record supports findings that spending time with the children was not a priority for Dan and that he could have spent much more time with the children. . . .

[However,] the District Court first found that the high cost of travel and the impossibility of scheduling a time which coordinated with the children's school schedule and Dan's work schedule would deprive Dan of meaningful custody and visitation. It also found that Dan was committed to being an active parent who was involved with his children as much as possible and that Cindy agreed with Dan that it was important for the children to visit with Dan. Based on these findings, the District Court ultimately found that moving to Kansas was not in the children's best interest.

Ample evidence supports the court's finding that the children's school schedule and Dan's work schedule would make scheduling Dan's two-month extended visitation during the summer impossible. Dan testified that he performs seasonal highway construction work from April through November in Montana and Idaho. He typically works twelve to eighteen hours a day, five or six days a week. He travels home to Corvallis on Friday, arriving sometime early Saturday morning. The remainder of his April through November weekends are spent doing laundry, catching up on sleep and, on Sunday afternoon, traveling back to the work site. Moreover, although Cindy acknowledged the importance of the children spending time with Dan, she conceded that the right to an extended visitation during the summer months—as she proposed in conjunction with her motion to relocate the children to Kansas—would be meaningless to Dan because of his work schedule. She also acknowledged that extended visitation during the winter months would be impossible from the children's standpoint because of their school schedules and that the relocation effectively would limit Dan's visitation to one week at Christmas.

The court also found that the high cost of travel would contribute to the impact Cindy's proposed move would have on Dan's ability to spend time with his children. Dan and Cindy approximated the airfare between Montana and Kansas at $1,000 and testified that neither of them makes a great deal of money. Dan stated that he could only afford one trip a year for the children to Montana. Cindy speculated that she could purchase one ticket per child per year, but did not commit to paying for any of the children's transportation for visitation.

The evidence also supported the court's determination that Dan is committed to being an active parent. The record reflects both Dan's belief in the importance of spending as much time as possible with his children and that he visited them nearly every other weekend and as often as permitted by his work schedule. Furthermore, Dan's concern about the children's welfare was supported by the fact that, although he has experienced financial difficulty, he continued to make child support payments and, at Cindy's request, paid the entire amount owed to the children's day care and school so they could continue attending.

We conclude that substantial evidence supports the District Court's finding that the proposed relocation to Kansas was not in the children's best interest.

Affirmed.

Notes

1. Primary Caretaker Presumption. Although the primary caretaker presumption has been favored by many academics, only three states have ever enacted it.[220] Did the West Virginia state supreme court apply the presumption accurately in the *Patricia Ann S.* case?

Is Ronald Henry correct that the primary caretaker test is too heavily weighted in favor of the functions usually performed by women? Is that a sufficient reason to abandon the test? What tasks are missing that ought to be on the list? Should wage-earning be a function that counts as "caretaking"? Note that Henry's charge takes the same form as claims made in favor of affirmative action, accommodations to pregnancy, initiatives to increase women's athletic opportunities, and other measures intended to achieve substantive goals, beyond formal equality. Underlying these efforts is an assumption that a rule neutral on its face is not neutral in fact if it produces skewed results. Analyze this assumption in the custodial context. Even if a primary caretaker presumption does not reflect gender preferences, is it a problem that the rule perpetuates them? Even without the presumption, primary caretaking figures strongly in custody decisions.[221] Is that a problem?

West Virginia replaced its primary caretaker presumption in 2000 in favor of a past caretaking standard. See note 3 below. Minnesota and Montana also tried the primary caretaker presumption, but neither retained it for long.

2. Joint Custody.   All states allow some form of joint custody, and some provide a presumption or preference in its favor. Most commonly, however, despite statutory language encouraging participation in the child's life by both parents,[222] joint custody is one among a number of custody alternatives and not necessarily the favored one. In states with a preference for joint custody, some narrow it to circumstances in which the parents jointly agree,[223] or allow the presumption to be overcome by a showing that joint custody would not be in the child's best interests, or would be detrimental to the child.[224] Iowa requires the court to order joint custody on the request of either parent, unless clear and convincing evidence indicates that such an arrangement is unreasonable and not in the child's best interests, but joint custody in Iowa does not necessarily mean joint physical care.[225] A few states explicitly disfavor joint custody awards.[226]

Critics of joint custody argue that to the extent it reduces gender stereotypes, it does so by sacrificing the custodial rights of mothers who have acted as primary parents in favor of fathers who have not earned those rights. Another concern is "custody blackmail"—that laws favoring joint custody provide additional bargaining leverage to men at divorce, who use it to exact financial concessions from mothers who fear litigation over parental rights. A third criticism is that it gives spouses opportunities to harass their former partner and to prevent them from relocating. Similar critiques are leveled against "friendly parent" custody standards, which take into account the willingness and ability of a parent to cooperate in contact between the child and the other parent.[227] For example, Florida requires courts to examine "the demonstrated capacity and disposition of each parent to facilitate and encourage a close and continuing parent-child relationship, to honor the time-sharing schedule, and to be reasonable when changes are required."[228] Critics of such provisions argue that they enable vindictive individuals to harass and manipulate their former spouses and discourage well-intentioned parents—usually mothers—from opposing joint custody for fear that this opposition might be used to label them as a "non-friendly" parent and therefore an inappropriate candidate for primary custodian. Fathers' rights advocates, by contrast, argue that mothers sometimes falsely claim abuse in order to obtain custody, and that such allegations can be difficult to refute.

The effects of joint custody on child support are open to dispute. Critics claim that shared arrangements may disadvantage women when courts assume that such joint parenting makes child support unnecessary. But often women have lower earnings and devote more time and expense to childrearing even when they share legal custody with their former husbands. Supporters of joint custody note that it results in greater child support compliance than other arrangements. However, researchers note that it is unclear whether joint custody encourages compliance or whether the kind of parents who seek joint custody are also the kind of parents who tend to take their child support obligations most seriously.

Whether joint custody benefits children appears to depend upon the family circumstances. Children generally do well under shared arrangements when parents are able to value each other's contribution and have good psychological functioning, high self-esteem, and a low level of anger. By contrast, when parents have intense hostility, low self-esteem, and a tendency to blame or punish their former spouse, the children are likely to suffer.[229]

3. The "Approximation" or "Past Caretaking" Standard. If the best interests test is too subjective, the primary caretaker presumption too unfair to primary breadwinners, and the joint custody alternative too unrealistic for many couples, is there a preferable alternative? Given the variety in circumstances in today's families and the importance of the actual custodial arrangements that parents make on their own, Elizabeth Scott suggests an alternative presumption, which she calls the "approximation standard." That standard calls for a custody arrangement that best approximates parenting patterns while the family was intact. Such an approach, she argues, promotes continuity and stability for children, encourages cooperative rather than adversarial behavior by parents, and provides incentives for both parents to invest in parenting before as well as after divorce.[230] This is also the approach taken by the American Law Institute, which calls it the "past caretaking standard."[231] Is this approach likely to have an effect on gender bias in custody decisions? In what direction? Does it unfairly penalize fathers who are primary breadwinners?

Another possibility is to give a custodial preference to the parent who is the same sex as the child. A few states have such a preference for children who are at or near adolescence; a few states expressly prohibit it.[232] Social science evidence on the benefits of such placements is mixed and may reflect gendered assumptions about what is healthy "sex role identification." Would you expect that successful role modeling depends upon sharing a primary residence with the same-sex parent?

4. Relocation. Most families relocate after divorce, giving rise to situations in which one parent or the other's relationship to the child necessarily changes, sometimes quite substantially. In such situations, what rules should govern whether a parent should be allowed to relocate with the child? On the one hand, depriving a custodial parent of the right to move with his or her children is a high price to pay for custody. It often seems unfair to make the parent who has borne the primary responsibility for the children during the marriage incur relocation limitations that the other parent does not incur at divorce. On the other hand, the noncustodial parent will often face significant, sometimes almost insurmountable constraints, in maintaining a close relationship to a child who resides a long distance away. Yet preventing both parents from relocating may impose significant economic as well as personal disadvantages. Did the court reach that regret in *Elser*? why or why not?

The law in this area has been unstable, but the clear trend has been toward increasing deference to the parent with whom the child has been primarily living. Typically, the kinds of reasons for relocation that courts view as acceptable are to take a significantly better job (or to allow a new spouse to take a significantly better job), to address significant health issues, to pursue educational opportunities not available in the original jurisdiction, to be close to other relatives, or to bring significant improvement in the family's quality of life.

Which of these reasons seem significant enough to deprive the noncustodial parent of frequent contact with the children?

Because most children of divorced families are in the physical custody of their mothers, the relocation standard a court applies will have a gender impact. Should that impact be taken into account? If one objective of custody law is to encourage parenting by fathers, should the standard prefer protecting the custodial/visitation rights of fathers or protecting only the caretaking roles already assumed during the marriage?

5. Fairness and Custody.   To what extent should fairness be a factor in custody rules? In *Patricia Ann S.*, for example, assume that (1) the children are more comfortable with their father and want to live with him; (2) the reason for this is that the father has physically and emotionally abused the mother, eliminating her self-esteem and impairing her parental abilities; and (3) it is a reasonable prediction that the mother will not be able to regain the confidence and trust of her children. In these circumstances (which represent one reading of the case), should fairness to the mother be a factor in her favor?

What about a father who remarries and the stepmother intends to stay at home and care for the child, while the biological mother, who was the primary caretaker during the marriage, has to return to full-time work? If a judge determines, in an otherwise close case, that staying at home with the stepmother is better for the child than institutional day care, is this a sufficient reason for decision? On what basis could a court make that determination? What role should the interests of a noncustodial father play when the custodial mother relocates for a better job? Again, should fairness to a parent be a major factor?

6. Marriage, Cohabitation, and the American Paradox.   In The Marriage-Go-Round, sociologist Andrew Cherlin notes that the United States is unlike any other country in the importance that it places both on marriage and on the ability to escape from marriage. Americans are more likely to marry and also to break up than couples in other nations. Cohabitation and its breakup are also more common in the United States.[233] Cohabiting couples are twice as likely to break up as married couples.[234] In short, the United States experiences exceptional social "turbulence—a coming and going of partners on a scale seen nowhere else."[235] This instability, many say, is not good for children. Cherlin, like other experts, concludes that families would be better off if parents were less quick to partner and repartner in marriage and cohabiting relationships. If that is true, does it have any implications for family law and policy?

Putting Theory Into Practice

2-25. Since the birth of her son, David, two years ago, Rhonda quit her job as an assistant office manager to care for her son at home and relied on support by her husband Hugh, who is a high school teacher. They are divorcing. Since Hugh does not make enough money to support two households, Rhonda has agreed that she must return to full-time employment and that David will have to be placed in day care. Rhonda seeks primary custody of David based on her primary caretaking role during the marriage. Hugh argues that he should have primary custody because his mother has agreed to take care of David while he works, which would be preferable to care by strangers. What rules should govern such a case? What further information should the court have to make its decision?

What if Hugh is about to remarry and his new wife is prepared to provide full-time, in-home care for David along with her own young child? Is this a stronger or weaker case for Rhonda?

2-26. When Janet and Mark divorced after an eight-year marriage, Janet had no job skills or training. During the marriage, she stayed at home to care for her three children, the first of whom was born almost immediately upon her graduation from high school. At the divorce, Janet decided to give up primary custody of the children, then ages 3, 5, and 8, to Mark, who was planning to remarry, so that Janet would have two years to attend community college full-time. Still, Janet had custody of the children every weekend and during school vacations, talked to them every night on the telephone, and continued to take primary responsibility for such things as doctor appointments, clothing, haircuts, birthday presents, and the like. Janet missed seeing the children every day, but felt the arrangement was the only way she would be able to make herself economically independent. The children were cared for during the day, when they weren't in school by their stepmother, who did not work outside the home.

The arrangement seemed to be working well, until one year into the arrangement, Mark announced that he had received a very large promotion and was moving to another state, 1,500 miles away. He intends to take the children with him. Should Janet be able to stop him from moving with the children? Under what general rule?

2-27. The No Child Left Behind Act allows children in "failing" schools to transfer to a non-failing school in the same school district. Eight-year-old Charlie lives with Vivian, his mother, at one end of the school district, served by a very poor elementary school, to which Charlie can walk. His father, George, lives at the other end of the district near a school that the court determines is better educationally. George seeks a change of custody, so that Charlie can live with him and attend the better school. The parents live only 10 miles apart, but the commute by city bus is 45 minutes, George could not do the commute alone, and neither parent's work schedules would allow them to accompany George back and forth to school from Vivian's house.

Should George get custody of Charlie? Is changing custody from Vivian to George fair to Vivian? Should fairness matter?

2-28. It is estimated that one-fifth of children haven't seen their father in the last year.[236] If making divorced men more involved in parenting is an important goal, how can it be achieved? What would you think of a requirement that each parent exercise approximately 50 percent of physical custody of his or her children? What are the advantages and disadvantages of such an approach?[237]

4. Unmarried Parents

One area in which many sex-based distinctions persist involves the rights of unmarried parents. The issue is increasingly important given the meteoric rise in nonmarital births. In 2010, more than 40 percent of all births in the United States were to unmarried women; as many as 70 percent in some racial groups.[238] At common law, the child of unmarried parents was filius nullius—the child of no one. In the nineteenth century, states began to recognize legal ties between unwed mothers and their children, but unwed fathers were generally denied parental rights (though not always parental obligations) well into the twentieth century.[239] That system crumbled beginning in the 1970s when the Supreme Court held, in a series of cases, that unwed fathers could not be categorically stripped of legal parentage without violating the Fourteenth Amendment's protections. These cases followed a series of cases recognizing the equal protection rights of illegitimate children not to be unfairly penalized by their parents' actions.[240]

In Stanley v. Illinois, the U.S. Supreme Court held that the state could not make the children of an unmarried father wards of the state at the death of the mother, on the assumption that he was unfit.[241] Peter Stanley had lived with his children for all their lives and with their mother for 18 years before her death. But because he was not married to their mother, he was not considered a legal parent under the applicable statute. The Court invalidated the statute on substantive and procedural due process grounds, holding that the children could not be removed from their father unless he was shown to be unfit. It found the state's proffered justifications—to protect "the moral, emotional, mental, and physical welfare of the minor and the best interests of the community" and to "strengthen the minor's family ties whenever possible"—to be undermined by cutting off custodial, biological fathers solely based on marital status.[242]

Although *Stanley* put an end to the categorical denial of unwed fatherhood, the Court considered in other cases the degree to which states could still differentiate between unmarried fathers and unmarried mothers. In Caban v. Mohammed, the Supreme Court decided that a stepparent could not adopt a child without the biological father's consent if the father had developed an ongoing, meaningful relationship with the child.[243] If state law would not allow the termination of a mother's rights in similar circumstances, the Court reasoned, it could not allow the termination of the rights of a father who had accepted his responsibilities as a parent. The Court rejected the state's justification that "a natural mother" usually has a "closer relationship with her child . . . than a father does."[244]

Finally, in Lehr v. Robertson, the Court considered an unwed father's rights to an infant before a substantial relationship has had time to develop.[245] The mother in that case married a man other than the biological father of her eight-month-old infant and petitioned for the stepfather to adopt the child when she was two. A court approved the adoption without notifying the biological father of the proceeding. New York maintained a "putative father registry" that allows men to notify the state of their intent to assert paternity over an actual or potential child. But the father had not registered, nor satisfied any other criteria such as listing on the birth certificate or living with the child that would entitle him to notice. The Court upheld the New York law, concluding that the father's biological tie to the child was not enough to justify full constitutional protection of his parental rights. While a "developed parent-child relationship" deserves robust protection, an undeveloped one is only protected if the father has grasped every opportunity to develop one.[246]

Together, these rulings allow states to grant legal parentage automatically to unwed mothers, but to impose preconditions on legal parentage for unwed fathers. Most states have adopted a system similar to the one endorsed by the Uniform Parentage Act, in which a man is the legal father of a child if one of several criteria is met, including marriage to the mother, adjudication or acknowledgement of paternity, open and notorious acknowledgment of fatherhood, or clear and convincing evidence of paternity.[247]

The federal government makes sex-based distinctions between unmarried mothers and unmarried fathers in circumstances that can produce harsh consequences. The Supreme Court has thrice upheld various provisions of immigration law that disallow citizen-fathers from passing citizenship to their offspring born abroad in situations when a citizen-mother could have transmitted citizenship.[248] In Nguyen v. Immigration and Naturalization Service, for example, the Supreme Court upheld a federal statute that sets forth different requirements for citizenship claimed through an American-born father than through the American-born mother.[249] Even though the child was abandoned by his Vietnamese mother, and raised exclusively by his American father in Texas, he was not eligible for citizenship because his father had not taken the right administrative steps within the allotted time to establish a legal parent-child relationship. Had his mother been the citizen, he would have inherited it automatically regardless of whether she actively participated in childrearing or took any affirmative steps to establish their relationship. But because his citizen-parent was his father, he was no longer eligible to apply for citizenship and was deported to Vietnam after conviction for a crime of moral turpitude. The Court upheld this gender differentiation against an equal protection challenge as justified by "a biological difference between the parents" because "the mother is always present at birth," but "the father need not be."[250]

Both lines of cases—considering the legality of state and federal distinctions between unwed mothers and fathers—are controversial. Some commentators argue that the rights of unmarried fathers and mothers should be identical; others claim that fathers and mothers are not similarly situated, and that the same rules should not apply. Justice Stevens has consistently followed the latter reasoning. Consider the following, from his dissent in Caban v. Mohammed:

> Men and women are different, and the difference is relevant to the question whether the mother may be given the exclusive right to consent to the adoption of a child born out of wedlock. Because most adoptions involve newborn infants or very young children, it is appropriate at the outset to focus on the significance of the difference in such cases.
>
> Both parents are equally responsible for the conception of the child out of wedlock. But from that point on through pregnancy and infancy, the differences between the male and the female have an important impact on the child's destiny. Only the mother carries the child; it is she who has the constitutional right to decide whether to bear it or not. In many cases, only the mother knows who sired the child, and it will often be within her power to withhold that fact, and even the fact of her pregnancy, from that person. If during pregnancy the mother should marry a different partner, the child will be legitimate when born, and the natural father may never even know that his "rights" have been affected. On the other hand, only if the natural mother agrees to marry the natural father during that period can the latter's actions have a positive impact on the status of the child; if he instead should marry a different partner during that time, the only effect on the child is negative, for the likelihood of legitimacy will be lessened.
>
> These differences continue at birth and immediately thereafter. During that period, the mother and child are together; the mother's identity is known with certainty. The father, on the other hand, may or may not be present; his

identity may be unknown to the world and may even be uncertain to the mother. These natural differences between unmarried fathers and mothers make it probable that the mother, and not the father or both parents, will have custody of the newborn infant.

In short, it is virtually inevitable that from conception through infancy the mother will constantly be faced with decisions about how best to care for the child, whereas it is much less certain that the father will be confronted with comparable problems. There no doubt are cases in which the relationship of the parties at birth makes it appropriate for the State to give the father a voice of some sort in the adoption decision. But as a matter of equal protection analysis, it is perfectly obvious that at the time and immediately after a child is born out of wedlock, differences between men and women justify some differential treatment of the mother and father in the adoption process.

Most particularly, these differences justify a rule that gives the mother of the newborn infant the exclusive right to consent to its adoption. Such a rule gives the mother, in whose sole charge the infant is often placed anyway, the maximum flexibility in deciding how best to care for the child. It also gives the loving father an incentive to marry the mother, and has no adverse impact on the disinterested father. Finally, it facilitates the interests of the adoptive parents, the child, and the public at large by streamlining the often traumatic adoption process and allowing the prompt, complete, and reliable integration of the child into a satisfactory new home at as young an age as is feasible. Put most simply, it permits the maximum participation of interested natural parents without so burdening the adoption process that its attractiveness to potential adoptive parents is destroyed.[251]

Consider also Justice Kennedy's plurality opinion in *Nguyen*:

To fail to acknowledge even our most basic biological differences—such as the fact that a mother must be present at birth but the father need not be—risks making the guarantee of equal protection superficial, and so disserving it. Mechanistic classification of all our differences as stereotypes would operate to obscure those misconceptions and prejudices that are real.[252]

Are Justices Stevens and Kennedy right? Granting the differences between mothers and fathers with respect to the birth process, should these differences have legal consequences? Does distinguishing between unmarried mothers and fathers promote, or undermine, gender equity?

Putting Theory Into Practice

2-29. Indiana law allows for the changing of a child's name, upon petition of a parent, if the change is in the child's best interest. Stephen Warren petitioned the court seeking to change the surname of his four-year-old child from his mother's surname to his own surname. Since birth, the child has had the surname of his mother, who was never married to his father. Warren argues that it is in the child's best interests to have his surname because (1) he is a Potowami Indian, and it is "relevant to the child's Indian heritage"; and (2) he pays child support, has visitation, and is involved in the child's life. The mother opposes the petition because (1) the child has had her surname since birth and would be confused by the change; (2) all of his records use her surname; and (3) he has siblings with the same surname.[253]

Should the court grant the petition? Explain your reasons.

2-30. Viet has just discovered that his former fiancée was pregnant before they ended their engagement, and that she has since given birth to the child and placed the child for adoption. Should she have been able to do so without Viet's consent? If not, should Viet have gotten automatic custody if he had wanted it (as unmarried mothers typically do), or should he have had to prove his fitness? What would formal equality require? What about substantive equality?

2-31. A newspaper article examining putative father registries concluded that "it's all smoke and mirrors. How can registries work if no one's heard of them? And it's just not reasonable to expect that men will register every time they have sex."[254] It also reported that, in Florida in 2004, 47 men signed up for the state's registry, while there were 89,436 out-of-wedlock births.[255] Do those numbers signal an equality problem? Should states have the obligation to educate men of the steps necessary to protect parental rights?

---

1. Fred Strebeigh, Equal: Women Reshape American Law 63 (2009).
2. Id.
3. Califano v. Webster, 430 U.S. 313, 317-318 (1977).
4. Peter T. Glick et al., Beyond Gender Prejudice as Simple Antipathy: Hostile and Benevolent Sexism Across Cultures, 79 J. Personality & Soc. Psychol. 763 (2000).
5. Catherine A. MacKinnon, Feminism Unmodified: Discourses on Life and Law 38 (1987).
6. See Schlesinger v. Ballard, 410 U.S. 498 (1975) (upholding policy).
7. For specific facts and figures, public opinion data, and related issues, see Faye J. Crosby, Affirmative Action Is Dead: Long Live Affirmative Action (2004).
8. City of Richmond v. J.A. Croson Co., 488 U.S. 469 (1989); Adarand Constructors, Inc. v. Pena, 515 U.S. 200 (1995).
9. United States v. Virginia, 518 U.S. 515, 524 (1996) (quoting Miss. Univ. for Women v. Hogan, 458 U.S. 718, 724 (1982)).
10. See, e.g., Ensley Branch, NAACP v. Siebels, 31 F.3d 1548, 1580 (11th Cir. 1994).
11. See Contractors Ass'n of Eastern Pennsylvania v. City of Philadelphia, 6 F.3d 990, 1010 (3d Cir. 1993) (affirmative action plan favoring women will pass intermediate scrutiny if it is shown to be "a product of analysis rather than a stereotyped reaction based on habit").
12. See Rosalie Berger Levinson, Gender-Based Affirmative Action and Reverse Gender Bias: Beyond *Gratz*, *Parents Involved*, and *Ricci*, 34 Harv. J. Law & Gender 1, 36 (2011) (arguing that although the race/gender anomaly is not justified, the incongruity should not be resolved by subjecting gender-based affirmative action to strict scrutiny).

13. For studies, see Loan Le & Jack Citrin, Affirmative Action, in Public Opinion and Constitutional Controversy 162, 171-176 (Nathaniel Persily et al. eds., 2008); see also Corey A. Ciocchetti & John Holcomb, The Frontier of Affirmative Action: Employment Preferences & Diversity in the Private Workplace, 12 U. Pa. J. Bus. L. 283, 285, 308-309 (2010); Crosby, supra note 7, at 138-141.

14. Susan W. Kaufmann, The History and Impact of State Initiatives to Eliminate Affirmative Action, 111 New Directions for Teaching and Learning 3, 5 (Fall 2007).

15. Id. at 7.

16. 539 U.S. 306 (2003).

17. 133 S. Ct. 2411 (2013).

18. See Liz Dwyer, Rejected from College: If You're a Woman, a Less-Qualified Man Probably Took Your Spot, Good Education, Apr. 15, 2011, found at http://www.good.is/post/rejected-from-college-if-you-re-a-woman-a-less-qualified-man-probably-took-your-spot.

19. Shirley M. Clark & Patricia S. Reed, Are We Losing the Best and the Brightest? Highly Achieved Women Leaving the Traditional Workforce, Final Report, at 9 (Nov. 2007), available at http://www.doleta.gov/reports/pdf/AreWeLosingThebest.pdf.

20. Dwyer, supra note 18.

21. EEOC v. Sears, Roebuck & Co., 628 F. Supp. 1264, 1307 (N.D. Ill. 1986), aff'd, 839 F.2d 302 (7th Cir. 1988).

22. Vicki Schultz, Telling Stories About Women and Work: Judicial Interpretations of Sex Segregation in the Workplace in Title VII Cases Raising the Lack of Interest Argument, 103 Harv. L. Rev. 1749, 1808 (1990).

23. See U.S. Bureau of Labor Statistics, Highlights of Women's Earnings in 2010, Report 1031, Table 2, at 10-35, July 2011, found at http://www.bls.gov/cps/cpswom2010.pdf.

24. 480 U.S. at 641 n.17.

25. 480 U.S. at 675 n.5 (Scalia, J., dissenting).

26. Ricci v. DeStefano, 557 U.S. 557 (2009).

27. Id. at 633 (Ginsburg, J., dissenting).

28. Susan Sturm & Lani Guinier, The Future of Affirmative Action: Reclaiming the Innovative Ideal, 84 Cal. L. Rev. 953, 957, 976-977 (1996). See also Lani Guinier & Susan Sturm, Trial by Firefighters, N.Y. Times, July 11, 2009, at A17 (*Ricci* case fails to question relevance of written tests for leadership skills).

29. See Jonathan D. Glater, Study Offers a New Test of Potential Lawyers, N.Y. Times, Mar. 10, 2009, at A22.

30. Deborah L. Rhode, Speaking of Sex: The Denial of Gender Equality 169 (1997).

31. Case C-407/98, 2000 E.C.R. I-5539. For recent cases, see Thomas Trelogan et al., Can't We Enlarge the Blanket and the Bed? A Comparative Analysis of Positive/Affirmative Action in the European Court of Justice and the United States Supreme Court, 28 Hastings Int'l & Comp. L. Rev. 39, 40-41 (2004); Christopher D. Totten, Constitutional Precommitments to Gender Affirmative Action in the European Union, Germany, Canada and the United States: A Comparative Approach, 21 Berkeley J. Int'l L. 27 (2003).

32. Louisa Peacock, EU Quotas Would "Patronise Women," The Telegraph, Mar. 5, 2012, at http://www.telegraph.co.uk/finance/jobs/9123991/EU-quotas-would-patronise-women.html; James Kanter, Europe to Study Quotas for Women on Boards, N.Y. Times, Mar. 15, 2012, at B3.

33. For a examination of the Norway model, established in Norway's Corporate Board Quota Law ("CBQ"), see Darren Rosenblum, Feminizing Capital: A Corporate Imperative, 6 Berkeley Bus. L.J. 55 (2009) (arguing for the CBQ to foster a productive symbiosis between the public and private spheres).

34. Peter Schuck, Diversity in America 164-165 (2003).

35. See Warren Farrell, Why Men Earn More: The Startling Truth About the Pay Gap—and What Women Can Do About It (2005).

36. See Kingsley Browne, Sex and Temperament in Modern Society: A Darwinian View of the Glass Ceiling and the Gender Gap, 37 Ariz. L. Rev. 971 (1995) (excerpted in Chapter 4).

37. Stephen J. Rose & Heidi I. Hartmann, Still a Man's Labor Market: The Long-Term Earnings Gap iii, 41 (Institute for Women's Policy Research, 2004).

38. U.S. Bureau of Labor Statistics, Highlights of Women's Earnings in 2011, at Table 1, at 9 (81.5 percent in 2010).

39. Id. at Table 2, at 15, 17, 33.

40. Clark & Reed, supra note 19, at 9.

41. Barry T. Hirsch, Why Do Part-Time Workers Earn Less? The Role of Worker and Job Skills, 58 Ind. & Lab. Rel. Rev. 525, 525-526 (2005).

42. U.S. Bureau of Labor Statistics, Women in the Labor Force: A Databook 2 (May 2005), at 73-76 (Table 20) (Feb. 2013).

43. In re Application of Mid-Florida Tel. Corp., 70 F.C.C.2d 281, 326 (Rev. Bd. 1978), set aside on other grounds, 87 F.C.C.2d 203 (1981).

44. See Lamprecht v. FCC, 958 F.2d 382 (D.C. Cir. 1992) (striking down broadcast preferences).

45. 414 U.S. 632 (1974). For a comprehensive history of pregnancy discrimination law, see Deborah Dinner, The Costs of Reproduction: History and the Legal Construction of Sex Equality, 46 Harv. C.R.-C.L. L. Rev. 415 (2011).

46. 417 U.S. 484, 496-497 n.20 (1974).

47. 429 U.S. 125, 133-140 (1976).

48. 42 U.S.C. §2000e(k) (2012).

49. Wendy W. Williams, The Equality Crisis: Some Reflections on Culture, Courts, and Feminism, 7 Women's Rts. L. Rep. 175, 191, 195-196 (1982).

50. Ruth Colker, Pregnancy, Parenting, and Capitalism, 58 Ohio St. L.J. 61, 80 (1997).

51. 186 F.3d 759 (7th Cir. 1999).

52. Id. at 767.

53. 42 U.S.C. §§12101-12213 (2012).

54. 42 U.S.C. §12102(1)(A) (2012).

55. See, e.g., Gorman v. Wells Mfg. Corp., 209 F. Supp. 2d 970, 976 (S.D. Iowa 2002) (noting that "the majority of federal courts hold that pregnancy-related complications do not constitute a disability under the ADA"); Gudenkauf v. Stauffer Commc'ns, Inc., 922 F. Supp. 465, 474 (D. Kan. 1996) (rejecting plaintiff's ADA claim because her "pregnancy was not unusual or abnormal" and the "conditions she experienced with the pregnancy were not outside the normal range").

56. 42 U.S.C. §12102(1)(A) (2012).

57. See EEOC Compliance Manual §902.2(c)(3) (2012); see also 29 C.F.R. §1630.2(j)(1)(ii) (2012). For detailed discussion of the law before and after the ADAAA, see Jeannette Cox, Pregnancy as "Disability" and the Amended Americans with Disabilities Act, 53 B.C. L. Rev. 443, 460-466 (2012).

58. Wiseman v. Wal-Mart Stores, Inc., 2009 U.S. Dist. LEXIS 62079 (D. Kan. June 9, 2009).

59. 446 F.3d 637 (6th Cir. 2006).

60. See, e.g., Urbano v. Cont'l Airlines, 138 F.3d 204 (5th Cir. 1998); Spivey v. Beverly Enterprises, Inc., 196 F.3d 1309 (11th Cir. 1999).

61. On this case, see Joanna L. Grossman, A Big Win for Pregnant Police Officers: A Jury Finds a New York County's Police Department Liable for Failing to Accommodate Pregnancy-Related Disability, FindLaw's Writ, June 27, 2006, available at http://writ.news.findlaw.com/grossman/20060627.html (describing jury's verdict in Lochren v. County of Suffolk, 2008 WL 2039458 (E.D.N.Y.)).

62. S. 942 (introduced May 14, 2013).

63. On the bill, see Joanna L. Grossman, The Pregnant Workers' Fairness Act: Accommodating the Needs of Pregnant Working Women, Justia's Verdict, May 11, 2012, available at http://verdict.justia.com/2012/05/11/the-pregnant-workers-fairness-act.

64. See Christine Jolls, Antidiscrimination and Accommodation, 115 Harv. L. Rev. 643 (2001).

65. Several of the relevant cases are collected in Joan C. Williams & Nancy Segal, Beyond the Maternal Wall: Relief for Family Caregivers Who Are Discriminated Against on the Job, 26 Harv. Women's L.J. 77, 134-136 (2003).

66. Joanna L. Grossman, Pregnancy, Work, and the Promise of Equal Citizenship, 98 Geo. L.J. 567, 615-617 (2010).

67. 208 U.S. 412, 419 n.1 (1908).

68. Mary E. Becker, From Muller v. Oregon to Fetal Vulnerability Policies, 53 U. Chi. L. Rev. 1219, 1238-1239 (1986).

69. See Cheryl L. Meyer, Video Display Terminals and Reproductive Complications: Regulatory Issues Concerning Health Care in the Workplace, 9 Wis. Women's L.J. 1 (1994).

70. David Kirp, Fetal Hazards, Gender Justice and the Justices: The Limits of Equality, 34 Wm. & Mary L. Rev. 101, 104-106 (1992).

71. See Michael Thomson, Reproductivity, the Workplace and the Gendering of the Body (Politic), 14 Cardozo Stud. L. & Lit. 565, 571 (2004).

72. 417 U.S. 484 (1974), excerpted supra pp. 168-69.

73. Young v. UPS, 707 F.3d 437 (4th Cir. 2013) (finding that UPS's denial of light duty was not pregnancy discrimination because Young was not similar in her inability to work to drivers who lost their licenses; it also found that the employer could distinguish based on source of injury unless Young could prove it was a pretext for discrimination).

74. See Chambers v. Omaha Girls Club, Inc., 834 F.2d 697 (8th Cir. 1987).

75. See Arlie Russell Hochschild, The Second Shift: Working Parents and the Revolution at Home (1989).

76. U.S. Department of Labor, Bureau of Labor Statistics, American Time Use Survey, 2005, available at http://www.bls.gov/tus; see also http://mothersandmore.org/press_room/statistics.shtml (citing studies).

77. W. Bradford Wilcox & Steven L. Nock, What's Love Got to Do with It? Equality, Equity, Commitment and Women's Marital Quality, 84 Soc. Forces 1338 (2006).

78. See Amy Kroska, Investigating Gender Differences in the Meaning of Household Chores and Child Care, 65 J. Marriage & Family 456, 463, 466 (May 2003) (women attribute more positive, powerful meanings than men to specific household chores such as baby care, meal preparation, and laundry, although women's time in paid labor is negatively related to these positive meanings); Rhona Mahony, Kidding Ourselves: Breadwinning, Babies, and Bargaining Power (1995) (discussing ways in which partners committed to equality end up with sexual division of labor).

79. Naomi Cahn, Gendered Identities: Women and Household Work, 44 Vill. L. Rev. 525, 532 (1999); Naomi Cahn, The Power of Caretaking, 12 Yale J.L. & Feminism 177 (2000).

80. Catherine Rampell, As Layoffs Surge, Women May Pass Men in the Job Force U.S., N.Y. Times, Feb. 6, 2009, at A15.

81. Id. (noting that, in 2008, women held 49 percent of the nation's jobs); see also Department of Labor, Women in Labor Force 2010, available at http://www.dol.gov/wb/factsheets/Qf-laborforce-10.htm (noting that women composed 47 percent of labor force in 2010).

82. Sylvia Ann Hewlett & Carolyn Buck Luce, Off Ramps and On Ramps: Keeping Talented Women on the Road to Success, Harv. Bus. Rev., Mar. 2005, at 43-45.

83. Claudia Wallis, The Case for Staying Home, Time, Mar. 22, 2004, at 51, 53.

84. Christine Percheski, Opting Out? Cohort Differences in Professional Women's Employment Rates from 1960 to 2005, 73 Am. Soc. Rev. 497 (2008).

85. Hewlett & Luce, supra note 82, at 45-47; Monica McGrath et al., Back in the Game—Returning to Business After a Hiatus: Experience and Recommendations for Women, Employers, and Universities (2005).

86. International Labor Organization, Breaking Through the Glass Ceiling: Women in Management (2004); Rana Foroohar, Myth and Reality: Forget All the Talk of Equal Opportunity. European Women Can Have a Job—But Not a Career, Newsweek International, Feb. 27, 2006.

87. Linda R. Hirshman, Get to Work 23, 24-25 (2006). For similar cases, see Sheryl Sandberg, Lean In: Women, Work, and the Will to Lead (2013).

88. Leslie Bennetts, The Feminine Mistake: Are We Giving Up Too Much? xxiii-xxiv (2007).

89. Hewlett & Luce, supra note 82; National Association of Women Lawyers, Retention and Promotion of Women in Law Firms (2006).

90. Tresa Baldas, EEOC Looks at Caregiver Bias, Nat'l L.J. May 21, 2007, at A1, A18 (quoting Stephanie Quincy).

91. Dee McAree, "Sex-Plus" Gender Bias Lawsuits on the Rise, Nat'l L.J., Mar. 7, 2005, at 4; see also Mary Still, Litigating the Maternal Wall: U.S. Lawsuits Charging Discrimination Against Workers with Family Responsibilities (2005), available at http://www.uchastings.edu/site_files/WLL/FRDreport.pdf (documenting rise in suits); Williams & Segal, Beyond the Maternal Wall, supra note 65.

92. EEOC, Enforcement Guidance: Unlawful Disparate Treatment of Workers with Caregiving Responsibilities, 915.002, May 23, 2007, available at http://www.eeoc.gov/policy/docs/caregiving.html.

93. 365 F.3d 107 (2d Cir. 2004).

94. Id.

95. Lust v. Sealy, 383 F.3d 580, 583 (7th Cir. 2004).

96. Stephen Benard et al., Cognitive Bias and the Motherhood Penalty, 59 Hastings L.J. 1359 (2008).

97. Knussman v. Maryland, 272 F.3d 625, 629-630 (4th Cir. 2001).

98. EEOC, Employer Best Practices for Workers with Caregiving Responsibilities (2009), available at http://www.eeoc.gov/policy/docs/caregiver-best-practices.html.

99. Joan Williams, Do Women Need Special Treatment? Do Feminists Need Equality?, 9 J. Contemp. Legal Issues 279, 285-296 (1998).

100. Williams & Segal, Beyond the Maternal Wall, supra note 65, at 79. See also Barbara Kellerman & Deborah L. Rhode eds., Women and Leadership: The State of Play and Strategies for Change 16 (2007) (documenting the "business case for work/family policies"); James T. Bond et al., The 2002 National Study of the Changing Workforce 34-35 (Families and Work Institute, 2002) (finding that employees with greater access to flexible work arrangements are more committed and have lower attrition and higher satisfaction rates than employees who lack such opportunities).

101. Hewlett & Luce, supra note 82, at 43.

102. Catherine R. Albiston, Bargaining in the Shadow of Social Institutions: Competing Discourses and Social Change in the Workplace Mobilization of Civil Rights, 39 Law & Soc'y Rev. 11, 23-27, 31-38 (2005).

103. See Joanna L. Grossman, Job Security Without Equality: The Family and Medical Leave Act of 1993, 15 Wash. U. J.L. & Pol'y 17 (2004) (noting negligible impact of FMLA on caretaking leaves by men).

104. Sarah Fass, Paid Leave in the States: A Critical Support for Low-Wage Workers and Their Families (2009); see also Gillian Lester, A Defense of State Paid Family Leave, 28 Harv. J.L. & Gender 1, 3 (2005).

105. 538 U.S. 721 (2003).

106. Id. at 728-731.

107. 132 S. Ct. 1327 (2012).

108. Id. at 1345 (Ginsburg, J., dissenting).

109. See Rebecca Ray, A Detailed Look at Parental Leave Policies in 21 OECD Countries, Center for Economic Policy and Research, at 10, 22-23, 27-28 (Sept. 2008), available at http://www.lisdatacenter.org/wp-content/uploads/parent-leave-details1.pdf; Jan Tormod Dege & Erik Aas, Norway, in Employment Law in Europe 710, 714 (Susan Mayne & Susan Maylon eds., 2001).

110. Id. at 713. See also Ray, supra note 109, at 19 (noting that in Japan although "maternity leave is nearly universally guaranteed, maternity pay is not").

111. Steven Erfors, Sweden, in Employment Law in Europe, supra note 109, at 710, 830; see also Ray, supra note 109, at 27-28; Elina Pylkkhanen & Nina Smith, OECD Study, Career Interruptions Due to Parental Leave: A Comparative Study of Denmark and Sweden 11 (2003); Katrin Bennhold, In Sweden, Men Can Have it All, N.Y. Times, June 9, 2010, at A6.

112. See surveys discussed in Ira Mark Ellman, Marital Roles and Declining Marriage Rates, 41 Fam. L.Q. 455, 482 (2007).

113. E.g., Michael Selmi, Family Leave and the Gender Wage Gap, 78 N.C. L. Rev. 707 (2000) (proposing six-week paid leave to both men and women that can be claimed only on an all-or-nothing basis); Lester, supra note 104, at 80-81 (listing various proposals made by others, including required parental leave for fathers, linking federal contract eligibility of family leave uptake rates by male employees, and public awareness campaigns).

114. Symposium, Unbending Gender: Why Family and Work Conflict and What to Do About It, 49 Am. U. L. Rev. 901, 904 (2000) (transcript, quoting Joan Williams).

115. Joan Williams, Toward a Reconstructive Feminism: Reconstructing the Relationship of Market Work and Family Work, 19 N. Ill. U. L. Rev. 89, 150-151 (1998). On the feminist campaign for universal child care, see Deborah Dinner, The Universal Childcare Debate: Rights Mobilization, Social Policy, and the Dynamics of Feminist Activism, 1966-1974, 28 Law & Hist. Rev. 577 (2010).

116. For a comprehensive study of the relevant federal programs, eligibility requirements, funding trends, waiting lists, and differences among the state programs through which federal funds are distributed, see Karen Schulman & Helen Blank, Child Care Assistance Policies 2005: States Fail to Make Up Lost Ground, Families Continue to Lack Critical Supports (National Women's Law Center Issue Brief, Sept. 2005).

117. U.S. Bureau of Labor Statistics, National Compensation Survey: Employee Benefits in Private Industry in the United States, Mar. 2005, at 26, Table 22.

118. See Heather S. Dixon, National Daycare: A Necessary Precursor to Gender Equality with Newfound Promise for Success, 36 Colum. Hum. Rts. L. Rev. 561 (2005).

119. Joan Williams, Unbending Gender: Why Family and Work Conflict and What to Do About It 51 (2000).

120. Id.

121. Robin Wilson, Family Science, Chron. of Higher Educ., July 22, 2005, at A6, A7-A8.

122. Sheila M. Rothman, Woman's Proper Place 40 (1978); see also Deborah L. Rhode, Association and Assimilation, 81 Nw. U. L. Rev. 106, 131-132 (1986); Deborah L. Rhode, Justice and Gender 291-292 (1989).

123. 458 U.S. 718 (1982).

124. Id. at 739 n. 5 (Powell, J., dissenting).

125. See United States v. Virginia, 518 U.S. 515, 523 (1996).

126. Faulkner v. Jones, 10 F.3d 226 (4th Cir. 1993).

127. Valorie K. Vojdik, Gender Outlaws: Challenging Masculinity in Traditionally Male Institutions, 17 Berkeley Women's L.J. 68, 71 (2002). Poor physical conditioning was also a factor. See Citadel's First Female Case Tells of the Stress of Her Court Fight, N.Y. Times, Sept. 10, 1995, A1, at 36.

128. See, e.g., Diane H. Mazur, A Call to Arms, 22 Harv. Women's L.J. 39, 76-77 (1999).

129. Faulker v. Jones, 858 F. Supp. 552 (D.S.C. 1994), aff'd as modified and remanded by Faulkner v. Jones, 51 F.3d 440 (4th Cir. 1995).

130. Katharine T. Bartlett, Unconstitutionally Male?: The Story of United States v. Virginia, in Women and the Law Stories 133, 167 (Elizabeth Schneider & Stephanie Wildman eds., 2011).

131. Id. at 174. See also Vojdik, supra note 127, at 98-99 (describing the culture of hyper-masculinity at The Citadel).

132. Bartlett, supra note 130.

133. See Mary Anne Case, Two Cheers for Cheerleading: The Noisy Integration of VMI and the Quiet Success of Virginia Women in Leadership, 1999 U. Chi. Legal F. 347, 349, 378.

134. Elizabeth Weil, Teaching to the Testosterone, N.Y. Times Mag., Mar. 3, 2008, at 39, 40; Jennifer Medina, Schools Try Separating Boys from Girls, N.Y. Times, Mar. 10, 2009; Tamar Lewin, Single-Sex Education Is Assailed in Report, N.Y. Times, Sept. 22, 2011, at A19.

135. Pub. L. No. 107-110, 115 Stat. 1425 (2002).

136. 34 C.F.R. §106.34(b)(4) (2012).

137. Survey, American Ass'n of Univ. Women, Shortchanging Girls, Shortchanging America 4 (1991).

138. Judith Kleinfeld, The Myth That Schools Shortchange Girls: Social Science in the Service of Deception (Women's Freedom Network 1998); see Kingsley R. Browne, Sex and Temperament in Modern Society, supra note 36, at 1032.

139. See, e.g., Michelle Conlin, The New Gender Gap: From Kindergarten to Grad School, Boys Are Becoming the Second Sex, Bus. Wk. Online, May 26, 2003, available at http://www.businessweek.com/magazine/content/03_21/b3834001_mz001.htm; Christina Hoff Sommers, The War Against Boys: How Misguided Feminism Is Harming Our Young Men (2000).

140. For reviews of the evidence, see Rebecca A. Kiselewich, In Defense of the 2006 Title IX Regulations for Single-Sex Public Education: How Separate Can Be Equal, 49 B.C. L. Rev. 217, 229-230 (2008); Sara Mead, The Evidence Suggests Otherwise: The Truth About Boys and Girls (2006), available at www.educationsector.org.

141. See William Raspberry, Same-Sex Schools Work—Sometimes, Wash. Post, Mar. 16, 1998, at A21.

142. Elizabeth Weil, Teaching Boys and Girls Separately, N.Y. Times Mag., Mar. 2, 2008, at 8. See also U.S. Dep't of Educ., Early Implementation of Public Single-Sex Schools: Perceptions and Characteristics (2008).

143. Diane F. Halpern et al., The Pseudoscience of Single-Sex Schooling, 333 Science 1706 (2011); see also Rosalind C. Barnett & Caryl Rivers, The Truth About Girls and Boys (2011) (analyzing international research on single-sex education and reaching conclusions similar to Halpern's).

144. For a summary of the debate on these issues, see Rosemary Salomone, Feminist Voices in the Debate over Single-Sex Schooling: Finding Common Ground, 11 Mich. J. Gender & L. 63 (2004). See also Gary J. Simson, Separate But Equal and Single-Sex Schools, 90 Cornell L. Rev. 443, 452-453 (2005).

145. AAUW, Position on Single-Sex Education, available at http://www.aauw.org/act/issue_advocacy/actionpages/singlesex.cfm.

146. ACLU, Preliminary Findings of ACLU "Teach Kids, Not Stereotypes" Campaign, Aug. 20, 2012, at 3, available at https://www.aclu.org/files/assets/doe_ocr_report2_0.pdf. (quoting Michael Gurian & Arlette Ballew, The Boys and Girls Learn Differently Action Guide for Teachers 100 (2003)); see also Feminist Majority Foundation, The State of Public School Sex Segregation in the United States (June 26, 2012), available at http://www.feminist.org/research/fmf.asp (finding, in study of single-sex education in public schools from 2007-2010, widespread non-compliance with Title IX and the Equal Protection Clause).

147. Tamar Lewin, Girls' Gains Have Not Cost Boys, Report Says, N.Y. Times, May 20, 2008, at A17.

148. Michael Gurian & Arlette Ballew, The Boys and Girls Learn Differently Action Guide for Teachers (2003); Leonard Sax, Why Gender Matters: What Parents and Teachers Need to Know About the Emerging Science of Sex Differences (2006); National Association for Single Sex Public Education, Advantages for Girls and Advantages for Boys (2006); Rosemary Salomone, Same, Different, Equal: Rethinking Single Sex Education (2003).

149. 775 F. Supp. 1004 (E.D. Mich. 1991).

150. Michael Meyers, The Non-Viability of Single-Race, Single-Sex Schools, 21 N.Y.U. Rev. L. & Soc. Change 663, 665-666 (1994-1995).

151. Note, Inner-City Single-Sex Schools: Educational Reform or Invidious Discrimination? 105 Harv. L. Rev. 1741, 1743-1744 (1992).

152. City of Richmond v. J.A. Croson Co., 488 U.S. 469 (1989).

153. Michael Bronski, Rethinking the Harvey Milk School: Not-So-Fast Times at Queermont High, The Boston Phoenix, News & Features, Aug. 8-14, 2003, available at http://www.bostonphoenix.com/boston/news_features/other_stories/documents/03073221.asp. For further information about the school, see www.hmi.org.

154. See Virginia: Separate-Sex Classes, N.Y. Times, Aug. 11, 2005, at A19.

155. See Melana Zyla Vickers, Where the Boys Aren't: The Gender Gap on College Campuses, in The Weekly Standard, Jan. 2, 2006, available at http://www.weeklystandard.com/Content/Public/Articles/000/000/006/531ffoaa.asp.

156. Jennifer Delahunty Britz, To All the Girls I've Rejected, N.Y. Times, Mar. 23, 2006, at A25.

157. Alex Kingsbury, Many Colleges Reject Women at Higher Rates Than for Men, U.S. News & World Report online, June 17, 2007 (quoting Henry Broaddus, director of admissions at William & Mary).

158. 34 C.F.R. § 106.41(b).

159. See, e.g., Kleczek v. R.I. Interscholastic League, 768 F. Supp. 951 (D.R.I. 1991) (holding that hockey is a contact sport and thus exempt from Title IX).

160. See, e.g., Adams v. Baker, 919 F. Supp. 1496 (D. Kan. 1996); see also cases reviewed in Eileen McDonagh & Laura Pappano, Playing with the Boys: Why Separate Is Not Equal in Sports, 137-144 (2008).

161. Robin Wilson, Oklahoma Hold 'Em, Chron. of Higher Educ., Apr. 4, 2008, at A8; see also Deborah L. Brake, Wrestling with Gender, 13 Nev. L.J. 486 (2013) (analyzing the phenomenon of match forfeitures as a form of gender backlash in response to the assertion of equality from the presence of girls in the sport).

162. See Petrie v. Illinois High Sch. Ass'n, 394 N.E.2d 855 (Ill. App. Ct. 1979); Williams v. Sch. Dist., 998 F.2d 168 (3d Cir. 1993).

163. Williams v. Sch. Dist. of Bethlehem, 998 F.2d 168 (3d Cir. 1993); Atty. Gen. v. Mass. Interscholastic Athletic Ass'n, Inc., 393 N.E.2d 284 (Mass. 1979). For a discussion of this case, see Deborah L. Brake, Getting in the Game: Title IX and the Women's Sports Revolution 58 (2010).

164. Rick Reilly, Not Your Average Skirt Chaser, CNN/SI.com, Nov. 21, 2001. See also Mike Wise, High School Sports in Field Hockey, a Twist on Title IX, N.Y. Times, Oct. 18, 2001, at S1, at http://www.timesunion.com/sports/article/Boy-wants-to-play-girls-field-hockey-3541070.php.

165. See, e.g., O'Connor v. Bd. of Educ., 545 F. Supp. 376 (N.D. Ill. 1982); cf. Thomka v. Mass. Interscholastic Ath. Ass'n, 22 Mass. L. Rep. 263 (Super. Ct. 2007).

166. See evidence reviewed in McDonagh & Pappano, supra note 158, at 53-68.

167. Katherine M. Franke, The Central Mistake of Sex Discrimination Law: The Disaggregation of Sex from Gender, 144 U. Pa. L. Rev. 1, 37-38 (1995).

168. McDonagh & Pappano, supra note 158, at 8.

169. Id. at 7.

170. Brake, Getting in the Game, supra note 163, at 16-17.

171. Kathleen McCrone, Sport and the Physical Emancipation of English Women 1870-1914, at 6-7 (1988); Helen Lenskyi, Out of Bounds, Women, Sport, and Sexuality 38 (1986).

172. Deborah Brake, Revisiting Title IX's Legacy: Moving Beyond the Three-Part Test, 12 Am. U. J. Gender Soc. Pol'y & L. 453, 458 (2004).

173. Title IX Facts Everyone Should Know, June 10, 2002, available at http://www.womenssportsfoundation.org/cgi-bin/iowa/issues/geena/record.html?record=862.

174. See Betsey Stevenson, Title IX and the Evolution of High School Sports, 25 Contemporary Economic Policy 486 (2007) (analyzing Title IX's impact statistically).

175. National Federation of State High School Associations, 2010-11 High School Athletics Participation Survey 52 (2011), available at www.nfhs.org.

176. See NCAA Sports Sponsorship and Participation Rates Report, 1981-82–2010-11, at 69, available at http://www.ncaapublications.com/productdownloads/PR2012.pdf.

177. See, e.g., Gonyo v. Drake Univ., 879 F. Supp. 1000 (S.D. Iowa 1995); Kelley v. Board of Trustees, 35 F.3d 265 (7th Cir. 1994); Miami Univ. Wrestling Club v. Miami Univ., 302 F.3d 608 (6th Cir. 2002).

178. See, for example, Horner v. Kentucky High School Athletic Ass'n, 43 F.3d 265 (6th Cir. 1994); Education Department Reaches Settlements of Title IX Athletics Complaints Against Four Districts, NSBA: Legal Clips, July 12, 2012, available at http://legalclips.nsba.org/?p=15271.

179. NSBA: Legal Clips, supra note 178.

180. Office for Civil Rights, Additional Clarification of Intercollegiate Athletics Policy: Three Part Test–Part Three (2005).

181. Don Sabo & Christine H. B. Grant, Limitations of the Department of Education's Online Survey Method for Measuring Athletic Interest and Ability on U.S.A. Campuses (Center for Research on Physical Activity, Sport and Health, D'Youville College, 2005).

182. Office for Civil Rights, Intercollegiate Athletics Policy Clarification: The Three-Part Test–Part Three (2010). For a discussion of the relevant history, see Brake, Getting in the Game, supra note 163, at 219-221.

183. See, for example, B. Glenn George, Forfeit: Opportunity, Choice, and Discrimination Theory Under Title IX, 22 Yale J.L. & Feminism 1 (2010); Dionne L. Koller, Not Just One of the Boys: A Post-Feminist Critique of Title IX's Vision for Gender Equity in Sports, 43 Conn. L. Rev. 401 (2010).

184. Deborah Brake, The Struggle for Sex Equality in Sport and the Theory Behind Title IX, 34 U. Mich. J.L. Reform 13, 74-122 (2001).

185. Janet S. Fink & Linda J. Kensicki, An Imperceptible Difference; Visual and Textual Constructions of Femininity in Sports Illustrated and Sports Illustrated for Women, 5 Mass Communication and Society 317 (2002).

186. Brake, Revising Title IX's Legacy, supra note 172, at 481.

187. McDonagh & Pappano, supra note 158, at 252-255.

188. See Jay Larson, Note, All Sports Are Not Created Equal: College Football and a Proposal to Amend the Title IX Proportionality Prong, 88 Minn. L. Rev. 1598 (2004).

189. National Coalition for Women and Girls in Athletics, Title IX Policies 23 (2007).

190. Id.

191. See McCormick v. Sch. Dist. of Mamaroneck, 370 F.3d 275 (2d Cir. 2004).

192. Vivian Acosta & Linda Carpenter, Women in Intercollegiate Sports: A Longitudinal, National Study—Thirty-Five Year Update: 1977-2012 (2012), available at http://acostacarpenter.org/AcostaCarpenter2012.pdf.

193. Paula Wasley, Education Dept. Ignores Rife Errors in Gender-Equity Data in College Sports Programs, USA Today Reports, Chron. of Higher Educ., Today's News, Oct. 20, 2005.

194. Deborah L. Rhode & Christopher J. Walker, Gender Equity in College Athletics: Women Coaches as a Case Study, 4 Stan. J. C.R. & C.L. 1, 23 (2008) (quoting surveyed coach).

195. Women's Sports Foundation, Title IX Facts Everyone Should Know, supra note 173.

196. Jerome Solomon, Title IX, 30 Years Later: Sexes Still Unequal in Athletics, Houston Chron., June 23, 2002, at A1.

197. See Brake, Getting in the Game, supra note 163, at 170.

198. Office for Civil Rights, Dear Colleague Letter, June 25, 2007, http://www.ed.gov/about/offices/list/ocr/letters/colleague-20070625.html.

199. NCAA Division I and II Bylaw 15, §3.4.3; see also Bylaw 15, §3.2.2.

200. NCAA, Pregnant and Parenting Student-Athletes: Resources and Model Policies (2008), available at http://www.ncaa.org/documents/NCAAParentingHandbook.pdf.

201. See Deborah L. Brake & Verna L. Williams, The Heart of the Game: Putting Race and Educational Equity at the Center of Title IX, 7 Va. Sports & Ent. L.J. 199 (2008).

202. Jennifer Butler & Donna A. Lopiano, Women's Sports Foundation, Title IX and Race in Intercollegiate Sport (2003).

203. Brake, Getting in the Game, supra note 163, at 112-118.

204. See Regina Austin, Super Size Me and the Conundrum of Race/Ethnicity, Gender, and Class for the Contemporary Law-Genre Documentary Filmmaker, 40 Loyola of L.A. L. Rev. 710 (2007); Katie Thomas, A City Team's Struggle Shows Disparity in Girls' Sports, N.Y. Times, June 14, 2009, at A1.

205. See, e.g., Mary A. Boutilier & Lucinda SanGiovanni, The Sporting Woman 173-176 (1983); Murray Sperber, College Sports Inc.: The Athletic Department vs. The University 322-332 (1990).

206. Boy Wants to Play Girls' Field Hockey, timesunion.com, May 7, 2012.

207. See Matthew McKeever & Nicholas H. Wolfinger, Reexamining the Economic Costs of Marital Disruption for Women, 82 Soc. Science Q. 202, 207 (Mar. 2001).

208. Matthew McKeever & Nicholas H. Wolfinger, Shifting Fortunes in a Changing Economy, in Fragile Families and the Marriage Agenda 127, 149 (Lori Kowaleski-Jones & Nicholas H. Wolfinger eds., 2005).

209. See, e.g., Saff v. Saff, 402 N.Y.S.2d 690 (App. Div. 1978), appeal dismissed, 415 N.Y.S.2d 829 (N.Y. 1979). On the changes to the American family and family law over the course of the twentieth century, see Joanna L. Grossman & Lawrence M. Friedman, Inside the Castle: Law and the Family in 20th Century America (2011).

210. American Law Institute, Principles of the Law of Family Dissolution, Chapter 4 (2002).

211. For an overview, see Ira Mark Ellman & Tara O'Toole Ellman, The Theory of Child Support, 45 Harv. J. Legislation 107 (2008).

212. Ira Mark Ellman et al., Intuitive Lawmaking: The Example of Child Support, 6 J. Empirical Legal Studies 69, 104-105 (2009).

213. Julie Bosman, Fighting over Child Support After the Pink Slip Arrives, N.Y. Times, Mar. 29, 2009, at A1.

214. Landon Thomas, Jr., Lawyer to Stars' Ex-Wives Has Never Been Busier, N.Y. Times, May 26, 2009, at B1 (quoting Brian Meyerson).

215. Judith H. Dobrzynski, "A Corporate Wife Holds Out for a 50-50 Split of Assets," N.Y. Times, Jan. 24, 1997 (discussing divorce between Gary and Lorna Wendt); Wendt v. Wendt, 1998 Conn. Super. LEXIS 1023, pp. 55-56 (awarding wife $20 million in equitable distribution).

216. J.S. v. J.S., 19 Misc. 3d 634, 857 N.Y.S.2d 427 (2008). For discussion of other trends and reaction to the case, see Wendy N. Davis, 'Til Death Do Us Pay, ABA J., Sept. 2008, at 18.

217. See U.S. Census Bureau, Current Population Reports, Custodial Mothers and Fathers and Their Child Support 2 & Table 4 (Dec. 2011).

218. See Katharine T. Bartlett, Preference, Presumption, Predisposition, and Common Sense: From Traditional Custody Doctrines to the American Law Institute's Family Dissolution Project, 36 Fam. L.Q. 11 (2002).

219. See Hoover v. Hoover, 764 A.2d 1192, 1194 (Vt. 2000). According to the dissenting judge, time was credited to the father for activities such as helping with schoolwork in which the mother also engaged but for which she was not given credit.

220. See, e.g., Martha Albertson Fineman, The Illusion of Equality: The Rhetoric and Reality of Divorce Reform 180-185 (1991) (for all children); David L. Chambers, Rethinking the Substantive Rules for Custody Disputes in Divorce, 83 Mich. L. Rev. 477 (1985) (for children between six months and five years).

221. See, e.g., In re Custody of Kali, 792 N.E.2d 635 (Mass. 2003); In re McBrayer, 83 P.2d 936 (Or. Ct. App. 2004).

222. See, e.g., Colo. Rev. Stat. §14-10-124(1) (West 2012).

223. See, e.g., Cal. Fam. Code §3080 (West 2012).

224. See, e.g., D.C. Code Ann. §16-914(a)(2) (West 2012); Fla. Stat. Ann. §61.13(2) (c)(2) (West 2012).

225. Iowa Code Ann. §598.41(2) & (5) (West Supp. 2012).

226. Oregon, for example, prohibits an order unless both parents agree. Or. Rev. Stat. §107.169(3) (2012); see also Vt. Stat. Ann. tit. 15, §665(a) (2012) (when parents cannot agree, court must order primary or sole custody to one parent).

227. See Margaret K. Dore, The "Friendly Parent" Concept: A Flawed Factor for Child Custody, 6 Loy. J. Pub. Int. L. 41 (2004).

228. Fla. Stat. Ann. §61.13(3)(a) (West 2012).

229. See Muriel Brotsky et al., Joint Custody Through Mediation: A Longitudinal Assessment of the Children, in Joint Custody and Shared Parenting 167 (1991).

230. Elizabeth S. Scott, Pluralism, Parental Preference, and Child Custody, 80 Cal. L. Rev. 615 (1992).

231. American Law Institute, Principles of the Law of Family Dissolution §2.08 (2002).

232. Alabama appears to allow a same-sex parent preference, by statute. Other states, such as Arizona and Maine, explicitly prohibit it. See Ariz. Rev. Stat. Ann. §25-403.01(A) (West 2012); Me. Rev. Stat. Ann. tit. 19-A, §1653(4) (West 2012) ("court may not apply a preference for one parent over the other . . . because of a parent's gender or the child's age or gender"). In a few jurisdictions, including Illinois and North Dakota, courts have allowed a preference for a parent of the same sex during or right

before adolescence on various role-modeling hypotheses. The majority rule, however, is that courts may not prefer a parent because he or she is the same sex as the child.

233. Andrew Cherlin, The Marriage-Go-Round: The State of Marriage and the Family in America Today, 4, 18 (2009).

234. Lisa Selin Davis, Everything But the Ring, Time, May 25, 2009, at 58.

235. Cherlin, supra note 233, at 4.

236. Stephen Perrine, Keeping Divorced Dads at a Distance, N.Y. Times, June 16, 2006, at E13.

237. See Ariel Ayanna, From Children's Interests to Parent Responsibility: Degendering Parenthood Through Custodial Obligation, 19 UCLA Women's L.J. 1 (2012).

238. Brady E. Hamilton et al., Births: Preliminary Data for 2010, 60.2 Nat'l Vital Statistics Report 1, 4 (Nov. 17, 2011).

239. See Mary Ann Mason, From Father's Property to Children's Rights: The History of Child Custody in the United States 24 (1994).

240. See, e.g., Levy v. Louisiana, 391 U.S. 68 (1968). On the development of rights for unwed fathers, see Joanna L. Grossman, The New Illegitimacy: Tying Parentage to Marital Status for Lesbian Co-Parents, 20 J. Gender, Soc. Pol'y & L. 101, 122-132 (2012).

241. 405 U.S. 645 (1972).

242. Id. at 652.

243. 441 U.S. 380 (1979).

244. Id. at 388.

245. 463 U.S. 248 (1983).

246. Id. at 250-262.

247. Unif. Parentage Act. §204, 9B U.L.A. 22-23 (Supp. 2011).

248. See Miller v. Albright, 523 U.S. 420 (1998) ; Nguyen v. INS, 533 U.S. 53 (2001); United States v. Flores-Villar, 131 S. Ct. 2312 (2011) (affirming without opinion, by a vote of 4-4, the appellate ruling, 536 F.3d 990 (9th Cir. 2008)).

249. *Nguyen*, 533 U.S. at 53.

250. Id. at 64.

251. Caban v. Mohammed, 441 U.S. 380, 404-408 (1979) (Stevens, J., dissenting).

252. 533 U.S. at 73.

253. See In re Paternity of Tibbitts, 668 N.E.2d 1266 (Ind. 1996).

254. Tamar Lewin, Unwed Fathers Fight for Babies Placed for Adoption by Mothers, N.Y. Times, Mar. 19, 2006; see also Lehr v. Robertson, 463 U.S. 248 (1983) (upholding New York's putative father registry against a constitutional challenge). Public information about using the registry is available at http://www.ocfs.state.ny.us/main/publications/pub5040.pdf.

255. See Ben Stevens, How Can a Man Protect His Paternity Rights if the Mother Wants to Place the Child for Adoption?, at http://www.scfamilylaw.com/how-can-a-man-protect-his-paternity-rights-if-the-mother-wants-to-place-the-child-for-adoption.

CHAPTER 3

Nonsubordination

A nonsubordination perspective shifts the focus of attention from whether women and men are the same or different, to whether a rule or practice serves to subordinate women to men. This perspective, sometimes referred to as dominance theory, sees sex differences as part of a larger conceptual system designed to legitimate the power imbalance between men and women. Leading feminist legal theorist Catharine MacKinnon calls this theory feminism "unmodified," because it analyzes the situation of all women *as women* and abandons "gender-neutral absolutes, such as difference and sexuality and speech and the state" that, according to MacKinnon, are characteristic of liberal feminism.[1]

This chapter introduces nonsubordination theory by pairing John Stuart Mill's description of women's nineteenth-century "subjection" as a "solitary breach" in the fundamental laws of modern civilization with Catharine MacKinnon's characterization of women's legal subordination as the ability of those with power—men—to identify their own point of view, systematically, as universal "point-of-viewlessness." The remainder of the chapter explores nonsubordination theory's claim that the law defines sex and sexual difference in ways that naturalize women's relative powerlessness in this society, primarily through legal materials relating to sexual harassment, pornography, domestic violence, and heterosexuality.

It is no accident that most of the topics of this chapter relate to sexual behavior—particularly inside families, workplaces, and educational institutions. This is largely because the sexual realm is where dominance theory has the most to offer. Traditional formal equality analysis has achieved significant improvements for women in employment, education, and other public benefits (although nonsubordination theorists tend to see these improvements as marginal exceptions—mostly on behalf of privileged women who fit the male profile). However, equality analysis is insufficient, MacKinnon argues, to address the central inequalities faced by women—sexual harassment, violence against women, poverty, and control of women's sexuality. To address these problems, MacKinnon contends that we must move beyond questions

291

of sameness and difference to the construction of women's sexuality that underpins these more central inequalities. As you study the materials in this chapter, consider what nonsubordination theory contributes to the equality principles studied this far. Is it a supplement, a full replacement, or something else?

A. WOMEN'S RIGHTS AND POWER IN THE LIBERAL STATE

In the readings below, John Stuart Mill—the leading spokesman for nineteenth-century liberalism—finds the subordination of women an aberrational blind spot of liberalism. Catharine MacKinnon, on the other hand, finds the subordination of women a more or less inevitable consequence of liberalism's emphasis on the individual, its claim to objectivity, and its idealism. These two starting points frame much of the material in this chapter.

Reading Questions

1. How significant are the differences in approach represented by these two readings? What consequences follow from them?
2. How important is sex equality to liberalism? How should it be weighed in relation to other liberal values, such as free speech, on issues like pornography and sexual harassment?

John Stuart Mill, The Subjection of Women

Three Essays by John Stuart Mill 427-428, 443-444, 449-450
(World's Classics edition 1912) (1869)

[T]he principle which regulates the existing social relations between the two sexes—the legal subordination of one sex to the other—is wrong in itself, and now one of the chief hindrances to human improvement; . . . it ought to be replaced by a principle of perfect equality, admitting no power or privilege on the one side, nor disability on the other.

The . . . difficulty . . . is that which exists in all cases in which there is a mass of feeling to be contended against. So long as an opinion is strongly rooted in the feelings, it gains rather than loses in stability by having a preponderating weight of argument against it. For if it were accepted as a result of argument, the refutation of the argument might shake the solidity of the conviction; but when it rests solely on feeling, the worse it fares in argumentative contest, the more persuaded its adherents are that their feeling must have some deeper ground, which the arguments do not reach; and while the feeling remains, it is always throwing up fresh entrenchments of argument to repair any breach made in the old. And there are so many causes tending to make the feelings connected with this subject the most intense and most deeply-rooted of all those which gather round and protect old institutions and customs, that we need not wonder to find them as yet less undermined and loosened than any of the rest by the progress of the great modern spiritual and social transition; nor suppose that the barbarisms to which men cling longest must be less barbarisms than those which they earlier shake off.

All causes, social and natural, combine to make it unlikely that women should be collectively rebellious to the power of men. They are so far in a position different from all other subject classes, that their masters require something more from them than actual service. Men do not want solely the obedience of women, they want their sentiments. All men, except the most brutish, desire to have, in the woman most nearly connected with them, not a forced slave but a willing one; not a slave merely, but a favorite. They have therefore put everything in practice to enslave their minds. The masters of all slaves rely, for maintaining obedience, on fear; either fear of themselves, or religious fears. The masters of women wanted more than simple obedience, and they turned the whole force of education to effect their purpose. All women are brought up from the very earliest years in the belief that their ideal of character is the very opposite to that of men; not self-will, and government by self-control, but submission, and yielding to the control of others. All the moralities tell them that it is their nature, to live for others; to make complete abnegation of themselves, and to have no life but in their affections. And by their affections are meant the only ones they are allowed to have—those to the men with whom they are connected, or to the children who constitute an additional and indefeasible tie between them and a man. When we put together three things—first, the natural attraction between opposite sexes; secondly, the wife's entire dependence on the husband, every privilege or pleasure she has being either his gift, or depending entirely on his will; and lastly, that the principal object of human pursuit, consideration, and all objects of social ambition, can in general be sought or obtained by her only through him—it would be a miracle if the object of being attractive to men had not become the polar star of feminine education and formation of character. And, this great means of influence over the minds of women having been acquired, an instinct of selfishness made men avail themselves of it to the utmost as a means of holding women in subjection, by representing to them meekness, submissiveness, and resignation of all individual will into the hands of a man, as an essential part of sexual attractiveness. . . .

The social subordination of women thus stands out an isolated fact in modern social institutions; a solitary breach of what has become their fundamental law; a single relic of an old world of thought and practice exploded in everything else, but retained in the one thing of most universal interest.

Catharine A. MacKinnon, Feminism Unmodified: Discourses on Life and Law

32-38, 40-41 (1987)

The mainstream doctrine of the law of sex discrimination . . . is, in my view, largely responsible for the fact that sex equality law has been so utterly ineffective at getting women what we need and are socially prevented from having on the basis of a condition of birth: a chance at productive lives of reasonable physical security, self-expression, individuation, and minimal respect and dignity. . . .

. . . Two alternate paths to equality for women emerge within [the] dominant approach. . . . The leading one is: be the same as men. This path is termed gender neutrality legally and the single standard philosophically. . . . To women who want equality yet find that you are different, the doctrine provides an alternate route: be different from men. This equal recognition of difference is termed the special benefit rule or the special protection rule legally, the double standard philosophically. . . .

Under the sameness standard, women are measured according to our correspondence with man, our equality judged by our proximity to his measure. Under the difference standard, we are measured according to our lack of correspondence with him, our womanhood judged by our distance from his measure. Gender neutrality is thus simply the male standard, and the special protection rule is simply the female standard, but do not be deceived: masculinity, or maleness, is the referent for both. . . .

As applied, the sameness standard has mostly gotten men the benefit of those few things women historically had — for all the good they did us. Almost every sex discrimination case that has been won at the Supreme Court level has been brought by a man. . . .

In reality, which this approach is not long on because it is liberal idealism talking to itself, virtually every quality that distinguishes men from women is already affirmatively compensated in this society. Men's physiology defines most sports, their needs define auto and health insurance coverage, their socially designed biographies define workplace expectations and successful career patterns, their perspectives and concerns define quality in scholarship, their experiences and obsessions define merit, their objectification of life defines art, their military service defines citizenship, their presence defines family, their inability to get along with each other — their wars and rulerships — defines history, their image defines god, and their genitals define sex. For each of their differences from women, what amounts to an affirmative action plan is in effect, otherwise known as the structure and values of American society. But whenever women are, by this standard, "different" from men and insist on not having it held against us, whenever a difference is used to keep us second class and we refuse to smile about it, equality law has a paradigm trauma and it's crisis time for the doctrine. . . .

The women that gender neutrality benefits, and there are some, show the suppositions of [the difference] approach in highest relief. They are mostly women who have been able to construct a biography that somewhat approximates the male norm, at least on paper. They are the qualified, the least of sex discrimination's victims. When they are denied a man's chance, it looks the most like sex bias. The more unequal society gets, the fewer such women are permitted to exist. Therefore, the more unequal society gets, the less likely the difference doctrine is to be able to do anything about it, because unequal power creates both the appearance and the reality of sex differences along the same lines as it creates its sex inequalities. . . .

There is an alternative approach, one that threads its way through existing law and expresses, I think, the reason equality law exists in the first place. . . . In this approach, an equality question is a question of the distribution of power. Gender is also a question of power, specifically of male supremacy and female subordination. The question of equality, from the standpoint of what it is going to take to get it, is at root a question of hierarchy, which—as power succeeds in constructing social perception and social reality—derivatively becomes a categorical distinction, a difference. Here, on the first day that matters, dominance was achieved, probably by force. By the second day, division along the same lines had to be relatively firmly in place. On the third day, if not sooner, differences were demarcated, together with social systems to exaggerate them in perception and in fact, because the systematically differential delivery of benefits and deprivations required making no mistake about who was who. Comparatively speaking, man has been resting ever since. Gender might not even code as difference, might not mean distinction epistemologically, were it not for its consequences for social power.

I call this the dominance approach. . . . The goal of this dissident approach is not to make legal categories trace and trap the way things are. It is not to make rules that fit reality. It is critical of reality. . . . The dominance approach centers on the most sex-differential abuses of women as a gender, abuses that sex equality law in its difference garb could not confront. It is based on a reality about which little of a systematic nature was known before 1970. . . . This new information includes not only the extent and intractability of sex segregation into poverty, which has been known before, but the range of issues termed violence against women, which has not been. It combines women's material desperation, through being relegated to categories of jobs that pay nil, with the massive amount of rape and attempted rape . . . which is apparently endemic to the patriarchal family; the battery of women that is systematic in one quarter to one third of our homes; prostitution, women's fundamental economic condition, what we do when all else fails, and for many women in this country, all else fails often; and pornography, an industry that traffics in female flesh, making sex inequality into sex to the tune of eight billion dollars a year in profits largely to organized crime.

These experiences have been silenced out of the difference definition of sex equality largely because they happen almost exclusively to women.

Understand: for this reason, they are considered not to raise sex equality issues. Because this treatment is done almost uniquely to women, it is implicitly treated as a difference, the sex difference, when in fact it is the socially situated subjection of women. The whole point of women's social relegation to inferiority as a gender is that for the most part these things aren't done to men. . . .

B. SEXUAL HARASSMENT

1. Sexual Harassment in the Workplace

The term "sexual harassment" did not come into use until the mid-1970s, and was not fully articulated as a form of discrimination based on sex until 1979, with the publication of Catharine MacKinnon's The Sexual Harassment of Working Women, excerpted below, and the 1980 development of guidelines by the Equal Employment Opportunity Commission (EEOC) prohibiting sexual harassment. The first recognition by the United States Supreme Court that sexual harassment is a form of sex discrimination came in the 1983 case of Meritor Savings Bank v. Vinson.[2] The case distinguished between: (1) *quid pro quo* harassment, in which the harasser requires sexual contact or favors as a condition of employment or advancement; and (2) hostile environment harassment, based on unwelcome conduct of a sexual nature that "has the purpose or effect of unreasonably interfering with an individual's work performance or creating an intimidating, hostile, or offensive" work environment.[3] Harris v. Forklift Systems, set forth below, clarified that hostile environment discrimination is to be judged from the perspective of a reasonable person, and that a showing of the victim's psychological or physical injury is not required to establish discrimination against the victim.

Estimates of how many women have experienced sexual harassment range from 30 to 80 percent, depending upon who is asked, and how sexual harassment is defined.[4] The prevalence of harassment has not changed much since researchers started collecting data in the late 1970s, despite the development of legal doctrine making it unlawful and imposing liability on employers.[5] Although formal complaints of sexual harassment have doubled over the last decade, victims only report about 5 to 15 percent of instances of harassment, and less than 3 percent end up in litigation. Major barriers to reporting include guilt, shame, fears of reprisal or blacklisting, an unwillingness to jeopardize working relationships or to be known as a humorless whiner, concerns about loss of privacy, and doubts that an effective response to a complaint would be forthcoming. Women of color experience disproportionate rates of abuse: they account for 16 percent of the female labor force, but 33 percent of women's sexual harassment claims. Women of color are ten times less likely to report harassing incidents internally than their white counterparts. Men account for about 16 percent of claims, up from approximately 9 percent of claims in 1992.[6]

The extension of sexual harassment law to same-sex harassment has been spotty, in part because courts have routinely held that Title VII does not prohibit discrimination based on sexual orientation. Oncale v. Sundowner Offshore Servs., Inc., however, opened the door to same-sex harassment claims as long as the plaintiff could prove the misconduct occurred "because of sex." The issue of sexual orientation harassment is developed more fully later in the chapter.

As the doctrine of sexual harassment has evolved, theorists have developed a number of different theories to try to understand why sexual harassment constitutes unlawful discrimination. Some of the leading samples of this theory follow in this section.

Reading Questions

1. Formal equality defines discrimination based on sex as treating men and women differently because they are men or women. Substantive equality looks to see whether rules and practices, even when they are gender-neutral in the formal sense, disadvantage women as a result of their materially different circumstances. In what sense is sexual harassment a form of sex discrimination?
2. What is the primary harm of sexual harassment? Is it the psychological injury? The impact on the performance of a victim's job? The exclusion of women from certain male dominated workplaces? The assault on a victim's dignity? Anything else?
3. Why do harassers harass? Is it a desire for sex, or control? A lack of sexual restraint? Incivility? A strategy for economic dominance in the workplace? An exhibition of a more general need to dominate? Does the reason matter for antidiscrimination law?
4. If sexual harassment is a male system of domination over women, can men be victims? Is the sexual harassment of gays and lesbians discrimination "because of sex"?

Catharine A. MacKinnon, Sexual Harassment of Working Women

1, 9-10 (1979)

Intimate violation of women by men is sufficiently pervasive in American society as to be nearly invisible. Contained by internalized and structural forms of power, it has been nearly inaudible. Conjoined with men's control over women's material survival, as in the home or on the job, or over women's learning and educational advancement in school, it has become institutionalized. . . .

Sexual harassment, most broadly defined, refers to the unwanted imposition of sexual requirements in the context of a relationship of unequal power.

Central to the concept is the use of power derived from one social sphere to level benefits or impose deprivations in another. The major dynamic is best expressed as the reciprocal enforcement of two inequalities.

When one is sexual, the other material, the cumulative sanction is particularly potent. American society legitimizes male sexual dominance of women and employer's control of workers. . . .

[T]he sexual harassment of women can occur largely because women occupy inferior job positions and job roles; at the same time, sexual harassment works to keep women in such positions. Sexual harassment, then, uses and helps create women's structurally inferior status.

Kathryn Abrams, *Gender Discrimination and the Transformation of Workplace Norms*

42 Vand. L. Rev. 1183, 1207-1209 (1989)

[S]exually oriented behavior in the workplace produces at least two responses among women that contribute to their subordination. . . . One response is a fear of sexual coercion. Sexually oriented behavior brings into the workplace echoes of a context in which men and women often are radically unequal. A woman struggling to establish credibility in a setting in which she may not be, or may not feel, welcome, can be swept off balance by a reminder that she can be raped, fondled, or subjected to repeated sexual demands. Her employment setting, already precarious, can be transformed instantly into an unwanted sexual encounter in which she is likely to feel even less control, a transformation that can cast shadows even when demands are not being made. The feelings of anxiety, fear, or vulnerability produced by the spectre of sexual coercion prevent women from feeling, or being viewed as, the equals of their male counterparts in the workplace.

But a woman need not be threatened with sexual coercion to feel, and to be perceived as, unequal in the workplace. Sexual inquiries, jokes, remarks, or innuendoes sometimes can raise the spectre of coercion, but they more predictably have the effect of reminding a woman that she is viewed as an object of sexual derision rather than as a credible co-worker. A woman who is continuously queried by male colleagues about her sexual preferences, referred to by co-workers as "the fucking flag girl," or depicted on the walls of men's restrooms in sexual poses is being told that she is not, first and foremost, a credible colleague and an equal. This message would be disturbing to any worker, even one who felt comfortable and secure in the workplace. For a woman worker, who may not have been socialized to feel comfortable in that role, and who may have faced numerous men who have difficulty viewing women as workers rather than wives or dates, this message can be devastating. Treatment that sexualizes women workers prevents them from feeling, and prevents others from perceiving them, as equal in the workplace.

L. Camille Hébert, *The Economic Implications of Sexual Harassment for Women*

3 Kan. J.L. & Pub. Pol'y 41, 47-50 (Spring 1994)

A common view is that sexual harassment . . . is motivated by sexual desire and that women are targets of sexual harassment because they are sexually attractive to their harasser. . . .

Existing patterns of sexual harassment in the workplace, however, are difficult to explain as caused by only sexual desire—even nonmutual, one-sided sexual desire.

One aspect of the pattern of sexual harassment in the workplace that suggests sexual harassment is motivated, or at least caused, by economic considerations is the profile of the women who are most often subjected to harassment. One characteristic common among women who report sexual harassment is economic vulnerability. . . .

[M]any women who report sexual harassment are very dependent on their jobs, which would make them economically vulnerable to sexual harassment. Women with low seniority and those in low-status and low-skill jobs are more frequently subjected to sexual harassment than women in higher status and higher skill jobs. Women in trainee positions and women on probation are also more frequently subjected to sexual harassment. There is no reason to expect that these women are more sexually attractive or desirable than women who are not in these jobs. . . .

[W]omen who are members of minority groups are more likely to be sexually harassed than nonminority women. . . .

. . . Highly educated women appear to be more likely to be sexually harassed than other women; similarly, women moving into nontraditional jobs—jobs traditionally dominated by men—frequently are subjected to sexual harassment. There is no reason to believe that such women are more sexually attractive than other women.

Nor, however, are these women necessarily more economically vulnerable than other women. In fact, the converse is likely to be true. . . . This does not mean, however, that sexual harassment against these women is not the result of economic factors. In these situations, economic factors other than economic vulnerability appear to be at work, such as the desire of men to ensure continued economic dominance over women in the workplace by discouraging women from entering jobs in which they would compete with men.

Some commentators have argued that sexual harassment is motivated by factors other than power imbalances by pointing to the fact that sexual harassment most often occurs among co-workers rather than between a supervisor and a subordinate. Such a contention, however, fails to recognize that forms of economic power other than supervisory power exist in the workplace. Males may be able to exert economic power over female co-workers by withholding information and training necessary to job performance, particularly when women are moving into jobs that traditionally have been held by men. Men may also be able to assert economic power over female co-workers by threatening to sabotage work or job performance. Finally, men, because of their longer job tenure (and because of their maleness), may simply have more authority with supervisors than newer female employees and thereby be able to influence the supervisor's perception of the women's job performance.

Sexual harassment in the workplace may even be motivated by the frustration some men feel over the loss of economic power in the workplace. . . . Some men feel threatened, both socially and economically, by the advancement of women; some of these men react to these women with hostility.

It is not surprising that this hostility would manifest itself in abusive sexual activity directed toward women. Because of both biological and social factors, men often have, or believe themselves to have, power over women in their sexual relationships. Some men may resort to sexual harassment in the workplace to assert power in a sexual context, in which they believe they have an advantage over women, and to express frustration over their loss or lack of relative power over women in the workplace context. . . .

A final reason to doubt the sexual attractiveness theory of sexual harassment is that women surveyed in sexual harassment studies report that their harassers also harass others at work. This finding suggests that sexual harassment is more a pattern of abusive behavior than the result of "isolated instances of personal sexual attraction."

Kathryn Abrams, The New Jurisprudence of Sexual Harassment

83 Cornell L. Rev. 1169, 1206-1208 (1998)

In some cases, sexual harassment has emerged as a means of preserving male control over the workplace, particularly where the entry of women into a particular workforce appears to call that control into question. A prime example is sexual harassment directed at women who have entered predominantly male fields. Some types of harassment within this category are particularly flagrant, including physical or sexual aggression or persistent, targeted verbal abuse so severe as to serve unequivocal notice that women are not welcome. Women targeted in this way are often compelled to leave the workplace or transfer to a job with different co-workers or another supervisor. Even when they stay, it is clear that they remain at the sufferance of their male co-workers; they have no hope of getting sufficient purchase on the workplace to make it in any sense their own.

Other forms of harassment aimed at preserving male control are slightly subtler. Supervisors or co-workers may sexualize women employees by either propositioning them directly or treating them in a manner that highlights their sexuality, as opposed to other, work related characteristics. Supervisors may demand that women workers conform to dominant feminine stereotypes that operate outside the workplace by making repeated comments or suggestions regarding the employees' physical appearance, or through instructions to behave in a feminine manner. In some cases, it may be applied categorically to signal that women are not taken seriously: that they are considered sex objects or "pets" instead of competent workers. These latter forms of harassment may not be sufficient to compel all women to leave any particular workplace. Yet they make clear—to women and the men who work with them—that mere presence is not equal to influence or control. These forms of harassment suggest that whatever professional goals women pursue, they will continue to be viewed and judged by reference to more traditional female roles and whatever careers they enter, they still will occupy subordinate roles.

Vicki Schultz, Reconceptualizing Sexual Harassment

107 Yale L.J. 1683, 1755, 1761, 1801 (1998)

Contrary to the assumption of the cultural-radical feminist tradition that inspired the development of harassment law, men's desire to exploit or dominate women sexually may not be the exclusive, or even the primary, motivation for harassing women at work. Instead, a drive to maintain the most highly rewarded forms of work as domains of masculine competence underlies many, if not most, forms of sex-based harassment on the job. . . . [B]y portraying women as less than equal at work, men can secure superior jobs, resources, and influence—all of which afford men leverage over women at home and everyplace else. . . . [The focus of legal inquiry should be whether the conduct at issue has] the purpose or effect of undermining women's "right to participate in the workplace on [an] equal footing."

Katherine M. Franke, What's Wrong with Sexual Harassment

49 Stan. L. Rev. 691, 693, 696 (1997)

According to the theory I develop . . . , the sexual harassment of a woman by a man is an instance of sexism precisely because the act embodies fundamental gender stereotypes: men as sexual conquerors and women as sexually conquered, men as masculine sexual subjects and women as feminine sexual objects. . . . Sexual harassment is a technology of sexism. It is a disciplinary practice that inscribes, enforces, and polices the identities of both harasser and victim according to a system of gender norms that envisions women as feminine, (hetero)sexual objects, and men as masculine, (hetero)sexual subjects. . . .

On my account, sexual harassment—between any two people of whatever sex—is a form of sex discrimination when it reflects or perpetuates gender stereotypes in the workplace. I suggest a reconceptualization of sexual harassment as gender harassment. Understood in this way, sexual harassment is a kind of sex discrimination not because the conduct would not have been undertaken if the victim had been a different sex, not because it is sexual, and not because men do it to women, but precisely because it is a technology of sexism. That is, it perpetuates, enforces, and polices a set of gender norms that seek to feminize women and masculinize men. . . .

Similarly, sexual harassment operates as a means of policing traditional gender norms particularly in the same-sex context when men who fail to live up to a societal norm of masculinity are punished by their male co-workers through sexual means.

Harris v. Forklift Systems, Inc.

510 U.S. 17 (1993)

Justice O'CONNOR delivered the opinion of the Court.

In this case we consider the definition of a discriminatorily "abusive work environment" (also known as a "hostile work environment") under Title VII. . . .

I

Teresa Harris worked as a manager at Forklift Systems, Inc., an equipment rental company, from April 1985 until October 1987. Charles Hardy was Forklift's president.

The Magistrate found that, throughout Harris' time at Forklift, Hardy often insulted her because of her gender and often made her the target of unwanted sexual innuendos. Hardy told Harris on several occasions, in the presence of other employees, "You're a woman, what do you know" and "We need a man as the rental manager"; at least once, he told her she was "a dumb ass woman." . . . Again in front of others, he suggested that the two of them "go to the Holiday Inn to negotiate [Harris'] raise." . . . Hardy occasionally asked Harris and other female employees to get coins from his front pants pocket. He threw objects on the ground in front of Harris and other women, and asked them to pick the objects up. . . . He made sexual innuendos about Harris' and other women's clothing.

In mid-August 1987, Harris complained to Hardy about his conduct. Hardy said he was surprised that Harris was offended, claimed he was only joking, and apologized. . . . He also promised he would stop, and based on this assurance Harris stayed on the job. But in early September, Hardy began anew: While Harris was arranging a deal with one of Forklift's customers, he asked her, again in front of other employees, "What did you do, promise the guy . . . some [sex] Saturday night?" . . . On October 1, Harris collected her paycheck and quit.

Harris then sued Forklift, claiming that Hardy's conduct had created an abusive work environment for her because of her gender. The United States District Court for the Middle District of Tennessee, adopting the report and recommendation of the Magistrate, found this to be "a close case," . . . but held that Hardy's conduct did not create an abusive environment. The court found that some of Hardy's comments "offended [Harris], and would offend the reasonable woman," . . . but that they were not "so severe as to be expected to seriously affect [Harris'] psychological well-being." A reasonable woman manager under like circumstances would have been offended by Hardy, but his conduct would not have risen to the level of interfering with that person's work performance. "Neither do I believe that [Harris] was subjectively so offended that she suffered injury. . . . Although Hardy may at times have genuinely offended [Harris], I do not believe that he created a working environment so poisoned as to be intimidating or abusive to [Harris]." . . . The United States Court of Appeals for the Sixth Circuit affirmed. . . .

II

Title VII . . . makes it "an unlawful employment practice for an employer . . . to discriminate against any individual with respect to his compensation, terms, conditions, or privileges of employment, because of such individual's race, color, religion, sex, or national origin." As we made clear in Meritor Savings Bank v. Vinson, this language "is not limited to 'economic' or 'tangible' discrimination. The phrase 'terms, conditions, or privileges of employment' evinces a congressional intent 'to strike at the entire spectrum of disparate treatment of men and women' in employment," which includes requiring people to work in a discriminatorily hostile or abusive environment. When the workplace is permeated with "discriminatory intimidation, ridicule, and insult," that is "sufficiently severe or pervasive to alter the condition of the victim's employment and create an abusive working environment," Title VII is violated.

This standard, which we reaffirm today, takes a middle path between making actionable any conduct that is merely offensive and requiring the conduct to cause a tangible psychological injury. As we pointed out in *Meritor*, "mere utterance of an . . . epithet which engenders offensive feelings in an employee," . . . does not sufficiently affect the conditions of employment to implicate Title VII. Conduct that is not severe or pervasive enough to create an objectively hostile or abusive work environment—an environment that a reasonable person would find hostile or abusive—is beyond Title VII's purview. Likewise, if the victim does not subjectively perceive the environment to be abusive, the conduct has not actually altered the conditions of the victim's employment, and there is no Title VII violation.

But Title VII comes into play before the harassing conduct leads to a nervous breakdown. A discriminatorily abusive work environment, even one that does not seriously affect employees' psychological well-being, can and often will detract from employees' job performance, discourage employees from remaining on the job, or keep them from advancing in their careers. Moreover, even without regard to these tangible effects, the very fact that the discriminatory conduct was so severe or pervasive that it created a work environment abusive to employees because of their race, gender, religion, or national origin offends Title VII's broad rule of workplace equality. . . .

We therefore believe the District Court erred in relying on whether the conduct "seriously affect[ed] plaintiff's psychological well-being" or led her to "suffe[r] injury." . . . Certainly Title VII bars conduct that would seriously affect a reasonable person's psychological well-being, but the statute is not limited to such conduct. So long as the environment would reasonably be perceived, and is perceived, as hostile or abusive, *Meritor*, there is no need for it also to be psychologically injurious.

This is not, and by its nature cannot be, a mathematically precise test. We need not answer today all the potential questions it raises. . . . But we can say that whether an environment is "hostile" or "abusive" can be determined only by looking at all the circumstances. These may include the frequency of the discriminatory conduct; its severity; whether it is physically threatening or humiliating, or a mere offensive utterance; and whether it unreasonably interferes with an employee's work performance. The effect on the employee's psychological well-being is, of course, relevant to determining whether the plaintiff actually found the environment abusive. But while psychological harm, like any other relevant factor, may be taken into account, no single factor is required. . . .

We therefore reverse the judgment of the Court of Appeals, and remand the case for further proceedings consistent with this opinion.

Justice SCALIA, concurring. . . .

"Abusive" (or "hostile," which in this context I take to mean the same thing) does not seem to me a very clear standard—and I do not think clarity is at all increased by adding the adverb "objectively" or by appealing to a "reasonable person's" notion of what the vague word means. Today's opinion does list a number of factors that contribute to abusiveness, . . . but since it neither says how much of each is necessary (an impossible task) nor identifies any single factor as determinative, it thereby adds little certitude. As a practical matter, today's holding lets virtually unguided juries decide whether sex-related conduct engaged in (or permitted by) an employer is egregious enough to warrant an award of damages. One might say that what constitutes "negligence" (a traditional jury question) is not much more clear and certain than what constitutes "abusiveness." Perhaps so. But the class of plaintiffs seeking to recover for negligence is limited to those who have suffered harm, whereas under this statute "abusiveness" is to be the test of whether legal harm has been suffered, opening more expansive vistas of litigation.

Be that as it may, I know of no alternative to the course the Court today has taken. One of the factors mentioned in the Court's nonexhaustive list—whether the conduct unreasonably interferes with an employee's work performance—would, if it were made an absolute test, provide greater guidance to juries and employers. But I see no basis for such a limitation in the language of the statute. Accepting *Meritor*'s interpretation of the term "conditions of employment" as the law, the test is not whether work has been impaired, but whether working conditions have been discriminatorily altered. I know of no test more faithful to the inherently vague statutory language than the one the Court today adopts. For these reasons, I join the opinion of the Court.

Justice GINSBURG, concurring.

Today the Court reaffirms the holding of Meritor Savings Bank v. Vinson . . . : "[A] plaintiff may establish a violation of Title VII by proving that discrimination based on sex has created a hostile or abusive work environment." The critical issue, Title VII's text indicates, is whether members of one sex are exposed to disadvantageous terms or conditions of employment to which members of the other sex are not exposed. . . . As the Equal Employment Opportunity Commission emphasized . . . the adjudicator's inquiry should center, dominantly, on whether the discriminatory conduct has unreasonably interfered with the plaintiff's work performance. To show such interference, "the plaintiff need not prove that his or her tangible productivity has declined as a result of the harassment." . . . It suffices to prove that a reasonable person subjected to the discriminatory conduct would find, as the plaintiff did, that the harassment so altered working conditions as to "ma[k]e it more difficult to do the job." . . .

The Court's opinion, which I join, seems to me in harmony with the view expressed in this concurring statement.

Oncale v. Sundowner Offshore Servs., Inc.

523 U.S. 75 (1998)

Justice SCALIA delivered the opinion of the Court.

This case presents the question whether workplace harassment can violate Title VII's prohibition against "discrimination . . . because of . . . sex" when the harasser and the harassed employee are of the same sex.

I

The District Court having granted summary judgment for respondent, we must assume the facts to be as alleged by petitioner Joseph Oncale. The precise details are irrelevant to the legal point we must decide. . . . In late October

1991, Oncale was working for respondent Sundowner Offshore Services on a Chevron U.S.A., Inc., oil platform in the Gulf of Mexico. He was employed as a roust about on an eight-man crew which included respondents John Lyons, Danny Pippen, and Brandon Johnson. Lyons, the crane operator, and Pippen, the driller, had supervisory authority. On several occasions, Oncale was forcibly subjected to sex-related, humiliating actions against him by Lyons, Pippen and Johnson in the presence of the rest of the crew. Pippen and Lyons also physically assaulted Oncale in a sexual manner, and Lyons threatened him with rape.

Oncale's complaints to supervisory personnel produced no remedial action; in fact, the company's Safety Compliance Clerk, Valent Hohen, told Oncale that Lyons and Pippen "picked [on] him all the time too," and called him a name suggesting homosexuality. Oncale eventually quit—asking that his pink slip reflect that he "voluntarily left due to sexual harassment and verbal abuse." When asked at his deposition why he left Sundowner, Oncale stated, "I felt that if I didn't leave my job, that I would be raped or forced to have sex."

Oncale filed a complaint against Sundowner in the United States District Court for the Eastern District of Louisiana, alleging that he was discriminated against in his employment because of his sex. . . . [T]he district court held that "Mr. Oncale, a male, has no cause of action under Title VII for harassment by male co-workers." On appeal, a panel of the Fifth Circuit . . . affirmed. We granted certiorari.

II . . .

Title VII's prohibition of discrimination "because of . . . sex" protects men as well as women, and in the related context of racial discrimination in the workplace we have rejected any conclusive presumption that an employer will not discriminate against members of his own race. "Because of the many facets of human motivation, it would be unwise to presume as a matter of law that human beings of one definable group will not discriminate against other members of that group." Castaneda v. Partida, 430 U.S. 482 (1977). In Johnson v. Transportation Agency, Santa Clara Cty., 480 U.S. 616 (1987), a male employee claimed that his employer discriminated against him because of his sex when it preferred a female employee for promotion. Although we ultimately rejected the claim on other grounds, we did not consider it significant that the supervisor who made that decision was also a man. If our precedents leave any doubt on the question, we hold today that nothing in Title VII necessarily bars a claim of discrimination "because of . . . sex" merely because the plaintiff and the defendant (or the person charged with acting on behalf of the defendant) are of the same sex.

Courts have had little trouble with that principle in cases like Johnson, where an employee claims to have been passed over for a job or promotion. But when the issue arises in the context of a "hostile environment" sexual harassment claim, the state and federal courts have taken a bewildering variety of stances. Some, like the Fifth Circuit in this case, have held that same-sex sexual harassment claims are never cognizable under Title VII. Other decisions say that such claims are actionable only if the plaintiff can prove that the harasser is homosexual (and thus presumably motivated by sexual desire). Still others suggest that workplace harassment that is sexual in content is always actionable, regardless of the harasser's sex, sexual orientation, or motivations.

We see no justification in the statutory language or our precedents for a categorical rule excluding same-sex harassment claims from the coverage of Title VII. As some courts have observed, male-on-male sexual harassment in the workplace was assuredly not the principal evil Congress was concerned with when it enacted Title VII. But statutory prohibitions often go beyond the principal evil to cover reasonably comparable evils, and it is ultimately the provisions of our laws rather than the principal concerns of our legislators by which we are governed. Title VII prohibits "discrimination . . . because of . . . sex" in the "terms" or "conditions" of employment. Our holding that this includes sexual harassment must extend to sexual harassment of any kind that meets the statutory requirements.

Notes

1. **Finding the Legal Line Between Ordinary Social Exchange and Sexual Harassment.** Courts have struggled with finding the line between "ordinary" social behavior between men and women and actionable sexual harassment, requiring that the conduct be sufficiently severe or pervasive, offensive (not only to the plaintiff, but to a reasonable person in the plaintiff's position), and unwelcome. Does the prohibition against sexual harassment leave room for ordinary sexual banter between men and women in the workplace? Under nonsubordination analysis, the ordinary is the problem—i.e., sex has been defined so that what has come to be accepted as everyday behavior, in fact, subordinates women. The ordinariness of sexual subordination makes it invisible, and thus all the more effective.

Those who have resisted recognizing sexual harassment as a wrong, on the other hand, see the law as a clumsy tool for restraining what is a "natural" attraction between the sexes. In one early case, in which defendant president of a company kissed the plaintiff, touched her breasts and buttocks, and put his hands up her dress, the court noted:

> It is important to point out that one of the traditional places where man meets woman is at the work place. Such meetings often result in dating, blossom into love, and eventually into marriage. . . . If civil liability is implanted on an employer for its employees['] natural interaction between the genders, either the collapse of our commercial system or the end of the human race can be foreseen. No employer could safely employ both males and females, and the number of marriages with children will be substantially decreased. There should be nothing wrong with a man, even a supervisor, telling a female that

she looks nice. Nor can there be anything wrong with a man, even a supervisor, asking a female out [on] a date. In doing so the man should not have to gamble on civil liability on her "yes" response.[7]

In another widely publicized case, the plaintiff introduced the following evidence of harassment: (1) her supervisor referred to her as a "pretty girl," as in "There's always a pretty girl giving me something to sign off on." (2) Once when she commented on how hot his office was, he raised his eyebrows and said, "Not until you stepped your foot in here." (3) Once when the announcement "may I have your attention, please" was broadcast over the public-address system, the supervisor stopped at her desk and said, "You know what that means, don't you? All pretty girls run around naked." (4) The supervisor once told her that his wife had told him "I had better clean up my act" and "better think of you as Ms. Anita Hill." (5) Once when she complained that his office was "smoky" from cigarette smoke, the supervisor replied, "Oh really? Were we dancing, like in a nightclub?" (6) When she asked him whether he had gotten his wife a Valentine's Day card, he responded that he had not but he should because it was lonely in his hotel room, at which point he looked ostentatiously at his hand with a gesture suggesting masturbation. Judge Richard Posner analyzed this conduct as follows:

> He never touched the plaintiff. He did not invite her, explicitly or by implication, to have sex with him, or to go out on a date with him. He made no threats. He did not expose himself, or show her dirty pictures. He never said anything to her that could not be repeated on prime time television. The comment about Anita Hill was the opposite of solicitation, the implication being that he would get into trouble if he didn't keep his distance. . . . Some of his repartee, such as "not until you stepped your foot in here," or, "Were we dancing, like in a nightclub?," has the sexual charge of an Abbott and Costello movie. The reference to masturbation completes the impression of a man whose sense of humor took final shape in adolescence. It is no doubt distasteful to a sensitive woman to have such a silly man as one's boss, but only a woman of Victorian delicacy—a woman mysteriously aloof from contemporary American popular culture in all its sex-saturated vulgarity—would find [his] patter substantially more distressing than the heat and cigarette smoke of which the plaintiff does not complain.[8]

Do you agree?

2. Sexual Harassment as Discrimination "Because of Sex"? As discussed in *Oncale*, sexual harassment is a form of discrimination under Title VII as long as it occurs *because of* sex. Given its foundation in equality analysis, under what circumstances should abusive or degrading behavior be considered actionable sexual harassment?

For example, what if a supervisor treats every worker in exactly the same way—abusively, and as a sexual object? Can this still be sex discrimination? Courts have not been consistent. Some have applied a comparative equality analysis and only recognized as discriminatory vulgar language, pictures, and jokes and other behaviors that affected plaintiffs in a particular way, or to a greater degree, because of their sex.[9] Other courts have concluded that a harasser cannot insulate him- or herself from a sexual harassment charge simply because his or her conduct is sufficiently egregious as to offend everyone.[10] For still other courts, the "because of sex" dimension is satisfied by the sexual nature of the offending behavior — in essence abandoning the equality paradigm in favor of a model that sees anything sexual as sex-based. To address the harms of sexual harassment, which approach makes most sense?

What if a supervisor's abusive conduct is not sexual or gendered in nature, but is targeted only at women? In EEOC v. National Education Ass'n,[11] the Ninth Circuit allowed plaintiffs to proceed with a hostile environment harassment lawsuit on the basis of their supervisor's bullying. While his conduct did not include sexual advances or comments, he yelled at the plaintiffs with "little or no provocation," and his shouting rants were often accompanied by aggressive physical gestures like lunging, pumping fists, and grabbing plaintiffs while barking commands or complaints at them. The bulk of evidence in the record showed that he behaved this way only toward women. The court held that this comparative evidence could satisfy the "because of sex" requirement as elucidated in *Oncale*.

What if, in contrast, the conduct *is* very sexual in nature, but not targeted at anyone in particular or even women in general? In Lyle v. Warner Brothers Television Productions, a writer's assistant for the long-running sitcom *Friends* alleged she had been sexually harassed by being forced to be present and take notes during meetings where the comedy writers engaged in sexually explicit conversation, gestures (including pantomimed masturbation), and cartoon drawings.[12] The plaintiff complained especially about the writers' discussions of their own sexual preferences and experiences and their fantasies about the sex lives of the actresses on the show, as well as other topics like anal sex and naked cheerleaders. The defendant offered "creative necessity" as a defense, arguing that comedy writers needed to have "frank sexual discussions and tell colorful jokes and stories (and even make expressive gestures) as part of the creative process."[13] The California Supreme Court, interpreting a state law provision similar to Title VII, concluded that while there is no categorical defense to sexual harassment lawsuits for creative workplaces, the plaintiff could not prevail because she did not prove that the conduct was either targeted at her directly or created hostility for women in general. To be actionable, the court held, undirected conduct must be even more severe and pervasive than targeted conduct. It also held that workplace context is relevant to determining whether actionable harassment occurred.

What if the sexual conduct is consensual between a supervisor and employee, but unfair to other employees? So-called sexual favoritism complaints have not fared well under Title VII generally due to the "because of sex" requirement. If a male supervisor has an affair with a female subordinates, other employees, both male and female, may have a grievance if the supervisor treats his subordinate more favorably than he treats them, but those effects are not obviously because of sex. But what if it was clear to women that employees who slept with the boss would be treated more favorably? Does that create an implied *quid pro quo* for other female employees or create a hostile environment? The EEOC issued a policy guidance in 1990 stating the agency's position that while isolated incidents of sexual favoritism do not violate Title VII, widespread favoritism can create a hostile environment, as well as support an implicit *quid pro quo* claim.[14]

The California Supreme Court, interpreting state antidiscrimination law, followed this guidance in a 2005 case, Miller v. Department of Corrections, which presents a textbook case of sexual favoritism.[15] There, the warden at a women's prison had sexual relationships with at least three female subordinates, often involving public displays of affection and emotional fights among the women over competing affairs. He admittedly treated these women more favorably than other employees, defending the decision to give one of them a promotion over more qualified applicants because he had no choice lest she "take him down" by revealing "every scar on his body." Plaintiffs claimed that female employees repeatedly questioned whether this was the type of workplace where they would have to 'F' my way to the top."[16] The court ruled that sexual favoritism is a valid claim when it is "sufficiently widespread" such that "the demeaning message is conveyed to female employees that they are viewed by management as 'sexual playthings' or that the way required for women to get ahead in the workplace is by engaging in sexual conduct with their supervisors or management." If you were an employer, what steps would you take to avoid liability for sexual favoritism? Must all office romance be prohibited?

Under MacKinnon's theory, can men ever be victims of sexual harassment? If sexual harassment is viewed primarily as a means of reinforcing gender subordination, what accounts for cases in which women harass male subordinates or co-workers? Although cases with male plaintiffs have been rare, they have resulted in some of the largest verdicts, including the first $1 million damage award in a sexual harassment case.[17] Most of these cases involve *quid pro quo* harassment. Do these claims support the suspicion that sexual harassment charges are sometimes simply an act of revenge following a romantic attraction that ends badly? Or do they indicate that women, no less than men, are capable of abusing power in the workplace? Men have also received unusually high verdicts for the harm of being wrongly accused in sexual harassment cases. A jury awarded one executive $26 million after he was fired by the company based on repeated charges of sexual harassment. One such charge included his description of a racy episode of *Seinfeld* to an offended female co-worker. The award was later overturned on appeal on the grounds that the fired executive had not proven that he was entitled to any damages, let alone that amount.[18]

3. The Standard for Determining Hostile Work Environment. *Harris* imposes both an objective and a subjective standard for determining a hostile work environment. The plaintiff must have been actually offended, and the offense taken must have been reasonable. A longstanding issue is whether "reasonable" should be interpreted in light of the plaintiff's sex—i.e., can conduct that would not be offensive to a male employee, if the tables were turned, be sufficiently offensive to the female plaintiff to be actionable as sexual harassment? Only the Ninth Circuit Court of Appeals has specifically applied a "reasonable woman" standard.[19] *Harris* and subsequent U.S. Supreme Court cases have firmly established the standard that the "objective severity of harassment should be judged from the perspective of a reasonable person in the plaintiff's position, considering 'all the circumstances.'"[20] In *Oncale*, Justice Scalia reaffirmed that the "objective severity of harassment should be judged from the perspective of a reasonable person in the plaintiff's position, considering 'all the circumstances.'" Is this broad enough to encompass a "reasonable woman" standard if the plaintiff is female? Must a jury take that perspective?

Should sexual harassment standards take into account research showing that women are more likely than men to perceive certain behaviors, such as unsolicited invitations for sex, as harassing?[21] Does a reasonable person standard ignore the perspectives of women, and legitimate behaviors that many female workers find offensive?[22] Or would women be harmed more than helped by the assumption that they are all alike, and easily offended?[23] Although this issue initially divided feminists, it has grown less important in light of recent social science surveys suggesting that men and women do not significantly vary in their interpretations of conduct serious enough to trigger legal liability.[24]

The trial court in *Harris* applied a "reasonable woman" standard and found the circumstances to be a "close case" that did not ultimately justify liability. By contrast, the Supreme Court, using "reasonable person" language, concluded that the facts may have been sufficient to state a case of sexual harassment. This may suggest that the exact formulation of the standard is not as important as who is applying it. Indeed, altering the legal standard from reasonable person to reasonable woman has little effect in mock jury studies; the most comprehensive study, involving five different methods and close to 2000 participants, found that the changes in the standard accounted for only about 2 percent of the variance in perceptions of hostile work environments.[25]

How should courts determine what acts are sufficiently pervasive and abusive to justify liability? Consider the proposal of Gillian K. Hadfield, who would define sex-based harassment as "sex-based non-job-related workplace conduct that would lead a rational woman to alter her workplace behavior—such as by refusing overtime, projects, or travel that will put her in contact with a harasser, requesting a transfer, or quitting. . . ." In Hadfield's view, "[b]ecause Title VII targets sex discrimination . . . the issue is whether a workplace practice has systematically negative consequences for women vis-à-vis men. Even if significant numbers of women enjoy an atmosphere in which sexual jokes abound, if systematically more women than men find this costly, then the practice is discriminatory. . . ." This approach would also eliminate the need for individual plaintiffs to prove that the behavior was unwelcome (see Note 4, below), since "those behaviors that rational women would be willing to pay to avoid are by definition unwelcome." Such a standard, however, would place "the onus on men, employers, and organizations to become educated about what behavior on their subordinates' part would prompt employment changes by a rational female employee. The test rejects the notion that men are entitled to the protection of their misimpressions about how such behavior is interpreted by women."[26] Is Hadfield's approach consistent with equality analysis? Would it be desirable?

4. When Is Sexual Conduct "Unwelcome"?   The plaintiff in a hostile environment sexual harassment case must prove that the conduct was "unwelcome." One function of this requirement is to prevent parties from using sexual harassment charges to punish each other when a consensual relationship fails. Critics have argued that, as in the case of proving rape, this requirement often seems to put on trial the plaintiff, whose sexually provocative speech or dress was thought by Justice Rehnquist in *Meritor* to be "obviously relevant." Evaluating it also, according to Louise Fitzgerald and others, reinforces double standards of morality that treat women's sexual expression more harshly than men's.[27] The Federal Rules of Evidence impose some limits on the evidence of dress or lifestyle that will be admissible: such evidence must be more probative than prejudicial.[28]

Probative evidence is evidence that helps to prove or disprove a point in issue.
Prejudicial evidence is evidence that promotes a bias, or a preconceived judgment about a point in issue.

Evidence of the plaintiff's participation in workplace banter has been still more controversial. Court decisions concerning the relevance of such evidence are divided. In one case, plaintiff admitted at trial that she cursed and used vulgar language while at work. Her co-workers also testified that she often made jokes about sex, including jokes about "screwing her boss," and that she participated in frequent discussions and bantering about sex. In light of this testimony, the trial judge concluded that "[a]ny harassment plaintiff received . . . was prompted by her own actions, including her tasteless joking. Considering plaintiff's contribution to and apparent enjoyment of the situation, it cannot be said that the defendants created 'an intimidating, hostile, or offensive working environment.'"[29] Other courts, however, have found that a plaintiff who has participated in some of the exchanges involving foul language and sexual innuendo do not lose all protection to be free from sexual harassment.[30]

What, besides consent to sexual advances, might explain an employee's participation in such conduct? Research suggests that such behavior might sometimes serve as a survival technique—a way to achieve acceptance or defuse a potentially unpleasant situation.[31] A similar motive might explain situations in which a plaintiff discounts the significance of harassing behavior as "[not] that big of a deal" or maintains friendly relations with the harasser. Yet courts have sometimes considered such responses as proof that the conduct was not sufficiently abusive to establish liability.[32] Do such outcomes "ignore[] the reality of what women must do to make life bearable in an all-male workplace"?[33]

The most obvious way for an employee to signal that particular behavior is offensive and unwelcome is to complain about it. Courts have increasingly required such complaints, but questions remain about when an employee must register objections: After the first instance? When conditions have become intolerable? Somewhere in between? Note, again, the potential catch-22 situation: if the woman complains too early, she is hypersensitive, humorless, and unreasonable; if she waits too long, she may have difficulty proving the behavior was unwelcome.[34] Should it matter that surveys show filing a formal complaint to be the least likely response of a victim of workplace harassment?

Is there a preferable alternative to the "unwelcome" test? Should "sexual attention in the workplace . . . be presumed to be unwelcome"?[35] Would this be fair to defendants? Several commentators have also suggested that certain kinds of conduct, such as sexual slurs, pornographic photos, or sexual contact not preceded by an expression of interest, should be presumed unwelcome, without evidence of the plaintiff's reaction.[36] Would this approach lead to an unduly sanitized workplace, discussed in Note 7, below? Or would it prevent the kind of victimization of victims that prevents women from making complaints?

Pretrial discovery is the process by which parties in civil litigation obtain information about their opponents' cases in order to prepare for trial and assess settlement offers. Over 90 percent of civil cases settle prior to trial.

According to surveyed practitioners, a primary problem in litigating harassment claims is not the unwelcomeness requirement itself, but the intrusive pretrial discovery practices that it permits. Defense lawyers are often able to question employees about issues such as their sex lives with other employees or their use of profanity, ostensibly to reveal any "seediness" in their background but also to discourage plaintiffs from going forward.[37] According to defense counsel, such questioning is an appropriate way to deter frivolous complaints; it keeps plaintiffs with inappropriate motives from assuming that "making a sexual harassment complaint will be a breeze."[38]

Is this a legitimate concern? How might it be accommodated without also discouraging meritorious complaints?

5. Sexual Harassment as an Offense Against Dignity. A European Union Recommendation on the Protection of Dignity of Women and Men at Work defines the issue in terms of workplace dignity, rather than sex discrimination. Western European countries generally recognize harassment as an offense whether or not it is based on sex. "Bullying" is an actionable tort that includes everything from verbal harangues to social ostracism.[39] In the last several years, 13 states have considered legislation that would make unlawful behaviors that are threatening, intimidating, or humiliating. Some commentators have recommended remedies for harassment by extending current tort law concepts of intentional infliction of emotional distress. Such a remedy would allow victims to sue the persons responsible, rather than just the employer, and would encompass conduct that is not sexual or aimed at only certain groups.[40]

A 2010 national survey found that about one-third of surveyed American workers reported bullying behavior, defined as verbal or psychological forms of aggressive (hostile) conduct that persists for at least six months. About 40 percent of the bullies were female, and more than 80 percent of their targets were other women.[41]

What conclusions do you draw from this research? Is the dignity approach preferable to the discrimination approach as a response to workplace harassment? Some critics worry that such legislation would encompass too much trivial behavior and impose undue legal costs. Others believe that it would prove largely meaningless since few victims could afford the costs of proceeding except in egregious cases. What is your view?

6. Employer Liability. Sexual harassment law involves two separate questions: (1) did actionable harassment occur; and (2) can the employer be held liable for it? Individual harassers cannot be held liable under Title VII, thus employer liability is crucial to providing a remedy to discrimination victims.[42]

Vicarious liability exists when an employer is responsible for the actionable conduct of an employee because of the supervisory relationship between the two parties.

Through a series of cases, the Supreme Court has defined the circumstances in which the employer is liable for harassment by its employees. In Faragher v. City of Boca Raton, a college student who worked as a lifeguard for Boca Raton alleged that her supervisors had created a "sexually hostile atmosphere" by repeatedly subjecting female lifeguards to " 'uninvited and offensive touching,' by making lewd remarks, and by speaking of women in offensive terms."[43] One lifeguard allegedly told her, "Date me or clean the toilets for a year." Although the city had a sexual harassment policy, it was not distributed to her supervisors, and they were unaware of its requirements. The Supreme Court held that an employer is "vicariously liable" for a hostile environment created by one of its employees if the employee suffers an adverse employment action such as discharge or demotion. An employee who has not suffered this kind of adverse action can still establish a claim for sexual harassment, but the employer will have a defense if it can show, in the words of the case:

> (a) that the employer exercised reasonable care to prevent and correct promptly any sexually harassing behavior, and (b) that the plaintiff employee unreasonably failed to take advantage of any preventive or corrective opportunities provided by the employer or to avoid harm otherwise. While proof that an employer had promulgated an antiharassment policy with complaint procedure is not necessary in every instance as a matter of law, the need for a stated policy suitable to the employment circumstances may appropriately be addressed in any case when litigating the first element of the defense. And while proof that an employee failed to fulfill the corresponding obligation of reasonable care to avoid harm is not limited to showing an unreasonable failure to use any complaint procedure provided by the employer, a demonstration of such failure will normally suffice to satisfy the employer's burden under the second element of the defense. No affirmative defense is available, however, when the supervisor's harassment culminates in a tangible employment action, such as discharge, demotion, or undesirable reassignment.[44]

In Burlington Industries v. Ellerth, the plaintiff was a salesperson who alleged that she was subjected to constant sexual harassment by her supervisor, a mid-level manager. The misconduct consisted of "repeated boorish and offensive remarks and gestures," including repeated warnings to "loosen up" in response to sexual comments and pressure to meet him at a hotel lounge under the threat that "you know, Kim, I could make your life very hard or very easy at Burlington."[45] The plaintiff never reported her supervisor's conduct to her employer, despite being aware that it had a policy against sexual harassment. The Court adopted the same legal standard for employer liability, but remanded Ellerth's case for application of it. The employer was likely to prevail given that she failed to take advantage of an available internal grievance procedure.

In two later cases, the Court further established that where an employee resigns as a result of conditions that have become intolerable (constructive discharge), the employer may avoid liability by showing that there was an effective remedial process that the employee unreasonably failed to use.[46]

Under the affirmative defense, employers who wish to avoid accountability must make prompt and thorough investigations and take remedial actions reasonably calculated to prevent further harassment and to protect the complainant. Thus, *Faragher* and *Ellerth* spurred many employers to adopt formal, written anti-harassment policies and procedures; some also adopted anti-harassment training programs. But there has been considerable litigation over what types of responses are required of employers and complainants under the affirmative defense. For example, what constitutes a reasonable remedial action? Case law suggests that employers may be able to avoid liability if they transfer complainants out of range of the harasser unless that involves a less desirable assignment.[47] As long as employers take some responsive measures, failure to stop the harassment is not necessarily fatal to the employer's proof of the affirmative defense.[48] As interpreted by lower courts, the law does not require employers to be very proactive. A survey of some 200 post-*Faragher* and post-*Ellerth* cases found that as long as the employer had a viable anti-harassment policy and a grievance procedure that allows an employee to bypass a harassing supervisor, *Ellerth* and *Faragher* "did little to change employer incentives to reduce the incidence of sexual harassment by supervisors in the workplace."[49]

Another set of questions focuses on victim behavior. When is a victim's failure to complain unreasonable? Most women, including disproportionate numbers of women of color, fail to report harassment out of concerns for retaliation, blacklisting, loss of privacy, and doubts that effective responses will be forthcoming.[50] Although employers must demonstrate that a victim's failure to complain was unreasonable, judges have been skeptical of plaintiffs' reasons for delaying or failing to complain. A "generalized fear of retaliation" is insufficient. As one circuit court put it, "the bringing of a retaliation claim, rather than failing to report harassment, is the proper method for dealing with retaliation."[51] Courts have imposed strict standards on plaintiffs, ruling in one case that a new employee who complained on her eighth day at a new job that she had been harassed daily since the first day had waited too long.[52] Yet the majority of surveyed victims say that complaints make the situation worse.[53] Studies support this perception, finding that as many as 60 percent of employees who complain about harassment are subjected to retaliation.[54] How can the law take account of this reality while providing adequate incentives for employees to provide notice of harassing conditions?[55]

Critics of the current law have charged that having an anti-harassment policy and a grievance process is not enough to change behaviors in the workplace. The law generally fails to require more proactive measures, such as training, and reporting hotlines, and some management experts advise against strategies that would encourage reporting.[56] About 40 percent of surveyed businesses have no training, and many programs that are in place have demonstrated no long-term positive effect on attitudes or behaviors.[57] Internal complaint mechanisms are often structured in ways that inadvertently discourage their use and diminish their ability to address underlying discrimination issues. For example, because employers cannot promise confidentiality during investigation of a complaint, many victims are unwilling to come forward.[58] Moreover, because internal grievance procedures tend to focus on individual problem solving and preserving harmonious working relationships, experts have noted that they fail to address broader systemic conditions that perpetuate discrimination, such as gender segregation and stratification in the workforce.[59]

7. Harassment Prevention Policies: Do They Go Too Far?   While some believe that harassment policies do not effectively address discriminatory behaviors in the workplace, others argue that the current liability structure gives employers too great an incentive to regulate harmless behaviors, including "trivial" sexual conduct. According to Vicki Schultz:

> [T]he federal agency and the lower courts charged with interpreting Title VII define[d] harassment primarily in terms of sexual advances and other sexual conduct—an approach I call the sexual model. . . . [T]his sexual model is too narrow, because the focus on sexual conduct has obscured more fundamental problems of gender-based harassment and discrimination that are not primarily "sexual" in content or design. . . . [T]he sexual model is also too broad, because . . . [it is] leading *companies* to prohibit a broad range of relatively harmless sexual conduct, even when that conduct does not threaten gender equality on the job. . . . Many firms are banning or discouraging intimate relationships between their employees. Worst of all, companies are disciplining (and even firing) employees for these perceived sexual transgressions without bothering to examine whether they are linked to sex discrimination in purpose or effect.[60]

Schultz worries, in addition, that both employers and employees use trivial examples of sexual conduct as a pretext for other concerns. Employers, for example, have seized on harassment as a convenient cover for discharges that are motivated by age, race, sexual orientation, or performance issues, while employees have made frivolous harassment claims in an effort to insulate themselves from "retaliation" when there are in fact valid justifications for their demotion or dismissal.[61]

Critics also claim that liability concerns have encouraged employers to promulgate overly broad categorical prohibitions on sexual expression. In Robinson v. Jacksonville Shipyards, Inc., the plaintiff established a "hostile environment" in a workplace pervaded by pornographic pictures and repeated sexual and demeaning remarks and jokes.[62] The court found that the employer had condoned this conduct and issued an order enjoining such behaviors. The decree required the employer to prohibit the display, reading, or viewing of pictures, posters, calendars, graffiti, and other materials that were "sexually suggestive, sexually demeaning, or pornographic."[63]

Does such an order raise First Amendment issues? The court concluded it did not, because (1) the employer had "no intention to express itself through the sexually-oriented pictures" and had banned other speech as well (such as political campaign literature and buttons); (2) pictures and verbal harassment were "not protected speech [when] they act as discriminatory conduct in the form of a hostile work environment"; (3) "regulation of discriminatory speech in the workplace constitutes nothing more than time, place, and manner regulation of speech"; (4) "female workers were a captive audience in relation to the speech that comprised the hostile work environment"; (5) even if the speech is "treated as fully protected by the First Amendment," the governmental interest in "cleansing the workplace of impediments to the equality of women is . . . a compelling interest that permits [a regulation] . . . narrowly drawn to serve this interest"; and (6) even a governmental employer has the power to enforce workplace rules impinging on free speech rights, in order to maintain discipline and order in the workplace.[64]

Schultz maintains that efforts to "sanitize the workplace" will "induce[] social stigma and enforce[] sexual conformity in a way that impoverishes life for everyone." In her view, what women need is a "sexually open" and "gender egalitarian" workplace.[65] She would reform sexual harassment law to eliminate its focus on sexual content; courts under her proposal would prohibit any harassment that occurs because of sex and impose lesser standards of liability on workplaces that were gender-integrated at all levels, because these have been shown to have a lower incidence of offensive conduct.

Eugene Volokh and Kingsley Browne, both strong critics of restrictions on workplace expression, argue that harassment laws should target only offensive conduct directed at a particular employee; they worry that broader vaguer prohibitions will encourage employers to avoid liability by unduly limiting workplace speech.[66] What is your view? Is the standard adopted by the court in Lyle v. Warner Bros. (the case involving *Friends*) a fair compromise?

Schultz, along with other commentators, is also critical of the growing tendency of employers to become "cupid cops." The limited research available suggests that somewhere between 20 to 40 percent of companies have policies or clear norms on workplace romances, and that the vast majority prohibit or discourage such relationships.[67] Most prohibitions target relationships between supervisors and their subordinates, and some policies that do not ban these relationships demand that they be disclosed to managers who can monitor the situation. Underlying these policies are concerns about the coercive potential for those in situations of unequal power, the fact or perception of favoritism, and the problems that can arise if the relationship sours.

Critics of prohibitions on workplace romances worry that attempts to enforce them are often ineffective and intrusive, and likely to drive relationships underground. Enforcement is also likely to have gender-biased results; those in subordinate positions, typically women, are the ones typically transferred or dismissed.

Do categorical bans on workplace relationships ignore courtship realities? For a growing number of employees, the increasing length of workweeks means that they have less time to find potential partners outside of the workplace. In representative surveys, 40 to 50 percent of employees had dated someone at work, one-fifth had dated a subordinate, over a quarter ended up marrying a colleague, and three-quarters felt that they should be able to date anyone they wished.[68]

In an effort to accommodate competing concerns, some organizations allow romantic relationships but ask, or require, the parties to sign a "love contract." A typical agreement acknowledges that the relationship is consensual and welcome and that the supervisor will under no circumstances allow it to affect a subordinate's job or their working relationship.[69] Is this a reasonable approach? Would you recommend it for the organization where you intend to work? Should chief executives who have secret affairs with employees be forced to resign, as has happened in some widely publicized cases? Or should employers drop these "date and tell" requirements and focus instead on prohibiting coercive relationships and favoritism of any form, whether sexually motivated or not?

8. Street Harassment.   How should the law handle "street hassling" — i.e., crude behaviors such as wolf whistles, leers, catcalls, grabs, pinches, and sexual invitations?[70] Some feminists have proposed liability for such conduct under tort doctrine or misdemeanor statutes.[71] What problems and benefits do you see from such efforts? An anti-harassment campaign has been launched on Philadelphia transit, featuring ads such as "Nice a** is not a compliment," and "In a perfect world, what would your sister/daughter, girlfriend hear as she walks to the subway? Hey sexy? Can I have a smile? What, you gay? Good morning!"[72] Are public awareness campaigns such as this one likely to change attitudes or behavior (or both)?

9. Race and Sexual Harassment.   Although research finds that women of color are especially vulnerable to sexual harassment, some courts seem unresponsive to combined power of racial and sexual abuse. In one such case, the trial judge granted summary judgment against the plaintiff whose claims included an incident where a co-worker dropped his pants and ordered her to "suck my dick, you black bitch." Another co-worker told the woman that he wanted to hang her in a cornfield, and she also encountered a Ku Klux Klan card posted on a factory beam. The court concluded that the behavior was "deplorable, and even offensive, humiliating, and threatening," but insufficiently severe and pervasive to alter the terms of employment.[73]

Some commentators have suggested that standards of what is offensive may be affected by cultural expectations, including those based on race. Consider the highly publicized Senate confirmation hearing in which Clarence Thomas, nominated to serve on the U.S. Supreme Court, faced accusations of sexual harassment. Anita Hill, a former staff attorney under Thomas' supervision at the EEOC, claimed that she had been subject to repeated and unwelcome sexual comments and advances. In assessing Hill's claims, Harvard sociologist Orlando Patterson argued that "what constitutes proper and effective male-female relations varies across gender, class, ethnicity, and religion." To "most American feminists . . . an obscenity is always an obscenity . . . ; to everyone else . . . an obscene expression . . . has to be understood in context." With his "mainstream cultural guard down," Thomas may have engaged in conduct that might be offensive to some but not to others like Hill. To those of African-American southern working class backgrounds, such conversation might have seemed reflective of a "down home style of courting." Patterson also claimed that "[i]f women are to break through the glass ceiling, they must escape the trap of neo-Puritan feminism with its reactionary sacralization of women's bodies."[74]

What is your view? Should the racial or cultural background of the parties ever affect what constitutes harassment in the workplace?

Putting Theory Into Practice

3-1. Analyze each of the following situations to determine whether it establishes a case of "discrimination based on sex." What theories of sex discrimination help you make the determination?

(a) An employee uses obscene language and tells sexually explicit jokes, which are offensive to some co-workers, both male and female.

(b) A supervisor berates all of his subordinate staff, both men and women; he refers to male associates who are insufficiently combative as wimps and pussies, and he refers to assertive women as castrating bitches.

(c) A bisexual employee makes unwanted sexual advances to both male and female workers. After they refuse him twice, he stops, but his presence makes them uncomfortable.

(d) An employee widely assumed to be gay invites a male co-worker to dance at the office Christmas party, stares at his anatomy in the restroom, and hangs around the co-worker's desk for no obvious work-related reason.

(e) At an all-female mortgage company office, female employees make lewd jokes, ask each other about their sexual experiences, discuss whose breasts are bigger, and change clothes in front of one another. One administrative assistant is offended, and claims that it interferes with her work.

(f) A secretary who works in a physician's office announces that she is pregnant. The doctor's wife believes her husband was having an affair with the secretary and that the child might be his. After other measures to alleviate his wife's fears, the doctor fires his secretary to save his marriage. Does it matter whether they were actually having an affair?[75]

(g) Two first-year associates complain to their law firm managing partner that one of their colleagues, an attractive single woman, has consistently received better assignments than they have from the supervising partner in the litigation section. That partner is in the midst of a messy divorce and has made a point of including their colleague in evening strategy sessions and out-of-town depositions on a major case. The managing partner raises the issue with the supervisor, who responds that he is not having an affair with the associate, although he is seeing her "socially." He has channeled assignments to her because she is more available in the evening and for travel than her married colleagues. As long as the relationship is consensual, he views it as "none of the firm's business."

(h) A Christian employee association of a government office posted a flyer stating "seeking to preserve our workplace integrity . . . with respect for the Natural Family, Marriage and Family values." A lesbian worker has complained that the flyer makes her feel targeted and excluded. The office head removed the flyer and the association sued. How should the court rule?[76]

3-2. You are your employer's ombudsperson, or impartial advisor, for sexual harassment claims. You have received several complaints about an informal e-mail distribution list for staff who wish to exchange x-rated humor. All members of the list have requested to be on it, and e-mails come with a warning that they should be viewed behind closed doors. The messages mainly involve sexually explicit jokes and graphics. Several female secretaries have walked in on male attorneys while they were viewing the e-mails, and they are now uncomfortable about continuing to work with these attorneys. How should you respond?

3-3. Of the things that a male boss might ask of a female employee, which is the most objectionable: (a) to kiss him, (b) to babysit his kids, or (c) to be responsible for serving coffee at staff meetings?[77] What specifically makes each request objectionable? Does the law reflect your opinion?

3-4. A woman brings a sex discrimination lawsuit under Title VII when she is not promoted to a supervisory position. She offers evidence that because she did so many personal tasks for her boss at his request, such as buying presents for his wife, picking up his dry cleaning, and talking through problems he was having as a father, her boss and others in the office did not perceive her as having managerial or executive abilities.[78] Is she likely to succeed?

3-5. A Minneapolis woman works as a cashier in a sex-toy shop. Day in, day out, she hears lewd conversations by co-workers. Does she have a hostile environment claim against her employer, for failing to stop, or shield her from, these conversations?[79]

3-6. A warehouse foreman in a workplace requiring heavy lifting stated repeatedly that he believed women were incapable of performing work in the warehouse and that he would never hire a woman. Although he was not found to have committed any discriminatory personnel action, he was demoted for violating the organization's nondiscrimination policy by expressing beliefs that reflected a discriminatory attitude. He challenges that disciplinary action. Should he be reinstated?[80]

2. Sexual Harassment in Educational Institutions

The law on sexual harassment in the educational setting is less developed than the law governing harassment in the workplace. The following section outlines the issues in three specific areas relating to educational institutions: (a) schools' legal liability for sexual harassment; (b) speech and conduct codes intended to eliminate offensive conduct in schools; and (c) faculty-student dating.

a. School Legal Liability for Sexual Harassment

Title IX of the Education Amendments of 1972, discussed in Chapter 2, broadly prohibits sex discrimination by educational institutions that receive any federal funding.[81] Although it is most closely associated with gender equity in athletics, Title IX has had substantial application in the sexual harassment context. The Supreme Court has interpreted Title IX to prohibit *quid pro quo* harassment and hostile environment harassment as forms of intentional sex discrimination and to permit lawsuits for money damages.[82] The standards of liability, however, are more favorable to educational institutions than to employers under Title VII. In Gebser v. Lago Vista Independent School District, parents of a female student sued the school district after police found that their daughter was having a sexual affair with one of her teachers.[83] By a 5-4 vote, the Court held that schools are not liable for harassment of a student by an employee unless officials had actual notice of the specific misconduct and responded with "deliberate indifference." The school's failure in that case to have a nondiscrimination policy and internal grievances procedure, which are both required by Title IX's implementing regulations, was not sufficient to render it liable for the harassment. This sort of violation, however, can trigger enforcement and penalties by the Department of Education's Office for Civil Rights, the agency charged with implementing Title IX.

In explaining the result in *Gebser*, Justice O'Connor's majority opinion reasoned that any stricter standard would be at odds with the overall compliance scheme of Title IX, which requires federal enforcement agencies to provide notice of any violation of nondiscrimination requirements before initiating enforcement actions. The "central purpose" of this notice is to "avoid diverting education funding from beneficial uses where a recipient was unaware of discrimination in its programs and is willing to institute prompt corrective measures." Justice Stevens' dissenting opinion noted that the Court's opinion creates incentives to avoid the knowledge that should trigger corrective action. According to some commentators, the liability standard in *Gebser* may encourage the see-no-evil/hear-no-evil attitudes already in place in many education districts. "When ignorance is bliss, and a defense to legal judgments, why should schools establish effective complaint strategies?"[84] To some, this double standard for educational and employment settings seems perverse. "Students often have fewer options for avoiding an abusive situation than an adult employee, their capacities for resistance are less developed, and their values are more open to influence. Schools are powerful socializing institutions and their failure to address harassment perpetuates the attitudes that perpetuate problems."[85] What is your view?

Harassment by peers adds another layer of problems. About four-fifths of elementary and secondary students experience harassment, but only 7 percent report it.[86] In coeducational environments, the abuse takes multiple forms.

> Subtle oppression by boys, who act obviously bored, sighing, groaning and rolling their eyes, sends a powerful message when a girl contributes in

class. . . . Boys verbally abuse girls in and outside the classroom. In addition to the constant attack on the intellectual and academic abilities of girls, boys degrade girls with language that is pejorative of women. . . . In addition to purposeful abuse, boys oppress girls by monopolizing physical space. . . . [T]eachers in England . . . found that while boys occupy the total area surrounding schools by playing football, girls observe from benches or wander in the periphery of the "boys' space."[87]

A 2011 survey of students in grades 7–12 found that harassment is "part of everyday life."[88] Girls are more likely to be harassed (56 percent), especially physically, but boys are not immune (40 percent). Boys describe being called "gay" as the worst type of harassment, while girls respond that unwelcome sexual comments, jokes, or gestures are the most troubling and online sexual rumors are the second most troubling. The impact of harassment on students includes a variety of physical, emotional, and educational consequences, including, most frequently, a desire not to go to school.

At the college level, 61 percent of male and 62 percent of female students report experiencing harassment, defined as unwanted and unwelcome sexual behavior that interferes with one's life. Conduct includes sexual comments, rumors, grabbing, and propositions. Men are more likely to be called homophobic names; women are more likely to be adversely affected.[89] Only 7 percent report such conduct to a faculty or school official, largely because they don't believe it is sufficiently serious. However, cases that are reported pose significant concerns: sexual harassment is now the largest source of liability claims against higher educational institutions.[90]

In Davis v. Monroe County Board of Education, a divided Supreme Court clarified the standards for schools' liability for peer harassment.[91] There, a fifth-grade female student alleged repeated acts of harassment by one of her male classmates, including verbal and physical assaults such as attempts to touch her genital area. Despite several complaints by the girl's mother to the teacher, principal, and, eventually, the school board, the school failed to take adequate remedial action. Even though the boy pled guilty to criminal sexual battery, the school took three months to even agree to change the girl's seat so she would not have to sit next to him in every class. The majority in Davis held that a school district's "deliberate indifference to known acts of harassment" by students could give rise to liability, but only when the district "exercises substantial control over the harasser and the context in which the known harassment occurs" and the conduct is so "severe, pervasive, and objectively offensive that it can be said to deprive the victims of access to the educational opportunities or benefits provided by the school."[92] In assessing the adequacy of remedial responses, courts should not expect that administrators can entirely "purg[e] their schools of actionable peer harassment" and "should refrain from second-guessing [administrators'] disciplinary decisions."[93] The Court remanded the case, which ultimately settled for an undisclosed amount of damages.

Critics found Davis problematic on the same grounds as Gebser, in that it creates an incentive for educators to avoid knowledge that might subject them to legal accountability. Given the reluctance of students to complain to anyone, reporting requirements are said to create an unrealistic limitation on accountability where other, less senior school personnel have knowledge of a problem and fail to take reasonable remedial action. School officials have generally opposed stricter liability standards on the ground that they have limited control over abusive conduct, especially by student peers. While other employers can dismiss workers who persist in harassment, administrators believe that they have fewer options in the face of recalcitrant students or even faculty who have their own due process rights. Where facts are contested or ambiguous, officials feel "caught in the middle. . . . We weren't doing the harassing. We're the entity with the deep pockets."[94] How would you respond?

While plaintiffs have generally had difficulty meeting the *Gebser/Davis* standard, a few cases have found it to be satisfied. In Simpson v. University of Colorado Boulder, for example, the plaintiff female students claimed they were sexually assaulted by the university's football players and recruits for the team.[95] The football's "ambassador program" paired high school senior recruits with female students who were supposed to "show them a good time." Many complaints of forcible assault and rape arose from the program. The district court in the case determined that the university's knowledge did not satisfy the "deliberate indifference" test. The Tenth Circuit Court of Appeals, however, reversed, concluding that the football coach was aware of the assaults but nevertheless maintained an unsupervised player-host recruitment program to entice recruits to matriculate. School officials also may be liable under another civil rights law, Section 1983, which creates liability for deprivations of constitutional rights. In Fitzgerald v. Barnstable School Committee, the Supreme Court held that parents could sue school officials for sex discrimination under that statute when they allegedly failed to respond to serious harassment of their daughter by another classmate.[96] The standard for school liability under this statute has yet to be determined in the harassment context.

In addition to the traditional litigation route, enforcement activities by the federal Office for Civil Rights (OCR) has exerted pressure on colleges and universities to be more proactive about and responsive to sexual violence on campus. OCR initiated enforcement proceedings, for example, against Eastern Michigan University based on the institution's issuance of a misleading statement about a student who was sexually assaulted and murdered in her dorm room by a fellow student—a statement that there was "no evidence of foul play." During the investigation, OCR discovered several sexual assault and harassment complaints that had been inadequately investigated or resolved. The University entered a voluntary resolution in which it agreed to take a number of proactive measures to educate students and staff about the problem of sexual assault, to widely disseminate information about the policies and procedures for dealing with it, and to develop procedures to assist victims.[97] The University was also fined under the Jeanne Clery Disclosure of Campus Security Policy and Campus Crime Statistics Act, which is designed to force disclosure of certain crimes on campus, including sexual assault.[98]

In 2011, OCR issued a "Dear Colleague" letter (DCL) to remind institutions covered by Title IX of their obligations in dealing with complaints of sexual violence. OCR shared data from a National Institute of Justice report finding that "1 in 5 women are victims of completed or attempted sexual assault while in college," and, during the 2007–2008 school year, there were 800 reported incidents of rape and attempted rape and 3,800 reports of other sexual batteries at public high schools.[99] The letter emphasizes the deleterious effects on education experienced by victims of sexual violence and the need for prompt and effective investigations of complaints. It provides step-by-step guidance for schools who receive complaints, emphasizing, for example, that schools can neither await the outcome of criminal investigations before initiating their own investigations, nor impose a heightened "clear and convincing" evidentiary standard.[100]

Has the law struck the right balance between avoiding undue liability and providing incentives for schools to prevent or remedy harassment? How proactive should schools be? Is there a danger of overreaction? How would you respond to proposals to ban sexually suggestive cheerleading routines?[101]

b. Speech and Conduct Codes to Prevent Harassment

One approach to addressing sexual and racial harassment in educational institutions, especially at the college and university level, has been speech codes that prohibit "verbal conduct" or "expression" that interferes with a student's ability to benefit from the educational environment. Some proposals relate specifically to the Internet and e-mail systems. These codes have drawn fierce criticism from free speech advocates, who consider them a form of censorship and urge that the appropriate remedy for hurtful speech is not less, but more, speech. By contrast, advocates of regulation argue that in a sexist, racist society, "free speech" is available only to those with the power to use it, and that anti-harassment codes are critical to protect the dignity and integrity of individuals who cannot effectively "fight back" with counterspeech. In the university setting, racist and sexist speech is said to prevent some students from participating fully in the university community and from developing their psychological and intellectual potential.[102]

The tension between schools' interests in both preventing harassment and protecting expression has provoked increasing disputes, but no Supreme Court decision. Speech codes have not fared well, for the most part, in the lower courts. For example, a federal appellate court struck down as vague and overbroad a policy defining harassment as "verbal, written or physical conduct which offends, denigrates or belittles an individual . . . [including] unsolicited derogatory remarks, jokes, demeaning comments or behaviors, slurs, mimicking, name calling, graffiti, innuendo, gestures, physical conduct, stalking, [and] threatening [or] bullying [conduct]."[103] When such codes have been used against classroom behavior by professors, courts have been similarly protective of First Amendment concerns. For example, one federal trial court held that a university could not impose sanctions under a policy prohibiting "verbal or physical conduct of a sexual nature," against a writing professor who made frequent references to sex (such as comments about belly dancing and vibrators), often as analogies to the writing process.[104]

The law has developed in Canada in a direction more supportive of speech codes. There, the Supreme Court of Canada upheld a statute penalizing the communication of statements that willfully promote hatred against any identifiable racial, religious, or ethnic group, as applied to a high school teacher who expressed anti-Semitic views, including the belief that the Holocaust was a myth.[105]

How should academic institutions deal with offensive speech? Are strategies other than prohibitions preferable, such as student protests, negative course evaluations, and open forums?

c. Faculty-Student Dating

Faculty-student dating has been another subject of campus concern. The limited available data suggest that such relationships are not uncommon. The conventional assumption is that broad prohibitions are unnecessary, unenforceable, or unduly paternalistic. Common views include:

> "Being sexually propositioned . . . is a normal and healthy part of life. (The real psychological and emotional tragedy probably befalls those who are not). . . .
> It is hardly self-evident that the 'power imbalance' in such [relationships] favors the teacher. . . . If matters turn out badly, his career is finished."[106]

> "You can't legislate love."[107]

> A prohibition on faculty-student sexual relations "portrays students as timid and in need of protection." "It's like saying I can't make choices about who I want to date."[108]

> "It would take cult-like reprogramming to stop professors and students from dating. 'From everything we know sociologically, anthropologically, and biologically, males tend to be attracted to nubile potential mates, and women tend to be attracted to older men who . . . are successful and represent symbols of power.'"[109]

Feminist literary critic Jane Gallop acknowledges that women are at a "disadvantage" in a faculty-student relationship, but believes that "denying women the right to consent further infantilizes us."[110] Law professor Sherry Young similarly maintains:

> Feminists should not be in the business of reducing the range of choice available to women, no matter how much they may question the wisdom of some of the choices that are made. . . . Feminists should not promote an image of women as helpless victims incapable of functioning under conditions of

inequality of power. . . . The most pernicious idea to emerge from the debate on consensual relationship policies is the notion that feminists should be in the business of questioning the capacity of women, limiting the choices available to women, or urging institutions to disregard the testimony of women about their lives, their aspirations, and their emotional commitments.[111]

Compare Robin West's analysis:

Smart male students view themselves as all sorts of things, including young intellectuals. A good male student will often attach himself to a brilliant professor, and will aspire to be like him. . . . Unlike the male student, [the good female student] is more likely to be attracted to the brilliant professor, and aspire not to be like him, but to give herself to him. . . . For the female student, the intellectual self must fight the giving self, both in external and internal reality. The women who lose this battle have lost far more than the women who lost the A to which they were entitled, and so has the world. . . .

"Falling-in-love" with high school teachers, college professors, or research assistants really does destroy the productivity, the careers, the earning potential, and eventually the self-respect of many gifted women. Smart women drop out of high school, college and graduate school (and pretty women are at the highest risk) to date, marry, to help, and to serve those they perceive as intellectual giants. Eventually they learn boredom, the weariness of inactivity, and the self-contempt of nonproductivity.[112]

Other feminists agree. In part, their concerns are based on students' own accounts of sexual overtures by faculty. In one representative study, almost three-quarters of those who rejected a professor's advances considered them coercive and about half of those who had sexual relationships believed that some degree of coercion was involved.[113] Moreover, "faculty whose self-image and self-interest are at stake may underestimate the pressures that students experience. Regardless of the teacher's own intentions, students may believe that their acceptance or rejection of sexual overtures will have academic consequences. Given the power disparities involved, even relationships that appear consensual at the outset may become less so over time."[114] Except in egregious cases, however, few students have been willing to file complaints, and few institutions have been willing to impose serious sanctions. Even where the rules are clear, the evidence often is not. Moreover, most campus enforcement structures address only those faculty-student sexual relationships that meet conventional definitions of sexual harassment. Yet the harms to both individuals and institutions can be significant even in the absence of an explicit *quid pro quo* or a pervasive hostile environment. In relationships where the professor has any advisory or supervisory authority over the student, both the fact and the appearance of academic integrity are at risk.[115]

A growing number of institutions attempt to discourage faculty-student relationships. A few, such as William & Mary, ban all "amorous relations between faculty and undergraduates," or between graduate students and their supervisors.[116] Other schools counsel against such relationships and place a heavy burden on the faculty member to establish consent if a student complains. Some institutions prohibit faculty-student relationships where the professor has direct academic responsibility for the student. If a relationship arises, the faculty member must make other arrangements for supervision of the student's work. What kind of policy would you recommend for your own school?

Putting Theory Into Practice

3-7. For each of the following problems, consider (1) whether the conduct constitutes sexual harassment; (2) whether it would be appropriate for a university to prohibit the conduct through rules and regulations; and (3) if the conduct is undesirable, what strategies short of prohibition might be appropriate.

(a) A male college student repeatedly pursues a female student for a date. He calls her frequently on the phone and approaches her in person when he sees her on campus. She continues to refuse and finally demands that he leave her alone and stop calling. He does so, but then a month later asks again in the hopes she has changed her mind. He has never touched her.

(b) One fraternity on campus has an annual "red light district" party. All female students who attend are required to dress as prostitutes. At the party, the male students simulate "pick-ups" of the prostitutes. Invariably, some "mock" solicitations develop during that evening into actual seductions. Another fraternity invites a stripper to perform on campus the routine she offers at a local club.

(c) A university professor finds himself attracted to one of his students, who he feels is also attracted to him. Aware of the problems that can arise with faculty-student dating, he attempts to put his feelings of attraction aside. After picking up more and more "signals" that the student would welcome some initiative on his part, however, he finally asks her out for coffee. Her acceptance leads to more invitations to accompany him to campus events.

(d) Students post anatomically explicit and derogatory remarks on a male-only computer bulletin board. Other students circulate a poster with a nude caricature of a woman candidate for office of a student organization and send to an e-mail list of 20 friends a parody titled "Top 75 Reasons Why Women [Bitches] Should Not Have Freedom of Speech."[117]

(e) Male students claim that an openly gay male professor has come on to them sexually by leering at them after class and by including favorable references to same-sex relationships in his lectures on ancient Greece. One student claims that the professor brushed his buttocks when leaving class in a crowded corridor.

3-8. A state university recruited a basketball player whom it knew to have a history of past sexual misconduct. As a student at the university, the basketball player had consensual sex with a female student in his room, while one of his teammates hid in the closet. Afterwards, the teammate attempted, unsuccessfully, to have sex with her. During the scuffle, the first basketball player invited other team members to the room, telling them that they were "running a train" on (i.e., gang-raping) the woman. A third teammate then raped the woman. Should the university be liable, under Title IX, for recruiting the athlete knowing of his history and failing to adequately supervise him?[118]

C. DOMESTIC VIOLENCE

1. Domestic Violence: Legal Strategies for Protecting Victims

According to William Blackstone, the husband at English common law was legally entitled to use some physical force to provide his wife with "moderate correction."[119] So too, under early American common law, a husband, as master of his household, could subject his wife to "chastisement" short of permanent physical injury.[120] By the end of the Civil War, partly through efforts by early feminists, the American legal system had repudiated the doctrine of chastisement. However, during the Reconstruction Era, a new body of common law emerged under which judges concluded that "the legal system should not interfere in cases of wife beating, in order to protect the privacy of the marriage relationship and to promote domestic harmony."[121]

By the end of the nineteenth century, wife beating was viewed as a crime, but increasingly characterized as solely the practice of "lawless or unruly men of the 'dangerous classes,'" particularly African American men and men from low-status immigrant ethnic groups such as German and Irish Americans. Domestic violence among the economically and racially privileged classes disappeared from view.[122] By the 1920s, the victims of wife beating and child abuse had been transferred from "protection societies," which sought to provide women and children a safe haven from abusive men, to "child welfare agencies," which attempted to regulate domestic life more broadly. In the process, women were increasingly seen as part of the problem, and "domestic trouble cases" often became an occasion to help wives "master the habits of cleanliness, nutrition, and child care."[123] The goal of the new family court system was to keep the family intact; accordingly, judges encouraged battered women to accept responsibility for their role in provoking the violence and discouraged them from filing criminal charges. Those views, and the perception of domestic violence as a private matter, lasted well into the 1970s.

Beginning in the 1960s, the women's movement sought to make "private" violence a public issue. Feminists created shelters to protect the health and safety of battered women and children. Activists also undertook public education campaigns to call attention to male violence and state inaction. So, too, advocates began using legal strategies to reform how law enforcement officials responded to cases of intimate abuse.

As the legal landscape has changed, so has the language used to describe it. Battered women's advocates initially introduced the term "domestic violence" to replace more colloquial terms such as "wife beating." More recently, the terms "intimate violence" or "intimate partner violence" serve to encompass the abuse of elders, children, and siblings. Descriptions of such violence also are evolving. The popular meaning of "battering" is physical assault, but many researchers now argue that the quest for control, and not physical violence per se, best captures an abusive relationship, and can involve threats, isolation, and control over necessities. Indeed, some evidence suggests that psychological abuse can be at least or more harmful to victims as physical assaults.[124]

It is estimated that one-quarter to one-third of women in the United States have experienced physical or sexual violence by an intimate partner or acquaintance at some point in their lifetime.[125] Slightly over one-quarter of men are estimated to have experienced such violence.[126] Approximately 16 percent of women and 5 percent of men have experienced stalking from which they felt very fearful, or believed that they or someone close to them would be harmed as a result.[127] Nearly half of all homeless women and children have fled violence.[128]

Most systematic studies conclude that women are significantly more likely to be the victim of intimate violence than men. One survey found that females were the victims in 72 percent of intimate murders and the victims in about 85 percent of the non-lethal intimate violence.[129] Other research suggests that women are at least as physically aggressive as men, but less likely to inflict serious injury. According to a 2008 report from the Centers for Disease Control and Prevention, domestic violence is a leading cause of death for women ages 15 to 44, and the leading cause of death of pregnant women. Over 90 percent of female homicide victims are killed by men with whom they have had a relationship.[130] African American women and Native American women are at the highest risk of intimate partner homicide.[131]

Women are most likely to be injured in an intimate relationship in the course of trying to end it. One study found that married women who lived apart from their husbands were nearly four times more likely to report that their husbands had raped, physically assaulted, and/or stalked them than women who lived with their husbands (20 percent and 5.4 percent, respectively).[132]

Some 37 percent of American Indian and Alaska Native women are victims of rape, physical assault, or stalking in their lifetimes by an intimate partner, as compared to 29 percent of African American women, 25 percent of white women, and 15 percent of Asian/Pacific Islander women.[133] Partly as a result of negative perceptions or experiences involving law enforcement and social service agencies, African American women are also more reluctant to report violence than are white women.[134] Studies that have investigated the incidence of domestic violence across class consistently find a link between poverty and abuse. Women in rural communities often face disproportionate dangers both because of the inaccessibility of shelters and support services, and the persistence of "old boy networks" that trivialize abuse.[135] Poor women are particularly vulnerable to violence because their lack of financial resources and employment skills traps them in abusive relationships.[136] By the same token, violence impairs individuals' ability to find and retain work, which perpetuates economic dependence. Some research indicates that when the violence rates are controlled for class-related variables, such as family income and occupation, the incidence of abuse is lower for African Americans than for whites, and equivalent for Hispanics.[137]

Research on lesbian and gay domestic violence has been limited. The National Violence Against Women Survey conducted by the Center for Policy Research and co-sponsored by the National Institute of Justice and the Centers for Disease Control and Prevention found that women who were cohabiting with men were nearly twice as likely to report victimization as were women cohabiting with women (20 percent versus 11 percent). Same-sex cohabiting men were nearly twice as likely to report abuse by their male partners as were opposite-sex cohabiting men by their female partners (15 percent and 8 percent). The authors of this study conclude that intimate partner violence is perpetrated primarily by men, whether against male or female partners.[138]

For much of the last decade, domestic violence deaths have been in decline for several reasons: (1) the increased provision of legal services for victims of intimate partner abuse, (2) improvements in women's economic status, and (3) demographic trends, most notably the aging of the population.[139] Researchers note that domestic violence programs enable many women to leave relationships before they feel that they need to use deadly force in self-protection.[140] However, the recent economic recession may have increased risks of serious injury, both because of the heightened stress and reduced economic options associated with unemployment, and cutbacks in some government-funded support services.[141]

On the law enforcement side, activists have pushed for mandatory policies because a majority of domestic violence reports resulted in no arrest and arrests often resulted in no prosecution. Should the victim be able to control whether or not her abuser should be arrested, or prosecuted? Stevenson v. Stevenson, excerpted below, raises the related question of who should control the continuation of a restraining order. The case concludes that dissolution of a restraining order in a domestic violence case is at the court's discretion and should depend upon a showing of good cause.

Reading Questions

1. What legal strategies for addressing domestic violence make the most sense?
2. What does it mean to treat domestic violence as a public problem rather than a private issue?
3. How much autonomy should victims have in deciding how to handle a case of domestic violence? Does the "public" nature of domestic violence mean that it is the state, rather than victims, that should have the final word on how a case is resolved? Should Mrs. Stevenson have been able to make her own decision about whether she still needed protection from her husband?

Karla Fischer, Neil Vidmar & René Ellis, *The Culture of Battering and the Role of Mediation in Domestic Violence Cases*

46 SMU L. Rev. 2117, 2121-2130, 2133, 2136-2138, 2141 (1993)

The culture of battering refers to the relationship context of an abusive relationship. The first of the three elements of the culture of battering is the abuse, which includes at least one of the following types: physical, emotional, sexual, familial, and property. Professionals have increasingly recognized non-physical forms of abuse as harmful to domestic violence victims. The second element is the systematic pattern of domination and control that the batterer exerts over his victim. This pattern may be initiated by the batterer's gradual imposition of a series of rules that his victim must follow or be punished for violating. Over time, victims may censor their own behavior in anticipation of yet-unexpressed rules. The abuser's rein on the members of the household is enhanced by the use of emotional abuse and financial and social isolation, all of which help keep the victim in fear of impending abuse. Victims may engage in episodes of rebellion or resistance to the rules, which are nearly always met with more serious violence. Even separating from the abuser, an act of rebellion by itself, does not secure the end of the abuse; rather, it frequently escalates it. The third element, hiding, denying, and minimizing the abuse, refers to typical coping strategies that battered women use to reduce the psychological impact of the abuse. Each of these elements to some degree must be present in order for a culture of battering to be established. . . .

As sociologist Liz Kelly has noted, the prevailing stereotype about domestic violence is that assaults are "physical, frequent, and life threatening." Yet, the reality of battered women's lives does not conform solely to this image. Advocates for battered women have long noted that financial abuse and property abuse are forms of emotional abuse inflicted upon women. Abusers frequently restrict women's access to money and destroy their personal property in an effort to gain control over them or keep them in a state of fear. Emotional and sexual abuse may be even more common. Forms of emotional abuse include acts that do not constitute overt threats of injury or violence, such as constant humiliation, insults, degradation, and ridicule. Of course, explicit threats to harm or kill, including those attached to vivid descriptions of the method the abuser would use to carry it out, also have emotional consequences. The abuser may extend threats of harm to the victim's extended family or her children. . . .

Battered women have frequently reported that abusers are extremely controlling of the everyday activities of the family. This domination can be all encompassing: as one of the batterers from Angela Browne's study was fond of stating, "[y]ou're going to dance to my music . . . be the kind of wife I want you to be." Charlotte Fedders' account of the escalating rules imposed by her husband [who was a prominent lawyer and high-level government official] over the course of their seventeen year, extremely violent marriage is particularly illuminating about the range of control that abusers can exert. Her husband insisted that no one (including guests and their toddler children) wear shoes in the house, that the furniture be in the same indentations in the carpet, that the vacuum marks in the carpet be parallel, and that any sand spilled from the children's sandbox during their play be removed from the surrounding grass. Charlotte was not allowed to write checks from their joint checking account. Any real or perceived infraction of these rules could result in her husband beating her, or at the very least, the expression of his irritation that was frequently a harbinger to a beating.

Typically, battered women talk to the men about the abuse, partly as an attempt to concretize the rules that are connected to the absence of abuse. In turn, many abusers promise to stop the abuse. One abuser in Browne's study formalized such discussions into a written document, where he set forth a list of conditions that his victim was to agree to in exchange for cessation of his violence. These conditions were: (1) the children were to keep their rooms clean without being told; (2) the children could not argue with each other; (3) he was to have absolute freedom to come and go as he wished, and could have a girlfriend if he wanted one; (4) she would perform oral sex on him anytime he requested; and (5) she would have anal sex with him. He enforced this document shortly after she "agreed" to it and continued to sexually assault her until his death. This abuser simply made explicit the rules in the relationship and made it obvious that abuse was the punishment for violating the rules.

In many abusive relationships, however, the rules do not need to be verbally expressed to create a family atmosphere controlled by the batterer. . . . What fuels this . . . process is the responsibility the victim feels, both as a woman socialized into believing that making relationships work is her job, and the responsibility added by the abuser, who blames her for the "failure" of the relationship, as evidenced by the occurrence of abuse. Women are taught in our society to care for others, to make decisions around what is best for other people, even if it denigrates their own needs. Batterers reinforce this societal message by consistently blaming women for everything that goes awry in their lives. The end result is manifested in frantic attempts by the woman to be the perfect wife, mother, and homemaker. . . .

The pattern of rule-making and rule-enforcing, nested within the control and domination exerted by the batterer over his family, is frequently interspersed with episodes of rebellion by the victims. . . . These resistance incidents are not initiated with ignorance on the part of victims, and they are very much aware that any type of challenge to the batterer is likely to result in further, perhaps escalating, violence. . . .

Fischer specifically asked the battered women in her study who had obtained court protective orders about the methods they had employed in attempting to stop the violence. Of the thirty-one strategies described, the women in her sample had tried an average of thirteen different strategies, including talking to the abuser about the abuse, consulting family and friends, calling the police, leaving him, and seeking counseling or legal advice. Fischer concluded that the number and variety of strategies tried suggests that battered women continue over time to increase their help-seeking rather than to decrease it and become passive. . . .

Our argument that abuse occurs within a relationship context of control and domination is an explicit rejection of the popular belief that abuse is simply a logical extension of a heated argument or disagreement. . . . Battered women's narratives of the context of abuse suggest quite the opposite of conflict. Women are typically beaten in a variety of situations that could hardly be classified as conflict: while sleeping, while using the toilet, and while in another room that the batterer suddenly entered to begin his beating. The usual scenario women describe is that at one moment all is calm and in the next, there is a major, seemingly untriggered explosion. . . .

In addition to the information about context, batterers' behavior during abusive incidents does not support an image that these men are out of control with anger. Women have reported deliberate, calculating behavior, ranging from searching for and destroying a treasured object of hers to striking her in areas of her body that do not show bruises (e.g. her scalp) or in areas where she would be embarrassed to show others her bruises.

Anger and conflict may be frequently confused with violence because both can be a proxy for abuse. The abuser may in fact be angry when he beats his victim or a conflict over what she has served for dinner may have developed before the incident of violence. But this simple coexistence in time does not mean that the anger or conflict has caused the violence. Lurking underneath the surface anger or conflict is the batterer's need to express his power over his victim. Even if the anger is controlled and all sources of conflict are removed from the relationship, violence still occurs. After all, batterers are usually involved in other social relationships, at work or elsewhere, where they become angry or have conflicts with others that they do not abuse. Their ability to cope with anger in some situations but not at home suggests that conflict and anger are not at the root of domestic violence. Perhaps the best evidence, however, that abuse is not about anger or conflict is that violence continues to occur, frequently escalating, after women leave their abusers.

Stevenson v. Stevenson

714 A.2d 986 (N.J. Super. Ct. 1998)

COOK, J.S.C. . . .

In what appears as a matter of first impression in New Jersey, this case presents the question whether a final restraining order issued under the Prevention of Domestic Violence Act . . . must be dissolved in all cases where the plaintiff so requests. For the reasons expressed below, this court determines that dissolution of a final restraining order at the request of plaintiff is not mandatory. Rather, dissolution in such cases is at the court's discretion, and should depend upon a showing of good cause, with an independent finding by the court based upon the facts presented in each case. . . .

On November 6, 1997, the parties appeared before this court for a hearing on plaintiff's complaint charging defendant with numerous violations of the Prevention of Domestic Violence Act (the Act). The testimony of plaintiff, the photographic exhibits offered by her counsel, and the graphic appearance at the hearing of the residual effects of the severe physical injuries she suffered, established by a clear preponderance of the evidence that defendant was guilty of attempted criminal homicide, aggravated assault, terroristic threats, criminal restraint and burglary, all in violation of the Act. These violations arose from a brutal, sadistic and prolonged attack by defendant on his wife during the late evening and early morning hours of October 29-30, 1997.

Plaintiff, who appeared at the hearing with two black and severely swollen eyes, testified that on the late evening of October 29, 1997, defendant came into the marital bedroom, went into a total rage, punched plaintiff with both fists, held her down with his knees, kicked her in the back and ribs, and continued beating her there for approximately 25 minutes. Defendant then dragged her by her hair down the stairs and out of the house, and shoved her into his van, saying that they were going to go to a friend's house. Plaintiff was bleeding from her ears, nose and mouth. She got out of the van, ran to a neighbor's house and banged on the door. Defendant chased her, screaming he would kill her, and that he should have killed her before. She was "petrified." He caught up to her outside the neighbor's house, and choked her with both hands around her throat. He then dragged her down the street and pushed her back into the van. She escaped again and ran to another neighbor's house. At that point, defendant's vicious attack on his wife had been going on for 45 minutes. She went inside the neighbor's house and asked her neighbor to call the police, while she went into a powder room, closed the door, and tried to hide from defendant. Defendant went into the neighbor's house and proceeded to rip the powder room door off its hinges. The door landed on plaintiff. He dragged her out of the house, and back towards their house. Plaintiff grabbed onto trees along the way, trying to resist. He was furious because she had asked her neighbor to call the police. Finally, he let go of her, got into the van and left.

She was badly injured and very scared. A neighbor came with a blanket and rendered first aid. She was rushed by ambulance to the Emergency Room . . . [and] medevac'd by helicopter to the Cooper Hospital Trauma Center. She had a fractured skull, a concussion, four broken ribs, and a punctured lung (pneumothorax), in addition to the injuries noted above. She remained hospitalized at Cooper for several days, and was still under medical care at the time of the hearing on November 6, 1997.

At the hearing, the court had the opportunity not only to hear the testimony of plaintiff, but to observe her injuries and review the photographic exhibits submitted by her counsel as well. . . . The photographic exhibits submitted by plaintiff's counsel depicted her injuries, as well as the powder room door that defendant ripped off its hinges in the neighbor's home where plaintiff sought refuge. The photos, including those of plaintiff's facial and head injuries, and the hole in her chest where a tube was inserted to re-inflate her punctured lung, depicted a severally beaten and battered woman.

Plaintiff testified she was in fear of defendant. She related a prior history of domestic violence on his part, including previous assaults. She was afraid he would take their ten year-old son and leave the area, noting that he would do anything and everything to get physical custody and keep their son away from her. She added that their ten year-old son was in the house throughout the forty-five minute period that the beating of his mother took place.

Defendant, who was represented by counsel at the hearing, did not testify. No evidence was presented to controvert plaintiff's testimony, or the domestic violence charges she made against him. . . .

Because of (1) the barbaric conduct of the defendant during the nightmarish incident of October 29-30, 1997; (2) the evidence of his drunkenness that night and in the past; (3) his prior history of domestic violence; and (4) plaintiff's clearly expressed fear that defendant would take her son away if not restrained, a final restraining order was entered. The order prohibited any further acts of domestic violence, and barred him from having any contact or communication with the plaintiff and from harassing or stalking her. The order also required defendant to undergo substance abuse and psychological evaluations, and restricted him to supervised visitation only. He was also ordered to pay plaintiff's attorneys' fees of $2,400 by December 12, 1997; child and spousal support; all household expenses; and other expenses enumerated in the order.

At the hearing on plaintiff's request that the court dissolve the final restraining order, several violations of the order came to light. For example, it appeared that the defendant has engaged in *unsupervised visitation* with the child, including trips out-of-state. He has continually attempted to contact plaintiff. He has not abided by the psychotherapy recommendations of the Steininger Center, nor with the substance abuse recommendations of Segaloff. Both of those reports are discussed below. He has not paid any of the attorney's fees he was ordered to pay. In short, the defendant has flouted and violated the final restraining order. . . .

At the hearing on March 13, 1998, plaintiff asked the court to dissolve the final restraining order. She claimed she had reconsidered her relationship with the defendant and wanted him to be involved with their son's life. She requested that the restraints be dissolved, but only on the condition that he commit no future violence.

The final restraining order permitted *supervised visitation only*, pending a risk assessment and further order of the court. Risk assessment evaluations, substance abuse evaluations, and psychological evaluations of defendant were received by the court. At the request of and by agreement of both parties, through their counsel, copies of those evaluation reports were provided to the parties and their counsel. Plaintiff testified she had read the reports. . . .

Those reports include (1) a psychological evaluation of defendant by Dr. Stuart Kurlansik, Chief Psychologist, The Steininger Center; and (2) a drug and alcohol abuse evaluation of defendant by Patricia Thurman, a substance abuse counsellor. . . .

Dr. Karlansik reported inter alia that:

When asked to describe the events which resulted in his referral to this office, Mr. Stevenson reported that "I assaulted my wife. I beat her up very badly."
. . .

He reported prior fights with his wife, but "nothing to this degree." He claimed that *every time they fought, he was drunk*. He stated that she never had to go to the hospital in previous fights. He stated that the previous fights involved punching, although not to the face. He stated that he bruised her in prior fights, but then claimed that she bruises easily. He reported that he had been in fights with other people during the period of his marriage as well. He stated that he boxes and plays hockey, and fought during the course of a game. He stated that he has had a few fights outside of the sport events, however. He then said there had been a handful, the most recent occurring [a year ago] at a roller rink [when] the other coach had been a poor sport, and "we ended up in a physical confrontation." . . . Another time, four years ago, he stated that he was a spectator at an ice hockey [game] in which his son was playing. He stated that a parent of one of his teams' children became involved in a fight with three of the opposing team's parents, and he "intervened." *He reported having a fight five years ago in a bar, and stated that he was intoxicated at the time.* He stated that he had played a game of pool for twenty dollars and the other person lost the game, and did not want to pay, "so I hit him." . . .

He denied any arrests as a result of fighting as an adult. As a juvenile, he stated that he was incarcerated at Glen Mills for a total of three years, and stated that "we could go on for hours" regarding juvenile incidents. He stated that he was at Glen Mills twice—once at age thirteen for assault, and the second time at age fourteen for robbery.

His current marriage has been his only marriage. He married on December 28, 1986. The most recent separation occurred October 29, 1997. He reported one other separation, two years ago. He stated that "things just weren't working well." This separation lasted about three months.

He reported that he has a *short temper*, although "not now." He claimed that the experience which brought him here has changed his life and a short temper is "not gonna be a trait for me anymore." . . .

An objective measure of personality functioning, the Million Clinical Multiaxial Inventory—III, was administered. . . . [T]he interpretive report stated that "on the basis of the test data (assuming denial is not present), it may be reasonable to assume that the patient is exhibiting psychological dysfunction of mild to moderate severity." An Axis I (an "acute" disorder) diagnosis of Generalized Anxiety Disorder is suggested, while Axis II (enduring features of an individual's personality, and therefore more "chronic") diagnosis of: *"Antisocial Personality Traits," "Passive-Aggressive Personality Traits," "Avoidant Personality Traits,"* and *"Sadistic Personality Feature"* are suggested. The NCS report hypothesizes . . . that he may manifest (among other things) a lack of empathy, intolerance, and display "impulsive and quixotic emotionality." It goes on to state that *individuals with his profile can "be easily provoked into sudden and unpredictable reactions," which "may be punctuated periodically by angry outbursts."*

Recommendations:

It is strongly urged that Mr. Stevenson participate in psychotherapy, to help him learn to control his anger (and to find more appropriate ways of expressing it), as well as to reduce his anxiety. Psychotherapy might also address what appears to be an issue with *excessive use of alcohol at times.*

In her substance abuse evaluation of the defendant, Ms. Thurman, a substance abuse counsellor . . . reported that: . . .

Robert, a 34 year-old white male, was interviewed on November 29, 1997, at 8:30 a.m. Eye contact was fair, affect closed, guarded and *very accusatory toward his estranged wife, Melody.*

When asked about his use of drugs and alcoholic beverages, Mr. Stevenson states he's never used drugs of any kind and attempts to portray himself as a modest drinker, however, says the day he was charged *"I had a little too much to drink."* . . . But, Robert was quick to defend his actions by blaming the problem on "I caught my wife trying to buy drugs on the phone" and sees no relationship between his drinking and his current family problems. . . .

Concluding, based upon the limited information available to us, we strongly suspect Mr. Stevenson is drinking more than he reports and we feel he would greatly benefit from outpatient counseling to enable him to cease drinking and evaluate his family problems in a drug free state. The fact the client admits he was under the influence at the time of the altercation with his wife prompts us to question the severity of his drinking and its relationship to his family problems. . . . If Mr. Stevenson is not already in treatment for substance abuse, *we would then recommend he be mandated to complete at least 3 months in substance abuse treatment.* . . .

At a risk assessment conference with a Family Court staff therapist, plaintiff expressed concern over defendant's *"need for control,"* and again said she feared he would flee with their son, perhaps to Arizona. . . . She also said that on more than one occasion, defendant has threatened that he "will do anything and everything he has to" in order to gain custody of his son. Plaintiff requested that supervised visitation continue.

There remain several criminal charges pending against defendant as a result of his sadistic attack on his wife, including criminal attempt — murder; aggravated assault; burglary; criminal mischief; threatened violence; and criminal restraint. He is reportedly free on $75,000 cash bail, and is awaiting further proceedings in the criminal case.

When considering a plaintiff's request to dissolve the Final Restraining Order, a court must not forget that it is the public policy of the State of New Jersey, expressed by the Legislature in the Act, *that victims of domestic violence must be assured the maximum protection from abuse the law can provide; that the official response to domestic violence, including that of the courts, shall communicate the attitude that domestic violent behavior will not be excused or tolerated; and that it is the responsibility of the courts to protect victims of domestic violence* by ordering those remedies and sanctions that are *available to assure the safety of the victims and the public.* . . .

In addition, the Legislature has mandated that a final restraining order cannot be dissolved [or modified], *unless good cause is shown.* . . . Even where good cause is shown, the language of the statute, [the Act] expressly makes dissolution *discretionary*, not mandatory (". . . final order *may* be dissolved").

Plaintiff's dissolution request, made despite the latest brutal beating she suffered at the hands of a drunken husband who has a past history of wife-beating and an alcohol abuse problem, is consistent with phase three of "the battered woman's syndrome." That phase of the battering cycle is characterized by a period of loving behavior by the batterer, during which pleas for forgiveness and protestations of devotion are often mixed with promises to seek counselling, stop drinking and refrain from further violence. A period of relative calm may last as long as several months, but in a battering relationship the affection and contrition of the batterer will eventually fade, and phases one and two, the "tension-building" phase and the "acute battering incident" phase, will start anew. . . . Plaintiff has gone through the battering cycle with defendant at least twice. Through this dissolution request she seeks to remain in the situation. She thus meets the definition of a "battered woman." . . . The New Jersey Legislature recognized the plight of battered women when it enacted the Act and provided battered women with the remedy of *permanent* restraining orders against wife-beaters and other batterers of women.

Obviously, if there were no basis at all for plaintiff to fear further violence — as most certainly there is, given the nature and extent of this attack and defendant's past history of violence, including domestic violence against plaintiff; then there would be no need to condition dissolution on the absence of further violence. But there is that inherent fear, a fear that this court and any reasonable person viewing this situation would certainly share.

[Because fear is vital to the continuance of power and control in a domestic violence relationship, and this fear can impact the victim's ability to act in the best interests of her child], it is important to consider the victim's fear of the defendant. When considering the question of fear of defendant, . . . the test should not be the victim's subjective fear. Rather, the test is one of objective fear, i.e., that fear which a reasonable victim similarly situated would have under the circumstances. . . .

When considering a victim's application to dissolve, and whether there is good cause to do so, a court must determine whether objective fear can be said to continue to exist, and also whether there is a real danger of domestic violence recurring, in the event the restraining order is dissolved. . . . Whether or not this plaintiff would agree, it is clear that *from the standpoint of objective fear*, that a reasonable victim of such a brutal beating by a husband, who has assaulted her in the past and has a history of other violent behavior, and is the subject of experts' findings of uncontrolled anger and excessive use of alcohol, would have a reasonable fear that future violence by her husband would occur, were the restraining order dissolved.

Even in cases of reconciliation, the court must still make *an independent finding* that continued protection is unnecessary before vacating a restraining order. . . . In this case, given the uncontroverted evidence of defendant's brutality against his wife, his history of violence both within and without the domestic arena, his alcohol abuse and uncontrolled assaultive behavior when under the influence, and the reports before the court, including those of The Steininger Center and Segaloff, a reasonable, objective and independent determination of the facts leads to the inescapable conclusion that a real threat of recurrence of domestic violence by defendant upon his battered wife will exist, if the Final Restraining Order is dissolved. This court will not be an accomplice to further violence by this defendant, by wholly dissolving at this point the restraints that have been entered against him. Accordingly, and for lack of good cause shown, plaintiff's application to dissolve the Final Restraining Order is denied.

The court does find cause to modify the Final Restraining Order with respect to certain matters concerning the child of the parties, as follows. The final restraining order shall remain in full force and effect, except that contact or communication between plaintiff and defendant relating to supervised visitation, and to the safety, health, education, welfare, status or activities of the minor child of the parties, shall be permitted. There shall be no further modification of the final restraining order, without application to and with the express approval of the court.

Defendant shall promptly undergo psychotherapy as recommended in the report of Dr. Kurlansik of The Steininger Center. He shall also promptly undergo at least three months of substance abuse treatment. . . . Upon completion of psychotherapy and substance abuse treatment, the court will consider unsupervised visitation.

Notes

1. The Violence Against Women Act. The Violence Against Women Act of 1994 (VAWA), which Congress periodically reauthorizes, responded to domestic violence on multiple fronts. For example, it tightened sanctions by requiring courts to sentence first-time offenders to prison or probation, rather than to deferred or diverted prosecution program, and to condition probation on participation in an approved nonprofit rehabilitation program. Assault with intent to rape, sexual abuse, and an attempt or solicitation to commit these offenses qualify as "serious violence felonies" under the federal "three strikes and you're out" sentencing structure. The Safe Homes for Women Act, created under VAWA, provides law enforcement personnel with the authority to enforce civil protection orders from other states, and requires databases and technical assistance to courts handling domestic violence. VAWA also expanded the State Justice Institute's authority and mission to study and eliminate gender bias in all criminal justice and court systems. On issues related to women of color, VAWA provided for the improvement of delivery services to racial, cultural, ethnic, and language minorities. It also expanded the remedies available to battered immigrant women, which had been broadened in the 2005 VAWA reauthorization legislation. Finally, VAWA created new substantive law, making it a federal crime to cross state lines for the purpose of, or in the course of, "harassing, intimidating, or injuring a spouse or intimate partner."[142]

Spurred by federal assistance, states have also expanded services for victims of domestic violence. However, in most jurisdictions, the need substantially exceeds the programs available. Even before budget cutbacks during the recent economic crisis, an estimated 7700 requests for services were unmet on a daily basis.[143] In 2010, one Philadelphia shelter reported turning down 5,000 requests a year, three times the number before the downturn.[144]

2. Mandatory Arrest, Prosecution, and Reporting Policies. Mandatory or pro-arrest policies require police officers to arrest a suspect if there is probable cause to believe that an assault or battery has occurred, or that a domestic restraining order has been violated, without regard to the victim's consent or objection. These policies began to appear in the wake of a landmark Minneapolis study showing that arrest lowered recidivism rates in domestic violence cases. This study, along with several high-profile lawsuits against unresponsive police departments, helped launch policies now in force in about half of the states.[145] These policies have dramatically increased arrest rates. Other changes have complemented and strengthened these policies, such as creation of offender databases, mandatory documentation of domestic violence incidents, and the development of specialized domestic violence police teams, prosecution units, and courts.[146]

Another initiative has been mandatory or no-drop prosecution policies, which require prosecutors to prosecute domestic violence cases regardless of the victim's wishes. The limited evidence available suggests that the vast majority of victims are reluctant to testify against an abuser due to fear of retaliation, financial dependence, emotional attachment, or family and community pressure.[147] An estimated 60 to 80 percent of victims either recant their testimony or refuse to testify.[148] Under these circumstances, prosecutors may use strategies similar to those used in murder cases where victims are unavailable: introducing spontaneous statements made by the victim at the time of arrest, police officers' testimony, and videos or photographs taken at the time of the injury in lieu of the victim's testimony. However, while evidence given by the victim in an effort to obtain help are admissible, evidence collected by the police as part of their investigation (known as "testimonial evidence") is not admissible against a criminal defendant unless the witness who made the statements at issue is unavailable and the defendant had a prior opportunity for cross-examination. Except in cases involving serious documented injuries, juries tend to be reluctant to convict if victims are uncooperative.[149] But prosecutors in many of these cases are able to obtain plea agreements at least to misdemeanors by charging defendants with more serious offenses, or by threatening to prosecute violations of restraining orders.

Mandatory medical reporting laws are another form of intervention. Over four-fifths of the states require reporting by health care providers if the patient has an injury that appears to have resulted from a deadly weapon.[150] A few states have laws that specifically address intimate partner violence. Advocates of these laws see them as a way to ensure early law enforcement intervention when women's lives and health are at risk, and note that women are more likely to visit doctors than call the police.

Proponents of mandatory arrest and prosecution strategies argue that these strategies are the best way to force law enforcement officials to take domestic violence seriously. By taking the decision to proceed away from victims, they contend, a mandatory approach can deter future abuse, reduce the exposure of victims to pressure and retaliation from the abuser, and enable them to receive much needed services.[151]

These policies have, however, been subject to considerable criticism. Evidence concerning their effectiveness is mixed. Some evidence indicates that some police officers remain unresponsive even under mandatory policies because they retain discretion to determine the existence of probable cause to believe that domestic violence has occurred.[152] Many studies find little deterrent impact, increased risk of retaliation, and increased likelihood that victims will fail to contact police or service providers.[153] Recent research finds that mandatory arrest policies increase the frequency of arrests, but not successful prosecutions or victim safety.[154] Research also indicates that arrest and prosecution works best with those who have the most to lose from criminal sanctions, and that the risks of violence escalate for those who have the least to lose: those who are unemployed, poorly educated, unmarried, and who already have a criminal record.[155]

Critics also charge that interventions over which victims have no control compound victims' trauma and erode their sense of efficacy, autonomy, and self-esteem — all aspects of their lives that are already weakened by the violence itself. In some jurisdictions, victims have even been jailed for refusing to testify after filing an abuse complaint. Critics also stress the likelihood that arrest and prosecution will remain more frequent in African-American and Latino communities, which are already disproportionately targeted by law enforcement officials.

Similar problems arise when courts refuse victims' requests to dissolve restraining orders or to issue protection orders that permit non-abusive ongoing contact. Practices vary; in some jurisdictions, courts defer to victims' preferences, in others they make independent inquiries concerning coercion and risks, and in some instances they deny requests as a matter of policy. However, pressure is hard to assess, and when in doubt many judges err on the side of keeping protections in place; no one wants to be the one who dissolved an order for a woman "found face down in the morning."[156] Yet refusing to defer to women's own risk assessments may discourage them from filing requests for restraining orders in the first instance, and deny her bargaining leverage that may help end the abuse.[157]

As to medical interventions, critics worry that women whose history of abuse makes them aware of reporting requirements may be deterred from seeking treatment.[158] The American Medical Association opposes mandatory reporting out of concerns for patients' safety, confidentiality, and autonomy.

Given these problems, some feminists conclude that strategies providing women with material resources such as housing, food, clothing, or money should take priority over policies that merely seek greater accountability by batterers.[159] They also propose that law enforcement agencies should make victims' long-term safety the preeminent concern and promote more outreach to victims to ensure that protective orders are effective. A "survivor-centered" approach also calls for flexible policies that permit dropping charges where victims are at high risk for retaliation and abusers are unlikely to get lengthy sentences or where an alternative like completion of a substance abuse and counseling program might assist the parties more than prosecution. The limited available evidence suggests that focusing on women's needs increases their willingness to cooperate with prosecutors and reduces their exposure to repeated abuse.[160]

The most systematic attempts to determine the preferences of battered women find that most want their batterer prosecuted.[161] One survey of women in shelters found that about three-quarters supported mandatory arrest and medical reporting laws, and about two-thirds favored no-drop policies. Only 15 to 20 percent believed that these policies would not benefit them and that they personally would be less likely to seek medical or law enforcement assistance in communities that had such requirements.[162] Taken together, such findings may suggest the need to improve rather than eliminate aggressive arrest, prosecution, and reporting policies through better training and education of police officers, and limits on coercion of victims.[163]

Some feminists today argue that mandatory strategies to combat domestic violence, including arrests, bail, plea bargaining, and domestic protection orders, separate the abuser from the victim in a way that amounts to an unwanted, "de facto divorce," and otherwise reduces the victim's family privacy and autonomy.[164] If you were in a decisionmaking role, would you support mandatory policies and the policy strategies described in this section? If you were a domestic violence judge, what evidence would be relevant to your decision about whether to honor a woman's decision to dissolve a restraining order? How might the presence of children affect your answers?

3. Criminal and Civil Enforcement. Domestic violence reform efforts have centered not only on promoting greater compliance with existing laws, but also on enacting new criminal prohibitions and expanding civil enforcement strategies. For example, all states now have anti-stalking laws, and almost all have criminal statutes that make violating a protection order a criminal offense. A minority of states make protective orders available for nonviolent forms of domestic abuse, and some commentators believe that all states should do so.[165] As these commentators note, research suggests that women find psychological abuse more painful than physical abuse, and psychological abuse often leads to physical abuse.[166] Restricting women's freedom or access to money, sabotaging their attempts to find or keep a job, and isolating them from friends and families are part of patterns of domination that experts believe should be subject to restraining orders.

Should victims of abuse ever be held accountable for violating a restraining order? Some judges have imposed fines or jail sentences for a battered woman's contempt of a civil protection order. For example, Kentucky Judge Megan Lake Thornton fined an impoverished woman $100 for reconciling with her husband a few days after she had obtained a protective order. Thornton explained, "I find that offensive. It drives me nuts when people just decide to do whatever they want." Like a vocal minority of family court judges, she has made it clear that no-contact orders apply equally to abusers and targets of abuse. "People are ordered to follow them and I don't care which side you are on."[167] Domestic violence advocates view this kind of formalistic egalitarian approach as unrealistic, unjust, and "a barrier that stops abused women from seeking protection of the court."[168] They believe that victims should be able to request orders that do not bar all contact. When parties have children, financial difficulties, or continuing love for their abusers, "[i]t's pretty hard to say, 'Never speak again.'"[169]

4. Civil Damage Claims. Another legal resource for survivors of intimate violence is the civil damages suit. VAWA had created a federal civil rights remedy for "crimes of violence motivated by gender," but the U.S. Supreme Court in United States v. Morrison determined that such a right of action was up to the states to create, and was beyond Congress's constitutional authority.[170] Although state tort law generally provides remedies for assault, many jurisdictions have barriers to spouses suing each other.

Beginning in the 1980s, some leading decisions also allowed actions under Section 1983 of the Federal Civil Rights Act against municipalities whose police were grossly negligent in responding to domestic violence complaints. However, in 2005, the U.S. Supreme Court limited such remedies. In Castle Rock v. Gonzales, the Court held that a jurisdiction's mandatory arrest policy does not create the necessary "special relationship" with the state or an entitlement under the Due Process Clause that would justify liability under Section 1983. There, Jessica Gonzales repeatedly requested the local police to arrest her ex-husband for violation of a civil restraining order after he abducted their three daughters who were playing in the family's front yard.[171] According to the facts in the complaint, which the Court accepted for purposes of the decision, the respondent contacted the police six times between 7:30 p.m. and 1:00 a.m. the next morning. She even went to the police station to file an incident report and begged the officers to look for her husband, who had a history of instability and violence. The officer who took the report made "no reasonable effort to enforce the [restraining order] or locate the three children. Instead he went to dinner." Shortly after 3:00 a.m., the husband arrived at the police station and opened fire. Officers shot back, killing him in the exchange, and then discovered the dead bodies of his daughters in his pick-up truck.

Colorado has a mandatory arrest law for violations of restraining orders. It provides that:

(a) Whenever a protection order is issued, the protected person shall be provided with a copy of such order. A peace officer shall use every reasonable means to enforce a protection order.

(b) A peace officer shall arrest, or, if an arrest would be impractical under the circumstances, seek a warrant for the arrest of a restrained person when the peace officer has information amounting to probable cause that [the order has been violated].

Speaking for the majority, Justice Scalia reasoned that these statutory provisions have not "truly made enforcement of restraining orders mandatory. A well-established tradition of police discretion has coexisted with apparently mandatory arrest statutes." Moreover, even if Gonzales had been entitled to enforcement, the majority concluded that such an entitlement would not constitute a property interest protected by the Due Process Clause and enforceable under Section 1983. Justice Souter, joined by Justice Breyer, concurred in the judgment but wrote separately to emphasize the concern that finding a property right to enforcement would in effect "federalize every mandatory state-law direction to executive officers whose performance on the job can be vitally significant to individuals affected." Justice Stevens, joined by Justice Ginsburg, dissented. As he read the statute, in light of its legislative history, "the police were required to provide enforcement. They lacked the discretion to do nothing."[172]

Following that decision, the mother brought a suit before the Inter-American Commission on Human Rights, affiliated with the Organization of American States. In essence, she claimed that the United States violated her rights under the American Declaration of the Rights and Duties of Man, namely her right to be free from gender-based violence and discrimination. State department lawyers countered that the Declaration imposes no duty to prevent crimes inflicted by private individuals and that the state acted reasonably on the information it had available. In rejecting that argument, the Commission found that the State failed to act with "due diligence" to protect the Gonzales children and their mother from domestic violence, which violated "the State's obligation not to discriminate and to provide for equal protection before the law under the American Declaration." The Commission also found that the state failed to undertake reasonable measures to protect the lives of the children, in violation of their right to life under the Declaration. Under the Commission's analysis, the "state apparatus was not duly organized, coordinated, and ready to protect these victims from domestic violence by adequately and effectively implementing the restraining order at issue . . . [which] constituted a form of discrimination in violation of Article II of the American Declaration."[173] Based on those conclusions, the Commission made recommendations to the United States, including that:

- it undertake a "serious, impartial and exhaustive investigation" into the deaths of the Gonzales children and the failures to enforce Jessica Lenahan's protection order, and hold those responsible accountable;
- it offer full reparations to Jessica Lenahan; and
- it adopt multifaceted legislation at the federal and state levels, or reform existing legislation to protect women and children from imminent violence and to ensure effective implementation mechanisms.[174]

How would you evaluate the Commission's ruling?

5. Stalking and Domestic Violence in the Workplace. According to Bureau of Justice reports, about 3.4 million individuals, three-quarters of them women, report being subject to stalking, defined as conduct causing reasonable persons to fear for their safety.[175] Estimates also suggest that anywhere between 75 to 95 percent of those who are subject to domestic violence experience related problems at work.[176] Problems include assaults, stalking, and harassing or threatening phone calls; destruction of work products; and lateness or absenteeism due to physical injuries, legal proceedings, and disruption of childcare and transportation arrangements. American companies are losing an estimated three to five billion dollars annually in absenteeism, lost productivity, turnover, and medical expenses.[177] Too often employers respond by penalizing or terminating employees who are victims, which compounds their problems and reinforces economic dependence on abusers. Workplaces that do not provide adequate security force many women to leave their jobs out of safety concerns.

Although about half of domestic violence victims report losing a job after the violence, only a small number of states have laws protecting them from job discrimination.[178] However, in some instances, employees may also be able to sue their employers for wrongful termination. Workers have won or settled a number of such cases. In one Oregon proceeding, the plaintiff and her abusive partner worked at the same company. After he began harassing her at work, vandalizing her car, and threatening to kill her if the employer did not fire her, the employer gave in to the threat without taking any disciplinary action against the abuser. The woman sued under Title VII and Oregon's antidiscrimination statute, and the case settled.[179] In another Massachusetts case, a woman who was terminated for taking time off from work to enforce a civil protection order successfully settled a claim for wrongful termination.[180]

Some employees have also sued for their employers' failure to take reasonable measures in response to foreseeable violence. These cases include tort claims for negligence in security, hiring, retention, and supervision. These are difficult cases to win. In Carroll v. Shoney's, for example, the court denied relief to the estate of a murdered woman who sued her restaurant employer for negligence.[181] The woman was a counter worker on the evening shift who had been beaten by her husband. She informed her assistant manager about the abuse and asked him to call the police if her husband came to the restaurant. When the husband arrived and made threats, the police escorted him from the premises, but released him after the restaurant did not press charges. The following day, management rejected the woman's requests to be excused from work and promised to call the police if the man showed up. He did, and shot her in the head before law enforcement officials could be alerted. The majority of the Alabama Supreme Court held that the restaurant was not liable because the murder was not foreseeable. The dissent, by contrast, claimed that the standard under prior cases was not "that the particular consequences should have been anticipated, but rather that some general harm or consequence could have been anticipated."[182] Such harm was "expectable" as the dissent viewed the facts, and the defendant had amplified the risks by placing the woman at the front counter.

Strategies to increase workplace protections are proceeding on several fronts. The Corporate Alliance to End Partner Violence brings together companies across the country to collaborate on ways to increase awareness among employers and to support policy initiatives.[183] These initiatives include laws that ban discrimination based on domestic violence and provide unpaid leave for employees to deal with violence-related concerns. About half of the states have enacted laws explicitly granting unemployment benefits in some circumstances, such as where loss of employment reflects individuals' reasonable actions to protect themselves or their families from domestic violence. Congress has also considered federal legislation, such as the Victims' Economic Security and Safety Act and the Victim's Employment Sustainability Act, which would prohibit discrimination based on domestic violence, guarantee eligible employees time off to address domestic violence issues, and ensure unemployment compensation for those who lose employment due to domestic violence.[184]

What strategies do you believe are most essential to deal with workplace violence? What stands in the way? How would you respond to the employers' legitimate concerns? Would it be appropriate, for example, to require individuals who are under a restraining order to wear global positioning satellite devices that track their location and alert police when they enter a prohibited zone?[185]

6. Domestic Violence and Housing Discrimination. A related issue involves housing discrimination based on domestic violence, which has only recently gained attention. A typical case involved Tiffani Alvera, who obtained a temporary restraining order against her husband after a brutal beating. She presented a copy of the order to the manager of her apartment complex, a federally subsidized cluster of residences for low-income tenants. Instead of sympathy, she received a notice of eviction. The management company for the complex maintained a policy of "zero tolerance for violence" that required eviction of any household with a member who posed a risk to the safety and well-being of other tenants. Alvera filed a complaint with the federal Department of Housing and Urban Development (HUD), which then brought a sex discrimination suit on her behalf under state and federal fair housing law. Because women constituted the majority of victims subject to eviction for domestic violence, the complaint alleged that "no-violence" policies had a gender-based disparate impact. The case ultimately settled under a consent decree requiring the management company to cease evicting or otherwise discriminating against victims of domestic violence and to provide training to its employees concerning the policy. Other cases have reached similar results.[186]

Battered women face other forms of housing discrimination in addition to evictions. For example, landlords often conduct criminal record checks of potential renters, and exclude both complainants and victims charged with domestic violence under mandatory arrest policies. In some instances, only the batterer's name appears on the lease agreement, which causes landlords to assert that they cannot evict the abuser and allow the victim to continue occupancy. Public housing authorities often lack procedures allowing battered women to transfer to another residence to escape a batterer.[187] Families that lose their housing due to domestic violence are generally too low in federal priorities to qualify for homeless shelters, given policies favoring chronically homeless single individuals.[188]

7. Domestic Violence and Child Custody. Children often give partners additional ways to exercise domination and abuse. A mother is all the more reluctant to leave her batterer if by doing so she jeopardizes the safety and economic support of her children. Moreover, victims' psychological profiles or reluctance to cooperate with an abuser may work against them in the victims' efforts to secure permanent custody of their children, and the victims may even be blamed for failing to protect children from abuse.[189] Visitation rights and joint custody arrangements may also give batterers the ability to continue their abuse. Battered mothers who escape a relationship and leave children behind may jeopardize their safety and their own future ability to regain custody.

In principle, at least, family law has recognized such problems. At least 17 states have a rebuttable presumption of some form against awarding custody to a parent who has perpetrated domestic violence, and many other states direct the court to take domestic violence into account in making custody and visitation decisions.[190] However, critics claim that judges and experts who make custody evaluations often fail to accord significant weight to evidence of domestic violence, and discount incidents as "occasional," provoked, uncorroborated, or unlikely to recur.[191] The existence of "friendly parent" provisions, discussed in Chapter 2 at p. 272, can further complicate the matter by penalizing a battered mother who "alienates" the child from the abuser.

Another difficult issue in battering relationships is allocating culpability when the children themselves are abused. If children are present when police arrive at the home of a domestic violence incident, in some jurisdictions "the officers, as mandated reporters of child maltreatment, will routinely report not only the perpetrator, but also the victim to the child protection agency"; the government may then "charge a victim with 'failure to protect' her children by permitting domestic violence to occur while they are living in the home."[192] Such practices can deter women from reporting violence.

The tragic case of Andrea Yates raises issues of whether fathers are subject to the same standard as mothers concerning child protection. Yates, who had a history of serious mental health difficulties and suicidal tendencies, drowned her five children in a bathtub. Shortly before the killings, her husband recognized that she was no longer taking needed medication, and was exhibiting signs of serious dysfunction. He contacted a mental health facility to request her admission and asked his mother to stay at the family home to minimize his wife's time alone with the children. He did not, however, take other measures to prevent abuse. After the killings, prosecutors concluded that there was insufficient evidence to press charges against the husband. Shelby Moore disagrees, and argues that the case reflects the double standards underpinning the abuse and neglect system, which faults abused mothers for failure to intervene when they have fewer and more dangerous options than fathers.[193] As Moore and other scholars note, men also are not held liable for neglecting children whom they abandon to the care of the mother. Should the law require less of mothers or more of both parents?[194]

Finally, how should the law respond when a battered woman flees with the children—or when an abuser does? Various federal statutes seek to protect victims of abduction and promote coordination among states.[195] When abductors flee the United States altogether, the Hague Child Abduction Convention mandates the return of children to their place of "habitual residence" for a custody determination unless their return would pose a "grave risk of harm."[196]

Judicial remedies known as "undertakings" can return families to the country of origin to arrange custody. Whether courts have interpreted the Convention in ways responsive to domestic violence that prompts abduction remains open to dispute. Some commentators charge that courts do not consider violence directed only against mothers when assessing harm. If their children are subject to return, these mothers may accompany them and become vulnerable to further abuse.[197]

Putting Theory Into Practice

3-9. Immigrant women face special difficulties in escaping abusive relationships due to lack of language ability, cultural backgrounds that tolerate violence, unfamiliarity with the U.S. legal system and local social services, and dependence on husbands for financial support and for eligibility for resident status. Some of these women come to the United States as "mail-order brides." What special measures would you recommend for protecting these women?[198] Should they have a right to legal assistance and adequate court services, including interpreters and referrals to appropriate social services, even if these are not available to other individuals who need them?

3-10. Rendez-Vous is a small, upscale eating establishment that caters to the Manhattan theater crowd. One of its best waitresses is being stalked by an ex-boyfriend who has come to the restaurant several times to harass her and has occasionally prevented her from arriving on time. After one loud abusive incident in which the owner had to call the police, he fires the waitress. "I don't need this," he tells her. "Business is bad enough as it is." Would it be fair to the employer to hold him liable for firing her? The boyfriend also has stalked her apartment complex, and his violent actions have alarmed other tenants. Should the landlord be able to evict her if she does not get a no-contact protective order? If not, what remedies should be available to him? If these responses to partner violence should be unlawful, how would you respond to concerns of employers and landlords?

2. Domestic Violence and Substantive Criminal Law

Under long-standing Anglo-American law, killing in the "sudden heat of passion" is not murder, but rather the lesser crime of voluntary manslaughter; the theory is that "adequate provocation" by the victim may cause a reasonable man to lose his reason.[199] Catching one's spouse in the act of adultery traditionally has been described as the quintessential example of adequate provocation. Sexual taunting, as in People v. Berry, excerpted below, provides a contemporary example. Until the 1960s, juries in some states also recognized an "unwritten law" of "honor defense" that allowed for acquittal of a defendant who killed his wife or his wife's lover out of sexual jealousy.

The **Model Penal Code** is a set of recommended criminal law statutes proposed to states by the prestigious American Law Institute, a long-standing elected body of distinguished judges, academics, and practicing lawyers. The code, which was first issued in 1962 and last updated in 1981, although now under review, has been the basis for many state laws.

Under the Model Penal Code (MPC), a homicide that would otherwise be murder may be reduced to manslaughter if defendants can show that they acted under the influence of "extreme mental or emotional disturbance for which there is reasonable explanation or excuse." Whether there is such an explanation or excuse for the disturbance is to be judged from the point of view of "a person in the actor's situation under the circumstances as he believes them to be." The intention of the MPC drafters was to focus on the defendant's disturbed state of mind, rather than on the existence of justifying circumstances. *Berry* reflects this approach, holding that the jury should have received instructions on voluntary manslaughter because the killing could have occurred in the heat of passion. The Donna Coker reading analyzes this doctrine through a nonsubordination lens.

Another criminal law doctrine that applies in some domestic violence cases is the law of self-defense. This doctrine exonerates a killing when reasonably necessary to save oneself from imminent death or great bodily harm. This is the law at issue in State v. Norman, excerpted below, where the court refused to find that a woman acted in self-defense because she killed the victim while he was sleeping.

Reading Questions

1. Both cases below concern the effect of a "cooling off period." In *Berry*, some time elapsed between the victim's provocation of the defendant and the defendant's violent acts. Should that eliminate his defense of provocation? In *Norman*, time had elapsed between the defendant's last abusive acts and her violent response. Should the passage of time eliminate her claim of self-defense?
2. What are the North Carolina Supreme Court's concerns in *Norman* about a rule that excuses Judy Norman's killing of her husband? Are these concerns legitimate?

People v. Berry

556 P.2d 777 (Cal. 1976)

SULLIVAN, Justice.

Defendant Albert Joseph Berry was charged by indictment with one count of murder and one count of assault by means of force likely to produce great bodily injury. . . . The assault was allegedly committed on July 23, 1974, and the murder on July 26, 1974. In each count, the alleged victim was defendant's wife, Rachel Pessah Berry. A jury found defendant guilty as charged and determined that the murder was of the first degree. Defendant was sentenced to state prison for the term prescribed by law. He appeals from the judgment of conviction.

Defendant contends that there is sufficient evidence in the record to show that he committed the homicide while in a state of uncontrollable rage caused by provocation and flowing from a condition of diminished capacity and therefore that it was error for the trial court to fail to instruct the injury on voluntary manslaughter as indeed he had requested. . . .

Defendant, a cook, 46 years old, and Rachel Pessah, a 20-year-old girl from Israel, were married on May 27, 1974. . . .

After their marriage, Rachel lived with defendant for only three days and then left for Israel. Immediately upon her return to San Francisco she told defendant about her relationship with and love for Yako. This brought about further argument and a brawl that evening in which defendant choked Rachel and she responded by scratching him deeply many times. Nonetheless they continued to live together. Rachel kept taunting defendant with Yako and demanding a divorce. She claimed she thought she might be pregnant by Yako. She showed defendant pictures of herself with Yako. Nevertheless, during a return trip from Santa Rosa, Rachel demanded immediate sexual intercourse with defendant in the car, which was achieved; however upon reaching their apartment, she again stated that she loved Yako and that she would not have intercourse with defendant in the future.

On the evening of July 22d defendant and Rachel went to a movie where they engaged in heavy petting. When they returned home and got into bed, Rachel announced that she had intended to make love with defendant, "But I am saving myself for this man Yako, so I don't think I will." Defendant got out of bed and prepared to leave the apartment, whereupon Rachel screamed and yelled at him. Defendant choked her into unconsciousness.

Two hours later defendant called a taxi for his wife to take her to the hospital. He put his clothes in the Greyhound bus station and went to the home of his friend Mrs. Berk for the night. The next day he went to Reno and returned the day after. Rachel informed him by telephone that there was a warrant for his arrest as a result of her report to the police about the choking incident. On July 25th defendant returned to the apartment to talk to Rachel, but she was out. He slept there overnight. Rachel returned around 11 a.m. the next day. Upon seeing defendant there, she said, "I suppose you have come here to kill me." Defendant responded, "yes," changed his response to "no," and then again to "yes," and finally stated "I have really come to talk to you." Rachel began screaming. Defendant grabbed her by the shoulder and tried to stop her screaming. She continued. They struggled and finally defendant strangled her with a telephone cord.

Dr. Martin Blinder, a physician and psychiatrist, called by the defense, testified that Rachel was a depressed, suicidally inclined girl and that this suicidal impulse led her to involve herself ever more deeply in a dangerous situation with defendant. She did this by sexually arousing him and taunting him into jealous rages in an unconscious desire to provoke him into killing her and thus consummating her desire for suicide. Throughout the period commencing with her return from Israel until her death, that is from July 13 to July 26, Rachel continually provoked defendant with sexual taunts and incitements, alternating acceptance and rejection of him. This conduct was accompanied by repeated references to her involvement with another man; it led defendant to choke her on two occasions, until finally she achieved her unconscious desire and was strangled. Dr. Blinder testified that as a result of this cumulative series of provocations, defendant at the time he fatally strangled Rachel, was in a state of uncontrollable rage, completely under the sway of passion.

We first take up defendant's claim that on the basis of the foregoing evidence he was entitled to an instruction on voluntary manslaughter as defined by statute which is "the unlawful killing of a human being, without malice . . . upon a sudden quarrel or heat of passion." [In an earlier case the court approved the following quotation of the law:] "[T]he fundamental of the inquiry is whether or not the defendant's reason was, at the time of his act, so disturbed or obscured by some passion — not necessarily fear and never, of course, the passion for revenge — to such an extent as would render ordinary men of average disposition liable to act rashly or without due deliberation and reflection, and from this passion rather than judgment."

We further held . . . that there is no specific type of provocation required . . . and that verbal provocation may be sufficient. [In a previous case] in the course of explaining the phrase "heat of passion" used in the statute defining manslaughter we pointed out that "passion" need not mean "rage" or "anger" but may be any "[v]iolent, intense, high-wrought or enthusiastic emotion" and concluded there "that defendant was aroused to a heat of 'passion' by a series of events over a considerable period of time. . . ." Accordingly we there declared that evidence of admissions of infidelity by the defendant's paramour, taunts directed to him and other conduct, "supports a finding that defendant killed in wild desperation induced by [the woman's] long continued provocatory conduct." We find this reasoning persuasive in the case now before us. Defendant's testimony chronicles a two-week period of provocatory conduct by his wife Rachel that could arouse a passion of jealousy, pain and sexual rage in an ordinary man of average disposition such as to cause him to act rashly from this passion. It is significant that both defendant and Dr. Blinder testified that the former was in the heat of passion under an uncontrollable rage when he killed Rachel.

The Attorney General contends that the killing could not have been done in the heat of passion because there was a cooling period, defendant having waited in the apartment for 20 hours. However, the long course of provocatory conduct, which had resulted in intermittent outbreaks of rage under specific provocation in the past, reached its final culmination in the apartment when Rachel began screaming. . . .

. . . There was no clear direction to the jury to consider the evidence of Rachel's course of provocatory conduct so as to determine whether defendant, as an ordinary man of average disposition, having been exposed to such conduct, was provoked into committing the homicide under a heat of passion. [The failure to give the jury proper instructions on this question was prejudicial error and requires us to reverse the conviction of murder of the first degree.]

Donna K. Coker, Heat of Passion and Wife Killing: Men Who Batter/Men Who Kill

2 S. Cal. Rev. L. & Women's Stud. 71, 93-94, 116, 117-120, 123, 128 (1992)

[H]omicide law divides sane individuals who intentionally kill into two major categories: those who premeditate murder and those who act in the heat of passion. Social stereotypes of wife-killing that characterize the killer as a previously non-violent man who "snapped" under pressure, roughly parallel the understandings which underlie heat-of-passion doctrine. However, this social stereotype is grossly inaccurate when applied to men who are identified as "batterers" and when applied to the general category of husband-wife killings. Violence perpetrated by abusive men is purposeful, not spontaneous; the majority of men who kill their wives have a documented history of violent assaults. Furthermore, one would expect to find empirical evidence of wife-killers who fit the stereotype of the heat-of-passion killer in those reports of forensic psychiatrists whose job it is to aid defense counsel, yet these reports seem to confirm that men who kill and men who batter have remarkably similar personality traits and similar motivations. While further research is needed before we can determine whether or not the "impassioned" wife-killer exists, if he does exist, he is apparently part of a very small group of wife-killers. . . .

. . . The case of People v. Berry appears in many criminal law textbooks as well as legal treatises, generally for the proposition that the question of "cooling off" is a jury question. . . .

The defense needed Blinder's testimony for two different, but equally critical, reasons. First, the fact that Berry had a prior conviction for stabbing and injuring his second wife had already been ruled admissible. Blinder's testimony was required to neutralize this damaging fact, but, in fact, Blinder went one step better by explaining that Berry's past violence resulted from his repeated emotional victimization at the hands of women. Second, Blinder's testimony was needed most obviously in order to cast the killing as a heat of passion killing and, in particular, to explain the 20-hour wait in Rachel's apartment as a result of cumulative passion and not premeditation and lying-in-wait. The result was psychiatric testimony that brilliantly—if tautologically—turned facts about Berry that suggested the antithesis of a "heat of passion killer"—i.e., a proclivity for violence, a history of serious prior assaults on the victim identical in kind to the fatal assault, Berry's stabbing of his ex-wife under remarkably similar circumstances, and a psychological profile fitting that of an abuser—into evidence of Berry's increasing provocation as the result of Rachel's relentless "taunting." . . .

In essence, Berry's defense was that he was the sort of man who abused women—but the twist was Blinder's psychiatric explanation that Berry's violence was a result of his choosing women who enraged him and provoked him to violence. The fact that Berry had a prior conviction for assaulting his ex-wife with a butcher knife, that in past relationships with other women he had destroyed their property, forcing former girlfriends to "put him out of the house, locking the door," indicated to Blinder the personality of the women with whom Berry involved himself, more than it demonstrated Berry's dangerous and abusive nature. Blinder testified that these women "offer[ed] him the promise of comfort but ultimately deliver[ed] emotional pain." Yet Blinder's testimony provides a classic portrait of an abuser. Berry was most dangerous when women threatened to leave him. Berry was "emotionally dependent" on wives and girlfriends; he threatened physical violence in order to control women; he destroyed women's property; and he had a history of violent relationships with wives and lovers. The Supreme Court's opinion read Dr. Blinder's testimony to focus narrowly on the effect of Rachel's "provocative" behavior on Berry's mental state. Dr. Blinder's testimony, however, refers to a cumulative rage resulting from the provocation of all the women in Berry's entire life:

Q: . . . How would you characterize [Berry's] state of mind . . . [at the time of the homicide]?

A: . . . I would say that he was in a state of uncontrollable rage which was a product of having to contend with what seems to me an incredibly provacative [sic] situation, an incredibly provacative [sic] young woman, and that this immediate situation was superimposed upon Mr. Berry having encountered the situation time and time again. So that we have a cumulative effect dating back to the way his mother dealt with him. . . .

Q: . . . [Y]ou say that the situation involving Rachel Berry and Albert Berry . . . was the product of . . . cumulative . . . provocations. Now, specifically, what would you base your opinion as to provocations on? . . .

A: . . . We have two factors here. . . . The past history, that is, the history of this man well in advance of his meeting the deceased. And then the history of his relationship with her. And I think the two go together. . . . After 15 years [of marriage to his second wife] and five children, his wife leaves him for . . . another man. . . . They continued to live together, during which time his wife taunted him about her boyfriend. . . .

One night while they were having sex, his wife [called him by the name of her boyfriend]. Despondent and enraged at the same time, he went into the kitchen, obtained a knife, and stabbed his wife in the abdomen. And she was not serious [sic]. He only got to spend a year in jail for that. . . .

So we have this pattern of enormous dependency on these women and then rupture of the relationship with tremendous rage, almost

> uncontrollable. I think in one instance he put his foot through the stereo . . .
> he had purchased for one of these girls [sic]. . . .
>> So we see a succession of women, beginning with his mother, who
>> offer the promise of comfort but ultimately deliver indifference and emo-
>> tional pain. . . .

The irony of this defense . . . [is that] Berry's past abuse of other women was used to strengthen his claim of Rachel's provocative nature: Berry had a pattern of involvement with emotionally abusive women; his violence was in response to their "abuse" — never the other way around. . . .

The California Supreme Court opinion repeatedly echoes the tenor of Blinder's words — using terms such as "the result" or "culmination" — terms that diffuse responsibility and make Berry's violence seem inevitable and uncontrollable. . . .

Though Blinder's testimony focused on Rachel's "provocative" sexual behavior, the truth is that Berry didn't kill Rachel until it appeared that she might make good on her threat to leave him. . . . Blinder's testimony completely ignores this fact. Not surprisingly, perhaps, Blinder's testimony is completely from Berry's perspective: the relationship dynamics continue, even though Rachel has rejected attempts at reconciliation and has filed a police report. Of course, a defense witness tells it from the perspective of the accused, but in this circumstance, the defendant's perspective is largely that of the Court and that of the Law, as well. That perspective, as identified in this article, suggests that a woman's "abandonment" of a husband is provocative — and that a woman's preference of another lover is provocation of the worst sort.

State v. Norman

378 S.E.2d 8 (N.C. 1989)

MITCHELL, Justice.

. . . At trial, the State presented the testimony of Deputy Sheriff R.H. Epley of the Rutherford County Sheriff's Department, who was called to the Norman residence on the night of 12 June 1985. Inside the home, Epley found the defendant's husband, John Thomas Norman, lying on a bed in a rear bedroom with his face toward the wall and his back toward the middle of the room. He was dead. . . . A later autopsy revealed three gunshot wounds to the head, two of which caused fatal brain injury. The autopsy also revealed a .12 percent blood alcohol level in the victim's body.

Later that night, the defendant related an account of the events leading to the killing. . . . The defendant told Epley that her husband had been beating her all day and had made her lie down on the floor while he slept on the bed. After her husband fell asleep, the defendant carried her grandchild to the defendant's mother's house. The defendant took a pistol from her mother's purse and walked the short distance back to her home. She pointed the pistol at the back of her sleeping husband's head, but it jammed the first time she tried to shoot him. She fixed the gun and then shot her husband in the back of the head as he lay sleeping. After one shot, she felt her husband's chest and determined that he was still breathing and making sounds. She then shot him twice more in the back of the head. The defendant told Epley that she killed her husband because "she took all she was going to take from him so she shot him."

The defendant presented evidence tending to show a long history of physical and mental abuse by her husband due to his alcoholism. At the time of the killing, the thirty-nine-year-old defendant and her husband had been married almost twenty-five years and had several children. The defendant testified that her husband had started drinking and abusing her about five years after they were married. His physical abuse of her consisted of frequent assaults that included slapping, punching and kicking her, striking her with various objects, and throwing glasses, beer bottles and other objects at her. The defendant described other specific incidents of abuse, such as her husband putting her cigarettes out on her, throwing hot coffee on her, breaking glass against her face and crushing food on her face. Although the defendant did not present evidence of ever having received medical treatment for any physical injuries inflicted by her husband, she displayed several scars about her face which she attributed to her husband's assaults.

The defendant's evidence also tended to show other indignities inflicted upon her by her husband. Her evidence tended to show that her husband did not work and forced her to make money by prostitution, and that he made humor of that fact to family and friends. He would beat her if she resisted going out to prostitute herself or if he was unsatisfied with the amounts of money she made. He routinely called the defendant "dog," "bitch" and "whore," and on a few occasions made her eat pet food out of the pets' bowls and bark like a dog. He often made her sleep on the floor. At times, he deprived her of food and refused to let her get food for the family. During those years of abuse, the defendant's husband threatened numerous times to kill her and to maim her in various ways.

The defendant said her husband's abuse occurred only when he was intoxicated, but that he would not give up drinking. She said she and her husband "got along very well when he was sober," and that he was "a good guy" when he was not drunk. She had accompanied her husband to the local mental health center for sporadic counseling sessions for his problem, but he continued to drink.

In the early morning hours on the day before his death, the defendant's husband, who was intoxicated, went to a rest area off I-85 near Kings Mountain where the defendant was engaging in prostitution and assaulted her. While driving home, he was stopped by a patrolman and jailed on a charge of driving while impaired. After the defendant's mother got him out of jail at the defendant's request later that morning, he resumed his drinking and abuse of the defendant.

The defendant's evidence also tended to show that her husband seemed angrier than ever after he was released from jail and that his abuse of the defendant was more frequent. That evening, sheriff's deputies were called to the Norman residence, and the defendant complained that her husband had been beating her all day and she could not take it anymore. The defendant was advised to file a complaint, but she said she was afraid her husband would kill her if she had him arrested. The deputies told her they needed a warrant before they could arrest her husband, and they left the scene.

The deputies were called back less than an hour later after the defendant had taken a bottle of pills. The defendant's husband cursed her and called her names as she was attended by paramedics, and he told them to let her die. A sheriff's deputy finally chased him back into his house as the defendant was put into an ambulance. The defendant's stomach was pumped at the local hospital, and she was sent home with her mother.

While in the hospital, the defendant was visited by a therapist with whom she discussed filing charges against her husband and having him committed for treatment. Before the therapist left, the defendant agreed to go to the mental health center the next day to discuss those possibilities. The therapist testified at trial that the defendant seemed depressed in the hospital, and that she expressed considerable anger toward her husband. He testified that the defendant threatened a number of times that night to kill her husband and that she said she should kill him "because of the things he had done to her."

The next day, the day she shot her husband, the defendant went to the mental health center to talk about charges and possible commitment, and she confronted her husband with that possibility. She testified that she told her husband later that day: "J.T., straighten up. Quit drinking. I'm going to have you committed to help you." She said her husband then told her he would "see them coming" and would cut her throat before they got to him.

The defendant also went to the social services office that day to seek welfare benefits, but her husband followed her there, interrupted her interview and made her go home with him. He continued his abuse of her, threatening to kill and to maim her, slapping her, kicking her, and throwing objects at her. At one point, he took her cigarette and put it out on her, causing a small burn on her upper torso. He would not let her eat or bring food into the house for their children.

That evening, the defendant and her husband went into their bedroom to lie down, and he called her a "dog" and made her lie on the floor when he lay down on the bed. Their daughter brought in her baby to leave with the defendant, and the defendant's husband agreed to let her baby-sit. After the defendant's husband fell asleep, the baby started crying and the defendant took it to her mother's house so it would not wake up her husband. She returned shortly with the pistol and killed her husband.

The defendant testified at trial that she was too afraid of her husband to press charges against him or to leave him. She said that she had temporarily left their home on several previous occasions, but he had always found her, brought her home and beaten her. Asked why she killed her husband, the defendant replied: "Because I was scared of him and I knowed when he woke up, it was going to be the same thing, and I was scared when he took me to the truck stop that night it was going to be worse then he had ever been. I just couldn't take it no more. There ain't no way, even if it means going to prison. It's better than living in that. That's worse hell than anything."

The defendant and other witnesses testified that for years her husband had frequently threatened to kill her and to maim her. When asked if she believed those threats, the defendant replied: "Yes. I believed him; he would, he would kill me if he got a chance. If he thought he wouldn't a had to went to jail, he would a done it." . . .

Two expert witnesses in forensic psychology and psychiatry who examined the defendant after the shooting, Dr. William Tyson and Dr. Robert Rollins, testified that the defendant fit the profile of battered wife syndrome. This condition, they testified, is characterized by such abuse and degradation that the battered wife comes to believe she is unable to help herself and cannot expect help from anyone else. She believes that she cannot escape the complete control of her husband and that he is invulnerable to law enforcement and other sources of help.

Dr. Tyson, a psychologist, was asked his opinion as to whether, on 12 June 1985, "it appeared reasonably necessary for Judy Norman to shoot J.T. Norman?" He replied: "I believe that . . . Mrs. Norman believed herself to be doomed . . . to a life of the worst kind of torture and abuse, degradation that she had experienced over the years in a progressive way; that it would only get worse, and that death was inevitable. . . ." Dr. Tyson later added: "I think Judy Norman felt that she had no choice, both in the protection of herself and her family, but to engage, exhibit deadly force against Mr. Norman, and that in so doing, she was sacrificing herself, both for herself and for her family."

Dr. Rollins, who was the defendant's attending physician at Dorothea Dix Hospital when she was sent there for evaluation, testified that in his opinion the defendant was a typical abused spouse and that "[s]he saw herself as powerless to deal with the situation, that there was no alternative, no way she could escape it." Dr. Rollins was asked his opinion as to whether "on June 12th, 1985, it appeared reasonably necessary that Judy Norman would take the life of J.T. Norman?" Dr. Rollins replied that in his opinion, "that course of action did appear necessary to Mrs. Norman."

Based on the evidence that the defendant exhibited battered wife syndrome, that she believed she could not escape her husband nor expect help from others, that her husband had threatened her, and that her husband's abuse of her had worsened in the two days preceding his death, the Court of Appeals concluded that a jury reasonably could have found that her killing of her husband was justified as an act of perfect self-defense. The Court of Appeals reasoned that the nature of battered wife syndrome is such that a jury could not be precluded from finding the defendant killed her husband lawfully in perfect self-defense, even though he was asleep when she killed him. We disagree.

The right to kill in self-defense is based on the necessity, real or reasonably apparent, of killing an unlawful aggressor to save oneself from *imminent* death or great bodily harm at his hands. . . . Our law has recognized that self-preservation under such circumstances springs from a primal impulse and is an inherent right of natural law. . . .

The killing of another human being is the most extreme recourse to our inherent right of self-preservation and can be justified in law only by the utmost real or apparent necessity brought about by the decedent. For that reason, our law of self-defense has required that a defendant claiming that a homicide was justified and, as a result, inherently lawful by reason of perfect self-defense must establish that she reasonably believed at the time of the killing she otherwise would have immediately suffered death or great bodily harm. Only if defendants are required to show that they killed due to a reasonable belief that death or great bodily harm was imminent can the justification for homicide remain clearly and firmly rooted in necessity. The imminence requirement ensures that deadly force will be used only where it is necessary as a last resort in the exercise of the inherent right of self-preservation. . . .

The term "imminent," as used to describe such perceived threats of death or great bodily harm as will justify a homicide by reason of perfect self-defense, has been defined as "immediate danger, such as must be instantly met, such as cannot be guarded against by calling for the assistance of others or the protection of the law." . . .

The evidence in this case did not tend to show that the defendant reasonably believed that she was confronted by a threat of imminent death or great bodily harm. The evidence tended to show that no harm was "imminent" or about to happen to the defendant when she shot her husband. The uncontroverted evidence was that her husband had been asleep for some time when she walked to her mother's house, returned with the pistol, fixed the pistol after it jammed and then shot her husband three times in the back of the head. The defendant was not faced with an instantaneous choice between killing her husband or being killed or seriously injured. Instead, *all* of the evidence tended to show that the defendant had ample time and opportunity to resort to other means of preventing further abuse by her husband. . . .

Dr. Tyson . . . testified that the defendant "believed herself to be doomed . . . to a life of the worst kind of torture and abuse, degradation that she had experienced over the years in a progressive way; that it would only get worse, and that death was inevitable." Such evidence of the defendant's speculative beliefs concerning her remote and indefinite future, while indicating she had felt generally threatened, did not tend to show that she killed in the belief—reasonable or otherwise—that her husband presented a threat of imminent death or great bodily harm. . . .

The reasoning of our Court of Appeals in this case . . . proposes justifying the taking of human life not upon the reasonable belief it is necessary to prevent death or great bodily harm—which the imminence requirement ensures—but upon purely subjective speculation that the decedent probably would present a threat to life at a future time and that the defendant would not be able to avoid the predicted threat. . . .

. . . The relaxed requirements for perfect self-defense proposed by our Court of Appeals would tend to categorically legalize the opportune killing of abusive husbands by their wives solely on the basis of the wives' testimony concerning their subjective speculation as to the probability of future felonious assaults by their husbands. Homicidal self-help would then become a lawful solution, and perhaps the easiest and most effective solution, to this problem. . . . It has even been suggested that the relaxed requirements of self-defense found in what is often called the "battered woman's defense" could be extended in *principle to any type of case* in which a defendant testified that he or she subjectively believed that killing was necessary and proportionate to any perceived threat. . . .

In conclusion, we decline to expand our law of self-defense beyond the limits of immediacy and necessity which have heretofore provided an appropriately narrow but firm basis upon which homicide may be justified. . . .

Reversed.

MARTIN, Justice, dissenting.

At the outset it is to be noted that the peril of fabricated evidence is not unique to the trials of battered wives who kill. The possibility of invented evidence arises in all cases in which a party is seeking the benefit of self-defense. Moreover, in this case there were a number of witnesses other than defendant who testified as to the actual presence of circumstances supporting a claim of self-defense. This record contains no reasonable basis to attack the credibility of evidence for the defendant. . . .

Evidence presented by defendant described a twenty-year history of beatings and other dehumanizing and degrading treatment by her husband. In his expert testimony a clinical psychologist concluded that defendant fit "and exceed[ed]" the profile of an abused or battered spouse, analogizing this treatment to the dehumanization process suffered by prisoners of war under the Nazis during the Second World War and the brainwashing techniques of the Korean War. The psychologist described the defendant as a woman incarcerated by abuse, by fear, and by her conviction that her husband was invincible and inescapable:

> Mrs. Norman didn't leave because she believed, fully believed that escape was totally impossible. There was no place to go. He, she had left before; he had come and gotten her. She had gone to the Department of Social Services. He had come and gotten her. The law, she believed the law could not protect her; no one could protect her, and I must admit, looking over the records, that there was nothing done that would contradict that belief. . . .

. . . For the battered wife, if there is no escape, if there is no window of relief or momentary sense of safety, then the next attack, which could be the fatal one, is imminent. In the context of the doctrine of self-defense, "imminent" is a term the meaning of which must be grasped from the defendant's point of view. Properly stated, the second prong of the question is not whether the threat was in fact *imminent*, but whether defendant's belief in the impending nature of the threat, given the circumstances as she saw them, was reasonable in the mind of a person of ordinary firmness.

Defendant's intense fear, based on her belief that her husband intended not only to maim or deface her, as he had in the past, but to kill her, was evident in the testimony of witnesses who recounted events of the last three days of the decedent's life. This testimony could have led a juror to conclude that defendant reasonably perceived a threat to her life as "imminent," even while her husband slept. . . .

From this evidence of the exacerbated nature of the last three days of twenty years of provocation, a juror could conclude that defendant believed that her husband's threats to her life were viable, that serious bodily harm was imminent, and that it was necessary to kill her husband to escape that harm. And from this evidence a juror could find defendant's belief in the necessity to kill her husband not merely reasonable but compelling. . . .

Notes

1. "Heat of Passion" Manslaughter and the Reasonable "Man."   Victoria Nourse compiled heat of passion cases from across several jurisdictions. She found that a woman's attempt to leave the relationship, or the man's belief in her infidelity, was the most common "provocation" when men killed women and sought reduction of their crime to manslaughter. In jurisdictions that follow the Model Penal Code, she found that there were three times as many infidelity cases reporting separation as cases of infidelity in a continuing relationship. Nourse asks: "If intimate homicide frequently involves separated couples why does our canonical legal image still revolve around sexual infidelity?"[200] In another study of separation assaults, jealousy was a major factor; male partners frequently warned women whom they later killed, "If I can't have you, nobody can."[201] Doctrines such as "heat of passion," along with similar cultural attitudes, result in lesser sentences for wife killers. In one review of Bureau of Justice statistics, only one-fifth of female spousal murders resulted in a conviction for first-degree murder and only 13 percent of those convicted received life imprisonment; only 2 percent were sentenced to death.[202] Gender biases may also affect expert testimony that influences judicial and jury decisions.

Is it relevant that Dr. Binder, who testified in the *Berry* case, had a troubled marital history? Two of his wives committed suicide; one assaulted him before taking her own life, perhaps fueled by jealousy.[203]

2. Heat of Passion and Sex Equality.   For three centuries, English courts reserved the heat of passion defense to men, and early American law followed suit. Before the 1960s, many states retained laws that allowed a husband to kill his wife's lover, but made no concession for the wife who killed her husband or his lover. Although the current heat of passion doctrine is gender neutral in form, women rarely assert the defense, perhaps because women are socialized to respond less aggressively than men to most provocation, including infidelity.[204]

Are juries likely to react the same way to women and men who invoke the heat of passion defense? No statistical evidence is available, but some experts cite representative examples to suggest gender bias. A case in point is that of Houston dentist Clara Harris, who killed her husband after he failed to keep his promise to end his extramarital affair with his office's receptionist. Harris confronted her husband and his mistress at a hotel, and the two women became involved in a violent fight. Hotel employees separated them, and Harris, still enraged, got in her car and ran over her husband twice in the parking lot. She was convicted of murder, despite her testimony that she was "in a fog" at the time, and that it was a "blackout" period, a "crazy time." Eye witnesses reported that after she had hit her husband, she jumped from the car, asked him repeatedly whether he was "okay" and screamed, "I am sorry." The jury convicted her of murder, and of using a deadly weapon, which enhanced the offense. During the sentencing phase, the jury also found that she had acted in the heat of passion, but imposed the maximum sentence of 20 years.[205] During the trial, both sides capitalized on gender stereotypes. The prosecution painted Harris as a wife who ignored her husband's needs and who was a selfish spendthrift. The defense painted the mistress as an unscrupulous and promiscuous woman with a history of "abnormal relationships," including an alleged lesbian affair.[206]

Compare the result in *Harris* with Maryland v. Peacock.[207] There, the defendant shot and killed his wife when he discovered her having sex with another man. He pleaded guilty to manslaughter and was sentenced to three years, with immediate eligibility for work release and possible home detention. In justifying the sentence, the judge explained that the "betrayal" was "almost unmanageable." "I seriously wonder how many married men would have the strength to walk away, but without inflicting some corporeal punishment. . . . I shudder to think what I would do. . . ."[208]

What message do sentences like those in *Harris* and *Peacock* send? Are there differences in the cases that justify the differences in sentences? What sentences would you impose? Should "hot-blooded" separation murders and assaults be seen as deserving of less culpability? Or would you favor the approach of Minnesota, which authorizes a finding of first-degree murder based on repeated abuse?[209]

If equality is a goal in these cases, is it best achieved by restricting the heat of passion doctrine or by enlarging it to mitigate women's killings, such as those described below?

3. The Battered Woman's Syndrome. Every year, some 500 women kill their abuser and many invoke a defense based on the battered woman's syndrome (BWS).[210] BWS is a subcategory of post-traumatic stress disorder involving "thoughts, feelings, and actions that logically follow a frightening experience that one expects could be repeated." The syndrome is associated with three major symptom clusters, each of which can be accompanied by neurochemical and other physical changes. These clusters are (1) cognitive disturbances, including repetitive memories that cause battered women to reexperience previous abusive incidents and that increase their perception of danger; (2) high arousal symptoms that cause battered women to be nervous and hypervigilant to cues of potential danger; and (3) avoidance symptoms, including depression, denial, minimization, and repression, often leading to isolation as the batterer exerts his power and control needs over the woman.[211] BWS researchers offer two psychological theories to help juries understand the syndrome: learned helplessness and the cycle theory of violence. The theory of learned helplessness was first developed by experimental psychologist Marvin Seligman to explain the fact that dogs and other animals subjected to electric shocks that they are powerless to control will soon stop trying to escape or to avert the shocks. In the context of battered women, Lenore E. A. Walker pioneered the theory of learned helplessness to explain a cycle that traps women in abusive relationships. That cycle includes a tension-building phase, an acute battering incident, and a period of loving-contrition or absence of tension. The pattern leads the battered woman to believe that she is unable to help herself, that others cannot help her, and that the batterer might in fact reform.

In this state of learned helplessness, what causes a battered woman to turn on her batterer? Many abused women do not, but others at some point experience a "turning point." The turning point may come when there is a marked increase in the severity of the abuse, when the abuse becomes visible to others who question the woman's denial or rationalizations, or when the "loving-contrition" phase becomes increasingly short or disappears altogether. At that point, the victim moves from the state of learned helplessness to a state of the "victimized self," who concludes that she must either assert herself or be killed. For some victims, this means finally being able to leave their batterers; others stay; a few kill.

4. The Battered Woman in Self-Defense Law: Substantive and Procedural Proposals.

The most common criticism of the law of self-defense in the battered woman context is that it reflects patterns of male aggression: a "fair fight" between physical equals meeting in a single, discrete confrontation. Critics say that this approach fails to take into account the realities of battered women. Its "objective" standard of reasonableness ignores the special circumstances facing women in abusive relationships, and fails to consider the risk that verbal threats may convey in light of the history of battering. Requirements of "imminence" and proportionate force also discount women's lesser strength, which may make delay and deadly force seem necessary.[212] Do these criticisms seem justified in the context of *Norman*? If so, do they support some critics' call for a "reasonable woman" or a "reasonable battered woman" standard? Assuming that expert testimony on battered woman's syndrome should have gone to the jury in *Norman*, should the defendant's circumstances constitute a justification, exonerating her from guilt, or merely an excuse or mitigating factor affecting the degree of crime or the sentence?

In cases of **self-defense**, many states require that victims be in imminent danger of serious bodily harm and that they respond only with force that is proportional to the threat that they face. If either of these requirements are lacking because victims have a chance to escape or use force greater than necessary, their self-defense claim will usually fail.

---

5. Concerns About the Battered Woman's Syndrome.   Uneasiness about use of the battered woman's syndrome reflects various concerns. The *Norman* court's objection was that such evidence could be too easily manipulated, and might encourage opportunistic premeditated killings. To test the validity of this concern, one scholar collected the data from numerous studies comparing battered women who killed their husbands to those who did not. He concluded that women who kill their husbands suffer from far more frequent, more severe, and more prolonged abuse than other battered women; they have less ability to support themselves and thus to escape from their situations; they are more likely to have children who are also being abused by the batterer; and they are more likely to live in an environment where a gun is present and where the batterer abuses alcohol or other drugs.[213] Other research indicates that some groups of women are more likely than others to respond with force. African-American women are disproportionately likely to resort to physical violence in part because they have less access to services than more affluent white women; they feel pressure not to shame or force imprisonment of a "black brother"; and they do not "really trust" law enforcement officials to help them.[214] Lesbians also have disproportionately high rates of violent responses because they too lack confidence that police and courts would be responsive, and because they experience bias based on sexual orientation from police, judges, and service providers.[215] A reluctance to come out publicly as a lesbian or to expose violence in the lesbian community, along with greater comfort and capacity in fighting back, also help to explain the use of force rather than other strategies of resistance.[216] What are the reform implications of these conclusions?

David L. Faigman and Amy J. Wright assert that "[t]he battered woman syndrome illustrates all that is wrong with the law's use of science."[217] They and other critics note that Walker's research, based on a small group of racially homogenous women, failed to establish either the duration of the cycle of violence or that all subjects experienced all three stages. The relevance of research on dogs to battered women is also problematic, particularly given that the dogs exhibited total passivity, while battered women generally resist in some form, including instances in which they assault or kill their batterers.

Moreover, when invoked in court, the battered woman's syndrome implies an excuse through mitigation based on the woman's passivity, while self-defense generally requires justification based on the reasonableness of the defendant's behavior. Women who do not match the BWS profile may be assumed (by themselves as well as others) as failing to meet standards for self-defense. The risk appears particularly great for African-American and lesbian women; their resistance, viewed through the lens of racial and homophobic stereotypes, is inconsistent with the image of helpless victim.[218] A final concern is that the syndrome will reinforce the view of woman as passive, dysfunctional, powerless, and victimized, a view from which so many negative consequences flow, especially in child custody contexts.

How could these harms be mitigated? To what extent would more accurate testimony about battered women help in cases like *Norman*? Would it be enough to show that a "reasonable" person, in the face of past experiences of abuse and no certain options for escaping it, might respond with deadly force? Could a defendant reasonably claim that "a sleeping abuser is merely seconds away from being an awakened abuser" who poses an imminent threat?[219]

6. Post-Conviction Strategies for Battered Women Who Kill. After Judy Norman had served four years of her six-year sentence, the state governor commuted her sentence to time served. He gave no reasons.[220] What would you have done as governor, or as a member of her jury? What did she deserve?

Systematic efforts for clemency on behalf of convicted women in over 20 other states have also yielded similar results. Estimates suggest that about 125 women convicted of killing an abuser have been freed since 1978. However, the trend toward clemency has slowed. Almost all the petitions were granted during the 1980s and early 1990s. In some states, no requests have ever been successful, even in cases where defendants were convicted before expert testimony on battered women was available at trial.[221]

Men's rights groups generally oppose efforts to mitigate penalties for battered women. According to Warren Farrell, feminists argue " 'there's never an excuse for violence against women.' Now they [are] saying 'but there's always an excuse for violence against men.' "[177] How would you respond to Farrell's argument? What criteria would you advise governors to apply in considering clemency requests by battered women convicted of killing their abusers?

7. Domestic Violence and the Public/Private Dichotomy. Regulating domestic violence has been traditionally viewed as private, and therefore at best a state, rather than a federal, matter. It was on this basis that the U.S. Supreme Court invalidated the federal civil rights remedy for sex-based violence enacted under VAWA (see Note 4, in Section C1, above).[222]

Critics have long criticized the traditional dichotomy between public and private, on the ground that it leaves women unprotected where they are most vulnerable. Victims experience abuse, and the conditions that perpetuate it—lack of income, family and cultural expectations—on a very personal level. Yet as MacKinnon notes, the resources that are available to the battered woman and how others expect her and her batterer to act reflect broader social and political forces.[223]

What follows from this critique of the public/private distinction? Is the exercise of public power represented in the *Stevenson* case, or reflected in mandatory no-drop prosecution policies, any better? Are there contexts in which greater public control over private violence compounds the power imbalances it seeks to address? Are there realms that the law should not reach? Consider this issue in light of the following discussion of pornography, reproductive rights, and same-sex relationships.

8. Domestic Violence as a Basis for Asylum. Whether domestic violence should be treated as a human rights violation has arisen in several contexts including asylum. The issue came to the fore in the United States in June 1999, when a federal immigration appeals panel overturned a grant of asylum to Rodi Alvarado Pena, a Guatemalan woman seeking refuge in the United States because the Guatemalan legal system had failed to protect her from her abusive husband.[224] The decision created a public outcry and seemingly flew in the face of Immigration and Naturalization Service guidelines promulgated in 1995 that recognized rape, domestic abuse, and other forms of violence against women as possible grounds for asylum. The opinion was later sent back for reconsideration.[225]

In the United States, the right to asylum is governed by the international definition of a "refugee." The United Nations Convention Relating to the Status of Refugees defines a refugee in part as any person who "owing to a well-founded fear of being persecuted for reasons of race, religion, national origin, membership in a particular social group or political opinion, is outside the country of his nationality and is unable or, owing to such fear, is unwilling to avail himself of the protection of that country." Victims of domestic violence have generally based their claims for asylum on the "membership in a particular social group."[226]

In a recent case, the Department of Homeland Security (DHS) stipulated to asylum for a Mexican woman who suffered years of abuse and rape at gunpoint. Her efforts to obtain assistance from the police were unsuccessful because of her husband's influence in the community, and other evidence suggested that the Mexican government was unable or unwilling to protect victims from abuse.[227] Experts hope that the DHS will adopt a rule clarifying that the test for asylum in domestic violence cases is whether the victim has adequate access to state protection.

Other international documents also provide support for treating domestic violence as a human rights issue. The Declaration on the Elimination of Violence Against Women and the UNHCR Guidelines on the Protection of Refugee Women recognize domestic violence as a form of gender discrimination, and thus a human rights violation. The UN Convention Against Torture is another possible foundation for asylum claims when women flee domestic violence. The United Nations Special Rapporteur on Violence Against Women has "recommended that bodies that report on human rights abuses and violence against women and treaty bodies consider treating domestic violence as an internationally proscribed form of torture."[228] Should all women fleeing domestic violence in their home countries be entitled to claim asylum in the United States?

9. Prevention and Treatment.   Although most domestic violence initiatives have focused on assisting victims and punishing perpetrators, many experts believe that more attention needs to center on prevention and rehabilitation. Since the late 1970s, many jurisdictions have adopted batterer treatment programs in prisons or as alternatives to incarceration. Such programs aim to change attitudes and improve anger management skills. Yet despite the prevalence of such initiatives, there is surprisingly little data on their long-term effectiveness, and much of the research available is conflicting or hampered by small and non-random samples. As one expert put it, "the field of batterer intervention is still in its infancy."[229] Particularly given the significant backlash against domestic violence programs among men's rights groups, there is an urgent need for better data on what can promote changes in male attitudes and behaviors.[230]

What might account for the failure to learn how to target interventions most effectively? What might be done to address it?

Putting Theory Into Practice

3-11. Child welfare authorities removed Sharon's three children from her home based on findings that her husband had subjected them to repeated abuse, such as cursing and beating them. A mental health evaluation of Sharon showed that she did not always put the needs of the children first, that her parenting skills were weak, and that she was a battered wife who had a history of relationships with batterers. Her social profile and personality type suggested that she was particularly vulnerable to abuse. The child welfare authorities now seek to terminate Sharon's parental rights to her children on the theory that even if she leaves her current husband, she is likely to enter into another relationship that will be dangerous to the children.

Under your state's abuse and neglect law, parental rights can be terminated on a showing that a parent has failed to prevent another person from abusing a child and that it is reasonably likely that the child will be abused if returned to the parent.

As Sharon's lawyers, what arguments would you make against termination of her parental rights? Should she win?

3-12. Debra and Terrance are cocaine addicts, arrested for the commission of several armed robberies. Debra admits the crimes, but claims a defense of duress, which is unlawful threat or coercion creating an immediate threat of injury that causes someone to act as she or he would not otherwise act. Debra argues that she participated in the robberies out of fear that Terrance would kill her if she did not. In support of her defense, Debra seeks to present expert testimony indicating that she suffers from battered woman's syndrome; she has a history of physical and emotional abuse that escalated every time she tried to leave Terrance.

Evidence of battered woman's syndrome has been admitted in the jurisdiction in cases in which a battered woman has killed her batterer and claims self-defense. Duress in the criminal law ordinarily does not exonerate a defendant but it can reduce the severity of the crime or the sentence. Should the defense of duress be available in Debra's circumstances? In any felony case?

3-13. What would you do if you had been Laura Beth Lamb, an attorney who fraudulently took the bar exam in her husband's place, after he physically abused her and threatened to kill both her and her unborn child if she did not take the exam? She pled guilty to felony impersonation, and received probation on condition of paying a fine and completing 200 hours of community service. The California Bar then recommended disbarment. If you were a justice on the California Supreme Court, how would you respond?[231]

3-14. A recent, highly publicized case of battering involved Barbara Sheehan, who shot and killed her husband after 17 years of physical and emotional abuse. He was a retired New York police officer and, according to testimony at trial by Sheehan and her children, his abuse included throwing boiling pasta sauce in her face and punching her in the face on the evening before the killing. Sheehan told the jury that on the day of the shooting, she took a loaded revolver that belonged to her husband and attempted to sneak out of the house following an argument in which he threatened to kill her if she continued to refuse to accompany him on a Florida vacation. As she passed by the bathroom where her husband was shaving, he tried to stop her by taking a semiautomatic pistol and aiming it at her head. She then shot him, and he reportedly fell to the floor and screamed that he was going to kill her. As he reached for his pistol, she then shot him ten more times.[232] Prosecutors attempted to characterize Sheehan as a pathological liar who murdered her husband because she despised him after years of a dysfunctional marriage and then cloaked herself in a false story of chronic abuse. They also claimed that her fatal shot occurred after her husband presented no real threat, and that Sheehan had not sought help from the police or from family members living close by.

Jurors had the option of convicting her for anything ranging from second degree murder (with a possible sentence of 25 years) to unlawful possession of a firearm (with a possible sentence of 3½ to 5 years), or acquitting her on all charges. If you were on the jury, how would you vote? How would you respond to other jurors with a different view?

D. PORNOGRAPHY

Sex sells. That has always been true, but increased technological innovations have created increased opportunities for private consumption of pornography. Adult theaters, rental videos, pay-per-view movies on cable and world-sites, phone sex, and Internet websites are estimated to generate somewhere between $10 billion and $14 billion annually. Americans spend more on pornography than on all other movies, performing arts, and professional football, basketball, and baseball combined.[233] Nielsen ratings indicated that about a quarter of all Internet users in the United States, some 60 million users, visited a pornography website. Two-thirds of these viewers were male.[234]

Since the early 1980s, some feminists have joined with religious conservatives and other activists to combat pornography on several fronts. While the conservative case against pornography focuses on the corruption of morals and erosion of "family values," the feminist rationale emphasizes the role of pornography in subordinating women through objectifying and degrading images, and erotizing abuse.

The traditional legal approach to pornography is encompassed within obscenity doctrine. The leading case, Miller v. California, permits the government to ban material if, under contemporary community standards, the work as a whole appeals to the "prurient interest," depicts sex in a "patently offensive" way, and lacks serious literary, artistic, political, or scientific value.[235] Feminists charge that this standard cannot be effective in challenging pornographic materials because it incorporates the very community standards that have made subordination sexually appealing. Moreover, it asks judges to admit to an uncomfortable psychological state of finding material both sexually arousing *and* patently offensive.[236]

One effort to combat pornography took the form of local ordinances that prohibited trafficking in pornography and provided monetary damages from the maker or seller to anyone injured by pornography. Such an ordinance was struck down in American Booksellers Association, Inc. v. Hudnut, excerpted below. The campaign against pornography has proven controversial among feminists, and this section explores the reasons.

Reading Questions

1. Is pornography an example of sex-based discrimination? In what sense?
2. Would you have upheld the ordinance challenged in *Hudnut*? Why or why not?
3. Is pornography damaging just to women, or to men as well?
4. If you think that pornography causes significant harms, should it be prohibited by law? What other strategies might be effective? How would antipornography activists evaluate those options?
5. Is it possible to reconcile the ordinance in *Hudnut* with the First Amendment? Is pornography different from other restrictions on speech, such as laws prohibiting libel or sexual harassment? How so?

1. The Feminist Critique of Pornography

Catharine A. MacKinnon, Feminism Unmodified: Discourses on Life and Law

171-172 (1987)

Pornography sexualizes rape, battery, sexual harassment, prostitution, and child sexual abuse; it thereby celebrates, promotes, authorizes and legitimizes them. More generally, it eroticizes the dominance and submission that is the dynamic common to them all. It makes hierarchy sexy and calls that "the truth about sex" or just a mirror of reality. Through this process pornography constructs what a woman is as what men want from sex. . . .

The content of pornography is one thing. There, women substantively desire dispossession and cruelty. We desperately want to be bound, battered, tortured, humiliated, and killed. . . . What pornography does goes beyond its content: it eroticizes hierarchy, it sexualizes inequality. It makes dominance and submission into sex. Inequality is its central dynamic; the illusion of freedom coming together with the reality of force is central to its working. . . .

From this perspective, pornography is neither harmless fantasy nor a corrupt and confused misrepresentation of an otherwise natural and healthy sexual situation. It institutionalizes the sexuality of male supremacy, fusing the eroticization of dominance and submission with the social construction of male and female. To the extent that gender is sexual, pornography is part of constituting the meaning of that sexuality.

Catharine A. MacKinnon, Pornography as Defamation and Discrimination

71 B.U. L. Rev. 793, 796-797, 801-802 (1991)

Pornography has a central role in actualizing . . . [a] system of subordination in the contemporary West, beginning with the conditions of its production. Women in pornography are bound, battered, tortured, harassed, raped, and sometimes killed; or in the glossy men's entertainment magazines, "merely" humiliated, molested, objectified, and used. In all pornography, women are prostituted. . . . It is done because someone who has more power than they do, someone who matters, someone with rights, a full human being and a full citizen, gets pleasure from seeing it, or doing it, or seeing it as a form of doing it. In order to produce what the consumer wants to see, it must first be done to someone, usually a woman, a woman with few real choices. . . .

The evidence shows that the use of pornography makes it impossible for men to tell when sex is forced, that women are human, and that rape is rape. Pornography makes men hostile and aggressive toward women, and it makes women silent. While these effects are not invariant or always immediate, and do not affect all men to the same degree, there is no reason to think they are not acted upon and every reason and overwhelming evidence to think that they are—if not right then, then sometime, if not violently, then through some other kind of discrimination. . . . When men use pornography, they experience in their bodies, not just their minds, that one-sided sex—sex between a person (them) and a thing (it)—is sex, that sexual use is sex, sexual abuse is sex, sexual domination is sex. This is the sexuality that they then demand, practice, purchase, and live out in their everyday social relations with others. Pornography works by making sexism sexy.

2. The Judicial, First Amendment Response

American Booksellers Association, Inc. v. Hudnut

771 F.2d 323 (7th Cir. 1985), aff'd mem., 475 U.S. 1001, reh'g denied, 475 U.S. 1132 (1986)

EASTERBROOK, Circuit Judge.

Indianapolis enacted an ordinance defining "pornography" as a practice that discriminates against women. "Pornography" is to be redressed through the administrative and judicial methods used for other discrimination. The City's definition of "pornography" is considerably different from "obscenity," which the Supreme Court has held is not protected by the First Amendment.

To be "obscene" under Miller v. California, . . . "a publication must, taken as a whole, appeal to the prurient interest, must contain patently offensive depictions or descriptions of specified sexual conduct, and on the whole have no serious literary, artistic, political, or scientific value." . . . Offensiveness must be assessed under the standards of the community. Both offensiveness and an appeal to something other than "normal, healthy sexual desires" are essential elements of "obscenity."

"Pornography" under the ordinance is "the graphic sexually explicit subordination of women, whether in pictures or in words, that also includes one or more of the following: (1) Women are presented as sexual objects who enjoy pain or humiliation; or (2) Women are presented as sexual objects who experience sexual pleasure in being raped; or (3) Women are presented as sexual objects tied up or cut up or mutilated or bruised or physically hurt, or as dismembered or truncated or fragmented or severed into body parts; or (4) Women are presented as being penetrated by objects or animals; or (5) Women are presented in scenarios of degradation, injury, abasement, torture, shown as filthy or inferior, bleeding, bruised, or hurt in a context that makes these conditions sexual; or (6) Women are presented as sexual objects for domination, conquest, violation, exploitation, possession, or use, or through postures or positions of servility or submission or display." . . . The statute provides that the "use of men, children, or transsexuals in the place of women in paragraphs (1) through (6) above shall also constitute pornography under this section." . . . The Indianapolis ordinance does not refer to the prurient interest, to offensiveness, or to the standards of the community. It demands attention to particular depictions, not to the work judged as a whole. It is irrelevant under the ordinance whether the work has literary, artistic, political, or scientific value. The City and many amici point to these omissions as virtues. They maintain that pornography influences attitudes, and the statute is a way to alter the socialization of men and women rather than to vindicate community standards of offensiveness. And as one of the principal drafters of the ordinance has asserted, "if a woman is subjected, why should it matter that the work has other value?" . . .

The plaintiffs are a congeries of distributors and readers of books, magazines, and films. . . . Civil rights groups and feminists have entered this case as amici on both sides. Those supporting the ordinance say that it will play an important role in reducing the tendency of men to view women as sexual objects, a tendency that leads to both unacceptable attitudes and discrimination in the workplace and violence away from it. Those opposing the ordinance point out that much radical feminist literature is explicit and depicts women in ways forbidden by the ordinance and that the ordinance would reopen old battles. It is unclear how Indianapolis would treat works from James Joyce's Ulysses to Homer's Iliad; both depict women as submissive objects for conquest and domination. . . .

"If there is any fixed star in our constitutional constellation, it is that no official, high or petty, can prescribe what shall be orthodox in politics, nationalism, religion, or other matters of opinion or force citizens to confess by word or act their faith therein." . . . Under the First Amendment the government must leave to the people the evaluation of ideas. Bald or subtle, an idea is as powerful as the audience allows it to be. A belief may be pernicious—the beliefs of Nazis led to the death of millions, those of the Klan to the repression of millions. A pernicious belief may prevail. Totalitarian governments today rule much of the planet, practicing suppression of billions and spreading dogma that may enslave others. One of the things that separates our society from theirs is our absolute right to propagate opinions that the government finds wrong or even hateful. . . .

Under the ordinance graphic sexually explicit speech is "pornography" or not depending on the perspective the author adopts. Speech that "subordinates" women and also, for example, presents women as enjoying pain, humiliation, or rape, or even simply presents women in "positions of servility or submission or display" is forbidden, no matter how great the literary or political value of the work taken as a whole. Speech that portrays women in positions of equality is lawful, no matter how graphic the sexual content. This is thought control. It establishes an "approved" view of women, of how they may react to sexual encounters, of how the sexes may relate to each other.

Those who espouse the approved view may use sexual images; those who do not, may not.

Indianapolis justifies the ordinance on the ground that pornography affects thoughts. Men who see women depicted as subordinate are more likely to treat them so. Pornography is an aspect of dominance. It does not persuade people so much as change them. It works by socializing, by establishing the expected and the permissible. In this view pornography is not an idea; pornography is the injury.

There is much to this perspective. Beliefs are also facts. . . . Depictions of subordination tend to perpetuate subordination. The subordinate status of women in turn leads to affront and lower pay at work, insult and injury at home, battery and rape on the streets. In the language of the legislature, "[p]ornography is central in creating and maintaining sex as a basis of discrimination. Pornography is a systematic practice of exploitation and subordination based on sex which differentially harms women. The bigotry and contempt it produces, with the acts of aggression it fosters, harm women's opportunities for equality and rights [of all kinds]."

Yet this simply demonstrates the power of pornography as speech. All of these unhappy effects depend on mental intermediation. Pornography affects how people see the world, their fellows, and social relations. If pornography is what pornography does, so is other speech. Hitler's orations affected how some Germans saw Jews. . . . Racial bigotry, anti-semitism, violence on television, reporters' biases — these and many more influence the culture and shape our socialization. None is directly answerable by more speech, unless that speech too finds its place in the popular culture. Yet all is protected as speech, however insidious. Any other answer leaves the government in control of all of the institutions of culture, the great censor and director of which thoughts are good for us. . . .

Much of Indianapolis's argument rests on the belief that when speech is "unanswerable," and the metaphor that there is a "marketplace of ideas" does not apply, the First Amendment does not apply either. The metaphor is honored; Milton's Areopagitica and John Stewart [sic] Mill's On Liberty defend freedom of speech on the ground that the truth will prevail, and many of the most important cases under the First Amendment recite this position. The Framers undoubtedly believed it. As a general matter it is true. But the Constitution does not make the dominance of truth a necessary condition of freedom of speech. To say that it does would be to confuse an outcome of free speech with a necessary condition for the application of the amendment.

A power to limit speech on the ground that truth has not yet prevailed and is not likely to prevail implies the power to declare truth. At some point the government must be able to say (as Indianapolis has said): "We know what the truth is, yet a free exchange of speech has not driven out falsity, so that we must now prohibit falsity." If the government may declare the truth, why wait for the failure of speech? Under the First Amendment, however, there is no such thing as a false idea, . . . so the government may not restrict speech on the ground that in a free exchange truth is not yet dominant. . . .

We come, finally, to the argument that pornography is "low value" speech, that it is enough like obscenity that Indianapolis may prohibit it. Some cases hold that speech far removed from politics and other subjects at the core of the Framers' concerns may be subjected to special regulation. . . . These cases do not sustain statutes that select among viewpoints, however. In [one case], the FCC sought to keep vile language off the air during certain times. The Court held that it may; but the Court would not have sustained a regulation prohibiting scatological descriptions of Republicans but not scatological descriptions of Democrats, or any other form of selection among viewpoints.

At all events, "pornography" is not low value speech within the meaning of these cases. Indianapolis seeks to prohibit certain speech because it believes this speech influences social relations and politics on a grand scale, that it controls attitudes at home and in the legislature. This precludes a characterization of the speech as low value. True, pornography and obscenity have sex in common. But Indianapolis left out of its definition any reference to literary, artistic, political, or scientific value. The ordinance applies to graphic sexually explicit subordination in works great and small. The Court sometimes balances the value of speech against the costs of its restriction, but it does this by category of speech and not by the content of particular works. . . . Indianapolis has created an approved point of view and so loses the support of these cases.

Any rationale we could imagine in support of this ordinance could not be limited to sex discrimination. Free speech has been on balance an ally of those seeking change. Governments that want stasis start by restricting speech. Culture is a powerful force of continuity; Indianapolis paints pornography as part of the culture of power. Change in any complex system ultimately depends on the ability of outsiders to challenge accepted views and the reigning institutions. Without a strong guarantee of freedom of speech, there is no effective right to challenge what is.

. . . The offense of coercion to engage in a pornographic performance . . . has elements that might be constitutional. Without question a state may prohibit fraud, trickery, or the use of force to induce people to perform—in pornographic films or in any other films. Such a statute may be written without regard to the viewpoint depicted in the work. New York v. Ferber . . . suggests that when a state has a strong interest in forbidding the conduct that makes up a film (in *Ferber* sexual acts involving minors), it may restrict or forbid dissemination of the film in order to reinforce the prohibition of the conduct. A state may apply such a rule to non-sexual coercion (although it need not). . . .

But the Indianapolis ordinance, unlike our hypothetical statute, is not neutral with respect to viewpoint . . . .

[The judgment of the district court finding the ordinance unconstitutional is affirmed.]

Nan D. Hunter & Sylvia A. Law, Brief Amici Curiae of Feminist Anti-Censorship Taskforce et al., in American Booksellers Association, Inc. v. Hudnut

21 U. Mich. J.L. Reform 69, 126-131 (Fall 1987-Winter 1988)

The [Indianapolis] ordinance . . . implies that sexually explicit images of women necessarily subordinate and degrade women and perpetuates stereotypes of women as helpless victims and people who could not seek or enjoy sex.

The ordinance also reinforces sexist stereotypes of men. It denies the possibility that graphic sexually explicit images of a man could ever subordinate or degrade him. It provides no remedy for sexually explicit images showing men as "dismembered, truncated or fragmented" or "shown as filthy or inferior, bleeding, bruised or hurt." . . .

The ordinance reinforces yet another sexist stereotype of men as aggressive beasts. Appellants assert:

> By conditioning the male orgasm to female subordination, pornography . . . makes the subordination of women pleasurable and seemingly legitimate. Each time men are sexually aroused by pornography, they learn to connect a woman's sexual pleasure to abuse and a woman's sexual nature to inferiority. They learn this in their bodies, not just their minds, so that it becomes a natural physiological response. At this point pornography leaves no more room for further debate than does shouting "kill" to an attack dog.

Men are not attack dogs, but morally responsible human beings. The ordinance reinforces a destructive sexist stereotype of men as irresponsible beasts, with "natural physiological responses" which can be triggered by sexually explicit images of women, and for which the men cannot be held accountable. Thus, men are conditioned into violent acts or negative beliefs by sexual images; women are not. Further, the ordinance is wholly blind to the possibility that men could be hurt and degraded by images presenting them as violent or sadistic.

The ordinance also reinforces sexist images of woman as incapable of consent. It creates a remedy for people "coerced" to participate in the production of pornography. . . .

In effect, the ordinance creates a strong presumption that women who participate in the creation of sexually explicit material are coerced. . . . Women are judged incompetent to consent to participate in the creation of sexually explicit material and condemned as "bad" if they do so. . . .

This provision does far more than simply provide a remedy to women who are pressured into the creation of pornography which they subsequently seek to suppress. It functions to make all women incompetent to enter into legally binding contracts for the production of sexually explicit material. When women are legally disabled from making binding agreements, they are denied power to negotiate for fair treatment and decent pay. Enforcement of the ordinance would drive production of sexually explicit material even further into an underground economy, where the working conditions of women in the sex industry would worsen, not improve. . . .

The ordinance damages individuals who do not fit the stereotypes it embodies. It delegitimates and makes socially invisible women who find sexually explicit images of women "in positions of display" or "penetrated by objects" to be erotic, liberating, or educational. These women are told that their perceptions are a product of "false consciousness" and that such images are so inherently degrading that they may be suppressed by the state. At the same time, it stamps the imprimatur of state approval on the belief that men are attack dogs triggered to violence by the sight of a sexually explicit image of a woman. It delegitimates and makes socially invisible those men who consider themselves gentle, respectful of women, or inhibited about expressing their sexuality.

Even worse, the stereotypes of the ordinance perpetuate traditional social views of sex-based difference. By defining sexually explicit images of women as subordinating and degrading to them, the ordinance reinforces the stereotypical view that "good" women do not seek and enjoy sex. As applied, it would deny women access to sexually explicit material at a time in our history when women have just begun to acquire the social and economic power to develop our own images of sexuality. Stereotypes of hair-trigger male susceptibility to violent imagery can be invoked as an excuse to avoid directly blaming the men who commit violent acts.

Finally, the ordinance perpetuates a stereotype of women as helpless victims, incapable of consent, and in need of protection.

Deborah L. Rhode, *Speaking of Sex: The Denial of Gender Inequality*

133-137 (1997)

[Some categories of harm] involve the use of pornography as a blueprint for sexual violence and degradation. . . . But . . . we have no gauge of frequency. Nor do we know whether pornography actually *causes* violence, or only influences its form. . . .

Two decades of laboratory research . . . [has] consistently found that exposure to sexually violent material increases viewers' expressed willingness to commit rape and decreases their sensitivity to its damage. Yet such research cannot adequately demonstrate the degree or duration of pornography's effects in the real world. Most experts believe that changes in the viewers' attitudes following laboratory experiments reflect the violence more than the sex. Although this distinction can be difficult to draw, many experts estimate that violent materials account for well under 10 percent of the pornography market. Sex offenders do not differ significantly from other individuals in their exposure or response to pornography. These offenders are more likely to be readers of *Field and Stream* than of sexually explicit material.

Other efforts to measure the harms of pornography by comparing changes over time or across cultures have been even more inconclusive. . . . Some countries with high pornography consumption have low rates of reported violence against women. Other countries that heavily censor sexual expression are scarcely feminist meccas; middle-eastern Muslim societies have little pornography *or* gender equality.

Yet it is a mistake to conclude, as do many civil libertarians, that there is no demonstrable link between sexual expression, sexual attitudes and sexual violence. In a nation that spends some $130 billion each year in advertising, it should not be necessary to belabor the point that images matter. A quarter-century's research leaves no doubt that aggression is in large part learned behavior, and that at least part of the learning process involves words and images. In short the real question is not whether there is some link between pornography and social harms, but whether it is strong enough to justify the risks of regulation. . . .

[One concern] is the absence of any logical limiting principle for legislation targeting subordination. . . . A further concern is that provisions distinguishing between "good" and "bad" forms of sexual pleasure will reinforce sexist stereotypes. Some recent studies suggest that . . . almost half of surveyed women report watching pornographic films regularly. . . . Even if such enjoyment is the product of sexist conditioning, it does not follow that women need more "sexual shame, guilt, and hypocrisy — this time served up as feminism. . . ."

. . . For many individuals, nonviolent erotica can provide a safe outlet for channeling sexual domination, treating sexual dysfunctions, and fantasizing about practices that they would not attempt in real life. . . .

Even if our society's ultimate goal is to reduce the presence of pornographic material, censorship has never been adequate to the task. Suppression generally increases the appeal of sexually arousing materials. . . . Yet it does not follow that all line drawing is futile, or that all anti-pornography regulation would carry the same risks as recent initiatives. For example, some First Amendment scholars propose banning only sexually explicit visual portrayals of force or violence that lack redeeming literary, artistic, political or scientific value. Such a standard would sweep far less broadly than either prevailing obscenity laws or alternatives focused on subordination, and would target only material that is most clearly harmful.

Notes

1. Pornography and the First Amendment. Some commentators have argued that regulation of pornography is consistent with the First Amendment, in that pornography is like other forms of speech that can be regulated because of their low value (such as advertising) or their social harm (such as libel, fraud, and sexual harassment). They also claim that pornography ordinances are no less vague than existing obscenity law. MacKinnon further claims that

> while the First Amendment supports pornography on the belief that consensus and progress are facilitated by allowing all views, however divergent and unorthodox, it fails to notice that pornography . . . is not at all divergent or unorthodox. It is the ruling ideology. Feminism, the dissenting view, is suppressed by pornography.[237]

How effectively does *Hudnut* respond to these claims?

Legislation somewhat similar to the Indianapolis ordinance has been upheld by the Canadian Supreme Court. In Regina v. Butler, the court sustained a statute that criminalizes "any publication a dominant characteristic of which is the undue exploitation of sex, or of sex and any one or more of the following subjects, namely crime, horror, cruelty and violence." The Court interprets the statute to prohibit any "materials that subordinate, degrade or dehumanize women."[238] In determining that the restriction of speech expression was justified, the Court concluded that the legislation "seeks to enhance respect for all members of society and nonviolence and equality in their relations with each other."[239] Is this a desirable approach? Is your view affected by the fact that the first targets of the legislation included a lesbian magazine, and two books by antipornography activist Andrea Dworkin?[240]

Another alternative is the approach of some sexually progressive societies that ban portrayals of "extreme abuse," such as rape, bestiality, and pedophilia.[241] Would such an approach be constitutional under the obscenity doctrine and the First Amendment? Desirable?

2. Evaluating the Harm of Pornography.   Evidence concerning the harms of pornography remains conflicting and contested. In 2004, the Subcommittee on Science, Technology, and Space of the Senate Committee on Commerce held a hearing on The Science Behind Pornography Addiction.[242] The hearing included evidence that prolonged exposure to pornography promotes sexual callousness, increases proclivity to rape, promotes adverse perceptions of women, and erodes trust and honesty in intimate relationships. Other experts at the hearing and in subsequent reports claimed that frequent viewing of pornography leads to unrealistic expectations concerning female appearance and behavior, greater acceptance of sexual harassment, and difficulties in forming sexually satisfying relationships.[243] In a Kaiser Family Foundation study, about half of the 15- to 24-year-olds surveyed believed that adolescents who see pornography on the Internet are more likely to have sex before they are ready and that such material promotes bad attitudes toward women.[244] A study of battered women also found that pornography use by the batterer was correlated with an increased likelihood of sexual as well as physical abuse.[245]

By contrast, other experts maintain that the vast majority of pornography viewers are occasional, recreational users, not addicts, and that such use can be beneficial in sparking desire and enhancing satisfaction. As the preceding excerpt from Rhode indicates, many researchers also believe that the causal relationships between pornography and sexual violence have not been established. Critics claim that the 2004 Hearings were stacked to exclude researchers who would have provided more credible evidence than the pornography opponents who testified.[246]

An equally contested issue is what kinds of explicit sexual imagery are most damaging. The premise of an Indianapolis-style ordinance is that violent pornography is more harmful and therefore more appropriate for regulation than nonviolent pornography. By contrast, some feminists contend that the most adverse effects on women's self-image come from nonviolent mainstream images that appear acceptable and normal.[247] In a sense, this point is fully consistent with one principle of dominance theory, which is that legal rules proscribing only the most severe forms of certain behaviors thereby legitimize the remainder. Would tighter controls on violent pornography further eroticize violence against women? Is the answer to regulate more, or less?

Many scholars argue for less regulation, both because they do not believe that violent pornography causes the harms that opponents cite, and because, even if it did, trying to prevent it through legal regulation would be counterproductive. On the latter point, David Cole agrees:

> Sexual expression . . . inevitably confounds society's attempts to regulate it. It subverts every taboo by making it a fetish. The forbidden is simultaneously eroticized. As a result, attempts to regulate sexual expression are doomed to failure; by creating taboos to transgress, regulation only adds to sexual expression's appeal.[248]

Is it possible that pornography has beneficial effects? Does a more open attitude toward pornography enable more open discussions generally about such topics as safe sex, sexual identity, and domestic violence?[249]

Consider also the following, from a former porn star:

> I'm just very happy with what I've done. On a social level, I think these movies are helping people's lives. A lot of our crowd, our audience, is made up of guys who maybe aren't the best-looking dudes in town. Maybe they're dorks or disabled or something like that, and there's no chance they're ever going to get laid. And I think the adult business definitely gives those guys an outlet. Otherwise, they'll explode.
>
> And lately, a lot of couples are benefiting from our films as well. . . . There are so many people who are so unhappy sexually. But now, because of the way sex has become so important in the media and so open, and people are finally talking about stuff and showing stuff sexually, people are realizing how unhappy they are and doing something about it. For the guys to bring these movies home to their spouses or girlfriends, sometimes it can really stimulate their relationship. Sometimes it works, sometimes it doesn't. But at least if a guy is unhappy with the way his wife is performing, he can watch porno and jerk off maybe, rather than have an affair. Everyone can disagree, but I think it's definitely at least an outlet for guys.[250]

By contrast, sociologist Michael Kimmel's *Guyland*, a study of young men and masculinity, finds a less benign function of pornography. For his subjects, "porn gives guys a world in which no one has to take no for an answer." It serves as a "refuge from the harsh reality of a more gender equitable world. . . . It's about anger at the loss of privilege." Escape into this world, Kimmel argues, fosters attitudes "that won't serve [men] in the long term. . . . They're missing out on developing the skills, sexual and otherwise, that might help them to sustain relationships with women in the real world," relationships that demand "at least a modicum of dignity, respect, and care."[251] What is your view?

3. Pornography and Individual Agency.   At the heart of the debate over pornography regulation is the extent to which people are capable of defining their own sexuality. Those favoring regulation of pornography assume that its proliferation prevents women from being independent agents; women's choices appear constrained by the ways in which sex has been defined in *men's* interests. Those opposing regulation assume that women have the capacity to think and act for themselves, and to know what they want. Many young "third wave" feminists and gays and lesbians have taken this approach and stressed the subversive and self-expressive aspects of pornography.[252] What is your view?

Is there some "natural" set of sexual drives and desires that pornography, advertising, and other social forces distort? Or is sexuality always socially constructed? If the latter, how could society promote the most healthy understandings of sex and sexuality?

4. Pornography, the Internet, and Children.   The increasingly accessible Internet has expanded opportunities for the creation and distribution of sexually explicit images. Online pornography poses special challenges for regulation. The first problem is detection. The sheer size of cyberspace makes it difficult to police. A second problem is accountability. Even if illegal content is discovered online, the responsible party may be impossible to track. Both of these difficulties are exacerbated by encryption technology, which allows parties to disguise their identities. A third problem is how can courts exercise authority over out-of-state providers. Other difficulties arise in determining which "community standards" govern online materials that can be downloaded anywhere. The Internet's decentralized structure also resists regulation by permitting users to reroute access around "blocks." In addition, users can post messages anonymously through the use of remailers, making it difficult to suspend privileges or identify senders.

The vast majority of nations prohibit the sale of pornography to children but find such prohibitions difficult to enforce. The same technologies that make it easy for individuals to disguise their identity make it equally easy to disguise their age. The first congressional attempt to cope with this problem, the Communications Decency Act, criminalized transmissions of "obscene or indecent" and "patently offensive" messages to a minor. The Supreme Court struck down these provisions as overly broad restrictions on speech.[253]

A subsequent act, the Child Online Protection Act (COPA), imposed criminal penalties on those who knowingly make available to minors through the Internet commercial materials "harmful to minors." Commercial websites that include such material must use age verification mechanisms such as credit cards or adult identification numbers. This statute, too, was eventually invalidated, on the grounds that plausible, less restrictive alternatives than criminal penalties were available, such as filtering and blocking software.[254]

However, the Supreme Court upheld a related law—the Children's Internet Protection Act (CIPA)—that requires publicly funded elementary schools, secondary schools, and libraries that provide Internet access to (1) block or filter adults' access to visual depictions of obscenity or child pornography and (2) block or filter children's access to obscenity, child pornography, or other material that is "harmful to minors." The American Library Association challenged the Act. In upholding CIPA, the Court's decision left open the possibility of later challenge if, as applied, software erroneously blocked constitutionally protected material and librarians were not willing, or able, to unblock it.[255]

The Child Pornography Prevention Act (CPPA) prohibits the production, transportation, receipt, or distribution of visual depictions that involve the use of a minor (any person under the age of 18) engaged in sexually explicit conduct, where the producer or distributor knows or has reason to know, that the depiction was or will be transported in interstate commerce or was created using a camera (or the like) that had traveled in interstate commerce. Visual depictions include computer-generated or "morphed" images that appear to be a minor engaged in sexually explicit conduct, as well as images that are adults promoted as children. Supporters of CPPA argued that these images are flooding the market and present just as great a risk of harm to children as pornography using live underage models. When the statute came before the Supreme Court for argument, Justice Scalia questioned whether there would in fact be "radical tragic consequences" for First Amendment jurisprudence if audiences could not see "minors copulating." When Justice Stevens smilingly interjected a reference to Romeo and Juliet, Justice Scalia responded, "you've seen a different version of that play than I have."[256] In Ashcroft v. Free Speech Coalition, the Court held that the statute proscribed material that was neither obscene nor child pornography, and violated the First Amendment.[257] In so ruling, the Court rejected the government's argument that such works could be banned because they contributed to child abuse when pedophiles used them to stimulate an appetite for sexual contact or to lure children into criminal acts. In the Court's view, child pornography had not been demonstrated to be "intrinsically related" to child abuse and the link between abuse and virtual child pornography was only "contingent and indirect."

The PROTECT Act, passed in 2003, attempts to curb the spread of child pornography on the Internet by making it a crime to offer or solicit sexually explicit images of children. The PROTECT Act applies even if the material at issue consists solely of computer-generated images or digitally altered photographs of adults, as well as to fraudulent offers of child pornography in which the material does not exist at all. Parts of this statute have also been found to be unconstitutional.[258]

Two other issues that recently have divided federal courts involve sentences for possession of child pornography. Some courts have revised sentences downward for individuals convicted of possession or distribution of child pornography on the ground that it is a victimless offense and that offenders are themselves victims of mental health disorders.[259] By contrast, other courts have viewed such offenses more seriously and have required even those convicted only of possessing pornography to pay restitution to victims in amounts ranging from $3,000 to $150,000.[260] VAWA authorizes restitution to victims who are harmed as a result of commission of a crime involving sexual exploitation of children.[261] Courts have divided over whether possession alone is enough to trigger liability, because the number of potential victims and offenders is "staggering," the amount of losses directly attributable to a single owner is difficult to calculate, and inconsistent verdicts are likely.[262]

What is your view? How serious is the crime of possession of pornography? Is a life sentence appropriate for a 26-year-old man convicted of 454 counts of possessing child pornography?[263] If restitution is appropriate, how should damages be measured? Should a lawyer convicted of possession be disbarred if the material he owned was legally made in the country in which he purchased it?[264]

5. Sexting. An issue gaining increased attention is sexting—sending nude or seminude pictures over cell phones. About a fifth of teens reported sending or receiving such pictures and almost half of boys in coed high schools had seen a nude picture of a female classmate.[265] Students have been expelled or suspended or denied the right to participate in school activities in response to such offenses.[266] Prosecutors in several states also have filed or threatened child pornography charges against students involved in sending or forwarding such photos. Sanctions for such offenses could include long prison terms and 10 to 20 years registration as a sex offender. In one case, the parents of two 15-year-old girls who circulated provocative photos of themselves wearing bras sued the district attorney. He had threatened prosecution of the girls if they did not attend a 10-hour class dealing with pornography and sexual violence. The American Civil Liberties lawyer representing the families denounced the "nuclear-weapon-type-charge like child pornography against kids who have no criminal intent and are merely doing stupid things."[267] Prosecutors, by contrast, defend the charges as a way to "protect these kids from themselves" and from acting in ways that can "follow them for the rest of their lives."[268]

Particularly where students have ignored school warnings not to engage in the practice, local district attorneys have viewed criminal charges, with the possibility of a suspended sentence, as a useful deterrent. Courts, however, have imposed limits on the sanctions that can be imposed. In Miller v. Mitchell, the Third Circuit Court of Appeals granted a preliminary injunction against requiring a student to attend an educational class on sexting on the grounds that it infringed her parent's autonomy and her own right of free expression.[269]

Sexting has evolved against a growing cultural backdrop of sexualization of adolescents.[270] Girls often use sexting as a form of "relationship currency"; it also serves to initiate or sustain intimacy, as well as to entertain friends and humiliate enemies.[271] Girls are more likely to send sexualized photos than boys, feel more pressure to do so, and suffer more adverse consequences. A common perception is that girls who sext are sluts, while boys are studs. Consequences for victims range from minor embarrassment to bullying, sexual harassment, stigma, psychological trauma, and even suicide.[272]

How would you respond to "sexting" as a parent, principal, or prosecutor? Are there legitimate issues of sexual self-expression and agency at issue? Should you punish those who send sexts as part of a relationship, or only those who forward them or pressure others to engage in the practice?[273] Should lawmakers create a separate misdemeanor offense of sexting and specify fines and counseling as the sanctions?[274]

Putting Theory Into Practice

3-15. You are a university lawyer who is contacted by the campus women students' organization. The group is offended by the practices of several fraternities, which show porn films and invite strippers to perform on campus at all-male parties. The students believe that these practices encourage date rape. They also protest the fraternity's practice of circulating provocative photos that members receive from their girlfriends. The fraternity officers believe that their members are entitled to exercise their First Amendment rights. How would you respond? What strategies would you propose?

3-16. You are a state legislator who has been contacted by the U.S. Attorney General in connection with a campaign to increase criminal penalties for possession of child pornography from a misdemeanor to a felony. Advocates of reform argue that such penalties are necessary to discourage demand. Opponents respond that felony convictions are inappropriate for first-time offenders who simply view images of sexual conduct by minors. What is your view?[275]

3-17. You are the Dean of Humanities at a university that offers a student-devised course on "Male Sexuality." The course includes a field trip to a gay strip club, class discussion of photographs of the students' genitals, and a requirement that each student produce a sexually explicit work. Adverse publicity has led to demands that the university cease offering the course. How should this be handled?[276]

E. SEXUAL ORIENTATION DISCRIMINATION

No legal rules or social norms have changed as quickly in modern society as the rules and norms relating to sexual orientation. Traditionally, a person was not entitled to any legal protection as a result of his or her sexual orientation. Same-sex sexual desires and behaviors were considered deviant and punishable by law, and discrimination against gay, lesbian, bisexual, and transgender individuals in employment and other spheres of life was widespread and without legal recourse. Faced with challenges to laws that penalized homosexual behaviors or discriminated on the basis of sexual orientation, courts denied both due process protections, on the grounds that legal protection for homosexuality was not deeply rooted in this nation's traditions, and equal protection rights, on the grounds that discrimination on the basis of sexual orientation did not warrant a heightened standard of constitutional review. In a number of areas, legal definitions operated to deny even the fact of sexual orientation discrimination. Homosexuals were not denied the right to marry, for example, because the definition of marriage requires a union of one man and one woman; gay partners who raised children together could not both be parents, since the law of parenthood limits children to one mother and one father.

The law changed first with respect to private sexual conduct. In the 2003 case of Lawrence v. Texas,[277] the U.S. Supreme Court reversed a 1986 opinion, Bowers v. Hardwick,[278] and held that private sexual conduct between consenting adults, including conduct between homosexuals, was constitutionally protected under the Due Process Clause. The following decade has seen intense public debate over gay rights, focused on same-sex marriage, the rights of gay and lesbian parents, and equal access to employment, including nondiscrimination in the U.S. military. United States v. Windsor, set forth below, marks a major turning point in this debate and, with the rapid change in public acceptance of gay rights, the case is a likely harbinger of further erosion in the traditional legal landscape with respect to gay, lesbian, bisexual, and transgender individuals.

1. Can Same-Sex Couples Marry?

Jones v. Hallahan, excerpted below, represents the traditional view that same-sex relationships cannot meet the definition of marriage. As of the time of this printing, all but 17 states and the District of Columbia continue to limit marriage to one man and one woman, but the trend is clearly in the direction of allowing same-sex marriage.

Reading Questions

1. Should courts or legislatures decide who has the right to marry? Why?
2. What is the legal reasoning of Justice Kennedy's opinion in *Windsor*? Is the point that states should be defining marriage for their own citizens? Or that federal *or state* restrictions on gay marriage are unconstitutional?
3. Why do you think same-sex marriage has been an important focus of the gay rights movement in this country? Is access to marriage necessary for achieving equality for gays and lesbians? Or would it make more sense to develop alternative family models? Are these mutually exclusive goals?

Jones v. Hallahan

501 S.W.2d 588 (Ky. 1973)

VANCE, Commissioner.

The appellants, each of whom is a female person, seek review of a judgment of the Jefferson Circuit Court which held that they were not entitled to have issued to them a license to marry each other.

Appellants contend that the failure of the clerk to issue the license deprived them of three basic constitutional rights, namely, the right to marry; the right of association; and the right to free exercise of religion. They also contend that the refusal subjects them to cruel and unusual punishment.

The sections of Kentucky statutes relating to marriage do not include a definition of that term. It must therefore be defined according to common usage.

Webster's New International Dictionary, Second Edition, defines marriage as follows:

> A state of being married, or being united to a person or persons of the opposite sex as husband or wife; also, the mutual relation of husband and wife; wedlock; abstractly, the institution whereby men and women are joined in a special kind of social and legal dependence, for the purpose of founding and maintaining a family. . . .

Black's Law Dictionary, Fourth Edition, defines marriage as:

> The civil status, condition or relation of one man and one woman united in law for life, for the discharge to each other and the community of the duties legally incumbent upon those whose association is founded on the distinction of sex.

Kentucky statutes do not specifically prohibit marriage between persons of the same sex nor do they authorize the issuance of a marriage license to such persons.

Marriage was a custom long before the state commenced to issue licenses for that purpose. For a time the records of marriage were kept by the church. Some states even now recognize a common-law marriage which has neither the benefit of license nor clergy. In all cases, however, marriage has always been considered as the union of a man and a woman and we have been presented with no authority to the contrary.

It appears to us that appellants are prevented from marrying, not by the statutes of Kentucky or the refusal of the County Court Clerk of Jefferson County to issue them a license, but rather by their own incapability of entering into a marriage as that term is defined.

In substance, the relationship proposed by the appellants does not authorize the issuance of a marriage license because what they propose is not a marriage.

The judgment is affirmed.

United States v. Windsor

133 S. Ct. 2675 (2013)

Justice KENNEDY delivered the opinion of the Court. . . .

I

In 1996, as some States were beginning to consider the concept of same-sex marriage, see, e.g., Baehr v. Lewin [1993] and before any State had acted to permit it, Congress enacted the Defense of Marriage Act (DOMA). DOMA contains two operative sections: Section 2, which has not been challenged here, allows States to refuse to recognize same-sex marriages performed under the laws of other States.

Section 3 is at issue here. It amends the Dictionary Act in Title 1, §7, of the United States Code to provide a federal definition of "marriage" and "spouse." Section 3 of DOMA provides as follows:

> In determining the meaning of any Act of Congress, or of any ruling, regulation, or interpretation of the various administrative bureaus and agencies of the United States, the word "marriage" means only a legal union between one man and one woman as husband and wife, and the word "spouse" refers only to a person of the opposite sex who is a husband or a wife. 1 U.S.C. §7.

The definitional provision does not by its terms forbid States from enacting laws permitting same-sex marriages or civil unions or providing state benefits to residents in that status. The enactment's comprehensive definition of marriage for purposes of all federal statutes and other regulations or directives covered by its terms, however, does control over 1,000 federal laws in which marital or spousal status is addressed as a matter of federal law. . . .

Edith Windsor and Thea Spyer met in New York City in 1963 and began a long-term relationship. Windsor and Spyer registered as domestic partners when New York City gave that right to same-sex couples in 1993. Concerned about Spyer's health, the couple made the 2007 trip to Canada for their marriage, but they continued to reside in New York City. The State of New York deems their Ontario marriage to be a valid one. . . .

Spyer died in February 2009, and left her entire estate to Windsor. Because DOMA denies federal recognition to same-sex spouses, Windsor did not qualify for the marital exemption from the federal estate tax, which excludes from taxation "any interest in property which passes or has passed from the decedent to his surviving spouse." . . . Windsor paid $363,053 in estate taxes and sought a refund. The Internal Revenue Service denied the refund, concluding that, under DOMA, Windsor was not a "surviving spouse." Windsor commenced this refund suit in the United States District Court for the Southern District of New York. She contended that DOMA violates the guarantee of equal protection, as applied to the Federal Government through the Fifth Amendment.

While the tax refund suit was pending, the Attorney General of the United States notified the Speaker of the House of Representatives . . . that the Department of Justice would no longer defend the constitutionality of DOMA's §3. Noting that "the Department has previously defended DOMA against . . . challenges involving legally married same-sex couples," the Attorney General informed Congress that "the President has concluded that given a number of factors, including a documented history of discrimination, classifications based on sexual orientation should be subject to a heightened standard of scrutiny." . . .

In response to the notice from the Attorney General, the Bipartisan Legal Advisory Group (BLAG) of the House of Representatives voted to intervene in the litigation to defend the constitutionality of §3 of DOMA. The Department of Justice did not oppose limited intervention by BLAG. . . .

On the merits of the tax refund suit, the District Court ruled against the United States. It held that §3 of DOMA is unconstitutional and ordered the Treasury to refund the tax with interest. Both the Justice Department and BLAG filed notices of appeal, and the Solicitor General filed a petition for certiorari before judgment. Before this Court acted on the petition, the Court of Appeals for the Second Circuit affirmed the District Court's judgment. It applied heightened scrutiny to classifications based on sexual orientation, as both the Department and Windsor had urged. . . .

III

When at first Windsor and Spyer longed to marry, neither New York nor any other State granted them that right. After waiting some years, in 2007 they traveled to Ontario to be married there. It seems fair to conclude that, until recent years, many citizens had not even considered the possibility that two persons of the same sex might aspire to occupy the same status and dignity as that of a man and woman in lawful marriage. For marriage between a man and a woman no doubt had been thought of by most people as essential to the very definition of that term and to its role and function throughout the history of civilization. That belief, for many who long have held it, became even more urgent, more cherished when challenged. For others, however, came the beginnings of a new perspective, a new insight. Accordingly some States concluded that same-sex marriage ought to be given recognition and validity in the law for those same-sex couples who wish to define themselves by their commitment to each other. The limitation of lawful marriage to heterosexual couples, which for centuries had been deemed both necessary and fundamental, came to be seen in New York and certain other States as an unjust exclusion.

Slowly at first and then in rapid course, the laws of New York came to acknowledge the urgency of this issue for same-sex couples who wanted to affirm their commitment to one another before their children, their family, their friends, and their community. And so New York recognized same-sex marriages performed elsewhere; and then it later amended its own marriage laws to permit same-sex marriage. New York, in common with, as of this writing, 11 other States and the District of Columbia, decided that same-sex couples should have the right to marry and so live with pride in themselves and their union and in a status of equality with all other married persons. . . .

Against this background of lawful same-sex marriage in some States, the design, purpose, and effect of DOMA should be considered as the beginning point in deciding whether it is valid under the Constitution. By history and tradition the definition and regulation of marriage, as will be discussed in more detail, has been treated as being within the authority and realm of the separate States. Yet it is further established that Congress, in enacting discrete statutes, can make determinations that bear on marital rights and privileges. Just this Term the Court upheld the authority of the Congress to pre-empt state laws, allowing a former spouse to retain life insurance proceeds under a federal program that gave her priority, because of formal beneficiary designation rules, over the wife by a second marriage who survived the husband. . . .

Other precedents involving congressional statutes which affect marriages and family status further illustrate this point. In addressing the interaction of state domestic relations and federal immigration law Congress determined that marriages "entered into for the purpose of procuring an alien's admission [to the United States] as an immigrant" will not qualify the noncitizen for that status, even if the noncitizen's marriage is valid and proper for state-law purposes. . . . And in establishing income-based criteria for Social Security benefits, Congress decided that although state law would determine in general who qualifies as an applicant's spouse, common-law marriages also should be recognized, regardless of any particular State's view on these relationships. . . .

Though these discrete examples establish the constitutionality of limited federal laws that regulate the meaning of marriage in order to further federal policy, DOMA has a far greater reach; for it enacts a directive applicable to over 1,000 federal statutes and the whole realm of federal regulations. And its operation is directed to a class of persons that the laws of New York, and of 11 other States, have sought to protect.

In order to assess the validity of that intervention it is necessary to discuss the extent of the state power and authority over marriage as a matter of history and tradition. State laws defining and regulating marriage, of course, must respect the constitutional rights of persons, see, e.g., Loving v. Virginia [1967]; but, subject to those guarantees, "regulation of domestic relations" is "an area that has long been regarded as a virtually exclusive province of the States." . . .

The recognition of civil marriages is central to state domestic relations law applicable to its residents and citizens. See Williams v. North Carolina [1942] ("Each state as a sovereign has a rightful and legitimate concern in the marital status of persons domiciled within its borders"). The definition of marriage is the foundation of the State's broader authority to regulate the subject of domestic relations with respect to the "[p]rotection of offspring, property interests, and the enforcement of marital responsibilities." . . . "[T]he states, at the time of the adoption of the Constitution, possessed full power over the subject of marriage and divorce . . . [and] the Constitution delegated no authority to the Government of the United States on the subject of marriage and divorce." . . .

Consistent with this allocation of authority, the Federal Government, through our history, has deferred to state-law policy decisions with respect to domestic relations. In De Sylva v. Ballentine [1956] for example, the Court held that, "[t]o decide who is the widow or widower of a deceased author, or who are his executors or next of kin," under the Copyright Act "requires a reference to the law of the State which created those legal relationships" because "there is no federal law of domestic relations." . . . In order to respect this principle, the federal courts, as a general rule, do not adjudicate issues of marital status even when there might otherwise be a basis for federal jurisdiction. . . . Federal courts will not hear divorce and custody cases even if they arise in diversity because of "the virtually exclusive primacy . . . of the States in the regulation of domestic relations." . . .

The significance of state responsibilities for the definition and regulation of marriage dates to the Nation's beginning; for "when the Constitution was adopted the common understanding was that the domestic relations of husband and wife and parent and child were matters reserved to the States. . . . Marriage laws vary in some respects from State to State. For example, the required minimum age is 16 in Vermont, but only 13 in New Hampshire. . . . Likewise the permissible degree of consanguinity can vary (most States permit first cousins to marry, but a handful . . . prohibit the practice). But these rules are in every event consistent within each State.

Against this background DOMA rejects the long-established precept that the incidents, benefits, and obligations of marriage are uniform for all married couples within each State, though they may vary, subject to constitutional guarantees, from one State to the next. . . . DOMA, because of its reach and extent, departs from this history and tradition of reliance on state law to define marriage. . . .

In acting first to recognize and then to allow same-sex marriages, New York was responding "to the initiative of those who [sought] a voice in shaping the destiny of their own times." . . . These actions were without doubt a proper exercise of its sovereign authority within our federal system, all in the way that the Framers of the Constitution intended. The dynamics of state government in the federal system are to allow the formation of consensus respecting the way the members of a discrete community treat each other in their daily contact and constant interaction with each other.

The States' interest in defining and regulating the marital relation, subject to constitutional guarantees, stems from the understanding that marriage is more than a routine classification for purposes of certain statutory benefits. Private, consensual sexual intimacy between two adult persons of the same sex may not be punished by the State, and it can form "but one element in a personal bond that is more enduring." Lawrence v. Texas [2003]. By its recognition of the validity of same-sex marriages performed in other jurisdictions and then by authorizing same-sex unions and same-sex marriages, New York sought to give further protection and dignity to that bond. For same-sex couples who wished to be married, the State acted to give their lawful conduct a lawful status. This status is a far-reaching legal acknowledgment of the intimate relationship between two people, a relationship deemed by the State worthy of dignity in the community equal with all other marriages. It reflects both the community's considered perspective on the historical roots of the institution of marriage and its evolving understanding of the meaning of equality.

IV

DOMA seeks to injure the very class New York seeks to protect. By doing so it violates basic due process and equal protection principles applicable to the Federal Government. . . . The Constitution's guarantee of equality "must at the very least mean that a bare congressional desire to harm a politically unpopular group cannot" justify disparate treatment of that group. Department of Agriculture v. Moreno [1973]. In determining whether a law is motived by an improper animus or purpose, " '[d]iscriminations of an unusual character' " especially require careful consideration (quoting Romer v. Evans [1996]). DOMA cannot survive under these principles. The responsibility of the States for the regulation of domestic relations is an important indicator of the substantial societal impact the State's classifications have in the daily lives and customs of its people. DOMA's unusual deviation from the usual tradition of recognizing and accepting state definitions of marriage here operates to deprive same-sex couples of the benefits and responsibilities that come with the federal recognition of their marriages. This is strong evidence of a law having the purpose and effect of disapproval of that class. The avowed purpose and practical effect of the law here in question are to impose a disadvantage, a separate status, and so a stigma upon all who enter into same-sex marriages made lawful by the unquestioned authority of the States.

The history of DOMA's enactment and its own text demonstrate that interference with the equal dignity of same-sex marriages, a dignity conferred by the States in the exercise of their sovereign power, was more than an incidental effect of the federal statute. It was its essence. The House Report announced its conclusion that "it is both appropriate and necessary for Congress to do what it can to defend the institution of traditional heterosexual marriage. . . . H.R. 3396 is appropriately entitled the 'Defense of Marriage Act.' The effort to redefine 'marriage' to extend to homosexual couples is a truly radical proposal that would fundamentally alter the institution of marriage." . . . The House concluded that DOMA expresses "both moral disapproval of homosexuality, and a moral conviction that heterosexuality better comports with traditional (especially Judeo–Christian) morality." . . . The stated purpose of the law was to promote an "interest in protecting the traditional moral teachings reflected in heterosexual-only marriage laws." . . . Were there any doubt of this far-reaching purpose, the title of the Act confirms it: The Defense of Marriage.

The arguments put forward by BLAG are just as candid about the congressional purpose to influence or interfere with state sovereign choices about who may be married. As the title and dynamics of the bill indicate, its purpose is to discourage enactment of state same-sex marriage laws and to restrict the freedom and choice of couples married under those laws if they are enacted. The congressional goal was "to put a thumb on the scales and influence a state's decision as to how to shape its own marriage laws." . . . The Act's demonstrated purpose is to ensure that if any State decides to recognize same-sex marriages, those unions will be treated as second-class marriages for purposes of federal law. This raises a most serious question under the Constitution's Fifth Amendment.

DOMA's operation in practice confirms this purpose. When New York adopted a law to permit same-sex marriage, it sought to eliminate inequality; but DOMA frustrates that objective through a system-wide enactment with no identified connection to any particular area of federal law. DOMA writes inequality into the entire United States Code. The particular case at hand concerns the estate tax, but DOMA is more than a simple determination of what should or should not be allowed as an estate tax refund. Among the over 1,000 statutes and numerous federal regulations that DOMA controls are laws pertaining to Social Security, housing, taxes, criminal sanctions, copyright, and veterans' benefits.

DOMA's principal effect is to identify a subset of state-sanctioned marriages and make them unequal. The principal purpose is to impose inequality, not for other reasons like governmental efficiency. Responsibilities, as well as rights, enhance the dignity and integrity of the person. And DOMA contrives to deprive some couples married under the laws of their State, but not other couples, of both rights and responsibilities. By creating two contradictory marriage regimes within the same State, DOMA forces same-sex couples to live as married for the purpose of state law but unmarried for the purpose of federal law, thus diminishing the stability and predictability of basic personal relations the State has found it proper to acknowledge and protect. By this dynamic DOMA undermines both the public and private significance of state-sanctioned same-sex marriages; for it tells those couples, and all the world, that their otherwise valid marriages are unworthy of federal recognition. This places same-sex couples in an unstable position of being in a second-tier marriage. The differentiation demeans the couple, whose moral and sexual choices the Constitution protects, see *Lawrence*, and whose relationship the State has sought to dignify. And it humiliates tens of thousands of children now being raised by same-sex couples. The law in question makes it even more difficult for the children to understand the integrity and closeness of their own family and its concord with other families in their community and in their daily lives.

Under DOMA, same-sex married couples have their lives burdened, by reason of government decree, in visible and public ways. By its great reach, DOMA touches many aspects of married and family life, from the mundane to the profound. It prevents same-sex married couples from obtaining government healthcare benefits they would otherwise receive. . . . It deprives them of the Bankruptcy Code's special protections for domestic-support obligations. . . . It forces them to follow a complicated procedure to file their state and federal taxes jointly. . . . It prohibits them from being buried together in veterans' cemeteries. . . .

For certain married couples, DOMA's unequal effects are even more serious. The federal penal code makes it a crime to "assaul[t], kidna[p], or murde[r] . . . a member of the immediate family" of "a United States official, a United States judge, [or] a Federal law enforcement officer," with the intent to influence or retaliate against that official. Although a "spouse" qualifies as a member of the officer's "immediate family," DOMA makes this protection inapplicable to same-sex spouses.

DOMA also brings financial harm to children of same-sex couples. It raises the cost of health care for families by taxing health benefits provided by employers to their workers' same-sex spouses. And it denies or reduces benefits allowed to families upon the loss of a spouse and parent, benefits that are an integral part of family security.

DOMA divests married same-sex couples of the duties and responsibilities that are an essential part of married life and that they in most cases would be honored to accept were DOMA not in force. For instance, because it is expected that spouses will support each other as they pursue educational opportunities, federal law takes into consideration a spouse's income in calculating a student's federal financial aid eligibility. . . . Same-sex married couples are exempt from this requirement. The same is true with respect to federal ethics rules.

Federal executive and agency officials are prohibited from "participat[ing] personally and substantially" in matters as to which they or their spouses have a financial interest. A similar statute prohibits Senators, Senate employees, and their spouses from accepting high-value gifts from certain sources, and another mandates detailed financial disclosures by numerous high-ranking officials and their spouses. Under DOMA, however, these Government-integrity rules do not apply to same-sex spouses.

The power the Constitution grants it also restrains. And though Congress has great authority to design laws to fit its own conception of sound national policy, it cannot deny the liberty protected by the Due Process Clause of the Fifth Amendment.

What has been explained to this point should more than suffice to establish that the principal purpose and the necessary effect of this law are to demean those persons who are in a lawful same-sex marriage. This requires the Court to hold, as it now does, that DOMA is unconstitutional as a deprivation of the liberty of the person protected by the Fifth Amendment of the Constitution.

The liberty protected by the Fifth Amendment's Due Process Clause contains within it the prohibition against denying to any person the equal protection of the laws. While the Fifth Amendment itself withdraws from Government the power to degrade or demean in the way this law does, the equal protection guarantee of the Fourteenth Amendment makes that Fifth Amendment right all the more specific and all the better understood and preserved.

The class to which DOMA directs its restrictions and restraints are those persons who are joined in same-sex marriages made lawful by the State. DOMA singles out a class of persons deemed by a State entitled to recognition and protection to enhance their own liberty. It imposes a disability on the class by refusing to acknowledge a status the State finds to be dignified and proper. DOMA instructs all federal officials, and indeed all persons with whom same-sex couples interact, including their own children, that their marriage is less worthy than the marriages of others. The federal statute is invalid, for no legitimate purpose overcomes the purpose and effect to disparage and to injure those whom the State, by its marriage laws, sought to protect in personhood and dignity. By seeking to displace this protection and treating those persons as living in marriages less respected than others, the federal statute is in violation of the Fifth Amendment. This opinion and its holding are confined to those lawful marriages.

The judgment of the Court of Appeals for the Second Circuit is affirmed.

Chief Justice ROBERTS, dissenting.

I agree with Justice Scalia . . . that Congress acted constitutionally in passing the Defense of Marriage Act (DOMA). Interests in uniformity and stability amply justified Congress's decision to retain the definition of marriage that, at that point, had been adopted by every State in our Nation, and every nation in the world.

The majority sees a more sinister motive, pointing out that the Federal Government has generally (though not uniformly) deferred to state definitions of marriage in the past. That is true, of course, but none of those prior state-by-state variations had involved differences over something—as the majority puts it—"thought of by most people as essential to the very definition of [marriage] and to its role and function throughout the history of civilization." That the Federal Government treated this fundamental question differently than it treated variations over consanguinity or minimum age is hardly surprising—and hardly enough to support a conclusion that the "principal purpose," of the 342 Representatives and 85 Senators who voted for it, and the President who signed it, was a bare desire to harm. Nor do the snippets of legislative history and the banal title of the Act to which the majority points suffice to make such a showing. At least without some more convincing evidence that the Act's principal purpose was to codify malice, and that it furthered *no* legitimate government interests, I would not tar the political branches with the brush of bigotry.

But while I disagree with the result to which the majority's analysis leads it in this case, I think it more important to point out that its analysis leads no further. The Court does not have before it, and the logic of its opinion does not decide, the distinct question whether the States, in the exercise of their "historic and essential authority to define the marital relation," may continue to utilize the traditional definition of marriage. . . .

Justice SCALIA, with whom Justice THOMAS joins, and with whom the Chief Justice joins as to Part I, dissenting.

. . . We have no power . . . to invalidate this democratically adopted legislation. . . .

I . . .

As I have observed before, the Constitution does not forbid the government to enforce traditional moral and sexual norms [see Lawrence v. Texas [2003] (Scalia, J., dissenting),] much as it neither requires nor forbids us to approve of no-fault divorce, polygamy, or the consumption of alcohol.

The majority concludes that the only motive for this Act was the "bare . . . desire to harm a politically unpopular group." Bear in mind that the object of this condemnation is not the legislature of some once-Confederate Southern state (familiar objects of the Court's scorn, . . . but our respected coordinate branches, the Congress and Presidency of the United States. Laying such a charge against them should require the most extraordinary evidence, and I would have thought that every attempt would be made to indulge a more anodyne explanation for the statute. The majority does the opposite—affirmatively concealing from the reader the arguments that exist in justification. It makes only a passing mention of the "arguments put forward" by the Act's defenders, and does not even trouble to paraphrase or describe them. I imagine that this is because it is harder to maintain the illusion of the Act's supporters as unhinged members of a wild-eyed lynch mob when one first describes their views as *they* see them.

To choose just one of these defenders' arguments, DOMA avoids difficult choice-of-law issues that will now arise absent a uniform federal definition of marriage. . . . Imagine a pair of women who marry in Albany and then move to Alabama, which does not "recognize as valid any marriage of parties of the same sex." When the couple files their next federal tax return, may it be a joint one? Which State's law controls, for federal-law purposes: their State of celebration (which recognizes the marriage) or their State of domicile (which does not)? (Does the answer depend on whether they were just visiting in Albany?) Are these questions to be answered as a matter of federal common law, or perhaps by borrowing a State's choice-of-law rules? If so, *which* State's? . . . DOMA avoided all of this uncertainty by specifying which marriages would be recognized for federal purposes. That is a classic purpose for a definitional provision.

Further, DOMA preserves the intended effects of prior legislation against then-unforeseen changes in circumstance. When Congress provided (for example) that a special estate-tax exemption would exist for spouses, this exemption reached only *opposite-sex* spouses—those being the only sort that were recognized in *any* State at the time of DOMA's passage. When it became clear that changes in state law might one day alter that balance, DOMA's definitional section was enacted to ensure that state-level experimentation did not automatically alter the basic operation of federal law, unless and until Congress made the further judgment to do so on its own. That is not animus—just stabilizing prudence. Congress has hardly demonstrated itself unwilling to make such further, revising judgments upon due deliberation. See, *e.g.*, Don't Ask, Don't Tell Repeal Act of 2010 . . .

. . . [T]o defend traditional marriage is not to condemn, demean, or humiliate those who would prefer other arrangements, any more than to defend the Constitution of the United States is to condemn, demean, or humiliate other constitutions. To hurl such accusations so casually demeans *this institution*. In the majority's judgment, any resistance to its holding is beyond the pale of reasoned disagreement. To question its high-handed invalidation of a presumptively valid statute is to act (the majority is sure) with *the purpose* to "disparage," "injure," "degrade," "demean," and "humiliate" our fellow human beings, our fellow citizens, who are homosexual. All that, simply for supporting an Act that did no more than codify an aspect of marriage that had been unquestioned in our society for most of its existence—indeed, had been unquestioned in virtually all societies for virtually all of human history. It is one thing for a society to elect change; it is another for a court of law to impose change by adjudging those who oppose it *hostes humani generis,* enemies of the human race. . . .

The penultimate sentence of the majority's opinion is a naked declaration that "[t]his opinion and its holding are confined" to those couples "joined in same-sex marriages made lawful by the State." I have heard such "bald, unreasoned disclaimer[s]" before. When the Court declared a constitutional right to homosexual sodomy [in Lawrence v. Texas], we were assured that the case had nothing, nothing at all to do with "whether the government must give formal recognition to any relationship that homosexual persons seek to enter." Now we are told that DOMA is invalid because it "demeans the couple, whose moral and sexual choices the Constitution protects," with an accompanying citation of *Lawrence*. It takes real cheek for today's majority to assure us, as it is going out the door, that a constitutional requirement to give formal recognition to same-sex marriage is not at issue here—when what has preceded that assurance is a lecture on how superior the majority's moral judgment in favor of same-sex marriage is to the Congress's hateful moral judgment against it. I promise you this: The only thing that will "confine" the Court's holding is its sense of what it can get away with.

. . . . [T]he view that *this* Court will take of state prohibition of same-sex marriage is indicated beyond mistaking by today's opinion. As I have said, the real rationale of today's opinion, whatever disappearing trail of its legalistic argle-bargle one chooses to follow, is that DOMA is motivated by "'bare . . . desire to harm'" couples in same-sex marriages. How easy it is, indeed how inevitable, to reach the same conclusion with regard to state laws denying same-sex couples marital status. . . .

[T]hat Court which finds it so horrific that Congress irrationally and hatefully robbed same-sex couples of the "personhood and dignity" which state legislatures conferred upon them, will of a certitude be similarly appalled by state legislatures' irrational and hateful failure to acknowledge that "personhood and dignity" in the first place. As far as this Court is concerned, no one should be fooled; it is just a matter of listening and waiting for the other shoe.

By formally declaring anyone opposed to same-sex marriage an enemy of human decency, the majority arms well every challenger to a state law restricting marriage to its traditional definition. Henceforth those challengers will lead with this Court's declaration that there is "no legitimate purpose" served by such a law, and will claim that the traditional definition has "the purpose and effect to disparage and to injure" the "personhood and dignity" of same-sex couples. The majority's limiting assurance will be meaningless in the face of language like that, as the majority well knows. That is why the language is there. The result will be a judicial distortion of our society's debate over marriage—a debate that can seem in need of our clumsy "help" only to a member of this institution.

As to that debate: Few public controversies touch an institution so central to the lives of so many, and few inspire such attendant passion by good people on all sides. Few public controversies will ever demonstrate so vividly the beauty of what our Framers gave us, a gift the Court pawns today to buy its stolen moment in the spotlight: a system of government that permits us to rule *ourselves*. Since DOMA's passage, citizens on all sides of the question have seen victories and they have seen defeats. There have been plebiscites, legislation, persuasion, and loud voices—in other words, democracy. Victories in one place for some, see North Carolina Const., Amdt. 1 (providing that "[m]arriage between one man and one woman is the only domestic legal union that shall be valid or recognized in this State") (approved by a popular vote, 61% to 39% on May 8, 2012),[6] are offset by victories in other places for others, see Maryland Question 6 (establishing "that Maryland's civil marriage laws allow gay and lesbian couples to obtain a civil marriage license") (approved by a popular vote, 52% to 48%, on November 6, 2012).[7] Even in a *single State*, the question has come out differently on different occasions. Compare Maine Question 1 (permitting "the State of Maine to issue marriage licenses to same-sex couples") (approved by a popular vote, 53% to 47%, on November 6, 2012)[8] with Maine Question 1 (rejecting "the new law that lets same-sex couples marry") (approved by a popular vote, 53% to 47%, on November 3, 2009).[9]

In the majority's telling, this story is black-and-white: Hate your neighbor or come along with us. The truth is more complicated. It is hard to admit that one's political opponents are not monsters, especially in a struggle like this one, and the challenge in the end proves more than today's Court can handle. Too bad. A reminder that disagreement over something so fundamental as marriage can still be politically legitimate would have been a fit task for what in earlier times was called the judicial temperament. We might have covered ourselves with honor today, by promising all sides of this debate that it was theirs to settle and that we would respect their resolution. We might have let the People decide.

But that the majority will not do. Some will rejoice in today's decision, and some will despair at it; that is the nature of a controversy that matters so much to so many. But the Court has cheated both sides, robbing the winners of an honest victory, and the losers of the peace that comes from a fair defeat. We owed both of them better. I dissent.

Justice ALITO, with whom Justice THOMAS joins as to Parts II and III, dissenting.

Our Nation is engaged in a heated debate about same-sex marriage. That debate is, at bottom, about the nature of the institution of marriage. Respondent Edith Windsor, supported by the United States, asks this Court to intervene in that debate, and although she couches her argument in different terms, what she seeks is a holding that enshrines in the Constitution a particular understanding of marriage under which the sex of the partners makes no difference. The Constitution, however, does not dictate that choice. It leaves the choice to the people, acting through their elected representatives at both the federal and state levels. . . .

6. North Carolina State Board of Elections, Official Results: Primary Election of May 8, 2012, Constitutional Amendment.

7. Maryland State Board of Elections, Official 2012 Presidential General Election Results for All State Questions, Question 06.

8. Maine Bureau of Elections, Nov. 3, 2009, Referendum Tabulation (Question 1).

9. Maine Bureau of Elections, Nov. 6, 2012, Referendum Election Tabulations (Question 1).

II . . .

Same-sex marriage presents a highly emotional and important question of public policy—but not a difficult question of constitutional law. The Constitution does not guarantee the right to enter into a same-sex marriage. Indeed, no provision of the Constitution speaks to the issue.

The Court has sometimes found the Due Process Clauses to have a substantive component that guarantees liberties beyond the absence of physical restraint. And the Court's holding that "DOMA is unconstitutional as a deprivation of the liberty of the person protected by the Fifth Amendment of the Constitution" suggests that substantive due process may partially underlie the Court's decision today. But it is well established that any "substantive" component to the Due Process Clause protects only "those fundamental rights and liberties which are, objectively, 'deeply rooted in this Nation's history and tradition,'" Washington v. Glucksberg [1997]. . . .

It is beyond dispute that the right to same-sex marriage is not deeply rooted in this Nation's history and tradition. In this country, no State permitted same-sex marriage until the Massachusetts Supreme Judicial Court held in 2003 that limiting marriage to opposite-sex couples violated the State Constitution. See Goodridge v. Department of Public Health [2003]. Nor is the right to same-sex marriage deeply rooted in the traditions of other nations. No country allowed same-sex couples to marry until the Netherlands did so in 2000.[4]

What Windsor and the United States seek, therefore, is not the protection of a deeply rooted right but the recognition of a very new right, and they seek this innovation not from a legislative body elected by the people, but from unelected judges. Faced with such a request, judges have cause for both caution and humility.

The family is an ancient and universal human institution. Family structure reflects the characteristics of a civilization, and changes in family structure and in the popular understanding of marriage and the family can have profound effects. Past changes in the understanding of marriage—for example, the gradual ascendance of the idea that romantic love is a prerequisite to marriage—have had far-reaching consequences. But the process by which such consequences come about is complex, involving the interaction of numerous factors, and tends to occur over an extended period of time.

We can expect something similar to take place if same-sex marriage becomes widely accepted. The long-term consequences of this change are not now known and are unlikely to be ascertainable for some time to come.[5] There

4. Curry–Sumner, A Patchwork of Partnerships: Comparative Overview of Registration Schemes in Europe, in Legal Recognition of Same-Sex Partnerships 71, 72 (K. Boele-Woelki & A. Fuchs eds., rev. 2d ed., 2012).

5. As sociologists have documented, it sometimes takes decades to document the effects of social changes—like the sharp rise in divorce rates following the advent of no-fault divorce—on children and society. See generally J. Wallerstein, J. Lewis, & S. Blakeslee, The Unexpected Legacy of Divorce: The 25 Year Landmark Study (2000).

are those who think that allowing same-sex marriage will seriously under-mine the institution of marriage. See, e.g., S. Girgis, R. Anderson, & R. George, What is Marriage? Man and Woman: A Defense 53–58 (2012); Finnis, Marriage: A Basic and Exigent Good, 91 The Monist 388, 398 (2008). Others think that recognition of same-sex marriage will fortify a now-shaky institution. See, e.g., A. Sullivan, Virtually Normal: An Argument About Homosexuality 202–203 (1996); J. Rauch, Gay Marriage: Why It Is Good for Gays, Good for Straights, and Good for America 94 (2004).

At present, no one — including social scientists, philosophers, and historians — can predict with any certainty what the long-term ramifications of wide-spread acceptance of same-sex marriage will be. And judges are certainly not equipped to make such an assessment. The Members of this Court have the authority and the responsibility to interpret and apply the Constitution. Thus, if the Constitution contained a provision guaranteeing the right to marry a person of the same sex, it would be our duty to enforce that right. But the Constitution simply does not speak to the issue of same-sex marriage. In our system of government, ultimate sovereignty rests with the people, and the people have the right to control their own destiny. Any change on a question so fundamental should be made by the people through their elected officials.

III

Perhaps because they cannot show that same-sex marriage is a fundamen-tal right under our Constitution, Windsor and the United States couch their arguments in equal protection terms. They argue that §3 of DOMA discrimi-nates on the basis of sexual orientation, that classifications based on sexual orientation should trigger a form of "heightened" scrutiny, and that §3 cannot survive such scrutiny. They further maintain that the governmental interests that §3 purports to serve are not sufficiently important and that it has not been adequately shown that §3 serves those interests very well. The Court's hold-ing, too, seems to rest on "the equal protection guarantee of the Fourteenth Amendment," although the Court is careful not to adopt most of Windsor's and the United States' argument. . . .

By asking the Court to strike down DOMA as not satisfying some form of heightened scrutiny, Windsor and the United States are really seeking to have the Court resolve a debate between two competing views of marriage.

The first and older view, which I will call the "traditional" or "conjugal" view, sees marriage as an intrinsically opposite-sex institution. BLAG notes that virtually every culture, including many not influenced by the Abrahamic religions, has limited marriage to people of the opposite sex. . . . And BLAG attempts to explain this phenomenon by arguing that the institution of mar-riage was created for the purpose of channeling heterosexual intercourse into a structure that supports child rearing. Others explain the basis for the institution in more philosophical terms. They argue that marriage is essen-tially the solemnizing of a comprehensive, exclusive, permanent union that is intrinsically ordered to producing new life, even if it does not always do so. . . . While modern cultural changes have weakened the link between marriage and procreation in the popular mind, there is no doubt that, throughout human history and across many cultures, marriage has been viewed as an exclusively opposite-sex institution and as one inextricably linked to procreation and biological kinship.

The other, newer view is what I will call the "consent-based" vision of marriage, a vision that primarily defines marriage as the solemnization of mutual commitment—marked by strong emotional attachment and sexual attraction—between two persons. At least as it applies to heterosexual couples, this view of marriage now plays a very prominent role in the popular understanding of the institution. Indeed, our popular culture is infused with this understanding of marriage. Proponents of same-sex marriage argue that because gender differentiation is not relevant to this vision, the exclusion of same-sex couples from the institution of marriage is rank discrimination.

The Constitution does not codify either of these views of marriage (although I suspect it would have been hard at the time of the adoption of the Constitution or the Fifth Amendment to find Americans who did not take the traditional view for granted). The silence of the Constitution on this question should be enough to end the matter as far as the judiciary is concerned. Yet, Windsor and the United States implicitly ask us to endorse the consent-based view of marriage and to reject the traditional view, thereby arrogating to ourselves the power to decide a question that philosophers, historians, social scientists, and theologians are better qualified to explore. Because our constitutional order assigns the resolution of questions of this nature to the people, I would not presume to enshrine either vision of marriage in our constitutional jurisprudence. . . .

All that §3 does is to define a class of persons to whom federal law extends certain special benefits and upon whom federal law imposes certain special burdens. In these provisions, Congress used marital status as a way of defining this class—in part, I assume, because it viewed marriage as a valuable institution to be fostered and in part because it viewed married couples as comprising a unique type of economic unit that merits special regulatory treatment. Assuming that Congress has the power under the Constitution to enact the laws affected by §3, Congress has the power to define the category of persons to whom those laws apply.

I respectfully dissent.

Notes

1. Same-Sex Marriage Litigation: An Overview.   Litigation over the constitutionality of restrictions against same-sex marriage began with Baehr v. Lewin, cited in *Windsor,* in which the Hawaii Supreme Court held that Hawaii's denial of the right to marriage to same-sex couples constituted sex discrimination. Under the court's reasoning, the state constitution's equal protection clause required the government to show a compelling interest in denying marriage licenses to gay and lesbian couples.[279] The court remanded the case to the trial court for resolution of that issue, but before that occurred, Hawaii voters approved an amendment to the state constitution providing that "[t]he legislature shall have the power to reserve marriage to opposite-sex couples." Similarly, a state court decision in Alaska found that the state's ban on same-sex marriage violated the state constitutional right to privacy provisions, only to be later superseded by constitutional amendment.[280] By the time *Windsor* was decided, however, 12 states and the District of Columbia had legalized same-sex marriage, either through court decision on due process or equal protection grounds (or both), legislative enactment, or popular referendum.[281]

On the same day as the *Windsor* case was decided, the Supreme Court declined to decide on the merits a challenge to a Ninth Circuit Court of Appeals ruling, Perry v. Brown.[282] *Perry* had invalidated a voter referendum in California, Proposition 8, which amended the California state constitution to ban same-sex marriages.[283] To decide *Perry* on the merits, the Court would have had to face the question it avoided in *Windsor*—i.e., the constitutionality of state bans on same-sex marriage. Instead, the Court held that the proponents of Proposition 8 lacked standing to defend it (the State of California itself, much like the Department of Justice in *Windsor*, refused to defend the law beyond trial). The effect of dismissing the case for lack of standing was to reinstate the lower court rulings that Proposition 8 was unconstitutional on both due process and equal protection grounds. With the addition of California to the states recognizing same-sex marriage, over one-third of the U.S. population now lives in a jurisdiction where same-sex marriage exists.

Windsor concerned the constitutionality of Section 3 of the Defense of Marriage Act (DOMA), enacting a federal definition of marriage as one man and one woman, for purposes of federal benefits and entitlements. After *Windsor*, the U.S. Department of Treasury ruled that same-sex couples legally married in any U.S. state, the District of Columbia, a U.S. territory, or a foreign country will be recognized as married for federal tax purposes, even if the couple is not living in a state that recognizes same-sex marriage. The same is now true regarding immigration status and federal employee benefits. Further, the Attorney General announced that the federal government will recognize same-sex marriages in other matters over which it has jurisdiction, including bankruptcies, prison benefits, and the right to refuse to testify against a spouse in federal court proceedings. While the federal government continues to expand the situations in which it will recognize same-sex marriages, it should be noted that Section 2 of DOMA, which permits states to decline to recognize same-sex marriages from other states, remains as yet untouched. Nor does the *Windsor* decision reach the constitutionality of state bans on same-sex marriage.

While the trend in favor of same-sex marriage is clear, as Justice Scalia notes in his dissent in *Windsor*, opinion in some states remains firmly opposed to same-sex marriage. Most notably, on May 8, 2012, voters in North Carolina passed a constitutional ban against same-sex marriage by 61 percent to 39 percent. Same-sex marriage opponents say that they can use the Court's "overstepping" in *Windsor* to reverse the trend in favor of same-sex marriage. Is this likely, in your view, or do the fault-lines divide on generational grounds, making it, at most, just a matter of time before same-sex marriage is well accepted?

2. *Windsor* Grounds.   What exactly is Justice Kennedy's reasoning in *Windsor*? Is it primarily a matter of federalism—i.e., states have the right to define marriage, to which the federal government should ordinarily defer? Or is the "equal dignity of same-sex marriage" also constitutionalized? If the latter, is it the case, as Justice Kennedy suggests, that the Court has left open the question whether states can constitutionally ban same-sex marriage? Or is Justice Scalia correct that the reasoning of the case also puts in jeopardy state laws banning same-sex marriage?

In previous state cases, the equal protection issue raised by challenges to state bans on same-sex marriage was whether discrimination based on sexual orientation is a form of discrimination "based on sex."[284] The argument was that a person banned from marrying someone of the same sex is being denied a privileged based on the sex of that person. The argument to the contrary was that there is no equal protection violation based on sex because men and women are equally barred from marrying someone of the same sex. To the extent that, in *Windsor*, the equal protection issue was triggered by the plaintiff's sexual orientation, not whether she or her partner is male or female, the law has shifted ground significantly. How rigorous should judicial review be of rules that disfavor persons based on their sexual orientation? As much as sex-based rules and practices? Race-based rules and practices? This issue is further discussed in Note 3 to Section 3, at p. 421-22.

One of the issues in *Windsor* is whether Congress was motivated by anti-gay animus when it passed DOMA. What exactly is the disagreement between Justice Kennedy and Justice Scalia on this issue? Justice Kennedy relies, in part, on Romer v. Evans,[285] in which the Court held that the state of Colorado could not single out a politically unpopular group—gays and lesbians—for special disfavor, by prohibiting state and local laws banning discrimination against members of that group. Is that decision applicable in *Windsor*? Does Justice Scalia effectively rebut the charge that Congress acted with antigay animus? Should it matter whether they did or not?

3. Domestic Partnership Benefits.   Even without recognition of same-sex marriage, recognition of same-sex relationships is growing. Many states and local jurisdictions allow same-sex partners and their dependents to benefit from employee fringe benefit plans, and a majority of the largest employees provide health benefits to the domestic partners of their employees.[286]

4. Resistance to Same-Sex Marriage.   What is the source of resistance to marriage for gay and lesbian couples? In supporting a constitutional amendment to prohibit such marriages, then President George Bush stated, without further explanation, that "changing the definition of marriage would undermine the family structure." The California Proposition 8 campaign to prevent same-sex marriage was organized and funded by religious groups that raised a number of concerns, such as:

> Children in public schools will have to be taught that same sex marriage is just as good as traditional marriage.
>
> Churches may be sued over their tax exempt status if they refuse to allow same-sex ceremonies in their religious buildings open to the public.
>
> Religious agencies will be challenged . . . to give up their long-held right to place children only in homes with both a mother and a father.
>
> Religious leaders may be sued for personally refusing to perform same sex marriage.[287]

How would you respond to such claims? To what extent do the dissenters in *Windsor* appear to share these concerns, and to what extent is the issue for them simply one of deferring to the judgment of Congress when it acts on such concerns?

What is the significance of the religious objections to same-sex marriage? Consider Mary Anne Case's suggestion:

> In my view, the following is the best explanation of the opposition to legal recognition of same-sex marriage on the part of evangelical Protestant religious conservatives who claim such recognition would undercut their own marriages: Unlike observant Jews and Roman Catholics, who clearly understand that civil marriage and marriage within their faith are not the same, such that one can be married in the eyes of the state and not the faith and vice versa, Protestant denominations in the United States have essentially abdicated the definition, creation and, above all the dissolution of marriage to the state. There is, for example, nothing like the get or annulment available to or required of Protestants. This leaves religiously conservative Protestants far more dependent on the state's regulation of marriage, far less able to distinguish conceptually between marriage as their religion defines it and as state law does and, unsurprisingly, far more opposed on a percentage basis to same-sex marriage than conservative Catholics and Jews who otherwise, according to poll data, share their opposition to homosexuality. . . . According to survey results released by the Pew forum in October 2004, 55% of Jews supported same-sex marriage, while opposition reached 48% among white Roman Catholics, 52% among Latino Catholics, 71% among Latino Protestants, 72% among Black Protestants and 75% among white evangelical Protestants.[288]

In California, Proposition 8 won 52 percent of the popular vote but 84 percent of the votes of adults who attended religious services on a regular basis.[289] Case concludes that the best solution would be "marriage licenses in the plural"—state licenses on minimal grounds, and licenses issued by religious institutions for those seeking a religious endorsement. Other commentators have argued for same-sex marriage or civil union legislation and court decisions that specifically include religious exemptions, and many current bills and judicial rulings have done so.[290]

Which branch of government should make the decision on same-sex marriage? About two-thirds of surveyed Americans think it should be the legislature.[291] Researchers find that primary factors that produce backlash to court decisions are the increased salience of the issue after a judicial ruling and anger over judicial activism.[292] What will be the likely effect of increased salience about gay marriage?

5. Is Marriage Worth Fighting For?   The LGBT community has not universally supported the campaign for same-sex marriage. Supporters argue that recognition of such marriages would ensure full legal benefits that are not available now, even under domestic partnership statutes. In addition, recognition of same-sex marriage would help to "normalize" the status of gays and lesbians, which could both stabilize those relationships and reduce the prejudice based on sexual orientation in society at large.

By contrast, some gays and lesbians have expressed reluctance to embrace an institution that has traditionally oppressed women. This argument has been raised less often by gays than lesbians, who worry that replicating the model of heterosexual unions will weaken the broader, extended relationships within lesbian communities; encourage possessive, patriarchal-style patterns of submission and dominance; and cultivate unacceptable distinctions between married and unmarried lesbians. Consider the following:

> [M]arriage will not liberate us as lesbians and gay men. In fact, it will constrain us, make us more invisible, force our assimilation into the mainstream, and undermine the goals of gay liberation. [A]ttaining the right to marry will not transform our society from one that makes narrow, but dramatic, distinctions between those who are married and those who are not married to one that respects and encourages choice of relationships and family diversity. Marriage runs contrary to two of the primary goals of the lesbian and gay movement: the affirmation of gay identity and culture; and the validation of many forms of relationships. . . .
>
> Justice for gay men and lesbians will be achieved only when we are accepted and supported in this society despite our differences from the dominant culture and the choices we make regarding our relationships. Being queer is more than setting up house, sleeping with a person of the same gender, and seeking state approval for doing so. It is an identity, a culture with many variations. It is a way of dealing with the world by diminishing the constraints of gender roles which have for so long kept women and gay people oppressed and invisible. Being queer means pushing the parameters of sex, sexuality, and family, and in the process transforming the very fabric of society. . . .
>
> The moment we argue, as some among us insist on doing, that we should be treated as equals because we are really just like married couples and hold the same values to be true, we undermine the very purpose of our movement

and begin the dangerous process of silencing our different voices. As a lesbian, I am fundamentally different from non-lesbian women. That's the point. Marriage, as it exists today, is antithetical to my liberation as a lesbian and as a woman because it mainstreams my life and voice. I do not want [to] be known as "Mrs. Attached-To-Somebody-Else." Nor do I want to give the state the power to regulate my primary relationship.[293]

Even if same-sex marriage is worth fighting for, is it the only thing? A report by a coalition of LGBT activists, educators, and writers, Beyond Same-Sex Marriage, concludes that "marriage is not the only worthy form of family or relationship, and it should not be economically privileged above all others."[294] Given that a majority of Americans no longer live in nuclear families, the coalition recommends legal recognition for a wide variety of relationships, including access to "vital government support programs." Would you support such recognition? Who might oppose it, and what arguments could be marshaled for and against?

The founder of an all-woman's community charges that the current generation has lost the vision of a more ideal society. It just "wants to fit in. Gays in the military and gay marriage? This is what [your generation] has come up with?" How would you respond?[295]

Putting Theory Into Practice

3-18. Military chaplains, among their many duties, sometimes provide marital counseling for servicemembers. Gay military members have requested this counseling, but not all chaplains will provide it. A group named Chaplain Alliance for Religious Liberty claims that many chaplains object to same-sex marriage as a matter of their religious faith and that these chaplains have a religious liberty interest in not being required to provide counseling to gay couples. They seek a religious conscience exemption from Congress.[296]

How should this issue be handled? Should military chaplains be required to counsel gay couples? Should the military fire any chaplain who refuses to counsel gay couples? Should the military be obligated to hire chaplains who are willing and able to counsel gay couples?

3-19. A public notary in Brazil sparked an outcry when she granted a civil union license to a trio — one man and two women — who she thought deserved recognition as a stable family unit.[297] Does recognition of "polyfidelitous unions," as the notary labeled them, present the same policy issues as recognition of same-sex unions? Does polygamy threaten women's rights in the family? If a state in the United States decides to legalize polyfidelitous marriages, should the federal government to required to recognize those marriages?

2. Lesbian Parents

Custody has been a focal point in many states for claims by lesbians who have served as co-parents for their partner's children and then sought to establish custody or visitation rights when the couple separated. The *Alison D.* case represents the traditional approach, denying the visitation claim on the grounds that the partner does not meet the state's definition of "parent." However, just as the law has moved rapidly on the same-sex marriage issue over the past decade, it is also changing with respect to recognition of parental rights by individuals who have raised children with their same-sex partners. Some of the more recent cases are explored in the notes that follow.

Reading Questions

1. Should a person who is not a biological or adoptive parent ever have custody or visitation rights to a child? Under what, if any, circumstances?
2. What policy justifications are most persuasive in determining custody rights for same-sex couples?

In the Matter of Alison D. v. Virginia M.

569 N.Y.S.2d 586 (N.Y. 1991)

PER CURIAM.

At issue in this case is whether petitioner, a biological stranger to a child who is properly in the custody of his biological mother, has standing to seek visitation with the child. . . . Petitioner relies on both her established relationship with the child and her alleged agreement with the biological mother to support her claim that she has standing. We agree with the Appellate Division . . . that, although petitioner apparently nurtured a close and loving relationship with the child, she is not a parent within the meaning of [New York law].

I

Petitioner Alison D. and respondent Virginia M. established a relationship in September 1977 and began living together in March 1978. In March 1980, they decided to have a child and agreed that respondent would be artificially inseminated. Together, they planned for the conception and birth of the child and agreed to share jointly all rights and responsibilities of child-rearing. In July 1981, respondent gave birth to a baby boy, A.D.M., who was given petitioner's last name as his middle name and respondent's last name became his last name. Petitioner shared in all birthing expenses and, after A.D.M.'s birth, continued to provide for his support. During A.D.M.'s first two years, petitioner and respondent jointly cared for and made decisions regarding the child.

In November 1983, when the child was 2 years and 4 months old, petitioner and respondent terminated their relationship and petitioner moved out of the home they jointly owned. Petitioner and respondent agreed to a visitation schedule whereby petitioner continued to see the child a few times a week. Petitioner also agreed to continue to pay one half of the mortgage and major household expenses. By this time, the child had referred to both respondent and petitioner as "mommy." Petitioner's visitation with the child continued until 1986, at which time respondent bought out petitioner's interest in the house and then began to restrict petitioner's visitation with the child. In 1987 petitioner moved to Ireland to pursue career opportunities, but continued her attempts to communicate with the child. Thereafter, respondent terminated all contact between petitioner and the child, returning all of petitioner's gifts and letters. No dispute exists that respondent is a fit parent. Petitioner commenced this proceeding seeking visitation rights. . . .

II

. . . Although the Court is mindful of petitioner's understandable concern for and interest in the child and of her expectation and desire that her contact with the child would continue, she has no right under [the law] to seek visitation and, thereby, limit or diminish the right of the concededly fit biological parent to choose with whom her child associates. She is not a "parent" within the meaning of [the law].

Petitioner concedes that she is not the child's "parent"; that is, she is not the biological mother of the child nor is she a legal parent by virtue of an adoption. Rather she claims to have acted as a "de facto" parent or that she should be viewed as a parent "by estoppel." Therefore, she claims she has standing to seek visitation rights. These claims, however, are insufficient. . . . Traditionally, in this State it is the child's mother and father who, assuming fitness, have the right to the care and custody of their child, even in situations where the nonparent has exercised some control over the child with the parents' consent. . . . To allow the courts to award visitation—a limited form of custody—to a third person would necessarily impair the parents' right to custody and control. . . .

De facto means "actual" or existing in fact, even though not formally or legally recognized.

. . . While one may dispute in an individual case whether it would be beneficial to a child to have continued contact with a nonparent, the Legislature did not . . . give such nonparent the opportunity to compel a fit parent to allow them to do so. . . .

KAYE, Judge (dissenting).

The Court's decision, fixing biology as the key to visitation rights, has impact far beyond this particular controversy, one that may affect a wide spectrum of relationships—including those of longtime heterosexual stepparents, "common-law" and nonheterosexual partners such as involved here, and even participants in scientific reproduction procedures. Estimates that more than 15.5 million children do not live with two biological parents, and that as many as 8 to 10 million children are born into families with a gay or lesbian parent, suggest just how widespread the impact may be. . . .

[The] impact of today's decision falls hardest on the children of those relationships, limiting their opportunity to maintain bonds that may be crucial to their development. The majority's retreat from the courts' proper role—its tightening of rules that should in visitation petitions, above all, retain the capacity to take the children's interests into account—compels this dissent. . . .

The relevant facts are amply described in the Court's opinion. Most significantly, Virginia M. agrees that, after long cohabitation with Alison D. and before A.D.M.'s conception, it was "explicitly planned that the child would be theirs to raise together." It is also uncontested that the two shared "financial and emotional preparations" for the birth, and that for several years Alison D. actually filled the role of coparent to A.D.M., both tangibly and intangibly. In all, a parent-child relationship—encouraged or at least condoned by Virginia M.—apparently existed between A.D.M. and Alison D. during the first six years of the child's life.

While acknowledging that relationship, the Court nonetheless proclaims powerlessness to consider the child's interest at all, because the word "parent" in the statute imposes an absolute barrier to Alison D.'s petition for visitation. . . . Other State Legislatures, in comparable statutes, have defined "parent" specifically . . . and that definition has of course bound the courts. . . . Significantly, [New York law] contains no such limitation. Indeed, it does not define the term "parent" at all. That remains for the courts to do, as often happens when statutory terms are undefined.

. . . The Legislature has made plain an objective . . . to promote "the best interest of the child" and the child's "welfare and happiness." Those words should not be ignored by us in defining standing for visitation purposes—they have not been in prior case law. . . .

Apart from imposing upon itself an unnecessarily restrictive definition of "parent," and apart from turning its back on a tradition of reading [the law] so as to promote the welfare of the children, in accord with the parens patriae power, the Court also overlooks the significant distinction between visitation and custody proceedings.

While both are of special concern to the State, custody and visitation are significantly different. . . . Custody disputes implicate a parent's right to rear a child—with the child's corresponding right to be raised by a parent. . . . Infringement of that right must be based on the fitness—more precisely the lack of fitness—of the custodial parent.

Visitation rights also implicate a right of the custodial parent, but it is the right to choose with whom the child associates. . . . Any burden on the exercise of that right must be based on the child's overriding need to maintain a particular relationship. . . . Logically, the fitness concern present in custody disputes is irrelevant in visitation petitions, where continuing contact with the child rather than severing of a parental tie is in issue. . . .

Of course there must be some limitation on who can petition for visitation. [New York law] specifies that the person must be the child's "parent," and the law additionally recognizes certain rights of biological and legal parents. Arguments that every dedicated caretaker could sue for visitation if the term "parent" were broadened, or that such action would necessarily effect sweeping change throughout the law, overlook and misportray the Court's role in defining otherwise undefined statutory terms to effect particular statutory purposes, and to do so narrowly, for those purposes only. . . .

. . . [R]ecent decisions from other jurisdictions, for the most part concerning visitation rights of stepparents [have] fashioned a test for "parental status" or "in loco parentis" requiring that the petitioner demonstrate actual assumption of the parental role and discharge of parental responsibilities. It should be required that the relationship with the child came into being with the consent of the biological or legal parent, and that the petitioner at least has had joint custody of the child for a significant period of time. . . . Other factors likely should be added to constitute a test that protects all relevant interests.

Notes

1. Sexual Orientation and Custody Disputes.   Even biological parents may face difficult custody issues if they are gay, lesbian, bisexual, or transgendered. Under the traditional view, homosexuality was sufficient to render a parent unfit to have custody of a child. The stated rule in a growing number of jurisdictions is that the sexual orientation of a parent may not be taken into account in a custody determination unless harm to the child is affirmatively demonstrated in a particular case.

Generally, under this harm or "nexus" standard, real or imagined stigma from having a homosexual parent is insufficient. The following analysis is increasingly typical:

> [O]ne of life's realities is that one of his parents is homosexual. In the absence of evidence that the homosexuality in some way harms the boy, limiting [his] relationship with that parent fails to permit him to confront his life situation, however unconventional it may be. . . . [The child's] best interest is served by exposing him to reality and not fostering in him shame or abhorrence for his mother's non-traditional commitment.[298]

Nonetheless, even under the nexus standard, many courts continue to assume that having a gay or lesbian parent is harmful to a child.[299] Only one jurisdiction, the District of Columbia, has a statutory prohibition on considering a parent's sexual orientation as the sole basis for denying child custody or visitation rights.[300] Would you support such a prohibition in your state?

2. Lesbian Co-Parents.   In its time, *Alison D.* represented the clear majority approach to lesbian co-parent cases. Almost all courts denied visitation and custody rights to lesbians who were de facto nonbiological parents, either because they lacked standing or because they failed to meet the substantive criteria for parenthood under the state's custody statute. The New York Court of Appeals affirmed *Alison D.*'s rejection of de facto parentage in a 2010 case, Debra H. v. Janice R.[301] But in the intervening two decades, several other states began to recognize lesbian co-parentage in similar cases. In 1995, a Wisconsin case adopted a doctrine variously labeled de facto parentage, equitable parenthood, parenthood by estoppel, or in loco parentis (taking on all or some responsibilities of a parent). Under that doctrine, the court awarded visitation rights to a lesbian co-parent who had raised the child on an equal basis with the biological parent, with that parent's approval.[302] Other courts have applied this approach in a variety of cases, some of them involving children conceived through artificial insemination.[303] Courts have also imposed support obligations on members of same-sex couples who assumed a parental role.[304] Courts in several states, however, have continued to reject de facto parentage, citing concerns about intruding on the biological mother's constitutionally protected parental rights and the lack of certainty about parental status that arises from a functional approach.[305]

An **equitable doctrine** refers to a legal rule developed by courts of equity in England and carried over today to common law jurisdictions. Most equitable doctrines relate to remedies that are available not as a matter of right, but as a matter of judicial discretion. Injunctions and estoppel are equitable concepts. **Estoppel** is the doctrine that a person who has contributed to another person's expectations (often benefiting from the arrangement creating those expectations) may not later assert a claim or defense contrary to those expectations.

Increasingly, lesbian co-parents are able to adopt the child they are (or intend to be) co-parenting, notwithstanding the traditional prohibition against a child having more than one mother (or more than one father), and even when same-sex marriage is prohibited. Over a dozen states allow "second-parent adoptions."[306] When the California Supreme Court ruled in favor of same-sex second-parent adoptions in 2003, more than 20,000 such adoptions had already been granted by family court judges.[307] But the national landscape on second-parent adoptions is still very mixed. The North Carolina Supreme Court, for example, ruled against second-parent adoption in 2010, invalidating not only a final adoption decree that had been previously granted in that particular case, but thousands more as well.[308] Utah bars adoptions by all unmarried couples, and Mississippi bars adoption by same-sex couples whether married or not.[309] Arkansas voters passed a referendum in 2008 to preclude adoption by any individual who was unmarried and "cohabiting with a sexual partner."[310] The state's supreme court struck down the referendum, however, as a violation of the state constitutional right to privacy. Only Florida had an outright prohibition on adoptions by gay or lesbian individuals, but the statute was held unconstitutional by an appellate court in 2010, and the state chose not to appeal.[311]

3. The Resistance to Gay and Lesbian Parenting. Among the most deeply held beliefs about lesbian and gay parents is that they are bad role models and that their children are not well adjusted. One concern is that children raised by gay and lesbian parents are exposed to premature sexualization or inappropriate sexual practices. Although the adequacy of research in this area has been questioned, most experts agree that children of homosexuals do not differ significantly in their psychosocial development from children in heterosexual families, and that gay and lesbian adults are no more likely to molest children than heterosexual adults.[312] The American Academy of Pediatrics supports same-sex co-parent adoptions.[313]

What if it *is* established that being raised by a homosexual parent makes a child more likely to be a homosexual? Two researchers have concluded, from a comparative longitudinal study, that while there is no significant difference in sexual attraction to someone of the same gender between those raised by lesbian single mothers and those raised by heterosexual single mothers, children raised in lesbian families are more likely to consider, and to have, homosexual involvement than are their peers raised by heterosexual mothers.[314] Should these findings play any role in custody decisions?

Putting Theory Into Practice

3-20. At a custody trial between biological parents, the father offers evidence to show that a lesbian mother snuggles with her children and her female companion in bed, has the children march with her in a gay and lesbian rights parade, and has her children participate in a "commitment ceremony" with her companion. Her children also have an "astonishing grasp of anatomical terminology." Is this evidence proof of harm to the children? What are the arguments on each side?[315]

3-21. Thomas orally agreed with a lesbian couple to provide sperm that would inseminate one of them and that he would forgo all parental rights to any child born as a result. They also agreed that Thomas would be available to meet the child if she became curious about her origins. A child was born, and when she was about five years old, the couple contacted Thomas so that she could meet him. For the next five or six years, Thomas visited with the child several times and developed a relationship with her, with the permission of the child's mothers. The parties eventually began to disagree, however, about the length and terms of the visits. Thomas files an action seeking court-ordered visitation. Should he succeed? Should advocates of the custodial rights of gay and lesbian parents favor Thomas' claim? If so, what access to the child should Thomas be allowed?

3. Employment and Other Forms of Discrimination Based on Sexual Orientation

There is no federal law that expressly prohibits discrimination on the basis of sexual orientation. Likewise, the U.S. Constitution has been consistently interpreted not to protect gays, lesbians, bisexuals, and transsexuals who experience employment discrimination by public employers.[316] This section explores state and federal laws governing sexual orientation discrimination by employers, the military, and private associations.

Reading Questions

1. Is sexual orientation a form of sex discrimination prohibited by Title VII? Does it matter whether the discrimination involves gender-role stereotyping?
2. What special problems worry an employer about being required to hire gays, lesbians, bisexuals, and transsexuals to be (a) FBI agents; (b) members of the attorney general staff; (c) army staff sergeants? Are any of these reasonable concerns?
3. One justification sometimes given for employment policies against hiring homosexuals is that they can be easily blackmailed—arguably a special problem in high-security positions such as the FBI.[260] Is blackmail against homosexual individuals less likely if gays can be fired for homosexuality, or is it more likely?
4. Which, if any, of the reasons for heightened constitutional scrutiny apply to gays, lesbians, bisexuals, and transsexuals? If constitutional protection is extended to same-sex marriage in all states, will these reasons be sufficient, even without heightened scrutiny?

Simonton v. Runyon

225 F.3d 122 (2d Cir. 2000)

WALKER, JR. Circuit Judge:

Plaintiff-appellant Dwayne Simonton sued the Postmaster General and the United States Postal Service . . . under Title VII of the Civil Rights Act of

1964 ("Title VII") for abuse and harassment he suffered by reason of his sexual orientation. The United States District Court for the Eastern District of New York . . . dismissed Simonton's complaint . . . for failure to state a claim, reasoning that Title VII does not prohibit discrimination based on sexual orientation. We agree. . . .

We must accept all facts alleged in the complaint as true. . . . The facts of this case are all too familiar in their general form. Simonton was employed as a postal worker in Farmingdale, New York, for approximately twelve years. He repeatedly received satisfactory to excellent performance evaluations. He was, however, subjected to an abusive and hostile work environment by reason of his sexual orientation. The abuse he allegedly endured was so severe that he ultimately suffered a heart attack.

For the sake of decency and judicial propriety, we hesitate before reciting in detail the incidents of Simonton's abuse. Nevertheless, we think it is important both to acknowledge the appalling persecution Simonton allegedly endured and to identify the precise nature of the abuse so as to distinguish this case from future cases as they arise. We therefore relate some, but not all, of the alleged harassment that forms the basis for this suit.

Simonton's sexual orientation was known to his co-workers who repeatedly assaulted him with such comments as "go fuck yourself, fag," "suck my dick," and "so you like it up the ass?" Notes were placed on the wall in the employees' bathroom with Simonton's name and the name of celebrities who had died of AIDS. Pornographic photographs were taped to his work area, male dolls were placed in his vehicle, and copies of Playgirl magazine were sent to his home. Pictures of an erect penis were posted in his work place, as were posters stating that Simonton suffered from mental illness as a result of "bung hole disorder." There were repeated statements that Simonton was a "fucking faggot."

There can be no doubt that the conduct allegedly engaged in by Simonton's co-workers is morally reprehensible whenever and in whatever context it occurs, particularly in the modern workplace. Nevertheless, as the First Circuit recently explained in a similar context, "we are called upon here to construe a statute as glossed by the Supreme Court, not to make a moral judgment." Higgins v. New Balance Athletic Shoe, Inc. . . . The law is well-settled in this circuit and in all others to have reached the question that Simonton has no cause of action under Title VII because Title VII does not prohibit harassment or discrimination because of sexual orientation.

I

The Equal Employment Opportunity Act of 1972 extended Title VII's protections to certain federal employees, including U.S. postal service employees. Section 2000e-16(a) provides, in part, that all personnel actions affecting covered employees "shall be made free from any discrimination based on race, color, religion, sex, or national origin." Id. Simonton argues that discrimination based on "sex" includes discrimination based on sexual orientation. We disagree.

Admittedly, we have "little legislative history to guide us in interpreting the Act's prohibition against discrimination based on 'sex.' " Meritor Sav. Bank v. Vinson. But we are informed by Congress's rejection, on numerous occasions, of bills that would have extended Title VII's protection to people based on their sexual preferences. See, e.g., Employment Nondiscrimination Act of 1996, S. 2056, 104th Cong. (1996). . . . Although congressional inaction subsequent to the enactment of a statute is not always a helpful guide, Congress's refusal to expand the reach of Title VII is strong evidence of congressional intent in the face of consistent judicial decisions refusing to interpret "sex" to include sexual orientation.

Moreover, we are not writing on a clean slate. In DeCintio v. Westchester County Med. Ctr., 807 F.2d 304 (2d Cir. 1986), we reversed a plaintiff's verdict in a Title VII suit alleging that a male employer had passed over several male applicants for a promotion in order to hire a woman with whom the employer had a romantic relationship. Interpreting the definition of "sex," we held that

> the other categories afforded protection under Title VII refer to a person's status as a member of a particular race, color, religion or nationality. "Sex," when read in this context, logically could only refer to membership in a class delineated by gender, rather than sexual activity regardless of gender. . . . The proscribed differentiation under Title VII, therefore, must be a distinction based on a person's sex, not on his or her sexual affiliations.

Id. at 306-307. Because the term "sex" in Title VII refers only to membership in a class delineated by gender, and not to sexual affiliation, Title VII does not proscribe discrimination because of sexual orientation.

Simonton argues that Oncale v. Sundowner Offshore Services, Inc. permits us to revisit our holding in DeCintio. We disagree that such an opportunity presents itself here. In Oncale, the Supreme Court rejected a per se rule that same-sex sexual harassment was non-cognizable under Title VII. . . . Oncale did not suggest, however, that male harassment of other males always violates Title VII. Oncale emphasized that every victim of such harassment must show that he was harassed because he was male.

Subsequent to the Supreme Court's decision in Oncale, the First Circuit has reaffirmed the inapplicability of Title VII to discrimination based on sexual orientation. See Higgins, 194 F.3d at 259 ("We regard it as settled law that, as drafted and authoritatively construed, Title VII does not proscribe harassment simply because of sexual orientation."). We likewise do not see how Oncale changes our well-settled precedent that "sex" refers to membership in a class delineated by gender. The critical issue, as stated in Oncale, "is whether members of one sex are exposed to disadvantageous terms or conditions of employment to which members of the other sex are not exposed." Oncale, 523 U.S. at 80. Simonton has alleged that he was discriminated against not because he was a man, but because of his sexual orientation. Such a claim remains non-cognizable under Title VII.

II

Simonton argues in the alternative that the harassment he suffered could be construed as discrimination based on sex rather than sexual orientation. He raises three arguments in this vein. Simonton first argues that, if the plaintiff's case in *Oncale* was sufficient to withstand summary judgment, he has pled facts sufficiently similar to those in *Oncale* to withstand dismissal. We disagree.

We are mindful that this case comes to us after a dismissal pursuant to Rule 12(b)(6), and that "generally a complaint that gives full notice of the circumstances giving rise to the plaintiff's claim for relief need not also correctly plead the legal theory or theories and statutory basis supporting the claim." Nevertheless, there is no basis to infer from the complaint that the harassment Simonton suffered was because of his sex and not, as he urges throughout his complaint, because of his sexual orientation. In the context of male-female sexual harassment, involving more or less explicit sexual proposals, it is easy to infer discrimination because of sex since "it is reasonable to assume those proposals would not have been made to someone of the same sex." *Oncale*, 523 U.S. at 80. And, as the Supreme Court stated, "the same chain of inference would be available to a plaintiff alleging same-sex harassment, if there were credible evidence that the harasser was homosexual." Id. But since Simonton does not offer "direct comparative evidence about how the alleged harasser treated members of both sexes in [his] mixed-sex workplace" (id. at 80-81) and does not allege a basis for inferring gender-based animus, we are unable to infer that the alleged conduct would not have been directed at a woman. Accepting as true all the facts that Simonton has pled, the only inference we can draw is that he was harassed because of his sexual orientation. As we have explained, such harassment is not cognizable under Title VII.

Simonton also argues that discrimination because of sexual orientation is discrimination based on sex because it disproportionately affects men. We decline to adopt a reading of Title VII that would also "achieve by judicial 'construction' what Congress did not do and has consistently refused to do on many occasions," *DeSantis*, 608 F.2d at 330. Therefore, this argument is unavailing.

Simonton next relies on Price Waterhouse v. Hopkins, to argue that the abuse he suffered was discrimination based on sexual stereotypes, which may be cognizable as discrimination based on sex. We find this argument more persuasive but not sufficiently pled in this case.

The plaintiff in *Price Waterhouse* filed suit after having been denied partnership in an accounting firm, in part because she was "macho." She was advised that she could improve her chances for partnership if she would "walk more femininely, talk more femininely, dress more femininely, wear make-up, have her hair styled, and wear jewelry." Justice Brennan, writing for the plurality, held that this was impermissible sex discrimination, and that "in the specific context of sex stereotyping, an employer who acts on the basis of a belief that a woman cannot be aggressive, or that she must not be, has acted on the basis of gender." Other courts have suggested that gender discrimination—discrimination based on a failure to conform to gender norms—might be cognizable under Title VII.

The same theory of sexual stereotyping could apply here. Simonton argues that the harassment he endured was based on his failure to conform to gender norms, regardless of his sexual orientation. The Court in *Price Waterhouse* implied that a suit alleging harassment or disparate treatment based upon nonconformity with sexual stereotypes is cognizable under Title VII as discrimination because of sex. This would not bootstrap protection for sexual orientation into Title VII because not all gay men are stereotypically feminine, and not all heterosexual men are stereotypically masculine. But it would plainly afford relief for discrimination based upon sexual stereotypes.

We do not reach the merits of this issue, however, as Simonton has failed to plead sufficient facts for our consideration of the issue. We do not have sufficient allegations before us to decide Simonton's claims based on stereotyping because we have no basis in the record to surmise that Simonton behaved in a stereotypically feminine manner and that the harassment he endured was, in fact, based on his non-conformity with gender norms instead of his sexual orientation. . . .

For the reasons set forth above, the judgment of the district court is affirmed.

Nichols v. Azteca Restaurant Enterprises, Inc.

256 F.3d 864 (9th Cir. 2001)

GOULD, Circuit Judge

Antonio Sanchez brought this action against his former employer, Azteca Restaurant Enterprises, Inc., alleging, among other claims, sexual harassment and retaliation in violation of Title VII of the Civil Rights Act of 1964 ("Title VII") and its state law counterpart, the Washington Law Against Discrimination ("WLAD"). Sanchez claimed that he was verbally harassed by some male co-workers and a supervisor because he was effeminate and did not meet their views of a male stereotype. Sanchez further asserted that he was terminated in retaliation for opposing the harassment. Following a bench trial, the district court entered judgment in favor of Azteca on all claims. . . .

We agree with Sanchez that the behavior of his co-workers and supervisor violated Title VII and WLAD. We further agree that Azteca failed to take adequate steps to remedy the harassment. . . . We affirm the judgment of the district court with respect to Sanchez's retaliation claim.

I

Azteca operates a chain of restaurants in Washington and Oregon. It employed Sanchez from October 1991 to July 1995. Sanchez at first worked as a host in Azteca's Burien restaurant, and later worked as a food server at the Southcenter restaurant.

Throughout his tenure at Azteca, Sanchez was subjected to a relentless campaign of insults, name-calling, and vulgarities. Male co-workers and a supervisor repeatedly referred to Sanchez in Spanish and English as "she" and "her." Male co-workers mocked Sanchez for walking and carrying his serving tray "like a woman," and taunted him in Spanish and English as, among other things, a "faggot" and a "fucking female whore." The remarks were not stray or isolated. Rather, the abuse occurred at least once a week and often several times a day.

This conduct violated company policy. Since 1989, Azteca has expressly prohibited sexual harassment and retaliation and has directed its employees to bring complaints regarding such conduct directly to the attention of the corporate office. . . . Upon receipt of a complaint, Azteca's policy is to conduct a thorough investigation, the results of which are reviewed by the company's EEO Board, which is then responsible for implementing an appropriate remedy.

In addition to this policy, Azteca has a bilingual (English and Spanish) training program about sexual harassment. This training, which all employees attend when hired, and annually thereafter, defines sexual harassment and instructs employees how to report complaints.

Sanchez attended Azteca's sexual harassment training and was familiar with the company's anti-harassment policy and reporting procedures. Yet he never complained to the corporate EEO officer or the area manager about the harassment he experienced, as required by the corporate policy. This is not to say, however, that Sanchez ignored the harassment. Indeed, the general manager of the Southcenter restaurant . . . testified that Sanchez complained about being called names, and an assistant manager testified that Sanchez made similar complaints to him. . . .

In response, Serna proposed the following solution: (1) Sanchez was to report any further harassment to the Southcenter general manager, who promised to address the issue; and (2) Serna was to follow up with "spot checks" over a two-week period to ensure that the harassment would stop. During the four or five spot checks that followed, Serna spoke with Sanchez only once and was told that conditions were improving. Serna replied that if the situation took a turn for the worse, Sanchez should tell the Southcenter general manager or call Serna directly. Sanchez made no further complaints.

On July 29, 1995, a couple of months after his meeting with Serna, Sanchez became involved in a heated argument with an assistant manager, and walked off the job. He was fired for leaving work in the middle of his shift. A month later, Sanchez filed a charge of discrimination with the EEOC. Thereafter, he initiated this lawsuit. . . .

Following a bench trial, the district court concluded that Sanchez had not been subjected to a hostile environment. . . . Sanchez timely appealed. . . . [Section II omitted.]

III

Under Title VII, it is unlawful for an employer "to discriminate against any individual with respect to his compensation, terms, conditions, or privileges of employment, because of . . . sex." It is by now clear that sexual harassment in the form of a hostile work environment constitutes sex discrimination.

To prevail on his hostile environment claim, Sanchez was required to establish a "pattern of ongoing and persistent harassment severe enough to alter the conditions of employment." To satisfy this requirement, Sanchez needed to prove that his workplace was "both objectively and subjectively offensive, one that a reasonable person would find hostile or abusive, and one that the victim in fact did perceive to be so." In addition, Sanchez was required to prove that any harassment took place "because of sex." . . . [The court runs through the three prong — (A) objectively hostile environment; (B) subjectively hostile environment; and (C) "because of sex" — and finds for Sanchez on each prong.]

[In its analysis of the "because of sex" prong, the court states:] *Price Waterhouse* sets a rule that bars discrimination on the basis of sex stereotypes. That rule squarely applies to preclude the harassment here. The only potential difficulty arises out of a now faint shadow cast by our decision in DeSantis v. Pacific Telephone & Telegraph Co., Inc. *DeSantis* holds that discrimination based on a stereotype that a man "should have a virile rather than an effeminate appearance" does not fall within Title VII's purview. This holding, however, predates and conflicts with the Supreme Court's decision in *Price Waterhouse*. And, in this direct conflict, *DeSantis* must lose. To the extent it conflicts with *Price Waterhouse*, as we hold it does, *DeSantis* is no longer good law. Under *Price Waterhouse*, Sanchez must prevail.[7]

Following *Price Waterhouse*, we hold that the verbal abuse at issue occurred because of sex. Because we hold that Sanchez has established each element of his hostile environment claim, we further hold that the conduct of Sanchez's co-workers and supervisor constituted actionable harassment under both Title VII and WLAD, and reverse the district court's contrary conclusion. . . .

Notes

1. Same-Sex Harassment and Sex-Stereotyping. Since the Supreme Court's ruling in Oncale v. Sundowner Offshore Services,[317] it has been clear that male-on-male harassment can violate Title VII as long as the plaintiff can prove the harassment occurred "because of sex." The Court in that case reasoned that a sexual harassment claim should not be precluded simply because the complainant and the harasser are of the same sex. In *Oncale*, the harassers

---

7. We do not imply that all gender-based distinctions are actionable under Title VII. For example, our decision does not imply that there is any violation of Title VII occasioned by reasonable regulations that require male and female employees to conform to different dress and grooming standards.

appear to have thought that the complainant was gay, although he claimed he was straight. In contrast, *Nichols* involved an openly gay complainant, and the Ninth Circuit Court of Appeals, while citing *Oncale* at length, adopted a theory not discussed in *Oncale* and not yet adopted by the Supreme Court in a sexual harassment case—the theory of sex stereotyping. This theory posits that men often harass other men to enforce "the traditional heterosexual male gender role" by encouraging "stereotypical forms of 'masculine' behavior" and punishing or devaluing "feminine" conduct. Mary Anne Case provides this analysis:

> By examining the similarity of the taunts typically hurled at both women and gay or effeminate men in hostile environments, taunts that stress feminine sexual passivity . . . [it is apparent] that the sexual harassment inflicted on all three groups may have in common the desire of certain "active" masculine males to drive out of the workplace those they see as contaminating it with the taint of feminine passivity. Such harassment is, therefore, a form of gender discrimination against the feminine, one with serious effects on the job performance and security of its victims, who should have a legal remedy against it regardless of their sex.[318]

One of the reasons for moving to the sex stereotyping theory was that many courts, before and after *Oncale*, have rejected sexual harassment claims by gays and lesbians, on the grounds that Congress intended the term "sex" to mean "biological male or female" and not one's sexuality or sexual orientation.[319] Should discrimination based on sexual orientation constitute discrimination because of sex? Does the sex stereotyping theory go further than the equality paradigm?

Given the reasoning cited above from the *Oncale* decision, is there a risk, as commentators like Janet Halley have warned, that recognition of harassment based on sexual orientation may expose gays and lesbians to unwarranted claims of harassment by individuals who are threatened by any display of homosexual conduct in the workplace?[320]

2. Legislative Efforts to Create Legal Rights Based on Sexual Orientation and Gender Identity.   Courts have uniformly ruled, as the court did in *Simonton*, that sexual orientation is not a form of sex discrimination under Title VII. Some gay and lesbian plaintiffs have been successful where they have been able to prove that the discrimination was rooted in their nonconformity with gender stereotypes, a theory successfully deployed in *Nichols*, although not accepted in many cases. The effort to pass broader federal legislation explicitly prohibiting discrimination based on sexual orientation has been largely unsuccessful. The first bill to include such protections was introduced by Congresswoman Bella Abzug in 1974. The bill proposed broad protection for gays and lesbians against discrimination in employment, housing, and public accommodations. Similar bills were introduced at regular intervals throughout the 1970s and 1980s, but none was passed into law. In 1994, the first version of the Employment Non-Discrimination Act (ENDA) was introduced in the Senate, which held hearings on the bill. ENDA was narrower than the unsuccessful bills of earlier decades, focusing only on employment. It has been proposed in different forms on multiple occasions since then, most recently in 2013. In its most common version, ENDA would prohibit employers from taking any employment action on the basis of sexual orientation or from retaliating against any individual who sought to enforce these protections. Although similar to Title VII, the proposed statute expressly exempts military and religious organizations and disallows disparate impact claims. It would not permit affirmative action based on sexual orientation and would not require benefits for domestic partners.

In addition to opposition from conservatives, ENDA has provoked heated controversy among gay rights advocates over whether to include protection for transgender persons. A version of ENDA that included protection against gender identity discrimination was introduced into the House of Representatives in 2007, but a sexual orientation–only version was the one that passed in the House. The Senate has never passed any version of ENDA, but the most recently introduced versions in both Houses of Congress include gender identity protection.[321] In 1998, President Clinton issued Executive Order 13087, which prohibits discrimination based on sexual orientation in the civilian federal workforce.

Gay rights advocates have met with greater success at the state level. As of 2013, 22 states had enacted laws prohibiting sexual orientation discrimination in various contexts, including employment, housing, and public accommodations; 16 of these expressly cover gender identity discrimination.[322] Increasing numbers of Fortune 500 companies also prohibit discrimination based on sexual orientation and gender identity.[323] Despite such protections, surveys find that between one-quarter and two-thirds of LGBT employees report experiencing discrimination at work.[324]

3. Sexual Orientation and Heightened Scrutiny. Constitutional challenges have been brought in cases involving discrimination against gays and lesbians by public employers, such as the U.S. military. The recently repealed "Don't Ask, Don't Tell" policy of the U.S. military (discussed in Note 5 below) was subjected to several such challenges during its 18-year lifespan. In Witt v. Department of the Air Force, the Ninth Circuit applied heightened scrutiny to DADT and concluded, under that standard, that the policy violated the due process/liberty interests of gay and lesbian service members.[325] More recently, under the Equal Protection Clause, it applied the same heightened scrutiny in reviewing the use of a peremptory challenge to exclude a gay man from a jury in a case concerning HIV drug pricing.[326] That is a more rigorous standard than the rational basis test applied in most of the other cases challenging this policy, although not as demanding as the strict scrutiny applied in cases involving racial classifications or marital privacy.

Gay rights advocates have frequently attempted to establish that homosexuals as a class have the characteristics required for special constitutional protection under the equal protection clause: (1) a history of discrimination;

(2) exhibition of obvious, immutable, or distinguishing characteristics that define them as members of a discrete group; and (3) political powerlessness, or the burdening of a fundamental right. How would you apply these criteria to LGBT populations? Is there any doubt, after the *Windsor* case, that a high level of constitutional protection is now required?

4. Discrimination on the Basis of Sexual Orientation by "Private" Associations.   A divided Supreme Court in Boy Scouts of America v. Dale upheld the right of the Boy Scouts to exclude members based on sexual orientation.[327] The case involved James Dale, who joined the Scouts at age 8 and for the next 12 years was an exemplary member. He earned 25 merit badges and the honored status of Eagle Scout. Shortly after being appointed an assistant troop leader, Dale enrolled at Rutgers University, where he became co-president of the Lesbian and Gay Alliance. His membership in the Scouts was revoked after a Newark newspaper identified him as president and quoted comments that he made in connection with a seminar on health needs of gay and lesbian teens.

Dale then filed a complaint under New Jersey public accommodation law, which bars discrimination based on characteristics such as race, ethnicity, and sexual orientation. The New Jersey Supreme Court upheld his claim, and in a 5-4 decision, the U.S. Supreme Court reversed. Writing for the majority, Chief Justice Rehnquist concluded that the New Jersey law violated the Boy Scouts' rights of speech and association. Under the Court's analysis, "the presence of a gay rights activist would force the organization to send a message that the Boy Scouts accepts homosexual conduct." According to Scout leadership, such a message would be inconsistent with its oath and laws requiring Scouts to be "morally straight" and "clean" in body and mind.

In upholding the Scouts' policy, the majority relied heavily on its prior decision in Hurley v. Irish-American Gay, Lesbian and Bisexual Group of Boston, Inc.[328] In *Hurley*, the Court ruled that organizers of a St. Patrick's Day parade could not be compelled by Massachusetts public accommodation law to let gays and lesbians march behind a LGBT banner. Just as those parade organizers had the right "not to propound a particular point of view," the Boy Scouts had a right not to convey the message of legitimacy that Dale's membership would imply.[329]

Justice Stevens, writing for himself and three other Justices, took issue with the majority's analysis of both the facts and the law.

> [N]either one of [the Scouts' guiding] principles—"morally straight" and "clean"—says the slightest thing about homosexuality. Indeed, neither term in the Boy Scouts' Law and Oath expresses any position whatsoever on sexual matters.
>
> BSA's published guidance on that topic underscores this point. Scouts, for example, are directed to receive their sex education at home or in school, but not from the organization. . . .

Several principles are made perfectly clear by [the Court's past cases in this area]. First, to prevail on a claim of expressive association in the face of a State's antidiscrimination law, it is not enough simply to engage in some kind of expressive activity. . . . Second, it is not enough to adopt an openly avowed exclusionary membership policy. . . . Third, it is not sufficient merely to articulate some connection between the group's expressive activities and its exclusionary policy. . . .

Rather, [the question is whether an anti-discrimination law] "impose[s] any serious burdens" on the group's "collective effort on behalf of [its] shared goals. . . ."

The evidence before this Court makes it exceptionally clear that BSA has, at most, simply adopted an exclusionary membership policy and has no shared goal of disapproving of homosexuality.[330]

The *Dale* holding has been controversial among constitutional scholars, policymakers, and the general public. Some commentators have viewed the decision as inconsistent with prior cases involving discrimination by private associations (discussed in Chapter 1). They are also troubled by granting First Amendment protection to an organization that discriminates on the basis of status not conduct: heterosexual troop leaders who support gay rights were not dismissed.

What is your view? Does it make sense that the Jaycees and Rotary Club cannot exclude women, while the Boy Scouts may exclude gays? In 2013, the Boy Scouts dropped the ban on gay members, although the ban on Scout leaders continues. How significant is this change of policy? Following the *Dale* decision, related disputes surfaced about whether public entities like schools and police departments should eliminate their support of Boy Scout activities. Today, many churches that oppose homosexuality are debating whether to drop their sponsorships of Boy Scout troops.[331] Should public support for, or against, allowing gay boys to join the Boy Scouts be relevant to the legal question of whether a private organization should be allowed to discriminate?

5. Sexual Orientation and Military Policy. Over 14,500 service members have lost their jobs because of the Don't Ask, Don't Tell policy.[332] The policy was enacted in 1993 under former President Bill Clinton, ironically as an attempt to bring about equality for gay service members by ending the long-standing outright ban on homosexuals serving in the military.[333] However, this supposed compromise resulted in the firing of service members across all branches, and a disproportionate number of the discharges were women. For example, in 2009, women made up 14 percent of the Army, but 48 percent of discharges. Women were 20 percent of the Air Force in that year, but 51 percent of the discharges under the policy.[334]

In enacting DADT, Congress found that combat effectiveness requires "high morale, good order and discipline, and unit cohesion" and that the ban on open homosexuals continues to be imperative because of "the unique circumstances of military service" and the threat that open homosexuals would pose to military morale, unity, and discipline. Those claims have been largely accepted by courts in challenges brought to the military's exclusion of gays and lesbians. A representative conclusion is that:

> The presence in the military environment of persons who engage in homosexual conduct or who, by their statements, demonstrate a propensity to engage in homosexual conduct, seriously impairs the accomplishment of the military mission. The presence of such members adversely affects the ability of the Military Services to maintain discipline, good order, and morale; to foster mutual trust and confidence among service members[;] to ensure the integrity of the system of rank and command; to facilitate assignment and worldwide deployment of service members who frequently must live and work under close conditions affording minimal privacy; to recruit and retain members of the Military Services; to maintain the public acceptability of military service; and to prevent breaches of security.[335]

How do you respond to this rationale?

During his campaign for the presidency, President Obama stated his intention to abolish the DADT policy. Congress considered proposals to end the ban, with the support of important figures like General Colin Powell.[336] While the legislation was under consideration, a federal district court ruled, in a case brought by the Log Cabin Republicans, that DADT violated the Fifth Amendment's guarantee of due process and the First Amendment's guarantee of freedom of speech.[337] While appeal was pending, Congress repealed DADT during a lame-duck session in December 2010.[338] Issues remain respecting the legal rights of gay and lesbian military personnel, but *Windsor* paved the way for their access to almost 100 dependency benefits that require legal marriage.[339]

Putting Theory Into Practice

3-22. For decades, a therapy known as conversion or reparative therapy has been used in an effort to reduce homosexual desires. At one time, this therapy involved electric shocks and nausea-inducing drugs, but today, it involves use of aversive stimuli (e.g., asking the patient to imagine receiving electric shocks, or vomiting) to suppress erotic stimulation in connection with homosexual imagery, and positive stimuli to encourage erotic responses to heterosexual imagery. A defender of the therapy says that it can be especially beneficial in reducing homosexual urges of young boys whose homosexual thoughts are connected with prior sex abuse. California now bans use of such therapy for minors, and other states are considering bills to make the practice illegal.[340] What are the arguments for and against such bans? Does your answer depend upon the quality of the science supporting such therapy, or should the practice be banned even if it "works"?

3-23. A study of soldiers who served in Iraq and Afghanistan found that almost three-quarters were personally comfortable interacting with gays and lesbians.[341] Should the opinions of current service members be relevant? If so, is three-quarters enough? Whose interests are at stake? Gay service members? All service members? The public at large?

3-24. The FBI has worried that homosexual agents will be too easily blackmailed, thus risking government secrets.[342] How would you respond to this concern?

3-25. Now that DADT has been repealed, what obstacles do you foresee to implementing this new, nondiscriminatory policy? One author suggests that even with DADT fully repealed, gays and lesbians continue to be harassed and denied opportunities for advancement.[343] What measures do you think might help gays and lesbians achieve equality in the military?

F. WOMEN IN THE MILITARY

Throughout the nation's history, cultural expectations and legal restrictions have severely limited female involvement in the armed forces. Until the early 1970s, women constituted less than 2 percent of the American military, and discrimination in placement and promotion was widespread, particularly for women of color. Enrollment was limited through quotas on female applicants; exclusion from combat positions, military academies, and training programs; and disqualification of women who became pregnant or had minor children. The prevailing view was apparent in one 1968 federal district court opinion: "In providing for involuntary service for men and voluntary service for women, Congress followed the teachings of history that if a nation is to survive, men must provide the first line of defense while women keep the home fires burning."[344]

In the mid-1970s, many of these restrictions were modified or withdrawn, without judicial intervention. As a result, female participation in the armed forces substantially increased, reaching 10 percent by the late 1980s, 13 percent by the turn of the century, and 15 percent by 2009. Currently, women serve in 93 percent of all army occupations and make up approximately 14 percent of the active Army.[345] Still, women's service in the military remains controversial, especially with respect to combat positions.

Reading Questions

1. What are the most significant concerns about women serving in combat? How do they compare to concerns about gays, lesbians, and bisexuals?

2. Is *Rostker* (discussed in Note 1, below) rightly decided? By what theory could it be defended or challenged?

3. What are the most likely objections to the service of women in combat positions?

Kingsley R. Browne, Women at War: An Evolutionary Perspective

49 Buff. L. Rev. 51, 54-57 (2001)

To date, the argument in favor of including women in [combat and close combat support] positions has proceeded under three fundamental assumptions: (1) that warfare in this modern age is fundamentally different from the warfare experienced by our fathers and our more distant ancestors; thus prior experience is no guide to future conduct; (2) that men and women are essentially identical in combat-relevant ways, other than (most would agree) in physical strength, a trait they view as largely irrelevant; thus, men and women are for the most part interchangeable in military positions; and (3) that the primary impediments to integration of women are male "attitudes" operating at a cognitive level; thus, only the lack of proper leadership stands in the way of overcoming this "ideology of masculinism."

All three of these assumptions are subject to serious question and have led to an under-appreciation of the costs and difficulty of sexual integration. The first assumption . . . is based upon a misunderstanding of modern warfare, a misunderstanding made considerably more acute by the lopsided experience of the allies in the Gulf War and the even more lopsided NATO air assault against the Serbs. Yet the business of war is still killing and risking being killed, often at short ranges. Many combat tasks, even in this technological age, have not changed that much from earlier times, and many continue to require physical strength, a trait that virtually everyone agrees is differentially distributed between the sexes.

The second assumption . . . overlooks a vast literature on temperamental and cognitive sex differences. Traits that are important to combat personnel include physical aggressiveness; willingness to kill strangers; willingness to expose oneself to physical risk; and cognitive skills, such as the three-dimensional spatial ability that is so critical to the "situational awareness" of fighter pilots. The questions raised by sex differences in these attributes are primarily whether they can be efficiently tested in advance of actual combat and whether there is enough overlap between the sexes to warrant considering women as well as men for combat positions.

The third assumption . . . overlooks the possibility of predispositions rooted deep in the psyches of both males and females that may stand as an obstacle to integration. Thus, even though some women as individuals possess as much strength, aggressiveness, and inclination to take risks as many men, there may still be reasons for excluding them from combat service. The relevant issue is "femaleness qua femaleness" rather than the individualized attributes of the women in question. Some of the questions that must be answered are whether men have an innate predisposition to resist introduction of women into certain all-male groups; whether introduction of women will disrupt cohesion by creating competition among men for the attentions of women; whether introduction of women will impair effectives by causing men to be overprotective of women; whether women can elicit following behavior in men to the same extent that other men can; and whether introduction of women will diminish the willingness of men to risk their lives and make the military less attractive to potential male "warriors." These questions involve not the capacity of women as individuals to be soldiers but rather the social dynamic that results from mixing men and women under what are often very trying conditions. This set of issues is more difficult to analyze than the former, because it is generally easier to measure traits of individuals than it is to measure social interactions between them. . . .

Is it really true that warfare has changed so much as to reverse the almost unanimous conclusion of human history that defense of the community and external projections of force should rest with men?

Notes

1. Legal Challenges. The most significant case to reach the Supreme Court concerning sex discrimination in the military was Rostker v. Golberg. At issue was a claim by a male plaintiff that the military's compulsory draft registration system, which included only men, constituted a violation of the Equal Protection Clause. Speaking for the majority, Justice Rehnquist rejected that claim.

> No one could deny that under Craig [v. Boren], the Government's interest in raising and supporting armies is an "important governmental interest." Congress and its Committees carefully considered and debated . . . alternative means of furthering that interest. . . .
>
> Congress was fully aware not merely of the many facts and figures presented to it by witnesses who testified before its Committees, but [also] of the current thinking as to the place of women in the Armed Services. . . .
>
> This case is quite different from several of the gender-based discrimination cases we have considered in that, despite appellees' assertions, Congress did not act "unthinkingly" or "reflexively and not for any considered reason." . . . The question of registering women for the draft not only received considerable national attention and was the subject of wide-ranging public debate, but also was extensively considered by Congress in hearings, floor debate, and in committee. . . .
>
> [T]he decision to exempt women from registration was not the "'accidental by-product of a traditional way of thinking about females.'" . . .

The purpose of registration [historically], therefore was to prepare for a draft of combat troops.

Women as a group, however, unlike men as a group, are not eligible for combat. . . . Congress specifically recognized and endorsed the exclusion of women from combat in exempting women from registration. In the words of the Senate Report:

The principle that women should not intentionally and routinely engage in combat is fundamental, and enjoys wide support among our people. It is universally supported by military leaders who have testified before the Committee. . . . Current law and policy exclude women from being assigned to combat in our military forces, and the Committee reaffirms this policy. . . .

The Senate Report specifically found that "[w]omen should not be intentionally or routinely placed in combat positions in our military services." . . . The President expressed his intent to continue the current military policy precluding women from combat. . . .

The existence of combat restrictions clearly indicates the basis for Congress' decision to exempt women from registration. The purpose of registration was to prepare for a draft of combat troops. Since women are excluded from combat, Congress concluded that they would not be needed in the event of a draft, and therefore decided not to register them.[346]

Because the plaintiff in *Rostker* had not challenged the constitutionality of the combat exemption, the Court found it unnecessary to resolve that issue, although the tenor of the decision left little doubt that a majority of Justices were prepared to defer to Congress on this matter. Justice Marshall, joined by Justice Brennan, dissented. As they read the record, the government had not sustained the burden of showing that a gender-based classification substantially furthered the goal of military preparedness. Even assuming the legitimacy of excluding women from combat, their exclusion from registration did not follow. According to government estimates, about one-third of those drafted during a national mobilization would not need combat skills. The registration system at issue included non-combat-eligible males, and the Joint Chiefs of Staff had been united in their desire to include females as well. Although some cost would be involved in registering more women than necessary in a system that precluded their combat service, the dissent noted that Supreme Court decisions had often rejected administrative expense as a rationale for gender classifications.[347]

Justice Rehnquist's opinion emphasized that the exclusion of women was not an accidental by-product "of a traditional way of thinking about females." In your mind, does its intentionality make it more acceptable?

2. Current Status of, and Views About, Women in Combat. By 1994, Congress had repealed all statutory bans on women's participation in military combat, leaving the decision to the secretary of defense, who can make changes with sufficient notice to Congress. The 1994 Direct Ground Combat rule served as the primary restriction on women's service for the last two decades, although the secretaries of each branch of the military also had discretion to impose certain further restrictions. As of 2012, women were generally excluded from ground combat and from occupational specialties. Only the Coast Guard allowed women to occupy positions in all of its occupational categories, although 99 percent of the positions within the Air Force were open to women. The other branches have fewer positions open to women—Army (66 percent), Marine Corps (68 percent), and Navy (88 percent).[348] Women's active military participation is still relatively small compared with men's. Currently, women account for 19 percent of active Air Force positions, 13 percent of Army positions, 7 percent of Marine Corps positions, and 16 percent of Navy positions.[349] Yet even these small percentages represent a dramatic increase in women's participation in the enlisted force from 42,000 in 1973 to 167,000 in 2010; during the same span, the enlisted force as a whole dropped by 738,000 members.[350] According to a Pew Research survey, the female force is more racially diverse than the male force, just as likely to experience the "struggles and benefits of service upon discharge," and more likely than their male counterparts to be critical of the wars in Iraq and Afghanistan.[351]

In 2012, the Department of Defense (DOD) conducted a review of gender restrictions in the military and issued a report notifying Congress of modest changes to allow women closer to the front lines.[352] One major change is to allow women to be assigned to direct combat units at the battalion level (smaller than the brigade level previously allowed) in the occupational specialties already open to women. Women are still barred from infantry as a specialty, but this change will still open up many new positions. A second change is to open up over 13,000 positions in Army units that are "co-located" with combat units. The DOD recommended against changes to rules that (1) exclude women from long-range reconnaissance operations or Special Operations Forces and (2) exclude women from positions with physically demanding tasks that the vast majority of them would not be able to perform.

Despite the modest recommendations in the 2012 report, Secretary of Defense Leon Panetta announced in January 2013 that the longstanding restriction on women in combat would be lifted. In declaring the new policy, Panetta observed that women have "shown great courage and sacrifice on and off the battlefield, contributed in unprecedented ways to the military's mission and proven their ability to serve in an expanding number of roles."[353] Allowing women access to combat positions, he explained, will help "ensure that the mission is met with the best-qualified and most capable people, regardless of gender." Panetta announced the military's intention to phase out *all* combat restrictions involving women by 2016. Now, if any branch of the military wants to retain any type of exclusion of women, it must come forward with its justification for doing so before the implementation date.

Legislative debates about women's participation in the military, particularly in combat positions, reflect an extended array of assumptions about women's physical and psychological unfitness for fighting and the cultural costs of seeing the nation's nurturers as "cannon fodder." Many military and congressional leaders remain convinced that actual "fighting is a man's job" and that most female soldiers lack sufficient strength, endurance, aggressiveness, or ability to "kill impersonally" in combat. Some maintain that aggression is "an intrinsic male" quality, and one author concludes that regardless of whether women are "innately less aggressive and combative than men" or "victims of cultural conditioning that represses their natural warlike instincts to levels below those typical of males," women are less qualified for combat missions.[354]

Opponents of women in combat also raise a host of concerns about pregnancy, promiscuity, and "gender-norming"—the practice of adjusting strength and fitness standards to reflect sex-based differences. According to these commentators, the military's effort to accommodate women is fostering resentment, diluting performance requirements, creating double standards, inspiring inappropriate chivalry, compromising morale, impairing recruitment, and diverting attention from more central goals of combat preparedness. Underlying these concerns have been a host of symbolic issues about masculinity, manhood, and dominance. General William Westmoreland expressed a common attitude with uncommon candor: "No man with any gumption wants a woman to fight his nation's battles."[355]

Proponents of equality treatment for women point out that the most comprehensive studies conclude that with appropriate training the vast majority of women can meet the physical demands of combat, and that their presence does not cause declines in unit cohesiveness.[356] As in civilian contexts, military positions requiring particular levels of strength, endurance, or agility can be allocated under gender-neutral guidelines that match individual capabilities with job requirements. Moreover, as many experts have noted, technological changes in warfare have reduced the relevance of physical strength in combat and eroded the distinctions between combat and combat-related positions. Federal judge Richard Posner puts it this way: "We live in an age of push-button warfare. Women can push buttons as well as men."[357]

The combat exclusion became less effective over time due to both technical loopholes and changes in styles of warfare. For example, commanders can get around a ban on assigning women to a particular combat unit by using a temporary assignment or by "attaching" her to a unit rather than assigning her. Moreover, in wars like the ones in Iraq and Afghanistan, the lack of a defined front line and insurgents' guerilla tactics have exposed female troops in many support positions to deadly situations despite their exclusion from front-line combat. As of early 2012, 144 women had been killed and 865 wounded while deployed to Iraq and Afghanistan.[358] As one Army lt. colonel put it, in Iraq, every soldier is "in harm's way." "The dynamics of the modern-day battlefield are non-linear," the secretary of defense noted in the 2012 report, "meaning there are no clearly defined front line and safer rear area where combat support operations are performed within a low-risk environment."[359] The result, according to an analyst at the Women's Research and Education Institute, is "[t]his is the first time in U.S. history that women are allowed to shoot back."[360] Females have also proved critical in combat support roles in enabling the military to respect cultural sensitivities, for example by searching female Iraqis at checkpoints.[361]

Whether to challenge sex-based policies, particularly exclusion of women from combat and draft registration systems, has been a matter of long-standing dispute among women's advocates. Those favoring equal treatment approaches argue that protective policies disserve women's interests by excluding them from positions of greatest power, status, and reward. Lack of combat eligibility restricts women's job opportunities, credibility, and career advancement in the military and limits their ability to capitalize on wartime service in other political and employment contexts. Double standards in the military also carry other costs in reinforcing traditional gender roles and stereotypes. In this vein, Mary Becker notes:

> Exclusion of women from militia service in combat denies women the obligations of full citizenship. This denial inevitably translates into disadvantaging women as citizens by depriving them of power they would otherwise share more equally with men. . . .
>
> [K]eeping women out of combat maintains the image of the male warrior, who is superior to physically passive women who need his protection and cannot resist his violence. . . . The military trains men to operate within a macho culture with the belief that they are superior to women. . . .
>
> [K]eeping women out of combat positions . . . supports the taboo against women using force, especially lethal force. . . . Maintaining male control of lethal force clearly preserves male interests both with respect to control of the military itself (a powerful institution in its own right) and with respect to men's power over women through physical intimidation throughout society. . . . [362]

If service in the military is a responsibility of citizenship, should women feel obligated to serve? Some feminists argue that women should seek to challenge military culture, not to assimilate within it. In opposing proposals for gender-neutral draft registration, a New Haven women's group issued the following response:

> • Women have traditionally fought for peace, and there is no reason for us to abandon that position now.
> • Our quest for equality must not lead us to embrace blindly all the standards and values of male institutions. . . . The conscription of women will not change the structure of power in the military or in this country. Why should we bide by a decision over which we have had no say? Once we are drafted, who will decide where we will serve? . . . These decisions will be made as they have always been made, by the *men* in the Pentagon and the White House, men who have refused to fight for equal rights for women, men who have on countless occasions demonstrated their disregard for the

legitimate grievances and sovereign rights of oppressed people all over the world. . . .[363]

Is it fair, as Ellen Goodman asks, if we see "[m]ore women . . . on the front lines than in the inner circle"?[364]

Can women have it both ways—that is, have the right to serve in combat without the obligation? If not, which way should they seek to have it? What formulation of gender equality is most consistent with your answer?

3. Sexual Abuse in the Armed Forces.   Of long-standing and increasing concern involving women and the military is sexual abuse. Certain characteristics of military life increase the risks of sexual misconduct: a highly masculine culture that reinforces aggression; strict hierarchies and limited opportunities for subordinates to escape abusive circumstances; stresses caused by lack of privacy and dangerous or onerous living conditions; separation from spouses or partners; and traditions of hazing for new or "deviant" recruits. The result has been a high level of domestic violence, sexual harassment, and rape during wartime.

A steady succession of scandals concerning sexual assault in the military has prompted studies, hearings, and reports—over 20 in the last two decades. Since the early 1990s, the Uniform Code of Military Justice has declared zero-tolerance for sexual harassment, but its frequency is hard to gauge, given the barriers to reporting. In Defense Department surveys, about one-third of women and 6 percent of men reported experiencing sexual harassment. In a 2010 survey of active-duty military personnel, 4.4 percent of women and 0.9 percent of men reported experiencing unwanted sexual contact.[365] Of those, 71 percent of women and 85 percent of men chose not to report it. Reasons included concerns about confidentiality, fear of retaliation, and a perceived futility of filing a complaint.[366] One study of military reserve members found that of those who had been subject to harassment, 67 percent of women and 78 percent of men did not report it. Of the women who reported, 41 percent were satisfied with the treatment of their complaints, and 23 percent indicated that they had suffered retaliation.[367] In 2011, the military received 3,192 complaints of sexual assault (involving 3,393 victims), a 1 percent increase over the prior year.[368] Over half of the reports alleged service member-on-service member attacks, and two-thirds involved rape, sodomy, or aggravated sexual assault.[369] Army estimates suggest that one-quarter of women in the military report experiencing a sexual assault during their service and that rates of domestic violence are estimated as three to five times higher among military couples than civilian couples.[370] Responses to both domestic violence and sexual assault have been strongly criticized on grounds that the armed forces have often failed to investigate complaints, protect complainants, and impose serious sanctions.[371] The problem is mirrored in the persistent incidents of sexual abuse in military academies.[372]

The reasons for individuals' reluctance to come forward were well illustrated by a highly publicized case in which Lt. General Claudia Kennedy, the

Army's highest-ranking woman, revealed that she had been harassed four years earlier by an officer subsequently chosen for the position of deputy inspector general, whose responsibilities would have included the investigation of sexual harassment. The appointment was withdrawn, but coverage of the incident suggested that women are reluctant to open their personal lives to investigation for fear of being blamed for inviting a sexual advance. In commenting on Lt. General Kennedy's dilemma, one female officer noted, "Now instead of being remembered as the first woman to earn three stars in the Army, she is going to be remembered as that woman with the sex complaint."[373]

In 2005 and 2006, various reforms led to broader definitions of rape, improved reporting procedures, including the possibility of a "confidential reporting option," new investigatory protocols, and a centralized system for responding to the needs of sexual assault victims. Some believe that the military has gone "too far" in trying to respond to sexual assault.[374] Others claim that it has not gone far enough. One National Guard staff sergeant who served in Iraq complained that women who were risking their lives were also counseled not to walk alone at night on the base: "You deploy me here and tell me it's not safe for me to walk alone to get a bite to eat because I'll probably get raped by one of our own?"[375]

A 2010 survey of active duty members of the Armed Forces found that 93 percent of service members had received sexual assault training in the previous 12 months, and 92 percent felt they had developed a good understanding of what constitutes sexual assault, how alcohol might exacerbate its likelihood, and how to avoid victimization. Eighty-five percent of women and 88 percent of men found the training moderately or very effective.[376] Only 26 percent of women and 39 percent of men, however, thought sexual assault had become less of a problem in the military than it was four years earlier.[377]

The recent focus of debates over sexual abuse in the military is who should have the authority for dealing with sexual abuse complaints. Traditionally, such complaints were handled within the usual "chain of command," —i.e., internally. Many claim that the command leadership simply does not take sexual abuse seriously. As a result, women believe that reporting is pointless, and abuse continues. Efforts in Congress to relocate responsibility elsewhere have, to date, not been successful, in face of the argument that removing authority within the chain of command undermines military effectiveness.[378] Does this sound familiar? Persuasive?

Putting Theory Into Practice

3-26. Rush Limbaugh summarizes a widespread view:

What will feminists seek in the military, first and foremost? Equality. Fairness. Gender quotas. Well, the military's chief goal is excellence. We shouldn't emasculate (pun intended) by shackling it with the demands of every silly social movement that is currently fashionable in society. The military has a job to do. . . . Its success will always be measured by its ability to destroy and decimate; not by whether it has a requisite percentage of women in foxholes, in daycare centers, or flying F-16s. I know this sounds harsh, but that's the way war is. Frankly, I don't believe that women should be in combat roles even if they can do the job. Why? You ask. Simple. Women have a civilizing role in society. War is that cruel last option in human relations. It isn't about career opportunities. Women have definite societal roles that are crucial to the continuation of mankind. They establish enduring values that are handed down from generation to generation. Women are the ones who give birth, without which the propagation of the species would not be perpetuated.

I just don't believe that we have to subject women to the horrors and rigors of war. . . . [I]t's bad enough that men come home in body bags. Why do we need to put women in them as well?[379]

Do you agree? If not, how do you respond, and to which theories would you point? If you agree, which theories (if any) support Limbaugh's argument?

---

1. See Catharine A. MacKinnon, Feminism Unmodified: Discourses on Life and Law 16 (1987).
2. 477 U.S. 57 (1986).
3. 29 C.F.R. §1604.11(a)(1)-(3) (1980).
4. See, e.g., Heather Antechol & Deborah Cobb-Clark, The Changing Nature of Employment-Related Sexual Harassment: Evidence from the U.S. Federal Government, 1978-1994, 57 Indus. & Lab. Rel. Rev. 443 (2004) (44 percent of women and 19 percent of men had experienced harassment); Theresa M. Beiner, Gender Myths v. Working Realities: Using Social Science to Reformulate Sexual Harassment Law 1 (2004) (citing studies finding 40 percent to 80 percent); Joanna L. Grossman, The First Bite Is Free: Employer Liability for Sexual Harassment, 61 U. Pitt. L. Rev. 671, 673-674 (2000) (citing studies and case histories).
5. Joanna Grossman, The Culture of Compliance: The Final Triumph of Form Over Substance in Sexual Harassment Law, 26 Harv. Women's L.J. 3, 5-7 (2003) (citing surveys, studies, and cases showing little change in the prevalence of harassment over three decades).
6. U.S. Equal Employment Opportunity Comm'n, Sexual Harassment Charges: EEOC & FEPAs Combined: FY 1997–FY 2011, at http://www.eeoc.gov/eeoc/statistics/enforcement/sexual _harassment.cfm; Tresa Baldas, More Men Filing Workplace Lawsuits, Nat'l L.J., July 28, 2008, at A1. See also Tanya Kateri Hernandez, A Critical Race Feminism Empirical Research Project: Sexual Harassment and the Internal Complaints Black Box, 39 U.C. Davis L. Rev. 1235, 1255-1260 (2006); Tanya K. Hernandez, The Next Challenge in Sexual Harassment Reform: Racial Disparity, 23 Women's Rts. L. Rep. 227 (2002).
7. Jones v. Wesco Invs., Inc., 846 F.2d 1154, 1157 n.6 (8th Cir. 1988).
8. Baskerville v. Culligan Int'l Co., 50 F.3d 428, 431 (7th Cir. 1995).
9. See, e.g., Holman v. Indiana, 211 F.3d 399, 403 (7th Cir.) ("Title VII does not cover the 'equal opportunity' or 'bisexual' harasser, then, because such a person is not discriminating on the basis of sex. He is not treating one sex better (or worse) than the other; he is treating both sexes the same (albeit badly).").
10. McDonnell v. Cisneros, 84 F.3d 256, 260 (7th Cir. 1996) ("It would be exceedingly perverse if a male worker could buy his supervisors and his company immunity from Title VII liability by taking care to harass sexually an occasional male worker, although his preferred targets were female.").
11. 422 F.3d 840 (9th Cir. 2005).

12. 132 P.3d 211 (Cal. 2006).

13. Lyle v. Warner Bros. Television Prods., 117 Cal. App. 4th 1164, 1175 (2004).

14. Policy Guidance on Employer Liability Under Title VII for Sexual Favoritism (Jan. 12, 1990), No. N-915-048, 2 EEOC Compliance Manual §615.

15. 115 P.3d 77 (Cal. 2005).

16. Id. at 82.

17. See Man Wins Sex-Harassment Suit Against a Woman, N.Y. Times, May 21, 1993, at A12.

18. Mackenzie v. Miller Brewing Co., 623 N.W.2d 739 (Wis. 2001).

19. See Steiner v. Showboat Operating Co., 25 F.3d 1459, 1464 (9th Cir. 1994).

20. See Oncale v. Sundowner Offshore Servs., Inc., 523 U.S. 75, 81 (1998).

21. See Jeremy A. Blumenthal, The Reasonable Woman Standard: A Meta-Analytic Review of Gender Differences in Perceptions of Sexual Harassment, 22 Law & Hum. Behav. 33, 71 (1998); Richard L. Wiener et al., Perceptions of Sexual Harassment: The Effects of Gender, Legal Standard, and Ambivalent Sexism, 21 Law & Hum. Behav. 71 (1997).

22. Caroline A. Forrell & Donna M. Mathews, A Law of Her Own: The Reasonable Woman as a Measure of Man 35-58 (2000).

23. See Linda Kelly Hill, The Feminist Misspeak of Sexual Harassment, 57 Fla. L. Rev. 133, 172-180 (2005) (arguing that the "reasonable woman" standard raises concerns of "victimization, essentialism, and judicial neutrality").

24. Theresa Beiner, Gender Myths v. Working Realities: Using Social Science to Reformulate Sexual Harassment Law 57-59 (2004).

25. Barbara A. Gutek et al., The Utility of the Reasonable Woman Standard in Hostile Environment Sexual Harassment Cases: A Multimethod Multistudy Examination, 5 Psychol. Pub. Pol'y & L. Rev. 596, 623 (1999).

26. Gillian K. Hadfield, Rational Women: A Test for Sex-Based Harassment, 83 Cal. L. Rev. 1151, 1182, 1185-1186 (1995).

27. Louise Fitzgerald, Who Says? Legal Psychological Construction of Women's Resistance to Sexual Harassment, in Directions in Sexual Harassment Law 94, 102 (Catharine A. MacKinnon & Reva B. Siegel eds., 2004).

28. See Theresa M. Beiner, Sexy Dressing Revisited: Does Target Dress Play a Part in Sex Harassment Cases?, 14 Duke J. Gender L. & Pol'y 125, 149 (2007).

29. Loftin-Boggs v. City of Meridian, 633 F. Supp. 1323, 1327 (S.D. Miss. 1986), aff'd, 824 F.2d 971 (5th Cir. 1987).

30. See, e.g., Carr v. Allison Gas Turbine Div., Gen. Motors Corp., 32 F.3d 1007, 1011 (7th Cir. 1994) (plaintiff's vulgar language and dirty jokes could not justify a barrage of derogatory language, pranks, and graffiti); Spencer v. Gen. Elec. Co., 697 F. Supp. 204 (E.D. Va. 1988), aff'd, 894 F.2d 651 (4th Cir. 1990), overruled on other grounds by Farrar v. Hobby, 506 U.S. 103 (1992) (joining in milder forms of sexual horseplay that occurred in the office did not waive plaintiff's protection against sexual harassment).

31. See Beth A. Quinn, The Paradox of Complaining: Law, Humor, and Harassment in the Everyday Work World, 25 Law & Soc. Inquiry 1151, 1179-1181 (2000).

32. Highlander v. K.F.C. Nat'l Mgmt. Co., 805 F.2d 644 (6th Cir. 1986); Scott v. Sears, Roebuck & Co., 798 F.2d 210, 212-214 (7th Cir. 1986).

33. Wendy Pollack, Sexual Harassment: Women's Experience vs. Legal Definitions, 13 Harv. Women's L.J. 35, 72-73 (1990).

34. See Reed v. Shepard, 939 F.2d 484, 492 (7th Cir. 1991) (female police officer's receptiveness to co-workers' sexually suggestive jokes and activities because she wanted to be accepted by others on the police force was fatal to her sexual harassment claim).

35. Louise Fitzgerald et al., Why Didn't She Just Report Him? The Psychological and Legal Implications of Women's Responses to Sexual Harassment, 51 J. Soc. Issues 117, 134 (1995).

36. See, e.g., Janine Benedet, Hostile Environmental Sexual Harassment Claims and Unwelcome Influence of Rape Law, 3 Mich. J. Gender & L. 125, 166, 173-174 (1995).

37. Grace S. Ho, Not Quite Rights: How the Unwelcomeness Element in Sexual Harassment Law Undermines Title VII's Transformative Potential, 20 Yale J.L. & Feminism 13, 151 (2008) (quoting defense attorney).

38. Id.

39. See generally Susanne Baer, Dignity or Equality?: Responses to Workplace Harassment in European, German, and U.S. Law, in Directions in Sexual Harassment Law 582 (Catharine A. MacKinnon & Reva B. Siegel eds., 2004).

40. Wendy N. Davis, No Putting Up with Put Downs, AVA J., Feb. 2008, at 16; Martha Chamallas, Discrimination and Outrage: The Migration from Civil Rights to Tort Law, 48 Wm. & Mary L. Rev. 2115 (2007).

41. Workplace Bullying Inst., Results of the 2010 and 2007 WBI U.S. Workplace Bullying Survey, http://www.workplacebullying.org/wbiresearch/2010-wbi-national-survey.

42. See, e.g., Williams v. Banning, 72 F.3d 552, 555 (7th Cir. 1995); Grossman, The Culture of Compliance, supra note 5, at 9 n.25.

43. 524 U.S. 775.

44. 524 U.S. at 792, 802.

45. 524 U.S. 742, 748-749 (1998).

46. Pennsylvania State Police v. Suders, 542 U.S. 129 (2004).

47. Compare Robinson v. Sappington, 351 F.3d 317 (2003) (reassignment not a defense) with Sparks v. Reg'l Med. Ctr. Bd., 792 F. Supp. 735 (N.D. Ala. 1992) (reassignment a defense).

48. See cases cited in Joanna L. Grossman, The First Bite Is Free: Employer Liability for Sexual Harassment, 61 U. Pitt. L. Rev. 671, 699 (2000).

49. Anne Lawton, Operating in an Empirical Vacuum: The *Ellerth* and *Faragher* Affirmative Defense, 13 Colum. J. Gender & L. 197, 210 (2004). See also David Sherwyn et al., Don't Train Your Employees and Cancel Your "1-800" Harassment Hotline: An Empirical Examination and Correction of the Flaws in the Affirmative Defense to Sexual Harassment Charges, 69 Fordham L. Rev. 1265, 1304 (2001) (survey of 100 federal cases supports conclusion that in order to minimize liability, employers "should not engage in or should eliminate extensive preventive efforts such as expensive sexual harassment sensitivity training, or more particularly, harassment-reporting hotlines").

50. Vicki Schultz, The Sanitized Workplace, 112 Yale L.J. 2061, 2140 (2003); Hernandez, A Critical Race Feminism, supra note 6, at 1262-1268.

51. Matvia v. Bald Head Island Mgmt., Inc., 259 F.3d 261, 270 (4th Cir. 2001).

52. Marsicano v. American Soc'y of Safety Engineers, No. 97-C7819, 1998 WL 603128 (N.D. Ill.).

53. Fitzgerald, Why Didn't She Just Report Him, supra note 35, at 100.

54. See id. at 122-123 (describing the results of a study of state employees finding that 62 percent of women who reported sexual harassment experienced retaliation, with the most assertive responses often triggering the harshest response); see also Deborah L. Brake & Joanna L. Grossman, The Failure of Title VII as a Rights-Claiming System, 86 N.C. L. Rev. 859, 902-905 (2008) (summarizing retaliation data).

55. See Brake & Grossman, supra note 54, at 879-884 (analyzing the way in which prompt complaint doctrines interfere with the ability of discrimination victims to enforce substantive rights).

56. Sherwyn et al., supra note 49, at 1304.

57. Train Right Solutions, EE Compliance Practices Benchmarking (2006); Deborah L. Rhode, Social Research and Social Change: Meeting the Challenge of Gender Inequality and Sexual Abuse, 30 Harv. J.L. & Gender 11, 14 (2007).

58. See Grossman, The Culture of Compliance, supra note 5, at 61-63; Schultz, supra note 50, at 2140.

59. See Grossman, The Culture of Compliance, supra note 5, at 42-47; Susan Bisom Rapp, An Ounce of Prevention Is a Poor Substitute for a Pound of Cure: Confronting the Developing Jurisprudence of Education and Prevention in Employment Discrimination Law, 22 Berkeley J. Emp. & Lab. L. 1 (2001); Susan Sturm, Second Generation Employment Discrimination: A Structural Approach, 101 Colum. L. Rev. 458, 483 (2001).

60. Schultz, supra note 50, at 2065.

61. Id. at 2113-2116, 2156.

62. 760 F. Supp. 1486 (M.D. Fla. 1991).

63. Id. at 1542 (Appendix).

64. Id. at 1534-1536.

65. Schultz, supra note 50, at 2146, 2164.

66. See Eugene Volokh, What Speech Does "Hostile Work Environment" Restrict?, Sexual Harassment: Cases, Case Studies, and Commentary 180, 202 (Paul I. Weizer ed., 2002); Kingsley Browne, The Silenced Workplace: Employer Censorship Under Title VII, in Directions in Sexual Harassment Law, supra note 27, at 399.

67. Schultz, supra note 50, at 2129.

68. Office Romances Rarely Kept Secret, CNN.com, Feb. 12, 2008 (in Career Builder survey, 40 percent had dated a colleague, 29 percent had married one, and 27 percent had dated a superior); Mireya Navarro, Love the Job? What About Your Boss?, N.Y. Times, July 24, 2005, at A1 (summarizing

surveys finding over half had dated a colleague, one-fifth had dated a subordinate, and the vast majority preferred no dating policies).

69. Schultz, supra note 50, at 2126; see also Phred Dvorak et al., Firms Confront Boss-Subordinate Love Affairs, Wall St. J., Oct. 27, 2008; Leslie Wang, Boeing Chief Is Ousted After Admitting Affair, N.Y. Times, Mar. 8, 2005, at A1.

70. For a comprehensive description of the problem, including video clips, and resources to combat it, see http://www.stopstreetharassment.org.

71. Olatokunbo Olukemi Laniya, Street Smut: Gender, Media, and the Legal Power Dynamics of Street Harassment, or "Hey Sexy" and Other Verbal Ejaculations, 14 Colum. J. Gender & L. 91 (2005); Cynthia Grant Bowman, Street Harassment and the Informal Ghettoization of Women, 106 Harv. L. Rev. 517 (1993).

72. Details of the SEPTA campaign can be found at http://www.stopstreetharassment.org/2013/04/septaads.

73. EEOC v. Champion Int'l Corp., No. 93C20279, 1995 WL 488333, at *2 (N.D. Ill.).

74. Orlando Patterson, Race, Gender and Liberal Fallacies, N.Y. Times, Oct. 10, 1991, at A15.

75. Mittl v. N.Y. State Div. of Human Rights, 794 N.E.2d 660 (N.Y. 2003); see also Kahn v. Objective Solutions, Int'l, 86 F. Supp. 2d 377 (S.D.N.Y. 2000).

76. See Good News Emp. Ass'n v. Hicks, 223 Fed. Appx. 734, 784 (9th Cir. 2007).

77. These examples are taken from Laura Rosenbury, Work Wives, 36 Harv. J.L. & Gender 345 (2013).

78. Id.

79. Gerald D. Skoning, 2000 Ten Wackiest Employment Lawsuits, Nat'l L. R., Apr. 2, 2001, at A21.

80. See Holland v. Dep't of the Air Force, 31 F.3d 1118 (Fed. Cir. 1994).

81. 20 U.S.C. §1681 (2012).

82. See Franklin v. Gwinnett County Public Schools, 503 U.S. 60 (1992).

83. 524 U.S. 274 (1998).

84. Deborah L. Rhode, Sex in Schools: Who's Minding the Adults, in Directions in Sexual Harassment Law, at 290, 297 (Catharine A. MacKinnon & Reva B. Siegel eds., 1999).

85. Id.

86. See American Association of University Women Educational Foundation, "The Failure of Title VII as a Rights-Claiming System" Hostile Hallways: Bullying, Teasing, and Sexual Harassment in School 4, 7 (2001).

87. Laurie LeClair, Note, Sexual Harassment Between Peers Under Title VII and Title IX: Why Girls Just Can't Wait to Be Working Women, 16 Vt. L. Rev. 303, 325-327 (1991).

88. See American Association of University Women, Crossing the Line: Sexual Harassment at School (2011).

89. American Association of University Women, Drawing the Line: Sexual Harassment on Campus (2005).

90. John L. Pulley, Risk Management Lawyer Says Boom in Sexual Harassment Lawsuits Should Make Colleges Handle Cases Carefully, Chron. of Higher Educ., Sept. 28, 2005 available at http://jobs.chronicle.com/article/Risk-Management-Lawyer-Says/120170/.

91. 526 U.S. 629 (1999).

92. Id. at 633.

93. Id. at 648.

94. Guy W. Horsley, quoted in Robin Wilson, William and Mary Seeks to Shift Liability for Damages to Professor in Federal Sexual Harassment Case, Chron. of Higher Educ., June 9, 1995, at A20.

95. 500 F.3d 1170 (10th Cir. 2007).

96. 555 U.S. 246 (2009).

97. Resolution, OCR Docket #15-09-6002, available at http://www2.ed.gov/about/offices/list/ocr/docs/investigations/15096002-a.pdf.

98. 20 U.S.C. §1092f (2012).

99. Office for Civil Rights, Dep't of Educ., Dear Colleague Letter, Apr. 4, 2011, available at http://www.whitehouse.gov/sites/default/files/dear_colleague_sexual_violence.pdf.

100. On litigation in the wake of Gebser and Davis, see Nancy Chi Cantalupo, Burying Our Heads in the Sand: Lack of Knowledge, Knowledge Avoidance, and the Persistent Problem of Campus Peer Sexual Violence, 43 Loy. U. Chi. L.J. 205 (2011).

101. Texas House to Cheerleaders: Don't Shake It, Reuters, May 5, 2005, at http://www.unexplained-mysteries.com/forum/index.php?showtopic=40043 (describing legislation that would empower the

Texas Education Agency power to sanction schools that allow "overtly sexually suggestive" routines at athletic events).

102. Compare Nadine Strossen, Defending Pornography: Free Speech, Sex, and the Fight for Women's Rights (1995) with Mari J. Matsuda et al., Words That Wound: Critical Race Theory, Assaultive Speech, and the First Amendment (1993).

103. Saxe v. State Coll. Area School Dist., 240 F.3d 200 (3d Cir. 2001); see also UWM Post, Inc. v. Bd. of Regents of Univ. of Wisconsin, 774 F. Supp. 1163 (E.D. Wis. 1991) (striking down a Wisconsin code that prohibited conduct that "create[s] an intimidating, hostile, or demeaning environment for education").

104. Silva v. Univ. of New Hampshire, 888 F. Supp. 293 (D.N.H. 1994).

105. See Regina v. Keegstra, 3 S.C.R. 697 (1990).

106. Edward Greer, What's Wrong with Faculty-Student Sex? Response I, 47 J. Legal Educ. 437, 438 (1997).

107. Dan Blatt, quoted in University of Virginia Considers Wide Ban on Intimate Teacher-Student Ties, N.Y. Times, Apr. 14, 1993, at A22.

108. Sara Rimer, Love on Campus: Trying to Set Rules for the Emotions, N.Y. Times, Oct. 1, 2003, at A21 (quoting Berkeley student newspaper editorial and Berkeley student journalist Virginia Griffey).

109. Tanya Shevitz, Dating Rule Was Defined at Cal, S.F. Chron., Dec. 3, 2001, at A25 (quoting Barry Dan, Professor of Sociology).

110. Jane Gallop, Feminism and Harassment Policy, Academe, Sept.-Oct. 1994, at 16, 22. See also Jane Gallop, Feminist Accused of Sexual Harassment 41-43 (1997).

111. Sherry Young, Getting to Yes: The Case Against Banning Consensual Relationships in Higher Education, 4 Am. U. J. Gender & L. 269, 298, 302 (1996).

112. Robin L. West, The Difference in Women's Hedonic Lives: A Phenomenological Critique of Feminist Legal Theory, 3 Wis. Women's L.J. 81, 109-111 (1987).

113. See surveys discussed in Caroline Forrell, What's Wrong with Faculty-Student Sex? The Law School Context, 47 J. Legal Educ. 47 (1997).

114. Rhode, Sex in Schools, supra note 84, at 296.

115. Forrell, supra note 113; see also Carol Sanger, Consensual Sex and the Limits of the Law, in Directions in Sexual Harassment Law, supra note 27, at 86-87; Neal Hutchens, The Legal Effect of College and University Policies Prohibiting Romantic Relationships between Students and Professors, 32 J.L. & Educ. 411 (2003); Paul M. Secunda, Getting to the Nexus of the Matter: A Sliding Scale Approach to Faculty-Student Consensual Relationship Policies in Higher Education, 55 Syracuse L. Rev. 55 (2004).

116. See www.wm.edu/about/administration/provost/documents/consensual_relations.pdf (rev. Apr. 2008).

117. Thomas J. De Loughry, Colleges Criticized for Response to Offensive Electronic Speech, Chron. of Higher Educ., Dec. 1, 1995, available at courses.cs.vt.edu/cs3604/lib/Censorship/Offensive.Speech.html.

118. See Williams v. Bd. of Regents, 477 F.3d 1282 (11th Cir. 2007).

119. William Blackstone, 1 Commentaries on the Laws of England 432-433 (1765).

120. Reva B. Siegel, "The Rule of Love": Wife Beating as Prerogative and Privacy, 105 Yale L.J. 2117, 2118 (1996).

121. Id. at 2120.

122. Id. at 2137-2139.

123. Evan Stark, Re-Presenting Woman Battering: From Battered Woman Syndrome to Coercive Control, 58 Alb. L. Rev. 973, 992-993 (1995). For further historical accounts of violence against women in Anglo-American social life and efforts to control it, see Linda Gordon, Heroes of Their Own Lives: The Politics and History of Family Violence (1988); Elizabeth Pleck, Domestic Tyranny: The Making of Social Policy Against Family Violence from Colonial Times to the Present (1987).

124. Margaret E. Johnson, Balancing Liberty, Dignity, and Safety: The Impact of Domestic Violence Lethality Screening, 32 Cardozo L. Rev. 519, 526 (2010); Jennifer Langhinrichsen-Rohling, Top 10 Greatest "Hits": Important Findings and Future Directions for Intimate Partner Violence Research, 20 J. of Interpersonal Violence 108, 113 (2005).

125. Hilary G. Harding & Marie Helwig-Larsen, Perceived Risk for Future Intimate Partner Violence Among Women in Domestic Violence Shelter, 24 J. Fam. Violence 75, 76 (2009) (quarter); National Center for Injury Prevention and Control, Centers for Disease Control, The National Intimate Partner and Sexual Violence Survey, 2010 Summary Report 1, 39 (2010) (a third experienced some violence; a quarter experienced severe violence).

126. The National Intimate Partner and Sexual Violence Survey, supra note 125, at 39.

127. Id. at 29.

128. Kimberly Bailey, Lost in Translation: Domestic Violence, "The Personal is Political," and the Criminal Justice System, 100 J. Criminal Law & Criminology 1255, 1281-1282 (2010).

129. See Callie Marie Rennison & Sarah Welchans, Bureau of Justice Statistics, Special Report: Intimate Partner Violence (NCJ 178247), May 2000, at 1, available at http://www.ojp.usdoj.gov/bjs/pub/pdf/ipv.pdf.

130. Jacqueline C. Campbell, Prediction of Homicide of and by Battered Women in Assessing Dangerousness: Violence by Batterers and Child Abusers 85, 86, (Jacqueline C. Cambell ed., 2d ed., 2007).

131. Marie Tessier, Intimate Violence Remains a Big Killer of Women, Women's eNews, July 25, 2008, available at http://www.womensenews.org/article.cfm/dyn/aid/3683; Elizabeth M. Schneider, Domestic Violence Law Reform in the Twenty-First Century: Looking Back and Looking Forward, 42 Fam. L.Q. 353, 361 (2008).

132. Patricia Tjaden & Nancy Thoennes, Full Report of the Prevalence, Incidence, and Consequences of Violence Against Women, findings from the National Violence Against Women Survey, Nov. 2000, available at http://www.ncjrs.org.

133. Id. at 37.

134. See Robert Hampton et al., Domestic Violence in the African American Community—An Analysis of Social and Structural Features, 9 Violence Against Women 533, 534 (2003).

135. Sara R. Benson, Failure to Arrest: A Pilot Study of Police Response to Domestic Violence in Rural Illinois, 17 Am. J. Gender Soc. Pol'y & L. 685, 697-699 (2009).

136. Angelo M. Moe & Myrtle Bell, Abject Economics: The Effects of Battering and Violence on Women's Work and Employability, 10 Violence Against Women 29, 35-36 (2004) (citing surveys such as those finding that between one- and two-thirds of women on welfare experience violence).

137. See Noel A. Cazenave & Murray A. Straus, Race, Class, Network Embeddedness, and Family Violence: A Search for Potent Support Systems, 10 J. Comp. Family Studies 281, 336 (1979).

138. Tjaden & Thoennes, supra note 132, at 30.

139. Amy Farmer & Jill Tiefenthaler, Explaining the Recent Decline in Domestic Violence, 21 Contemp. Econ. Pol'y 158 (Apr. 2003).

140. Laura Dugan, Explaining the Decline in Intimate Partner Homicide: The Effects of Changing Domesticity, Women's Status, and Domestic Violence Resources, 3 Homicide Stud. 187 (1999).

141. Michelle Chen, The Economic Crisis Hits Home, Ms., Fall 2010, at 15; Justine Andronici & Debra Katz, Save Your Life, Save Your Livelihood, Ms., Spring 2010, at 43.

142. VAWA was passed as part of the Violent Crime Control and Law Enforcement Act of 1994, Pub. L. No. 103-322, 108 Stat. 1796 (codified as amended in scattered sections of 8 U.S.C., 16 U.S.C., 18 U.S.C., 28 U.S.C., and 42 U.S.C.).

143. Tessier, Intimate Violence Remains a Big Killer of Women, supra note 131 (citing studies by the National Network to End Domestic Violence); Elizabeth M. Schneider, Domestic Violence Law Reform in the Twenty-First Century, supra note 131, at 361.

144. Michelle Chen, The Economic Crisis Hits Home, supra note 141 at 15.

145. Atinuke O. Awoyomi, The State-Created Danger in Domestic Violence Cases: Do We Have a Solution in Okin v. Village of Cornwall-on-Hudson Police Department?, 20 Colum. J. Gender & L., 1, 9 (2010).

146. See Schneider, Domestic Violence Law Reform in the Twenty-First Century, supra note 131, at 355; Emily J. Sack, Battered Women and the State: The Struggle for the Future of Domestic Violence Policy, 2004 Wis. L. Rev. 1657, 1671.

147. Keith Guzik, The Forces of Conviction: The Power and Practice of Mandatory Prosecution upon Misdemeanor Domestic Battery Suspects, 32 Law & Soc. Inquiry 41, 48 (2007); Nancy R. Rhodes & Eva Baranoff McKenzie, Why Do Battered Women Stay?: Three Decades of Research, 3 Aggression and Violent Behavior 391 (1998). See also National Coalition Against Domestic Violence, Statistics, available at http://www.ojp.usdoj.gov/bjs/intimate/report.htm (finding 15 percent of women want to protect batterers).

148. Bailey, Lost in Translation, supra note 128, at 1257.

149. Guzik, supra note 147, at 49.

150. Linda K. Bledsoe et al., Understanding the Impact of Intimate Partner Violence Mandatory Reporting Law, 10 Violence Against Women 536, 544 (2004).

151. Christopher D. Maxwell et al., National Institute of Justice, Research in Brief: The Effects of Arrest on Intimate Partner Violence: New Evidence from the Spousal Assault Replication Program (2001).

152. Bailey, supra note 128, at 1273; Benson, supra note 135, at 698-700.

153. For an overview, see Sally F. Goldfarb, Reconceiving Civil Protection Orders for Domestic Violence: Can Law Help End the Abuse Without Ending the Relationship?, 29 Cardozo L. Rev. 1511, 1537 (2008).

154. Leigh Goodmark, Autonomy Feminism: An Anti-Essentialist Critique of Mandatory Interventions in Domestic Violence Cases, 37 Fla. State U. L. Rev. 1, 35 (2009).

155. See Guzik, supra note 147, at 44; Deborah Epstein et al., Transforming Aggressive Prosecution Policies: Prioritizing Victims' Long-Term Safety in the Prosecution of Domestic Violence Cases, 12 Am. U. J. Gender Soc. Pol'y & L. 465, 476-477 (2003).

156. Tamara L. Kuennen, Analyzing the Impact of Coercion on Domestic Violence Victims; How Much Is Too Much?, 22 Berkeley J. Gender, L. & Justice 2, 25 (2007).

157. Goldfarb, supra note 153, at 1501-1505, 1523 (citing evidence that only a small minority of women subject to physical assault obtain protective orders, and that many women want protection without ending the relationship).

158. Michael A. Rodriguez et al., Mandatory Reporting of Intimate Violence to Police: Views of Physicians in California, 89 Am. J. Pub. Health 575, 577 (1999) (reporting that 60 percent of physicians would not report if the patient objected because notification could worsen the violence).

159. Schneider, Domestic Violence Law Reform in the Twenty-First Century, supra note 131, at 358; Donna Coker, Shifting Power for Battered Women: Law, Material Resources, and Poor Women of Color, 33 U.C. Davis L. Rev. 1009 (2000).

160. Epstein, supra note 155, at 486-498.

161. Hillary Potter, Battle Cries: Black Women and Intimate Partner Abuse 84 (2008); Alisa Smith, It's My Decision, Isn't It?, 6 Violence Against Women 1384, 1395-1396 (2000).

162. Smith, supra note 161 , at 1395-1396.

163. Sack, supra note 146, at 1722.

164. See Jeannie Suk, At Home in the Law: How the Domestic Violence Revolution Is Transforming Privacy (2009).

165. Margaret E. Johnson, Redefining Harm, Reimagining Remedies, and Reclaiming Domestic Violence Law, 42 U.C. Davis L. Rev. 1107, 1133-1137 (2009).

166. Id. at 1113, 1121.

167. Francis X. Clines, Judge's Domestic Violence Ruling Creates an Outcry in Kentucky, N.Y. Times, Jan. 8, 2002, at A14 (quoting Thornton). For other examples, see Debora L. Threedy, Legal Archeology and Feminist Legal Theory: A Case Study of Gender and Domestic Violence, 29 Women's Rts. L. Rep. 171, 189 (2008).

168. Clines, supra note 167, at A14 (quoting Carol Jordan, director of the Kentucky Governor's Office of Child Abuse and Domestic Violence).

169. Id. at A14 (quoting Sherry Currens, Executive Director of the Kentucky Domestic Violence Association).

170. United States v. Morrison, 529 U.S. 598 (2000). The case arose from a sexual assault by two college football players. One of them, after raping the victim, told her that "You better not have any fucking diseases." He later announced in the dormitory's dining room that "I like to get girls drunk and fuck the shit out of them."

171. 545 U.S. 748 (2005).

172. Id. at 760; Id. at 772 (Souter, J., concurring in the judgment); Id. at 784-785 (Stevens, J., dissenting).

173. Jessica Lenahan (Gonzales) et al. v. United States, Report No. 80/11, Case 12.626, paragraphs 5 & 60 (Merits, July 21, 2011).

174. Id. ¶201.

175. Elizabeth Olson, Though Many Are Stalked, Few Report It, Study Finds, N.Y. Times, Feb. 5, 2009, at A1.

176. See Family Violence Prevention Fund, The Facts on the Workplace and Domestic Violence, available at http://endabuse.org/userfiles/file/Workplace/Workplace.pdf; Marie Tessier, More States Give Abuse Victims Right to Time Off, Jan. 18, 2005, available at www.womensenews.org.

177. Julie Leopold, Execs Aware of Domestic Violence Costs, Feb. 3, 2003, available at www .womensenews.org; Angela M. Moe & Myrtle Bell, Abject Economics: The Effects of Battering and Violence on Women's Work and Employability, 10 Violence Against Women 29, 34 (2004).

178. Alison Bowen, Battered New Yorker Sues Employer for Firing Her, July 26, 2007, available at www.womensenews.org.

179. See She's Fired For His Abuse, In Brief, NOW Legal Defense and Education Fund, Winter 2000, available at http://web.archive.org/web/20000816095919/http://www.nowldef.org/html/news/ib/win00.shtml.

180. See Apessos v. Memorial Press Group, 15 Mass. L. Rptr. 322, 2002 WL 31324115 (Mass. Super. 2002) (rejecting defendant's motion to dismiss a claim for wrongful termination).

181. 775 So. 2d 753 (Ala. 2000).

182. Id.

183. See Laila Karamally, Companies Try to Bring Domestic Violence Issues into the Open, 83 Workforce Mgmt. 60 (Sept. 2004).

184. Andronici & Katz, Save Your Life, Save Your Livelihood, supra note 141, at 44.

185. Jennifer Hahn, Tracking the Abusers, Ms., Summer 2008, at 18 (noting that such devices are widely used to track parolees and sex offenders but only seven states permit it for domestic violence cases).

186. Tamar Lewin, Zero Tolerance Policy Is Challenged, N.Y. Times, July 11, 2001, at A10; see also Lenora M. Lapidus, Doubly Victimized: Housing Discrimination Against Victims of Domestic Violence, 11 Am. U. J. Gender Soc. Pol'y & L. 377, 378-382 (2003); see also Bouley v. Young-Sabourin, discussed in Vivian Berger, Don't Evict Victims, Nat'l L.J., June 6, 2005, at B3.

187. Susan A. Reif & Lisa Krisher, Subsidized Housing and the Unique Needs of Domestic Violence Victims, 34 Clearinghouse Rev. 20, 28 (2000); Lapidus, supra note 186, at 384-386.

188. Brad Paul, Women and Children Last, Ms., Fall 2006, at 18-19.

189. See Nicholson v. Scoppetta, 820 N.E.2d 840 (N.Y. 2004) (holding that a policy of removing children from their mother's custody was not justified where the only allegation of neglect was that the child witnessed the mother's abuse; the reasonableness of the mother's action must be considered in light of all the circumstances).

190. See American Law Institute, Principles of the Law of Family Dissolution: Analysis and Recommendations, §2.11, and Comment (c) to §2.11, at 255-256, 261-267 (2002).

191. Schneider, Domestic Violence Law Reform in the Twenty-First Century, supra note 131, at 360 (describing inadequate consideration of violence in custody cases); Leigh Goodmark, When Is a Battered Women Not a Battered Woman? When She Fights Back, 20 Yale J.L. and Feminism 75, 116 (2008) (describing judicial belief that women fabricate claims to gain custody leverage); Joan S. Meier, Domestic Violence, Child Custody, and Child Protection: Understanding Judicial Resistance and Imagining the Solutions, 11 Am. U. J. Gender Soc. Pol'y & L. 657, 673-674 & n.50 (2003) (citing cases); Wellesley Center for Women, Battered Mothers Speak Out: A Human Rights Report on Domestic Violence and Child Custody in the Massachusetts Family Courts (2002), available at http://www.wcwonline.org/wrn/batteredreport.html (women claiming abuse characterized as unreasonable or "hysterical").

192. Sack, supra note 146, at 1684. See also The "Failure to Protect" Working Group, Charging Battered Mothers with "Failure to Protect": Still Blaming the Victim, 27 Fordham Urb. L.J. 849, 849-857 (2000); Family Violence Prevention Fund, The Case for Violence Prevention, available at www.enddnabuse.org/programs.

193. Shelby A. D. Moore, Understanding the Connection Between Domestic Violence, Crime, and Poverty: How Welfare Reform May Keep Battered Women from Leaving Abusive Relationships, 12 Tex. J. Women & L. 451, 484 (2003).

194. See Dorothy E. Roberts, Mothers Who Fail to Protect Their Children: Accounting for Private and Public Responsibility, in Mother Troubles: Rethinking Contemporary Maternal Dilemmas 31 (Julia E. Hanigsberg & Sara Ruddick eds., 1999).

195. The Uniform Child Custody Jurisdiction and Enforcement Act (UCCJEA) generally favors the "home state" of the child and custodial parent. Other relevant statutes are the Parental Kidnapping Prevention Act (PKPA), and the full faith and credit requirements of the Violence Against Women Act (VAWA).

196. Hague Convention of October 25, 1980, on the Civil Aspects of Child Abduction, Article 13(b).

197. Merle H. Weiner, Using Article 20, 38 Fam. L.Q. 583 (2004).

198. See discussion in Chapter 5, at pp. 577-580; Deanna Kwong, Removing Barriers for Battered Immigrant Women: A Comparison of Immigrant Protections Under VAWA I & II, 17 Berkeley Women's L.J. 137 (2002); Sarah M. Wood, VAWA's Unfinished Business: The Immigrant Women Who Fall Through the Cracks, 11 Duke J. Gender L. & Pol'y 141 (2004).

199. See Joshua Dressler, Understanding Criminal Law §31.07[A], [B], at 527-528 (3d ed. 2001).

200. Victoria Nourse, Passion's Progress: Modern Law Reform and the Provocation Defense, 106 Yale L.J. 1331, 1345 (1997).

201. Ruth E. Fleury et al., When Ending the Relationship Does Not End the Violence, 6 Violence Against Women 1363, 1365 (2000).

202. Myrna S. Raeder, The Admissibility of Prior Acts of Domestic Violence: Simpson and Beyond, 69 S. Cal. L. Rev. 1463, 1477 (1996).

203. Mike Weiss, Mayhem Shadowed Therapist's Life: Expert on Relationships Examines Why Many of His Ended Badly, San Fran. Chron., May 22, 2001, at A1.

204. See Christine R. Harris, A Review of Sex Differences in Sexual Jealousy, Including Self-Report Data, Psychosociological Responses, Interpersonal Violence, and Morbid Jealousy, 2 Personality & Soc. Psychol. Rev. 102 (2003).

205. Nick Madigan, Wife Testifies She Was "In a Fog" Just Before Her Car Struck Husband, N.Y. Times, Feb. 8, 2003, at A11; Ron Nissamov, Parham Shares Views on Harris, Houston Chron., Feb. 16, 2003, at 33.

206. Lucas Wall, Common Link in Uncommon Lives: Clara Harris: Mother of Twins Kept to Herself, Houston Chron., Aug. 4, 2002, at 37; Ruth Rendon, "I Could Kill Him," Harris Told Teen: Defense Says Words Taken Out of Context, Houston Chron., Jan. 17, 2003, at 36.

207. No. 94-CR-0943 (Balt. Cty. Ct., Oct. 17, 1994).

208. Quoted in Catharine A. MacKinnon, Sex Equality 730-731 (2d ed. 2007).

209. See Minn. Stat. Ann §609.185(6) (West 2012) (defining murder in the first degree as, among other things, causing "death of a human being while committing domestic abuse, when the perpetrator has engaged in a past pattern of domestic abuse upon the victim or upon another family or household member and the death occurs under circumstances manifesting an extreme indifference to human life").

210. Kirstin Cole, Barbara Sheehan on What Happened the Day of the Shooting, PIX11. com, Oct. 28, 2011.

211. Lenore E.A. Walker, Battered Women Syndrome and Self-Defense, 6 Notre Dame J.L. Ethics & Pub. Pol'y 321, 327-328 (1992).

212. See Walter Steele & Christine Sigman, Reexamining the Doctrine of Self-Defense to Accommodate Battered Women, 18 Am. J. Crim. L. 169, 175-180 (1991).

213. See Charles Patrick Ewing, Battered Women Who Kill: Psychological Self-Defense as Legal Justification 23-40 (1987).

214. Goodmark, When Is a Battered Women Not a Battered Woman?, supra note 191, at 96-98.

215. Id. at 102.

216. Id.; Janice L. Ristock, No More Secrets: Violence in Lesbian Relationships 99 (2002); Adele M. Morrison, Queering Domestic Violence to Straighten out Criminal Law: What Might Happen When Queer Theory and Practice Meet Criminal Law's "Conventional" Responses to Domestic Violence, 13 S. Cal. L. & Women's Stud. 8, 147 (2003); Sheila M. Seelau & Eric P. Seelau, Gender-Role Stereotypes and Perceptions of Heterosexual, Gay, and Lesbian Domestic Violence, 20 J. Fam. Violence 363, 363 (2005).

217. David L. Faigman & Amy J. Wright, The Battered Woman's Syndrome in the Age of Science, 39 Ariz. L. Rev. 67, 68 (1997).

218. Goodmark, supra note 191, at 120-122; Alafair S. Burke, Rational Actors, Self-Defense and Duress: Making Sense, Not Syndrome out of the Battered Woman, 81 N.C. L. Rev. 212, 230-247 (2002); Adele M. Morrison, Changing the Domestic Violence (Dis)course: Moving Away from White Victim to Multi-Cultural Survivor, 39 U.C. Davis L. Rev. 1061 (2006).

219. Joan Krause, Distorted Reflections of Women Who Kill: A Response to Professor Dressler, 4 Ohio State J. Crim. L. 555, 563 (2007); Burke, supra note 218, at 266.

220. Elizabeth Leland, Abused Wife's Sentence Commuted, Charlotte Observer, July 8, 1989, at B1.

221. See Burke, supra note 218.

222. See United States v. Morrison, 529 U.S. 598 (2000).

223. Catharine A. MacKinnon, Disputing Male Sovereignty: On United States v. Morrison, 114 Harv. L. Rev. 135, 170 (2002).

224. In re R-A, 22 I & N Dec. 906 (A.G. 2001; B.I.A. 1999).

225. See also Aguirre-Cervantes v. INS, 242 F.3d 1169 (9th Cir. 2001) (overturning Board of Immigration Appeals and granting asylum to a woman who, along with other members of her immediate family, had been abused by her father).

226. See Andrea Binder, Gender and the "Membership in a Particular Social Group" Category of the 1951 Refugee Convention, 10 Colum. J. Gender & L. 167 (2001).

227. L.R. v. United States (B.I.A. 2010), discussed in Julia Preston, Asylum Granted to Mexican Woman in Case Setting Standard on Domestic Abuse, N.Y. Times, Aug. 13, 2010, at A14 and Elsa M.

Bullard, Insufficient Government Protection; The Inescapable Element in Domestic Violence Asylum Cases, 95 Minn. L. Rev. 1867, 1867-1868 (2010).

228. Amanda Blanck, Domestic Violence as a Basis for Asylum Status: A Human Rights Based Approach, 22 Women's Rts. L. Rep. 47, 72 (2001).

229. Suzanne Batchelor, Programs for Batterers Changing Their Focus, Jan. 1, 2006, available at www.womensenews.org (quoting Shelly Jackson).

230. Molly Dragiewicz, Equality with a Vengeance: Men's Rights Groups, Battered Women, and Antifeminist Backlash (2011).

231. See In re Lamb, 776 P.2d 765 (Cal. 1989).

232. Cole, supra note 210. See also Dan Bilefsky, Queens Woman Testifies She Killed Her Husband in Self-Defense, N.Y. Times, Sept. 19, 2011, available at http://www.nytimes.com/2011/09/20/nyregion/at-murder-trial-barbara-sheehan-testifies-she-killed-her-husband-in-self-defense.html. See also Bilefsky's follow-up articles on Oct. 6 and Oct. 12, 2011.

233. Frank Rich, Naked Capitalists, N.Y. Times Mag., May 20, 2001, at 51.

234. Natasha Vargas-Cooper, Hard Core, Atlantic, Jan./Feb. 2011, available at http://www.the-atlantic.com/magagazine/print/2011/01/hard-core.

235. 413 U.S. 15 (1973).

236. Deborah L. Rhode, Speaking of Sex: The Denial of Gender Equality 130-135 (1997).

237. Catharine A. MacKinnon, Toward a Feminist Theory of the State 205 (1989).

238. 89 D.L.R.4th 449 (S.C.C. 1992).

239. Id. at 488.

240. Nadine Strossen, A Feminist Critique of "the" Feminist Critique of Pornography, 79 Va. L. Rev. 1099, 1145-1146 (1993).

241. International Center for Missing and Exploited Children, Child Pornography: Model Legislation and Global Review (6th ed. 2010).

242. The Science Behind Pornography Addiction, Hearing on S. 2056, 108th Cong. (2004).

243. Id.; Report of the American Psychological Association Task Force on the Sexualization of Girls 29, 31, 34 (2006).

244. Pamela Paul, The Porn Factor, Time, Jan. 19, 2004, at 99.

245. Janet Hinson Shope, When Words Are Not Enough: The Search for the Effect of Pornography on Abused Women, 10 Violence Against Women 56, 67-68 (2004).

246. Pamela Paul, The Porn Factor, Time, Jan. 19, 2004, at 99; Clay Calvert, The First Amendment, the Media, and Cultural Wars: Eight Important Lessons from 2004 About Speech, Censorship, Science, and Public Policy, 41 Cal. W. L. Rev. 325, 344 (2005).

247. Carlin Meyer, Sex, Sin, and Women's Liberation: Against Porn Suppression, 72 Tex. L. Rev. 1097 (1994).

248. David Cole, Playing by Pornography's Rules: The Regulation of Sexual Expression, 143 U. Pa. L. Rev. 111, 116 (1994).

249. See Mary C. Dunlap, Sexual Speech and the State: Putting Pornography in Its Place, 17 Golden Gate U. L. Rev. 359 (1987).

250. Brad Armstrong, Porn Star, in Gig: Americans Talk About Their Jobs at the Turn of the Millennium 359, 364 (John Bowe et al. eds., 2000).

251. Michael Kimmel, Guyland 173, 177, 188 (2008).

252. Vargas-Cooper, supra note 234; Bridget J. Crawford, Toward a Third-Wave Feminist Legal Theory: Young Women, Pornography and the Praxis of Pleasure, 14 Mich. J. Gender & Law 99, 139-152 (2007); Jeffrey G. Sherman, Love Speech: The Social Utility of Pornography, 47 Stan. L. Rev. 661 (1995).

253. Reno v. ACLU, 521 U.S. 844 (1997).

254. Ashcroft v. ACLU, 542 U.S. 656 (2004); ACLU v. Gonzales, 478 F. Supp. 775 (E.D. Pa. 2007).

255. 539 U.S. 194 (2003).

256. Tony Mauro, Virtual Reality Check, American Lawyer, Dec. 2001, at 70 (quoting Justice Scalia).

257. 535 U.S. 234 (2002).

258. United States v. Williams, 553 U.S. 285 (2008).

259. United States v. Irey, 612 F.3d 1160 (11th Cir. 2010) (en banc) (reversing a district court's sentence of 17 years for having sex with children and distributing the images and imposing a 30-year sentence). For other examples and a critique, see Kathryn A. Kimball, Losing Our Soul: Judicial Discretion in Sentencing Child Pornography Offenders, 63 Fla. L. Rev. 1515 (2011).

260. Dina McLeod, Section 2259 Restitution Claims and Child Pornography Possession, 109 Mich. L. Rev. 1327 (2011).

261. 18 U.S.C. §2259 (2012).

262. McLeod, supra note 260, at 1342 (noting that each year there are about 200 victims of child pornography and 3,000 prosecutions for possession, and that some offenders collect thousands of images).

263. Jacob Carpenter, East Naples Man's Life Sentence for Child Porn Too Harsh, Attorney Says, Naplesnews.com, Nov. 3, 2011.

264. In re Boudreau, 815 So. 2d 76 (La. 2002) (the models were of legal age in Norway).

265. Jane Bailey & Mouna Hanna, The Gendered Dimensions of Sexting: Assessing the Applicability of Canada's Child Pornography Provision, Canadian Journal of Women & Law, 405, 409-410 (2011) (reviewing surveys). Tamar Lewin, Rethinking Sex Offender Laws for Youth: Showing Off Online, N.Y. Times, Mar. 21, 2010, available at http://www.nytimes.com/2010/03/21/us/21sexting.html?pagewanted=all; see also Andrea Lenhart, Teens and Sexting (2009).

266. Bailey & Hanna, supra note 265, at 413-414 (2011).

267. Sean D. Hamill, Students Sue Prosecutors in Cellphone Photos Case, N.Y. Times, Mar. 26, 2009, at A18. (quoting Witold J. Walczak).

268. Comments of Michal McAlexander, Chief Deputy, Prosecutor's Office, Allen County, PA, in Racy Teen Messaging Could Be Illegal, Talk of the Nation, NPR, Feb. 18, 2009.

269. 598 F.3d 139 (3d Cir. 2010). The class would have required the student to write an essay about what was wrong with what she did.

270. M. Gigi Durham, The Lolita Effect: The Media Sexualization of Young Girls and What We Can Do About It (2008).

271. Lenhart, supra note 265; Alex Morris, They Know What Boys Want, N.Y. Mag. Jan. 30, 2011, available at http://nymag.com/news/features/70977/; Jim Hoffman, Girl's Nude Photo and Altered Life, N.Y. Times, Mar. 27, 2011, at A1.

272. Bailey & Hanna, supra note 265, at 407, 411-421.

273. See id. at 439-441 (arguing against compounding the adverse consequences for girls who naively trust an intimate partner not to share sexualized representations).

274. See National Conference of State Legislators, 2011 Legislation Related to Sexting, http://www.ncsl.org/default.aspx?tabid=22127.

275. Amanda Bronstad, Light Terms for Child Porn Blasted, Nat'l L.J., Jan. 15, 2007, at A1.

276. See Cathy Young, Skin Flicks 101: What Porn Studies Profs Don't Get About Sex, 35 Reason 20 (May 2003).

277. 539 U.S. 558 (2003).

278. 478 U.S. 186 (1986).

279. 852 P.2d 44 (Haw. 1993).

280. Same-Sex Marriage People's Veto, Question 1 (2009). Voters in Alaska then passed a referendum to authorize same-sex marriage in the November 2012 election.

281. See Windsor, 133 S. Ct. at 2690.

282. 671 F.3d 1052 (9th Cir. 2012).

283. Hollingsworth v. Perry, 133 S. Ct. 2652 (2013). On remand, the appeal was dismissed by the Ninth Circuit. Perry v. Brown, 725 F.3d 1140 (9th Cir. 2013).

284. See, e.g., Baehr v. Lewin, 852 P.2d 44 (Haw. 1993).

285. 517 U.S. 620 (1996).

286. See http://www.hrc.org/issues/pages/benefits, for continually updated information.

287. Protect Marriage Coalition et al., Unsigned Letter, Six Consequences the Coalition Has Identified If Proposition 8 Fails, and Joint Statement to California Religious Leaders Regarding Proposition 8, available at www.protectmarriage.com/files.

288. Mary Anne Case, Marriage Licenses, 89 Minn. L. Rev. 1758, 1795-1796 (2005).

289. Robert P. Jones & Daniel Cox, California's Proposition 8 and Religious Voters 2 (Public Religion Research 2009).

290. David Blankenhorn & Jonathan Rauch, A Reconciliation on Gay Marriage, N.Y. Times, Feb. 21, 2009, at Wk 11. See Goodrich v. Department of Public Health, 798 N.E. 2d 941, 965 n.29 (Mass. 2003); An Act Implementing the Guarantee of Equal Protection Under the Constitution of the State for Same-Sex Couples, G.A. 899, Section 7, 2009 Leg. Sess. Section (Conn. 2009). Some commentators argue that such exemptions are unnecessary since respect for religious leaders' and institutions' practices is already constitutionally required. See Robin Fretwell Wilson, Matters of Conscience: Lessons for Same-Sex Marriage from the Healthcare Context, in Same-Sex Marriage and Religious Liberty 77, 89 (Douglas Laycock et al. eds., 2008).

291. Patrick Egan et al., Gay Marriage, Public Opinion, and the Courts, In Public Opinion and Constitutional Controversy (Nathaniel Persily et al. eds., 2008).

292. Michael J. Klarman, *Brow* and *Lawrence* (and *Goodridge*), 104 Mich. L. Rev. 431, 473 (2005).

293. Paula L. Ettelbrick, Since When Is Marriage a Path to Liberation, 2 Out/Look, Nat'l Gay & Lesbian Q. 9, 14 (Fall 1989). For a related view, see Katha Pollitt, Gay Marriage? Don't Say I Didn't Warn You, in Subject to Debate: Sense and Dissents on Women, Politics, and Culture 109 (Katha Pollitt ed., 2001).

294. Beyond Same-Sex Marriage: A New Strategic Vision for All Our Families and Relationships (July 26, 2006).

295. Ariel Levy, Lesbian Nation, New Yorker, Mar. 2, 2009, at 37 (quoting Lamar Van Dyke).

296. See http://www.alliancealert.org/tag/group-chaplain-alliance-for-religious-liberty.

297. Mariano Castillo, Unprecedented Civil Union United Brazilian Trio, CNN.com (Aug. 31, 2012), available at http://www.cnn.com/2012/08/31/world/americas/brazil-polyfaithful-union/index.html?hpt=hp_t3.

298. Blew v. Verta, 617 A.2d 31, 36 (Pa. Super. Ct. 1992); see also Jacoby v. Jacoby, 763 So. 2d 410, 413 (Fla. Dist. Ct. App. 2000) (law cannot give effect to private biases, which in any event "flow not from the fact that the children were living with a homosexual mother, but from the fact that she is a homosexual").

299. For examples of cases, see Nancy D. Polikoff, Custody Rights of Lesbian and Gay Parents Redux: The Irrelevance of Constitutional Principles, 60 UCLA Rev. Disc. 226 (2013).

300. See D.C. Code Ann. §16-914(a)(1)(A) (2012).

301. 930 N.E.2d 184 (N.Y. 2010).

302. In re Marriage of H.S.H.-K., 533 N.W.2d 419 (Wis. 1995).

303. See, e.g., A.H. v. M.P., 857 N.E.2d 1061 (Mass. 2006); C.E.W. v. D.E.W., 845 A.2d 1146 (Me. 2004); Rubano v. DiCenzo, 759 A.2d 959, 974 (R.I. 2000); V.C. v. M.J.B., 748 A.2d 539 (N.J. 2000); In re Parentage of M.F., 170 P.3d 601 (Wash. Ct. App. 2007); In re E.L.M.C., 100 P.3d 546, 559-560 (Colo. Ct. App. 2004). See also William B. Turner, The Lesbian De Facto Parent Standard in Holtzman v. Knott: Judicial Policy Innovation and Diffusion, 22 Berkeley J. Gender L. & Just. 135 (2007).

304. Elisa B. v. Superior Court, 117 P.3d 660, 663 (Cal. 2005).

305. See, e.g., Janice M. v. Margaret K., 948 A.2d 73 (Md. 2008); Jones v. Barlow, 154 P.3d 808, 809-810 (Utah 2007); White v. White, 293 S.W.3d 1 (Mo. Ct. App. 2009).

306. Courtney G. Joslin, The Legal Parentage of Children Born to Same-Sex Couples, 39 Fam. L.Q. 683, 691 (2005).

307. Sharon S. v. Superior Court, 73 P.3d 554, 568 (Cal. 2003).

308. Boseman v. Jarrell, 704 S.E.2d 494 (N.C. 2010).

309. Miss. Code Ann. §93-17-3(5) (2012); Utah Code Ann. §78B-6-117 (2012).

310. Ark. Code Ann. §9-8-204 (2012), invalidated by Dep't of Human Servs. v. Cole, 2011 Ark. 145 (2011).

311. In re Matter of Adoption of X.X.G. & N.R.G., 45 So. 3d 79, 81 (Fla. Dist. Ct. App. 2010).

312. Four of the most recent studies are described in William Meezan & Jonathan Rauch, Gay Marriage, Same-Sex Parenting, and America's Children, in Marriage and Child Well-Being, 15 The Future of Children 97, 105-106 (Fall 2005). Critics of custody by gay and lesbian parents argue that the studies purporting to show no harm are methodologically flawed. See Lynn D. Wardle, Considering the Impacts on Children and Society of "Lesbigay" Parenting, 23 Quinnipiac L. Rev. 541, 550 (2004).

313. American Academy of Pediatrics, Co-Parent or Second Parent Adoption by Same-Sex Parents, 109 Pediatrics 339 (2002).

314. See Judith Stacey & Timothy J. Biblarz, (How) Does the Sexual Orientation of Parents Matter?, 66 Am. Soc. Rev. 159 (2001); Susan Golombok & Fiona Tasker, Do Parents Influence the Sexual Orientation of Their Children? Findings from a Longitudinal Study of Lesbian Families, 32 Dev. Psychol. 3, 7 (1996); Fiona Tasker & Susan Golombok, Growing Up in a Lesbian Family: Effects on Child Development 102-114 (1997).

315. See Hertzler v. Hertzler, 908 P.2d 946 (Wyo. 1995).

316. See, e.g., Shahar v. Bowers, 114 F.3d 1097 (11th Cir. 1997) (en banc); Padula v. Webster, 822 F.2d 97 (D.C. Cir. 1987).

317. 523 U.S. 75 (1998).

318. Mary Anne Case, Disaggregating Gender from Sex and Sexual Orientation: The Effeminate Man in the Law and Feminist Jurisprudence, 105 Yale L.J. 1, 7 (1995). See also Craig R. Waldo et al., Are Men Sexually Harassed? If So by Whom?, 22 Law & Hum. Behav. 59, 61 (1998).

319. See, e.g., DeSantis v. Pacific Telephone & Telegraph Co., 608 F.2d 327 (9th Cir. 1979); Bibby v. Phila. Coca-Cola Bottling Co., 260 F.3d 257 (3d Cir. 2001).

320. Janet Halley, Split Decisions: How and Why to Take a Break from Feminism 293-296 (2006).

321. See S. 815, A Bill to Prohibit Employment Discrimination on the Basis of Sexual Orientation or Gender Identity, 112th Cong., 1st Sess. (2011); H.R. 1397, A Bill To Prohibit Employment Discrimination on the Basis of Sexual Orientation or Gender Identity, 112th Cong., 1st Sess. (2011).

322. National Gay and Lesbian Task Force, State Nondiscrimination Laws in the U.S. (2012), available at http://www.thetaskforce.org/downloads/reports/issue_maps/non_discrimination_1_12_color.

323. See Human Rights Campaign, Corporate Equality Index 2012: Rating American Workplaces on Lesbian, Gay, Bisexual and Transgender Equality.

324. Catalyst, Making Change: LGBT Inclusion—Understanding the Challenges 18 (2007); Brad Sears & Christy Mallory, The Williams Institute, Evidence of Employment Discrimination on the Basis of Sexual Orientation in State and Local Government (2011); Brad Sears & Christy Mallory, The Williams Institute, Documented Evidence of Employment Discrimination and its Effects on LGBT People (2011).

325. 527 F.3d 806 (9th Cir. 2008). Contrast Cook v. Gates, 528 F.3d 42 (1st Cir. 2008) (rejecting both substantive due process claim and equal protection claims to "Don't Ask, Don't Tell" applying rational basis review).

326. Smithkline Beecham Corp. v. Abbott Laboratories, 2014 U.S. App. LEXIS 1128 (9th Cir. Jan. 21, 2014).

327. 530 U.S. 640 (2000).

328. 515 U.S. 557 (1995).

329. Boy Scouts of America v. Dale, 530 U.S. 640, 651, 653, 655-656 (2000).

330. Id. at 668-669, 682-684.

331. See, e.g., http://www.usatoday.com/story/news/nation/2013/06/11/baptists-consider-dropping-boy-scouts/2413471.

332. About "Don't Ask, Don't Tell," Servicemembers Legal Def. Network, http://www.sldn.org/pages/about-dadt.

333. National Defense Authorization Act of 1994, Pub. L. No. 103-160, 107 Stat. 1547 §571, codified as amended at 10 U.S.C. §654 (2006).

334. See Andrea Stone, "Don't Ask, Don't Tell" Discharges Hit Lesbians Hardest (Aug. 16, 2010), http://www.aolnews.com/2010/08/ask-don't-tell-discharges-hit-lesbians-hardest.

335. Steffan v. Cheney, 780 F. Supp. 1, 10 (D.D.C. 1991), aff'd sub nom. Steffan v. Perry, 41 F.3d 677 (D.C. Cir. 1994) (en banc).

336. Military Readiness Enhancement Act (MREA) of 2007, H.R. 1246, 110th Cong., 1st Sess. (Feb. 28, 2007). Rep. Martin Meehan (D-Mass.) first introduced the MREA in the 109th Congress in March 2005; the bill gained 122 bipartisan cosponsors but failed to get past the House Armed Services Committee. See H.R. 1059, 109th Cong., 1st Sess. (Mar. 2, 2005). Rep. Meehan became Chairman of the House Armed Services Personnel Subcommittee and reintroduced the bill with 110 original cosponsors.

337. Log Cabin Republicans v. United States, 716 F. Supp. 2d 884 (C.D. Cal. 2010).

338. Don't Ask, Don't Tell Repeal Act of 2010, Pub. L. No. 111-321, §2(a)(2)(C), 124 Stat. 3515 (2010).

339. See Amanda Terkel, DOMA Bars Gay Military Families from Nearly 100 Benefits, at http://www.huffingtonpost.com/2013/02/11/doma-military-benefits_n_2662752.html; United States v. Windsor, 133 S. Ct. 2675 (2013).

340. See Peter Weber, The End of "Ex-Gay" Conversion Therapy, The Week, June 20, 2013, at http://theweek.com/article/index/245893/the-end-of-ex-gay-conversion-therapy. An advocacy group supporting this therapy, Exodus International, has recently disbanded. Id. A Christian-based organization named Restored Hope Network advocates counseling methods to those "struggling" with "sexual confusion." See http://www.restoredhopenetwork.com.

341. Aaron Belkin, "Don't Ask, Don't Tell": Does the Gay Ban Undermine the Military's Reputation, 34 Armed Forces & Society 276, 278, 285 (2008).

342. See, e.g., Padula v. Webster, 822 F.2d 97 (D.C. Cir. 1987) (upholding denial of employment of homosexuals because, among other things, having FBI agents who engage in conduct criminalized in half the states would undermine the FBI's law enforcement credibility, and agents would be subject to blackmail in performing their counterintelligence activities).

343. Ashley Behre, Note, Coming Out to Fight for Our Country: Achieving Equality for Gay Service Members in a Post-"Don't Ask, Don't Tell" Military, 29 Hof. Lab. & Emp. L.J. 189 (2011).

344. United States v. St. Clair, 291 F. Supp. 122, 125 (S.D.N.Y. 1968).

345. For current data, see Women in the U.S. Army, http://www.army.mil/women/today.html.

346. 453 U.S. 57, 70-72, 74, 76-77 (1981).

347. Id. at 85 (Marshall, J., dissenting).

348. Department of Defense, Report to Congress on the Review of Laws, Policies and Regulations Restricting the Service of Female Members in the U.S. Armed Forces at 2 (Feb. 2012), available at http://www.defense.gov/news/WISR_Report_to_Congress.pdf.

349. Id.

350. Eileen Patten and Kim Parker, Pew Social & Demographic Trends, Women in the U.S. Military: Growing Share, Distinctive Profile 2 (2011), available at www.pewsocialtrends.org.

351. Id.

352. Id.

353. Information about the policy change is available at http://www.defense.gov/releases/release .aspx?releaseid=15784; http://www.defense.gov/transcripts/transcript.aspx?transcriptid=5183; and http://www.defense.gov/news/WISRImplementationPlanMemo.pdf.

354. See sources quoted in Arnulfo Urias, The Politics of Biology: Evolutionary Biology and the Exclusion of Women from Combat, 14 S. Cal. Rev. L. & Women's Stud. 83, 101-102 (2004).

355. William Westmoreland, quoted in Judith Wagner Decrew, The Combat Exclusion and the Role of Women in the Military, Hypatia, Winter 1995, at 62.

356. See, e.g., J. Michael Brower, Undermining Old Taboos: U.S. Studies Say Women Can Meet Physical Demands of Combat, Armed Forces J. Int'l, May 1996, at 13 (reporting on studies sponsored by the Army Research Institute and the British Ministry of Defense); Martha McSally, Women in Combat: Is the Current Policy Obsolete?, 14 Duke J. Gender L. & Pol'y 1011, 1029-1040 (2007); Blythe Leszkay, Feminism on the Front Lines, 14 Hastings Women's L.J. 133, 161 (2003).

357. Richard Posner, Overcoming Law 55 (1995). Maia Goodell argues that the physical-strength rationale for excluding women from combat is clearly traceable to ideology rather than biology. See Maia Goodell, Physical-Strength Rationales for De Jure Exclusion of Women from Military Combat Positions, 34 Seattle U. L. Rev. 17 (2010).

358. Craig Whitlock, Pentagon to Ease Ban on Women in Some Combat Roles, Wash. Post, Feb. 10, 2012, at A3.

359. DOD Report to Congress, supra note 348, at 3.

360. Mona Iskander, Female Troops in Iraq Redefine Combat Roles, July 5, 2004, available at www .womensenews.org; Tim McGirk, World, Time, Feb. 27, 2006, at 38 (quoting Lory Manning).

361. Female Troops in Iraq Exposed to Combat, CNN, June 28, 2005, available at http://www.cnn .com/2005/WORLD/meast/06/25/women.combat.

362. Mary E. Becker, The Politics of Women's Wrongs and the Bill of "Rights": A Bicentennial Perspective, 59 U. Chi. L. Rev. 453, 496-498 (1992). See also Diane H. Mazur, A Call to Arms, 22 Harv. Women's L.J. 39 (1999) (arguing that feminists are not in a position to criticize the military's treatment of servicewomen until they accept responsibility of participation in the military).

363. Feminist Opposition to the Draft, quoted in Catharine MacKinnon, Sex Equality 270-271 (2001)

364. Ellen Goodman, Value Judgments 158-59 (1993).

365. Lindsay M. Rock and Rachel N. Lipari, 2010 Workplace and Gender Relations Survey of Active Duty Members: Overview Report on Sexual Assault iv (March 2011).

366. Id. at vi.

367. Id. at 40, 42; see also Department of Defense, Annual Report on Sexual Assault in the Military Fiscal Year 2011 vii (2012).

368. Department of Defense, Annual Report on Sexual Assault in the Military, supra note 367, at 32.

369. Id. at 36-38.

370. Marie Tessier, Sexual Assault Pervasive in the Military, Experts Say, Mar. 31, 2003, available at www.womensenews.org; Cathleen Lutz, Living Room Terrorists, Women's Rev. of Books, Feb. 2004, at 17-18.

371. Lutz, supra note 370, at 17-18; Tessier, supra note 370.

372. See Department of Defense, Annual Report on Sexual Harassment and Violence at the Military Service Academies (Dec. 2011).

373. Elizabeth Becker, Women in Military Say Silence on Harassment Protects Careers, N.Y. Times, May 12, 2000, at A1.

374. See Jessica L. Cornett, The U.S. Military Responds to Rape: Will Recent Changes Be Enough, 29 Women's Rts. L. Rep. 99, 107-113 (2008).

375. Amy Herdy, Bite the Bullet, Ms., Spring 2009, at 80 (reviewing Helen Benedict, The Lonely Soldier: The Private War of Women Serving in Iraq, and quoting Liz O'Herrin).

376. Rock & Lipari, 2010 Gender Relations Survey, supra note 365, at vi-vii.

377. Id. at vii.

378. See Jennifer Steinhauer, Complex Fight in Senate Over Curbing Military Sex Assaults, at http://www.nytimes.com/2013/06/15/us/politics/in-senate-complex-fight-over-curbing-sexual-military-assaults.html?pagewanted=all&_r=0.

379. Rush Limbaugh III, The Way Things Ought to Be 200-201 (1992).

CHAPTER *4*

Difference

Formal equality assumes a basic sameness between men and women, and the obligation of law to respect that sameness. Substantive equality assumes some meaningful differences and seeks to eliminate the disadvantages of those differences through various legal strategies. Nonsubordination theory treats sameness and difference both as artificial constructs, designed to keep women in their place.

Difference theory (also referred to as cultural feminism, relational feminism, or the ethic of care) offers still another perspective on gender and the law. Like substantive equality, difference theory underscores important differences between women and men. Unlike substantive equality, however, difference theory sees at least some of these differences not as problems to be overcome but rather as potentially valuable resources that might provide a better model for legal and social institutions than do "male" characteristics and values. Within this theory, women tend to be associated with the values of relationship, protection of the vulnerable, and context-based reasoning, while men are identified with autonomy, individualism, and risk-taking. This chapter investigates the nature of these claimed differences and their implications for the law.

Feminist theorists often view difference theory with suspicion because of the risk that attributing certain traditional virtues to women will reinforce the stereotypes upon which ideologies of subordination rest. At the same time, it is generally assumed that the increasing presence of women in law schools, legal practice, elected office, juries, and the judiciary will affect how law is created, taught, practiced, and applied. This chapter explores the tension between the embrace of gender differences as a means of improving legal institutions and the rejection of gender stereotypes.

A. THE ETHIC OF CARE AND ITS LEGAL IMPLICATIONS

This section sets forth the basic case for difference theory: that women have distinctive traits and values that should be affirmatively valued in the public as well as private realm of private relationships and family.

449

Some of those who have helped develop difference theory in law were influenced by Carol Gilligan's 1982 publication, In a Different Voice: Psychological Theory and Women's Development. This work challenged a widely accepted model of moral development articulated by psychologist Lawrence Kohlberg, a model that charted a progression in moral thinking through increasingly abstract levels of reasoning. Gilligan argued that this model missed the more contextualized, relationship-sensitive style of reasoning more typical of girls. In one of her most well-known studies, Gilligan compared how boys and girls responded to "Heinz's dilemma," in which Heinz's wife is dying of cancer and requires a drug that Heinz cannot afford to purchase from the local pharmacist. The children are asked whether Heinz should steal the drug. Summarizing Gilligan's findings, Carrie Menkel-Meadow explains:

> Jake, an eleven-year-old boy, sees the problem as one of "balancing rights," like a judge who must make a decision or a mathematician who must solve an algebraic equation. Life is worth more than property, therefore Heinz should steal the drug. For Amy, an eleven-year-old girl, the problem is different. Like a "bad" law student who "fights the hypo" she wants to know more facts. Have Heinz and the druggist explored other possibilities, like a loan or credit transaction? Why couldn't Heinz and the druggist simply sit down and talk it out so that the druggist would come to see the importance of Heinz's wife's life? In Gilligan's terms, Jake explores the Heinz dilemma with the "logic of justice" while Amy uses the "ethic of care." Amy scores lower on the Kohlberg scale because she sees the problem rooted in the persons involved rather than in the larger universal issues posed by the dilemma.[1]

It is important to note that Gilligan did not reject abstract reasoning; rather, she believed that the more contextualized form of reasoning (at which girls were more likely to excel) was no less valuable or advanced a way of thinking. In appropriating Gilligan's research, however, feminist legal scholars have tended to be highly critical of "masculine" values and forms of reasoning and strong advocates for "feminine" alternatives.[2]

Leslie Bender argues that unlike the ethic of justice, the ethic of care "focuses attention on the unique context of the dispute and the parties' on-going relationships and interdependencies."[3] Along similar lines, Mary Becker explains that "[w]e need to target both the overvaluation or masculine qualities and the cultural undervaluation of feminine qualities." "Relational feminism stresses the need to value community, relationships, and traditional feminine qualities because these valuable qualities have been so undervalued in our overly individualistic and masculinist culture."[4]

If certain characteristics are sex-related, where did these differences come from? Robin West argues that connectedness is biologically and materially rooted in such experiences as pregnancy, heterosexual penetration, menstruation, and breastfeeding.[5] Philosopher Sara Ruddick locates gender differences in the social practice of mothering, in which boys develop their identities by separating from their differently gendered mothers, which reinforces for boys the values of separation and individualism, while girls develop by identifying with their mothers, to whom they remain connected, which reinforces for girls the values of relationship and communal identity.[6] Are these theories mutually exclusive? Difference theory has been deployed in support of a variety of legal reform proposals. As the following reading by Leslie Bender illustrates, it can be used to support the expansion of legal obligations, such as the "duty to rescue" in tort law, or, as developed in Part B of this chapter, a greater obligation on the part of the state to support families. At the same time, the premises of difference theory, as the following reading by Kingsley Browne demonstrates, can be used to explain why women invest less in their own human market capital than men, choose the jobs they do, and thus earn less.

Reading Questions

1. Robin West finds the basis for women's difference in her bodily capacity to reproduce and breastfeed. Is this convincing? How does it apply to childless women?
2. Should women try to "own" and promote the characteristics attributed to women in this section?
3. Is there a "female" experience of the world? If so, does it matter whether it is based in biology or social practice?
4. What would it mean for society to be organized and governed according to an ethic of care, cooperation, and interpersonal responsibility? Is difference theory essentially conservative?

Robin West, Jurisprudence and Gender

55 U. Chi. L. Rev. 1, 1-3, 14-15, 58-59 (1988)

[V]irtually all modern American legal theorists, like most modern moral and political philosophers, either explicitly or implicitly embrace what I will call the "separation thesis" about what it means to be a human being: a "human being," whatever else he is, is physically separate from all other human beings. I am one human being and you are another, and that distinction between you and me is central to the meaning of the phrase "human being." . . .

[B]y virtue of their shared embrace of the separation thesis, all of our modern legal theory . . . is essentially and irretrievably masculine. . . . [T]he cluster of claims that jointly constitute the "separation thesis"—the claim that human beings are, definitionally, distinct from one another, the claim that the referent of "I" is singular and unambiguous, the claim that the word "individual" has an uncontested biological meaning, namely that we are each physically individuated from every other, the claim that we are individuals "first," and the claim that what separates us is epistemologically and morally prior to what connects us—while "trivially true" of men, [is] patently untrue of women. Women are not essentially, necessarily, inevitably, invariably, always, and forever separate from other human beings: women, distinctively, are quite clearly "connected" to another human life when pregnant. In fact, women are in some sense "connected" to life and to other human beings during at least four recurrent and critical material experiences: the experience of pregnancy itself; the invasive and "connecting" experience of heterosexual penetration, which may lead to pregnancy; the monthly experience of menstruation, which represents the potential for pregnancy; and the post-pregnancy experience of breast-feeding. Indeed, perhaps the central insight of feminist theory of the last decade has been that women are "essentially connected," not "essentially separate," from the rest of human life, both materially, through pregnancy, intercourse, and breast-feeding, and existentially, through the moral and practical life. . . .

The "connection thesis" is simply this: Women are actually or potentially materially connected to other human life. Men aren't. This material fact has existential consequences. While it may be true for men that the individual is "epistemologically and morally prior to the collectivity," it is not true for women. The potential for material connection with the other defines women's subjective, phenomenological and existential state, just as surely as the inevitability of material separation from the other defines men's existential state. Our potential for material connection engenders pleasures and pains, values and dangers, and attractions and fears, which are entirely different from those which follow, *for men*, from the necessity of separation. Indeed, it is the rediscovery of the multitude of implications from this material difference between men and women which has enlivened (and divided) both cultural and radical feminism in this decade. . . . As Carol Gilligan notes, this development is somewhat paradoxical: during the same decade that liberal feminist political activists and lawyers pressed for equal (meaning same) treatment by the law, feminist theorists in the non-legal disciplines rediscovered women's differences from men. . . .

By the claim that modern jurisprudence is "masculine," I mean two things. First, I mean that the values [and] the dangers that characterize women's lives are not reflected at any level whatsoever in contracts, torts, constitutional law, or any other field of legal doctrine. The values that flow from women's material potential for physical connection are not recognized as values by the Rule of Law, and the dangers attendant to that state are not recognized as dangers by the Rule of Law.

Mary Becker, Care and Feminists

17 Wis. Women's L.J. 57, 60 (2002)

The goal of relational feminism is a society in which all human beings, women as well as men, can find human fulfillment and happiness. We need to target *both* the cultural *over*-valuation of masculine qualities and the cultural *under*-valuation of feminine qualities, the cultural focus on men and their needs and the concomitant tendency to see women as less than fully human and their injuries or needs as the result of their own (unfortunate) choices. We must also target the cultural insistence that women and men are essentially different. In the ideal world of relational feminists, women and men would have access to the support and opportunities necessary for human fulfillment and happiness; valuable traits would be valued whether masculine or feminine and whether displayed by women or men. Relational feminism stresses the need to value community, relationships, and traditional feminine qualities because these valuable qualities have been so under-valued in our overly individualistic and masculinist culture.

Leslie Bender, A Lawyer's Primer on Feminist Theory and Tort

38 J. Legal Educ. 3, 31-36 (1988)

Negligence law could begin with Gilligan's articulation of the feminine voice's ethic of care—a premise that no one should be hurt. We could convert the present standard of "care of a reasonable person under the same or similar circumstances" to a standard of "conscious care and concern of a responsible neighbor or social acquaintance for another under the same or similar circumstances." . . .

In the law of **negligence**, individuals are held to a defined **standard of care** in which they are responsible for exercising (at least) the degree of prudence that a reasonable person would use under the same circumstances.

The recognition that we are all interdependent and connected and that we are by nature social beings who must interact with one another should lead us to judge conduct as tortious when it does not evidence responsible care or concern for another's safety, welfare, or health. Tort law should begin with a premise of responsibility rather than rights, of interconnectedness rather than separation, and a priority of safety rather than profit or efficiency. The masculine voice of rights, autonomy, and abstraction has led to a standard that protects efficiency and profit; the feminine voice can design a tort system that encourages behavior that is caring about others' safety and responsive to others' needs or hurts, and that attends to human contexts and consequences. . . .

One of the most difficult areas in which questions of duty and the standard of care arise is the "no duty to rescue" case. The problem is traditionally illustrated by the drowning-stranger hypothetical and the infamous case of Yania v. Bigan.[117] . . .

Each year that I teach torts I watch again as a majority of my students initially find this legal "no duty" rule reprehensible. After the rationale is explained and the students become immersed in the "reasoned" analysis, and after they take a distanced, objective posture informed by liberalism's concerns for autonomy and liberty, many come to accept the legal rule that intuitively had seemed so wrong to them. They are taught to reject their emotions, instincts, and ethics, and to view accidents and tragedies abstractly, removed from their social and particularized contexts, and to apply instead rationally-derived universal principles and a vision of human nature as atomistic, self-interested, and as free from constraint as possible. They are also taught that there are legally relevant distinctions between acts and omissions.

How would this drowning-stranger hypothetical look from a new legal perspective informed by a feminist ethic based upon notions of caring, responsibility, interconnectedness, and cooperation? If we put abstract reasoning and autonomy aside momentarily, we can see what else matters. In defining duty, what matters is that someone, a human being, a part of us, is drowning and will die without some affirmative action. That seems more urgent, more imperative, more important than any possible infringement of individual autonomy by the imposition of an affirmative duty. If we think about the stranger as a human being for a moment, we may realize that much more is involved than balancing one person's interest in having his life saved and another's interest in not having affirmative duties imposed upon him in the absence of a special relationship, although even then the balance seems to me to weigh in favor of imposing a duty or standard of care that requires action. The drowning stranger is not the only person affected by the lack of care. He is not detached from everyone else. He no doubt has people who care about him — parents, spouse, children, friends, colleagues; groups he participates in — religious, social, athletic, artistic, political, educational, work-related; he may even have people who depend upon him for emotional or financial support. He is interconnected with others. If the stranger drowns, many will be harmed. It is not an isolated event with one person's interests balanced against another's. When our legal system trains us to understand the drowning-stranger story as a limited event between two people, both of whom have interests at least equally worth protecting, and when the social ramifications we credit most are the impositions on personal liberty of action, we take a human situation and translate it into a cold, dehumanized algebraic equation. We forget that we

117. . . . . Yania was a business competitor of Bigan and had gone into Bigan's land to speak with him. Both men were involved in strip-mining, and Bigan was working at a deep trench partially filled with water. Although the facts are ambiguous, there was testimony that Bigan dared or cajoled Yania to jump into the pit, in which he drowned as Bigan looked on. It is equally possible that Yania jumped into the pit to demonstrate to Bigan his expertise in solving the problem there. In either case, Yania drowned and Yania's widow sued Bigan. She lost. The Pennsylvania Supreme Court refused to impose an affirmative duty on one party to rescue or aid another.

are talking about human death or grave physical harms and their reverberating consequences when we equate the consequences with such things as one person's momentary freedom not to act. People are decontextualized for the analysis, yet no one really lives an acontextual life. . . .

If instead we impose a duty of acting responsibly with the same self-conscious care for the safety of others that we would give our neighbors or people we know, we require the actor to consider the human consequences of her failure to rescue. . . .

The duty to act with care for another's safety, which under appropriate circumstances would include an affirmative duty to act to protect or prevent harm to another, would be shaped by the particular context. One's ability to aid and one's proximity to the need would be relevant considerations. Whether one met that duty would not be determined by how a reasonable person would have acted under the circumstances but by whether one acted out of a conscious care and concern for the safety, health, and well-being of the victim in the way one would act out of care for a neighbor or friend. . . . This seemingly minor change would transform the core of negligence law to a human, responsive system.

Richard A. Posner, Conservative Feminism

1989 U. Chi. Legal F. 191, 214

[Most] people are what they are; most neighbors are not caring, and most accident victims are not neighbors. Human nature will not be altered by holding injurers liable for having failed to take the care that a caring neighbor would have taken. The only effect of adopting Bender's proposal would be to shift negligence liability in the direction of strict liability. Her "caring neighbor" is an unnecessary step in the analysis. Bender might as well argue directly for strict liability on the ground that it is the more altruistic regime than negligence.

Is it? Strict liability is sometimes defended on the ground that it provides more compensation to more accident victims. This is a partial analysis. Strict liability can also result in higher prices, and the burden may be borne by consumers. The net distributive impact is unclear. If these complications are ignored, maybe a feminine outlook on law could be expected to stress compensation—obviously Bender associates altruism with women. On the other hand, strict liability is more rule-like, less standard-like, less contextualist, less sensitive to the particulars of the individual accident, than negligence is; in that respect it is the more masculine standard.

Strict liability is a tort doctrine, applied only in certain carefully defined circumstances, in which someone can be liable for damages even if not proved to have been at fault or to have caused the damages.

Kingsley R. Browne, Sex and Temperament in Modern Society: A Darwinian View of the Glass Ceiling and the Gender Gap

37 Ariz. L. Rev. 971, 984, 1016, 1065-1066, 1071, 1081-1082 (1995)

It is my central thesis that much of what we call the glass ceiling and gender gap is the product of basic biological sex differences in personality and temperament. These differences have resulted from differential reproductive strategies that have been adopted by the two sexes during human history and are every bit as much a product of natural selection as our bipedal locomotion and opposable thumbs. Although these temperamental traits evolved in our hunting-and-gathering ancestral environment, they remain with us today whether or not they remain adaptive. . . .

Evolutionary theory predicts that men will tend to exhibit greater status-seeking, competitiveness, and risk-taking than women, and that women will exhibit more nurturance and affiliative behavior. These predictions are borne out in every known human society. With respect to all of these traits, the differences are statistical, in the sense that they are generalizations that do not hold true for all individuals. However, even relatively small between-group differences can have a dramatic effect on the sex ratio at the extremes. Moreover, since the glass ceiling and the gender gap in compensation are themselves both group-based phenomena, it seems appropriate to seek an explanation for them in terms of group-based traits. . . .

It is a common observation—sometimes a complaint—that in order for women to attain the highest levels of success in the working world they must "be like men." Prominent among the qualities of successful female executives are the "male" traits of aggressiveness, ambition and drive, strong career orientation ("a passion for success"), and risk-taking. Women are consistently perceived to have a lesser level of these traits than men. Even apart from commitment to children, women as a class differ in important temperamental ways from men. Combined with women's greater commitment to families these temperamental differences have a powerful effect. . . .

If a substantial contributor to the "glass ceiling" is the fact that women tend not to display, to the same degree that men do, the temperamental traits and accompanying behaviors that result in achieving the highest levels, then in order for women to achieve parity, something must change: either the job requirements or women themselves. Many students of the glass ceiling have advocated both changes: employers should stop rewarding driven and ambitious people, and girls should be socialized to manifest the same drive and ambition as males. For a whole host of reasons, both of these suggestions are unlikely to bear fruit.

It seems unlikely in the extreme that employers will cease rewarding employees who exhibit a high degree of commitment to the employer. All else being equal—and in the absence of some prohibition—an employer will generally prefer a worker who puts in more hours to one who puts in fewer; it will prefer a worker who will travel or relocate to one who will not; and it will prefer a worker whose career is not interrupted by lengthy absences from the labor market to one whose is. Those employees are simply more valuable. Moreover, it is a fact of life in modern America that men work more hours, are more willing to travel and relocate, and are less likely to leave the labor force for extended periods. . . .

[T]he simplistic observation that men and women have different average earnings tells one very little, but the fact that earnings are easier to quantify and compare than other important job attributes has led to an undue focus on wage disparities. To the extent that compensation differences are due to the kinds of differences described above, it is not clear why there should be societal intervention. The studies described above suggest that if women make the same kinds of human-capital investments and occupational choices as men, their compensation will be much more similar to men's than it is now. If they choose to work fewer hours, seek less job-related training, and select jobs that have advantages that for them outweigh the lower pay, it is difficult to see why there is any need for correction. Preventing employers from giving higher pay to employees who work more hours, have greater job-related training, or occupy riskier jobs seems foolish.

Kathryn Abrams, The Second Coming of Care

76 Chi.-Kent L. Rev. 1605, 1607-1608, 1610-1611 (2001)

In its first incarnation, the feminist legal focus on care was part of a larger project of characterizing women, differentiating them from men, and challenging the institutional structures to which women had gained access both as participants and as interpreters. Carol Gilligan may have offered her pathbreaking analysis to challenge the unitary conceptual structure of developmental psychology. But, as taken up in law, Gilligan's thesis represented a way of articulating those attributes of women that were specific to the sex, rather than inherent in the universal legal subject (a subject who was formally unmarked, but, to feminists, increasingly recognizable as male). Care was an emanation from women, an expression of their essence that was not, in this early period, analyzed in its concrete particulars. Women's orientation toward care was manifested in a series of paradigmatic settings: nurturing a child, placing concern for others above concern for oneself, performing tasks collaboratively rather than competitively or individualistically, and analyzing problems relationally rather than hierarchically or in zero-sum fashion. . . .

These features of early accounts of care ultimately created difficulties for their feminist legal proponents. The essentialism of first-generational arguments about care was the most frequent target, although this objection took various forms. Some feminists observed that this ostensibly far-reaching characterization did not apply to them: they did not have children; they did not count care or sacrifice for others among the central activities of their lives; they did not experience in their daily lives the relational thinking or the warm, soft-focus glow of collaborative connection that leading theories of care ascribed them. The acontextuality of many discussions of care also fueled an anti-essentialist critique. Black feminists since Sojourner Truth had suggested that the dichotomy between care and work had never applied to the lives of women of color or working-class white women, whose caregiving activities were not permitted to be the predominant focus of their lives. . . .

. . . MacKinnon argues that women learned to value care because caring for men was what they were valued for. . . . The dominance approach succeeded not only in curtailing discussion of care-based difference, but in shifting the substantive focus from questions such as workplace accommodation of childrearing, to issues such as sexual harassment, rape, and pornography. . . .

Yet while the claims and critiques of dominance theory were preoccupying feminist legal scholars, feminist scholars in other fields were shifting emphases and addressing defects in earlier arguments about care. Theorists such as philosopher Sara Ruddick characterized care not as an emanation from or essence of women, but as a practice in which many women and some men engaged, that formed particular habits of mind and orientations toward others through the activities of nurturance of and concern for particular others. Other scholars, such as political theorist Joan Tronto, worked to concretize and situate care, by describing systematic ways in which various categories of caregivers had been marginalized. . . .

By the mid 1990s a concern with care began to resurface among feminist legal scholars. This focus coincided with growing analytical and practical doubts about dominance feminism as a fully adequate vehicle for addressing women's oppression. Not only had the dominance approach been problematized as essentialist and as understating women's potential for agency, but its persistent focus on sexuality was also challenged as inadequate to address a range of issues that reflected the gendering and the oppression of women, foremost among them the care of children and other dependents.

Notes

1. Mainstreaming the Ethic of Care in the Law. As both a critique of existing "male" law and a substantive reform agenda, difference theory or the "ethic of care" has been applied to virtually every area of law. For example, over 25 years ago Kathleen Lahey and Sarah Salter challenged the "patriarchal nature of the dominations upon which corporate culture depends" and urged legal reforms in corporate law that reflect "the ethics of care, responsibility, connection, and sharing" that are organized around the "values of contextuality, continuity, and holistic participation."[7] More recently, Joan MacLeod Heminway argues that because women and men use different factors and processes in deciding whom to trust, greater gender diversity on corporate boards will enhance "trust diversity" and hence the independence of corporate boards.[8] Marjorie Kornhauser has defended progressive income tax rules from a "female voice" perspective that emphasized interdependence and altruism.[9] Aviva Orenstein has proposed a new "apology exception" to evidentiary rules relating to admissions by party-opponents based on feminist relational values.[10] Judith Resnik has criticized the relegation of mundane, fact-specific cases, such as prisoner petitions and Social Security cases, to Article I judges or state courts, as well as the treatment of "the complex and messy activity of interacting with litigants, witnesses, and lawyers" as "mere housekeeping." She urges "[r]etrieving—without romanticizing—the importance of 'humble' activities" that may be "repetitive and non-engaging," but nonetheless necessary to maintain the daily maintenance of a judicial system.[11]

Since the 1990s, proposals along these lines have largely vanished. Can you think of a reason?

2. The Feminist Critique of Difference Theory and an Ethic of Care. The primary feminist criticism of difference theory, referred to in the Abrams reading, is that the values that it seeks to redeem and celebrate are the same as those that have been used to justify women's subordination to men. Catharine MacKinnon argues, for example, that the theory "mak[es] it seem as though [women's] attributes, with their consequences, really are somehow ours, rather than what male supremacy has attributed to us for its own use. For women to affirm difference, when difference means dominance, as it does with gender, means to affirm the qualities and characteristics of powerlessness."[12] Does she have a point?

Linda McClain, after reviewing the dangers of difference theory, concludes that the voice of care is important but is better attributed to liberal humanist values than specifically "female" values. Liberalism has plenty of room for these values, she argues. Rather than forcing a "stark pick between mothering and contract, or care and justice, or connection and separation," feminists should engage in dialogue about how their insights about interdependency, connection, and responsibility can be incorporated within the liberal legal system. "[P]rinciples of justice, equality, and autonomy can coexist with and inform care and responsibility, just as care and connection, for both liberals and feminists, aid in the pursuit of justice."[13] Joan Tronto echoes this theme, arguing that "we need to stop talking about 'women's morality' and start talking instead about a care ethic that includes the values traditionally associated with women."[14]

Is this gender-neutral approach appealing? Consider Leslie Bender's objection:

[W]hile I am sympathetic to feminists who make this argument, I believe it is politically, theoretically, and factually unsound to move women from center stage in this proposed reconstruction of legal and ethical discourse based on an ethic of care. Interpersonal caregiving is something that women have specialized in for years. We have special knowledge and insights to offer. After

many, many years of being submerged, we have finally come above the surface and caught our long-awaited breath. The air tastes good. A change to
"humanism," I fear, will ultimately press us under water again.[15]

What is your view? What is gained and lost by a gender-neutral strategy?

3. The Normative Implications of the Evolutionary Thesis.   The extent
to which differences between men and women, including characteristics ordinarily viewed as social, are rooted in biology has produced an extensive scientific literature—too extensive to permit a representative sampling. Without
the opportunity to fully explore the research, the question for this chapter
will have to be not *whether* the premises of evolutionary biology (also called
"developmental biology" and "sociobiology") are true, but rather *what follows*
if they are true.

To Richard Epstein and other conservative scholars, different personality
types and social roles are a matter of efficiency—nature's efficiency. Efforts to
change the instincts that have emerged as adaptive behaviors are simply inefficient.[16] Kingsley Browne, while stating that there are no "necessary" implications in finding a biological basis for women's difference, makes it clear that
once the "glass ceiling" or the gender gap in women's earnings is explained
as a product of natural selection processes, there is no longer sex discrimination for which a legal remedy is necessary. Elsewhere he states that efforts to
prohibit sexual harassment are doomed, insofar as they go "against the grain"
of human psychology.[17]

George Gilder takes another tack. According to Gilder, women who abandon traditional, biology-created gender roles do so at the expense of both children who need their care and also men, whose sexual energies and aggressions
will be directed either toward the long-term goal of providing for their families or toward various dangerous, anti-social pursuits.

> A man without a woman has a deep inner sense of dispensability, perhaps
> evolved during the millennia of service in the front lines of tribal defense.
> He is sexually optional. Several dominant males could impregnate all the
> women and perpetuate the tribe. It is this sense of dispensability that makes
> young men good fighters, good crusaders, good martyrs. But it also weakens
> the male ability to care deeply and long and stunts young men's sense of the
> preciousness of human beings. Because the woman has always been directly
> responsible for infants and almost always exclusively responsible, she is dubi-
> ous about the dying and killing that have surrounded male activities.
>
> Once the man marries he can change. He has to change, for his wife will not
> long have him if he remains in spirit a single man. He must settle his life, and
> commit it to the needs of raising a family. He must exchange the moral and
> spiritual rhythms of the hunt for a higher, more extended mode of sexual life.
> He must submit, ethically and sexually, to the values of maternal morality and
> futurity.[18]

How do you respond?

4. Evolutionary Biology: The Critique.   In response to the claims of scholars like Epstein and Browne, some feminists have observed that even if sex-based differences exist, they do not account for the full range of occupational segregation and wage differentials that exist. Deborah Weiss argues, for example, that "heritable" (i.e. genetic) differences interact with various forms of discrimination, including unconscious discrimination, irrational discrimination, and structural discrimination, in ways that are impossible to untangle. Because the effects of sex-based differences are indeterminate, antidiscrimination policies remain fully necessary, even if the goal of evenly distributing women throughout all labor markets is unjustified.[19]

More broadly, legal scholar Amy Wax argues that even if gender differences exist based on the sexually dimorphic scramble to keep one's genes alive, society still has a choice about what behaviors to promote. Thus, despite human biological urges, society develops moral codes to discourage drunk driving, teen pregnancy, and sexual violence, and it likewise may undertake policies to encourage a "greater impulse for 'nurturing' or a diminished attraction to competition in the male population."[20] The significance of sociobiological findings, according to Wax, is that when desired behavior goes "against nature," it must be furthered by building a sense of moral duty and social obligation, rather than by trying to transform feelings or attitudes. Sociobiology does not mean, however, that biological differences must be embraced.

> [M]an does indeed have tendencies, some stronger, more pervasive, and more "hard wired" than others. To say that, however, is not to say that the tendencies cannot be curbed or overcome by the forces of culture or morality.[21]

Feminist scholars June Carbone and Naomi Cahn make a similar point:

> The most critical development in our evolutionary past may be not so much the development of any particular behavior or trait, but the ability to reshape our behavior with others. As our biological knowledge grows, we are almost certain to find that our genes create the capacity for various behaviors and virtues, with love, loyalty, and commitment among them, but that these values do not happen automatically. Instead, the right conditions in childhood, including parent-child attachment, family stability, appropriate role models, and education, prime the neural pathways that allow[] some behavior to develop and become deeply ingrained. Over longer periods of time, the prevalence of certain norms within a group can favor the passing on of the genes associated with that behavior, so that these genes, whether they are the genes that control the ability to learn, the discipline to conform behavior to norms, or the tendency to [do] so with a minimum of external coercion, become more common over time.[22]

One could differ, of course, about which moral principles should guide society's response to the biological givens—i.e., whether they should be guided by Gilder's sense of gender role order, for example, or Carbone's and Cahn's "virtues" of love, loyalty, and commitment. Does sociobiological analysis add anything to the choice between social ideals?

Putting Theory Into Practice

4-1. In a highly publicized incident, Harvard President Lawrence Summers attributed women's underrepresentation in science and engineering partly to their inferior ability at the high end of the performance range. Although he would like "nothing better than to be proved wrong," Summers indicated that his reading of the data revealed biological sex-based differences in intrinsic science and math aptitude. In support of his hypothesis, Summers referred specifically to a study that found that half as many female as male twelfth graders scored in the top 5 percent of math and science aptitude tests. He also found it telling that his two-and-a-half-year-old twin daughters, when given trucks, concluded that the daddy truck is carrying the baby truck.[23] Is Summers wrong? How would you respond to him?

4-2. Michael Mattioli is a 66-year-old retired psychologist. For over 30 years, he lived in a Manhattan apartment complex owned by New York University. He then moved "temporarily" to Rochester to care for his mother, age 95, and his father, age 99, so that they would be spared the "indignity of dying in a nursing home." His mother died four years later, but his father lived on. New York University sought to evict Mattioli from his Manhattan apartment on the basis of a statute allowing eviction of tenants who do not use the premises as their primary residence. Mattioli believed he should be able to keep his apartment, since he intended to return there as soon as his father no longer needed him. "I'm sure that at N.Y.U.'s medical school and law school and nursing school, they're teaching about the problems of the elderly," he said. "I don't think they're teaching that people who are taking responsibility for their own parents should be driven out of their apartments."[24]

Should the circumstances of Mattioli's departure from his apartment and his intention to return sometime in the indefinite future provide a defense to the eviction action? Is difference theory relevant?

4-3. Choose an area of law—like corporate law or environmental law—and explain how an ethic of care might make a difference. How would you evaluate that difference?

B. WORK AND FAMILY

Chapter 2 examined issues of work and family from the point of view of equality for women. This chapter focuses on values beyond equality that might support greater subsidies for families. Difference theorists draw attention to the needs of society's dependents—especially children, the disabled, and the elderly. They tend to view the responsibility for addressing these needs as not simply a private responsibility, but a public one as well, and they see caretaking as a public good, not simply a private consumption choice.

How does looking at work and family issues through this lens change the picture? In this section, Martha Fineman argues that caretaking creates a "collective or societal debt," to which the state needs to be more responsive, with state resources that recognize that caretaking interferes with the caretaker's ability to invest in market employment. Vicki Schultz contends that both women, and society more broadly, benefit most when caretakers are able to pursue both family obligations and paid market work. Dorothy Roberts questions traditional assumptions about both female domesticity and women's participation in market employment by highlighting the race and class subordination that these assumptions often ignore, particularly with respect to paid domestic help.

Reading Questions

1. To what extent should adults without families have to subsidize workplace accommodations for adults with families? In the cost of paid family leaves? In the higher taxes required for better state support of families? In disproportionate evening and weekend work so other employees can have time with their children?
2. Is the better policy emphasis on providing women sufficient support to care for their dependents, or on helping them gain the employment skills that would enable them to support their families without state assistance?

Martha Albertson Fineman, Cracking the Foundational Myths: Independence, Autonomy, and Self-Sufficiency

8 Am. U. J. Gender Soc. Pol'y & L. 13, 18-22, 26-27 (2000)

It is puzzling, as well as paradoxical, that the term dependency has such negative connotations [in political discourse]. Its very existence prompts and justifies mean spirited and ill-conceived political responses, such as the recent welfare "reform." Far from being pathological, avoidable, and the result of individual failings, dependency is a universal and inevitable part of the human development. It is inherent in the human condition.

All of us were dependent as children, and many of us will be dependent as we age, become ill, or suffer disabilities. In this sense, dependency is "inevitable" and not deserving of condemnation or stigma. Note that the examples I have chosen to illustrate this category of inevitable dependency are biological or physical in nature. Biological dependencies, however, do not exhaust the potential range of situations of dependence. For example, in addition to biological dependence, one may be psychologically or emotionally dependent on others. In fact, these other forms of dependence may even accompany the physiological or biological dependence, which I have labeled inevitable. But economic, psychological, and emotional dependency are not generally under-stood to be universally experienced. As a result, assertions about their inevita-bility in each individual's life would be controversial. It is the characteristic of universality (which indisputably accompanies inevitable dependence) that is central to my argument for societal or collective responsibility. In other words, the realization that biological dependency is both inevitable and universal is theoretically important. Upon this foundational realization is built my claim for justice—the demand that society value and accommodate the labor done by the caretakers of inevitable dependents.

I argue that the caretaking work creates a collective or societal debt. Each and every member of society is obligated by this debt. Furthermore, this debt transcends individual circumstances. In other words, we need not be elderly, ill, or children any longer to be held individually responsible. Nor can we sat-isfy or discharge our collective responsibility within our individual, private families. Merely being financially generous with our own mothers or duly supporting our own wives will not suffice to satisfy our share of the societal debt generally owed to all caretakers.

My argument that the caretaking debt is a collective one is based on the fact that biological dependency is inherent to the human condition, and there-fore, of necessity of collective or societal concern. Just as individual depen-dency needs must be met if an individual is to survive, collective dependency needs must be met if a society is to survive and perpetuate itself. The mandate that the state (collective society) respond to dependency, therefore, is not a matter of altruism or empathy (which are individual responses often resulting in charity), but one that is primary and essential because such a response is fundamentally society-preserving.

If infants or ill persons are not cared for, nurtured, nourished, and perhaps loved, they will perish. We can say, therefore, that they owe an individual debt to their individual caretakers. But the obligation is not theirs alone—nor is their obligation confined only to their own caretakers. A sense of social justice demands a broader sense of obligation. Without aggregate caretaking, there could be no society, so we might say that it is caretaking labor that produces and reproduces society. Caretaking labor provides the citizens, the workers, the voters, the consumers, the students, and others who populate society and its institutions. The uncompensated labor of caretakers is an unrecognized subsidy, not only to the individuals who directly receive it, but more signifi-cantly, to the entire society. . . .

The assignment of responsibility for the burdens of dependency to the family in the first instance, and within the family to women, operates in an unjust manner because this arrangement has significant negative material con-sequences for the caretaker. This obvious observation allows me to introduce an additional, but often overlooked, form of dependency into the argument—"derivative dependency." Derivative dependency arises on the part of the per-son who assumes responsibility for the care of the inevitable dependent person. I refer to this form of dependency as derivative to capture the very simple point that those who care for others are themselves dependent on resources in order to undertake that care. Caretakers have a need for monetary or material resources. They also need recourse to institutional supports and accommodation, a need for structural arrangements that facilitate caretaking.

Currently, neither the economic nor the structural supports for caretaking are adequate. Many caretakers and their dependents find themselves impoverished or severely economically compromised. Some of their economic problems stem from the fact that within families, caretaking work is unpaid and not considered worthy of social subsidies. There are also, however, direct costs associated with caretaking. Caretaking labor interferes with the pursuit and development of wage labor options. Caretaking labor saps energy and efforts from investment in career or market activities, those things that produce economic rewards. There are foregone opportunities and costs associated with caretaking, and even caretakers who work in the paid labor force typically have more tenuous ties to the public sphere because they must also accommodate caretaking demands in the private. These costs are not distributed among all beneficiaries of caretaking (institutional or individual). Unjustly, the major economic and career costs associated with caretaking are typically borne by the caretaker alone.

Further, most institutions in society remain relatively unresponsive to innovations that would lessen the costs of caretaking. Caretaking occurs in a larger context and caretakers often need accommodation in order to fulfill multiple responsibilities. For example, many caretakers also engage in market work. Far from structurally accommodating or facilitating caretaking, however, workplaces operate in modes incompatible with the idea that workers also have obligations for dependency. Workplace expectations compete with the demands of caretaking—we assume that workers are those independent and autonomous individuals who are free to work long and regimented hours.

In discussing the costs and impediments associated with undertaking the tasks of caretaking, it is important to emphasize that, unlike inevitable dependency, derivative dependency is not a universal experience. In fact, many people in our society totally escape the burdens and costs that arise from assuming a caretaking role, perhaps even freed for other pursuits by the caretaking labor of others. The status of derivative dependency is structured by and through existing societal institutions, culturally and socially assigned according to a script rooted in ideologies, particularly those of capitalism and patriarchy. These scripts function at an unconscious (and therefore, unexamined) level, and channel our beliefs and feelings about what is considered natural and what are appropriate institutional arrangements. When individuals act according to these scripts, consistent with prevailing ideology and institutional arrangements, we say they have chosen their path from the available options. The construction of this notion of individual choice allows us to avoid general responsibility for the inequity and justify the maintenance of the status quo. We ignore the fact that individual choice occurs within the constraints of social conditions. These constraints include ideology, history, and tradition, all of which funnel decisions into prescribed channels and often operate in a practical and symbolic manner to limit options.

As it now stands in this society, derivative dependents are expected to get both economic and structural resources within the family. The market is unresponsive and uninvolved, and the state is perceived as a last resort for financial resources, the refuge of the failed family. A caretaker who must resort to governmental assistance may do so only if she can demonstrate that she is needy in a highly stigmatized process. . . .

In order to move from our current situation to a more just resolution for the dilemma of caretaking and dependency, we will need more than a responsive state. The state will also have to be an active participant in shaping and monitoring other societal institutions. One fundamental task will be monitoring and preventing the exploitation and appropriation of the labor of some citizens through institutional and ideological arrangements. This must be prevented even when the justification for the labor's appropriation and exploitation is that it is used for the good of the majority. Further, it must be prevented even in contexts where social constraints and conventions coerce consent from the laborer.

In this endeavor, the state must use its regulatory and redistributive authority to ensure that those things that are not valued or are undervalued in market or marriage are, nonetheless, publicly and politically recognized as socially productive and given value. Conferral of value requires the transfer of some economic resources from the collective society to caretakers through the establishment of mechanisms that tax those who receive the benefits of caretaking in order to compensate those who do the caretaking. Other societies do this in a variety of ways, such as using tax revenues to provide childcare allowances and universal benefits that assist caretakers, or through a basic income guarantee. Money, however, is not enough. The active state must also structure accommodation of the needs of caretaking into society's institutions.

Vicki Schultz, Life's Work

100 Colum. L. Rev. 1881, 1883-1886, 1900-1905 (2000)

[T]he concept of a "life's work" [describes] some of the central elements of a utopian vision in which women and men from all walks of life can stand alongside each other as equals, pursuing our chosen projects and forging connected lives. In the process, we come to view each other as equal citizens and human beings, each entitled to equal respect and a claim on society's resources because of our shared commitments and contributions. As individuals, our work provides us with a forum to realize at least some of our aspirations, to form bonds with others, to serve society, and to project ourselves into the larger world beyond our own families and friends. It also provides us with the wherewithal to sustain ourselves, economically and socially, so that we may enter into intimate relationships with the security that permits us to love (and leave) freely, without need of recompense. This world of equal citizenship, stable community, and a strong, secure selfhood for everyone is the world I believe feminism was born to bring into being.

Recently, however, a number of feminists and liberals have begun to move away from such a vision; some even associate an emphasis on equal work with conservatism. Some feminist legal scholars now advocate paying women to care for their own families in their own households; many seem to have given up on achieving genuine gender integration of the work done in both households and workplaces. Some liberal thinkers urge that we provide everyone a guaranteed income or capital allotment; they believe tying the distribution of social goods to work interferes with individual freedom and choice. The presence of these discourses has moved me to articulate a feminist vision of the significance of paid work to the good life, to equality, and to women. I agree that it is vitally important to create society-wide mechanisms for allocating the costs of household labor and for allowing people to realize their preferences. But, unless we pay attention to the institutional contexts through which housework is valued and individual choice realized, stubborn patterns of gender inequality will continue to reassert themselves—including the gender-based distribution of work that is at the root of women's disadvantage. In the search for social justice, separatism simply won't suffice. . . .

In my view, a robust conception of equality can be best achieved through paid work, rather than despite it. Work is a site of deep self-formation that offers rich opportunities for human flourishing (or devastation). To a large extent, it is through our work—how it is defined, distributed, characterized, and controlled—that we develop into the "men" and "women" we see ourselves and others see us as being. Because law's domain includes work and its connection to other spheres of existence, the prospect of who we become as a society, and as individuals, is shaped profoundly by the laws that create and control the institutions that govern our experiences as workers. I believe that it is only by recognizing the formative power of such forces that we can imagine and invent ourselves as full human agents. . . .

Paid work has the potential to become the universal platform for equal citizenship it has been imagined to be, but only if we ensure meaningful participation in the workforce by attending to the specific needs of various social groups and individuals. In the past, legal efforts to achieve equality focused on protecting people from identity-based discrimination; we have tended to take the number and quality of jobs, job-holding services, wages, and working conditions produced by the market as a neutral baseline to which no one is to be denied access because of group status. But in order to make paid work the basis for equal citizenship, we will have to take steps to ensure that what the market produces is both substantively adequate and universally available for everyone. This means that, in the future, we will have to supplement employment discrimination law with measures like job-creation programs, wage subsidies, universal child care and health care programs, enhanced employee representation, and a reduced workweek for everyone. To achieve such reforms, feminists must move beyond an identity politics that presses for cultural recognition and revaluation of "women's experience." We must join forces with a broad array of groups—including the labor movement—not simply to advance each other's interests, but to fashion a shared interest in creating a social order in which work is consistent with egalitarian conceptions of citizenship and care. . . .

It is vitally important to acknowledge the hidden labor that is performed in households, and to create society-wide mechanisms for allocating its costs rather than continuing to impose them on individual family members (too often, women). One method of doing so is already being implemented on a massive scale: collectivizing housework by converting it into employment. A great deal of work once performed in private households has been handed over to day-care providers, cleaning services, home health aides, landscapers, and the like. Feminists could think creatively about how to capitalize on this trend by supporting efforts to upgrade the pay, promotional prospects, and working conditions associated with work once performed by at-home spouses. Compared to marriage and intimate relationships, labor markets and workplaces are spaces in which it is easier for workers to mobilize to obtain public accountability and protection. By transforming at least some forms of household work into paid employment, we could more easily protect those who do the work from discrimination, unfair labor practices, wage and hour violations, adverse working conditions, health and safety threats, and other problems on the job. We could also make it easier for those who perform household labor to engage in collective action to improve their situation. The recent victory of 70,000 California home health care workers in organizing a union, for example, holds promise for highlighting—and upgrading—the value of service work. Such victories continue the work started by the comparable worth campaigns of the 1980s.

Converting household work into paid employment not only provides jobs for many people who need them, it also frees those who provide unpaid family labor to pursue more fully for pay the work that suits them best. Countless middle- and working-class families buy time or convenience by purchasing such things as child care, cleaning services, dinners from McDonald's, lawn mowing, haircuts, car repair, and other services that should count as commercialized forms of household labor. There may, of course, be some forms of household labor that cannot or should not be commodified. There may also be some services that average- or low-income people cannot afford. But, there is no reason why a commercialization strategy must be limited to pure market forces. Some services could be subsidized for those who cannot afford them, or even made available for free to everyone (like public schooling, a now universal service that was once provided exclusively within the family setting).

Despite the fact that converting household labor into paid work collectivizes it and renders it more visible and publicly accountable, feminists in the movement to value housework tend to shun this approach. Instead, these feminists are proposing schemes to compensate women for performing household labor in private homes. Some legal feminists argue that (heterosexual) women's household labor provides their male partners with the time and resources to specialize in market work, and thus the men should compensate the women. These feminists propose marriage-based "joint property" schemes that redistribute income from husbands (or sometimes higher wage-earners, assumed to be husbands) to wives (or lower wage-earners, assumed to be wives) at divorce. Other feminists promote state-based "welfare" strategies in which the government pays caregiver stipends that are not tied to paid employment, but are instead intended to permit women to choose full-time or near full-time homemaking and child care. In joint property proposals the source of funding is the husband, while in welfare approaches it is the state. But both strategies channel funds through the family unit to pay women to keep house and care for our own kin.

Wittingly or unwittingly, advocates of these family-based approaches replicate some of the same conservative assumptions that have been used traditionally to justify women's disadvantage. Indeed, feminists in this movement tend to rely on the human capital literature to assert that it is women's disproportionate responsibility for housework and child care that accounts for our lower wages and our inferior position in the workforce. Unfortunately, many of these feminists seem unaware of (or uninformed about) the body of sociological work that casts doubt on the validity of human capital theory. Within the social sciences, the debate is between conventional economists — who pin women's plight on our family roles — and feminist sociologists (and sociologically-inclined economists) — who have produced evidence that discriminatory workplace dynamics are a more fundamental cause. The sociological literature points toward a more contextual approach that rejects static family-based conceptions of women's difference; it shows instead that socially-constructed features of the workworld help create the very gender differences (manifested in work aspirations, employment patterns, and familial divisions of labor) that human capital theory attributes to women themselves. Such an approach creates greater possibilities for change. If the sources of women's disadvantage lie not in sociobiological forces that commit women more heavily to child care and housework but instead in the political economy of paid work, we can challenge the sex bias in allegedly gender-neutral forces in labor markets and work places. We can create more empowering gender arrangements by demanding work and working conditions that will give women more economic security, more political clout, more household bargaining power, and perhaps even more personal strength with which to pursue our dreams.

[Additional portions of this article are set forth in Chapter 5.]

Dorothy Roberts, Spiritual and Menial Housework

9 Yale J.L. & Feminism 51, 55-59 (1997)

The "cult of domesticity" legitimized the confinement of women to the private sphere by defining women as suited for motherhood (and unsuited for public life) because of their moral or spiritual nature. Thus, the very idealization of women's spirituality bolstered the opposition between maternal nurturing in the home and masculine work in the cutthroat marketplace.

Household labor, however, is not all spiritual. It involves nasty, tedious physical tasks—standing over a hot stove, cleaning toilets, scrubbing stains off of floors and out of shirts, changing diapers and bedpans. The notion of a purely spiritual domesticity could only be maintained by cleansing housework of its menial parts. The ideological separation of home from market, then, dictated the separation of spiritual and menial housework. Housework's undesirable tasks had to be separated physically and ideologically from the moral aspects of family life.

This dichotomy has two important consequences. First, women may delegate housework's menial tasks to others while retaining their more valuable spiritual duties. Second, this fragmentation fosters a hierarchy among women because the menial aspects of housework are typically delegated by more privileged women to less privileged ones. At the same time, the availability of a class of menial workers, sustained by race and class subordination, makes this division of women's housework possible. Although women's participation in the market is now widely accepted, the assignment of household work to women and the distinction between spiritual and menial housework both persist. In the hit movie *The First Wives' Club*, the character played by Diane Keaton complains to her friends about the work she did for her ex-husband: "I washed his shorts, I ironed them, and I starched them." "You did?" her friends respond in amazement. "Well, I supervised," Keaton clarifies. This scene conveys the spiritual housewife's relationship to menial housework: she supervises the labor of less privileged women.

An early example of the distinction between spiritual and menial housework is embodied in the relationship between Mammy and her mistress. The image of Mammy was that of a rotund, handkerchiefed house servant who humbly nursed her master's children. Mammy was both the perfect mother and the perfect slave; whites saw her as a "passive nurturer, a mother figure who gave all without expectation of return, who not only acknowledged her inferiority to whites but who loved them." It is important to recognize, however, that Mammy did not reflect any virtue in Black motherhood. The ideology of Mammy placed no value in Black women as the mothers of their own children. Rather, whites claimed Mammy's total devotion to the master's children, without regard to the fate of Mammy's own offspring. Moreover, Mammy, while caring for the master's children, remained under the constant supervision of her white mistress. She had no real authority over either the white children she raised or the Black children she bore. Mammy's domestic labor is the perfect illustration of menial housework; her mistress, on the other hand, performed the spiritual work in the house.

Today, the spiritual/menial split enables many professional women to go to work without disturbing the sexual division of housework or relinquishing their role as spiritual housekeepers. In her study of domestics and the women who employ them, Judith Rollins found that middle-class women's entry in the workplace did not change their attitudes toward their role in the home. According to Rollins, "The middle-class women I interviewed were not demanding that their husbands play a greater role in housekeeping; they accepted the fact that responsibility for domestic maintenance was theirs, and they solved the problem of their dual responsibilities by hiring other women to assist." Female employers usually view their maids as an extension of the more menial part of themselves rather than as autonomous employees. Hiring a domestic worker leaves the employer free both to work outside the home and to devote herself to the spiritual aspects of being a wife and mother.

The modern household worker's job is defined in a way that prevents its interference with the female employer's spiritual prerogatives. Even if a child spends the entire day with her nanny while her mother is at work, the hour of "quality time" mother and child share at bedtime is considered most important. Of course, the mother expects the nanny to develop a warm and caring relationship with the child. She wants the nanny to treat the child as a special person, and not as a chore. But the mother nevertheless desires her own relationship with her child to be superior to—closer, healthier, and more influential than—the relationship the child has with the nanny. . . .

These incompatible motives parallel another dilemma that mothers face in delegating child care to a less privileged employee. In another study of private child care arrangements, Julia Wrigley discovered that parents were torn between their desire to hire a high-status substitute mother and their preference for a manageable subordinate. "They would like caregivers who share their child-rearing values and who operate independently," Wrigley explains, "but they also want inexpensive, reliable, controllable employees." Parents often resolve this dilemma by relying on their spiritual supervision of the low-status employees' menial work. For example, one employer commented that "sometimes it was better to accept 'dumb' employees who are under the parents' control rather than deal with cocky ones." In both studies, employers resolved their contradictory desires by distinguishing between their own spiritual and the employees' menial housework.

Thus, the mother's spiritual moments with her child are far more valuable than the long hours the nanny spends caring for the child. Moreover, the working mother might not be able to devote quality time to her child at all if she came home to face the chores that the nanny took care of during the day. Some working mothers also hire another woman, who has even lower status, to clean the house and run errands. By delegating work to a nanny and/or maid, affluent women can fulfill their spiritual calling as mother despite their career in the market.

What is wrong with distinguishing between the roles played by the mother and by the woman she hires to care for her children? Would we not expect to find a difference between a child's relationship with her parents and with the paid household help? My point is not that we should eradicate all distinctions among people who perform housework, but to demonstrate how the distinction made between spiritual and menial housework fosters both a gendered and racialized devaluation of this type of labor. By separating spiritual from menial housework, both the mother and the nanny continue to be undercompensated for their work in the home despite working women's supposed liberation from domestic confinement.

Notes

1. Substantive Equality vs. Difference Theory as a Basis for Legal Reform.   Both substantive equality and difference theory support greater public responsibility for children and family leave policies, as well as better employer policies governing flexible and reduced schedules. However, while substantive equality models justify supportive measures as necessary to eliminate the disadvantages women experience, and thus to equalize the sexes' legal and economic status, difference theory justifies such measures as part of a better, more nurturing world for everyone. Which approach seems more politically viable? Is there an advantage to characterizing these measures as a positive, societal ideal, rather than as an accommodation to women's "difference"?

2. Furthering "Family Values": What Needs to Change?   Fineman's assertion that caretaking is a public good, and therefore a collective social responsibility, tracks arguments of other feminist thinkers. Economist Nancy Folbre, for example, argues that the "invisible hand" of the market cannot function without the "invisible heart" of care: "Markets cannot function effectively outside the framework of families and communities built on values of love, obligation, and reciprocity."[25] Many feminists have pointed out that caretaking has traditionally been performed without pay by women, but now that women are flooding into paid work, societies must find some other equitable way to provide caretaking services.[26]

What might greater state support for caretaking look like? Income supplements for families with dependents, greater tax subsidies for child care expenses, and mandatory paid leave are examples. These reforms, discussed in Chapter 2, leave existing employment and family patterns relatively intact, with government assistance to lessen their burdens.

For some feminists, adequate support for caretaking requires a fundamental rethinking of "the family." Martha Fineman, for example, argues that the state has a legitimate interest in caring for dependents, but no legitimate interest in the kinds of intimate relationships adults form with one another. Therefore, she concludes, marriage should be abolished as a legal category, or at least as the unit through which state supports for caregiving should flow.

Fineman argues that the paradigm of the caregiving family should be the dyad of Mother/Child rather than Husband/Wife, and that state support should flow accordingly to "caregiving families," understood as dependents and the people who nurture them.[27]

Vicki Schultz, who favors decent work for all, believes that only participation in the paid work force can bring women full citizenship. Her approach points toward reforms of the workplace rather than the family or government programs.[28]

Are these positions necessarily at odds with one another? Or are the state's obligations to support caretakers and the woman's participation in the work force complementary feminist goals?

3. Is Caretaking a Public Good? From an equality perspective, the debate over caretaking is about the disadvantages women experience when the family is organized to give them primary responsibility for their "private" decision to have children, while the "ideal worker" in the workplace is assumed to be available full time, and unburdened by significant family responsibilities.[29] Theorists such as Martha Fineman stress that caretaking is not just a private consumption decision, but also a public good, upon which society depends.

A number of feminist theorists resist the premise that caretaking is a public good. Katherine Franke's primary concern is the further privileging of reproduction, along with its various cultural associations and a sexual division of labor that oppresses women.

> Reproduction has been so taken for granted that only women who are not parents are regarded as having made a choice—a choice that is constructed as nontraditional, nonconventional, and for some, non-natural.[30]

Franke also raises fairness issues about the public support for an activity over which the public retains so little control.

> The politics of public value, public subsidy, but private accountability with respect to raising children is revealed to be quite paradoxical under close examination. . . . [For example, a] large number of home schoolers are fundamentalist christian families who . . . "are no longer fighting against the mainstream—they're 'dropping out' and creating their own private America." Many families . . . are heeding the call of Paul Weyrich, a founder of the Christian Right, to "drop out of this culture, and find places . . . where we can live godly, righteous, and sober lives." Not coincidentally, these families, and many others like them, are also making the loudest demands for public subsidies or vouchers that will finance home-schooling as well as private, parochial school tuition for families that seek to remove their children from the public school system. It must be worth at least thinking about the carte blanche we give the privatized family to refuse to teach "our" future citizens public norms of tolerance, equality, and humanity—or worse. . . .
>
> What also strikes me as worthy of examination is the degree to which parenting is described as productive society activity while, in many regards,

parenting has become as much or more about consumption than production. Sylvia Anne Hewlett, the founder of the National Parenting Association, mused in a recent op-ed piece . . . about how the public fails to recognize the financial sacrifices that mothers make to raise children. What with "therapy, summer camp, computer equipment and so on," kids are just darn expensive, she argued. The "and so on" explicitly entails Pokemon accessories, My Little Pony dolls, Barbies, fancy sneakers, and other expensive articles of consumption that are aggressively marketed to children these days. While I don't think that children of any economic class should be deprived of the toys and other items that bring joy into their lives, I am concerned about the bourgeois framing of an issue that gives the larger public the tab for the marketing-induced "needs" of children. And all in the name of "society-preserving work." That children want things, or their parents wish to provide them to their children, is an insufficient justification for shifting the costs of those needs to the public.[31]

Another critic, Mary Anne Case, focuses on the unfairness of shifting the burden of caretaking to those who choose not to have children.

> The difficulty I have experienced goes beyond privileging certain kinds of family over others, and more broadly extends to a privileging of family matters over an employee's other life concerns.
>
> . . . [I]f the premise of some parents' advocates really is one of strong equality of result (i.e., that parent should, in effect, be held harmless in time and money from their decision to have children; that their decision to have children should be made as close as possible to costless), then we really are talking, if not quite about a zero-sum game, then at least about a massive redistribution from nonparents to parents, one which, on grounds, *inter alia*, of inequity to people like myself, I would strongly oppose.[32]

Even if caretaking is a public good, is there a reason why it should be singled out for priority over other public goods such as health care or the environment? Is there such a thing as too much caretaking? What about the "helicopter parent" phenomenon?[33]

How far should caretaking obligations extend? In his influential 2009 book, The Life You Can Save, Princeton philosopher Peter Singer argues that if relatively well off individuals can save the lives of starving children in other nations with little harm to themselves, they have a moral obligation to do so. Do you think that feminists like Fineman and Bender agree? Is there a logical stopping point to an ethic of care?

4. Dependent Care and the Market in Domestic Workers.   The primary approach to child and elder care in the United States has been to treat it as a "private" issue to be negotiated by individual women. Government involvement has largely been limited to providing mothers with resources to track down "deadbeat dads." Women who must work but cannot afford high-quality in-home assistance or day care look to their own relatives, to babysitters, or to low-cost, frequently unlicensed family day-care centers that feature frequent turnover and poorly trained workers. Those workers are 93 percent female and poorly paid.[34] And, as Dorothy Roberts argues, the convergence of gender roles, racial norms, and market forces has meant that a disproportionate part of that undervalued labor force is nonwhite. Similar patterns characterize care for the elderly, a problem that is rapidly increasing as the baby boom generation ages. Women make up almost 90 percent, and women of color, 30 percent of this workforce, which is characterized by low wages, high turnover, and often unsafe or exploitative working conditions.[35]

Domestic work also lacks effective legal protections. It is explicitly excluded from coverage under the National Labor Relations Act (which guarantees the right to organize and engage in collective bargaining). It is also outside the protection of the Occupational Safety and Health Act, Title VII, and most state workers' compensation acts. Domestic workers typically have only limited eligibility for unemployment benefits. Collective action is difficult for domestic workers because they are isolated from one another, and enforcement of applicable laws and regulations is a serious problem, particularly when workers are undocumented. Many of these workers lack entitlement to overtime or health benefits, unemployment or disability benefits, or social security when they retire.

How might a true "ethic of care" restructure the market for caretaking? What mix of organizing strategies, government subsidies, tax incentives, and statutory protections would be most helpful?[36]

Putting Theory Into Practice

4-4. What are the implications of difference theory for laws relating to women's reproductive rights? Would the state be entitled or compelled, for example, to take greater control over the mother's risk-taking behavior during pregnancy, to express a stronger "ethic of care"?

4-5. How do you plan to cope with the challenges involved in balancing personal and professional commitments? Do you expect to work full time throughout your career? If so, how do you expect to meet family needs? Do you plan to have children? If so, who will take care of them? What accommodations do you think are fair to expect from your employer?

C. WOMEN IN THE JUSTICE SYSTEM

Women participate in the justice system in every respect—as parties, judges, lawyers, and witnesses. This section examines both the ways in which women's different voice is and is not heard, and the ways in which the legal system might look different if it were more deliberately shaped around an "ethic of care."

Reading Questions

1. Would you expect women to bring different values to the judging process, or are the generalizations in this section about women judges the product of stereotyping? If so, what would these values be?

2. Are lawyers and judges likely to bring gender biases to the courtroom, or to be subject to such biases in the workplace? Are jurors likely to bring systematic gender biases to the jury room? If so, how should the legal system respond?

3. How important is the uniform sentencing of people convicted of the same crime? Are there factors other than the crime and its severity that should be taken into account in setting a criminal sentence? The degree of misery caused to the victim and his or her family? Whether the defendant is pregnant, or the primary caretaker of children? Whether the defendant grew up highly disadvantaged with respect to parenting or economic resources?

1. Women in Legal Practice

American Bar Association Commission on Women in the Profession, Fair Measure: Toward Effective Attorney Evaluations

17-23 (2d ed. 2008)

B. Specific Types of Gender Bias . . .

(i) *The maternal wall: how stereotypes link motherhood and part-time work with lack of competence and commitment* . . .

Negative competence assumptions. A 2004 study found that adding the words "has a two-year-old child" to a woman's resume led evaluators to rate a woman as less capable and skillful and to decrease their interest in training and promoting her. Mothers were held to higher performance and time commitment standards than nonmothers, although fathers were held to lower performance and time commitment standards than nonfathers. A 2007 study found that mothers were 79% less likely to be hired, 100% less likely to be promoted, offered an average of $11,000 less in salary, and held to higher punctuality and performance standards. Mothers were seen as less suitable for hire, promotion, and management training, and deserving of lower salaries. It is often noted that "when men need time off to handle family matters, people think it reflects well on them. When women need time off to handle family matters, it is seen as a lack of commitment or a weakness." Women's absence (but not men's) often is attributed to lack of commitment. This is an example of *attribution bias*: note how the stereotype that women, but not men, lack commitment drives different interpretations of men's and women's behavior.

The pregnancy plummet. Job evaluations of managers "plummeted," according to one study, when they became pregnant. Pregnant women, the study found, tend to be viewed as "overly emotional, often irrational . . . and less committed to their jobs. They were not seen as valued or dependable employees." . . .

The good mother v. the norm of work devotion. While "the good father" and "the good mother" share many attributes, one important difference emerges: the good mother (but not the good father) is "always available to her children." The implicit stereotype of "the good mother" is a married mother who "will do anything for [her] children (e.g., children come first, always on call, wants the best for her kids)." This ideal clashes with the ideal of a lawyer who is always available for clients. The notion that a lawyer with a "good work ethic" is always on call reflects "the norm of work devotion," which requires that professionals "manifest singular 'devotion to work,' unencumbered with family responsibilities." When "[t]ime becomes a proxy for dedication and excellence," lawyers who need to place limits on their availability for work tend to be judged as lacking in both commitment and competence. . . .

"Killing moms with kindness." Benevolent prescriptive stereotyping, in a kinder and gentler tone of voice, enforces employers' sense of how mothers should behave. An example: A husband and wife worked for the same law firm. After they had a baby, the mother was sent home promptly at 5:30, on the assumption that she had a baby to care for. The father was kept later than ever, on the assumption that he had a family to support. Note how the employer, in effect, is pressuring the family into traditional gender roles. For a lawyer, such well-intended actions could lead to exclusion from challenging assignments or beneficial client contacts, and ultimately to denial of partnership. This is stereotyping, despite the good intentions: the better approach is simply to ask each parent what he or she wants.

"Role incongruity." Role incongruity sends the message that one cannot be a good mother and hold a certain job. For example, in one Fourth Circuit case, a supervisor told a lawyer that she needed to decide if she wanted to be "a successful mommy or a successful lawyer." In a Massachusetts case, an investigation revealed that a managing partner said that a woman with children was not a suitable candidate for a full-time position because her priorities lay "elsewhere."

Giving the benefit of the doubt to others, but not mothers. "The rule appears to be, when judgments are uncertain, give an in-group member the benefit of the doubt." Merit reviews have been found to be particularly vulnerable to stereotyping of this kind, called *leniency bias*. An example from an in-house lawyer who is a mother: "[B]efore I went part-time, people sort of gave me the benefit of the doubt. They assumed that I was giving them as fast a turnaround as was humanly possible. After I went part-time, this stopped, and they assumed that I wasn't doing things fast enough because of my part-time schedule." The vast majority of attorneys working flexible work schedules are women, and they do so for childcare reasons. The combination of being a woman and working a flexible schedule makes motherhood salient, which may well trigger leniency bias.

Mothers are assumed to be uncommitted. As noted above, part-time work can trigger maternal wall bias by making gender salient. The mother quoted in the previous section continued, "[B]efore I went part-time, when people called and found I was not at my desk, they assumed that I was elsewhere at a business meeting. But after I went part-time, the tendency was to assume that I was not there because of my part-time schedule—even if I was out at a meeting." This again is *attribution bias*: note how the lawyer's absence was attributed to a work reason while she was full time, but to a family reason once her part-time status triggered the schema of the "good mother" who is always available to her children. . . .

Double jeopardy. Studies that inquire whether women of color encounter different kinds of maternal wall stereotypes are few and far between. One found that African-American mothers are even less likely to be promoted than white mothers. Another reported that white women are sometimes offered flexible work arrangements that are not offered to women of color.

(ii) Double standards: why women have to work harder to prove competence . . .

The common saying "women must try twice as hard to achieve half as much" is documented by more than a quarter century of social science. Women are judged as less competent than men in traditionally masculine domains such as the law.

Studies document that women need to provide more evidence of job-related skills (relative to white men) before evaluators feel confident of their competence and that this has an effect on performance evaluations. Not only do women have to work harder to establish competence; they also can make fewer mistakes than men before they are judged incompetent.

The following are basic patterns of descriptive stereotyping that can make it harder for women to establish competence, driven by unspoken stereotypes that associate competence with men.

He's skilled, she's lucky. Men's successful performance of masculine tasks tends to be attributed to stable personality traits (he has the right stuff) while women's successes tend to be attributed to transitory situational factors (she lucked out or drew a receptive judge).

He's busy, she has trouble with deadlines. Conversely, men's failures tend to be attributed to situational factors (he's busy working on other matters), while women's tend to be attributed to stable personality traits (she has trouble with deadlines).

Are men given larger rewards for the same accomplishments? When men's successes are attributed to personality traits while women's are attributed to transitory factors, men will be seen as deserving of larger rewards than women for the same accomplishment. . . .

Do women need to prove their competence over and over again? Stereotypes are resistant to disconfirming information. Thus women may have to prove their competence over and over while men do not, because men's good performance is consistent with their assumed competence, whereas women's good performance is inconsistent with the stereotype of them as less competent at masculine tasks and in predominantly male work environments. . . .

Are women's mistakes remembered long after men's are forgotten? Similarly, stereotype-consistent information is recalled better than stereotype-inconsistent information, so that women's mistakes (confirming their lack of competence) are remembered long after men's are forgotten.

Are men judged on their potential and women strictly on their achievements? The tendency to judge men on their potential but women strictly on their achievements again reflects the automatic assumption (until proven otherwise) that men are competent. . . .

Presto change-o. In one study, subjects preferred an educated candidate over an experienced one when the male candidate had outstanding educational credentials. But this "education advantage" disappeared when the female candidate was better educated. Then many respondents stressed experience over education—and still favored the male over the female. In the evaluation context, criteria may be given different weight depending on the gender of the person being evaluated.

Double jeopardy. A 2006 study found that women lawyers of color reported being perceived less favorably than their counterparts in almost every one of the 14 categories covered in a survey. . . . Extensive literature documents the negative competence assumptions triggered by race for African-Americans. One study found that a favorable letter of recommendation for a black candidate was interpreted by third parties as indicating a less objectively good performance than a similar recommendation for a white candidate because of competence assumptions. Another study found that white women were seen as significantly more competent and more intelligent than black women. A third found that, when subjects were given identical resumes—one with a white-sounding name and the other with an African-American sounding name—African-Americans had to have eight years more experience than whites in order to receive the same number of callbacks. . . .

The evidence on Asian-American women is both scarcer and more mixed. On the one hand, Asians are seen as "too competent, too ambitious, too hard-working," which might be expected to mitigate the stereotypes of women (and racial minorities) as less competent. On the other hand, one stereotype of Asian-American women is that they are deferential and passive, a characterization that might be expected to trigger negative competence assumptions.

(iii) Double-binds and "deference-challenged" women: when the job requires a "go-getter" but assertive women are disliked . . .

Whereas descriptive stereotyping impacts assessments of competence, "deference-challenged" women often encounter prescriptive stereotyping that faults them for their failure to conform to feminine norms of selflessness and sensitivity to the comfort of others. (These are the interpersonal skills that are felt to be lacking.) . . .

Moreover, many behaviors considered inappropriate for women are precisely those deemed necessary in order to be seen as competent in a traditionally male job, thereby creating a double bind. If women behave in traditionally feminine ways, their competence is undervalued, whereas if they behave in traditionally masculine ways, their interpersonal skills are derogated and their mental health questioned. "Because advancement in organizations depends not only on competence but also on social acceptance and approval," negative reactions to women who seek to achieve in "areas that traditionally are off-limits to them can be lethal when they strive to get ahead."

What a witch. Some women are unpleasant; others lack inter-personal skills. That said, studies show that behavior that would be accepted in men often is considered unacceptable in women. When a woman in a traditionally masculine job is called a "witch" or "too ambitious" in situations where a man would be characterized as "hard-driving," "having a temper," or "not suffering fools lightly," the unspoken prescription that women should be "helpful, warm, understanding, and kind" is at work. Decades of studies document that behavior that is praised and applauded in men often is regarded as unattractive in women, and that women who do not display feminine characteristics often are judged less psychologically healthy and evaluated less favorably than those who do. Women who violate the mandates of femininity are often viewed as "aggressive, selfish, greedy and cold." In some workplaces, women are seen either as "likable, dependent . . . traditional women" who are nice but not competent or as "dominant, competent, nontraditional women" (e.g., career women, feminists) who are competent, but are disliked for violating unspoken norms that women should be inclusive and nurturing. This pattern is called *ambivalent sexism*.

He's incisive; she's abrasive. Ambivalent sexism also lies behind the finding that the "same critical remark was found to be abrasive coming from a woman, but incisive and direct coming from a man."

She's a shameless self-promoter; he knows his own worth. Hiding one's light under a bushel is not a promising strategy for success. Not surprisingly, self-promotion enhances performance ratings and thus impacts evaluations. Yet self-promotion in women is often viewed with distaste. One study found, in the context of a masculine job, that women who "spoke in a direct, self-confident manner, highlighted past accomplishments," and attributed successes to skill rather than luck were viewed less positively than women who were more modest about skills and accomplishments and included disclaimers ("I'm no expert") and hedges ("Don't you think?"). Another found that women had "to show that they were not seeking status at the expense of other group members." Self-promotion in women flouts the norm that "women cooperate, men compete," and that women are selfless and supportive of others.

Notes

1. Women's Representation in the Legal Profession.   By the turn of the twentieth century, various political, legal, and social forces had coalesced to secure women's rights to admission to the bar in about half the states, and by 1920, formal barriers were largely removed. But informal obstacles remained substantial. One District of Columbia judge captured widespread attitudes: "Bring on as many women lawyers as you choose, I do not believe they will be a success."[37]

Since the 1960s, the representation of women in the American legal profession has increased from about 3 to 31 percent, and since the turn of the twenty-first century, women have constituted almost half of entering law students. Yet female practitioners remain underrepresented at the top and overrepresented at the bottom in terms of status, power, and financial reward. Women account for only 19 percent of law firm partners, 20 percent of Fortune 500 company general counsels, about 23 percent of federal judges, and 27 percent of state judges.[38] The gap widens for women of color, who account for less than 5 percent of law firm partners, general counsel, and state and federal judges.[39] Minority representation in the bar lags behind that in most other professions, as well as in the labor force generally. According to the most recent available data, minorities constituted about 25 percent of the civilian labor force, 25 percent of physicians, 23 percent of computer scientists, 20 percent of accountants, and 18 percent of academics, compared to 10 percent of lawyers. Women account for a higher percentage of minority lawyers than white lawyers (44 percent compared to 30 percent).[40] A substantial gender pay gap also persists. Overall, women attorneys earned a median 22 percent less than men. In private practice, the gap is smaller; for women associates it is 4 percent and for equity partners, 13 percent.[41] Gaps persist even for female partners who are equally productive as their male colleagues in generating revenue for their firms.[42]

One main challenge in achieving gender equity in the legal profession involves retention and promotion. The problem is not simply that women have not been in the pipeline long enough to achieve substantial representation at the highest levels. In studies comparing women's and men's likelihood of making partner, "the rate for men ranges from two to five times greater than for women. Even women who never take time out of the labor force and who work long hours have a lower chance of partnership than similarly situated men."[43] Minority men account for twice as many partners as minority women.[44] The disparities are most pronounced at the highest levels, such as managing partners and senior government officials; women account for only 5 percent of those partners.[45] Similar gender disparities are apparent in most other European and Anglo-American nations.[46] Underrepresentation is greatest for women of color. Their proportion of equity partners remains stuck at around 2 percent and they have "a nearly 100 percent attrition rate from law firms at the end of eight years."[47] Factors contributing to these attrition rates are professional and social isolation, unconscious bias, and lack of access to flexible schedules, mentors, and quality work assignments.[48]

Sex-based differences in career paths affect women's underrepresentation, but these differences have been narrowing over time. Men and women are now similarly distributed in most legal settings, although women are disproportionately underrepresented in business (which accounts for 12.3 percent of female lawyers and 14.6 percent of male lawyers) and overrepresented in public interest positions (which account for 7.8 percent of female lawyers and 4.2 percent of male lawyers). In private practice, the ratio of female to male lawyers is 51 percent to 55.4 percent. In government, men and women are evenly represented (both around 13 percent).[49]

2. Women Lawyers: Seeking a Different Professional Life? Should it be of concern that women do not occupy the same status as men in private practice, and that they are grossly underrepresented in large firms? Consider Carrie Menkel-Meadow's observation:

> Achievement of high-status and lucrative positions in large law firms represents the liberal feminist achievement of the American Dream. But is it a dream or a nightmare? Monetary and prestige measures of success, drawn from conventional male-constructed sociology, all too often are taken as the measure of women's progress in the profession, even where there is some evidence women themselves look to other measures, like doing socially useful work or having meaningful relationships at work with clients and co-workers. Both cultural and more radical feminist critiques remind us that becoming surrogate males is not the feminist-humanist transformative vision. Committing many hours to routinized tasks, within a highly stratified hierarchy, on cases and transactions with debatable social utility, while leaving one's children in the care of low-income women is hardly the feminist vision of a more humane world. . . . Women want to be in the workforce but may want to reconstruct what it means to be a productive worker.[50]

Does this suggest a different "women's" vision of a professional life? Discrimination? Or both? Studies of career change reflect similar gender differences. For example, in one in-depth Colorado bar study, virtually all men moved up in status over the course of the 12 years surveyed. That was true of only about half of women. Male lawyers' primary explanation for leaving their last job was new opportunities in law (46 percent); the second most common reason was unhappiness with compensation (23 percent). Women were slightly more likely to cite dissatisfaction with compensation (26 percent), and far less likely to cite new opportunities in law (27 percent). Women also gave reasons that almost no men report: lifestyle concerns (10 percent), unhappiness with legal practice (6 percent), and opportunities outside of law (4 percent).[51] These findings are consistent with a number of earlier studies and with patterns in most European nations, where women move "sideways not up."[52]

Satisfaction rates also reveal a substantial gender gap. [A]though female lawyers report about the same overall career satisfaction as their male colleagues, women also experience greater dissatisfaction with most dimensions of practice: salary, level of responsibility, recognition for work, content of work, chances for advancement, and control over their work lives. . . . [In an ABA survey of large firm lawyers] [w]hite men graded their career satisfaction as A; white women and minority men graded theirs as B, and minority women hovered between B minus and C plus.[53] Women of color are the least satisfied of all lawyers with almost all aspects of their workplaces.[54]

In attempting to account for this "paradox of success," theorists suggest two explanations.

> One involves values. Women may ascribe less significance to aspects of their work environment on which they are disadvantaged, such as compensation and promotion, than to other factors such as intellectual challenge, which evokes greater satisfaction among female than male attorneys. A second theory is that women have a lower sense of entitlement, in part because their reference group is other women or because they "have made peace with second best."[55]

What implications do you draw from these differences? Is Kingsley Browne right in his article excerpted earlier in this chapter: there is no glass ceiling, only different career paths? Or is Deborah Rhode right that "female lawyers' dissatisfaction with certain aspects of practice, which is reflected in disproportionate rates of attrition, should be cause for concern in a profession committed to diversity and equity"?[56] What do women want from a career in law? Is it different from what men want? Is it possible to generalize about either group on the issues that matter most? What would success in the law look like in a "more humane world"? Is it possible that women's different priorities largely explain their underrepresentation and call for no institutional remedies?

3. Structural Bias and Unconscious Bias.   More significant than conscious bias against women in legal practice are structural barriers and unconscious attitudes and assumptions. This bias is apparent in law schools themselves, some argue. Studies in the 1980s and 1990s found that female students received lower grades than their male classmates, given predictions based on test scores and college performance, and that they also participated less in class, held fewer leadership positions, and received less mentoring.[57] More recent studies have shown more mixed results, but at many institutions, male students talk more in class and receive higher grades.[58] In national surveys, women are underrepresented on law reviews and write fewer law review notes and articles.[59] Other studies have shown a persistent gap in the most prestigious judicial clerkships.[60] Women law students also have higher rates of dissatisfaction, disengagement, and self-doubt than men.[61]

What implications should be drawn from these findings? To what extent are women themselves responsible for the gender disparities that persist? In commenting on the lower class participation rates of women at Harvard Law School, an editorial in the student newspaper faulted women for "consciously choosing to let their male peers do most the talking" and asserted that female students had a "duty" to speak up.[62] Another commentator, in response to feminists' arguments that the aggressive, competitive atmosphere of law school classrooms silences women, claims that such assertions revive nineteenth-century stereotypes about women's inability to engage in the "hot strifes of the bar."[63]

As for additional structural features of the legal world that may contribute to an unequal playing field for women, in hearings before the ABA Commission on Women in the Profession, the most commonly cited obstacle was legal employers' failure to accommodate family responsibilities.[64] Two central problems are the excessive hours in many practice settings, and the inadequacy of part-time options, parental leave, and flexible schedule arrangements. Although the vast majority of legal employers provide paid maternity leave, the duration is often insufficient and only about 10 to 15 percent of surveyed employers provide the same opportunities for men. So too, while over 90 percent of law firms report offering part-time policies, only about 4 percent of lawyers actually use them.[65] Women who take advantage of part-time policies often report "schedule creep" and second-class status in work assignments and advancement possibilities; their reduced hours aren't respected, and they fall off the partnership track. Few law firms have followed the lead of major corporations and accounting firms in providing help to employees in securing affordable, quality child care and elder care, particularly for emergencies, weekends, and evenings. Such failures carry significant costs in recruitment, retention, absenteeism, and job-related stress.[66]

Another commonly cited obstacle involves the exclusion of women, particularly women of color, from challenging work assignments and informal networks of support, mentoring, and business development. ABA research finds that

- Fifty-five percent of white women and 43 percent of women of color in law firms, compared with 3 percent of white men and 24 percent of men of color, reported limited access to client development opportunities.
- Thirty-nine percent of white women and 44 percent of women of color in law firms, compared with 2 percent of white men and 25 percent of men of color, reported being passed over for desirable assignments.[67]

More mixed findings emerged from a 2009 study by the Minority Corporate Counsel Association. There, the vast majority of minority lawyers and female associates in large firms believed that their firm's leadership was committed to diversity (81 percent and 79 percent, respectively). Still higher numbers of whites (90 percent) and male partners (94 percent) had similar assessments. Only 13 to 14 percent of minority partners and female associates reported experiencing discrimination. Yet many also reported substantially less satisfaction than their white male counterparts concerning assignments, mentoring, and business development.[68] As one woman of color noted, "There are subtle forms of 'discrimination' that are difficult to truly pinpoint or detail. . . . [H]ow is one to know whether missed opportunities are a result of a racial or gender bias . . . ? However, it is very apparent that being of the same race, ethnicity or gender as a powerful partner" can be an advantage when it makes the partner "fee[l] comfortable with the associate."[69] Some minority female lawyers also reported feeling like "tokens" when they were included on teams just to make the firm's "numbers" look good for corporate clients.[70]

By contrast, some white male lawyers objected to efforts at " 'diversity' and 'inclusion' [as] pernicious forms of racial . . . discrimination." In their view, "reverse discrimination" fostered a "victim mentality and an expectation that success does not need to be earned."[71] How would you respond?

Strategies for addressing these obstacles fall into two categories. One is to assist women, particularly women of color, to compete on a playing field that is not yet equal. These strategies include formal mentoring programs and women's initiatives that provide opportunities for support, guidance, and business development. Many bar associations and women's organizations are also active in providing research, educational materials, training, and programs. So, for example, a 2008 study by Catalyst, an organization for advancing professional women, catalogs "unwritten rules" that are critical in career development. The most important rules cited by survey participants were to

- network and build relationships within and outside the organization (71 percent);
- find ways to become visible (51 percent);
- communicate effectively and ask for frequent feedback (43 percent);
- perform well and produce results (35 percent);
- find a mentor, coach, or sponsor (32 percent);
- work long hours (29 percent); and
- develop a good career plan (20 percent).[72]

A second set of strategies aims at reforming institutional structures to create fairer evaluation, assignment, and reward systems, as well as more effective work/family policies. A 2008 report by the National Association of Women Lawyers identified the following strategies for breaking down gender barriers:

- ensure a broadened selection of leaders by diversifying the nominating process; publicizing explicit selection criteria; and holding partners accountable for achieving diversity;
- correct for hidden biases by tracking retention, increasing the objectivity of evaluation processes, and ensuring diverse representation in high-profile teams and leadership positions;
- promote meaningful mentoring through strategies such as training and reward systems; and
- promote workplace flexibility by offering customized schedules to all lawyers, employing a balanced-life coordinator; and monitoring the usage and impact of reduced hour schedules on retention and promotion.[73]

The Minority Corporate Counsel Association's report echoes many of these recommendations and also proposes that law firms implement "360-degree feedback loops" to provide bottom-up evaluations and gather information from all lawyers concerning their experiences and opportunities.[74]

Other commentators have recommended that legal employers centralize responsibility for diversity initiatives, obtain buy-in from leaders, and ensure accountability for developing and monitoring those initiatives.[75] Further proposals are that bar associations support "no glass ceiling" campaigns in which participating law firms adopt goals and timetables for women in leadership; that clients direct business only to firms with demonstrable commitments to diversity; and that students pressure employers through groups like Building a Better Legal Profession and the Yale Law Women's Association, which rank firms on their diversity and family-friendly policies.[76] How would you evaluate these strategies? What stands in their way?

4. Women in the Legal Profession: A Different Voice?   Matthew Hale Carpenter, in unsuccessfully defending the right of Myra Bradwell to become a member of the Illinois Bar, argued that while some cases may require the "rough qualities possessed by men, . . . [t]here are many causes in which the silver voice of a woman would accomplish more than the severity and sternness of man could achieve."[77] Do women bring any special qualities to legal practice?

Among contemporary lawyers, perceptions of gender differences are widely shared. In a representative ABA Journal poll, only 8 percent of women lawyers believed that male and female lawyers had the same strengths, and only 18 percent believed that they had the same weaknesses. Slightly under half of male lawyers believed that men and women had the same strengths and weaknesses. Women lawyers were thought to have greater empathy and "better people skills," but insufficient assertiveness and aggressiveness.[78] Lawyers in other nations often hold similar views.[79]

Many commentators have similarly argued that women lawyers practice in a "different voice," more sensitive to values of care, compassion, and cooperation than prevailing legal norms.[80] Such differences are assumed to account for sex-linked differences in choice of specialties, such as women's disproportionate representation among family lawyers, family court judges, and teachers of family law.[81] Some commentators have also associated greater openness to different perspectives and a recognition of the contingency and partiality of claims to "truth" and certainty to "feminist" legal methods.[82] Do these differences reflect women's "different voice," or simply the legacy of gender stereotypes?

Recent social science research does not confirm the sharp gender-linked variations in male and female lawyering that many practitioners and commentators assume. For example, a sophisticated survey by William Felstiner and colleagues finds no measurable differences in clients' perception of male and female lawyers; both sexes are seen as friendly, polite, organized, confident, and trustworthy. Nor does the sex of lawyers matter in terms of whether a client would be willing to recommend them or use them again.[83] Similarly, Lynn Mather's empirical study of divorce attorneys in three New England states finds that male and female lawyers both prefer amicable settlements. The gender differences were generally minor and some ran contrary to conventional stereotypes. Women tended to place slightly more value than men on being a sensitive listener (4.5 on scale of 5, compared to 4.18). However, female lawyers were also more likely than their male colleagues to say that they discouraged clients from talking about emotional and personal problems. Female lawyers also were more likely to be seen as unreasonable, aggressive, hard-nosed advocates, who were willing to pursue unreasonable client objectives. In interpreting such findings, Mather notes that women attorneys were disproportionately likely to represent women clients, and may have been willing to fight harder on "small points" because they realized the importance that financial concessions might have for their clients' well-being. Mather, like other contemporary commentators, stresses the importance of context, and concludes that gender is only one of the factors that influence lawyers' working styles.[84] Such accounts are consistent with the most recent, comprehensive social science research that finds few characteristics on which men and women consistently differ along gender lines. Even on these characteristics, gender typically accounts for only about 5 percent of the variation.[85] Contextual forces and other factors like race, ethnicity, and sexual orientation can be equally significant.

Similarly, surveys of leadership styles and decisionmaking behavior have reached mixed results. Some research based on small-scale laboratory experiments and individuals' self-descriptions finds that women display greater interpersonal skills and adopt more participatory, democratic styles, while men rely on more directive and task-oriented approaches. Yet many large-scale studies find no such differences, particularly those based on evaluations of leaders by supervisors, subordinates, and peers in real-world settings.[86] In accounting for these disparate results, researchers note that gender stereotypes and socialization patterns push women to behave, and to describe their own behavior, in ways that comport with traditional standards of femininity. Yet the force of these standards is constrained in organizational settings where advancement requires some measure of conformity to traditionally masculine styles of leadership.

Another context in which gender differences have been extensively researched involves negotiating behavior. Over the past two decades, a large body of theoretical and empirical research has attempted to determine whether men and women have different negotiating styles and effectiveness. One summary of this work finds

> conflicting claims and widely disparate results—such as the most recent studies' conclusions that "men negotiate significantly better outcomes than women" . . . ; "women behave more cooperatively than men" . . . ; "women may obtain lower joint outcomes in integrative bargaining because of a higher

level of concern for the other" . . . , but also that "there are no statistically significant differences in negotiation outcomes and performance between men and women."[87]

In accounting for these conflicting results, it may be significant that gender is mediated by other aspects of the negotiating context that vary across research settings. These other aspects include the relative social status, perceived power, and attitudes toward conflict of the participants. Whether negotiators are the same sex, whether they have ongoing relationships, and whether they are acting for themselves or as representatives for someone else also matters. One of the few findings of gender difference that holds up across multiple studies is that women seem to feel less confident than men even when there are no objective differences in outcome.[88]

It is possible, of course, to argue for more caring and cooperative approaches to legal practice on the basis of feminist commitments, not feminine characteristics. Much recent work by feminists as well as other commentators concludes that nonadversarial collaborative and problem-solving techniques may be more effective than conventional adversarial methods and that more participatory, less hierarchical lawyering styles can improve representation of clients.[89]

To what extent can it be expected that women will change the profession? In summarizing research from around the globe, Ulrike Schultz concludes that although women in the legal profession do not speak in a collective voice or form a distinctive culture, they have altered the conditions of work and the laws affecting women.[90] Is that true of this country as well? Is it more likely that the profession will change women than that women will change the profession?

Putting Theory Into Practice

4-6. Have you observed any gender patterns in class participation in the course for which you have been reading this book? Analyze these dynamics. How does one get recognition in your class? What factors seem to affect who gets called on, who asks questions, and who stays after class to ask questions? Is this class typical? How would you assess the climate for women in your law school? What about women of color?

To the extent that female students participate less in class and feel more alienated from the educational process, what strategies should law professors consider to address these disparities? How would you evaluate these strategies in terms of the different perspectives examined in this course?

4-7. Leila Robinson, the first woman lawyer in Massachusetts, counseled her female colleagues: "Do not take sex into the practice. Don't be 'lady lawyers.' Simply be lawyers and recognize no distinction between yourselves and the other members of the bar."[91] Is that still good advice?

Why or why not? What strategies would be most effective in building coalitions for change within the legal profession?

4-8. The Austin Manifesto on Women in Law, adopted at a 2009 Women's Power Summit on Law and Leadership, maintained that "[a] critical mass of women lawyers is a significant element in providing a work environment that is hospitable and nurturing to women lawyers."[92] Yet the preceding year, a study by the American Bar Association found that a majority of women lawyers under 40 preferred male supervisors, who received higher marks than women for constructive criticism and keeping confidences. In explaining the survey results, consultants noted that women expect more nurturing from other women than from men and so are more readily disappointed when it is not forthcoming. Competition among women for credit and power is also particularly likely to be divisive.[93] How should legal employers and women's initiatives respond to these findings?

2. Judging

Judith Resnik, On the Bias: Feminist Reconsiderations of the Aspirations for Our Judges

61 S. Cal. L. Rev. 1877, 1879, 1921-1926 (1988)

A vast body of legal literature addresses the question of what qualifies a person to be a judge. We speak about seeking individuals who will be "impartial," "disengaged," "independent," and who will hear both sides and judge fairly. . . .

. . . A touchstone of feminism is connection; over and over again, feminist theories speak about our interrelatedness, our interdependencies, our selves and others as impossible of comprehension in isolation. . . .

At one level, what is missing [in the ideal of judging] is evident: We do not, but we could, demand that those who hold power do so with attentive love, with care, with nurturance, with a responsible sense of one's self as connected to and dependent upon those who are being judged. . . . But there are (at least) three difficulties. The first is one of domination. Assuming that we could alter the aspirations for judging, what would happen if the list of judicial qualifications were simply enlarged by adding the qualities feminist theories have helped us learn to value? . . . Stirring a bit of connection and responsible nurturance in the pot of powerful disengagement of our judges is hardly the kind of transformative response that feminist insights demand. A revised, rather than an expanded, list of attributes, is required.

A second problem is one of enthusiasm. How sure can we be that connection and care are qualities we want for our judges? . . . How, one might ask, could an empathic judge sentence another-in-whom-one-sees-oneself to years of incarceration? How could judges impose economic burdens on struggling individuals or entities? For those of us who might applaud a possible reduction in criminal penalties which such intimacy and empathy might foster, we must recognize that our empathic judges would not simply experience connection with defendants, but also with victims. Might such judges respond with too harsh condemnations? Or with paralysis from being torn in too many directions?

. . . In our current world, in which we do not ask judges to recognize their connectedness to those before them, some judges impose harsh sentences and some more lenient ones; some judges impose obligations upon litigants without much apparent stress while others appear reluctant to sanction. The length of judicial opinions and the energy of some dissents bear testimony to the tugs and pulls of contemporary judging, complete with its claims of dispassion and disinterest.

. . . Perhaps if we learned to speak of judging as a terrible and terrifying job, as a burden of inflicting pain by virtue of judgment, we might develop modes of resolution different from those so readily accepted today. We might seek more communal modes of decision-making, insisting upon groups of two, three, or four judges to share the honor, the obligation, and the pain of decision. When we recognize the burden and the pain of judging, we might uncover one element of adjudication that exists but is relatively unacknowledged: Much "adjudication" is not a win/lose proposition but an effort at accommodation, with judges and juries responding to both sides but currently without vocabulary or permission to express empathy with competing claims. Many verdicts allocate victory to both sides, but our tradition is to mask that allocation rather than to endorse the practice of seeing multiple claims of right. Feminism may help bolster our trust in practice and permit us to remove the facades of total victory and defeat.

A third problem with revising the list of aspirations for our judges is one of meaning and application. Care, connection, nurturance, identification are distinct qualities, each in need of contextual examination. If we simply stipulate to an expanded list of qualities for judges, we slip back into the universalism that feminist vantage points have taught us to suspect. Moreover, courts have claimed to be nurturant in the past; the juvenile court and intermediate sentencing were both based upon arguments of an obligation to be responsive to the needs of the populations presumably being served. Maternal thinking is appealing as a model, but many accounts of juvenile court and intermediate sentencing suggest that parenting modes are profoundly disabling to those parented. . . .

Notes

1. Gender Differences in Judging. Some legal scholars once claimed that there is a "feminine" jurisprudence that is apparent even among relatively conservative female judges such as Justice Sandra Day O'Connor. This assertedly feminine jurisprudence is characterized by a focus on responsibility and human interdependence and reflects understanding of gender discrimination.[94] The claim has been widely disputed, however, and a comparison in 2003 revealed that while Justice O'Connor and Justice Ginsburg voted for the same result approximately 75 percent of the time, Justice O'Connor agreed with relatively conservative Justice Kennedy 83 percent of the time, and Justice Ginsburg agreed with liberal Justices Breyer and Souter 94 percent.[95] Does this disprove the thesis? How relevant is it that, as Justice Ginsburg notes, they have voted the same on gender discrimination cases?[96] Consider Justice O'Connor's assertion that questions concerning women's "different voice" in judging are "dangerous and unanswerable."[97] She and Justice Ginsburg have been fond of quoting the observation that "[a]t the end of the day, a wise old man and a wise old woman reach the same decision."[98] Yet they both have strongly supported the appointment of more women on the Court, and argued that their presence increases the legitimacy and quality of the decisionmaking process.

Empirical studies of gender differences in judicial voting behaviors have reached varying results. Some have found that women judges were more sympathetic to divorced wives and gay rights plaintiffs; others have found no significant differences or more male support for women's rights issues.[99] One study of state supreme court justices found that female justices after 1991 (but not before) were more likely to rule for the criminal defendants.[100] Yet another study reports that increasing the number of female judges in a district is associated with lower sex disparities in sentencing for serious crimes, possibly because female offenders benefit from the paternalistic biases of male judges.[101]

Since the 1990s, however, the vast majority of studies have found some relationship between a judge's gender and voting behavior in gender-related cases.[102] For example, one study concluded that (1) having a female judge increased the probability of a finding for the plaintiff by 86 percent (from 22 percent to 41 percent) in sexual harassment cases and by 65 percent (from 17 percent to 28 percent) in sex discrimination cases, and (2) having a female on the panel more than doubled the probability that a male judge, regardless of his ideology, rules for the plaintiff in sexual harassment cases (increasing the probability from 16 percent to 35 percent) and nearly tripled the probability in sex discrimination cases (increasing it from 11 percent to 30 percent).[103]

What could explain these results? The author of the study explores four possible explanations: (1) female judges influence male judges through simple deliberation; (2) male judges defer to female judges in sex discrimination cases; (3) male judges make implicit strategic bargains with female judges for their votes in future cases; and (4) female judges cause male judges to moderate their anti-plaintiff preferences.[104] Which explanation(s), if any, seem plausible to you?

A recent survey of federal and state appellate decisions found that female judges were significantly more likely than male judges to rule in favor of gay and lesbian rights. The difference was significant when controlling for factors including age and party affiliation. Female law students are also more liberal than male students on gay rights issues. However, public opinion research finds no significant differences in men's and women's attitudes on the morality of same-sex relationships, although highly educated women are much more likely than highly educated men to believe that same-sex couples should have the right to marry.[105] Extrapolating from such findings, Fred Smith argues that the women who attend law school and become eligible for judgeships are more highly educated and have less traditional views of gender roles than the general public, which helps account for differences in judicial voting behavior on gay rights issues.[106]

Research on women judges in other countries have found "isolated cases of gender-specific approaches to the judicial task."[107] A study of the Canadian Supreme Court found that increasing the number of women justices also increased the likelihood that male justices would vote with their female colleagues in support of civil liberties and against criminal defendants.[108] However, the results in other nations are not always consistent with gender stereotypes. For example, in divorce cases involving spousal maintenance, women judges in some countries are less likely than their male colleagues to favor housewives, perhaps because these women "apply their own personal professional standards."[109] However, studies of state supreme court decisions in American divorce cases found that female judges were more supportive of women after controlling for political party affiliation.[110]

2. Diversity on the Bench.   Currently, women account for about 22 percent of federal judgeships and 27 percent of state judgeships. Three out of nine Justices on the U.S. Supreme Court are women. Women of color constitute about 5 percent of federal judges and 3 percent of state judges.[111] Women's representation in other countries averages about 25 percent, but the proportion varies considerably by country, ranging from 63 percent in Poland to 5 percent in Japan.[112]

What evidence would be required to make the case for "affirmative action" in the selection and confirmation of judges? Are there symbolic values in having a judiciary that is representative of the public irrespective of the extent to which women or minority judges have an identifiable, group-linked perspective? Are there any special considerations in this regard for the legitimacy of international courts?[113]

To what extent is the case for female judges based on an expectation that they will favor women's interests? In Blank v. Sullivan & Cromwell, Judge Constance Baker Motley denied a motion seeking her recusal in a gender discrimination case on grounds that her sex and prior experience as a civil rights attorney would bias her in favor of the plaintiff.[114] In rejecting that motion, the court ruled that if the "background or sex or race of each judge were, by definition, sufficient grounds for removal, no judge on this court could hear this case, or many others."[115] Does the motion make any more sense than one to recuse a male judge in such a case?

A **recusal** is a decision by a judge to remove (or disqualify) himself from a case and have another judge replace him. The most common basis for a judge's recusal is a conflict of interest, which creates the likelihood or appearance of bias. For example, a judge could not be expected to fairly judge a case if she or a family member has a financial interest in the outcome.

Consider a 2003 case in which an attorney requested recusal of a female judge in a case involving allegations that the defendant had groped a female nurse and used vulgar language. The attorney could not see how a woman judge "would be fair because of the nature of the allegations."[116] Can you? Would a male judge necessarily be more "fair"? To what extent do we want judges to build on their experience of group membership in deciding cases? Where is the line between empathy and partiality? (See Note 3 below.) Is it coherent to claim both that women have a "different voice" *and* that they bring no bias to their own decisionmaking?

In 2005, when Justice O'Connor announced her retirement, leaving only one woman on the Supreme Court, a Gallup poll found that only 15 percent of Americans thought it was essential to appoint another woman, 33 percent thought it was a good idea, and 49 percent said it didn't matter.[117] What is your view? What difference do you think it makes whether there is a woman on the Supreme Court, or how many? Would it have helped to appoint a woman who had a history of not supporting women's issues?[118]

3. Judicial Values: Empathy vs. Detached Neutrality.   What is the guarantee of impartiality in the courts—judges who are detached and objective, or empathetic and understanding of other perspectives? In 2009, when a vacancy on the Court opened, President Obama announced his views on the qualities of the Justice that he would appoint:

> I will seek somebody with a sharp and independent mind and a record of excellence and integrity. I will seek someone who understands that justice isn't about some abstract legal theory or footnote in a casebook. It is also about how our laws affect the daily realities of people's lives—whether they can make a living and care for their families; whether they feel safe in their homes and welcome in their own nation. I view that quality of empathy, of understanding and identifying with people's hopes and struggles as an essential ingredient for arriving at just decisions and outcomes.[119]

Commentators from the right were quick to condemn the President's statement. On Fox *Forum*, S. E. Cupp noted:

> The word *empathy*, according to its Greek derivation, means "physical affection, passion, and partiality." I thought Aristotle said the law is reason free from passion? And, if justice is blind, I'm fairly certain she's also impartial. But more importantly, who is on the receiving end of [empathy] by Obama's definition?[120]

Karl Rove echoed similar themes in criticizing "empathy" as too

> amorphous a basis on which to pick a justice. Should the "empathy stan-
> dard" apply to the unborn? How about gun owners? . . . What Mr. Obama
> wants in a nominee isn't really "empathy" and "understanding." He wants
> a liberal. . . .[121]

Thomas Sowell claimed that the "very idea of the rule of law becomes meaningless when it is replaced by the empathies of judges."[122] Senator Orrin Hatch of Utah weighed in that empathy is a "code word for an *activist* judge."[123] By contrast, two-thirds of surveyed Americans assigned empathy the highest degree of importance in selecting a Supreme Court Justice, and those most knowledgeable about the Court were particularly likely to value empathy. The most commonly desired characteristic, endorsed by three-quarters of Americans, was that justices "[u]phold the values of those who wrote the Constitution long ago." Are those positions always consistent, particularly on women's rights issues?[124]

What is the alternative to "empathy"? Is detachment possible? Desirable? Are empathy and objectivity compatible? Drawing on research concerning regulation of emotions, Terry Maroney argues that it is unrealistic and counterproductive to expect judges to put feelings aside in their decisionmaking. Rather, she proposes a model of engagement in which judges anticipate and respond thoughtfully to emotions and integrate lessons from those emotions into their future decisionmaking processes.[125] Susan Bandes similarly argues that empathy is both inevitable and essential to good judging; it enables judges to understand conflicting claims, but it does not dictate how they should be resolved. Thus, in her view, "it is misleading to discuss whether judges should exercise empathy . . . the questions are for whom they exercise it, how accurately they exercise it, how aware they are of their own limitations and blind spots, and what they do to correct for those blind spots."[126]

In the context of non-judicial conflict resolution, Susan Sturm and Howard Gadlin question the assumption that " 'detached neutrality' is the only or even the best way to achieve impartiality and reduce the expression of bias." They offer as an alternative the ideal of "multi-partiality," which they define as the ability to "critically analyz[e] a conflict from multiple vantage points—as a way to check the inevitable biases in decision making that have to be continually surfaced and corrected."[127]

Are any of these models preferable for judicial decisionmaking?

4. Gender Bias in the Courtroom.

Gender bias in the courtroom has not vanished. In one New York case, for example, Judge Robert Hamley resigned after stating that domestic violence cases were a "waste of the court's time" and that most women asked to get "smacked around."[128]

Beginning in 1982, courts began establishing gender bias task forces to respond to such conduct by all participants in the justice system. Some jurisdictions also established separate commissions on racial and ethnic bias or gave one commission responsibility to consider all diversity-related issues. By the turn of the twenty-first century, some 65 state and federal courts had issued reports on bias in the justice system. The ABA Commission on Women in the Profession summarizes the problems exemplified by these studies and the reforms necessary to address them:

> Between two-thirds and three-quarters of women report experiencing bias, while only a quarter to a third of men report observing it and far fewer report experiencing it. Women are also more likely than men to believe that bias is a significant problem and that female attorneys are treated less favorably than male attorneys by judges and opposing counsel. Two-thirds of African American lawyers, but less than a fifth of white lawyers, report witnessing racial bias in the justice system in the last three years. About forty percent of surveyed lawyers report witnessing or experiencing sexual orientation bias in professional settings, even in jurisdictions that have ordinances prohibiting it. Between about a quarter to a half of lawyers with disabilities also experience various forms of bias in the legal system. . . .
>
> Demeaning conduct takes a variety of forms. To be sure, gender bias rules and educational programs have reduced the most egregious problems. Female lawyers no longer routinely cope with labels such as "pretty girl," "little lady," "lawyerette," "baby doll," "sweetie" and "attorney generalette." . . . However, some of these problems persist, particularly those involving disrespectful forms of address. Female lawyers, administrative personnel, and witnesses are still addressed by their first names, while male counterparts are not. . . .
>
> Women also report recurring instances of being ignored, interrupted, or mistaken for nonprofessional support staff. And support staff, for their part, often experience similarly demeaning comments and have been expected to perform menial personal services, such as making coffee or running non-work related errands. . . .
>
> When men observe such incidents, they often seem like isolated, idiosyncratic, or inadvertent slights. A common reaction is that women should just "grow up and stop whining." Such reactions both silence and stigmatize complainants. Many women are unwilling to jeopardize a client's case or their own career prospects by antagonizing decision makers or earning a reputation as "humorless," "oversensitive," or a "troublemaker." . . .
>
> A common finding of gender bias studies is that the credibility of female lawyers, litigants, and witnesses is often discounted. Examples range from the occasional overt comment, such as "Shut up. Let's hear what the men have to say," to the much more common and subtle patterns of devaluation, such as openly ignoring or trivializing claims.
>
> In some instances, judicial attitudes are tied to perceptions about the substantive rights or injuries at issue. Claims involving violence, acquaintance rape, sexual harassment, and employment discrimination face special skepticism. In New Jersey's recent follow-up survey of gender bias, about 60 to 70 percent of women (compared with about a quarter of men) reported that victims of domestic violence and sex harassment had less credibility than other victims.[129]

How serious are these problems? If you were a lawyer encountering demeaning comments, how would you respond?

The ABA has taken some steps to attempt to address these issues, amending both the ABA Model Code of Judicial Conduct, Section 3B(6), and the Model Rules of Professional Conduct, Rule 8.4, to include prohibitions on gender bias in the courtroom. The Model Code of Judicial Conduct was revised in 1990 to provide:

> A judge shall perform judicial duties without bias or prejudice . . . and shall not permit staff, court officials and others subject to the judge's direction and control to do so. . . .
>
> A judge shall require lawyers in proceedings before the judge to refrain from manifesting, by words or conduct, bias or prejudice . . . against parties, witnesses, counsel or others. This Section does not preclude legitimate advocacy when race, sex, religion, national origin, disability, age, sexual orientation, or socioeconomic status, or other similar factors, are issues in the proceeding. . . .

In 1998, the ABA added the following Comment to Rule 8.4:

> A lawyer who, in the course of representing a client, knowingly manifests by words or conduct, bias or prejudice based upon race, sex, religion, national origin, disability, age, sexual orientation or socioeconomic status violates [this rule] when such actions are prejudicial to the administration of justice. Legitimate advocacy respecting the foregoing factors does not violate [this rule].

Putting Theory Into Practice

4-9. In France, 80 percent of new judges are female. As in other civil law countries, the judiciary is a separate career track. To become a member of the bench, individuals apply for positions at a special college either directly from law school or from positions in the bar. Applicants are selected based on performance on an exam. In recent years, about three-quarters of the applicants have been women, and they do slightly better on the exam; their pass rate has been 11 percent compared to 8 percent for men. Part of the explanation for the disparities in applications is that judges average three times less income than lawyers, and occupy a relatively low status in the profession.

The current concern is that men, who are 80 percent of defendants in the courts, might lose confidence in a system dominated by women judges. According to the French Justice Minister, quotas might be necessary if the current trends continue. Women judges have been highly critical of the suggestion. As the vice president of the Magistrates Union noted, "No one ever talked about quotas when the judiciary was dominated by men."[130]

Should quotas be imposed or should qualified men be given preference in the selection process?

4-10. A Ugandan woman with the first name Jane came before a Massachusetts immigration judge seeking asylum. Her claim was based on incidents of torture and rape in her homeland. Before denying her request, the judge quipped, "Jane, Come Here. Me Tarzan."[131]

In a hearing in Orange County, California, the judge opened the proceedings by asking the female lawyer of record for her business card to substantiate the fact that she was an attorney. The court then inquired of the woman, who was wearing maternity clothes, "Are you ready to have your baby? Is it momentarily?" He then added, "Well, your appearance, Ms. Roberson, leaves a lot to be desired, as far as your clothing is concerned."[132]

If you had been the lawyer in either of these cases, how would you have responded? If you had a filed a formal complaint, how should either of the judges have been subject to sanctions?

4-11. Ginnah Muhammad, a conservative Muslim, wore a full veil that left only her eyes exposed when she appeared in a Michigan small claims court to resolve a dispute over a rental car. The judge asked her to remove her veil before testifying. As he explained:

> One of the things I need to do as I am listening to testimony is I need to see your face and I need to see what's going on and unless you take that off, I can't see your face and I can't tell whether you're telling me the truth and I can't see certain things about your demeanor and temperament that I need to see in a court of law.

Muhammad responded: "I'm a practicing Muslim. . . . I wish to respect my religion and so I will not take off my clothes."

In an effort to clarify his concern, the judge explained that he wasn't asking her to take off her clothes but just to "take off the part that's covering your face [while] . . . you testify, and then you can put the veil back on."

"Well, your honor with all due respect," Muhammad responded, "this is part of my clothes."

The court then noted that the issue had come up before in his courtroom, and that practicing Muslims had told him that veiling was not a "religious thing. . . . It's a custom thing."

Muhammad responded, "Well, that's not correct."

The court dismissed the complaint.[133] Should the dismissal be reversed? Should the judge be subject to a reprimand? Would your answer be affected by research showing that the ability to recognize deception through demeanor is rare, even among trained professionals? When one set of tests was given to judges, police officers, trial lawyers, psychotherapists, and CIA agents, no group was able to do better than 50 percent in weeding out deceit, the same success rate that would come through random guessing.[134]

4-12. The chief justice of the Delaware Supreme Court used his state e-mail account to send to 38 male colleagues a video depicting a professional-looking young woman in a bar competing with a glamorous blonde for the attention of a man by simulating oral sex with a wine bottle. One critic observed: "[The woman] in the video could be a clerk in the court, a stenographer, a secretary. She's a woman in professional garb. It's a classic theme in porn. She's being ignored by men. She's unworthy of attention except to give men [oral sex]." The justice, who said he has daughters who are professionals and a businesswoman wife, said he felt the video showed "assertive" women in their "own right."[135]

Does this violate the state judicial rules of conduct, which requires judges to "avoid impropriety and the appearance of impropriety"? Does it suggest he cannot be fair to women in his court? Should the justice resign? Face other sanctions?

3. Juries

The jury system reflects a tension between the right to be judged by one's peers, and the right to an impartial tribunal. The *J.E.B.* case, which follows, discusses the history of women's exclusion from juries, and concludes that it is unconstitutional to use peremptory challenges to discriminate in jury selection on the basis of sex, regardless of whether a peremptory challenge involves a man or woman.

A **peremptory strike** (or **peremptory challenge**) is the elimination of a juror from the panel without the need to give a reason. Jurors may also be eliminated for "cause" where there is a basis for believing that they would be unable to reach an impartial decision.

Typically, each side in a criminal case is entitled to unlimited challenges for cause, and a certain number of peremptory challenges. The issue in *J.E.B.* is whether, even though peremptory challenges ordinarily require no reason, gender as a reason is unacceptable. A prior case, Batson v. Kentucky,[136] had held that peremptory strikes could not be used to eliminate jurors on the basis of race.

Reading Questions

1. As a practical matter, can gender bias be eliminated from jury selection? Will *J.E.B.* simply penalize bad lawyering by practitioners who are unable to come up with a plausible neutral reason for disqualifying potential jurors based on race or sex?
2. Is there any truly "gender-neutral" frame of reference in evaluating issues like enforcement of child support or protective orders?

J.E.B. v. Alabama ex rel. T.B.

511 U.S. 127 (1994)

Justice BLACKMUN delivered the opinion of the Court[, in which STEVENS, O'CONNOR, SOUTER, and GINSBURG, JJ., joined].

I

On behalf of [the mother of a minor child], respondent State of Alabama filed a complaint for paternity and child support against petitioner J.E.B. in the District Court of Jackson County, Alabama. . . . The trial court assembled a panel of 36 potential jurors, 12 males and 24 females. After the court excused three jurors for cause, only 10 of the remaining 33 jurors were male. The State then used 9 of its 10 peremptory strikes to remove male jurors; petitioner used all but one of his strikes to remove female jurors. As a result, all the selected jurors were female.

Before the jury was empaneled, petitioner objected to the State's peremptory challenges on the ground that they were exercised against male jurors solely on the basis of gender, in violation of the Equal Protection Clause. . . . Petitioner argued that the logic and reasoning of Batson v. Kentucky, which prohibits peremptory strikes solely on the basis of race, similarly forbids intentional discrimination on the basis of gender. The court rejected petitioner's claim and empaneled the all-female jury. The jury found petitioner to be the father of the child and the court entered an order directing him to pay child support. . . .

. . . Today we reaffirm what, by now, should be axiomatic: Intentional discrimination on the basis of gender by state actors violates the Equal Protection Clause, particularly where, as here, the discrimination serves to ratify and perpetuate invidious, archaic, and overbroad stereotypes about the relative abilities of men and women.

II

Discrimination on the basis of gender in the exercise of peremptory challenges is a relatively recent phenomenon. Gender-based peremptory strikes were hardly practicable for most of our country's existence, since, until the 19th century, women were completely excluded from jury service. So well-entrenched was this exclusion of women that in 1880 this Court, while finding that the exclusion of African-American men from juries violated the Fourteenth Amendment, expressed no doubt that a State "may confine the selection [of jurors] to males." Strauder v. West Virginia [1880].

Many States continued to exclude women from jury service well into the present century, despite the fact that women attained suffrage upon ratification of the Nineteenth Amendment in 1920. States that did permit women to serve on juries often erected other barriers, such as registration requirements and automatic exemptions, designed to deter women from exercising their right to jury service. . . .

. . . In this country, supporters of the exclusion of women from juries tended to couch their objections in terms of the ostensible need to protect women from the ugliness and depravity of trials. Women were thought to be too fragile and virginal to withstand the polluted courtroom atmosphere. . . .

This Court in Ballard v. United States [1946], first questioned the fundamental fairness of denying women the right to serve on juries. Relying on its supervisory powers over the federal courts, it held that women may not be excluded from the venire in federal trials in States where women were eligible for jury service under local law. In response to the argument that women have no superior or unique perspective, such that defendants are denied a fair trial by virtue of their exclusion from jury panels, the Court explained:

> It is said . . . that an all male panel drawn from the various groups within a community will be as truly representative as if women were included. The thought is that the factors which tend to influence the action of women are the same as those which influence the action of men—personality, background, economic status—and not sex. Yet it is not enough to say that women when sitting as jurors neither act nor tend to act as a class. Men likewise do not act like a class. . . . The truth is that the two sexes are not fungible; a community made up exclusively of one is different from a community composed of both; the subtle interplay of influence one on the other is among the imponderables. To insulate the courtroom from either may not in a given case make an iota of difference. Yet a flavor, a distinct quality is lost if either sex is excluded. . . .

Fifteen years later, however, the Court still was unwilling to translate its appreciation for the value of women's contribution to civic life into an enforceable right to equal treatment under state laws governing jury service. In Hoyt v. Florida [1961], the Court found it reasonable, "despite the enlightened emancipation of women," to exempt women from mandatory jury service by statute, allowing women to serve on juries only if they volunteered to serve. The Court justified the differential exemption policy on the ground that women, unlike men, occupied a unique position "as the center of home and family life." . . .

In 1975, the Court finally repudiated the reasoning of *Hoyt* and struck down, under the Sixth Amendment, an affirmative registration statute nearly identical to the one at issue in *Hoyt*. We explained: "Restricting jury service to only special groups or excluding identifiable segments playing major roles in the community cannot be squared with the constitutional concept of jury trial." The diverse and representative character of the jury must be maintained "'partly as assurance of a diffused impartiality and partly because sharing in the administration of justice is a phase of civic responsibility.'" [Taylor v. Louisiana (1975).]

III

Taylor relied on Sixth Amendment principles, but the opinion's approach is consistent with the heightened equal protection scrutiny afforded gender-based classifications. . . .

While the prejudicial attitudes toward women in this country have not been identical to those held toward racial minorities, the similarities between the experiences of racial minorities and women, in some contexts, "overpower those differences." . . .

Certainly, with respect to jury service, African-Americans and women share a history of total exclusion, a history which came to an end for women many years after the embarrassing chapter in our history came to an end for African-Americans. . . . Under our equal protection jurisprudence, gender-based classifications require "an exceedingly persuasive justification" in order to survive constitutional scrutiny. . . .

Far from proffering an exceptionally persuasive justification for its gender-based peremptory challenges, respondent maintains that its decision to strike virtually all the males from the jury in this case "may reasonably have been based upon the perception, supported by history, that men otherwise totally qualified to serve upon a jury might be more sympathetic and receptive to the arguments of a man alleged in a paternity action to be the father of an out-of-wedlock child, while women equally qualified to serve upon a jury might be more sympathetic and receptive to the arguments of the complaining witness who bore the child." . . .

We shall not accept as a defense to gender-based peremptory challenges "the very stereotype the law condemns." . . . Respondent's rationale, not unlike those regularly expressed for gender-based strikes, is reminiscent of the arguments advanced to justify the total exclusion of women from juries. Respondent offers virtually no support for the conclusion that gender alone is an accurate predictor of juror's attitudes; yet it urges this Court to condone the same stereotypes that justified the wholesale exclusion of women from juries and the ballot box. Respondent seems to assume that gross generalizations that would be deemed impermissible if made on the basis of race are somehow permissible when made on the basis of gender.

Discrimination in jury selection, whether based on race or on gender, causes harm to the litigants, the community, and the individual jurors who are wrongfully excluded from participation in the judicial process. The litigants are harmed by the risk that the prejudice which motivated the discriminatory selection of the jury will infect the entire proceedings. . . . The community is harmed by the State's participation in the perpetuation of invidious group stereotypes and the inevitable loss of confidence in our judicial system that state-sanctioned discrimination in the courtroom engenders.

When state actors exercise peremptory challenges in reliance on gender stereotypes, they ratify and reinforce prejudicial views of the relative abilities of men and women. Because these stereotypes have wreaked injustice in so many other spheres of our country's public life, active discrimination by litigants on the basis of gender during jury selection "invites cynicism respecting the jury's neutrality and its obligation to adhere to the law." . . . The potential for cynicism is particularly acute in cases where gender-related issues are prominent, such as cases involving rape, sexual harassment, or paternity. . . .

In recent cases we have emphasized that individual jurors themselves have a right to nondiscriminatory jury selection procedures. . . . Contrary to respondent's suggestion, this right extends to both men and women. . . . All persons, when granted the opportunity to serve on a jury, have the right not to be excluded summarily because of discriminatory and stereotypical presumptions that reflect and reinforce patterns of historical discrimination. Striking individual jurors on the assumption that they hold particular views simply because of their gender is "practically a brand upon them, affixed by law, an assertion of their inferiority." Strauder v. West Virginia [1880]. It denigrates the dignity of the excluded juror, and, for a woman, reinvokes a history of exclusion from political participation. The message it sends to all those in the courtroom, and all those who may later learn of the discriminatory act, is that certain individuals, for no reason other than gender, are presumed unqualified by state actors to decide important questions upon which reasonable persons could disagree.

IV

Our conclusion that litigants may not strike potential jurors solely on the basis of gender does not imply the elimination of all peremptory challenges. . . . Parties still may remove jurors whom they feel might be less acceptable than others on the panel; gender simply may not serve as a proxy for bias. . . .

V

Equal opportunity to participate in the fair administration of justice is fundamental to our democratic system. It not only furthers the goals of the jury system. It reaffirms the promise of equality under the law—that all citizens, regardless of race, ethnicity, or gender, have the chance to take part directly in our democracy. . . .

Justice O'CONNOR, concurring.

I agree with the Court that the Equal Protection Clause prohibits the government from excluding a person from jury service on account of that person's gender. . . . But today's important blow against gender discrimination is not costless. I write separately to discuss some of these costs, and to express my belief that today's holding should be limited to the government's use of gender-based peremptory strikes.

The principal value of the peremptory is that it helps produce fair and impartial juries. Moreover, "[t]he essential nature of the peremptory challenge is that it is one exercised without a reason stated, without inquiry and without being subject to the court's control." . . . Indeed, often a reason for it cannot be stated, for a trial lawyer's judgments about a juror's sympathies are sometimes based on experienced hunches and educated guesses, derived from a juror's responses at voir dire or a juror's "bare looks and gestures." That a trial lawyer's instinctive assessment of a juror's predisposition cannot meet the high standards of a challenge for cause does not mean that the lawyer's instinct is erroneous. . . . Our belief that experienced lawyers will often correctly intuit which jurors are likely to be the least sympathetic, and our understanding that the lawyer will often be unable to explain the intuition, are the very reason we cherish the peremptory challenge. But, as we add, layer by layer, additional constitutional restraints on the use of the peremptory, we force lawyers to articulate what we know is often inarticulable.

In so doing we . . . increase the possibility that biased jurors will be allowed onto the jury, because sometimes a lawyer will be unable to provide an acceptable gender-neutral explanation even though the lawyer is in fact correct that the juror is unsympathetic. Similarly, in jurisdictions where lawyers exercise their strikes in open court, lawyers may be deterred from using their peremptories, out of the fear that if they are unable to justify the strike the court will seat a juror who knows that the striking party thought him unfit. Because I believe the peremptory remains an important litigator's tool and a fundamental part of the process of selecting impartial juries, our increasing limitation of it gives me pause.

Nor is the value of the peremptory challenge to the litigant diminished when the peremptory is exercised in a gender-based manner. We know that like race, gender matters. A plethora of studies make clear that in rape cases, for example, female jurors are somewhat more likely to vote to convict than male jurors. . . . Moreover, though there have been no similarly definitive studies regarding, for example, sexual harassment, child custody, or spousal or child abuse, one need not be a sexist to share the intuition that in certain cases a person's gender and resulting life experience will be relevant to his or her view of the case. "Jurors are not expected to come into the jury box and leave behind all that their human experience has taught them." . . . Individuals are not expected to ignore as jurors what they know as men — or women.

Today's decision severely limits a litigant's ability to act on this intuition, for the import of our holding is that any correlation between a juror's gender and attitudes is irrelevant as a matter of constitutional law. But to say that gender makes no difference as a matter of law is not to say that gender makes no difference as a matter of fact. . . . Today's decision is a statement that, in an effort to eliminate the potential discriminatory use of the peremptory, . . . gender is now governed by the special rule of relevance formerly reserved for race. Though we gain much from this statement, we cannot ignore what we lose. In extending *Batson* to gender we have added an additional burden to the state and federal trial process, taken a step closer to eliminating the peremptory challenge, and diminished the ability of litigants to act on sometimes accurate gender-based assumptions about juror attitudes.

These concerns reinforce my conviction that today's decision should be limited to a prohibition on the government's use of gender-based peremptory challenges. The Equal Protection Clause prohibits only discrimination by state actors. . . .

Accordingly, I adhere to my position that the Equal Protection Clause does not limit the exercise of peremptory challenges by private civil litigants and criminal defendants. . . . This case itself presents no state action dilemma, for here the State of Alabama itself filed the paternity suit on behalf of petitioner. But what of the next case? Will we, in the name of fighting gender discrimination, hold that the battered wife—on trial for wounding her abusive husband—is a state actor? Will we preclude her from using her peremptory challenges to ensure that the jury of her peers contains as many women members as possible? I assume we will, but I hope we will not.

Justice KENNEDY, concurring in the judgment.

I am in full agreement with the Court.

The importance of individual rights to our analysis prompts a further observation concerning what I conceive to be the intended effect of today's decision. We do not prohibit racial and gender bias in jury selection only to encourage it in jury deliberations. Once seated, a juror should not give free rein to some racial or gender bias of his or her own. The jury system is a kind of compact by which power is transferred from the judge to jury, the jury in turn deciding the case in accord with the instructions defining the relevant issues for consideration. The wise limitation on the authority of courts to inquire into the reasons underlying a jury's verdict does not mean that a jury ought to disregard the court's instructions. A juror who allows racial or gender bias to influence assessment of the case breaches the compact and renounces his or her oath.

In this regard, it is important to recognize that a juror sits not as a representative of a racial or sexual group but as an individual citizen. Nothing would be more pernicious to the jury system than for society to presume that persons of different backgrounds go to the jury room to voice prejudice. . . . The jury pool must be representative of the community, but that is a structural mechanism for preventing bias, not enfranchising it. . . . Thus, the Constitution guarantees a right only to an impartial jury, not to a jury composed of members of a particular race or gender. . . .

Justice SCALIA, with whom THE CHIEF JUSTICE and Justice THOMAS join, dissenting.

Today's opinion is an inspiring demonstration of how thoroughly up-to-date and right-thinking we Justices are in matters pertaining to the sexes (or as the Court would have it, the genders), and how sternly we disapprove the male chauvinist attitudes of our predecessors. . . . The parties do not contest that discrimination on the basis of sex[1] is subject to what our cases call "heightened scrutiny." . . .

The core of the Court's reasoning is that peremptory challenges on the basis of any group characteristic subject to heightened scrutiny are inconsistent with the guarantee of the Equal Protection Clause. That conclusion can be reached only by focusing unrealistically upon individual exercises of the peremptory challenge, and ignoring the totality of the practice. Since all groups are subject to the peremptory challenge (and will be made the object of it, depending upon the nature of the particular case) it is hard to see how any group is denied equal protection. . . . That explains why peremptory challenges coexisted with the Equal Protection Clause for 120 years. This case is a perfect example of how the system as a whole is even-handed. While the only claim before the Court is petitioner's complaint that the prosecutor struck male jurors, for every man struck by the government petitioner's own lawyer struck a woman. To say that men were singled out for discriminatory treatment in this process is preposterous. The situation would be different if both sides systematically struck individuals of one group, so that the strikes evinced group-based animus and served as a proxy for segregated venire lists. . . . The pattern here, however, displays not a systemic sex-based animus but each side's desire to get a jury favorably disposed to its case. That is why the Court's characterization of respondent's argument as "reminiscent of the arguments advanced to justify the total exclusion of women from juries" is patently false. Women were categorically excluded from juries because of doubt that they were competent; women are stricken from juries by peremptory challenge because of doubt that they are well disposed to the striking party's case. . . . There is discrimination and dishonor in the former, and not in the latter — which explains the 106-year interlude between our holding that exclusion from juries on the basis of race was unconstitutional, Strauder v. West Virginia, and our holding that peremptory challenges on the basis of race were unconstitutional, Batson v. Kentucky.

Although the Court's legal reasoning in this case is largely obscured by anti-male-chauvinist oratory, to the extent such reasoning is discernible it invalidates much more than sex-based strikes. . . . [The Court's analysis] places all peremptory strikes based on any group characteristic at risk, since they can

1. Throughout this opinion, I shall refer to the issue as sex discrimination rather than (as the Court does) gender discrimination. The word "gender" has acquired the new and useful connotation of cultural or attitudinal characteristics (as opposed to physical characteristics) distinctive to the sexes. That is to say, gender is to sex as feminine is to female and masculine to male. The present case does not involve peremptory strikes exercised on the basis of femininity or masculinity (as far as it appears, effeminate men did not survive the prosecution's peremptories). The case involves, therefore, sex discrimination plain and simple.

all be denominated "stereotypes." Perhaps, however (though I do not see why it should be so), only the stereotyping of groups entitled to heightened or strict scrutiny constitutes "the very stereotype the law condemns"—so that other stereotyping (e.g., wide-eyed blondes and football players are dumb) remains OK. Or perhaps when the Court refers to "impermissible stereotypes," it means the adjective to be limiting rather than descriptive—so that we can expect to learn from the Court's peremptory/stereotyping jurisprudence in the future which stereotypes the Constitution frowns upon and which it does not. . . .

[M]ake no mistake about it: there really is no substitute for the peremptory. Voir dire (though it can be expected to expand as a consequence of today's decision) cannot fill the gap. The biases that go along with group characteristics tend to be biases that the juror himself does not perceive, so that it is no use asking about them. It is fruitless to inquire of a male juror whether he harbors any subliminal prejudice in favor of unwed fathers. . . .

In order, it seems to me, not to eliminate any real denial of equal protection, but simply to pay conspicuous obeisance to the equality of the sexes, the Court imperils a practice that has been considered an essential part of fair jury trial since the dawn of the common law. The Constitution of the United States neither requires nor permits this vandalizing of our people's traditions.

For these reasons, I dissent.

NOTE ON EQUALITY AND IMPARTIALITY IN THE JURY CONTEXT

As Justice O'Connor notes, there are some cases in which gender does make a difference. Does pretending otherwise improve the accuracy of the jury system? What exactly does impartiality mean in the context of a jury of peers? Is it that a potential juror should have no views on any relevant subject? Or that jury perspectives in some sense should be drawn from a cross-section of the community, and "not arbitrarily skewed for or against any particular group or characteristic"? Should the goal be proportional representation on juries?

Although *J.E.B.* has met with considerable support in theory, it has proven more problematic in practice. Part of the difficulty, Charles Ogletree notes, is that while gender may be an imperfect proxy for relevant attitudes, it is not an entirely irrational one. The stereotypes that influence lawyers in jury selection may also be ones that "affect the behavior of men and women in the jury box."[137] Moreover, inventive lawyers can always summon nondiscriminatory reasons for a challenge, and most trial courts are reluctant to reject them as pretextual unless they are patently implausible or clearly incorporate impermissible stereotypes. Appellate courts are similarly reluctant to reverse lower court rulings, which often turn on factual determinations of credibility. Lawyers who feel ethically obligated to gain sympathetic hearings for their clients may be equally reluctant to acknowledge—even to themselves—the role that impermissible stereotypes play in their juror selections. Experienced litigators and jury consultants believe that concerns such as race, sex, ethnicity, and religion routinely figure in juror selection.[138]

Given these evidentiary hurdles, it is perhaps unsurprising that claims of gender discrimination in peremptory challenges are relatively rare. A survey of cases in the first five years under *J.E.B.* found only 127 reported complaints and 23 reversals in all state and federal systems. Clearly the ruling has not been as burdensome as critics predicted. But neither has it been as effective as supporters hoped. Surveyed cases include numerous examples of peremptories that have been sustained despite the stereotypes underlying them. Women have been struck for being "timid," "not assertive," "weak," "vacillating," overweight, and single mothers.[139] One particularly striking case, Talley v. State, involved a battered woman on trial for murder of her husband. The state used all 13 of its strikes against women, and the court upheld the exclusions. Among the reasons that the prosecutor offered were that a female prospective juror had "heard of the battered woman syndrome," "agree[d] with feminists ideals and goals," or had read romance novels, "indicating that she did not look at life as it is."[140]

A recent case from the Ninth Circuit Court of Appeals concerned the standard to be applied to the use of a peremptory challenge to exclude a gay man from a jury in a trial relating to the pricing of HIV medications. The Ninth Circuit panel granted a new trial in the case, holding that heightened scrutiny applied to challenges based on sexual orientation discrimination.[141]

Putting Theory Into Practice

4-13. In the trial of O.J. Simpson for murder of his battered white wife, jury consultants for both sides found that black women were the group most likely to vote for acquittal; they were least likely to credit the domestic violence evidence, or to respond favorably to Marcia Clark, the white woman lead prosecutor.[142] Although the judge submitted a detailed 79-page questionnaire to prospective jurors concerning possible sources of bias, defense counsel still believed that it was in their interest to use peremptory challenges to increase black women's representation on the jury.

If you had been one of the defense lawyers in the *Simpson* case, what would you have done? If your team had used its peremptory challenges to exclude men and white women, is it likely that the prosecution could have established a constitutional violation?

4-14. How should courts deal with strikes based on an individual's sexual orientation? Should lawyers be entitled to ask jurors questions about their living arrangements and about conduct that might suggest a lesbian or gay identity?

4-15. The defendant was on trial for violating a restraining order that protected his battered wife. The prosecutor used her three peremptory challenges to strike the first three jurors on the panel who had indicated prior involvement with a protective order. The defendant was convicted

and appealed, claiming gender bias in jury selection. Although the prosecutor had not omitted from her exclusions any women who had prior
involvement with a protective order, she admitted that she assumed that
the men involved in such a dispute would likely have been defendants
rather than complainants.

Should the conviction be reversed? What if the prosecutor had been
less forthcoming about her assumption?[143]

4-16. A prosecutor uses his three peremptory challenges to exclude
three overweight African-American women from the jury. In explaining
his decision to the court, he cites their dress and hairstyles, as well as their
youth. Two women had braided hair, which he had always regarded "as
somewhat radical." One was "grossly overweight and . . . [wearing] a little
tiny skirt that doesn't fit her . . . a skirt that's hiked halfway up her thighs
when she stands, and then when she sits, you can see everything that God
gave the woman." That made him "uncomfortable" trusting her with a
case of "this seriousness."[144] Are these constitutionally permissible reasons for exclusion?

In comments to a reporter outside of court, the prosecutor acknowledged, "Young, obese, black women are really dangerous to me. . . . I've
never liked young obese black women and I think that they sense that."[145]
If he had made that statement in court, should that have affected the legitimacy of his peremptory challenges?

4. Criminal Sentencing

Traditionally, judges considered the individual circumstances of defendants
when determining punishment. Women generally received more lenient sentences than men who committed similar crimes partly because they had more
family and community ties and less extensive criminal records, and because
male judges were often motivated by chivalry or paternalism.[146] Other sentencing disparities reflected racial and gender bias and idiosyncratic views of judges.

During the 1980s, in a general effort to promote more consistency and
proportionality in punishment, Congress passed the Sentencing Reform Act,
which attempted to prescribe uniform sentences for similar conduct. The
Federal Sentencing Commission established the Federal Sentencing Guidelines
in order to shift the focus of punishment away from the characteristics of the
defendant to the characteristics of the crime. The Guidelines prohibited consideration of traditional "individualizing" factors, except in "extraordinary" situations, and specified that family ties and responsibilities were not ordinarily
relevant. Supreme Court decisions have determined that Federal Sentencing
Guidelines cannot be mandatory, although they remain as advisory. States,
which handle the vast majority of criminal cases, have their own guidelines.

Despite these guidelines, most research reveals significant gender, racial,
and ethnic differences. Women are generally treated more leniently than men,

controlling for the severity of the offense and their prior criminal record, and white defendants are treated more leniently than nonwhites. Gender dispari-ties appear partly attributable to assumptions that women are less dangerous, more remorseful, more open to reform, more likely to be victims themselves, and more likely to have family responsibilities and community ties.[147] However, women who commit particularly egregious crimes tend to receive even harsher sentences than men, probably in part because they deviate so far from accepted notions of femininity.[148]

The Federal Guidelines permit a downward adjustment for family circum-stances only in truly exceptional circumstances. Being a single parent is not generally viewed as an exceptional circumstance. A primary concern is that greater discretion for family circumstances would reward women for their sta-tus as mothers or, alternatively, penalize women who do not have children. It would say in effect, "you have violated the criminal law, but we'll overlook that so you can do what you are supposed to do—care for your children."[149] The same goes for pregnant women. One court noted that "pregnancy of con-victed female felons is neither atypical nor unusual," and that giving a down-ward departure for pregnancy would send "an obvious message to all female defendants that pregnancy is 'a way out.' "[150]

Despite the Guidelines, research indicates that judges in practice tend to give mothers with children and pregnant women lighter sentences.[151] Is that fair? Or does it constitute sex discrimination? Some commentators argue that it does not.

> The purpose of just punishment emphasizes consistency in sentencing. If the "same" sentence has an inconsistent impact on two different defendants, then considering the two sentences as equivalent is unjust. An incarcerative sentence may have a distinctly different impact on a parent than it has on a non-parent. For example, in many states incarceration constitutes a ground for termination of parental rights. A two year prison sentence does not equal two years in prison accompanied by permanent loss of child custody. . . .[152]

What is your view?

Some countries have not tried so hard to be sex-neutral. On June 27, 1994, President Nelson Mandela of the Republic of South Africa signed a Presidential Act providing an early release from prison for certain categories of prisoners, including "all mothers in prison on 10 May 1994, with minor children under the age of twelve (12) years." Fathers were not included. In his statement in support of the Act, President Mandela stated that he was motivated predomi-nantly by a concern for children who had been deprived of the nurturing and care that their mothers would ordinarily have provided.

> Having spent many years in prison myself, I am well aware of the hardship which flows from incarceration. I am also well aware that imprisonment inev-itably has harsh consequences for the family of the prisoner. . . . Account was taken of the special role I believe that mothers play in the care and nurturing of younger children. . . . I have had an on-going concern about the general

plight of young children in South Africa. . . . In my experience there are only a minority of fathers who are actively involved in nurturing and caring for their children. . . . [153]

A father, with a child under the age of 12, who was not entitled to early release under the order challenged his exclusion under the anti-discrimination provisions of the interim South African Constitution. Is there any question about how this case would be decided in the United States? A majority of the South African Constitutional Court rejected the challenge on the grounds that the early release order was not "unfair discrimination." One justice dissented, and another determined that although the Act constituted "unfair discrimination," it was justified.[154]

In the United States, one of the factors "not ordinarily relevant" to determining whether to depart from the federal Sentencing Guidelines is a defendant's mental or emotional condition, but prior abuse has been considered by some courts if the defendant can establish a nexus between the abuse and the offense. In 1994, only two weeks after receiving custody of her two young sons, Susan Smith loaded them into her car, drove to a nearby lake, pointed the car toward the lake, released the hand brake and jumped out. She told the police that she and her children had been abducted by an African-American carjacker. After a fruitless nine-day search for the offender, Smith confessed. Her capital murder trial was short, and during the penalty phase, her attorneys argued for leniency based on a history of depression brought on in large part by sexual abuse she suffered as a child. The jury sentenced her to life imprisonment, sparing her the death penalty.[155] Does this seem appropriate?

In a more recent, well-publicized case, Andrea Yates, who suffered from severe postpartum depression, drowned her five children, ages six months to seven years, in the family bathtub. She was convicted for the murders of three of the children. A jury deliberated for 40 minutes before sentencing her to life in prison instead of the death penalty. Her conviction was subsequently reversed. On trial, she was found not guilty by reason of insanity and sentenced to an indefinite civil commitment.

What facts would you need before deciding on guilt and sentencing in the Yates case? One commentator explains:

The "baby blues," or "blues," occurs in fifty to seventy percent of women in the first six to eight weeks after birth; symptoms include crying, general depression, and fatigue. The "blues" does not impair a mother's judgment and is probably not a disorder or disease. Postpartum depression occurs in ten to twenty percent of women and may persist for one year. It is categorized as a type of reaction depression and involves feelings of hopelessness, inadequacy, anxiety, and moodiness. Although studies are few, the level of support that the mother receives from the father and family is more determinative of the depression than are demographic and biological factors. Postpartum psychosis occurs in one to two of every one thousand births and can lead to suicide or infanticide. It involves a major deviation from the normal processes of thinking, behavior, and emotion. Emotional reactions may be inappropriate to the circumstances, and actions may not be related to facts. For example, a mother may say that she sees the room upside down, express concern that a small pimple on her child's face is a misplaced testis, or fear that the hospital staff is part of a conspiracy to kill the baby. Anxiety can lead to panic attacks; a mother often has obsessive thoughts about harming the baby by putting it in the oven, drowning it, cutting off its body parts, or dropping it from an elevated surface. Hospitalization is necessary for the protection of both the mother and the child.[156]

Is compassion appropriate in the Andrea Yates case? Does it matter that postpartum depression is a female-specific defense? One study of 24 cases in which postpartum psychosis was offered as a defense found that 8 women were acquitted and 4 were given probation, while 10 were sentenced to between 3 and 20 years, and 2 received life sentences.[157] Are those disparities defensible?

Prior abuse was not presented as a factor in the Yates case but, as noted above, it was an important part of Susan Smith's sentencing hearing. In federal courts, past victimization has been found as a basis for downward departure from the Sentencing Guidelines as well. In one case, the court found that a history of abuse so severe that the defendant was "virtually a mind puppet" was extraordinary and that a downward departure was not forbidden by the Guidelines.[158]

Should sentencing be affected by a woman's involvement in a controlling relationship? This issue arises sometimes in the context of drug conspiracies. A significant number of women charged in these conspiracies—sometimes called "women of circumstance"—are "wives, mothers, sisters, daughters, girlfriends, and nieces, who become involved in crime because of their financial dependence on, fear of, or romantic attachment to male drug traffickers."[159] Many are "desperate, unsuspecting or coerced women who often have no prior criminal history and serve as the sole caretakers of young children," charged with conspiracy and subject to harsh sentencing laws.[160] Women may also suffer disproportionate sentences, either because they refuse to snitch, out of loyalty or fear, or because they do not know enough valuable information to obtain a reduced sentence as a cooperating witness. A "safety valve" in the federal Violent Crime Control and Drug Enforcement Act of 1994 provides relief to nonviolent, low-level drug offenders who cooperate with the authorities, but this will not help women too fearful to cooperate or too uninformed to provide valuable evidence. Nor does it assist women facing state charges.[161]

Kemba Smith was a student at Hampton University with no prior criminal record. She became involved with a man eight years older, who was the ringleader of a cocaine enterprise. By the time Smith realized her boyfriend was a drug dealer, he was abusing her, and she feared retaliation (he eventually killed his best friend for informing on him). Smith never handled any of the drugs, but she received a 24-year prison sentence for conspiracy to distribute cocaine. President Clinton pardoned her after six years of incarceration and a mass media campaign.[162] What sentence would have been appropriate?

Will recognition of women's subjugation by boyfriends or husbands reinforce stereotypical assumptions about female dependence and passivity? Consider the case of the "Miss America Bandit," United States v. Mast.[163] There, a young woman was convicted of a string of bank robberies. At sentencing, the judge ordered a downward departure based on the defendant's domination by her boyfriend, even though there were no indications of physical abuse. The judge's comments during the sentencing hearing included: "men have exercised traditional control over the activities of women, and I'm not going to ignore that, no matter how much flak I get from women's lib"; and "I think it's a fact of life that men can exercise a Svengali influence over women"; and "women are a soft touch, particularly if sex is involved."[164] Is this judge taking the social reality of the defendant into consideration, or is he instead imposing his own views of reality—reminiscent of stereotypes—on the situation?

Putting Theory Into Practice

4-17. Most states remove infants from imprisoned mothers almost immediately after birth, and women do not have the opportunity to nurse or bond with their newborns. Children of imprisoned parents are five to six times as likely as their peers to end up behind bars, and 10 percent land in foster care.[165] In 2002, Jodie received a four-year sentence for a fourth offense of operating a motor vehicle while intoxicated and fleeing an officer. She placed her two-year-old son with her mother, but in 2004, her mother was no longer able to take care of the child. At that point, the state moved to permanently terminate Jodie's rights to her son so that he could be adopted into a stable family. What should the law do about this issue?[166]

4-18. Tammy is convicted of conspiracy to distribute and possession with intent to distribute cocaine. She concedes her involvement in her boyfriend's drug dealing, but says that she was drawn into the conspiracy through her romantic attachment to a drug dealer. Since then, she has cooperated fully with the authorities, which led to the arrest and guilty pleas of several drug co-conspirators. Under the Federal Sentencing Guidelines, Tammy's prison sentence should be between 70 and 87 months. Is this an appropriate case for a downward reduction? If so, how much? What are the policy considerations for and against a sentence reduction?[167]

4-19. Jody Arias was accused of killing her Mormon boyfriend who had jilted her. Circumstantial evidence provided motive and opportunity. She first denied that she was at the murder scene, but when the evidence showed that she had been there, she changed her story, claiming that she was there but alleging that the victim was killed by intruders while she hid in the closet. When later evidence showed that she was holding a camera while the victim was murdered, Arias eventually confessed to killing the victim, but claimed that it was in self-defense, after a long history of domestic abuse and manipulation by the victim. As part of her defense, Arias claimed that the victim had an appetite for deviant sex acts, and enjoyed viewing child pornography. If you were Arias' defense counsel, how would you pick a jury? Would the gender of a potential juror be relevant to you?

---

1. Carrie Menkel-Meadow, Portia in a Different Voice: Speculations on a Women's Lawyering Process, 1 Berkeley Women's L.J. 39, 46 (1985). For an overview of the "connection thesis" literature, see Patricia W. Hatamyar & Kevin M. Simmons, Are Women More Ethical Lawyers? An Empirical Study, 31 Fla. St. L. Rev. 785, 839-841 (2004).

2. See, e.g., Leslie Bender, From Gender Difference to Feminist Solidarity: Using Carol Gilligan and an Ethic of Care in Law, 15 Vt. L. Rev. 1 (1990).

3. Id. at 37.

4. Mary Becker, Care and Feminists, 17 Wis. Women's L.J. 57, 60 (2002).

5. Robin West, Jurisprudence and Gender, 55 U. Chi. L. Rev. 1 (1988).

6. Sara Ruddick, Maternal Thinking: Toward a Politics of Peace (1989).

7. Kathleen A. Lahey & Sarah W. Salter, Corporate Law in Legal Theory and Legal Scholarship: From Classicism to Feminism, 23 Osgoode Hall L.J. 543, 555-556. 570 (1985). See also Kellye Y. Testy, Capitalism and Freedom—For Whom?: Feminist Legal Theory and Progressive Corporate Law, 67 L. & Contemp. Probs. 87, 99 (2004) (urging a union of progressive corporate law and feminist legal theory, which articulates "a normative vision of the relationship between life and law, one that prescribes a moral vision for social ordering, based upon the principles of equality and human flourishing"); Theresa A. Gabaldon, Assumptions About Relationships Reflected in the Federal Securities Laws, 17 Wis. Women's L.J. 215 (2002) (examining the role of relationships in the context of federal securities laws); Barbara Ann White, Feminist Foundations for the Law of Business: One Law and Economics Scholar's Survey and (Re)View, 10 UCLA Women's L.J. 39 (1999) (urging feminist methods of recognizing the excluded voice and the feminist ethic of care in business law).

8. See Joan MacLeod Heminway, Sex, Trust, and Corporate Boards, 18 Hast. Women's L.J. 173 (2007).

9. Marjorie Kornhauser, The Rhetoric of the Anti-Progressive Income Tax Movement: A Typical Male Reaction, 86 Mich. L. Rev. 464 (1987).

10. Aviva Orenstein, Apology Excepted: Incorporating a Feminist Analysis into Evidence Policy Where You Would Least Expect It, 28 Sw. U. L. Rev. 113 (1999). See also Kit Kinports, Evidence Engendered, 1991 U. Ill. L. Rev. 413 (criticizing evidence law for characteristics such as abstractness, formality, hierarchy, and adversarialness, that tend both to institutionalize female disadvantage in concrete cases and to reinforce values that are not congenial to many women); Rosemary C. Hunter, Gender in Evidence: Masculine Norms vs. Feminist Reforms, 19 Harv. Women's L.J. 127, 129 (1996) (criticizing rules of evidence for, among other things, privileging "fact over value, reason over emotion, presence over absence, physical over psychological, perception over intuition").

11. See Judith Resnik, Housekeeping: The Nature and Allocation of Work in Federal Trial Courts, 24 Ga. L. Rev. 909, 945, 960-961 (1990).

12. Catharine A. MacKinnon, Feminism Unmodified: Discourses on Life and Law 38-39 (1987).

13. Linda C. McClain, "Atomistic Man" Revisited: Liberalism, Connection, and Feminist Jurisprudence, 65 S. Cal. L. Rev. 1171, 1196-1202, 1263 (1992).

14. Joan C. Tronto, Moral Boundaries: A Political Argument for an Ethic of Care 3 (1993).

15. Leslie Bender, From Gender Difference to Feminist Solidarity: Using Carol Gilligan and an Ethic of Care in Law, 15 Vt. L. Rev. 1, 40 (1990).

16. Richard A. Epstein, Gender Is for Nouns, 41 DePaul L. Rev. 981, 989-990 (1992).

17. See Kingsley R. Browne, An Evolutionary Perspective of Sexual Harassment: Seeking Roots in Biology Rather Than Ideology, 8 J. Contemp. Legal Issues 5 (1997); see also Kingsley R. Browne, Women at War: An Evolutionary Perspective, 49 Buff. L. Rev. 51, 56 (2001) (using evolutionary psychology and the literature of sex-linked cognitive and behavioral differences to challenge the assumption that "all it will take to integrate women into combat roles is educating men out of their ideology of masculinism").

18. George F. Gilder, Men and Marriage 15-16 (1986). Other scholarship based on the evolutionary perspective includes Owen D. Jones & Timothy H. Goldsmith, Law and Behavioral Biology, 105 Colum. L. Rev. 405 (2005); Owen D. Jones, Law and the Biology of Rape: Reflections on Transitions, 11 Hastings L.J. 151 (2000); Owen D. Jones, Sex, Culture, and the Biology of Rape: Toward Explanation and Prevention, 87 Cal. L. Rev. 827 (1999); see also Symposia, Biology and Sexual Aggression, 39 Jurimetrics 133, 243 (Fall & Winter 1999).

19. See Deborah Weiss, The Annoyingly Indeterminate Effects of Sex Differences, 19 Tex. J. Women & Law 99 (2010).

20. Amy L. Wax, Against Nature—On Robert Wright's "The Moral Animal," 63 U. Chi. L. Rev. 307, 355-356 (1996).

21. Id. at 329-330.

22. See, e.g., June Carbone & Naomi Cahn, The Biological Basis of Commitment: Does One Size Fit All?, 25 Women's Rts. L. Rep. 223, 247-248 (2004).

23. Lawrence H. Summers, Remarks at the National Bureau of Economic Research, Diversifying the Science and Engineering Workforce, Jan. 14, 2005, summarized at http://harvardmagazine .com/2005/03/gender-gap.html.

24. David Margolick, At the Bar, N.Y. Times, July 10, 1992, at B8.

25. Nancy Folbre, The Invisible Heart: Economics and Family Values xi (2001).

26. Joan Williams, Unbending Gender: Why Family and Work Conflict and What to Do About It (2000).

27. Martha Albertson Fineman, The Neutered Mother, the Sexual Family, and Other Twentieth Century Tragedies 228-236 (1995).

28. Deborah L. Rhode, Balanced Lives, 102 Colum. L. Rev. 834, 836, 846 (2002).

29. Williams, supra note 26, at 274.

30. Katherine Franke, Theorizing Yes: An Essay on Feminism, Law, and Desire, 101 Colum. L. Rev. 181, 186-187 (2001).

31. Id. at 191-192.

32. Mary Anne Case, How High the Apple Pie? A Few Troubling Questions About Where, Why, and How the Burden of Care for Children Should Be Shifted, 76 Chi.-Kent L. Rev. 1753, 1767, 1771 (2001). For a rich historical analysis of how feminism came to "abandon" the interests of single women, see Rachel F. Moran, How Second-Wave Feminism Forgot the Single Woman, 33 Hofstra L. Rev. 223 (2004).

33. See Judith Warner, Perfect Madness: Motherhood in the Age of Anxiety 220 (2005).

34. Full-time child-care workers in private households earned, on average, $398 per week. U.S. Bureau of Labor Statistics, Highlights of Women's Earnings in 2010, Report 1031, at 20 (July 2011).

35. Peggie R. Smith, Aging and Caring in the Home: Regulating Paid Domesticity in the 21st Century, 92 Iowa L. Rev. 1835, 1848 (2007).

36. Peggie R. Smith, Welfare, Child Care and the People Who Care: Union Representation of Family Child Care Providers, 55 Kan. L. Rev. 321 (2006); Peggie R. Smith, The Publicization of Home-Based Care Work in State Labor Law, 92 Minn. L. Rev. 1390 (2008).

37. Belva Lockwood, My Efforts to Become a Lawyer, in Women and the American Economy: A Documentary History 1675-1929, at 297-301 (W. Elliot Brownlee & Mary M. Brownlee eds., 1976).

38. ABA Commission on Women in the Profession, A Current Glance at Women in the Law 2011 (2011); Minority Corporate Counsel Association (MCCA), Sustaining Pathways to Diversity: A Comprehensive Examination of Diversity Demographics, Initiatives, and Policies in Corporate Legal Departments (2011); Report of the Center for Women in Government and Civil Society, University at Albany State University of New York (Spring 2011).

39. For law firms, see NALP, Women and Minorities in Law Firms by Race and Ethnicity (2010). For general counsel, see MCCA, Sustaining Pathways to Diversity, supra note 38. For women of color on the judiciary, see http://www.afj.org/judicial_selection_resources/selection_database/ byCourtRaceGender.asp.

40. Elizabeth Chambliss, Miles to Go: Progress of Minorities in the Legal Profession (Commission on Racial and Ethnic Diversity in the Legal Profession, 2005).

41. For median weekly earnings of lawyers, see Bureau of Labor Statistics, Table 39, "Median weekly earnings of full-time wage and salary workers by detailed occupation and sex," available at http://www.bls.gov/cps/cpsaat39.pdf. For private practice salaries, see National Association of Women Lawyers (NAWL), Report of the Sixth Annual National Survey on Retention and Promotion of Women in Law Firms, Oct. 2011, at 19. See also Kenneth G. Dau-Schmidt et al., Men and Women of the Bar: An Empirical Study of the Impact of Gender on Legal Careers, 16 Mich. J. Gender & Law 49, 104, 123 (2009) (finding 15 years after law school, women on average earn approximately $100,000 less than men; women with childcare responsibilities show the most negative impact on income, although they enjoy higher career satisfaction).

42. Marina Angel et al., Statistical Evidence on the Gender Gap in Law Firm Partner Compensation 2 (Temple Univ. Beasley Sch. of Law, Paper No. 2010-24), available at http://works.bepress.com/cgi/viewcontent.cgi?article=1001&context=marina_angel; Theresa M. Beiner, Some Thoughts on the State of Women Lawyers and Why Title VII Has Not Worked for Them, 44 Ind. L. Rev. 685, 688 (2011).

43. Deborah L. Rhode, From Platitudes to Priorities: Diversity and Gender Equity in Law Firms, 24 Geo. J. Legal Ethics 1041, 1043 (2011).

44. Jessica Faye Carter, Leave None Behind, Nat'l L.J., Dec. 8, 2008, at 23 (noting that women of color account for 30 percent of adult female population but a lower percent of female partners).

45. NAWL, supra note 41, at 2; Vanessa Blum, Report Offers Detailed Look at DOJ Lawyers; Many Women, Minorities Find Jobs in Lower Ranks, But Not at Top, Legal Times, Oct. 27, 2003, at 1 (of some 9,000 lawyers working for U.S. Justice Department, men are 50 percent more likely to be in the most senior posts than women, and white men are more than three times as likely to be in such posts than minority women).

46. See Ulrike Schultz, Introduction: Women in the World's Legal Profession: Overview and Synthesis, in Women in the World's Legal Profession xxv, xliv (Ulrike Schultz & Gisela Shaw eds., 2003) (noting that even when women achieve partnership, they lack the same degree of power, independence, and decisionmaking authority as men).

47. For partnerships, see Women and Minorities at Law Firms—By Race and Ethnicity, http://www.nalp.org/minoritieswomen. For attrition, see ABA Commission on Women in the Profession, From Visible Invisibility to Visibly Successful 7 (2009). See also Deepali Bagati, Women of Color in U.S. Law Firms 1-2 (Catalyst, 2009).

48. Chambliss, supra note 40, at 34; Tom McCann, Partnership and Management Remain Elusive Goals for Minority Lawyers, Chicago Lawyer, July 2003, at 8; David B. Wilkins, Partners Without Power?: A Preliminary Look at Black Partners in Corporate Law Firms, 2 J. Inst. for Study of Leg. Ethics 15 (1999).

49. Catalyst, Women in Law in the U.S. 5 (July 2012), available at http://www.catalyst.org/file/706/qt_women_in_law_in_the_us.pdf.

50. Carrie Menkel-Meadow, Exploring a Research Agenda of the Feminization of the Legal Profession: Theories of Gender and Social Change, 14 Law & Soc. Inquiry 289, 307-308 (1989).

51. Nancy Reichman & Joyce S. Sterling, Gender Penalties Revisited, 14-15, 25 (Colorado Bar Association, 2004).

52. Schultz, supra note 46, at xlv. See Paul W. Mattessich & Cheryl W. Heilman, The Career Paths of Minnesota Law School Graduates: Does Gender Make a Difference?, 9 Law & Ineq. J. 59, 85 (1990) (finding that women were less likely to cite advancement-related reasons for leaving a job); American Bar Association Commission on Women in the Profession, Options and Obstacles: A Survey of the Studies of the Careers of Women Lawyers (July 1994) (citing studies).

53. Rhode, From Platitudes to Priorities, supra note 43, at 1044, 1046.

54. See Theresa M. Beiner, Not All Lawyers Are Equal: Difficulties That Plague Women and Women of Color, 58 Syracuse L. Rev. 317, 329 (2008); Ronit Dinovitzer et al., After the JD: First Results of a National Study of Legal Careers 3, 58, 64-65 (2004).

55. Rhode, From Platitudes to Priorities, supra note 43, at 1044.

56. Id.

57. The findings were especially pronounced for lesbian and gay students and students of color. Some basic studies include: Linda F. Wightman, Law School Admission Council Research Report Series, Women in Legal Education: A Comparison of the Law School Performance and Law School Experience of Women and Men 25 (1996); Lani Guinier, Michael Fine & Jane Balin, Becoming Gentlemen 41 (1997); Elizabeth Mertz et al., What Difference Does Difference Make: The Challenge for Legal Education, 48 J. Legal Educ. 1 (1998); Janice L. Austin et al., Results from a Survey: Gay, Lesbian, and Bisexual Students' Attitudes About Law School, 48 J. Legal Educ. 157 (1998).

58. See Alice Shih, Yale Law School Faculty & Students Speak Up About Gender: Ten Years Later, Apr. 25, 2012, available at http://ms-jd.org/blog/article/yale-law-school-faculty-students-speak-about-gender-ten-years-later (finding that men were responsible for 57 percent of class participation, a rate higher than in 2002, and a perception that women may be penalized socially for participating more than average); The Study on Women's Experiences at Harvard Law School (2004), discussed in "Women's Experience" Raises Concerns, Harvard L. S. Record, Feb. 26, 2004, at 1 (noting that male students were 50 percent more likely to speak voluntarily at least once during a class meeting than female students, and that female students constituted a significantly smaller proportion of "frequent talkers"); Yale Law Women, Yale Law School Faculty, and Students Speak About Gender (2002), available at http://www.yale.edu/ylw, discussed in Sari Bashi & Maryana Iskander, Methodology Matters, 53 J. Legal Educ. 505, 505-506 (2003); Felice Batlan et al., Not Our Mother's Law School? A Third Wave Feminist Study of Women's Experiences in Law School, 39 U. Balt. L. Forum 124, 129-131, 140 (2009) (reviewing studies finding lower grades and participation rates for women).

59. Jennifer Mullins & Nancy Leong, The Persistent Gender Disparity in Student Note Publication, 23 Yale J. Law & Feminism 385 (2011) (finding that women accounted for almost half of law students but only 39 percent of note writers, and were underrepresented on law reviews); Minna Kotkin, Of Authorship and Authority: An Empirical Study of Gender Disparity and Prestige in the "Top Ten" Law Reviews, 31 Women Rights L. Rep. 385 (2010) (finding women wrote fewer articles than men and that the disparity was greatest in the most prestigious journals).

60. Batlan et al., supra note 58, at 129-130; see also D. H. Kaye & Joseph L. Gastwirth, Where Have All the Women Gone? The Gender Gap in Supreme Court Clerkships, 49 Jurimetrics 411 (2009).

61. Batlan et al., supra note 58, at 131; Elizabeth Mertz, Inside the Law School Classroom: Toward a New Legal Realist Pedagogy, 60 Vand. L. Rev. 483, 509 (2007); Adam Neufield, Costs of an Outdated Pedagogy? Study on Gender at Harvard Law School, 13 J. Gender, Social Pol'y & L. 511, 516-517, 530-539 (2005); Bashi & Iskander, supra note 58, at 404-413; Claire G. Schwab, A Shifting Gender Divide: The Impact of Gender on Education at Columbia Law School in the New Millennium, 36 Colum. J. L. & Soc. Probs. 229, 325 (2003).

62. Women's Experience, supra note 58, at 1.

63. John O. McGinnis, At Law School, Unstrict Scrutiny, Wall St. J., July 27, 2005, at D10 (discussing Dan Subotnik, Toxic Diversity (2005)).

64. American Bar Association [ABA], Hearings to Identify Current Obstacles, Opportunities Facing Women Lawyers (May 7, 2003), available at http://abanet.org/lpm/lpt/articles/mgt05041.html.

65. Rhode, From Platitudes to Priorities, supra note 43, at 1056.

66. See American Bar Association Commission on Women in the Profession, Legal Progeny: A Guide to Providing Child Care Benefits for Legal Employers, Lawyers, and Bar Associations 2-3 (2003). For recommendations and examples of model workplace policies, see Cynthia Alvert et al., Project for Attorney Retention, Reduced Hours, Full Success: Part Time Partners in U.S. Law Firms (2009); Deborah L. Rhode, Balanced Lives: Changing the Culture of Workplace Practices (ABA Commission on Women in the Profession, 2001); Joan Williams et al., Better on Balance? The Corporate Counsel Work/Life Report, 10 Wm. & Mary J. Women & L. 367 (2004).

67. See ABA Commission on Women in the Profession, Visible Invisibility: Women of Color in Law Firms 19, 21 (2006).

68. MCCA, Sustaining Pathways to Diversity, supra note 38, at 13, 23-30.

69. Id. at 20.

70. Id. at 14.

71. Id. at 25.

72. Laura Sabattini, Unwritten Rules: What You Don't Know Can Hurt Your Career 5 (Catalyst, 2008).

73. National Association of Women Lawyers, Actions for Advancing Women into Law Firm Leadership (2008).

74. MCCA, Sustaining Pathways to Diversity, supra note 38, at 38-39.

75. Rhode, From Platitudes to Priorities, supra note 43, at 1072-1073; Beiner, Some Thoughts on the State of Women Lawyers, supra note 42, at 697.

76. Deborah L. Rhode & Barbara Kellerman, Women and Leadership: The State of Play, in Women and Leadership: The State of Play and Strategies for Change 1, 30-34 (Barbara Kellerman & Deborah L. Rhode eds., 2008); Judith S. Kaye & Ann C. Reddy, The Progress of Women Lawyers at Big Firms: Steadied or Simply Studied?, 76 Fordham L. Rev. 1941, 1969-1970 (2008); Rachel Breitman, Women's

Group Names Top 10 Family Friendly Firms, Nat'l L.J., Oct. 20, 2008, at S12 (giving credit for extended parental leave policies, on-site child care, telecommuting options, and leadership opportunities for women and minorities); Peter Schmidt, Advocates of Diversity Grasp for Ways to Drive Change in the Legal Profession, Chron. Higher Ed., Nov. 29, 2009, at 2007 (discussing Building a Better Legal Profession).

77. Bradwell v. Illinois, 83 U.S. 130, 137 (1872).

78. Terry Carter, Paths Need Paving, ABA J., Sept. 2000, at 34.

79. See Hilary Sommerlad & Peter Sanderson, Gender, Choice, and Commitment (1998) (describing male barristers' perception of male colleagues as powerful, aggressive, logical, tough, strong, and dominant and female colleagues as vulnerable, intuitive, empathetic, emotional, and subjective, and barristers' belief that male characteristics were more professionally desirable); Schultz, supra note 46, at lvii (describing small-scale studies that find differences in women's working styles, such as being more generous with their time and more concerned with client relations than their male counterparts).

80. See, e.g., Rand Jack & Dana Crowley Jack, Moral Vision and Professional Decisions: The Changing Values of Women and Men Lawyers (1989); Susan P. Sturm, From Gladiators to Problem-Solvers: Connecting Conversations About Women, the Academy, and the Legal Profession, 4 Duke J. Gender L. & Pol'y 119 (1997); Carrie Menkel-Meadow, Portia in a Different Voice: Speculations on a Women's Lawyering Process, 1 Berkeley Women's L.J. 39 (1985).

81. See Schultz, supra note 46, at xxxvii (practitioners and judges); Lynn Mather, Gender in Context: Women in Family Law, in Women in the World's Legal Professions, supra note 46, at 33, 35; Marjorie E. Kornhauser, Rooms of Their Own: An Empirical Study of Occcupational Segregation By Gender Among Law Professors, 73 UMKC L. Rev. 293 (2005)(law professors); Deborah Jones Merritt & Barbara F. Reskin, Sex, Race, and Credentials: The Truth About Affirmative Action in Law Faculty Hiring, 97 Colum. L. Rev. 199, 258-259 (1997) (law professors).

82. See, e.g., Katharine T. Bartlett, Feminist Legal Methods, 103 Harv. L. Rev. 829 (1990); Tracy E. Higgins, "By Reason of Their Sex": Feminist Theory, Postmodernism, and Justice, 80 Cornell L. Rev. 1536 (1995).

83. William Felstiner et al., The Effect of Lawyers' Gender on Client Perceptions of Lawyers, in Schultz, supra note 46, at 23, 26.

84. Mather, supra note 81, at 39-40; Schultz, supra note 46, at lvii.

85. See sources cited in Deborah L. Rhode, Speaking of Sex: The Denial of Gender Equality 21-42 (1997).

86. For an overview, see Deborah L. Rhode, The Difference "Difference" Makes, in The Difference "Difference" Makes: Women and Leadership 3, 18-20 (Deborah L. Rhode ed., 2003).

87. Carrie Menkel-Meadow, Teaching About Gender and Negotiation: Sex, Truths, and Videotape, 16 Negotiation J. 357 (Oct. 2000).

88. For reviews of multiple studies, see id.; Carol Watson, Gender vs. Power as a Predictor of Negotiation Behavior and Outcomes, 10 Negotiation J. 117 (1994); Sandra R. Farber & Monica Rickenberg, Under-Confident Women and Over-Confident Men: Gender and a Sense of Competence in a Simulated Negotiation, 11 Yale J.L. & Feminism 271, 286, 301 (1999).

89. See Carrie Menkel-Meadow, The Limits of Adversarial Ethics, in Ethics in Practice: Lawyers' Roles, Responsibilities, and Regulation (Deborah L. Rhode ed., 2000); Deborah L. Rhode, In the Interests of Justice 49-115 (2001); Sturm, supra note 80, at 127-128, 135-137.

90. Schultz, supra note 46, at ix.

91. Letter from Leila J. Robinson [Sawtelle] to the Equity Club (Apr. 9, 1887), reprinted in Women Lawyers and the Origins of Professional Identity in America: The Letters of the Equity Club, 1887 to 1890, 66 (Virginia G. Drachman ed., 1993).

92. Austin Manifesto on Women in Law, available at http://www.utexas.edu/law/academics/centers/cwl/summit/Austin_manifesto.pdf.

93. Via Chen, The End of Sisterhood, American Lawyer, May 1, 2009, available at http://amlawdaily.typepad.com/amlawdaily/2009/04/the-end-of-sisterhood.html.

94. See Brenda Kruze, Women on the Highest Court: Does Gender Bias or Personal Life Experience Influence Their Opinions?, 36 U. Tol. L. Rev. 995 (2005); Suzanna Sherry, Civil Virtue and the Feminine Voice in Constitutional Adjudication, 72 Va. L. Rev. 543 (1986).

95. Tony Mauro, O'Connor & Ginsburg, Together and Apart, Legal Times, June 9, 2003, at 15.

96. Joan Biskupic, Ginsburg: The Court Needs Another Woman, USA Today, May 6, 2009, at 2.

97. Sandra Day O'Connor, Portia's Progress, 66 N.Y.U. L. Rev. 1546, 1557 (1991).

98. Biskupic, supra note 96, at 2 (quoting Ginsburg).

99. Deborah L. Rhode & Barbara Kellerman, Women and Leadership: The State of Play, in Women and Leadership: The State of Play and Strategies for Change 1, 51-52, n.104 (Barbara Kellerman &

Deborah L. Rhode eds., 2008); Theresa M. Beiner, Female Judging, 36 U. Tol. L. Rev. 821, 821-829 (2005); Fred O. Smith, Jr., Gendered Justice: Do Male and Female Judges Rule Differently on Questions of Gay Rights? 57 Stan. L. Rev. 2087, 2089-2091 (2005).

100. See Madhavi McCall & Michael A. McCall, How Far Does the Gender Gap Extend? Decision Making on State Supreme Courts in Fourth Amendment Cases, 1980-2000, 44 Soc. Sci. J. 67 (2007); Madhavi McCall, Structuring Gender's Impact: Judicial Voting Across Criminal Justice Cases, 36 Am. Pol. Res. 264 (2007).

101. See Max Schanzenbach, Racial and Sex Disparities in Prison Sentences: The Effect of District-Level Judicial Demographics, 24 J. Legal Stud. 57 (2005).

102. Rosalind Dixon, Female Justices, Feminism, and the Politics of Judicial Appointment: A Re-Examination, 21 Yale J.L. & Feminism 297, 312 (2010).

103. Jennifer L. Peresie, Female Judges Matter: Gender and Collegial Decisionmaking in the Federal Appellate Courts, 114 Yale L.J. 1759, 1776, 1778 (2005). See also Christina L. Boyd et al., Untangling the Causal Effects of Sex on Judging, 54 Amer. J. Poli. Sci. 389 (2010) (probability of judge deciding in favor of plaintiff in a discrimination case decreases about 10 percent when the judge is male, and increases when a woman serves on a panel with men). For a collection of analysis of many of the studies of the impact of gender on case outcomes and the influence of female judges on their colleagues, see Fiona Kay & Elizabeth Gorman, Women in the Legal Profession, 4 Ann. Rev. Law Soc. Sci. 299, 321-323 (2008).

104. Peresie, supra note 103, at 1781-1786.

105. Smith, supra note 99, at 2097, 2111, 2114, 2116, 2120.

106. Id. at 2097.

107. Schultz, supra note 46, at xxv, li. For an overview, see Dermot Feenan, Women Judges: Gender Judging, Justifying Diversity, 35 J. Law & Soc. 490, 493-494 (2008).

108. Nadia A Jilani et al., Gender, Consciousness Raising, and Decision Making on the Supreme Court of Canada, 94 Judicature 59, 61, 69 (2010).

109. Feenan, supra note 107, at 493-494.

110. See Elaine Martin & Barry Pyle, State High Courts and Divorce: The Impact of Judicial Gender, 36 U. Tol. L. Rev. 923 (2005).

111. See Twenty Years of Legal Ethics: Past, Present and Future, 20 Geo. J. Legal Ethics 321, 339 (2007) (remarks by Mary Clark).

112. Schultz, supra note 46, at li.

113. Nienke Grossman, Sex on the Bench: Do Women Judges Matter to the Legitimacy of International Courts, 12 Chi. J. Int'l L. 648 (2012).

114. 418 F. Supp. 1 (S.D.N.Y. 1975).

115. Id. at 4.

116. Lynn Hecht Schafran, Not from Central Casting: The Amazing Rise of Women in the American Judiciary, 36 U. Tol. L. Rev. 953, 959 (2005).

117. Joan Biskupic, High Court Just a 1-Woman Show, USA Today, Jan. 26, 2007, at 6A.

118. See Dixon, supra note 102, at 338, arguing that feminists should reconsider the priority they place on symbolic versus substantive concerns in the judicial appointment process, and if forced to choose, should prefer a man who is sympathetic to feminist views to a woman who is not.

119. President Barack Obama, Remarks by the President on Justice David Souter, May 1, 2009, available at http://www.whitehouse.gov/the_press_office/Remarks-By-The-President-On-Justice-David-Souter.

120. S. E. Cupp, Obama's Wacky Supreme Court Vision, Fox Forum, at FoxNews.com., available at http://foxforum.blogs.foxnews.com/2009/05/05/cupp_supreme_court.

121. Karl Rove, Op. Ed., Republicans and Obama's Court Nominees, Wall St. J., May 7, 2009, available at http://online/wsj.com/article/SB124165369700093881.html.

122. Thomas Sowell, "Empathy" vs. Law, National Review Online, May 5, 2009.

123. William Safire, On Language, N.Y. Times Magazine, May 17, 2009, at 26.

124. James L. Gibson, Expecting Justice and Hoping for Empathy, Miller-McCune Online (2010), http://www.miller-mccune.com/legal-affairs/expecting-justice-and-hoping-for empathy-17677 (defining empathy as being able to understand how the law hurts or helps people).

125. Terry A. Maroney, Emotional Regulation and Judicial Behavior, 99 Cal. L. Rev. 1485 (2011).

126. Susan A. Bandes, Empathetic Judging and the Rule of Law, Cardozo L. Rev. De Novo 133, 135-136 (2009).

127. Susan Sturm & Howard Gadlin, Conflict Resolution and Systemic Change, 3 J. Dispute Resolution 1, 4 (2007).

128. Joan Dempsey Klein, Remarks, 36 U. Tol. L. Rev. 918 (2005).

129. ABA Commission on Women in the Profession, The Unfinished Agenda 20-21 (2001). For a comprehensive bibliography, see National Center for State Courts, Racial and Ethnic Bias in the Courts: Bibliography, prepared for the National Consortium of Task Forces and Commissions on Racial and Ethnic Bias in the Courts (2002).

130. Adam Sage, Women on Top in Race to Sit on the Bench, London Times, June 3, 2003, at 3 (quoting Veronique Imbert).

131. Gail Diane Cox, And as Cheetah . . . , Nat'l L.J., Aug. 11, 2003, at 3.

132. Anthony P. Capozzi, Gender Bias Is Alive and Well, Cal. Bar J., June 2004, at 9.

133. The transcript is quoted in Stephen Lubet, Lawyer's Poker 150-153 (2006), and available at http://volokh.com/posts/1166121763.shtml.

134. Id. at 151-152.

135. See Maureen Milford, Supreme Court Chief Justice Sent Racy Video to Colleagues, The News Journal, April 30, 2009, available at http://m.delawareonline.com/detail.jsp?key=204334&rc=ne&full=1. A complaint was dismissed in a confidential order.

136. 476 U.S. 79 (1986).

137. Charles Ogletree, Just Say No! A Proposal to Eliminate Racially Discriminatory Uses of Peremptory Challenges, 31 Am. Crim. L. Rev. 1099, 1104 (1994).

138. See Leonard Post, A Loaded Box of Stereotypes, Nat'l L.J., Apr. 25, 2005, at A1, A18.

139. Susan Hightower, Sex and the Peremptory Strike: An Empirical Analysis of J.E.B. v. Alabama's First Five Years, 52 Stan. L. Rev. 895, 924-926 (2000).

140. Talley v. State 687 So. 2d 1261, 1267 (Ala. Crim. App. 1996).

141. Smithkline Beecham Corp. v. Abbott Laboratories, 2014 U.S. App. LEXIS 1128 (Jan. 21, 2014).

142. Albert W. Alshuler, How to Win the Trial of the Century: The Ethics of Lord Brougham and the O. J. Simpson Defense Team, 29 McGeorge L. Rev. 311, 312 (1998).

143. State v. Jensen, 76 P.3d 188 (Utah Ct. App. 2003); Debora L. Threedy, Legal Archeology and Feminist Legal Theory: A Case Study of Gender and Domestic Violence, 29 Women's Rts. L. Rep. 171 (2008).

144. People v. Galbert, 1995 WL 108696, at *2 (Cal. App.), discussed in Sondra Solovay, Tipping the Scales of Justice: Fighting Weight-Based Discrimination 94-95 (2000).

145. Galbert v. Merkle, 1997 U.S. Dist. LEXIS 2081, at *3 (N.D. Cal. Feb. 24, 1997); Tanya Schevitz, Appeals Court Backs Banning of Fat Juror, San Francisco Examiner, Feb. 8, 1995, at A1, A12 (quoting William Tingle).

146. See Nancy Gertner, Women, Justice and Authority: How Justice Affects Women: Women Offenders and the Sentencing Guidelines, 14 Yale J.L. & Feminism 291, 292 (2002); Amy Farrell, Geoff Ward, & Danielle Rousseau, Intersections of Gender and Race in Federal Sentencing: Examining Court Contexts and the Effects of Representative Court Authorities, 14 J. Gender, Race, & Justice 85, 89-90 (2010).

147. Farrell, Ward, & Rousseau, supra note 146, at 91-92; Ryan Elias Newby, Evil Women and Innocent Victims: The Effect of Gender on California Sentences for Domestic Homicide, 22 Hastings Women's L.J. 113, 117-119 (2011). For commentators' justifications, see Carissa Bryne Hessick, Race and Gender as Explicit Sentencing Factors, 14 J. Gender, Race, & Justice 127, 139-140 (2010).

148. Newby, supra note 147, at 119-120, 155, 156.

149. Ilene H. Nagel & Barry L. Johnson, Gender Issues and the Criminal Law: The Role of Gender in a Structured Sentencing System: Equal Treatment, Policy Choices, and the Sentencing of Female Offenders Under the United States Sentencing Guidelines, 85 J. Crim. L. & Criminology 181, 208 (1994).

150. United States v. Pozzy, 902 F.2d 133, 138-139 (1st Cir. 1990).

151. See, e.g., United States v. Mateo, 299 F. Supp. 2d 201, 212-213 (S.D.N.Y. 2004) (giving a lighter sentence to a mother who did not have a spouse to care for her newborn child); see also Sean B. Berberian, Protecting Children: Explaining Disparities in the Female Offender's Pretrial Process, and Policy Issues Surrounding Lenient Treatment of Mothers, 10 Hastings Women's L.J. 369 (1999) (finding that women with children were significantly more likely to receive pretrial release and lower bail/bond amounts).

152. Eleanor Bush, Considering the Defendant's Children at Sentencing, 2 Fed. Sent'g Rep. 194, 194 (1990). See also Myrna Raeder, Gender and Sentencing: Single Moms, Battered Women, and Other Sex-Based Anomalies in the Gender-Free World of the Federal Sentencing Guidelines, 20 Pepp. L. Rev. 905, 961 (1993) (blindly imposing equal treatment on parents at sentencing when the rest of society does not "makes a mockery of so-called gender neutrality in sentencing").

153. President of the Republic of South Africa v. Hugo, 1997 (4) SA 1 (CC).

154. Id.

155. See Chris Burritt & Jack Warner, The Susan Smith Trial, Atlanta Const., July 22, 1995, at C8; Jurors in Susan Smith Trial Say They Don't Have Any Regrets, Atlanta Const., Aug. 28, 1995, at C6.

156. Michele Connell, The Postpartum Psychosis Defense and Feminism: More or Less Justice for Women?, 63 Case W. Res. L. Rev. 143, 146-147 (2002).

157. Id. at 147-148.

158. 976 F.2d 1216, 1218 (9th Cir. 1992).

159. Shimica Gaskins, Note, "Women of Circumstance" — The Effects of Mandatory Minimum Sentencing on Women Minimally Involved in Drug Crimes, 41 Am. Crim. L. Rev. 1533, 1534 (2004).

160. Id. at 1536.

161. Id. at 1547.

162. See id. at 1535.

163. No. CR-88-0720-AAH-1 (C.D. Cal. 1989), rev'd on other grounds, 925 F.2d 1472 (9th Cir. 1991).

164. See John Griffith, Woman Faces Counts in Bank Case, Oregonian, Feb. 4, 1992, at C8; Kim Murphy, "Soft Touch" Bandit Gets a Break from Judge on Term, L.A. Times, May 13, 1989, available at http://articles.latimes.com/1989-05-10/local/me-2905_1_women-are-soft-touches-sentencing-guidelines-svengali-relationship

165. For an overview of problems, see Susan F. Sharp & M. Elaine Eriksen, Imprisoned Mothers and Their Children, in Women in Prison: Gender and Social Control (Barbara H. Zaitzow & Jim Thomas eds., 2003).

166. Kenosha County Dep't of Human Services v. Jodie W., 716 N.W.2d 845 (Wis. 2006) (reversing the permanent termination of Jodie's parental rights).

167. See United States v. Guiro, 887 F. Supp. 66 (E.D.N.Y. 1995) (upholding sentence of eight months of home confinement and 500 hours of community service). See also United States v. Naylor, 735 F. Supp. 928 (D. Minn. 1990) (upholding downward departure because of defendant's romantic relationship with a manipulative, much older co-defendant); United States v. Thomas, 181 F.3d 870 (7th Cir. 1999) (denying downward departure for female defendant who claimed she committed tax fraud because of the abuse she suffered at the hands of her husband and because of her dependent personality).

CHAPTER 5

Autonomy

For women's rights advocates, equality is a critical value, but so, too, is autonomy. This chapter shifts the emphasis from women having what men have, to women being able to stand on their own, make their own decisions, and pursue their own notion of a life well lived.

The concept of autonomy is woven deeply into Anglo-American liberal legal principles. The law governing contracts, torts, and crimes typically assumes that the individual is capable of formulating a specific "intent" to act, of exercising free "choice" or "consent," and of behaving as a "reasonable" person. Women's rights advocates make similar assumptions when they argue that women should have freedom to control their own lives and make their own reproductive choices.

Contemporary social theory has challenged the Enlightenment view of the self as autonomous and capable of acting independently of external influence. Today, the individual is more often understood as constituted through multiple sources of identity and as subject to social, institutional, and ideological forces that construct and constrain individuals' desires, choices, and perceptions of reality. This more complex view of autonomy reveals the limitations of the traditional liberal concept and points toward pragmatic strategies for overcoming these limitations. From this vantage point, freedom is a relative concept rather than an absolute one, but the assumption remains that, in most matters, more is better than less.

Another complexity arises from different views about the subject of the autonomy interest. Typically, autonomy is thought to reside in the individual person, and means the right to be free from interference by others. The contemporary women's rights movement, however, has often considered relationships as the foundation of autonomy rights and has argued for concepts of autonomy that encompass the freedom to flourish in a positive sense, not just freedom from the interference of others. This chapter explores these themes in contexts in which autonomy, choice, and consent are most deeply implicated—rape, prostitution, pregnancy, abortion, and welfare.

A. SEX AND CONSENT

1. "Statutory" Rape: The (Ir)relevance of Consent

One of the most difficult and contested issues in the law of rape is that of consent. The chapter begins with the law of statutory rape, which presumes the lack of consent to sex by victims below a certain age. Traditionally, only a woman could be the victim of statutory rape, and only a man could be charged with the crime. The *Michael M.* case, below, upholds the sex-based statutory scheme, justifying the law not in the traditional terms of female incapacity, but rather as a measure to further the state's interest in preventing unwed teenage pregnancies.

Statutory rape is sexual intercourse or assault with a person under the legal age of consent. This age is set by statute and varies from state to state. Typically, the crime of statutory rape has different degrees, depending on such factors as the age of the victim and the age and power of the perpetrator. In contrast to conventional rape, lack of consent is not a requirement of statutory rape; a person under a certain age is presumed to lack capacity to consent.

Reading Questions

1. Consider the factual complexities that underpin the Justices' different conclusions. Did Sharon consent to sex with Michael? Is the account by Justice Rehnquist consistent with the facts reported in the footnote to the Justice Blackmun concurrence? If Sharon did consent to sex, should it have been a crime? By whom?
2. Should the law distinguish between males and females for purposes of defining crimes of rape? Is the law upheld in *Michael M.* based on outmoded stereotypes? Is the law "good" for women?
3. Do the potential benefits to women of statutory rape laws outweigh the negative implications of relying on stereotypes?

Michael M. v. Superior Court of Sonoma County

450 U.S. 464 (1981)

Justice REHNQUIST announced the judgment of the Court and delivered an opinion, in which THE CHIEF JUSTICE, Justice STEWART, and Justice POWELL joined.

The question presented in this case is whether California's "statutory rape" law . . . violates the Equal Protection Clause of the Fourteenth Amendment.

Section 261.5 defines unlawful sexual intercourse as "an act of sexual intercourse accomplished with a female not the wife of the perpetrator, where the female is under the age of 18 years." The statute thus makes men alone criminally liable for the act of sexual intercourse.

In July 1978, a complaint was filed in the Municipal Court of Sonoma County, Cal., alleging that petitioner, then a 17-year-old male, had had unlawful sexual intercourse with a female under the age of 18, in violation of §261.5. The evidence, adduced at a preliminary hearing showed that at approximately midnight on June 3, 1978, petitioner and two friends approached Sharon, a 16-year-old female, and her sister as they waited at a bus stop. Petitioner and Sharon, who had already been drinking, moved away from the others and began to kiss. After being struck in the face for rebuffing petitioner's initial advances, Sharon submitted to sexual intercourse with petitioner. Prior to trial, petitioner sought to set aside the information on both state and federal constitutional grounds, asserting that §261.5 unlawfully discriminated on the basis of gender. The trial court and the California Court of Appeal denied petitioner's request for relief and petitioner sought review in the Supreme Court of California. . . .

The justification for the statute offered by the State, and accepted by the Supreme Court of California, is that the legislature sought to prevent illegitimate teenage pregnancies. That finding, of course, is entitled to great deference. . . .

We are satisfied not only that the prevention of illegitimate pregnancy is at least one of the "purposes" of the statute, but also that the State has a strong interest in preventing such pregnancy. At the risk of stating the obvious, teenage pregnancies, which have increased dramatically over the last two decades, have significant social, medical, and economic consequences for both the mother and her child, and the State. Of particular concern to the State is that approximately half of all teenage pregnancies end in abortion. And of those children who are born, their illegitimacy makes them likely candidates to become wards of the State.

We need not be medical doctors to discern that young men and young women are not similarly situated with respect to the problems and the risks of sexual intercourse. Only women may become pregnant, and they suffer disproportionately the profound physical, emotional and psychological consequences of sexual activity. The statute at issue here protects women from sexual intercourse at an age when those consequences are particularly severe.

The question thus boils down to whether a State may attack the problem of sexual intercourse and teenage pregnancy directly by prohibiting a male from having sexual intercourse with a minor female. We hold that such a statute is sufficiently related to the State's objectives to pass constitutional muster.

Because virtually all of the significant harmful and inescapably identifiable consequences of teenage pregnancy fall on the young female, a legislature acts well within its authority when it elects to punish only the participant who, by nature, suffers few of the consequences of his conduct. It is hardly unreasonable for a legislature acting to protect minor females to exclude them from punishment. Moreover, the risk of pregnancy itself constitutes a substantial deterrence to young females. No similar natural sanctions deter males. A criminal sanction imposed solely on males thus serves to roughly "equalize" the deterrents on the sexes.

We are unable to accept petitioner's contention that the statute is impermissibly under-inclusive and must, in order to pass judicial scrutiny, be *broadened* so as to hold the female as criminally liable as the male. It is argued that this statute is not *necessary* to deter teenage pregnancy because a gender-neutral statute, where both male and female would be subject to prosecution, would serve that goal equally well. The relevant inquiry, however, is not whether the statute is drawn as precisely as it might have been, but whether the line chosen by the California Legislature is within constitutional limitations.

In any event, we cannot say that a gender-neutral statute would be as effective as the statute California has chosen to enact. The State persuasively contends that a gender-neutral statute would frustrate its interest in effective enforcement. Its view is that a female is surely less likely to report violations of the statute if she herself would be subject to criminal prosecution. In an area already fraught with prosecutorial difficulties, we decline to hold that the Equal Protection Clause requires a legislature to enact a statute so broad that it may well be incapable of enforcement. . . .

There remains only petitioner's contention that the statute is unconstitutional as it is applied to him because he, like Sharon, was under 18 at the time of sexual intercourse. Petitioner argues that the statute is flawed because it presumes that as between two persons under 18, the male is the culpable aggressor. We find petitioner's contentions unpersuasive. Contrary to his assertions, the statute does not rest on the assumption that males are generally the aggressors. It is instead an attempt by a legislature to prevent illegitimate teenage pregnancy by providing an additional deterrent for men. The age of the man is irrelevant since young men are as capable as older men of inflicting the harm sought to be prevented.

In upholding the California statute we also recognize that this is not a case where a statute is being challenged on the grounds that it "invidiously discriminates" against females. To the contrary, the statute places a burden on males which is not shared by females. But we find nothing to suggest that men, because of past discrimination or peculiar disadvantages, are in need of the special solicitude of the courts. Nor is this a case where the gender classification is made "solely for . . . administrative convenience," . . . or rests on "the baggage of sexual stereotypes." . . . As we have held, the statute instead reasonably reflects the fact that the consequences of sexual intercourse and pregnancy fall more heavily on the female than on the male.

Accordingly, the judgment of the California Supreme Court is Affirmed.

Justice BLACKMUN, concurring in the judgment.

I think . . . that it is only fair, with respect to this particular petitioner, to point out that his partner, Sharon, appears not to have been an unwilling participant in at least the initial stages of the intimacies that took place the night of June 3, 1978.* Petitioner's and Sharon's nonacquaintance with each other before the incident; their drinking; their withdrawal from the others of the group; their foreplay, in which she willingly participated and seems to have encouraged; and the closeness of their ages (a difference of only one year and 18 days) are factors that should make this case an unattractive one to prosecute

* Sharon at the preliminary hearing testified as follows: "Q. [by the Deputy District Attorney]. On June the 4th, at approximately midnight—midnight of June the 3rd, were you in Rohnert Park?" A. [by Sharon]. Yes. "Q. Is that in Sonoma County?" A. Yes. "Q. Did anything unusual happen to you that night in Rohnert Park?" A. Yes. "Q. Would you briefly describe what happened that night? Did you see the defendant that night in Rohnert Park?" A. Yes. "Q. Where did you first meet him?" A. At a bus stop. "Q. Was anyone with you?" A. My sister. "Q. Was anyone with the defendant?" A. Yes. "Q. How many people were with the defendant?" A. Two. "Q. Now, after you met the defendant, what happened?" A. We walked down to the railroad tracks. "Q. What happened at the railroad tracks?" A. We were drinking at the railroad tracks and we walked over to this bush and he started kissing me and stuff, and I was kissing him back, too, at first. Then, I was telling him to stop— "Q. Yes." A.—and I was telling him to slow down and stop. He said, 'Okay, okay.' But then he just kept doing it. He just kept doing it and then my sister and two other guys came over to where we were and my sister said—told me to get up and come home. And then I didn't— "Q. Yes." A.—and then my sister and— "Q. All right." A.—David, one of the boys that were there, started walking home and we stayed there and then later— "Q. All right." A.—Bruce left Michael, you know. "The Court: Michael being the defendant?" The Witness: Yeah. We was lying there and we were kissing each other, and then he asked me if I wanted to walk him over to the park; so we walked over to the park and we sat down on a bench and then he started kissing me again and we were laying on the bench. And he told me to take my pants off. I said, 'No,' and I was trying to get up and he hit me back down on the bench and then I just said to myself, 'Forget it,' and I let him do what he wanted to do and he took my pants off and he was telling me to put my legs around him and stuff—
"Q. Did you have sexual intercourse with the defendant?" A. Yeah. "Q. He did put his penis into your vagina?" A. Yes. "Q. You said that he hit you?" A. Yeah. "Q. How did he hit you?" A. He slugged me in the face. "Q. With what did he slug you?" A. His fist. "Q. Where abouts in the face?" A. On my chin. "Q. As a result of that, did you have any bruises or any kind of an injury?" A. Yeah. "Q. What happened?" A. I had bruises. "The Court: Did he hit you one time or did he hit you more than once?" The Witness: He hit me about two or three times.
"Q. Now, during the course of that evening, did the defendant ask you your age?" A. Yeah. "Q. And what did you tell him?" A. Sixteen. "Q. Did you tell him you were sixteen?" A. Yes. "Q. Now, you said you had been drinking, is that correct?" A. Yes. "Q. Would you describe your condition as a result of the drinking?" A. I was a little drunk.' . . .
CROSS-EXAMINATION "Q. Did you go off with Mr. M. away from the others?" A. Yeah. "Q. Why did you do that?" A. I don't know. I guess I wanted to. "Q. Did you have any need to go to the bathroom when you were there." A. Yes. "Q. And what did you do?" A. Me and my sister walked down the railroad tracks to some bushes and went to the bathroom. "Q. Now, you and Mr. M., as I understand it, went off into the bushes, is that correct?" A. Yes. "Q. Okay. And what did you do when you and Mr. M. were there in the bushes?" A. We were kissing and hugging. "Q. Were you sitting up?" A. We were laying down. "Q. You were lying down. This was in the bushes?" A. Yes. "Q. How far away from the rest of them were you?" A. They were just bushes right next to the railroad tracks. We just walked off into the bushes; not very far.
"Q. So your sister and the other two boys came over to where you were, you and Michael were, is that right?" A. Yeah. "Q. What did they say to you, if you remember?" A. My sister didn't say anything. She said, 'Come on, Sharon, let's go home.' "Q. She asked you to go home with her?" A. (Affirmative nod.) "Q. Did you go home with her?" A. No. "Q. You wanted to stay with Mr. M.?" A. I don't know. "Q. Was this before or after he hit you?" A. Before.

at all, and especially to prosecute as a felony, rather than as a misdemeanor chargeable under §261.5. But the State has chosen to prosecute in that manner, and the facts, I reluctantly conclude, may fit the crime.

Justice BRENNAN, with whom Justices WHITE and MARSHALL join, dissenting. . . .

[E]ven assuming that prevention of teenage pregnancy is an important governmental objective and that it is in fact an objective of §261.5 . . . , California still has the burden of proving that there are fewer teenage pregnancies under its gender-based statutory rape law than there would be if the law were gender neutral. To meet this burden, the State must show that because its statutory rape law punishes only males, and not females, it more effectively deters minor females from having sexual intercourse.[5]

The plurality assumes that a gender-neutral statute would be less effective than §261.5 in deterring sexual activity because a gender-neutral statute would create significant enforcement problems. . . . However, a State's bare assertion that its gender-based statutory classification substantially furthers an important governmental interest is not enough to meet its burden of proof under Craig v. Boren. . . .

The State has not produced such evidence in this case. Moreover, there are at least two serious flaws in the State's assertion that law enforcement problems created by a gender-neutral statutory rape law would make such a statute less effective than a gender-based statute in deterring sexual activity.

"Q. What happened in the five minutes that Bruce stayed there with you and Michael?" A. I don't remember. "Q. You don't remember at all?" A. (Negative head shake.) "Q. Did you have occasion at that time to kiss Bruce?" A. Yeah. "Q. You did? You were kissing Bruce at that time?" A. (Affirmative nod.) "Q. Was Bruce kissing you?" A. Yes. "Q. And were you standing up at this time?" A. No, we were sitting down.

"Q. Okay. So at this point in time you had left Mr. M. and you were hugging and kissing with Bruce, is that right?" A. Yeah. "Q. And you were sitting up." A. Yes. "Q. Was your sister still there then?" A. No. Yeah, she was at first. "Q. What was she doing?" A. She was standing up with Michael and David. "Q. Yes. Was she doing anything with Michael and David?" A. No, I don't think so. "Q. Whose idea was it for you and Bruce to kiss? Did you initiate that?" A. Yes. "Q. What happened after Bruce left?" A. Michael asked me if I wanted to go walk to the park. "Q. And what did you say?" A. I said, 'Yes.' "Q. And then what happened?" A. We walked to the park.

"Q. How long did it take you to get to the park?" A. About ten or fifteen minutes. "Q. And did you walk there?" A. Yes. "Q. Did Mr. M. ever mention his name?" A. Yes. . . .

5. Petitioner has not questioned the State's constitutional power to achieve its asserted objective by criminalizing consensual sexual activity. However, I note that our cases would not foreclose such a privacy challenge. The State is attempting to reduce the incidence of teenage pregnancy by imposing criminal sanctions on those who engage in consensual sexual activity with minor females. We have stressed, however, that "[i]f the right of privacy means anything, it is the right of the individual, married or single, to be free from unwarranted governmental intrusion into matters so fundamentally affecting a person as the decision whether to bear or beget a child." Eisenstadt v. Baird, [1972]. Minors, too, enjoy a right of privacy in connection with decisions affecting procreation. Carey v. Population Services International, [1977]. Thus, despite the suggestion of the plurality to the contrary . . . , it is not settled that a State may rely on a pregnancy-prevention justification to make consensual sexual intercourse among minors a criminal act.

First, the experience of other jurisdictions, and California itself, belies the plurality's conclusion that a gender-neutral statutory rape law "may well be incapable of enforcement." There are now at least 37 States that have enacted gender-neutral statutory rape laws. Although most of these laws protect young persons (of either sex) from the sexual exploitation of older individuals, the laws of Arizona, Florida, and Illinois permit prosecution of both minor females and minor males for engaging in mutual sexual conduct. California has introduced no evidence that those States have been handicapped by the enforcement problems the plurality finds so persuasive.[7] Surely, if those States could provide such evidence, we might expect that California would have introduced it.

In addition, the California Legislature in recent years has revised other sections of the Penal Code to make them gender-neutral. For example [other California criminal law statutes], prohibiting sodomy and oral copulation with a "person who is under 18 years of age," could cause two minor homosexuals to be subjected to criminal sanctions for engaging in mutually consensual conduct. Again, the State has introduced no evidence to explain why a gender-neutral statutory rape law would be any more difficult to enforce than those statutes.

The second flaw in the State's assertion is that even assuming that a gender-neutral statute would be more difficult to enforce, the State has still not shown that those enforcement problems would make such a statute less effective than a gender-based statute in deterring minor females from engaging in sexual intercourse. Common sense, however, suggests that a gender-neutral statutory rape law is potentially a greater deterrent of sexual activity than a gender-based law, for the simple reason that a gender-neutral law subjects both men and women to criminal sanctions and thus arguably has a deterrent effect on twice as many potential violators. Even if fewer persons were prosecuted under the gender-neutral law, as the State suggests, it would still be true that twice as many persons would be subject to arrest. The State's failure to prove that a gender-neutral law would be a less effective deterrent than a gender-based law, like the State's failure to prove that a gender-neutral law would be difficult to enforce, should have led this Court to invalidate §261.5.

III

Until very recently, no California court or commentator had suggested that the purpose of California's statutory rape law was to protect young women from the risk of pregnancy. Indeed, the historical development of §261.5

---

7. There is a logical reason for this. In contrast to laws governing forcible rape, statutory rape laws apply to consensual sexual activity. Force is not an element of the crime. Since a woman who consents to an act of sexual intercourse is unlikely to report her partner to the police—whether or not she is subject to criminal sanctions—enforcement would not be undermined if the statute were to be made gender neutral. . . .

demonstrates that the law was initially enacted on the premise that young women, in contrast to young men, were to be deemed legally incapable of consenting to an act of sexual intercourse.[9] Because their chastity was considered particularly precious, those young women were felt to be uniquely in need of the State's protection.[10] In contrast, young men were assumed to be capable of making such decisions for themselves; the law therefore did not offer them any special protection.

It is perhaps because the gender classification in California's statutory rape law was initially designed to further these outmoded sexual stereotypes, rather than to reduce the incidence of teenage pregnancies, that the State has been unable to demonstrate a substantial relationship between the classification and its newly asserted goal. . . .

I would hold that §261.5 violates the Equal Protection Clause of the Fourteenth Amendment, and I would reverse the judgment of the California Supreme Court.

Justice STEVENS, dissenting.

Local custom and belief—rather than statutory laws of venerable but doubtful ancestry—will determine the volume of sexual activity among unmarried teenagers. The empirical evidence cited by the plurality demonstrates the futility of the notion that a statutory prohibition will significantly affect the volume of that activity or provide a meaningful solution to the problems created by it. Nevertheless, as a matter of constitutional power, unlike my Brother Brennan . . . , I would have no doubt about the validity of a state law prohibiting all unmarried teenagers from engaging in sexual intercourse. The societal interests in reducing the incidence of venereal disease and teenage pregnancy are sufficient, in my judgment, to justify a prohibition of conduct that increases the risk of those harms.

My conclusion that a nondiscriminatory prohibition would be constitutional does not help me answer the question whether a prohibition applicable to only half of the joint participants in the risk-creating conduct is also valid. It cannot be true that the validity of a total ban is an adequate justification for a

9. California's statutory rape law had its origins in the Statutes of Westminster enacted during the reign of Edward I at the close of the 13th century. . . . The age of consent at that time was 12 years, reduced to 10 years in 1576. . . . This statute was part of the common law brought to the United States. Thus, when the first California penal statute was enacted, it contained a provision . . . that proscribed sexual intercourse with females under the age of 10. In 1889, the California statute was amended to make the age of consent 14. . . . In 1897, the age was advanced to 16. . . . In 1913 it was fixed at 18, where it now remains. . . .

Because females generally have not reached puberty by the age of 10, it is inconceivable that a statute designed to prevent pregnancy would be directed at acts of sexual intercourse with females under that age. . . .

10. Past decisions of the California courts confirm that the law was designed to protect the State's young females from their own uninformed decision making. . . . It was only in deciding *Michael M.* that the California Supreme Court decided for the first time in the 130-year history of the statute, that pregnancy prevention had become one of the purposes of the statute.

selective prohibition; otherwise, the constitutional objection to discriminatory rules would be meaningless. The question in this case is whether the difference between males and females justifies this statutory discrimination based entirely on sex. . . .

In my judgment, the fact that a class of persons is especially vulnerable to a risk that a statute is designed to avoid is a reason for making the statute applicable to that class. The argument that a special need for protection provides a rational explanation for an exemption is one I simply do not comprehend. . . .

If pregnancy or some other special harm is suffered by one of the two participants in the prohibited act, that special harm no doubt would constitute a legitimate mitigating factor in deciding what, if any, punishment might be appropriate in a given case. But from the standpoint of fashioning a general preventive rule—or, indeed, in determining appropriate punishment when neither party in fact has suffered any special harm—I regard a total exemption for the members of the more endangered class as utterly irrational.

In my opinion, the only acceptable justification for a general rule requiring disparate treatment of the two participants in a joint act must be a legislative judgment that one is more guilty than the other. The risk-creating conduct that this statute is designed to prevent requires the participation of two persons—one male and one female. In many situations it is probably true that one is the aggressor and the other is either an unwilling, or at least a less willing, participant in the joint act. If a statute authorized punishment of only one participant and required the prosecutor to prove that that participant had been the aggressor, I assume that the discrimination would be valid. Although the question is less clear, I also assume, for the purpose of deciding this case, that it would be permissible to punish only the male participant, if one element of the offense were proof that he had been the aggressor, or at least in some respects the more responsible participant in the joint act. The statute at issue in this case, however, requires no such proof. The question raised by this statute is whether the State, consistently with the Federal Constitution, may always punish the male and never the female when they are equally responsible or when the female is the more responsible of the two.

It would seem to me that an impartial lawmaker could give only one answer to that question. The fact that the California Legislature has decided to apply its prohibition only to the male may reflect a legislative judgment that in the typical case the male is actually the more guilty party. Any such judgment must, in turn, assume that the decision to engage in the risk-creating conduct is always—or at least typically—a male decision. . . . But the possibility that such a habitual attitude may reflect nothing more than an irrational prejudice makes it an insufficient justification for discriminatory treatment that is otherwise blatantly unfair. For, as I read this statute, it requires that one, and only one, of two equally guilty wrongdoers be stigmatized by a criminal conviction. . . .

[I do not] find at all persuasive the suggestion that this discrimination is adequately justified by the desire to encourage females to inform against their male partners. Even if the concept of a wholesale informant's exemption were an acceptable enforcement device, what is the justification for defining the exempt class entirely by reference to sex rather than by reference to a more neutral criterion such as relative innocence? Indeed, if the exempt class is to be composed entirely of members of one sex, what is there to support the view that the statutory purpose will be better served by granting the informing license to females rather than to males? If a discarded male partner informs on a promiscuous female, a timely threat of prosecution might well prevent the precise harm the statute is intended to minimize.

Finally, even if my logic is faulty and there actually is some speculative basis for treating equally guilty males and females differently, I still believe that any such speculative justification would be outweighed by the paramount interest in evenhanded enforcement of the law. A rule that authorizes punishment of only one of two equally guilty wrongdoers violates the essence of the constitutional requirement that the sovereign must govern impartially.

I respectfully dissent.

Notes

1. Consent and Statutory Rape. Technically, lack of consent is not an element of statutory rape. Yet the extent to which Sharon participated willingly seems important to the Justices. Note that Justice Rehnquist and Justice Blackmun reach the same conclusion in the case, but apparently based on different views about Sharon's level of consent. From Justice Rehnquist, all we know is that Sharon was "struck in the face" for "rebuffing" Michael's advances and that then she "submitted" to sexual intercourse. Under Justice Blackmun's detailed reading of the facts, Sharon's participation was "not unwilling." Which rationale for statutory rape laws does each narrative support? In what sense, if any, did Sharon lack capacity? Was she taken advantage of because of her age? If Sharon was "willing," what does this say about the majority's justification for the sex-based statute — that the fear of pregnancy is an effective deterrent?

What does it mean for a teenage girl to "consent" to sex? Michelle Oberman argues:

> [E]ven assuming that girls do experience sexual pleasure and desire, these are only two of a multiplicity of factors which induce their consent to sex.
>
> The stories girls tell about the "consensual" sex in which they engage reflect a poignant subtext of hope and pain. Girls express longing for emotional attachment, romance, and respect. At the same time, they suffer enormous insecurity and diminished self-image. These two factors are clearly interrelated — the worse girls feel about themselves, the more they look to males for ratification of the women that they are becoming. The importance of being attractive to males takes on a central role in many girls' lives. . . . Girls want boyfriends, relationships, or somebody who will hold them and tell them that they are wanted.

Girls negotiate access to the fulfillment of these emotional needs by way of sex. A girl who wants males to find her attractive, who wants acceptance and popularity, might reasonably consent to sex with a popular boy, to multiple popular boys, or with any partner who can persuade her that she is attractive and desirable. Males recognize, and occasionally exploit, girls' insecurity. . . . Modern statutory rape law . . . classifies intercourse as either consensual sex or rape. However, from the girl's vantage point, her consent may have been so fraught with ambivalence that it was meaningless. . . .

If girls' autonomy is to be taken seriously, the law must evaluate the sexual decisions they make, and formulate a legal response which enhances the likelihood that those decisions are autonomous ones.[1]

If Oberman is right, what would such a legal response look like? Consider Wendy Williams' comment about statutory rape laws:

At this point, we need to think as deeply as we can about what we want the future of women and men to be. Do we want equality of the sexes—or do we want justice for two kinds of human beings who are fundamentally different?[2]

Which do we want?

2. Statutory Rape Laws.   At one time, the legal age of sexual consent was ten or younger. The nineteenth-century reformers who succeeded in persuading states to increase the statutory age were motivated both by a desire to protect young women from sexual exploitation, and to control their burgeoning sexuality.[3]

The legal consent age now ranges from 12 to 18, the most common being 16. The statutory rape laws of all states except Idaho are now sex-neutral. The move to neutrality appears to have had less to do with a recognition of female sexual autonomy than with a recognition of male vulnerability to sexual exploitation. Recent well-publicized cases involving the solicitation of sex from underage boys by priests, teachers, and coaches have dramatically altered social attitudes. (See Note 4, below.)

Many state statutes now focus on the number of years that separate the parties, either ignoring relationships between adolescents of similar ages, or making these interactions less serious. In California, for example, any person who engages in unlawful sexual intercourse with a minor who is not more than three years older or three years younger than the perpetrator is guilty of a misdemeanor, whereas any person over the age of 21 years who engages in unlawful sexual intercourse with a minor under 16 years of age may be guilty of either a misdemeanor or a felony.[4] Laws that treat sexual acts between teenagers more leniently, or ignore them altogether, are sometimes called "Romeo and Juliet laws."

One issue under Romeo and Juliet laws is whether they apply to sexual conduct between persons of the same sex. One Kansas case involved an 18-year-old young man who was charged with sodomy involving a 15-year-old boy. If the younger boy had been a girl, the longest prison sentence the

Kansas Romeo and Juliet Law allowed would have been 15 months. Because the law was expressly limited to opposite-sex cases, the defendant was sentenced to more than 17 years in prison. The sentence was reversed on appeal, on state and federal equal protection grounds and due process grounds.[5]

3. Statutory Rape Enforcement.   Beginning in the mid-1990s, California and several other states, in order to reduce teenage pregnancy and welfare costs, launched a campaign to toughen enforcement of statutory rape laws and to publicize the illegality of sex with minors. Congress encouraged such policies in the Personal Responsibility and Work Opportunity Act of 1996. This Act, discussed more fully in a later section of this chapter, advises criminal and welfare agencies to "aggressively enforce statutory rape laws." The 1996 Amendments to the Federal Child Abuse Prevention and Treatment Act authorized grants to states for programs relating to investigation and prosecution of statutory rape that involve caretakers or family members.

States typically require certain service providers to reports acts of child abuse. These mandatory reporting laws vary by state. Should they apply to cases of statutory rape? In 2003, the attorney general of Kansas wrote an opinion letter stating that any sexual activity by a minor younger than 16 is inherently injurious and that the reporting statute therefore requires, among other things, that abortion providers report to state authorities every minor who seeks an abortion. How would you evaluate this approach? In 2004, a U.S. district court temporarily enjoined the opinion, writing that the approach violates minors "right to information privacy concerning personal sexual matters that might be revealed through mandatory reporting."[6] The Tenth Circuit Court of Appeals vacated the injunction and remanded for further proceedings.[7] On remand, the district court issued a permanent injunction against enforcement of the mandatory reporting statute in accordance with the opinion letter, declining to interpret the statute to make all underage sexual activity inherently injurious, and to impose a reporting duty only where the reporter has reason to suspect injury, as well as illegal sexual activity. The court concluded that some minors would face irreparable harm if the opinion letter was followed.[8] What kind of injury do you think the court was referring to?[9]

How should prosecutors decide whether to pursue statutory rape violations? How important is the apparent consent of the victim, the ages of the parties, or the fact that sexual intercourse led to pregnancy? Should adults in special trust relationships such as teachers or athletic coaches be especially targeted irrespective of the other party's age and consent? What about men who father children who end up on welfare? Should lawmakers be concerned that teenage girls may be reluctant to seek reproductive health care out of fear it may lead to rape prosecutions?

How should courts and/or legislatures respond to a practice of allowing men arrested for statutory rape to marry their pregnant partners in lieu of jail time? In Orange County, California, it is reported that "young teenage girls, some even at the age of thirteen, have been permitted to marry the adult men who statutorily raped or molested them. The permission to engage in these marriages comes from juvenile court judges on the advice of welfare agency officials, and provides the statutory rapist with an affirmative defense to any possible pending statutory rape charge."[10] The issue was brought to greater public attention when, in May 2005, 22-year-old Matthew Koso married his 14-year-old pregnant girlfriend, whom he began dating when she was 12. The couple lived in Nebraska, but were able to cross state lines and marry in Kansas, which allows boys as young as 14 to marry girls as young as 12, as long as the parents of the minor permit. Should the case be prosecuted as statutory rape in Nebraska? The editorial staff of the *New York Times* thought so, arguing that "neither parental nor state approval makes it right to tie a girl as young as 12 to another person in what is supposed to be a lifetime commitment."[11]

Do you agree? Consider the following:

> [D]o not get caught up in the notion that the [New York] Times has taken a principled stand on the inability of underage girls to properly decide what is right for themselves even with parental consultation. For more than a decade, the Times has assumed the strong editorial position that parental notification laws for underage girls getting abortions—even for those who cross state lines—are wrong.[12]

Is this point well taken? A number of states allow underage pregnant teenagers to consent to marriage but not to sex. In a few celebrated cases, prosecutions have been brought against the older spouse. Do such laws or such prosecutions make sense?[13]

4. Gender Neutrality and Differential Treatment of Male and Female Offenders.   Most countries with legal traditions similar to the United States, such as Great Britain, Canada, and Australia, have adopted gender-neutral statutory rape laws.[14] However, many prosecutors, judges, and juries, as well as society generally, tend to view the crime differently when the victims are male, particularly when the offenders are female. In justifying gender-specific language in the Model Penal Code, its commentators claim that the "potential consequences of coerced intimacy [for males] does not seem so grave. For one thing there is no prospect of unwanted pregnancy. And however devalued virginity has become for the modern woman, it would be difficult to believe that its loss constitutes comparable injury to the male."[15] Is this right? Should the sex of the victim affect the penalties?

Double standards regarding statutory rape remain common. A widespread attitude is that underage men welcome the encounter; otherwise they would not be physically capable of engaging in the sexual act. However, research indicates that male sexual responses are stimulated not only by desire, but sometimes fear and anger.[16] Boys may often be reluctant to acknowledge sexual abuse by women because the culture conditions them to view such encounters as "getting lucky."[17] Many male adolescents fear that resistance will make them look like a "sissy" or a "fag," and that complaints will result in disbelief or ridicule. However, even victims who repress their sense of injury may suffer psychological harm.[18]

The culture's persistent double standards concerning sexual victimization help explain the harsher sentences that male sex offenders normally receive.[19] However, in some cases, female offenders are beginning to receive harsh treatment if it appears that they exploited an underage male. One of the most well-known cases was a Seattle grade school teacher, Mary Kay Letourneau, who at age 35 had sex with her 13-year-old student, for which she received a 7-1/2 year prison sentence. All but six months of the sentence was suspended conditional upon her entering a sex-offender treatment program and refraining from contact with the boy. Shortly thereafter, her sentence was reinstated after she was found in his company. She had one child with the boy prior to sentencing and conceived another during her brief release. The couple married once the boy became of age. Other cases include female teachers in Tennessee and Florida. Lisa Lynette Clark of Georgia was impregnated by her son's 15-year-old friend, whom she married a day before she was arrested. Another woman was sentenced to 30 years in 2005 for having sex with teenagers, to whom she provided drugs and alcohol.[20] Are these cases any different from the more traditional statutory rape of girls by men?

Female sexual offenders have varying profiles. Some are teachers who fall in love with young students and pursue them in the hope that they will return their affection. Others were victims of child sexual abuse or experienced other intergenerational abuse.[21] Should such different background circumstances matter to criminal liability?

Putting Theory Into Practice

5-1. A law in State X defines statutory rape as sexual intercourse with a child under the age of 16. Colleen, age 20, gives birth to a baby fathered by 16-year-old Shane, who at the time of conception was 15. Colleen was, for several years, Shane's babysitter, and Shane never complained to his parents about the sexual liaison with Colleen. Colleen is charged with statutory rape, but pleads to the lesser crime of contributing to a child's misconduct. After the child's birth, Colleen applies for public assistance, whereupon the Department of Social Services petitions the court to order Shane to contribute to the child's financial support. The Parentage Act of State X, which mandates that parents provide support for their children, makes no exception for parents who are minors. Does this make sense? Should Shane be liable for child support?

5-2. Under the Federal Sentencing Guidelines, discussed in Chapter 4, a sentence for a crime may be enhanced if the defendant has a prior conviction for a violent crime, which is defined as a felony that either involves force, attempted force, or threat of force, or involves conduct that presents a serious potential risk of physical injury to the victim. Should statutory rape be considered a violent crime, or its own type of enhancing crime, for purposes of the Guidelines?[22]

5-3. Victims of statutory rape can sue third parties for negligence in permitting the act to occur. A girl who was a guest at a horse farm sued the farm's owner for failure to prevent her sexual assault by the owner's boyfriend. The owner claims that the sex was consensual and that the victim had hid her relationship with the boyfriend from her parents for several years.

Should the consent defense be allowed? The lawyer for the owner claims that the girl's complicity, not the owner's negligence, was responsible for the rape and the jury should hear the evidence about the girl's conduct. The lawyer for the girl claims that allowing consent defenses will discourage minors from coming forward for fear that they will be blamed for their own assaults. Which way would you rule?[23]

2. Defining and Explaining Rape: Distinguishing Consent and Nonconsent

According to governmental and crime center research, about 16 to 18 percent of American women and 1 to 3 percent of American men have experienced an attempted or completed rape. Rates for African-American women are slightly higher (22 percent) and rates for Hispanic women are slightly lower (14 percent) than rates for white women (18 percent). About 12 percent of victims are 10 years old or younger; 30 percent are 11 to 17 years old; and 37 percent are 18 to 24 years old.[24] Estimates of the frequency of prison rape vary. According to a 2012 Department of Justice report, about 10 percent of adult former state prisoners reported being sexually victimized during their most recent period of confinement. About 5 percent reported an incident that involved facility staff.[25]

Explanations for rape fall along three main dimensions: individual, sociobiological, and cultural. At the individual level:

> Profiles of rapists indicate that many are primarily attracted to power; they want the feeling of domination, adventure, and self-esteem that comes from coercive sex. Other men emphasize anger; rape is a means to punish or avenge some wrong by a particular woman, women in general, or another adversary. Most rapists blame their victims, and some stress situational influences such as peer pressure or drug and alcohol abuse. Exposure to family violence during childhood increases the likelihood that men will engage in sexually violent activities as adults.[26]

The sociobiological explanation is that, at an evolutionary level, men having intercourse with a large number of fertile females has "favorable reproductive consequences." For men who have difficulty attracting willing partners, coercive sex is "adaptive" and likely to be favored by natural selection.[27] Critics of this account note that they do not explain the substantial variation in rape rates across time and culture, or the frequency of sexual assaults involving non-vaginal intercourse or female victims too young or too old to bear children.

Cultural explanations stress the eroticization of male aggression in popular films, television, fiction, and video games, as well as gender stereotypes in media coverage of sexual assault.[28] Such frameworks also underscore the role of male-dominated institutions such as the military, fraternities, and athletic teams in fostering attitudes that legitimate male sexual aggression.

How to tell whether women have consented to sex is a highly charged issue. Catharine MacKinnon, in the reading excerpted below, criticizes the traditional distinction between sex and rape. Is it possible to draw the line between coercive and consensual sex in a culture in which violence and domination are eroticized? Consent issues often appear in the form of questions about what evidence should be admissible to prove (or disprove) rape. The *Alberts* decision, below, exemplifies the legal debate over when arguably provocative behavior by the alleged victim should be considered consent, and admissible to exonerate a defendant charged with rape.

An issue related to the complainant's consent is the accused's culpability if he was confused about what the complainant intended. Ordinarily, criminal law holds people responsible only for what they knowingly or intentionally do, although they may be liable for a lesser offense when they act negligently; for example, someone who negligently causes a fatal automobile accident usually will be charged with manslaughter or homicide, not murder. The law of rape, however, generally does not recognize the lesser offense of negligent rape.

Beyond the questions raised by defining rape are issues with respect to proving it. For example, the law generally prohibits the introduction of evidence of the victim's past sexual behavior. Why do you suppose that is? The issue in the *Alberts* case was whether an episode of skinny-dipping constituted "past sexual behavior"; if it was, the state's rape shield law would normally exclude the evidence from trial unless it fell under an exception, such as to attack the credibility of the complainant. The appellate court found that the episode did qualify as past sexual behavior, but remanded the case for a determination of whether the victim made a *false* statement about the incident, which would make the evidence relevant to her credibility.

A **rape shield statute** is an evidentiary rule prohibiting the introduction of prior sexual behavior by the complainant under specified circumstances. Under Federal Rule of Evidence 412, such evidence is inadmissible in any civil or criminal proceeding except to prove that (1) a person other than the accused was the source of semen, injury, or other physical evidence, or (2) to show behavior with the accused that is offered to prove consent to the sexual activity. The evidence is also admissible if excluding it would violate the defendant's constitutional rights.

Reading Questions

1. What makes the line between consent and coercion so difficult to draw? Have you ever had an experience where you had difficulty seeing the difference?
2. Does previous skinny-dipping fit your conception of "past sexual behavior"? Should a jury hear about it? Does it seem reasonable that if it was sexual behavior the jury doesn't hear about it, but that if it wasn't, evidence of it is admissible? Should otherwise inadmissible evidence of past sexual behavior be considered if it establishes that the complainant lied about it?
3. Compare the treatment of complainants' provocative sexualized banter under rape shield laws and under sexual harassment doctrine. Does it make sense to view the conduct as relevant in determining whether harassment occurred but not whether rape occurred? Should the standards be more similar?
4. Should all of the "rape myths" explored in this section be presumed to be untrue?
5. What steps is it fair to require that a man take before he engages in sexual activity with someone to make sure that there is true consent?

Catharine A. MacKinnon, Toward a Feminist Theory of the State

172-174 (1989)

Under law, rape is a sex crime that is not regarded as a crime when it looks like sex. . . .

Rape cases finding insufficient evidence of force reveal that acceptable sex, in the legal perspective, can entail a lot of force. This is both a result of the way specific facts are perceived and interpreted within the legal system and the way the injury is defined by law. The level of acceptable force is adjudicated starting just above the level set by what is seen as normal male sexual behavior, including the normal level of force, rather than at the victim's, or women's, point of violation. In this context, to seek to define rape as violent not sexual is as understandable as it is futile. . . .

The point of defining rape as "violence not sex" has been to claim an ungendered and nonsexual ground for affirming sex (heterosexuality) while rejecting violence (rape). The problem remains what it has always been: telling the difference. . . . To know what is wrong with rape, [we must] know what is right about sex. . . . Perhaps the wrong of rape has proved so difficult to define because the unquestionable starting point has been that rape is defined as distinct from intercourse, while for women it is difficult to distinguish the two under conditions of male dominance. . . .

Susan Estrich, Rape

95 Yale L.J. 1087, 1102-1105 (1986)

My view is that . . . a "negligent rapist" should be punished, albeit—as in murder—less severely than the man who acts with purpose or knowledge, or even knowledge of the risk. First, he is sufficiently blameworthy for it to be just to punish him. Second, the injury he inflicts is sufficiently grave to deserve the law's prohibition.

The traditional argument against negligence liability is that punishment should be limited to cases of choice, because to punish a man for his stupidity is unjust and, in deterrence terms, ineffective. Under this view, a man should only be held responsible for what he does knowingly or purposely or at least while aware of the risks involved. . . .

If inaccuracy or indifference to consent is [the best that a man can do] because he lacks the capacity to act reasonably, then it might well be unjust and ineffective to punish him for it. But such men will be rare . . . at least as long as voluntary drunkenness is not equated with inherent lack of capacity. More common is the case of the man who could have done better but didn't; could have paid attention, but didn't; heard her say no, or saw her tears, but decided to ignore them. Neither justice nor deterrence argues against punishing this man.

Certainly, if the "reasonable" attitude to which a male defendant is held is defined according to a "no means yes" philosophy that celebrates male aggressiveness and female passivity, there is little potential for unfairness in holding men who fall below *that* standard criminally liable. Under such a low standard of reasonableness, only a very drunk man could honestly be mistaken as to a woman's consent, and a man who voluntarily sheds his capacity to act and perceive reasonably should not be heard to complain here—any more than with respect to other crimes—that he is being punished in the absence of choice.

But even if reasonableness is defined—as I argue it should be—according to a rule that "no means no," it is not unfair to hold those men who violate the rule criminally responsible, provided that there is fair warning of the rule. I understand that some men in our society have honestly believed in a different reality of sexual relations, and that many may honestly view such situations differently than women. But, it is precisely because men and women may perceive these situations differently, and because the injury to women stemming from the different male perception may be grave, that it is necessary and appropriate for the law to impose a duty upon men to act with reason, and to punish them when they violate that duty.

In holding a man to such a standard of reasonableness, the law signifies that it considers a woman's consent to sex to be significant enough to merit a man's reasoned attention. In effect, the law imposes a duty on men to open their eyes and use their heads before engaging in sex—not to read a woman's mind, but to give her credit for knowing her own mind when she speaks it. The man who has the inherent capacity to act reasonably, but fails to do so, has made the blameworthy choice to violate this duty. While the injury caused by purposeful conduct may be greater than that caused by negligent acts, being negligently sexually penetrated without one's consent remains a grave harm, and being treated like an object whose words or actions are not even worthy of consideration adds insult to injury. This dehumanization exacerbates the denial of dignity and autonomy which is so much a part of the injury of rape, and it is equally present in both the purposeful and negligent rape.

By holding out the prospect of punishment for negligence, the law provides an additional motive for men to "take care before acting, to use their faculties and draw on their experience in gauging the potentialities of contemplated conduct." We may not yet have reached the point where men are required to ask verbally. But if silence does not negate consent, at least the word "no" should, and those who ignore such an explicit sign of non-consent should be subject to criminal liability.

The deeper problem is that women are socialized to passive receptivity; may have or perceive no alternative to acquiescence; may prefer it to the escalated risk of injury and the humiliation of a lost fight; submit to survive. Also, force and desire are not mutually exclusive under male supremacy. So long as dominance is eroticized, they never will be. Some women eroticize dominance and submission; it beats feeling forced. Sexual intercourse may be deeply unwanted, the woman would never have initiated it, yet no force may be present. So much force may have been used that the woman never risked saying no. Force may be used, yet the woman may prefer the sex — to avoid more force or because she, too, eroticizes dominance. Women and men know this. Considering rape as violence not sex evades, at the moment it most seems to confront, the issue of who controls women's sexuality and the dominance/submission dynamic that has defined it. When sex is violent, women may have lost control over what is done to them, but absence of force does not ensure the presence of that control. Nor, under conditions of male dominance, does the presence of force make an interaction nonsexual. If sex is normally something men do to women, the issue is less whether there was force than whether consent is a meaningful concept.

State v. Alberts

722 N.W.2d 402 (Iowa 2006)

STREIT, Justice.

Is skinny-dipping a form of sexual behavior? Michael John Alberts allegedly sexually assaulted R.M., his nephew's twenty-two-year-old girlfriend. Alberts was convicted of third-degree sexual abuse following a jury trial in Johnson County, Iowa. . . . Because we find the district court erred by failing to determine whether R.M. made a prior false allegation of sexual misconduct relating to a skinny-dipping incident, we reverse the district court judgment on this error and remand for further proceedings.

On the night of October 19, 2003, R.M. attended a bachelorette party at a Cedar Rapids bar named Borrowed Bucks. Alberts was also at the bar, and the two struck up a conversation. Alberts and R.M. knew each other through R.M.'s boyfriend, Jesse Goeller. Alberts is Jesse's forty-two-year-old uncle. R.M. attended a half dozen or so family gatherings with Jesse where Alberts was present.

Additionally, a few weeks prior to the bachelorette party, Jesse, R.M., and a friend of R.M. ran into Alberts at Borrowed Bucks. There, the four of them danced as a group and at times Alberts and R.M. danced together in a provocative manner. When the bar closed, R.M. and Jesse sat with Alberts in the cab of Alberts' semi-truck. R.M.'s friend waited in the car. R.M. and Alberts smoked marijuana. Before leaving, R.M. unhooked her bra under her shirt and hung it on Alberts' rearview mirror. R.M. left the cab and Jesse followed a couple minutes later after Alberts handed Jesse R.M.'s bra.

During the bachelorette party, R.M. drank several beers and a shot of tequila. At closing time, R.M. went with Alberts to his family's lake house instead of remaining with the bachelorette group. When they arrived at the lake house, R.M. ate some food, headed for the bathroom, and vomited. She then told Alberts she felt "like crap" and needed to "sleep this off." Alberts followed R.M. into one of the bedrooms and sat next to her on the bed. With Alberts still in the room, R.M. took off her skirt and climbed into bed.

Sometime later, R.M. woke to find Alberts sucking her breasts. According to R.M., she did not respond to his actions. Alberts then performed oral sex on her and had intercourse with her. R.M. claims she pretended to be asleep during the entire episode. Alberts thereafter left to sleep in another bedroom.

The next morning, Alberts drove R.M. to her home. R.M. showered as soon as she got there. Jesse, the boyfriend, who had been visiting friends in Ames, returned home early in the afternoon. After speaking with R.M. about the previous night's events, Jesse took R.M. to the hospital.

At the hospital, R.M. told the nurse she needed to report a rape. A sexual assault examination ensued. The nurse found semen inside her vagina, but did not observe any evidence of trauma or injury. Police officers spoke with R.M. at the hospital and told her she had the option to press charges, which she did three days later. . . .

Because Alberts had elicited statements from witnesses during depositions regarding R.M.'s flirtatious nature, her past sexual comments, and prior allegation of being trapped by a man during a skinny-dipping incident, the State filed a motion in limine asking the court to determine whether such evidence was admissible. The State contended such testimony was either inadmissible under the Iowa rape-shield law or irrelevant to the case at hand.

In the unreported pretrial hearing, the State pointed to several incidents involving R.M. it considered inadmissible and irrelevant. One specific instance was a Fourth of July party where Jesse's brother Josh discovered R.M. skinny-dipping with Chris Slach. In his deposition, Josh described how he saw R.M. with her arms around Slach in the Cedar River. Josh said he "busted them" because R.M. was supposed to be dating his brother. According to Josh, R.M. came out of the water crying. She told Josh "[t]hank God you saw me. I didn't know what to do out there. . . . I couldn't get away from him. I didn't know what to do." R.M. later explained that nothing sexual had happened between the two. Slach was also prepared to testify it was R.M.'s idea to go skinny-dipping and there was no sexual contact between the two.

Alberts argued the rape-shield law was not applicable to this situation because there was no sexual contact and therefore no "past sexual behavior." Alternatively, he argued that if this was sexual activity or sexual behavior, then it was admissible under the false-claim exception to the rape-shield law.

A **motion *in limine*** is a request by a party to the court, usually before the start of a trial, to exclude evidence the other side intends to present. It is heard by the judge, without the jury, in order to shield the jury from evidence that the judge may rule would be harmful, prejudicial, or otherwise inadmissible.

The district court sustained most of the State's motion *in limine* and specifically excluded any evidence pertaining to the skinny-dipping incident. The court also excluded any testimony which described R.M.'s character as flirtatious or promiscuous. However, the court allowed the jury to hear evidence that R.M. had engaged in "dirty dancing" with Alberts a few weeks before the alleged sexual abuse, smoked marijuana with him in the cab of his semi-truck, and removed her bra and hung it on his rear-view mirror. . . .

Alberts claimed the district court erred when it ruled he could not present evidence about the skinny-dipping incident or question R.M. about the incident during cross-examination. . . .

Rule 5.412 prohibits introduction of reputation or opinion evidence of a complainant's "past sexual behavior" and substantially limits admissibility of evidence of specific instances of a complainant's past sexual behavior. Rule 5.412(d) defines "past sexual behavior" as "sexual behavior other than the sexual behavior with respect to which sexual abuse is alleged." We recently clarified this definition:

> "past sexual behavior" means a volitional or non-volitional physical act that the victim has performed for the purpose of the sexual stimulation or gratification of either the victim or another person or an act that is sexual intercourse, deviate sexual intercourse or sexual contact, or an attempt to engage in such an act, between the victim and another person. . . .

In his brief to the district court, Alberts argued the skinny-dipping incident was not "past sexual behavior" and "not a claim of prior sexual activity because no actual sexual contact occurred." In support of this argument, Alberts offered the deposition testimony of both skinny-dippers.

When questioned at her deposition about the incident, R.M. denied any sexual activity occurred:

> We were skinny dipping in the river together, and he got close to me and asked me if he could kiss me, and I said, "No, I have a boyfriend."

Slach corroborated R.M.'s testimony that she declined his request for a kiss. Both parties expressly denied any sexual activity occurred. . . .

At the outset, we concede the difficulty in determining what sexual behavior is for purposes of our rape-shield law. [In a prior case, the court held that nude posing was not sexual conduct *per se* but in some circumstances could be determined to be so.]

Just like nudity alone is not sexual, skinny-dipping in and of itself is not sexual behavior. But in this case, the skinny-dipping incident should be deemed sexual behavior based on the circumstances described. Slach testified he was at a Fourth of July party drawing a beer from the keg when R.M. approached him and asked him if he would like to go swimming. It was approximately midnight and the two of them had never previously spoken. At his deposition, Slach said:

> I didn't see any reason to decline her. I wasn't seeing anybody at the time, and I just assumed from the way that she come up to me that she was somewhat interested, and it didn't appear to be at the time that she was attached to anybody either.

According to Slach, R.M. took her clothes off first and encouraged him to do the same. He recalls both of them being completely naked. While they were in the river, R.M. put her arms around Slach's shoulders, which prompted him to ask for permission to kiss her. Slach stated "it kind of seemed to me like she was coming on to me." After R.M. declined the kiss, the two of them continued to have their arms around each other for another five minutes until Josh interrupted them, causing them to get out of the water.

Based on these facts, the skinny-dipping was likely a precursor to sexual activity. This is evidenced by Slach asking for a kiss. To say it was not sexual behavior would be to say a circumstance where the complaining witness was thwarted in her attempt to meet someone for an amorous rendezvous was not sexual behavior. Such a result would be contrary to the purpose of the rape-shield law, which is to protect the victim's privacy, encourage the reporting and prosecution of sex offenses, and prevent the parties from delving into distractive, irrelevant matters. . . . Thus, this particular episode of skinny-dipping is covered by the rape-shield law unless R.M. made a related false allegation of sexual misconduct. . . .

[T]he court failed to take the additional step of determining whether R.M. made a false claim of sexual misconduct relating to the incident, which would make the rape-shield law not applicable. . . .

In her deposition, R.M. stated Slach never "forced himself" on her while they were skinny-dipping. However, at the time of the incident, R.M. allegedly came out of the water crying. According to Josh, the person who discovered R.M. and Slach skinny-dipping, R.M. said: "Thank God you saw me. I didn't know what to do out there. . . . I couldn't get away from him. I didn't know what to do." R.M.'s statements to Josh, if she did say them, are relevant for two reasons. First, they reflect on her credibility as a witness. Second, the alleged statements may reveal a motive to lie. If a fact finder were to conclude she made untruthful statements to preserve her boyfriend's perception of her virtue when she was discovered skinny-dipping with another man, the fact finder might reasonably conclude she's also untruthful with respect to her allegations that Alberts raped her for the same reason.

Even if the evidence was relevant, it may still "be excluded if its probative value is substantially outweighed by danger of unfair prejudice, confusion of the issues, or misleading the jury, or by considerations of undue delay, waste of time, or needless presentation of cumulative evidence." . . .

Under Rule 5.403, the primary focus is not upon the witness, but the interests of the defendant and the right of the defendant to present a defense. . . . Based on the record before us, we do not find any of the aforementioned dangers potentially outweighed the probative value of this evidence. This evidence would not have been confusing to the jury, nor would it have been cumulative or a waste of time. Moreover, the evidence would not have been misleading to the jury because R.M. would have had ample opportunity to deny or explain her allegedly untruthful statements. Finally, while it may have been embarrassing for R.M. to testify about going skinny-dipping, this is not the kind of unfair prejudice that will outweigh the probative value of clearly relevant evidence. This is especially true when the countervailing right of a defendant to present a defense to a criminal charge is at stake. . . .

We find the trial court abused its discretion by excluding evidence of the skinny-dipping incident without first giving Alberts the opportunity to prove . . . that R.M. made a prior false claim of sexual misconduct involving the man with whom she went skinny-dipping. For the sake of judicial economy, we remand for a hearing to determine whether R.M. made these statements and if so, whether they are false. If the trial court finds Alberts meets the threshold showing set forth in this opinion, then a new trial shall be granted. If Alberts fails to make such a showing, then his conviction stands. This matter is remanded to the trial court for proceedings consistent with this opinion.

Notes

1. Rape Law Reform.   Rape law reform in this country has come in two waves: (1) the Model Penal Code (MPC) revision of the 1950s, intended to "modernize" the criminal law, and (2) laws responding to the critique of rape laws (including the MPC) by women's advocates, which began in the 1970s. The MPC, which stimulated statutory reform in many states, abolished a common provision requiring the victim to offer the "utmost" or "reasonable" resistance to her attacker. This reform refocused the crime from the consent of the woman to the conduct of the defendant. To increase the likelihood of convictions and to reduce the scope for idiosyncratic or biased judgments, the MPC also divided rape into three categories. First-degree felony rape was reserved for life-threatening conduct where the parties were strangers or where the defendant inflicted serious bodily harm. Life-threatening rape between acquaintances was a second-degree felony. Less serious abuses were grouped under a new third-degree felony of "gross sexual imposition." The choice continues to raise subtle questions about naming the crime. In what sense does it matter what term is used?

The **Model Penal Code** is a series of model criminal statutory provisions written by the American Law Institute over the course of more than a decade and completed in 1962. It was intended to function as a compilation of American law and serve as a guide for national reform. Most notable was its categorization of the mens rea or mental state of a criminal act into four realms (purpose, knowledge, recklessness, and negligence), its equal treatment of inchoate and completed crimes, its focus on utilitarian justice, and its then-revolutionary approach to rape. States have since adopted the code to varying degrees.

The next wave of law reform brought new legislation, such as rape shield statutes, seeking to protect victims, encourage reporting, and exclude prejudicial evidence. By the close of the 1990s, all states had such provisions. In addition, in 1994, Congress enacted Federal Rules of Evidence 413 and 415, which make evidence of the defendant's prior instances of sexual violence admissible in federal cases, even if relevant only to the *defendant*'s disposition or propensity to engage in such conduct. The rules have been controversial. Advocates see them as necessary to convict repeat offenders, particularly in child molestation cases. Critics object because these rules carve out an exception to the usual doctrine that prior similar acts are inadmissible to show propensity, and because defendants have been subject to intrusive pretrial discovery in cases where evidence of the claimed assault is dubious.

Other reforms spurred by women's rights advocates included reformulation of statutory provisions with gender-neutral language, elimination or relaxation of the marital rape exemption, alterations in the substantive requirements of force and nonconsent, and the expansion of federal crime statistics reporting requirements to include sex without consent even if force is not used.[29]

2. Marital Rape.   Early common law assumed that a married woman gave her irrevocable consent to intercourse with her husband. This assumption followed from the law's treatment of married women as their husbands' property. When this rationale became outdated, other justifications emerged for the marital exemption from rape law. According to the Model Penal Code, courts should not intrude on the "privacy" of the family relationship; forced sex by a husband is not as harmful as other sexual assaults; and spousal rape would be too easy to charge, too hard to disprove, and too readily available for blackmail. In many countries in Africa and the Middle East, attitudes toward marital rape still mirror those that sustained traditional exemption in Anglo-American law.[30]

About half the states and the District of Columbia have abolished marital immunity for sexual offenses, either by judicial decision or by statute. In the remaining states, forcible rape is unlawful under at least some circumstances; but many make marriage a defense for lesser degrees of sexual assault, such as sex with someone who is incapacitated or unconscious.[31] Fifteen states grant immunity unless requirements such as prompt complaint, extreme force, and separation are met. Often spouses lack protection if they have not met strict statutory criteria for being "separated."[32] Some legislative reforms have actually broadened, rather than narrowed, the marital rape exemption. A few states, such as Connecticut, recognize a qualified exemption for parties living together but not legally married to one another.[33]

Is there a convincing justification for treating marital rape with greater leniency than other sexual assault? The traditional arguments for the exemption is that legal intervention undermines marital intimacy, that marital sex fosters reconciliation, and that the rape exemption protects defendants from "vindictive wives" who might use fabricated claims of assault to gain leverage in divorce cases.[34] No research, however, finds that wives are prone to make false charges.[35] What the evidence does show is that the greatest adverse psychological effects on women who have been raped are those resulting from sexual assaults by a husband or a relative. In one study, 52 percent of women raped by a husband and 52 percent of women raped by a relative reported long-term effects on their lives. For women raped by a stranger, the figure was 39 percent; for women raped by an acquaintance, 25 percent; and for women raped by a friend, date, or lover, 22 percent.[36] Based on such evidence, a few courts have specifically rejected the rationale that marital rape is less traumatic than stranger rape. Does it follow that the criminal law should treat marital rape the same as other forms of sexual assault?

   3. Consent.   Nowhere in the law are issues of consent, or lack of consent, as divisive as in the context of rape. Perspectives range from the traditional assumption that consent can be inferred from "evidence of public displays of general interest in sexual activity"[37] to Catharine MacKinnon's claim that consent is merely a label that the law places on the kind of sex acceptable under conditions of gender inequality. Note that the traditional view presupposes the greatest amount of female self-control, MacKinnon's the least. Which understanding is likely to lead to rules that promote women's sexual autonomy?

   Much of the contemporary debate on rape law has centered on how or whether to redefine consent and how much importance to attach to it. Only 16 states criminalize nonconsensual sex without the additional element of force. Only six of those states define it as rape; in the remainder, nonconsent without force is a misdemeanor.[38] In none of those jurisdictions are there any reported cases of prosecutions involving nonphysical coercion in academic or workplace settings.[39] Is this a problem?

How would you define "consent"? Susan Estrich proposes that the law should focus on the reasonableness of the defendant's intent and should assume that a reasonable man understands "no" to mean "no." Does it go too far? Far enough? What about a woman who is frightened into passivity? Should a "yes" be required?

Stephen Schulhofer and Joan McGregor argue that the focus of criminal prohibitions should be protecting women's autonomy — her physical integrity and her capacity to choose, unconstrained by impermissible pressures. To that end, Schulhofer proposes a crime of nonviolent sexual misconduct for invading women's bodily integrity in the face of ambivalence, objection, or silence. "No" would mean "no," whether or not a defendant used physical force. Such a statute would encompass economic pressure or other coercive behavior to obtain sex.[40] McGregor believes that the law should require affirmative consent.[41] Would such statutes conform to popular understandings of sexual assault?[42] Should that — the public's understandings — be the test?

An influential academic proposes pushing the law in the opposite direction. Professor Jed Rubenfeld argues that lack of consent should not be sufficient to prove rape: force should also be shown. Rubenfeld's argument is that since the law does not consider it to be rape to deceive a woman into having sex through false promises or misrepresentations, then it is not really the woman's consent (or autonomy) that the law is trying to protect, but rather freedom from physical force or coercion.[43] How would you respond?

4. Rape Shield Laws and Defendant's Rights.   All states have enacted rape shield laws. The majority of these laws prohibit admission of evidence of prior sexual conduct subject to one or more legislated exceptions, such as where the evidence would show prior sexual conduct between the complainant and the accused; an alternative source of semen, pregnancy, or injury; bias or motive to fabricate; a pattern of prior sexual conduct like prostitution; a mistaken belief by the accused in the complainant's consent; and prior false accusations of sexual assault by the complainant. Some states allow judicial discretion, and others have a catchall provision allowing evidence where necessary to protect the defendant's constitutional rights. At least four states determine the admissibility of a woman's sexual history based on the purpose for which the evidence is offered. In California and Delaware, sexual history offered to prove the complainant's consent to sexual intercourse is prohibited, but sexual history offered to attack her credibility is admissible. Just the reverse is the standard in Nevada and Washington.[44]

Rape shield statutes have drawn criticism from all sides. Civil libertarians and criminal defense counsel often claim that the protections compromise defendants' rights to a fair trial. As stated by one defense counsel:

Now a public-policy decision designed to correct vestiges of Victorian-era morality has stacked the deck against every citizen accused of a sex crime. . . .

Our justice system depends on the belief that a randomly drawn jury, culled only for prejudice and partiality, can detect truth and falsity. But if a jury is given a skewed presentation of the facts, or if important facts are withheld from a jury, we cannot expect it to do justice.

Most rape cases that turn on whether a sex act was consensual . . . [will] ultimately come down to a "he said/she said" contest between the accused and the accuser. But how can a jury accurately judge the credibility of the two parties if the accused has been presented in the worst possible light while the accuser is enshrouded in a cloak of purity?[45]

By contrast, many women's advocates claim that the exemptions compromise complainants' rights to privacy and deter other victims from reporting the crime. The problem is particularly acute for prostitutes, who are frequently vulnerable to sexual assault.[46] Shield laws do not prevent police and prosecutors from considering sexual history, nor do they prevent nongovernmental actors and the media from publicizing such behavior.[47] One commentator, reviewing many cases, suggests that rape shield laws have not been effective in undermining the unofficial but pervasive "chastity requirement" imbedded in traditional rules of credibility and consent.[48] Is the *Alberts* case an example of such ineffectiveness? Or is the complainant's credibility always relevant?

A similar debate has surfaced over defendant's rights. One issue involves the admission of prior sexual misconduct. Prior bad acts are ordinarily not admissible in a criminal trial, because they are thought to be overly prejudicial.[49] The justifications for allowing evidence of prior sexual conduct in rape cases are that sexual offenders are more likely to re-offend than other criminals, false accusations of rape are rare, and sexual offenses are particularly hard to prove. However, as a Report by the Judicial Conference noted, "the overwhelming majority of judges, lawyers, law professors and legal organizations" have opposed the admission of prior sexual misconduct.[50] As experts have noted, recidivism rates are not disproportionately high for sex offenses except those involving specialized interests (e.g., pedophilia) and those reflecting other antisocial tendencies.[51] Although the frequency of false charges is difficult to measure, it is noteworthy that one-third of convicted defendants who have been exonerated by DNA evidence were individuals convicted of rape.[52] So too, some commentators claim that the effects of laws requiring registration of sex offenders and limitations on where they can live and work are excessive and ineffective forms of punishment.[53]

Another potential difficulty, illustrated especially in celebrity trials, is that the media is able, through leaks and paid investigators, to publish compromising information that would be inadmissible in trial. A case involving a Los Angeles Lakers basketball star, Kobe Bryant, illustrates some of the difficulties surrounding current shield provisions. A hotel clerk whom Bryant invited to his room claimed that he threw her over a chair, put his hands around her neck, and raped her. Bryant claimed that they had consensual sex, that the "strangling thing" was something that he did during consensual sex (as a girlfriend would confirm), and that the complainant's vaginal bruising could have occurred during consensual sex that she had with other partners around the time in question.[54] Media coverage of the case was extensive. The victim's name, address, and telephone number as well as details about her sex life quickly surfaced, as did a prom picture of her raising her dress to show a garter. She was the target of several death threats and frequent harassment.

In applying Colorado's shield law, the trial judge determined that the complainant's sexual activity around the time of the assault (within approximately 72 hours preceding the assault and her physical examination) could be admitted as evidence. On three occasions, court clerks mistakenly released transcripts of closed hearings to the press, and the defense attorney inadvertently referred to the complainant by name in open court, in violation of court order. In Colorado v. Bryant,[55] the media challenged an order preventing publication of the pretrial transcripts mistakenly released to the media. The transcripts included details about the victim's sexual conduct that might be ruled inadmissible under the state's rape shield laws. The media argued, and the dissent agreed, that the information had already become available through other sources so that the order was an unjustifiable prior restraint on publication. The majority, however, stressed not only the injury to the victim in the Bryant case, but also the message that would be sent to other sexual assault victims, who might be deterred from reporting the offense if they believed that the shield statute would not be enforced. How would you assess the competing concerns?[56] If the information was already available from other sources, does that lessen the media's interest in publication?

In response to the harassment, threats, and humiliating coverage, the victim indicated that she would not testify and the prosecutor subsequently dropped the charges. She then filed a civil suit. Bryant issued a carefully crafted apology, and the case settled.[57] In a *New York Times* op-ed, Dahlia Lithwick offered this assessment of the Bryant prosecution:

> Enacted with the best of intentions, rape shield statutes don't work, particularly in high-profile cases. . . . There is a class of cases that are simply beyond the ability of the legal system to resolve, both because some truths are ultimately unknowable, and because it isn't "justice" when everyone emerges from a trial so damaged that it hardly matters who won.[58]

Even so, is there some value to rape shield laws that merits their existence?

5. Rape and Scientific Evidence. Following a sexual assault, women victims often agree to an exam that yields a "rape kit"—a collection of hair, semen, and skin cell samples. The DNA extracted from these kits can be checked against databases of DNA from violent criminals and a match can lead to successful prosecutions. Because the average rapist commits between 8 and 16 sexual assaults before being caught, and serial offenders account for the vast majority of rapes, kit evidence can be a crucial law enforcement tool. However, between 180,000 and 400,000 kits remain unanalyzed due to lack of resources.[59] Some women's rights advocates argue that processing most of these kits should not be a high priority because the vast majority of cases involve acquaintances where the defense focuses on consent, so DNA would be irrelevant.[60] Other advocates point out that even acquaintances might be serial offenders, so the evidence would still be useful. How should women's rights groups respond?

6. The Rape Crisis Counselor Privilege.   A related issue is whether a rape complainant should have the right to shield disclosures made to rape crisis counselors. About half of the states and the District of Columbia have enacted privilege statutes that protect such information. The Federal Rules of Evidence do not provide such protection.

The justifications for the privilege are self-evident. Victims of sexual assault are likely to obtain higher quality counseling if confidentiality can be assured, and without that assurance, the injuries of a sexual assault may be compounded by public disclosure of intimate details from therapeutic sessions. Rape crisis centers are often the primary source of assistance for victims, and failure to protect confidential disclosures to counselors at these centers, whether or not they are licensed physicians, would compromise treatment and reporting, particularly consequential for individuals who cannot afford to pay for assistance from psychiatrists who can assert the privilege.[61]

The justifications for allowing defendants access to therapeutic records are equally apparent. In some rape cases, the boundaries of consent and coercion are blurred at best, and subtle, even unintended, encouragement by rape counselors to define an interaction as rape may affect how a complainant later recalls the event.[62] Other relevant details in therapeutic records may include the complainant's prior involvement with the accused and a history of mental health problems.

Given the enormous costs to the defendant of an unjust conviction, is some relinquishment of the complainant's privacy interests reasonable? How would you strike the balance?

7. Cultural Attitudes and "Rape Myths."   Although estimates of conviction rates for rape vary widely, almost all indicate that they are substantially lower than for other felonies. Some research suggests that fewer than 10 percent of sexual assaults will result in a conviction.[63] Of all the major felonies, rape is the least reported, least indicted, and least likely to end in conviction.[64] Major factors affecting likelihood of conviction include the degree of acquaintance between the victim and accused; the appearance and reputation of the victim; the availability of physical evidence; and the presence and degree of intoxication.[65] Low conviction rates are often attributed to "myths" about rape shared by judges, juries, and law enforcement personnel: (1) only certain women (i.e., those with "bad" reputations) are raped; (2) only certain men (i.e., psychopaths) rape; (3) women invite or deserve rape by their appearance and behavior; and (4) women fantasize or fabricate rape, motivated by desire, revenge, blackmail, jealousy, guilt, or embarrassment.[66]

Consider the following examples:

- Missouri Congressman Todd Akin, opposing an exception for rape in an anti-abortion statute, argues that pregnancy from rape is rare because "if it's legitimate rape, the female body has ways to try to shut the whole thing down."[67]
- A survey of public allegations of sexual assault against 168 prominent athletes found that one-third resulted in no charges and another one-fifth in charges that were dismissed.[68] Women who accuse stars like Kobe Bryant and Mike Tyson receive death threats and harassment for being "gold diggers" who needlessly destroy revered role models for conduct that they invite by going to athletes' hotel rooms alone.[69]
- A juror who voted to acquit William Kennedy Smith of the rape of a woman he picked up in a bar explained that "he's too charming and too good-looking to have to resort to violence for a night out."[70]
- Jurors voted to acquit three St. John's University fraternity brothers in a widely publicized rape of a woman they had gotten intoxicated. She failed to protest as she drifted in and out of consciousness, and one juror later justified the acquittal on the grounds that, "Hell hath no fury like a woman scorned."[71]
- Camille Paglia argues that a "girl who lets herself get dead drunk at a fraternity party is a fool. A girl who goes upstairs alone with a brother at a fraternity party is an idiot. Feminists call this 'blaming the victim.' I call it common sense." Paglia and other commentators argue that women must "take responsibility" for their choices and clearly communicate their sexual desires and nonconsent.[72]

A Toronto police officer told a group of college women that if they wanted to avoid sexual assault, they should avoid dressing like "sluts." In response, young women have marched in "slutwalks" in more than 70 cities around the world, dressed in bras, halter tops, and garter belts.[73] Two recent, highly publicized cases highlight the costs for complainants in celebrated cases. One involved the prosecution of WikiLeaks Founder Julian Assange. According to a confidential Swedish police report, one woman claimed that Assange prevented her from reaching for a condom while they were having sex. A second woman claimed that after having protected sex with Assange, she woke to find him having sex with her without a condom. When the two women discovered that they both had unprotected sex, they decided to insist that Assange get tested for sexually transmitted diseases. They went to a police station for advice, and gave statements that led prosecutors to charge Assange with third-degree rape. The women have been vilified on the Internet and face regular death threats. A former equal opportunities ombudsman who is representing them explained that it was common for men who force sex on women without a condom to be subject to prosecution in Sweden: "It's a violation of sexual integrity and it can be seen as rape."[74] Do you agree?

A second celebrated case involved claims by a Guinean hotel maid, Nafissatou Diallo, that she was raped by the director of the International Monetary Fund, Dominique Strauss-Kahn. According to the maid's account, she was in the room of the upscale Sofitel Hotel in New York City, which had been reported as ready for cleaning, when Strauss-Kahn emerged naked, forced her onto the bed, tore off her clothes, and forced her to have oral sex. She asked him to stop and told him she didn't want to lose her job, to which he allegedly responded, "You're not going to lose your job."[75] After he left the suite and Diallo resumed cleaning, she encountered her supervisor in the hall. When asked why she was upset, Diallo described the rape, and the hotel subsequently called 911. Forensic evidence at the scene confirmed the sexual encounter, and police moved to arrest Dominique Strauss-Kahn while he was on a plane heading for Europe. In order to continue holding Strauss-Kahn, the New York district attorney had to file an indictment within five days. He did so, but shortly thereafter, troubling inconsistencies and lies in the victim's account began to surface. She had claimed a fictional child on her tax return to get an extra deduction; she had understated her income in order to obtain cheap housing; and she had lied about being gang raped on her asylum application. She had also given inconsistent accounts of the Sofitel incident to police, prosecutors, and media. In a taped conversation that she had with a friend who had been convicted of a sting operation, she reportedly stated something to the effect that Strauss-Kahn "had a lot of money" and she "knew what she was doing."[76] Such compromising and inconsistent statements convinced the district attorney to drop the charges. In its motion to dismiss, prosecutors wrote, "If we do not believe her beyond a reasonable doubt, we cannot ask a jury to do so."[77] Was the dismissal appropriate?

Does this case have the potential to reinforce rape myths? Another example is the case of Jody Arias, who was accused of killing her ex-boyfriend. Arias, after several previous inconsistent stories including that she was not at the murder scene, settled on a claim of self-defense, admitting that she killed her boyfriend but claiming that she had been the victim of a long history of coerced sex and emotional abuse. An expert testified that she was the victim of sexual abuse, but that testimony was based primarily on interviews of Arias, who had proved to be unreliable. There was extensive evidence of Arias' initiation of sexual activity with her boyfriend, even after they had broken up. There was also extensive evidence that she had planned the crime in advance, and the viciousness of the killing undermined her claim that it was a reasonable and spontaneous response to a plausible threat. The jury convicted her of first-degree murder.[78] What myths does this case help to reinforce? If it happens, are they myths?

In the aftermath of the Strauss-Kahn case, women's rights advocates expressed concerns that victims would be more reluctant to report rapes. Since an estimated 60 percent of rapes are already not reported, women's worries that they would be "dragged through the mud" could add to the difficulties of holding rapists accountable.[79] Is there anything that prosecutors could have done to prevent such results?

8. Rape Trauma Syndrome. In the course of improving clinical treatment for rape victims, researchers have developed a profile known as the "rape trauma syndrome." The syndrome is characterized by two phases: Phase I, the "acute phase," is a period of disorganization in which the victim is either emotionally out of control—crying, sobbing, restless, or tense—or extraordinarily controlled—calm, composed, or subdued. Headaches, fatigue, and gastrointestinal or sleep disturbances are common during this period. Phase II, the "long-term reorganization process," is a period of nightmares, phobic reactions, sexual fears, and changes in routine.[80]

Some courts have approved use of expert testimony about rape trauma syndrome to help prove that a forcible assault, rather than consensual sex, occurred. However, disputes about the scientific basis for the theory have encouraged limitation of its use to rehabilitating the victim's credibility rather than proving the prosecution's case-in-chief. In both contexts, expert testimony regarding rape trauma syndrome may be effective in dispelling rape myths regarding victim's behavior after the rape. In one New York case, the court noted:

> [T]he reaction of a rape victim in the hours following her attack is not something within the common understanding of the average lay juror. Indeed, the defense would clearly want the jury to infer that because the victim was not upset following the attack, she must not have been raped. This inference runs contrary to the studies cited earlier, which suggest that half of all women who have been forcibly raped are controlled and subdued following the attack. . . .
> Thus, we conclude that evidence of this type is relevant to dispel misconceptions that jurors might possess regarding the ordinary responses of rape victims in the first hours after their attack.[81]

Some feminists have been concerned that rape trauma evidence focuses too much on the behavior of the victim rather than the accused, and that it might be misused to show that an alleged victim's behavior was atypical, and thus inconsistent with claims of rape. The Indiana Supreme Court, for example, held that it was an abuse of discretion to exclude expert testimony that the victim's conduct in returning to the bar where the rape allegedly had taken place was inconsistent with that of a person who had been forcibly raped.[82] Is it fair for women's rights advocates to support admission of rape trauma evidence only when it helps female complainants, not when it exculpates male defendants?

9. Racial Bias. At one time, rape of a non-white woman was not a crime.[83] By contrast, the rape of a white woman by a black man was long considered the most horrific sexual offense and provided the most common justification for lynching. At various times, the law required that blacks convicted of raping white women be castrated.[84]

Although most rapes, like most other crimes, are intraracial rather than interracial, rapes in which black men are the perpetrators and white women the victims continue to receive the greatest attention and the most serious sanctions. In one study of cases involving no weapons, prosecutors were over four times as likely to file charges if the victim was white.[85] In explaining their decisions, prosecutors often claim that jurors are less willing to convict in cases involving poor and minority victims.[86] How might these prejudices be addressed?

A controversial case involving racial dynamics involved a young African American exotic dancer who claimed that she was raped by several white members of the Duke University lacrosse team that had asked her to perform as a stripper. A medical exam showed evidence of forcible sex. There was evidence that the dancer had been subject to racial epithets. Several of the university's athletic teams had a history of alcohol-related offenses, and town-gown relations were complicated by class and racial tensions. The immediate media and community reaction was to assume that rape had occurred at the party, a reaction fueled by the white prosecutor who was facing a difficult election campaign. Bringing charges gained him the support from the black community necessary for victory. The university administration, in the wake of considerable adverse media coverage, fired the coach and prevented the team from competing for the remainder of the season.

It soon became apparent, however, that there were considerable inconsistencies in the victim's account and other critical weaknesses in the case. Although the victim picked out players she said were her attackers from pictures of those present at the party, the photo spread did not conform to accepted practice because it included no other pictures that might have produced a false identification. One of the players whom the woman identified had photographic and telephone records that placed him elsewhere. DNA tests on the woman's underwear showed traces of sperm and other material that failed to match any of the lacrosse players. The prosecutor maintained that despite these weaknesses, he had enough evidence to put the matter to a jury. He also failed to disclose exculpatory DNA evidence to the defense and falsely claimed to the court that he was unaware of any such evidence. That conduct subsequently resulted in his disbarment. The rape charges were dropped, and the players sued the city and the university alleging various breaches of duty in connection with the case. The case generated several books and months of media coverage, much of which emphasized the gullibility of the public toward accusations of rape.[87] Does the case prove that rape "myths" are sometimes true? That race can work both ways? That race and rape are still a volatile combination?

Putting Theory Into Practice

5-4. At Richard's trial for rape, witnesses testified that they saw him in the bar that evening with the complainant, Candice, who was sitting on his lap and "making out with Richard and a few others." Richard testified that he had felt Candice's breasts and bottom while at the bar and she had been rubbing his crotch. When she finally left the bar with him, witnesses said that she was "hanging all over" him like she had been hanging all over others earlier in the evening. Richard and Candice went from the bar to his trailer where they engaged in sex. Before they left Richard's trailer, the woman with whom Richard lived came home unexpectedly and saw them together. She became enraged and dragged Candice out of the trailer by the hair. Candice returned immediately to town, at which point she went to the police and charged Richard with rape.[88]

Should evidence of Candice's activity with other men on the evening of the events in question be admissible in Richard's rape trial? How about the fact that Candice was wearing skimpy clothing? That she was making out with Richard, including rubbing his crotch?

5-5. Some defendants have sought to prevent terms such as "rape," "attack," and "victim" from being used in court on the grounds that they express legal conclusions. Should they succeed?

In one such case, which resulted in a hung jury, the complainant refused to testify on retrial if she could not use the terms "attack" or "rape," on the grounds that it made her less credible and denied her right to testify to the "truth of what happened."[89] What is your view?

5-6. Might sexual intercourse under the following circumstances be viewed as nonconsensual? Should it constitute a crime? Are there additional facts that you would need to answer the question?

(a) A welfare-dependent mother of three young children who can't make ends meet has unwanted sex with her landlord in order to persuade him not to evict her.

(b) A struggling student has sex with a fellow student in order to persuade him to allow her to join his study group.

(c) A woman has sex with her boyfriend to keep him from leaving her.[90]

5-7. J.L. drives home from a party with two men she has just met. She testifies that they told her to give them oral sex and that she could leave the car "as soon as we're done." One of them says, "I don't want to rape you," and she responded that he could go ahead as long as he "stops when I tell him to." When he inserted his penis into her vagina, "it hurt," and she told him to stop. He did so only after he continued for "about five seconds," apparently long enough for him to reach orgasm.[91] Can he be prosecuted for rape? Should he be?

3. Acquaintance Rape

According to U.S. government statistics, about seven in ten rapes or sexual assaults against women are by a relative, a friend, or an acquaintance. The National Crime Victimization Survey found that the average annual rate of rape/sexual assault was 3.8 per 1000 college students (6 of 1000 female students and 1.4 of 1000 male students). About four-fifths of the rapes/sexual assaults involved acquaintances and almost 90 percent involved no weapon. Over one-quarter of some 4,000 surveyed college-age women had experienced rape, attempted rape, unwanted sexual contact, or stalking during the seven-month period preceding the survey. Almost half the women whose experiences met the legal definition of rape did not label them as rape. Only a small percentage reported them. Over 40 percent did not report the assault because they did not think it was serious and were not sure a crime had been committed. An additional 13 percent did not know how to make a report. Another 20 percent who were raped did not report it because they anticipated harsh or dismissive treatment by others in the justice system. Women had been taking drugs or alcohol in about 40 percent of the rape cases.[92]

The major issue concerning acquaintance rape is, again, how to distinguish coercive from consensual sex. The difficulties are compounded by the use of drugs and alcohol and a social context in which ambiguous and inconsistent understandings coexist.

Reading Questions

1. What rules should govern sex on dates? How do these rules compare with the rules on your campus? How is your campus policy enforced?
2. How much responsibility do women have for what happens to them? When, if ever, is "blaming the victim" appropriate?
3. When male and female perspectives differ, who should bear the risk of misunderstood signals? How can such misunderstandings be minimized?
4. When rape occurs under circumstances in which the accused is impaired by alcohol, should the consequences be less severe? What impact should the victim's voluntary intoxication have on a rape charge?

Karen M. Kramer, Note, Rule by Myth: The Social and Legal Dynamics Governing Alcohol-Related Acquaintance Rapes

47 Stan. L. Rev. 115, 141-143 (1994)

[The following account is taken from a supplemental report prepared by Detective Tim Frecceri in the case of State v. Thomas.]

Anne had arrived as a freshman at [Stanford] University a few days before the incident. While meeting other residents in her dorm, Anne stopped in

Thomas's room because she heard him playing music she liked. After visiting other people, she returned to his room later that evening and Thomas offered her a beer. Although Anne had only drunk alcohol once before, she accepted the beer. Other students who had been in Thomas's room when Anne arrived left for a different party. In the period of two hours, Thomas gave Anne half a beer and eight drinks of peppermint schnapps, all of which she drank. Anne asked Thomas, "if he was trying to get her drunk, but he told her he was not, and assured her that everything was O.K."

After consuming the alcohol, Anne "didn't feel too good, so she laid down . . . on his bed." When asked if she had any intention of teasing or seducing Thomas, she emphatically said, "no." To the contrary, "because of alcohol's effect on her, she had to lay down and didn't do a lot of talking." After a while, she and Thomas began to kiss; soon he had completely undressed her.

In her conversation with the detective, Anne explained that she didn't feel any pressure from the suspect, and that he didn't make any verbal threats to her as he undressed her. However, she said, she felt a certain coercion from [Thomas'] presence, coupled with the fact that her condition and judgment had been impaired by alcohol. She mentioned [Thomas'] physical size as part of this coercion, estimating that he is at least 6'04" or more, and has a muscular build. She also mentioned the manner in which [Thomas] spoke to her as part of this coercion, recalling that from when he began providing her with alcohol to when they were having sexual intercourse, he kept saying to her in a calm, soothing voice, statements like, "It's O.K. You can do what you want, no one has to know, I won't hurt you," among other things. . . . When she became aware that things were going beyond holding and kissing, she indicated to [Thomas] that he should stop. . . . [Anne] told him, "I can't do this, I have a boyfriend." [Thomas] responded by saying, "It's O.K., he doesn't have to know." [Anne] then told [Thomas] that she was a virgin and that she was only seventeen years old. [Thomas] responded by saying something similar to, "It's O.K. No one has to know, your family doesn't have to find out, this can be between you and me. If you want it, it's O.K. I won't hurt you." [Anne] recalled that she protested more than once; she is certain that she told [Thomas] several times that she couldn't do it because she was a virgin and because she was only seventeen years old. [However, Thomas] proceeded to have sexual intercourse with [her]. . . . [Anne] felt sharp vaginal pain and said, "Ow, stop." [Thomas] stopped for a minute or so and continued to lay next to [Anne], kissing and touching her. As she became aware that he was preparing to have sexual intercourse again, she again told the suspect, "I can't, I'm a virgin." . . . Nevertheless, [Thomas] positioned himself above [Anne], as she lay on her back, and again inserted his erect penis into her vagina. Once again, after a few moments of [Thomas] pushing his penis into [Anne's] vagina, she felt a sharp vagina[l] pain, so she said, "Ow, stop." [Anne] thinks she might have told [Thomas], "that hurts," as well. . . . [Thomas] then asked her, "If you don't want it in you, will you at least kiss it?" [Anne] complied. . . . She could not recall her frame of mind at this time, though she did feel somewhat obligated to do this to the suspect. She indicated that because she was intoxicated and had impaired judgment, because [Thomas] was unable to continue intercourse with her, due to her vagina[l] pain, and because of his physical presence, she was aware of implied coercion.

After Thomas had an orgasm, Anne dressed and left the room, leaving behind several personal items, including her wallet, glasses, and shoes.

Notes

1. Consent and Responsibility. Surveys of college students find that neither men nor women have complete confidence that a woman's "no" means "no" in a sexual situation. In the article excerpted above, Karen Kramer reports that in a survey by the Stanford University Rape Education Project, "[t]he 1,190 male and female students who responded overwhelmingly reported that when they say 'no' in a sexual situation, they mean it. Yet both men and women rated a 'no' from others as less meaningful than their own. Particularly striking was the belief among women that they mean no when they say 'no,' but that other women often do not." Indeed, some college women admit to engaging in "token resistance," defined as saying no when they mean yes. Does this fit your own experience? How should the law respond?

Commentator John Leo reflects widespread concerns when he objects to the "no means no" formula for consent on the ground that "no can mean 'maybe,' 'convince me,' 'back off a while,' or 'get lost.' The mating game does not proceed by words alone." In Leo's view, the "demonization" of men that is common in feminists' writing on date rape is profoundly unjust. If women cannot be clear about their preferences, men should not pay the price.[93]

Other commentators worry that broadening definitions of rape will reinforce traditional views of women as dependent and passive. According to Katie Roiphe:

> By protecting women against verbal coercion, [rape-crisis] feminists are promoting the view of women as weak-willed, alabaster bodies, whose virtue must be protected from the cunning encroachments of the outside world. The idea that women can't withstand verbal or emotional pressure infantilizes them. The suggestion lurking behind this definition of rape is that men are not just physically but intellectually and emotionally more powerful than women. . . .

> Allowing verbal coercion to constitute rape is a sign of tolerance toward the ultra feminine stance of passivity. The brand of "low self-esteem" [described by these feminists] should not be tolerated, it should be changed. Whether or not we feel pressured, regardless of our level of self-esteem, the responsibility for our actions is still our own.[94]

Another complaint is that overly aggressive definitions of rape give women unreasonable control to define, after the fact, what is or is not acceptable, consensual sex.[95] Stephen J. Schulhofer argues that intercourse, without a clear declaration of consent by the woman, should be punishable as "nonviolent sexual misconduct."[96] Would this new criminal prohibition solve or compound the problems that Roiphe discusses? Would such a law be enforceable? Would women feel under pressure to give explicit consent to sex that they did not desire? How should the law deal with misunderstandings, mistakes of fact, or the ambivalence noted in the surveys above?

In the case described by Kramer, the police detective investigating the case recommended that the district attorney prosecute Thomas on several charges, including statutory rape and a California statute defining an act as rape when "a person is prevented from resisting by any intoxicating or anesthetic substance, or any controlled substance, administered by or with the privity of the accused." The district attorney concluded that there was insufficient evidence to charge forcible rape and decided to charge Thomas only with statutory rape. If the woman had been over 18, should Thomas have been convicted under California law? Would Schulhofer's proposal make more sense? If so, what penalties would be appropriate?

Do the issues of consent and coercion in acquaintance rape mask other cultural dynamics? Some commentators argue that alcohol is "often used to create a gray area, a realm of plausible deniability where no one supposedly has to take responsibility for what he (or she) wanted to do."[97] Should alcohol abuse be a mitigating factor for the perpetrator (he wasn't fully in control of his actions) and/or an aggravating factor for the complainant (she shouldn't have put herself in that position)? In some cases, women students who have reported rapes have been charged with violating school drinking and drug policies.[98] Do defendants need to know that victims' intoxication make them incapable of consent? Or should it be enough for the prosecution just to prove such intoxication?[99]

Andrew Taslitz argues that a primary explanation for acquaintance rape is male self-deception:

> The common thread in all the relevant types of self-deception is that semiconscious or unconscious processes, motivated by serving an overriding self-interest, suppress from the conscious mind certain thoughts and feelings that might work against that interest, thereby permitting us to act contrary to our sincerely professed conscious principles.[100]

Drawing on social science research, Taslitz explores cognitive biases and semiconscious or unconscious self-deception ranging from willful ignorance, systematic ignoring, emotional detachment, and rationalization (semiconscious), which reinforce self-interest.

> Self-deception can be overcome by sustained efforts. . . . A "reasonableness" standard that is defined by jurors as a duty of reasonable inquiry to determine an intended sexual partner's desires is an effective way to combat male self-deception. . . . Because self-deception in this area is morally worse than the simple ignorance involved in ordinary criminal negligence, self-deceptive negligence . . . merits more severe punishment than is generally accorded to crimes of negligence.[101]

If Taslitz's diagnosis is correct, is criminal punishment the right prescription? Is "education" or peer pressure likely to be effective?[102]

The Canadian Criminal Code, Section 273(b), provides that the accused's belief that the complainant consented to sex is not a defense if that belief involved "recklessness or willful blindness," or the accused did not take "reasonable steps . . . to ascertain that the complainant was consenting." Is this a satisfactory solution? Canadian law also incorporates an affirmative consent standard. Consent is defined as "the voluntary agreement of the complainant to engage in the sexual activity in question." Consent is not present if "the accused induces the complainant to engage in the activity by abusing a position of trust, power or authority."[103]

According to some experts, a major barrier to progress in dealing with sexual assaults is the mismatch between prevalent media images of shocking, violent rapes, and the kinds of sexual coercion common in most rapes, which involve acquaintances.[104] How might this discontinuity be addressed? Would it make sense to try to educate jurors on the factors that motivate rapes that do not involve violence?

2. Male Rape.   The frequency with which men are victimized by rape is hard to assess, in part because until 2012, it was excluded from the federal definitions of rape for national reporting purposes. However, research by the Centers for Disease Control and Prevention found that 1.4 percent of men said they had been raped, over a quarter before they were age 10; 11.7 percent reported unwanted sexual contact.[105] The Department of Justice put the figure for rape at 3 percent of men, and other experts believe it is much higher.[106] Men subject to sexual abuse are at increased risk for physical and psychological problems, as well as substance abuse, and many feel that their masculinity has been called into question. Humiliation and self-blame, together with an absence of resources for men at rape crisis centers, discourage reporting of the offense. In military contexts, men also worry about retaliation. In 2013, the Pentagon estimated that over half of the 26,000 service members who experienced unwanted sexual contact in the preceding year were male.[107] A Department of Defense anonymous survey of men who had experienced but had not reported sexual crimes found that the predominant reasons were not wanting anyone to know (about a half), not believing that anything would be done (about a third), and fearing reprisals (close to a third).[108]

In 2011, a scandal emerged involving alleged sexual abuse of young boys by a coach affiliated with Penn State University's football program. Jerry Sandusky was indicted for multiple counts of sexual assault of boys that he had worked with through a charity. According to the grand jury's presentment, many of the alleged assaults, which included forced oral sex and anal rape, occurred in the locker room and showers of the football building. On at least one occasion, a low-ranking member of the coaching staff saw Sandusky anally raping a preadolescent boy. He reported the incident to the head coach, Joe Paterno, the "winningest" coach in college football history. Paterno passed along some version of the report to upper-level university officials, but the incident was never reported to the police and no action was taken against Sandusky, although he was told not to bring children to university facilities and his keys to the locker room were assertedly taken away. When the scandal became public in 2011, Paterno and the university president were fired for their failure to respond appropriately to what they had been told about Sandusky. But witnesses differed on how specific the information was that reached them. In an interview with the Washington Post, Paterno said the eyewitness was reluctant to "get specific" about the nature of the abuse and suggested that it might have been "inappropriate . . . fondling." And, Paterno stated, "To be frank with you, I don't know that it would have done any good, because I never heard of, of rape and a man."[109] Is this credible? What might be done to increase awareness of male rape?

3. Institutional Responsibilities.   What are the responsibilities of educational institutions to prevent and remedy sexual assault? In 1990, as part of an effort to increase accountability for student safety, Congress passed the Campus Security Act. It requires all colleges and universities receiving federal funds to report campus crime statistics, including all forcible or nonforcible sexual offenses. Despite this requirement, many sexual assaults are said to go unreported, partly because institutions are reluctant to disclose anything that would alarm prospective students and their families. Schools have an additional reason to avoid reporting when an incident of sexual assault involves a star athlete whose eligibility might be compromised or when the defendant threatens to sue for violation of his own due process rights. A case in point involved Christy Brzonkala, the student whose claim under the Violence Against Women Act resulted in Supreme Court review.[110] Virginia Tech failed to disclose her complaint of rape by two prominent football players and attempted to dissuade her from making any public disclosures.

Should Congress amend the Campus Security Act to include a private right of action for monetary damages if a school negligently fails to report abuse? If the rapes occur in connection with official athletic events, such as recruiting parties, could the institution be liable for sexual harassment under Title IX for creating a hostile environment?[111] Does your institution have effective rape education programs?

Putting Theory Into Practice

5-8. In 2002, Harvard University adopted a new policy requiring victims of sexual assault by peers to produce "sufficient independent corroboration," as a requirement for the investigation of the complaint. After substantial protest and a complaint by a student alleging that the policy constituted sex discrimination in violation of Title IX of the Civil Rights

Act, the University altered the policy to require the student victim to provide "as much information as possible," which the federal Office of Civil Rights found acceptable.[112] Is this a better policy?

5-9. A fraternity mails invitations to women stating "Hey ladies. Whether you're dressing up as a slutty nurse, a slutty doctor, a slutty school girl or just a total slut, we invite you. . . ." A female student goes to the party dressed as a slutty school girl. Everyone present expects to get drunk, and does. The student wakes up in the morning next to someone she does not ever remember meeting, under circumstances in which it is clear that she had sex. He claims that she consented and was not incapacitated at the time. If she files a charge of rape with the university, should she prevail?[113] Should the university itself have any liability? What strategies should the university pursue in addressing fraternity parties and other events on and off campus that often lead to alcohol-induced sex, often among near-strangers?[114]

5-10. In 2011, Stanford University considered changes to its procedures for violations of the Stanford conduct code, including provisions regarding sexual harassment and assault. The code required proof by clear and convincing evidence, which the federal Office of Civil Rights noted was inconsistent with the preponderance of evidence standard established under Title IX for violations of civil rights law.[115] Law students opposed to changing Stanford's standard have circulated comments, including the following:

- So we enhance the seriousness of a crime by making it easy to be convicted of it?
- Doesn't the question come down to what kind of citizens we want universities to create?
- Do we want to train them to assume guilt . . . [and cast] away a student on 50 percent plus one preponderance standard in a classic "he said, she said" case?
- Making it easy to get a false conviction does not improve the safety of accusers or others on campus. It makes us all vulnerable to being punished based on false accusations.[116]

How would you respond?

4. Rape, War, and the Military: Violence Against Women as a Human Rights Issue

Women have long been targets of mass rape during wartime.[117] Accounts of brutalization are common in the literature of ancient Greece and Rome. The Old Testament similarly chronicles the invasion of Canaan by Hebrew tribes, whose spoils of war included "sheep, cattle, asses, and thirty-two thousand girls who had had no intercourse with a man."

As Susan Brownmiller notes, the degradation of women has traditionally served to enhance the degradation of men:

> Rape by a conqueror is compelling evidence of the conquered's status of masculine impotence. . . . Rape by a conquering soldier destroys all remaining illusions of power and property for men of the defeated side. The body of a raped woman becomes a ceremonial battlefield . . . a message passed between men. . . .[118]

Early prohibitions on such abuse were largely unenforced. In the United States, initial prohibitions on rape in wartime appeared in the 1863 military code for the Union Army, which codified early humanitarian law protecting non-combatants. At the international level, Article 46 of the Hague Convention of 1907 outlawed rape during occupations, and the Geneva Convention of 1929, which governed treatment of prisoners of war, guaranteed female prisoners all the regard "due their sex."

These prohibitions did little to deter massive rapes during World War II. The most notorious cases involved Japanese soldiers' "comfort facilities" or brothels, staffed by "comfort women." Most of these women were disfavored ethnicities, such as Koreans and Filipinos, who were abducted or otherwise coerced into sexual slavery. An estimated 200,000 women were involved, often listed in official military documents as "military supplies"; almost three-quarters died from their treatment. Most of those who survived the camps were murdered or abandoned in dangerous areas at the close of the war.[119] Although the International Military Tribunal of the Far East gathered evidence on these abuses, its charter did not include sexual offenses and its proceedings (the Tokyo Trials) largely ignored them except when they were coupled with other offenses.[120] In Germany, rape was subsumed under crimes against humanity but was not included in a single indictment. The Allies who ran the Nuremberg Tribunal also ignored atrocities committed by their own soldiers, including an estimated rape of some 100,000 to 800,000 women in the Soviet capture of Berlin.

After World War II, international law began to include explicit prohibitions on rape during wartime. Article 27 of the 1949 Geneva Conventions, and subsequent Protocols of 1977, protect women against rape, enforced prostitution, or any form of indecent assault. More recently, the 1998 Rome Statute, which defines the jurisdiction of the International Criminal Court (ICC), defines "rape, sexual slavery, enforced prostitution, forced pregnancy, enforced sterilization, or any other form of sexual violence of comparable gravity" as crimes against humanity, war crimes, and potentially part of genocide. Although the United States is not currently a signatory to the Rome Statute, U.S. courts have provided civil relief to victims of wartime rape under the Alien Torts Claim Act. In 1995, for example, the Second Circuit Court of Appeals held that Radovan Karadzic, leader of the Bosnian-Serb territory, could be held accountable for rape as an act of genocide and other war crimes committed during the

Yugoslav conflict. A jury subsequently awarded the plaintiffs $745 million in compensatory and punitive damages.[121]

The international community first began to prosecute rape as a human rights violation largely in response to the atrocities committed in Rwanda and Yugoslavia in the early 1990s. Estimates of the number of rapes that occurred during the Yugoslavian conflict range from 20,000 to 50,000. What made these rapes distinctive was their role in ethnic cleansing. For example, Muslim and Croatian women were raped in order to make women tainted and therefore unmarriageable within their cultures as well as to produce Serbian babies. Many women were murdered after rape, or held in camps where they were raped repeatedly, often until they died.[122] In Rwanda, an estimated 250,000 to 535,000 Tutsi women were raped, and some 200,000 murdered. Most of those who survived are now HIV-positive.[123]

What also distinguishes these mass rapes is the response of the international community, prompted by women's rights advocates. Their efforts have been critical in chronicling the abuses, drawing attention to the cultural context that legitimated them, and establishing rape as a crime against humanity within the jurisdiction of the International Criminal Tribunal for the former Yugoslavia (ICTY) and the International Criminal Tribunal for Rwanda (ICTR). For the first time, an international tribunal recognized rape as a tool of genocide and a crime against humanity and indicted a former head of government, Slobodan Milosevic, for mass rapes constituting such a crime.[124] Women's groups have also pressured the Japanese government to contribute to the Asian Women's Fund, which has also raised $4 million in non-governmental funds to compensate former comfort women. Some of these women have refused to accept such reparations on the grounds that this approach allows Japan to continue to avoid issuing a formal apology.[125]

Other efforts on the international front have centered on preventing gender violence from occurring in future conflicts. One involves implementation of command responsibility, which is now codified in the Rome Statute, which establishes that military and non-military leaders can be held responsible for crimes under the ICC's jurisdiction. Another initiative involved the establishment of an unofficial Women's International War Crimes Tribunal, which heard testimony and passed judgment on high-ranking Japanese military and political leaders for their role in authorizing sexual slavery. Although the judgment carried no binding force, it has served an important role in clarifying international law and gaining compensation for comfort women.

Despite these efforts, rape remains common in armed conflict. Amnesty International estimates that more women have been raped in the Democratic Republic of the Congo (DRC) than in any other conflict. Recent estimates have put the number at about 2 million, with one woman raped per minute.[126] Armed bands of soldiers have developed a "signature" form of rape: local defense forces (known as Mai Mai) use branches or bayonets, and Rwandans gang rape their victims. An estimated 30 percent of women raped during the conflict are HIV-positive as a consequence.[127] In war-torn Liberia, 92 percent of surveyed women had experienced sexual violence.[128] Convictions for these crimes are rare. The International Rescue Committee rape centers in Sierra Leone have treated more than 9,000 survivors since 2003 and fewer than one-half of 1 percent of those rapes have resulted in criminal convictions.[129] In many other conflicts, rape victims also die from attempted abortions and lack of health care during childbirth. Those who survive are often subject to permanent injuries or infertility, social ostracism, and desertion by their husbands. In Libya, where female chastity is highly valued, Moammar Gadhafi's troops raped women on a massive scale, and some survivors were subject to honor killings for bringing shame on their families.[130] More resources are urgently needed for organizations such as HEAL Africa, which attempts to help victims with medical assistance and social services, including basic education and job skills.

United Nations peacekeeping forces have not only been often ineffective in preventing sexual abuse, they have also contributed to the problem. In the UN mission in the Congo, soldiers have coerced sex, often with minors, by offering money, food, or employment. Going rates are said to be as little as $1 or $2. Victims rarely report abuse due to concerns of ostracism by their families and communities.[131] According to a former commander of U.N. peacekeeping forces in the eastern Congo, "[i]t has probably become more dangerous to be a woman than a soldier in armed conflict."[132]

Rape is also a significant problem in the United States armed services. Surveys find that between 20 to 30 percent of women serving in the military have experienced sexual assault or rape, although 80 percent remain unreported, largely due to concerns about retaliation and ostracism.[133] At the 2008 Hearings before the House Committee on Oversight and Reform, Representative Jane Harman noted that "women serving in the U.S. military are more likely to be raped by a fellow solider than killed by enemy fire in Iraq."[134] In response to these statistics, the Department of Defense has mobilized a Task Force on Sexual Assault in the Military Services to survey military installations around the world and make recommendations for reform. Despite such efforts, the number of complaints has continued to increase at double digits annually.[135] In 2011, 17 victims, representing all branches of the armed forces, sued the secretary of defense for a "systematic failure to stop rape and sexual assault."[136] In 2013, estimates that 6 percent of active duty women reported experiencing sexual assault in the previous year led to calls for major overhaul in the military justice system.[137] Male-on-male sexual assault in the previous year is also problematic, especially given the concerns of shame and retaliation that prevents reports.[138]

What do you think accounts for the pervasiveness of rape in military and wartime settings? How might it be more effectively addressed?

5. Prostitution: Consent Under Conditions of Constraint

Prostitution has been a common practice across time and culture, but in the United States, it remained relatively invisible until the antebellum period.

With industrialization, urbanization, and western migration, markets for sex increased and provoked significant challenge. The first major initiatives, variously characterized as "moral reform" and "social purity" campaigns, began in the 1830s and resurfaced in the late nineteenth and early twentieth centuries. At the outset, the leaders were mainly male clergy and philanthropists, but women's organizations soon joined the crusade. Their goals were to reform prostitutes and to discourage men from employing or recruiting them. These efforts led to expanded criminal prohibitions and enforcement strategies.

The criminalization of prostitution has been justified on multiple grounds: promoting morality, protecting public health, avoiding public nuisance, and preventing sexual exploitation and abuse. Class, race, and ethnic prejudice also underpinned many of the early "antivice" campaigns. Moral reformers were particularly concerned by the vision of husbands of white women consorting with lower-class immigrants and women of color.

Today, the legal status of prostitution varies widely around the world. Most countries either prohibit or regulate the sale of sex, but the scope of permissible behavior, the severity of penalties, and the practices of enforcement agencies differ considerably.

In the United States, every state but Nevada prohibits engaging in sexual intercourse for money or offering to do so. Every state but Nevada also makes it a crime to knowingly encourage or compel a person to sell sex for money (pandering) or to receive "something of value" knowing that it was earned through an act of prostitution (pimping).[139] Most jurisdictions classify first-time offenses as misdemeanors, but typically punish repeat behavior as a felony. About half of all states have a "patron clause," which subjects customers to the same penalty as prostitutes. Other jurisdictions classify purchase of sex as a less serious offense.[140] New York is the only state that has higher penalties for the customer than the prostitute.[141]

Nevada permits prostitution in counties with populations under 200,000 persons, subject to highly restrictive licensing conditions. Prostitutes must be registered and fingerprinted by the police and must work in brothels where they typically have no control over their hours or customers.[142] County police have broad discretion to regulate the conditions under which commercial sex is permissible. For example, prostitutes generally may not have their children live in the same community in which they work, drive a car in city limits, or appear on the streets after 5 p.m. In the areas surrounding brothels, this system has effectively reduced street solicitation and incidental crime and has largely eliminated the risks of sexually transmitted diseases. However, it has failed to curtail illegal prostitution elsewhere in the state. About a thousand women work in 33 licensed brothels and account for only a small percentage of prostitutes estimated to be working in Nevada.[143]

Most anti-prostitution statutes in this country are sex-neutral in form but sex-biased in practice. Law enforcement officials generally prosecute only prostitutes, not customers or pimps, who are overwhelmingly male. Current policies are expensive and largely ineffective deterrents. Thousands are spent prosecuting women offenders, who typically return almost immediately to the streets.[144] In one study, almost two-thirds of incarcerated prostitutes reported at least five arrests, and their jail time increased the intensity and duration of women's involvement in streetwalking.[145] Although some evidence suggests that most streetwalkers would like to quit, a variety of forces make exit difficult: lack of education and employment skills, the stigma of an arrest record, substance abuse and mental health problems, and control by pimps.[146]

The criminal approach also increases women's vulnerability to physical abuse and economic coercion. Studies of streetwalkers typically find that about two-thirds to four-fifths are subject to physical assault and to extremely high rates of rape, murder, and post-traumatic stress disorders.[147] Women are reluctant to report abuses that could lead to prostitution charges, and police systematically fail to pursue complaints by sex workers. Arrest records heighten women's difficulties in moving to alternative work and often force them to rely on pimps and middlemen to screen customers or provide money for bail and fines.

Those who work in high-end escort services typically incur fewer risks either of arrest or physical abuse, and often make substantial sums. Details of such services emerged in 2007, with the arrest of the "D.C. Madam," and in 2008, with the forced resignation of New York governor Eliot Spitzer, who patronized the Emperor's Club, a service charging between $1,000 and $5,000 an hour.[148]

Most European countries have repealed prohibitions on engaging in prostitution but have retained laws against soliciting, pimping, pandering, running a disorderly house, or transporting a woman across national boundaries for purposes of prostitution. Other restrictions range from fairly laissez-faire approaches in countries like Denmark and the Netherlands, to tightly controlled zoning systems for licensed brothels in many German cities. Sweden criminalizes the purchase but not the sale of sex.[149] Even where commercial sex is legal and taxable, workers often lack basic rights and benefits, such as pensions, health insurance, and unemployment assistance. The same is true in Nevada, where prostitutes are classified as independent contractors rather than employees.[150]

In other countries, particularly those in Asia, South America, and the Mideast, prostitution remains a criminal offense. The prohibitions in some tradition-oriented societies are quite severe. In other nations, a de facto licensing system has evolved despite formal prohibitions. Through de facto or de jure licensing structures, a growing number of Asian and European countries are also developing sex tourism industries.

Dorchen Leidholdt, Prostitution: A Violation of Women's Human Rights

1 Cardozo Women's L.J. 133, 135-138 (1993)

Prostitution is not about women making money. It is about other people—usually men—making money off women's bodies. Pimps, brothel owners, club owners, hotel chains, travel agencies, pornographers, organized crime syndicates, and governments are the real economic beneficiaries of the sex trade in women. . . .

Prostitution is not about individuals. It is an institution of male dominance, and it is also a global industry in which the prostituting of women is constantly being packaged in new ways, using new forms of technology, tapping new markets: sex-tourism, mail-order bride selling, sex entertainment, sex immigration, dial-a-porn, computer pornography.

Just as prostitution isn't about individuals, it isn't about choice. Instead, prostitution is about the absence of meaningful choices; about having alternative routes to survival cut off or being in a situation where you don't have options to begin with. . . . [T]he majority of women in prostitution in the country—most studies estimate 60-70 percent—have histories of sexual abuse in childhood. . . . Add to this the reality that the population targeted by pimps and traffickers is teenagers. It becomes clear that the majority of prostitutes are socialized into "sex work" in childhood and adolescence when consent is meaningless and choice an illusion.

Then there are the related factors of poverty, lack of education, and homelessness. Women in prostitution, with few exceptions, are not people who debated between the advantages of going to law school or working at the X-tasy Massage Parlor. The average education level of a sample of Portland, Oregon [prostitutes] was tenth grade. . . .

Choice vanishes when, in order to endure the prostitution, women become addicted to alcohol or drugs, or become prostitutes to support their addiction. In the Portland, Oregon, study, 85% of the women were drug or alcohol abusers.

Nor is choice present when a woman is so traumatized by having stranger after stranger use her body as a seminal spittoon that she accepts prostitution as her destiny.

Just as prostitution is not about choice, it's not about work. Or if it is, it is work in the same way that slavery or bonded labor is work—work that violates human dignity and every other human right. What other kind of work has as job training years of being sexually abused in childhood? What other job has as its working conditions: rape . . . beatings . . . and premature death and murder.

Margaret Jane Radin, The Pragmatist and the Feminist

63 S. Cal. L. Rev. 1699, 1699-1701 (1990)

If the social regime permits buying and selling of sexuality . . . , thereby treating [it] as a fungible market commodit[y] given the capitalistic understandings of monetary exchange, there is a threat to the personhood of women, who are the "owners" of these "commodities." The threat to personhood from commodification arises because essential attributes are treated as severable fungible objects, and this denies the integrity and uniqueness of the self. But if the social regime prohibits this kind of commodification it denies women the choice to market their sexual . . . services, and given the current feminization of poverty and lack of avenues for free choice for women, this also poses a threat to the personhood of women. The threat from enforced noncommodification arises because narrowing women's choices is a threat to liberation, and because their choices to market sexual . . . services, even if nonideal, may represent the best alternatives available to those who would choose them.

Thus the double bind: both commodification and noncommodification may be harmful. Harmful, that is, under our current social conditions. Neither one need be harmful in an ideal world. The fact that money changes hands need not necessarily contaminate human interactions of sharing, nor must the fact that a social order makes nonmonetary sharing its norm necessarily deprive or subordinate anyone. That commodification now tends toward fungibility of women and noncommodification now tends toward their domination and continued subordination are artifacts of the current social hierarchy. In other words, the fact of oppression is what gives rise to the double bind.

Thus, it appears that the solution to the double bind is not to solve but to dissolve it: remove the oppressive circumstances. But in the meantime, if we are practically limited to those two choices, which are we to choose? I think that the answer must be pragmatic. We must look carefully at the nonideal circumstances in each case and decide which horn of the dilemma is better (or less bad), and we must keep re-deciding as time goes on.

To generalize a bit, it seems that there are two ways to think about justice. One is to think about justice in an ideal world, the best world that we can now conceive. The other is to think about nonideal justice; given where we now find ourselves, what is the better decision? In making this decision, we think about what actions can bring us closer to ideal justice. For example, if we allow commodification, we may push further away any ideal of a less commodified future. But if we enforce noncommodification, we may push further away any ideal of a less dominated future. In making our decisions of nonideal justice, we must also realize that these decisions will help to reconstitute our ideals. For example, if we commodify all attributes of personhood, the ideal of personhood we now know will evolve into another one that does not conceive fungibility as bad. The double bind, then, is a problem involving nonideal justice, and I think its only solution can be pragmatic. There is no general solution; there are only piecemeal, temporary solutions.

Notes

1. Alternative Regulatory Structures. The alternatives to the existing criminal approach to prostitution are:

- full decriminalization, i.e., removal of penalties from all consensual sexual activities and related commercial practices;

- partial decriminalization, i.e., removal of penalties from the sale of sexual services but not from other related activities such as purchasing, pimping, pandering, soliciting, or advertising; and
- regulation, i.e., removal of penalties from activities that meet state-imposed requirements, such as zoning restrictions, licensing regulations, and health exams.

Most women's rights advocates and sex workers agree on two points: criminal penalties for workers are not appropriate, and more strategies are necessary to ensure their safety. From this perspective, many feminists point out that the best way for society to minimize the harms associated with prostitution is to maximize women's other employment choices, increase their access to social services, and reduce the safety risks and social stigma associated with consensual commercial sex.

Most women's rights advocates and sex workers are also united in opposing regulation as an alternative to decriminalization. Workers generally object to the highly restrictive conditions imposed by licensing structures and to the large share of profits taken by brothel owners (typically 50 percent). Counties in Nevada exclude women with criminal records or sexually transmitted diseases, brothels limit women's mobility and choices, and licensing structures permanently stigmatize women as sex workers. It is for these reasons that only a small percentage of Nevada's prostitutes work in licensed establishments, despite the relatively safe working conditions and substantial incomes available. Women in small brothels can net up to $1,500 a week after room and board, while women in larger ranches make substantially more. As independent contractors, prostitutes generally set their own prices for different services.[151] Although conditions can be better in worker-owned collectives, these are relatively rare in sex work.[152]

Windsor, Canada, offers a less stigmatized model. There, the city sought to create a safe "adult entertainment destination" while respecting escorts' "right to self determination in their work." Sex work is licensed, advertised, and "normalized"; and workers are given information about health, safety, social services, and financial planning.[153] Experiences in other countries are more mixed. In Australia, legalization resulted in higher levels of illegal and child prostitution, organized crime, and trafficking.[154] In the Netherlands, brothels are legal, as is street prostitution in certain zones, and sex workers have access to pensions, Social Security benefits, and state-organized health care. However, illegal prostitution and trafficking remain problems, and many workers are unwilling to take advantage of benefits that would stigmatize them as prostitutes.[155]

To what extent would legalization of prostitution represent state collaboration in the exploitation and commodification of female sexuality? The public generally opposes decriminalization. Surveys over the last decade find that about 60 to 80 percent of voters are against legalized prostitution for consenting adults, with women less supportive than men.[156] Ballot initiatives to decriminalize sex work have been infrequent and unsuccessful. A 2008 initiative to legalize prostitution in San Francisco was defeated by a 58 to 42 percent margin, and a 2004 Berkeley, California, proposal to make prostitution the city's lowest law enforcement priority (along with marijuana possession) lost by a two-to-one margin. Voters and city leaders have often opposed such measures because they would insulate pimps, along with prostitutes, from prosecution and increase risks of public nuisance.[157]

More politically acceptable are diversion programs pioneered by a number of problem-solving courts, such as Hartford, Connecticut's Community Court and New York City's Midtown Community Court. These programs allow defendants who plead guilty to prostitution to avoid incarceration if they participate in individualized treatment plans. Such plans include social services designed to address underlying problems, such as substance abuse or lack of education and employment skills. These programs have substantially reduced recidivism rates, as have some similar efforts targeted at rehabilitating juvenile offenders.[158] Why do you think more communities have not adopted such approaches?

A final strategy, proposed by Andrea Dworkin in the 1980s, and supported by some contemporary women's rights advocates, is to decriminalize selling of sex by prostitutes but prohibit purchase of sex by customers, pimps, and traffickers. As noted earlier, Sweden has such a law, and the approach has also spread to Iceland and Norway. Swedish law imposes fines or prison of up to one year for those convicted and also provides aid to women seeking to leave sex work.[159] It is credited with reducing the frequency of street prostitution and trafficking and enjoys the support of about four-fifths of the public.[160] Although arrests are infrequent, the law has reduced the acceptability of purchasing sex.[161] However, sex workers oppose this approach on the ground that it makes their lives less safe by forcing them underground to protect patrons. When prostitution is invisible, workers are more vulnerable to violence and are less able to insist on condoms and to seek health and safety services.[162]

What is your view? Does the Swedish partial decriminalization approach seem preferable or politically plausible for the United States? Is it fair that women like Deborah Jeane Palfrey, known as the D.C. Madam, faced a 55-year prison term for arranging sexual liaisons for powerful men, while her male customers faced no prosecution, and some retained influential government positions?[163]

What constitutes effective enforcement strategies? Some municipalities have attempted to crack down on customers by publishing the names and photos of those convicted (Denver, Detroit, Dallas, Minneapolis, Philadelphia, Richmond); impounding vehicles or taking away the driving licenses of those convicted of solicitation from their cars (Detroit, Oakland, United Kingdom); posting on the Internet videos of men soliciting prostitutes (Winnipeg). Would you recommend any of these strategies? In surveys in England, Scotland, and the United States, men agreed that being placed on a sex offender registry would be the most effective deterrent to their purchase of sex. Other effective deterrents would be prison time and public exposure.[164]

How should laws and law enforcement be reformed? What stands in the way of reforms?

2. Prostitution and the Autonomy of Women. At issue in debates over prostitution are fundamental issues about the meaning of consent and the nature of sexual expression. Among the most divisive issues are whether women who engage in commercial sex have made truly free choices to do so, and whether commercial sex is work like any other.

What complicates the debate is the diversity of stories among women engaged in commercial sex and the inadequate or conflicting data concerning their experiences. As one worker put it, "[s]ome [women] feel they are victims. Some *are* victims. And then there are others who say that they have made that choice and celebrate that choice."[165] Some prostitutes claim that the first time they felt powerful was the first time they turned a trick.[166] According to one worker:

> [B]eing able to earn [a substantial income] is a blessing. . . . I have no regret for
> my experiences. Prostitution brought me social life, money, sex and entertain-
> ment. . . . I was alone in college, on welfare with a son. He wanted football
> clothes. He got them.[167]

One prostitute who had previously worked in a male-dominated occupation servicing telephone lines recalled that "I came home exhausted every day plus I was harassed by guys on the job. Working as a prostitute in a massage parlor is far less draining and I still get that kick of being an assertive woman."[168] The prominent Hollywood Madam, Heidi Fleiss, "wouldn't recommend prostitution as a career because it doesn't have great long-term prospects." But in the short term, the money can help someone finish school, start a business, or do something else "positive with her life."[169]

One Stanford law school graduate, Cristina Schultz Warthen, appears to have pursued such a strategy by working as an escort during her legal education. Her Internet site featured topless photos and listed rates ranging from $1250 for two hours to $3000 for six hours. According to one posting on the site, "I have paid off 100 percent of my student loans and I have tried to send a positive message to SF escorts re: assumptions about the nature and social status of women in the business."[170] In another posting, Schultz states, "During my education, I was continually taught to question paradigms and assumptions. I never understood, however, why this questioning had to stop when it bumped up against accepted social and sexual norms. I never understood why you had to be a down-to-earth educated chaste career-girl or a sexual, sensual adventuress or temptress."[171] On a confidential escort-rating site, some 82 men claimed to have had sex with her. She eventually pled guilty to tax evasion and agreed to pay $243,000 and serve a year of home detention and three years of probation.[172] Was this an appropriate result? If Schultz eventually applies to the bar, could she ever satisfy the standard requiring applicants to demonstrate "good moral character"?

Even for well-compensated sex workers, however, many feminists, such as Dorchen Leidholdt in the reading above, question whether prostitution represents the kind of free, informed, individual choice that is worthy of respect. If the average age of entry into prostitution is between 12 and 14, as research suggests,[173] that is hardly a point at which capacities for autonomous decision-making are well developed. So too, Catharine MacKinnon notes, "[i]f prostitution is a free choice, why are the women with the fewest choices the ones most often found doing it?"[174] In her view, "[u]nderstood as a practice of sexual exploitation, prostitution cannot be made safe."[175]

According to some sociologists, when prostitutes give favorable accounts of their experience, they are engaging in "neutralizing techniques":

> Sociologists use the term to describe the way in which socially despised and marginalized groups survive their marginal condition. Such techniques may be employed because the only alternative available may be the painful one of self-contempt. The idea that prostitution is freely chosen is such a technique.[176]

By contrast, defenders of sex work are offended by the dismissal of their own perceptions as false consciousness. As members of one Canadian organization of sex workers put it:

> When you are a prostitute that says, "Well, I don't agree with the way you're interpreting my life, I don't feel oppressed or I don't feel exploited in the way that you're saying," they say things like "she's too blinded to her own oppression to see her experience for what it really is, and it really is the patriarchy." They find it necessary to interpret prostitutes' experience of their lives and then feed it back to the prostitutes to tell them what's really happening, whereas they wouldn't dare be so condescending or patronizing with any other group of women.[177]

In a world of true equality, would commercial sex be inherently exploitative? Are the degrading aspects of current prostitution largely attributable to its social and legal status rather than to its intrinsic nature? Consider these views:

> Anonymous sex has validity in its own right. Since when is sex only acceptable and valid and good sex if it's linked to love or linked to someone that they have invested in, in terms of a relationship? There are a lot of people who feel unwilling or reluctant or unable to express a lot of pockets of their sexuality and their sexual needs unless it is with someone they don't have to look at afterwards. There's an excitement that goes with a new person, a novelty. Needing novelty is perfectly acceptable around other needs that we have. . . . Humanity benefits from giving legitimacy to all kinds of needs as long as they're consensual. . . . [Prostitutes'] ideal situation is like anybody else's—that we have control over our work environment. . . .[178]

> Legal and illegal sex businesses are places where men can commit sexual . . . exploitation without fear and where they are socialized to inflict those same acts on other women in their lives. When prostitution is tolerated or legalized by the state, sexual predation is normalized. . . .[179]

We need to reflect on whether romantic love is really the only valid foundation for sexual interaction; to question the view that "legitimate" sexual intimacy must be tied to spiritual connection. All too many of us seem to have swallowed wholesale this ideology: we abhor . . . "impersonal" sex; we yearn for intimate "pillow talk"; we disdain the prostitute for engaging in sex without "real connection." (Which of us hasn't engaged in sex without connection? It wasn't prostitutes who told their daughters to "close your eyes and think . . . [of the Empire]"). . . . Must we all learn to see the subjects of our sexual desire as whole, equal, non-partial, and unsegmented? Even were it desirable, *can* we eliminate inequality in the realm of the intimate? Can we do so before we eliminate pervasive economic and social inequality? And if not, what do we do in the meantime?[180]

Does women's purchase of sex from men stand on the same footing as men's purchase from women? The limited available evidence suggests that women tend to "shy away from straightforward cash for sex transactions" and prefer at least the illusion of affection and romance.[181] Does a romantic façade make the transaction any less exploitative? Are men's purchases of sex from men different from women's purchases of sex from men? Is it the nature of the act, the working conditions, or the social context that should be most critical in shaping our cultural norms and legal policies?

3. Trafficking. After drugs, sex trafficking is the most profitable activity of organized crime, with annual profits around $32 billion.[182] The International Labor Organization estimates that some 12 million individuals are in forced or bonded labor or sexual servitude.[183] Four-fifths are women and children.[184] The United States government estimates that about 17,500 individuals are trafficked into the United States each year, largely from Southeast Asia, Eastern Europe, Latin America, and the independent states of the former Soviet Union, including Russia.[185]

Trafficking encompasses a range of crimes, including sex tourism, debt bondage, involuntary servitude, forced prostitution, and rape. The 2000 United Nations Convention Against Transnational Organized Crime; Protocol to Prevent, Suppress, and Punish Trafficking in Persons, Especially Women and Children, includes as trafficking "the recruitment, transportation, transfer, harboring or receipt of persons, by means of the threat or use of force or other forms of coercion, of abduction, of fraud, of deception, of the abuse of power or of a position of vulnerability or of the giving or receiving of payments or benefits to achieve the consent of a person having control over another person, for the purposes of exploitation." Exploitation includes "the prostitution of others or other forms of sexual exploitation, forced labor or services, slavery, or practices similar to slavery, servitude, or the removal of organs." The United States has adopted a similar, although somewhat narrower, definition in the Victims of Trafficking and Violence Protection Act of 2000. The Act prohibits:

(A) sex trafficking in which a commercial sex is induced by force, fraud, or coercion, or in which the person induced to perform such an act has not attained 18 years of age; or

(B) the recruitment, harboring, transportation, provision, or obtaining a person for labor or services, through the use of force, fraud, or coercion for the purpose of subjection to involuntary servitude, peonage, debt bondage, or slavery.

A significant part of the current trafficking industry involves deception, kidnapping, or outright purchase of women and girls for work in the sex trade. Some women or their families are duped by advertisements or agents promising jobs such as waitresses, au pairs, sales clerks, actresses, and exotic dancers. Other women voluntarily accompany a new husband or a boyfriend to another country where they are sold into bondage.[186] Women and children are also drugged or kidnapped and smuggled across state lines. Many are then sold into child marriages or to brothels and kept against their will by a variety of methods.[187] Typically, they are taken to a city or foreign country where they lack marketable skills and familiarity with the language and legal culture. Their passports and other forms of identification are removed, and they are threatened with assault, murder, or prosecution by local authorities if they try to escape. Some are told that if they do manage to leave, their family members will suffer retaliation. Female refugees displaced by war or disasters may also land in "survival sex."[188] Once women have entered the sex trade, the social stigma that they encounter further restricts their employment and marriage options; many face ostracism if they return to their original communities.[189] Children who are abused or orphaned as a result of HIV and armed conflict may also end up in brothels.[190]

Some women are promised freedom after they have earned enough to repay their travel, purchase price, room and board, and interest on these debts. Often, however, such promises are not kept or the costs remain prohibitive. Women who refuse to work may be raped, physically assaulted, denied food, or forcibly restrained from leaving houses of prostitution.[191] Many prostitutes have 10- to 18-hour shifts in squalid conditions with no choice of customers and little birth control or health care. The rising rate of sexually transmitted disease, coupled with longstanding beliefs about the value of intercourse with virgins, has heightened demand for ever-younger partners of both sexes, and purchase of preteens and adolescents has become increasingly common. A representative account appears in a State Department Trafficking Report:

> Neary grew up in rural Cambodia. Her parents died when she was a child, and, in an effort to give her a better life, her sister married her off when she was 17. Three months later they went to visit a fishing village. Her husband rented a room in what Neary thought was a guest house. But when she woke the next morning, her husband was gone. The owner of the house told her she had been sold by her husband for $300 and that she was actually in a brothel.

> For five years, Neary was raped by five to seven men every day. In addition to brutal physical abuse, Neary was infected with HIV and contracted AIDS. The brothel threw her out when she became sick, and she eventually found her way to a local shelter. She died of HIV/AIDS at the age of 23.[192]

Nicholas Kristof's *New York Times* profile of Long Pross, a Thai 13-year-old sold into slavery, is still more horrific. She was painfully stitched up to look like a virgin four times and subjected to electric shocks and beatings if she protested. When recovering from a painful second abortion, she pled for rest and enraged the brothel owner, who gouged out her eye. It was only the resulting infection and disfigurement that finally enabled her escape.[193]

Trafficking also supports the rapidly increasing sex tourism industry. A growing number of companies offer "sex tours" to countries such as Thailand and the Philippines, where purchasers have ready access to bars and brothels.[194] A California travel agency ad reads: "Sex Tours to Thailand, Real Girls, Real Sex, Real Cheap. These women are the most sexually available in the world. Did you know you can actually buy a virgin girl for as little as $200? You could fuck a different girl for the rest of your life." The agency offers a prize to the man who has sex with the most girls on the tour. "Travel and the Single Male" offers its customers a "sexual Disneyland" capable of fulfilling their most exotic fantasies.[195]

Such prostitution reflects racist as well as sexist dynamics. Male tourists can convince themselves that women and children from other races and nationalities are hyper-sexed, exotic "others" who willingly cater to sexual fantasies and benefit economically from doing so. Children are particularly attractive because they are easily exploited and relatively cheap. A 2007 FBI study found that men traveling to Central America typically paid underage prostitutes less than $5. In rationalizing his sexual transactions with 14- and 15-year-old girls in Mexico and Colombia, one retired school teacher noted: "If they don't have sex with me, they may not have enough food. If someone has a problem with me doing this, let UNICEF feed them. I've never paid more than $20 to these young women, and that allows them to eat for a week."[196] Similar rationalizations, along with the other revenue and corruption generated by sex tourism, encourage officials in many impoverished countries to tolerate child prostitution.[197]

The U.S. State Department, as well as most experts in the field, has advocated a three-pronged approach to human trafficking: prevention, punishment, and protection. Prevention approaches would focus on challenging the cultural devaluation of women, expanding their education and employment opportunities, providing shelters and services for victims, reducing poverty in the countries that supply the global trade, and providing better information to vulnerable groups about the strategies of traffickers and the legal remedies available.[198]

Some experts have criticized these approaches as well intentioned in principle but ineffective in practice. Inadequate resources have been available for prevention and protective strategies, and inadequate attention has been focused on forced labor that does not include sexual exploitation.[199]

In an effort to combat the most egregious forms of trafficking, about a hundred agencies from 18 countries have signed the global Code of Conduct for the Protection of Children from Sexual Exploitation in Travel and Tourism.[200]

It requires ethical policies and contract clauses repudiating the sexual exploitation of children, training for personnel, and annual reporting on compliance. Activists also support more consumer pressure, including airport protests aimed at sex-tour participants.

The inadequacy of resources, training, and penalties are partly responsible for making the global sex trade an expanding vehicle for international crime. Sex traffickers, who procure women for compulsory sex and assist their imprisonment, have received sentences as light as one to four years.[201] In many foreign countries, enforcement of anti-trafficking laws remains grossly inadequate due to lack of funding, corruption of police and immigration officials, and governmental ambivalence about curtailing profitable sex tourism activities.

The Trafficking Victims Protection Act (TVPA) of 2000, reauthorized in 2003 and 2008, attempts to respond to these problems by increasing the maximum penalties for trafficking to 20 years, providing a civil damages remedy for victims, increasing assistance to international law enforcement efforts, and giving the President discretionary power to impose sanctions on nations that fail to meet minimum standards for enforcement of anti-trafficking prohibitions. In addition, the TVPA establishes an annual Trafficking in Persons (TIP) Report, published by the State Department, that separates countries into Tier 1 countries, which meet the minimum standards set by the U.S. government for eliminating trafficking; Tier 2 countries, which do not comply with the minimum standards but are making "significant efforts to bring themselves into compliance"; and Tier 3 countries, which do not comply with the minimum standards and are not making "significant efforts to bring themselves into compliance." The United States will not provide "nonhumanitarian, non-trade-related foreign assistance" to Tier 3 countries and will also direct the International Monetary Fund to vote against "any loan or other utilization of the funds of the respective institution to that country." However, in the first five years under the Act, only three countries were subject to sanctions, despite widespread evidence of noncompliance.[202]

To combat child sexual tourism, Congress, in 2003, passed the Prosecutorial Remedies and Other Tools to End the Exploitation of Children Today (PROTECT) Act and the Trafficking Victims Reauthorization Act, which increase penalties to a maximum of 30 years imprisonment for engaging in child sexual trafficking. However, relatively few criminal prosecutions have been brought. In the first action against a U.S. tourist agency, the New York Attorney General obtained a restraining order against Big Apple Oriental Tours, which allegedly employed tour guides to negotiate sexual services for American customers in the Philippines. In the first five years after passage of PROTECT, prosecutors secured only 47 convictions of the sex tourism provisions.[203]

The 2000 Trafficking Act also addresses the third area in which increased efforts are necessary: protection of victims. Traditionally, the targets of trafficking have been subject to immediate deportation, which deters reporting and cooperation with enforcement efforts. Under the Act, some 5,000

"T" visas, as well as social services, are available each year for women who are assisting investigators and who would "suffer extreme hardship" if deported. However, in the first seven years of the act, only about 1,000 persons were granted visas and certified for benefits. Principal barriers include victims' inability to provide usable information to law enforcement and their fear that they or their families will be subject to retaliation if they cooperate.[204]

At the international level, the United Nations Protocol to Prevent, Suppress, and Punish Trafficking in Persons, Especially Women and Children (supplementing the United Nations Convention Against Transnational Organized Crime) directs signatory nations to consider implementing measures to assist victims, such as medical, psychological, and counseling services, and employment, education, and training opportunities. To that end, the United States has pledged financial assistance to groups that work against trafficking and provide assistance to its victims. However, there has been controversy over the government's decision to target the funds only to domestic and international groups that oppose prostitution. Some women's rights activists see that decision as analogous to the recently withdrawn global gag rule, which denied U.S. assistance to groups that provide abortion-related information or services. The New York–based women's rights organization, Equality Now, opposes the anti-prostitution policy on the grounds that it interferes with legitimate advocacy and support services on behalf of women involved in the sex trade.

In 2011, opponents of such restrictions won a major victory when the United States agreed to support a recommendation of a report by the United Nations Human Rights Council Working Group as part of the Universal Periodic Review of human rights records of member states. In response to Recommendation 86, the U.S. Department of State report agreed that "no one should face violence or discrimination in access to public services based on sexual orientation or their status as a person in prostitution."[205] Following the State Department report, a coalition of groups titled Human Rights for All recommended repeal of the anti-prostitution policy. By contrast, supporters of restricted funding argue that it is more effective to assist organizations that "see trafficking and prostitution as both inextricably mixed and socially harmful."[206] Which position would you support?

4. International Matchmaking. Another practice with the potential for sexual abuse involves "mail-order brides." International matchmaking involves two primary forms. One is pen pal clubs. These organizations offer information to and about men and women for free. An estimated 10,000 foreign women looking for marriage or a relationship belong.[207] The second type of organization is the mail-order bride agency, which generally recruits and screens potential candidates from economically disadvantaged communities through newspaper and magazine advertisements. Most recruits come from Asia, Latin America, Eastern Europe, and the former Soviet Union. These agencies market catalogs to men that include women's names, pictures, and biographical data including physical measurements and personal interests.

The World Association of Introduction Agencies recognizes some 2,700 agencies worldwide, which broker an estimated 8,000 to 16,000 American marriages annually.[208] Close to 2 million websites provide information on mail-order brides.[209] This industry represents a modern variation on an earlier tradition of picture brides, a system in which individual families arranged marriages between their daughters and men of the same racial or ethnic groups abroad using only pictures and recommendations. That practice was encouraged by restrictive immigration laws, such as U.S. anti-Asian exclusion acts, which largely limited legal immigration status to male laborers and prevented them from traveling back and forth to their native lands to arrange their own marriages. Once a man selected a picture bride, the marriage would be legalized in Asia, and the wife would be eligible to immigrate to the United States. The practice died out in the mid-twentieth century as a result of the repeal of the exclusion acts and the growth of the Asian population in the United States. However, a superficially similar practice resurfaced in the 1970s, partly due to the Vietnam War, and the experience of American soldiers with Asian prostitutes. Former military personnel are prominent founders of modern bridal agencies and constitute a large percentage of their customers.[210]

Mail-order bride catalogs are highly salable in and of themselves, as they feature attractive women and provide a fantasy for American men who have been "unlucky in love." The women are typically portrayed as exotic, dutiful, and accommodating. A 2008 website listing for Brides 4U describes Asian brides as "attractive physically, very feminine, petite and slender, . . . gentle and polite, . . . charming and attentive to their partner, . . . and respecting [of] traditions." Latin brides are described as having "exotic beauty, refreshingly sunny disposition[s] . . . and traditional upbringings where old fashioned values and family virtues remain a vital way of life." Cherry Blossoms portrays Filipinos who are "subservient and docile." A typical entry reads: "Maria Claire (19) Philippines/5'3"; 105; hospital attendant (nursing aide grad). Catholic. I'm kind, honest, and humble to everybody and most of all loving and caring. Never been touch and never been kiss except to the one I'm looking to."[211] The website of Chance for Love maintains: "The Russian woman has not been exposed to the world of rampant feminism that asserts its rights in America. She is the weaker gender and knows it."[212]

The catalogs target men from industrialized countries such as the United States, Australia, and Canada. The typical client is white, older than the potential bride, financially well off, and politically conservative. Most have at least two years of college and have been divorced at least once.[213] Many consider American women too independent, selfish, and career-oriented. Broker services reinforce and accommodate this view. One website, Goodwife.com, features images of scantily clad homemakers in sexually provocative poses while cooking and cleaning. The site explains:

> We, as men, are more and more wanting to step back from the types of women
> we meet now. With many women taking on the "me first" feminist agenda

and the man having to take a back seat to her desire for power and control, many men are turned off by this and look back to having a more traditional woman as our partner.[214]

For a fee, men buy the addresses of the women they select from the catalogs. Some agencies also offer video presentations, and services such as private investigators and clinical psychologists. Customers then mail letters to potential brides or join a group tour that allows members to interview potential applicants. Typically, the man travels to the home country of the potential bride, often through arrangements made by the agency. If, after meeting, the couple agrees to marry, the wedding occurs in the woman's home country or the husband-to-be applies for a fiancée visa, which allows the prospective bride to travel to the man's country. United States immigration law requires the couple to marry within 90 days. Once they are married, the bride obtains resident status on a two-year conditional basis. Ninety days before the expiration of the two-year period, the couple must jointly petition for unrestricted permanent residency status for the wife. The burden of proof is on the couple to establish that the marriage is viable and was not fraudulently arranged to evade immigration restrictions.

Expectations are frequently disappointed. Although the practice appeals to men seeking submissive wives, the women who participate are sufficiently independent and resourceful to leave their country and often do not fit the stereotype of the docile helpmate. So too, many women's knowledge of American society comes from romanticized media portrayals, encouraging the belief that American husbands treat their wives better than husbands in their home countries.[215] When asked why they are seeking an American to marry, women generally say that they believe that Americans make good husbands while men from their own country do not.[216] However, the men seeking foreign brides frequently have negative attitudes toward women. Many have experienced a bitter divorce or break-up, and a substantial number become physically, sexually, and emotionally abusive toward new wives who do not fulfill their fantasies.[217] For some women, a risk of such abuse may seem the necessary price of immigration. According to a report for Congress, "There is no question that many of the alien women who advertise for U.S. husbands are far more interested in gaining permanent residence alien status than in gaining a good marriage."[218]

The extent of domestic violence in mail-order marriages is impossible to estimate with any accuracy since police records do not reveal this information, and women have well-documented reasons not to report abuse. They frequently fear further retaliation against themselves or their children and loss of economic support. These concerns are common in any violent relationship but are especially prominent among mail-order wives for multiple reasons. These women typically have no family or support network on which they can rely and lack the language and employment skills for financial independence. Few have funds to seek legal assistance or to return to their native country. Many fear deportation and the cultural stigma of divorce. Those who come from nations with a tradition of gender subordination may also see some abuse as a standard feature of marital relationships. In one study, mail-order brides were six times more likely to experience domestic violence than other women.[219]

In response to these problems, the U.S. Immigration and Nationality Act, the Violence Against Women Act, and the Battered Immigrant Women Protection Act provide for a waiver of the joint petition requirement for permanent residency in certain circumstances, including spousal abuse.[220] The International Marriage Broker Regulation Act became part of the 2005 Violence Against Women Reauthorization Act.[221] It provides prospective brides with information about the immigration process, domestic violence resources, and their prospective husband's prior marital and criminal records. The Act also limits the number of fiancée visas that an American can seek within a particular time period in order to prevent serial abuse. Claims that the statute represents unconstitutional discrimination against men seeking brides abroad have been rejected on the ground that higher risks of violence justify such background checks.[222] Some countries of origin have also attempted to restrict abuses. The Philippines, for example, makes it illegal to broker mail-order marriages.[223]

Other proposed reforms include precluding customers with a history of domestic violence from obtaining fiancée visas for a prescribed number of years and a civil liability cause of action against marriage brokers. In the first successful matchmaker lawsuit, Nataliya Fox obtained a $430,000 award against Encounters International for failing to screen customers for violence, misstating deportation risks, and omitting required disclosures about the legal rights of domestic-violence victims. She suffered severe physical abuse from her husband, who had a prior history of battering. He eventually divorced Nataliya, paid her $110,000 in a settlement, and obtained a new mail-order bride.[224]

Putting Theory Into Practice

5-11. Would you support an ordinance to decriminalize the purchase and sale of sex in your community? Why or why not? What about criminalizing only the purchase? Would you include licensing or zoning requirements?

5-12. A group of women students at a state law school decide to organize a conference to draw attention to the harmful effects of prostitution and the extent to which it perpetuates gender subordination. The organizers have lined up a number of highly prominent participants, all of whom oppose decriminalization of most prostitution-related activities. The students also intend to ask some well-known scholars to present alternative points of view on prostitution, including support of decriminalization. The leading anti-prostitution speakers refuse to participate if "pro-prostitution" advocates are present. They also demand removal of sexually explicit footage in an exhibit by an artist who supports decriminalization. When complaints are made about censorship of speech, one professor responds: "I don't see this as a fight within feminism but a fight between those who wish to end male supremacy and those who wish to do better under it."[225]

How would you have handled the incident if you had been one of the student leaders? If the students agree, how should the dean and university legal counsel respond to First Amendment claims?

5-13. The Shady Lady Ranch brothel, two and a half hours northwest of Las Vegas, offers male prostitutes to female customers.[226] In what respect, if any, does this business reflect progress for women? In what respect is it bad for women?

B. PREGNANCY AND AUTONOMY

1. Control of Conception and Other Aspects of Women's Health

Woman's role in reproduction has always been a factor in limiting her life choices and opportunities. Thus, contraception, pregnancy, abortion, and other reproductive issues have been central to controversial debates about women's autonomy.

Women's reproductive choices were not broadly regulated in the United States until the nineteenth century. The momentum for legal control of women's options came largely from moral reformers and physicians who, in response to the increased demand by women for contraception and abortion, wanted to assert technical, ethical, and social superiority over their competitors, particularly midwives. In 1873, Congress passed the Comstock Law, which prohibited dissemination of information about abortion and contraception. While the early efforts to overturn this regulation asserted women's right to control their own bodies, feminist pioneers such as Margaret Sanger also used eugenic arguments in favor of birth control. Reflecting this mix of motivations, throughout the early twentieth century fertility control emerged as a right for the privileged and a duty for the poor. By the middle of the twentieth century, more liberal sexual mores, opportunities for women in paid employment, economic pressure within families to control fertility, and the availability of oral contraception helped liberalize public attitudes and practices, but many state laws banning contraception remained on the books.[227]

The first case recognizing constitutional protection for women's reproductive choice was Griswold v. Connecticut. The case remains famous in the field of constitutional law for its decisional grounding. The Supreme Court's use of substantive due process theories to invalidate protective labor legislation in the early twentieth century had been subject to considerable criticism and had made judges wary of second-guessing legislative judgments on the basis of non-explicit constitutional guarantees. *Griswold* represented a departure from that judicial restraint. Finding nowhere a specific constitutional provision that protected the right of the married couple to use contraceptives, the Court based the right in the "penumbras" of the guarantees of the First, Third, Fourth, Fifth, and Ninth Amendments. Taken together, these guarantees were said to encompass a broader right of privacy, which has been subsequently extended to include a right to use contraceptives by unmarried persons (Eisenstadt v. Baird, discussed below), the right to an abortion (Roe v. Wade, discussed in the next section), and the right to sexual intimacy among homosexual partners (Lawrence v. Texas, discussed in Chapter 4).

Griswold concerns limits to state laws restricting access to contraception. A host of other issues concern state or private obligations to ensure access. Erickson v. Bartell Drug Co., for example, addresses whether insurance carriers can exclude contraception from otherwise comprehensive health care coverage.

Reading Questions

1. Should there be a constitutional right of privacy? If so, how broadly should it be defined?
2. What is the relationship between a woman's right to privacy and her right to equality?
3. How important was marriage as a grounding for the privacy right in *Griswold*? Is the result in *Eisenstadt* consistent with this grounding?
4. Even if the state cannot prohibit access to contraceptives, should pharmacists be allowed to refuse to dispense them? Should insurers be allowed to refuse to include contraception in otherwise comprehensive health care coverage?

Griswold v. Connecticut

381 U.S. 479 (1965)

Mr. Justice DOUGLAS delivered the opinion of the court.

[Appellants, Planned Parenthood personnel who prescribed contraceptives for "married persons," were charged as accessories to the violation of the Connecticut statute prohibiting the use of contraceptives. The Court first held that they had standing to assert their patients' privacy rights.]

[W]e are met with a wide range of questions that implicate the Due Process Clause of the Fourteenth Amendment. . . . We do not sit as a super-legislature to determine the wisdom, need, and propriety of laws that touch economic problems, business affairs, or social conditions. This law, however, operates directly on an intimate relation of husband and wife and their physician's role in one aspect of that relation.

The association of people is not mentioned in the Constitution nor in the Bill of Rights. The right to educate a child in a school of the parents' choice—whether public or private or parochial—is also not mentioned. Nor is the right to study any particular subject or any foreign language. Yet the First Amendment has been construed to include certain of those rights. . . . In other words, the First Amendment has a penumbra where privacy is protected from governmental intrusion. . . .

The foregoing cases suggest that specific guarantees in the Bill of Rights have penumbras, formed by emanations from those guarantees that help give them life and substance. Various guarantees create zones of privacy. The right of association contained in the penumbra of the First Amendment is one, as we have seen. The Third Amendment in its prohibitions against the quartering of soldiers "in any house" in time of peace without the consent of the owner is another facet of that privacy. The Fourth Amendment explicitly affirms the "right of the people to be secure in their persons, houses, papers, and effects, against unreasonable searches and seizures." The Fifth Amendment in its Self-Incrimination Clause enables the citizen to create a zone of privacy which government may not force him to surrender to his detriment. The Ninth Amendment provides: "The enumeration in the constitution, of certain rights, shall not be construed to deny or disparage others retained by the people." . . . We have had many controversies over these penumbral rights of "privacy and repose." These cases bear witness that the right of privacy which presses for recognition here is a legitimate one.

The present case, then, concerns a relationship lying within the zone of privacy which, in forbidding the use of contraceptives rather than regulating their manufacture or sale, seeks to achieve its goals by . . . having a maximum destructive impact upon that relationship. Such a law cannot stand in light of the familiar principle, so often applied by the Court, that a "governmental purpose to control or prevent activities constitutionally subject to state regulation may not be achieved by means which sweep unnecessarily broadly and thereby invade the area of protected freedoms." NAACP v. Alabama [1964]. Would we allow the police to search the sacred precincts of marital bedrooms for telltale signs of the use of contraceptives? The very idea is repulsive to the notions of privacy surrounding the marriage relationship.

We deal with a right of privacy older than the Bill of Rights—older than our political parties, older than our school system. Marriage is a coming together for better or worse, hopefully enduring, and intimate to the degree of being sacred. It is an association that promotes a way of life, not causes; a harmony in living, not political faiths; a bilateral loyalty, not commercial or social projects. Yet it is an association for as noble a purpose as any involved in our prior decisions.

Reversed.

Mr. Justice GOLDBERG, whom THE CHIEF JUSTICE and Mr. Justice BRENNAN join, concurring. . . .

[I]t should be said of the Court's holding today that it in no way interferes with a State's proper regulation of sexual promiscuity or misconduct. As my Brother Harlan so well stated in his dissenting opinion in Poe v. Ullman [1961]:

> Adultery, homosexuality and the like are sexual intimacies which the State forbids . . . but the intimacy of husband and wife is necessarily an essential and accepted feature of the institution of marriage, an institution which the State not only must allow, but which always and in every age it has fostered and protected. It is one thing when the State exerts its power either to forbid extra-marital sexuality . . . or to say who may marry, but it is quite another when, having acknowledged a marriage and the intimacies inherent in it, it undertakes to regulate by means of the criminal law the details of that intimacy.

In sum, I believe that the right of privacy in the marital relation is fundamental and basic — a personal right "retained by the people" within the meaning of the Ninth Amendment.

Erickson v. Bartell Drug Co.

141 F. Supp. 2d 1266 (W.D. Wash. 2001)

Robert S. LASNIK, Judge.

The parties' cross-motions for summary judgment in this case raise an issue of first impression in the federal courts whether the selective exclusion of prescription contraceptives from defendant's generally comprehensive prescription plan constitutes discrimination on the basis of sex.[1] In particular, plaintiffs assert that Bartell's decision not to cover prescription contraceptives such as birth control pills, Norplant, Depo-Provera, intra-uterine devices, and diaphragms under its Prescription Benefit Plan for non-union employees violates Title VII. . . .

This matter is proceeding as a class action on behalf of "all female employees of Bartell who at any time after December 29, 1997, were enrolled in Bartell's Prescription Benefit Plan for non-union employees while using prescription contraceptives."

---

1. Bartell's benefit plan is self-insured and covers all prescription drugs, including a number of preventative drugs and devices, such as blood-pressure and cholesterol-lowering drugs, hormone replacement therapies, prenatal vitamins, and drugs to prevent allergic reactions, breast cancer, and blood clotting. The plan specifically excludes from coverage a handful of products, including contraceptive devices, drugs prescribed for weight reduction, infertility drugs, smoking cessation drugs, dermatologicals for cosmetic purposes, growth hormones, and experimental drugs.

A. APPLICATION OF TITLE VII . . .

In 1978, Congress had the opportunity to expound on its view of sex discrimination by amending Title VII to make clear that discrimination because of "pregnancy, childbirth, or related medical conditions" is discrimination on the basis of sex. . . . The amendment, known as the Pregnancy Discrimination Act ("PDA"), was not meant to alter the contours of Title VII: rather, Congress intended to correct what it felt was an erroneous interpretation of Title VII by the United States Supreme Court in General Elec. Co. v Gilbert, 429 U.S. 125 (1976). In *Gilbert*, the Supreme Court held that an otherwise comprehensive short-term disability policy that excluded pregnancy-related disabilities from coverage did not discriminate on the basis of sex. . . .

Although this litigation involves an exclusion for prescription contraceptives rather than an exclusion for pregnancy-related disability costs, the legal principles established by *Gilbert* and its legislative reversal govern the outcome of this case. An employer has chosen to offer an employment benefit which excludes from its scope of coverage services which are available only to women. All of the services covered by the policy are available to both men and women, so, as was the case in *Gilbert*, "there is no risk from which men are protected and women are not. Likewise, there is no risk from which women are protected and men are not." *Gilbert*, 429 U.S. at 135 (quoting Geduldig v. Aiello, 417 U.S. 484, 496-97 (1974). Nevertheless, the intent of Congress in enacting the PDA, even if not the exact language used in the amendment, shows that mere facial parity of coverage does not excuse or justify an exclusion which carves out benefits that are uniquely designed for women. . . .

The PDA is not a begrudging recognition of a limited grant of rights to a strictly defined group of women who happen to be pregnant. Read in the context of Title VII as a whole, it is a broad acknowledgment of the intent of Congress to outlaw any and all discrimination against any and all women in the terms and conditions of their employment, including the benefits an employer provides to its employees. Male and female employees have different, sex-based disability and healthcare needs, and the law is no longer blind to the fact that only women can get pregnant, bear children, or use prescription contraception. The special or increased healthcare needs associated with a woman's unique sex-based characteristics must be met to the same extent, and on the same terms, as other healthcare needs. Even if one were to assume that Bartell's prescription plan was not the result of intentional discrimination,[7] the exclusion of women-only benefits from a generally comprehensive prescription plan is sex discrimination under Title VII.

7. There is no evidence or indication that Bartell's coverage decisions were intended to hinder women in their ability to participate in the workforce or to deprive them of equal treatment in employment or benefits. The most reasonable explanation for the current state of affairs is that the exclusion of women-only benefits is merely an unquestioned holdover from a time when employment-related benefits were doled out less equitably than they are today. The lack of evidence of bad faith or malice toward women does not affect the validity of plaintiffs' Title VII claim. Where a benefit plan is discriminatory on its face, no inquiry into subjective intent is necessary. . . .

Title VII does not require employers to offer any particular type or category of benefit. However, when an employer decides to offer a prescription plan covering everything except a few specifically excluded drugs and devices, it has a legal obligation to make sure that the resulting plan does not discriminate based on sex-based characteristics and that it provides equally comprehensive coverage for both sexes. . . . In light of the fact that prescription contraceptives are used only by women, Bartell's choice to exclude that particular benefit from its generally applicable benefit plan is discriminatory.

B. SPECIFIC ARGUMENTS RAISED BY DEFENDANT-EMPLOYER . . .

An underlying theme in Bartell's argument is that a woman's ability to control her fertility differs from the type of illness and disease normally treated with prescription drugs in such significant respects that it is permissible to treat prescription contraceptives differently than all other prescription medicines. The evidence submitted by plaintiffs shows, however, that the availability of affordable and effective contraceptives is of great importance to the health of women and children because it can help to prevent a litany of physical, emotional, economic, and social consequences. See Sylvia A. Law, Sex Discrimination and Insurance for Contraception, 73 Wash. L. Rev. 363, 364-368 (1998).

. . . [T]he adverse economic and social consequences of unintended pregnancies fall most harshly on women and interfere with their choice to participate fully and equally in the "marketplace and the world of ideas." Stanton v. Stanton, 421 U.S. 7, 14-15 (1975). See also Planned Parenthood v. Casey, 505 U.S. 833, 856 (1992) ("The ability of women to participate equally in the economic and social life of the nation has been facilitated by their ability to control their reproductive lives."). . . .

The fact that prescription contraceptives are preventative appears to be an irrelevant distinction in this case: Bartell covers a number of preventative drugs under its plan. The fact that pregnancy is a "natural" state and is not considered a disease or illness is also a distinction without a difference. Being pregnant, though natural, is not a state that is desired by all women or at all points in a woman's life. Prescription contraceptives, like all other preventative drugs, help the recipient avoid unwanted physical changes. As discussed above, identifying and obtaining an effective method of contraception is a primary healthcare issue throughout much of a woman's life and is, in many instances, of more immediate importance to her daily healthcare situation than most other medical needs. . . . Although there are some distinctions that can be drawn between prescription contraceptives and the other prescription drugs covered by Bartell's plan, none of them is substantive or otherwise justifies the exclusion of contraceptives from a generally comprehensive healthcare plan. . . .

Bartell also suggests that it should be permitted to limit the scope of its employee benefit programs in order to control costs. Cost is not, however, a defense to allegations of discrimination under Title VII. See Los Angeles Dept. of Water & Power v. Manhart, 435 U.S. 702, 716-717 (1978). . . . While it is undoubtedly true that employers may cut benefits, raise deductibles, or otherwise alter coverage options to comply with budgetary constraints, the method by which the employer seeks to curb costs must not be discriminatory. Bartell offers its employees an admittedly generous package of healthcare benefits, including both third-party healthcare plans and an in-house prescription program. It cannot, however, penalize female employees in an effort to keep its benefit costs low. The cost savings Bartell realizes by excluding prescription contraceptives from its healthcare plans are being directly borne by only one sex in violation of Title VII. . . .

Prescription contraceptives are not the only drugs or devices excluded from coverage under Bartell's benefit plan. Bartell argues that it has chosen to exclude from coverage all drugs for "family planning," and that this exclusion is neutral and non-discriminatory. There is no "family planning" exclusion in the benefit plan, however, and the contours of such a theoretical exclusion are not clear. On the list of excluded drugs and devices, contraceptive devices and infertility drugs are the two categories which might be considered "family planning" measures. Contrary to defendant's explanation, there appear to be some drugs which fall under the "family planning" rubric which are covered by the plan. Prenatal vitamins, for example, are frequently prescribed in anticipation of a woman becoming pregnant and are expressly covered under the plan. And although both parties agree that Bartell's plan excludes coverage for Viagra, an impotency drug, it is not clear that it falls into any of the excluded categories. . . .

Plaintiffs' motion for summary judgment on their disparate treatment claim is granted. Bartell is hereby ordered to cover each of the available options for prescription contraception to the same extent, and on the same terms, that it covers other drugs, devices, and preventative care for non-union employees. It is further ordered that Bartell shall offer coverage for contraception-related services, including the initial visit to the prescribing physician and any follow-up visits or outpatient services, to the same extent, and on the same terms, as it offers coverage for other outpatient services for its non-union employees. . . .

Notes

1. The Constitutional Right to Contraception. The right in *Griswold* was based squarely on the special status of marriage in this society. In Eisenstadt v. Baird, the Court extended *Griswold* to prevent Massachusetts from barring distribution of contraceptives to unmarried persons. In so ruling, the Court reasoned that "the goals of deterring premarital sex and regulating the distribution of potentially harmful articles cannot reasonably be regarded as legislative aims of [the contraception law]" since it would be irrational to make an unwanted child the "punishment for fornication." In the Court's view: "If the right of privacy means anything, it is the right of the individual, married or single, to be free from unwarranted governmental intrusion into matters so fundamentally affecting a person as the decision whether to bear or beget a child."[228]

How far should this right extend? Should it apply to minors? How about a constitutional right to have sex? Although, in Carey v. Population Servs. Int'l, the Court invalidated a New York law that, among other things, restricted the sale of contraceptives to minors younger than 16, it sidestepped the question whether minors have a constitutional right of access to contraception.[229] Similarly, in striking down a Texas statute prohibiting same-sex sodomy in Lawrence v. Texas, the Supreme Court cited Eisenstadt and Carey for the proposition that the liberty interest protected sexual decisions by unmarried persons, but stopped short of declaring a fundamental right to all sexual activity between consenting adults.[230]

Popular acceptance of Griswold has been deep and wide, despite the fact that many scholars at one time questioned its grounding as a matter of constitutional law.[231] Support has been so strong, in fact, that one nominee to a seat of the U.S. Supreme Court, Robert Bork, was defeated in 1987 largely because of his opposition to the ruling.[232]

Nevertheless, the 2012 campaign for the Republican nomination for president exposed considerable backlash on the issue, reflecting a growing conservatism about issues dealing with women's control of their reproductive lives. Proposed federal legislation that would have permitted any employer to omit coverage for contraceptives from its employee health insurance plans based on any moral or religious objection was narrowly defeated by a vote of 51 to 48 in a Democratic-controlled Senate.[233] Even the most moderate of the four men then seeking the Republican nomination, Mitt Romney, said he supported the legislation.[234] When a female Georgetown law student was denied the opportunity to testify about the proposed legislation, she told the press that she would have talked about the women who have been affected by Georgetown's failure to include contraception in its student health plan.[235] In response to her statements, Rush Limbaugh called her a "slut" and a "prostitute" on his national radio show, repeatedly telling listeners that the student has "so much sex she can't afford it" and that she seeks someone to pay her for having sex.[236] Outrage over those statements caused over 100 advertisers to pull ads from his program. Public opinion polling at the time of the controversy indicated that eight in ten Democrats supported requiring employers to include coverage for contraceptives in their employer-based health insurance plans, but that only four in ten Republicans did.[237]

2. Contraception and Women's Autonomy. Do women benefit from being the ones primarily responsible for birth control? On the one hand, of course, female contraception allows women to maintain greater control over their reproductive lives. On the other hand, some believe that making contraception a "woman's responsibility" has its disadvantages. Consider Catharine MacKinnon's argument:

So long as women do not control access to our sexuality, abortion facilitates women's heterosexual availability. In other words, under conditions of gender inequality, sexual liberation in this sense does not free women; it frees male sexual aggression. The availability of abortion removes the one remaining legitimized reason that women have had for refusing sex besides the headache.[238]

Does access to contraception and abortion actually reduce women's autonomy?

Does the practice of contraception reproduce, or at least reflect, underlying class and gender ideologies? Historian Linda Gordon underlines these class dimensions of birth control, explaining how men, particularly those of lower socio-economic status, tend to associate masculinity with sexual images of virility. This identity is undercut by the use of contraception "because it introduces calculation and negotiation with women into sexual relations." Among the prosperous, masculinity is associated to a greater extent with earning power, responsibility, children's high achievement, and other goals that tend to be served by contraceptive use. Race and ethnicity are further complicating factors. At various times and circumstances, racial and ethnic pride might stimulate fertility, or it might stimulate greater use of contraception. Race and ethnicity also affect the availability of competing opportunities to motherhood and thus the motivation to reproduce.[239]

Male condom use has increased dramatically. Ten percent of women of reproductive age rely on their partners' use of condoms, 17 percent of women rely on female sterilization, 17 percent use birth control pills, 6 percent rely on male sterilization, and 8 percent use injectable contraceptives, diaphragms, or IUDs.[240] The remaining 42 percent rely on various levels of abstinence or do not use any form of contraception. Significantly, of course, female contraceptive alternatives do not protect against HIV/AIDS and other sexually transmitted diseases.

3. Emergency Contraception, Abortion, and Conscience Laws. Of the 3 million unintended pregnancies that occur in the United States each year, estimates suggest that access to emergency contraception could prevent 1.5 million pregnancies, of which half now end in abortion.[241] The "morning-after pill" designed to address emergency contraception needs, however, has been highly controversial. Some people who believe that life begins at conception consider emergency contraception to be similar to abortion because it may prevent implantation. Supporters argue, on the other hand, that it is different from abortion because it does not destroy an embryo. The Federal Drug Administration (FDA) has taken the latter view.

Among the issues are whether there should be age restrictions to availability of the morning-after pill and whether it should be available over the counter or only by prescription. A 2009 court decision ordered that Plan-B One-Step be available to anyone of any age, without prescription, but the pill retails between $40 and $50 dollars, and the court decision does not apply to generics, which tend to be $10 to $20 less expensive.[242] The Obama administration continues to oppose the easy availability of generics to young teenagers, and the controversy continues.

A further issue is the right of pharmacists and hospitals to refuse to dispense contraceptives. In small communities, pharmacists' refusals to fill prescriptions or make referrals have undermined access to this medication. Eleven states have laws permitting either pharmacists or pharmacies to refuse filling contraceptive prescriptions on ethical or religious grounds, and many others are considering such legislation.[243] Federal law enables institutions and individuals to refuse to provide birth control services that are "contrary to [their] religious beliefs or moral principles,"[244] and the 2005 Weldon Amendment prohibits federal funding for any federal, state, or local agency that discriminates against any "health care entity" that does not provide or offer referrals or insurance coverage for abortions. Catholic hospitals follow the National Conference of Bishops Ethical and Religious Directives for Catholic Health Care Services, which prohibit all forms of contraceptive services and counseling, medical and surgical abortions, sterilizations, and even emergency contraception to victims of rape.[245] Some hospitals prohibit affiliated doctors from performing similar medical procedures elsewhere. The impact of these restrictions has increased with the trend of religiously affiliated health care facilities merging with non-sectarian institutions. What is the right approach to this issue? Since 1998, the American Pharmacists Association has had a policy supporting members' right to "refuse to dispense medication" while encouraging pharmacies to provide alternative arrangements for ensuring that prescriptions are filled. Is this a good compromise?

Efforts have failed to enact federal legislation that would require hospitals to provide access to a full range of reproductive services. About 18 states and the District of Columbia, however, require all hospitals to provide either information about emergency contraception, a referral for the morning-after pill, or on-site emergency contraception treatment, which means that "conscience clauses" apply only to procedures such as abortion, sterilization, and artificial insemination, and not to emergency contraception.[246] California's Women's Contraception Equity Act requires Catholic institutions, including hospitals, to provide their employees with contraceptive coverage if they provide prescription drug coverage.[247]

4. The Fight for Contraceptive Equity Insurance and Women's Health. Is *Erickson* correctly decided? What exactly is the nature of the discrimination? Does it matter whether the insurance plan covers drugs used only by men, such as Viagra? *Erickson* is just one of several cases challenging the exclusion of coverage for prescription contraceptives in employment-based insurance plans. Plaintiffs in these cases have urged that access to contraception is an issue of sex equality.[248] The district courts have split on whether such exclusions constitute unlawful discrimination under Title VII, as amended by the PDA.[249] Only one federal appellate court has considered this issue. The Eighth Circuit, in Standridge v. Union Pacific Railroad Company, held that it was neither pregnancy nor sex discrimination for the employer to exclude coverage for all forms of contraception, including sterilization. The court concluded that contraception is not a "related medical condition" under the terms of the PDA, even though the Supreme Court held in *Johnson Controls*, discussed in Chapter 2, that "potential pregnancy" is covered by that same language.[250] The *Standridge* court found "unpersuasive" a decision from the EEOC that interpreted the PDA to require coverage of prescription contraceptives for women if they cover "other prescription drugs and devices, or other types of services that are used to prevent the occurrences of other medical conditions."[251] It also concluded that the employer's plan was gender-neutral because it excluded coverage for male contraception (condoms) and sterilization.

The impact of these rulings both in favor of and against contraceptive equity has lessened over the last decade, as the number of employers providing insurance with contraceptive benefits has dramatically increased. Nine out of ten employer-provided insurance plans cover prescription contraceptives, compared with only three in ten a decade earlier.[252] This change came about primarily through state adoption of contraceptive coverage mandates. Twenty-eight states have some type of mandated benefit law for prescription contraceptives.[253]

Since 1998, health plans participating in the Federal Employees Health Benefit Program have been required to provide prescription contraceptive coverage if other prescription drugs are covered.[254] Contraceptive coverage will become all but universal, as regulations implemented under the 2010 Patient Protection and Affordable Care Act would nationalize the mandate that all employer-sponsored health care plans must include certain contraceptive services.[255] The new regulations do contain a narrow exception for certain religious employers, however, and some plans are at least temporarily "grandfathered" and permitted to maintain existing exclusions. The exception still requires non-profit religious employers to provide contraceptive coverage, but it permits them to seek reimbursement from the government in many cases so as to avoid paying for something that violates the religious principles upon which the entity is based. In one pending challenge, a Roman Catholic order filed suit on the grounds that filing the form to request reimbursement could be construed as authorizing the provision of contraceptives.[256] A federal judge ruled in favor of the order, and the U.S. Supreme Court issued a stay pending appeal, which allows the order to refuse to provide contraceptive coverage until the issue is resolved.[257] Other pending cases raise the question whether a for-profit company can refuse to provide contraceptive benefits because doing so violates the religious beliefs of the owners, in violation of the Religious Freedom Restoration Act.[258] After conflicting decisions in the Tenth and Third Circuits, the U.S. Supreme Court granted certiorari and will review the cases.[259] Do you think an employer should be allowed to exclude contraception coverage from its health insurance coverage for religious reasons? For further discussion of the tension between religious freedom and gender equality, see Chapter 6, at 742.

5. Access to Treatment for Infertility. Women have also challenged their employers' response to infertility as a form of sex discrimination. The CDC estimates that as many as 7 million women suffer some degree of infertility.[260] With advances in reproductive technology, women have many more options for treating infertility. Twelve percent of women of childbearing age have sought medical help for infertility or prevention of miscarriage.[261] Because most treatments for infertility are expensive, prohibitively so for many women, insurance coverage is an important issue. By and large, however, plaintiffs have not succeeded in litigation challenging insurance exclusions under Title VII and the PDA. In Krauel v. Iowa Methodist Medical Center, the Eighth Circuit Court of Appeals held that infertility is not a "related medical condition" under the PDA because both men and women can suffer from it. It is thus unlike the "potential pregnancy" recognized in *Johnson Controls*, which is unique to women.[262] The Second Circuit in Saks v. Franklin Covey Co. rejected a similar claim, ruling that it was neither pregnancy nor sex discrimination for an employer to deny insurance coverage for surgical impregnation procedures (such as artificial insemination and in vitro fertilization) performed only on women.[263] The court noted that including "infertility within the PDA's protection as a 'related medical condition[]' would result in the anomaly of defining a class that simultaneously includes equal numbers of both sexes and yet is somehow vulnerable to sex discrimination."[264] To fall under the PDA, the court concluded, the condition "must be unique to women." The Seventh Circuit, however, held in Hall v. Nalco that an employer could not fire a woman because she requested time off to undergo in vitro fertilization without violating the PDA. If her allegations were true, the plaintiff "was terminated not for the gender-neutral condition of infertility, but rather for the gender-specific quality of childbearing capacity."[265] Employees "terminated for taking time off to undergo IVF—just like those terminated for taking time off to give birth or receive other pregnancy-related care—will always be women."[266] Can *Saks* and *Hall* be reconciled? Which one has the better reading of *Johnson Controls*?

6. Gender Bias in Health Care. Health concerns about female contraception are part of a broader set of issues related to gender bias in health care. Some of these complaints concern the failure to provide adequate warnings and instructions for contraceptives, and to provide research and treatment for women with conditions such as heart disease, renal disease, and lung cancer, for which men receive better health care.[267]

One representative study found that emergency rooms incorrectly sent home a disproportionate number of women and blacks who had warning signs of heart attacks.[268] Other problems concern the overuse of certain invasive procedures or restrictive instructions. Such biases may be related to the fact that, at one time, women were disproportionately excluded from medical research and drug test trials.[269] To rectify such exclusions, the NIH Revitalization Act of 1993 required the National Institutes of Health of the Department of Health and Human Services to ensure that women and minorities were among the subjects of clinical research.

Concerns about the lack of attention to women's health have been fueled by the discovery of numerous drugs and other products that, as in the case of some contraceptives, have turned out to be medically unsafe for women. Examples have included the Dalkon Shield contraceptive; DES, a synthetic estrogen hormone prescribed for miscarriages, later linked to cancer and birth defects; and Bendectin, an anti-nausea medication also found to cause birth defects. Concerns have also been raised about silicone breast implants. In the 1990s, the makers of the implants spent more than 6 billion dollars settling about 370,000 claims for arthritic and autoimmune disorders claimed to have resulted from the rupture and leakage of silicone from the implants. During this time, the FDA withdrew approval of the implants except for "urgent need" patients who had had mastectomies, at which point saline implants dominated the market. Subsequently, in 2006, a new type of silicone implant was approved, with the requirement of 10 years of follow-up study.[270] In 2012, half of the almost 300,000 breast augmentation procedures performed in the United States made use of silicone implants.[271] Based on five years of post-approval studies, the FDA determined that silicone implants "have a reasonable assurance of safety and effectiveness when used as labeled" and "despite frequent local complications and adverse outcomes, the benefits and risks . . . are sufficiently well understood for women to make informed decisions about their use."[272]

A new women's health care controversy centers on whether states should require or promote vaccination of school-age girls with Gardasil, a vaccine designed to protect against four strands of the human papilloma virus (HPV). HPV is the most common sexually transmitted disease with which 79 million people are currently infected.[273] It is responsible for almost all cervical cancers, as well as a significant percentage of cancers of the vulva, vagina, penis, anus, mouth, and throat, and 90 percent of genital warts. There are about 12,000 new cervical cancer cases every year and about 4,000 deaths from the disease. Black and Hispanic women have disproportionately high rates of cervical cancer and face worse outcomes.[274] In 2006, the FDA approved Gardasil for females ages 9 to 26.[275] Conservative groups like the Family Research Council have opposed the vaccine because female adolescents could see it as "license to engage in premarital sex."[276] Such opposition has helped block proposed legislation in about half of the states to require vaccination, as well as efforts to require its coverage in insurance policies.[277]

In 2009, the FDA approved Gardasil for use in boys 9 through 26 years of age.[278] In 2011, an advisory committee of the FDA recommended that all boys of the requisite ages receive the vaccine. In support of the recommendation, the committee stated: "HPV vaccination of males offers an opportunity to decrease the burden of HPV related disease in both males and females. In addition to providing direct benefit to boys by preventing future genital warts or anal cancer there is also the potential that vaccinating boys will reduce the spread of HPV from males to females and reduce some of the HPV–related burden that women suffer from."[279] As a legislator, would you support a mandate for both boys and girls to receive the vaccine? If so, how would you respond to conservative critics who object to mandatory use of a vaccine to prevent sexually transmitted disease?

7. Sterilization.   Sterilization is currently the second-most widely used birth control technique. Almost 17 percent of women rely on female sterilization for contraception, and nearly 6 percent of women rely on the sterilization of their male partners.

Sterilization has an unbecoming history, due to its compulsory application to poor, minority, and mentally disabled women. In a 1927 case permitting such sterilization, Justice Oliver Wendell Holmes infamously declared: "Three generations of imbeciles is enough."[280] The view of the Supreme Court toward compulsory sterilization ultimately changed,[281] but some states continue to authorize sterilization for certain offenses such as child sexual abuse.[282]

Sterilization for poor and minority women as a condition of receiving welfare has led to federal and state regulations designed to prevent such coercion. However, as forced sterilization laws tightened, it became more difficult for parents and guardians to obtain the procedure for developmentally disabled women whose best interests—including their autonomy—might benefit from sterilization. Attention then shifted to how sterilization standards should both protect women, but also enable them to live richer, sexually active lives. Some jurisdictions such as Connecticut attempt to accommodate these competing concerns by allowing courts to authorize sterilization if presented with clear and convincing evidence that it is in the best interests of the individual or that the individual would choose it for herself if able.[283] Is this a good balance?

Putting Theory Into Practice

5-14. The Women's Health and Cancer Rights Act of 1998 was passed to require that insurance plans that include coverage for mastectomy also cover reconstruction of the removed breast, and also the other breast in order to produce a symmetrical appearance. Is this entitlement best viewed as a gender equality issue? An autonomy issue? Does it serve to reinforce the concept of women as sexual objects? Or does it expand their life choices in a positive way?

5-15. You have been appointed the guardian ad litem for Beth, an 18-year-old woman who has the mental function of an 8 year old. Beth is able to work in a sheltered workshop setting and to take care of her own basic, physical needs, but she is not able to cook, drive, read, balance a checkbook, or follow complicated instructions. She would like to move from her parents' home to a supervised group-home setting with people her own age. Her parents are agreeable to the move, as long as she has a tubal ligation first so that, if she becomes sexually active, she cannot become pregnant. Because she is incompetent, state law requires a judicial order authorizing the procedure. Your role is to make a recommendation to the court about whether the procedure is in Beth's best interests.

What will you recommend to the court? What additional evidence, if any, would you need to gather to support your recommendation?

5-16. A 2005 Executive Order in Illinois provided that "[u]pon receipt of a valid, lawful prescription for a contraceptive, a pharmacy must dispense the contraceptive, or a suitable alternative permitted by the prescriber, to the patient . . . without delay, consistent with the normal time frame for filling any other prescription."[284] Pursuant to this order, Walgreens requires its pharmacists to sign statements promising to fill contraceptive prescriptions. It suspended four pharmacists who refused to do so based on their religious beliefs.

Columnist Ellen Goodman argues that "the pharmacist's license does not include the right to dispense morality."[285] Should state law or pharmacy boards dictate policy in this area? Or should we let the market decide?

Should pharmacists who morally oppose contraception (especially the morning-after pill, which opponents consider a form of abortion) be protected from adverse employment action for acting on their consciences? Should states enact laws protecting them from such consequences? Is there a compromise position?[286]

2. Abortion

Access to abortion has been the most contested site for women's claims to reproductive autonomy. As noted in the prior section, the legal regulation of abortion began in earnest in the nineteenth century. Physicians advocated the criminalization of abortion using arguments that related not only to protecting potential life, but also to ensuring women's performance of marital and maternal obligations, preserving the ethnic character of the nation, and maintaining the social order.[287] By the 1960s, about 1 million abortions were being performed annually, most of them illegally. Because of their illegality, many abortions were performed under unsafe conditions by unskilled practitioners. Between 1,000 and 10,000 individuals died each year of botched abortions, who were disproportionately poor and minority women. These human costs were a catalyst of reform activity.[288]

While attitudes about abortion were changing in the 1960s and about one-third of states liberalized their statutes, at the time of the Roe v. Wade decision in 1973, half the states still prohibited termination of pregnancy except where necessary to preserve maternal life.[289] In Roe v. Wade, the U.S. Supreme Court recognized a constitutional right to obtain an abortion, a right that has continued to expand and contract in subsequent decisions. The two most important of these—Planned Parenthood v. Casey and Gonzales v. Carhart—are excerpted in this section.

Reading Questions

1. As the law has evolved, the legal grounds for the abortion right has shifted, as well as the arguments advocates have taken on both sides of the debate. Which do you find most persuasive?
2. Is it true, as the majority in Roe maintains, that the Court can resolve disputes over abortion without also resolving the "difficult question of when life begins"?
3. What rights, if any, should a woman's husband have concerning reproductive issues such as abortion and adoption? Does giving the woman the full power to make the abortion decision undermine efforts to increase men's responsibility for contraception and childrearing?
4. What role should parents play in the decisions of a pregnant minor?
5. Should the public fund abortions that poor women or minors cannot afford?
6. Does it matter whether the abortion right is grounded in a right of privacy or autonomy, in equal protection, or in an ethic of responsibility?

Roe v. Wade

410 U.S. 113 (1973)

Justice BLACKMUN delivered the opinion of the Court. . . .

[Texas law makes] it a crime to "procure an abortion," as therein defined, or to attempt one, except with respect to "an abortion procured or attempted by medical advice for the purpose of saving the life of the mother." Similar statutes are in existence in a majority of the States. . . .

Three reasons have been advanced to explain historically the enactment of criminal abortion laws in the 19th century and to justify their continued existence.

It has been argued occasionally that these laws were the product of a Victorian social concern to discourage illicit sexual conduct. Texas, however, does not advance this justification in the present case. . . .

A second reason is concerned with abortion as a medical procedure. When most criminal abortion laws were first enacted, the procedure was a hazardous one for the woman. . . . Modern medical techniques have altered this situation. . . .

The third reason is the State's interest—some phrase it in terms of duty—in protecting prenatal life. Some of the argument for this justification rests on the theory that a new human life is present from the moment of conception. The State's interest and general obligation to protect life then extends, it is argued, to prenatal life. . . .

The Constitution does not explicitly mention any right of privacy. In a line of decisions, however going back perhaps as far as [1891], the Court has recognized that a right of personal privacy, or a guarantee of certain areas or zones of privacy, does exist under the Constitution. In varying contexts, the Court or individual Justices have, indeed, found at least the roots of that right in the First Amendment . . . ; in the Fourth and Fifth Amendments . . . ; in the penumbras of the Bill of Rights . . . ; or in the concept of liberty guaranteed by the first section of the Fourteenth Amendment. . . . These decisions make it clear that only personal rights that can be deemed "fundamental" or "implicit in the concept of ordered liberty," . . . are included in this guarantee of personal privacy. They also make it clear that the right has some extension to activities relating to marriage, Loving v. Virginia [1967]; procreation, Skinner v. Oklahoma [1942]; contraception, Eisenstadt v. Baird [1972]; family relationships, Prince v. Massachusetts [1944]; and child rearing and education, Pierce v. Society of Sisters [1925], Meyer v. Nebraska [1923].

This right of privacy, whether it be founded in the Fourteenth Amendment's concept of personal liberty and restrictions upon state action, as we feel it is, or, as the District Court determined, in the Ninth Amendment's reservation of rights to the people, is broad enough to encompass a woman's decision whether or not to terminate her pregnancy. The detriment that the State would impose upon the pregnant woman by denying this choice altogether is apparent. Specific and direct harm medically diagnosable even in early pregnancy may be involved. Maternity, or additional offspring, may force upon the woman a distressful life and future. Psychological harm may be imminent. Mental and physical health may be taxed by child care. There is also the distress, for all concerned, associated with the unwanted child, and there is the problem of bringing a child into a family already unable, psychologically and otherwise, to care for it. In other cases, as in this one, the additional difficulties and continuing stigma of unwed motherhood may be involved. All these are factors the woman and her responsible physician necessarily will consider in consultation. . . .

We, therefore, conclude that the right of personal privacy includes the abortion decision, but that this right is not unqualified and must be considered against important state interests in regulation. . . .

The appellee and certain *amici* argue that the fetus is a "person" within the language and meaning of the Fourteenth Amendment. In support of this, they outline at length and in detail the well-known facts of fetal development. If this suggestion of personhood is established, the appellant's case, of course, collapses, for the fetus' right to life would then be guaranteed specifically by the Amendment. . . .

The Constitution does not define "person" in so many words. Section 1 of the Fourteenth Amendment contains three references to "person.". . . . None indicates, with any assurance, that it has any possible pre-natal application.

All this, together with our observation . . . that throughout the major portion of the 19th century prevailing legal abortion practices were far freer than they are today, persuades us that the word "person," as used in the Fourteenth Amendment, does not include the unborn. . . .

. . . We need not resolve the difficult question of when life begins. When those trained in the respective disciplines of medicine, philosophy, and theology are unable to arrive at any consensus, the judiciary, at this point in the development of man's knowledge, is not in a position to speculate as to the answer. . . .

[W]e do not agree that, by adopting one theory of life, Texas may override the rights of the pregnant woman that are at stake. [The State does, however,] have an important and legitimate interest in preserving and protecting the health of the pregnant woman, whether she be a resident of the State or a nonresident who seeks medical consultation and treatment there, and [it] has still *another* important and legitimate interest in protecting the potentiality of human life. These interests are separate and distinct. Each grows in substantiality as the woman approaches term and, at a point during pregnancy, each becomes "compelling."

With respect to the State's important and legitimate interest in the health of the mother, the "compelling" point, in the light of present medical knowledge, is at approximately the end of the first trimester. This is so because of the now-established medical fact . . . that until the end of the first trimester mortality in abortion may be less than mortality in normal childbirth. It follows that, from and after this point, a State may regulate the abortion procedure to the extent that the regulation reasonably relates to the preservation and protection of maternal health. Examples of permissible state regulation in this area are requirements as to the qualifications of the person who is to perform the abortion[,] . . . the facility in which the procedure is to be performed . . . ; and the like.

This means, on the other hand, that, for the period of pregnancy prior to this "compelling" point, the attending physician, in consultation with his patient, is free to determine, without regulation by the State, that, in his medical judgment, the patient's pregnancy should be terminated. If that decision is reached, the judgment may be effectuated by an abortion free of interference by the State.

With respect to the State's important and legitimate interest in potential life, the "compelling" point is at viability. This is so because the fetus then presumably has the capability of meaningful life outside the mother's womb. State regulation protective of fetal life after viability thus has both logical and biological justifications. If the State is interested in protecting fetal life after viability, it may go so far as to proscribe abortion during that period, except when it is necessary to preserve the life or health of the mother.

Measured against these standards, [Texas law], in restricting legal abortions to those "procured or attempted by medical advice for the purpose of saving the life of the mother," sweeps too broadly. The statute makes no

distinction between abortions performed early in pregnancy and those performed later, and it limits to a single reason, "saving" the mother's life, the
legal justification for the procedure. The statute, therefore, cannot survive the
constitutional attack made upon it here. . . .

Planned Parenthood of Southeastern Pennsylvania v. Casey

505 U.S. 833 (1992)

Justice O'CONNOR, Justice KENNEDY, and Justice SOUTER announced the
judgment of the Court and delivered the opinion of the Court [with Justice
BLACKMUN and Justice STEVENS joining in certain parts of the opinion].

I

Liberty finds no refuge in a jurisprudence of doubt. Yet 19 years after our
holding that the Constitution protects a woman's right to terminate her pregnancy in its early stages, Roe v. Wade [1973], that definition of liberty is still
questioned. Joining the respondents as amicus curiae, the United States, as it
has done in five other cases in the last decade, again asks us to overrule *Roe.* . . .

At issue in these cases are five provisions of the Pennsylvania Abortion
Control Act of 1982 as amended in 1988 and 1989. . . .

After considering the fundamental constitutional questions resolved by
Roe, principles of institutional integrity, and the rule of *stare decisis*, we are led
to conclude this: the essential holding of Roe v. Wade should be retained and
once again reaffirmed.

It must be stated at the outset and with clarity that *Roe*'s essential holding,
the holding we reaffirm, has three parts. First is a recognition of the right of the
woman to choose to have an abortion before viability and to obtain it without
undue interference from the State. Before viability, the State's interests are not
strong enough to support a prohibition of abortion or the imposition of a substantial obstacle to the woman's effective right to elect the procedure. Second
is a confirmation of the State's power to restrict abortions after fetal viability,
if the law contains exceptions for pregnancies which endanger a woman's life
or health. And third is the principle that the State has legitimate interests from
the outset of the pregnancy in protecting the health of the woman and the life
of the fetus that may become a child. These principles do not contradict one
another; and we adhere to each.

II . . .

[T]he reservations any of us may have in reaffirming the central holding
of *Roe* are outweighed by the explication of individual liberty we have given
combined with the force of *stare decisis*. . . .

Stare decisis is the concept that once a legal principle has been decided, its precedent should be followed in subsequent cases. The principle is premised on the benefits of stability and reliability in legal decisionmaking, as well as other considerations listed in the *Casey* case.

. . . [F]or two decades of economic and social developments, people have organized intimate relationships and made choices that define their views of themselves and their places in society, in reliance on the availability of abortion in the event that contraception should fail. The ability of women to participate equally in the economic and social life of the Nation has been facilitated by their ability to control their reproductive lives. . . . The Constitution serves human values, and while the effect of reliance on *Roe* cannot be exactly measured, neither can the certain cost of overruling *Roe* for people who have ordered their thinking and living around that case be dismissed. . . .

IV . . .

The trimester framework no doubt was erected to ensure that the woman's right to choose not become so subordinate to the State's interest in promoting fetal life that her choice exists in theory but not in fact. We do not agree, however, that the trimester approach is necessary to accomplish this objective. A framework of this rigidity was unnecessary and in its later interpretation sometimes contradicted the State's permissible exercise of its powers.

Though the woman has a right to choose to terminate or continue her pregnancy before viability, it does not at all follow that the State is prohibited from taking steps to ensure that this choice is thoughtful and informed. Even in the earliest stages of pregnancy, the State may enact rules and regulations designed to encourage her to know that there are philosophic and social arguments of great weight that can be brought to bear in favor of continuing the pregnancy to full term and that there are procedures and institutions to allow adoption of unwanted children as well as a certain degree of state assistance if the mother chooses to raise the child herself. "[T]he Constitution does not forbid a State or city, pursuant to democratic processes, from expressing a preference for 'normal childbirth.'" . . . It follows that States are free to enact laws to provide a reasonable framework for a woman to make a decision that has such profound and lasting meaning. This, too, we find consistent with *Roe*'s central premises, and indeed the inevitable consequence of our holding that the State has an interest in protecting the life of the unborn. . . .

Numerous forms of state regulation might have the incidental effect of increasing the cost or decreasing the availability of medical care, whether for abortion or any other medical procedure. The fact that a law which serves a valid purpose, one not designed to strike at the right itself, has the incidental effect of making it more difficult or more expensive to procure an abortion cannot be enough to invalidate it. Only where state regulation imposes an undue burden on a woman's ability to make this decision does the power of the State reach into the heart of the liberty protected by the Due Process Clause. . . .

A finding of an undue burden is a shorthand for the conclusion that a state regulation has the purpose or effect of placing a substantial obstacle in the path of a woman seeking an abortion of a nonviable fetus. A statute with this purpose is invalid because the means chosen by the State to further the interest in potential life must be calculated to inform the woman's free choice, not hinder it. . . .

Some guiding principles should emerge. What is at stake is the woman's right to make the ultimate decision, not a right to be insulated from all others in doing so. Regulations which do no more than create a structural mechanism by which the State, or the parent or guardian of a minor, may express profound respect for the life of the unborn are permitted, if they are not a substantial obstacle to the woman's exercise of the right to choose. . . . Unless it has that effect on her right of choice, a state measure designed to persuade her to choose childbirth over abortion will be upheld if reasonably related to that goal. Regulations designed to foster the health of a woman seeking an abortion are valid if they do not constitute an undue burden. . . .

These principles control our assessment of the Pennsylvania statute, and we now turn to the issue of the validity of its challenged provisions.

V . . .

Except in a medical emergency, the statute requires that at least 24 hours before performing an abortion a physician inform the woman of the nature of the procedure, the health risks of the abortion and of childbirth, and the "probable gestational age of the unborn child." The physician or a qualified nonphysician must inform the woman of the availability of printed materials published by the State describing the fetus and providing information about medical assistance for childbirth, information about child support from the father, and a list of agencies which provide adoption and other services as alternatives to abortion. An abortion may not be performed unless the woman certifies in writing that she has been informed of the availability of these printed materials and has been provided them if she chooses to view them. . . .

To the extent [two prior Supreme Court cases] find a constitutional violation when the government requires, as it does here, the giving of truthful, nonmisleading information about the nature of the procedure, the attendant health risks and those of childbirth, and the "probable gestational age" of the fetus, those cases go too far, are inconsistent with *Roe*'s acknowledgment of an important interest in potential life, and are overruled. . . . It cannot be questioned that psychological well-being is a facet of health. Nor can it be doubted that most women considering an abortion would deem the impact on the fetus relevant, if not dispositive, to the decision. In attempting to ensure that a woman apprehend the full consequences of her decision, the State furthers the legitimate purpose of reducing the risk that a woman may elect an abortion,

602   Chapter 5. Autonomy

only to discover later, with devastating psychological consequences, that her decision was not fully informed. If the information the State requires to be made available to the woman is truthful and not misleading, the requirement may be permissible.

We also see no reason why the State may not require doctors to inform a woman seeking an abortion of the availability of materials relating to the consequences to the fetus, even when those consequences have no direct relation to her health. An example illustrates the point. We would think it constitutional for the State to require that in order for there to be informed consent to a kidney transplant operation the recipient must be supplied with information about risks to the donor as well as risks to himself or herself. . . .

The idea that important decisions will be more informed and deliberate if they follow some period of reflection does not strike us as unreasonable, particularly where the statute directs that important information become part of the background of the decision. The statute, as construed by the Court of Appeals, permits avoidance of the waiting period in the event of a medical emergency and the record evidence shows that in the vast majority of cases, a 24-hour delay does not create any appreciable health risk. In theory, at least, the waiting period is a reasonable measure to implement the State's interest in protecting the life of the unborn, a measure that does not amount to an undue burden.

Whether the mandatory 24-hour waiting period is nonetheless invalid because in practice it is a substantial obstacle to a woman's choice to terminate her pregnancy is a closer question. The findings of fact by the District Court indicate that because of the distances many women must travel to reach an abortion provider, the practical effect will often be a delay of much more than a day because the waiting period requires that a woman seeking an abortion make at least two visits to the doctor. The District Court also found that in many instances this will increase the exposure of women seeking abortions to "the harassment and hostility of anti-abortion protestors demonstrating outside a clinic." . . . As a result, the District Court found that for those women who have the fewest financial resources, those who must travel long distances, and those who have difficulty explaining their whereabouts to husbands, employers, or others, the 24-hour waiting period will be "particularly burdensome."

These findings are troubling in some respects, but they do not demonstrate that the waiting period constitutes an undue burden. We do not doubt that, as the District Court held, the waiting period has the effect of "increasing the cost and risk of delay of abortions," but the District Court did not conclude that the increased costs and potential delays amount to substantial obstacles. . . .

[One provision] of Pennsylvania's abortion law provides, except in cases of medical emergency, that no physician shall perform an abortion on a married woman without receiving a signed statement from the woman that she has notified her spouse that she is about to undergo an abortion. The woman has the option of providing an alternative signed statement certifying that her husband is not the man who impregnated her; that her husband could not be located; that the pregnancy is the result of spousal sexual assault which she has reported; or that the woman believes that notifying her husband will cause him or someone else to inflict bodily injury upon her. A physician who performs an abortion on a married woman without receiving the appropriate signed statement will have his or her license revoked, and is liable to the husband for damages.

[The District Court found that the reasons some women do not consult their husbands about the decision to obtain an abortion include domestic violence, sexual abuse, rape, and sexual mutilation.] . . .

[T]he District Court's findings reinforce what common sense would suggest. In well-functioning marriages, spouses discuss important intimate decisions such as whether to bear a child. But there are millions of women in this country who are the victims of regular physical and psychological abuse at the hands of their husbands. Should these women become pregnant, they may have very good reasons for not wishing to inform their husbands of their decision to obtain an abortion. Many may have justifiable fears of physical abuse, but may be no less fearful of the consequences of reporting prior abuse to the Commonwealth of Pennsylvania. Many may have a reasonable fear that notifying their husbands will provoke further instances of child abuse; these women are not exempt from [the] notification requirement. Many may fear devastating forms of psychological abuse from their husbands, including verbal harassment, threats of future violence, the destruction of possessions, physical confinement to the home, the withdrawal of financial support, or the disclosure of the abortion to family and friends. These methods of psychological abuse may act as even more of a deterrent to notification than the possibility of physical violence, but women who are the victims of the abuse are not exempt from [the] notification requirement. And many women who are pregnant as a result of sexual assaults by their husbands will be unable to avail themselves of the exception for spousal sexual assault, because the exception requires that the woman have notified law enforcement authorities within 90 days of the assault, and her husband will be notified of her report once an investigation begins. If anything in this field is certain, it is that victims of spousal sexual assault are extremely reluctant to report the abuse to the government; hence, a great many spousal rape victims will not be exempt from the notification requirement. . . .

The spousal notification requirement is thus likely to prevent a significant number of women from obtaining an abortion. It does not merely make abortions a little more difficult or expensive to obtain; for many women, it will impose a substantial obstacle. We must not blind ourselves to the fact that the significant number of women who fear for their safety and the safety of their children are likely to be deterred from procuring an abortion as surely as if the Commonwealth had outlawed abortion in all cases. . . .

This conclusion is in no way inconsistent with our decisions upholding parental notification or consent requirements. . . . Those enactments, and our judgment that they are constitutional, are based on the quite reasonable assumption that minors will benefit from consultation with their parents and that children will often not realize that their parents have their best interests at heart. We cannot adopt a parallel assumption about adult women.

We recognize that a husband has a "deep and proper concern and interest . . . in his wife's pregnancy and in the growth and development of the fetus she is carrying." . . . With regard to the children he has fathered and raised, the Court has recognized his "cognizable and substantial" interest in their custody. . . . If this case concerned a State's ability to require the mother to notify the father before taking some action with respect to a living child raised by both, therefore, it would be reasonable to conclude as a general matter that the father's interest in the welfare of the child and the mother's interest are equal.

Before birth, however, the issue takes on a very different cast. It is an inescapable biological fact that state regulation with respect to the child a woman is carrying will have a far greater impact on the mother's liberty than on the father's. The effect of state regulation on a woman's protected liberty is doubly deserving of scrutiny in such a case, as the State has touched not only upon the private sphere of the family but upon the very bodily integrity of the pregnant woman. . . . The Court has held that "when the wife and the husband disagree on this decision, the view of only one of the two marriage partners can prevail. Inasmuch as it is the woman who physically bears the child and who is the more directly and immediately affected by the pregnancy, as between the two, the balance weighs in her favor." . . .

Women do not lose their constitutionally protected liberty when they marry. The Constitution protects all individuals, male or female, married or unmarried, from the abuse of governmental power, even where that power is employed for the supposed benefit of a member of the individual's family. These considerations confirm our conclusion that [the spousal notification provision] is invalid.

[The Court also upheld a provision requiring consent to an abortion, except in a medical emergency, for an unemancipated minor under 18, unless the court determines that that she is mature and capable of giving informed consent, or that an abortion would be in her best interests.]

Justice BLACKMUN, concurring in part, concurring in the judgment in part, and dissenting in part. . . .

State restrictions on abortion violate a woman's right of privacy. . . .

A State's restrictions on a woman's right to terminate her pregnancy also implicate constitutional guarantees of gender equality. State restrictions on abortion compel women to continue pregnancies they otherwise might terminate. By restricting the right to terminate pregnancies, the State conscripts women's bodies into its service, forcing women to continue their pregnancies, suffer the pains of childbirth, and in most instances, provide years of maternal care. The State does not compensate women for their services; instead, it assumes that they owe this duty as a matter of course. This assumption — that women can simply be forced to accept the "natural" status and incidents of motherhood—appears to rest upon a conception of women's role that has triggered the protection of the Equal Protection Clause. See, e.g., Mississippi Univ. for Women v. Hogan [1982]; Craig v. Boren [1976]. The joint opinion recognizes that these assumptions about women's place in society "are no longer consistent with our understanding of the family, the individual, or the Constitution." . . .

Justice SCALIA, with whom THE CHIEF JUSTICE, Justice WHITE, and Justice THOMAS join, concurring in the judgment in part and dissenting in part. . . .

The States may, if they wish, permit abortion-on-demand, but the Constitution does not require them to do so. The permissibility of abortion, and the limitations upon it, are to be resolved like most important questions in our democracy: by citizens trying to persuade one another and then voting. . . .

That is, quite simply, the issue in this case: not whether the power of a woman to abort her unborn child is a "liberty" in the absolute sense; or even whether it is a liberty of great importance to many women. Of course it is both. The issue is whether it is a liberty protected by the Constitution of the United States. I am sure it is not. I reach that conclusion not because of anything so exalted as my views concerning the "concept of existence, of meaning, of the universe, and of the mystery of human life." . . . Rather, I reach it for the same reason I reach the conclusion that bigamy is not constitutionally protected—because of two simple facts: (1) the Constitution says absolutely nothing about it, and (2) the longstanding traditions of American society have permitted it to be legally proscribed. . . .

In truth, I am as distressed as the Court is . . . about the "political pressure" directed to the Court: the marches, the mail, the protests aimed at inducing us to change our opinions. How upsetting it is, that so many of our citizens (good people, not lawless ones, on both sides of this abortion issue, and on various sides of other issues as well) think that we Justices should properly take into account their views, as though we were engaged not in ascertaining an objective law but in determining some kind of social consensus. The Court would profit, I think, from giving less attention to the fact of this distressing phenomenon, and more attention to the *cause* of it. That cause permeates today's opinion: a new mode of constitutional adjudication that relies not upon text and traditional practice to determine the law, but upon what the Court calls "reasoned judgment," . . . which turns out to be nothing but philosophical predilection and moral intuition. . . .

As long as this Court thought (and the people thought) that we Justices were doing essentially lawyers' work up here—reading text and discerning our society's traditional understanding of that text—the public pretty much left us alone. Texts and traditions are facts to study, not convictions to demonstrate about. But if in reality our process of constitutional adjudication consists primarily of making *value judgments* . . . then a free and intelligent people's attitude towards us can be expected to be (*ought* to be) quite different. The people know that their value judgments are quite as good as those taught in any law school—maybe better. If, indeed, the "liberties" protected by the Constitution are, as the Court says, undefined and unbounded, than the people *should* demonstrate, to protest that we do not implement their values instead of *ours*. . . .

We should get out of this area, where we have no right to be, and where we do neither ourselves nor the country any good by remaining.

Reva Siegel, Reasoning from the Body: A Historical Perspective on Abortion Regulation and Questions of Equal Protection

44 Stan. L. Rev. 261, 267, 361-363 (1992)

Social forces play a powerful part in shaping the process of reproduction. Social forces define the circumstances under which a woman conceives a child, including how voluntary her participation in intercourse may be. Social forces determine whether a woman has access to methods of preventing and terminating a pregnancy, and whether it is acceptable for her to use them. Social forces determine the quality of health care available to a woman during pregnancy, and they determine whether a pregnant woman will be able to support herself throughout the term of gestation, or instead will be forced to depend on others for support. Social relations determine who cares for a child once it is born, and what resources, rewards, and penalties attend the work of gestating and nurturing human life. . . .

[T]oday, as in the nineteenth century, legislators enacting restrictions on abortion may act from judgments about the sexual and maternal conduct of the women they are regulating, and not merely from a concern about the welfare of the unborn. Legislators may condemn abortion because they assume that any pregnant woman who does not wish to be pregnant has committed some sexual indiscretion properly punishable by compelling pregnancy itself. Popular support for excusing women who are victims of rape or incest from the proscriptions of criminal abortion laws demonstrates that attitudes about abortion do indeed rest on normative judgments about women's sexual conduct. Opinion polls like Louisiana's suggest that the public assumes a woman can be coerced into continuing a pregnancy because the pregnancy is her sexual "fault."

Along distinct, but related lines, legislators may view abortion as repellant because it betrays a lack of maternal solicitude in women, or otherwise violates expectations of appropriately nurturing female conduct. If legislators assume that women are "child-rearers," they will take for granted the work women give to motherhood and ignore what it takes from them, and so will view women's efforts to avoid some two decades of life-consuming work as an act of casual expedience or unseemly egoism. Thus, they will condemn women for seeking abortion "on demand," or as a mere "convenience," judging women to be unnaturally egocentric because they do not give their lives over to the work of bearing and nurturing children—that is, because they fail to act like mothers, like normal women should. . . .

Even if state actors have adopted restrictions on abortion out of a genuine and single-minded concern for the welfare of the unborn, archaic or stereotypical assumptions about women may nonetheless deeply bias their deliberations, making fetal life-saving by compelled pregnancy seem reasonable where otherwise it would not. A legislature's attitudes about women may cause it to underestimate or disregard the burdens it would impose on them by compelling pregnancy. A latent assumption that motherhood is women's "normal" condition can easily render state actors oblivious to the life-consuming consequences of forcing women to perform its work—just as a latent assumption that motherhood is women's "deserved" condition will cause indifference to the burdens the legislation will inflict. In short, a legislature may not decide that it is reasonable to save unborn life by compelling pregnancy, "but for" the archaic or stereotypic assumptions about women it holds. If restrictions on abortion are adopted in these circumstances, they offend constitutional guarantees of equal protection. . . .

[S]tate action restricting abortion injures women. . . . First, restrictions on abortion do not merely force women to bear children; powerful gender norms in this society ensure that almost all women who are forced to bear children will raise them as well, a result that legislatures adopting restrictions on abortion both desire and expect. Second, the work legislatures would force women to perform defines women's social status along predictable, gender-delineated lines. Women who perform the socially essential labor of bearing and rearing children face diverse forms of stigmatization and injury, none of which is ordained by the physiology of gestation, and all of which is the doing of the society that would force women to bear children. Third, when states adopt restrictions on abortion, they compel women to become mothers, while in no respect altering the conditions that make the institution of motherhood a principal cause of women's subordinate social status. When the gender-based impositions of abortion-restrictive regulation are considered in light of the forms of gender bias that may animate it, it is clear abortion-restrictive regulation is and remains caste legislation which subordinates women in ways that offend constitutional guarantees of equal protection. . . .

Gonzales v. Carhart

550 U.S. 124 (2007)

Justice KENNEDY delivered the opinion of the Court.

These cases require us to consider the validity of the Partial-Birth Abortion Ban Act of 2003 (Act), a federal statute regulating abortion procedures. [The

Act is more specific and precise than the Act addressed in Stenberg v. Carhart [2000], which the court found to be unconstitutional.] . . .

The operative provisions of the Act provide in relevant part:

(a) Any physician who, in or affecting interstate or foreign commerce, knowingly performs a partial-birth abortion and thereby kills a human fetus shall be fined under this title or imprisoned not more than 2 years, or both. This subsection does not apply to a partial-birth abortion that is necessary to save the life of a mother whose life is endangered by a physical disorder, physical illness, or physical injury, including a life-endangering physical condition caused by or arising from the pregnancy itself. This subsection takes effect 1 day after the enactment.

(b) As used in this section —

(1) the term 'partial-birth abortion' means an abortion in which the person performing the abortion —

(A) deliberately and intentionally vaginally delivers a living fetus until, in the case of a head-first presentation, the entire fetal head is outside the body of the mother, or, in the case of breech presentation, any part of the fetal trunk past the navel is outside the body of the mother, for the purpose of performing an overt act that the person knows will kill the partially delivered living fetus; and

(B) performs the overt act, other than completion of delivery, that kills the partially delivered living fetus. . . .

[The District Courts in these two cases each found the Act to be unconstitutional, one because it lacked an exception where necessary for the health of the mother and because it covered not merely intact D&E but also certain other D&Es, and the other because it imposed an undue burden on a woman's ability to choose a second-trimester abortion, was unconstitutionally vague, and lacked a health exception. The decisions were upheld on appeal.] . . .

The Act proscribes a method of abortion in which a fetus is killed just inches before completion of the birth process. Congress stated as follows: "Implicitly approving such a brutal and inhumane procedure by choosing not to prohibit it will further coarsen society to the humanity of not only newborns, but all vulnerable and innocent human life, making it increasingly difficult to protect such life." . . .

The Act's ban on abortions that involve partial delivery of a living fetus furthers the Government's objectives. No one would dispute that, for many, D&E is a procedure itself laden with the power to devalue human life. . . .

Respect for human life finds an ultimate expression in the bond of love the mother has for her child. The Act recognizes this reality as well. Whether to have an abortion requires a difficult and painful moral decision. . . . While we find no reliable data to measure the phenomenon, it seems unexceptionable to conclude some women come to regret their choice to abort the infant life they once created and sustained. . . . Severe depression and loss of esteem can follow. . . .

In a decision so fraught with emotional consequence some doctors may prefer not to disclose precise details of the means that will be used, confining themselves to the required statement of risks the procedure entails. From one standpoint this ought not to be surprising. Any number of patients facing imminent surgical procedures would prefer not to hear all details, lest the usual anxiety preceding invasive medical procedures become the more intense. This is likely the case with the abortion procedures here in issue. . . .

It is, however, precisely this lack of information concerning the way in which the fetus will be killed that is of legitimate concern to the State. . . . The State has an interest in ensuring so grave a choice is well informed. It is self-evident that a mother who comes to regret her choice to abort must struggle with grief more anguished and sorrow more profound when she learns, only after the event, what she once did not know: that she allowed a doctor to pierce the skull and vacuum the fast-developing brain of her unborn child, a child assuming the human form.

It is a reasonable inference that a necessary effect of the regulation and the knowledge it conveys will be to encourage some women to carry the infant to full term, thus reducing the absolute number of late-term abortions. The medical profession, furthermore, may find different and less shocking methods to abort the fetus in the second trimester, thereby accommodating legislative demand. The State's interest in respect for life is advanced by the dialogue that better informs the political and legal systems, the medical profession, expectant mothers, and society as a whole of the consequences that follow from a decision to elect a late-term abortion.

It is objected that the standard D&E is in some respects as brutal, if not more, than the intact D&E, so that the legislation accomplishes little. What we have already said, however, shows ample justification for the regulation. Partial-birth abortion, as defined by the Act, differs from a standard D&E because the former occurs when the fetus is partially outside the mother to the point of one of the Act's anatomical landmarks. It was reasonable for Congress to think that partial-birth abortion, more than standard D&E, "undermines the public's perception of the appropriate role of a physician during the delivery process, and perverts a process during which life is brought into the world." . . .

The Act's furtherance of legitimate government interests bears upon, but does not resolve, the next question: whether the Act has the effect of imposing an unconstitutional burden on the abortion right because it does not allow use of the barred procedure where " 'necessary, in appropriate medical judgment, for [the] preservation of the . . . health of the mother.'" . . . The prohibition in the Act would be unconstitutional, under precedents we here assume to be controlling, if it "subject[ed] [women] to significant health risks." . . . The evidence presented in the trial courts and before Congress demonstrates both sides have medical support for their position.

Respondents presented evidence that intact D&E may be the safest method of abortion. . . . Respondents, in addition, proffered evidence that intact D&E

was safer for women with certain medical conditions or women with fetuses that had certain anomalies. . . .

The Court has given state and federal legislatures wide discretion to pass legislation in areas where there is medical and scientific uncertainty. . . . Considerations of marginal safety, including the balance of risks, are within the legislative competence when the regulation is rational and in pursuit of legitimate ends. When standard medical options are available, mere convenience does not suffice to displace them; and if some procedures have different risks than others, it does not follow that the State is altogether barred from imposing reasonable regulations. The Act is not invalid on its face where there is uncertainty over whether the barred procedure is ever necessary to preserve a woman's health, given the availability of other abortion procedures that are considered to be safe alternatives. . . .

[T]he judgments of the Courts of Appeals are reversed.

Justice GINSBURG, with whom Justice STEVENS, Justice SOUTER, and Justice BREYER join, dissenting. . . .

Seven years ago, in Stenberg v. Carhart, . . . the Court invalidated a Nebraska statute criminalizing the performance of a medical procedure that, in the political arena, has been dubbed "partial-birth abortion." With fidelity to the Roe-Casey line of precedent, the Court held the Nebraska statute unconstitutional in part because it lacked the requisite protection for the preservation of a woman's health.

Today's decision is alarming. It refuses to take Casey and Stenberg seriously. It tolerates, indeed applauds, federal intervention to ban nationwide a procedure found necessary and proper in certain cases by the American College of Obstetricians and Gynecologists (ACOG). It blurs the line, firmly drawn in Casey, between previability and postviability abortions. And, for the first time since Roe, the Court blesses a prohibition with no exception safeguarding a woman's health. . . .

I

As Casey comprehended, at stake in cases challenging abortion restrictions is a woman's "control over her [own] destiny." . . . "There was a time, not so long ago," when women were "regarded as the center of home and family life, with attendant special responsibilities that precluded full and independent legal status under the Constitution." . . . Those views, this Court made clear in Casey, "are no longer consistent with our understanding of the family, the individual, or the Constitution." . . . Women, it is now acknowledged, have the talent, capacity, and right "to participate equally in the economic and social life of the Nation." Their ability to realize their full potential, the Court recognized, is intimately connected to "their ability to control their reproductive lives." . . . Thus, legal challenges to undue restrictions on abortion procedures do not seek to vindicate some generalized notion of privacy; rather, they center on a woman's autonomy to determine her life's course, and thus to enjoy equal citizenship stature. . . .

In keeping with this comprehension of the right to reproductive choice, the Court has consistently required that laws regulating abortion, at any stage of pregnancy and in all cases, safeguard a woman's health. . . .

In *Stenberg*, we expressly held that a statute banning intact D&E was unconstitutional in part because it lacked a health exception. . . . We noted that there existed a "division of medical opinion" about the relative safety of intact D&E, . . . but we made clear that as long as "substantial medical authority supports the proposition that banning a particular abortion procedure could endanger women's health," a health exception is required. . . .

In 2003, a few years after our ruling in *Stenberg*, Congress passed the Partial-Birth Abortion Ban Act—without an exception for women's health. . . . The congressional findings on which the Partial-Birth Abortion Ban Act rests do not withstand inspection, as the lower courts have determined and this Court is obliged to concede. . . .

Many of the Act's recitations are incorrect. . . . For example, Congress determined that no medical schools provide instruction on intact D&E. . . . But in fact, numerous leading medical schools teach the procedure. . . .

More important, Congress claimed there was a medical consensus that the banned procedure is never necessary. . . . But the evidence "very clearly demonstrate[d] the opposite." . . .

Similarly, Congress found that "[t]here is no credible medical evidence that partial-birth abortions are safe or are safer than other abortion procedures." . . . But the congressional record includes letters from numerous individual physicians stating that pregnant women's health would be jeopardized under the Act, as well as statements from nine professional associations, including ACOG, the American Public Health Association, and the California Medical Association, attesting that intact D&E carries meaningful safety advantages over other methods. . . . No comparable medical groups supported the ban. In fact, "all of the government's own witnesses disagreed with many of the specific congressional findings."

In contrast to Congress, the District Courts made findings after full trials at which all parties had the opportunity to present their best evidence. The courts had the benefit of "much more extensive medical and scientific evidence . . . concerning the safety and necessity of intact D&Es." . . .

During the District Court trials, "numerous" "extraordinarily accomplished" and "very experienced" medical experts explained that, in certain circumstances and for certain women, intact D&E is safer than alternative procedures and necessary to protect women's health. . . .

According to the expert testimony plaintiffs introduced, the safety advantages of intact D&E are marked for women with certain medical conditions, for example, uterine scarring, bleeding disorders, heart disease, or compromised immune systems. . . . Further, plaintiffs' experts testified that intact D&E is significantly safer for women with certain pregnancy-related conditions, such as placenta previa and accreta, and for women carrying fetuses with certain abnormalities, such as severe hydrocephalus. . . .

Intact D&E, plaintiffs' experts explained, provides safety benefits over D&E by dismemberment for several reasons: *First,* intact D&E minimizes the number of times a physician must insert instruments through the cervix and into the uterus, and thereby reduces the risk of trauma to, and perforation of, the cervix and uterus—the most serious complication associated with nonintact D&E. . . . *Second,* removing the fetus intact, instead of dismembering it *in utero,* decreases the likelihood that fetal tissue will be retained in the uterus, a condition that can cause infection, hemorrhage, and infertility. . . . *Third,* intact D&E diminishes the chances of exposing the patient's tissues to sharp bony fragments sometimes resulting from dismemberment of the fetus. . . . *Fourth,* intact D&E takes less operating time than D&E by dismemberment, and thus may reduce bleeding, the risk of infection, and complications relating to anesthesia. . . .

Today's opinion supplies no reason to reject [the District Courts'] findings. Nevertheless, despite the District Courts' appraisal of the weight of the evidence, and in undisguised conflict with *Stenberg,* the Court asserts that the Partial-Birth Abortion Ban Act can survive "when . . . medical uncertainty persists." . . . This assertion is bewildering. Not only does it defy the Court's longstanding precedent affirming the necessity of a health exception, with no carve-out for circumstances of medical uncertainty, . . . it gives short shrift to the records before us, carefully canvassed by the District Courts. . . .

The law saves not a single fetus from destruction, for it targets only a *method* of performing abortion. . . . And surely the statute was not designed to protect the lives or health of pregnant women. . . . In short, the Court upholds a law that, while doing nothing to "preserv[e] . . . fetal life," . . . bars a woman from choosing intact D&E although her doctor "reasonably believes [that procedure] will best protect [her]." . . .

As another reason for upholding the ban, the Court emphasizes that the Act does not proscribe the nonintact D&E procedure. . . . But why not, one might ask. Nonintact D&E could equally be characterized as "brutal," . . . involving as it does "tear[ing] [a fetus] apart" and "ripp[ing] off" its limbs. . . . "[T]he notion that either of these two equally gruesome procedures . . . is more akin to infanticide than the other, or that the State furthers any legitimate interest by banning one but not the other, is simply irrational." . . .

Delivery of an intact, albeit nonviable, fetus warrants special condemnation, the Court maintains, because a fetus that is not dismembered resembles an infant. . . . But so, too, does a fetus delivered intact after it is terminated by injection a day or two before the surgical evacuation, . . . a fetus delivered through medical induction or cesarean. . . . Yet, the availability of those procedures—along with D&E by dismemberment—the Court says, saves the ban on intact D&E from a declaration of unconstitutionality. . . . Never mind that the procedures deemed acceptable might put a woman's health at greater risk. . . .

Ultimately, the Court admits that "moral concerns" are at work, concerns that could yield prohibitions on any abortion. . . . Notably, the concerns expressed are untethered to any ground genuinely serving the Government's interest in preserving life. By allowing such concerns to carry the day and case, overriding fundamental rights, the Court dishonors our precedent. . . .

Revealing in this regard, the Court invokes an antiabortion shibboleth for which it concededly has no reliable evidence: Women who have abortions come to regret their choices, and consequently suffer from "[s]evere depression and loss of esteem." . . . Because of women's fragile emotional state and because of the "bond of love the mother has for her child," the Court worries, doctors may withhold information about the nature of the intact D&E procedure. . . . The solution the Court approves, then, is *not* to require doctors to inform women, accurately and adequately, of the different procedures and their attendant risks. . . . Instead, the Court deprives women of the right to make an autonomous choice, even at the expense of their safety.

This way of thinking reflects ancient notions about women's place in the family and under the Constitution—ideas that have long since been discredited. . . .

One wonders how long a line that saves no fetus from destruction will hold in face of the Court's "moral concerns." . . . The Court's hostility to the right *Roe* and *Casey* secured is not concealed. Throughout, the opinion refers to obstetrician-gynecologists and surgeons who perform abortions not by the titles of their medical specialties, but by the pejorative label "abortion doctor." . . . A fetus is described as an "unborn child," and as a "baby," . . . ; second-trimester, previability abortions are referred to as "late-term," . . . ; and the reasoned medical judgments of highly trained doctors are dismissed as "preferences" motivated by "mere convenience." . . . Instead of the heightened scrutiny we have previously applied, the Court determines that a "rational" ground is enough to uphold the Act. . . . And, most troubling, *Casey*'s principles, confirming the continuing vitality of "the essential holding of *Roe*," are merely "assume[d]" for the moment, . . . rather than "retained" or "reaffirmed." . . .

. . . In candor, the Act, and the Court's defense of it, cannot be understood as anything other than an effort to chip away at a right declared again and again by this Court—and with increasing comprehension of its centrality to women's lives. . . .

Jeannie Suk, The Trajectory of Trauma: Bodies and Minds of Abortion Discourse

110 Colum. L. Rev. 1193-1201 (2010)

The idea of women traumatized by abortion has recently acquired a constitutional foothold. . . . Justice Kennedy, writing for the Court, said it was "unexceptionable to conclude" that some women who have abortions later feel "regret" resulting in "severe depression and loss of esteem." Then he noted that some who undergo the late-term procedure at issue may be unaware of its details (piercing and vacuuming the skull of the fetus before removing its intact body) at the time. Finally, he thought it was "self-evident that a mother who comes to regret her choice to abort must suffer grief more anguished and sorrow more profound when she learns, only after the event, what she once did not know. . . .

Justice Ginsburg's dissent . . . called the Court's reference to abortion regret "an antiabortion shibboleth" that assumes "women's fragile emotional state." Though she acknowledged that "for most women, abortion is a painfully difficult decision," she pointedly suggested that the weight of scientific authority resisted "post-abortion syndrome"—purportedly a kind of post-traumatic stress disorder. The court's reasoning, she said, "reflects ancient notions about women's place in the family and under the Constitution—ideas that have long since been discredited."

The strong rejoinder to Justice Kennedy's salvo presents this battle of ideas as having a clear, rightful winner: On one side are modern constitutional ideals of right-thinking people heeding scientific evidence; on the other side are retrograde stereotypes supported by ideologically tainted junk science. The supposition is that defenders of abortion rights value the autonomy of women, while those undermining the right reveal latent sexism in depicting women as regretful beings who must be protected from themselves. There is perhaps an understandable desire, in an ideological war, to discredit a line of reasoning that threatens to gain ground. Critics of the notion of women suffering after abortion thus emphasize the connection between today's concern for such emotional pain and age-old sexism. . . .

I argue, however, that rather that representing such a departure, . . . [the Kennedy reasoning] continues a legal discourse of trauma around women's bodies and sexuality. This intellectual context, which has been all but ignored, gives important meaning to the present discourse of women's psychological pain in our legal system. . . .

Variations now abound in legal contexts in which we routinely see claims of psychological disorder arising from traumatic experiences. Battered Woman Syndrome and Rape Trauma Syndrome, for example, have gained acceptance as traumatic disorders considered relevant for some legal purposes. Trauma resulting from violation of the body has been a focus in feminist legal reform, particularly in domestic violence, rape, sex abuse, and sexual harassment. The concern for abortion trauma is a recognizable outgrowth of legal thinking of psychological trauma as a core of women's experience. . . .

Abortion trauma is a notion with which those committed to abortion rights are deeply uncomfortable. To some, the idea that women might suffer from psychological harm that can trace to their abortions may be more alarming than the argument that abortion is murder. If the idea is indeed threatening, it is not merely because it revisits old sexism that we all know to be outmoded.

Rather it is because it resonates so profoundly with now common legal sensibilities of more recent vintage: feminist visions of women with bodies violated and minds traumatized.

Notes

1. Grounding the Abortion Right. The reasoning of *Roe* has probably received more criticism than any other single example of constitutional jurisprudence. Critics have pointed to the lack of a constitutional basis for the right,[290] as well as the failure of *Roe*'s trimester system to fully acknowledge the state's interest in protecting unborn life.[291] Some scholars support *Roe* but believe, as exemplified in the excerpt by Reva Siegel, that an equality framework would better capture the important social dimensions of women's reproductive choice. These scholars also underscore the meaninglessness of a privacy right for women who have insufficient social support and resources to exercise it.[292]

The equality principle has become the theoretical foundation for abortion preferred by many feminists, including Justice Ginsburg before she joined the Court. Equality arguments figured in Justice Blackmun's concurring opinion in *Casey*, but they have not been accepted by the Court. Is Siegel's analysis a sound application of equality analysis? Formal or substantive equality? Is nonsubordination theory more apt? Or can a woman's right to choose an abortion rest entirely on the equality principle?

Is it necessary to choose between the privacy and equality rationales? One scholar reasons that both analyses are necessary; equality analysis is necessary to understand that the right to make reproductive decisions is fundamentally a problem of unequal power, but the end goal remains autonomous decision-making.[293] Is this right? As a practical matter, does it matter whether the right to have an abortion is based on privacy or equality?

Marjorie M. Shultz worries that the "uncritical embrace of extreme autonomy rhetoric and *exclusively* woman-regarding positions . . . undermine[s] our persuasiveness, [renders] us vulnerable on grounds of principle, and [damages] our aspirations for a humane and responsible world." Shultz also raises concerns that, on principle, an unrestricted autonomy-based right would affect other legal principles in an undesirable way, such as undercutting the responsibility of doctors and employers to take reasonable measures to protect the safety of a fetus.[294] Linguist and political analyst George Lakoff argues that proponents of women's rights should avoid terms like choice, which are too consumer-oriented, and even abortion, which sounds negative. They should instead focus on personal freedom from government interference and the lack of support for contraception and sex education.[295] William Saletan goes further: "What we need is an explicit pro-choice war on the abortion rate." Activists should concede that abortion is wrong but focus on reducing its necessity while avoiding dragging the criminal law into "personal tragedies."[296]

By contrast, commentators like Linda McClain caution against autonomy-based theories for the abortion right, whether strategic or principled, on the ground that such theories will trigger too much second-guessing of women's decisions, without adequate societal or governmental commitment to family support and reproductive health. It will also leave women vulnerable to charges of irresponsibility. Even the most compelling cases of constraint will still be found by some abortion opponents to be instances of mere "convenience."[297]

Groups such as Feminists for Life of America (FFL), who base their opposition to the woman's right to an abortion on the principles of relational feminism, illustrate McClain's argument. FFL rejects the argument that abortion rights are necessary for women's equality and opposes abortion as a "quick fix," as oppressive of women, and as discriminatory against unborn children whom it is in women's interests to protect. The group's "Women Deserve Better" campaign has argued that most women are coerced into abortions because of a lack of financial and emotional support.[298] The Justice Foundation's Operation Outcry campaign similarly collects affidavits from women who regret their abortion and features them on satellite networks reaching 10 million homes.[299] How might Siegel respond to these approaches? How would Catharine MacKinnon respond? How do you?

In explaining their decision to have an abortion, three-fourths of surveyed women say they cannot afford a child; three-fourths say that having a baby would interfere with work, school or the ability to care for dependents; and half say they do not want to be a single parent or are having problems with their husband or partner.[300] What legal and policy implications do you draw from those reasons?

2. *Stare Decisis*, Reliance, and Autonomy.   Part of *Casey*'s rationale for preserving *Roe* is that women have come to rely upon the right to choose abortion. In what sense is this true? One possibility is that they are accustomed to relying on abortion as a backup if they fail to use other forms of contraception or those methods fail. Can this be what the three Justices of the lead opinion in *Casey* have in mind? An alternative view is that women have come to see themselves as having some control and autonomy in personal decisionmaking, which *Roe* has come to symbolize, and it is this autonomy that enables them to plan their lives in long-range terms. Is *this* what the plurality of Justices had in mind? If so, this reasoning is specifically rejected by Justice Rehnquist in his *Casey* dissent, which is joined by four other Justices:

> The joint opinion . . . turns to what can only be described as an unconventional—and unconvincing—notion of reliance, a view based on the surmise that the availability of abortion since *Roe* has led to "two decades of economic and social developments that would be undercut if the error of *Roe* were recognized." . . . The joint opinion's assertion of this fact is undeveloped and totally conclusory. In fact, one can not be sure to what economic and social developments the opinion is referring. Surely it is dubious to suggest that women have reached their "places in society" in reliance upon *Roe*, rather than as a result of their determination to obtain higher education and

compete with men in the job market, and of society's increasing recognition of their ability to fill positions that were previously thought to be reserved only for men.[301]

What different assumptions about individual autonomy and choice do the authors of the dissent and the plurality opinion make?

Abortion is fairly widely accepted, at least in some circumstances. In a 2012 Quinnipiac University poll, 64 percent of respondents said that they agree with Roe v. Wade, and only 14 percent say that abortion should be illegal in all cases—numbers that have remained relatively constant since 2005.[302] What are the implications of these statistics? Do they support the Court's reliance rationale in *Casey*? Should the abortion issue be decided by popular vote?

3. "Informed Consent" Requirements.   State legislatures continue to pass more and more restrictive abortion regulation, making it difficult to keep up with the current state of the law. A frequently updated website on abortion regulation state by state is http://www.guttmacher.org/sections/abortion.php.

As of July 2013, 35 states require that women receive counseling before they obtain an abortion. Twenty-six of these states specify what information a woman must be given—usually information about the gestational age of the fetus and the extent of fetal development, and often about the ability of a fetus to feel pain. In addition, some states require information about the medical and psychological risks of abortion.[303] Some argue that these kinds of requirements violate the legal and ethical boundaries of medical informed consent by expressing their preference for children over abortion in a way that serves to unduly influence a woman's choice.[304] In fact, many state-required disclosures have been found to misrepresent medical knowledge.[305] A few of them have been successfully challenged, but litigation on this issue has been infrequent.[306] A survey by the House Committee on Oversight and Government Reform found that 87 percent of federally funded centers gave out false information concerning the link between abortion, breast cancer, infertility, depression, and stress disorder.[307] Proposed federal legislation, the Stop Deceptive Advertising for Women's Services Act, would require the Federal Trade Commission to enforce truth-in-advertising standards for organizations claiming to offer reproductive services.[308]

Twenty-three states regulate the provision of ultrasound by abortion providers, with nine of these mandating that an abortion provider perform an ultrasound of each woman seeking an abortion and requiring the provider to offer the woman the opportunity to view the image.[309] Is this useful information for the pregnant woman? Or is it unduly coercive?[310] Taking it one step further, Texas enacted a law requiring vaginal ultrasound in order to pick up a fetal heartbeat sound earlier than with a standard abdominal ultrasound procedure. Some advocates argued that this was state-imposed rape.[311] Several newspapers pulled a cartoon strip about the Texas law after it went viral.[312] In Virginia, after strong public protest, a similar law was withdrawn.[313]

Twenty-six states require a woman seeking an abortion to wait a specified period of time between when she receives counseling and the procedure, usually 24 hours.[314] Two studies have examined the effects of mandatory delay laws in Mississippi. The Mississippi law requires that women seeking an abortion receive information in person from a health care provider 24 hours before the procedure. One study found that the total rate of abortions for Mississippi residents decreased by approximately 16 percent; that the proportion of Mississippi residents traveling to other states to obtain abortions increased 37 percent; and that the proportion of second-trimester abortions among all Mississippi women obtaining abortions increased 40 percent. A second study found that the rate of second-trimester abortions in Mississippi after enactment of the law increased by 53 percent among women whose closest health care provider is in-state, but only 8 percent among women living close to an out-of-state provider.[315] What role should such studies play in challenges to mandatory wait laws?

4. Restrictions on Late-Term Abortions.   Eighty-eight percent of abortions occur before the end of the first trimester. Women who obtain "late-term" abortions—i.e. after the first trimester—are disproportionately young and victims of physical abuse or rape.[316] Seventy percent of women who seek late-term abortions did not realize earlier that they were pregnant, 48 percent had difficulty making arrangements (often because of restrictive laws intended to reduce abortion), and 33 percent were afraid to tell their parents or partner. Other reasons include pressure not to have an abortion and discovery of fetal abnormalities that will lead to death in the womb or soon after birth.[317]

The "partial-birth" abortion regulation at issue in *Carhart* is part of a larger body of regulation aimed at restricting abortions after the first trimester. Forty-one states prohibit at least some abortions after a certain point in pregnancy, often fetal viability or a particular gestational age such as 24 weeks. The circumstances in which later-term abortions are permitted vary by state. In 26 states, late-term abortion is permitted to preserve the life or health of the woman. Some states require the involvement of a second physician for late-term abortions, including 12 states that require that a second physician attend the procedure to treat a fetus if it is born alive, and 9 states that require that a second physician certify that the abortion is medically necessary. Four states prohibit abortion altogether in the third trimester, except to save the life of the mother.[318]

Are states right to put more limits on late-term abortions? If so, what should those limits be?

5. Abortion "Regret."   Is the ban on partial-birth abortions consistent with *Roe*'s expression of the increasing state interest in the pregnancy as it progresses? Or does it reflect increasing ambivalence about the procedure generally, and the success of anti-abortion advocates to reframe the issue as protection for women?

Criticism of the gender paternalism reflected in the *Carhart* decision was extensive. Reva Siegel documents the growing use of claims about post-abortion syndrome (or PAS) as an anti-abortion strategy that would attract broader support for the fetal rights argument. She quotes David Reardon, an anti-abortion activist:

> While committed pro-lifers may be more comfortable with traditional "defend the baby" arguments, we must recognize that many in our society are too morally immature to understand this argument. They must be led to it. And the best way to lead them to it is by first helping them to see that abortion does not help women, but only makes their lives worse.[319]

Is it true, as Justice Ginsburg states, that abortion-regret arguments are paternalistic stereotypes and anti-woman rhetoric? Or is Jeannie Suk right that post-abortion syndrome fits the pattern of explanations of women's victimization used by legal reformers to secure more protection for women in other areas, such as sexual violence and harassment? Could both analyses be correct?

Susan Appleton sees a connection between the abortion-regret reasoning of *Carhart* and its use by courts and legislations in addressing such matters as adoption, surrogacy arrangements, the disposition of frozen embryos, and the status of sperm donors. Appleton argues that regret jurisprudence legitimates the transfer of power from the individual to the state in the arena of family, sex, and reproduction, which is supposed to be a domain of personal liberty. It also involves the state in producing regret and making regret seem natural and self-generated through the gendered assumptions it conveys about sexual experience, autonomy, and family.[320] In adoption-surrender cases, for example, women's regret often functions "as a legally sanctioned 'price of pleasure.'"[321] What do you think of this analysis? Does a decision like *Carhart* reflect and reinforce attitudes that create regret?

What research, if any, would affect your views on whether, and to what extent, abortion harms women? In 2009, one set of researchers concluded that, compared to women who had never had an abortion, women who had had an abortion were at increased risk of several anxiety, mood, and substance abuse disorders.[322] Subsequent research using the same data but controlling for prior mental health difficulties and experience of violence found no such anxiety and mood disorders, although it did find an association with substance abuse, which the researchers attributed to the likelihood they had been unable to control for other relevant risk factors.[323] On what facts does Justice Kennedy rely?

6. Anti-Abortion Activism.　Anti-abortion advocates have long sought to dissuade women from obtaining an abortion through clinic pickets and protest activities. After the U.S. Supreme Court found civil rights statutes inapplicable to protect clinic access, Congress passed the Freedom of Access to Clinic Entrances Act (FACE).[324] FACE allows for civil remedies and/or criminal penalties against anyone who "by force or threat of force or by physical obstruction, intentionally injures, intimidates or interferes with or attempts to injure,

... or intimidate such person from, obtaining or providing reproductive health services." Violators are subject to one year in prison or up to $10,000 in fines, or both, for the first violation, and up to three years in prison and up to $25,000 in fines for the second. If bodily injury or death results, other penalties are possible. The Act also authorizes a private right of action in favor of physicians, clinic staff, and patients who are injured by conduct proscribed by the Act. Critics of FACE have argued that it violates the First Amendment, the Eighth Amendment, the Tenth Amendment, and the Religious Freedom Restoration Act, but the Act has survived numerous constitutional attacks at the federal appellate level.

State laws also provide some protection for health care providers and for women seeking abortions. These include general trespass laws and actions for tortious interference with business, false imprisonment, and intentional infliction of emotional distress. Fifteen states and the District of Columbia prohibit certain specified actions. For example, some state laws provide specific protections such as "bubble zones" around clinics, within which protesters may not approach clinic workers and clients. Some states prohibit excessive noise outside a clinic, possessing or having access to a weapon during a demonstration at a medical facility, threatening or intimidating staff, or blocking the entrance to a clinic.[325]

In 2000, the U.S. Supreme Court upheld a Colorado statute making it unlawful for demonstrators within 100 feet of a health-care facility to "knowingly approach" within 8 feet of another person, without that person's consent, in order to pass a leaflet or handbill to, display a sign to , or engage in oral protest, education, or counseling with that person.[326] At the time of this printing, 14 year later, the Supreme Court considers a similar challenge to a 2007 Massachusetts statute creating a 35-foot buffer zone around abortion clinics, enacted after a history of violence at Massachusetts clinics.[327]

Anti-abortion activists sometimes target doctors' homes (Operation Housecall) and use media ads and websites. In one campaign, radio ads proclaimed: "Some doctors deliver babies. Some doctors kill babies."[328] In another instance, the American Coalition of Life Activists portrayed a medical provider and its affiliated doctors on a website, in posters with the physicians' names and addresses labeled "GUILTY," "Deadly Dozen GUILTY," and "Nuremberg Files." This campaign followed in the wake of the murder of other doctors who had been identified in a series of posters labeled "WANTED" and "UNWANTED." In an action against the website developers under both FACE and the Racketeer Influenced and Corrupt Organizations Act (RICO), plaintiffs won an injunction shutting down the website and a verdict of $4.8 million (reduced from $108 million at the trial level).[329]

The vilification of abortion providers can often have tragic consequences, such as the 2009 murder of a Wichita doctor, George Tiller, in his church sanctuary. An Operation Rescue "Tiller Watch" web page had featured vitriolic postings, and pro-life leaders had denounced him as "a baby killer" and "mass murderer."[330] The doctor who attempted to take Dr. Tiller's place has faced harassment and a number of threats, including a letter from an anti-abortion activist who befriended the killer of Dr. Tiller, warning the doctor to check under her car for explosives before turning the key.[331]

7. Spousal Notice and Consent Provisions.   Is *Casey* right to find spousal consent provisions unconstitutional? At a time when many feminists are urging measures to encourage fathers to be more engaged in childrearing, does it make sense to deny them the right to participate in the abortion decision? In a widely circulated *New York Times* op-ed piece, Dalton Conley argues that "if we want to make fathers relevant, they need rights too. If a father is willing to legally commit to raising a child with no help from the mother, he should be able to obtain an injunction against the abortion of the fetus he helped create."[332] Similarly, Glenn Sacks objects to the "anti-male double standards" that require men to be responsible for child support if the woman carries an unplanned pregnancy to term, but gives them "no say" in that decision or the decision to terminate the pregnancy.[333] How would you respond?

8. Parental Consent and Notification Requirements.   *Casey* upheld provisions requiring minors to have parental consent before obtaining an abortion, as long as the state made available a bypass procedure permitting exemptions from the consent requirement. Under that procedure, a judge must allow an abortion for a minor who has demonstrated that she is mature and capable of giving informed consent, or has shown that the abortion would be in her best interests. This holding was consistent with the Court's prior and subsequent decisions upholding both parental consent and parental notification requirements, despite evidence that they resulted in delays causing health risks, financial costs, trauma, and unwanted births.[334]

Thirty-eight states now require parental involvement in a minor's decision to have an abortion. Of these, 12 require only parental notification, 21 require only parental consent (3 of these requiring consent of both parents), and 5 require both notification and consent. Exceptions are typically available for a medical emergency, and 15 states make an exception in cases of abuse, assault, incest, or neglect. All but 1 of the 38 states provide an alternative judicial bypass procedure; 13 of these states require judges to use the clear and convincing evidence standard in determining that the minor is mature and that the abortion is in her best interests.[335] Courts in a few states have struck down parental consent or parental notification statutes under their own state constitutional provisions, although anti-abortion advocates in one state have sought repeatedly to overrule one such decision through a constitutional amendment, most recently in 2012.[336] Proposed federal legislation requires all minors who travel outside their home state for an abortion to obtain parental consent and wait 24 hours.[337]

At one time, it seemed that most minors who pursued a bypass procedure obtained judicial permission to obtain an abortion.[338] However, a recent study involving interviews of professionals from every state with a bypass provision found numerous difficulties by minors in pursuing bypass petitions, including the inability of minors to obtain helpful and reliable information, pay the costs, and find a judge who will hear the petition. Minors who are in state custody face additional problems, including confusion within the system about who is authorized to provide consent. Once a petition is before the court, abuse of judicial discretion is also a problem. Some judges grill the minors on their sex lives, or deliver stern lectures on the need for parental consultation.[339] Is this appropriate? Does it make sense to presume that a minor is unable to make reproductive decisions without parental consultation, and that parents act presumptively in their children's best interests?

9. Federal Policy Relating to Minors and Abortion.   The federal government in recent decades has provided various funding programs to support pregnancy prevention for teenagers. Since 1997, the funds have been available only for programs that met stringent requirements premised on abstinence as the sole prevention strategy. Thus, qualifying programs have been required to teach that abstaining from sex "is the only certain way to avoid out-of-wedlock pregnancy, sexually transmitted diseases, and other associated health problems," that a "mutually faithful monogamous relationship in context of marriage is the expected standard of human sexual activity," and that "sexual activity outside of marriage is likely to have harmful physical and psychological effects."[340] Much of the funding for these programs expired in 2009 and 2010 but then was renewed as part of the Patient Protection and Affordable Care Act signed into law by President Obama in 2010.[341]

The political popularity of these abstinence-only programs has not been matched by any demonstration of effectiveness. The vast majority of abstinence-only curricula include errors and distortions, and none have been found to delay sexual activity.[342] By contrast, other research finds that two-thirds of comprehensive sex education programs have had a positive impact on behavior and have not encouraged sexual activity.[343] The consequences of inadequate sex education are substantial. According to data from the Centers for Disease Control and Prevention, one in four teenage girls has a sexually transmitted infection (STI), and African American girls are at more than twice the risk of white girls. HIV/AIDS is the gravest risk of unprotected sexual activity, and right now people under the age of 25 are the fastest-growing category of new HIV infections.[344] One study showed that students who take virginity pledges—a common feature of abstinence-only programs—delayed sexual activity slightly, but when they did have sex, they used condoms less frequently and were less likely to be tested for STIs. Students who take part in abstinence-only programs are also more likely to believe, incorrectly, that condoms do not protect against STIs.[345]

Critics of abstinence-only programs generally do not object to approaches that encourage teens to resist unwanted sex, but believe that teens should also have accurate information about sexual activity and birth control. Some critics also argue that abstinence-only initiatives violate minors' constitutional rights concerning health and procreation decisions, and that some federally funded programs include religious material in violation of the First Amendment Establishment Clause, which requires separation between church and state. One federal court struck down a Louisiana program on that ground.[346] Another concern involves the focus on monogamous marriage as the cultural norm, which may reinforce prejudice against gay and lesbian students.

   10. The Class and Race Dimensions of the Abortion Right.   Underfunding of family planning programs may also restrict poor women's reproductive choices and increase the number of abortions. Nearly half of pregnancies are unintended, and 43 percent of those pregnancies are terminated by abortion. Poor women are more than five times more likely to have an unintended pregnancy than women at the highest income levels, and this disparity continues to grow. Black women have double the unintended pregnancies of non-Hispanic white women.[347]

   It is estimated that between about one-fifth to one-third of women poor enough to qualify for government-funded health care cannot obtain the abortions they seek because of lack of resources.[348] Federal funding legislation, known as the "Hyde Amendment," limits federal reimbursement for abortions to very narrow exceptions, such as when necessary to save the life of the mother or to end pregnancies resulting from rape or incest. The restriction applies to funding provided through the Department of Health and Human Services and primarily affects Medicaid. The Supreme Court has sustained such legislation on the ground that it does not impose an unconstitutional condition on women's exercise of their fundamental right to an abortion but simply leaves them in the same place they would be absent any federal funding program.[349] Although some states provide funds for indigent women, only 4 states voluntarily provide funds for all or most medically necessary abortions, with 13 additional states providing funds pursuant to court order.[350] Already, in anticipation of the 2014 effective date of the federal requirement under the Patient Protection and Affordable Care Act for the establishment of state-level health care exchanges to assist individuals and small businesses to purchase a private health insurance plan, 8 states restrict insurance coverage of abortion in *all* private insurance plans written in the state, and 23 states restrict abortion coverage in plans that will be offered through the insurance exchanges.[351] Women of limited means living in rural areas are particularly affected by abortion restrictions, given the difficulties of transportation and the lack of confidentiality in small communities.[352]

   Access to abortion in the United States is also constrained by the number of physicians prepared to perform them. Only 46 percent of residency training programs in obstetrics and gynecology provide training in first-trimester abortion, and only 15 percent of chief residents in family medicine programs know how to perform the procedures. Since 1982, the number of abortion providers has fallen by one-third, and over 85 percent of U.S. counties have none.[353] One reason is the violence and abuse directed at abortion providers, described in Note 6, above.

On the international front, poor women's access to reproductive services increased when in 2009 the Obama administration rescinded the "Global Gag Rule." Under that policy, which had been in place under both Bush administrations, foreign non-governmental organizations could not receive U.S. family-planning funds if they used their own resources to provide abortions, or abortion counseling, and referrals. Repeated efforts to reinstate the gag rule have, as yet, been unsuccessful.[354]

11. Personhood Amendments.   At one time, it seemed possible, as the majority in *Roe* maintained, that legal issues about abortion could be decided without having to resolve the "difficult question of when life begins." One of the strategies being increasingly pursued by anti-abortion advocates, however, is proposed legislation or constitutional amendments providing that life begins at conception. As of 2012, measures in 20 different states would declare that personhood begins at conception. In November 2011, voters in Mississippi narrowly defeated an amendment of its Bill of Rights that would define "persons" to include "every human being from the moment of fertilization, cloning, or the functional equivalent thereof."[355] A bill in Oklahoma declares that life begins at conception and affords all unborn children "at every stage of development all the rights, privileges, and immunities available to other persons, citizens, and residents of this state."[356] The Oklahoma Supreme Court declared the amendment unconstitutional.[357] Still, these initiatives serve as an organizing force for anti-abortion advocates, and the legislation they have motivated may trigger eventual review of Roe v. Wade by the U.S. Supreme Court.[358] One such piece of legislation, also from Oklahoma, bans the use of the drug misoprostol to induce abortions. After the Oklahoma State Supreme Court found the law to be unconstitutional, the U.S. Supreme Court agreed to hear the case, but then sent it back to the Oklahoma court to certify whether the statute banned the use of misoprostol even when used under a protocol approved by the Food and Drug Administration.[359]

If a "Personhood Amendment" becomes law, what would be its effect? It would certainly ban abortion (its declared primary purpose) and probably eliminate any potential exceptions in the case of rape or incest. Would any miscarriage necessitate a state murder investigation? How would it affect frozen embryos? Would a pregnant woman be able to declare her fetus as a dependent for tax purposes? Would she be entitled to welfare benefits immediately upon becoming pregnant?

In a satirical effort to draw attention to the gender implications of the efforts to expand the definition of personhood, Oklahoma state representative Constance Johnson introduced a bill to amend the "Personhood" bill introduced in the Oklahoma legislature to say: ". . . provided, however, any action in which a man ejaculates or otherwise deposits semen anywhere but in a woman's vagina, shall be interpreted and construed as an action against an unborn child."[360] Is this just silly, or does it identify a real problem in this kind of legislation?

12. The Impact of Increasing Abortion Restrictions.   Many states have positioned themselves in the event that the Supreme Court overturns Roe v. Wade. As of February 2014, 20 states had either pre-*Roe* laws or post-*Roe* laws that would immediately ban abortion if *Roe* were overturned.[361] If the Supreme Court were to eliminate the constitutional right of a woman to choose to have an abortion, the result would be a patchwork of regulations, with some states completely denying abortion rights except to protect maternal life, and others providing stringent regulations. Those most adversely affected would be low-income women who could not afford travel to permissive jurisdictions (see Note 10), and who would be more likely to resort to an illegal, dangerous, underground procedure, comparable to what existed prior to *Roe*.

More restrictive abortion laws do not necessarily mean fewer abortions. Abortion rates are lower in countries where it is legal; for example, in Western Europe, where abortions are broadly available, the abortion rate is 12 per 1,000 women. Countries with highly restrictive abortion laws tend to have higher abortion rates; in Latin America, for example, the rate is 32 per 1,000 women. Abortions are also safer where they are legal because of the methods used, the sanitary conditions, and the later gestational age at which women seek illegal abortions. In South Africa, the annual number of abortion-related deaths fell by 91 percent after the liberalization of the abortion law. Worldwide, although abortion rates declined significantly between 1995 and 2003, they have now leveled off at 28 per 1,000 women between ages 15 and 44.[362]

Putting Theory Into Practice

5-17. Research shows consistently that most families prefer boys to girls, especially as first or only children.[363] In China, the combination of a restrictive "one child" population control policy and a cultural preference for sons has resulted in an increasingly skewed sex ratio; in 2005, 121 boys were born for every 100 girls. Similar ratios occur in India, leading both countries to ban the use of ultrasounds for sex determination (although enforcement of these bans is extremely difficult). Many scholars predict that a skewed male-female ratio will result in increased violence and crime.[364]

Illinois law prohibits abortions that are performed "with knowledge that the pregnant woman is seeking the abortion solely on account of the sex of the fetus."[365] Pennsylvania law provides that "[no] abortion which is sought solely because of the sex of the unborn child shall be deemed a necessary abortion."[366] Are these laws constitutional? Are they enforceable, or wise? What about laws to prohibit sex selection in in-vitro fertilization?

5-18. There are more than 4,000 centers, sometimes called Crisis Pregnancy Centers, that purport to offer comprehensive services to women with unwanted pregnancies. Typically these centers advertise by offering free pregnancy tests and counseling. They then attempt to dissuade women from obtaining an abortion, often with false claims relating abortion to sterility, breast cancer, and other harms. These centers, which do not provide abortions, are not regulated or licensed.[367] Should they be? Would it be appropriate to require that these centers post signs disclosing the limitations of their services, or encouraging women to consult with a health care provider?[368]

5-19. A bill in Kansas would, if passed, make it illegal for any state employee to perform an abortion, and would thereby, among other things, preclude abortion training to medical students or medical residents in the University of Kansas Medical Center.[369] Is this bill constitutional? Should it be?

5-20. A Michigan father defended against a paternity suit in which he was ordered to pay $500 per month in child support, on the grounds the law on which it was based constituted sex discrimination. The father, represented by the National Center for Men, argued that he had been deprived of the right to avoid parenthood. He claimed that the mother had falsely assured him that she was unable to get pregnant due to a medical condition, and that she was using birth control just in case. The state also denied him any right to determine whether the pregnancy would be carried to term.[370] Should his defense be accepted?

5-21. A 1997 Louisiana law provides that "[a]ny person who performs an abortion is liable to the mother of the unborn child for any damage occasioned or precipitated by the abortion." A signed consent may reduce damages, but not eliminate them.[371] A group of abortion providers and their patients brought suit. What should be the outcome?[372] Are tort remedies a logical extension of the regret analysis in *Carhart*, or do they violate the U.S. Constitution?[373]

5-22. Some abortion protestors photograph and videotape women entering abortion clinics; the photographs are later posted on the Internet, in some cases along with age, height, and location. Protestors hope that the increased publicity will deter women from seeking abortions and claim that the postings are protected under the First Amendment. Should these postings be allowed? If not, what remedies should be available to women whose photographs are published?

3. Pregnancy and Contractual Autonomy

Beyond issues of contraception and abortion are a host of reproductive issues implicating women's autonomy. This section addresses what legal rules should govern women who are willing to bear children for someone else, as a surrogate, or through other arrangements arising from nontraditional methods of reproduction. In this area, the law has been unable to keep up with either medical technology or evolving social practice. This new frontier presents crucial challenges for women's autonomy and public policy.

Reading Questions

1. In cases like *Baby M*, excerpted below, are women's autonomy and reproductive freedom served best by enforcing, or not enforcing, private agreements?
2. Is equality a useful principle in these cases? For example, if men can sell their sperm, why can't women sell their gestational capacities?
3. What would equality mean in a dispute between a couple over their frozen embryos? How important is biology in these cases?
4. Should the surrogate mother's right to change her mind and keep the child depend upon whether the child is biologically hers or the egg came from another woman?

In re Baby M

537 A.2d 1227 (N.J. 1988)

WILENTZ, C.J.

In this matter the Court is asked to determine the validity of a contract that purports to provide a new way of bringing children into a family. For a fee of $10,000, a woman agrees to be artificially inseminated with the semen of another woman's husband; she is to conceive a child, carry it to term, and after its birth surrender it to the natural father and his wife. The intent of the contract is that the child's natural mother will thereafter be forever separated from her child. The wife is to adopt the child, and she and the natural father are to be regarded as its parents for all purposes. The contract providing for this is called a "surrogacy contract," the natural mother inappropriately called the "surrogate mother."

We invalidate the surrogacy contract because it conflicts with the law and public policy of this State. While we recognize the depth of the yearning of infertile couples to have their own children, we find the payment of money to a "surrogate" mother illegal, perhaps criminal, and potentially degrading to women. Although in this case we grant custody to the natural father, the evidence having clearly proved such custody to be in the best interests of the infant, we void both the termination of the surrogate mother's parental rights and the adoption of the child by the wife/stepparent. We thus restore the "surrogate" as the mother of the child. We remand the issue of the natural mother's visitation rights to the trial court. . . .

We find no offense to our present laws where a woman voluntarily and without payment agrees to act as a "surrogate" mother, provided that she is not subject to a binding agreement to surrender her child. . . .

I. FACTS

In February 1985, William Stern and Mary Beth Whitehead entered into a surrogacy contract. It recited that Stern's wife, Elizabeth, was infertile, that they wanted a child, and that Mrs. Whitehead was willing to provide that child as the mother with Mr. Stern as the father.

The contract provided that through artificial insemination using Mr. Stern's sperm, Mrs. Whitehead would become pregnant, carry the child to term, bear it, deliver it to the Sterns, and thereafter do whatever was necessary to terminate her maternal rights so that Mrs. Stern could thereafter adopt the child. Mrs. Whitehead's husband, Richard, was also a party to the contract; Mrs. Stern was not. Mr. Whitehead promised to do all acts necessary to rebut the presumption of paternity under the Parentage Act. Although Mrs. Stern was not a party to the surrogacy agreement, the contract gave her sole custody of the child in the event of Mr. Stern's death. . . .

Mr. Stern, on his part, agreed to attempt the artificial insemination and to pay Mrs. Whitehead $10,000 after the child's birth, on its delivery to him. In a separate contract, Mr. Stern agreed to pay $7,500 to the Infertility Center of New York ("ICNY"). The Center's advertising campaigns solicit surrogate mothers and encourage infertile couples to consider surrogacy. ICNY arranged for the surrogacy contract by bringing the parties together, explaining the process to them, furnishing the contractual form, and providing legal counsel.

The history of the parties' involvement in this arrangement suggests their good faith. William and Elizabeth Stern were married in July 1974, having met at the University of Michigan, where both were Ph.D. candidates. Due to financial considerations and Mrs. Stern's pursuit of a medical degree and residency, they decided to defer starting a family until 1981. Before then, however, Mrs. Stern learned that she might have multiple sclerosis and that the disease in some cases renders pregnancy a serious health risk. Her anxiety appears to have exceeded the actual risk, which current medical authorities assess as minimal. Nonetheless that anxiety was evidently quite real, Mrs. Stern fearing that pregnancy might precipitate blindness, paraplegia, or other forms of debilitation. Based on the perceived risk, the Sterns decided to forego having their own children. The decision had special significance for Mr. Stern. Most of his family had been destroyed in the Holocaust. As the family's only survivor, he very much wanted to continue his bloodline.

Initially the Sterns considered adoption but were discouraged by the substantial delay apparently involved and by the potential problem they saw arising from their age and their differing religious backgrounds. They were most eager for some other means to start a family.

The paths of Mrs. Whitehead and the Sterns to surrogacy were similar. Both responded to advertising by ICNY. . . . Mrs. Whitehead's response apparently resulted from her sympathy with family members and others who could have no children (she stated that she wanted to give another couple the "gift of life"); she also wanted the $10,000 to help her family.

Both parties, undoubtedly because of their own self-interest, were less sensitive to the implications of the transaction than they might otherwise have been. Mrs. Whitehead, for instance, appears not to have been concerned about whether the Sterns would make good parents for her child; the Sterns, on their part, while conscious of the obvious possibility that surrendering the child might cause grief to Mrs. Whitehead, overcame their qualms because of their desire for a child. At any rate, both the Sterns and Mrs. Whitehead were committed to the arrangement; both thought it right and constructive.

. . . On February 6, 1985, Mr. Stern and Mr. and Mrs. Whitehead executed the surrogate parenting agreement. After several artificial inseminations over a period of months, Mrs. Whitehead became pregnant. The pregnancy was uneventful and on March 27, 1986, Baby M was born. . . .

Mrs. Whitehead realized, almost from the moment of birth, that she could not part with this child. She had felt a bond with it even during pregnancy. . . . She apparently broke into tears and indicated that she did not know if she could give up the child. . . .

Nonetheless, Mrs. Whitehead was, for the moment, true to her word. Despite powerful inclinations to the contrary, she turned her child over to the Sterns on March 30 at the Whiteheads' home.

The Sterns were thrilled with their new child. They had planned extensively for its arrival, far beyond the practical furnishing of a room for her. It was a time of joyful celebration—not just for them but for their friends as well. The Sterns looked forward to raising their daughter, whom they named Melissa. . . .

Later in the evening of March 30, Mrs. Whitehead became deeply disturbed, disconsolate, stricken with unbearable sadness. She had to have her child. She could not eat, sleep, or concentrate on anything other than her need for her baby. The next day she went to the Sterns' home and told them how much she was suffering.

The depth of Mrs. Whitehead's despair surprised and frightened the Sterns. She told them that she could not live without her baby, that she must have her, even if only for one week, that thereafter she would surrender her child. The Sterns, concerned that Mrs. Whitehead might indeed commit suicide, not wanting under any circumstances to risk that, and in any event believing that Mrs. Whitehead would keep her word, turned the child over to her. . . .

The struggle over Baby M began when it became apparent that Mrs. Whitehead could not return the child to Mr. Stern. Due to Mrs. Whitehead's refusal to relinquish the baby, Mr. Stern filed a complaint seeking enforcement of the surrogacy contract. . . .

The Whiteheads immediately fled to Florida with Baby M. They stayed initially with Mrs. Whitehead's parents, where one of Mrs. Whitehead's children had been living. For the next three months, the Whiteheads and Melissa lived at roughly twenty different hotels, motels, and homes in order to avoid apprehension. From time to time Mrs. Whitehead would call Mr. Stern to discuss the matter; the conversations, recorded by Mr. Stern on advice of counsel, show an escalating dispute about rights, morality, and power, accompanied by threats of Mrs. Whitehead to kill herself, to kill the child, and falsely to accuse Mr. Stern of sexually molesting Mrs. Whitehead's other daughter.

Eventually the Sterns discovered where the Whiteheads were staying, commenced supplementary proceedings in Florida, and obtained an order requiring the Whiteheads to turn over the child. Police in Florida enforced the order, forcibly removing the child from her grandparents' home. She was soon thereafter brought to New Jersey and turned over to the Sterns. . . .

The trial took thirty-two days over a period of more than two months. . . . [The trial court] held that the surrogacy contract was valid; ordered that Mrs. Whitehead's parental rights be terminated and that sole custody of the child be granted to Mr. Stern; and, after hearing brief testimony from Mrs. Stern, immediately entered an order allowing the adoption of Melissa by Mrs. Stern, all in accordance with the surrogacy contract. . . .

II. INVALIDITY AND UNFORCEABILITY OF SURROGACY CONTRACT . . .

A. Conflict with Statutory Provisions

The surrogacy contract conflicts with: (1) laws prohibiting the use of money in connection with adoptions; (2) laws requiring proof of parental unfitness or abandonment before termination of parental rights is ordered or an adoption is granted; and (3) laws that make surrender of custody and consent to adoption revocable in private placement adoptions.

(1) Our law prohibits paying or accepting money in connection with any placement of a child for adoption. Violation is a high misdemeanor. Excepted are fees of an approved agency (which must be a non-profit entity) and certain expenses in connection with childbirth.

Considerable care was taken in this case to structure the surrogacy arrangement so as not to violate this prohibition. . . . Nevertheless, it seems clear that the money was paid and accepted in connection with an adoption. . . .

Mr. Stern knew he was paying for the adoption of a child; Mrs. Whitehead knew she was accepting money so that a child might be adopted; the Infertility Center knew that it was being paid for assisting in the adoption of a child. The actions of all three worked to frustrate the goals of the statute. . . .

. . . The evils inherent in baby-bartering are loathsome for a myriad of reasons. The child is sold without regard for whether the purchasers will be suitable parents. The natural mother does not receive the benefit of counseling and guidance to assist her in making a decision that may affect her for a lifetime. In fact, the monetary incentive to sell her child may, depending on her financial circumstances, make her decision less voluntary. Furthermore, the adoptive parents may not be fully informed of the natural parents' medical history. . . .

(2) The termination of Mrs. Whitehead's parental rights, called for by the surrogacy contract and actually ordered by the court, fails to comply with the stringent requirements of New Jersey law. . . .

In order to terminate parental rights under the private placement adoption statute, there must be a finding of "intentional abandonment or a very substantial neglect of parental duties without a reasonable expectation of a reversal of that conduct in the future." . . .

Our statutes, and the cases interpreting them, leave no doubt that where there has been no written surrender to an approved agency or to DYFS, termination of parental rights will not be granted in this state absent a very strong showing of abandonment or neglect. . . . It is clear that a "best interests" determination is never sufficient to terminate parental rights; the statutory criteria must be proved.

In this case a termination of parental rights was obtained not by proving the statutory prerequisites but by claiming the benefit of contractual provisions. . . . [A] contractual agreement to abandon one's parental rights, or not to contest a termination action, will not be enforced in our courts. . . .

(3) The provision in the surrogacy contract stating that Mary Beth Whitehead agrees to "surrender custody . . . and terminate all parental rights" contains no clause giving her a right to rescind. It is intended to be an irrevocable consent to surrender the child for adoption—in other words, an irrevocable commitment by Mrs. Whitehead to turn Baby M over to the Sterns and thereafter to allow termination of her parental rights. . . .

. . . Such a provision, however, making irrevocable the natural mother's consent to surrender custody of her child in a private placement adoption, clearly conflicts with New Jersey law. . . .

The[] strict prerequisites to irrevocability constitute a recognition of the most serious consequences that flow from such consents: termination of parental rights, the permanent separation of parent from child, and the ultimate adoption of the child. Because of those consequences, the Legislature severely limited the circumstances under which such consent would be irrevocable. The legislative goal is furthered by regulations requiring approved agencies, prior to accepting irrevocable consents, to provide advice and counseling to women, making it more likely that they fully understand and appreciate the consequences of their acts. . . .

The provision in the surrogacy contract whereby the mother irrevocably agrees to surrender custody of her child and to terminate her parental rights conflicts with the settled interpretation of New Jersey statutory law. . . .

B. Public Policy Considerations

The surrogacy contract's invalidity . . . is further underlined when its goals and means are measured against New Jersey's public policy. The contract's basic premise, that the natural parents can decide in advance of birth which one is to have custody of the child, bears no relationship to the settled law that the child's best interests shall determine custody. . . .

The surrogacy contract guarantees permanent separation of the child from one of its natural parents. Our policy, however, has long been that to the extent possible, children should remain with and be brought up by both of their natural parents. . . . This is not simply some theoretical ideal that in practice has no meaning. The impact of failure to follow that policy is nowhere better shown than in the results of this surrogacy contract. A child, instead of starting off its life with as much peace and security as possible, finds itself immediately in a tug-of-war between contending mother and father.

The surrogacy contract violates the policy of this State that the rights of natural parents are equal concerning their child, the father's right no greater than the mother's. . . . The whole purpose and effect of the surrogacy contract was to give the father the exclusive right to the child by destroying the rights of the mother.

The policies expressed in our comprehensive laws governing consent to the surrender of a child stand in stark contrast to the surrogacy contract and what it implies. Here there is no counseling, independent or otherwise, of the natural mother, no evaluation, no warning. . . .

Under the contract, the natural mother is irrevocably committed before she knows the strength of her bond with her child. She never makes a totally voluntary, informed decision, for quite clearly any decision prior to the baby's birth is, in the most important sense, uninformed, and any decision after that, compelled by a pre-existing contractual commitment, the threat of a lawsuit, and the inducement of a $10,000 payment, is less than totally voluntary. . . .

Although the interest of the natural father and adoptive mother is certainly the predominant interest, realistically the only interest served, even they are left with less than what public policy requires. They know little about the natural mother, her genetic makeup, and her psychological and medical history. Moreover, not even a superficial attempt is made to determine their awareness of their responsibilities as parents.

Worst of all, however, is the contract's total disregard of the best interests of the child. There is not the slightest suggestion that any inquiry will be made at any time to determine the fitness of the Sterns as custodial parents, of Mrs. Stern as an adoptive parent, their superiority to Mrs. Whitehead, or the effect on the child of not living with her natural mother.

This is the sale of a child, or, at the very least, the sale of a mother's right to her child, the only mitigating factor being that one of the purchasers is the father. Almost every evil that prompted the prohibition on the payment of money in connection with adoptions exists here. . . .

The main difference [between adoption and surrogacy], that the unwanted pregnancy is unintended while the situation of the surrogate mother is voluntary and intended, is really not significant. Initially, it produces stronger reactions of sympathy for the mother whose pregnancy was unwanted than for the surrogate mother, who "went into this with her eyes wide open." On reflection, however, it appears that the essential evil is the same, taking advantage of a woman's circumstances (the unwanted pregnancy or the need for money) in order to take away her child, the difference being one of degree.

Intimated, but disputed, is the assertion that surrogacy will be used for the benefit of the rich at the expense of the poor. In response it is noted that the Sterns are not rich and the Whiteheads not poor. Nevertheless, it is clear to us that it is unlikely that surrogate mothers will be as proportionately numerous among those women in the top 20 percent income bracket as among those in the bottom twenty percent. Put differently, we doubt that infertile couples in the low-income bracket will find upper income surrogates. . . .

The long-term effects of surrogacy contracts are not known, but feared — the impact on the child who learns her life was bought, that she is the offspring of someone who gave birth to her only to obtain money; the impact on the natural mother as the full weight of her isolation is felt along with the full reality of the sale of her body and her child; the impact on the natural father and adoptive mother once they realize the consequences of their conduct. . . .

The surrogacy contract is based on principles that are directly contrary to the objectives of our laws. It guarantees the separation of a child from its mother; it looks to adoption regardless of suitability; it totally ignores the child; it takes the child from the mother regardless of her wishes and her maternal fitness; and it does all of this, it accomplishes all of its goals, through the use of money.

Beyond that is the potential degradation of some women that may result from this arrangement. In many cases, of course, surrogacy may bring satisfaction, not only to the infertile couple, but to the surrogate mother herself. The fact, however, that many women may not perceive surrogacy negatively but rather see it as an opportunity does not diminish its potential for devastation to other women. . . .

IV. CONSTITUTIONAL ISSUES

Both parties argue that the Constitutions — state and federal — mandate approval of their basic claims. . . . The right asserted by the Sterns is the right of procreation; that asserted by Mary Beth Whitehead is the right to the companionship of her child. We find that the right of procreation does not extend as far as claimed by the Sterns. As for the right asserted by Mrs. Whitehead, since we uphold it on other grounds . . . , we need not decide that constitutional issue. . . .

. . . The right to procreate very simply is the right to have natural children, whether through sexual intercourse or artificial insemination. It is no more than that. Mr. Stern has not been deprived of that right. Through artificial insemination of Mrs. Whitehead, Baby M is his child. The custody, care, companionship, and nurturing that follow birth are not parts of the right to procreation; they are rights that may also be constitutionally protected, but that involve many considerations other than the right of procreation. To assert that Mr. Stern's right of procreation gives him the right to the custody of Baby M would be to assert that Mrs. Whitehead's right of procreation does not give her the right to the custody of Baby M; it would be to assert that the constitutional right of procreation includes within it a constitutionally protected contractual right to destroy someone else's right of procreation. . . .

Mrs. Whitehead . . . claims the right to the companionship of her child. This is a fundamental interest, constitutionally protected. . . . By virtue of our decision Mrs. Whitehead's constitutional complaint—that her parental rights have been unconstitutionally terminated—is moot. . . .

V. CUSTODY

. . . Our reading of the record persuades us that the trial court's decision awarding custody to the Sterns (technically to Mr. Stern) should be affirmed. . . .

Our custody conclusion is based on strongly persuasive testimony contrasting both the family life of the Whiteheads and the Sterns and the personalities and characters of the individuals. The stability of the Whitehead family life was doubtful at the time of trial. Their finances were in serious trouble. . . . Mr. Whitehead's employment, though relatively steady, was always at risk because of his alcoholism, a condition that he seems not to have been able to confront effectively. Mrs. Whitehead had not worked for quite some time, her last two employments having been part-time. . . . Certain of the experts noted that Mrs. Whitehead perceived herself as omnipotent and omniscient concerning her children. She knew what they were thinking, what they wanted, and she spoke for them. As to Melissa, Mrs. Whitehead expressed the view that she alone knew what that child's cries and sounds meant. Her inconsistent stories about various things engendered grave doubts about her ability to explain honestly and sensitively to Baby M—and at the right time—the nature of her origin. . . . In short, while love and affection there would be, Baby M's life with the Whiteheads promised to be too closely controlled by Mrs. Whitehead. The prospects for wholesome, independent psychological growth and development would be at serious risk.

The Sterns have no other children, but all indications are that their household and their personalities promise a much more likely foundation for Melissa to grow and thrive. There is a track record of sorts—during the one-and-a-half years of custody Baby M has done very well, and the relationship between both Mr. and Mrs. Stern and the baby has become very strong. The household is stable, and likely to remain so. Their finances are more than adequate, their circle of friends supportive, and their marriage happy. Most important, they are loving, giving, nurturing, and open-minded people. They have demonstrated the wish and ability to nurture and protect Melissa, yet at the same time to encourage her independence. . . . All in all, Melissa's future appears solid, happy, and promising with them. . . .

VI. VISITATION

The trial court's decision to terminate Mrs. Whitehead's parental rights precluded it from making any determination on visitation. . . . We therefore remand the visitation issue to the trial court for an abbreviated hearing. . . .

We also note the following for the trial court's consideration: First, this is not a divorce case where visitation is almost invariably granted to the non-custodial spouse. . . . Mrs. Whitehead spent the first four months of this child's life as her mother and has regularly visited the child since then. Second, she is not only the natural mother, but also the legal mother, and is not to be penalized one iota because of the surrogacy contract. Mrs. Whitehead, as the mother (indeed, as a mother who nurtured her child for its first four months—unquestionably a relevant consideration), is entitled to have her own interest in visitation considered. . . .

In all of this, the trial court should recall the touchstones of visitation: that it is desirable for the child to have contact with both parents; that besides the child's interests, the parents' interests also must be considered; but that when all is said and done, the best interests of the child are paramount. . . .

While probably unlikely, we do not deem it unthinkable that, the major issues having been resolved, the parties' undoubted love for this child might result in a good faith attempt to work out the visitation themselves, in the best interests of their child.

Conclusion

This case affords some insight into a new reproductive arrangement: the artificial insemination of a surrogate mother. . . .

We have found that our present laws do not permit the surrogacy contract used in this case.

. . . [T]he Legislature remains free to deal with this most sensitive issue as it sees fit, subject only to constitutional constraints.

If the Legislature decides to address surrogacy, consideration of this case will highlight many of its potential harms. We do not underestimate the difficulties of legislating on this subject. In addition to the inevitable confrontation with the ethical and moral issues involved, there is the question of the wisdom and effectiveness of regulating a matter so private, yet of such public interest. Legislative consideration of surrogacy may also provide the opportunity to begin to focus on the overall implications of the new reproductive biotechnology—in vitro fertilization, preservation of sperm and eggs, embryo implantation and the like. The problem is how to enjoy the benefits of the technology—especially for infertile couples—while minimizing the risk of abuse. The problem can be addressed only when society decides what its values and objectives are in this troubling, yet promising, area. . . .

Notes

1. Decisional Autonomy. One justification for the court's ruling in *Baby M* was a concern that women may irrevocably consent to relinquishing a child without fully understanding and appreciating the consequences of their acts.

When providing guidance to the lower court on visitation for Mrs. Whitehead, the court offered this view:

> It seems to us that given her predicament, Mrs. Whitehead was rather harshly judged — both by the trial court and by some of the experts. She was guilty of a breach of contract, and indeed, she did break a very important promise, but we think it is expecting something well beyond normal human capabilities to suggest that this mother should have parted with her newly born infant without a struggle. Other than survival, what stronger force is there?

Is this accurate, condescending, or both? What assumptions about women's ability to make decisions, particularly those involving reproduction, underlie the court's view? Do similar ones underlie the U.S. Supreme Court's ruling in Gonzales v. Carhart, excerpted in the prior section, that Congress can constitutionally prohibit a particular method of abortion in part to save "a mother who comes to regret her choice to abort" from "grief more anguished and sorrow more profound" when she learns later how the abortion was performed?[374] Are empirical studies, which tend to show that most surrogates are happy with the experience and would do it again, relevant to the legal questions about surrogacy?

2. Gestational Surrogacy.   In *Baby M*, Mary Beth Whitehead was the child's biological mother because of her genetic contribution to the child. The agreement entailed what is now referred to as "traditional surrogacy." Because she was the mother, after the New Jersey Supreme Court determined that her rights could not be terminated on the basis of a contract signed before the birth of the child, the custody of the child was adjudicated between her and the child's biological father under the customary test applied in custody disputes between biological parents — i.e., the best interests of the child.

When the genetic and gestational functions are separated, the issue becomes more complicated. With "gestational surrogacy," the surrogate provides the womb, but not the egg. With sperm and egg provided either by the intended parents or donors, conception is achieved through in vitro fertilization. Today, almost all surrogacy arrangements are done this way. In Johnson v. Calvert, the gestational mother asserted parental rights against the intended parents, who were also both the genetic parents of the child.[375] The California Supreme Court interpreted the state's version of the Uniform Parentage Act to permit a finding of parenthood on either genetic or gestational grounds, concluding that "when the two means do not coincide in one woman, she who intended to procreate the child — that is, she who intended to bring about the birth of a child that she intended to raise as her own — is the natural mother under California law."[376] As for the concern expressed by *Baby M* court about when a pre-birth contract could be truly voluntary, the court responded:

> The argument that a woman cannot knowingly and intelligently agree to gestate and deliver a baby for intending parents carries overtones of the reasoning that for centuries prevented woman from attaining equal economic rights

and professional status under the law. To resurrect this view is both to fore-close a personal and economic choice on the part of the surrogate mother, and to deny intending parents what may be their only means of procreating a child of their own genes.[377]

In a subsequent California case involving another surrogate who was not the genetic mother, it was the intended father who changed his mind; he no longer wished to be either married or a father. In this case, as well, the court held that the party's original intent should be controlling and that the father would remain responsible for child support.[378]

Some commentators have criticized approaches that give gestational carriers fewer rights to change their minds than those surrogates who are also genetic mothers. The concern is that this both devalues the care invested during gestation and also encourages more couples to undergo egg extraction, a prolonged and difficult process that results in more high-risk pregnancies, so that the surrogate will only have a gestational and not genetic relationship to the infant.[379] If these are valid concerns, what follows?

Matters can become even more complicated when neither claimant is the genetic mother. In one egg donor case, a Pennsylvania court voided a surrogacy contract and declared that the legal mother of triplets was the gestational surrogate, not the contracting couple. The court determined that the egg donor was comparable to a sperm donor.[380]

Several cases involving lesbian parents and nontraditional reproductive procedures have recognized the parental status of both women.[381] Issues involving lesbian parents are explored more fully in Chapter 3.

3. The Regulation of Surrogacy.   The *Baby M* ruling thrust the surrogacy issue into the public eye. In the year after the ruling, legislatures all over the country considered bills to permit, prohibit, or regulate surrogacy. Most did not become law, but several states, including New York, have since banned surrogacy.[382] In the absence of controlling statutory authority, state court rulings have produced mixed results. The rulings reflect a variety of different approaches, including (1) an intent-based approach, which seeks to fulfill the intentions of the parties (*Calvert*); (2) the genetic contribution test, which looks to the genetic tie between parent and child (*Baby M*); and (3) the gestational primacy test, giving preference to the mother who gestated and bore the child.[383]

The legal landscape for surrogacy remains quite checkered. A handful of jurisdictions treat surrogacy agreements as void and unenforceable. Another group of states allow surrogacy under some but not all circumstances. The most common restrictions are prohibitions or limits on what can be paid. Some states, such as Virginia, require that the surrogate mother be married and already have a child. Other jurisdictions require prior court approval. Of the 11 states that allow surrogacy, 7 of them require that the prospective parents be married.[384]

The world community reflects similar divisions in legal approaches, with all preconception arrangements prohibited in most Middle Eastern countries, China, Denmark, Norway, Switzerland, Costa Rica, and Germany, and only unpaid surrogacy allowed in Korea and Australia. In Great Britain, surrogacy agreements are unenforceable, and it is illegal to advertise for or broker surrogacy arrangements.[385] Surrogacy has increasingly become a feature of "reproductive tourism," in which couples from countries like the United States and England hire surrogate carriers in places like India, where it can be done more cheaply and without legal regulation.[386] Surrogacy in the United States can cost between $40,000 and $100,000, of which about $25,000 is paid to the surrogate. Surrogacy in India costs between $5,000 and $12,000, with the surrogate receiving only $3,000–$6,000 for her services. International surrogacy arrangements, however, have led to conflicts about parentage, citizenship, and other matters when the surrogate and the intended parents come from countries with conflicting laws.[387] Does it also heighten concerns about the potential exploitation of women (see Note 5)?

4. The Practice of Surrogacy Today.   The legislative and judicial developments in this area reflect the rising demand for surrogacy. As many as 7 million American women suffer some degree of infertility. Advances in reproductive technology have provided many more options for treating infertility, and many women take advantage of this technology. Worldwide it is estimated that approximately 7 million children have been born through some means of assisted reproductive technology.[388] Surrogacy is one option for infertile couples, although the cost is often prohibitive. Gay male couples also sometimes turn to surrogacy in order to have a child with a genetic tie to one partner. Exact numbers on surrogacy are hard to get, but the American Society for Reproductive Medicine estimates that there were approximately 600 births a year to gestational surrogates between 2003 and 2007.[389] The vast majority of surrogacy contracts are honored by both parties whether or not they are legally enforceable.

5. Feminist Responses to Surrogacy.   Feminist scholars have divided over the issue of surrogacy in general and its implications for autonomy in particular. When the trial court in *Baby M* ordered the surrogacy agreement enforced (a ruling later overturned), Betty Friedan saw "frightening implications for women" and a "terrifying denial of what should be basic rights for women."[390] The principal feminist defense of surrogate contracts credits the surrogate's expression of intent that her role will be limited to gestation and legitimates the contracting father's intent to play an equal parental role. According to Marjorie Shultz:

> Rules that would determine legal parenthood on the basis of individual intentions about procreation and parenting—at least in the context of reproductive technology—would recognize, encourage and reinforce men's choices to nurture children. By adopting a sex-neutral criterion such as intention, the law would partially offset the biological disadvantages men experience in

accessing child-nurturing opportunities. The result would parallel recent legal efforts to offset the burdens that childbearing imposes on women who seek equal access to market employment.[391]

Of what significance to the debate over surrogacy arrangements are the economic pressures that might lead a surrogate to enter into an arrangement? Toward which legal approach does recognition of these pressures lead? Margaret Radin is concerned about the "commodification of personhood" that surrogacy represents.[392] By contrast, Judge Richard Posner takes an economic efficiency approach in arguing that the financial constraints that push a woman toward becoming a surrogate are no different and no more objectionable than the considerations that motivate all kinds of decisionmaking throughout the economy.[393] This is essentially the framework applied by one court:

> Although common sense suggests that women of lesser means serve as surrogate mothers more often than do wealthy women, there has been no proof that surrogacy contracts exploit poor women to any greater degree than economic necessity in general exploits them by inducing them to accept lower-paid or otherwise undesirable employment.[394]

Who is right? Can women give meaningful consent to act as surrogates without any future parental rights, or are these arrangements unacceptably exploitative? Consider the words of one woman, who served as a surrogate for a gay male couple, in an essay entitled "Mutual Exploitation":

> The obvious assumption is the possibility of exploitation by the intended parents towards the surrogate. However, the reverse is just as easily possible and likely much more prevalent than people realize. In fact, the process may work best when there is mutual exploitation, to a degree. . . . [T]he experience was absolutely ideal. I had amazing people doting on me constantly, and I had the enjoyable pregnancy I had previously missed. It was a spiritual experience to be able to help create a life for two people who so desired a child, and I got to play the nurturing role. . . . On top of all this, I was compensated, and after it all, my life went back to being my life. So I can say, with absolute certainty, that any construed exploitation done "against" me was equally matched.[395]

Critics of surrogate contracts like Nancy Ehrenreich have also emphasized how surrogacy arrangements support ideological messages about having a child "of one's own" that have reinforced male dominance and women's sense of obligation to bear children:

> Given the discourse surrounding this issue, which treats infertility as a human tragedy of immense proportions and child rearing as an inviolable right, enforcing such contracts would seem to suggest that it is absolutely essential for women to become mothers by whatever means possible.[396]

Do you agree? Is there another way to read women's desire for surrogacy arrangements? What about men's desire? Is the intended father acting out of a male chauvinist vanity in "wanting a child that is 'his,' or is he expressing a male commitment to nurturing a child?"[397]

Is there a race component to surrogacy arrangements? Consider Anita Allen's concern:

Minority women increasingly will be sought to serve as "mother machines" for embryos of middle and upper-class clients. It's a new, virulent form of racial and class discrimination. Within a decade, thousands of poor and minority women will be used as a "breeder class" for those who can afford $30,000 to $40,000 to avoid the inconvenience and danger of pregnancy.[398]

April Cherry and Dorothy Roberts also worry that such reproductive technologies reinforce racial hierarchy, particularly in light of current estimates of the cost of the procedure, ranging from $30,000 to $70,000.[399] How should policymakers respond?

Lori B. Andrews, who has vigorously defended surrogacy contracts, is concerned about the implications of assuming that women cannot make responsible reproductive decisions. If gestation gives rise to "special rights" for surrogates to change their minds, could it not also justify "special responsibilities," such as a woman's responsibility to have a Caesarean section if doctors believe it would be beneficial to the child. Andrews concludes:

Some feminists have criticized surrogacy as turning participating women, albeit with their consent, into reproductive vessels. I see the danger of the anti-surrogacy arguments as potentially turning all women into reproductive vessels, without their consent, by providing government oversight for women's decisions and creating a disparate legal category for gestation.[400]

What is your view? What regulations do you believe should govern surrogacy arrangements?

6. Frozen "Pre-Embryos": Balancing Wanted and Unwanted Parenthood. There are currently over 400,000 embryos in frozen storage, with little clear law on how to resolve disputes that arise about their use. In one Tennessee case, Davis v. Davis, a couple had planned on using frozen embryos to start a family, but divorced before a pregnancy had been achieved. At divorce, the wife sought custody of the embryos for possible future implantation and the husband sought authority to prevent implantation.

On appeal to the state supreme court, the wife changed her position, deciding that rather than use the embryos to become pregnant herself, she wanted to donate them to a childless couple. The court rejected the approaches of both the trial court and the court of appeals, holding that "preembryos are not, strictly speaking, either 'persons' or 'property,' but occupy an interim category that entitles them to special respect because of their potential for human life." The court stated that, if possible, a contest over pre-embryos should be resolved according to prior agreement. Where no such agreement exists, each party's constitutional privacy interests require that their individual positions, burdens, and interests be weighed against the other's, with the court choosing the disposition that avoids the most harm. In *Davis*, the court balanced the interests as follows:

Beginning with the burden imposed on Junior Davis, we note that the consequences are obvious. Any disposition which results in the gestation of the preembryos would impose unwanted parenthood on him, with all of its possible financial and psychological consequences. The impact that this unwanted parenthood would have on Junior Davis can only be understood by considering his particular circumstances, as revealed in the record.

Junior Davis testified that he was the fifth youngest of six children. When he was five years old, his parents divorced, his mother had a nervous breakdown, and he and three of his brothers went to live at a home for boys run by the Lutheran Church. . . . From that day forward, he had monthly visits with his mother but saw his father only three more times before he died in 1976. Junior Davis testified that, as a boy, he had severe problems caused by separation from his parents. He said that it was especially hard to leave his mother after each monthly visit. He clearly feels that he has suffered because of his lack of opportunity to establish a relationship with his parents and particularly because of the absence of his father.

In light of his boyhood experiences, Junior Davis is vehemently opposed to fathering a child that would not live with both parents. Regardless of whether he or Mary Sue had custody, he feels that the child's bond with the non-custodial parent would not be satisfactory. He testified very clearly that his concern was for the psychological obstacles a child in such a situation would face, as well as the burdens it would impose on him. Likewise, he is opposed to donation because the recipient couple might divorce, leaving the child (which he definitely would consider his own) in a single-parent setting.

Balanced against Junior Davis's interest in avoiding parenthood is Mary Sue Davis's interest in donating the preembryos to another couple for implantation. Refusal to permit donation of the preembryos would impose on her the burden of knowing that the lengthy IVF procedures she underwent were futile, and that the preembryos to which she contributed genetic material would never become children. While this is not an insubstantial emotional burden, we can only conclude that Mary Sue Davis's interest in donation is not as significant as the interest Junior Davis has in avoiding parenthood. If she were allowed to donate these preembryos, he would face a lifetime of either wondering about his parental status or knowing about his parental status but having no control over it. He testified quite clearly that if the preembryos were brought to term he would fight for custody of his child or children. Donation, if a child came of it, would rob him twice—his procreational autonomy would be defeated and his relationship with his offspring would be prohibited.

The case would be closer if Mary Sue Davis were seeking to use the preembryos herself, but only if she could not achieve parenthood by any other reasonable means. We recognize the trauma that Mary Sue has already experienced and the additional discomfort to which she would be subjected if she opts to attempt IVF again. Still, she would have a reasonable opportunity, through IVF, to try once again to achieve parenthood in all its aspects—genetic, gestation, bearing, and rearing.

Further, we note that if Mary Sue Davis were unable to undergo another round of IVF, or opted not to try, she could still achieve the child-rearing aspects of parenthood through adoption. The fact that she and Junior Davis pursued adoption indicates that, at least at one time, she was willing to forego genetic parenthood and would have been satisfied by the childrearing aspects of parenthood alone.[401]

Is this analysis consistent with the principle of equality? Is it an application of the "ethic of care"? Pragmatism? Stereotyped thinking? Resistance to stereotypes?

Mary Sue Davis was unable to conceive children through the usual means because, after six painful tubal pregnancies, both of her fallopian tubes were inoperative. Each of the six IVF attempts involved a month of subcutaneous injections and five anesthetizations for the aspiration procedure. Should this painful series of treatments have been considered in the balancing of interests? Is it clear to you why Junior Davis's strong feelings—about not fathering children he could not raise himself in a nuclear family—weighed more heavily than Mary Sue Davis's wish to succeed in her efforts to produce one or more children for herself or for others?

While the law is still emerging in this area, the trend in this context favors the right not to procreate over the right to procreate, as the court did in *Davis*. This approach usually means that the agreement the couple signed before the assisted reproductive procedures is unenforceable.[402] Some commentators have criticized this trend, arguing that there is no convincing evidence of psychological harm from involuntary genetic parenthood, and that whatever interest individuals have in avoiding genetic parenthood should be waivable in advance.[403] A few states have enacted statutes addressing the status or use of cryopreserved pre-embryos. For example, Florida requires couples and IVF programs to agree in advance about the disposition of pre-embryos in the event of a divorce or the death of a spouse.[404] Louisiana requires the treatment of pre-embryos as "juridical persons" and prohibits the destruction of pre-embryos or their use for research purposes.[405] How would you resolve the competing concerns? Is there a single "feminist" answer?

Putting Theory Into Practice

5-23. In the surrogacy contract signed by the parties in *Baby M*, Mrs. Whitehead agreed not to abort any fetus conceived with Mr. Stern's sperm unless necessary to preserve her physical health. She also agreed, in the event prenatal testing revealed "that the fetus is genetically or congenitally abnormal," to "abort the fetus upon demand of Williams Stern" and accept a reduced payment of $1,000 rather than the $10,000 upon the birth of a child. Are these provisions enforceable?

5-24. In 2011, a gay male couple sues in New Jersey state court to enforce a surrogacy agreement under which one man's sister would carry a child for the couple who was conceived using his partner's sperm and a donor egg. The couple asks the court to rule that *Baby M.* does not apply to cases of gestational surrogacy.[406] How should the court rule? Why?

5-25. In 2002, Congress authorized the spending of nearly $1 million to promote the donation of frozen embryos to recipients who intend to use the embryos to bear and raise a child. Is this a good policy?

5-26. Dr. Eleanora Porcu, who helped to develop the technology for freezing of eggs (or oocyte cryopreservation), saw the possibility of freezing unfertilized eggs as a way of sidestepping the Roman Catholic Church's ban on freezing embryos, which the Church deems immoral. However, she is opposed to giving healthy women the opportunity to freeze their eggs so that they can postpone childbearing for their own convenience. This practice is harmful to feminism, she says, because "[i]t means that we're accepting a mentality of efficiency in which pregnancy and motherhood are marginalized." "We've demonstrated that we are able to do everything like men. . . . Now we have to do the second revolution, which is not to become dependent on a technology that involves surgical intervention. We have to be free to be pregnant when we are fertile and young."[407] Do you agree?

5-27. Would enactment of a "personhood amendment," discussed in the previous section, have an effect on surrogacy? On the regulation of cryopreserved pre-embryos or embryos?

4. The Pregnant Woman and Fetus as Adversaries

A different kind of control of pregnant women concerns their prosecution and confinement for abusing drugs or engaging in other behaviors detrimental to the fetus.

Reading Questions

1. As between women's autonomy interests and the safety of fetuses or children, is it clear whose interests should prevail?
2. If children's interests should be paramount, what about other regulation of pregnant women? Should they be allowed to smoke? Drink alcoholic beverages? Drive without a seat belt? Live with an abusive spouse?

Ferguson v. City of Charleston

532 U.S. 67 (2001)

Justice STEVENS delivered the opinion of the Court.

In this case, we must decide whether a state hospital's performance of a diagnostic test to obtain evidence of a patient's criminal conduct for law enforcement purposes is an unreasonable search if the patient has not consented to the procedure. More narrowly, the question is whether the interest in using the threat of criminal sanctions to deter pregnant women from using cocaine can justify a departure from the general rule that an official nonconsensual search is unconstitutional if not authorized by a valid warrant.

I

In the fall of 1988, staff members at the public hospital operated in the city of Charleston by the Medical University of South Carolina (MUSC) became concerned about an apparent increase in the use of cocaine by patients who were receiving prenatal treatment. In response to this perceived increase, as of April 1989, MUSC began to order drug screens to be performed on urine samples from maternity patients who were suspected of using cocaine. If a patient tested positive, she was then referred by MUSC staff to the county substance abuse commission for counseling and treatment. However, despite the referrals, the incidence of cocaine use among the patients at MUSC did not appear to change.

Some four months later, Nurse Shirley Brown, the case manager for the MUSC obstetrics department, heard a news broadcast reporting that the police in Greenville, South Carolina, were arresting pregnant users of cocaine on the theory that such use harmed the fetus and was therefore child abuse. Nurse Brown discussed the story with MUSC's general counsel, Joseph C. Good, Jr., who then contacted Charleston Solicitor Charles Condon in order to offer MUSC's cooperation in prosecuting mothers whose children tested positive for drugs at birth.

After receiving Good's letter, Solicitor Condon took the first steps in developing the policy at issue in this case. He organized the initial meetings, decided who would participate, and issued the invitations, in which he described his plan to prosecute women who tested positive for cocaine while pregnant. The task force that Condon formed included representatives of MUSC, the police, the County Substance Abuse Commission and the Department of Social Services. Their deliberations led to MUSC's adoption of a 12-page document entitled "POLICY M-7," dealing with the subject of "Management of Drug Abuse During Pregnancy."

The first three pages of Policy M-7 set forth the procedure to be followed by the hospital staff to "identify/assist pregnant patients suspected of drug abuse." The first section, entitled the "Identification of Drug Abusers," provided that a patient should be tested for cocaine through a urine drug screen if she met one or more of nine criteria. It also stated that a chain of custody should be followed when obtaining and testing urine samples, presumably to make sure that the results could be used in subsequent criminal proceedings. The policy also provided for education and referral to a substance abuse clinic for patients who tested positive. Most important, it added the threat of law enforcement intervention that "provided the necessary 'leverage' to make the policy effective." That threat was, as respondents candidly acknowledge, essential to the program's success in getting women into treatment and keeping them there.

The threat of law enforcement involvement was set forth in two protocols, the first dealing with the identification of drug use during pregnancy, and the second with identification of drug use after labor. Under the latter protocol, the police were to be notified without delay and the patient promptly arrested. Under the former, after the initial positive drug test, the police were to be notified (and the patient arrested) . . . [unless she consented] to substance abuse treatment.

The last six pages of the policy contained forms for the patients to sign, as well as procedures for the police to follow when a patient was arrested. The policy also prescribed in detail the precise offenses with which a woman could be charged, depending on the stage of her pregnancy. If the pregnancy was 27 weeks or less, the patient was to be charged with simple possession. If it was 28 weeks or more, she was to be charged with possession and distribution to a person under the age of 18—in this case, the fetus. If she delivered "while testing positive for illegal drugs," she was also to be charged with unlawful neglect of a child. Under the policy, the police were instructed to interrogate the arrestee in order "to ascertain the identity of the subject who provided illegal drugs to the suspect." Other than the provisions describing the substance abuse treatment to be offered to women who tested positive, the policy made no mention of any change in the prenatal care of such patients, nor did it prescribe any special treatment for the newborns.

II

Petitioners are 10 women who received obstetrical care at MUSC and who were arrested after testing positive for cocaine. . . .

Petitioners' complaint challenged the validity of the policy under various theories, including the claim that warrantless and nonconsensual drug tests conducted for criminal investigatory purposes were unconstitutional searches. Respondents advanced two principal defenses to the constitutional claim: (1) that, as a matter of fact, petitioners had consented to the searches; and (2) that, as a matter of law, the searches were reasonable, even absent consent, because they were justified by special non-law-enforcement purposes. The District Court rejected the second defense because the searches in question "were not done by the medical university for independent purposes. [Instead,] the police came in and there was an agreement reached that the positive screens would be shared with the police." [The Fourth Circuit Court of Appeals reversed on the grounds that the searches were reasonable under the "special needs" exception.]

We granted certiorari . . . to review the appellate court's holding on the "special needs" issue.

III

Because MUSC is a state hospital, the members of its staff are government actors, subject to the strictures of the Fourth Amendment. . . . Moreover, the urine tests conducted by those staff members were indisputably searches within the meaning of the Fourth Amendment. . . . Neither the District Court nor the Court of Appeals concluded that any of the nine criteria used to identify the women to be searched provided either probable cause to believe that they were using cocaine, or even the basis for a reasonable suspicion of such use. . . . The reasonable expectation of privacy enjoyed by the typical patient undergoing diagnostic tests in a hospital is that the results of those tests will not be shared with nonmedical personnel without her consent. . . .

In this case, . . . the central and indispensable feature of the policy from its inception was the use of law enforcement to coerce the patients into substance abuse treatment. This fact distinguishes this case from circumstances in which physicians or psychologists, in the course of ordinary medical procedures aimed at helping the patient herself, come across information that under rules of law or ethics is subject to reporting requirements, which no one has challenged here. . . .

Respondents argue in essence that their ultimate purpose—namely, protecting the health of both mother and child—is a beneficent one. . . . While the ultimate goal of the program may well have been to get the women in question into substance abuse treatment and off of drugs, the immediate objective of the searches was to generate evidence for law enforcement purposes in order to reach that goal. The threat of law enforcement may ultimately have been intended as a means to an end, but the direct and primary purpose of MUSC's policy was to ensure the use of those means. In our opinion, this distinction is critical. Because law enforcement involvement always serves some broader social purpose or objective, under respondents' view, virtually any nonconsensual suspicionless search could be immunized under the special needs doctrine by defining the search solely in terms of its ultimate, rather than immediate, purpose. Such an approach is inconsistent with the Fourth Amendment. Given the primary purpose of the Charleston program, which was to use the threat of arrest and prosecution in order to force women into treatment, and given the extensive involvement of law enforcement officials at every stage of the policy, this case simply does not fit within the closely guarded category of "special needs."

Accordingly, the judgment of the Court of Appeals is reversed, and the case is remanded for further proceedings consistent with this opinion.

Dissenting opinion by Justice SCALIA, with whom THE CHIEF JUSTICE and JUSTICE THOMAS join as to Part II.

There is always an unappealing aspect to the use of doctors and nurses, ministers of mercy, to obtain incriminating evidence against the supposed objects of their ministration—although here, it is correctly pointed out, the doctors and nurses were ministering not just to the mothers but also to the children whom their cooperation with the police was meant to protect. But whatever may be the correct social judgment concerning the desirability of what occurred here, that is not the issue in the present case. The Constitution does not resolve all difficult social questions, but leaves the vast majority of them to resolution by debate and the democratic process—which would produce a decision by the citizens of Charleston, through their elected representatives, to forbid or permit the police action at issue here. The question before us is a narrower one: whether, whatever the desirability of this police conduct, it violates the Fourth Amendment's prohibition of unreasonable searches and seizures. In my view, it plainly does not....

II . . .

The conclusion of the Court that the special-needs doctrine is inapplicable rests upon its contention that respondents "undertook to obtain [drug] evidence from their patients" not for any medical purpose, but "for the specific purpose of incriminating those patients." In other words, the purported medical rationale was merely a pretext; there was no special need. . . . This contention contradicts the District Court's finding of fact that the goal of the testing policy "was not to arrest patients but to facilitate their treatment and protect both the mother and unborn child." . . . This finding is binding upon us unless clearly erroneous. . . .

The cocaine tests started in April 1989, neither at police suggestion nor with police involvement. Expectant mothers who tested positive were referred by hospital staff for substance-abuse treatment—an obvious health benefit to both mother and child. . . . And, since "infants whose mothers abuse cocaine during pregnancy are born with a wide variety of physical and neurological abnormalities," . . . which require medical attention, . . . the tests were of additional medical benefit in predicting needed postnatal treatment for the child. Thus, in their origin—before the police were in any way involved—the tests had an immediate, not merely an "ultimate" . . . purpose of improving maternal and infant health. . . .

[I]t is not the function of this Court—at least not in Fourth Amendment cases—to weigh petitioners' privacy interest against the State's interest in meeting the crisis of "crack babies" that developed in the late 1980's. I cannot refrain from observing, however, that the outcome of a wise weighing of those interests is by no means clear. The initial goal of the doctors and nurses who conducted cocaine-testing in this case was to refer pregnant drug addicts to treatment centers, and to prepare for necessary treatment of their possibly affected children. When the doctors and nurses agreed to the program providing test results to the police, they did so because (in addition to the fact that child abuse was required by law to be reported) they wanted to use the sanction of arrest as a strong incentive for their addicted patients to undertake drug-addiction treatment. And the police themselves used it for that benign purpose, as is shown by the fact that only 30 of 253 women testing positive for cocaine were ever arrested, and only 2 of those prosecuted. . . . It would not be unreasonable to conclude that today's judgment, authorizing the assessment of damages against the county solicitor and individual doctors and nurses who participated in the program, proves once again that no good deed goes unpunished.

Notes

1. Criminal Prosecutions of Drug-Abusing Pregnant Women. According to the Department of Health and Human Services, approximately 4.5 percent of pregnant women in 2009 and 2010 used illicit drugs.[408] Drug abuse by a pregnant woman, especially crack cocaine, enhances certain serious risks to the unborn child, including growth retardation, smaller head circumference, impaired motor development, greater difficulty with tasks that require visual attention and focus, and higher incidences of depression, anxiety, attention-deficit disorders, and delinquent and aggressive behaviors. Boys appear to be more vulnerable than girls to behavior problems. However, the long-term damage does not appear to be as serious as was once thought. A study based on 4,419 cocaine-exposed children showed that I.Q. scores averaged only about 4 points lower than those of unexposed children, and that children outgrow some of the effects in terms of brain and body size.[409] New research suggests that in utero exposure to methamphetamine is a growing problem and may pose similar or ever greater dangers than cocaine.[410]

In response to growing concern about the risks of fetal damage from drug use, prosecutors in at least 36 states have charged drug-addicted pregnant women under various criminal statutes prohibiting delivery of a controlled substance to a minor, child abuse or endangerment, and homicide.[411] Many charges have been rejected, at least on appeal, on the grounds that the statutes under which charges were brought were not intended to apply to unborn children as victims. The Kentucky Supreme Court, for example, reversed a criminal conviction of a woman whose baby tested positive for cocaine at birth. In construing the child endangerment law to exclude a pregnant woman's conduct, the court relied in part on the state's Maternal Health Act of 1992, in which the legislature stated that "punitive actions taken against pregnant alcohol or substance abusers would create additional problems, including discouraging these individuals from seeking the essential prenatal care and substance abuse treatment necessary to deliver a healthy newborn."[412] Substance abuse by pregnant women, according to the Kentucky legislature, should be treated "solely as a public health issue."[413] To the same end, the South Carolina Supreme Court in 2008 overturned the conviction of a defendant for homicide by child abuse, on grounds of ineffective counsel. Although the defendant's fetus was stillborn and tested positive for cocaine, the court concluded that the state relied upon "outdated" research about the consequences of cocaine use on the fetus, and that defendant's counsel had failed to call experts who would have testified about "recent studies showing that cocaine is no more harmful to a fetus than nicotine use, poor nutrition, lack of prenatal care, or other conditions commonly associated with the urban poor."[414]

There is little doubt that statutes specifically targeted at drug abuse by pregnant women would be constitutional and enforceable, and legislatures in a number of states have begun to pass such laws. One example that has become a model for other states is a Utah law enacted in 2010 that makes it criminal homicide for a woman to engage in conduct that intentionally or knowingly causes a miscarriage.[415] Is this a reasonable statute?[416] A 2006 Alabama law prohibits a "responsible person" from "exposing a child to an environment in which he or she . . . knowingly, recklessly or intentionally causes or permits a child to be exposed to, to ingest or inhale, or to have contact with a controlled substance, chemical substance or drug paraphernalia." The law was intended to protect children from the dangers of methamphetamine labs, but prosecutors have expanded the law's definition of "child" to mean "fetus" and interpreted the term "environment" to also mean the "womb." According to the *New York Times*, there have been approximately 60 chemical-endangerment prosecutions of new mothers since the law was passed. The minimum sentence under the law is 10 years.[417] Is this a reasonable approach?

In an Indiana case, a despondent pregnant woman who was 33-weeks pregnant swallowed rat poison in an effort to end her life after her boyfriend abandoned her. Although the woman lived, the baby, who was delivered by emergency C-section, did not. She was convicted of murder, and the conviction was upheld by the Indiana Court of Appeals.[418] Is a murder prosecution reasonable under these circumstances?[419] In the 2-1 decision, the dissenting judge suggested that holding the woman's actions covered by Indiana's feticide statute could result in the criminalization of pregnant women who smoke, drink, or take over-the-counter cold remedies and sleep aids. The majority responded that the statute requires the intention to terminate a pregnancy.[420] Is this a satisfactory distinction?

According to the Department of Health and Human Services, 10.8 percent of pregnant women use alcohol during pregnancy, and 16.3 percent use tobacco—two to three times, respectively, the number of pregnant women who abuse illegal drugs.[421] An upstate New York woman was charged with child endangerment after she delivered a baby whose blood alcohol was 0.18 percent; the charges were later dismissed on the grounds that the state's child-endangerment statute was not intended to apply to the unborn.[422] If the state amended the statute to include such conduct, what penalties would be appropriate? What about pregnant women who drive too fast, fail to use seat belts, or work extended hours against the advice of their doctors?

The effects of substance abuse can interact with other risk factors and cultural biases. For example, research shows that among women who drink at the same rate, children born to low-income women have a 70.9 percent rate of fetal alcohol syndrome, compared to a 4.5 percent rate for those of upper-income women. Better nutrition is the difference. A Northwestern University study suggests that outcomes in pregnancies complicated by cocaine abuse may be improved by comprehensive prenatal care.[423] Race and class also affect how service providers respond to high-risk factors. One study found that despite similar rates of substance abuse, black women are ten times more likely than white women to be reported to government authorities.[424]

Should a pregnant woman who is in an abusive relationship and does not leave her batterer be prosecuted under a child abuse statute? Her abuser is subject to additional penalties. Federal legislation criminalizes harm caused to a "child in utero" during the course of other specified offenses. So, for example, a man who assaults his pregnant partner can also be guilty of a separate crime under federal law if he causes injury to the fetus.

Some courts have ordered female offenders with a history of substance abuse to avoid becoming pregnant, as a term of probation. Such probationary conditions have generally been overturned because they are not deemed to be reasonably related to the crime committed (which often has nothing to do with childrearing) or to the goal of rehabilitation. However, some trial courts have ordered women who have been convicted of child abuse not to become pregnant as a condition of probation. Many of these cases, too, have been overturned on appeal.[425] Should the option be preserved?

2. Civil Alternatives to Criminal Prosecution. What about a form of "civil commitment" (not requiring a criminal conviction) for women who are in grave danger of drug abuse during a pregnancy? In 1998, South Dakota became the first state to require pregnant women who abuse alcohol or drugs to be taken into custody and to undergo mandatory rehabilitation. Wisconsin soon followed, and several other states have considered adopting a similar approach.[426] Would you support such legislation? Does it present different concerns than treatment required as a condition of probation?

The Canadian Supreme Court considered this issue. In Winnipeg Child and Family Services v. G.D.F., a trial court granted an order to confine a pregnant woman who was addicted to glue sniffing, which can damage the fetal nervous system. Two of the woman's previous children were born permanently disabled and were wards of the state. The Canadian Supreme Court held that the court lacked authority to order confinement to protect the unborn under its *parens patriae* jurisdiction, which sometimes allows courts to step into the shoes of the parent to safeguard the best interests of a child. In so holding, the Court expressed concerns not only about the restriction of women's rights, but also the possibility that confinement would "drive the problem underground" by deterring women from seeking prenatal care. Two dissenting Justices would have permitted intervention to prevent "abusive activity that will cause serious and irreparable harm to the [fetus]," where the remedy was the "least intrusive option" and the process was procedurally fair. In the dissent's view, "when a woman chooses to carry a fetus to term, she must accept some responsibility for its well-being and the state has an interest in trying to ensure the child's health."[427] What is your view? Should it matter whether the woman chose not to take advantage of voluntary treatment programs?

State child abuse and neglect statutes provide another response to the problem. These civil statutes are available only if a court concludes that they were intended to apply to prenatal conduct. Civil child abuse laws in more than a dozen states apply to substance abuse during pregnancy.[428]

In Florida, Samantha Burton was hospitalized without her consent after she was admitted to the hospital in her seventh month of pregnancy on a false alarm of premature labor. Her doctor argued that she was risking a miscarriage if she didn't quit smoking immediately and stay on bed rest in the hospital, and a judge agreed.[429] Should a second opinion have been required, at least?

If drug abuse during pregnancy constitutes child neglect, what governmental responses are most appropriate? Removal of the child from the parent and in some cases termination of parental rights are the most likely options, but is that a good option for the child?

Every leading medical organization, including the American Medical Association and the American College of Obstetrics and Gynecologists, has concluded that the best response to substance abuse during pregnancy is education and treatment rather than punishment.[430] Although most states have provided some resources for such approaches, many programs come nowhere close to meeting the need.[431] Several of the pregnant addicts facing well-publicized prosecutions for criminal child abuse had sought treatment, but found either that waiting lists were long or that the programs available would not accept pregnant women. In New York City, 87 percent of drug treatment programs reject pregnant Medicaid patients addicted to crack cocaine, and yet these are the women most likely to be targeted for prosecution.[432]

In partial response to this problem, Congress passed the Alcohol, Drug Abuse, and Mental Health Administration Reorganization Act.[433] This legislation expands block grants provided to states for drug treatment programs, including money targeted at addressing the particular needs of pregnant, drug-addicted women. A number of states have enacted legislation to prohibit drug treatment facilities from discriminating against pregnant women.[434]

Putting Theory Into Practice

5-28. A non-profit organization founded as Children Requiring a Caring Kommunity (C.R.A.C.K.), later renamed Project Prevention, was established to provide "effective prevention measures to reduce the tragedy of numerous drug-affected pregnancies." The Project offers $300 to drug-abusing females who promise to be sterilized or to receive long-term birth control. As of August 2011, 3,848 addicts or alcoholics had taken advantage of the offer. Of those whose race is noted, 42 percent are black or Hispanic.[435] Is Project Prevention a good approach? Is its approach any more, or less, defensible than court-mandated probation conditions?

5-29. To be eligible for Medicaid-subsidized prenatal care in New York, a pregnant woman is compelled by law to be interviewed by a battery of professionals, including nurses, health educators, financial officers, HIV counselors, and social workers. The questions include personal details about any past and current romantic relationships, experience with domestic violence, use of alcohol and drugs, mental illness, eating habits, earning capacity, and the earning capacity of any boyfriends.[436] Is this appropriate? Are poor, pregnant women entitled to any privacy with respect to their personal relationships and habits, or is divulging this information a reasonable quid pro quo for public assistance?

5-30. Wisconsin State Senator Glenn Grothman has proposed SB507, which provides for statewide education and public awareness campaigns about child abuse and neglect. The bill specifies that "[i]n promoting these campaigns and materials, the [Child Abuse and Neglect Prevention Board] shall emphasize nonmarital parenthood as a contributing factor to child abuse and neglect."[437] How would you respond to this proposed legislation?

5-31. Research has established that a regimen of AZT treatment is successful in reducing the rate of HIV transmission from mother to child by approximately two-thirds.[438] Should AZT treatment be required for pregnant women who are HIV-positive? Should HIV testing be required? In 2006, the CDC issued a recommendation that HIV-testing be universal in early pregnancy, but that allows for individuals to opt-out of the testing.[439] A handful of states have adopted mandatory HIV-testing laws for pregnant women, following either an opt-out or opt-in model. A few states mandate HIV-testing for newborns.[440] Should mandates regarding testing or treatment be limited by the constitutional right to refuse medical treatment?[441]

5-32. In India, there are 927 girls for every 1,000 boys (as compared to the worldwide ratio of 1,050 girls to 1,000 boys). The country is considering cash incentives of $5,000 (plus free health insurance) to the families of baby girls in an effort to limit the number of sex-selective abortions in favor of boys.[442] Is this a justifiable form of sex discrimination? Are there other preferable approaches?

5-33. Marlise Numoz of Texas was 14 weeks pregnant when, after collapsing on her kitchen floor, doctors pronounced her brain dead and the fetus non-viable. Her family agreed that she did not want to have machines to keep her body alive, but hospital officials concluded that a Texas law stating that "[a] doctor may not withdraw or withhold life-sustaining treatment from a pregnant patient" required them to continue life-sustaining treatment against the will of her family. After the father sued the hospital for "cruel and obscene mutilation of a corpse," the court ordered the termination of life support.[443] How would you evaluate the statute? If the fetus had been viable, should the result have been different? An adult clearly has the right to have respected her wish not to have life-sustaining medical intervention. Should the rule be different for pregnant women?

5-34. A 28-year-old woman from Salt Lake City failed to follow medical advice to have a Cesarean section. As a result, one of her twins was stillborn, although he could have been saved if the mother had undergone the procedure. She was arrested for first-degree criminal homicide and child endangerment. What defenses could be raised on her behalf? Should her conduct be criminalized? The woman later pled guilty to two counts of child endangerment and the homicide charge was dropped.[444] Is this an appropriate outcome? Should the failure of a mother to consent to a medically recommended Caesarean section be an appropriate factor to consider in a subsequent abuse and neglect action on behalf of the child, even if the vaginal birth was successful?[445]

5-35. A mother who already had six children ages seven and under became pregnant with octuplets through an artificial insemination process supervised by a doctor. The prospects for eight healthy children in one pregnancy are very remote, and each additional fetus lowers the chances for each other fetus to be born without severe problems. Should the state intervene? When? How? Against whom?[446]

5-36. Two weeks before her sentencing hearing on a forgery conviction, Yuriko wrote to the judge telling him that she was pregnant and wished to have an abortion. The judge offered her a deal: if she agreed to bring the fetus to term, he would give her probation instead of a prison sentence.[447] Should this kind of plea bargain be permissible?

C. ECONOMIC AUTONOMY AND WOMEN'S POVERTY

One of the most significant impairments of women's autonomy is not primarily legal, but economic. The final section of this chapter explores the welfare system and its impact on poverty among women and their children.

Welfare began in the United States as part of state "mother's pensions" programs for destitute families. Use of the term "pension" implied that the payment was a substitute for money that might otherwise be received in paid employment. Implicit in these early programs was the understanding that childrearing was work and that a mother's devotion to the care of her children was important.[448] The initial purpose was to relieve impoverishment caused by mothers having been widowed or abandoned by their husband—i.e., "worthy" mothers. From the very beginning, blacks, immigrants, and unwed mothers were systematically excluded, either by the failure to establish programs in locations where these populations were concentrated or through discriminatory eligibility requirements, including residency and moral character requirements. In 1931, the first national survey of mother's pensions, broken down by race, found that only 3 percent of recipients were black.[449]

With the civil rights movement of the 1960s came successful legal challenges to welfare criteria that excluded racial and ethnic minorities. As a result, an increasing proportion of welfare recipients were never married, non-Caucasian, and adolescent. By 1992, over 60 percent of welfare recipients were women of color. As this demographic transformation occurred, so too did the image of women on welfare, who were often viewed as lazy, promiscuous, and socially irresponsible. Accordingly, attention began to focus less on child welfare and more on mothers' sexual and procreative practices.

In 1996, national welfare policy shifted significantly. Rather than a potentially long-term public entitlement of support for poor, single-parent families, it became a time-limited benefit that assumed that every able-bodied parent should work to support his or her own children. This section examines this shift, as well as broader questions concerning autonomy and welfare policy. The reading by Judith Koons describes the Personal Responsibility Work Opportunity Act (PRWORA), drawing attention to the moral dimensions of the Act. Readings by Martha Fineman and Vicki Schultz then outline the ongoing debate about whether economic vulnerability of primary caretakers should be addressed through public support, as prior welfare policy assumed, or through their paid employment as PRWORA mandates.

Reading Questions

1. In what way does the goal of promoting economic self-sufficiency conflict with the goal of providing adequate support for children and their caretakers? Which is the more important objective?
2. Does the emphasis on work serve women well, or is Fineman's model of public subsidy for care of dependents a better emphasis?
3. To what extent should the federal government promote marriage as a means of ensuring stability (including economic stability) for children?

Judith Koons, Motherhood, Marriage and Morality: The Pro-Marriage Moral Discourse of American Welfare Policy

19 Wis. Women's L.J. 1, 2-3, 6-8, 10-14, 20-24, 41-42 (2004)

During a campaign speech in 1991, Bill Clinton vowed to "put an end to welfare as we know it." Five years later, with the adoption of the Personal Responsibility and Work Opportunity Reconciliation Act (PRWORA), that promise was given effect. . . . Yet, the means adopted in TANF to "put an end to welfare"—work requirements, time requirements, state and local autonomy, and family values—have been components for many centuries of Euro-American policies on social provisioning. The "new tools" of welfare reform are part of an old, old story that is deeply etched with considerations of gender, race, and class. In that story, the single mother is "a hideous monster" to whom social policy gives two options: get a man or a low-wage job. . . .

Welfare reform in the mid-1990s arose out of the appearance of a consensus on policy across party lines. Among the key provisions of the PRWORA were the Food Stamp Program, the Child Care and Development Block Grant, and the Temporary Aid to Needy Families Block Grant. In the Food Stamp Program, eligibility criteria were tightened and welfare families were no longer automatically enrolled in the program. Many programs for children were reworked in the PRWORA. Various food and childcare programs were consolidated into the Child Care and Development Block Grant. Funding was reduced or eliminated for child nutrition and meals programs. Child support enforcement efforts were bolstered. The Supplemental Security Income (SSI) definition of disability for children was narrowed.

Aid to Families with Dependent Children (AFDC), which had been construed to provide welfare assistance as a matter of statutory entitlement, was replaced by TANF, a fixed block grant program. With the adoption of the PRWORA, the framework for welfare was changed from a "statutory entitlement model" to a "devolved contractual model." Given flexibility to design work-oriented, transitional assistance programs, states were permitted to use TANF funds for cash assistance, childcare, education, training, and transportation. . . .

For the central work requirement, the federal government required a welfare-reliant mother to engage in an approved work activity within two years of receiving her first welfare check or face sanctioning. The work activity requirement was slated to increase . . . to thirty hours per week in 2000. Optional individual responsibility plans were designed to move welfare recipients into the work force as quickly as possible. . . .

Traditional "family values" were asserted in the PRWORA in five interrelated ways. First, the PRWORA explicitly expressed a purpose of promoting two-parent families. Construing the purpose as one of promoting marriage, a number of states adopted pro-marriage programs for welfare recipients. For example, Oklahoma announced a $10 million marriage initiative, financed by "unspent" TANF funds, to reduce the state's divorce rate by one-third by 2010. Arizona established a Marriage and Communication Skills Commission and appropriated TANF funds for marriage skills training vouchers. West Virginia adopted the "first unambiguous cash incentive for marriage," a $100 monthly marriage bonus for TANF recipients who are married. A growing Marriage Movement endorsed these and other pro-marriage and "responsible fatherhood" initiatives.

Second, the purpose of the PRWORA explicitly discouraged out-of-wedlock pregnancies. States were required to track out-of-wedlock pregnancy rates and to take steps to reduce illegitimate births. Bonuses for "Illegitimacy Reduction" were established for states that achieved the highest decreases of out-of-wedlock births without increases in abortions. In an effort to encourage abstinence and prevent teen pregnancy, federal funds were allocated to three different abstinence education programs.

Third, the PRWORA regulated non-marital sexuality by allowing states to impose "family caps" on recipient households. Under "family cap" legislation, a family could not receive additional benefits due to the birth of a child who was conceived during a period in which the family was eligible for TANF. Four states adopted family caps under federal waivers in the early 1990s. As of December 2003, twenty-four states had some form of family cap policy in place.

Fourth, the PRWORA opened the door for states to promote family planning and to encourage welfare-reliant mothers to relinquish their children for adoption. In fifteen states, family planning information and counseling initiatives were integrated into the TANF program. Three states devised programs to encourage mothers who receive welfare to give up children for adoption. In addition to offering services such as "positive information" about adoption, two states provided cash incentives for relinquishing newborns.

Fifth, the PRWORA demonstrated that welfare is a site of sexual regulation by mandating paternity identification as well as child support enforcement cooperation. Under the PRWORA, states were required to ensure that recipients cooperate with paternity identification and child support enforcement provisions. Furthermore, and with far-reaching consequences, the domestic violence exception to these procedures became optional. In addition, the PRWORA directed states to sanction uncooperative clients and, at the same time, expanded administrative powers and decreased judicial review.

With these measures, the PRWORA sought to codify—at the national and state levels—a conservative family values agenda. However, in the ensuing years, the rhetorical pitch has been elevated to advocate for more aggressive pro-marriage welfare policies. The PRWORA helped states over the threshold "toward what could become a robust and multi-front attack on the problem of family composition." . . .

The rhetoric of welfare retrenchment of the late twentieth and early twenty-first centuries is, without question, a discourse of heterosexual marriage and conservative morality. That welfare retrenchment in the 1990s was, at heart, a marriage-based discourse is clearly reflected in the PRWORA's statement of purpose. Of the four purposes, three of them pointed toward marriage. Moreover, the structure of the section underscored the marital impetus of the PRWORA and the double-bind that it erected for poor women.

In subsection one, the purpose was to allow children to be "cared for in their own homes." However, subsection two created a critical inconsistency because "dependence of needy parents on government benefits" was to be ended. The contradiction was thus set: children should be cared for in their homes, but poor women must leave their homes and enter the low-wage labor market. Subsection four provided the answer to the conundrum—poor women should marry and become part of two-parent families so they may have the resources to care for their children. . . .

Moral reform continues to be offered as the solution to poverty. The prominent conservative view is that single motherhood and teenage pregnancy, by themselves, are causes of poverty and dependency. Into the twenty-first century, marriage is being proposed as the ideal anti-poverty program. In fact, the welfare system is seen as a result of "the collapse of marriage." Marriage is characterized as a "social good under attack." The reasons recited for the weakness of marriage are instructive. According to marriage advocates, over the past forty years there has been an "extraordinary shift in cultural norms concerning sex, marriage, and childbearing," including the advent of birth control, the entry of more women into the labor force, and the increasing acceptability of cohabitation outside of wedlock. Widened opportunities for women, including alternatives to marriage that were the fruits of the women's and civil rights movements are constitutive of this normative shift. . . .

Within the aligned "culture of poverty" rhetoric, structural economic factors—such as employment opportunities, the sex-segregated occupational structure, the shift from an industrial to a service- and technology-based economy, gendered pay inequity, access to education and training, and availability of child care—play an insignificant role in poverty. . . . Forcing women back into the marital fold is advanced as the means to end the economic misery of low-income women and to re-establish the social order. . . .

The pro-marriage rhetoric of welfare retrenchment is a package of loaded social symbols. Unbound, the discourse reveals the relic of the "good mother" from sixteenth-century Reformation Europe, the image of the "deserving" pauper of seventeenth-century colonial America, the deliberately split persona of the "independent" wage laborer and the "dependent" mother of the New Deal, and the icon of the "illegitimate" African-American mother and infant of the welfare rights era.

In pieces, the discourse shows that welfare retrenchment is a vehicle for the oppression of poor women in the labor market. The "bridefare or workfare" framework of welfare retrenchment exploits the labor of women, by mandating either unpaid work in the home or low-wage employment in the secondary labor market. In addition, welfare retrenchment is clearly redistributive, directing resources away from poor mothers and children and toward a newly valorized class of workers that is serving the middle and upper classes.

Martha Albertson Fineman, Cracking the Foundational Myths: Independence, Autonomy, and Self-Sufficiency

8 Am. U. J. Gender Soc. Pol'y & L. 13, 22-23, 25-26 (2000)

In popular and political discourse, the idea of "subsidy" is viewed as an equally negative companion to dependence, the opposite of the ideal of self-sufficiency. But a subsidy is nothing more than the process of allocating collective resources to some persons or endeavors rather than other persons or endeavors because a social judgment is made that they are in some way "entitled" or the subsidy is justified. . . .

Typically, subsidy is thought of as the provision of monetary or economic assistance. But subsidy can also be delivered through the organization of social

structures and norms that create and enforce expectations. Taking this observation into account, along with the earlier discussion of inevitable and derivative dependency, it seems obvious that we must conclude that subsidy is also
universal. We all exist in context, in social and cultural institutions, such as
families, which facilitate, support and subsidize us and our endeavors.

. . . We all live subsidized lives. Sometimes the benefits we receive are public and financial, such as in governmental direct transfer programs to certain
individuals like farmers or sugar growers. Public subsidies can also be indirect, such as the benefits given in tax policy. Private economic subsidy systems
work in the forms of foundations, religions and charities. But a subsidy can
also be non-monetary, such as the subsidy provided by the uncompensated
labor of others in caring for us and our dependency needs.

It seems clear that all of us receive one or the other or both types of subsidy
throughout our lives. The interesting question in our subsidy shaped society,
therefore, has to be why only some subsidies are differentiated and stigmatized while others are hidden. In substantial part, subsidies are hidden when
they are not called subsidy (or welfare, or the dole), but termed "investments,"
"incentives," or "earned" when they are supplied by government, and called
"gifts," "charity," or the product of familial "love" when they are contributions of caretaking labor. . . .

As a result of such discussion, the very terms of independence and
self-sufficiency might well be redefined or re-imagined in the public mind.
Independence is not the same as being unattached. Independence from subsidy and support is not attainable, nor is it desirable—we want and need the
contexts that sustain us. A different understanding of independence is needed
and attainable. Independence is gained when an individual has the basic
resources that enable her or him to act consistent with the tasks and expectations imposed by the society. This form of independence should be every
citizen's birthright, but independence in this sense can only be achieved when
individual choices are relatively unconstrained by inequalities, particularly
those inequalities that arise from poverty. Independence, as well as justice,
requires that those who are assigned a vital societal function are also provided
with the wherewithal to do those tasks. This is a state or collective responsibility and may not be relegated to potentially exploitative private institutions.

Vicki Schultz, Life's Work

100 Colum. L. Rev. 1881, 1914-1915, 1928-1935 (2000)

[T]raditional welfare strategies can be detrimental to women. . . . Joint property approaches [whereby individual men pay their partners for taking care of
the house and children] rely on individual breadwinners to fund household
labor, while welfare strategies rely on the state. State funding is advantageous
for women, because it frees them from serving individual men and sheds class

bias by funding household work at a uniform level regardless of the earnings of the family members who support it. Nonetheless, by paying women to stay home with their children rather than providing real support for parents (especially single parents) to work at paid jobs, welfare strategies still encourage women to invest in homemaking and caregiving to the exclusion of their job skills—which may harm women and their families in the long run. . . .

I realize that work alone is no panacea. It is the platform on which equal citizenship should be built, not the entire edifice. Still, the importance of work to the future cannot be overemphasized; abandoning work as a political and cultural ideal would be a serious mistake. People need more than money or property: We need life projects. We need goals and activities to which we can commit our hearts, minds, and bodies. We need to struggle with our capacities and our limits, in sustained ways in stable settings. We need to work alongside others in pursuit of common goals. We need to feel that we are contributing to something larger than ourselves and our own families. Most of us even need something that requires regular rhythms and structure, and provides a mechanism for deferring gratification. We need to feel that we are earning our keep—that we have a source of wherewithal that is our own. We also need public recognition for our labors. It is difficult to imagine any single activity that can fulfill all these purposes for the vast majority of people other than working. We have seen what happens to people when they don't have work to give life structure and meaning, and it is not exemplary. There is a reason why democratic societies have organized themselves as employment societies. Paid work is the only institution that can be sufficiently widely distributed to provide a stable foundation for a democratic order. It is also one of the few arenas—perhaps the only one—in which diverse groups of people can come together and develop respect for each other through shared experience. Can we think of a society anywhere in the world we would want to emulate in which most people do not work for a living? . . .

The emphasis on work has been crucial to Second Wave feminism, which was born in part out of the recognition that even relatively well-off, white middle-class women were united with their minority, poor, and working-class sisters in the experience of being marginalized in the world of work—which in turn disempowered them in politics and in private life. . . . Older Americans have also demanded recognition as valid workers, and they won it in the Age Discrimination in Employment Act (ADEA). . . . The disability rights movement has also emphasized access to work, and they won an important victory with the Americans with Disabilities Act (ADA). . . .

We can also view the transition from welfare to work as part of this trend. I realize that the impetus for welfare-to-work programs has come from the political right, who may not have the best interests of poor people at heart. But it would be a mistake to attribute all of the new emphasis on work to conservatives alone. Some of the demand has come from members of the working poor who do not receive welfare, and who do not have the luxury of keeping a parent at home to take care of their own children. . . .

Poor single parents have long expressed a desire for work that will allow them to support their children; they know that a decent job is the only path that provides real hope for their empowerment in the long run. Most people who receive welfare payments have been working for pay all along, as they must in order to ensure the survival of their families. But, partly because so many of them are women and racial minorities, single parents have not been perceived as "authentic" workers who have the capacity to contribute to productive endeavors beyond raising their own children. Women who draw on welfare are overrepresented among classic contingent workers, who fare worse on a variety of dimensions than people in more permanent employment. . . .

Even if many welfare-to-work programs have been adopted for the wrong reasons, their existence does provide a political opening to turn things around. Not only is paid work important to people's ability to get ahead and their sense of community and self-esteem; it is also a more easily politicized setting than the privatized home. By creating social systems that allow poor (and other) parents to combine caregiving with stable employment, we enable them to move into the workforce—a space in which they can more easily engage in collective action to improve their situation. . . .

Viewed from this perspective, the best welfare-to-work programs push in the direction of a more expansive set of social programs that guarantee and support a right to work for everyone. If work is to provide the foundation for citizenship (as welfare-to-work programs imply), then everyone must have access to a suitable job, as well as the training and education needed to do the job. There is no reason to find or create jobs exclusively for people who have drawn on welfare, when so many others are struggling to find jobs, often under fiercely competitive conditions. The goal should be to ensure that everyone—mothers on welfare, fathers struggling to pay child support, poor women and men without children, people with disabilities, middle-class homemakers or divorcees, people in temporary jobs who want steady employment, older people, youth who are trying to finance continuing education, and, yes, even well educated displaced workers—has work.

Notes

1. Poverty, Gender, and Race.   Poverty is strongly correlated with gender, race, ethnicity, and marital status. Official Census Bureau figures put the poverty rate at about 15.2 percent, while a new supplemental formula, which takes account of noncash benefits and essential expenditures, put the rate at 16.1 percent.[450] The figure is highest among households headed by a single mother (31.6 percent) and lowest among two-parent households (6.2 percent). For non-Hispanic whites, the rate was 9.9 percent; for blacks, it was 27.4 percent, for Hispanics it was 26.6 percent, and for Asians, it was 12.1 percent.[451] Among 21 developed nations with comparable data, the United States has the second highest rate of poverty.[452]

2. Challenges to the Welfare System.   During the 1980s and 1990s, American conservatives launched a sustained challenge to the traditional welfare system on the grounds that it entrenched, rather than reduced, poverty. In this view, the poor make rational choices based on the existing incentive structures. Welfare discourages work and rewards out-of-wedlock childrearing. Critics like Charles Murray not only called for ending the entitlement-based welfare system, but also supported shaming those dependent upon welfare and praising self-sufficiency. Without a distinction between the deserving and the undeserving poor, Murray argued that indigent parents would have no reason to take responsibility for providing for themselves and their families.[453]

Individual agency figures strongly in this line of analysis. Those critical of public welfare tend to assume that the poor could work if only they chose to, and that they choose instead to take government benefits. Others describe an economic structure in which the opportunities for self-sufficiency are steadily worsening for the "have-nots." According to some observers, one silver lining of this reform is that recipients are no longer demonized as shirkers; they are now part of the working poor and their poverty cannot simply be attributed to their own shiftlessness.[454] In your view, is this correct? Was the reform worth the price?

3. The Impact of Welfare Reform.   The Koons reading describes the major overhaul of the U.S. welfare system that occurred with the passage of the Personal Responsibility and Work Opportunity Reconciliation Act of 1996. The impact of welfare reform has been mixed. In the first decade following welfare reform, the number of welfare recipients has declined, and paid employment and earnings among low-income single mothers increased. Twelve years after caseloads peaked in the pre-reform era at 5.1 million families, the number of families on cash assistance dropped to 1.9 million. It is, however, difficult to tell how much of that improvement was the result of general gains in the economy during the first five years following welfare reform. Positive trends have slowed since 2001.[455]

The economic downturn that began in 2008 increased the economic vulnerability of the poor while posing new challenges for the welfare system. Because the federal block grant system provides no additional funding to meet increased need and many state and local governments confront declining revenue, they have been unable to address soaring unemployment and economic hardship. The central premise of welfare reform that all able-bodied parents should work has proven impossible to accommodate in the declining job market. The hardships are reaching across the economic spectrum as a growing number of formerly middle-class parents are unable to meet basic subsistence needs although they often have too many assets to qualify for aid.[456]

By 2011, the fifteenth anniversary of welfare reform, benefit levels in all but two states were below the level in 1996, adjusted for inflation, and the poverty rate for children and families were about the same (20.7 and 12.5 percent). Benefits fell below 50 percent of the poverty line in all states.[457] Yet while poverty and unemployment rates for single mothers are at their highest levels in at least 20 years, the percentage of families on assistance has declined.[458] Welfare caseloads have fallen 60 percent since 1996.[459] The result is that only 28 percent of the poor are receiving welfare, compared with 75 percent in 1995.[460] The human costs are substantial. Many families report insufficient food, housing, utilities, and health care, and the inadequacy of assistance keeps women trapped in violent relationships.[461]

Studies of what happens to poor families after they leave welfare show that most remain poor.[462] Average earnings for these families are below poverty levels for a family of three.[463] Studies show that between 50 and 75 percent of those who left the welfare rolls remained poor two years after leaving welfare. One reason is that many states do not consider college attendance as meeting work requirements; the number of recipients enrolled in college has dropped since reform.[464] Difficulties in understanding and complying with welfare requirements pose other problems. About half of those eligible for some benefits don't get them, partly because those who do not receive cash assistance are unaware that they may qualify for child-care help, health insurance, and food stamps.[465] Because welfare subsidies come nowhere close to meeting most recipients' sustenance needs, most rely on unreported income, which, if detected, can subject them to substantial penalties, including extended or permanent bans from further assistance.[466] For those on the bottom rung of the income scale, an estimated 10 to 20 percent of recipients, the situation has worsened since reform. These "disconnected" parents have problems of substance abuse, mental health or learning disabilities, domestic violence, inadequate education, and criminal records, which make getting a living wage impossible.[467] Children of parents who are working also may suffer due to the lack of supervision and additional responsibilities in caring for younger siblings. Poorer school performance is the consequence.[468]

Angie Jobe offers a case history. Jason DeParle's *American Dream* chronicles Jobe's life for seven years as she transitioned from welfare to work. By official accounts, she looks to be a success story. She earns $11 an hour as a nurse assistant and supports her family without government assistance. But she has an extended commute, beginning at 5:30 a.m., often needs to work double shifts and overtime, and sometimes still cannot pay her utility bill. Her daughter, who spent much of her childhood caring for siblings, got pregnant and dropped out of school at age 17. She is now in a similar situation as her mother, working at a low-wage job as a checkout clerk.[469]

Yet despite such hardships, the political climate for increased welfare support is unpromising. Cash-strapped states and a deficit-conscious Congress have shown little support for enhancing the safety net of the poor, who have little leverage in the political process.[470] How might these obstacles be addressed?

4. Drug Testing of Welfare Recipients. In 2011, a beneficiary contested Florida's new requirement of drug tests for all TANF applicants. A former

Navy veteran who has sole custody of his son sued to enjoin the law as an unreasonable search and seizure.[471] A federal district court issued an injunction that the state is appealing. According to the governor, the measure is a valid means of saving revenue and ensuring that benefits accomplish their intended purpose. "Welfare is for the benefit of children, and the money should go to the benefit of children," he stated. "This makes all the sense in the world."[472] However, only about 2.5 percent of applicants have failed the test, a rate that compares favorably to the estimated 8.7 percent of Americans who use drugs.[473] As a consequence, the state has saved only $98,000 in denied benefits.[474] Nonetheless, public opinion polls show strong support for drug testing where public funds are involved.[475] If you were the lawyer for the state, what arguments would you make in support of the law? If you were the ACLU lawyer challenging the law, how would you respond?

5. Welfare Reform and the Promotion of Marriage. An important objective of PRWORA is the reduction of out-of-wedlock pregnancies and childbirths. Proponents of marriage-based programs point to studies that have shown that children who grow up with both of their biological parents are more successful across a broad range of outcomes than children who grow up with only one parent, including higher educational attainment, better behavioral outcomes, and mental health. However, it is not clear to what extent these positive outcomes are due to pre-existing characteristics of the parents who choose to marry (and also choose not to divorce) rather than to marriage itself.[476]

Since 2002, the federal government has funded A Healthy Marriage Initiative, designed to promote stable marriages and responsible fatherhood. Activities include marriage education programs, public service announcements, and courses in relationships skills for adults and adolescents.[477] The vast majority of states have changed their rules to eliminate pre-1996 welfare eligibility barriers to two-parent families. Bonuses of as much as $25 million are also available to states that meet targets in reducing out-of-wedlock births and abortions.[478]

Critics of the "healthy marriage" approach to welfare reform charge that, even if marriage is a legitimate government goal, marriage alone is not sufficient to lift couples out of poverty. These critics argue that the approach reflects an unduly narrow definition of healthy families, and that the money would be better spent on programs that are critically underfunded, such as child care. Marriage promotion is particularly problematic for black and Latino families, given the ways in which incarceration and joblessness have narrowed the pool of eligible men, and the extended family patterns that are common in these racial groups.[479] The Center for Law and Social Policy proposes "Marriage Plus" as an alternative, which would include not only marriage counseling and relationship training, but pregnancy prevention, mental health support, greater childcare services, reform of the child support system, and job training and placement.[480]

Other critics, such as Anna Marie Smith, have challenged the priority given to heterosexual marriages over other household arrangements. In her view, a just society would ensure that every person is "equally valued and respected," and would recognize that caretakers irrespective of marital status have a "special claim to public support," given their contributions to the nurture of dependents and the "good of the community." These individuals should have an entitlement to support equivalent to a living wage, and should enjoy the "same right to determine their intimate lives that privileged citizens take for granted."[481]

Do you agree? Is marriage promotion a legitimate governmental objective? Is it a better use of federal funds than childcare subsidies? What data might you need to answer that question?

6. Welfare and Autonomy.   To what extent should autonomy be a goal for the welfare system? Can the views of Fineman, Smith, and Schultz be reconciled? Is it possible that the emphasis on women's autonomy actually has undermined their well-being? Consider this further analysis by Fineman:

> Rejection of the idea that there is some collective responsibility for dependency is not surprising in a society such as ours. American political ideology offers an iconic construct of the autonomous individual and trusts the abstraction of an efficiency-seeking market as an ordering mechanism. We have an historic and highly romanticized affair with the ideals of the private and the individual, as contrasted with the public and the collective, as the appropriate units of focus in determining social good. . . .

> The theory of dependency I set forth develops a claim of "right" or entitlement to support and accommodation from the state and its institutions on the part of caretakers — those who care for dependents. Their labor should be treated as equally productive even if unwaged, and should be measured by its societal value, not by economic or market indicators. The fact that dependency work has been un- or under-valued in the market is an argument *for* governmental intervention and restructuring to mandate adjustment and market accommodation, as well as more direct reparations.[482]

7. Income Inequality.   In 2011, the Occupy Wall Street Movement drew national attention to the growing inequality in American society. Spin-off groups such as Women Occupying Wall Street (WOW), Occupy Patriarchy, and Women Occupy have underscored the way that women, because they are overrepresented among the poor, have borne the brunt of this inequality.[483] Since the 1980s, the after-tax income of the top 1 percent of the nation's income recipients nearly tripled, while the after-tax income of the bottom 80 percent declined.[484] Even within that top 1 percent, wealth has grown more concentrated. The 400 richest Americans now have more money than the bottom 50 percent of all Americans combined.[485] Defenders of such inequalities claim that they are the natural and inevitable product of a market system; people differ in how hard they work, how talented they are, and how much risk they assume, and should be rewarded accordingly. Critics respond that the current level of inequality raises concerns of equal opportunity and political participation.

Income affects many factors that affect equal opportunity, such as education, nutrition, health, housing, and physical safety. As a consequence, the accident of birth is highly predictive of life chances. Upward mobility is less common in the United States than in most other industrial nations. A child born in the bottom one-fifth of the socioeconomic spectrum in the United States has only about a 17 percent chance of making it into the upper two-fifths.[486]

A second reason for concern about growing inequalities in wealth is that they translate into inequalities in political power. Money buys access and influence, and the result is to entrench existing entitlements. Much of the gap in life prospects is due to laws, institutions, and tax policies that reflect the interests of the rich, rather than the vast majority of Americans. Two-thirds of the public believes that wealth is unfairly distributed.[487] What is your view? If you believe that current income inequalities are unjust, what responses would you propose?

Putting Theory Into Practice

5-36. Your state legislator proposes a measure to give low-income individuals and couples who periodically attend parenting classes an annual tax deduction (or cash benefits if they do not pay taxes). Is this a good idea? Should schools be required to offer marriage relationship skills and fatherhood classes? How about giving poor couples an annual cash "bonus" for staying married? If, as a practical matter, welfare programs inhabit a "zero-sum fiscal environment" in which dollars spent on marriage and fatherhood initiatives take away from other crucial support programs, which strategies should take priority?[488]

5-37. You are chairing a coalition of women's rights organizations that is advising Congress on changes to the welfare program in light of the economic crisis that started in 2008. What reforms would you propose?

5-38. You are a single mother with two children under five. You have a minimum-wage job at a local grocery store. It does not provide health benefits. Prepare a budget based on living expenses in your locality. Could you manage without welfare assistance? If not, what benefits would be most critical? With welfare assistance, could you meet basic subsistence needs?

---

1. Michelle Oberman, Turning Girls into Women: Re-Evaluating Modern Statutory Rape Law, 85 J. Crim. L. & Criminology 15, 70 (1994).
2. Wendy W. Williams, The Equality Crisis: Some Reflections on Culture, Courts, and Feminism, 7 Women's Rights L. Rep. 175, 200 (1982).

3. See J. Shoshanna Ehrlich, You Can Steal Her Virginity But Not Her Doll: The Nineteenth Century Campaign to Raise the Legal Age of Sexual Consent, 15 Cardozo J.L. & Gender 229, 231 (2009).

4. Cal. Penal Code §261.5 (West 2012).

5. See State v. Limon, 122 P.3d 22 (Kan. 2005).

6. See Aid for Women v. Foulston, 327 F. Supp. 2d 1273 (D. Kan. 2004).

7. Aid for Women v. Foulston, 441 F.3d 1101 (10th Cir. 2006).

8. Aid for Women v. Foulston, 427 F. Supp. 2d 1093 (D. Kan. 2006).

9. Id. (accepting testimony that minors might not continue to seek timely medical care if all illegal sexual activity is immediately reported).

10. Kelly C. Connerton, The Resurgence of the Marital Rape Exemption: The Victimization of Teens by Their Statutory Rapists, 61 Alb. L. Rev. 237, 256 (1997).

11. What's the Matter with Kansas?, N.Y. Times, Aug. 31, 2005, at A18; Jodi Wilgoren, Rape Charge Follows Marriage to a 14-Year-Old, N.Y. Times, Aug. 30, 2005, available at http://www.nytimes.com/2005/08/30/national/30baby.html?pagewanted=all&_r=0. In the wake of bad publicity about this case, Kansas raised its minimum age for marriage to 16 (with parental consent). See Kan. Stat. Ann. §23-106 (2012).

12. Mark E. Hyman, The Times Crosses State Lines, The American Spectator, Sept. 9, 2005, available at http://spectator.org/articles/48065/times-crosses-state-lines.

13. Claire Bushey, Age of Consent Muddles Law on Marriage vs. Rape, Women's eNews, June 7, 2007, available at http://womensenews.org/story/the-courts/070607/age-consent-muddles-law-marriage-vs-rape#.UysV3hD4Klo.

14. Philip N.S. Rumney, In Defense of Gender Neutrality Within Rape, 6 Seattle J. Soc. Just. 481, 486 (2007).

15. Kay L. Levine, No Penis, No Problem, 33 Fordham Urban L.J. 357, 363 (2006).

16. Id. at 364.

17. Alicia Graham, Simply Sexual: The Discrepancy in Treatment Between Male and Female Sex Offenders, 7 Whittier J. Child. & Fam. Advoc. 145, 160 (2007).

18. Levine, supra note 15, at 404.

19. Graham, supra note 17, at 153.

20. Kate Zernike, The Siren Song of Sex with Boys, N.Y. Times, Dec. 11, 2005, at SR3 (Sunday Week in Review).

21. Levine, supra note 15, at 395.

22. United States v. Shannon, 110 F.3d 382 (7th Cir. 1996), cert. denied, 522 U.S. 888 (1997).

23. Tresa Baldas, Courts Split on "Consent Defense for Minors" in Civil Trials, Nat'l L.J., Oct. 22, 2007, at A3.

24. National Center for Injury Prevention and Control, CDC, National Intimate Partner and Sexual Violence Survey (2010); surveys cited in Testimony of Susan B. Carbon, Director, Office on Violence Against Women, Rape in the United States, Testimony before the Subcommittee on Crime and Drugs, Committee on the Judiciary, United States Senate, Sept. 14, 2010, http://w.judiciary-senate.gov/hearings/hearing-search.cfm.

25. Department of Justice, Nearly 10 Percent of Former State Prisoners Reported Being Sexually Victimized During Confinement, available at http://www.ojp.usdoj.gov/newsroom/pressreleases/2012/ojppr051712.pdf.

26. Deborah L. Rhode, Speaking of Sex: The Denial of Gender Equality 121 (1997).

27. See Owen D. Jones & Timothy H. Goldsmith, Law and Behavioral Biology, 105 Colum. L. Rev. 405 (2005).

28. See Helen Benedict, Virgin or Vamp: How the Press Covers Sex Crimes (1992).

29. The definition updated in 2012 eliminates the word "forcible" and defines rape as "the penetration . . . of the vagina or anus with any body part or object, or oral penetration by a sex organ of another person without the consent of the victim." U.S. Department of Justice, Attorney General Holder Announces Revisions to the Uniform Crime Reports Definition of Rape, http://www.fbi.gov/news/pressrel/press-releases/attorney-general-eric-holder-announces-revisions-to-the-uniform-crime-reports-definition-of-rape.

30. See Michelle J. Anderson, Marital Immunity, Intimate Relationships, and Improper Inferences: A New Law on Sexual Offenses by Intimates, 54 Hastings L.J. 1465, 1468-1473, nn.8-12, 1557-1574 (2003).

31. Id. at 1470-1471. For provisions in these states see the Appendix in id. at 1537-1574.

32. Id. at 1471-1473.

33. Conn. Gen. Stat. Ann. §53(a)-67(b) (West 2012).

34. Jill Elaine Hasday, Contest and Consent: A Legal History of Marital Rape, 88 Cal. L. Rev. 1373, 1486-1489 (2000).

35. Id. at 149.

36. Diana E. H. Russell, Rape in Marriage 192-193 (rev. ed. 1990).

37. See State v. Colbath, 540 A.2d 1212 (N.H. 1988) (opinion by now-retired Justice Souter).

38. Michal Buchhandler-Raphael, The Failure of Consent: Re-Conceptualizing Rape as Sexual Abuse of Power, 18 Mich. J. Gender & L., 147, 158 (2011).

39. Id. at 167.

40. Stephen Schulhofer, Unwanted Sex: The Culture of Intimidation and the Failure of Law (2000).

41. Joan McGregor, Is It Rape?: On Acquaintance Rape and Taking Women's Consent Seriously 190-193 (2005).

42. Susan Caringella, Addressing Rape Reform in Law and Practice (2009) (arguing that a society that can scarcely accept "no means no" is unlikely to adapt to "only yes means yes").

43. Jed Rubenfeld, The Riddle of Rape-by-Deception and the Myth of Sexual Autonomy, 122 Yale L.J. 1372 (2013).

44. For a state-by-state catalog of all rape shield statutes as of 2011, see http://www.ndaa.org/pdf/NCPCA%20Rape%20Shield%202011.pdf. For an older but more detailed description of the differences in state approaches, see Michelle J. Anderson, From Chastity Requirement to Sexuality License: Sexual Consent and a New Rape Shield Law, 70 Geo. Wash. L. Rev. 51 (2002).

45. Barry Tarlow, Criminal Justice: Rape Suspects' Uphill Road, L.A. Times, Aug. 17, 2003, at M3.

46. Michele Alexander, "Girls Gone Wild" and Rape Law: Revising the Contractual Concept of Consent and Ensuring an Unbiased Application of "Reasonable Doubt" When the Victim Is Nontraditional, 17 Am. U. J. Gender Soc. Pol'y & L. 41 (2009).

47. Aya Gruber, Rape, Feminism, and the War on Crime, 84 Wash. L. Rev. 581, 646-647 (2009).

48. Anderson, supra note 44, at 74-75, 94-95.

49. Federal Rules of Evidence 413-415.

50. Report of the Judicial Conference of the United States on the Admission of Character Evidence in Certain Sexual Assault Cases (1995).

51. Charles H. Rose, III, Should the Tail Wag the Dog?: The Potential Effects of Recidivism Data on Character Evidence Rules, 36 N.M. L. Rev. 341, 344 (2006); R. Karl Hanson & Kelly Morton-Bourgon, Predictors of Sexual Recidivism: An Updated Meta-Analysis (2004), available at http://ww2.ps-sp.gc.ca/publications/corrections/pdf/200402_e.pdf; U.S. Bureau of Justice, Recidivism Rates of Prisoners Released in 1994 (2002).

52. Samuel L. Gross et al., Exonerations in the United States, 95 J. Crim. L. & Criminology 523, 529 (2005).

53. Roger Lancaster, Sex Offenders: The Last Pariahs, N.Y. Times, Aug. 21, 2011, at SR6.

54. The transcript of preliminary hearing is available at http://www.thesmokinggun.com/archive/0924041kobea1.html.

55. 94 P.3d 624 (Colo. 2004).

56. See, e.g., Deborah L. Forman, Embryo Disposition, Divorce & Family Law Contracting: A Model for Enforceability, 24 Colum. J. Gender & Law 378 (2013).

57. Kirk Johnson, As Accuser Balks, Prosecutors Drop Bryant Rape Case, N.Y. Times, Sept. 2, 2004, available at http://query.nytimes.com/gst/fullpage.html?res=9D07E0DB1231F931A3575AC0A9629C8B63; Bill Saporito, Kobe Rebounds, Time, Sept. 13, 2004, at 72.

58. Dahlia Lithwick, The Shield That Failed, N.Y. Times, Aug. 8, 2004, at SR11.

59. Stephanie Hallett, How to Stop a Serial Rapist, Ms., Summer 2011, at 33; Katherine Prevost O'Connor, Eliminating the Rape Kit Backlog: Bringing Necessary Changes to the Criminal Justice System 72 UMKC L. Rev. 193, 194-196 (2003).

60. Wendy Murphy, Most Rape Cases Are About Consent, Not DNA, Women's eNews, Feb. 9, 2011.

61. Jennifer Bruno, Pitfalls for the Unwary: How Sexual Assault Counselor-Victim Privileges May Fall Short of Their Intended Protections, 2002 U. Ill. L. Rev. 1373.

62. See Rachel Capoccia, Piercing the Veil of Tears: The Admission of Rape Crisis Counselors' Records in Acquaintance Rape Trials, 68 S. Cal. L.J. 1335, 1342 (1995).

63. Francis X. Shen, How We Still Fail Rape Victims: Reflecting on Responsibility and Legal Reform, 22 Colum. J. Gender & L. 1, 8 (2011).

64. See Ilene Seidman & Susan Vickers, The Second Wave: An Agenda for the Next Thirty Years of Rape Law Reform, 38 Suffolk U. L. Rev. 467, 472 (2005).

65. Shen, supra note 63, at 14-27; Henry F. Fradell & Kagan Brown, The Effects of Using Social Scientific Rape Typologies on Juror Decisions to Convict, 31 Law & Psych. Rev. 1, 1-16 (2007).

66. For examples, see Rose Corrigan, Up Against a Wall: Rape Reform and the Failure of Success 5, 83-109 (2013).

67. John Eligon & Michael Schwirtz, Senate Candidate Provokes Ire with "Legitimate Rape" Comment, N.Y. Times, Aug. 19, 2012, at A13.

68. Sports Figures, Cases Involving Athletes and Sexual Assault, USA Today, Dec. 22, 2003, at A1, A5.

69. See Saporito, supra note 57.

70. Lynn Hecht Schafran, The Importance of Voir Dire in Rape Trials, Trial, Aug. 1992, at 26.

71. Peggy Reeves Sanday, A Woman Scorned: Acquaintance Rape on Trial 238 (1996).

72. Camille Paglia, Sex, Art, and American Culture 51 (1992); McGregor, supra note 41, at 77.

73. Rebecca Traister, Ladies, We Have a Problem, N.Y. Times Mag., July 24, 2011, at 9.

74. John Burns, Confidential Swedish Police Report Details Allegations Against WikiLeaks Founder, N.Y. Times, Dec. 19, 2010, at A9, A12.

75. Christopher Dickey & John Solomon, The Maid's Tale, Newsweek, Aug. 1 & 8, 2011, 26, 28 (quoting Diallo).

76. Id. at 31.

77. Scott Turow, Reasonable Doubt and the Strauss-Kahn Case, N.Y. Times, Aug. 28, 2011, at SR4.

78. See http://www.huffingtonpost.com/news/jodi-arias.

79. Cara Buckley, After Strauss-Kahn, Fear of Rape Victim Silence, N.Y. Times, Aug. 24, 2011, at A21.

80. See Ann Wolbert Burgess & Lynda Lytle Holmstrom, Rape Trauma Syndrome, in Forcible Rape: The Crime, the Victim, and the Offender 315 (Duncan Chappell et al. eds., 1977).

81. People v. Taylor, 552 N.E.2d 131, 138 (N.Y. 1990).

82. Henson v. State, 535 N.E.2d 1189 (Ind. 1989).

83. See George v. State, 37 Miss. 316 (1859).

84. See A. Leon Higginbotham, Jr., & Anne F. Jacobs, The "Law Only as an Enemy": The Legitimization of Racial Powerlessness Through the Colonial Laws of Virginia, 70 N.C. L. Rev. 969, 1055-1060 (1992).

85. Cassia Spohn & David Holleran, Prosecuting Sexual Assault: A Comparison of Charging Decisions in Sexual Assault Cases Involving Strangers, Acquaintances, and Intimate Partners, 18 Just. Q. 651, 680 (2001).

86. Jeffrey J. Pokorak, Rape as a Badge of Slavery: The Legal History of, and Remedies for, Prosecutorial Race of Victim Charging Disparities, 7 Nev. L.J. 1, 39 (2006).

87. The prosecutor argued that despite the inconsistencies, he had an "obligation" to put the victims' positive identification to the jury. Bennett L. Gershman & Joel Cohen, "No Gatekeeper of Justice," Nat'l L.J., Feb. 19, 2007, at A22 (quoting Michael Nifong). For critical accounts, see Race to Injustice: Lessons Learned from the Duke Lacrosse Rape Case (Michael L. Siegel ed., 2009); Stuart Taylor & K.C. Johnson, Until Proven Innocent: Political Correctness and the Shameful Injustices of the Duke Lacrosse Rape Case (2007).

88. See State v. Colbath, 540 A.2d 1212 (N.H. 1988).

89. Vesna Jaksic, Playing with the Power of Words, Nat'l L.J., July 23, 2007, at A1, A26 (describing Nebraska v. Safi, No. CR 05-87 (Dist. Ct. Lancaster Co. Neb. 2007)).

90. For a discussion of these and related hypotheticals, see Stephen Schulhofer, Taking Sexual Autonomy Seriously, 11 Law & Phil. 35 (1992).

91. State v. Baby, 946 A.2d 463, 467 (2008).

92. National Crime Victimization Study, Violent Victimization of College Students (1995-2002), available at www.bjs.gov/content/pub/pdf/vvcs02.pdf. See also Christopher P. Krebs et al., The Campus Sexual Assault Study: Final Report xiii, xviii (Oct. 2007), available at http://www.ncjrs.gov/pdf-files1/nij/grants/221153.pdf (finding that one in five women are victims of attempted or completed sexual assault during their college years and that the majority of assaults occur when women are incapacitated by alcohol or other substances).

93. John Leo, Two Steps Ahead of the Thought Police 247 (1994).

94. Katherine Roiphe, The Morning After: Fear, Sex, and Feminism on College Campuses 66-68 (1993).

95. See Neil Gilbert, The Phantom Epidemic of Sexual Assault, 103 Pub. Int. 54 (Spring 1991).

96. Michael Kimmel, Guyland 220 (2007); see also Stephen Schulhofer, Taking Sexual Autonomy Seriously, 11 Law & Phil. 35, 77 (1992).

97. Caroline Knapp, Drinking: A Love Story (1996).

98. See Michelle J. Anderson, The Legacy of the Prompt Complaint Requirement, Corroboration Requirement, and Cautionary Instructions on Campus Sexual Assault, 84 B.U. L. Rev. 945, 1010 (2004).

99. State v. Jones, 2011 Lexis 119 (2011) (requiring knowledge).

100. Andrew E. Taslitz, Willfully Blinded: On Date Rape and Self-Deception, 28 Harv. J.L. & Gender 381, 394 (2005).

101. Id. at 434, 446.

102. For analysis of other cognitive biases that may incline individuals, particularly women with hierarchical world views, to be highly judgmental of complainants' conduct in acquaintance rape cases, see Dan M. Kahan, Culture, Cognition and Consent: Who Perceives What, and Why, in Acquaintance Rape Cases, 158 U. Penn. L. Rev. 728 (2010).

103. Criminal Code, R.S.C. 1985, C-46 §273. See Buchhandler-Raphael, supra note 38, at 169-170.

104. Corey Rayburn, To Catch a Sex Thief: The Burden of Performance in Rape and Sexual Assault Trials, 15 Colum. J. Gender & L. 437 (2006).

105. National Center for Injury Prevention and Control of the Centers for Disease Control and Prevention, National Intimate Partner and Sexual Violence Survey, 2010 Summary Report 1, 2 (2011); see also Bennett Capers, Real Rape Too, 99 Cal. L. Rev. 1259 (2011).

106. United States Department of Justice, Criminal Victimization in the United States 2008, Table 2 (2011); Roni Caryn Rabin, As Victims, Men Struggle for Rape Awareness, N.Y. Times, Jan. 24, 2012, at D4.

107. See James Dao, When Victims of Military Sex Assaults are Men, N.Y. Times, June 24, 2013, available at http://www.nytimes.com/2013/06/24/us/in-debate-over-military-sexual-assault-men-are-overlooked-victims.html.

108. Jesse Ellison, The Military's Secret Shame, Newsweek, Apr. 11, 2011, at 42.

109. Sally Jenkins, "I Just Did What I Thought Was Best," Wash. Post, Jan. 15, 2012, at A1 (quoting Paterno). Paterno died shortly after the scandal broke; Sandusky was convicted by a jury of multiple counts of child sexual assault; and Louis Freeh, hired by Penn State to conduct an independent investigation into the scandal, issued a scathing indictment of the university for failing to act on its prior knowledge of Sandusky's conduct. Freeh's report is available on http://www.thefreehreportonpsu.com. See also Richard Goldstein, Joe Paterno, Longtime Penn State Coach, Dies at 85, N.Y. Times, Jan. 23, 2012, at A1; Joe Drape, Sandusky Guilty of Sexual Abuse of 10 Young Boys, N.Y. Times, June 22, 2012, at A1.

110. United States v. Morrison, 529 U.S. 598 (2000).

111. See discussion of Simpson v. University of Colorado in Chapter 3 at p. 324; Kimmel, supra note 96, at 233 (describing million-dollar settlement of Simpson case).

112. Eric Hoover, Harvard's Sexual Assault Policy Does Not Violate Students' Rights, U.S. Inquiry Finds, Chron. Higher Educ., Apr. 3, 2003, at A1. See Sarah M. Seltzer, Leaning Committee Signals Major Changes in Sexual Assault Policy, Harv. Crimson, June 5, 2003, available at http://www.thecrimson.com/article.aspx?ref=348399. See also Stephanie Schmidt, A Perfunctory Change? Harvard University's New Sexual Misconduct Complaint Procedure: Lessons from the Frontlines of Campus Adjudication Systems, 18 Berkeley Women's L.J. 165 (2005).

113. Elizabeth Armstrong, et al., Sexual Assault on Campus: A Multilevel Integrative Approach to Party Rape, 53 Soc. Probs. 483, 491, 496 (2006).

114. See Lisa Belkin, After Class, Skimpy Equality, N.Y. Times, Aug. 26, 2011, at ST1.

115. The letter to Stanford is available at http://www2.ed.gov.about/offices/list/ocr/letters/colleague-201104.pdf.

116. Postings to lawtalk@lists.stanford.edu (Dec. 2011) (available on request from authors).

117. For an overview, see Sexual Violence in Conflict Zones: From the Ancient World to the Era of Human Rights (Elizabeth D. Heineman ed., 2011).

118. Susan Brownmiller, Against Our Will: Men, Women and Rape 35 (1976).

119. Shellie K. Park, Broken Silence: Redressing the Mass Rape and Sexual Enslavement of Asian Women by the Japanese Government in an Appropriate Forum, 3 Asian-Pac. L. & Pol'y J. 2, 28 (2002).

120. Kelly D. Askin, A Decade of the Development of Gender Crimes in International Courts and Tribunals: 1993 to 2003, 11 (No. 3) Hum. Rts. Brief 16, 16 (2004).

121. Kadic v. Karadzic, 70 F. 3d 232 (2d Cir. 1995).

122. Lynda E. Boose, Crossing the River Drina: Bosnian Rape Camps, Turkish Impalement, and Serb Cultural Memory, 28 Signs 71, 73-74 (Autumn 2002).

123. Jennifer M. Hentz, The Impact of HIV on the Rape Crisis in the African Great Lakes Region, 12 (No. 2) Hum. Rts. Brief 12, 13 (2005).

124. See Adrienne Kalosieh, Consent to Genocide?: The ICTY's Improper Use of the Consent Paradigm to Prosecute Genocidal Rape in FOCA, 24 Women's Rts. L. Rep. 121, 129 (2003).

125. Afreen R. Ahmed, The Shame of Hwang v. Japan: How the International Community Has Failed Asia's "Comfort Women," 14 Tex. J. Women & L. 121, 147 (2004).

126. Jeffrey Gettleman, Congo Study Sets Estimates for Rapes Much Higher, N.Y. Times, May 11, 2011, available at http://www.nytimes.com/2011/05/12/world/africa/12congo.html. Also see the study on which Gettleman's article is based: Amber Peterman et al., Estimates and Determinants of Sexual Violence Against Women in the Democratic Republic of Congo, 101 Am. J. of Pub. Health, June 2011, No. 6, at 1060.

127. Hentz, supra note 123, at 13.

128. Office of the High Commissioner of Human Rights, Rape: Weapon of War, http://www.oohchr.org/EN/NewsEvents/Pages/RapeWeaponWar.aspx.

129. Nicholas D. Kristof, In This Rape Center, the Patient Was 3, N. Y. Times, Oct. 8, 2011, available at http://www.nytimes.com/2011/10/09/opinion/sunday/kristof-In-This-Rape-Center-the-Patient-Was-3.html.

130. Hilmi M. Zawati, Hidden Deaths of Libyan Rape Survivors, Nat'l L.J., Jan 9, 2012.

131. Investigation of the Office of Internal Oversight Services into Allegations of Sexual Exploitation and Abuse, United Nations Organization Mission in the Democratic Republic of Congo (Jan. 2005); Marc Lacey, In Congo War, Even Peacekeepers Add to Horror, N.Y. Times, Dec. 18, 2004, at A1.

132. Office of the High Commissioner for Human Rights (quoting Major-General Patrick Cammaert). See Melissa Goldenberg Goldstoff, Security Council Resolution 1820: An Imperfect But Necessary Resolution to Protect Civilians from Rape in War Zones, 16 Cardozo J.L. & Gender 491 (2010).

133. Helen Benedict, The Scandal of Military Rape, Ms., Fall 2008, at 42.

134. Id. (quoting Harman).

135. Andrea Stone, 17 Victims Sue Pentagon Over Plague of Sexual Violence, aol.com, Feb. 15, 2011, http://www.aolnews.com/2011/02/15/17-victims-sue-pentagon-over-plague-of-sexual-violence.com.

136. Id. (quoting complaint). Cioca v. Rumsfeld, Docket No. 1:11-cv-00151-L0-TCB (E.D. Va. 2011).

137. Jennifer Steinhauer, Sexual Assaults in Military Raise Alarm in Capital, N.Y. Times, May 8, 2013, at A1.

138. Jesse Ellison, The Military's Secret Shame, Newsweek, Apr. 11, 2011, at 40, 42.

139. Sylvia Law, Commercial Sex: Beyond Decriminalization, 73 S. Cal. L. Rev. 523, 530 (2000).

140. See Joann Miller, Prostitution in Contemporary American Society, in Sexual Coercion: A Sourcebook on Its Nature, Causes and Prevention 45 (Elizabeth Grauerholz & Mary Koralewski eds., 1991).

141. U.S. Federal and State Prostitution Laws, ProCon.org (2010), http://prostitution.procon.org/view.resource.php?resourceID=000119#2.

142. Law, supra note 139, at 543, 552-554.

143. Id. at 560.

144. San Francisco Task Force on Prostitution, Final Report Submitted to the Board of Supervisors of the City and County of San Francisco (1996), available at http://www.baysman. org/SFTFP.html.

145. Maureen A. Norton-Hawk, The Counterproductivity of Incarcerating Female Street Prostitutes, 22 Deviant Behav. 403, 405 (2001).

146. C. Aaron McNeece & Elizabeth Mayfield Arnold, Program Closure: The Impact on Participants in a Program for Female Prostitutes, 12 Res. Soc. Work Prac. 159, 168 (2002) (reporting that 90 percent of interviewees expressed desire to leave). For other research, see Catharine MacKinnon, Trafficking, Prostitution, and Inequality, 46 Harv. Civ. Rights-Civ. Lib. L. Rev. 271, 290 (2011).

147. See MacKinnon, Trafficking, supra note 146, at 282; Catharine A. MacKinnon, Sex Equality 1233-1240 (2d ed. 2007); Melissa Farley, Prostitution, Trafficking, and Cultural Amnesia: What We Must Not Know in Order to Keep the Business of Sexual Exploitation Running Smoothly, 18 Yale J.L. & Feminism 109, 113-116 (2006).

148. Eric Lipton, Women in Escort Case Plans to Name Names in Defense, N.Y. Times, Apr. 29, 2007, at A20; Stefano Esposito et al., "I Offer an Authentic Experience": Prostitute Says Going Rate Here Is Only $700 to $800 an Hour, Chicago Sun-Times, Mar. 16, 2008, available at http://redlightchicago.wordpress.com/2008/03/16/prostitute-says-rate-here-is-700-to-800/.

149. MacKinnon recounts the legislative history of the law and considers it "sex equality in inspiration and effect." Mackinnon, Trafficking, supra note 146, at 301.

150. Law, supra note 139, at 543, 552-554.

151. Rebecca Mead, American Pimp, New Yorker, Apr. 23 & 30, 2001, at 74, 82; Alexa Albert, Mustang Ranch and Its Women (2001).

152. For a model of a peep show that is worker-owned, see Kim Price-Glynn, Strip Club 21 (2010).

153. Eleanor Maticka-Tyndale et al., Making a Place for Escort Work: A Case Study, 42 J. Sex. Res. 1, 2, 7-8 (2005).

154. Mary Sullivan, What Happens When Prostitution Becomes Work? An Update on Legalization of Prostitution in Australia 23 (2005), available at http://action.web.ca/home/catw/readingroom .shtml?x=84641.

155. Janet Halley et al., From the International to the Local in Feminist Legal Responses to Rape, Prostitution/Sex Work, and Sex Trafficking: Four Studies in Contemporary Governance Feminism, 29 Harv. J.L. & Gender 335, 398 (2006); MacKinnon, Trafficking, supra note 146, at 304-306; Janice G. Raymond, Ten Reasons for Not Legalizing Prostitution (2003), available at http://www.rapereliefshelter .bc.ca/issues/prostitution_legalizing.html.

156. Quinnipiac University Poll (2008), available at http://www.quinnipiac.edu/polling.xml; Social Science Research Center (1995) (81 percent of adults, and 74 percent of males oppose legalization), available at http://www.prostitution procon.org./poll.htm (62 percent of New Yorkers, 54 percent of men, and 68 percent of women oppose legalization).

157. See Johnny California, Measure K in California Defeated—Prostitution Laws Still Enforced, Nov. 6, 2008, available at http://johnnycalifornia.com/?p=1145; Jess McKinley, San Francisco's Prostitutes Support a Proposition, N.Y. Times, Oct. 31, 2008, at A10; Rebecca W. Turek, Prostitutes' Rights Measure Defeated in Berkeley, available at http://journalism.berkeley.edu/projects/election2004/ archives/berkeley; Chip Johnson, A Look Back at the Year's News Stories, San Francisco Chron., Dec. 31, 2004, at B1.

158. Christina Hoag, New Laws Treat Teen Prostitutes as Abuse Victims, AP and ABC News, Apr. 18, 2009; Bernice Yeung, Throw Away Girls, Cal. Law., Nov. 2003, at 59.

159. Roger Mathews, Prostitution, Politics, and Policy, 113 (2008); Sweden Unveils Tougher Penalties for Buying Sex, The Local: Sweden's News in English, Jan. 27, 2011, http://www .thelocalse/31680/20110127.

160. Farley, Prostitution, Trafficking and Cultural Amnesia, supra note 147, at 138; Gunilla S. Ekberg, The Swedish Law That Prohibits the Purchase of Sexual Services, 10 Violence Against Women 1187, 1189-1193 (2004); Fact Sheet on Violence Against Women, http:// www.prostitutionresearch.com/ swedish.html; Sheila Jeffreys, The Industrial Vagina: The Global Sex Trade 203 (2009). Street prostitution has reportedly declined by 50 percent since the law's passage. Sweden's Law a Success: Report, The Local: Sweden's News in English, July 3, 2010, http://www.thelocfal.se/27580/201007303. For a comprehensive review of the mixed evidence on Sweden's law, see Katie Beran, Revisiting the Prostitution Debate: Uniting Liberal and Radical Feminism in Pursuit of Policy Reform, 30 J. Law & Ineq, 19, 49-53, 55 (2012).

161. Beran, supra note 160, at 51, 53.

162. Aziza Ahmed, Feminism, Power, and Sex Work in the Context of HIV/AIDs Consequences for Women's Health, 34 Harv. J.L. & Gender 225, 255 (2011).

163. Mark Benjamin, Fall Girls, Ms., Summer 2008, at 37. Palfrey committed suicide after being convicted of racketeering and money laundering. For politicians alleged to have been customers, including Louisiana Senator David Vitter, see id.

164. Melissa Farley, Julie Bindel, & Jacqueline M. Golding, Men Who Buy Sex: Who They Buy and What They Know 26 (2009).

165. Sex Trade Workers and Feminists: Myths and Illusions, in Good Girls/Bad Girls: Feminists and Sex Trade Workers Face to Face 202 (Laurie Bell ed., 1987).

166. Gail McPherson, The Whore Stigma: Female Disorder and Male Unworthiness, 37 Soc. Text 39, 54 (1993).

167. Anonymous, Prostitution: A Narrative by a Former "Call Girl," 1 Mich. J. Gender & L. 105 (1993).

168. McPherson, supra note 166, at 57.

169. Heidi Fleiss, as told to Nadya Labi, In Defense of Prostitution, Legal Affairs, Sept./Oct. 2003, available at http://www.legalaffairs.org/issues/September-October-2003/feature_Fleiss_sepoct03 .asp.

170. Dan Reed, Stanford Law Grad, U.S. Clash over Cache of Cash, San Jose Mercury News, Oct. 6, 2004, at B1.

171. John Roemer, Degree of Flexibility: Stanford Law Grad Turned Escort Says Her Legal Training Taught Her to Question Assumptions, San Francisco Daily J., Oct. 25, 2004, at A1; Howard Mintz, Stanford Law School Grad Pleads Guilty to Running Escort Service, San Jose Mercury News, posted Jan. 26, 2009, available at http://www.lawschool.com/Brazil.htm.

172. Mintz, supra note 171; She Works Hard for the Money, Playboy, Feb. 1, 2005, at 49.

173. U.S. Department of Child Exploitation and Obscenity, http://www.justice.gov/criminal/ceos/prostitution.html.

174. Catharine MacKinnon, Prostitution and Civil Rights, 1 Mich. J. Gender & L. 13, 27-28 (1996).

175. MacKinnon, Trafficking, supra note 146, at 299.

176. Sheila Jeffreys, The Idea of Prostitution 137 (1997).

177. Realistic Feminists: An Interview with Valerie Scott, Peggy Miller, and Ryan Hotchkiss of the Canadian Organization for the Rights of Prostitutes, in Good Girls/Bad Girls 204, 213 (Laurie Bell ed., 1987).

178. Id. at 206, 209.

179. Farley, Prostitution, Trafficking and Cultural Amnesia, supra note 147, at 142.

180. Carlin Meyer, Decriminalizing Prostitution: Liberation or Dehumanization?, 1 Cardozo Women's L.J. 105, 117 (1993).

181. Mireya Navarro, The West Gets Wilder, N.Y. Times, Jan. 8, 2006, at S2 (quoting Amalia Cazebas).

182. U.S. Dep't of Health and Human Services, About Human Trafficking, 2012, http://www.acf .hhs.gov/trafficking/about/index.html; Report of the Director-General Global Alliance Against Forced Labor, paragraph 265 and Table 2.1, International Labor Conference (June 6, 2005).

183. U.S. Dep't of State, Trafficking in Persons Report 8 (2009).

184. U.N. Office on Drugs and Crime, Global Report on Trafficking in Persons Report 8 (2009).

185. Civil Rights Div., U.S. Dep't of Justice, Report on Activities to Combat Human Trafficking: Fiscal Years 2001-2005, at 9 (2006).

186. U.S. Dep't of State, Trafficking in Persons Report, supra note 183, at 6-11; see also Alexandra V. Orlova, Trafficking of Women and Children for Exploitation in the Commercial Sex Trade: The Case of the Russian Federation, 6 Geo. J. Gender & L. 157 (2005); Peter Landsman, The Girls Next Door, N.Y. Times Mag., Jan. 25, 2004, at 32.

187. For child marriages, see Jane Kim, Trafficked: Domestic Violence, Exploitation in Marriage, and the Foreign-Bride Industry, 51 Va. J. Int'l L. 443, 454-465 (2011).

188. Gaiutra Bahadur, Survival Sex, Ms., Summer 2008, at 28-29.

189. See U.S. Dep't of State, Trafficking in Persons Report, supra note 183, at 6-11.

190. Julia O'Connell Davidson, Children in the Global Sex Trade (2005).

191. Id. at 8-9 (reporting rates of rape between 60 and 75 percent, and rates of physical assault between 70 and 95 percent).

192. Id. at 6.

193. Nicholas Kristof, If This Isn't Slavery, What Is?, N.Y. Times, Jan. 4, 2009, at SR8.

194. Luchina Fisher, Judge to Rule on Ground-Breaking Sex Tourism Case, Sept. 22, 2003, available at www.womensenews.org.

195. Davidson, supra note 190, at 130.

196. Federal Bureau of Investigation, 76 FBI Law Enforcement Bulletin 1, 16-21 (2007). For customers' views, see Kathy Steinman, Sex Tourism and the Child: Latin America's and the United States' Failure to Prosecute Sex Tourists, 13 Hastings Women's L.J. 53, 62 (2002).

197. Steinman, supra note 196, at 65.

198. U.S. Dep't of State, Trafficking in Persons Report, supra note 183, at 20-36.

199. Jonathan Todres, Taking Prevention Seriously: Developing a Comprehensive Response to Child Trafficking and Sexual Exploitation, 43 Vand. J. Transnational L. 1 (2010); Robert Uy, Blinded by Red Lights: Why Trafficking Discourse Should Shift Away from Sex and the "Perfect Victim Paradigm," 26 Berkeley J. Gender, L. & Justice 204 (2011).

200. Code of Conduct for the Protection of Children from Sexual Exploitation in Travel and Tourism, TheCode.org, http://www.thecode.org.

201. See United States v. Casteneda, 239 F.3d 978 (9th Cir. 2001). For the inadequacy of resources, see Rebecca Clarren, The Invisible Ones, Ms., Summer 2007, at 45; April Riger, Missing the Mark: Why the Trafficking Victims Protection Act Fails to Protect Trafficking Victims in the United States, 30 Harv. J.L. & Gender 231, 246 (2007).

202. Susan W. Tiefenbrun, Updating the Domestic and International Impact of the U.S. Victims of Trafficking Protection Act of 2000: Does Law Deter Crime?, 38 Case W. Res. J. Int'l L. 249, 286 (2006).

203. Camelia M. Tepelus, Social Responsibility and Innovation on Trafficking and Child Sex Tourism: Morphing of Practice into Sustainable Tourism Policies?, 8 Tourism and Hospitality Research 98, 103 (2008); Operation Predator Website (2008), available at http://www.ice.gov/pi/news/factsheets/operationpredator.htm.

204. Lise Olsen, Sex Trafficking Victims Live in Visa Limbo, Houston Chron., Nov. 24, 2008, available at http://www.chron.com/news/houston-texas/article/Visa-problems-put-sex-trafficking-victims-lives-1768768.php; Jayrashri Srikantiah, Perfect Victims and Real Survivors: The Iconic Victim in Domestic Human Trafficking Law, 87 B.U. L. Rev. 157, 178-180 (2007).

205. U.S. Dep't of State, Report of the United States of America, Submitted to the U.N. High Commissioner for Human Rights, in Conjunction with the Universal Periodic Review, Responses to the U.N. Human Rights Council Working Group Report, para. 5 (Mar. 10, 2011).

206. Jennifer Friedlin, Debate Roars over Anti-Trafficking Funds, Apr. 16, 2004, available at www.womensenews.org (quoting Kent Hill, assistant administrator for U.S. Agency for International Development).

207. Vanessa Brocato, Profitable Proposals: Explaining and Addressing the Mail-Order Bride Industry Through International Human Rights Law, 5 San Diego Int'l L.J. 225, 230 (2004).

208. Arin Greenwood, For Mail Order Brides: Happily Ever After, ABA J., Jan. 2008, at 14; Kate O'Rourke, To Have and to Hold: A Postmodern Feminist Response to the Mail-Order Bride Industry, 30 Denv. J. Int'l L. & Pol'y 475, 476 (2002). The industry doubled in size between 1997 and 2004. Kirsten Lindee, Love, Honor or Control: Domestic Violence, Trafficking, and the Question of How to Regulate the Mail Order Bride Industry, 16 Colum. J. Gender & L. 551, 552 (2007).

209. Kim, supra note 187, at 468.

210. Donna R. Lee, Mail Fantasy: Global Sexual Exploitation in the Mail-Order Bride Industry and Proposed Legal Solutions, 5 Asian L.J. 139, 160 (1998).

211. Beverly Encarguez Perez, Woman Warrior Meets Mail-Order Bride: Finding an Asian American Voice in the Women's Movement, 18 Berkeley Women's L.J. 211, 221 (2003); Cherry Blossoms, Nov./Dec. 1995. For catalogs, see the Cherry Blossoms website at http://www.blossoms.com.

212. David Crary, Protecting Mail-Order Brides, Ariz. Rep., July 6, 2003, at A2.

213. U.S. Citizenship & Immigr. Servs., International Matchmaking Organizations: A Report to Congress (1999).

214. Kim, supra note 187, at 470-471 (quoting GoodWife.com).

215. Perez, supra note 211, at 221.

216. Robert J. Scholes, with Anchalee Phataralaoha, The "Mail-Order Bride" Industry and its Impact on U.S. Immigration, Report to Congress (2006), http://www.aila.org/content/fileviewer.aspx?docid=13775&linkid=151742.

217. For examples of violence and sexual exploitation, see Kim, supra note 187, at 471.

218. Scholes, supra note 216, at 5.

219. Peter Clough, Mail-Order Bride Phenomenon—Conclusion of a Series: Internet Brides Roll the Dice for Love or Misery, Vancouver Province (Canada), Oct. 31, 2004, available at 2004 WLNR 11829049.

220. Immigration and Nationality Act, June 27, 1952, ch. 477, 66 Stat. 163 (8 U.S.C. 1101 et seq.); Violence Against Women Act of 2000, Pub. L. 106-386, div. B, Oct. 28, 2000, 114 Stat. 1491; Battered Immigrant Women Protection Act of 2000, Pub. L. 106-386, div. B, title V, Oct. 28, 2000, 114 Stat. 1518.

221. International Marriage Broker Regulation Act of 2005, Pub. L. 109-162, title VIII, subtitle D (Sec. 831 et seq.), Jan. 5, 2006, 119 Stat. 3066; Violence Against Women Reauthorization Act of 2005, Pub. L. 109-162, Sec. 3, titles I to IX, Jan. 5, 2006, 119 Stat. 2964-3077.

222. See, e.g., European Connections & Tours, Inc. v. Gonzales, 480 F. Supp. 2d 1355 (N.D. Ga. 2007).

223. Rep. Act No. 6955 (1990) (Phil.); Rep. Act No. 9208 (2003) (Phil.).

224. Mail-Order Brides Beware, Asia Intelligence Wire, Dec. 6, 2004, available at 2004 WLNR 13401738.

225. Tamar Lewin, Furor on Exhibit at Law School Splits Feminists, N.Y. Times, Nov. 13, 1992, at B9.

226. Hollywood Madame Heidi Fleiss Abandons Plan for Stud Farm, Fox News, Feb. 10, 2009. For her former plans, see Navarro, supra note 181, at S1.

227. Deborah L. Rhode, Justice and Gender 202-207 (1989). For a comprehensive history of the regulation of contraception, see Linda Gordon, Woman's Body, Woman's Right: Birth Control in America (revised 1990).

228. 405 U.S. 438, 453 (1972).

229. 431 U.S. 678 (1977).

230. 539 U.S. 558 (2003).

231. See, e.g., Robert P. George & David L. Tubbs, The Bad Decision That Started It All, National Review, July 18, 2005, at 39-40.

232. See Mark Gitenstein, Matters of Principle: An Insider's Account of American's Rejection of Robert Bork's Nomination to the Supreme Court (1992). For Bork's view of Griswold, see Robert H. Bork, Neutral Principles and Some First Amendment Problems, 47 Ind. L.J. 1, 7-12 (1971) (arguing that Griswold was an unprincipled decision).

233. 158 Cong. Rec. S. 1162 (Mar. 1, 2012); Robert Pear, Senate Rejects Step Targeting Coverage of Contraception, N.Y. Times, Mar. 1, 2012, available at http://www.nytimes.com/2012/03/02/us/politics/senate-kills-gop-bill-opposing-contraception-policy.html?pagewanted=all.

234. See Romney Clarifies His Position on Blunt Amendment, The Miami Herald, Feb. 29, 2012.

235. See Sarah Kiff, Meet Sandra Fluke: The Woman You Didn't Hear at Congress' Contraceptives Hearing, Feb. 16, 2012, at http://www.washingtonpost.com/blogs/ez-ra-klein/post/meet-sandra-fluke-the-woman-you-didnt-hear-at-congress-contraceptives-hearing/2012/02/16/gIQAJh57HR_blog.html.

236. See Matt Negrin, Sandra Fluke Says Rush Limbaugh's Apology Doesn't Change Anything, OTUS News, Mar. 5, 2012, at http://abcnews.go.com/Politics/OTUS/rush-limbaugh-apologizes-calling-sandra-fluke-slut/story?id=15841687#.T1fasPUyF8E.

237. Erik Eckholm, Poll Finds Divisions Over Requiring Coverage, N.Y. Times, March 1, 2012, at A15.

238. Catharine MacKinnon, Feminism Unmodified: Discourses on Life and Law 99 (1987).

239. Gordon, supra note 227, at 480-481, xix-xxi.

240. See William D. Mosher, National Center for Health Statistics, Use of Contraception and Use of Family Planning Services in the United States: 1982-2008, 23 Vital and Health Statistics 29, at Table 4 (Aug. 2010).

241. Deana Pisoni, Ninth Annual Review of Gender and Sexuality Law: Health Law Chapter: Access to Contraceptives, 9 Geo. J. Gender & L. 1125, 1131 (2008).

242. See http://www.npr.org/blogs/health/2013/06/11/190742896/administrations-plan-for-morning-after-pill-pleases-no-one.

243. See Guttmacher Institute, State Policies in Brief: Emergency Contraception, as of Feb. 1, 2014, available at http://www.guttmacher.org/statecenter/spibs/spib_EC.pdf.

244. See, e.g., 42 U.S.C. §300a-7(c)(B) (2011).

245. Available at http://www.usccb.org/bishops/directives.shtml.

246. See Guttmacher Institute, State Policies in Brief: Emergency Contraception, supra note 243.

247. For an overview, see Guttmacher Institute, Rights vs. Responsibilities: Professional Standards and Provider Refusals (2005).

248. Cornelia T.L. Pillard articulates an equality-based theory for contraceptive access in Our Other Reproductive Choices: Equality in Sex Education, Contraceptive Access, and Work-Family Policy, 56 Emory L.J. 941, 963-977 (2007).

249. Compare Stocking v. AT&T Corp., 436 F. Supp. 2d 1014 (W.D. Mo. 2006) (PDA requires coverage) and EEOC v. UPS, 141 F. Supp. 2d 1216 (D. Minn. 2001) (exclusion constitutes sex discrimination under Title VII) with Cummins v. Illinois, 2005 U.S. Dist. LEXIS 42634 (S.D. Ill. Aug. 30, 2005) (PDA does not require coverage).

250. 479 F.3d 936, 942 (8th Cir. 2007).

251. Id. at 943 (citing EEOC Commission Decision on Coverage of Contraception (Dec. 14, 2000), available at http://www.eeoc.gov/policy/docs/decision-contraception.html).

252. Guttmacher Institute, Facts on Contraceptive Use in the United States, Aug. 2013, available at http://www.guttmacher.org/pubs/fb_contr_use.html.

253. Guttmacher Institute, Insurance Coverage of Contraceptives, as of Feb. 1, 2014 (analyzing state contraceptive coverage mandates), available at http://www.guttmacher.org/statecenter/spibs/spib_ICC.pdf.

254. See Pub. L. 108-7, 117 Stat. 474 (2003).

255. See Patient Protection and Affordable Care Act, Public Law 111-148 (Mar. 23, 2010); 45 C.F.R. Part 147 (2011); DHHS Press Release, Jan. 20, 12012, available at http://www.hhs.gov/news/press/2012pres/01/20120120a.html.

256. See Little Sisters of the Poor Home for the Aged v. Sebelius, 2013 U.S. Dist. LEXIS 180867 (D. Colo.); see also Roman Catholic Archbishop of Wash. v. Sebelius, 2013 U.S. Dist. LEXIS 179317 (D.D.C. 2013).

257. See Little Sisters of the Poor Home for the Aged v. Sebelius, 134 S. Ct. 893 (2013).

258. See, e.g., Gilardi v. DHHS, 733 F.3d 1208 (D.C. Cir. 2013); Beckwith Elec. Co. v. Sebelius, 2013 U.S. Dist. LEXIS 94056 (M.D. Fla. 2013).

259. Conestoga Wood Specialties v. Sebelius; Sebelius v. Hobby Lobby Stores, Inc., 134 S. Ct. 678 (U.S. 2013). The rulings below are at Sebelius v. Hobby Lobby Stores, Inc., 723 F.3d 1114 (10th Cir. 2013) (holding injunction against regulations is warranted); Conestoga Wood Specialties Corp., et al., v. Sebelius, 724 F.3d 377 (3d Cir. 2013) (affirming denial of the injunction).

260. CDC, Vital Health Statistics, Fertility, Family Planning, and Reproductive Health of U.S. Women 23/25, at 21-22 (Dec. 2005).

261. Id. at 29-30.

262. 95 F.3d 674, 679-80 (8th Cir. 1996).

263. 316 F.3d 337, 346-49 (2d Cir. 2003).

264. Id. at 346.

265. 534 F.3d 644, 649 (7th Cir. 2008)

266. Id. at 648-649.

267. See Mary Crossley, Infected Judgment: Legal Responses to Physician Bias, 48 Vill. L. Rev. 195, 225, 227-229 (2003) (citing studies); Sandra C. Gan et al., Treatment of Acute Myocardial Infarction Among Men and Women, 343 New Eng. J. Med. 8 (July 2000).

268. J. Hector Pope et al., Missed Diagnoses of Acute Cardiac Ischemia in the Emergency Department, 342 New Eng. J. Med. 1163 (Apr. 2000). See also Crossley, supra note 267, at 211-223; Lisa C. Ikemoto, Racial Disparities in Health Care and Cultural Competency, 48 St. Louis U. L.J. 75 (2003).

269. Crossley, supra note 267, at 224 (citing studies).

270. See FDA Approves Silicone Gel-Filled Breast Implants After In-Depth Evaluation, available at http://www.fda.gov/bbs/topics/news/2006/new01512.html. On the history of breast implants, see Florence Williams, Breasts: A Natural and Unnatural History (2012).

271. See FDA Update on the Safety of Silicone Gel-Filled Breast Implants at 3 (June 2011), available at http://www.fda.gov/downloads/MedicalDevices/ProductsandMedical-Procedures/Implantsand Prosthetics/BreastImplants/UCM260090.pdf.

272. Id. at 34.

273. See Centers for Disease Control and Prevention (CDC), HPV Vaccine Information for Clinicians—Fact Sheet, available at http://www.cdc.gov/std/HPV/STDFact-HPV.htm.

274. See Centers for Disease Control and Prevention, Cervical Rates by Race and Ethnicity, available at http://www.cdc.gov/Features/dsCervicalCancer/.

275. See http://www.fda.gov/BiologicsBloodVaccines/Vaccines/ApprovedProducts/ UCM094042.htm.

276. Nancy Gibbs, Defusing the War over the "Promiscuity" Vaccine, Time, June 21, 2006 (quoting Bridget Maher), available at http://content.time.com/time/nation/article/0,8599,1206813,00.html.

277. Women in Government, the State of Cervical Cancer Prevention in America 7-8 (2008) (noting that only one state requires vaccination and five require coverage). Arguing for broader access to Gardasil, see Micah Globerson, Gardasil a Year Later: Cervical Cancer as a Model of Inequality of Access to Health Services, 15 Cardozo J. Law & Gender 247 (2009).

278. See http://www.fda.gov/BiologicsBloodVaccines/Vaccines/ApprovedProducts/ucm186991.htm.

279. CDC, Online Newsroom Press Briefing Transcript, www.cdc.gov/media/releases/2011/ t1025_hpv_12yroldvaccine.html.

280. Buck v. Bell, 274 U.S. 200, 207 (1927).

281. See Skinner v. Oklahoma, 316 U.S. 535 (1942).

282. See, e.g., Cal. Penal Code §645 (West 2012) (authorizing hormone suppression treatment for parolees convicted of certain sexual offenses); Wash. Rev. Code §9.92.100 (West 2012) (authorizing sterilization for persons convicted of sex with female under age ten).

283. Conn. Gen. Stat. §45a-699(b) (2012).

284. 68 Ill. Admin. Code §1330.91(j) (2005). The order was the subject of a state and federal lawsuit, see Menges v. Blagojevich, 451 F. Supp. 2d 992 (C.D. Ill. 2006) and Morr-Fitz, Inc. v. Blagojevich, 901 N.E.2d 373 (Ill. 2008), and subsequently repealed. 33 Ill. Reg. 12992 (2009).

285. Ellen Goodman, Pharmacists and Morality, Boston Globe, Apr. 14, 2005, at A14.

286. For the "market" argument, see Robert K. Vischer, Conscience in Contest: Pharmacist Rights and the Eroding Moral Marketplace, 17 Stan. L. & Pol'y Rev. 83, 119 (2006) (if "moral pluralism is going to mean anything in our society it has to mean something at Walgreen's").

287. Reva Siegel, Reasoning from the Body: A Historical Perspective on Abortion Regulation and Questions of Equal Protection, 44 Stan. L. Rev. 261, 279 (1992).

288. Deborah L. Rhode, Justice and Gender 207 (1989) (citing sources).

289. Id. at 208.

290. A classic critique by a scholar who supported abortion as a matter of policy but thought it had no constitutional basis is John Hart Ely, The Wages of Crying Wolf, 82 Yale L.J. 920 (1973).

291. See, e.g., Patrick Lee & Robert P. George, The Wrong of Abortion, in Abortion, in Contemporary Debates in Applied Ethics 13 (Andrew Cohen & Christopher Heath Wellman eds. 2005).

292. See, e.g., Sylvia A. Law, Rethinking Sex and the Constitution, 132 U. Pa. L. Rev. 955 (1984).

293. See Schnably, Beyond Griswold: Foucauldian and Republican Approaches to Privacy, 23 Conn. L. Rev. 861, 932-934 (1991). For a similar argument that emphasizes the importance of viewing women's reproductive rights from the point of view of women's experiences, not as analogs to or derivations from men's experiences, see Jennifer S. Hendricks, Body and Soul: Equality, Pregnancy, and the Unitary Right to Abortion, 45 Harv. C.R.-C.L. L. Rev. 329 (2010).

294. Marjorie Shultz, Abortion and the Maternal-Fetal Conflict: Broadening Our Concerns, 1 S. Cal. Rev. L. & Women's Stud. 79, 81 (1992).

295. George Lakoff, The Foreign Language of Choice, posted on Alternet, reviewed in Katha Pollitt, If the Frame Fits, The Nation, July 11, 2005, available at http://advocatesforpregnantwomen.org/file/if%20the%20frame%20fits-%20the%20Nation.pdf.

296. William Saletan, Three Decades After Roe, An Abortion War We Can All Support, N.Y. Times, Jan. 22, 2006, at E17.

297. Linda C. McClain, The Poverty of Privacy?, 3 Colum. J. Gender & L. 119, 173 (1992). See also Pamela S. Karlan & Daniel R. Ortiz, In a Diffident Voice: Relational Feminism, Abortion Rights, and the Feminist Legal Agenda, 87 Nw. U. L. Rev. 858 (1993) (expressing concern over relational feminism in the abortion context).

298. See http://www.feministsforlife.org.

299. See Emily Bazelon, Is There A Post-Abortion Syndrome?, N.Y. Times Mag., Jan. 21, 2007, at 43; http://www.operationoutcry.org/articles_view.asp?articleid=14856&columnid=2073.

300. Lawrence B. Finer et al., Reasons U.S. Women Have Abortions: Quantitative and Qualitative Perspectives, 37 Perspectives on Sexual and Reproductive Health 110, 113 (2005).

301. Planned Parenthood v. Casey, 505 U.S. at 956, 957 (1992) (Rehnquist, C.J., dissenting).

302. This poll and others with comparable findings can be found at http://www.pollingreport.com/abortion.htm.

303. For a state-by-state breakdown of laws relating to mandatory counseling and waiting periods, see Guttmacher Institute, Counseling and Waiting Periods for Abortion, as of Feb. 1, 2014, at http://www.guttmacher.org/statecenter/spibs/spib_MWPA.pdf.

304. See Jennifer Y. Seo, Raising the Standard of Abortion Informed Consent: Lessons to Be Learned from the Ethical and Legal Requirements for Consent to Medical Experimentation, 21 Colum. J. Law & Gender 357, 358 (2011).

305. Researchers at the Guttmacher Institute conclude that five states require information that overstates the risk to future fertility, and seven states require information that asserts an inaccurate link between abortion and breast cancer. See Chinue Turner Richardson & Elizabeth Nash, Misinformed Consent: The Medical Accuracy of State-Developed Abortion Counseling Materials, Guttmacher Pol'y Rev. Fall 2006, Vol. 9, No. 4, found at http://www.guttmacher.org/pubs/gpr/09/4/gpr090406.html.

306. Harper Jean Tobin, Confronting Misinformation on Abortion: Informed Consent, Deference and Fetal Pain Laws, 17 Colum. J. Gender & L. 112, 114 (2008).

307. Bazelon, supra note 299, at 45-46, 62; Nancy Gibbs, 1 Woman at a Time, Time, Feb. 25, 2007, at 25, 28.

308. For a description of the Act, see http://www.opencongress.org/bill/112-h2543/show.

309. Guttmacher Institute, Requirements for Ultrasound, as of February 1, 2014, at http://www.guttmacher.org/statecenter/spibs/spib_RFU.pdf.

310. For an argument that mandatory ultrasound intrudes upon the woman's decisionmaking by confusing medically informed consent with a moral question and forcing her to conceptualize the fetus as a child, see Carol Sanger, Seeing and Believing: Mandatory Ultrasound and the Path to a Protected Choice, 56 UCLA L. Rev. 351 (2008).

311. See, e.g., Nicholas D. Kristof, When States Abuse Women, Mar. 3, 2012, at SR11.

312. See Jamie Frevele, Several Newspapers Pull Doonesbury Strip About Texas' Transvaginal Ultrasound Law, Mar. 11, 2012, at http://www.themarysue.com/newspapers-pull-doonesbury-strip/.

313. See Jessica Grose, Virginia Gov. Bob McDonnell Backs Off the Invasive Ultrasound Law, Feb. 22, 2012, at http://www.slate.com/blogs/xx_factor/2012/02/22/virginia_gov_bob_mcdonnell_changes_his_mind_about_ultrasound_law.html.

314. Guttmacher Institute, Counseling and Waiting Periods for Abortion, as of February 1, 2014, at http://www.guttmacher.org/statecenter/spibs/spib_MWPA.pdf.

315. See Theodore Joyce et al., The Impact of Mississippi's Mandatory Delay Law on Abortions and Births, 278 JAMA 653, 655 (1997); Ted Joyce & Robert Kaestner, The Impact of Mississippi's Mandatory Delay Law on the Timing of Abortion, 32 Family Planning Perspectives 4 (2000).

316. Stephanie Pappas, Study Reveals Who Gets Late-Term Abortions, Dec. 16, 2011, at http://www.livescience.com/17529-trimester-abortions.html.

317. See Aida Torres & Jacqueline Darroch Forrest, Why Do Women Have Abortions, 20(4) Family Planning Perspectives 169 (1988).

318. See Guttmacher Institute, State Policies on Later Abortions, as of February 1, 2014, at http://www.guttmacher.org/statecenter/spibs/spib_PLTA.pdf.

319. Reva B. Siegel, Dignity and the Politics of Protection: Abortion Restrictions Under *Casey*/*Carhart*, 117 Yale L.J. 1695, 1718-1719 (2008) (quoting David Reardon, Politically Correct vs. Politically Smart: Why Politicians Should be Both Pro-Woman and Pro-Life, 2 Post-Abortion Rev., Fall 1994, at 3).

320. Susan Appleton, Reproduction and Regret, 23 Yale J. Law & Feminism 255, 258-259 (2011).

321. Id. at 325.

322. See Priscilla K. Coleman et al., Induced Abortion and Anxiety, Mood, and Substance Abuse Disorders: Isolating the Effects of Abortion in the National Comorbidity Survey, 43 J. Psychiatric Research 770 (2009).

323. See Julia R. Steinberg & Lawrence B. Finer, Examining the Association of Abortion History and Current Mental Health: A Reanalysis of the National Comorbidity Survey Using a Common-Risk-factors Model, 72 Social Sci. & Medicine 72 (2011).

324. See, e.g., Bray v. Alexandria Women's Health Clinic, 506 U.S. 263 (1993) (holding that Section 1985 of the Civil Rights Statutes did not provide a federal cause of action to stop demonstrations at abortion clinics based on a violation of the civil rights of women). For FACE, see 18 U.S.C. §248(a)(1) (2012).

325. See Guttmacher Institute, Protecting Access to Clinics, as of February 1, 2014, found at http://www.guttmacher.org/statecenter/spibs/spib_PAC.pdf.

326. Colorado v. Hill, 530 U.S. 703 (2000).

327. McCullen v. Coakley, 708 F.3d 1 (1st Cir. 2013) (affirming denial of challenge), cert. granted, 133 S. Ct. 2857 (2013).

328. Eyal Press, My Father's Abortion War, N.Y. Times Mag., Jan. 22, 2006, at 59.

329. See Planned Parenthood of the Columbia/Willamette, Inc. v. American Coalition of Life Activists, 422 F.3d 949 (9th Cir. 2005).

330. See http://www.operationrescue.org/category/tiller-watch.

331. Jenny Deam, Doctor Struggles to Fill Role of Slain Kansas Abortion Provider, L.A. Times, Mar. 5, 2012, found at http://www.latimes.com/news/nationworld/nation/la-na-kansas-abortion-20120305,0,2466363.story?track=lat-pick.

332. Dalton Conley, A Man's Right to Choose, N.Y. Times, Dec. 1, 2005, at A35.

333. Glenn Sacks, Alito and the Rights of Men, L.A. Times, Nov. 1, 2005, at B11.

334. The most recent U.S. Supreme Court decision on the subject is Ayotte v. Planned Parenthood of Northern New England, 546 U.S. 320 (2006). For a continuously updated state-by-state survey of parental consent laws, see http://www.guttmacher.org/statecenter/spibs/spib_PIMA.pdf.

335. Rachel Rebouche, Parental Involvement Law and New Governance, 34 Harv. J. Law & Gender 175, 179-183 (2011); Guttmacher Institute, Parental Involvement in Minors' Abortions, as of February 1, 2014, found at http://www.guttmacher.org/statecenter/spibs/spib_PIMA.pdf.

336. See http://ballotpedia.org/wiki/index.php/California_Parental_Notification_Before_a_Minor%27s_Abortion_%282012%29.

337. See Editorial, Yet Another Curb on Abortion, Mar. 12, 2012, at A24; Federal Parental Notification Law Introduced, Mar. 18, 2011, at http://www.feminist.org/news/news-byte/uswirestory.asp?id=13015.

338. A 10-year study in Massachusetts cited by a state appellate judge in 1997 showed that all bypass petitions but 13 were granted, and of these 13, all but 1 were reversed on appeal; in the remaining case, the parents eventually gave consent. See American Academy of Pediatrics v. Lungren, 940 P.2d 797, 836 n.12 (Cal. 1997) (Kennard, J., dissenting).

339. Rebouche, supra note 335, at 188-196.

340. 42 U.S.C. §710(b)(2) (2012). For a history of the federal programs, see No More Money: Abstinence-Only-Until-Marriage Funding, found at http://www.nomoremoney.org/index.cfm?pageid=947.

341. 42 U.S.C. §710.

342. Staff of H. Comm. on Gov't Reform, The Content of Federally Funded Abstinence-Only Education Programs (Dec. 2004), http://www.democrats.reform.house.gov/Documents/20041201102153-50247.pdf (prepared by minority staff, finding distortions such as exaggerated condom failure rates and suggestions that abortion causes cancer); Christopher Trenholm et al., Mathematica Policy Research, Inc., Impacts of Four Title V, Section 510 Abstinence Programs Final Report 17 (2007), available at http://www.mathematica-mpr.com/publications/pdfs/impactabstinence.pdf.

343. Douglas Kirby, National Campaign to Prevent Teen and Unplanned Pregnancy, Emerging Answers: Research Findings on Programs to Reduce Teen Pregnancy and Sexually Transmitted Diseases 15-16 (2007).

344. Julie F. Kay, What's Not Being Said About Sex and Who It's Hurting, available at http://www.americanprogress.org/issues/2008/03/abstinence_only.html.

345. Id.

346. ACLU of Louisiana v. Foster, 2002 U.S. Dist. LEXIS 13778 (E.D. La. July 24, 2002).

347. See Guttmacher Institute, Facts on Unintended Pregnancy in the United States, December 2013, found at http://www.guttmacher.org/pubs/FB-Unintended-Pregnancy-US.html.

348. Allison Stevens, Hyde's Exit Leaves His Amendment Open to Challenge, Women's eNews, Jan. 7, 2007. For an inventory of state statutes relating to Medicaid funding for abortions, as well as an analysis of the Hyde Amendment's impact on the timing of poor women's abortions, see http://www.guttmacher.org/statecenter/spibs/spib_SFAM.pdf.

349. Harris v. McRae, 448 U.S. 297 (1980).

350. Guttmacher Institute, State Funding of Abortion Under Medicaid, as of Feb. 1, 2014, found at http://www.guttmacher.org/statecenter/spibs/spib_SFAM.pdf.

351. Guttmacher Institute, Restricting Insurance Coverage of Abortion, as Feb. 1, 2014, found at http://www.guttmacher.org/statecenter/spibs/spib_RICA.pdf.

352. Lisa R. Pruitt, Toward a Feminist Theory of the Rural, 2 Utah L. Rev. 421, 470-473 (2007).

353. See Sarah Kliff, Has Violence Deterred Doctors From Performing Abortions?, Wash. Post, March 6, 2012, at www.washingtonpost.com/blogs/ezra-klein/post/has-violence-deterred-doctors-from-performing-abortions/2012/03/06/gIQAU7A6uR_blog.html.

354. See, e.g., Laura Bassett, Abortion "Gag Rule" Could Cut AIDS Assistance to Poor Countries, Huffington Post, July 22, 2011, found at http://www.huffingtonpost.com/2011/07/22/abortion-gag-rule_n_907407.html.

355. See Miss. Initiative 26 (2011), discussed in Christopher R. Green, A Textual Analysis of the Possible Impact of Measure 26 on the Mississippi Bill of Rights, 81 Supra 39 (2011).

356. This bill and numerous initiatives from other states are described at the Personhood USA website, at http://www.personhoodusa.com.

357. In re Initiative Petition, No. 395 State Question No. 761, 286 P.3d 637 (Okla. 2012), cert. denied, Personhood Okla. v. Barber, 133 S. Ct. 528 (2012).

358. In acknowledgment of the potential unconstitutionality of such amendments, Virginia's proposed legislation is "subject . . . to the laws and constitutions of Virginia and the United States." See Va. H.B. 1 Unborn children; construing the word "person" under Virginia law to include. (introduced Nov. 2011), available at http://leg1.state.va.us/cgi-bin/legp504.exe?121+sum+HB1.

359. Cline v. Okla. Coalition for Reprod. Justice, 133 S. Ct. 2887 (2013). The state case is Okla. Coalition v. Cline, 292 P.3d 27 (Okla. 2012).

360. See Constance Johnson, About My "Spilled Semen" Amendment to Oklahoma's Personhood Bill, The Guardian, Feb. 9, 2012, at http://www.guardian.co.uk/commentisfree/cifamerica/2012/feb/09/spilled-semen-amendment-oklahoma-personhood-bill. For examples of legislative and judicial actions that elevate sperm to potential life, see Harvey L. Riser & Paula K. Garrett, Life Begins at Ejaculation: Legislating Sperm as the Potential to Create Life and the Effects on Contracts for Artificial Insemination, 21 Am. U. J. Gender & Soc. Pol'y 39 (2012).

361. Guttmacher Institute, Abortion Policy in the Absence of *Roe*, as of Feb. 1, 2014, found at http:// www.guttmacher.org/statecenter/spibs/spib_APAR.pdf. This website reviews many other types of abortion-related restrictions on a state-by-state basis.

362. See Guttmacher Institute, Facts on Induced Abortion Worldwide, Jan. 2012, available at http://www.guttmacher.org/pubs/fb_IAW.html.

363. See Frank Newport, Americans Prefer Boys to Girls, Just as They Did in 1941, June 23, 2011, available at http://www.gallup.com/poll/148187/americans-prefer-boys-girls-1941.aspx (in 2011 polling, 40 percent of respondents would prefer a boy if they are only going to have one child, while 28 percent would prefer a girl, as compared to 38 to 24 percent in 1941).

364. See Therese Hesketh, The Consequences of Son Preference and Sex-Selective Abortion in China and Other Asian Countries, 183 Canadian Medical Association J. 1374 (Sept. 6, 2011); Jeff Jacoby, Choosing to Eliminate Unwanted Daughters, The Boston Globe, Apr. 6, 2008 , available at http://www.boston.com/bostonglobe/editorial_opinion/oped/articles/2008/04/06/choosing_to _eliminate_unwanted_daughters.

365. 720 Ill. Ann. Stat. §510/6(8) (2012).

366. 18 Pa. Cons. Stat. Ann. §3204(a) & (c) (2012).

367. For different views, see http://www.prochoiceamerica.org/what-is-choice/abortion/ abortion-crisis-pregnancy-centers.html, with http://www.aul.org/2012/12/americans-united-for-life -leaderhead-to-richmond-virginia-for-free-speech-case-arguments-in-the-4th-circuit-court-of-appeals.

368. In Greater Baltimore Center for Pregnancy Concerns v. Mayor and City Council of Baltimore, 683 F.3d 539 (4th Cir. 2012) and Centro Tepeyac v. Montgomery Cnty., 683 F.3d 591 (4th Cir. 2012), the Fourth Circuit Court of Appeals ruled that local ordinances along these lines violate the First Amendment. The cases were reheard before the entire court, en banc, and on July 3, 2013, the same result was reached.

369. See Doctor Training at Issue in Kansas Abortion Bill, The Kansas City Star, Mar. 8, 2012, found at http://www.kansascity.com/2012/03/08/3478488/doctor-training-at-issue-in-kansas.html.

370. Dubay v. Wells, 506 F.3d 422 (6th Cir. 2007).

371. La. Rev. Stat. Ann. §9:2800.12 (2012).

372. Okpalobi v. Foster, 244 F.3d 405 (5th Cir. 2001) (en banc) (dismissed on standing grounds); Women's Health Clinic v. State, 825 So. 2d 1210 (La. Ct. App. 2002) (same).

373. See Maya Manian, Privatizing Bans on Abortion: Eviscerating Constitutional Rights Through Tort Remedies, 80 Temple L. Rev. 123 (2007).

374. 550 U.S. 124, 159-160 (2007).

375. 19 Cal. Rptr. 2d 494 (Cal. 1993).

376. Id. at 500.

377. Id. at 503.

378. In re Marriage of Buzzanca, 61 Cal. Rptr. 2d 280 (Ct. App. 1998).

379. Jennifer Hendricks, Essentially a Mother, 13 William & Mary J. Women & L. 429, 477 (2007).

380. J.F. v. D.B., 66 Pa. D. & C. 4th 1 (Pa. Ct. Comm. Pl. 2004).

381. See, e.g., K.M. v. E.G., 117 P.3d 673 (Cal. 2005) (recognizing rights of former lesbian partner, who supplied ova; court declined to treat partner like semen donor); In re Parentage of L.B., 122 P.3d 161 (Wash. 2005) (recognizing standing of lesbian co-parent to seek custody rights to child conceived by her partner through artificial insemination).

382. N.Y. Dom. Rel. §123 (2012). Other states that ban paid surrogacy include Arizona, Indiana, Louisiana, Michigan, Nebraska, North Dakota, and Utah. On *Baby M*'s influence, see Elizabeth S. Scott, Surrogacy and the Politics of Commodification, 72 L. Contemp. Prob. 109 (2009). On the role of brokers, see Carol Sanger, Developing Markets in Baby-Making: In the Matter of Baby M, 29 Harv. J.L. & Gender 67 (2007).

383. On competing approaches, see Browne C. Lewis, Three Lies and a Truth: Adjudicating Maternity in Surrogacy Disputes, 49 U. Louisville L. Rev. 371 (2011).

384. See Elizabeth Meltzer, Eighth Annual Review of Gender and Sexuality Law: Health Care Law Chapter: Assisted Reproductive Technologies, 8 Geo. J. Gender & L. 807, 821-824 (2007).

385. See Jill Elaine Hasday, Intimacy and Economic Exchange, 119 Harv. L. Rev. 491 (2005); Margaret Foster Riley, with Richard A. Merrill, Regulating Reproductive Genetics: A Review of American Bioethics Commissions and Comparison to the British Human Fertilization and Embryology Authority, 6 Colum. Sci. & Tech. L. Rev. 1, 4 (2005).

386. See Debora Spar, Reproductive Tourism and the Regulatory Map, 352 New Eng. J. Med. 531-533 (2005); Debora Spar, The Baby Business: How Money, Science, and Politics Drive the Commerce of

Conception (2006); Nilanjana S. Roy, Protecting the Rights of Surrogate Mothers in India, N.Y. Times, Oct. 4, 2011, available at http://www.nytimes.com/2011/10/05/world/asia/05iht-letter05.html.

387. See Permanent Bureau of the Hague Conference on Private International Law, Private International Law Issues Surrounding the Status of Children, Including Issues Arising from International Surrogacy Arrangements, available at http://www.hcch.net/upload/wop/genaff2011pd11e.pdf.

388. Emily Galpern, Assisted Reproductive Technologies: Overview and Perspective Using a Reproductive Justice Framework, Dec. 2007, available at http://geneticsandsociety.org/downloads/ART.pdf.

389. Sara Rimer, No Stork Involved, but Mom and Dad Had Help, N.Y. Times, July 12, 2009, at A1.

390. James Barron, Views on Surrogacy Harden After Baby M Ruling, N.Y. Times, Apr. 2, 1987, at A1.

391. Marjorie Maguire Shultz, Reproductive Technology and Intent-Based Parenthood: An Opportunity for Gender Neutrality, 1990 Wis. L. Rev. 297, 302-303.

392. Margaret Jane Radin, Market Inalienability, 100 Harv. L. Rev. 1849, 1885 (1987).

393. Richard Posner, The Ethics and Economics of Enforcing Contracts of Surrogate Motherhood, 5 J. Contemp. Health L. & Pol'y 21, 26 (1989) (just as only wealthy people can afford butlers and expensive cars, so only wealthy people will be able to afford surrogate mothers).

394. Johnson v. Calvert, 19 Cal. Rptr. 494, 503 (Cal. 1993).

395. Beth Jones, Mutual Exploitation: A Response, in Pregnant Man? A Conversation, 22 Yale J.L. & Feminism 207, 257 (2010).

396. Nancy Ehrenreich, Surrogacy as Resistance? The Misplaced Focus on Choice in the Surrogacy and Abortion Funding Contexts, 41 DePaul L. Rev. 1369, 1376 (1992).

397. Shultz, supra note 391, at 353.

398. Anita L. Allen, The Black Surrogate Mother, 8 Harv. Blackletter J. 17, 30 (1991).

399. April L. Cherry, Nurturing the Service of White Culture: Racial Subordination, Gestational Surrogacy, and the Ideology of Motherhood, 10 Tex. J. Women & L. 83 (2001); Dorothy E. Roberts, Race and the New Reproduction, 47 Hastings L.J. 935 (1996). For costs, see Alex Kuczynski, Her Body, My Baby, N.Y. Times Mag., Nov. 30, 2008, at 45.

400. Lori Andrews, Surrogate Motherhood: The Challenge for Feminists, 16 Law, Med. & Health Care 72, 78 (1988).

401. Davis v. Davis, 842 S.W.2d 588, 597 (Tenn. 1992).

402. See, e.g., J.B. v. M.B., 783 A.2d 707 (N.J. 2001) (at divorce, wife entitled to have frozen embryos destroyed, notwithstanding agreement in contract to relinquish them to in vitro fertilization program if their marriage dissolved, because such contracts are contrary to public policy); Dahl v. Angle, 194 P.3d 834 (Or. App. 2008) (embryos destroyed pursuant to agreement, over objection of husband who wanted another couple to be able to use them). For a discussion of the cases, see Mark P. Strasser, You Take the Embryos But I Get the House (and the Business): Recent Trends in Awards Involving Embryos upon Divorce, 57 Buffalo L. Rev. 1159 (2009) (discussing Davis).

403. Glenn Cohen, The Constitution and the Right Not to Procreate, 60 Stan. L. Rev. 1135 (2008). For other commentary, see Jessica Berg, Owning Persons: The Application of Property Theory to Embryos and Fetuses, 40 Wake Forest L. Rev. 159, 161 (2005).

404. Fla. Stat. Ann. §742.17 (West 2012).

405. La. Rev. Stat. §9:121 et seq. (West 2012).

406. See A.G.R. v. D.R.H. & S.H., No. FD-09-001838-07 (N.J. Super. Ct. Ch. Div. Dec. 13, 2011).

407. Rachel Lehmann-Haupt, Why I Froze My Eggs, Newsweek, May 11 & 18, 2009, at 50-51.

408. DHHS, Results from the 2010 National Survey on Drug Use and Health: Summary of National Findings 20 (2010).

409. Susan Okie, The Epidemic That Wasn't, N.Y. Times, Jan. 26, 2009, found at http://www.nytimes.com/2009/01/27/health/27coca.html?_r=1.

410. Linda L. LaGasse et al., Prenatal Methamphetamine Exposure and Childhood Behavior Problems at 3 and 5 Years of Age, 129 Pediatrics 680 (2012).

411. See Julie B. Ehrlich, Breaking the Law by Giving Birth: The War on Drugs, The War on Reproductive Rights, and the War on Women, 32 N.Y.U. Rev. Law & Soc. Change 381, 383 n.15 (2008).

412. Cochran v. Commonwealth, 315 S.W.3d 325, 329 (Ky. 2010).

413. Maternal Health Act of 1992, 1992 Ky. Acts, ch. 442 (H.B. 192) (preamble).

414. McKnight v. State, 661 S.E.2d 354 (S.C. 2008). McKnight appeared to mark a shift from an earlier decision in South Carolina, Whitner v. State, 492 S.E.2d 777 (S.C. 1997), which rejected an ineffective counsel claim and upheld a criminal child neglect conviction under the child endangerment law, based

on the conclusion that a viable fetus is a "child" and that proof of cocaine metabolites in the infant at birth proved endangerment by the mother in the last trimester.

415. See 2010 Ut. HB 462.

416. See Lynn M. Paltrow & Farah Diaz-Tello, Caution: Pregnancy May Be Hazardous to Your Liberty, at Huffington Post, Mar. 2, 2010, found at http://www.huffingtonpost.com/lynn-m-paltrow/caution-pregnancy-may-be-_b_483131.html (arguing "no," and citing a number of other state law examples).

417. See Ada Calhoun, The Criminalization of Bad Mothers, N.Y. Times Mag., Apr. 25, 2012, available at http://www.nytimes.com/2012/04/29/magazine/the-criminalization-of-bad-mothers.html?pagewanted=a.

418. See Bei Bei Shuai v. State, 2012 Ind. App. LEXIS 43 (Feb. 8, 2012). For a news video account of the case, see http://www.theindychannel.com/news/27215238/detail.html.

419. For the argument that such prosecutions "fly in the face of medical and public health recommendations regarding the most effective and appropriate ways to respond to suicide attempts and drug-dependency disorders," see Lynn Paltrow, Is Locking Up Pregnant Women the New Cure for State Financial Woes and Mental Health Problems?, at RH Reality Check, Mar. 30, 2011, found at http://www.rhrealitycheck.org/blog/2011/03/30/locking-pregnant-women-cure-state-financial-woes-mental-health-problems.

420. Id.

421. See DHHS, supra note 408, at 29, 43.

422. Jordan Carleo, Evangelist, Charge Dropped in Drunken Baby Case, Albany Times Union, Apr. 9, 2004, at B1.

423. Dorothy E. Roberts, Race and the New Reproduction, 47 Hastings L.J. 935, 953-954 (1996).

424. Id. at 947-948.

425. See, e.g., Trammell v. State, 751 N.E.2d 283 (Ind. Ct. App. 2001) (no-pregnancy condition excessively infringes on defendant's privacy rights and serves no rehabilitative purpose).

426. See Christa J. Richer, Note, Fetal Abuse Law: Punitive Approach and the Honorable Status of Motherhood, 50 Syracuse L. Rev. 1127 (2000); Guttmacher Institute, Substance Abuse During Pregnancy, Mar. 1, 2012, available at http://www.guttmacher.org/statecenter/spibs/spib_SADP.pdf. On the Wisconsin law, and a pending lawsuit challenging its constitutionality, see Erik Eckholm, Case Explores Rights of Fetus Versus Mother, N.Y. Times, Oct. 23, 2013, at A1.

427. 3 S.C.R. 925 (1997).

428. See, e.g., Fla. Stat. Ann. §415.503(9)(g)(1) (West 2012); 705 Ill. Comp. Stat. Ann. §405/2-18(2)(c) & (d) (2012); Nev. Rev. Stat. Ann. §432B.330(1)(b) (2012).

429. See Bill Kaczor, Florida Woman Fights Ruling That Kept Her in Hospital, Jan. 26, 2010, found at http://apnews.myway.com/article/20100126/D9DFDKO0.html.

430. Lynn M. Paltrow & Julie B. Ehrlich, Pregnant Addicts Aren't Child Abusers, in Women's eNews, Sept. 26, 2006, available at http://www.alternet.org/story/41917. See also Linda C. Fentiman, The New "Fetal Protection": The Wrong Answer to the Crisis of Inadequate Health Care for Women and Children, 84 Denv. U. L. Rev. 537, 594-597 (2006) (proposing a more aggressive battle against poverty, universal health care, expanded and targeted substance abuse programs for pregnant women, improved environmental and workplace health laws, and a no-fault program to compensate children who suffer prenatal harm).

431. David C. Brody & Heidee McMillin, Combating Fetal Substance Abuse and Governmental Foolhardiness Through Collaborative Linkages, Therapeutic Jurisprudence, and Common Sense: Helping Women Help Themselves, 12 Hastings Women's L.J. 243, 268 (2001).

432. Rachel Roth, Making Women Pay: The Hidden Costs of Fetal Rights 140 (2000).

433. Pub. L. No. 102-321, 106 Stat. 323 (codified as amended in scattered sections of 42 U.S.C.A. §§201-300 (West Supp. 2012)).

434. See Jean Reith Schroedel & Pamela Fiber, Punitive Versus Public Health Oriented Responses to Drug Use by Pregnant Women, 1 Yale J. Health Pol'y L. & Ethics 217 (2001).

435. See http://www.projectprevention.org/statistics.html. See also Lynn Paltrow, Why Caring Communities Must Oppose C.R.A.C.K./Project Prevention: How C.R.A.C.K. Promotes Dangerous Propaganda and Undermines the Health and Well Being of Children and Families, 5 J.L. Soc'y 11, 13-15 (2003) (challenging negative racial and gender stereotypes that the program promotes).

436. For details about the New York State Prenatal Assistance Program, see Khiara M. Bridges, Privacy Rights and Public Families, 34 Harv. J. Law & Gender 113 (2011). For discussion of the larger

issue of what conditions the state may place on public assistance, see Dorothy Roberts, The Only Good Poor Woman: Unconstitutional Conditions and Welfare, 72 Denv. U. L. Rev. 931 (1995).

437. Glenn Grothman, Wisconsin Senator, Proposes Law That Declares Single Parenthood Child Abuse, Huffington Post, Mar. 2, 2012, found at http://www.huffingtonpost.com/2012/03/02/glenn-grothman-wisconsin-law-single-parenthood-child-abuse_n_1316834.html?ref=politics&ir=Politics/.

438. See David Lowe, HIV Study Raises Ethical Concerns for the Treatment of Pregnant Women, 10 Berkeley Women's L.J. 176, 178 (1995).

439. Centers for Disease Control, Revised Recommendations for HIV Testing of Adults, Adolescents, and Pregnant Women in Health-Care Settings (2006), available at http://www.cdc.gov/mmwr/preview/mmwrhtml/rr5514a1.htm.

440. Jeremy W. Peters, New Jersey Requires H.I.V. Test in Pregnancy, N.Y. Times, Dec. 27, 2007, available at http://www.nytimes.com/2007/12/27/nyregion/27hiv.html.

441. See Cruzan v. Director, Missouri Dep't of Health, 497 U.S. 261 (1990).

442. See Gagandeep Kaur, India's Anti-Feticide Plan Frustrates Leading Critic, in Women's eNews, Oct. 1, 2008, available at http://www.wunrn.com/news/2008/10_08/09_29_08/092808_india2.htm.

443. See Wade Goodwyn, The Strange Case of Marlise Munoz and John Peter Smith Hospital, NPR, Jan. 28, 2014, at http://www.npr.org/blogs/health/2014/01/28/267759687/the-strange-case-of-marlise-munoz-and-john-peter-smith-hospital.

444. See Monica K. Miller, Refusal to Undergo a Cesarean Section: A Woman's Right or a Criminal Act?, 15 Health Matrix 383 (2005).

445. See N.J. Div. of Youth & Family Servs. v. V.M., 974 A.2d 448 (N.J. Super. Ct. App. Div. 2009) (yes), discussed critically in Jessica L. Waters, In Whose Best Interest? New Jersey Division of Youth and Family Services v. V.M. and B.G. and the New Wave of Court-Controlled Pregnancies, 34 Harv. J. Law & Gender 81 (2011).

446. For some provocative views, see Kate Zernike, And Baby Makes How Many?, N.Y. Times, Feb. 9, 2009, at ST1; Lisa Belkin, How Many Children Is Too Many? N.Y. Times, Feb. 9, 2009, at http://parenting.blogs.nytimes.com/2009/02/09/how-many-children-is-too-many.

447. The facts were taken from Cleveland Bar Association v. Clearly, 754 N.E.2d 235 (Ohio 2001), described and critiqued in April L. Cherry, The Detention, Confinement, and Incarceration of Pregnant Women for the Benefit of Fetal Health, 16 Colum. J. Gender & L. 147 (2007).

448. See Jill Duerr Berrick, From Mother's Duty to Personal Responsibility: The Evolution of AFDC, 7 Hastings Women's L.J. 257, 258-259 (1996); Bridgette Baldwin, Stratification of the Welfare Poor: Intersections of Gender, Race & "Worthiness" in Poverty Discourse and Policy, 6 Modern American 4, 4-5 (2010).

449. See Linda Gordon, Pitied But Not Entitled: Single Mothers and the History of Welfare 48 (1994). General sources on women and welfare include Mimi Abramovitz, Regulating the Lives of Women: Social Welfare Policy from Colonial Times to the Present (1988); Jill Quadagno, The Color of Welfare: How Racism Undermined the War on Poverty (1994); Dorothy E. Roberts, Welfare and the Problem of Black Citizenship, 105 Yale L.J. 1563 (1996).

450. U.S. Census Bureau, The Research Supplemental Poverty Measure: 2010 at 5 (2011), http://www.census.gov/propd/www/abs/p.60.html. See Theresa Tritch, Reading Between the Poverty Lines, N.Y. Times, Nov. 19, 2011 at SR2.

451. U.S. Census Bureau, Income, Poverty and Health Insurance Coverage in the United States: 2010 at 14 (Sept. 2011).

452. Timothy M. Smeeding, Poorer by Comparison, Pathways, Winter 2008, at 3.

453. Charles Murray, Losing Ground: American Social Policy 1950-1980, at 154-162, 178-181 (1984).

454. Marissa Chappell, The War on Welfare: Family, Poverty, and Policies in Modern America 247 (2010). But see Full Transcript of the Mitt Romney Secret Video, Mother Jones, Sept. 19, 2012, at www.motherjones.com/politics/2012/09/full-transcript-mitt-romney-secret-video (leveraging negative ideas about recipients of federal aid into broad critique of President Obama and his supporters).

455. Robert Pear & Erik Eckholm, A Decade After Welfare Overhaul, a Fundamental Shift in Policy and Perception, N.Y. Times, Aug. 21, 2006, at 12.

456. Amy Goldstein, Welfare Rolls See First Climb in Years, Wash. Post, Dec. 17, 2008, at A1; Molly Hennessy-Fiske, Middle-Class Jobless Run into a Welfare Wall, L.A. Times, Mar. 26, 2009, at A1.

457. Ife Finch & Liz Schott, TANF Benefits Fell Further in 2011 and Are Worth Much Less Than in 1996 in Most States (Center on Budget and Policy Priorities, Nov. 21, 2011).

458. For poverty and unemployment rates, see Diana Spatz, The End of Welfare as I Knew It, Nation, Jan. 2, 2012, at 22.

459. Diana Brazzell, Welfare Reform at 15, The Policy Brief, Aug. 25, 2011, http://thepolicybrief
.wordpress.com/2011/08/25/welfare-reform-at-15.

460. Jake Blumgart, Happy Birthday, Welfare Reform, American Prospect, Aug. 19, 2011, http://
prospect.org/article/happy-birthday-welfare-reform.

461. Legal Momentum, Welfare Reform at Age 15: A Vanishing Safety Net for Women and Children,
Apr. 2011, at 7, https://www.legalmomentum.org/resources/welfare-reform-age-15-vanishing-safety
-net-women-and-children.

462. Chappell, supra note 454, at 245.

463. Legal Momentum, supra note 461, at 5.

464. Noah Zatz, What Welfare Requires from Work, 54 UCLA L. Rev. 373, 415 (2006) (citing state
definitions); Juliette Terzieff, Study: Welfare Clock Should Stop for College Moms, womenenews.org,
Apr. 20, 2006 (noting that only 10 percent of single mothers hold a degree and number has dropped
since reform), available at http://womensenews.org/story/education/060420/study-welfare-clock
-should-stop-college-moms#.Uys1vxD4Klo.

465. Richard Wolf, How Welfare Reform Changed America: 10 Years Later, Success Stories
Common But Many Families Still Struggle to Get By, U.S.A. Today, July 18, 2006, at A1. See also Kaaryn
S. Gustafson, Public Assistance and the Criminalization of Poverty 124-145 (2011).

466. Gustafson, supra note 465, at 67-69, 141, 143, 160.

467. Wolf, supra note 465; Pear & Eckholm, supra note 465, Erik Eckholm, A Welfare Law Milestone
Finds Many Left Behind, N.Y. Times, Aug. 22, 2006, at 13; Rebecca M. Blank, Improving the Safety Net
for Single Mothers Who Face Serious Barriers to Work, 17 The Future of Children 183, 184 (Fall 2007).

468. Pamela Morris et al., Effects of Welfare Reform and Employment Policies on Young Children
(Society for Research in Child Development 2005).

469. Jason DeParle, The American Dream 338 (2004).

470. Blumgart, supra note 460.

471. Lebrun v. Florida Dep't of Children and Families (M.D. Fla. No. 11-1473, 2011) (enjoining Fla.
Stat. §414.0652).

472. Michael C. Bender, Drug Test Law Faces Challenge, St. Petersburg Times, Sept. 8, 2011, at A1
(quoting Rick Scott).

473. Id. (citing the National Survey on Drug Use and Health).

474. Harper's Index, Harper's Mag., Nov. 2011, available at http://harpers.org/archive/2011/
11/0083663.

475. Bender, supra note 472 (noting that 78 percent of Floridians supported drug tests for state
workers, a policy also subject to legal challenge).

476. See Sara McLanahan, Fragile Families and the Marriage Agenda, Center for Research on Child
Wellbeing Working Paper # 03-16-FF, Dec. 2003, available at http://www.olin.wustl.edu/macarthur/
bio/mclanahan.htm; Kimberly A. Yuracko, The Meaning of Marriage: Does Marriage Make People
Good or Do Good People Marry?, 42 San Diego L. Rev. 889 (2005).

477. See Julia M. Fisher, Marriage Promotion Policies and the Working Poor: A Match Made in
Heaven?, 25 B.C. Third World L.J. 475, 485 n.71 (2005).

478. Marnie Eisenstadt, Birth Figures Deliver Bonus: State Receives $25 Million in Federal Money
as Out-of-Wedlock Births Decline, The Post-Standard (Syracuse, New York), Oct. 14, 2004, at A8. For
a state-by-state listing of marriage promotion efforts, see Theodora Ooms et al., Center for Law and
Social Policy, Beyond Marriage Licenses: Efforts in States to Strengthen Marriage and Two-Parent
Families, Apr. 2004, available at http://www.clasp.org/publications/beyond_marr.pdf.

479. Angela Onwuachi-Willig, The Return of the Ring: Welfare Reform's Marriage Cure as the
Revival of Post-Bellum Control, 93 Cal. L. Rev. 1647, 1690 (2005).

480. For the Marriage Plus proposal, see Ooms et al., supra note 478. See also Linda McClain, The
Place of Families 85-115 (2006).

481. Anna Marie Smith, Welfare Reform and Sexual Regulation 228, 230, 248 (2007).

482. Martha Albertson Fineman, The Autonomy Myth: A Theory of Dependency xiii-xv (2004).

483. Sarah Seltzer, We Are the Many, Not the Few, Ms., Winter 2012, at 34.

484. Hendrik Hertzberg, Occupational Hazards, The New Yorker, Nov. 7, 2011, at 24 (summarizing a 2011 report of the Congressional Budget Office); Congressional Budget Office, Trends in the
Distribution of Household Income Between 1979 and 2007 (Oct. 2011).

485. Rob Reich & Debra Satz, Ethics and Inequality, Boston Review, Nov. 28, 2011, available at
http://www.bostonreview.net/BR36.6/rob_reich_debra_satz_occupy_movement_future_php.

486. Julia B. Isaacs, Isabel V. Sawhill, & Ron Haskins, Getting Ahead or Losing Ground: Economic Mobility in America, The Brookings Institution, Feb. 2008, at 19, available at http://www.pewstates .org/uploadedFiles/PCS_Assets/2008/PEW_EMP_GETTING_AHEAD_FULL(2).pdf; Rana Foroohar, Whatever Happened to Upward Mobility, Time, Nov. 14, 2011, at 28.

487. Montopoli, Brian. Poll: 43 percent agree with views of "Occupy Wall Street," CBS News, Oct. 25, 2011, available at http://www.cbsnews.com/8301-503544_162-20125515-503544/poll-43 -percent-agree-with-views-of-occupy-wall-street/?tag=cbsnewsMainColumnArea.

488. Smith, supra note 481, at 311.

CHAPTER *6*

Identity

This final chapter examines a series of issues relating to gender and identity. The first involves the interrelationships of a person's multiple identities. Do characteristics such as race, ethnicity, age, disability, or sexual orientation interact with gender in ways that make discrimination more difficult to recognize than when only one characteristic is at issue? Do they amplify the experience of inequality, or transform it? What implications does the interaction of these characteristics have for law and policy?

A second issue concerns fundamental factors involving the definition of male and female. Is the difference natural, biological (or "essential")? Or is it psychological, or social? One focus for examining this question is transgender identity. Transgender individuals challenge the law's assumption that an individual's identity as man or woman is fixed. What should follow? Should a transgender female be able to marry a male? A female? Is discrimination against transgender persons discrimination "because of sex"?

This chapter also addresses masculinity. Most of this book is focused on the interests of women, but gender also constrains opportunities for men. What is masculinity and what attention does it demand from women?

Finally, who speaks for "women's" interests? To what extent do claims on behalf of a group marginalize some of its members? Do feminists presuppose as the background norm a white, middle-class, heterosexual woman? When Western feminists criticize cultural practices of other nations or religions that contribute to sexual inequality, are they being arrogant, or even "imperialist"?

Readings in the other chapters of this book tend to take for granted various identity assumptions—what a woman is, what sex is, and what it means that a law or practice is (or is not) in women's interests. The identity issues raised in this chapter challenge some of these assumptions. In an important sense, much of the material in this chapter could be viewed as a form of self-critique. Do they go too far? Far enough?

A. DIFFERENCES AMONG WOMEN

The term "women" is used freely throughout the book. To what extent do differences among women complicate the use of this term? This section examines two problems related to diversity among women. First, the combination of a person's gender and other characteristics such as race, class, or ethnicity may mask the existence of discrimination based on any single characteristic or the way those characteristics work together to create a different discriminatory dynamic. Second, speaking of women as if they were all the same tends to "essentialize" women, or reduce them to a set of common denominators—usually white, middle class, heterosexual, and able-bodied. Both of these problems are cases of unrecognized discrimination—the former unrecognized by employers, say, or courts, and the latter unrecognized by those, including feminists, seeking reform of the law. As you consider each of these problems, consider whether or how they can be avoided. From a legal perspective, should each disadvantaging characteristic and every combination thereof be a separate category of analysis? From a political perspective, to what extent does acknowledging differences among women undercut group-based arguments on their behalf?

This section focuses the debate with excerpts by Devon Carbado and Mitu Gulati and Angela Harris. These excerpts highlight the ways in which black women might experience work differently from other blacks and from other women. This experience of multiple, interacting identities is often referred to as a problem of intersectionality. For consideration also is a response to the essentialism critique by Catharine MacKinnon, clarifying the central commitments of feminism and the way the essentialism critique weakens the ability of feminists to pursue those commitments.

Intersectionality refers to the interactions among more than one source of identity.

Reading Questions

1. Are there claims in this book that have overlooked certain groups of women?
2. With so many differences within groups, do gender and other categories make sense?
3. Is it possible to avoid generalizations? Won't every generalization be inaccurate as to someone?
4. What does it mean to "perform identity"?
5. Is the essentialism critique a "tool of woman-bashing"?

Devon W. Carbado & Mitu Gulati, The Fifth Black Woman

11 J. Contemp. Legal Issues 701, 710-715, 717-720 (2001)

Consider the following hypothetical. Mary, a black woman, works in an elite corporate firm. There are eighty attorneys at the firm, twenty of whom are partners. Only two of the partners are black, and both are men. The firm has three female partners, and all three are white. There are no Asian American, Native American, or Latina/o partners. The firm is slightly more diverse at the associate rank. There are fifteen female associates: three, including Mary, are black, two are Asian American, and one is Latina. The remaining female associates are white. Of the forty-five male associates, two are black, two are Latino, three are Asian American, and the rest are white.

Mary is a seventh-year associate at the firm. She, along with five other associates, is up for partnership this year. Her annual reviews have been consistently strong. The partners for whom she has worked praise her intellectual creativity, her ability to perform well under pressure, her strong work ethic, her client-serving skills, and her commitment to the firm. She has not brought in many new clients, but, as one of the senior partners puts it, "that is not unusual for a person on the cusp of partnership."

For the past three years, the Chair of the Associate's Committee, the committee charged with making partnership recommendations to the entire partnership, has indicated to Mary that she is "on track." Being "on track" was important to Mary because, were she not on track, she would have seriously explored the option of moving either to another firm with better partnership prospects for her or in-house to an investment bank that provided greater job security. It was generally understood, however, and the Chair made sure to make it clear that "being on track is not a guarantee that you will ultimately make partner." . . .

The Associate Committee recommends that the firm promote all six. However, the partners vote only four into the partnership: one black man, one Asian American male, one white man, and one white woman. They deny partnership to Mary and a white male associate. The partnership's decision to depart from the Associate Committee's recommendation is not unusual. . . . [I]t accepts the committee's positive recommendation only half of the time.

Subsequently, Mary brings a disparate treatment discrimination suit under Title VII. She advances three separate theories: race discrimination, sex discrimination, and race and sex discrimination. She does not, however, have any direct evidence of animus against her on the part of the employer. In other words, Mary can point to no explicit statements such as "We don't like you because you are a woman," or "We think that you are incompetent; all blacks are." The evidence is all circumstantial: Mary was highly qualified, but was rejected for a position that was arguably open.

> A **motion for summary judgment** is a request to the court by the defendant to dismiss a particular cause of action by the plaintiff on the grounds that even if all of the facts alleged were proved, they would be insufficient to support a legal claim.

The court, ruling in favor of the firm's summary judgment motion, rejects all three of Mary's claims. With respect to the race discrimination claim, the court reasons that it is not supported by evidence of intentional or animus-based discrimination. According to the court, there is no evidence that the firm dislikes (or has a taste for discrimination against) blacks. In fact, argues the court, the evidence points in the other direction. The very year the firm denied partnership to Mary, it extended partnership to another African-American. Further, within the past five years, the firm had promoted two other African-Americans to the partnership. The court notes that both of these partners participated in the deliberations as to whether Mary would be granted partnership, and neither has suggested that the firm's decision to deny Mary partnership was discriminatorily motivated. The court concludes that the simple act of denying one black person a promotion is, especially when other blacks have been promoted, insufficient to establish discrimination.

The court disposes of Mary's gender discrimination claim in a similar way. That is, it concludes that the fact that the firm has in the past promoted women to the partnership, that the partners who voted to deny partnership to Mary extended partnership to another woman, and that women participated in the firm's deliberations as to whether Mary would be promoted, and none of these women have claimed that Mary was treated unfairly because she is a woman, suggests that the firm did not engage in sex-based discrimination against Mary.

The court concludes its dismissal of Mary's compound discrimination claim (the allegation of discrimination based on her race and sex) with an argument about cognizability. . . . According to the court, there is no indication in the legislative history of Title VII that the statute intended "to create a new classification of 'black women' who would have greater standing than, for example, a black male." According to the court, "the prospect of the creation of new classes of protected minorities, governed only by mathematical principles of permutation and combination, clearly raises the prospect of opening the hackneyed Pandora's box."

The foregoing hypothetical articulates the classic intersectionality problem wherein black women fall through an anti-discrimination gap constituted by black male and white female experiences. The problem can be framed in terms of essentialism. Consider first the court's response to Mary's race discrimination claim. In determining whether Mary experienced race discrimination, the court assumes that there is an essential black experience that is unmodified by gender. The court's adjudication of Mary's race discrimination claim conveys the idea that racism is necessarily total. It is a particular kind of animus that reaches across gender, and affects men and women in the same way. It is about race—a hostility against all black people. . . .

Consider now the court's adjudication of Mary's sex discrimination. Here, too, the court's analysis reflects essentialism. The essentialism in this context conveys the idea that women's experiences are unmodified by race. The court assumes that if a firm engages in sex discrimination, such discrimination will negatively affect all women—and in the same way. . . .

Finally, consider the court's rejection of Mary's compound discrimination claim. Here, the court doctrinally erases black women's status identity as black women. Its conclusion that this identity status is not cognizable means that, for purposes of Title VII, black women exist only to the extent that their experiences comport with the experiences of black men or white women. Under the court's view, and in the absence of explicit race/gender animus, black women's discriminatory experiences as black women are beyond the remedial reach of Title VII. . . .

To appreciate the identity performance problem, assume again that Mary is an African American female in a predominantly white elite corporate law firm. As before, Mary is up for partnership and her evaluations have been consistently strong. Stipulate now that four other black women are up for partnership, as are two white women and two white men. The Associate's Committee recommends that the firm extends partnership to all nine associates. The members of the partnership, however, decide to depart from this recommendation. They grant partnership to four of the black women. The fifth black woman, Mary, does not make partner. Of the four white associates, the firm extends partnership to one of the men and one of the women.

The partnership's decision creates a buzz around the firm. The firm had never before granted partnership to so many non-white attorneys. Moreover, in the firm's fifty year history, it had only ever promoted two black people to partnership. Both of these partners are men, and the firm promoted both of them in the mid-1980s, a period during which the firm, along with many others, had enjoyed a high level of prosperity.

Prior to 1980, the firm had never hired a black female associate. Furthermore, most of those who were hired after that date left within two to three years of their arrival. Given the history of black women at the firm—low hiring rate, high attrition rate, low promotion rate—associates at the firm dubbed this year the "year of the black woman."

Mary, however, does not agree. Subsequent to the partnership decision, she files a Title VII discrimination suit, alleging (1) race and sex compound discrimination, i.e., discrimination against her on account of her being a black woman, and (2) discrimination based on identity performance. The firm moves for summary judgment on two theories. First, it argues that Mary may not ground her discrimination claim on her race and sex. According to the firm, Mary may separately assert a race discrimination claim and/or a sex discrimination claim; however, she may not, under Title VII, advance a discrimination claim combining race and sex. Second, the firm contends that whatever identity Mary invokes to ground her claim, there is simply no evidence of intentional discrimination.

With respect to the first issue, the court agrees with Mary that a discrimination claim combining race and sex is, under Title VII, legally cognizable. The court has read, and understood, and it agrees with the literature on intersectionality. Under the court's view, black women should be permitted to ground their discrimination claims on their specific status identity as black women. According to the court, failing to do so would be to ignore the complex ways in which race and gender interact to create social disadvantage: a result that would be inconsistent with the goals of Title VII.

With respect to second issue, the court agrees with the firm. The court reasons that recognizing Mary's status identity does not prove that the firm discriminated against her because of that identity. It explains that the firm promoted four associates with Mary's precise status identity—that is, four black women. Why, the court rhetorically asks, would a racist/sexist firm extend partnership to these women? The court suggests that when there is clear evidence of non-discrimination against the identity group within which the plaintiff is situated, that produces an inference that the plaintiff was not the victim of discrimination.

The court rejects the plaintiff's arguments that Title VII itself and the Supreme Court's interpretation of Title VII focuses on protecting individuals, not groups, from discrimination. . . .

The problem with the court's approach is that it fails to consider whether Mary was the victim of an intra-racial (or intra-gender) distinction based not simply on her identity status as a black woman but on her performance of that identity. In effect, the court's approach essentializes the identity status "black female." More specifically, the court assumes that Mary and the other four black women are similarly situated with respect to their vulnerability to discrimination. However, this might not be the case. The social meaning of being a black woman is not monolithic and static but contextual and dynamic. An important way in which it is shaped is by performance. In other words, how black women present their identity can (and often does) affect whether and how they are discriminated against.

Consider, for example, the extent to which the following performance issues might help to explain why Mary was not promoted, but the other black women were.

Dress. While Mary wears her hair in dreadlocks, the other black women relax their hair. On Casual Fridays, Mary sometimes wears West African influenced attire. The other black women typically wear khaki trousers or blue jeans with white cotton blouses.

Institutional Identity. Mary was the driving force behind two controversial committees: the committee for the Recruitment and Retention of Women and Minorities and the committee on Staff/Attorney Relations. She has been critical of the firm's hiring and work allocation practices. Finally, she has repeatedly raised concerns about the number of hours the firm allocates to pro bono work. None of the other four black women have ever participated on identity-related or employee relations-related committees. Nor have any of them commented on either the racial/gender demographics of the firm or the number of hours the firm allocates for pro bono work.

Social Identity. Mary rarely attends the firm's happy hours. Typically, the other four black women do. Unlike Mary, the four black women each have hosted at least one firm event at their home. All four play tennis, and two of them play golf. Mary plays neither. Finally, while all four black women are members of the country club to which many of the partners belong, Mary is not.

Educational Affiliations. Two of the other four black women graduated from Harvard Law School, one graduated from Yale, and the other graduated from Stanford. Mary attended a large local state law school at the bottom of the second tier of schools.

Marital Status. All four of the other black women are married. Two are married to white men and each of them is married to a professional. Mary is a single mother.

Residence. Each of the other four black women lives in predominantly white neighborhoods. Mary lives in the inner city, which is predominantly black.

Professional Affiliation. Mary is an active member of the local black bar association, the Legal Society Against Taxation, and the Women's Legal Caucus. None of the four black women belongs to any of these organizations. One of them is on the advisory board of the Federalist Society. One of the four black women is a Catholic, two are Episcopalian, and the other does not attend church. Mary is a member of the Nation of Islam. . . .

Intersectionality does not capture this form of preferential treatment. While intersectionality recognizes that institutions make intra-group distinctions, that understanding is situated in an anti-discrimination context that is buttressed by a status conception of identity.

Assuming the foregoing performance issues obtain in Mary's case, do they reflect impermissible discrimination? The answer is not obviously yes. Perhaps the partners simply do not like Mary. Based on the description of how Mary performs her identity, could one not reasonably conclude the following: She does not attend happy hours, she creates trouble, she is not a team player, she does not dress or act professionally. Redescribing Mary's performance in this way makes the employer's decision to deny her partnership appear non-discriminatory (and even legitimate). After all, working and succeeding in an organization is not only about doing work. It is also about getting along with people and getting them to like you. An argument can be made that Mary simply did not do much work in the direction of getting the people who mattered to like her. The other four black women did; and they got promoted. On its face some—perhaps—will see this as fair. Those who do the extra work of making people like them should get promoted. Given our claim that this line of reasoning is flawed, the question is: What exactly is the relationship between identity performance and workplace discrimination? . . .

Broadly speaking, there are two ways to make the point that intra-group distinctions based on identity performance implicate workplace discrimination. The first is to focus on the preferred group members. In our hypothetical, they are the four black women. The second way is to focus on the disfavored group members. Mary, the fifth black woman, falls into this category. . . .

In a prior article, *Working Identity* [85 Cornell L. Rev. 1259 (2000)], we argued that an employee's awareness that identity-based assumptions about her are at odds with the institutional norms and criteria of a firm creates an incentive for that employee to work her identity. There are a number of ways an employee might do this. The employee might laugh in response to, or engage in racist humor (signaling collegiality). She might socialize with her colleagues after work (signaling that she can fit in; is one of the boys). She might avoid contact with other employees with negative workplace standing (signaling that she is not really "one of them"). The list goes on. The point is that whatever particular strategy the employee deploys, her aim will likely be to comfort her supervisors/colleagues about her negative workplace standing. Specifically, the employee will attempt to signal that she can fit in, that she is not going to make her supervisors/colleagues uncomfortable about her identity—or theirs—and, at bottom, that the negative stereotypes that exist about her status identity are inapplicable to her. *Working Identity* refers to these strategies collectively as "comfort strategies." These strategies are constituted by identity performances.

Stipulate that the four black women in the hypothetical performed comfort strategies. The claim that the performance of such strategies constitutes discrimination is based on the idea that people with negative workplace standing (e.g., people of color) have a greater incentive to perform comfort strategies than people with positive workplace standing. This means that identity performances burden some employees (e.g., blacks) more than others (e.g., whites). Without more, this racial distribution of identity performances is problematic. The problem is compounded by the fact that identity performances constitute work, a kind of "shadow work." This work is simultaneously expected and unacknowledged. Plus, it is work that is often risky. Finally, this work can be at odds with the employee's sense of her identity. That is, the employee may perceive that she has to disassociate from or disidentify with her identity in order to fit in. To the extent the employee's continued existence and success in the workplace is contingent upon her behaving in ways that operate as a denial of self, there is a continual harm to that employee's dignity.

Recall that the claim is that the firm's discrimination against Mary derives from an intra-group distinction based on Mary's dress, institutional identity, marital status, professional and educational affiliations, and residence. The question becomes, why is this discrimination impermissible? The short answer is that the distinction creates an intra-racial and an inter-racial problem. The problem is that the firm draws a line between black people who do (or whom the firm perceives as performing) identity work to fit in at the firm and black people who do not perform (or whom the firm perceives as not performing) such work. The interracial problem is that white people are not subject to this subcategorization.

Angela P. Harris, *Race and Essentialism in Feminist Legal Theory*

42 Stan. L. Rev. 581, 588-589, 595 (1990)

[T]he story [feminists] tell about "women," despite its claim to universality, seems to black women to be peculiar to women who are white, straight, and socioeconomically privileged—a phenomenon Adrienne Rich terms "white solipsism." . . .

The notion that there is a monolithic "women's experience" that can be described independent of other facts of experience like race, class, and sexual orientation is one I refer to . . . as "gender essentialism." A corollary to gender essentialism is "racial essentialism"—the belief that there is a monolithic "Black Experience," or "Chicano Experience." The source of gender and racial essentialism (and all other essentialisms, for the list of categories could be infinitely multiplied) is the . . . voice that claims to speak for all. The result of essentialism is to reduce the lives of people who experience multiple forms of oppression to addition problems: "racism + sexism = straight black women's experience," or "racism + sexism + homophobia = black lesbian experience." Thus, in an essentialist world, black women's experience will always be forcibly fragmented before being subjected to analysis, as those who are "only interested in race" and those who are "only interested in gender" take their separate slices of our lives. . . .

[T]he "nuance theory" approach to the problem of essentialism . . . [is to offer generalization] about "all women" while qualifying statements, often in footnotes, supplement the general account with the subtle nuances of experience that "different" women add to the mix. Nuance theory thus assumes the commonality of all women—differences are a matter of "context" or "magnitude"; that is, nuance.

The problem with nuance theory is that by defining black women as "different," white women quietly become the norm, or pure, essential woman.

Catharine A. MacKinnon, *Women's Lives, Men's Laws*

87-88, 90 (2005)

Discerning commonalities in experience is not the same as searching for an "essence." The socially constructed "woman" has no "essence." If women "as women" are social and concrete, they must encompass all of women's experiences of social hierarchy, because race, class, and sexual orientation (for instance) contribute to making women's concrete situation and status as women be what it is. A genuinely feminist method is thus open to real women in the social world and builds its category, "women," from them. . . .

[F]eminism does not take the view that gender is all there is. It takes the view that gender is almost never not there. Feminism claims not that all women are affected the same by male power or are similarly situated under it. It claims that no woman is unaffected by it. Feminism does not see all women as the same; it criticizes this view. It claims that all women are seen and treated as women in some way under male supremacy. This is not to say that feminism is always practiced, even by feminists. This is not to say that feminism does not need to be more race-conscious; it does. Neither is it to say that some work, claiming to be feminist, has not been racist; it has. It is to say that some of the feminist analysis that has been dismissively tagged with what has become the academic epithet of "essentialism," as exemplary of the "straight, white, and economically privileged," is not. . . .

The "essentialism" charge has become a sneer, a tool of woman-bashing, with consequences that far outrun its merits. The widespread acceptance of the claim seems due more to its choice of target than its accuracy in hitting it. Male power is ecstatic; its defenders love the accusation that feminism is "essentialist," even though they don't really know what this means. They do know that it has divided women, which sure takes a lot of heat off. The charge brings the moral authority of opposition to racism to the support of male dominance. "Essentialist" name-calling has become a weapon of choice against those who oppose pornography, prostitution, cliterectomy, dowry burning, and other misogynist cultural practices, practices that target women as women across cultures, although often in culturally specific forms. Avoiding "essentialism" has become a politically and intellectual respectable pretext for dismissing and ignoring gender and the realities of sexual politics. . . .

Anti-"essentialism," as practiced, thus corrodes group identification and solidarity and leaves us with one-at-a-time personhood; liberal individualism. What a coincidence. With the inability to assert a group reality—an ability that only the subordinated need—comes the shift away from realities of power in the world and toward the search for "identity," excuse me, "identities." It changes the subject, as it were, or tries to. But who wins? Can a postmodern humanism be far behind? "Identity" in its currently psychologically shrunk sense is not women's problem. Reality is: a reality of group oppression that exists whether we identify with our group or not.

Notes

1. Racial Tensions in the First Wave of Feminism.   Nineteenth-century suffragettes exploited both the civil rights principles underlying abolition and the racism that persisted after the Civil War. Elizabeth Cady Stanton, for example, claimed both affinity with Negro slaves and superiority over them, reminding white political leaders of the obvious injustice that black men could vote while white women could not: "[Y]ou place the [N]egro, so unjustly degraded by you, in a superior position to your own wives and mothers," she complained.[1] Later suffragettes used even more explicitly racist arguments asserting the desirability of diluting the Negro vote as a rationale for supporting women's suffrage. For example, one Southern suffragist at a 1903 convention of the National American Women Suffrage Association claimed that "[t]he enfranchisement of women would insure immediate and durable white supremacy, honestly attained."[2]

Does any of this sound familiar? Recall the concern expressed by Dorothy Roberts about privileged women's exploitative delegation of menial tasks to low-income women of color.[3] Does white women's equality continue to depend upon the inequality of minority women? Do white women feel entitled, at least unconsciously, to status and income at least as high as minority women? What is to be done? Joan Williams writes:

> Domesticity divides women against themselves. Until feminists acknowledge this dynamic and diffuse it, alliances among women will remain fragile and difficult. Gender wars are not limited to conflicts between employed women and homemakers, for American women are not divided into two dichotomous groups. Instead, they are on a continuum. Some are as work-primary as "high-powered" men; others do no market work. But most American women lie somewhere in the middle, or shift between various points on the continuum at different stages of their lives. These infinite gradations are divisive, as each woman judges women more work-centered than herself as insensitive to their children's needs, and those less work-centered as having "dropped out," or "given up." . . .
>
> Gender has always seemed the most important axis of social power for privileged white women because it is the only one that blocks their way, privileged as they are by class and race. This is not to say that the injustice meted out to them is not injustice. It is. But if privileged women want others to join their struggles, they must re-imagine themselves in ways that take into account the perspective of their proposed allies.[4]

2. The Intersectionality Critique. An older case that helped to stimulate the intersectionality critique involved a challenge by a black woman to an airline grooming policy prohibiting employees from wearing a braided hairstyle. The court held that because the policy applied to all employees—women and men, black and white—it was not discrimination on the basis of either race or gender. In rejecting claims that the style was crucial to black women, the judge pointed out that the plaintiff did not begin to wear the hairstyle until just after a white actress, Bo Derek, popularized corn rows in the movie "10," rather than several years earlier when Cicely Tyson wore the hairstyle at the Academy Awards.[5]

Critics attacked the case for ignoring "intersectionality"—or the interrelationships between race and gender. According to Paulette Caldwell:

Wherever they exist in the world, black women braid their hair. They have done so in the United States for more than four centuries. African in origin, the practice of braiding is as American—black American—as sweet potato pie. A braided hairstyle was first worn in a nationally-televised media event in the United States—and in that sense "popularized"—by a black actress, Cicely Tyson, nearly a decade before the movie "10." More importantly Cicely Tyson's choice to popularize (i.e., to "go public" with) braids, like her choice of acting roles, was a political act made on her own behalf and on behalf of all black women.

The very use of the term "popularized" to describe Bo Derek's wearing of braids—in the sense of rendering suitable to the majority—specifically subordinates and makes invisible all of the black women who for centuries have worn braids in places where they and their hair were not overt threats to the American aesthetic.[6]

How compelling is this critique? Consider Richard Ford's response.

Suppose some black women employed by American Airlines wished to wear cornrows and advance the political message they ostensibly embody, while others thought cornrows damaged the interests of black women in particular and reflected badly on the race as a whole (given the cultural politics of black America in the mid-to-late 1970s, there almost certainly were such black women employed by American Airlines and even more certainly there were such black women among its customers). Suppose further that the management of American Airlines, either formally or informally, sought out and considered the opinions of its employees as well as of its customers and made its grooming policies based at least in part on such information. Now Rogers's claim is no longer plausibly described as a claim on behalf of black women. Instead it is a claim on behalf of some black women over the possible objections of other black women.

Rogers and her supporters might object: "What business is it of other black women whether we wear braids—no one will be forced to wear them." But this individualistic account of the stakes of the case flatly contradicts the proffered rationale for conceiving of the hairstyle as a legal right: cornrows are the "cultural essence," not of one black *woman*. If this claim is to be taken seriously then cornrows cannot be the cultural essence of only those black women who choose to wear them—they must be the cultural essence of *all* black women. And in this case *all* black women have a stake in the rights claim and the message about them that it will necessarily send—not only those who support the political and cultural statement conveyed by cornrows but also those who oppose that statement.

We'd need a fairly detailed account of the cultural and political stakes of cornrows to have a real sense of the political dimensions of this legal conflict. Does the wearing of cornrows track social class (are most cornrow wearers working class "authentics" or bourgeois trendies?) or ideological splits (nationalist v. integrationist?) within the black community? Do cornrows reflect a sophisticated racial politics in which the essentialist message is subordinate, ambiguous or even ironic or is a crude essentialism a central or indispensable part of the politics of cornrows? Is the symbolism of cornrows widely shared and well understood at least within some subset of American society or is it ambiguous?[7]

Is Ford right? How would you have decided the *Rogers* case? What evidence would have been relevant to your decision?

As the basic intersectionality critique has become accepted within feminist legal theory, it has reached increasingly beyond race to include other dimensions of oppression, including age, class, disability, and sexual orientation.[8] As this scholarship has matured, a broad range of empirical research has begun to substantiate some of the intersectionality claims. For example, one study of harassment charges brought under the Americans with Disabilities Act found that disabled individuals who are female, the member of a racial minority, older, or work for a small or a very large company are at higher risk of experiencing disability harassment than others.[9] Another study examining a sample of judicial opinions in federal courts from 1965 through 1999 concluded, among other things, that plaintiffs who make intersectional claims in discrimination cases are only half as likely to win their cases as plaintiffs who allege a single basis of discrimination.[10] What are the possible explanations?[11] Other research is beginning to show how differences within groups, like the differences described in the Carbado and Gulati excerpt, affect the nature of discrimination.[12]

3. The Essentialism Critique.　To what extent do the theoretical perspectives examined in this book assume, as Angela Harris charges, that the "women" who would be aided by the perspective are white, middle-class, able-bodied individuals? Harris's claim is that with respect to some experiences, like rape, being black is not simply additive, but that it transforms the experience.

> [T]he paradigm experience of rape for black women has historically involved the white employer in the kitchen or bedroom as much as the strange black man in the bushes. During slavery, the sexual abuse of black women by white men was commonplace. Even after emancipation, the majority of working black women were domestic servants for white families, a job which made them uniquely vulnerable to sexual harassment and rape.
>
> Moreover, as a legal matter, the experience of rape did not even exist for black women. During slavery, the rape of a black woman by any men, white or black, was simply not a crime. Even after the Civil War, rape laws were seldom used to protect black women against either white or black men, since black women were considered promiscuous by nature. In contrast to the partial or at least formal protection white women had against sexual brutalization, black women frequently had no legal protection whatsoever. "Rape," in this sense, was something that only happened to white women; what happened to black women was simply life.
>
> Finally, for black people, male and female, "rape" signified the terrorism of black men by white men, aided and abetted, passively (by silence) or actively

(by "crying rape"), by white women. . . . [S]ocial activist Ida B. Wells . . . saw that both the law of rape and Southern miscegenation laws were part of a patriarchal system through which white men maintained their control over the bodies of all black people: "[W]hite men used their ownership of the body of the white female as a terrain on which to lynch the black male." Moreover, Wells argued, white women, protected by the patriarchal idealization of white womanhood, were able to remain silent, unhappily or not, as black men were murdered by mobs. . . .

[T]he experience of rape for black women includes not only a vulnerability to rape and a lack of legal protection radically different from that experienced by white women, but also a unique ambivalence. Black women have simultaneously acknowledged their own victimization and the victimization of black men by a system that has consistently ignored violence against women while perpetrating it against men.[13]

Can you think of other examples where race transforms the experience of sexual subordination, rather than merely intensifying it? In the critique above, does Harris herself overgeneralize or "essentialize" black women? Does Paulette Caldwell's analysis of the importance of hair to African American women essentialize them? Do many gender critiques essentialize men?

Is MacKinnon right that an overobsession with essentialism "corrodes group identification and solidarity" and thus the political basis for changing women's reality of subordination? Is there a middle ground that recognizes the need for both the critical edge that MacKinnon's dominance theory provides and caution about claims made on behalf of all women?[14]

4. Intersectionality and the Problem of Categorization. To what extent are the problems of intersectionality and essentialism an inevitable result of the inadequacy of *all* categories, magnified in the case of multiple categories? Linda Krieger outlines how difficult the problem is, even from the standpoint of a single category:

Every person, and perhaps even every object that we encounter in the world, is unique, but to treat each as such would be disastrous. Were we to perceive each object *sui generis*, we would rapidly be inundated by an unmanageable complexity that would quickly overwhelm our cognitive processing and storage capabilities. Similarly, if our species were "programmed" to refrain from drawing inferences or taking action until we had complete, situation-specific data about each person or object we encountered, we would have died out long ago. To function at all, we must design strategies for simplifying the perceptual environment and acting on less-than-perfect information. A major way we accomplish both goals is by creating categories. . . .

What happens when we group objects into categories? First, we tend to perceive members of the same category as being more similar to each other, and members of different categories as more dissimilar to each other, than when all the objects are viewed in aggregate. The same results adhere when the "objects" we categorize are other human beings. . . .

Second, although some debate exists on this issue, it appears that we create a mental prototype, often visual, of the "typical" category member. To determine whether an item is a member of a particular category, we match the object perceived with the category prototype and determine the "distance" between the two. We experience an object first as a member of its "basic" category—the category most accessible at the moment. Only with additional mental processing do we identify it as a member of its superordinate or subordinate categories. . . .

But the price of this cognitive economy is that categorical structures—whether prototypes, stereotypes, or schemas—bias what we see, how we interpret it, how we encode and store it in memory, and what we remember about it later. In intergroup relations, these biases, mediated through perception, inference, and judgment, can result in discrimination, whether we intend it or not, whether we know it or not.[15]

Carbado and Gulati suggest that categorization based on multiple categories leads not only to discriminatory decisionmaking by employers of the sort Krieger describes but also to pressure on individuals to emphasize, or suppress, key aspects of their identity. As legal theorists like Kenji Yoshino note, members of subordinate groups have to choose when to assert their identity and when to "cover" their differences to fit within the dominant culture.[16] This choice constrains "intersectionals" in ways that others are not constrained.[17] Does this concept help to explain the conduct of some of the female lawyers in the Carbado and Gulati excerpt? If so, what follows? Does everyone perform their gender and their race in some way, or is this only an issue for racial minorities and women? Is there a legal fix to the pressures to conform to (subordinating) expectations?

Putting Theory Into Practice

6-1. Reconsider Problem 2-8, involving the unmarried pregnant woman fired from her job at the YWCA because of concern that she would be a poor role model for the teenagers served by the YWCA programs. What, if anything, does the intersectionality critique add to your analysis of her case?

6-2. As a gift for her mother, Seandria purchased the Miracle Morning package from an Elizabeth Arden Red Door Salon and Spa in suburban Washington D.C., which included a facial, massage, manicure, and lunch. While her mother, who is African American, was at the salon, she asked that the salon also color and style her hair. The receptionist refused, telling her that the salon "did not do black people's hair."[18] Is this unlawful discrimination?

B. WHAT IS A WOMAN? THE SPECIAL CASES OF TRANSGENDER AND INTERSEX

Throughout this book, male and female are assumed (for the most part) to be clear, fixed, and easily ascertainable categories. This section examines the challenge that transgender individuals and people with an intersex condition make to this assumption and to the law generally.

The San Francisco Human Rights Commission defines "transgender" as "an umbrella term that includes male and female cross dressers, transvestites, female and male impersonators, pre-operative and post-operative transsexuals, and transsexuals who choose not to have genital reconstruction, and all persons whose perceived gender and anatomic sex may conflict with the gender expression, such as masculine-appearing women and feminine-appearing men. All other terms — cross-dresser, transvestite, transsexual — are subsets of the umbrella term transgender." The term "intersex" is used to describe "anyone with a congenital condition whose sex chromosomes, gonads, or internal or external sexual anatomy do not fit clearly into the binary male/female norm."[19]

Transgender individuals and people with an intersex condition challenge the law's assumption that a person is either male or female, and that a sexual designation is permanent. Most legal cases involving transgender arise with respect to marital status and employment rights.

This section includes two cases that take diametrically opposed positions on the law and policy implications of transgender. Kantaras v. Kantaras illustrates the traditional commitment to an unalterable, biological definition of sex. It holds that a marriage entered into by a post-operative female-to-male is not valid, and thus cannot end in a legal divorce, with rights such as property division or spousal support. *Kantaras* still represents the majority view in the marriage context.

Schroer v. Billington addresses the issue of transgender in the employment context. Traditionally, just as courts have held that discrimination based on an individual's sexual orientation is not discrimination "because of sex" under Title VII, Title VII has not generally been applied to transsexuals. *Schroer* represents a new emerging, but still minority, view that discrimination against transgender individuals violates Title VII, based both on a literal reading of the statute and on the sex stereotyping theory of Price Waterhouse v. Hopkins (excerpted in Chapter 1).

The first-person account by Elvia Arriola shows how transsexuals challenge some conventional feminist assumptions.

Reading Questions

1. Should the law consider Michael Kantaras as a man or a woman, for purposes of marriage? If same-sex marriage is allowed, will the *Kantaras* problem go away?

2. Are there contexts in which employers should not be required to include transgender individuals in their workforce? If so, what might they be? If not, why?

Kantaras v. Kantaras

884 So. 2d 155 (Fla. Dist. Ct. App. 2004)

FULMER, Judge, joined by COVINGTON and WALLACE, JJ., concurring.

Linda Kantaras appeals from a final judgment dissolving her marriage to Michael Kantaras. This appeal presents an issue of first impression in Florida: whether a postoperative female-to-male transsexual person can validly marry a female under the current law of this state. We hold that the law of this state does not provide for or allow such a marriage; therefore, we reverse the final judgment and remand for the trial court to declare the marriage of the parties void. . . .

In 1959 Margo Kantaras was born a female in Ohio. In 1986 Margo changed her name to Michael John Kantaras, and in 1987 Michael underwent sex reassignment, which included hormonal treatments, a total hysterectomy, and a double mastectomy. In 1988 Michael met Linda, and Linda learned of Michael's surgeries. Linda, who was pregnant by a former boyfriend, gave birth to a son in June 1989. Linda and Michael applied for a marriage license with Michael representing that he was male. The two married in July 1989 in Florida. In September 1989, Michael applied to adopt Linda's son, with Michael representing to the court that he was Linda's husband. Linda gave birth to a daughter in 1992 after Linda underwent artificial insemination with the sperm of Michael's brother.

In 1998 Michael filed a petition for dissolution of marriage seeking to dissolve his marriage to Linda and to obtain custody of both children. Linda answered and counterpetitioned for dissolution and/or annulment claiming that the marriage was void ab initio because it violated Florida law that bans same-sex marriage. Linda claimed that the adoption of her son was void because it violated Florida's ban on homosexual adoption, and she claimed that Michael was not the biological or legal father of her daughter. After a lengthy trial, the trial court entered an order finding that Michael was legally a male at the time of the marriage, and thus, the trial court concluded that the marriage was valid. The trial court also concluded that Michael was entitled to primary residential custody of the two children.

In outlining its reasons for determining that Michael was male at the time of the marriage, the trial court stated, in part:

> 24. Michael at the date of marriage was a male based on the persuasive weight of all the medical evidence and the testimony of lay witnesses in this case, including the following:

(a) As a child, while born female, Michael's parents and siblings observed his male characteristics and agreed he should have been born a "boy."

(b) Michael always has perceived himself as a male and assumed the male role doing house chores growing up, played male sports, refused to wear female clothing at home or in school and had his high school picture taken in male clothing.

(c) Prior to marriage he successfully completed the full process of transsexual reassignment, involving hormone treatment, irreversible medical surgery that removed all of his female organs inside of his body, including having a male reconstructed chest, a male voice, a male configured body and hair with beard and moustache, and a naturally developed penis.

(d) At the time of the marriage his bride, Linda was fully informed about his sex reassignment status, she accepted along with his friends, family and work colleagues that Michael in his appearance, characteristics and behavior was perceived as a man. At the time of the marriage he could not assume the role of a woman.

(e) Before and after the marriage he has been accepted as a man in a variety of social and legal ways, such as having a male driving license; male passport; male name change; male modification of his birth certificate by legal ruling; male participation in legal adoption proceedings in court; and as a male in an artificial insemination program, and participating for years in school activities with the children of this marriage as their father. All of this, was no different than what Michael presented himself as at the date of marriage.

25. Michael was born a heterosexual transsexual female. That condition [which] is now called "Gender Identity Dysphoria," was diagnosed for Michael in adulthood some twenty (20) years after birth. Today and at the date of marriage, Michael had no secondary female identifying characteristics and all reproductive female organs were absent, such as ovaries, fallopian tubes, cervix, womb, and breasts. The only feature left is a vagina which Dr. Cole testified was not typically female because it now had a penis or enlarged, elongated clitoris.

26. Michael after sex reassignment or triatic treatments would still have a chromosomal patter [sic] (XX) of a woman but that is a presumption. No chromosomal tests were performed on Michael during the course of his treatment at the Rosenberg Clinic.

27. Chromosomes are only one factor in the determination of sex and they do not overrule gender or self-identity, which is the true test or identifying mark of sex. Michael has always, for a lifetime, had a self-identity of a male. Dr. Walter Bockting, Dr. Ted Huang and Dr. Collier Cole, all testified that Michael Kantaras is now and at the date of marriage was medically and legally "male."

28. Under the marriage statute of Florida, Michael is deemed to be male, and the marriage ceremony performed in the Sandford [sic] County Court house on July 18, 1989, was legal.

The issue in this case involves the interplay between the Florida statutes governing marriage and the question of whether Michael Kantaras was legally male or female when he married Linda. We first address the relevant statutes and then discuss our reasons for concluding that the trial court erred in finding that Michael was male at the time of the marriage. . . .

In the case before us, the trial court relied heavily on the approach taken by [a 2001] Australian family court, which the trial court believed "correctly states the law in modern society's approach to transsexualism." In that case, the Australian court took the view that courts must recognize advances in medical knowledge and practice and found that a female-to-male transsexual should be considered a man for purposes of marriage. Australia prohibits same-sex marriage; nevertheless, the court ruled that a marriage between a woman and a postoperative female-to-male transsexual was valid. In affirming the trial court, the Family Court of Australia stated in its conclusion:

> Unless the context requires a different interpretation, the words "man" and "woman" when used in legislation have their ordinary contemporary meaning according to Australian usage. That meaning includes post-operative transsexuals as men or women in accordance with their sexual reassignment. . . .

We disagree.

The controlling issue in this case is whether, as a matter of law, the Florida statutes governing marriage authorize a postoperative transsexual to marry in the reassigned sex. We conclude they do not. We agree with the Kansas, Ohio, and Texas courts in their understanding of the common meaning of male and female, as those terms are used statutorily, to refer to immutable traits determined at birth. Therefore, we also conclude that the trial court erred by declaring that Michael is male for the purpose of the marriage statutes. Whether advances in medical science support a change in the meaning commonly attributed to the terms male and female as they are used in the Florida marriage statutes is a question that raises issues of public policy that should be addressed by the legislature. . . .

Schroer v. Billington

577 F. Supp. 2d 293 (D.D.C. 2008)

Opinion by Judge JAMES ROBERTSON.

Diane Schroer is a male-to-female transsexual. Although born male, Schroer has a female gender identity—an internal, psychological sense of herself as a woman. In August 2004, before she changed her legal name or began presenting as a woman, Schroer applied for the position of Specialist in Terrorism and International Crime with the Congressional Research Service (CRS) at the Library of Congress. The terrorism specialist provides expert policy analysis to congressional committees, members of Congress and their staffs. The position requires a security clearance.

Schroer was well qualified for the job. She is a graduate of both the National War College and the Army Command and General Staff College, and she holds masters degrees in history and international relations. During Schroer's twenty-five years of service in the U.S. Armed Forces, she held important command and staff positions in the Armored Calvary, Airborne, Special Forces and Special Operations Units, and in combat operations in Haiti and Rwanda. Before her retirement from the military in January 2004, Schroer was a Colonel assigned to the U.S. Special Operations Command, serving as the director of a 120-person classified organization that tracked and targeted high-threat international terrorist organizations. In this position, Colonel Schroer analyzed sensitive intelligence reports, planned a range of classified and conventional operations, and regularly briefed senior military and government officials, including the Vice President, the Secretary of Defense, and the Chairman of the Joint Chiefs of Staff. At the time of her military retirement, Schroer held a Top Secret, Sensitive Compartmented Information security clearance, and had done so on a continuous basis since 1987. After her retirement, Schroer joined a private consulting firm, Benchmark International, where, when she applied for the CRS position, she was working as a program manager on an infrastructure security project for the National Guard.

When Schroer applied for the terrorism specialist position, she had been diagnosed with gender identity disorder and was working with a licensed clinical social worker . . . to develop a medically appropriate plan for transitioning from male to female. The transitioning process was guided by a set of treatment protocols formulated by the leading organization for the study and treatment of gender identity disorders, the Harry Benjamin International Gender Dysphoria Association. Because she had not yet begun presenting herself as a woman on a full-time basis, however, she applied for the position as "David J. Schroer," her legal name at the time. In October 2004, two months after submitting her application, Schroer was invited to interview with three members of the CRS staff, [including Charlotte Preece, who] was the selecting official for the position. Schroer attended the interview dressed in traditionally masculine attire—a sport coat and slacks with a shirt and tie.

Schroer received the highest interview score of all eighteen candidates. In early December, Preece called Schroer, told her that she was on the shortlist of applicants still in the running, and asked for several writing samples and an updated list of references. After receiving these updated materials, the members of the selection committee unanimously recommended that Schroer be offered the job. In mid-December, Preece called Schroer, offered her the job, and asked, before she processed the administrative paper work, whether Schroer would accept it. Schroer replied that she was very interested but needed to know whether she would be paid a salary comparable to the one she was currently receiving in the private sector. The next day, after Preece confirmed that the Library would be able to offer comparable pay, Schroer accepted the offer, and Preece began to fill out the paperwork necessary to finalize the hire.

Before Preece had completed and submitted these documents, Schroer asked her to lunch on December 20, 2004. Schroer's intention was to tell Preece about her transsexuality. She was about to begin the phase of her gender transition during which she would be dressing in traditionally feminine clothing and presenting as a woman on a full-time basis. She believed that starting work at CRS as a woman would be less disruptive than if she started as a man and later began presenting as a woman.

When Schroer went to the Library for this lunch date, she was dressed in traditionally masculine attire. Before leaving to walk to a nearby restaurant, Preece introduced her to other staff members as the new hire who would soon be coming aboard. Preece also gave Schroer a short tour of the office, explaining where her new colleagues' offices were and describing Schroer's job responsibilities. As they were sitting down to lunch, Preece stated that they were excited to have Schroer join CRS because she was "significantly better than the other candidates." Schroer asked why that was so, and Preece explained that her skills, her operational experience, her ability creatively to answer questions, and her contacts in the military and in defense industries made her application superior.

About a half hour into their lunch, Schroer told Preece that she needed to discuss a "personal matter." She began by asking Preece if she knew what "transgender" meant. Preece responded that she did, and Schroer went on to explain that she was transgender, that she would be transitioning from male to female, and that she would be starting work as "Diane." Preece's first reaction was to ask, "Why in the world would you want to do that?" Schroer explained that she did not see being transgender as a choice and that it was something she had lived with her entire life. Preece then asked her a series of questions, starting with whether she needed to change Schroer's name on the hiring documentation. Schroer responded that she did not because her legal name, at that point, was still David. Schroer went on to explain the Harry Benjamin Standards of Care and her own medical process for transitioning. She told Preece that she planned to have facial feminization surgery in early January and assured her that recovery from this surgery was quick and would pose no problem for a mid-January start date. In the context of explaining the Benjamin Standards of Care, Schroer explained that she would be living full-time as a woman for at least a year before having sex reassignment surgery. Such surgery, Schroer explained, could normally be accomplished during a two-week vacation period and would not interfere with the requirements of the job.

. . . Because Schroer expected that there might be some concern about her appearance when presenting as a woman, she showed Preece three photographs of herself, wearing traditionally feminine professional attire. Although

Preece did not say it to Schroer, her reaction on seeing these photos was that Schroer looked like "a man dressed in women's clothing." . . .

Although Schroer initially thought that her conversation with Preece had gone well, she thought it "ominous" that Preece ended it by stating "Well, you've given me a lot to think about. I'll be in touch."

[After speaking with other Library of Congress personnel, Preece rescinded the job offer.] . . .

ANALYSIS

I.

None of the five assertedly legitimate reasons that the Library has given for refusing to hire Schroer withstands scrutiny. [These concerns included (1) Schroer's ability to maintain her contacts within the military because she is transgender; (2) Schroer's credibility when testifying before Congress; (3) Schroer's trustworthiness because she had not been up front about her transition from the beginning of the interview process; (4) Schroer's transition might distract her from her job; and (5) Schroer's ability to maintain her security clearance. All of these concerns were pretextual.]

II.

Schroer contends that the Library's decision not to hire her is sex discrimination banned by Title VII, advancing two legal theories. The first is unlawful discrimination based on her failure to conform with sex stereotypes. The second is that discrimination on the basis of gender identity is literally discrimination "because of . . . sex."

A. Sex stereotyping

Plaintiff's sex stereotyping theory is grounded in the Supreme Court's decision in Price Waterhouse v. Hopkins. In that case, a female senior manager was denied partnership in a large accounting firm in part because she was perceived to be too "macho" for a woman. Her employer advised that she would improve her chances at partnership if she would "take 'a course at charm school'" and would "'walk more femininely, talk more femininely, dress more femininely, wear make-up, have her hair styled, and wear jewelry.'" In ruling for the plaintiff, the Court held that Title VII reaches claims of discrimination based on "sex stereotyping." . . .

[D]iscrimination against a plaintiff who is transsexual—and therefore fails to act and/or identify with his or her gender—is no different from the discrimination directed against Ann Hopkins in Price Waterhouse, who, in sex-stereotypical terms, did not act like a woman. Sex stereotyping based on a person's gender nonconforming behavior is impermissible discrimination, irrespective of the cause of that behavior.

What makes Schroer's sex stereotyping theory difficult is that, when the plaintiff is transsexual, direct evidence of discrimination based on sex stereotypes may look a great deal like discrimination based on transsexuality itself, a characteristic that, in and of itself, nearly all federal courts have said is unprotected by Title VII. . . .

Ultimately, I do not think that it matters for purposes of Title VII liability whether the Library withdrew its offer of employment because it perceived Schroer to be an insufficiently masculine man, an insufficiently feminine woman, or an inherently gender-nonconforming transsexual. . . .

B. Discrimination because of sex

Schroer's second legal theory is that, because gender identity is a component of sex, discrimination on the basis of gender identity is sex discrimination. In support of this contention, Schroer adduced the testimony of Dr. Walter Bockting, a tenured associate professor at the University of Minnesota Medical School who specializes in gender identity disorders. Dr. Bockting testified that it has long been accepted in the relevant scientific community that there are nine factors that constitute a person's sex. One of these factors is gender identity, which Dr. Bockting defined as one's personal sense of being male or female.[1]

The Library adduced the testimony of Dr. Chester Schmidt, a professor of psychiatry at the Johns Hopkins University School of Medicine and also an expert in gender identity disorders. Dr. Schmidt disagreed with Dr. Bockting's view of the prevailing scientific consensus and testified that he and his colleagues regard gender identity as a component of "sexuality" rather than "sex." According to Dr. Schmidt, "sex" is made up of a number of facets, each of which has a determined biologic etiology. Dr. Schmidt does not believe that gender identity has a single, fixed etiology.

Resolving the dispute between Dr. Schmidt and Dr. Bockting as to the proper scientific definition of sex . . . is not within this Court's competence. More importantly (because courts render opinions about scientific controversies with some regularity), deciding whether Dr. Bockting or Dr. Schmidt is right turns out to be unnecessary.

The evidence establishes that the Library was enthusiastic about hiring David Schroer—until she disclosed her transsexuality. The Library revoked the offer when it learned that a man named David intended to become, legally, culturally, and physically, a woman named Diane. This was discrimination "because of . . . sex." . . .

---

1. The other eight factors . . . are chromosomal sex, hypothalamic sex, fetal hormonal sex, pubertal hormonal sex, sex of assignment and rearing, internal morphological sex, external morphological sex, and gonads.

Imagine that an employee is fired because she converts from Christianity to Judaism. Imagine too that her employer testifies that he harbors no bias toward either Christians or Jews but only "converts." That would be a clear case of discrimination "because of religion." No court would take seriously the notion that "converts" are not covered by the statute. Discrimination "because of religion" easily encompasses discrimination because of a change of religion. But in cases where the plaintiff has changed her sex, and faces discrimination because of the decision to stop presenting as a man and to start appearing as a woman, courts have traditionally carved such persons out of the statute by concluding that "transsexuality" is unprotected by Title VII. In other words, courts have allowed their focus on the label "transsexual" to blind them to the statutory language itself. . . .

For Diane Schroer to prevail on the facts of her case, however, it is not necessary to draw sweeping conclusions about the reach of Title VII. Even if the decisions that define the word "sex" in Title VII as referring only to anatomical or chromosomal sex are still good law—after that approach "has been eviscerated by Price Waterhouse,"—the Library's refusal to hire Schroer after being advised that she planned to change her anatomical sex by undergoing sex reassignment surgery was literally discrimination "because of . . . sex." . . .

In refusing to hire Diane Schroer because her appearance and background did not comport with the decisionmaker's sex stereotypes about how men and women should act and appear, and in response to Schroer's decision to transition, legally, culturally, and physically, from male to female, the Library of Congress violated Title VII's prohibition on sex discrimination.

Elvia R. Arriola, Law and the Gendered Politics of Identity: Who Owns the Label "Lesbian"?

8 Hastings Women's L.J. 1, 1-3, 5-6, 8-9 (1997)

Several years ago, I was a member of a predominantly lesbian women's support group. The group offered a "womanspace" for individuals who wanted to share their experiences, strength, and hope as survivors of rape and sexual abuse. On a weekly basis, anywhere from fifteen to thirty women of all racial, ethnic and social backgrounds, who knew each other only by first name, rented a meeting room from a community church and shared stories of sexual victimization and abuse, with the singular goal of healing themselves through mutual support. . . . In the company of other survivors, the women felt safe enough, sometimes for the first time in their adult lives, to weep or get angry; for in this safe space they trusted that their companions would not mock, negate, or minimize their feelings. Of course, the critical sense of safety was ensured by the practice of someone standing guard at the door to make sure no man accidentally walked into the rented rooms. If that happened, all talk would suspend until the man was gone. This ground rule grew out of the plainly obvious fact that this was a meeting for women healing from sexual abuse by the men in their lives; only an all-women atmosphere could guarantee an emotionally safe environment.

Imagine, then, the turmoil created in this "womanspace" when one day a tall, quiet woman who had shown up regularly at meetings for several weeks suddenly came out to the group as a transsexual female. Not only that, she was a transsexual female who identified as a lesbian. Suddenly "Micki," who had simply appeared as an unusually tall, rather quiet and professionally dressed woman, looked very different to the group's members. Some of the women were too involved with their own issues to take in immediately what had just happened. In the following weeks, however, a few women, both lesbian and not, reacted strongly, sharing that they felt threatened by Micki's continued presence. Micki's feminine appearance bore witness to the wonders of modern medicine, but to some she was nothing but a fake. Her revelation explained at last the slightly masculine build around the shoulders and neck: this supposed woman was a man, or at least had been born male. Further, although she had given up her male identity, Micki's self-confident demeanor betrayed residual hints of her socialization as a privileged white male.

Her chosen identity as a lesbian posed another gender and sexuality enigma. Having castrated "his" penis while leaving "his" sexual orientation unscathed, to what label was s/he entitled? The choice of a lesbian identity to express her (his) new identity as a "woman-loving-woman" communicated an unfamiliar sex and gender ambiguity. For some, the ambiguity only generated feelings of hostility and feelings of mockery for this once-man's appropriation of a label—lesbian—which they felt belonged only to "real women." In the conflict and confusion that surfaced for several weeks after her coming out, Micki encountered both support and prejudice from fellow members of the incest survivors' group. A few sought out Micki's friendship, trying to assure her that she was welcome. Others kept their distance and in private conversations voiced their distrust and interest in removing Micki from the group. They felt abandoned by their group, angry and enraged that not everyone agreed that Micki should leave. Too many individuals supported Micki to force a formal demand that she leave and not come back. The resistors expressed a sense of betrayal by the group's unwillingness to oust Micki, whose perceived crime was in once having had a penis and now being viewed as neither truly female, nor woman, nor lesbian. She was at best a not-man. Eventually, the conflict led to a split, as Micki's resistors formed their own group, with membership limited to women who had been born into a female body. Micki herself eventually left the group. She ultimately formed her own support group, focusing on gender identity and abuse issues. . . .

By leaving to form another support group, Micki opened the door for healing from incest and sexual abuse to other transsexual females. Yet, the women who separated from the original group never had to examine the source of their fears. No one thought to ask whether some of their reactions to Micki, based upon preconceived ideas about the meaning of sex, gender or sexuality, might have stemmed from the same hetero-patriarchal value system which accounted for their own sexual victimization. Certainly no one felt the need to understand or address the unique form of gender oppression that leads an individual to such a drastic measure as sex reassignment surgery (SRS). The fact that Micki's recovery involved stories of how s/he had been shamed and traumatized from the time of his (her) childhood for engaging in gender-nonconforming behavior did not interest her opponents. Yet I wonder how the group never questioned the inclusion of "butchy" lesbians, some of whom dressed in very masculine attire, and who described similar childhood examples of abusive treatment for their own gender-nonconforming behavior. I have asked and answered my own question: it is all gender-based oppression. . . .

I have often wondered what would have happened in that group if Micki had not left. In the few weeks she was there, did it make any difference for someone like Micki, who had been raised as a boy and had become a man, to hear the depth of anger experienced by women who had survived male rape or incest and who now felt desperate at being unable to escape even a hint of residual male energy in a transgender female? Was it unreasonable for the women-from-birth to see Micki as a burden, rather than as someone who might help their healing by vouching as a once-man for the reality of abusive male power, and affirming to them, "yes, this is what men do and you were unjustly violated"? Could either side have seen the source of their fears and their unjust experiences as rooted in societal attitudes based on male power and privilege which continue to induce heightened levels of female sexual victimization, or which so oppress some boys/men that their only escape is to castrate the physical signs of the male gender identity they were assigned at birth?

Notes

1. What Is a Woman? Was "Micki" a woman? Was Diane Schroer? Michael Kantaras? What factors should determine the answer to that question? In portions of the opinion deleted from the excerpt, the *Kantaras* case catalogs relevant case law on the subject, much of which looks to a person's genitalia at birth as the most objective criterion, simplest to apply. As one court cited in *Kantaras* states, "Every schoolchild, even of tender years, is confident he or she can tell the difference, especially if the person is wearing no clothes."[20] But is it that simple?

The rights of transgender individuals have become increasingly complicated as jurisdictions resolve the issue in different ways, particularly in the family law context. The complexity is exacerbated by the fact that the definition of sex often varies by legal context. A single state may define sex differently depending on whether the issue is marriage, parentage, employment discrimination, bathroom use, housing, or participation in athletics, to name just a few contexts in which the issue has been litigated. In her unsuccessful attempt to have the U.S. Supreme Court address the issue, Christine Lee

Littleton describes the confused landscape. As a male-to-female transsexual suing her husband's doctors for wrongful death, she noted that

> while in San Antonio, Texas, [she] is a male and has a void marriage; as she travels to Houston, Texas, and enters federal property, she is female and a widow; upon traveling to Kentucky she is female and a widow; but upon entering Ohio, she is once again male and prohibited from marriage; . . . if her travel takes her north to Vermont, she is male and may marry a female; if instead she travels south to New Jersey she may marry a male.[21]

Is this a significant problem? If so, what should be done about it?

The court ruled against Littleton, holding that only individuals with different chromosomes could marry.[22] The result was to allow lesbian couples to wed as long as one member had a Y chromosome, which is the case with transgender males to females and people born with conditions like androgen insensitivity syndrome. That ruling arguably made Texas one of the first jurisdictions to recognize same-sex marriage.[23] Does this result make sense? Who should transgender individuals be allowed to marry in jurisdictions that restrict marriage to a "man and a woman"?

2. "Intersex" Children. Consider the situation of those who, by medical definitions, are neither completely "male" nor "female." Estimates vary as to the percentage of the world's population with an intersex condition, in part because definitions of the condition also vary widely. With a broad definition, including anyone born with sex chromosomes, gonads, or internal or external sexual anatomy that do not neatly correspond with "male" or "female," the estimated intersex rate is 1 to 2 percent of the population.[24] A narrower definition focusing only on those with severe atypicalities, perhaps severe enough to warrant discussion with sex differentiation specialists and consideration of surgical alteration, produces estimates closer to 1 in 4,500 births.[25]

The issue of surgery to "correct" intersexed individuals as infants so that they are more clearly male, or female, is controversial. Reassignment surgery on intersex infants has been a standard protocol since the late 1950s and early 1960s. Clinicians have assured parents over the years that the surgical potential for normal-looking genitalia should dictate the child's gender and that any innate gender propensity of the child can be changed by careful upbringing. They have also counseled parents that children who do not have the surgery as infants become confused and distressed by their sexual ambiguity, are often teased and rejected by other children, and are not as successful in adapting to one sex or the other if they undergo surgery later on. For more than a decade, intersex advocacy groups have strongly opposed infant surgery, preferring to have parents raise their intersex children as social males or females, and then let the children decide for themselves at puberty whether they would like to change their social sex, with or without surgical assistance.[26] The delay prevents some "mistakes" from being made, although, as a practical matter, lack of financial resources, support networks, and safe educational environments often prevent exercise of free choice by the affected children.[27]

Feminists have found the intersex issue a difficult one. Nancy Ehrenreich explores the arguments on both sides, and concludes that intersex surgery is like female genital cutting and other genital surgeries in that both are cultural practices with the potential to reinforce misogynist gender norms.[28]

Why do we think that intersex individuals need to become identified either as male or female? Can you imagine a world in which one didn't need to be one or the other? In the state of Oaxaca in southern Mexico, the local Zapotec people have made room for a third category, which they call "muxes"—men who consider themselves women and live in a socially sanctioned netherworld between the two genders. Some dress as women and take hormones to change their bodies; others favor male clothes.[29] Do even the Muxe seem overly committed to a two-gender world? A similar model is represented in the Navajo recognition of the category "nadle" (or "nadleehe")—intersex individuals who are considered to be good luck to their families, greatly respected for being able to do the work of both men and women, and often the custodians of wealth.[30]

Australia now provides three gender options for passport applicants—male, female, and X. The "X" marker is available to those with medical certification that "the person has had, or is receiving appropriate clinical treatment for gender transition to a new gender, or that they are intersex and do not identify with the sex assigned to them at birth."[31] What would be the consequences of challenging the two-gender world for children without ambiguous genitalia? Two families have made headlines recently for refusing to reveal the gender of their babies—a Swedish baby named Pop, and a Canadian baby named Storm—and declaring their intent to raise them gender-free.[32]

3. Transgender and Discrimination "Because of Sex." Transgender individuals face intense employment discrimination and, until recently, they have had no legal protection.[33] Just as courts generally have held that discrimination based on sexual orientation is not discrimination based on sex, they have excluded transgender individuals, as well, from the protection of Title VII.[34] However, a growing number of courts have, as in *Schroer*, applied the sex stereotyping theory recognized in Price Waterhouse v. Hopkins to discrimination against transgender employees. As one federal appellate court put it in a case involving a transitioning fire department employee, "Sex stereotyping based on a person's gender non-conforming behavior is impermissible discrimination, irrespective of the cause of that behavior."[35] In a 2012 adjudication, the EEOC took this approach as well. In Macy v. Holder, the Commissioners concluded that discrimination against a transgender person "because that person is transgender is, by definition, discrimination 'based on . . . sex,' and such discrimination therefore violates Title VII."[36] The Eleventh Circuit applied the same reasoning to an equal protection challenge brought by a transgender public employee whose supervisor thought it was "unnatural" and "unsettling" for a biological male to appear at work dressed as a woman.[37]

One argument that persuaded the court in *Schroer* and the EEOC in *Macy* is that transgender discrimination is not based on sex, per se, but on an individual's decision to *change* sex. Paisley Currah and Shannon Minter analyze the distinction:

> [A]lthough it is difficult to see how an employer's decision to terminate an employee for undergoing sex-reassignment could plausibly be deemed anything other than a form of sex-based discrimination, courts have adopted the Orwellian notion that there is a meaningful legal distinction between discrimination because of sex and discrimination because of a change of sex. [I]n Underwood v. Archer Management Services, Inc. [D.D.C. 1994], [for example,] the plaintiff alleged that she had been terminated from her job because, as a transsexual woman, she retained some masculine traits. The court held that insofar as "she was discriminated against because . . . she transformed herself into a woman" rather than "because she is a woman," she had failed to state a viable sex discrimination claim.
>
> The incoherence of this purportedly meaningful distinction (between sex and change of sex) is apparent the moment one imagines a court applying a similar distinction in a case involving discrimination on any other ground. It is unlikely, for example, that an employer who terminated an employee for changing her religious affiliation or nationality would be absolved of liability on the ground that he did not object to the employee's new religion or national origin, but only to the change of religion or national origin. Yet, the only difference between these situations and that of a transsexual person is that while changing one's religion or nationality is generally considered to be a legitimate personal choice, "the very idea that one sex can change into another" is likely to engender "ridicule and horror."[38]

The proposed federal Employment Non-Discrimination Act (ENDA) has been plagued with controversy among advocates over whether it should protect against both sexual orientation and gender identity discrimination. Those who favored leaving transgender individuals out of the legislation thought, at one time, that passage is more likely without them. The latest version of the legislation, passed by the Senate in 2013 but not allowed to be introduced in the House, contains protection for transgender employees.[39]

Sixteen states and the District of Columbia prohibit gender identity discrimination in employment, housing, and/or public accommodations; another six prohibit such discrimination by public employers.[40] In addition, more than one hundred cities and counties have passed laws prohibiting gender identity discrimination. One such ordinance has become a test issue for conservative groups. In 2008, the Citizens for Responsible Government gathered sufficient signatures for a ballot initiative to overturn an action adding gender identity to the non-discrimination code of Montgomery County, Maryland. Among the key concerns of the citizens group was that "any man thinking that he has a particularly strong interest in women and children who are not related to him can put on makeup and a dress and wander into the women's restroom." The group cited an example of women in a gym locker room frightened by a masculine individual in makeup and a ruffled skirt.[41] Are these valid concerns? How should advocates for the transgendered community respond?

How should the restroom issue be handled? In Etsitty v. Utah Transit Authority, the Tenth Circuit Court of Appeals held that the Authority had a legitimate nondiscriminatory reason for firing a transitioning transsexual who intended to use a female restroom despite the fact that she still had male genitalia.[42] By contrast, a British Columbian court held that a bar was obligated to make reasonable accommodation for a transsexual transitioning from male to female.[43] Which approach makes more sense?

European courts generally have held that gender reassignment surgery does not alter an individual's sex for purposes of family law but that discrimination against transgender individuals is discrimination based on sex for purposes of human rights law. Canadian courts have taken the same position regarding discrimination,[44] and England's Gender Recognition Act of 2004 allows a transgender person to change legal sex and gain all the rights of the new sex, including those that relate to marriage and parentage.[45]

4. Transgender and Intersex Athletes. As awareness of transgender and intersex issues grows, so have controversies in athletics, where sex-segregation is the norm for most sports, at most levels. Title IX's application to sex-segregation in sports is discussed in Chapter 2. A controversy erupted at the World Track Championships in 2009 over a South African runner, Caster Semenya, whose gender was scrutinized after she won the 800 meters by 2.45 seconds.[46] Semenya was not stripped of her medal, but was ordered to undergo gender testing by the governing international body, which revealed that she is intersex. She has internal testicles, no ovaries, and no uterus. After a forced 11-month layoff, she was cleared to continue competing as a woman and later qualified for South Africa's 2012 Olympic team. In the London Olympics, she carried the flag for her country and won a silver medal in the 800 meters.[47]

In 2011, the NCAA adopted a new policy on transgender athletes, which allows student athletes to participate in sex-segregated sports in accordance with their gender identity as long as certain medical criteria are met. A trans male who has been treated with testosterone can compete only on men's teams. A trans female can continue to compete on men's teams, or can compete on women's teams following one calendar year of documented testosterone-suppression treatment.[48] These rules apply only to post-season play; individual schools have discretion in handling athlete placement during the regular season. The International Olympic Committee also adopted new rules on transgender athletes, permitting them to compete as the opposite sex after having undergone sex reassignment surgery, legally changing their sex, and completing two years of hormone therapy. What is the right approach to determining the sex of an athlete? Who should decide? Do these controversial cases suggest a problem with the overall system that segregates athletes by sex?

5. "Sex" and "Gender." Legal issues raised by transgender individuals re-invoke a whole line of questions about the distinction between "sex" and "gender." Feminist theorist Linda Nicholson argues that feminists have used the word "gender" in two distinct ways. On the one hand, gender was developed and is still often used as a contrasting term to sex, to depict that which is socially constructed as opposed to that which is biologically given. On this usage, gender is typically thought to refer to personality traits and behavior in distinction from the body. Here, gender and sex are thought to be distinct. On the other hand, gender has increasingly become used to refer to any social construction having to do with the male/female distinction, including those constructions that separate "female" bodies from "male" bodies. This latter usage emerged when many came to realize that society not only shapes personality and behavior, it also shapes the ways in which the body appears. But if the body is itself always seen through social interpretation, then sex is not something that is separate from gender but is, rather, that which is subsumable under it.[49]

Which conception of gender is more appropriate for feminism? Nicholson argues for the second. In her view, treating gender as something distinct from sex assumes that there is uniform sexual difference that is constant across cultures; this belief she calls "biological foundationalism." Nicholson argues that such a framework is inappropriate for feminists because it assumes without proof that all cultures experience sexual and bodily difference in the same way. Similarly, Katherine Franke argues that it is gender that determines sex, and not the other way around. In Franke's view, "sexual equality jurisprudence has uncritically accepted the validity of biological sexual differences. By accepting these biological differences, equality jurisprudence reifies as foundational fact that which is really an effect of normative gender ideology."[50] For example, physical differences that are assumed to have biological bases in fact are influenced by gendered cultural norms. It follows for Franke, and most other feminists, that discrimination against transgender people should be understood as a form of sex discrimination. Nicholson's and Franke's arguments seem to suggest that the distinction between "sex" and "gender" is not a useful one.

In contrast to Franke's focus on the primacy of social gender, Mary Anne Case argues that unless sex and gender are "disaggregated," forms of sex discrimination that turn on gender-role expectations rather than physical attributes will not be readily recognized. Case argues that *Price Waterhouse*, *VMI*, and the numerous cases in which effeminate men have been penalized for breaching gender norms are cases of gender, not sex, discrimination.[51] According to Case, "the world will not be safe for women in frilly pink dresses—they will not, for example, generally be as respected as either men or women in gray fannle suits—unless and until it is made safe for men in dresses as well."[52]

Judges as well as academic feminists disagree about the proper relationship between the concepts of "sex" and "gender." Some members of the Supreme Court use the terms "sex" and "gender" interchangeably. The issue became a matter of discussion between the justices in J.E.B. v. Alabama. The opinion for the Court written by Justice Blackmun, the separate concurring opinions by Justice O'Connor and Justice Kennedy, and the dissenting opinion by Justice Rehnquist all addressed whether use of peremptory strikes to exclude potential jurors because they are men or because they are women is "gender" discrimination. Justice Scalia explained why the term "sex discrimination" is more appropriate to the case:

> [G]ender is to sex as feminine is to female and masculine to male. The present case does not involve peremptory strikes exercised on the basis of femininity or masculinity (as far as it appears, effeminate men did not survive the prosecution's peremptories). The case involves, therefore, sex discrimination plain and simple.[53]

Justice Ginsburg had made the move from sex to gender by 1975, when she decided that the word "sex" was too disturbing in that it "may conjure up improper images" of what occurs in theaters showing pornography.[54] Similar issues have arisen in international human rights and refugee law.[55]

How should law use the terms "sex" and "gender"?

Putting Theory Into Practice

6-3. Marvin is a female-to-male transsexual who married Rosa in 2001. Rosa was aware that he was a transgender. They were unable to conceive children of their own but decided to use artificial insemination (using a sperm bank) to impregnate Rosa. It worked and a child was born, to whom Marvin became quite attached during the remaining two years in which they were together. At that point, Rosa attempts to annul the marriage, on the grounds that because Marvin was born a female, he cannot conduct a valid marriage with another female.

Applicable state law says that a child is conclusively presumed to be the child of the husband of the child's mother. Marvin wants shared custody rights to the child. Should he have them?[56]

6-4. The Equal Credit Opportunity Act prohibits banks and other credit institutions from denying credit based on sex. Jose is a cross dresser, and alleges that his requested loan application was denied because of that fact. Should he have a claim under the Act?

6-5. Frank is fired from his job as a police officer after he reveals to his supervisor that he will be undergoing the transition from male to female under the close supervision of his doctor and psychiatric counselor. Frank sues under Title VII, and the police department defends the lawsuit on the grounds that a transsexual will not have the "street credibility" necessary to maintain order in the tough community in which he works. Even if the approach in *Schroer* is followed and discrimination against transgender is viewed as discrimination because of sex, should the police department be required to retain Frank in this case?

6-6. A rape counseling organization employs only female volunteers and rejects a transgender person who had transitioned from being male to female. Although subject to a law prohibiting discrimination based on sexual identity, the organization claims that it has a compelling interest in having women who are sexually assaulted helped by those who have "suffered oppression from birth."[57] Should the organization be allowed to reject the transsexual applicant?

6-7. A transgender biologically male middle-school student seeks to wear female clothing. How would you advise the school board?[58]

6-8. Mikki, a woman with an intersex condition, was sentenced to 14 months in prison for writing bad checks. Where should she be housed? Is the prison within its rights to place her in solitary confinement rather than with the female population?

C. MASCULINITIES

The emphasis of this book, and of the study of gender and law more generally, is on women. Men, however, are getting more attention, both because of the gender stereotypes that limit them, and because of the relationship between those stereotypes and those that limit women. The readings below addresses this topic.

Reading Questions

1. To what extent are men the beneficiaries of feminism?
2. What is masculinity's relationship to femininity? Do the theories explored in other chapters of this book understate the distinctive burdens faced by men in a gendered society?
3. Do you think most men and women would agree on the problems associated with masculinity and the appropriate responses?

Nancy E. Dowd, Asking the Man Question: Masculinities Analysis and Feminist Theory

33 Harv. J. Law & Gender 415, 416-419 (2010)

Masculinities work can be used to understand more clearly how male privilege and dominance are constructed. It can make us see harms suffered by boys and men that we have largely ignored. It may also reinforce and strengthen the commitment to antiessentialism in feminist theory. Exposing the complexities and multiplicity of masculinities leads toward understanding intersection and multiple forms of discrimination more clearly. . . .

Masculinities analysis may also remind us to be attentive to different patterns of inequality and to our interpretation of those patterns. Where one sex is sole or dominant, dominance should be something that triggers scrutiny. This should matter both when the dominant sex benefits (as in occupying high paid jobs) or is harmed (as in occupying more prison cells). We should question not only why one sex fills or dominates the pattern, but also the gendered meaning of both who is present and who is absent. Oddly, when one sex is dominant, sometimes gender issues are rendered invisible. Examples of this are male predominance in the juvenile and adult criminal justice systems, and women's predominance in the welfare system. Invisibility is fostered by gender neutral language that covers the predominance of gender patterns, but also by the acceptance of the pattern as usual, normal, and taken-for-granted.

On the other hand, where both sexes are present, one or both may claim bias. We tend to frame competing claims of bias as requiring prioritization or hierarchy rather than seeing how they interconnect. We tend to argue over who has the more important issues to address or the most pressing "crisis." Resisting this "either/or" approach of a hierarchy of inequalities is critical. For example, in education there are inequality issues for both girls and boys, women and men. Rather than exclusively focusing on the issues of one sex to the exclusion of the other, as if only one can claim our focus or deserve our attention, we should see and insist on addressing both. Inequalities often interlock. A battle of the sexes, moreover, may only divert attention from more serious issues of race and class. Examining subordination in isolation undermines our understanding and our attack upon the interacting dynamic, even if gender-specific problem solving is needed. . . .

Raising issues about men when so many issues about women remain generates resistance and distrust. . . . Masculinities analysis needs to continually challenge itself to challenge the hegemony of men and male power. The project of imagining positive, affirming, egalitarian masculinities is ongoing, but it is absolute essential. . . .

These are what I have identified as core propositions [of masculinities scholarship]:

1. *Men are not universal or undifferentiated.*
2. *Men pay a price for privilege.*
3. *Intersections of manhood particularly with race, class and sexual orientation are critical to the interplay of privilege and disadvantage, to hierarchies among men, and factors that may entirely trump male gender privilege.*
4. *Masculinity is a social construction, and not a biological given.*
5. *Hegemonic masculinity recognizes that one masculinity norm dominates multiple masculinities.*
6. *The patriarchal dividend is the benefit that all men have from the dominance of men in the overall gender order.*
7. *The two most common pieces defining masculinity are, at all costs, to not be like a woman and not be gay.*
8. *Masculinity is as much about relation to other men as it is about relation to women.*

9. *Men, although powerful, feel powerless.*
10. *Masculinities study exposes how structures and cultures are gendered male.*
11. *The spaces and places that men and women daily inhabit and work within are remarkably different.*
12. *The role of men in achieving feminist goals is uncertain and unclear.*
13. *The asymmetry of masculinities scholarship and feminist theory reflects the differences in the general position of men and women.*

The implications of these teachings . . . are that feminists should "ask the man question."

Frank Rudy Cooper, "Who's the Man?": Masculinities Studies, Terry Stops, and Police Training

18 Colum. J. Gender & Law 671, 671-672, 674-676, 741 (2009)

We men have some strange rituals. One occurs on the basketball court. A player will make a move around a defender and score a basket. They he'll shout, "who's the man?" He wants his opponent to say, "*You* are the man." This episode is a paradigmatic description of how masculinities work. Men often act with the goal of impressing other men. We gain our masculine esteem and relative masculine stature from other men's acknowledgements of our masculinity. Sociologist Michael Kimmel puts it best: "[w]e are under the constant careful scrutiny of other men. Other men watch us, rank us, grant our acceptance into the realm of manhood. Manhood is demonstrated for other men's approval." . . .

How does masculinity affect policing? This is an important question, given that policemen have nearly unique powers to make others acknowledge them as "the man" while ostensibly merely performing their duties.

The short answer is that officers may get "macho" with civilians. Specifically, they may enact a command presence in situations where it only serves to boot the officer's masculine esteem. To enact command presence is to take charge of a situation. It involves projecting an aura of confidence and decisiveness. It is justified by the need to control dangerous suspects. A situation that does not justify enacting command presence is what I call a "masculinity contest." A masculinity contest is a face-off between men where one party is able to bolster his masculine esteem by dominating the other. A prototypical masculinity contest is a bar fight. Men will glare at each other and ratchet up their challenges until one party backs down or is subdued. Male police offers may sometimes be tempted to turn encounters with male civilians into masculinity contests.

The insight that policemen may sometimes enact command presence is order to stage masculinity contests and boost their masculine esteem is important because it helps explain patterns of law enforcement. . . . [S]cholars have long noted that officers sometimes use their Terry v. Ohio stop and frisk powers to racially profile. The usual explanation for that practice is racial animus.

However, concentrating sole on race as an explanation for police behaviors ignores the fact that the overwhelming majority of police officers are men and the overwhelming majority of those they stop are men. As David Sklansky says, "one train may hide another." I contend that the desire to boost one's masculine esteem is a train traveling behind, and obscured by, the desire to boost one's racial esteem in some officers' decision to disproportionately stop and frisk men belonging to racial minorities. . . .

If policemen are using *Terry* stops and frisks to play the game of "who's the man?" rather than just to gather evidence of crime, then we need to change the gender dynamics of policing. I propose that we do so by changing the cultures of police forces. This can be achieved by establishing extensive training programs designed to root out the attitudes and rituals that perpetuate a macho police culture. . . .

Aside from the question of whether policemen should bully civilians, we might ask whether such actions can ever actually sate the desire to prove one's masculinity. According to Kimmel, they cannot:

> [T]he bully is the *least* secure about his manhood, and so he is constantly trying to prove it. But he proves it by choosing opponents he is absolutely certain he can defeat; thus the standard taunt to a bully is to "pick one someone your own size." He can't, though, and after defeating a smaller and weaker opponent, which he was sure would prove his manhood, he is left with the empty gnawing feeling that he has not proved it after all, and he must find another opponent, again one smaller and weaker, that he can again defeat to prove it to himself. . . . When does it end? Never.
>
> So bullying is a counter-productive activity for the bully himself. . . .
>
> The bully's conundrum demonstrates that no one really benefits from the current structure of masculinity. Ultimately, hegemonic masculinity is the source of the problem of police harassment of men.

Michael Kimmel, *Integrating Men into the Curriculum*

4 Duke J. Gender L. & Pol'y 181, 181-182, 184, 186-188 (1997)

There is a general failure to see men, or more accurately masculinity, at every level of the educational endeavor—from what is taught, to who the teachers are, to the gender of the students, and to the gender of classroom dynamics. At every moment in the process, men are invisible.

"But wait," you will say, "men are not invisible. They are everywhere!" Quite true. Men are ubiquitous in universities, in professional schools, and in the public sphere in general. Most people would not dispute that men constitute an overwhelming majority of corporate executives and CEOs, attorneys and law professors, members of collegiate boards of trustees, and state, local, and national legislators. And of course it is true that in college curricula, every course that does not have the word women in the title is about men. For example, in the social sciences there may be courses called Women in Politics or Psychology of Women, but the courses with more generic titles like Social Change or Public Administration are courses in which the entire syllabus is organized around men. The course materials, however, focus almost exclusively on men in their public activities: men are discussed as political leaders, military heroes, scientists, writers, artists, and the like. By contrast, when women are discussed at all, the class almost always includes a discussion of femininity, about how the women's experiences as women influenced their experiences in their public activities. Can one imagine a literature course in which the experience of Jane Austen or the Brontes, or a physics course in which the experience of Marie Curie was discussed without a discussion of the lives of women, about how their femininity contributed to, affected, or even determined their work? Can one imagine that same British literature course examining Charles Dickens' or William Thackeray's experience of masculinity, or that physics course examining Albert Einstein's or Sir Isaac Newton's efforts to prove their masculinity? It is in this sense that men themselves are invisible as men. . . . Everywhere one turns, it seems, there are courses on men, but little or no information on masculinity. . . .

Most feminist scholars have properly focused their attention on women, primarily on the "omissions, distortions, and trivializations" of women's experiences, and the spheres to which women have historically been consigned, like private life and the family. . . . Now it is time to go a step further to include men as men. . . .

That scholars and students alike remain unaware of the centrality of gender in men's lives only helps to perpetuate inequalities based on gender in American society. This ignorance keeps in place the power of men over women, and the power of some men over other men, both of which are among the central mechanisms of power in our society. . . .

[W]hen gender is acknowledged, writers often endow manhood with a transcendental, almost mythic set of properties that still keep it invisible. For example, in the works of Robert Bly, Sam Keen, and other popular authors, manhood becomes an eternal, timeless essence that resides deep in the heart of every man. Manhood is thought of as a thing, a quality that one either has or does not have. Or manhood is considered innate, residing in the particular anatomical organization of the human male, or perhaps, as some transcendent tangible property that each man must manifest in the world, a reward presented with great ceremony to a young novice by his elders for having successfully completed an arduous initiation ritual. . . .

Definitions of masculinity, however, are not the manifestations of some inner essence, nor do they bubble up through biological composition. The search for a transcendent, timeless definition of manhood is itself a sociological phenomenon—society tends to search for the timeless and eternal during moments of crises, those points of transition when old definitions no longer work and new definitions are yet to be firmly established. It is important to think of manhood in a different way: as a constantly changing collection of meanings that are constructed through relationships with themselves, with other men, and with the world. A social constructionist perspective understands gender definitions as neither static nor timeless, but historically articulated within and through people's interactions with their worlds [that perspective notes the different meanings of manhood within and across time and cultures]. . . . Experiences depend, for example, on class, race, ethnicity, sexuality, age, even region of the country. . . . Masculinity [also] means different things to individual men as they age and develop. The issues confronting a man about proving himself and feeling successful, along with the social institutions in which he will attempt to enact those experiences, all will change throughout his life. . . .

Joan C. Williams, Femmes, Tomboys, and Real Men: Placing Masculinity at the Core of a Feminist Analysis

William E. Massey, Sr., Lecture in the History of American Civilization,
Harvard University, May 8, 2008

A powerful description of [professional male identity] is Marianne Cooper's "Being the 'Go-To Guy,'" an analysis of the paradigmatic white-collar workplace of the 21st century: Silicon Valley. . . . [Her study describes how] white-collar men also enact their chosen masculinity on the job. Silicon Valley engineers, to some extent, appear to internalize the image of themselves as mere "pencil pushers" ("It's not like being a brave firefighter" . . . .), making their need to prove their masculinity a pressing concern. This they do by turning long hours into a heroic activity. Noted Arlie Hochschild in 1989, "He talked about his long hours as if he were describing the hair on his chest." ("He's a real man; he works 90-hour weeks. He's a slacker; he works 50 hours a week.") Whereas blue-collar work is suffused with masculinity—it is dirty, and requires strength—white-collar work is clean, gender-neutral knowledge work unrelated to physical strength. This leaves white-collar men searching for ways to imagine their work as the appropriate arena in which to prove their manliness. "Though the essence of this masculinity is rooted in technical expertise," another key characteristic is "working a lot of hours." Said one engineer:

> Even under normal circumstances, when there are no extraordinary demands, you see people working 36 hours straight just because they are doing it to meet the deadline. They are going to get it done, and everybody walks around being proud of how exhausted they were last week and conspicuously putting in wild hours. It's a status thing to have pizza delivered to the office. So I don't know why it happens, but I really feel like it is kind of a machismo thing: I'm tough. I can do this. Yeah, I'm tired, but I'm on top of it. You guys don't worry about me. . . . The people who conspicuously overwork are guys, and I think it's usually for the benefit of other guys.

"There's this kind of machismo culture among the young male engineers that you just don't sleep," said one father of two who ultimately left that world to work from home. Denying oneself sleep is a way to turn a sedentary job into a test of physical endurance.

> It's an idea derived from the male tradition probably. Even as a contractor you have to live with it, too. You have to be part of the team. You can't fall out. If you get injured, you come back as fast as you can or you play with your injury whether it's emotional or physical.

"The successful enactment of this masculinity," notes Cooper, "involves displaying one's exhaustion, physically and verbally, in order to convey the depth of one's commitment, stamina, and virility." This norm is policed through language of community and mutual responsibility: one's refusal to sleep proves one's commitment to the team. "A prerequisite for being a committed team player is a devotion to work that borders on addiction," Cooper concludes, quoting one man who admitted, "I was just anxious as hell unless I was working." Ultimately, it took him "just years and 12-step programs" to escape a situation he had come to see as unhealthy.

Many studies have found that a worker's manliness is called into question when his family care obligations become salient at work, so that admitting one is taking time off for family life is seen as a loss of face. This situation prompts men either to avoid taking time off work, or to hide that they are, to preserve their "Go To" status. When one man's boss spoke enthusiastically of the need to hold a particular meeting as soon as possible, one engineer reacted with panic. "[S]weating like a horse," he called his secretary. "Hey, you gotta get me out of this, because my baby is getting christened and if I don't meet with the priest it's not going to happen and my family is going to kill me and my wife will divorce me and I won't have any kids and my life will be terrible." So the secretary lied for him, taking care to present the image that other work obligations prevented the early meeting his manager sought. The younger man resented the manager's demands, noting that the manager himself "doesn't have two kids and a wife, he has people that live in his house, that's basically what he has." But taking on this issue directly apparently seemed infeasible because he was dependent on the VP for good assignments and a future with the firm.

This shows how utterly unrealistic is the dominant conventional wisdom that the "stalled revolution"—reflecting men's failure to pick up their share of the housework—is best addressed by encouraging women to negotiate with their husbands. This strategy has clearly failed, and this analysis shows why. It rests on the assumption that *family* is "the gender factory," whereas *workplaces* in many ways are the gender factories that set the nonnegotiable terms within which women negotiate in family life. Recall the young couple who both worked for the same law firm, where the wife was sent home promptly at 5:30 after she had a baby, because she had a baby to take care of, whereas her husband was kept later than ever: because he had a family to support. This is a particularly dramatic example of workplaces' role in reproducing bread-winner/homemaker roles without regard to the preferences of the couple in question.

An additional factor is at work in this dynamic: the role of unceasing status negotiations in relationships among conventional men. This aspect of conventional masculinity is astutely observed by Deborah Tannen, who notes the importance, for men, of maintaining "the one-up position." Historians have noted that, when masculinity first became associated with breadwinner status in the 19th century, anxiety became men's heritage. "Sons had to compete for manhood in the market rather than grow into secure manhood by replicating fathers," noted a commentator in the 1920s. "Work is the institution that most defines the majority of adult males," noted a feminist man in the 1970s. "Many of us look to work for our most basic sense of worth."

This makes it difficult for men to challenge, or even question, the felt mandate to live up to workplace norms, even if that means disappointing their wives or partners. "I was talking to a friend of mine, a partner at a major San Francisco law firm," Derek Bok told me in 2001. "He was always complaining about how hard he worked, so I asked: 'Then why don't you just work 3/5 as hard and take 3/5 the salary?' He was tongue-tied. But of course the real reason he couldn't is that then he feared he wouldn't 'be a player.'"

These status negotiations that are so central a part of hegemonic masculinity mean that men feel they have a lot to lose if they "lose face." "Men are more likely to be on guard to prevent themselves from being put in a one-down position . . . ," notes Tannen. Because caregiving is not high-status—and because having a wife who takes care of all family matters is—many men are reluctant to admit at work that they have family responsibilities at home. This is true of both blue- and white-collar men. Indeed, my studies of union arbitrations show that men in unionized jobs more often get fired due to family responsibilities than women, because the men are extremely reluctant to admit that family responsibilities are the reason they need to leave work. Said Peter Richardson, an anthropologist who has both worked in factories and studied blue-collar men, "It would be embarrassing, like a loud fart in church."

There's some hope here. Some younger men are less willing than their elders to play by the old rules. The literature on Gen-X and Gen-Y men suggests that a critical mass of younger men—though by no means all—are seeking something different. Cooper cites Rich, the man who went into a panic at missing his child's baptism:

> The CEO of this start-up company had three kids—4, 7, 10—nice kids but he never ever sees them because he's at work 7 days a week. . . . And I'm thinking, his kids aren't going to have any idea who he is. He doesn't think these little moments matter, but they do. I mean, the guy was a real shit when it came to his kids. I'm sorry. He's 40, and he's bound and determined that he's going to make his multimillions, and he thinks he is doing the right thing for his kids, because he thinks he's doing all this for them, since one day they will be rich. They will be rich with money, but poor as people.

Rich makes short work of the traditionalist rationale: that workaholic fathers are selfless, doing it all for their children. The transparent flaws of this version of masculinity for Rich are hopeful — yet recall that Rich felt powerless to challenge this ideology at work, and in fact put his foot down only when his supervisor threatened to deprive him of attendance at a "set piece" — his child's baptism. As Arlie Hochschild pointed out long ago, ideal-worker men tend to think of childhood not in terms of day-in, day-out care, but in terms of set pieces such as performances. This is a long way from playing an equal role in a child's life.

But it is a start. . . .

[Their dissatisfaction with the ideal-worker model] is a powerful force for change, if feminists can engage with men to effect such change. Herein lies the challenge, as Cooper's essay makes clear. She ends her piece by discussing another Gen-X man who at one point "personified the Silicon Valley warrior." His log-in was Ali; but eventually the work ethic required to knock 'em out proved unappealing. He took off only a few days when his second child was born, "a sore point" with his wife, but taken for granted by his colleagues at work. Eventually Kirk quit, but in order to do so, "he had to renegotiate aspects of his identity." Kirk recognized that, "They need the job to come first, and I had spent a year letting a really crappy job come first. The family really suffered." But when he did quit, "I had to convince myself that it was okay to fail." He had to let go of being a player — the go-to guy.

Feminists can admire men with this kind of courage all we want, but we can't depend on them. Until feminists, in alliance with men like Kirk, create nonstigmatized career tracks that offer Gen-X and Gen-Y men good careers that allow time for family life, the revolution will remain stalled.

Here's the fact: femininity has changed a lot but masculinity has changed very little. True, the old schemas of reassuringly nice and feminine women persist, but now they exist alongside a much broader understanding of femininity that also includes deference-challenged women: Hillary not only bakes cookies; she also runs for president — with high negatives, but a credible campaign.

Changing femininity is not enough. Feminists need to work with men to deinstitutionalize "go-to guy" masculinity in the workplace, using the trend in employment law that prohibits employers from using stereotypes as job requirements. Part and parcel of this effort will be to help men invent a range of masculinities, so that it will not take such raw courage for men to refuse to be the go-to guy.

. . . [O]ne reason that allying with like-minded men is so important is because feminists seeking to restructure market work cannot assume that all women will join the fun. Women who perform as ideal workers typically have paid a higher price for doing so than men: most either gave up having children, or faced daily challenges as well as abiding fears that their absence from their children's lives means that they are "bad moms." These women, as a group, cannot realistically be expected to join with mothers to change the workplace — although some will. Women who are happily child-free, regretfully childless, or who have raised families as ideal workers won't be the shock troops for challenging the ideal-worker norm. It's not even fair to demand that of them. . . .

Darren Rosenblum, Unsex Mothering: Toward a New Culture of Parenting

35 Harv. J. Law & Gender 57, 58 (2012)

I was, until recently, a pregnant man. . . . My husband and I began the process of having a child several years ago when we hired a surrogacy agency that works primarily with gay male couples. After a complex process, we are now raising our daughter.

As a parent, I confront a far more sexed area of life than I have ever encountered before. Everyone congratulates my partner and me on being "fathers," even though within our home we share responsibilities and flip roles, including a mothering role, with some fluidity. The outside world, it seems, needs to box us into the "daddy" category as much as it invests women with the power of motherhood.

Some time ago, I was in a taxi with my daughter. . . . She fussed a bit and the driver said, "Where's the mother? Only the mother knows how to do this." Avoiding a complex explanation that I view myself as both mother and father, I said she has two dads. He still seemed perplexed that a man could know how to care for a child. I left the taxi and wiped a saliva-soaked Cheerio from my daughter's chin, feeling less of a parent because I was perceived as only a father, and not the primary parent—a mother. It is a feeling constantly reinforced for gay male parents I know who report that when in public, at markets, stores, and restaurants—they get asked by women: "Is it mommy's day off?" It is challenging to come up with a responsible response.

Notes

1. Masculinity.   Contemporary views about masculinity tend to divide into two broad normative categories: (1) the celebration of traditional masculine values, and (2) the desire to eliminate strict gender roles, for men as well as for women. Prominent advocates for traditional masculine values often appeal to biological understandings of masculinity. Harvard Professor Harvey Mansfield, for example, argues that men are by nature dominant, aggressive, self-confident risk takers. At its best, manliness encourages men to defend higher ends, and this role is threatened by "feminist nihilism." Although in the public sphere, the sexes should have equal rights, in the private sphere, Mansfield advocates respect for differences and wants society to stop trying to "feminize boys." "Men should be expected, not merely free to be manly."[59] Robert Bly, an active proponent of the "men's movement," urges men to "retreat from the world of women to temporary male sanctuaries in order to recapture some 'deep' or 'wild' masculinity that has become dormant in today's modern technological society in which women actively participate."[60]

Other commentators, while not necessarily supporting the movement to celebrate traditional male values, seek to put men's anxiety about their manhood in a sympathetic light. Susan Faludi, for example, argues that hypermasculine behavior is often a response to men's feeling of being "downsized," economically and emotionally, both by the rise in women's rights and the erosion of traditional male jobs.[61] Is she right? If so, what follows?

On the other side is a growing acceptance of more positive, androgynous visions of masculinity that are represented, in various ways, in the readings of this section. Many of these visions would enlist men in the same struggles against male violence, homophobia, and gender inequality in which feminists have engaged.[62] This effort builds on a long tradition that has included historic leaders such as John Stuart Mill, Frederick Douglass, and W. E. B. Dubois.[63] Others emphasize the ways in which men, as well as women, suffer from gender stereotypes, and highlight the particular penalties men sometimes pay for engaging in caregiving behavior.[64]

A large national survey by the Center for Work-Life Policy on the female "brain drain" in science, engineering, and technology documents the macho cultures that prevail in these fields.[65] Another study has documented how working conditions in the construction industry help produce hyper-masculinized behaviors of "manning up," risk taking, aggressiveness, and denigrating women, especially among undocumented immigrants.[66] Many men, including those in blue collar occupations, are caught in the "daddy double-bind"; they are expected to be both breadwinners and involved fathers in settings that provide inadequate support for that dual role.[67] How does this double-bind compare with burdens women face in being both parents and workers? Are different strategies called for, or is it really the same problem? How about for gay male parents?[68] Will they, too, be helped by laws such as Sweden has, entitling two employed parents to a combined 16 months of parental leave, but requiring that each parent take at least 2 months of the time allowance?[69]

Michael Kimmel cites a survey in which women and men were asked what they were most afraid of. "Women responded that they were most afraid of being raped and murdered. Men responded that they were most afraid of being laughed at."[70] Is one worse than the other? Does the asserted difference have potential legal and policy implications? For example, would the training Frank Cooper suggests be appropriate only for men, or for policewomen as well?

Much as feminist legal scholarship extended into virtually every area of the law, masculinity studies is reaching across many fields and doctrines. The Frank Cooper article on police practices, highlighting how masculinity asserts itself and harms men as well as women, is one example.[71] The Darren Rosenblum analysis of gay male parenting is another. Can you identify other domains where standards of masculinity constrain both men and women?

Another area of investigation, which illustrates the effects of masculinity norms on both men and women, has been the military.

What is the role of law, in the context of the military, in reinforcing stereotypes about men as courageous? Theoretically, female soldiers can be punished for cowardice, but, so far, none have, as though martial courage were only expected of men. On the other hand, two of the most publicized military cases in recent memory involve the first woman B-52 bomber pilot, Kelly Flinn, and Lt. Colonel Karen Tew, both court marshaled [sic], not for lacking the male virtue of courage, but for having sexual relations with male soldiers. The two female officers were thus punished for being absent the virtue that is chiefly ascribed to women—chastity.[72]

Which stereotypes are more damaging? Is it possible to say?

2. The Intersection of Gender and Race, Class, Ethnicity, and Sexual Orientation.   To what extent is it possible to generalize about the experience of men? Are there sufficient commonalities between African-American, Asian, and Hispanic men to justify claims on behalf of "men of color"? How might differences in class and sexual orientation complicate the question?

Are men's disadvantages feminist issues? For example, black men have disproportionate rates of unemployment and are concentrated in low-status, low-paid occupations. Black men also have higher rates of incarceration and substance abuse and lower rates of college attendance than black women.[73] Floyd Weatherspoon concludes that African-American men suffer from a combination of race and gender discrimination both in employment and in the criminal justice system.[74] By contrast, Devon Carbado asserts that "[h]eterosexual Black men occupy a privileged victim status in antiracist discourse."

A central project of antiracist discourse is to reveal the extent to which Black men are victims of a racist criminal justice system. Given the statistics for Black male incarceration and the problems of discrimination in the criminal justice system, this project is undeniably important.

Nevertheless, as a result of this focus on Black men without a similar focus on Black women, Black men are perceived to be significantly more vulnerable and significantly more "endangered" than Black women. Black men become the quintessential example of the effects of racial subordination. . . .

As a consequence of this myth of racial authenticity and the currency of the endangered Black male trope, when an individual Black man is on trial for some criminal offense, the Black community sees first and foremost his status as a racial victim. Furthermore, when the alleged crime involves violence against women, the fact that a Black female or a woman of any race may be the victim of Black male aggression is subordinate to the concern that a Black man may be the victim of a racist criminal justice system.[75]

Could Weatherspoon and Carbado both be correct? How should feminists conceptualize the relationship between women of color and men of color in a society that is both racist and sexist?

Putting Theory Into Practice

6-9. Mark, who is divorced from his ex-wife, Margaret, is charged with child sexual abuse, based on evidence that he (1) allowed his two-year-old daughter to sleep alone with him in bed; (2) let her walk into the bathroom while he was naked in the shower; and (3) in changing her diapers, often applied diaper cream to her vagina.[76] Part of Mark's defense is that Margaret also engaged in these behaviors, and yet she is not charged with child abuse. Can behavior that is not child sexual abuse if engaged in by mothers constitute child sexual abuse by fathers?

6-10. Can you think of other areas, besides those discussed in this section, in which a focus on masculinity could lead to insights not already produced by women-centered analysis? What are the policy implications of these insights?

6-11. Reconsider the issue examined in Chapter 2 of whether separate schools or classes should be allowed for boys. What about all-male, all-black schools?

D. THE PRIMACY OF GENDER

Do the theoretical approaches examined in this book unreasonably elevate women's interests above those of other subordinate groups? Are feminists too quick to judge the practices of other cultures on the basis of their own cultural assumptions?

These questions are explored by reference to practices known as "female circumcision," or "female genital mutilation" ("FGM")—terms that reveal their own normative assumptions. The case of Bah v. Mukasey concludes that FGM constitutes persecution against women, for purposes of U.S. asylum law. Amede Obiora, then, criticizes the "pre-judgment" that feminists have displayed in opposing all forms of FGM. By contrast, Madhavi Sunder questions whether Westerners have been overly tolerant of persecution based on religion and culture.

Reading Questions

1. To what extent can Western feminists be faulted for privileging issues of gender equality over other cultural values held by women?
2. Is it presumptuous or necessary for women's rights advocates from liberal democracies to judge other cultures by their own standards of freedom and equality?
3. To what extent should practices, ordinarily considered illegal, be tolerated because they are part of a religious or cultural tradition?

Bah v. Mukasey

529 F.3d 99 (2d Cir. 2008)

STRAUB, Circuit Judge:

Petitioners, three women from Guinea who underwent female genital mutilation in the past, petition for review of decisions of the Board of Immigration Appeals ("BIA") affirming, inter alia, the denial of their claims for withholding of removal and Convention Against Torture ("CAT") relief based on female genital mutilation. The agency held that because the genital mutilation had already occurred, the presumption that petitioners' lives or freedom would be threatened in the future was automatically rebutted by the fact that it had occurred. . . .

Because the agency committed significant errors in the application of its own regulatory framework for withholding of removal claims, we grant in part and dismiss in part the petitions for review. . . .

Female genital mutilation "is the collective name given to a series of surgical operations, involving the removal of some or all of the external genitalia, performed on girls and women primarily in Africa and Asia." . . . According to the World Health Organization, female genital mutilation can be classified into four different categories:

Type I Excision of the prepuce with or without excision of part or all of the clitoris.

Type II Excision of the prepuce and clitoris together with partial or total excision of the labia minora.

Type III Excision of part or all of the external genitalia and stitching/narrowing of the vaginal opening (infibulation).

Type IV Unclassified: Includes pricking, piercing or incision of clitoris and/or labia; stretching of clitoris and/or labia; cauterization by burning of clitoris and surrounding tissues; . . . scraping . . . of the vaginal orifice or cutting . . . of the vagina; Introduction of corrosive substances into the vagina to cause bleeding or herbs into the vagina with the aim of tightening or narrowing the vagina; any other procedure which falls under the definition of FGM. . . .

The U.S. Department of State has largely adopted this classification. . . .

Genital mutilation "is often performed under unsanitary conditions with highly rudimentary instruments." . . .

The procedure is carried out with special knives, scissors, scalpels, pieces of glass or razor blades [in] poor light and septic conditions. The procedures are usually carried out by an elderly woman of the village who has been specially designated for this task, or by traditional birth attendants. . . . Anaesthetics and antiseptics are not generally used. Assistants and/or family members hold down the girl to prevent her struggling. . . . Paste mixtures made of herbs, local porridge, ashes, or other mixtures are rubbed on to the wound to stop bleeding. . . .

Genital mutilation can have devastating, permanent effects on its victims, including immediate and long-term physical problems such as infection, difficulty during urination and menstruation, incontinence, and sexual dysfunction; complications during child birth such as fetal and maternal death, birth defects, and internal damage to the mother; and severe psychological problems....

In light of the long-lasting and severe consequences of genital mutilation, paired with the reasons for its infliction, the practice has been largely condemned by the international community.[77] . . . It has also been criticized and condemned by many activist groups within the countries where it is practiced.[78] Moreover, in recognition of the harmful effects of genital mutilation, the United States Congress has criminalized female genital mutilation of minors in the United States.[79]

Petitioner Salimatou Bah, . . . a native and citizen of Guinea, entered the United States without valid travel documents in June 2003, and in January 2005 was placed in removal proceedings by service of a Notice to Appear ("NTA"). She applied for asylum, withholding of removal, and relief under the CAT, alleging, inter alia, that as a young girl she "suffered" the "barbarous act" of female genital mutilation, and the event "still has dire consequences on [her] adult life."

In a statement accompanying her application, Salimatou explained that she belongs to the Fulani ethnic group, which strongly supports the practice of genital mutilation as "the best way to prevent the Fulani girls from having premarital sex," and "to force the Fulani girls to keep their virginity until the marriage." She claimed that at the age of eleven, her mother and aunt took her to a "small area fenced with wood and stuffed with coconut leaves." She was taken into a tent where five "old ladies" with knives and other tools undressed her and had her lie on the ground. Salimatou, "scared and shaking," tried to escape, but the women restrained her. She was then held down by two of the women while two others opened her legs so that a fifth could make a "deep cut of [her] 'private part'" without "any anesthetic or sanitary precaution." Salimatou screamed throughout the mutilation, and experienced "pain all over [her] body." She began "bleeding heavily" and feeling dizzy to the point where she was unable to stand on her own. After she was given "traditional medicines," she convalesced for weeks during which time she was "treated traditionally with dried leaves and some other local potions." Salimatou further stated that she later had "problems with [her] menstrual period," as well as complications during the deliveries of her children. She also stated that she "can barely feel any pleasure" during sexual intercourse with her husband. She sought asylum in order to "live free from that barbarous act still in practice" in Guinea....

Petitioner Mariama Diallo . . . is also a native and citizen of Guinea and a member of the Fulani ethnic group, was admitted into the United States in May 1992 on a nonimmigrant visa, which she overstayed. . . .

Mariama testified that she underwent genital mutilation, including "removal of [her] clitoris," when she was eight years old. According to

Mariama, her parents were opposed to the practice of FGM, but her aunt and grandmother arranged for her to undergo the mutilation without their knowledge. Mariama further testified that she was ill for a month after the mutilation, suffering constant pain, excessive bleeding, and loss of consciousness. Mariama testified that childbirth was extremely difficult for her, and that she experiences pain every time she engages in intercourse as a result of the genital mutilation. She further testified that she suffered two miscarriages. Finally, Mariama stated that she feared that her daughters would be subject to genital mutilation were she forced to return to Guinea. In support of her female genital mutilation claim, she submitted a gynecologist's report stating, inter alia: "Evaluation of the pelvis demonstrated a scarred anterior fourchette and surgically absent clitoris. The labia minora were rudimentary and anteriorly fused." The report further stated that Mariama "has compromised intimacy and sexual satisfaction," and that she "requires repetitive surgical correction of her anterior fourchette to accommodate vaginal deliveries." . . .

Petitioner Haby Diallo . . . is also a native and citizen of Guinea and member of the Fulani ethnic group. She applied for asylum, withholding of removal, and relief under the CAT, alleging that she had been subjected to female genital mutilation as a child, that she "totally opposed" the practice, and that she did not want her "future daughters" to be subjected to it. At her merits hearing, Haby testified that she was forced to undergo genital mutilation when she was eight years old. She testified that during a visit to her grandmother, she was taken by "three old women" to "the bush." There, one woman held her down while another spread her legs apart and the third performed the mutilation with a knife. Haby testified that she "suffered a lot" initially, and although she was bleeding heavily, she was not taken to a hospital. Instead, she was treated with "traditional medicine." She further testified that she has problems menstruating as a result of the genital mutilation, and that she does "not have any type of pleasure when [she is] having . . . sexual intercourse with a man." Finally, she testified that she is "definitely" against female genital mutilation. In support of her claim, she submitted an affidavit from a doctor stating that his physical examination yielded results "compatible with" her allegation of having been subject to genital mutilation in the past. . . .

Pursuant to 8 U.S.C. §1231(b)(3)(A), an alien may not be removed to a country if "the alien's life or freedom would be threatened in that country because of the alien's race, religion, nationality, membership in a particular social group, or political opinion." . . .

Here, the records below provide ample evidence that Guinean and/or Fulani women are routinely subjected to various forms of persecution and harm beyond genital mutilation. For example, the 2004 State Department Country Report on Human Rights Practices for Guinea states that "[d]omestic violence against women [is] common," and that "police rarely intervene[] in domestic disputes." . . . Moreover, the report states that women in Guinea are commonly subject, without recourse, to crimes such as rape and sex trafficking. . . . Under the regulations, once the petitioners established past persecution on account of a protected ground in the form of female genital mutilation, it should have been presumed that their lives or freedom would be threatened in the future.

L. Amede Obiora, Bridges and Barricades: Rethinking Polemics and Intransigence in the Campaign Against Female Circumcision

47 Case W. Res. L. Rev. 275, 288-290, 295-299, 316-317, 329 (1997)

Genital scarification and reconstruction are time-honored and worldwide practices. As extant cultural traditions, the practices are particularly prevalent in Africa where they are reported to occur in about twenty-six countries; the exact number of women affected is unknown, but it is estimated between 80 and 110 million. Within the African context, the age at which it is performed varies between localities and it is possible to distinguish at least four major forms of incidence. The ritualized marking of female genitalia begins with the mildest forms of the procedures, where the clitoris is barely nicked or pricked to shed a few drops of blood. This procedure is innocuous and has a strictly symbolic connotation.

The next range of surgeries extend to the removal of the clitoral prepuce, hood, or outer skin. This is the form that ritual Muslims refer to as sunna, and medical data indicates that it poses minimal health risks if scientifically performed and monitored. Sunna is most comparable to male circumcision and there is some suggestion that it may serve the purpose of hygiene and cleanliness. A more radical form of female genital surgeries is known as excision or clitorectomy. In this procedure, the clitoral glans and some of the nympha or labia minora, the narrow lip-like enclosures of the genital anatomy, are severed. The most extreme form of the surgeries is called infibulation, and it has been identified as the form that presents the most significant risks and hazards. This procedure entails scraping the labia majora, the two rounded folds of tissue that contour the external boundaries of the vulva, and stitching the remaining raw edges together in a manner that ensures that only a tiny opening will be left after the surgery heals. . . .

Describing a vital aspect of African cultural identity as "mutilation" has proven offensive, if not psychically mutilating, to critical African constituencies like the Premier Group des Femmes d'Afrique who prefer to employ the term "female circumcision." . . .

Female circumcision is embedded in an intricate web of habits, attitudes, and values, along with having both functional and symbolic connotations. In Africa, the practice is validated and undergirded by a wide spectrum of principles, in addition to temporal and spiritual beliefs. Recurring themes such as sexuality and fertility express preeminent indigenous values like solidarity among women, public recognition of lifecycle change, and procreation for social continuity. Some of these themes are not peculiar to cultures that practice circumcision. Adherence to rites of passage, for example, is an abiding phenomenon in the West.

[Obiora surveys a number of different symbolic meanings for female circumcision in different tribes, including circumcision as a test of courage; as a symbolic linking with tribal history; as a means of making the body symbolically fertile; as a sacrifice to a fertility deity; as a rite of purification; as a means of sex differentiation; as an aesthetic practice; as a symbol of individual identity; as a kind of cosmetic surgery akin to ear piercing; as a contraceptive device; as a means of inaugurating a girl into sexual womanhood; and finally as a way to discourage premarital sex. Obiora argues that it is this last function of female circumcision that Western critics have focused on to the exclusion of its other meanings and functions. She notes that female circumcision in the nineteenth-century West was primarily practiced for the control of female sexuality, and she suggests that Western observers therefore read their own cultural history onto the practice of female circumcision. Obiora also argues that Western academics tend to treat African people as lacking in agency, compelled by their "cultures" to behave in certain ways.] . . .

Through the years in Africa, outside interventionists, whether colonialist or missionary (and now feminist), continue to presume that it is their duty as the "advanced" to elevate and enlighten the "backward." It is characteristic of these interventionists to pay scant attention to crucial issues including the wishes and opinions of the supposed beneficiaries of their benevolence, the overall implications of intervention, and the possibility of more "benign" intervention. Not surprisingly, their campaigns, often couched in terms of virtual monopoly on good judgment, are perceived as unduly ethnocentric and presumptuous. Such campaigns conform to patterns and habits that have historically provoked righteous indignation and engendered cultural resistance to Western "missionary" exploits. Moreover, they tend to pre-judge and alienate the only forces—women, the "victims" and perpetrators—capable of facilitating or subverting meaningful change.

Leti Volpp, Framing Cultural Difference: Immigrant Women and Discourses of Tradition

22 differences: A Journal of Feminist Cultural Studies 90, 93-97, 106 (2011)

Tina Isa [was] a sixteen-year-old who was murdered by her parents, Palestinian émigrés in 1989. According to the [*People* magazine] rendition of the events, after the family moved to the United States from the West Bank in 1985, Tina quickly began to "assimilate to the anything but traditional values of American adolescence," which included working at Wendy's and dating an African American classmate. This was said to violate "long-standing Arab understandings concerning the appropriate behavior for young women" and bring "shame and dishonor on the family name." While Tina's father sought to arrange a marriage for her, which would have required "that she be a virgin," Tina resisted. The night of her murder, her father "accused her of shaming the family by virtue of her allegedly promiscuous behavior," and he stabbed her to death while her mother held her down. Both parents were convicted of first-degree murder and sentenced to death. . . .

[At the trial, the parents mounted] what is popularly known as a "cultural defense" with the assistance of an anthropologist, who testified that Tina had "offended her father's sense of honor" and that "[e]veryone growing up in the Middle East knows that being killed is a possible consequence of dishonoring the family." [Depictions of the crime suggest] that the murder was produced by "Palestinian" or "Arab" culture. Why was Tina Isa's murder not considered the consequence of individual pathology? In the words of journalist S. T. Meravi, "It would be a mistake to believe that [the father] is a typical Palestinian. He just happens to harbor a variety of pathologies that many often ascribe to Palestinians, and as such he embodies some of our worst fears." But why do self-serving claims of individual criminal defendants from certain communities slide so easily into broader assumptions about group-based cultural difference? Surely if the Isas were white, Tina Isa's murder would not have been condemned as the result of "white" culture; the Isas' acts would have been understood as individual and not the outcome of group-based determinism, and could not, therefore, represent "cultural difference." The conceptualization of Tina Isa's murder as produced by Palestinian or Arab culture reflects the selective blaming of culture.* . . .

According to the FBI, [however,] Tina Isa was aware of her father's association with [a terrorist organization]. Her parents, whose abuse she had reported to the State Department of Family Services, apparently believed she would no longer be under their jurisdiction when she turned seventeen, which is when she threatened to leave home. Thus, according to the FBI, Tina was murdered before she was able to expose the activities of the cell. . . . [W]e need to ask why the circumstances of her case are only partly remembered. In this example of competing narratives, the "cultural "explanation prevails. . . .

The traction given to particular narratives of cultural difference makes it all too easy to tell simple stories. . . . The simple story, which explains a murder solely as the result of traditional cultural values of extreme gender subordination, pushes us toward a simple "answer," namely, the binary debate that pits cultural relativism against universalism. . . . [This fails] to recognize Tina Isa—and her parents—beyond their stock roles in acting out a well-rehearsed script. . . .

If we recognize that gender subordination is not merely a practice engaged in by immigrants importing disorderly difference, and we recognize that anxiety about forms of gender subordination practiced in immigrant communities

---

* The father in this case was given a death sentence; he died of a heart attack in prison. The mother received a life sentence.

can function as a proxy for xenophobia, then we should think differently about culture and identity. . . .

The typical discussion relies on the pitching of a battle between the abstract principles of gender equality and respect for cultural norms. This framing creates a vacuum, whereby every factor but a warring traditional culture and modern feminism is absented from any given situation. Into our analysis must be inserted an understanding of culture that encompasses political and material forces and a more complicated vision of feminism. This vision of feminism would recognize the subjectivity of immigrant women . . . and would not presume that shedding culture is a precondition to emancipation. . . .

When culture and feminism are believed to be opponents in a zero-sum game, women will be presumed to be emancipated when they have abandoned their cultures. But what goes into shaping cultural practices is more than time-honored "tradition"; moreover, women's experiences of subordination will be shaped by factors beyond community-specific cultural practices. We should understand immigrant women to possess a complex subjectivity that is not reducible to cultural victimization. In thinking about particular cases, we must look to concrete instances and particular contexts, and avoid describing immigrant lives in a language of cultural difference that divides the traditional immigrant from the modern citizen.

Madhavi Sunder, *Piercing the Veil*

112 Yale L.J. 1399, 1401-1405 (2003)

The failure of the international community to intervene in Afghanistan prior to September 11th was more than a failure of politics. It was also a failure of law. To put it bluntly, human rights law has a problem with religion. In a postmodern world in which the nation-state has been deconstructed and eighteenth- and nineteenth-century notions of unmediated national sovereignty have been properly put to rest, religion—and its attendant category, culture—represent the New Sovereignty. Human rights abuses that since World War II are no longer acceptable when committed by states are paradoxically tolerated when justified in the name of religion or culture. September 11th crystallized this fact. The infamous Taliban regime in Afghanistan assumed power in 1996 and immediately began stripping women of fundamental human rights to education, healthcare, work, and movement. But war, not law, defeated what has been described as the world's most ruthless fundamentalist regime. For all its pomp and circumstance, international human rights had little to do with it.

Current scholarship posits an inherent conflict between women's rights and culture. But . . . religion qua religion is less the problem than is our traditional legal construction of this category. Premised on a centuries-old, Enlightenment compromise that justified reason in the public sphere by allowing deference to religious despotism in the private, human rights law continues to define religion in the twenty-first century as a sovereign, extralegal jurisdiction in which inequality is not only accepted, but expected. Law views religion as natural, irrational, incontestable, and imposed—in contrast to the public sphere, the only viable space for freedom and reason. Simply put, religion is the "other" of international law.

Today, fundamentalists are taking advantage of this legal tradition. Yet, contrary to law's centuries-old conception, religious communities are internally contested, heterogeneous, and constantly evolving over time through internal debate and interaction with outsiders. And this has never been so true as in the twenty-first century. Individuals in the modern world increasingly demand change within their religious communities in order to bring their faith in line with democratic norms and practices. Call this the New Enlightenment: Today, individuals seek reason, equality, and liberty not just in the public sphere, but also in the private spheres of religion, culture, and family. Current law, however, elides these claims for modernization. Failing to recognize cultural and religious communities as contested and subject to change, legal norms such as the "freedom of religion," the "right to culture," and the guarantee of "self-determination" defer to the claims of patriarchal, religious elites, buttressing their power over the claims of modernizers. Paradoxically, law's failure to question or revisit its old Enlightenment views is obstructing the emergence of the New Enlightenment. In short, human rights law, not religion, is the problem.

But on the ground, women's human rights activists are piercing the veil of religious sovereignty. [There is] a growing disconnect between human rights law and human rights practice. [A] close study of women's human rights activists working in Muslim communities and countries . . . demonstrates that, despite law's formal refusal to acknowledge claims of internal dissent, women are nonetheless claiming their rights to challenge religious and cultural authorities and to imagine religious community on more egalitarian and democratic terms. . . .

Scholars have failed to recognize the full significance of these efforts. By insisting, in the words of President George W. Bush, "if you're not with us, you're against us," scholars celebrate campaigns for women's rights in Muslim communities for their similarities to Western women's rights movements, but elide what is different in these claims. In fact, these campaigns present powerful critiques of current law, which offers women a right to religious freedom (on leaders' terms) or to equality (within the public sphere), but no right to both. Envisioning a third way, women human rights activists in Muslim communities are pursuing equality and freedom within the context of religion, not just without it.

We ignore these activists at our peril. In an era of rising fundamentalism in which women's—and men's—lives are increasingly governed by private, not public, laws, securing human rights requires deconstructing religion and culture. . . . Unmasking the politics and mutability of religion that traditional legal narratives have concealed, we must identify that part of religion that is a human or legal construction and thus requires justification and accountability. . . .

This is nothing less than a question of life or death. In Pakistan last summer, a mentally disturbed young man was stoned to death for alleged blasphemy, and a tribal council ordered that a young woman be raped as revenge for a crime allegedly committed by her brother—all on the basis of traditional Islamic Shari'a law. In Nigeria, another woman, Amina Lawal, awaits her fate after an appeals court in that country upheld a Shari'a court's ruling that Lawal be stoned to death because she gave birth to a child outside of marriage. Nigeria's Supreme Court may ultimately decide the case. But as it currently stands, there is no legal theory—either under Nigerian national law or international human rights law—for overturning the pronouncements of a religious court.

In such cases, law's conception of religion and culture matters. So long as law continues to hold a fundamentalist view of religion and culture, it will transfer more power to fundamentalists and traditionalists at the expense of human rights.

Notes

1. Female Genital "Surgeries." The World Health Organization estimates that over 100 million women have had some form of FGM. The practice primarily occurs in about 26 African nations.[80] Although 50 African nations have signed a protocol against FGM, and some reports suggest that it is declining, an estimated 2 million girls undergo the practice each year.[81]

In 1996, the United States became the second country in the world to ban female genital surgeries.[82] U.S. directors of international financial institutions are required to oppose non-humanitarian loans to countries where FGM is commonly practiced if local governments have not undertaken educational measures to combat the practice.[83] Federal legislation also makes it illegal to "knowingly circumcise[], excise[] or infibulate[] the whole or any part of the labia majora or labia minora or clitoris of another person who has not attained the age of 18 years." The maximum sentence is five years. The statute explicitly rejects the possibility of a cultural defense: "No account shall be taken of the effect on the person on whom the operation is to be performed of any belief on the part of that person, or any other person, that the operation is required as a matter of custom or ritual." Is this the right policy?

As Bah v. Mukasey makes evident, FGM is considered to be a form of persecution on the basis of group membership (i.e., women) that may support an asylum petition. Is this an example of Western ethno-centrism, as Obiora suggests, or does it exemplify the basic "universal obligation to protect human functioning and its dignity"?[84]

In addressing the role of criminal and human rights law in combating practices that subordinate women, Helen Stacy notes that legal prohibitions are most likely to be successful when they work in tandem with broader social movements. So, for example, laws against footbinding in China were not effective until anti-footbinding societies enlisted parents to take an oath that they would not bind their daughters' feet or allow their sons to marry a woman who had been subjected to the practice. By analogy, Stacy argues that courts that want to take some effective action against FGM could direct governments to establish programs that promulgate alternative, safe, coming of age rituals.[85] Does this strike you as a desirable approach? What other alternatives might be feasible?

2. Multiculturalism and the Veil. A related issue involves the practice of veiling by Muslim women. Here, as with the FGM practices described in the Obiora excerpt, veiling practices vary, with some cultural traditions calling for covering of the entire body (the jilbab or burkhah) and others for only headscarves (hijab). Islamic veiling is not just a religious practice, but also "a highly contested political symbol within Muslim societies and the global political arena."[86] Approaches to the issue vary. At one end of the spectrum, Turkey and France ban headscarves worn for religious purposes in all universities and government offices. The Turkish ban was upheld by the European Court of Human Rights.[87] In France, a veiled Muslim woman born in Morocco, who moved to France upon her marriage to a French national, was denied French citizenship on grounds of "insufficient assimilation." The decision was based on the threat her religious practices were seen to present to the French value of sex equality, represented not only by her veiling, but also by her "living in total submission to the men of her family."[88] The purposes of these bans range from the desire to assimilate other cultures into a single national identity, the belief that the headscarf is a symbol of female oppression and the totalitarian tendencies of Islamic groups, and concerns about security. Other countries, like the United States and Great Britain, believe that bans violate women's right to religious freedom.[89]

The reasons for veiling also vary. Some women engage in the practice as a form of identification with conservative, male-controlled Muslim communities. On the other hand, Ernest Gellner has argued that "[c]ontrary to what outsiders generally suppose, the typical Muslim woman in a Muslim city doesn't wear the veil because her grandmother did so, but because her grandmother did *not*."[90] Some Muslim women — who tend to be "young, urban, and typically the daughters of migrants from rural areas — deliberately embrace[] the choice to cover, challenging . . . both the secular construction of the headscarf as a means of Islamic male oppression [and] the Islamic masculinist construction of the veil as a protector of women's modesty and place in . . . the domestic sphere."[91] Many Muslim women also embrace the veil as a protection from sexual assault and harassment, as well as a challenge to Western imperialism and objectification of women's bodies. "Why is a veil more oppressive than a miniskirt?" asks one woman.[92] Is it?

3. The "Cultural Defense" in Criminal Law. At issue in the Tina Isa case discussed in the Leti Volpp reading is the controversial "cultural defense." This criminal law defense would permit evidence describing accepted practices in an immigrant defendant's native country in order to bolster a claim of justification or excuse. Advocates of the defense claim that it is consistent with principles of religious liberty, equal protection, and cultural pluralism.[93] Opponents argue that it reinforces stereotypes, legitimates gender subordination, invites anti-immigrant backlash, and promotes inconsistent treatment. "If you want to live here, live by our rules," is a common reaction.[94]

Two landmark examples are a New York case, People v. Chen, and a California case, People v. Wu.[95] In *Chen*, the defendant was a 54-year-old Chinese immigrant who killed his wife by smashing her skull with a claw hammer. Chen argued that he lacked the intent to kill but rather had acted under "extreme emotional disturbance" in part because of his Chinese cultural values. Chen had become suspicious that his wife was having an affair and attacked her after she admitted that she was seeing another man. Chen's attorney introduced an anthropologist who testified that, "[i]n general terms, I think that one could expect a Chinese to react in a much more volatile, violent way to those circumstances than someone from our own society. I think there's no doubt about it." According to this expert, social control is more strict and unchanging in China than in the West. A Chinese man whose wife had committed adultery would be dishonored, and both parties would have difficulty remarrying. In the United States, the anthropologist also claimed, a Chinese man whose wife had committed adultery would be considered a "pariah" among Chinese women and would have no chance of finding a white woman. On cross-examination, the expert contrasted Chinese people with "the average American," whom he described as a white professional male, and argued that Chinese immigrants assimilated into American society "very slowly, if ever." Impressed by this testimony, the trial judge found Chen guilty of manslaughter rather than murder and sentenced him to five years probation instead of time in prison.

In *Wu*, the defendant, Helen, who grew up in China, became romantically involved with a man, Gary Wu, who emigrated to the United States and married another woman. Many years later, however, he contacted Helen and told her he was unhappily married and that if Helen emigrated to the United States he would marry her, and she could bear a child for him. Helen did emigrate to the United States, but Gary did not offer to marry her, even after the two of them had a child, a son named Sidney. Gary did divorce his wife, but did not tell Helen.

Helen, who was unable to speak English or drive a car, was unhappy in the United States, and eventually told Gary she would return to Macau. She did so without Sidney, but for the next eight years repeatedly asked Gary to visit her with Sidney. Gary continually asked for money, at one point proposing marriage after Helen showed him a certificate of deposit for a million Hong Kong dollars. Finally, Helen and Gary were married in Las Vegas, but when pressed

Gary would not say whether he had married her for her money. Shortly thereafter, Helen saw Gary beating their son, and Sidney told her the house they were staying in belonged to another woman, Gary's girlfriend. At that point, Helen told Sidney she wanted to die and asked if he would go too. He clung to her neck and cried. Helen cut the cord off a window blind and strangled her son. She then attempted to kill herself by slashing her wrist with a kitchen knife, but she was revived at the local emergency room.

At the murder trial, the judge refused to instruct the jurors that they could choose to consider Helen's cultural background in determining the presence or absence of malice, and Wu was convicted of murder. On appeal, the California Court of Appeals reversed, holding that evidence of her cultural background was relevant to the issues of premeditation and deliberation and could potentially reduce the murder charge to one of voluntary manslaughter. The experts in this case were not anthropologists but "transcultural psychologists," who explained that Helen's behavior represented love and maternal altruism: ". . . in her own culture, in her own mind, there are no other options but to, for her at the time, but to kill herself and take the son along with her so that they could sort of step over to the next world where she could devote herself, all of herself to the caring of the son, caring of Sidney. . . . Her purpose . . . in many ways . . . is a benevolent one."

Leti Volpp's point in the excerpt about the Tina Isa case is that we should avoid the temptation to reduce the narratives in such cases to cultural stereotypes, which often serves merely to reassure ourselves that our culture is more advanced. The solution, she argues, is to simultaneously universalize the dynamics of subordination and particularize them. This means identifying not only the special role of cultural traditions in a gender-based crime, but also the ways in which these cases are similar to other cases of violence and gender subordination.[96]

There are hundreds of cases in which individuals have attempted to invoke a cultural defense. They involve a wide variety of cultural claims in a wide variety of contexts, including homicide, rape, drugs, custody, child abuse, animal cruelty, employment discrimination suits, and the treatment of the dead.[97] A disproportionate number of these cases involve Asian immigrants. In such proceedings, Daina Chiu argues, the debate over the "cultural defense" is in large part a debate over three different ways of "managing Asian difference" in American society. The first is the "exclusion" approach: it argues for a cultural defense as "special treatment" to protect immigrants and to preserve American identity as white. Chiu argues that this approach is particularly harmful to Asian women because it legitimates their traditional subordinate role in Asian culture. A second framework, the "assimilation" approach, rejects the defense and demands conformity to dominant norms. A third, intermediate position, which admits cultural evidence to show state of mind or mitigate punishment, reflects what Chiu calls "guilty liberalism." Chiu argues that this position enables "white society . . . to reinforce its prejudices through the other culture while purporting to act in tolerance of difference. In particular, this approach allows white society to reconstruct the subordination of women through the medium of another culture." Chiu argues that the *Chen* case is an example of guilty liberalism. The judge in that case, she argues, reduced Chen's culpability not because he was acting under "different" cultural values, but because he held the "same" cultural values as Americans: "The subordination of women and the privileging of the male sex-right are common to both cultures."[98] Cynthia Lee similarly argues that the defense is most likely to succeed when it is "culturally convergent" with patriarchal norms in our own society.[99] If these commentators are correct, what does it suggest about when cultural evidence should be admissible?

4. Religious Freedom and Gender Equality in the United States.   The potential conflict between religious freedom and nondiscrimination laws is especially apparent with respect to employment decisions made by religious organizations. In the unanimous 2012 decision of Hosanna-Tabor Evangelical Lutheran Church and School v. EEOC,[100] the United States Supreme Court held that both the Establishment Clause and the Free Exercise Clause bar employment discrimination lawsuits based on the termination of employees by a religious institution when that employee is a "minister" within the "ministerial exception" to nondiscrimination statutes. The Court determined that the plaintiff in *Hosanna-Tabor*, allegedly fired because of a disability in violation of the Americans with Disabilities Act, was a minister on the basis of her title ("Minister of Religion, Commissioned") and the fact that she taught religious as well as secular subjects.

Should the ministerial exception apply even when the religious institution's discrimination has nothing to do with a religious belief or practice? For example, a prior decision of the Ninth Circuit Court of Appeals had held that the ministerial exception did not extend to cases of sexual harassment, where the employer did not claim a religious purpose for the harassment.[101] On the one hand, the U.S. Supreme Court made clear in *Hosanna-Tabor* that the claimed discriminatory behavior need not be connected to a particular tenet of the religion: "The purpose of the exception is not to safeguard a church's decision to fire a minister only when it is made for a religious reason. The exception instead ensures that the authority to select and control who will minister to the faithful . . . is the church's alone."[102] At the same time, the Court limited the case to the church's decision to fire an employee[103] and did not discuss whether it might have broader application.

How similar is the Court's decision in *Hosanna-Tabor* to international law's tolerance of human rights abuses described by Sunder? Is a hands-off approach an unwarranted capitulation to religion? This issue is further examined in the context of accommodations to religious beliefs relating to abortion and contraception in Chapter 5.

Putting Theory Into Practice

6-12. In 1996, a group of Somali immigrants living in Seattle sought to persuade a hospital to perform largely symbolic circumcisions on their daughters, a procedure that involved simply pricking the clitoral hood and that was less intrusive than male circumcision. The parents presented this as an alternative to sending their daughters to Africa for a more extreme procedure. The hospital initially agreed but changed course when it was inundated with complaints.[104] What would you have done? Should such a procedure be banned given that circumcision is now performed on a majority of male newborns?[105]

6-13. A Hmong immigrant attempted to defend a charge of child sexual assault in Wisconsin on the grounds that he was married to the child, who was 14 years old at the time, according to Hmong custom.[106] How would you evaluate the defense?

6-14. Harvard University recently decided to set aside six hours a week in one of its gyms when only women would be admitted in order to accommodate female Muslim students. In the absence of such a policy, they would be unable to exercise in appropriate attire. The decision provoked considerable controversy. Critics viewed it as a concession to sexist cultural norms that included Shari'a and honor killings and invoked visions of women in veils and chadors on treadmills.[107] If you were an administrator at Harvard, how would you respond?

6-15. Alamo Rent-A-Car maintains a "Dress Smart Policy," which prohibits the wearing of any article of clothing not approved in the policy. A Muslim employee requested permission to wear a head covering during the holy month of Ramadan. Alamo told her that she could wear the head covering while working in the back of the office, but not while working at the rental counter. She was eventually suspended for wearing her head scarf at the counter in violation of the policy. Should she prevail in a Title VII case?[108]

6-16. In a number of different immigrant groups in the United States, parents are expected to arrange for their daughters' marriages. A survey of agencies throughout the world that had encountered forced marriage cases reported multiple forms of fraud, force, or coercion to make girls (some as young as 13) enter or stay in a forced marriage. Tactics included emotional blackmail, isolation, social ostracism, economic threats, and threats of physical violence and loss of immigration status.[109] Over half of the cases involve Muslim families.[110] Should forced marriages be banned in the United States or regulated in some manner, or should they be tolerated in the name of religious liberty?

The United Kingdom estimated that 5,000 to 8,000 forced marriages were reported across the country in 2009.[111] In response, the country has established a "Forced Marriage Unit" and national helpline, passed a law creating a special "forced marriage protective order" in family court, made changes to the visa sponsorship process, and has conducted overseas "rescue" operations as well as extensive community education, outreach, and training. Is this the right approach? Can you think of other measures that might be an appropriate part of a regulatory solution?

6-17. A teacher at a Catholic girls' school was dismissed after she lent her name to an advertisement supporting abortion rights on the 30th anniversary of Roe v. Wade. Title VII prohibits discrimination based on religion.[112] Does the teacher have a claim against the school?

6-18. Obama Abou Salama is a professor of botany at Cairo University and a member of the Muslim Brotherhood. Mr. Salama runs premarital counseling classes. "A woman," he teaches, "takes pleasure in being a follower and finds ease in obeying a husband who loves her." Female members of his classes agree readily. One of the advisors to Egyptian President Mohamed Morsi, Omaima Kamel, supports the Muslim Brotherhood's family values agenda. "Let's face it," she explains, "if your work took you away from your fundamental duties at home and if your success came at the cost of your family life and stability of your children, then you are the one who stands to lose."[113] Do Western feminists have a positive role to play in influencing such attitudes in Egypt? Or is this a matter for the Egyptian women themselves?

6-19. Mary Anne Case writes

> At a time when so many different religious fundamentalisms are coming to the foreground and demanding legal recognition, I want to vindicate something I have come to call feminist fundamentalism, by which I mean an uncompromising commitment to the equality of the sexes as intense and at least as worthy of respect as, for example, a religiously or culturally based commitment to female subordination or fixed sex roles.[114]

Evaluate this statement. What do you think Case means? What would change, if anything, if United States public policy fully reflected the values of feminist fundamentalism?

---

1. Elizabeth Cady Stanton, Address to the Legislature of the State of New York (Feb. 14, 1854).

2. Sara M. Evans, Born for Liberty: A History of Women in America 155 (1989). For discussion of how feminist advocates used the race analogy in complex ways, often in collaboration with African American women, to help secure women's rights, and also disaggregated race from sex when it became a liability, see Serena Mayeri, Reasoning from Race: Feminism, Law, and the Civil Rights Revolution (2011). See also bell hooks, Ain't I a Woman: Black Women and Feminism 127-139 (1981) (describing historical tensions over race within the women's movement).

3. Dorothy Roberts, Spiritual and Menial Housework, 9 Yale J.L. & Feminism 51 (1997), excerpted in Chapter 4.

4. Joan Williams, Implementing Anti-Essentialism: How Gender Wars Turn into Race and Class Conflict, 15 Harv. Blackletter L.J. 41, 43, 51 (1999).

5. Rogers v. American Airlines, 527 F. Supp. 229 (S.D.N.Y. 1981).

6. Paulette M. Caldwell, A Hair Piece: Perspectives on the Intersection of Race and Gender, 1991 Duke L.J. 365, 379.

7. Richard T. Ford, Racial Culture: A Critique 24-25 (2005).

8. See, e.g., Darren Lenard Hutchinson, Identity Crisis: "Intersectionality," "Multidimensionality," and the Development of an Adequate Theory of Subordination, 6 Mich. J. Race & L. 285, 309-316 (2001); Francisco Valdes, Beyond Sexual Orientation in Queer Legal Theory: Majoritarianism, Multidimensionality, and Responsibility in Social Justice Scholarship or Legal Scholars as Cultural Warriors, 75 Denv. U. L. Rev. 1409, 1415 (1998).

9. See Linda R. Shaw et al., Intersectionality and Disability Harassment: The Interactive Effects of Disability, Race, Age, and Gender, 55(2) Rehabilitation Bulletin 82, 88 (2012).

10. See Rachel Kahn Best et al., Multiple Disadvantages: An Empirical Test of Intersectionality Theory in EEO Litigation, 45 Law & Soc'y Rev. 991 (2011).

11. Suzanne Goldberg gives one explanation—that in insisting discrimination be established by comparison to someone else who does not have the characteristics of the plaintiff, courts are excluding plaintiffs who have been discriminated against based on more than one factor, or who are penalized for "performing" gender in an unacceptable way. See Suzanne B. Goldberg, Discrimination by Comparison, 120 Yale L.J. 718 (2011).

12. See, e.g., Ian Aryes & Richard Luedeman, Tops, Bottoms, and Versatiles: What Straight Views of Penetrative Preferences Could Mean for Sexuality Claims Under Price Waterhouse, 123 Yale L.J. 714 (2013) (demonstrating through online survey research that heterosexuals have different levels of aversion toward gay men depending upon those men's penetrative preferences).

13. Angela P. Harris, Race and Essentialism in Feminist Legal Theory, 42 Stan. L. Rev. 581, 601 (1990).

14. Examples of the broad range of efforts along these lines include Janet Halley, Split Decisions: How and Why to Take a Break from Feminism (2006) (arguing for a form of feminism that neither denies harm nor assumes guilt); Katharine T. Bartlett, Feminist Legal Methods, 103 Harv. L. Rev. 829, 880-885 (1990) (describing the "positional" stance that both commits to specific truths and values and acknowledges the importance of contingency and perspective); Kathryn Abrams, Feminist Lawyering and Legal Method, 16 Law & Soc. Inq'y 373 (1991) (describing concrete methodological innovations that avoid both absolute and relativistic assumptions).

15. Linda Hamilton Krieger, The Content of Our Categories, 47 Stan. L. Rev. 1161, 1188-1190 (1995).

16. Kenji Yoshino, Covering, 11 Yale L.J. 769, 772 (2002).

17. See Gowri Ramachandran, Intersectionality as "Catch 22": Why Identity Performance Demands are Neither Harmless Nor Reasonable, 69 Alb. L. Rev. 299 (2005).

18. See Denny v. Elizabeth Arden Salons, 456 F.3d 427 (4th Cir. 2006). The court ruled against the plaintiff on the Title II claim on the grounds that a beauty salon is not a place of public accommodation, but it remanded the case for trial on whether the salon had violated Section 1981's prohibition on race discrimination in the making of contracts. For a critique of the case, see Radiance A. Walters, Denny v. Elizabeth Arden Salons, Inc.: Condoning Race Discrimination in Resembling Places of Public Accommodation Under Title II, 8 U. Md. L.J. Race, Religion, Gender & Class 407 (2008).

19. Julie A. Greenberg, Health Care Issues Affecting People with an Intersex Condition or DSD: Sex or Disability Discrimination?, 45 Loy. L.A. L. Rev. 849, 853 (2012).

20. Littleton v. Prange, 9 S.W.3d 223, 223 (Tex. App. 1999); see also In re Estate of Gardiner, 22 P.3d 1086 (Kan. 2001) (invalidating marriage between man and transsexual woman on grounds that legal sex cannot be changed for purposes of marriage law).

21. Tina Kelley, Through Sickness, Health and Sex Change, N.Y. Times, Apr. 27, 2008, at Style, 1, 7. See also Helen B. Berrigan, Transsexual Marriage: A Trans-Atlantic Judicial Dialogue, 12 Law & Sex. 87 (2003).

22. Littleton, 9 S.W.3d at 230-231.

23. Jennifer Finney Boylan, Is My Marriage Gay?, N.Y. Times, May 12, 2009, at A23.

24. See Melanie Blackless et al., How Sexually Dimorphic Are We? Review and Synthesis, 12 Am. J. Hum. Biology 151, 161 (2000); see also Julie A. Greenberg, Defining Male and Female: Intersexuality and the Collision Between Law and Biology, 41 Ariz. L. Rev. 265, 267 (1999).

25. See Peter A. Lee et al., Consensus Statement on Management of Intersex Disorders, 118 Pediatrics 488 (2006).

26. E. J. Graff, The M/F Boxes, The Nation, Dec. 17, 2001, at 20, 21. For a survey of views on the question of how to respond to "ambiguous genitals," with some rich narratives, see Elizabeth Weil, What If It's (Sort of) a Boy and (Sort of) a Girl?, N.Y. Times Mag. Sept. 24, 2006 (available at http://www.nytimes.com/2006/09/24/magazine/24intersexkids.html); For a similar dilemma with respect to transgender minors, see Hanna Rosin, A Boy's Life, The Atlantic Online, Nov. 8, 2008 (available at http://www.theatlantic.com/doc/print/200811/transgender-children). Margaret Talbot, About a Boy: Transgender Surgery at Sixteen, The New Yorker, March 18, 2013, available at http://www.newyorker.com/reporting/2013/03/18/130318fa_fact_talbot?currentPage=all. The lead advocacy group today is Advocates for Informed Choice; information about this group is available at aiclegal.org. On the emerging intersex movement and legal issues affecting people with an intersex condition, see Julie A. Greenberg, Intersexuality and the Law: Why Sex Matters (2012).

27. See Amanda Kennedy, Because We Say So: The Unfortunate Denial of Rights to Transgender Minors Regarding Transition, 19 Hastings Women's L.J. 281 (2008).

28. Nancy Ehrenreich (with Mark Barr), Intersex Surgery, Female Genital Cutting, and the Selective Condemnation of "Cultural Practices," 40 Harv. C.R.-C.L. L. Rev. 71 (2005). For both medical and legal issues of gender assignment, see Greenberg, supra note 26; Legal Aspects of Gender Assignment, 13 Endocrinologist 277 (2003); Anne Tamar-Mattis, Exceptions to the Rule: Curing the Law's Failure to Protect Intersex Infants, 21 Berkeley J. Gender L. & Just. 59 (2006).

29. See Marc Lacey, A Lifestyle Distinct: The Muxe of Mexico, N.Y. Times Week in Review, Dec. 6, 2008, at 4.

30. See Alison Shaw, Is It a Boy, or a Girl? The Challenges of Genital Ambiguity, in Changing Sex and Bending Gender 20, 25-26 (Alison Shaw & Shirley Ardener eds., 2005); see also Jessica Knouse, Intersexuality and the Social Construction of Anatomical Sex, 12 Cardozo J. L. & Gender 135, 150 (2005).

31. The new policy is described at https://www.passports.gov.au/web/sexgenderapplicants.aspx.

32. See Swedish Parents Keep 2-Year-Old's Gender Secret, The Local, (Jun. 9, 2009), http://www.thelocal.se/20232/20090623. After five years, Pop's parents revealed that he is a boy. David Wilkes, Boy or Girl? The Parents Who Refused to Say for FIVE Years Finally Reveal Sex of Their 'Gender-Neutral' Child, The Daily Mail (Jan. 20, 2012), http://www.dailymail.co.uk/news/article-2089474/Beck-Laxton-Kieran-Cooper-reveal-sex-gender-neutral-child-Sasha.html (It's a boy).

33. Shanelle Matthews, Transgender Rights Run into Bathroom Politics, Women's eNews, Apr. 28, 2008; San Francisco Human Rights Commission, Economic Empowerment for the Lesbian, Gay, Bisexual, and Transgender Communities 10 (2000) (estimating unemployment rate of 70 percent); Shannon Minter & Christopher Daley, A Legal Needs Assessment of San Francisco's Transgender Communities (2003), available at http://www.ftmi.org/images/0TransFinal.pdf. See generally Transgender Rights (Paisley Currah et al. eds., 2006).

34. See, e.g., Etsitty v. Utah Transit Authority, 502 F.3d 1215, 1224 (10th Cir. 2007) (Title VII does not cover discrimination against transsexuals); Dobre v. National R.R. Passenger Corp., 850 F. Supp. 284 (E.D. Pa. 1993) (requiring male-to-female transition transsexual to use male washroom and dress in traditionally male attire is not discrimination "against a female because she is female"); James v. Rank Mart Hardware Inc., 881 F. Supp. 478 (D. Kan. 1995) (discrimination against male transvestite is permissible as long as female transsexuals are treated no better).

35. Smith v. Salem, 378 F.3d 566, 575 (6th Cir. 2004) (sexual harassment against transgender individual is discrimination because of sex and also sex stereotyping in violation of Price Waterhouse); see also Rosa v. Park W. Bank & Trust Co., 214 F.3d 213 (1st Cir. 2000); Lie v. Sky Publishing Corp., 15 Mass. L. Rptr. 412 (Super. 2002); Schwenk v. Hartford, 204 F.3d 1187 (9th Cir. 2000). On protection of transgender workers through sex discrimination laws, see L. Camille Hébert, Transforming Transsexual and Transgender Rights, 15 Wm. & Mary J. of Women & L. 535 (2009).

36. EEOC Appeal No. 0120120821 (Apr. 20, 2012), available at http://www.washingtonblade.com/content/files/2012/04/90910497-EEOC-Ruling.pdf. The significance of this ruling is discussed in Joanna L. Grossman, The EEOC Rules That Transgender Discrimination Is Sex Discrimination, Justia's Verdict, May 1, 2012, available at http://verdict.justia.com/2012/05/01/the-eeoc-rules-that-transgender-discrimination-is-sex-discrimination.

37. Glenn v. Brumby, 663 F.3d 1312 (11th Cir. 2011).

38. Paisley Currah & Shannon Minter, Unprincipled Exclusions: The Struggle to Achieve Judicial and Legislative Equality for Transgender People, 7 Wm. & Mary J. Women & L. 37, 40-41 (2000).

39. See http://www.transequality.org/ENDA; http://www.hrc.org/laws-and-legislation/federal-legislation/employment-non-discrimination-act.

40. A current map of relevant state laws is available at http://www.aclu.org/maps/non-discrimination-laws-state-state-information-map.

41. Matthews, supra note 33 (quoting Michelle Turner). The Maryland Court of Appeals later held that the referendum had been improperly certified because many of the signatures were invalid. See Doe v. Montgomery County Bd. of Elections, 962 A.2d 342 (Md. 2009).

42. 502 F.3d at 1224. On the restroom issue, see Terry S. Kogan, Transsexuals in Public Restrooms: Law, Cultural Geography and Etsitty v. Utah Transit Authority, 18 Temp. Pol. & Civ. Rts. L. Rev. 673 (2009).

43. Sheridan v. Sanctuary Investments Ltd., [1999] 33 C.H.R.R. D. 467.

44. See Laura Grenfell, Embracing Law's Categories: Anti-Discrimination Laws and Transgenderism, 15 Yale J.L. Feminism 51, 70-71, 78-81 (2003).

45. Gender Recognition Act, 2004, c. 7 (Eng.).

46. See Christopher Clarey, Gender Test After a Gold-Medal Finish, N.Y. Times, Aug. 19, 2009, at B13.

47. Peroshni Govender, South African Caster Semenya Cleared to Return, reuters.com, July 6, 2010, available at http://uk.reuters.com/article/2010/07/06/uk-athletics-semenya-idUKTRE 6652M520100706; Jeré Longman, Farah Wins 5,000 to Give Home Team Another Title, N.Y. Times, Aug. 11, 2012, at SP3. On the issues raised by Semenya's case, see Erin Buzuvis, Caster Semenya and the Myth of a Level Playing Field, 6 Am. U. Modern Am. 36 (2010).

48. See Marta Lawrence, Transgender Policy Approved (Sept. 13, 2011), available at http://www.ncaa.org/wps/wcm/connect/public/NCAA/Resources/Latest+News/2011/September/Transgender+policy+approved. On these issues, see Erin E. Buzuvis, Transgender Student-Athletes and Sex-Segregated Sport: Developing Policies of Inclusion for Intercollegiate and Interscholastic Athletics, 21 Seton Hall J. Sports & Ent. L. 1 (2011).

49. Linda Nicholson, Interpreting Gender, 20 Signs: Journal of Women in Culture and Society 79 (1994).

50. See Katherine M. Franke, The Central Mistake of Sex Discrimination Law: The Disaggregation of Sex from Gender, 144 U. Pa. L. Rev. 1, 2 (1995).

51. Mary Anne Case, Disaggregating Gender from Sex and Sexual Orientation: The Effeminate Man in the Law and Feminist Jurisprudence, 105 Yale L.J. 1 (1995).

52. Id. at 7.

53. 511 U.S. 127, 157 n.1 (1994) (Scalia, J., dissenting).

54. See Ruth Bader Ginsburg, Gender in the Supreme Court: The 1973 and 1974 Terms, 1975 Sup. Ct. Rev. 1, n.1.

55. See Valerie Oosterveld, The Definition of "Gender" in the Rome Statute of the International Criminal Court: A Step Forward or Back for International Criminal Justice? 18 Harv. Hum. Rts. J. 55, 66-71 (2005).

56. See In re Marriage of Simmons, 825 N.E.2d 303 (Ill. 2005).

57. Nixon v. Vancouver Rape Relief Society, 2002 C.L.L.C 230-009, 42 C.H.R.R. D/20.

58. See Doe v. Yunits, 2001 WL 664947 (Mass. Super. Ct. Feb. 26, 2001). This and related cases are discussed in Transgender Law and Policy Institute, Litigation: Case Law—Youth, at http://www.transgenderlaw.org/cases/index.htm#youth.

59. Harvey C. Mansfield, Manliness 244 (2006).

60. Michael S. Kimmel, Issues for Men in the 1990s, 46 U. Miami L. R. 671, 672, (1992), citing Robert Bly, Iron John: A Book About Men 6, 222-237, 244-249 (1990).

61. Susan Faludi, Stiffed: The Betrayal of the American Man (2000). In a similar, but more contentious vein, see Christina Hoff Sommers, The War Against Boys: How Misguided Feminism Is Harming Our Young (2000) (blaming feminists for men's sense of disempowerment and disadvantage).

62. For examples, see Handbook of Studies on Men & Masculinities (Michael S. Kimmel et al. eds., 2005); The Black Male Handbook (Kevin Powell ed., 2007); Michael Kimmel, Guyland (2008); R. W. Connell, The Men and the Boys (2000); R. W. Connell, Masculinities (1995); Michael Kimmel, Manhood in America: A Cultural History (1996).

63. Shira Tarrent, Men and Feminism 28-39 (2009); Against the Tide: Pro-Feminist Men in the United States 1776-1990, A Documentary History (Michael S. Kimmel & Thomas E. Mosmiller eds., 1991).

64. See, e.g., Keith Cunningham-Parmeter, Men At Work, Fathers at Home: Uncovering the Masculine Face of Caregiver Discrimination, 24 Colum. J. Gender & Law 253 (2013).

65. Sylvia Ann Hewlett, The Athena Factor: Reversing the Brain Drain in Science, Engineering, and Technology, Harvard Business Review Research Report (May 2008).

66. See Letitia M. Saucedo & Maria Christina Morales, Masculinities Narratives and Latino Immigrant Workers: A Case Study of the Las Vegas Residential Construction Trades, 33 Harv. J. Law & Gender 625 (2010).

67. Kari Palazzari, The Daddy Double-Bind: How the Family and Medical Leave Act Perpetuates Sex Inequality Across All Class Levels, 16 Colum. J. Gender & L. 429 (2008).

68. For an extended conversation between a dozen professors about gay male parenthood, see Rosenblum et al., Pregnant Man?: A Conversation, 22 Yale J. Law & Feminism 207 (2010).

69. The Swedish model is described in Darren Rosenblum, Unsex Mothering: Toward a New Culture of Parenting, 35 Harv. J. Gender & Law 57, 109-110 (2012).

70. Michael S. Kimmel, Masculinity as Homophobia: Fear, Shame, and Silence in the Construction of Gender Identity, in Theorizing Masculinities 119, 133 (Harry Brod & Michael Kaufman eds., 1994).

71. For other work in the criminal justice area, see Angela P. Harris, Gender, Violence, Race, and Criminal Justice, 52 Stan. L. Rev. 777 (2000).

72. John M. Kang, The Burdens of Manliness, 33 Harv. J. Law & Gender 477, 495 (2010).

73. Olatunde C. A. Johnson, Disparity Rules, 107 Colum. L. Rev. 374 (2007).

74. See Floyd D. Weatherspoon, Remedying Employment Discrimination Against African American Males, 36 Washburn L.J. 23 (1996); Floyd D. Weatherspoon, The Devastating Impact of the Justice System on the Status of African-American Males: An Overview Perspective, 23 Cap. U. L. Rev. 23 (1994).

75. Devon W. Carbado, Men in Black, 3 J. Gender Race & Just. 427, 429 (2000).

76. Cases involving these kinds of behaviors are discussed in Camille Gear Rich, Innocence Interrupted: Reconstructing Fatherhood in the Shadow of Child Molestation Law, 101 Cal. L. Rev. 609 (2013). Rich argues that the gendered interpretation of child molestation laws helps to reinforce gendered parenting norms. Id.

77. See, e.g., World Health Organization, Eliminating Female Genital Mutilation: An Interagency Statement OHCHR, UNAIDS, UNDP, UNECA, UNESCO, UNFPA, UNHCR, UNICEF, UNIFEM, WHO (2008), http://www.who.int/reproductive-health/publications/fgm/fgm_statement_2008.pdf; Committee on the Elimination of All Forms of Discrimination Against Women, Female Circumcision General Recommendation No. 14, U.N. GAOR, 45th Sess., Supp. No. 38 & Corr. 1, at 80, P 438, U.N. Doc. A/45/38 (1990); Declaration on the Elimination of Violence against Women, G.A. Res. 104, U.N. GAOR, 48th Sess., Art. 2(a), U.N. Doc. A/48/629 (1993).

78. See, e.g., Inter-African Committee on Traditional Practices Homepage, http://www.iac-ciaf.com.

79. See 18 U.S.C. §116(a) (2012).

80. Christopher Powell, New Study Shows Female Genital Mutilation Exposes Women and Babies to Significant Risk at Childbirth (June 2, 2006), available at http://www.who.int/mediacentre/news/releases/2006/pr30/en/index.html; U.S. State Department, Prevalence of the Practice of Female Genital Mutilation (2001).

81. UNFPA, State of the World Population 2006: Women and Migration; William Saletan, When Cutting Isn't Cruel, Wash. Post, Aug. 20, 2006, available at http://www.washingtonpost.com/wp-dyn/content/article/2006/08/18/AR2006081800981.html.

82. Federal Prohibition of Female Genital Mutilation Act, 18 U.S.C. §116 (2012).

83. 22 U.S.C. §262k-2 (2012).

84. Martha Nussbaum, Sex & Social Justice 29-30 (1999) (referring generally to international human rights). For general discussion of feminism and religious-based cultural practices that, from a Western viewpoint, violate women's basic human rights, see Patricia A. Broussard, Female Genital Mutilation: Exploring Strategies for Ending Ritualized Torture: Shaming, Blaming, and Utilizing the Convention Against Torture, 15 Duke J. Gender L. & Pol'y 19 (2008); International Law: Modern Feminist Approaches (Doris Buss & Ambreena Manji eds., 2005); Ayelet Shachar, Religion, State, and the Problem of Gender: New Modes of Citizenship and Governance in Diverse Societies, 50 McGill L.J. 49 (2005); Sally Engle Merry, Constructing a Global Law: Violence Against Women and the Human Rights System, 28 Law & Soc. Inquiry 941 (2003).

85. Helen M. Stacy, Human Rights for the 21st Century: Sovereignty, Civil Society, Culture 110, 177 (2009).

86. Valorie K. Vojdik, Politics of the Headscarf in Turkey: Masculinities, Feminism, and the Construction of Collective Identities, 33 Harv. J. Law & Gender 661, 661 (2010).

87. Sahin v. Turk., App. 44774/98, Eur. Ct. H.R. (Nov. 10, 2005); see also Vojdik, supra note 86.

88. Conseil d'Etat Decision in the case of Mme M, 286798, delivered June 27, 2008, described in Mary Anne Case, Feminist Fundamentalism as an Individual and Constitutional Commitment, 19 Am. U. J. Gender, Soc. Pol'y & L. 549, 550 (2011).

89. Vojdik, supra note 86, at 662 (citing examples and sources); see also Pnina Werbner, Veiled Interventions in Pure Space: Honour, Shame and Embodied Struggles Among Muslims in Britain and France, 24(2) Theory, Culture & Society 161 (2007) (comparing British and French approaches).

90. Quoted in Werbner, supra note 89, at 173.

91. Vojdik, supra note 86, at 664-665.

92. Estelle Freedman, No Turning Back 223-224 (2002). See Joan Scott, The Politics of the Veil (2007).

93. Alison Dundes Renteln, The Use and Abuse of the Cultural Defense, in Multicultural Jurisprudence: Comparative Perspectives on the Cultural Defense 62 (Marie Claire Foblets & Alison Dundes Renteln eds., 2009).

94. Steven E. Briggs, Letter to the Editor, California Bar Journal, Apr. 2009, at 9. For backlash, see Arthur R. Silen, Letter to the Editor, id.

95. People v. Chen, No. 87-7774 (N.Y. Sup. Ct. Dec. 2, 1988); People v. Wu, 286 Cal. Rptr. 868 (Ct. App. 1991). Both of these cases are explored in Leti Volpp, (Mis)Identifying Culture: Asian Women and the "Cultural Defense," 17 Harv. Women's L.J. 57 (1994).

96. Leti Volpp, Framing Cultural Difference: Immigrant Women and Discourses of Tradition, 22 Differences: A Journal of Feminist Cultural Studies 90, 101 (2011).

97. See generally Alison Dundes Renteln, The Cultural Defense (2004).

98. Daina C. Chiu, The Cultural Defense: Beyond Exclusion, Assimilation, and Guilty Liberalism, 82 Cal. L. Rev. 1053, 1057, 1114 (1994).

99. Cynthia Lee, Cultural Convergence: Interest Convergence Theory Meets the Cultural Defense, 49 Ariz. L. Rev. 911, 918 (2007).

100. Hosanna-Tabor Evangelical Lutheran Church and School v. EEOC, 132 S. Ct. 694 (2012).

101. Bollard v. California Province of the Soc'y of Jesus, 196 F.3d 940, 944 (9th Cir. 1999). Bollard was applied and reaffirmed in Elvig v. Calvin Presbyterian Church, 375 F.3d 941 (9th Cir. 2004) (holding that a supervising pastor's sexual harassment of a female minister was not related to the church's "constitutionally protected prerogative to choose its ministers" nor "a constitutionally protected religious practice," and therefore Title VII was applicable).

102. *Hosanna-Tabor*, 132 S. Ct. at 709.

103. Id. at 709 n.4 (citing *Bollard* with approval).

104. See Doriane Lambelet Coleman, The Seattle Compromise: Multicultural Sensitivity and Americanization, 47 Duke L.J. 717 (1998).

105. Child Trends Databank, Percentage of Newborn Males Circumcised in the Hospital (2003), available at http://www.childrensdatabank.org/pdf/85_PDF.pdf (56 percent, down from 63 percent in 2001).

106. See State v. Mong Lor, Appeal No. 2008AP852-CR, Wis. Ct. App. March 4, 2009, found at http://statecasefiles.justia.com/documents/wisconsin/court-of-appeals/2008AP000852-CR -%282009-03-04%29.pdf (holding that because Wisconsin does not recognize a "cultural marriage defense," the defendant did not have grounds to charge that his lawyer was ineffective in not raising the defense).

107. Katha Pollitt, Sweatin' to the Koran?, The Nation, Apr. 28, 2008, at 14.

108. See EEOC v. Alamo Rent-A-Car, 432 F. Supp.2d 1006 (D. Ariz. 2006) (employee should have been granted an exception because the possibility that other employees might request deviations was hypothetical and did not constitute undue hardship).

109. See Tahirih Justice Center, Forced Marriages in Immigrant Communities in the United States: 2011 National Survey Results, Sept. 2011, at 8, found at http://www.tahirih.org/site/wp-content/ uploads/2011/09/REPORT-Tahirih-Survey-on-Forced-Marriage-in-Immigrant-Communities-in-the -United-States-September-2011.pdf.

110. Id. at 11.

111. Id. at 7.

112. See Curay-Cramer v. Ursuline Academy of Wilmington Del., Inc., 344 F. Supp. 2d 923 (D. Del. 2004) (no, because it would require the court to become entangled in church doctrine, which would violate the First Amendment). See also Fassl v. Our Lady of Perpetual Help Roman Catholic Church, 2005 U.S. Dist. LEXIS 22546 (refusing to hear employee Family and Medical Leave Act complaint against a Catholic Church, on First Amendment grounds).

113. Mona El-Naggar, Family Life According to the Brotherhood, N.Y. Times, Sept. 4, 2012, available at http://www.nytimes.com/2012/09/05/world/middleeast/05iht-letter05.html.

114. Case, Feminist Fundamentalism as an Individual and Constitutional Commitment, supra note 88, at 550.

Table of Cases

Principal cases are in italics.

Table of Terms

*Page numbers indicate where the definition
box for each term can be found.*

Index

Aas, Erik, 284
AAUW. *See* American Association of University Women (AAUW)
ABA Commission on Women in the Profession, 139, 484, 514, 515, 516, 519
  bias in justice system, 495
  bias in legal practice, 476–480
Abortion, 595–626
  access to, 595
  adolescents, 622–623
  anti-abortion activism. *See* Anti-abortion activism
  autonomy-based theories, 615
  bypass procedures, 621–622
  Catholic hospitals, 590
  class and race dimensions, 623–624
  conscience laws, 589–590
  constitutional basis for abortion right, 615–616
  delay laws, 618
  disclosures, 618
  equality principle, 615
  father's rights, 621, 626
  federal funding, 623, 624
  Global Gag Rule, 624
  harm to women from, 619
  increasing restrictions, impact of, 625
  "informed consent" requirements, 617–618
  international issues, 624
  Internet postings, 620, 626
  judicial bypass procedures, 621–622
  late-term, restrictions on, 618
  legal framework, 596–626
  mandatory wait laws, 618
  minors, 621–623
  parental consent and notification, 621–622
  partial-birth, 607–615, 618
  personhood amendments, 624
  post-abortion syndrome, 619
  poverty and, 623–624
  providers, 620, 624
  public opinion and, 616, 617
  race and class dimensions, 623–624
  rape exception, 550
  rates, 625
  reasons for, 616
  regret, 618
  regulation of, 616, 617
  reliance interests, 616–617
  sex selection and, 625
  spousal notice and consent, 621
  stare decisis, 616
  state funding limits, 623
  waiting period, 618
Abramovitz, Mimi, 682
Abrams, Kathryn, 745
  ethic of care, 457–458
  sexual harassment, 298, 300–301
Abrams, Paul, 136
Abstinence-only programs, 622–623
Abuse
  of children. *See* Child abuse
  of inmates, 510
  of women. *See* Battered woman's syndrome; Domestic violence
Abzug, Bella, 420

765